# A HISTORY OF WESTERN SOCIETY

# A HISTORY OF WESTERN SOCIETY

## Second Edition

**John P. McKay**

**Bennett D. Hill**

**John Buckler**

University of Illinois, Urbana

Houghton Mifflin Company

Boston

Dallas    Geneva, Illinois

Hopewell, New Jersey    Palo Alto

London

## About the Authors

**John P. McKay**  A native of St. Louis, Missouri, John P. McKay received his B.A. from Wesleyan University (1961), his M.A. from the Fletcher School of Law and Diplomacy (1962), and his Ph.D. from the University of California, Berkeley (1968). He began teaching history at the University of Illinois in 1966 and became a professor there in 1976. John won the Herbert Baxter Adams Prize for his book *Pioneers for Profit: Foreign Entrepreneurship and Russian Industrialization, 1885-1913* (1970). He has also written *Tramways and Trolleys: The Rise of Urban Mass Transport in Europe* (1976) and has translated Jules Michelet's *The People* (1973). His research has been supported by fellowships from the Ford Foundation, the Guggenheim Foundation, and IREX. Recently named general editor of *Industrial Development and the Social Fabric: An International Series of Historical Monographs,* John continues to serve on the editorial board of the *Journal of Economic History.*

**Bennett D. Hill**  A native of Philadelphia, Bennett D. Hill earned an A.B. at Princeton (1956) and advanced degrees from Harvard (A.M., 1958) and Princeton (Ph.D., 1963). He is a professor of history at the University of Illinois at Urbana, where he served as chairman of the department from 1978 to 1981. He has published *English Cistercian Monasteries and Their Patrons in the Twelfth Century* (1968) and *Church and State in the Middle Ages* (1970); and articles in *Analecta Cisterciensia, The New Catholic Encyclopaedia, The American Benedictine Review,* and *The Dictionary of the Middle Ages.* His reviews have appeared in *The American Historical Review, Speculum, The Historian, The Catholic Historical Review,* and *Library Journal.* He has been a fellow of the American Council of Learned Societies, served on numerous committees for the National Endowment for the Humanities and the Woodrow Wilson Foundation, and is an associate editor of the *American Benedictine Review.*

**John Buckler**  Born in Louisville, Ky., John Buckler received his B.A. from the University of Louisville in 1967. Harvard University awarded him the Ph.D. in 1973. He is currently an associate professor at the University of Illinois, and is serving on the Subcommittee on Cartography of the American Philological Association. In 1980 Harvard University Press published his *The Theban Hegemony, 371-362 B.C.* His articles have appeared in journals both here and abroad, like the *American Journal of Ancient History, Classical Philology, Rheinisches Museum für Philologie, Classical Quarterly, Wiener Studien,* and *Symbolae Osloenses.*

**Text Credits**  Excerpts from S. N. Kramer, *The Sumerians* (Chicago: University of Chicago Press, 1964), copyright © by the University of Chicago. Reprinted by permission. Excerpts from "Sumerian Myths and Epic Tales," trans. S. N. Kramer; "Akkadian Myths and Epics," trans. E. Z. Speiser; "Laws from Mesopotamia and Asia Minor," trans. S. N. Kramer; and "Summarian Wisdom Text," trans. S. N. Kramer, in *Ancient Near Eastern Texts Relating to the Old Testament* by James B. Pritchard (ed.), 3rd ed. with Supplement (copyright © 1969 by Princeton University Press), pp. 44-590 (passim). Reprinted by permission of Princeton University Press. Excerpts from *Greek Elegy and Iambus,* trans. by J. M. Edmonds, Harvard University Press, 1931, reprinted by permission of the publisher and the Loeb Classical Library. Excerpts from Sappho reprinted by permission of Schocken Books Inc. from *Greek Lyric Poetry* edited by Willis Barnstone. Copyright © 1962, 1967 by Willis Barnstone. Excerpts from J. T. McNeil and H. Gamer, trans., *Medieval Handbooks of Penance,* Octagon Books, New York, 1965. Reprinted by permission of Columbia University Press. Riddle No. 44 from Michael Alexander, trans., *The Earliest English Poems* (London: Penguin Books Ltd, 1966), p. 99. Copyright © Michael Alexander, 1966. Reprinted by permission of Penguin Books Ltd. Excerpts from "Richard II," Act II, Scene I, and "Hamlet," Act III, Scene I, in *The Complete Plays and Poems of William Shakespeare* (edited by William A. Neilson and C. J. Hill). Copyright © 1942 by Houghton Mifflin Company. Copyright renewed, 1969. Portion of "The White Man's Burden" from *Rudyard Kipling's Verse: Definitive Edition.* Reprinted by permission of Doubleday & Company, Inc., The National Trust, and Eyre Methuen Ltd.

**Cover:**  The Hunt of the Unicorn. VI, The Unicorn is killed and brought to the castle. Silk, wool, silver and silver-gilt threads. Franco-Flemish. XVI Century, c. 1500. The Metropolitan Museum of Art, gift of John D. Rockefeller, Jr., The Cloisters Collection, 1937.

Printed in the U.S.A.

Library of Congress Catalog Card Number: 82-81316

ISBN: 0-395-32804-7

# CONTENTS

# MAPS

# PREFACE

*A HISTORY OF WESTERN SOCIETY* grew out of the authors' desire to infuse new life into the study of Western civilization. As we wrote in the preface to the first edition, "History is the study of change over time and historians have seen many changes in their own discipline in recent years. Imaginative questions and innovative research have opened up vast new areas of interest and increased historical knowledge rapidly." We noted that the pushing back of the frontiers of knowledge had been especially dramatic in European social history, but that similar advances had characterized economic and intellectual history, while new research and fresh interpretations were simultaneously revitalizing the study of the traditional mainstream of political, diplomatic, and religious development. Yet it seemed to us that although new discoveries and controversies were stimulating professional historians, both the broad public and the intelligentsia often appeared to be losing interest in the past. The distinguished mathematical economist of our acquaintance who smugly quipped "What's new in history?" – confident that the answer was nothing and that historians were as dead as the events they examine – was not alone.

It was our conviction, based on considerable experience introducing large numbers of students to the broad sweep of Western civilization, that a book reflecting current trends could excite readers and inspire a new interest in history and a heightened curiosity about our Western heritage. Our strategy was twofold. First, we made social history the core element of our work. Not only did we incorporate recent research by social historians, but also we sought to re-create the life of ordinary people in appealing human terms. At the same time we were determined to give the great economic, political, intellectual, and cultural developments the attention they unquestionably deserve. We wanted to give individual readers and instructors a balanced, integrated perspective, so that they could pursue on their own or in the classroom those themes and questions that they found particularly exciting and significant.

In preparing the second edition we have worked hard to build upon the favorable response to our efforts. Social history remains the core element of our work, and once again important recent research on such subjects as population, diet, women, and the family has been integrated into the text. At the same time we have expanded somewhat our treatment of major intellectual and cultural developments in order to realize fully the promise of the balanced approach of the first edition. Thus the discussion of such topics as Judaism, Islam, medieval philosophy, the baroque, romanticism, and nineteenth-century science has been substantially expanded, for example, while new material on ancient Egypt, medieval drama, Renaissance literature, French classicism, Descartes, Darwin, and realism has been woven into the work. Finally, every chapter of the book has been painstakingly reviewed for content and clarity, resulting in a wholly new chapter on the ancient Near East and in many small improvements, notably in the discussion of feudalism, the English Reformation, and the French Revolution. In all our endeavors the encouraging, constructive comments and suggestions of many readers have been greatly appreciated.

Other distinctive features from the first edition remain in the second. To help guide the reader toward historical understanding we have posed specific historical questions at the beginning of each chapter. These questions are then answered in the course of the chapter, each of which now concludes with a concise summary of the chapter's findings. Timelines, which students find useful, have been added in many chapters.

We have also tried to suggest how historians actually work and think. We have quoted rather extensively from a wide variety of primary sources and have demonstrated in our use of these quotations how historians sift and weigh evidence. We want the reader to realize that history is neither a list of cut-and-dried facts nor a senseless jumble of conflicting opinions. It is our further hope that the primary quotations, so carefully fitted into their historical context, will give the reader a sense that even in the earliest and most remote periods of human experience history has been shaped by individual men and women, some of them great aristocrats, others ordinary folk.

Each chapter concludes with several carefully selected suggestions for further reading. These suggestions are briefly described, in order to help readers know where to go to continue thinking and learning about the Western world. The chapter bibliographies have been expanded in order to keep them current with the vast and complex new work being done in many fields. In a number of areas each new journal or monograph may present fresh perspectives or challenge accepted views, and the best of these recent works have been singled out for citation.

The second edition has many new illustrations and all the illustrations in *A History of*

*Western Society* have been carefully selected to re-enforce both the book's social theme and its balanced treatment of all aspects of Western history. Artwork is an integral part of our book, for the past can speak in pictures as well as words. Maps and line drawings are also a fundamental part of the book and, as with illustrations, they carry captions to enhance their value.

Western civilization courses differ widely in chronological structure from one campus to another. To accommodate the various divisions of historical time into intervals that fit a two-quarter, three-quarter, or two-semester period, *A History of Western Society* is being published in three versions, each set embracing the complete work:

One-volume hardcover edition, A HISTORY OF WESTERN SOCIETY; two-volume paperback, A HISTORY OF WESTERN SOCIETY *Volume I: From Antiquity to the Enlightenment* (Chapters 1-17), *Volume II: From Absolutism to the Present* (Chapters 16-31); three-volume paperback, A HISTORY OF WESTERN SOCIETY *Volume A: From Antiquity to the Reformation* (Chapters 1-13), *Volume B: From the Renaissance to 1815* (Chapters 12-21), *Volume C: From the Revolutionary Era to the Present* (Chapters 21-31).

Note that overlapping chapters in both the two- and the three-volume sets permit still wider flexibility in matching the appropriate volume with the opening and closing dates of a course term. Furthermore, for courses beginning with the Renaissance rather than antiquity or the medieval period, the reader can begin study with Volume B.

*A History of Western Society* also has a study guide for students, as well as an instructor's manual. Both of these excellent aids have been written primarily by Professor James Schmiechen of Central Michigan University. Professor Schmiechen read all our drafts, from the first prospectus to the final typescript of the second edition, and he gave us many valuable suggestions in addition to his enthusiastic and warmly appreciated support. His *Study Guide* contains chapter summaries, chapter outlines, study questions, self-check lists of important concepts and events, and a variety of study aids and suggestions. An innovation in this revision of the *Study Guide* — one that we feel will be extremely useful to the student — is our step-by-step Reading with Understanding exercises, which take the reader by ostensive example through reading and studying activities like underlining, summarizing, identifying main points, classifying information according to sequence, and making historical comparisons. To enable both students and instructors to use the *Study Guide* with the greatest possible flexibility, the guide is available in two volumes, with considerable overlapping of chapters. Instructors and students who use only Volumes A and B of the text have all the pertinent study materials in a single volume, *Study Guide, Volume* 1 (Chapters 1–21); likewise, those who use only Volumes B and C of the text also have all the necessary materials in one volume, *Study Guide, Volume* 2 (Chapters 12–31).

It is also a pleasure to thank Roger Schlesinger, Washington State University; Charles Rearick, University of Massachusetts at Amherst; Donald Buck, DeAnza College; James Powell, Syracuse University; John M. Riddle, North Carolina State University; Laurence Lee Howe, University of Louisville; and Archibald Lewis, University of Massachusetts at Amherst, Jack R. Harlan, University of Illinois; Marc Cooper, Southwestern Missouri State University; and Lowell L. Blaisdell, Texas Tech University; Kevin K. Carroll, Arizona State University; Robert G. Clouse, Indiana State University; Albert A. Hayden, Wittenberg University; Harry M. Hutson, University of Tennessee at Martin; Dorothy Vogel Krupnik, Indiana University of Pennsylvania; Charles A. Le Guin, Portland State Univer-

sity; Carolyn C. Lougee, Stanford University; Paul J. Pinckney, University of Tennessee-Knoxville; C. Mary Taney, Glassboro State College; William M. Welch, Jr., Troy State University; and John C. White, University of Alabama-Huntsville, who read and critiqued the manuscript through its development.

Many of our colleagues at the University of Illinois kindly provided information and stimulation for our book, often without even knowing it. N. Frederick Nash, Rare Book Librarian, gave freely of his time and made many helpful suggestions for illustrations. Barbara Bohen, Director of the World Heritage Museum at the University, allowed us complete access to the sizable holdings of the museum. James Dengate kindly supplied information on objects from the museum's collection. Caroline Buckler took many excellent photographs of the museum's objects and generously helped us at crucial moments in production. Such wide-ranging expertise was a great asset for which we are very appreciative. Bennett Hill wishes to express his sincere appreciation to the Rt. Rev. James A. Wiseman, Abbot of St. Anselm's Abbey, Washington, D.C. for his support and understanding in the preparation of this second edition; and to William McKane for help with the maps.

Each of us has benefited from the generous criticism of his co-authors, although each of us assumes responsibility for what he has written. John Buckler has written the first six chapters; Bennett Hill has continued the narrative through Chapter 16; and John McKay has written Chapters 17 through 31. Finally, we warmly welcome any comments or suggestions for improvements from our readers.

JOHN P. MCKAY
BENNETT D. HILL
JOHN BUCKLER

# CHAPTER 1

## NEAR EASTERN ORIGINS

THE CULTURE of the modern Western world has its origins in places as far away as modern Iraq, Iran, and Egypt. In these areas human beings abandoned their life of roaming and hunting to settle in stable agricultural communities. From these communities grew cities and civilizations, societies that invented concepts and techniques that have become integral parts of contemporary life. Fundamental is the development of writing by the Sumerians in Mesopotamia, an invention that enables knowledge of the past to be preserved and facilitates the spread and accumulation of learning, lore, literature, and science. Mathematics, astronomy, and architecture were all innovations of the ancient Near Eastern civilizations. So too were the first law codes and religious concepts that still permeate daily life.

How did wild hunters become urban dwellers? How did the roots of Western culture establish themselves in far-off Mesopotamia, and what caused Mesopotamian culture to become predominant throughout most of the ancient Near East? What part did the Egyptians play in this vast story? Lastly, what did the arrival of the Hittites on the fringes of Mesopotamia and Egypt mean to the superior cultures of their new neighbors? These are the questions this chapter will explore.

On December 27, 1831, young Charles Darwin stepped aboard the H.M.S. *Beagle* to begin a voyage to South America and the Pacific Ocean. In the course of that five-year voyage he became convinced that species of animals and human beings had evolved from lower forms. At first Darwin was reluctant to make public his theories because they ran counter to the biblical account of creation, which claimed that God had made Adam in one day. Finally, however, in 1859 he published *On the Origin of Species.* In 1871 he followed it with *The Descent of Man,* in which he argued that human beings and apes are descended from a common ancestor. Even before Darwin had proclaimed his theories, evidence to support them had come to light. In 1856, the fossilized bones of an early form of man were discovered in the Neander valley of Germany. Called Neanderthal Man after the place of his discovery, he was physically more primitive than and anatomically a bit different from modern man (*Homo sapiens,* or thinking man). But he was clearly a human being and not an ape. He offered proof of Darwin's theory that *Homo sapiens* had evolved from less-developed forms.

The theories of Darwin, supported by the evidence of fossilized remains, ushered in a new scientific era, an era in which scientists and scholars have re-examined the very nature of human beings and their history. Men and women of the twentieth century have made new discoveries, solved some old problems, and raised many new ones. Since 1959, the anthropologists Louis and Mary Leakey and their son Richard, working in the Olduvai Gorge in East Africa, have uncovered fossilized bones of several very early types of human beings as well as species of advanced apes. The work of the Leakeys alone demonstrates how complex the course of human evolution has been.

Why did some human types become extinct while others thrived? More importantly, what are the links among the fossilized remains? The answers to these questions lie in the future. For the moment, perhaps the wisest and most humble answer is the observation of Loren Eiseley, a noted American anthropologist: "The human interminglings of hundreds of thousands of years of prehistory are not to be clarified by a single generation of archaeologists."[1]

Despite the enormous uncertainty surrounding human development, a reasonably clear picture can be had of two important early periods: the Paleolithic or Old Stone Age, and the Neolithic or New Stone Age. The immensely long Paleolithic Age, which lasted from about 400,000 B.C. until about 7000 B.C., takes its name from the crude stone tools the earliest hunters chipped from flint and obsidian, a black volcanic rock. During the much shorter Neolithic Age, which lasted from about 7000 B.C. to about 3000 B.C., human beings began using new types of stone tools and pursuing agriculture.

## THE PALEOLITHIC AGE

Life in the Paleolithic Age was perilous and uncertain at best. Survival depended largely on the success of the hunt, but the hunt often brought sudden and violent death. Paleolithic peoples hunted in a variety of ways, depending on the climate and the environment. Often the hunters stationed themselves at river fords and waterholes and waited for their prey to come to them. Paleolithic hunters were thoroughly familiar with the habits of the animals they relied upon, and paid close attention to their migratory habits. Other hunters trapped their quarry, and those who lived in open areas stalked and pursued game. Paleolithic peoples hunted a huge variety of animals, ranging from elephants in Spain to deer in China.

Success in the hunt often depended more on the quality and effectiveness of the hunters' social organization than on their bravery. Paleolithic hunters were organized – they hunted in groups. They used their knowledge of the animal world and their power of thinking to plan how to down their prey. The

ability to think and to act as an organized social group meant that Paleolithic hunters could successfully feed on animals that were bigger, faster, and stronger than themselves.

Paleolithic peoples also nourished themselves by gathering nuts, berries, and seeds. Just as they knew the habits of animals, so they had vast knowledge of the plant kingdom. Some Paleolithic peoples even knew how to plant wild seeds to supplement their food supply. Thus, they relied on every part of the environment for their survival.

Home for Paleolithic folk also varied according to climate and environment. Particularly in cold regions, they sought refuge in caves from the weather, predatory animals, and other people. In warmer climates and in open country they built shelters, some of them no more elaborate than temporary huts or sunscreens.

The basic social unit of Paleolithic societies was probably the family, but family bonds were no doubt stronger and more extensive than those of families in modern, urban, and industrialized societies. It is likely that the bonds of kinship were strong not just within the nuclear family of father, mother, and children, but throughout the extended family of uncles, aunts, cousins, nephews, and nieces. People in nomadic societies typically depend on the extended family for cooperative work and mutual protection. The ties of kinship probably also extended beyond the family to the tribe. A *tribe* was a group of families, led by a patriarch, who considered themselves to be descended from a common ancestor. Most tribes probably consisted of from thirty to fifty people.

As in the hunt, so too in other aspects of life – the members of the group had to cooperate in order to survive. The adult males normally hunted, and between hunts made their stone weapons. The realm of the women was probably the camp. There they made utensils, and were probably responsible for the invention of weaving. They fashioned skins into cloths, tents, and footwear. They left the camp to gather nuts, grains, and fruits to supplement the group's diet. Their unique function was the bearing of children, who were essential to the continuation of the group.

Women also had to tend the children, especially in their earliest and most helpless days. Part of women's work was tending the fire, which served for warmth and cooking and also for protection against wild animals.

Paleolithic peoples were also world travelers. Before the dawn of history bands of *Homo sapiens* flourished in Europe, Africa, and Asia, and had crossed into the continents of North and South America and Australia. By the end of the Paleolithic Age, there were very few "undiscovered" areas left in the world.

Some of the most striking accomplishments of Paleolithic peoples were intellectual. The development of the human brain made thought possible. Unlike animals, whose behavior is the result of instinct, Paleolithic peoples used reason to govern their actions. Thought and language permitted the lore and experience of the old to be passed on to the young. An invisible world also opened up to *Homo sapiens.* The Neanderthalers developed the custom of burying their dead and of leaving offerings with the body, perhaps in the belief that in some way life continued after death.

Paleolithic peoples produced the first art. They decorated the walls of their caves with paintings of animals and scenes of the hunt. They also began to fashion clay models of pregnant women and of animals. Many of the surviving paintings, such as those at Altamira in Spain and Lascaux in France, are located deep in the caves, in areas not easily accessible.

These areas were probably places of ritual and initiation, where young men were taken when they joined the ranks of the hunters. They were also places of magic. The animals depicted on the walls were either those hunted for food or those feared as predators. Many are shown wounded by spears or arrows; others are pregnant. The early artists may have been expressing the hope that the hunt would be successful and game plentiful. By portraying the animals as realistically as possible, the artists and hunters may have hoped to gain power over them. The statuettes of pregnant women seem to express a wish for fertile women to have babies and thus ensure the group's survival. The wall paintings and statuettes express human beings' earliest yearnings to control their environment.

Despite their many achievements, Paleolithic peoples were sometimes their own worst enemies. At times they fought each other for control of hunting grounds, and some early hunters wiped out less aggressive peoples. On occasion Paleolithic peoples seem to have preyed on one another, probably under the threat of starvation. One of the grimmest indications that Neanderthal Man was at times cannibalistic comes from a cave in Yugoslavia, where investigators found human bones burned and split open. Even so, cannibalism appears to have been rare. The overriding struggle of the Paleolithic Age was with an uncompromising environment.

## THE NEOLITHIC AGE

Hunting is at best a precarious way of life, even when the diet is supplemented with seeds and fruits. If the climate changed even slightly, the all-important herds might move to new areas. As recently as the late 1950s the

Caribou Eskimos of the Canadian Northwest Territories suffered a severe famine when the caribou herds, their only source of food and bone for weapons, changed their migration route. Paleolithic tribes either moved with the herds, and adapted themselves to new circumstances, or – like the Caribou Eskimos – perished. Several long ice ages – periods when huge glaciers covered vast parts of Europe – subjected small bands of Paleolithic hunters to extreme hardship.

Not long after the last Ice Age, around 7000 B.C., some hunters and gatherers began to rely chiefly on agriculture for their sustenance. This development has traditionally been called "the Agricultural Revolution." Yet the work of Jack R. Harlan, a leading scientist in the field of agronomy, has caused scholars to reappraise the origins of agriculture:

*Agriculture is not an invention or a discovery and is not as revolutionary as we had thought; furthermore, it was adopted slowly and with reluctance. The current evidence indicates that agriculture evolved through an extension and intensification of what people had already been doing for a long time.*[2]

Striking support for Harlan's view came in 1981 from an American archaeological expedition to the Nile valley in Egypt. Investigators found that for thousands of years nomads had planted wheat and barley in the silt left by the flooding of the Nile. These people, however, never shifted to a life of settled farming. Instead, the crops they grew were just another, though important, source of their food. In short, hunters and gatherers apparently long knew how to grow crops, but did not base their existence on them.

The real transformation of human life occurred when hunters and gatherers gave up their nomadic way of life to depend primarily on the grain they grew and the animals they domesticated. Agriculture made for a more stable and secure life. Neolithic peoples thus flourished, fashioning an energetic and creative era. They were responsible for many fundamental inventions and innovations that the modern world takes for granted. First, obviously, is systematic agriculture, the primary economic activity of the entire ancient world and the basis of all modern life. The settled routine of Neolithic farmers led to the evolution of towns and eventually cities. Neolithic farmers usually raised more food than they could consume, and their surpluses permitted larger and healthier populations. Since surpluses of food could also be bartered for other commodities, the Neolithic era witnessed the beginnings of large-scale trade. In time the increasing complexity of Neolithic societies led to the development of writing, prompted by the need to keep records and later by the urge to chronicle experiences, learning, and beliefs.

The transition to settled life also had a profound impact on the family. The shared needs and pressures that make for strong extended-family ties in nomadic societies are less prominent in settled societies. Bonds to the extended family weakened. In towns and cities, the nuclear family – father, mother, and children – was more dependent on its immediate neighbors than on kinfolk.

Meanwhile, however, the nomadic way of life and the family relationships it nurtured continued to flourish alongside settled agriculture. Even nomadic life changed. Neolithic nomads traveled with flocks of domesticated animals, which were their main source of wealth and food. Often farmers and nomads bartered peaceably with one another, each group trading its surpluses for those of the other. Although nomadic peoples continued

MAP 1.1 SPREAD OF CULTURES This map illustrates the spread of Mesopotamian and Egyptian culture through a semicircular stretch of land often called the "Fertile Crescent."

to exist throughout the Neolithic period and into modern times, the future belonged to the Neolithic farmers and their descendants. While the development of agriculture may not have been revolutionary, the changes that it ushered in certainly were.

Until recently, scholars thought that agriculture originated in the ancient Near East and gradually spread elsewhere. Contemporary work, however, points to a more complex pattern of development. For unknown reasons people in various parts of the world all seem to have begun domesticating plants and animals at roughly the same time, around 7000 B.C. Four main points of origin have been identified. In the Near East, sites as far apart as Tepe Yahya in modern Iran, Jarmo in Iraq, Jericho in Palestine, and Hacilar in modern

Turkey (see Map 1.1) raised wheat, barley, peas, and lentils. They also kept herds of sheep, pigs, and possibly goats. In western Africa, Neolithic farmers domesticated many plants, including millet, sorghum, and yams. In northeastern China, peoples of the Yangshao culture developed techniques of field agriculture, animal husbandry, potterymaking, and bronze metallurgy. Innovations in the New World were equally striking. Indians in Central and South America domesticated a host of plants, among them corn, beans, and squash. From these far-flung areas, knowledge of farming techniques spread to still other regions.

The first farmers gathered and planted the seeds of wild wheat, barley, and other plants. Later farmers learned to improve their crops.

The excavators of Tepe Yahya demonstrated in 1976 how specialization in farming could have led to a new species of grain: the Neolithic farmers of Tepe Yahya, preferring a particular species of wheat to others, planted only that species; when nearby wild grasses fertilized the wheat naturally, a new hybrid species resulted.

The deliberate planting of crops itself led to changes in their genetic structure. The plants and animals cultivated by Neolithic farmers gradually evolved to the point where most of them could no longer survive in the wild. Thus human beings and the plants and animals they domesticated depended on each other for survival. Contemporary work on the origins of farming has led to a chilling revelation: the genetic base of most modern domesticated plants, like wheat and corn, is so narrow that a new pest or plant disease could destroy much of it. The result would be widespread famine. Human society is depending on a precarious food base.

Once people began to rely on farming for their livelihood, they settled in permanent villages and built houses. The location of the village was crucial. Early farmers chose places where the water supply was constant and adequate for their crops and flocks. At first, villages were small, consisting of a few households. As the population expanded and prospered, villages usually developed into towns. Between 8000 and 7000 B.C., the community at Jericho grew to at least two thousand people. Jericho's inhabitants lived in mud-brick houses built on stone foundations, and they surrounded their town with a massive fortification wall. The Neolithic site of Catal Hüyük in Anatolia (modern Turkey) covered thirty-two acres. The outer houses of the settlement formed a solid wall of mud brick, which served as a bulwark against at-tack. At Tepe Yahya, too, the Neolithic farmers surrounded their town with a wall.

Walls offered protection and permitted a more secure and stable way of life than that of the nomad. They also prove that towns grew in size, population, and wealth, for these fortifications were so large that they could have been raised only by a large labor force. They also indicate that towns were developing social and political organization. The fortifications were the work of the whole community, and they would have been impossible without central planning.

One of the major effects of the advent of agriculture and settled life was a dramatic increase in population. No census figures exist for this period, but the number and size of the towns prove that Neolithic society was expanding. Early farmers found that agriculture provided a larger and much more dependable food supply than had hunting and gathering. No longer did the long winter months mean the immediate threat of starvation. Farmers raised more food than they could consume, and they learned to store the surplus for the winter. Because the farming community was better fed than ever before, it was also more resistant to diseases that kill people who are suffering from malnutrition. Thus Neolithic farmers were healthier and longer-lived than their predecessors. All these factors explain the growth of towns like Jericho and Jarmo.

The surplus of food had two other momentous consequences. First, grain became an article of commerce. The farming community traded surplus grain for items it could not produce itself. The community thus obtained raw materials such as precious gems and metals. In Mesopotamia the early towns imported copper from the north, and eventually copper replaced stone for tools and weapons. Trade also brought Neolithic communities

TOWER AT JERICHO *Photographed during excavation, this tower is a good example of the strong fortifications of Neolithic towns. The sheer size of the walls amply illustrates the huge amount of labor and central planning necessary to build them. (Consulate General of Israel)*

into touch with one another, making possible the spread of ideas and techniques.

Second, agricultural surplus made possible the division of labor. It freed some members of the community from the necessity of raising food. Artisans and craftsmen devoted their attention to making the new stone tools farming demanded — hoes and sickles for fieldwork and mortars and pestles for grinding the grain. Other artisans began to shape clay into pottery vessels, which were used to store grain, wine, and oil, and which served as kitchen utensils. Still other artisans wove baskets and cloth. People who could specialize in particular crafts produced more and better goods than any single individual could.

Prosperity and stable conditions nurtured other innovations and discoveries. Neolithic farmers improved their tools and agricultural techniques. They domesticated bigger, stronger animals, such as the bull and the horse, to work for them. To harness the power of these animals they invented tools like the plow, which came into use by 3000 B.C. The first plows had wooden shares and could break only light soils, but they were far more efficient than stone hoes. By 3000 B.C. the wheel had been invented, and farmers devised ways of hitching bulls and horses to wagons. These developments enabled Neolithic farmers to raise more food more efficiently and easily than ever before, simply because animals and machines were doing a greater proportion of the actual work.

In arid regions like Mesopotamia and Egypt, farmers learned to irrigate their land. By diverting water from rivers, they were able to open new land to cultivation. River waters flooding the fields deposited layers of rich mud, which increased the fertility of the soil. Thus the rivers, together with the manure of domesticated animals, kept replenishing the land. One result was a further increase in population and wealth. Irrigation, especially on a large scale, demanded group effort. The entire community had to plan which land to irrigate and how to lay out the canals. Then everyone had to help dig the canals. The demands of irrigation underscored the need for strong central authority within the community. Successful irrigation projects in turn strengthened such central authority by proving it effective and beneficial. Towns evolved corporate spirit and governments, to which individuals were subordinate. Here were the makings of urban life.

The development of systematic agriculture

was a fundamental turning-point in the history of civilization. Farming gave rise to stable settled societies, which enjoyed considerable prosperity. It made possible an enormous increase in population. Some inhabitants of the budding towns turned their attention to the production of goods that made life more comfortable. Settled circumstances and a certain amount of leisure made the accumulation and spread of knowledge easier. Finally, sustained farming prepared the way for urban life.

## MESOPOTAMIAN CIVILIZATION

Mesopotamia is the Greek name for the land between the Euphrates and Tigris rivers. Both rivers have their headwaters in the mountains of Armenia in modern Turkey. Both are fed by numerous tributaries, and the entire river system drains a vast mountainous region. Overland routes in Mesopotamia usually follow the Euphrates, because the banks of the Tigris are frequently steep and difficult. North of the ancient city of Babylon, the land levels out into a barren expanse. In 401 B.C., the Greek writer and adventurer Xenophon gave a vivid description of this area:

*In this area the land is a level plain just like the sea, full of wormwood. If there was any brush or reed there, it was invariably fragrant, like spices. Trees there were none, but wild animals of all sorts – a great many wild asses and many ostriches. There were also bustards and gazelles.*[3]

The desert continues south of Babylon, and in 1857 the English geologist and traveler W. K. Loftus depicted it in grim terms:

*There is no life for miles around. No river glides in grandeur at the base of its [the ancient city of Uruk] mounds; no green date groves flourish near its ruins. The jackal and the hyena appear to shun the dull aspect of its tombs. The king of birds never hovers over the deserted waste. A blade of grass or an insect finds no existence there. The shrivelled lichen alone, clinging to the weathered surface of the broken brick, seems to glory in its universal dominion upon those barren walls.*[4]

Farther south the desert gives way to a six-thousand square-mile region of marshes, lagoons, mudflats, and reed banks. At last, in the extreme south the Euphrates and the Tigris unite and empty into the Persian Gulf.

This forbidding area became the home of many folk and the land of the first cities. Bands of Semitic nomads occupied the region around Akkad (modern Baghdad). Into the south came the Sumerians, a people who probably migrated from the east. The Sumerians were farmers and city builders. By 3000 B.C. they had established a number of cities in the southernmost part of Mesopotamia, a region that became known as Sumer. As the Sumerians pushed north, they came into contact with the Semites, who readily adopted Sumerian culture, and turned to urban life. The Sumerians soon changed the face of the land and made Mesopotamia the "cradle of civilization" (see Map 1.1).

### ENVIRONMENT AND MESOPOTAMIAN CULTURE

From the outset geography had a profound effect on the evolution of Mesopotamian civilization. In this region agriculture is possible only with irrigation. Consequently, the Sumerians and later the Akkadians built their cities along the Tigris and Euphrates and their branches. The rivers supplied fish, a major element of the city dwellers' diet. The rivers also provided reeds and clay, which they used

MAP OF NIPPUR   *The oldest map in the world, dating to ca 1500 B.C., shows the layout of the Mesopotamian city of Nippur. Inscribed on a clay tablet, the map has enabled archaeologists to locate ruined buildings: (A) the ziggurat, (B) canal, (C) enclosure and gardens, (D) city gates, and (E) the Euphrates River. (From the photographic collections of the University Museum, The University of Pennsylvania)*

as building materials. Since this entire area lacks stone, mud-brick became the primary building-block of Mesopotamian architecture.

Although the rivers sustained life, they acted simultaneously as a powerful restraining force, especially on Sumerian political development. They made Sumer a geographical maze. Between the rivers, streams, and irrigation canals stretched open desert or swamp, where nomadic tribes roamed. Communication between cities was difficult and at times dangerous. City was isolated from city, each in its own locale. Thus each Sumerian city became a state, independent of the others and protective of its independence. Any city that tried to unify the country was resisted by the other cities. As a result, the political history of Sumer is one of almost constant warfare.

The experience of the city of Nippur is an example of how bad conditions could become. At one point in its history Nippur was conquered eighteen times in twenty-four years. Although Sumer was eventually unified, unification came late and was always tenuous.

The harsh environment fostered a grim, even pessimistic, spirit among the Mesopotamians. They especially feared the ravages of flood. The Tigris can bring quick devastation, as it did to Baghdad in 1831, when floodwaters destroyed seven thousand homes in a single night. The same tragedy occurred often in antiquity. The chronicle of King Hammurabi recorded years when floods wiped out whole cities. Vulnerability to natural disaster deeply influenced Mesopotamian religious beliefs.

The Mesopotamians considered natural catastrophes the work of the gods. At times the Sumerians described their chief god, Enlil, as "the raging flood which has no rival." The gods, they believed, even used nature to punish the Mesopotamians. According to the myth of the Deluge, which gave rise to the biblical story of Noah, the god Enki warned Ziusudra, the Sumerian Noah:

*A flood will sweep over the cult-centers;*
*To destroy the seed of mankind . . .*
*Is the decision, the word of the assembly of*
    *the gods.*[5]

The myth of Atrahasis describes the gods' annoyance at the prosperity of mankind and tells how Enlil complained to the other gods:

*Oppressive has become the clamor of mankind.*
*By their uproar they prevent sleep.*
*Let the flour be cut off for the people,*
*In their bellies let the greens be too few.*[6]

Enlil and the other gods decide to send a drought and then a flood to destroy human life. In the face of harsh conditions, the Mesopotamians considered themselves weak and insignificant as compared to the gods. This feeling was particularly strong among the Sumerians.

The Mesopotamians did not worship their deities because the gods were holy. Human beings were too insignificant to pass judgment on the conduct of the gods, and the gods were too superior to honor human morals. Rather, the Mesopotamians worshiped the gods because they were mighty. Likewise, it was not the place of men and women to understand the gods. The Sumerian Job once complained to his god:

*The man of deceit has conspired against me,*
*And you, my god, do not thwart him,*
*You carry off my understanding.*[7]

The motives of the gods were not always clear. In times of affliction one could only pray and offer sacrifices to appease them.

### SUMERIAN SOCIETY

The Sumerians sought to please and calm the gods, especially the patron deity of the city. In the center of each city the people erected a shrine and then built their houses around it. The best way to honor the god was to make the shrine as grand and as impressive as possible, for a god who had a splendid temple might think twice about sending floods to destroy the city.

The temple had to be worthy of the god, a symbol of his power, and it had to last. Special skills and materials were needed to build it. Only stone was suitable for its foundations and precious metals for its decoration. Since the Mesopotamians had to import both stone and metals, temple construction encouraged trade. Architects, engineers, craftsmen, and workers had to devote a great deal of thought, effort, and time to build the temple. By 2000

B.C. the result was Mesopotamia's first monumental architecture – the ziggurat, a massive stepped tower that dominated the city.

Once the ziggurat was built, a professional priesthood was needed to run it and to perform the god's rituals. The people of the city met the expenses of building and maintaining the temple and its priesthood by setting aside extensive tracts of land for that purpose. The priests took charge of the produce of the temple lands and the sacred flocks. Part of the yield went to the feeding and clothing of the priests and the temple staff, and for offerings to the gods. Part was sold or bartered to obtain goods, such as precious metals or stone, needed for construction, maintenance, and ritual.

Until recently, the dominant position and wealth of the temple had led historians to consider the Sumerian city-state an absolute theocracy, or government by an established priesthood. According to this view, the temple and its priests owned the city's land and controlled its economy. Newly discovered documents and recent works, however, have resulted in new ideas about the Sumerian city and its society. It is now known that the temple owned a large fraction, but not all, of the city's territory, and did not govern the city. A king, or *lugal,* exercised political power, and most of the city's land was the property of individual citizens.

Sumerian society was a complex arrangement of freedom and dependence and was divided into four categories: nobles, free clients of the nobility, commoners, and slaves. The nobility consisted of the king and his family, the chief priests, and high palace officials. The king originally rose to power as a war leader, elected by the citizenry, who established a regular army, trained it and led it into battle. The might of the king and the frequency of warfare in Mesopotamia quickly made him the supreme figure in the city, and kingship soon became hereditary. The symbol of his status was the palace, which rivaled the temple in grandeur.

The king and the lesser nobility held extensive tracts of land that were, like the estates of the temple, worked by slaves and clients. Clients were free men and women who were dependent on the nobility. In return for their labor the clients received small plots of land to work for themselves. Although this arrangement assured the clients of a livelihood, the land they worked remained the possession of the nobility or the temple. Thus, not only did the nobility control most — and probably the best — land, they also commanded the obedience of a huge segment of society. They were the dominant force in Mesopotamian society.

Commoners were free citizens. They were independent of the nobility; however, they could not rival the nobility in social status and political power. Commoners belonged to large patriarchal families that owned land in their own right. Commoners could sell their land, if the family approved, but even the king could not legally take their land without their approval. Commoners had a voice in the political affairs of the city and full protection under the law.

Until comparatively recent times, slavery has been a fact of life throughout the history of Western society. Some Sumerian slaves were foreigners and prisoners of war. Some were criminals, who had lost their freedom as punishment for their crimes. Still others served as slaves in repayment of debts. These were more fortunate than the others, because the law required that they be freed after three years. But all slaves were subject to whatever treatment their owners might mete out. They could be beaten and even branded. Yet they were not considered dumb beasts. Slaves engaged in trade and made profits. Indeed, many slaves bought their freedom. They could borrow money, and they received at least some protection under the law.

## THE SPREAD OF MESOPOTAMIAN CULTURE

The Sumerians established the basic social, economic, and intellectual patterns of Mesopotamia, but the Semites played a large part in spreading Sumerian culture far beyond the boundaries of Mesopotamia. Despite the cultural ascendancy of the Sumerians, their unending wars wasted their strength. In 2331 B.C., the Semitic chieftain Sargon conquered Sumer and created a new empire. The symbol of his triumph was a new capital, the city of Agade. Sargon, the first "world conqueror," led his armies to the Mediterranean Sea. Although his empire lasted only a few generations, it spread Mesopotamian culture throughout the Fertile Crescent, the belt of rich farmland that extends from Mesopotamia in the east up through Syria in the north and down to Egypt in the west (see Map 1.1).

Sargon's impact and the extent of Mesopotamian influence even at this early period have been dramatically revealed at Ebla in modern Syria. In 1964, archaeologists unearthed there a once-flourishing Semitic civilization that had assimilated political, intellectual, and artistic aspects of Mesopotamian culture. In 1975, the excavators uncovered thousands of clay tablets, which proved that the people of Ebla had learned the art of writing from the Mesopotamians. Eblaite artists borrowed heavily from Mesopotamian art but developed their own style, which in turn influenced Mesopotamian artists. The Eblaites transmitted the heritage of Mesopotamia to other Semitic centers in

Syria. In the process, a universal culture developed in the ancient Near East, a culture basically Mesopotamian but fertilized by the traditions, genius, and ways of many other peoples.

When the clay tablets of Ebla were discovered, many scholars confidently predicted that they would shed fresh light on the Bible. Some even claimed to recognize in them biblical names like Jerusalem and the "Five Cities of the Plain," which included Sodom and Gomorrah. Careful study since then suggests that these claims were more often optimistic than accurate: so far the Ebla tablets have added very little to biblical scholarship. Yet they are a goldmine of data on the ancient history of northern Syria. Some of them deal with Ebla's relations with neighboring peoples, while others provide detailed information on local agricultural production and the weaving industry. All confirm the existence and importance of direct contact between Mesopotamia and Syria as early as the third millennium B.C. Moreover, they demonstrate the early and widespread influence of Mesopotamian civilization far beyond its own borders.

*SARGON OF AKKAD   This bronze head, with elaborately worked hair and beard, portrays the great conqueror Sargon of Akkad. Originally the eyes were probably precious jewels, which have subsequently been gouged out. This head was found in the ruins of the Assyrian capital of Nineveh, where it had been taken as loot. (Directorate General of Antiquities, Baghdad, Iraq)*

## THE TRIUMPH OF BABYLON

Although the empire of Sargon was extensive, it was also short-lived. It was left to the Babylonians to unite Mesopotamia politically as well as culturally. The Babylonians were Amorites, a Semitic people who had migrated from Arabia and settled in the Sumerian city of Babylon. Babylon enjoyed an excellent geographical position, and it was ideally suited to be the capital of Mesopotamia. It dominated trade on the Tigris and Euphrates rivers: all commerce to and from Sumer and Akkad had to pass by its walls. It also looked beyond Mesopotamia. Babylonian merchants followed the Tigris north to Assyria and An-

atolia. The Euphrates led merchants to Syria, Palestine, and the Mediterranean. The city grew great because of its commercial importance and its power being soundly based.

Babylon was also fortunate in its far-seeing and able king Hammurabi (1792–1750 B.C.). Hammurabi set out to do three things: to make Babylon secure, to unify Mesopotamia, and to win for the Babylonians a place in Mesopotamian civilization. The first two he accomplished by conquering Assyria in the north and Sumer and Akkad in the south. Then he turned to his third goal.

Politically, Hammurabi joined in his kingship the Semitic concept of the tribal chieftain

| | Meaning | Pictograph | Ideogram | Phonetic sign |
|---|---|---|---|---|
| A | Star | | | |
| B | Woman | | | |
| C | Mountain | | | |
| D | Slave woman | | | |
| E | Water In | | | |

FIGURE 1.1 SUMERIAN WRITING (Excerpted from S. N. Kramer, The Sumerians: Their History, Culture and Character, *University of Chicago Press, Chicago, 1963, pp. 302–306*)

and the Sumerian idea of urban kingship. Culturally, he encouraged the spread of myths that explained how Marduk, the god of Babylon, had been elected king of the gods by the other Mesopotamian deities. Hammurabi's success in making Marduk the god of all Mesopotamians made Babylon the religious center of Mesopotamia. Through Hammurabi's genius the Babylonians made their own contribution to Mesopotamian culture — a culture vibrant enough to maintain its identity even while assimilating new influences. Hammurabi's conquests and the activity of Babylonian merchants spread this enriched culture north to Anatolia and west to Syria and Palestine.

## THE INVENTION OF WRITING AND THE FIRST SCHOOLS

Mesopotamian culture spread as rapidly as it did largely because of the invention and evolution of writing. Until recently, scholars have credited the Sumerians with the invention of writing. Recent work, however, suggests that the Sumerian achievement, a form of writing called cuneiform – from the Latin for wedge-shaped, which describes the strokes of the stylus – may have been a comparatively late stage in the development of writing. The origins of writing probably go back thousands of years earlier than previously thought. As early as the ninth millennium B.C., Near Eastern peoples used clay tokens as counters for recordkeeping. By the fourth millennium B.C., people had realized that drawing pictures of the tokens on clay was simpler than making tokens. This breakthrough in turn suggested that more information could be conveyed by adding pictures of still other objects. The result was a complex system of pictographs, in which each sign was a picture of an object. Pictographs were the forerunners of cuneiform writing.

How did this pictographic system work and how did it evolve into cuneiform writing? At first, if a scribe wanted to indicate a star, he simply drew a picture of it on a wet clay tablet (see line A of Figure 1.1), which became rock-hard when baked. Anyone looking at the picture would know what it meant and would think of the word for star. This complicated and laborious system had serious limitations. It would not represent abstract ideas or combinations of ideas. For instance, how could it depict a slave woman?

The solution appeared when the scribe discovered that he could combine signs to express meaning. To refer to a slave woman he used the sign for woman (line B) and the sign for mountain (line C) – literally, "mountain woman" (line D). Since the Sumerians regularly obtained their slave women from the mountains, this combination of signs was easily understandable.

The next step was to simplify the system. Instead of drawing pictures, the scribe made

conventionalized signs. Thus, the signs became ideograms: they symbolized ideas. The sign for star could also be used to indicate heaven, sky, or even god.

The real breakthrough came when the scribe learned to use signs to represent sounds. For instance, the scribe drew two parallel wavy lines to indicate the word *a,* or "water" (line E). Besides water, the word *a* in Sumerian also meant "in." The word *in* expresses a relationship that is very difficult to represent pictorially. Instead of trying to invent a sign to mean *in,* some clever scribe used the sign for water, because the two words sounded alike. This phonetic use of signs made possible the combining of signs to convey abstract ideas. The use of writing enabled merchants to keep complicated business records, inventories, and bills of lading. More important, the learning, lore, history, and philosophy of a culture could be recorded and preserved for unborn generations.

The Sumerian system of writing was so complicated that only professional scribes mastered it, and even they had to study it for many years. By 2500 B.C., scribal schools flourished throughout Sumer. Most students came from wealthy families, and it was largely a male profession. Each school had a master, teachers, and monitors. Discipline was strict, and students were caned for sloppy work and misbehavior. One graduate of a scribal school had few fond memories of the joy of learning. He described a typical day:

*My headmaster read my tablet, said:*
*"There is something missing," caned me.*
. . . . . . . . . . . . . . . . . .
*The fellow in charge of silence said:*
*"Why did you talk without permission," caned me.*
*The fellow in charge of the assembly said:*
*"Why did you stand at ease without permission,"*
*caned me.*[8]

The boy was so lax at his work that he was expelled. Only when his father wined and dined the headmaster was he allowed to return to school.

The Sumerian system of schooling set the educational standards of Mesopotamian culture, and the Akkadians and Babylonians adopted its practices and techniques. Students began by learning how to prepare clay tablets and make signs. They studied grammar and word lists, and they solved simple mathematical problems. Mesopotamian education always had a practical side, because of the economic and administrative importance of scribes. Most scribes took administrative positions in the temple or palace, where they kept records of business transactions, accounts, and inventories. But scribal schools did not limit their curriculum to business affairs. They were also centers of culture and learning. Topics of study included mathematics, botany, and linguistics. Advanced students copied and studied the classics of Mesopotamian literature. Talented students and learned scribes wrote compositions of their own. As a result of this work many literary, mathematical, and religious texts survive today, giving a surprisingly full picture of Mesopotamian intellectual and spiritual life.

## MESOPOTAMIAN THOUGHT AND RELIGION

The Mesopotamians made significant and sophisticated advances in mathematics, using a numerical system based on units of sixty. For practical purposes they also used factors of ten and six. They developed the concept of place value — that the value of a number depends on where it stands in relation to other numbers. Mesopotamian mathematical texts are of two kinds: tables and problems. Scribes compiled tables of squares and square roots,

cubes and cube roots, and reciprocals. They wrote texts of problems, which dealt not only with equations and pure mathematics but also with concrete problems, such as how to plan irrigation ditches. The Mesopotamians did not consider mathematics a purely theoretical science. The building of cities, palaces, temples, and canals demanded knowledge of geometry and trigonometry. The Mesopotamians solved the practical problems involved, but they did not turn their knowledge into theories. In this respect, they were quite different from the Greeks, who enjoyed theorizing.

Mesopotamian medicine was a combination of magic, prescriptions, and surgery. Mesopotamians believed that demons and evil spirits caused sickness and that incantations and magic spells could drive them out. Or, they believed, the physician could force the demon out by giving the patient a foul-tasting prescription. As medical knowledge grew, some prescriptions were found to work and thus were true medicines. The physician relied heavily on plants, animals, and minerals for his recipes, and he often mixed them with beer to cover their unpleasant taste. Surgeons practiced a dangerous occupation, and the penalties for failure were severe. One section of Hammurabi's law code decreed: "If a physician performed a major operation on a seignior with a bronze lancet and has caused the seignior's death, or he opened up the eye-socket of a seignior and has destroyed the seignior's eye, they shall cut off his hand."[9] No wonder that one medical text warned physicians to have nothing to do with a dying person.

Mesopotamian thought had its profoundest impact in theology and religion. The Sumerians originated many beliefs, and the Akkadians and Babylonians added to them. The American journalist H. L. Mencken once sug-

gested that "the theory that the universe is run by a single God must be abandoned and . . . in place of it we must set up the theory that it is actually ruled by a board of gods all of equal puissance and authority."[10] The Mesopotamians would have agreed that many gods run the world, but they did not consider all gods and goddesses equal to one another. Some deities had very important jobs, such as taking care of music, law, sex, and victory, while others had lesser tasks, such as overseeing leatherworking and basketweaving. The god in charge of metalworking was hardly the equal of the god of wisdom.

Divine society was a hierarchy. According to the Sumerians the air-god Enlil was the king of the gods, and he laid down the rules by which the universe was to be run. Enki, the god of wisdom, put Enlil's plans into effect. The Babylonians believed that the gods elected Marduk as their king, after which he assigned the lesser gods various duties to perform. Once the gods received their tasks, they carried them out forever.

Mesopotamian gods lived their lives much as human beings lived theirs. The gods were anthropomorphic, or human in form. Unlike men and women, they were powerful and immortal and could make themselves invisible. Otherwise, Mesopotamian gods and goddesses were very human: they celebrated with food and drink, and they raised families. They enjoyed their own "Garden of Eden," a green and fertile place. They could be irritable, and they were not always holy. Even Enlil was punished by other gods because he had once raped the goddess Ninlil.

The Mesopotamians had many myths and epics to account for the creation of the universe. According to one Sumerian myth, only the primeval sea existed at first. Genesis, the first book of the Old Testament, says precisely the same thing. The sea produced heaven and

earth, which were united. Heaven and earth gave birth to Enlil, who separated them and made possible the creation of the other gods.

Babylonian beliefs were similar. In the beginning was the primeval sea, the goddess Tiamat, who gave birth to the gods. When Tiamat tried to destroy the gods, Marduk killed her and divided her body:

*He split her like a shellfish into two parts:*
*Half of her he set up and ceiled as sky,*
*Pulled down the bar and posted guards.*
*He bade them not to let her waters escape.*[11]

These myths are the earliest known attempts to answer the question "how did it all begin?" The Mesopotamians obviously thought about these matters, as about the gods, in human terms. They never organized their beliefs into a philosophy, but their myths offered understandable explanations of natural phenomena. They were emotionally satisfying, and that was their greatest appeal.

Mesopotamian myths also explained the origin of human beings. In one myth the gods decided to make their lives easier by creating servants, whom they wanted made in their own image. Nammu, the goddess of the watery deep, brought the matter to Enki. After some thought, Enki instructed Nammu and the others:

*Mix the heart of the clay that is over the abyss.*
*The good and princely fashioners will thicken the*
*   clay.*
*You, do you bring the limbs into existence.*[12]

In Mesopotamian myth, as in Genesis, men and women were made in the divine image. However, human beings lacked godlike powers. The myth "The Creation of the Pickax" gives an excellent idea of their insignificance. According to this myth, Enlil drove his pickax into the ground, and out of the hole crawled the Sumerians, the first people.

As Enlil stood looking at them, some of his fellow gods approached him. They were so pleased with Enlil's work that they asked him to give them some people to serve them. Consequently, the Mesopotamians believed it their duty to supply the gods with sacrifices of food and drink and to house them in fine temples. In return, they hoped that the gods would be kind.

These ideas about the creation of the universe and of human beings are part of the Mesopotamian legacy to Western civilization. They spread throughout the ancient Near East and found a home among the Hebrews, who adopted much of Mesopotamian religious thought and made it part of their own beliefs. Biblical parallels to Mesopotamian literary and religious themes are many. Such stories as the creation of Adam, the Deluge, the Garden of Eden, and the tale of Job can be traced back to Mesopotamian originals. Through the Bible, Mesopotamian as well as Jewish religious concepts influenced Christianity and Islam. Thus these first attempts by women and men to understand themselves and their world are still alive today.

## DAILY LIFE IN MESOPOTAMIA

The law code of King Hammurabi offers a wealth of information about daily life in Mesopotamia. Hammurabi issued his code to "establish law and justice in the language of the land, thereby promoting the welfare of the people." His code may seem harsh, but it was no more harsh than the Mosaic law of the Hebrews, which it heavily influenced. Hammurabi's code inflicted such penalties as mutilation, whipping, and burning. Today in parts of the Islamic world these punishments are still in use. Despite its severity, a spirit of justice and a sense of responsibility pervade the code. Hammurabi genuinely felt that his

*LAW CODE OF HAMMURABI Hammurabi ordered his code to be inscribed on a stone pillar and set up in public. At the top of the pillar Hammurabi is depicted receiving the scepter of authority from the god Shamash. (Clichés des Musées Nationaux, Paris)*

duty was to govern the Mesopotamians as righteously as possible. He tried to regulate the relations of his people so that they could live together in harmony.

Hammurabi's code has two striking characteristics. First, the law differed according to the social status of the offender. Aristocrats were not punished as harshly as commoners, nor commoners as harshly as slaves. Even slaves had rights, however, and received some protection under the law. Second, the code demanded that the punishment fit the crime. Like the Mosaic law of the Hebrews, it called for "an eye for an eye, and a tooth for a tooth," at least among equals. However, an aristocrat who destroyed the eye of a commoner or slave could pay a fine instead of los-

ing his own eye. Otherwise, as long as the criminal and the victim shared the same social status, the victim could demand exact vengeance for his injury.

Hammurabi's code began with legal procedure. There were no public prosecutors or district attorneys, so individuals brought their own complaints before the court. Each side had to produce written documents or witnesses to support its case. In cases of murder, the accuser had to prove the defendant guilty: any accuser who failed to do so was put to death. This strict law was designed to prevent people from lodging groundless charges. The Mesopotamians were very worried about witchcraft and sorcery. Anyone accused of witchcraft, even if the charges were not proved, underwent an ordeal by water. The gods themselves would decide the case. The defendant was thrown into the Euphrates, which was considered the instrument of the gods. A defendant who sank was guilty; a defendant who floated was innocent. (In medieval Europe and colonial America accused witches also underwent ordeals by water, but they were considered innocent only if they sank.) Another procedural regulation covered the conduct of judges. Once a judge had rendered a verdict, he could not change it. Any judge who did so was fined heavily and deposed from his position. In short, the code tried to guarantee a fair trial and a just verdict.

Hammurabi expected his officials to do their duty and to protect his subjects. Governors and city officials were required to wipe out crime, and they paid personally for their failures to protect the innocent. If a person was robbed and the robber was not caught, the officials had to repay the victim. This law encouraged officials to keep order. Soldiers either carried out the king's commands or faced dire consequences. Any officer or private who tried to shirk his duty by hiring a substitute was put to death, as was any officer who illegally forced men to serve in the army. The law protected soldiers from abuse by their officers. Any officer who wronged a soldier or stole his property was put to death.

Consumer protection is not a modern idea; it goes back to Hammurabi's day. Merchants and businessmen had to guarantee the quality of their goods and services. A boatbuilder who did sloppy work had to repair the boat at his own expense. A boatman who lost the owner's boat or sank someone else's boat replaced it and its cargo. Housebuilders guaranteed their work with their lives. Careless work could result in the collapse of a house and the death of its inhabitants. If that happened, the builder himself was put to death. A merchant who tried to increase the interest rate on a loan forfeited the entire amount. A farmer who hired an overseer to cultivate his land had the right to order an incompetent overseer to be dragged through the fields. Hammurabi's laws tried to ensure that consumers got what they paid for and paid a just price.

Crime was a feature of Mesopotamian urban life just as it is in modern cities. Burglary was a serious problem, hard to control. Because houses were built of mud-brick, it was easy for an intruder to dig through the walls. Hammurabi's punishment for burglary matched the crime. A burglar caught in the act was put to death on the spot, and his body was walled into the breach he had made. The penalty for looting was also grim: anyone caught looting a burning house was thrown into the fire.

Mesopotamian cities had breeding places of crime. Taverns were notorious for being the haunts of criminals, especially since they often met at taverns to make their plans. Tavernkeepers were expected to keep order and arrest anyone overheard planning a crime.

Taverns were normally run by women, and they also served as houses of prostitution. Prostitution was disreputable but not illegal, and the law did not regulate it. Despite their social stigma, taverns were popular places, for Mesopotamians were fond of beer and wine. Tavernkeepers made a nice profit, but if they were caught increasing their profits by watering drinks, they were drowned.

The aim of all these statutes was to punish the criminal. Exact retribution gave the victim or the victim's family legal satisfaction and was intended to end the matter. To some degree the code protected society by eliminating people who had committed serious crimes. Beyond that it did not go.

Because farming was essential to Mesopotamian life, Hammurabi's code dealt extensively with agriculture. Tenant farming was widespread, and tenants rented land on a yearly basis. Instead of money they paid a proportion of their crops as rent. Unless the land was carefully cultivated, it quickly reverted to wasteland. Therefore tenants faced severe penalties for neglecting the land or not working it at all. Since irrigation was essential to grow crops, tenants had to keep the canals and ditches in good repair. Otherwise, the land would be subject to floods and farmers to crippling losses. Anyone whose neglect of the canals resulted in damaged crops had to bear all the expense of the lost crops. If the tenant could not pay the costs, he was sold into slavery.

The oxen farmers used for plowing and threshing grain were ordinarily allowed to roam the streets. If an ox gored a passer-by, its owner had to pad its horns, tie it up, or else bear the responsibility for future damages. Sheep raising was very lucrative because textile production was a major Mesopotamian industry. (Mesopotamian cloth was famous throughout the Near East.) The shepherd was a hired man with considerable responsibility. He was expected to protect the flock from wild animals, which were a standing problem, and to keep the sheep out of the crops. Since date palms were the only source of wood in Mesopotamia, wanton destruction of trees was a serious offense. This strict regulation of agriculture paid rich dividends. The Mesopotamians often enjoyed bumper crops, which fostered a large and thriving population.

Hammurabi gave careful attention to marriage and the family. As elsewhere in the Near East, marriage had aspects of a business agreement. The prospective groom and the father of the future bride arranged everything. The man offered the father a bridal gift, usually a sum of money. If the man and his bridal gift were acceptable, the father provided his daughter with a dowry. After marriage the dowry belonged to the woman (although the husband normally administered it) and was a means of protecting her rights and status. Once the two men agreed upon financial matters, they drew up a contract; no marriage was considered legal without one. Either party could break off the marriage, but not without paying a stiff penalty. Fathers often contracted marriages while their children were still young. The girl either continued to live in her father's house until she reached maturity or she went to live in the house of her father-in-law. During this time she was legally considered a wife. Once she and her husband became of age, they set up their own house.

The wife was expected to be rigorously faithful. The penalty for adultery was death. According to Hammurabi's code: "If the wife of a man has been caught while lying with another man, they shall bind them and throw them into the water."[13] The husband had the power to spare his wife by obtaining a pardon for her from the king. He could, however, ac-cuse his wife of adultery even if he had not caught her in the act. In such a case she could try to clear herself before the city council, which investigated. If she was found innocent, she could take her dowry and leave her husband. If a woman decided to take the direct approach and kill her husband, she was impaled.

The husband had virtually absolute power over his household. Like the later Roman *paterfamilias* (Chapter 5), he could even sell his wife and children into slavery to pay his debts. Sons did not lightly oppose their fathers, and any son who struck his father could have his hand cut off. A father was free to adopt children and include them in his will. Artisans sometimes adopted children to teach them the family trade. Although the father's power was great, he could not disinherit a son without just cause. Cases of disinheritance became matters for the city to decide, and the code ordered the courts to forgive a son for his first offense. Only if a son wronged his father a second time could he be disinherited.

Law codes are preoccupied with the problems of society, and provide a bleak view of things. Other Mesopotamian documents give a happier glimpse of life. Although Hammurabi's code dealt with marriage shekel by shekel, a Mesopotamian poem tells of two people meeting secretly in the city. Their parting is delightfully modern:

*Come now, set me free, I must go home,*
*Kuli-Enlil . . . set me free, I must go home.*
*What can I say to deceive my mother?*[14]

Countless wills and testaments show that husbands habitually left their estates to their wives, who in turn willed the property to their children. All this suggests happy family life. Hammurabi's code restricted married women from commercial pursuits, but financial documents prove that many women engaged in business without hindrance. Some carried on the family business, while others became wealthy landowners in their own right. Mesopotamians found their lives lightened by holidays and religious festivals. Traveling merchants brought news of the outside world, and swapped marvelous tales. Despite their pessimism, the Mesopotamians enjoyed a vibrant and creative culture, a culture that left its mark on the entire Near East.

## EGYPT, THE LAND OF THE PHARAOHS (3100–1200 B.C.)

The Greek historian and traveler Herodotus in the fifth century B.C. called Egypt the gift of the Nile River. No other single geographical factor had such a fundamental and profound impact on the shaping of Egyptian life, society, and history as the Nile. Unlike the rivers of Mesopotamia it rarely brought death and destruction. Its waters, even in flood times, seem almost tame when compared to the rampaging Tigris. The river was primarily a creative force. The Egyptians never feared the Nile in the way the Mesopotamians feared their rivers. Instead, they sang its praises:

*Hail to thee, O Nile, that issues from the earth*
*    and comes to keep Egypt alive! . . .*
*He that waters the meadows which Re created,*
*He that makes to drink the desert . . .*
*He who makes barley and brings emmer [wheat]*
*    into being . . .*
*He who brings grass into being for the cattle . . .*
*He who makes every beloved tree to grow . . .*
*O Nile, verdant art thou, who makest man and*
*    cattle to live.*[15]

In the mind of the Egyptians the Nile was the supreme fertilizer and renewer of the land. Each September the Nile floods its valley,

transforming it into a huge area of marsh or lagoon. By the end of November the water retreats, leaving behind a thin covering of fertile mud ready to be planted with crops.

The annual flood made the growing of abundant crops almost effortless, especially in southern Egypt. Herodotus, who was used to the rigors of Greek agriculture, was amazed by the ease with which the Egyptians raised their crops:

*For indeed without trouble they obtain crops from the land more easily than all other men. . . . They do not labor to dig furrows with the plough or hoe or do the work which other men do to raise grain. But when the river by itself inundates the fields and the water recedes, then each man, having sown his field, sends pigs into it. When the pigs trample down the seed, he waits for the harvest. Then when the pigs thresh the grain, he gets his crop.*[16]

As late as 1822, John Burckhardt, an English traveler, watched nomads sowing grain by digging large holes in the mud and throwing in seeds. The extraordinary fertility of the Nile valley made it easy to produce an annual agricultural surplus, which in turn sustained a growing and prosperous population.

Whereas the Tigris and Euphrates and their many tributaries carved up Mesopotamia into isolated areas, the Nile served to unify Egypt. The river was the principal highway, and promoted easy communication throughout the valley. As individual bands of settlers moved into the Nile valley, they created stable agricultural communities. By about 3100 B.C., there were some forty of these communities, which were in constant contact with one another. This contact, encouraged and facilitated by the Nile, virtually assured the early political unification of the country.

Egypt was fortunate in that it was nearly self-sufficient. Besides the fertility of its soil, Egypt possessed enormous quantities of stone,

## PERIODS OF EGYPTIAN HISTORY

| PERIOD | DATES | SIGNIFICANT EVENTS |
|--------|-------|--------------------|
| Archaic | 3100–2660 B.C. | Unification of Egypt |
| Old Kingdom | 2660–2180 B.C. | Construction of the pyramids |
| First Intermediate | 2180–2080 B.C. | Political chaos |
| Middle Kingdom | 2080–1640 B.C. | Recovery and political stability |
| Second Intermediate | 1640–1570 B.C. | Hyksos "invasion" |
| New Kingdom | 1570–1075 B.C. | Creation of an Egyptian empire |
| | | Akhenaten's religious policy |

which served as the raw material of architecture and sculpture. Abundant clay was available for pottery, as was gold for jewelry and ornaments. The raw materials that Egypt lacked were close at hand. The Egyptians could obtain copper from Sinai and timber from Lebanon. They had little cause to look to the outside world for their essential needs, which helps to explain the insular quality of Egyptian life.

Geography further encouraged isolation by closing Egypt off from the outside world. To the east and west of the Nile valley stretch grim deserts. The Nubian Desert and the cataracts of the Nile discourage penetration from the south. Only in the north did the Mediterranean Sea leave Egypt exposed. Thus geography shielded Egypt from invasion and from extensive immigration. Unlike the Mesopotamians, the Egyptians enjoyed centuries of peace and tranquillity, during which they could devote most of their resources to peaceful development of their distinctive civilization.

Yet Egypt was not completely sealed off. As early as 3250 B.C. Mesopotamian influences,

notably architectural techniques and materials and perhaps even writing, made themselves felt in Egyptian life. Still later, from 1680 to 1580 B.C., northern Egypt was ruled by foreign invaders, the Hyksos. Infrequent though they were, such periods of foreign influence fertilized Egyptian culture without changing it in any fundamental way.

### THE GOD-KING OF EGYPT

The geographic unity of Egypt quickly gave rise to political unification of the country under the authority of a king, whom the Egyptians called pharaoh. The details of this process have been lost, though some archaeologists recently made a startling suggestion. Tomb finds from the ancient region of Nubia, in modern Sudan, indicate that monarchy may have developed there earlier than in Egypt. If so, Egyptians may have developed the concept of kingship from their neighbors to the south.

The Egyptians themselves told of a great king, Menes, who united Egypt into a single kingdom around 3100 B.C. Thereafter the

Egyptians divided their history into dynasties, or families of kings. For modern historical purposes, however, it is more useful to divide Egyptian history into periods. The political unification of Egypt ushered in the period known as the Old Kingdom, an era remarkable for its prosperity and artistic flowering, and for the evolution of religious beliefs.

In the realm of religion, the Egyptians developed complex and often contradictory ideas about an afterlife. These beliefs were all rooted in the environment of Egypt itself. The climate of Egypt is so stable that change is cyclical and dependable: though the heat of summer bakes the land, the Nile always floods and replenishes it. The dry air preserves much that would decay in other climates. Thus there was an air of permanence about Egypt; the old lived on and became part of the present.

This cyclical rhythm permeated Egyptian religious beliefs. According to the Egyptians, the god Osiris, a fertility god associated with the Nile, dies each year, and each year his wife Isis brings him back to life. Osiris eventually became king of the dead, a god who weighed the hearts of human beings to determine whether they had lived justly enough to deserve everlasting life. Osiris's care for the dead was shared by Anubis, the jackal-headed god who annually helped Isis resuscitate Osiris. Anubis was the god of mummification, which was essential to Egyptian funerary rites.

The focal point of religious and political life in the Old Kingdom was the pharaoh, who commanded the wealth, resources, and the people of all Egypt. The pharaoh's power was such that the Egyptians considered him to be the falcon-god Horus in human form. He was a guarantee to his people, a pledge that the gods of Egypt (strikingly unlike those of Mesopotamia) cared for their people. The king's surroundings had to be worthy of

THE PYRAMIDS AT GIZA   *Giza was the burial place of the pharaohs of the Old Kingdom and of their aristocracy, whose rectangular tombs are visible behind the middle pyramid. The small pyramids at the foot of the foremost pyramid probably belong to the pharaoh's wives. (Courtesy, Museum of Fine Arts, Boston)*

a god. Only a magnificent palace was suitable for his home; in fact, the very word *pharaoh* means "great house." The king's tomb also had to reflect his might and exalted status. To this day the great pyramids at Giza near Cairo bear silent but magnificent testimony to the god-kings of Egypt. The pharaoh's ability to command the resources and labor necessary to build a huge pyramid amply demonstrates that the god-king was an absolute ruler.

The religious significance of the pyramid is as awesome as the political. The pharaoh as a god was the earthly sun, and the pyramid, which towered to the sky, helped him ascend

*EGYPTIAN FARM WORK   This tomb depicts the cycle of the agricultural year from ploughing to reaping. (Metropolitan Museum of Art, New York)*

the heavens after death. The pyramid provided the dead king with everything that he would need in the afterlife. His body had to be preserved from decay if his *ka,* an invisible counterpart of the body, was to live on. So the Egyptians developed an elaborate process of embalming the dead pharaoh and wrapping his corpse in cloth. As an added precaution, they carved a statue of the pharaoh out of hard stone; if anything happened to the fragile mummy, the pharaoh's statue would help keep his ka alive. The need for an authentic likeness accounts for the naturalism of Egyptian portraiture. Artistic renderings of the pharaohs combine accuracy and the abstract in the effort to capture the essence of the living person. This approach produced that haunting quality of Egyptian sculpture – portraits of lifelike people imbued with a solemn, ageless, and serene spirit.

To survive in the spirit world the ka needed everything that the pharaoh needed in life: food and drink, servants and armed retainers, costly ornaments, and herds of animals. In Egypt's prehistoric period, the king's servants and herdsmen and their flocks were slaughtered at the tomb to provide for the ka. By the time of the Old Kingdom, artists had substituted statues of scribes, officials, soldiers, and servants for their living counterparts. To remind the ka of daily life, artists covered the walls of the tomb with scenes of ordinary life, ranging from agricultural routines to banquets and religious festivities, from hunting parties to gardens and ponds. Designed to give joy to the ka, these paintings, models of furniture, and statuettes today provide an intimate glimpse of Egyptian life 4,500 years ago.

The humor and vivacity of Egyptian tomb paintings are striking, especially when they depict everyday scenes. The scene above, which dates only to about 1300 B.C. is remarkable chiefly because it is typical. This tomb painting shows an Egyptian couple at work in the fields. In the top band the couple reap wheat, while in the second band they harvest flax. To the right in the second band the couple is seen ploughing for the next year's crop. In the bottom two bands are an orchard of date palms and a garden filled with flowers and herbs. The wavy bands represent irrigation canals. The simple agricultural implements include a metal sickle and a light plough drawn by two oxen. Unfortunately, however, research published in 1982 suggests that many Egyptian farmers suffered from various parasites that thrived in the warm, stagnant water of the irrigation canals. Nonetheless, tomb scenes like this one preferred warmth to harsh realities. Other sources of information give a gloomier view of daily life.

## THE PHARAOH'S PEOPLE

Because the common folk stood at the bottom of the social and economic scale, they were always at the mercy of grasping officials. The arrival of the tax collector was never a happy occasion. One Egyptian scribe described the worst that could happen:

*And now the scribe lands on the river-bank and is about to register the harvest-tax. The janitors carry staves and the Nubians rods of palm, and they say, Hand over the corn, though there is none. The cultivator is beaten all over, he is bound and thrown into a well, soused and dipped head downwards. His wife has been bound in his presence and his children are in fetters.*[17]

That was an extreme situation. Nonetheless, taxes might amount to 20 percent of the harvest, and the collection of taxes could often be brutal.

On the other hand, everyone, no matter how lowly, had the right of appeal, and the account of one such appeal, "The Tale of the Eloquent Peasant," was a favorite Egyptian story. The hero of the tale, Khunanup, was robbed by the servant of the high steward, and Khunanup had to bring his case before the steward himself. When the steward delayed his decision, Khunanup openly accused him of neglecting his duty, saying, "The arbitrator is a spoiler; the peace-maker is a creator of sorrow; the smoother over of differences is a creator of soreness."[18] The pharaoh himself ordered the steward to give Khunanup justice, and the case was decided in the peasant's favor.

Egyptian society seems to have been a curious mixture of freedom and constraint. Slavery did not become widespread until the New Kingdom. There was neither a caste system nor a color bar, and humble people could rise to the highest positions if they possessed talent. The most famous example of social mobility (which, however, dates to the New Kingdom) is the biblical story of Joseph, who came to Egypt as a slave and rose to be second only to the pharaoh. On the other hand, most ordinary folk were probably little more than serfs, who could not easily leave the land of their own free will. Peasants were also subject to forced labor, just as they were in early modern France, and this labor included work on the pyramids and canals. Young men were drafted into the pharaoh's army, which served both as a fighting force and as a labor corps.

The vision of thousands of people straining to build the pyramids and countless artists adorning the pharaoh's tomb brings to the modern mind a distasteful picture of oriental despotism. Yet H. Frankfort, one of the most perceptive historians of ancient Egypt, has treated the matter in a purely Egyptian context:

*Nothing would be more misleading than to picture the Egyptians in abject submission to their absolute ruler. . . . Their polity was not imposed but evolved from immemorial predilections and was adhered to, without protest, for almost three thousand years. . . . If a god had consented to guide the nation, society held a pledge that the unaccountable forces of nature would be well disposed and bring prosperity and peace. . . . Truth, justice, were "that by which the gods live," an essential element in the established order. Hence, Pharaoh's rule was not tyranny, or his service slavery.[19]*

The Egyptian view of life and society is alien to those raised on the Western concepts of individual freedom and human rights. To the ancient Egyptians the pharaoh embodied justice and order — harmony among men and women, nature, and the divine. If the pharaoh was weak, or if he allowed anyone to challenge his unique position, he opened the way to chaos. Twice in Egyptian history the pharaoh failed to maintain rigid centralization. During those two eras, known as the First and Second Intermediate periods, Egypt was exposed to civil war and invasion. Yet even in the darkest times the monarchy survived, and in each period a strong pharaoh arose to crush the rebels or expel the invaders and restore order.

## THE HYKSOS IN EGYPT (1640–1570 B.C.)

While Egyptian civilization flourished behind its bulwark of sand and sea, momentous changes were taking place in the ancient Near East, changes that would leave their mark even on rich and insular Egypt. These changes involved enormous and remarkable movements of peoples, especially peoples who spoke Semitic languages.

The original home of the Semites was probably the Arabian peninsula. Some tribes

moved into northern Mesopotamia, others into Syria and Palestine, and still others into Egypt. Shortly after 1800 B.C., people whom the Egyptians called Hyksos, which means "Rulers of the Uplands," began to settle in the Delta. Egyptian tradition, as later recorded by the priest Manetho in the third century B.C., depicted the coming of the Hyksos as a brutal invasion:

*In the reign of Toutimaios — I do not know why — the wind of god blew against us. Unexpectedly from the regions of the east men of obscure race, looking forward confidently to victory, invaded our land, and without a battle easily seized it all by sheer force. Having subdued those in authority in the land, they then barbarously burned our cities and razed to the ground the temples of the gods. They fell upon all the natives in an entirely hateful fashion, slaughtering them and leading both their children and wives into slavery. At last they made one of their people king, whose name was Salitis. This man resided at Memphis, leaving in Upper and Lower Egypt tax collectors and garrisons in strategic places.[20]*

Although the Egyptians portrayed the Hyksos as a conquering horde, they were probably no more than nomads looking for good land. Their entry into the delta was probably gradual and generally peaceful, much like that of the Hebrews, who did not arrive until around 1500 B.C. Indeed, the Hebrews are typical of the Semitic movement. They were a pastoral people, organized in large tribes whose chiefs and patriarchs directed the life of the community.

The Hyksos "invasion" was one of the fertilizing periods of Egyptian history; it introduced new ideas and techniques into Egyptian life. The Hyksos brought with them the method of making bronze and casting it into tools and weapons. They thereby brought Egypt fully into the Bronze Age culture of the

Mediterranean world, a culture in which the production and use of bronze implements became basic to society. Bronze tools made farming more efficient than ever before because they were sharper and more durable than the copper tools they replaced. The Hyksos' use of bronze armor and weapons as well as horse-drawn chariots and the composite bow, made of laminated wood and horn and far more powerful than the simple wooden bow, revolutionized Egyptian warfare. However much the Egyptians learned from the Hyksos, Egyptian culture eventually absorbed the newcomers. The Hyksos came to worship Egyptian gods and modelled their monarchy on the pharaoh's.

## THE NEW KINGDOM: REVIVAL AND EMPIRE (1570-1200 B.C.)

Politically, Egypt was only in eclipse. The Egyptian sun shone again when a remarkable line of kings, the pharaohs of the Eighteenth Dynasty, arose to challenge the Hyksos. The pharaoh Ahmose (1558-1533 B.C.) pushed the Hyksos out of the Delta. Thutmose I (1512-1500 B.C.) subdued Nubia in the south, and Thutmose III (1490-1436 B.C.) conquered Palestine and Syria and fought inconclusively with the Hurrians' new kingdom of Mitanni on the upper Euphrates. These warrior-pharaohs inaugurated the New Kingdom – a period in Egyptian history characterized by enormous wealth and conscious imperialism. During this period, probably for the first time, widespread slavery became a feature of Egyptian life. The pharaoh's armies returned home leading hordes of slaves, who constituted a new labor force for imperial building projects. The Jews, who according to the Old Testament migrated into Egypt during this period to escape a drought, were soon en-slaved and put to work on imperial construction projects.

The kings of the Eighteenth Dynasty created the first Egyptian empire. They ruled Palestine and Syria through their officers, and they incorporated the African region of Nubia. Egyptian religion and customs flourished in Nubia, making a huge impact on African culture there and in neighboring areas. These warrior-kings celebrated their success with monuments on a scale unparalleled since the pharaohs of the Old Kingdom had built the pyramids. Even today the colossal granite statues of these pharaohs and the rich tomb objects of Tutankhamen ("King Tut") testify to the might, wealth, and splendor of the New Kingdom.

## AKHENATEN AND MONOTHEISM

One of the most extraordinary of this unusual line of kings was Akhenaten (1367-1350 B.C.), a pharaoh more concerned with religion than conquest. Nefertiti, his wife and queen, encouraged his religious bent. Akhenaten and Nefertiti were monotheists: that is, they believed that the sun-god Aton, whom they worshiped, was universal, the only god. They considered all other Egyptian gods and goddesses frauds, and forbade their worship.

The religious notions and actions of Akhenaten and Nefertiti were in direct opposition to traditional Egyptian beliefs. The Egyptians had long worshiped a host of gods, chief among whom was Amon-Re. Originally Amon and Re had been two distinct sun-gods, but the Egyptians merged them and worshiped Amon-Re as the king of the gods. Besides Amon-Re, the Egyptians honored such other deities as Osiris, Osiris's wife Isis, and his son Horus. Indeed, Egyptian religion had room for many gods and an easy tolerance for new gods.

THE TOMB OF "KING TUT" *The pharaoh Tu-tankhamun was buried in three coffins, one inside the other. Shown here is the removal of the second coffin from the other coffin. The innermost coffin was made of gold. (The Metropolitan Museum of Art. Photograph by Harry Burton)*

THE PHARAOH'S COFFIN *This magnificent coffin from the tomb of "King Tut" depicts the pharaoh in all of his glory. Crossed over his chest are a crook and a flail, which were the emblems of the god Osiris. Richly engraved on the coffin are figures representing both Lower and Upper Egypt. (Metropolitan Museum of Art, New York)*

Herodotus once remarked that the Egyptians "are excessively religious, more so than other men." Akhenaten's attack on the old gods threatened all Egyptians, for the old gods were crucial to the afterlife. Naturally, then, many Egyptians viewed Akhenaten's attack on Osiris, Isis, Anubis, and other gods as a threat to their own chances for immortality. Others were sincerely devoted to the old gods for different reasons. After all, had not Amon-Re driven out the Hyksos and brought Egypt a new era of happiness? To these genuine religious sentiments were added the motives of the traditional priesthood. Although many priests were genuinely scandalized by Akhenaten's monotheism, many others were more concerned about their own welfare. What were the priests of the outlawed gods to do? Akhenaten had destroyed their livelihood and their reason for existence. On grounds of pure self-interest, the established priesthood opposed Akhenaten. Opposition in turn drove the pharaoh to intolerance and persecution. With a vengeance he tried to root out the old gods and their rituals.

Akhenaten celebrated his break with the past by building a new capital, Akhetaten, the modern El-Amarna. There Aton was honored with an immense temple and proper worship. Worship of Aton focused on "truth" (as Akhenaten defined it) and a desire for the natural. The pharaoh and his queen demanded that the "truth" be carried over into art. Unlike Old Kingdom painting and sculpture, which blended the actual and the abstract, the art of this period became relentlessly realistic. Sculptors molded exact likenesses of Akhenaten, despite his ugly features and misshapen body. Artists portrayed the pharaoh in intimate family scenes, playing with his infant daughter or expressing affection to members of his family. On one relief Akhenaten appears gnawing a cutlet of meat, while on another he lolls in a chair. Akhenaten was being portrayed as a mortal man, not as the dignified pharaoh of Egypt.

Akhenaten's monotheism was imposed from above, and failed to find a place among the people. The prime reason for Akhenaten's failure is that his god had no connection with the past of the Egyptian people, who trusted the old gods and felt comfortable praying to them. Average Egyptians were no doubt distressed and disheartened when their familiar gods were outlawed, for they were the heavenly powers that had made Egypt powerful and unique. The fanaticism and persecution that accompanied the new monotheism were in complete defiance of the Egyptian tradition of tolerant polytheism, or worship of several gods. Thus, when Akhenaten died, his religion died with him.

## THE HITTITE EMPIRE

At about the time of the Hyksos entry into the Nile Delta, other parts of the Near East were also troubled by the arrival of newcomers. Two new groups of peoples, the Hurrians and Kassites, carved out kingdoms for themselves. Meanwhile the Hittites, who had long been settled in Anatolia (modern Turkey), became a major power in that region and began to expand eastward. Around 1595 B.C., a century and a half after Hammurabi's death, the Hittites and the Kassites brought down the Babylonian kingdom and established Kassite rule there. The Hurrians created the kingdom of Mitanni on the upper reaches of the Euphrates and Tigris.

The Hittites were an Indo-European people. The term *Indo-European* refers to a large family of languages that includes English, most of the languages of modern Europe,

MAP 1.2 BALANCE OF POWER IN THE NEAR EAST *This map shows the areas controlled by the Hittites and Egyptians at the height of their power.*

Greek, Latin, Persian, and Sanskrit, the sacred tongue of ancient India. During the eighteenth and nineteenth centuries, European scholars learned that peoples who spoke related languages had spread as far west as Ireland and as far east as central Asia. In the twentieth century, linguists deciphered the language of the Hittites, and the Linear B script of Mycenaean Greece. When both languages proved to be Indo-European, scholars were able to form a clearer picture of these vast movements. Archaeologists were able to date them roughly and put them into their historical context.

The original home of the Indo-Europeans remains to be identified. Judging primarily from the spread of the languages, linguists

have suggested that the migrations started from central Europe. Although two great waves began around 2000 B.C. and 1200 B.C., these migrations were typically sporadic and gradual. For instance, the Celtic-speaking Gauls did not move into modern France, Belgium, and Germany until the seventh century B.C., long after most Indo-Europeans had found new homes.

Around 2000 B.C., however, Indo-Europeans were on the move on a massive scale. Peoples speaking the ancestor of Latin pushed into Italy, and Greek-speaking Mycenaeans settled in Greece. The Hittites came into prominence in Anatolia, and other folk thrust into Iran, India, and central Asia. At first the waves of Indo-Europeans and others disrupted existing states, but in time the newcomers settled down.

## THE RISE OF THE HITTITES

Until recently, scholars thought that as part of these vast movements the Hittites entered Anatolia only around 1800 B.C. Current archaeological work and new documents, however, prove that Hittites had settled there at least as early as 2700 B.C. Nor did they overrun the country in a sweeping invasion, burning, looting, and destroying as they advanced. Their arrival and diffusion seems in fact to have been rather peaceful, accompanied by intermarriage and alliance with the native population. So well did the Hittites integrate themselves into the local culture of central Anatolia that they even adopted the worship of several native deities.

Although much uncertainty still surrounds the earliest history of the Hittites, their rise to prominence in Anatolia is quite well documented. During the nineteenth century B.C. the native kingdoms in the area engaged in suicidal warfare that left most of Anatolia's once-flourishing towns in ashes and rubble. In this climate of exhaustion the Hittite king Hattusilis I built a hill citadel at Hattusas, the modern Boghazköy, from which he led his Hittites against neighboring kingdoms. Hittite tradition recorded Hattusilis' achievements:

*And on whatever campaign he went, he also by his strength kept the hostile country in subjection. And he kept devastating countries, and he made the countries tremble; and he made them boundaries of the sea.*[21]

Hattusilis' grandson and successor Mursilis I extended the Hittite arms as far as Babylon. With help from the Kassites, Mursilis captured the city and snuffed out the dynasty of Hammurabi. While the Hittites carried off Babylonian loot, the Kassites took control of the territory. Upon his return home, the victorious Mursilis was assassinated by members of his own family, plunging the kingdom into confusion and opening the door to foreign invasion. The Hittites quickly lost substantial tracts of land in the east and south, and Hattusas itself prepared for attack. Mursilis' career is representative of the success and weakness of the Hittites. They were extremely vulnerable to attack by vigilant and tenacious enemies. Yet once united behind a strong king, they were a power to be reckoned with.

## HITTITE SOCIETY

The geography of central Anatolia encouraged the rise of self-contained agricultural communities. Each was probably originally ruled by a petty king, but under the Hittites a group of local officials known as the Elders handled community affairs. Besides the farming population, a well-defined group of artisans fashioned the pottery, cloth, leather goods, and metal tools needed by society. Documents also report that traveling merchants peddled goods and gossip, reminding individual communities that they were part of a larger world. Like many other societies, ancient and modern, the Hittites held slaves, who nonetheless enjoyed certain rights under the law.

At the top of Hittite society was the aristocracy, among whom the relatives of the king constituted a privileged group. The king's relations were a mighty and often unruly group who served as the chief royal administrators. The royal family was often a threat to the king, for some of them, like the assassin of Mursilis I, readily resorted to murder as a method of seizing power. Sons of the king traditionally served as governors of conquered provinces.

THE HITTITE GOD ATARLUHAS *This statue of the god Atarluhas, with two lions at his feet, was set up near the gateway of the Hittite city of Carchemish. A bird-headed demon holds the lions. In 1920 this statue was destroyed in a war between Turkey and Syria. (The British Museum)*

Just as the aristocracy stood at the head of society, so the king and queen stood above the aristocracy. The king was supreme commander of the army, chief judge, and supreme priest. He carried on all diplomatic dealings with foreign powers, and in times of war personally led the Hittite army into the field. The queen, who was highly regarded, held a strong, independent position. She had important religious duties to perform, and some queens even engaged in diplomatic correspondence with foreign queens.

The Hittites are typical of many newcomers

to the ancient Near East in that they readily assimilated the cultures that they found. On arriving in Anatolia, they adopted much of the local culture. Soon they fell under the far more powerful spell of the superior Mesopotamian culture. The Hittites adopted the cuneiform script for their own language. Hittite kings published law codes, just as Hammurabi had done. Royal correspondence followed Mesopotamian forms. The Hittites delighted in Mesopotamian myths, legends, and epics. Of Hittite art, one scholar has observed that "there is hardly a single Hittite monument which somewhere does not show traces of Mesopotamian influence."[22] To the credit of the Hittites, one must add that they used these Mesopotamian borrowings to create something of their own. Nonetheless, the huge debt of the Hittites and other invaders brilliantly illustrates the great attraction and strength of Mesopotamian culture.

## THE ERA OF HITTITE GREATNESS
### (CA 1475–CA 1200 B.C.)

The Hittites, like the Egyptians of the New Kingdom, eventually produced an energetic and capable line of kings who restored order and rebuilt Hittite power. Once Telepinus (1525–1500 B.C.) had brought the aristocracy under control, Suppiluliumas I (1380–1346 B.C.) secured central Anatolia and Mursilis II (1345–1315 B.C.) regained Syria. Around 1300 B.C. Mursilis' son stopped the Egyptian army of Rameses II at the battle of Kadesh in Syria. Having fought each other to a standstill, the Hittites and Egyptians first made peace, then an alliance. Alliance was followed by friendship, and friendship by active cooperation. The two greatest powers of the early Near East tried to make war between them impossible.

The Hittites exercised remarkable political

wisdom and flexibility in the organization and administration of their empire. Some states they turned into vassal-kingdoms, ruled by the sons of the Hittite king; the king and his sons promised each other mutual support in times of crisis. Still other kingdoms were turned into protectorates, whose native kings were allowed to rule their populations with considerable freedom. The native kings swore obedience to the Hittite king, and had to contribute military contingents to the Hittite army. Although they also sent tribute to the Hittites, the financial burden was moderate. The common people of these lands probably felt Hittite overlordship little if at all.

While the Hittites were often at war, owing to the sheer number of enemies surrounding them, they often sought diplomatic and political solutions to their problems. They were realistic enough to recognize the limits of their power and far-sighted enough to appreciate the value of peace and alliance with Egypt. Together the two kingdoms provided much of the ancient Near East with a precious interlude of peace.

## THE FALL OF EMPIRES (1200 B.C.)

This stable and generally peaceful situation endured until the cataclysm of the thirteenth century B.C., when both the Hittite and Egyptian empires were destroyed by invaders. The most famous of these marauders, called the "Sea Peoples" by the Egyptians, remain one of the puzzles of ancient history. Despite much new work, modern archaeology is still unable to identify the Sea Peoples satisfactorily. It is known, however, that they were part of a larger movement of peoples. Although there is serious doubt about whether the Sea Peoples alone overthrew the Hittites, they did

deal both the Hittites and the Egyptians a hard blow, making the Hittites vulnerable to overland invasion from the north and driving the Egyptians back to the Nile Delta. The Hittites fell under the external blows, but the Egyptians, shaken and battered, retreated to the Delta and held on.

In 1200 B.C., as earlier, both Indo-European and Semitic-speaking peoples were on the move. They brought down the old centers of power and won new homes for themselves. In Mesopotamia the Assyrians destroyed the kingdom of Mitanni and struggled with the Kassites; the Hebrews moved into Palestine; and another wave of Indo-Europeans penetrated Anatolia. But once again these victories were political and military, not cultural. The old cultures – especially that of Mesopotamia – impressed their ideas, values, and ideals on the newcomers. Although the chaos of the thirteenth century B.C. caused a serious material decline throughout the ancient Near East, the old cultures lived on through a dark age.

———◆———

In the long span of years covered by this chapter, human beings made astonishing strides, advancing from primitive hunters to builders of complex and sophisticated civilizations. By harnessing the plant and animal worlds for their welfare, human beings prospered dramatically. With their basic bodily needs more than satisfied, they realized even greater achievements, including more complex social groupings, metal technology, and long-distance trade. The intellectual achievements of these centuries were equally impressive. Ancient Near Eastern peoples created advanced mathematics, monumental architecture, and engaging literature. Although the societies of the Near East suffered stunning blows in the thirteenth century B.C., more persisted than perished. The great achievements of Mesopotamia and Egypt survived to improve and sustain the lives of those who came after.

## NOTES

1. L. Eiseley, *The Unexpected Universe,* Harcourt Brace Jovanovich, New York, 1969, p. 102.

2. J. R. Harlan, "The Plants and Animals That Nourish Man," *Scientific American* 235 (September 1976): 89.

3. Xenophon *Anabasis* 1.5.1.

4. W. K. Loftus, *Travels and Researches in Chaldaea and Susiana,* R. Carter & Brothers, New York, 1857, p. 163.

5. J. B. Pritchard, ed., *Ancient Near Eastern Texts,* 3rd ed., Princeton University Press, Princeton, 1969, p. 44. Hereafter called *ANET.*

6. Ibid., p. 104.

7. *ANET,* p. 590.

8. Quoted in S. N. Kramer, *The Sumerians,* University of Chicago Press, Chicago, 1964, p. 238.

9. *ANET,* p. 175.

10. H.L. Mencken, *A Mencken Chrestomathy,* Knopf, New York, 1949, p. 67.

11. *ANET,* p. 67.

12. Kramer, p. 150.

13. *ANET,* p. 171.

14. Kramer, p. 251.

15. *ANET,* p. 372.

16. Herodotus *The Histories* 2.14.

17. Quoted in A. H. Gardiner, "Ramesside Texts Relating to the Taxation and Transport of Corn," *Journal of Egyptian Archaeology* 27 (1941): 19–20.

18. A. H. Gardiner, "The Eloquent Peasant," *Journal of Egyptian Archaeology* 9 (1923): 17.

19. H. Frankfort, *The Birth of Civilization in the Near East,* Doubleday, New York, 1956, pp. 119–120.

20. Manetho *History of Egypt* fr. 42.75–77.

21. E. H. Sturtevant and G. Bechtel, *A Hittite Chrestomathy,* Linguistic Society of America, Philadelphia, 1935, p. 183.

22. M. Vieyra, *Hittite Art 2300–750 B.C.,* Alec Tiranti, London, 1955, p. 12.

## SUGGESTED READING

The continuing research on the evolution of mankind makes any book quickly outdated, but a commendable exception is R. Leakey and R. Lewin, *Origins* (1977). G. Clark, *Archaeology and Society: Reconstructing the Prehistoric Past,* 3rd ed. (1957), is a study in methodology, and his *The Stone Age Hunters* (1967) describes life and society in the Paleolithic Age. A convenient general treatment is G. Clark and S. Piggott, *Prehistoric Societies* (1965). F. Dahlberg, *Woman the Gatherer* (1981), demonstrates the importance to primitive society of women's role in gathering.

As the text suggests, the origins of agriculture and the Neolithic period have recently received a great deal of attention. Professor Harlan's conclusions, besides the article cited in note 2, are set out in a series of works including "Agricultural Origins: Centers and Noncenters," *Science* 174 (1971): 468–474, and *Crops and Man* (1975). The 1981 Egyptian expedition mentioned in the text is described by F. Wendorf and R. Schild, "The Earliest Food Producers," *Archaeology* 34 (September/October 1981): 30–36. A broad survey of the problem is M. N. Cohen, *The Food Crisis in Prehistory* (1977).

For the societies of Mesopotamia, see A. Leo Oppenheim, *Ancient Mesopotamia,* rev. ed. (1977); M. E. L. Mallowan, *Early Mesopotamia and Iran* (1965); and H. W. F. Saggs, *The Greatness That Was Babylon* (1962). E. Chiera, *They Wrote on Clay* (1938), offers a delightful glimpse of Mesopotamian life, as does H. W. F. Saggs, *Everyday Life in Babylonia and Assyria* (1965).

C. Aldred, *The Egyptians* (1961), provides a good, readable survey of Egyptian developments. More detailed is A. Gardiner, *Egypt of the Pharaohs*

(1961). A. Nibbi, *Ancient Egypt and Some Eastern Neighbors* (1981) looks at Egyptian history in a broad context. See also J. M. White, *Everyday Life in Ancient Egypt* (1963).

Recent general introductions to problems and developments shared by several Near Eastern societies come from D. H. Trump, *The Prehistory of the Mediterranean* (1980), and a series of studies edited by T. A. Wertime and J. D. Muhly, *The Coming of the Age of Iron* (1980). J. B. Pritchard, *The Ancient Near East,* 2 vols. (1958, 1976) is a fine synthesis by one of the world's leading Near Eastern specialists. A sweeping survey is C. Burney, *The Ancient Near East* (1977). Pioneering new work on the origins of writing appears in a series of pieces by D. Schmandt-Besserat, notably "An Archaic Recording System and the Origin of Writing," *Syro-Mesopotamian Studies* 1/2 (1977): 1–32, and "Reckoning before Writing," *Archaeology* 32 (May/June, 1979): 23–31.

O. R. Gurney, *The Hittites,* 2nd ed. (1954) is still a fine introduction by an eminent scholar. Good also is J. G. MacQueen, *The Hittites and Their Contemporaries in Asia Minor* (1975). The 1960s were prolific years for archaeology in Turkey. A brief survey by one of the masters of the field is J. Mellaart, *The Archaeology of Modern Turkey*

(1978), which also tests a great number of widely-held historical interpretations. The Sea Peoples have been the subject of two recent studies: A. Nibbi, *The Sea Peoples and Egypt* (1975), and N. K. Sandars, *The Sea Peoples* (1978).

For Near Eastern religion and mythology, good introductions are S. N. Kramer, ed., *Mythologies of the Ancient World* (1961); E. O. James, *The Ancient Gods: The History and Diffusion of Religion in the Ancient Near East and the Eastern Mediterranean* (1960); and J. Gray, *Near Eastern Mythology* (1969). A survey of Mesopotamian religion by one of the foremost scholars in the field is T. Jacobsen, *The Treasures of Darkness: A History of Mesopotamian Religion* (1976).

Surveys of Near Eastern art include H. Frankfort, *The Art and Architecture of the Ancient Orient* (1954), old but still very useful; R. D. Barnett and D. J. Wiseman, *Fifty Masterpieces of Ancient Near Eastern Art* (1969); and J. B. Pritchard's delightful *The Ancient Near East in Pictures,* 2nd ed. (1969). For literature, see S. Fiore, *Voices from the Clay: The Development of Assyro-Babylonian Literature* (1965); W. K. Simpson, ed., *The Literature of Ancient Egypt* (1973); and, above all, J. B. Pritchard, ed., *Ancient Near Eastern Texts* cited frequently in the Notes.

# CHAPTER 2

## SMALL KINGDOMS AND MIGHTY
## EMPIRES IN THE NEAR EAST

THE MIGRATORY INVASIONS that brought down the Hittites and stunned the Egyptians in the thirteenth century B.C. ushered in an era of confusion and weakness. Although much was lost in the chaos, the old cultures of the ancient Near East survived to nurture new societies. In the absence of powerful empires, the Phoenicians, Syrians, Hebrews, and many other peoples carved out small independent kingdoms, until the Near East was a patchwork of them. During this period Hebrew culture and religion evolved under the influence of urbanism, kings, and prophets.

In the ninth century B.C. this jumble of small states gave way to an empire that for the first time embraced the entire Near East. Yet the very ferocity of the Assyrian Empire led to its downfall only two hundred years later. In 550 B.C. the Persians and Medes, who had migrated into Iran, created a "world empire" stretching from Anatolia in the west to the Indus valley in the east. For over two hundred years the Persians gave the ancient Near East peace and stability.

How did Egypt, its political greatness behind it, pass on its cultural heritage to its African neighbors? How did the Jewish state evolve, and what was daily life like in Jewish society? What forces helped to shape Jewish religious thought, still powerfully influential in today's world? What enabled the Assyrians to overrun their neighbors, and how did their cruelty finally cause their undoing? Lastly, how did Iranian nomads create the Persian Empire? This chapter will seek answers to these questions.

## EGYPT, A SHATTERED KINGDOM

The invasions of the Sea Peoples ended the great days of Egyptian power. One scribe left behind a somber portrait of Egypt stunned and leaderless:

*The land of Egypt was abandoned and every man was a law to himself. During many years there was no leader who could speak for others. Central government lapsed, small officials and headmen took over the whole land. Any man, great or small, might kill his neighbor. In the distress and vacuum that followed ... men banded together to plunder one another. They treated the gods no better than men, and cut off the temple revenues.*[1]

No longer able to dream of foreign conquests, Egypt looked to its own security from foreign invasion. Egyptians suffered a four-hundred-year period of political fragmentation, a new dark age known to Egyptian specialists as the Third Intermediate Period (eleventh–seventh centuries B.C.).

The decline of Egypt was especially sharp in foreign affairs. Whereas the pharaohs of the Eighteenth Dynasty had held sway as far abroad as Syria, their weak successors found it unsafe to venture far from home. In the wake of the Sea Peoples, numerous small kingdoms sprang up in the Near East, each fiercely protective of its own independence. To them Egypt was a memory, and foreign princes often greeted Egyptian officials with suspicion or downright contempt. One Egyptian official, Wen-Amon, left a lively report of his reception in Phoenicia, on an official mission to buy wood. Instead of the respect and deference Wen-Amon expected, he was greeted by the thundering of the king of Byblos:

*If the ruler of Egypt were the lord of mine, and I were his servant also, he would not have to send silver and gold, saying: "Carry out the commission of Amon!" There would be no carrying of a royal-gift, such as they used to do for my father. As for me — me also — I am not your servant! I am not the servant of him who sent you either!*[2]

In the days of Egypt's greatness, no mere king of Byblos would have dared to speak so insolently to an Egyptian official.

Disrupted at home and powerless abroad, Egypt fell prey to invasion by its African neighbors. Libyans from North Africa filtered into the Nile Delta, where they established independent dynasties. Indeed, from 950 to 730 B.C. northern Egypt was ruled by Libyan pharaohs. The Libyans built cities, and for the first time a sturdy urban life grew up in the Delta. Although the coming of the Libyans changed the face of the Delta, the Libyans genuinely admired Egyptian culture, and eagerly adopted Egypt's religion and way of life.

In southern Egypt, meanwhile, the pharaoh's decline opened the way to the energetic Africans of Nubia, who extended their authority northward throughout the Nile valley. Nubian influence in these years, though pervasive, was not destructive. Since the imperial days of the Eighteenth Dynasty (see pages 29–31), the Nubians too had adopted many features of Egyptian culture. Now Nubian kings and aristocrats embraced Egyptian culture wholesale. The thought of destroying the heritage of the pharaohs would have struck them as stupid and barbaric. Thus the Nubians and the Libyans repeated an old Near Eastern phenomenon: new peoples conquered old centers of political and military power, but were themselves assimilated into the older culture.

The reunification of Egypt occurred late and unexpectedly. With Egypt distracted and disorganized by foreign invasions, an independent African state, the Kingdom of Kush, grew up in modern Sudan with its capital at Nepata. These Africans too worshiped Egyptian gods and used Egyptian hieroglyphs to write their language. In the eighth century B.C. their king Piankhy swept through the entire Nile valley from Nepata in the south to the Delta in the north. United once again, Egypt enjoyed a brief period of peace during which Egyptians continued to assimilate their African conquerors. In the Kingdom of Kush, Egyptian methods of administration and bookkeeping, Egyptian arts and crafts, and Egyptian economic practices became common, especially among the aristocracy. Nonetheless, reunification of the realm did not lead to a new Egyptian empire. In the centuries between the fall of the New Kingdom and the recovery of Egypt, several small but vigorous kingdoms had taken root and grown to maturity in the ancient Near East. By 700 B.C. Egypt was once again a strong kingdom, but no longer a mighty empire.

Yet Egypt's legacy to its African neighbors remained vibrant and rich. By trading and exploring southward along the coast of the Red Sea, the Egyptians introduced their goods and ideas as far south as the land of Punt, probably a region on the Somali coast. As early as the New Kingdom Egyptian pharaohs had exchanged gifts with the monarchs of Punt, and contact between the two areas persisted. Egypt was the primary civilizing force in Nubia, which became an African version of the pharaoh's realm, complete with royal pyramids and Egyptian deities, governmental procedures, and language. Egyptian religious beliefs penetrated as far south as Ethiopia. Just as Mesopotamian culture enjoyed wide appeal throughout the Near East, so Egyptian culture had a massive impact on northeastern Africa.

## THE CHILDREN OF ISRAEL

The fall of the Hittite Empire and Egypt's collapse created a vacuum of power in the western Near East that allowed for the rise of

MAP 2.1    SMALL KINGDOMS IN THE NEAR
EAST    This map illustrates the political fragmentation of the Near East after the great wave of thirteenth-century invasions.

tines, settled along the coast of modern Israel
(see Map 2.1). Establishing themselves in five
cities somewhat inland from the sea, the Philistines set about farming and raising flocks.

Another sturdy new culture was that of the
Phoenicians, a Semitic-speaking people who
had long inhabited several cities along the
coast of modern Lebanon. They had lived
under the shadow of the Hittites and Egyptians, but in this period the Phoenicians enjoyed full independence. (It was one of their
princes, the king of Byblos, who had given
Wen-Amon an unpleasant taste of the Phoenicians' newly found sense of freedom.) Unlike the Philistine newcomers, who turned
from seafaring to farming, the Phoenicians
took to the sea. They became outstanding
merchants and explorers. In their trading
ventures they sailed as far west as modern
Tunisia, where in 813 B.C. they founded the
city of Carthage, which would one day struggle with Rome for domination of the western
Mediterranean. Phoenician culture was urban,
based on the prosperous commercial centers
of Tyre, Sidon, and Byblos. The Phoenicians'
overwhelming cultural achievement was the
development of an alphabet, which they
handed on to the Greeks sometime in the late
eighth century B.C.

South of Phoenicia arose another small
kingdom, that of the Hebrews or ancient
Jews. Although smaller, poorer, less important, and less powerful than neighboring
kingdoms, the realm of the Hebrews was to
nourish religious ideas that underlie all of
Western civilization. Who were the Jewish
people, and what brought them to this new
land? Earlier Mesopotamian and Egyptian
sources refer to people called Habiru or Ha-
piru, which seems to mean a class of homeless, independent nomads. One such group of
Habiru were the biblical Hebrews. The original homeland of the Hebrews was probably

numerous small states. No longer crushed between the Hittites in the north and the Egyptians in the south, various peoples — some of
them newcomers — created homes and petty
kingdoms in Syria, Phoenicia, and Palestine.
After the Sea Peoples had raided Egypt, a
branch of them, known in the Bible as Philis-

northern Mesopotamia, and the most crucial event in their historical development was their enslavement in Egypt. According to the Old Testament, the Hebrews had followed their patriarch Abraham out of Mesopotamia into Canaan, and from there had migrated into the Nile Delta to escape a drought. Arriving during the imperial days of the Eighteenth Dynasty, the Hebrews were soon enslaved and forced to labor on building projects. The passing of Egypt's greatness was the Hebrews' opportunity.

The agent of the Hebrews' deliverance from slavery was Moses, a figure so towering in legendary stature that his actual existence has been doubted. According to the Old Testament, Yahweh – called Jehovah in the Bible – appeared in a burning bush and commanded Moses to lead the Hebrews out of Egypt into Canaan. Thus Moses, in obedience

to the injunctions of Yahweh, directed his people to undertake a political act in the name of their god. The biblical book of Exodus depicts Moses leading the liberated Hebrews from Egypt into Canaan, which was to be their new homeland.

Today archaeologists are trying to ascertain precisely what happened around the time of the Hebrew exodus, and in the process to assess the accuracy of the biblical account. The archaeological record indicates that the thirteenth century B.C. was a time of warfare, disruption, and destruction, and seems to confirm the biblical portrayal of the exodus as a long period of conflict and turmoil. Apparently, nomadic Hebrew tribes filtered into Palestine from Egypt. According to Exodus, the Hebrews at this time consisted of a loose political confederation of twelve disunited tribes, which they believed to be descended from the twelve great-grandsons of Abraham.

In a series of vicious wars and savage slaughters they slowly won a place for themselves in Palestine (see Map 2.1). Success was not automatic, and the Hebrews suffered defeats and setbacks, but gradually they spread their power northward. In some cases they assimilated themselves to the culture of the natives, even going so far as to worship Baal, an ancient Semitic fertility god. In other instances, they carved out little strongholds and enslaved the natives. Even after the conquest, nearly constant fighting was required to consolidate the Hebrews' position.

The greatest danger to the Hebrews came from the Philistines, whose superior technology and military organization at first made them invincible. In Saul (ca 1000 B.C.), a farmer of the tribe of Benjamin, the Hebrews found a champion and a spirited leader. Saul carried the war to the Philistines, often without success. Yet in the meantime he established a monarchy over the twelve Hebrew tribes. Thus, under the peril of the Philistines, the Hebrew tribes evolved from scattered independent units into a centralized political organization in which the king directed the energies of the people.

Saul's work was carried on by David of Bethlehem, who in his youth had followed Saul into battle against the Philistines. Through courage and cunning David became king of Judah, hurled back the Philistines, and waged war against his other neighbors. To give his kingdom a capital he captured the city of Jerusalem, which he enlarged, fortified, and made the religious and political center of his realm. David's military successes won the Hebrews unprecedented security, and his forty-year reign was a period of vitality and political consolidation. David spent his last days dawdling in his harem, and letting the

reins of power slip from his hands. Yet his ruin was not Israel's ruin. His work in consolidating the monarchy and enlarging the kingdom paved the way for his son Solomon.

Solomon (ca 965–925 B.C.) applied his energies to creating a nation out of a collection of tribes ruled by a king. He divided the kingdom, for purposes of effective administration, into twelve territorial districts cutting across the old tribal borders. To Solomon the twelve tribes of Israel were far less important than the Hebrew nation. He also yearned to bring his kingdom up to the level of its more sophisticated neighbors, and set about a building program to make Israel a respectable Near Eastern state. Work was begun on a magnificent temple in Jerusalem, on cities, palaces, fortresses, and roads. Solomon worked to bring Israel into the commercial mainstream of the world around it, and kept up good relations with Phoenician cities to the north. To pay for all this activity he imposed taxes far greater than any levied before, much to the displeasure of his subjects.

Solomon dedicated the temple in grand style, and made it the home of the Ark of the Covenant, the cherished chest that contained the holiest of Hebrew religious articles. As is recorded in the Old Testament:

*And they [the priests] brought up the ark of the lord, and the tabernacle of the congregation, and all the holy vessels that were in the tabernacle, even these did the priests and the Levites bring up. And king Solomon, and all the congregation of Israel, that were assembled unto him, were with him before the ark, sacrificing sheep and oxen, that could not be told nor numbered for multitude. And the priests brought in the ark of the lord unto his place, into the oracle of the house, to the most holy place.*[3]

The temple in Jerusalem was to be the religious heart of the kingdom and the symbol of

Hebrew unity. It also became the stronghold of the priesthood, for a legion of priests was needed to conduct religious sacrifices, ceremonies, and prayers. Yet Solomon's efforts were crowned with strife. He was too liberal in his ways, especially when it came to religion, to please some people, and the financial demands of his building program drained the resources of his people. His use of forced labor for his building projects further fanned popular resentment. However, Solomon had turned a rude kingdom into a state with broad commercial horizons and greater knowledge of the outside world. At his death, the Hebrews broke into two political halves (see Map 2.1). The northern part of the kingdom of David and Solomon became Israel, with its capital at Samaria. The southern half was Judah, and Solomon's city of Jerusalem remained its center. With political division went a religious rift: Israel, the northern kingdom, established rival sanctuaries to gods other than Yahweh. The Hebrew nation was divided, but at least it was divided into two far more sophisticated political units than before the time of Solomon. The Hebrews had taken their place in the increasingly cosmopolitan world of the Near East.

## THE EVOLUTION OF JEWISH RELIGION

Hand in hand with their political evolution from fierce nomads to urban dwellers, the Hebrews were evolving spiritual ideas that still permeate Western society. Their chief literary product, the Old Testament, has fundamentally influenced both Christianity and Islam and still exerts a compelling force on the modern world.

It was Moses, the man who led the Hebrews to the promised land, who declared to the Hebrews Yahweh's covenant with them. According to the Old Testament, Yahweh appeared to Moses during the Exodus from Egypt, and ordered Moses to tell the Hebrews that he would watch over them, his chosen people. In return the Jews were to obey the Ten Commandments, which enjoined them to worship Yahweh and no other god.

Yahweh was unique because he was a lone god. Unlike the gods of Mesopotamia and Egypt, Yahweh was not the son of another god, nor did he have a divine wife or family. Initially an anthropomorphic god, Yahweh gradually lost his human form and became totally spiritual. Although Yahweh could assume human form, he was not to be depicted in any form. Consequently, the Jews considered graven images — statues and other representations — idolatrous.

At first Yahweh was probably conceived of as no more than the god of the Jews, a god who sometimes faced competition from Baal and other gods in Palestine. Enlil, Marduk, Amon-Re, and the others sufficed for foreigners. In time, however, the Jews came to regard Yahweh as the only god who existed. This was the beginning of true monotheism.

Yahweh was considered the creator of all things; his name means "he causes to be." He governed the cosmic forces of nature, including the movements of the sun, moon, and stars. His presence filled the universe. At the same time Yahweh was a personal god. Despite his awesome power, he was not too mighty or aloof to care for the individual. The Jews even believed that he intervened in human affairs.

Unlike Akhenaten's monotheism, Jewish monotheism was not an unpopular religion imposed from above. It was the religion of a whole people, deeply felt and cherished. Yet the Jews did not consider it their duty to spread the belief in the one god. The Jews rarely proselytized, as later the Christians did. As the chosen people, the chief duty of the

Jews was to maintain the worship of Yahweh as he demanded.

The original form of Yahweh's covenant with the Jews, the Ten Commandments, embodied an ethical code of conduct. It forbade the Jews to steal, murder, lie, and commit adultery. The covenant was a constant force in Jewish life, and the Old Testament records one occasion when the entire nation formally reaffirmed it:

*And the king [of the Jews] stood by a pillar, and made a covenant before the lord, to walk after the lord, and to keep his commandments and his testimonies and his statutes with all their heart and all their soul, to perform the words of this covenant that were written in this book [Deuteronomy]. And all the people stood to the covenant.*[4]

From the Ten Commandments evolved Jewish law, a code of law and custom originating with Moses and built upon by priests and prophets. The earliest part of this code, the Torah or Mosaic law, was often as harsh as Hammurabi's code, which had a powerful impact upon it. Later tradition, largely the work of prophets who lived from the eleventh to the fifth centuries B.C., was more humanitarian. The work of the prophet Jeremiah (ca 626 B.C.) exemplifies this gentler spirit. According to Jeremiah, Yahweh demanded righteousness from his people and protection for the weak and helpless:

*For if ye thoroughly amend your ways and your doings; if ye thoroughly execute judgment between a man and his neighbor; if ye oppress not the stranger, the fatherless, and the widow, and shed not innocent blood in this place, neither walk after other gods to your hurt: then I will cause you to dwell in this place, in the land that I gave your fathers, for ever and ever.*[5]

Here the emphasis is on mercy and justice, on avoiding wrongdoing to others because it is displeasing to Yahweh. These precepts replaced the old law's demand for "an eye for an eye." Thus this passage is representative of a subtle and positive shift in Jewish thinking. Jeremiah proclaimed that the god of anger was also the god of forgiveness: "Return, thou backsliding Israel, saith the lord; and I will not cause mine anger to fall upon you; for I am merciful, saith the lord, and I will not keep anger forever."[6] Although Yahweh would punish wrongdoing, he would not destroy those who repented. One generation might be punished for its misdeeds, but Yahweh's mercy was a promise of hope for future generations.

The uniqueness of this phenomenon can be seen by comparing the essence of Hebrew monotheism with the religious outlook of the Mesopotamians. Whereas the Mesopotamians considered their gods capricious, the Jews knew what Yahweh expected of them. The Jews believed that their god would protect them and make them prosper if they obeyed his commandments. The Mesopotamians thought human beings insignificant as compared to the gods, so insignificant that the gods might even be indifferent to them. The Jews too considered themselves puny in comparison to Yahweh. Yet they were Yahweh's chosen people, and he had promised never to abandon them. Finally, though the Mesopotamians believed that the gods generally preferred good to evil, their religion did not demand ethical conduct. The Jews could please their god only by living up to high moral standards in addition to worshiping him.

The evolution of Hebrew monotheism resulted in one of the world's greatest religions, which deeply influenced the development of two others. Many parts of the Old Testament show obvious debts to Mesopotamian culture. Nonetheless, to the Jews goes the credit for developing a religion so emotionally satisfying and ethically grand that it has not only flourished but also profoundly influenced Christianity and Islam. Without Moses there could not have been Jesus or Mohammed. The religious standards of the modern West are deeply rooted in Judaism.

## DAILY LIFE IN ISRAEL

Historians generally know far more about the daily life of the aristocracy and the wealthy in ancient societies than about the conditions of the common people. Jewish society is an exception, simply because the Old Testament, which lays down laws for all Jews, has much to say about peasants and princes alike. Comparisons with the social conditions of Israel's ancient neighbors and modern anthropological work among Palestinian Arabs shed additional light on biblical practices. Thus the life of the common people in ancient Israel is better known than, for instance, the lives of ordinary Romans or ancient Chinese.

The nomadic Hebrews first entered Palestine as tribes, consisting of numerous families who thought of themselves as all related to one another. As the Jews consolidated their hold on Palestine, and as the concept of one Jewish nation gained a hold, the importance of the tribes declined.

At first good farm land, pasture land, and watering-spots were held in common by the tribe. Common use of land was – and still is – characteristic of nomadic peoples. Typically each family or group of families in the tribe drew lots every year to determine who worked what fields. But as formerly nomadic peoples turned increasingly to settled agriculture, communal use of land gave way to family ownership. In this respect the experience of the ancient Hebrews seems typical of many early peoples. Slowly but inevitably the shift

from nomad to farmer affected far more than just how people fed themselves. Family relationships reflected evolving circumstances. The extended family, organized in tribes, is even today typical of nomads. With the transition to settled agriculture, the tribe gradually becomes less important than the extended family. With the advent of village life, and finally full-blown urban life, the extended family in turn gives way to the nuclear family.

The family – people related to one another, all living in the same place – was the primary social institution among the Jews. At its head stood the father, who like the Mesopotamian father held great powers. The father was the master of his wife and children, with power of life and death over his family. By the eighth century B.C., the advent of full-blown urban life began to change the shape of family life again. The father's power and the overall strength of family ties relaxed. Much of the father's power passed to the elders of the town, especially the power of life and death over his children. One result of this general development was the liberation of the individual person from the tight control of the family.

Marriage was one of the most important and joyous events in the life of the Hebrew family. When the Jews were still nomads, a man could have only one lawful wife but any number of concubines. Settled life changed marriage customs and later Jewish law allowed men to be polygamous. Not only did kings David and Solomon have harems, but rich men might also have several wives. The chief reason for this custom, as in Mesopotamia, was the desire for children. Given the absence of medical knowledge and the rough conditions of life, women faced barrenness, high infant mortality, and rapid aging. Several women in the family led to some quarrelsome households; and the legal wife, if she were barren, could be scorned and ridiculed by her husband's concubines.

The common man was too poor to afford the luxury of several women in the home. The typical marriage in ancient Israel was monogamous, and a virtuous wife was revered and honored. Perhaps the finest and most fervent song of praise to the good wife comes from the book of Proverbs in the Old Testament:

*Who can find a virtuous woman? for her price is far above rubies ... Strength and honour are her clothing; and she shall rejoice in time to come. She openeth her mouth with wisdom; and in her tongue is the law of kindness. She looketh well to the ways of her household, and eateth not the bread of idleness. Her children arise up, and call her blessed; her husband also, and he praiseth her ... Favour is deceitful, and beauty is vain: but a woman that feareth the lord, she shall be praised.*[7]

The commandment "honor thy father and thy mother" was fundamental to the Mosaic law. The wife was a pillar of the family, and her work and wisdom were respected and treasured.

Betrothal and marriage were serious matters in ancient Israel. As in Mesopotamia, they were left largely in the hands of the parents. Boys and girls were often married when they were little more than children, and their parents naturally made the marriage arrangements. Rarely were the prospective bride and groom consulted. Marriages were often contracted within the extended family, and commonly among first cousins — a custom still found among Palestinian Arabs today. Although early Jewish custom permitted marriage with foreigners, the fear of alien religions soon led to restrictions against mixed marriages.

The father of the groom offered a bridal gift to the bride's father. This custom, the marriage price, also existed among the Mesopotamians and still survives among modern Palestinian Arabs. The gift was ordinarily money, the amount depending on the social status and wealth of the two families. In other instances, the groom could work off the marriage price by performing manual labor, as Jacob did for Leah and Rachel. At the time of the wedding the man gave his bride and her family wedding presents; unlike Mesopotamian custom, the bride's father did not provide her with a dowry.

As in Mesopotamia, marriage was a legal contract, not a religious ceremony. At marriage a woman left her family and joined the family and clan of her husband. The occasion when the bride joined her husband's household was festive. The groom wore a crown and his best clothes. Accompanied by his friends, also dressed in their finest and carrying musical instruments, the bridegroom walked to the bride's house, where she awaited him in her richest clothes, jewels, and a veil which she removed only later when the couple was alone. The bride's friends joined the group, and together they all marched in procession to the groom's house, their way marked by music and songs honoring the newlyweds. Though the wedding feast might last for days, the couple consummated their marriage on the first night; the next day the bloody linen was displayed to prove the bride's virginity.

Divorce was available only to the husband. He could normally end the marriage very simply and for any of a number of reasons:

*When a man hath taken a wife, and married her, and it come to pass that she find no favour in his eyes, because he hath found some uncleanness in her: then let him write her a bill of divorcement, and give it in her hand, and send her out of his house. And when she is departed out of his house, she may go and be another man's wife.*[8]

The right to initiate a divorce was denied the wife. Even adultery by the husband was not

necessarily grounds for divorce. Jewish law, like the Code of Hammurabi, generally punished adultery with death. Generally speaking, Jewish custom frowned on divorce, and the typical couple entered into marriage fully expecting to spend the rest of their lives together.

The newly married couple was expected to begin a family at once. Children, according to the book of Psalms, "are an heritage of the lord: and the fruit of the womb is his reward."[9] The desire for children to perpetuate the family was so strong that if a man died before he could sire a son, his brother was legally obliged to marry the widow. The son born of the brother was thereafter considered the offspring and heir of the dead man. If the brother refused, the widow had her revenge by denouncing him to the elders in public:

*Then shall his brother's wife come unto him in the presence of the elders, and loose his shoe from off his foot, and spit in his face, and shall answer and say, So shall it be done unto that man that will not build up his brother's house.*[10]

Sons were especially desired because they maintained the family bloodline and kept the ancestral property within the family. The first-born son had special rights, honor, and responsibilities. At his father's death he became the head of the household, and received a larger inheritance than his younger brothers. Daughters were less highly valued because they would eventually marry and leave the family. Yet in Jewish society, unlike other cultures, infanticide was illegal; Yahweh had forbidden it.

The Old Testament often speaks of the pain of childbirth. Professional midwives frequently assisted at deliveries. The newborn infant was washed, rubbed with salt, and wrapped in swaddling-clothes – bands of cloth that were wrapped around the baby. Normally the mother nursed the baby herself, and weaned the infant at about the age of three. The mother customarily named the baby immediately after birth, but children were free to change names after they grew up. Eight days after the birth of a son, the ceremony of circumcision – removal of the foreskin of the penis – took place. Circumcision signified that the boy belonged to the Jewish community, and according to Genesis was the symbol of Yahweh's covenant with Abraham.

As in most other societies, so in ancient Israel the early education of children was in the hands of the mother. It was she who taught her children right from wrong and gave them their first instruction in the moral values of their society. As boys grew older, they received more of their education from their fathers. Fathers instructed their sons in religion and the history of their people. Many children were taught to read and write, and the head of each family was probably able to write. Fathers also taught their sons the family craft or trade. Boys soon learned that inattention could be painful, for Jewish custom advised fathers to be strict: "He that spareth his rod hateth his son: but he that loveth him chasteneth him betimes."[11]

Once children grew to adulthood, they entered fully into economic and social life. For most that meant a life on the farm, whose demands and rhythm changed very little over time. Young people began with the lighter tasks. Girls traditionally tended flocks of sheep and drew water from the well for household use. The well was a popular meeting spot, where girls could meet other young people and even travelers passing through the country with camel caravans. After the harvest, young girls followed behind the reapers to glean the fields. Even this work was governed by law and custom: once the girls had gone through the fields, they were not to return, for Yahweh had declared that anything left behind belonged to the needy:

THE SEASONS OF THE YEAR *The Hebrew agricultural year, like that of other peoples, was tied to the sun, seasons, and stars. The center of this mosaic floor shows the sun in its chariot, pulled by four horses. In the outer circle are the signs of the zodiac, while the four seasons of the year peer at the viewer from the corners of the panel. (Consulate General of Israel)*

*When thou cuttest down thine harvest in thy field, and hast forgot a sheaf in the field, thou shalt not go again to fetch it: it shall be for the stranger, for the fatherless, and for the widow: that the lord thy God may bless thee in all the work of thine hands.*[12]

Boys also tended flocks, especially in wild areas. Like the young David, they practiced their marksmanship with slings and entertained themselves with music. They shared the lighter work, such as harvesting grapes and beating the limbs of olive trees to shake the fruit loose. Only when they grew to full strength did they perform the hard work of harrowing, ploughing, and harvesting.

The land was precious to the family, not simply because it provided a living, but also because it was a link to the past. It was the land of the family's forebears, and held their tombs. The family's feeling for its land was so strong that in times of hardship when land had to be sold, the nearest kin had first right to buy it. Thus the land might at least remain within the extended family.

Ironically, the success of the first Hebrew kings endangered the future of many family farms. With peace, more settled conditions, and increasing prosperity, some Jews began to amass larger holdings by buying out poor and struggling farmers. Far from discouraging this development, the kings created their own huge estates. In many cases slaves, both Jewish and foreign, worked these large farms and estates shoulder-to-shoulder with paid free men. Although the Old Testament called upon the royal and the rich to treat the slave and the laborer with justice and charity, there is no reason to think that Hebrew slavery was different from any other slavery. The prophet Jeremiah thundered against the exploiters:

*Woe unto him that buildeth his house by unrighteousness, and his chambers by wrong; that useth his neighbor's service without wages, and giveth him not for his work.*[13]

In still later times, rich landowners rented plots of land to poor, free families; the landowners provided the renters with seed and livestock, and normally took half the yield as rent. Although many Old Testament prophets denounced the destruction of the family farm, as the Gracchi were later to condemn the destruction of small Roman farms (Chapter 5), the trend continued toward large estates worked by slaves and hired free men.

The development of urban life among the Jews created new economic opportunities, especially in crafts and trades. People special-

ized in particular occupations, like milling flour, baking bread, making pottery, weaving cloth, and carpentry. All these crafts were family trades. Sons worked with their father; if the business prospered, they might be assisted by a few paid workers or slaves. The practitioners of a particular craft usually lived in a particular street or section of the town, a custom that is still prevalent in the Middle East today. By the sixth century B.C. craftsmen had formed guilds, intended like European guilds in the Middle Ages (Chapter 9) to protect their interests and aid their members. By banding together, craftsmen gained a corporate status within the community.

Commerce and trade developed later than crafts. In the time of Solomon, foreign trade was in the king's domain. Aided by the Phoenicians, who ranked among the leading merchants of the Near East, Solomon built a fleet to trade with ports on the Red Sea. Solomon also participated in the overland caravan trade. Otherwise, trade with neighboring countries was handled by foreigners, usually Phoenicians. Jews dealt mainly in local trade, and in most instances craftsmen and farmers sold directly to their customers. Only much later, after the great Exile – the period in the sixth century B.C., known as the Babylonian Captivity, when the Babylonians resettled the Jews in Mesopotamia – did Jews become merchants in large numbers. Many of Israel's wise men disapproved of commerce, and like the ancient Chinese, they considered it unseemly to profit from others' work.

Between the eclipse of the Hittites and Egyptians and the rise of the Assyrians, the Hebrews moved from nomadism to urban life and full participation in the mainstream of ancient Near Eastern culture. Retaining their unique religion and customs, they drew from the practices of other peoples and contributed to the lives of their neighbors.

## ASSYRIA, THE MILITARY MONARCHY

Small kingdoms like those of the Phoenicians and the Hebrews could exist only in the absence of a major power. The beginning of the ninth century B.C. saw the rise of such a power: the Assyrians of northern Mesopotamia, whose chief capital was at Nineveh on the Tigris river. The Assyrians were a Semitic-speaking people heavily influenced, like so many other peoples of the Near East, by the Mesopotamian culture of Babylon to the south. They were also one of the most warlike peoples in history, largely because throughout their history they were threatened by neighboring folk. Living in an open and exposed land, the Assyrians experienced frequent and devastating attacks by the wild war-loving tribes to their north and east and by the Babylonians to the south. The constant threat to the Assyrians' survival promoted political cohesion and military might.

For over two hundred years the Assyrians labored to dominate the Near East. In 859 B.C. the new Assyrian king Shalmaneser unleashed the first of a long series of attacks on the peoples of Syria and Palestine. Year after relentless year, Assyrian armies hammered at the peoples of the west. These ominous events inaugurated two turbulent centuries marked by Assyrian military campaigns, constant efforts by Syria and the two Jewish kingdoms to maintain or recover their independence, eventual Assyrian conquest of Babylonia and northern Egypt, and periodic political instability in Assyria itself, which prompted stirrings of freedom throughout the Near East.

Under the Assyrian kings Tiglath-pileser III (744-727 B.C.) and Sargon II (721-705 B.C.), both mighty warriors, the Near East trembled as never before under the blows of

Assyrian armies. The Assyrians stepped up their attacks in Anatolia, Syria, and Palestine. The kingdom of Israel and many other states fell; others, like the kingdom of Judah, became subservient to the warriors from the Tigris. In 717–716 B.C. Sargon led his army in a sweeping attack along the Philistine coast into Egypt. He defeated the pharaoh, who suffered the further ignominy of paying tribute to the foreign conquerors. Sargon also lashed out at Assyria's traditional enemies to the north, and then turned south against a renewed threat in Babylonia. By means of almost constant warfare, Tiglath-pileser III and Sargon carved out an Assyrian empire that stretched from east and north of the Tigris river to central Egypt (see Map 2.2).

An empire forged with so much blood and effort was vulnerable to revolt, and revolt provoked brutal retaliation. The Assyrian king Ashurbanipal (668–633 B.C.) left a grisly account of how he dealt with the Babylonians, who had conspired against him and perhaps earlier against his grandfather, King Sennacherib:

*I tore out the tongues of these whose slanderous mouths had uttered blasphemies against my god Ashur and had plotted against me, his god-fearing prince; I defeated them completely. The others, I smashed alive with the very same statues of protective deities with which they had smashed my own grandfather Sennacherib — now finally as a belated burial sacrifice for his soul. I fed their corpses, cut into small pieces, to dogs, pigs, zibu-birds, vultures, the birds of the sky and also to the fish of the ocean. After I had performed this and thus made quiet again the hearts of the great gods, my lords, I removed the corpses of those whom the pestilence had felled, whose leftovers after the dogs and pigs had fed on them were obstructing the streets, filling the places of Babylon, and of those who had lost their lives through the horrible famine.*[14]

Revolt against the Assyrians inevitably promised the rebels bloody battles, prolonged sieges accompanied by starvation, plague, and sometimes even cannibalism, and finally surrender followed by systematic torture and slaughter.

Though atrocity and terrorism struck unspeakable fear into Assyria's subjects, Assyria's success was actually due to sophisti-

THE KING OF ASSYRIA ON THE MARCH *The might of the Assyrian king and his retinue shines clearly in this relief. With almost photographic precision the artist has captured the details of the chariot's construction, the harness of the horses, and the weapons and equipment of the accompanying infantrymen. (Metropolitan Museum of Art, New York)*

cated, far-sighted, and effective military organization. By Sargon's time the Assyrians had invented the mightiest military machine the ancient Near East had ever seen. The mainstay of the Assyrian army, the soldier who ordinarily decided the outcome of battles, was the infantryman, armed with a spear and sword and protected by helmet and armor. The Assyrian army also featured archers, some on foot, others on horseback, still others in chariots – the latter ready to wield lances once they had expended their supply of arrows. Some infantry archers wore heavy armor, strikingly similar to the armor worn much later by William the Conqueror's Normans. These soldiers served as a primitive field artillery, whose job was to sweep the enemy's walls of defenders so that others could storm the defenses. Slingers also served as artillery in pitched battles. For mobility on the battlefield, the Assyrians organized a corps of chariots.

Assyrian military genius was remarkable for the development of a wide variety of siege machinery and techniques, including excavation to undermine city walls and battering-rams to knock down walls and gates. Never before in the Near East had anyone applied such technical knowledge to warfare. The Assyrians even invented the concept of a corps of engineers, who bridged rivers with pontoons or provided soldiers with inflatable skins for swimming. Furthermore, the Assyrians knew how to coordinate their efforts, both in open battle and in siege warfare. Sennacherib's account of his siege of Jerusalem in 701 B.C. is a vivid portrait of the Assyrian war machine in action:

*As to Hezekiah, the Jew, he did not submit to my yoke, I laid siege to 46 of his strong cities, walled forts and to the countless small villages in their vicinity, and conquered them by means of well-stamped earth-ramps, and battering rams brought thus near to the walls combined with the attack by foot soldiers, using mines, breaches as well as sapper work . . . Himself I made prisoner in Jerusalem, his royal residence, like a bird in a cage. I surrounded him with earthwork in order to molest those who were leaving his city's gate . . . Hezekiah himself, whom the terror-inspiring splendor of my lordship had overwhelmed and whose irregular and elite troops which he had brought into Jerusalem, his royal residence, in order to strengthen it, had deserted him, did send me, later, to Nineveh,*

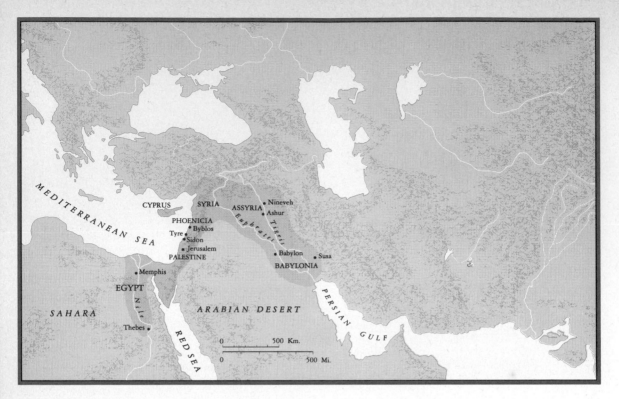

MAP 2.2 THE ASSYRIAN EMPIRE *The As-syrian Empire at its height included almost all of the old centers of power in the ancient Near East.*

*my lordly city, together with 30 talents of gold, 800 talents of silver . . . and all kinds of valuable treasures.*[15]

Hezekiah and Jerusalem shared the fate of many a rebellious king and capital, and were indeed lucky to escape severe reprisals. The Assyrians were too powerful and well organized and far too tenacious to be turned back by isolated strongholds, no matter how well situated or defended.

### ASSYRIAN RULE

Not only did the Assyrians know how to win battles; they also knew how to use their victories. As early as the reign of Tiglath-pileser III, the Assyrian kings began to organize their conquered territories into an empire. The lands closest to Assyria became provinces governed by Assyrian officials. Kingdoms beyond the provinces were not annexed, but became dependent states that followed Assyria's lead. The Assyrian king chose their rulers, either by regulating the succession of native kings or by supporting native kings who appealed to him. The Old Testament recounts how Ahaz, king of Judah, called for help from Tiglath-pileser, and in return for Assyrian support became his vassal:

*So Ahaz sent messengers to Tiglath-pileser king of Assyria, saying, I am thy servant and thy son: come up, and save me out of the hand of the king of Syria, and out of the hand of the king of Israel, which rise up against me. And Ahaz took the*

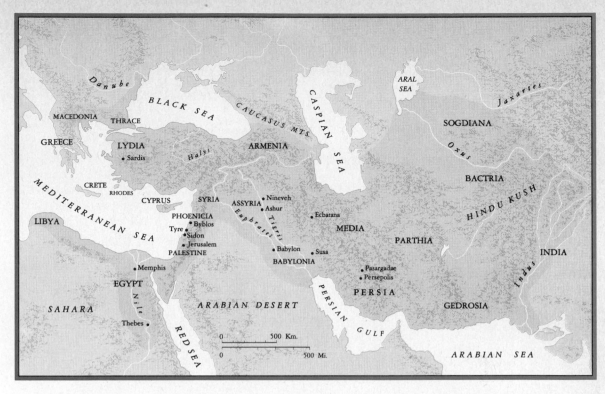

MAP 2.3   THE PERSIAN EMPIRE   *The Persian
Empire not only included more of the ancient Near
East than had the Assyrian Empire, but it also ex-
tended as far east as western India.*

*silver and gold that was found in the house of the
lord, and in the treasures of the king's house, and
sent it for a present to the king of Assyria.*[16]

Against still more distant states the kings
waged frequent war in order to conquer them
outright or to make their dependent states secure.

Royal roads and swift mounted messengers
linked the Assyrian empire, and Assyrian records describe how these royal messengers
brought the king immediate word of unrest
or rebellion within the empire. Because of
good communications, Assyrian kings could
generally move against rebels at a moment's
notice. Thus, though rebellion was common
in the Assyrian empire, it rarely got off the
ground before the king struck back hard.

In the seventh century B.C. Assyrian power
seemed secure. From their capitals at Nineveh,
Kalah, and Ashur on the Tigris river, the Assyrians ruled a vast empire. Good communications, an efficient army, and calculated
terrorism easily kept down the conquered
population. With grim efficiency they sacked
rebellious cities, leaving forests of impaled
prisoners or piles of severed heads to signal
their victory. Their ferocity horrified their
subjects and bred a vast hatred among them.

Yet the downfall of Assyria was swift and
complete. Babylon finally won its independence in 626 B.C. and joined forces with a new
people, the Medes, an Indo-European-speaking folk from Iran. Together the Babylonians
and the Medes destroyed the Assyrian empire
in 612 B.C., paving the way for the rise of the

Persians. The Hebrew prophet Nahum spoke for many when he proclaimed: "Nineveh is laid waste: who will bemoan her?".[17] Their cities destroyed and their power shattered, the Assyrians disappeared from history, remembered only as a cruel people of the Old Testament who oppressed the Hebrews. Two hundred years later, when the Greek adventurer and historian Xenophon passed by the ruins of Nineveh, he marvelled at their extent but knew nothing of the Assyrians. The glory of their empire was forgotten.

Yet modern archaeology has brought the Assyrians out of obscurity. In 1839 the intrepid English archaeologist and traveler A. H. Layard began to excavate Nineveh, then a mound of debris beside the Tigris. His findings electrified the world. In the course of a few years Layard's discoveries shed remarkable new light on Assyrian history. His excavations had an equally stunning impact on the history of art. Layard's workers unearthed masterpieces, including monumental sculpted figures – huge winged bulls, human-headed lions, and sphinxes – as well as brilliantly sculpted friezes. Equally valuable were the numerous Assyrian cuneiform documents, which ranged from royal accounts of mighty military campaigns to simple letters by common people.

Among the most renowned of Layard's finds were the Assyrian palace reliefs, whose number has been increased by the discoveries of twentieth-century archaeologists. Assyrian kings delighted in scenes of war, which their artists depicted in graphic detail. By the time of Ashurbanipal, Assyrian artists had hit upon the idea of portraying a series of episodes – in fact, a visual narrative – of events that had actually taken place. Scene followed scene in a continuous frieze, so the viewer could follow the progress of a military campaign from the time that the army marched out until the

enemy was conquered. So too with another theme of the palace reliefs – the lion hunt. Hunting lions was probably a royal sport, although some scholars have suggested a magical significance. They argue that the hunting scenes depict the king as the protector of his people, the one who wards off evil. In any case, here too the viewer proceeds in sequence, from preparations for the chase through the hunting itself to the killing of the lions. These reliefs, like those depicting warfare, tell a story in pictures, an artistic technique novel in the ancient Near East.

Assyrian art, like much of Egyptian art, was realistic, but the warmth and humor of the Egyptian scenes are absent from the Assyrian reliefs. Assyrian art is stark and often brutal in subject matter, yet marked by an undeniable strength and sophistication of composition. Assyrian realism is well represented by the illustration on page 57, a scene which portrays the climax of the royal lion hunt. The scene is like a photograph, snapped at the height of the action. The king, mounted on horseback, has already fired his arrows into two lions, who nonetheless are still full of fight. The wounded lion on the left has just pounced on a riderless horse, which in a moment will fall mortally wounded. Meanwhile, the king thrusts his spear into another lion, which has begun its spring. The artistic rendering of the figures is exciting and technically flawless. The figures are anatomically correct and in proper proportion and perspective. The whole composition conveys both action and tension. Assyrian art fared better than Assyrian military power. The techniques of Assyrian artists influenced the Persians, who adapted them to gentler scenes.

In fact, many Assyrian innovations, military and political as well as artistic, were taken over wholesale by the Persians. Although the memory of Assyria was hateful throughout

ROYAL LION HUNT *This relief from the palace of Ashurbanipal at Nineveh shows the king fighting two lions, and it is typical of the energy and artistic brilliance of Assyrian sculptors. (Reproduced by Courtesy of the Trustees of the British Museum)*

the Near East, the fruits of Assyrian organizational genius helped enable the Persians to bring peace and stability to the same regions where Assyrian armies had spread terror.

## THE EMPIRE OF THE PERSIAN KINGS

Like the Hittites before them, the Iranians were Indo-Europeans from central Europe and southern Russia who migrated into a land inhabited by more primitive peoples. Once settled in the area between the Caspian Sea and the Persian Gulf, the Iranians, like the Hittites, fell under the spell of the more sophisticated cultures of their Mesopotamian neighbors. Yet the Iranians went on to create one of the greatest empires of antiquity, one that encompassed hundreds of peoples and cultures. The Persians, the most important of the Iranian peoples, had a far-sighted conception of empire. They respected their subjects

and allowed them to practice their native customs and religions. Thus, the Persians gave the Near East political unity coupled with cultural diversity. Never before had any Near Eastern people viewed empire in such intelligent and humane terms.

### THE LAND OF MOUNTAINS AND PLATEAU

Persia – the modern country of Iran – is a stark land of towering mountains and flaming deserts, with a broad central plateau in the heart of the country (see Map 2.3). Iran stretches from the Caspian Sea in the north to the Persian Gulf in the south. Between the Tigris-Euphrates valley in the west and the Indus valley in the east rises an immense plateau, surrounded on all sides by lofty mountains that cut off the interior from the sea.

The central plateau is very high, a landscape of broad plains, scattered oases, and two vast deserts. The high mountains, which catch the moisture coming from the sea, generate ample rainfall for the plain. This semi-tropical area is very fertile, in marked contrast to the aridity of most of Iran. The mountains surrounding the central plateau are dotted with numerous oases, often very fertile, which have from time immemorial served as havens for small groups of people.

At the center of the plateau lies an enormous depression – a forbidding region devoid of water and vegetation, so glowing hot in summer that it is virtually impossible to cross. This depression forms two distinct grim and burning salt deserts, perhaps the most desolate spots on earth. These two deserts form a barrier between east and west.

Iran's geographical position and topography explain its traditional role as the highway between East and West. Throughout history wild, nomadic people migrating from the broad steppes of Russia and Central Asia have streamed into Iran. Confronting the uncrossable salt deserts, most have turned either eastward or westward, moving on until they reached the advanced and wealthy urban centers of Mesopotamia and India. When cities emerged along the natural lines of east-west communication, Iran became the area where nomads met urban dwellers, a meeting-ground of unique significance for the civilizations of both East and West.

## THE COMING OF THE MEDES AND THE PERSIANS

The history of human habitation in Iran is long and rich: traces of prehistoric peoples date back as far as 15,000–10,000 B.C. About the prehistoric period, historians and archaeologists still have much to learn. Perhaps the best recent account of prehistoric developments comes from one of the world's foremost experts on ancient Iran, the French scholar Roman Ghirshman:

*The arrival of the Iranians in the plateau was preceded by a long period of several millennia, during which there slowly developed the civilization of prehistoric man, who, coming down from his caves, established himself in the plains and valleys. Over the course of more than thirty centuries man acquired the knowledge of and developed agriculture, domesticated animals, took the first steps in metallurgy. His art of painted pottery, doubtless born in the plateau, underwent a rapid rise and extensive diffusion. Man organized his social life by creating villages, and, never remaining isolated, he established and enlarged his contacts with other human groups.*[18]

The Iranians entered this land around 1000 B.C. The most historically important of them were the Medes and the Persians, related peoples who settled in different areas. Both groups were part of the vast movement of Indo-European-speaking peoples whose wanderings led them into Europe, the Near East, and India in many successive waves (page 31). These Iranians were nomads, who migrated with their flocks and herds. Like their kinsmen the Aryans, who moved into India, they were also horse-breeders, and the horse gave them a decisive military advantage over the prehistoric peoples of Iran. The Iranians rode into battle in horse-drawn chariots or on horseback, and easily swept the natives before them. Yet because the influx of Iranians went on for centuries, there continued to be constant cultural interchange between conquering newcomers and conquered natives.

Excavations at Siyalk, some 125 miles south of present-day Tehran, provide a valuable glimpse of the encounter of Iranian and native. The village of Siyalk had been inhabited since prehistoric times before falling to the Iranians. The new lords fought all comers: natives, rival Iranians, and even the Assyrians, who often raided far east of the

Tigris. Under the newly-arrived Iranians, Siyalk became a fortified town with a palace and perhaps a temple, all enclosed by a circuit wall strengthened by towers and ramparts. The town was surrounded by fields and farms, for agriculture was the basis of this evolving society.

The Iranians initially created a patchwork of tiny kingdoms, of which Siyalk was one. The chieftain or petty king was basically a warlord who depended on his fellow warriors for aid and support. This band of noble warriors, like the Greek heroes of the *Iliad,* formed the fighting strength of the army. The king owned estates that supported him and his nobles; for additional income the king levied taxes, which were paid in kind and not in cash. He also demanded labor services from the peasants. Below the king and his warrior nobles were free people who held land and others who owned nothing. Artisans produced the various goods needed to keep society running. At the bottom of the social scale were slaves – probably both natives and new-comers – to whom fell the drudgery of hard labor and household service to the king and his nobles.

This early period saw some significant economic developments. The use of iron increased. By the seventh century B.C. iron farm implements had become widespread, leading to increased productivity, greater overall prosperity, and higher standards of living. At the same time Iranian agriculture saw the development of the small estate. Farmers worked small plots of land, and the general prosperity of the period bred a sturdy and free peasantry, who enjoyed greater freedom than their contemporaries in Egypt and Mesopotamia.

Kings exploited Iran's considerable mineral wealth, and Iranian iron, copper, and lapis lazuli attracted Assyrian raiding parties. Even

more important, mineral wealth and Iranian horse-breeding stimulated brisk trade with the outside world. Kings found that merchants, who were not usually Iranians, produced large profits to help fill the kings' coffers. Overland trade also put the Iranians in direct contact with their Near Eastern neighbors.

Gradually two groups of Iranians began coalescing into larger units. The Persians had settled in Persis, the modern region of Fars, in southern Iran. Their kinsmen the Medes occupied Media, the modern area of Hamádan in the north, with their capital at Ecbatana. The Medes were exposed to attack by nomads from the north, but their greatest threat was the frequent raids of the Assyrian army. Even though distracted by grave pressures from their neighbors, the Medes united under one king around 710 B.C., and extended their control over the Persians in the south. In 612 B.C. the Medes were strong enough to join the Babylonians in overthrowing the Assyrian Empire. With the rise of the Medes, the balance of power in the Near East shifted for the first time east of Mesopotamia.

## THE CREATION OF THE PERSIAN EMPIRE

In 550 B.C. Cyrus the Great (559–530 B.C.), king of the Persians and one of the most remarkable statesmen of antiquity, threw off the yoke of the Medes by conquering them and turning their country into his first satrapy, or province. In the short space of a single lifetime, Cyrus created one of the greatest empires of antiquity. Two characteristics lift Cyrus above the common level of warrior-kings. First, he thought of Iran, not just Persia and Media, as a state. His concept has survived a long, complex, and often turbulent history to play its part in the contemporary world.

Second, Cyrus held an enlightened view of

TOMB OF CYRUS  *For all of his greatness Cyrus retained a sense of perspective. His tomb, though monumental in size, is rather simple and unostentatious. Greek writers reported that it bore the following epitaph: "O man, I am Cyrus the son of Cambyses. I established the Persian Empire and was king of Asia. Do not begrudge me my memorial." (Oriental Institute, University of Chicago)*

empire. Many of the civilizations and cultures that fell to his armies were, he realized, far older, more advanced, and more sophisticated than his. Free of the narrow-minded snobbery of the Egyptians, the religious exclusiveness of the Hebrews, and the calculated cruelty of the Assyrians, Cyrus gave Near Eastern peoples and their cultures his respect, toleration, and protection. Conquered peoples continued to enjoy their institutions, religion, language, and way of life under the Persians. The Persian Empire, which Cyrus created, became a political organization sheltering many different civilizations. To rule such a vast area and so many diverse peoples demanded talent, intelligence, sensitivity, and a cosmopolitan view of the world. These qualities Cyrus and many of his successors possessed in abundance. Consequently, the Persians gave the

ancient Near East over two hundred years of peace, prosperity, and security.

Cyrus showed his magnanimity at the outset of his career. Once the Medes had fallen to him, Cyrus united them with his Persians. Ecbatana, the Median capital, became a Persian seat of power. Medes were honored with important military and political posts, and thenceforth helped the Persians to rule the expanding empire. Cyrus' conquest of the Medes resulted not in slavery and slaughter, but in the union of Iranian peoples.

With Iran united, Cyrus looked at the broader world. He set out to achieve two goals: first, to win control of the west, and thus of the terminal ports of the great trade routes that crossed Iran and Anatolia. Secondly, Cyrus strove to secure eastern Iran from the pressure of nomadic invaders. In 550 B.C. neither goal was easy. To the northwest was the young kingdom of Lydia in Anatolia, whose king Croesus was proverbial for his wealth. To the west was Babylonia, enjoying a new period of power now that the Assyrian Empire had been crushed. To the southwest was Egypt, still weak but sheltered behind its bulwark of sand and sea. To the east ranged tough, mobile nomads, capable of massive and destructive incursions deep into Iranian territory.

Cyrus turned first to Croesus' Lydian kingdom, which fell to him around 546 B.C. He established a garrison at Sardis, the capital of Lydia, and ordered his generals to subdue the Greek cities along the coast of Anatolia. Cyrus had thus gained the important ports that looked out to the Mediterranean world. And for the first time the Persians came into direct contact with the Greeks, a people with whom their later history was to be intimately connected.

From Lydia, Cyrus next marched to the far eastern corners of Iran. In a brilliant campaign he conquered the regions of Parthia, Bactria, and even the most westerly part of India. All of Iran was now Persian, from Mesopotamia in the west to the western slopes of the Hindu Kush in the east.

In 540 B.C. Cyrus moved against Babylonia, now isolated from outside help. When Persian soldiers marched quietly into Babylon the next year, the Babylonians welcomed Cyrus as a liberator. Cyrus described the event himself thus:

*When I made my gracious entry into Babylon, with rejoicing and pleasure I took up my lordly residence in the royal palace. Marduk, the great lord, turned the noble race of the Babylonians toward me, and I gave daily care to his worship. My numerous troops marched peacefully into Babylon. In all Sumer and Akkad I permitted no unfriendly treatment. The dishonoring yoke was removed from them. Their fallen dwellings I restored; I cleared out the ruins.*[19]

Cyrus won the hearts of the Babylonians with toleration of and adherence to Babylonian religion, humane treatment, and support of their efforts to refurbish their capital.

Cyrus was equally generous toward the Jews. He allowed them to return to Palestine, from which they had been deported by the Babylonians. He protected them, gave them back the sacred items they used in worship, and rebuilt the temple of Yahweh in Jerusalem. The Old Testament sings the praises of Cyrus, whom the Jews considered the shepherd of Yahweh, the lord's anointed:

*[Yahweh] that saith of Cyrus, he is my shepherd, and shall perform all my pleasure: even saying to Jerusalem, thou shalt be built; and to the temple, thy foundation shall be laid. Thus saith the lord to his anointed, to Cyrus, whose right hand I have holden, to subdue nations before him.*[20]

Rarely have conquered people shown such gratitude to their conquerors. Cyrus's benevolent policy created a Persian Empire in which the cultures and religions of its members were respected and honored. Seldom have conquerors been as wise, sensitive, and far-sighted as Cyrus and his Persians.

### THUS SPAKE ZARATHUSTRA

Iranian religion was originally simple and primitive. Ahuramazda, the chief god, was the creator and benefactor of all living creatures. Yet unlike Yahweh, he was not a lone god. The Iranians were polytheistic. Mithra the sun god, whose cult would later spread throughout the Roman Empire (page 187), saw to justice and redemption. Other Iranian deities personified the natural elements: moon, earth, water, and wind. As in ancient India, fire was a particularly important god. The sacred fire consumed the blood sacrifices that the early Iranians offered to all of their deities.

Early Iranian religion was close to nature and unencumbered by ponderous theological beliefs. A priestly class, the Magi, developed among the Medes to officiate at sacrifices, chant prayers to the gods, and tend the sacred flame. A fine, concise description of this early worship comes from the great German historian Eduard Meyer:

*Iranian religion knew neither divine images nor temples. On a hilltop one called upon god and his manifestations — sun and moon, earth and fire, water and wind — and erected altars with their eternal fire. But in other appropriate places one could, without further preparation, pray to the deity and bring him his offerings, with the assistance of the Magi, who in addition chanted the holy formulas.*[21]

In time the Iranians built fire temples for these sacrifices. As late as the nineteenth century, fire was still worshiped in Baku, a major city on the Russian-Iranian border.

Around 600 B.C. the prophet Zarathustra – or Zoroaster, as he is more generally known – breathed new meaning into Iranian religion. Of Zoroaster the man, as little is known as of Moses; like his Jewish counterpart, Zoroaster is remembered for his work, which long outlived him. Like Moses, Zoroaster preached a novel concept of divinity and human life. Life, he taught, is a constant battleground between two opposing forces, good and evil. Ahuramazda embodied good and truth but was opposed by Ahriman, a hateful spirit who stood for evil and falsehood. Ahuramazda and Ahriman were locked together in a cosmic battle for the human race, a battle that stretched over thousands of years. But, according to Zoroaster, people were not mere pawns in this struggle. Each person had to choose which side to join – whether to lead a life characterized by good behavior and truthful dealings with others or by wickedness and lies.

Zoroaster emphasized the responsibility of the individual in this decision. He taught that people possessed the free will to decide between Ahuramazda and Ahriman, and that people must rely on their own consciences to guide them through life. Their decisions were crucial, Zoroaster warned, for there would be a time of reckoning. He promised that Ahuramazda would eventually triumph over evil and lies, and that at death each person would stand before the tribunal of good. Ahuramazda, like the Egyptian god Osiris, would judge whether the dead had lived righteously and on that basis would weigh their lives in the balance. Then good and truth would conquer evil and lies. In short, Zoroaster taught the concept of a Last Judgment at which Ahuramazda would decide each person's eternal fate on the basis of that person's deeds in life.

In Zoroaster's thought the Last Judgment was linked to the notion of a divine kingdom after death for those who had lived according to good and truth. They would accompany Ahuramazda to a life of eternal truth in what Zoroaster called "the House of Song" and "the Abode of Good Thought." There they would dwell with Ahuramazda forever. Liars and the wicked, denied this blessed immortality, would be condemned to eternal pain, darkness, and punishment. Thus, Zoroaster preached a Last Judgment that led to a heaven or a hell.

Although tradition has it that Zoroaster met with opposition and coldness, his thought converted Darius (521–486 B.C.), one of the most energetic men ever to sit on the Persian throne. The Persian royal family adopted Zoroastrianism, though without trying to impose it on others. Under the protection of the Persian kings, Zoroastrianism swept through Iran, winning converts and sinking roots that sustained healthy growth for centuries. Zoroastrianism survived the fall of the Persian Empire to influence religious thought in the age of Jesus and to make a vital contribution to Manicheanism, a theology that was to spread through the Byzantine Empire and pose a significant challenge to Christianity. A handful of the faithful still follow the teachings of Zoroaster, whose vision of divinity and human life has transcended the centuries.

## PERSIA'S WORLD EMPIRE

Cyrus' successors rounded out the Persian conquest of the ancient Near East. In 525 B.C. Cyrus's son Cambyses (530–522 B.C.) subdued Egypt. Darius (521–486 B.C.) and his son Xerxes (486–464 B.C.) invaded Greece, but were fought to a standstill and forced to retreat (Chapter 3); the Persians never won a permanent foothold in Europe. Yet Darius

*DARIUS AND XERXES   This relief from the Persian capital of Persepolis shows King Darius and Crown Prince Xerxes in state. Behind them the royal bodyguard stands at attention, as the royal pair receives the guard's commander. (Oriental Institute, University of Chicago)*

carried Persian arms into India. Around 513 B.C. western India became the Persian satrapy, or province, of Hindush, which included the valley of the Indus river. Thus, within thirty-seven years the Persians transformed themselves from a subject people to the rulers of an empire that included Anatolia, Egypt, Mesopotamia, Iran, and western India. They had created a "world empire" encompassing all of the oldest and most honored kingdoms and peoples of the ancient Near East. Never before had the Near East been united in one such vast political organization (see Map 2.3).

The Persians knew how to use the peace that they had won on the battlefield. Unlike the Assyrians, they did not resort to royal terrorism to keep order. Like the Assyrians, however, they employed a number of bureaucratic techniques to bind the empire together. The sheer size of the empire made it impossible for one man to rule it effectively. Consequently the Persians divided the empire into some twenty huge satrapies — provinces measuring hundreds of square miles, many of

them kingdoms in themselves. Each satrapy had a governor, drawn from the Median and Persian nobility and often a relative of the king; the governor or satrap was directly responsible to the king. An army officer, also responsible to the king, commanded the military forces stationed in the satrapy. Still another official collected the royal taxes. Moreover, the king sent out royal inspectors to watch the satraps and other officials, a method of royal surveillance later used by the medieval king Charlemagne (Chapter 8).

Effective rule of the empire demanded good communications. To meet this need the Persians established a network of roads. The main highway, known as the Royal Road, spanned some 1677 miles from the Greek city of Ephesus on the coast of Asia Minor to Susa in western Iran. The distance was broken into 111 post-stations, each equipped with fresh horses for the king's messengers. Other roads branched out to link all parts of the empire, from the coast of Asia Minor to the valley of the Indus river. Along these roads royal

THE ROYAL PALACE AT PERSEPOLIS *King Darius began and King Xerxes finished building a grand palace worthy of the glory of the Persian Empire. Pictured here is the monumental audience hall,* *where the king dealt with ministers of state and foreign envoys. (Oriental Institute, University of Chicago)*

couriers sped so quickly that the Greek historian and traveler Herodotus marvelled at them:

*There is nothing which is mortal that arrives faster than these couriers ... For they say that as many days as the whole journey takes that many horses and men stand at intervals, a horse and man stationed at each daily segment of road. These neither snow nor rain nor heat nor night prevents from traversing their appointed run as fast as possible. The first courier hands over the dispatch to the second, the second to the third. Thereafter from one to another the dispatch passes on.*[22]

This system of communications enabled the Persian king to keep in intimate touch with his subjects and officials. He was able to rule efficiently, keep his ministers in line, and protect the rights of the peoples under his control. How effective Persian rule could be, even in small matters, is apparent in a letter from King Darius to the satrap of Ionia, the Greek region of Anatolia. The satrap had transplanted Syrian fruit trees in his province, an experiment Darius praised. Yet the king also learned that his governor had infringed on the rights granted to the sanctuary of the Greek god Apollo, an act that provoked the king to anger:

*The King of Kings, Darius the son of Hystaspes says this to Gadatas, his slave [satrap]. I learn that you are not obeying my command in every particular. Because you are tilling my land, transplanting fruit trees from across the Euphrates [Syria] to Asia Minor, I praise your project, and there will be laid up for you great favor in the king's house. But because you mar my dispositions towards the gods, I shall give you, unless you change your ways, proof of my anger when wronged. For you exacted payment from the sacred gardeners of the temple of Apollo, and you ordered them to dig up secular land, failing to understand the attitude of my forefathers towards the god, who told the Persians the truth.*[23]

Fruit trees and foreign gods — even such small matters as these were important to the man whom the world called "The King of Kings, the King of Persia, the King of the Provinces."[24] This document alone suggests the efficiency of Persian rule and the compassion of Persian kings. Conquered peoples, left free to enjoy their traditional ways of life, found in the Persian king a capable protector. No wonder that many Near Eastern peoples were, like the Jews, grateful for the long period of peace they enjoyed as the subjects of the Persian Empire.

———◆———

Between around 1200 and 500 B.C. the Near East passed from fragmentation to political unification under the Persian Empire. On the road from chaos to order, from widespread warfare to general peace, peoples in many areas wrought vast and enduring achievements. The Egyptians survived invasion to share their heritage with their African neighbors and later with the Greeks. The homeless Hebrews laboriously built a state and entered the broader world of their neighbors. Simultaneously, they evolved religious and ethical beliefs that permeate the modern West.

Although the Assyrians made the Near

East tremble in terror of their armies, they too contributed to the heritage of these long years. Their military and, particularly, political abilities gave the Persians the tools they needed to govern a host of different peoples. Those tools were to be well used. For over two hundred years Persian kings offered their subjects enlightened rule. The Persians gave the ancient Near East a period of peace and stability in which peoples enjoyed their native traditions and lived in concord with their neighbors.

Meanwhile to the west, another people — the Greeks — were slowly shaping cultural and political ideals that were to have an even greater impact on the future. Although Greece and the Near East would eventually become locked in a mighty conflict, the heritage of the East would blend with that of Greece to influence Western civilization in a fundamental way.

—————————————

## Notes

1. James H. Breasted, *Ancient Records of Egypt,* University of Chicago Press, Chicago, 1907, IV, paragraph 398.

2. J. B. Pritchard, ed., *Ancient Near Eastern Texts,* Princeton University Press, Princeton, 1950, p. 27.

3. 1 Kings 8:4-6.

4. 2 Kings 23:3.

5. Jeremiah 7:5-7.

6. Ibid. 3:12.

7. Proverbs 31:10, 25-30.

8. Deuteronomy 24:1-2.

9. Psalms 128:3.

10. Deuteronomy 25:9.

11. Proverbs 13:24.

12. Deuteronomy 24:19.

13. Jeremiah 23:13.

14. Pritchard, *op. cit.*, p. 288.

15. Ibid.

16. 2 Kings 16:7–8.

17. Nahum 3:7.

18. R. Ghirshman, *L'Iran des origines à l'Islam,* Albin Michel, Paris, 1976, p. 343.

19. Quoted from A. T. Olmstead, *A History of the Persian Empire,* University of Chicago Press, Chicago, 1963, p. 53.

20. Isaiah 44:28–45:1.

21. E. Meyer, *Geschichte des Altertums,* 7th ed., Vol. IV, Part I, Wissenschaftliche Buchgesellschaft, Darmstadt, 1975, pp. 114–115.

22. Herodotus 8.98.

23. R. Meiggs and D. M. Lewis, *A Selection of Greek Historical Inscriptions,* Clarendon Press, Oxford, 1969, no. 12.

24. Behistun Inscription col. 1.1.

## SUGGESTED READING

Although late Egyptian history is still largely a specialist's field, K. A. Kitchen, *The Third Intermediate Period in Egypt (1100–650 B.C.)* (1973) is a good synthesis of the period. Valuable too is M. L. Bierbrier's monograph, *Late New Kingdom in Egypt, c. 1300–664 B.C.* (1975). More general is R. David, *The Egyptian Kingdoms* (1975). H. S. Smith, *A Visit to Ancient Egypt: Life at Memphis and Saqqara (c. 500–30 B.C.* (1974) gives a picture of life during the period, and P. L. Shinnie, *Meroe: A Civilization of the Sudan* (1967), does the same for one of Egypt's most important southern neighbors. Those interested in the whole story of Wen-Amon's adventures should read H. Goedicke, *The Report of Wenamun* (1975). Sir A. H. Gardiner, ed., *Late Egyptian Stories* (1973) contains other pieces of late Egyptian literature.

D. Harden, *The Phoenicians,* 2nd ed. (1971) gives a good account of Phoenician history and life. More recently, G. Herm, *The Phoenicians: The Purple Empire of the Ancient World* (1975), treats Phoe-nician seafaring and commercial enterprises. A more general treatment of the entire area is R. Fedden, *Syria and Lebanon,* 3rd ed. (1965). Those interested in individual Phoenician cities should see N. Jidejian, *Byblos through the Ages,* 2nd ed. (1971), *Tyre through the Ages* (1969), and *Sidon through the Ages* (1971). For a history of Phoenicia written at the time of the Roman Empire, see A. I. Baumgarten, *The Phoenician History of Philo of Byblos* (1981).

The Jews have been one of the best studied people in the ancient world, and the reader can easily find many good treatments of Jewish history and society. A readable and balanced book is J. Bright, *A History of Israel,* 2nd ed. (1972). Somewhat older is A. S. Kapelrud, *Israel from Earliest Times to the Birth of Christ* (1966). Other useful general books include G. W. Anderson, *The History and Religion of Israel* (1966), which is a solid scholarly treatment of the subject. The archaeological exploration of ancient Israel is so fast-paced that nearly any book is quickly outdated. Nonetheless, A. Negev, *Archaeological Encyclopedia of the Holy Land* (1973), which is illustrated, is still a good place to start.

S. Yeivin, *The Israelite Conquest of Canaan* (1971), though a bit dated, is a good survey of the Jewish entry into Palestine. M. Pearlman, *In the Footsteps of Moses* (1974), a more popular account, also treats the period. R. de Vaux, *Ancient Israel, Its Life and Institutions,* 2nd ed. (1965), ranges across all eras of Jewish history, and is especially recommended because of its solid base in the ancient sources. The period of Jewish kingship has elicited a good deal of attention. Most recent is B. Halpern, *The Constitution of the Monarchy in Israel* (1981), which makes the significant point that the Jews are the only ancient Near Eastern people to have recorded the decision to adopt monarchy as a form of government. Also valuable in this connection is A. R. Johnson, *Sacral Kingship in Ancient Israel,* 2nd ed. (1967). Solomon's importance as a strong king and an innovator is underlined by a series of studies, especially T. N. Mettinger, *Solomonic State Officials: A Study of the Civil Service Officials of the Israelite Monarchy* (1971); E. W. Heaton, *Solomon's New Men: The*

*Emergence of Ancient Israel as a National State* (1974); and lastly J. Gutmann, *The Temple of Solomon* (1975).

More specific than de Vaux' splendid general work on Hebrew society is P. A. H. de Boer, *Fatherhood and Motherhood in Israelite and Judean Piety* (1974), which treats a fundamental aspect of Jewish religion and society. A fascinating and ambitious new study of myth and religion is J. O'Brien and W. Major, *In the Beginning: Creation Myths from Ancient Mesopotamia, Israel and Greece* (1981). Lastly, P. R. Ackroyd, *Israel under Babylon and Persia* (1970), gives an informative account of Jewish inability to resist expansion of the great monarchies.

The Assyrians, despite their achievements, have not attracted the scholarly attention that the ancient Jews and other Near Eastern peoples have. Even though outdated, A. T. Olmstead, *History of Assyria* (1928), still possesses the merit of being soundly based in the original sources. Olmstead was a rare scholar who attempted to understand the entire development of the ancient Near East. More recent and more difficult is J. A. Brinkman, *A Political History of Post-Kassite Babylonia, 1158–722 B.C.* (1968), which treats the Babylonian response to the rise of Assyria. M. Cogan, *Imperialism and Religion: Assyria, Judah and Israel in the Eighth and Seventh Centuries B.C.E.* (1973), traces the various effects of Assyrian expansion on the two Jewish kingdoms.

An informative look at the Assyrians themselves comes from J. Laessoe, *People of Ancient Assyria:*

*Their Inscriptions and Correspondence* (1963). Those who appreciate the vitality of Assyrian art should start with the masterful work of R. D. Barnett and W. Forman, *Assyrian Palace Reliefs,* 2nd ed. (1970), an exemplary combination of fine photographs and learned, though not difficult, discussion.

In addition to the works on Iran cited in the Notes, G. C. Cameron, *History of Early Iran* (1969); W. Culican, *The Medes and the Persians* (1965); and J. A. deGobineau, *The World of the Persians* (1971), which is illustrated with color plates, all provide introductions to Persian history. Vastly informative but difficult is E. Herzfeld, *The Persian Empire: Studies in the Geography and Ethnology of the Ancient Near East* (1968), a posthumous work by one of the world's leading authorities on the Persians. Very useful is J. D. Pearson, ed., *A Bibliography of Pre-Islamic Persia* (1975). S. A. Matheson, *Persia: An Archaeological Guide* (1972), is a good guide to Persian monuments. A good brief account of Cyrus the Great's career can be found in M. E. L. Mallowan, "Cyrus the Great (558–529 B.C.)," *Iran* 10 (1972), 1–17.

J. H. Moulton, *Early Zoroastrianism: The Origins, the Prophet, and the Magi* (1972), is a sound treatment of the beginnings and early spread of Zoroastrianism. R. C. Zaehner, *The Dawn and Twilight of Zoroastrianism* (1961) discusses the whole course of Zoroastrianism's history. Zaehner also provides a good introduction to the basic teachings of Zoroastrianism in his *Teachings of the Magi: A Compendium of Zoroastrian Beliefs* (1975).

# CHAPTER 3

## THE LEGACY OF GREECE

THE ANCIENT NEAR EAST was the seat of old cultures and rich empires, but the rocky peninsula of Greece was the home of the civilization that fundamentally shaped Western civilization. The Greeks were the first to explore most of the questions that continue to concern Western thinkers to this day. Going beyond mythmaking and religion, the Greeks strove to understand, in logical, rational terms, the universe and the position of men and women in it. The result was the birth of philosophy and science, which were far more important to most Greek thinkers than religion. The Greeks speculated on human beings and society and created the very concept of politics.

While the scribes of the ancient Near East produced king lists, the Greeks invented history to record, analyze, and understand how people and states functioned in time and space. In poetry, the Greeks spoke as individuals. In drama, they dealt with the grandeur and weakness of humanity and with the demands of society on the individual. The greatest monuments of the Greeks were not temples, statues, or tombs, but profound thoughts set down in terms as fresh and immediate today as they were some 2,400 years ago.

The history of the Greeks is divided into two broad periods: the Hellenic (the subject of this chapter), roughly the time between the arrival of the Greeks and the triumph of Philip of Macedon, and the Hellenistic, the age beginning with Alexander the Great and ending with the Roman conquest (the subject of Chapter 4).

What geographical factors helped to mold the evolution of the city-state and to shape the course of the Greek experience? How did the Greeks develop basic political forms – forms as different as democracy and tyranny – that have influenced all of later Western history?

MAP 3.1   ANCIENT GREECE   *In antiquity the home of the Greeks included the islands of the Aegean and the western shore of Turkey as well as the Greek peninsula itself.*

What did the Greek intellectual triumph entail? And, lastly, how and why did the Greek genius eventually fail? These profound questions, which can never be fully answered, are the themes of this chapter.

## THE LAND AND THE POLIS

Hellas, as the ancient Greeks called their land, encompassed the Aegean Sea and its islands as well as the Greek peninsula (see Map 3.1). The Greek peninsula itself is an extension of the Balkan system of mountains, stretching in the direction of Egypt and the Near East. Greece is mountainous; its rivers are never more than creeks, and most of them go dry in the summer. It is, however, a land blessed with good harbors, the most important of which look to the east. The islands of the Aegean continue to sweep to the east, and serve as steppingstones between the peninsula and Anatolia. As early as 1000 B.C., Greeks from the peninsula had settled along the coastline of Anatolia (Asia Minor); the heartland of these eastern Greeks was in Ionia. Thus, geography alone encouraged the Greeks to turn their attention to the old civilizations of Asia Minor and Egypt.

Despite the poverty of its soil, Greece is strikingly beautiful, as the eminent German historian K. J. Beloch has written:

*Greece is an alpine land, which rises from the waters of the Mediterranean sea, scenically probably the most beautiful region in southern Europe. The noble contours of the mountains, the bare,*

*rocky slopes, the dusty green of the conifer forests, the white cover of snow which envelops the higher summits for the greatest part of the year, added to which is the profound blue surface of the sea below, and above everything the diffused brightness of the southern sun; this gives a total picture, the charm of which impresses itself unforgettably on the soul of the observer.*[1]

The Greeks gloried in their land, and its beauty was one of the factors that elicited their loyalty to the soil of this hard peninsula. The climate of Greece is mild; though hot in summer, the air is dry and stirred by breezes. In winter snow may blanket the mountain slopes, but rarely covers the lowlands.

Simultaneously, geography acted as an enormously divisive force in Greek life. The mountains of Greece dominate the landscape. They cut the land into many small pockets, and isolate areas of inhabitation from one another. Innumerable peninsulas open to the sea, which is dotted with islands, most of them small and many uninhabitable. The geographical fragmentation of Greece encouraged political fragmentation. Furthermore, communications were extraordinarily poor. Rocky tracks were far more common than roads, and the few roads were unpaved. Usually they were nothing more than a pair of ruts cut into the rock to accommodate the wheels of vehicles. The small physical units of Greece discouraged the growth of great empires.

As in Sumer, the typical Greek political unit was the city-state, which the Greeks called the polis. Rarely did there occur the combination of extensive territory and political unity that allowed one polis to rise above others. Only three city-states were able to muster the resources of an entire region behind them (see Map 3.2): Sparta, which dominated the regions of Laconia and Messenia;

Athens, which united the large peninsula of Attica under its rule; and Thebes, which in several periods marshaled the resources of the fertile region of Boeotia. Otherwise, the political pattern of ancient Greece was one of many small city-states, few of which were much stronger or richer than their neighbors.

Physically, the term *polis* designated a city or town and its surrounding countryside. The typical polis consisted of people living in a compact group of houses within the city. The city's water supply came from public fountains and cisterns. By the fifth century B.C., the city was generally surrounded by a wall. The city contained a point, usually elevated, called the acropolis, and a public square or marketplace (agora). On the acropolis, which in the early period was a place of refuge, stood the temples, altars, public monuments, and various dedications to the gods of the polis. The agora was originally the place where the warrior assembly met, but it became the political center of the polis. In the agora were porticoes, shops, and public buildings, such as council and administrative buildings and courts.

The unsettled territory of the polis was typically the source of its wealth. This territory consisted of arable land, pastureland, and wasteland. Farmers left the city each morning to work their fields or tend their flocks of sheep and goats, and they returned to the city at night. On the wasteland men often quarried stone, mined for precious metals, or at certain times of the year obtained small amounts of fodder. Thus, the polis encompassed a combination of urban and agrarian life.

Regardless of its size or wealth, the polis was fundamental to Greek life. Aristotle, perhaps Greece's greatest thinker, could not envisage civilized life apart from the polis. "The

MAP 3.2  COLONIZATION OF THE MEDITER-
RANEAN  Although both the Greeks and Phoenicians colonized the Mediterranean basin at roughly
the same time, the Greeks spread over far greater
areas.

polis," he wrote, "exists by nature, and man is by nature a being of the polis."[2] Aristotle was summing up the Greek view that the life of men and women in the polis was the only way to live according to nature.

The polis was far more than a political institution. Above all, it was a community of citizens, and the affairs of the community were the concern of all citizens. The intimacy of the polis was an important factor, and one hard for modern city dwellers to imagine. The philosopher Plato thought that five thousand citizens constituted the right population for an ideal polis. Though utopian, Plato was not

in this case being unrealistic. Although population figures for Greece are mostly guesswork, because most city-states were small enough not to need a census, the polis of Thebes in Boeotia is a useful illustration of how small a Greek state was. When Alexander the Great destroyed Thebes in 335 B.C., he sold thirty thousand people into slavery. Some six thousand people had died in the fighting, and many others he spared. Thus the free population of Thebes had numbered between thirty and forty thousand at most, and Thebes was a large polis, a major power. Most city-states were far smaller.

THE SHAPE OF THE ATHENIAN POLIS    This quaint print, which depicts the Athenian acropolis and surrounding area, shows clearly the basic geographical requirements of the polis. Early Greeks desired an elevated spot, or acropolis, as a place of refuge. Later, in more secure times, the acropolis often became the main seat of the polis' temples. At the foot of the citadel spread the agora, public buildings, and private homes. (Photo: Caroline Buckler)

The mild climate of Greece meant that much of Greek life was spent outdoors. In a polis, as in a modern Greek village, a person might easily see most other citizens in the course of the day. Nearly everything that happened within the polis was known immediately and discussed at length. Any stranger who arrived with news from abroad found a large and talkative audience at once. Similarly, the citizen would normally see the public buildings and the temples of the polis daily. The monuments of past victories, the tombs of dead warriors, all these would be personal and familiar. In short, life in the polis was very public. The smallness of the polis enabled Greeks to see how the individual fitted into the overall system – how the human parts made up the social whole.

The customs of the community were at the same time the laws of the polis. Rome later created a single magnificent body of law, but the Greeks had as many law codes as they had city-states. Though the laws of one polis might be roughly similar to those of another polis, the law of any given polis was unique simply because the customs and the experience of each polis had been unique.

The polis also had a religious aspect. Although all Greeks customarily worshiped the great deities – Zeus, Hera, Apollo, Athena, and others, who supposedly lived on Mount Olympus – the citizens of each polis had their own particular cults for these gods. Besides the Olympian gods, each polis had its own minor deities, each with his or her own local cult. Participation in the cults and rituals was a civic duty. By honoring the gods and goddesses of the polis, the citizens honored the polis itself. But this civic religion, unlike the religion of the Hebrews, did not entail religious belief. What individuals believed was their own business. Citizens could be total atheists, but they were still expected to participate in the religion of the polis. Their participation did not brand them as hypocrites, but rather as loyal citizens.

The polis could be governed in any of several ways. First, it could be a monarchy, a term derived from the Greek for "the rule of one man." A king could represent the community, reigning according to law and respecting the rights of the citizens. Second, the aristocracy – those who owed their position to birth – could govern the state. Third, the running of the polis could be the duty and prerogative of an oligarchy, which literally means "the rule of a few" – a small group of wealthy citizens, regardless of their status at birth. Or the polis could be governed by a democracy, the rule of the people, which in Greece meant that all the citizens, without respect to birth or wealth, administered the workings of government. How a polis was governed depended on who had the upper hand. When the wealthy held power, they usually instituted oligarchies; when the people could break the hold of the rich, they established democracies. In any case, no polis ever had an iron-clad and unchangeable constitution.

Still another form of Greek government was tyranny. Under tyranny the polis was ruled by a tyrant, a man who had seized power by unconstitutional means. The Greeks did not in theory consider tyranny a legitimate form of government, but in practice it flourished from the seventh century B.C. to the end of the Classical Period. Although the earliest tyrants may have been popular figures, abuses of tyranny soon gave this type of government a bad name. One lasting effect of

tyranny, nevertheless, was to break the exclusive hold of the aristocracy on Greek government. Even so, the Greeks always considered tyranny a political perversion.

Ironically, the very integration of the polis proved to be one of its weaknesses. Because the bonds that held the polis together were so intimate, Greeks were extremely reluctant to allow foreigners to share fully in its life. An alien, even someone Greek by birth, could almost never expect to be made a citizen. Nor could women play a political role in the polis. Women participated in the civic cults, and they served as priestesses, but the polis had no room for them in state affairs. Thus, the exclusiveness of the polis doomed it to a limited horizon.

The individualism of the polis proved to be another serious weakness. The citizens of each polis were determined to remain free and autonomous. Rarely were the Greeks willing to unite in larger political bodies. When they did, they preferred leagues or confederations in which each polis insisted on its autonomy. The political result in Greece, as in Sumer, was almost constant warfare. The polis could dominate, but unlike Rome it could not incorporate.

## THE BRONZE AGE
### (2000 – 1100 B.C.)

Greek-speaking peoples did not enter the peninsula of Greece until the Bronze Age. Of these early years the ancient Greeks themselves remembered almost nothing. One of the sterling achievements of modern archaeology is the discovery of this lost past. In the nineteenth century, Heinrich Schliemann, a German businessman turned archaeologist, excavated the site of Mycenae in Greece and

| PERIOD | SIGNIFICANT EVENTS | MAJOR WRITERS |
|---|---|---|
| Bronze Age 2000–1100 B.C. | Arrival of the Greeks in Greece<br>Rise and fall of the Mycenaean kingdoms | |
| Dark Age 1100–800 B.C. | Greek migrations within the Aegean basin<br>Social and political recovery<br>Evolution of the polis<br>Rebirth of literacy | Homer<br>Hesiod |
| Lyric Age 800–500 B.C. | Rise of Sparta and Athens<br>Colonization of the Mediterranean basin<br>Flowering of lyric poetry<br>Development of philosophy and science in Ionia | Archilochus<br>Sappho<br>Tyrtaeus<br>Solon<br>Anaximander<br>Heraclitus |
| Classical Age 500–338 B.C. | Persian wars<br>Growth of the Athenian empire<br>Peloponnesian War<br>Rise of drama and historical writing<br>Flowering of Greek philosophy<br>Spartan and Theban hegemonies<br>Conquest of Greece by Philip of Macedon | Herodotus<br>Thucydides<br>Aeschylus<br>Sophocles<br>Euripides<br>Aristophanes<br>Plato<br>Aristotle |

the site of Troy in Asia Minor. He discovered the lost past of the Greek people, and to this past he gave the name Mycenaean.

The Mycenaeans entered Greece around 2000 B.C. and settled in central Greece and the Peloponnesus, the peninsula that forms the southernmost part of Greece (see Map 3.1). Mycenaean civilization was utterly unlike anything the later Greeks evolved. The political unit of the Mycenaeans was the kingdom, not the polis. The king and his warrior-aristocracy stood at the top of society. The symbol of the king's power and wealth was the palace, which was also the economic center of the kingdom. Within its walls royal craftsmen fashioned jewelry and rich ornaments, made and decorated fine pottery, forged weapons,

prepared hides and wool for clothing, and manufactured the goods needed by the king and his retainers. Palace scribes kept account of taxes and drew up inventories of the king's possessions. From the palace the king directed the lives of his subjects, and he tightly controlled society. About the king's subjects, almost nothing is known.

The Mycenaean kingdoms were in touch with each other and with the Bronze Age culture of the Minoans in Crete, but these contacts were often violent. The Minoans had established a vibrant and artistically gifted civilization, from which the Mycenaeans derived much of their art. The wealth of the Minoans tempted Mycenaean greed and ambition, and in about 1450 B.C. a band of Mycenaean raiders conquered Cnossus, the most important and the richest Minoan site. This attack was typical of the Mycenaeans, who were consistently a warlike and restless people.

Indeed, the entire history of Mycenaean Greece is a dreary tale of warfare. During the years 1300–1100 B.C., kingdom after kingdom suffered attack and destruction. But not one alien artifact has been found on any of these sites. There are no traces of invading peoples, nothing to suggest that these kingdoms fell to foreign invaders. Instead, the legends preserved by later Greeks told of grim wars between Mycenaean kingdoms and of the fall of great royal families. Apparently Mycenaean Greece destroyed itself in a long series of internecine wars, a pattern that would be repeated by Greeks of later ages.

The fall of the Mycenaean kingdoms ushered in a period of such poverty, disruption, and backwardness that historians usually call it the Dark Age of Greece (1100–800 B.C.). Even literacy was a casualty of the chaos. Yet even this period was important to the development of Greek civilization. It was a time of widespread movements of Greek-speaking peoples. Some Greeks sailed to Crete, where they established new communities. A great wave of Greeks spread eastward through the Aegean to the coast of Asia Minor. These immigrations turned the Aegean into a Greek lake. The people who stayed behind gradually rebuilt Greek society. They thus provided an element of continuity, a link between the Mycenaean period and the Greek culture that emerged from the Dark Age.

The movement of Greek-speaking peoples was not confined to the descendants of the Mycenaeans. During the Dark Age the last peoples who would help create Greek civilization of the historical period moved into Greece. The Boeotians entered Greece from

MINOAN SNAKE GODDESS   *This elegant statuette in many ways represents all of the difficulty of interpreting Minoan civilization. Although the Minoans left behind many brilliant pieces of art, they left no history or literature as guides for the understanding of them. Consequently, it is impossible to know what this goddess meant to the Minoans. (Museum of Fine Arts, Boston. Gift of Mrs. W. Scott Fitz)*

THE RETURN OF ODYSSEUS *This fine fifth-century relief portrays one of the most popular episodes from the* Odyssey: *the return of Odysseus from the Trojan War. Although his faithful wife, Penelope,* *and some poor retainers welcomed him eagerly (as this scene suggests), he had singlehandedly to defeat neighboring lords who coveted his kingdom. (Metropolitan Museum of Art, Fletcher Fund, 1930)*

Thessaly and settled in Boeotia. The Dorians, who were nomads, followed the Boeotians and settled in the Peloponnesus. Although the Dorians have traditionally been accused of overthrowing the Mycenaean kingdoms, recent archaeological work has proved that they entered Greece long afterwards. The common language of all these peoples, newcomers and survivors alike, was a bond between them.

## HOMER, HESIOD, AND THE HEROIC PAST (1100 – 800 B.C.)

The Greeks, unlike the Hebrews, had no sacred book that chronicled their past. Instead, they had the *Iliad* and the *Odyssey,* the epic poems created by Homer (eighth century B.C.) to describe a time when gods still walked the earth. And they learned the origin and the descent of the gods from the *Theogony,* an epic poem by Hesiod (ca 700 B.C.). For all their importance to Greek thought and literature, Homer and Hesiod were shadowy figures. Later Greeks knew little about them and were not even certain when they had lived. Although some later Greeks thought they had flourished in the tenth century B.C., the historian Herodotus (484-425 B.C.) gave a more accurate date:

*It seems to me that the age of Hesiod and Homer was no more than 400 years earlier than my time.*

*They are the poets who gave the Greeks the gene-alogy of the gods, and they distributed to the gods their honors and acts, and they declared their forms.*[3]

This uncertainty over the poets' dates is significant. It indicates that the Greeks remembered very little of their own past, especially the time before they entered Greece. They had also forgotten a great deal about the Bronze and Dark Ages.

Instead of authentic history the poems of Homer and Hesiod offered the Greeks an ideal past, a largely legendary Heroic Age. In terms of pure history these poems contain scraps of information about the Bronze Age, much about the early Dark Age, and some about the poets' own era. Chronologically, then, the Heroic Age falls mainly in the period between the collapse of the Mycenaean world and the rebirth of literacy. Yet it is a mistake to treat the *Iliad* and the *Odyssey* as history; they are magnificent blendings of legends, myth, and a little authentic tradition.

The *Iliad* recounts an expedition of Mycenaeans, whom Homer called Achaeans, to besiege the city of Troy in Asia Minor. The heart of the *Iliad,* however, is the quarrel between Agamemnon, the king of Mycenae, and Achilles, the tragic hero of the poem, and how their quarrel brought suffering to the Achaeans. Only when Achilles put away his anger and pride did he consent to come forward, face, and kill the Trojan hero Hector. The *Odyssey* narrates the adventures of Odysseus, one of the Achaean heroes who fought at Troy, during his voyage home from the fighting.

The splendor of these poems does not lie in their plots, though the *Odyssey* is a marvelous adventure story. Rather, both poems portray engaging but often flawed characters who are larger than life and yet typically human.

Achilles, the hero of the *Iliad,* is capable of mastering Trojan warriors but can barely control his own anger. Agamemnon commands kings, yet is a man beset by worries. Hector, the hero of the Trojans, is a formidable, noble, and likable foe. Odysseus, the hero of the *Odyssey,* trusts more to his wisdom and good sense than to his strength. Odysseus' wife Penelope faithfully endures the long years of war and separation, patiently waiting for her beloved husband to return from Troy.

Homer was strikingly successful in depicting the deeds of the great gods, who sit on Mount Olympus and watch the fighting at Troy as though they were spectators at a modern baseball game. Sometimes they even participate in the action. Homer's deities are reminiscent of the Mesopotamian gods and goddesses. Hardly a decorous lot, the Olympians are raucous, petty, deceitful, and splendid. In short, they are human. Zeus, the king of the gods, favors the Trojans, but Hera, his wife and queen of the gods, supports the Achaeans. To distract Zeus so that she can aid her favorites, Hera seduces him with wine and sex. Athena, the gray-eyed goddess of wisdom, squabbles with human beings as though she were a fishwife. In the *Odyssey,* Hephaestus, the god of fire, uses an invisible net to catch his wife, Aphrodite, the goddess of love, sleeping with Ares, the god of war. When Hephaestus summons the other gods to witness the scene, they laugh and joke about his catch. One god even wishes that someday he could be as unlucky as Ares.

Homer at times portrayed the gods in a serious vein, but he never treated them in a systematic fashion, as did Hesiod. Hesiod's epic poem, the *Theogony,* traces the descent of Zeus. Hesiod was influenced by Mesopotamian myths, which the Hittites had adopted and spread to the Aegean. Hesiod's poem claims that in the beginning there was chaos, the "yawning deep." From chaos came Gaea (Earth), who gave birth to Uranus (Heaven). Gaea and Uranus then gave birth to Cronus and Ocean (the deep-swelling waters). Cronus, the son of Earth and Heaven, like the Mesopotamian Enlil, separated the two and became king of the gods.

Like the Hebrews, Hesiod envisaged his cosmogony – that is, his account of the way the universe developed – in moral terms. Zeus, the son of Cronus, defeated his evil father and took his place as the king of the gods. He then sired Lawfulness, Right, Peace, and other powers of light and beauty. Thus, in Hesiod's conception, Zeus was the god of righteousness, a god who loved justice and hated wrongdoing.

In another epic poem, *Works and Days,* Hesiod wrote of his own time. He lived in the village of Ascra in Boeotia, a scenic place set between beautiful mountains and fertile plains, but Hesiod was a grim pessimist and did not think highly of his village: "Ascra, bad in winter, uncomfortable in summer, never good." Although sometimes portrayed as a common man, Hesiod was a wealthy farmer. He may not, however, have been an aristocrat. The matter of his social standing sets him apart, for all the other great writers of Greece – and, later, Rome – were members of the aristocracy, for only they had the wealth, leisure, and education to create literature. Naturally, then, ancient Greek and Roman literature always reflected the values, cares, and ambitions of the aristocracy. For this reason alone, the common people in Greco-Roman culture are largely unknown to the modern world. Hesiod opens a window to the other side of life.

Hesiod was the victim of injustice. In his will, Hesiod's father had divided his lands between Hesiod and his brother Perses. Perses bribed the aristocratic authorities to give him the larger part of the inheritance and then squandered his wealth. Undaunted by the injustice of the powerful, Hesiod thundered back in a voice reminiscent of Khunanup, the "Eloquent Peasant" (see page 27):

*Bribe-devouring lords, make straight
   your decisions,
Forget entirely crooked judgments.
He who causes evil to another harms himself.
Evil designs are most evil to the plotter.*[4]

The similarities are striking between the fictional Khunanup and Hesiod, both of whom were oppressed by the rich and powerful. Yet the differences are even more significant. Hesiod, unlike Khunanup, did not receive justice from the political authorities of the day, but he fully expected divine vindication. Hesiod's call for justice has gone ringing through the centuries, its appeal as fresh today as when he first uttered it more than two millennia ago. Hesiod spoke of Zeus as Jeremiah had spoken of Yahweh, warning that Zeus would see that justice was done and injustice punished. He cautioned his readers that Zeus was angered by those who committed adultery and those who harmed orphans and offended the aged. Hesiod's ethical concepts and his faith in divine justice were the product of his belief that the world was governed by the power of good.

Hesiod went on to advise Perses how to become a prosperous farmer. Hesiod's agricultural year was determined by the stars and the seasons. He advised Perses to plow when the constellation Pleiades set and to harvest when it rose. Wood was best cut in autumn, and the farmer should then begin building his plows and wagons and fashioning his tools. When the star Arcturus rose at dusk, it was time to prune the vines. Hesiod warned against doing field work during the time of biting cold, when

*all the immense wood roars;*
*Wild animals shiver and put their tails*
*between their legs,*
*Even those whose hide is covered with fur.*
*For now the cold wind blows through animals*
*even though they be shaggy-breasted.*[5]

In the heat of the summer, however, when the crops were stored in the barn, the farmer rested, sitting in the shade and sipping wine.

In *Works and Days* Hesiod also offered some hardheaded advice on how to live. Although his pessimism was pervasive, his advice was very practical. Hesiod was not theorizing; he was giving his readers tips on how to survive in a hard world. He recommended that a man get a house, an ox, and a slave woman to help with the field work. A man should not take a wife until he was around thirty years old. Then he should be very careful about his prospective bride: "He who trusts women trusts deceivers." Beware of the flirt because "she wants your barn." Marry, he advised, a fine maiden, "for a man gains nothing better than a good wife." Hesiod warned that a couple should have only one son; but if they have a second, they should do so late in life. He insisted upon the importance of good neighbors, because neighbors will help each other in times of trouble. The constant theme of Hesiod's philosophy is to live justly and uprightly, but never trust anyone.

## THE LYRIC AGE (800–500 B.C.)

Hesiod stood on the threshold of one of the most vibrant periods of Greek history, an era of extraordinary expansion geographically, ar-

tistically, and politically. Greeks ventured as far east as the Black Sea and as far west as Spain (see Map 3.2). With the rebirth of literacy, this period also witnessed a tremendous literary flowering as poets broke away from the heroic tradition and wrote about their own lives. The individualism of the poets typifies this age of adventure and exploration, and the term "Lyric Age" strikingly conveys the spirit of these years. Politically, these were the years when Sparta and Athens – the two poles of the Greek experience – rose to prominence.

### OVERSEAS EXPANSION

During the years 1100–800 B.C., the Greeks not only recovered from the breakdown of the Mycenaean world, but also grew in wealth and numbers. This new prosperity brought with it new problems. Greece is a small and not especially fertile country. The increase in population meant that many men and their families had very little land or none at all. Land hunger drove many Greeks to seek new homes outside of Greece. Other factors, largely intangible, played their part as well: the desire for a new start, a love of excitement and adventure, and natural curiosity about what lay beyond the horizon.

The Mediterranean offered the Greeks an escape valve, for they were always a seafaring people. To them the sea was a highway, not a barrier. Through their commercial ventures they had long been familiar with the rich areas of the western Mediterranean. Moreover, the geography of the Mediterranean basin favored colonization. The land and the climate of the Mediterranean region are remarkably uniform. Greeks could travel to new areas, whether to Cyprus in the east or to Malta in the west, and establish the kind of settlement they had had in Greece. They could also raise the same crops that they had raised in Greece. The move to a new home was not a move into totally unknown conditions. Once the colonists had established themselves in their new homes, they continued life essentially as they had lived it in Greece.

From about 750 to 550 B.C., Greeks from the mainland and from Asia Minor poured onto the coasts of the northern Aegean, the Ionian Sea, and the Black Sea, and into North Africa, Sicily, southern Italy, southern France, and Spain (see Map 3.2). Just as the migrations of the Dark Age had turned the Aegean into a Greek lake, this later wave of colonization spread the Greeks and their culture throughout the Mediterranean. Colonization on this scale had a profound impact on the course of Western civilization. It meant that the prevailing culture of the Mediterranean basin would be Greek, and to this heritage Rome would later fall heir.

One man can in many ways stand as the symbol of the vital and robust era of colonization. Archilochus was born on the island of Paros, the bastard son of an aristocrat. He knew that because of his illegitimacy he would never inherit his father's land, and this knowledge seems to have made him self-reliant. He was also a poet of genius, the first of the lyric poets who left an indelible mark on this age. Unlike the epic poets, who portrayed the deeds of heroes, Archilochus sang of himself. He knew the sea, the dangers of sailing, and the price that the sea often exacted. He spoke of one shipwreck in grim terms and even treated the god of the sea with irony: "Of fifty men gentle Poseidon left one, Koiranos, to be saved from shipwreck."

Together with others from Paros he took part in the colonization of Thasos in the northern Aegean. He described the island in less than glowing terms: "Like the spine of an ass it stands, crowned to the brim with a wild forest." His opinion of his fellow colonists was hardly kinder; about them he commented: "So the misery of all Greece came together in Thasos." Yet at Thasos he fell in love with a woman named Neoboule. They did not marry because her father opposed the match. In revenge, Archilochus seduced Neoboule's younger sister, railed at the entire family, and left Thasos to live the life of a mercenary.

His hired lance took him to Euboea, and he left a striking picture of the fighting there:

*Not many bows will be strung, nor slings be slung*
*When Ares begins battle in the plain.*
*There will be the mournful work of the sword:*
*For in this kind of battle are the spear-famed*
*Lords of Euboea experienced.*[6]

Through it all, however, Archilochus kept his sardonic humor. Commenting on the death of a relative, for example, he remarked, "I won't cure anything by weeping or make it worse by pursuing pleasures and festivities." For Archilochus the adventure of colonization had a happy, if unusual, ending. The people of Paros, overlooking his waywardness because of his poetic genius, welcomed him back. Later he was killed defending his homeland.

Archilochus exemplifies the energy, restlessness, self-reliance, and sense of adventure that characterizes this epoch. People like him broke old ties, faced homelessness and danger, and built new homes for themselves. They made the Mediterranean Greek.

### LYRIC POETS

Archilochus the colonist and adventurer is not nearly as important as Archilochus the lyric poet, whose individualism set a new tone in Greek literature. For the first time in Western civilization, men and women began to write of their own experiences. Their poetry reflected their belief that they had something precious to say about themselves. To them poetry did not belong only to the gods or to the great heroes on the plain of Troy. Some lyric poets used their literary talents for the good of their city-states. They stood forth as individuals and in their poetry urged their countrymen to be patriotic and just.

One of the most unforgettable of these writers is the poet Sappho. Unlike Archilochus, she neither braved the wilds nor pushed into the unknown, yet she was no less individual than he. Sappho was born in the seventh century B.C. on the island of Lesbos, a place of sun, sea, and rustic beauty. Her marriage produced a daughter, to whom she wrote some of her poems. Sappho's poetry is personal and intense. She delighted in her surroundings, which were those of aristocratic women, and she celebrated the little things around her. Hers was a world of natural beauty, of sacred groves, religious festivals, wedding celebrations, and noble companions. Sappho fondly remembered walks with a girlfriend:

*There was neither a hill nor a sanctuary*
*Nor a stream of running water*
*Which we failed to visit;*
*Nor when spring began any grove*
*Filled with the noise of nightingales.*[7]

The rising of Hesperus, the evening star, prompted her to welcome it:

*Hesperus, bringing back all things*
*  Which light-giving dawn disperses,*
*You bring back the sheep, you bring back the goat,*
*  You bring the child back to its mother.*[8]

Sappho is best known for erotic poetry, for she expressed her love frankly and without shame. She was bisexual, and much of her poetry dealt with her homosexual love affairs.

MOSAIC PORTRAIT OF SAPPHO *The Greek letters in the upper left corner identify this idealized portrait as that of Sappho. The mosaic, which was found at Sparta, dates to the late Roman Empire and testifies to Sappho's popularity in antiquity. (Photo: Caroline Buckler)*

In one of her poems she remembered the words of her lover:

*Sappho, if you don't come out,*
*Surely I will no longer love you.*
*O come to us and free your lovely*
*Strength from your bed.*
*Lifting off your Chian robe,*
*Bathe in the waters like a*
*Pure lily beside a spring.*[9]

In another poem Sappho described Aphrodite appearing to her in answer to her prayers. The goddess advised her to be patient: the girl she loved would return her love soon enough.

In antiquity Sappho's name became linked with female homosexual love. Today, the English word *lesbian* is derived from Sappho's island home. Yet to see Sappho as licentious is to misunderstand her and her world completely. The Greeks accepted bisexuality — that men and women could enjoy both ho-

*STATUE OF "LEONIDAS"* *Found at Sparta, this statue is thought by some to represent Leonidas, the Spartan king who was killed at Thermopylae. The statue, with its careful rendering of the muscles and the face, reflects the Spartan ideal of the strong, intelligent, and brave warrior. (Photo: Caroline Buckler)*

mosexual and heterosexual lovemaking. Homosexual relationships normally carried no social stigma. In her mature years Sappho was courted by a younger man who wanted to marry her. By then she had already proclaimed her love for several girls, yet the young man was not troubled by these affairs. As it turned out, Sappho refused to marry because she was past child-bearing age.

In their poetry Archilochus and Sappho reveal two sides of Greek life in this period.

Archilochus exemplifies the energy and adventure of the age, while Sappho expresses the intensely personal side of life. The common link is their individualism, their faith in themselves, and their desire to reach out to other men and women in order to share their experiences, thoughts, and wisdom.

## THE GROWTH OF SPARTA

During the Lyric Age the Spartans expanded the boundaries of their polis and made it the leading power in Greece. Like other Greeks, the Spartans faced the problems of overpopulation and land hunger. Unlike other Greeks, the Spartans solved these problems by conquest, not by colonization. To gain more land the Spartans set out in about 735 B.C. to conquer Messenia, a rich and fertile region in the southwestern Peloponnesus. This conflict, known as the First Messenian War, lasted for twenty years and ended in a Spartan triumph. The Spartans appropriated Messenian land and turned the Messenians into helots, or state serfs.

In about 650 B.C., Spartan exploitation and oppression of the Messenian helots led to a helot revolt so massive and stubborn that it became known as the Second Messenian War. The Spartan poet Tyrtaeus, a contemporary of these events, vividly portrayed the ferocity of the fighting:

*For it is a shameful thing indeed*
  *When with the foremost fighters*
*An elder falling in front of the young men*
  *Lies outstretched,*
*Having white hair and grey beard,*
*Breathing forth his stout soul in the dust,*
*Holding in his hands his genitals*
  *stained with blood.*[10]

Confronted with horrors such as this, Spartan enthusiasm for the war waned. To rally his countrymen Tyrtaeus urged the warriors to face the Messenians:

*And let each man coming near*
*  with his great spear or sword,*
*Wounding his man cut him down and take him;*
*And putting foot against foot and leaning shield*
*    against shield,*
*Crest upon crest and helmet upon helmet,*
*And chest to chest, drawing near,*
*  let him fight his man,*
*Taking him with the hilt of his sword*
*  or with his great spear.*[11]

Finally, after some thirty years of fighting, the Spartans put down the revolt. Nevertheless, the political and social strain caused by this war led to a transformation of the Spartan polis.

It took the full might of the Spartan people, aristocrat and commoner alike, to win the Second Messenian War. After the victory the nonnobles, who had done much of the fighting, demanded rights equal to those of the nobility. Their agitation disrupted society, until the aristocrats agreed to remodel the state. Although the Spartans later claimed that the changes brought about by this compromise were the work of Lycurgus, a legendary, semidivine lawgiver, they were really the work of the entire Spartan people.

The Lycurgan regimen, as these reforms were called, was a new political, economic, and social system. Political distinctions among the Spartans were eliminated, and all citizens became equal to one another. In effect, the Lycurgan regimen abolished the aristocracy and made the government an oligarchy. Actual governance of the polis was in the hands of two kings, who were primarily military leaders. The kings and twenty-eight elders made up a council that deliberated on foreign and domestic matters and prepared legislation for the assembly, which consisted of all Spartan citizens. The real executive power of the polis was in the hands of five *ephors,* or overseers. The ephors were elected from and by all the people.

To provide for their economic needs the Spartans divided the land of Messenia among all citizens. Helots worked the land, raised the crops, provided the Spartans with their living, and occasionally served in the army. The Spartans kept the helots in line by means of systematic terrorism, hoping to to beat them down and keep them quiet. Spartan citizens were supposed to devote their time exclusively to military training.

In the Lycurgan system every citizen owed primary allegiance to Sparta. Suppression of the individual, together with emphasis on military prowess, led to a barracks state. Family life itself was sacrificed to the polis. If an infant was deformed or handicapped at birth, the polis could demand that the parents put it out to die. In this respect the Spartans were no better or worse than other Greeks. Infanticide was common in ancient Greece and Rome, and many people resorted to it as a way of keeping population down. The difference is that in other Greek states the decision to kill a child belonged to the parents, not to the polis.

Once a Spartan boy reached the age of seven, he lived in barracks with other boys his age. Spartan youth all underwent rugged physical and military training until they reached twenty-four, when they became front-line soldiers. For the rest of their lives, Spartan men kept themselves prepared for combat. Their military training never ceased, and the older men were expected to be models of endurance, frugality, and sturdiness to the younger men. In battle Spartans were supposed to stand and die rather than retreat. An anecdote about one Spartan mother sums up Spartan military values. As her son was setting off to battle, the mother handed him his shield and advised him to come back either victorious carrying the shield or dead being carried upon it. In short, in the Lycurgan regimen Spartans were expected to train vigorously, disdain luxury and wealth, do with little and like it.

## THE EVOLUTION OF ATHENS

Like Sparta, Athens too faced pressing social and economic problems during the Lyric Age, but the Athenian response to them was far different from that of the Spartans. Instead of creating an oligarchy, the Athenians extended to all citizens the right and duty of governing the polis. Indeed, the Athenian democracy was one of the most thoroughgoing in Greece.

In the seventh century B.C., however, the aristocracy still governed Athens, as oppressively as the "bribe-devouring lords" against whom Hesiod had railed. The aristocrats owned the best land, met in an assembly to govern the polis, and interpreted the law. Noble landowners were forcing small farmers into economic dependence. Many families were being sold into slavery; others were exiled and their land pledged to the rich. Poor farmers who borrowed from their wealthy neighbors put up their land as collateral. If a farmer was unable to repay the loan, his creditor put a stone on the borrower's field to signify his indebtedness and thereafter took one-sixth of the annual yield until the debt was paid. If the farmer had to borrow again, he pledged himself and at times his family. If he was again unable to repay the loan, he became the slave of his creditor. Because the harvests of the poor farmer were generally small, he normally raised enough to live on but not enough to repay his loan.

The peasants, however, were strong in numbers, and they demanded reforms. They wanted the law to be published so that everyone would know its contents. Under pressure, the aristocrats relented and turned to Draco, a fellow aristocrat, to codify the law. In 621 B.C., Draco published the first law code of the Athenian polis. His code was thought harsh, but it nonetheless embodied the ideal that the law belonged to all citizens. The aristocrats hoped in vain that Draco's law code would satisfy the peasants. Many of the poor began demanding redistribution of the land, and it was obvious that broader reform was needed. Unrest among the peasants continued.

In many other city-states conditions such as those in Athens led to the rise of tyrants. The word *tyrant* brings to mind a cruel and bloody dictator, but the Greeks seem at first to have used the word to denote a leader who seized power without legal right. Many of the first tyrants, though personally ambitious, were men who kept the welfare of the polis in mind. They usually enjoyed the support of the peasants because they reduced the power of the aristocrats. Later tyrants were often harsh and arbitrary – hence the Greeks began to use the word in the modern sense – and when they were, peasants and aristocrats alike suffered.

Only one person in Athens had the respect of both aristocrats and peasants: Solon, himself an aristocrat and poet, but a man opposed to tyrants. Like Hesiod, Solon used his poetry to condemn the aristocrats for their greed and dishonesty. He stormed against

*those citizens who are persuaded*
*to destroy this great city*
*because they desire reckless wealth.*[12]

Solon recited his poems in the Athenian agora, where everyone could hear his relentless call for justice and fairness. The aristocrats realized that Solon was no crazed revolutionary, and the common people trusted him. Around 594 B.C., the aristocrats elected him *archon,* chief magistrate of the Athenian polis, and gave him extraordinary power to reform the state.

Solon immediately freed all people enslaved for debt, recalled all exiles, canceled all debts on land, and made enslavement for debt illegal. He also divided society into four legal groups on the basis of wealth. In the most influential group were the wealthiest citizens, but even the poorest and least powerful group enjoyed certain rights. Solon allowed them into the old aristocratic assembly, where they could take part in the election of magistrates.

In all his work, Solon gave thought to the rights of the poor as well as the rich. He gave the commoners a place in government and a voice in the political affairs of Athens. His work done, Solon insisted that all swear to uphold his reforms. Then, since many were clamoring for him to become tyrant, he left Athens to travel.

Although Solon's reforms solved some immediate problems, they did not bring peace to Athens. Some aristocrats attempted to make themselves tyrants, while others banded together to oppose them. In 546 B.C., Pisistratus, an exiled aristocrat, returned to Athens, defeated his opponents, and became tyrant. Pisistratus reduced the power of the aristocracy while supporting the common people. Under his rule Athens prospered, and his building program began to transform it into one of the splendors of Greece. His reign as tyrant promoted the growth of democratic ideas by arousing in the Athenians rudimentary feelings of equality.

Athenian acceptance of tyranny did not long outlive Pisistratus, for his son Hippias ruled harshly, and his excesses led to his overthrow. After a brief period of turmoil between factions of the nobility, Cleisthenes, a wealthy and prominent aristocrat, emerged triumphant in 508 B.C., largely because he won the support of the people. Cleisthenes created the Athenian democracy, and he did so with the full knowledge and approval of the Athenian people. He reorganized the state completely, but he presented every innovation to the assembly for discussion and ratification. All Athenian citizens had a voice in Cleisthenes' work.

Cleisthenes created a new local unit, the deme, to serve as the basis of his political system. Citizenship was tightly linked to the deme, for each deme kept the roll of those within its jurisdiction who were admitted to citizenship. Cleisthenes also created ten new tribes as administrative units. All the demes were grouped in tribes, which thus formed the link between the demes and the central government. The central government included an assembly of all citizens and a new council of five hundred members. The council prepared legislation for the assembly to consider, and it handled diplomatic affairs. The result of Cleisthenes' work was to make Athens a democracy with a government efficient enough to permit effective popular rule.

Athenian democracy was to prove an inspiring ideal in Western civilization. It demonstrated that a large group of people, not just a few, could efficiently run the affairs of state. By heeding the opinions, suggestions, and wisdom of all its citizens, the state enjoyed the maximum amount of good counsel. Since all citizens could speak their minds, they did not have to resort to rebellion or conspiracy to express their desires.

Athenian democracy must not, however, be thought of in modern terms. In Athens democracy meant a form of government in which poor men as well as rich enjoyed political power and responsibility. In practice, though, most important offices were held by aristocrats. Furthermore, Athenian democracy denied political rights to many people, including women and slaves. Foreigners were seldom admitted to citizenship. Unlike modern democracies, Athenian democracy did not mean that the citizen would merely vote for others who would then run the state. Instead, every citizen was expected to be able to perform the duties of most magistrates. In Athens citizens voted and served. The people were the government. It is this union of the individual and the state − the view that the state exists for the good of the citizen and that the duty of the citizen is to serve it well − that has made Athenian democracy so compelling an ideal.

## THE CLASSICAL PERIOD
### (500–338 B.C.)

In the years 500–338 B.C., Greek civilization reached its highest peak in politics, thought, and art. In this period the Greeks beat back the armies of the Persian Empire. Then, turning their spears against one another, they destroyed their own civilization in a century of warfare. Some thoughtful Greeks felt prompted to record and analyze these momentous events; the result was the creation of history. This era saw the flowering of philosophy, as thinkers in Ionia and on the Greek mainland began to ponder the nature and meaning of the universe and human experience. Not content to ask "why," they used their intellects to explain the world around them and to determine humanity's place in it.

The Greeks invented drama, and the Athenian tragedians Aeschylus, Sophocles, and Euripides explored themes that still inspire audiences today. Greek architects reached the zenith of their art and created buildings whose very ruins still inspire awe. Because Greek intellectual and artistic efforts attained their fullest and finest expression in these years, this age is called the Classical Period. Few periods in the history of Western society can match it in sheer dynamism and achievement.

### THE DEADLY CONFLICTS (499–404 B.C.)

One of the hallmarks of the Classical Period was warfare. In 499 B.C. the Ionian Greeks, with the feeble help of Athens, rebelled against the Persian Empire. In 490 B.C., the Persians struck back at Athens but were beaten off at the Battle of Marathon, a small plain in Attica. This failure only prompted the Persians to try again. In 480 B.C., the Persian king Xerxes led a mighty invasion force into Greece. In the face of this emergency the Greeks united and pooled their resources to resist the invaders. The Spartans provided the overall leadership and commanded the Greek armies. The Athenians, led by the wily Themistocles, provided the heart of the naval forces.

The first confrontation between the Persians and the Greeks occurred at the pass of Thermopylae and in the waters off Artemisium in northern Greece. At Thermopylae the Greek hoplites − the heavily armed troops − showed their mettle. Before the fighting began, a report came in that when the Persian archers shot their bows the arrows darkened the sky. One gruff Spartan merely replied, "Fine, then we'll fight in the shade." The Greeks at Thermopylae fought to the last man, but the Persians took the position. In their next two battles, the Greeks fared better. In 480 B.C., the Greek fleet smashed the Persian navy at Salamis, an island south of Athens. The following year, the Greek army destroyed the Persian forces at Plataea, a small polis at Boeotia.

The significance of these Greek victories is nearly incalculable. By defeating the Persians, the Greeks ensured that oriental monarchy would not stifle the Greek achievement. The Greeks were thus able to develop their particular genius in freedom. These decisive victories meant that Greek political forms and intellectual concepts would be the heritage of the West.

After turning back the invasion, the Greeks took the fight to the Persian Empire. In 478 B.C., the Greeks decided to continue hostilities until they had liberated the Ionians from Persian rule. To achieve that goal a strong navy was essential. The Greeks turned to Athens, the leading naval power in the Aegean, for leadership. Athens and other states, especially those in the Aegean, responded by establishing the Delian League. Athens controlled the Delian League, providing most of the warships for operations and determining how much money each member should contribute to the league's treasury.

Over the next twenty years Athens drove the Persians out of the Aegean and turned the Delian League into an Athenian empire. Athenian rule became severe, and the Athenian polis became openly imperialistic. Although all members of the Delian League were supposed to be free and independent states, Athens reduced them to the status of subjects. A sense of the harshness of Athenian rule can be gained from the regulations the Athenians imposed on their subject allies. After the Athenians had suppressed a revolt in Euboea, they imposed an oath on the people:

*I will not revolt from the people of Athens either by any means or devices whatsoever or by word or deed, nor will I be persuaded by anyone who does revolt. And I will pay the tribute to the Athenians that I can persuade the Athenians [to levy]. I will be to them the best and truest ally possible. I will help and defend the people of Athens if anyone wrongs them, and I will obey the people of Athens.* [13]

The Athenians dictated to the people of Erythrae, a polis on the coast of Asia Minor, their form of government:

*There will be a council of 120 men chosen by lot. . . . The [Athenian] overseers and garrison commander will choose the current council by lot and establish it in office. Henceforth the council and the [Athenian] garrison commander will do these things thirty days before the council goes out of office.* [14]

The Athenians also interfered with the economic affairs of the allies and decreed that they use Athenian coins, weights, and measures. The lengths to which the Athenians could go are exemplified in the oath they forced on the people of Colophon, another polis in Asia Minor: "And I will love the Athenian people, and will not desert them . . ." The Athenians were willing to enforce their demands by armed might, and they were ready both to punish violations and to suppress discontent.

The expansion of Athenian power and the aggressiveness of Athenian rule alarmed Sparta and its allies. While relations between Athens and Sparta cooled, Pericles (ca 494–429 B.C.) became the leading statesman in Athens. An aristocrat of solid intellectual ability, he turned Athens into the wonder of Greece. But like the democracy he led, Pericles was aggressive and imperialistic. He made

MAP 3.3 THE PELOPONNESIAN WAR *This map, which shows the alignment of states during the Peloponnesian War, vividly illustrates the large scale of the war and its divisive impact.*

no effort to allay Spartan fear and instead continued Athenian expansion. At last, in 459 B.C., Sparta and Athens went to war over conflicts between Athens and some of Sparta's allies. The war ended fourteen years later with no serious damage to either side and nothing settled. But this war had divided the Greek world between two great powers.

During the 440s and 430s, Athens continued its severe policies toward its subject allies and came into conflict with Corinth, one of Sparta's leading allies (see Map 3.3). Once again Athens and Sparta were drifting toward war. In 432 B.C., the Spartans convened a meeting of their allies, who complained of Athenian aggression and demanded that Athens be stopped. With a show of reluctance, the Spartans agreed to declare war. The real reason for war, according to the Athenian historian Thucydides, was very simple:

*The truest explanation, though the one least mentioned, was the great growth of Athenian power and the fear it caused the Lakedaimonians [Spartans], which drove them to war.*[15]

At the outbreak of this, the Peloponnesian War, a Spartan ambassador warned the Athenians: "This day will be the beginning of great evils for the Greeks." Few men have ever spoken more prophetically. The Peloponnesian War lasted a generation (431–404 B.C.) and brought in its wake fearful plagues, famine, civil wars, widespread destruction, and huge loss of life. Thucydides, the historian who also fought as a general in the war, described its cataclysmic effects:

*For never had so many cities been captured and destroyed, whether by the barbarians or by the Greeks who were fighting each other. . . . Never had so many men been exiled or slaughtered, whether in the war or because of civil conflicts.*[16]

As the war dragged on, old leaders like Pericles died and were replaced by men of the war generation. In Athens the most prominent of this new breed of politicians was Alcibiades (ca 450–404 B.C.), an aristocrat, a kinsman of Pericles, and a student of the philosopher Socrates. Alcibiades was brilliant, handsome, charming, and popular with the people. He was also self-seeking and egotistical; a shameless opportunist, his first thoughts were always for himself.

Alcibiades' schemes helped bring Athens down to defeat. Having planned an invasion of Sicily that ended in disaster, he deserted to the Spartans and plotted with the Persians, who had sided with Sparta, against his homeland. When his treachery had brought the Athenians to the brink of defeat, he struck a bargain with them. He promised to persuade Persia to throw its support to Athens, if the Athenians would allow him to return home. When they agreed, Alcibiades cheerfully double-crossed the Spartans and led the Athenians against Sparta's forces.

In the end, all of Alcibiades' intrigues failed. The Spartans defeated the Athenian

MOSAIC PORTRAIT OF ALCIBIADES *The artist has caught all the craftiness, intelligence, and quickness of Alcibiades, who became a romantic figure in antiquity. Besides the artistic merit of the portrait, the mosaic is interesting because Alcibiades' name in the upper right corner is misspelled. (Photo: Caroline Buckler)*

fleet in the Aegean and blockaded Athens by land and sea. Finally, in 404 B.C., the Athenians surrendered and watched helplessly while the Spartans and their allies destroyed the walls of Athens to the music of flute girls. The Peloponnesian War lasted twenty-seven years, and it dealt Greek civilization a serious blow.

## THE BIRTH OF HISTORICAL AWARENESS

One positive development grew out of the Persian and Peloponnesian wars: the beginnings of historical writing. Herodotus (ca 485–425 B.C.), known as "the Father of History," was born at Halicarnassus in Asia Minor. As a young man he traveled widely, visiting Egypt, Phoenicia, and probably Babylon. Later he migrated to Athens, which became his intellectual home. In the first lines of his book, *The Histories,* Herodotus explained his reasons for writing history:

*This is the publication of the researches of Herodotus of Halicarnassus – so that past deeds will not be forgotten by men through lapse of time – which points out the great and admirable achievements, both those of the Greeks and those of the barbarians, lest they be uncelebrated, and which points out why they waged war against each other.*[17]

This introduction bears some resemblance to that of the *Iliad,* and indeed *The Histories* has been called a prose epic. The basic difference is that Herodotus dealt with the real and factual, not with legend. He even gave history its name; his word *historia* originally meant "investigation." Only after his book appeared did the word *historia* gain its modern meaning.

Herodotus chronicled the rise of the Persian Empire, sketched the background of Athens and Sparta, and described the land and customs of the Egyptians and the Scythians, who lived in the region of the modern Crimea. The sheer scope of this work is awesome. Lacking newspapers, sophisticated communications, and easy means of travel, Herodotus nevertheless wrote a history that covered the major events of the Near East and Greece.

Perhaps Herodotus' most striking characteristic is his curiosity. He loved to travel, and like most travelers he accumulated a stock of fine stories. He was an excellent storyteller, and the customs of non-Greek peoples fascinated him. But tales and digressions never obscure the central theme of his work. Herodotus diligently questioned everyone who could tell him anything about the Persian wars. The confrontation between East and West unfolds relentlessly in *The Histories,* reaching its climax in the great battles of Salamis and Plataea.

In Herodotus' opinion the victory of the Greeks was due to their ability to live life simply, without luxury or wealth. He emphasized this point in describing a meeting between the Persian king Xerxes and a Greek deserter. Xerxes was about to invade Greece, so he questioned the deserter about the Greeks and their land. The deserter told him that

*in Greece poverty is ever-present, but excellence is acquired, attained from wisdom and hard law. By making use of them Greece wards off both poverty and despotism.*[18]

Herodotus turned to this thought again when he concluded his history with a moral: "Those accustomed to soft lands are themselves soft."

The outbreak of the Peloponnesian War prompted Thucydides (ca 460–ca 400 B.C.) to write a history of its course in the belief that

*it would be great and more noteworthy than previous wars, considering that both states were in the prime of all their preparations and seeing that the other Greeks were taking sides with one or the other, some immediately, others intending to do so. For this was the greatest movement among the Greeks and some of the barbarians, and so to speak among most of mankind.*[19]

A politician and a general, Thucydides saw action in the war until he was exiled for a defeat. Exile gave him the time and opportunity to question eyewitnesses about the details of events and to visit battlefields. Since he was an aristocrat and a prominent man, he had access to the inner circles of men who made the decisions.

Thucydides was intensely interested in human nature and how it manifested itself during the war. In 430 B.C., a terrible plague struck Athens. Thucydides described both the symptoms of the plague and the reactions of the Athenians in the same clinical terms. He portrayed the virtual breakdown of a society beset by war, disease, desperation, and despair. Similarly, he chronicled the bloody civil war on the island of Corcyra. Instead of condemning the injustice and inhumanity of the fighting, in which citizen turned on citizen and people ruthlessly betrayed their friends, he coolly observed that such things are normal as long as human nature is what it is.

Thucydides saw the Peloponnesian War as highly destructive to Greek character. He noted – with a visible touch of regret – that the old, the noble, and the simple fell before ambition and lust for power. Thucydides interpreted the war and its effects in purely human terms. He firmly rejected any notion that the gods intervened in human affairs. In his view the fate of men and women was, for good or ill, entirely in their own hands.

## ATHENIAN ARTS IN THE AGE OF PERICLES

In the last half of the fifth century B.C., Pericles turned Athens into the showplace of Greece. He appropriated Delian League funds to pay for a huge building program, planning temples and other buildings to honor Athena, the patron goddess of the city, and to display to all Greeks the glory of the Athenian polis. Pericles also pointed out that his program would employ a great many Athenians and bring economic prosperity to the city.

Thus began the undertaking that turned the Acropolis into a monument for all time. Construction of the Parthenon began in 447 B.C., followed by the Propylaea, the temple of Athena Nike (Athena the Victorious), and the Erechtheion. Even today in their ruined state they still evoke awe. Plutarch, a Greek writer who lived in the first century A.D., observed:

*In beauty each of them was from the outset antique, and even now in its prime fresh and newly made. Thus each of them is always in bloom, maintaining its appearance as though untouched by time, as though an ever-green breath and undecaying spirit had been mixed in its construction.*[20]

Even the pollution of modern Athens, although it is destroying the ancient buildings, cannot rob them of their splendor and charm.

The planning of the architects and the skill of the workmen who erected these buildings were both very sophisticated. Visitors approaching the Acropolis first saw the Propylaea, the ceremonial gateway, a building of complicated layout and grand design whose Doric columns seem to hold up the sky.

On the right was the small temple of Athena Nike, whose dimensions harmonize with those of the Propylaea. The temple was built to commemorate the victory over the Persians, and the Ionic frieze above its columns depicted the battle of the Greeks and the Persians. Here for all the world to see was a tribute to Athenian and Greek valor – and a reminder of Athens' part in the victory.

Ahead of the visitors as they stood in the Propylaea was the huge statue of Athena Promachus (the Front-Line Fighter), so gigantic that the crest of Athena's helmet and the point of her spear could be seen by sailors entering the harbor of Athens. This statue celebrated the Athenian victory at the battle of Marathon, and was paid for by the spoils taken from the Persians. To the left stood the Erechtheion, an Ionic temple that housed several ancient shrines. On its southern side is the famous Portico of the Caryatids, a porch whose roof is supported by statues of Athenian maidens. The graceful Ionic columns of the Erechtheion provide a delicate relief from

THE PARTHENON *Stately and graceful, the Parthenon symbolizes the logic, order, and sense of beauty of Greek architecture. The Parthenon was also the centerpiece of Pericles' plan to make Athens the artistic showcase of the Greek world. (Photo: Caroline Buckler)*

the prevailing Doric order of the massive Propylaea and Parthenon.

As visitors walked on they obtained a full view of the Parthenon, thought by many to be the perfect Doric temple. The Parthenon was the chief monument to Athena and her city. The sculptures that adorned the temple portrayed the greatness of Athens and its goddess. The figures on the eastern pediment depicted Athena's birth, those on the west the victory of Athena over the god Poseidon for the possession of Attica. Inside the Parthenon stood a huge statue of Athena, the masterpiece of Phidias, one of the greatest sculptors of all time.

The Parthenon appears to be all rectangle and triangle, yet it is a structure of curves. Both the pavement that supports the columns and the beam above the columns are curved to avoid the illusion of flatness. The columns themselves are gently curved from bottom to top. The Parthenon also appears rigorously regular, but it is actually a collection of irregularities, all designed to compensate for the effects of optical illusion. For instance, the columns are not regularly spaced, and they incline inward; those at the rear are stockier than those at the front end. In all these refinements the Athenian architect showed his knowledge of mathematics, optics, and design. The impression the Parthenon creates is one of perfection. Well might all Athenians, no matter how humble, feel a great burst of pride in themselves, their goddess, and their polis when they gazed on the Parthenon.

In many ways the Athenian Acropolis is

the epitome of Greek art and its spirit. Although the buildings were dedicated to the gods and most of the sculptures portrayed gods, these works nonetheless express the Greek fascination with the human and rational. Greek deities were anthropomorphic, and Greek artists portrayed them as human beings. While honoring the gods, Greek artists were thus celebrating human beings. In the Parthenon sculptures it is visually impossible to distinguish the men and women from the gods and goddesses. This aspect of Greek art made a powerful impression on the American novelist Mark Twain, who visited the Acropolis at night:

*As we wandered thoughtfully down the marble-paved length of this stately temple [the Parthenon] the scene about us was strangely impressive. Here and there in lavish profusion were gleaming white statues of men and women, propped against blocks of marble, some of them armless, some without legs, others headless — but all looking mournful in the moonlight and startlingly human!*[21]

The Acropolis also exhibits the rational side of Greek art. There is no violent emotion in this art, but instead a quiet intensity. Likewise, there is nothing excessive, for "nothing too much" was the canon of artist and philosopher alike. Greek artists portrayed action in a balanced, restrained, and sometimes even serene fashion, capturing the noblest aspects of human beings: their reason, dignity, and promise.

Other aspects of Athenian cultural life were as rooted in the life of the polis as were the architecture and sculpture of the Acropolis. The development of drama was tied to the religious festivals of the city. The polis sponsored the production of plays and required that wealthy citizens pay the expenses of their production. At the beginning of the year dramatists submitted their plays to the archon. He

chose those he considered best and assigned a theatrical troupe to each playwright. Although most Athenian drama has perished, enough has survived to prove that the archons had superb taste. Many plays were highly controversial, but the archons neither suppressed nor censored them.

The Athenian dramatists were the first artists in Western society to examine such basic questions as the rights of the individual, the demands of society on the individual, and the nature of good and evil. Conflict is a constant element in Athenian drama. The dramatists used their art to portray, understand, and resolve life's basic conflicts.

Aeschylus (525–456 B.C.), the first of the great Athenian dramatists, was also the first to express the agony of the individual caught in conflict. In his trilogy of plays, *The Oresteia*, Aeschylus deals with the themes of betrayal, murder, and reconciliation. *The Agamemnon*, the first play of the trilogy, depicts Agamemnon's return from the Trojan War and his murder by his wife Clytemnestra and her lover Aegisthus. In the second play, *The Libation Bearers*, Orestes, the son of Agamemnon and Clytemnestra, avenges his father's death by killing his mother and her lover. His act of vengeance is the work of a dutiful son, but the murder of his mother is a sin against his own blood.

The last play of the trilogy, *The Eumenides*, works out the atonement and absolution of Orestes. The Furies, goddesses who avenged murder and unfilial conduct, demand Orestes' death. Orestes stands trial at Athens, with Athena as judge and Apollo as counsel for the defense. When the jury casts six votes to condemn Orestes and six to acquit him, Athena casts the deciding vote in favor of mercy and compassion. Aeschylus used *The Eumenides* to urge reason and justice to reconcile fundamental conflicts. The play concludes with a prayer that civil dissension never be allowed to destroy the city and that the life of the city be one of harmony and grace.

Sophocles (496–406 B.C.) too dealt with matters personal and political. In *Antigone* he examined the relationship between the individual and the state by exploring a conflict between the ties of kinship and the demands of the polis. In the play Polynices has attacked his own state, Thebes, and has fallen in battle. Creon, the Theban king, refuses to allow Polynices' body to be buried. Polynices' sister Antigone is appalled by Creon's action because custom demands that she bury her brother's corpse. Creon is right in refusing to allow Polynices' body to be buried in the polis, but wrong to refuse any burial at all. He continues in his misguided and willful error. As the play progresses, Antigone comes to stand for the precedence of divine law over human defects. Sophocles touches upon the need for recognition of the law and adherence to it as a prerequisite for a tranquil state.

Sophocles' masterpieces have become classics of Western literature, and his themes have inspired generations of playwrights. Perhaps his most famous plays are *Oedipus the King* and its sequel, *Oedipus at Colonus. Oedipus the King* is the ironic story of a man doomed by the gods to kill his father and marry his mother. Try as he might to avoid his fate, Oedipus' every action brings him closer to its fulfillment. When at last he realizes that he has carried out the decree of the gods, Oedipus blinds himself and flees into exile. In *Oedipus at Colonus* Sophocles dramatizes the last days of the broken king, whose patient suffering and uncomplaining piety win him an exalted position. In the end the gods honor him for his virtue. The interpretation of these two plays has been hotly debated, but Sophocles seems to be saying that human beings should do the will of the gods, even without fully understanding it, for the gods stand for justice and order.

Euripides (ca 480–406 B.C.), the last of the three great Greek dramatists, also explored the theme of personal conflict within the polis and sounded the depths of the individual. With Euripides drama entered a new, and in many ways more personal, phase. To him the gods were far less important than human beings. Euripides viewed the human soul as a place where opposing forces struggle with each other, where strong passions such as hatred and jealousy come into conflict with reason. The essence of Euripides' tragedy is the flawed character – the men and women who bring disaster on themselves and their loved ones because their passions overwhelm reason. Although Euripides' plays were less popular in his own lifetime than those of Aeschylus and Sophocles, Euripides was a dramatist of genius, and his work later had a significant impact on Roman drama.

Writers of comedy treated the affairs of the polis bawdily and often coarsely. Even so, their plays too were performed at religious festivals. The comic playwrights dealt primarily with the political affairs of the polis and the conduct of its leading politicians. Best known are the comedies of Aristophanes (ca 445–386 B.C.), an ardent lover of his city and a merciless critic of cranks and quacks. He lampooned eminent generals, at times depicting them as morons. He commented snidely on Pericles, poked fun at Socrates and hooted at Euripides. He saved some of his strongest venom for Cleon, a prominent politician. It is a tribute to the Athenians that such devastating attacks could openly and freely be made on the city's leaders and foreign policy. Even at the height of the Peloponnesian War, Aristophanes proclaimed that peace was preferable to the ravages of war. Like Aeschylus, Sophocles, and Euripides, Aristophanes used his art to dramatize his ideas on the right conduct of the citizen and the value of the polis.

Perhaps never were art and political life so intimately and congenially bound together as at Athens. Athenian art was the product of deep and genuine love of the polis. It aimed at bettering the lives of the citizens and the quality of life in the state.

## DAILY LIFE IN PERICLEAN ATHENS

In sharp contrast with the rich intellectual and cultural life of Periclean Athens is the simplicity of its material life. The Athenians – and in this respect they were typical of Greeks in general – lived very happily with comparatively few material possessions. In the first place, there were very few material goods to own. The thousands of machines, tools, and gadgets considered essential for modern life had no counterpart in Athenian life. The inventory of Alcibiades' goods, which the Athenians confiscated after his desertion, is enlightening. His household possessions consisted of chests, beds, couches, tables, screens, stools, baskets, and mats. Other necessities of the Greek home included pottery, metal utensils for cooking, tools, luxury goods such as jewelry, and a few other things. These items they had to buy from craftsmen. Whatever else they needed, such as clothes and blankets, they produced at home.

The Athenian house was rather simple. Whether large or small, the typical house consisted of a series of rooms built around a central courtyard, with doors opening onto the courtyard. Many houses had bedrooms on an upper floor. Artisans and craftsmen often set aside a room to use as a shop or work area. The two principal rooms were the men's dining room and the room where the women worked wool. Other rooms included the kitchen and bathroom. By modern standards there was not much furniture. In the men's dining room were couches, a sideboard, and small tables. Cups and other pottery were often hung on the wall from pegs. Other household furnishings included items such as those confiscated from Alcibiades.

In the courtyard were the well, a small altar, and a washbasin. If the family lived in the country, the stalls of the animals faced the courtyard. The countryman kept oxen for plowing, pigs for slaughtering, sheep for wool, goats for cheese, and mules and donkeys for transportation. Even in the city, chickens and perhaps a goat or two roamed the courtyard together with dogs and cats.

Cooking, done over a hearth in the house, provided welcome warmth in the winter. Baking and roasting were done in ovens. Food consisted of various grains, especially wheat and barley, as well as lentils, olives, figs, and grapes. Garlic and onion were popular garnishes, and wine was always on hand. These foods were stored at home in large jars, and with them the Greek family ate fish, chicken, and vegetables. Women ground wheat into flour at home, baked it into bread, and on special occasions made honey or sesame cakes. The Greeks used olive oil for cooking, as families still do in modern Greece; they also used it as an unguent and as fuel for lamps.

By American standards the Greeks did not eat much meat. On special occasions, such as important religious festivals, the family ate the animal sacrificed to the god and gave the god the exquisite delicacy of the thighbone wrapped in fat. The only Greeks who consistently ate meat were the Spartan warriors. They received a small portion of meat each day, together with the infamous Spartan black broth, a ghastly concoction of pork cooked in blood, vinegar, and salt. One Greek, after tasting the broth, commented that he could easily understand why the Spartans were so willing to die.

In the city a man might support himself as a craftsman – a potter, bronzesmith, sailmaker, or tanner – or he could contract with the polis to work on public buildings, such as the Parthenon and Erechtheion. Men without skills worked as paid laborers but competed with slaves for work. Slaves – usually foreigners, both barbarian and Greek – were paid as much for their labor as were free men.

Slavery was commonplace in Greece, as it was throughout the ancient world. In its essentials Greek slavery resembled Mesopotamian slavery. Slaves received some protection under the law and could buy their freedom. On the other hand, masters could mistreat or neglect their slaves short of killing them, which was illegal. The worst-treated slaves were those of the silver mines at Laurium, who lived, worked, and died in wretchedness. Yet slavery elsewhere was not generally brutal. One crusty aristocrat complained that in Athens one could not tell the slaves from the free. Most slaves in Athens served as domestics and performed light labor around the house. Nurses for children, teachers of reading and writing, and guardians for young men were often slaves. The lives of these slaves were much like those of their owners. Other slaves were skilled workers, who could be found working on public buildings or in small workshops.

The importance of slavery in Athens must not be exaggerated. Apart from the owners of the Laurium mines, Athenians did not own huge gangs of slaves as did Roman owners of large estates. Slave labor competed with free labor and kept wages down, but it never replaced the free labor that was the mainstay of the Athenian economy.

Most Athenians supported themselves by agriculture, but unless the family was fortunate enough to possess holdings in a plain more fertile than most of the land, they found it difficult to reap a good crop from the soil. Wealthy landowners sold their excess produce in the urban marketplace, but many people must have consumed nearly everything they raised. The plow, though wooden, sometimes had an iron share, and was pulled by oxen. Attic farmers were free men. Though hardly prosperous, they were by no means destitute. Greek farmers could usually expect yields of five bushels of wheat and ten of barley per acre for every bushel of grain sown. A bad harvest meant a lean year. In many places farmers grew more barley than wheat because of the nature of the soil. Wherever possible farmers also cultivated vines and olive trees.

For sport both the countryman and the city dweller often hunted for rabbits, deer, or wild boar. A successful hunt supplemented the family's regular diet. Wealthy men hunted on horseback; most others hunted on foot with their dogs. Hunting also allowed a man to display to his fellows his bravery and prowess in the chase. If wild boar were the prey, the sport could be dangerous, as Odysseus discovered when a charging boar slashed open his foot.

The social condition of Athenian women has been the subject of much debate and little agreement. One thing is certain: the status of a free woman of the citizen class was strictly protected by law. Only her children, not those of foreigners or slaves, could be citizens. Only she was in charge of the household and the family's possessions. Yet the law protected her primarily to protect her husband's interests. Raping a free woman was a lesser crime than seducing her because seduction involved the winning of her affections. This law was not concerned with the husband's feelings but with ensuring that he need not doubt the legitimacy of his children.

Ideally, respectable women lived a secluded life in which the only men they saw were relatives. How far this ideal was actually put into practice is impossible to say. At least Athenian women seem to have enjoyed a social circle of other women of their own class. They also attended public festivals, sacrifices, and funerals. Nonetheless, prosperous and respectable women probably spent much of their time in the house. A white complexion – a sign that a woman did not have to work in the fields – was valued highly.

Courtesans lived the freest lives of all Athenian women. Although some courtesans were simply prostitutes, others added intellectual accomplishments to physical beauty. In constant demand, cultured courtesans moved freely in male society. Their artistic talents and intellectual abilities appealed to men who wanted more than sex. The most famous of all courtesans was Aspasia, mistress of Pericles and supposedly friend of Socrates. Under Pericles' roof, she participated in intellectual discussions equally with some of the most stimulating thinkers of the day. Yet her position, like that of most other courtesans, was precarious. After Pericles' death, Aspasia fended for herself, ending her days as the madam of a house of prostitution.

A woman's main functions were to raise the children, oversee the domestic slaves and hired labor, and together with her maids work wool into cloth. The women washed the wool in the courtyard and then brought it into the women's room, where the loom stood. They spun the wool into thread and wove the thread into cloth. They also dyed wool at home and decorated the cloth by weaving in colors and designs. The woman of the household either did the cooking herself or directed her maids. In a sense, poor women lived freer lives than did wealthier women. They performed manual labor in the fields or

sold goods in the agora, going about their affairs much as men did.

A distinctive feature of Athenian life, and Greek life in general, was acceptance of homosexuality. The distinguished English scholar K.J. Dover has succinctly described the difference between Greek and modern outlooks on human sexuality:

*Greek culture differed from ours in its readiness to recognize the alternation of homosexual and heterosexual preferences in the same individual, its implicit denial that such alternation or coexistence created peculiar problems for the individual or for society, its sympathetic response to the open expression of homosexual desire in words and behavior, and its taste for the uninhibited treatment of homosexual subjects in literature and the visual arts.*[22]

No one has satisfactorily explained how the Greek attitude toward homosexual love developed, or determined how common homosexual behavior was. Homosexuality was probably far more common among the aristocracy than among the lower classes. It is impossible to be sure, simply because most of what the modern world knows of ancient Greece and Rome comes from the writings of aristocrats. Since aristocratic boys and girls were often brought up separately, the likelihood of homosexual relationships was very great. This style of life was impossible for the common folk because every member of the family – husband and wife, son and daughter – got out and worked. Among the poorer classes the sexes mingled freely.

Even among the aristocracy attitudes toward homosexuality were complex and sometimes conflicting. Most people saw homosexual love affairs among the young as a stage in the development of a mature heterosexual life. Yet some Athenian aristocrats ridiculed homosexual practices. Comic writers habitually made fun of "boy-crazy men" and "effeminate youths." Others, such as the Spartans and the philosopher Plato, saw in homosexual relationships the opportunity for older men to train their juniors in practical wisdom. For them, the sexual element was supposed to give way to the benefits of education. In Sparta, as in Sappho's Lesbos, noble women loved girls for the same reasons. Warrior-aristocracies generally emphasized the physical side of the relationship in the belief that warriors who were also lovers would fight all the harder to impress each other. They would also be less likely to desert their lovers in battle. Whatever their intellectual and educational content, homosexual love affairs were also overtly sexual.

What effect did homosexual love have on the Greeks? An American psychologist has concluded that the "Greek adolescent ... ended up as a non-neurotic, completely (or predominantly) heterosexual adult."[23] Most of Sappho's young lovers went on to marry and raise families. They never regretted the homosexual loves of their past or thought them unusual. Their previous relationships did not prevent them from devoting their primary affection to their new mates. For many Greeks, homosexuality was a normal practice, and they treated it as straightforwardly and honestly as they did heterosexual love and other aspects of life.

Despite some modern speculation to the contrary, relations between Athenian husbands and wives were probably close. The presence of female slaves in the home could be a source of trouble; men were always free to resort to prostitutes; and some men and women engaged in homosexual love affairs. But basically husbands and wives depended on each other for mutual love and support. The wife's position and status in the household were guaranteed by her dowry, which

came from her father and remained her property throughout her married life. If the wife felt that her marriage was intolerable, she could divorce her husband far more easily than could a Mesopotamian wife.

To judge by the evidence of funerary reliefs, there seems to have been nothing radically odd about the relationships of Athenian wives and husbands. One scholar has noted that funerary reliefs express the sorrow of the entire household — husband, children, and slaves — at the death of a wife. An epitaph of the fourth or third century B.C. reads:

*Chaerestrate lies in this tomb. When she was alive her husband loved her. When she died he lamented.*[24]

## THE FLOWERING OF PHILOSOPHY

The myths and epics of the Mesopotamians are ample testimony that speculation about the origin of the universe and of mankind did not begin with the Greeks. The signal achievement of the Greeks was their willingness to treat these questions in rational rather than mythological terms. Although Greek philosophy did not fully flower until the Classical Period, Ionian thinkers had already begun in the Lyric Age to ask what the universe was made of. These men are called the Pre-Socratics, for their work preceded the philosophical revolution begun by the Athenian Socrates. Though they were born observers, the Pre-Socratics rarely undertook deliberate experimentation. Instead they took individual facts and wove them into general theories. Despite appearances, they believed, the universe was actually simple and subject to natural laws. Drawing upon their observations, they speculated about the basic building blocks of the universe.

The first of the Pre-Socratics, Thales (ca

600 B.C.), learned mathematics and astronomy from the Babylonians and geometry from the Egyptians. Yet there was an immense and fundamental difference between Near Eastern thought and the philosophy of Thales. The Near Eastern peoples considered such events as eclipses as evil omens. Thales viewed them as natural phenomena that could be explained in natural terms. In short, he asked *why* things happened. He believed the basic element of the universe to be water. Although he was wrong, the way in which he had asked the question was momentous: it was the beginning of the scientific method.

Thales' follower Anaximander continued his work. Anaximander was the first of the Pre-Socratics to use general concepts, which are essential to abstract thought. One of the most brilliant of the Pre-Socratics, a man of striking originality, Anaximander theorized that the basic element of the universe is "the boundless" or "endless" – something infinite and indestructible. In his view, the earth floats in a void, held in balance by its distance from everything else in the universe.

Anaximander even concluded that mankind had evolved naturally from lower organisms: "In water the first animal arose covered with spiny skin, and with the lapse of time some crawled onto dry land and breaking off their skins in a short time they survived."[25] This remarkable speculation corresponds crudely to Darwin's theory of evolution of species, which it predated by two-and-a-half millennia.

Another Ionian, Heraclitus (ca 500 B.C.) declared the primal element to be fire. He also declared that the world had neither beginning nor end: "This world, the world of all things, neither any god nor man made, but it always was and it is and it will be: an everlasting fire, measures kindling and measures going out."[26] Although the universe was eternal, according to Heraclitus, it changed constantly. An out-

growth of this line of speculation was the theory of Democritus that the universe is made of invisible, indestructible atoms. The culmination of Pre-Socratic thought was the theory that four simple substances make up the universe: fire, air, earth, and water.

With this impressive heritage behind them, the philosophers of the Classical Period ventured into new areas of speculation. This development was partly due to the work of Hippocrates (second half of the fifth century B.C.), the father of medicine.

Like Thales, Hippocrates sought natural explanations for natural phenomena. Basing his opinions on empirical knowledge, not on religion or magic, he taught that natural means could be employed to fight disease. In his treatise *On Airs, Waters, and Places*, he noted the influence of climate and environment on health. Hippocrates and his followers put forth a theory that was to prevail in medical circles until the eighteenth century. The human body, they declared, contains four humors, or fluids: blood, phlegm, black bile, and yellow bile. In a healthy body the four humors are in perfect balance; too much or too little of any particular humor causes illness. Hippocrates and his pupils shared the Ionian belief that they were dealing with phenomena that could be explained purely in natural terms. But Hippocrates broke away from the mainstream of Ionian speculation by declaring that medicine was a separate craft – just as ironworking was a craft – and that it had its own principles.

The distinction between natural science and philosophy, upon which Hippocrates insisted, was also promoted by the sophists, who traveled the Greek world teaching young men. Despite differences of opinion on philosophical matters, the sophists all agreed that human beings were the proper subject of study. They also believed that excellence could be taught, and used philosophy and rhetoric to prepare young men for life in the polis. The sophists laid great emphasis on logic and the meanings of words. They criticized traditional beliefs, religion, rituals, and myth, and even questioned the laws of the polis. In essence they argued that nothing is absolute, that everything – even the customs and constitution of the state – is relative. Hence, many Greeks of more traditional inclination considered them wanton and harmful, men who were interested in "making the worse seem the better cause."

One of those whose contemporaries thought him a sophist was Socrates (ca 470–399 B.C.), who sprang from the class of small artisans. Socrates spent his life in investigation and definition. Not strictly speaking a sophist, because he never formally taught or collected fees from anyone, Socrates shared the sophists' belief that human beings and their environment are the essential subjects of philosophical inquiry. Like the sophists, Socrates thought that excellence could be learned and passed on to others. His approach when posing ethical questions and defining concepts was to start with a general topic or problem and to narrow the matter to its essentials. He did so by continuous questioning, a running dialogue. Never did he lecture. Socrates thought that by constantly pursuing excellence, an essential part of which was knowledge, human beings could approach the supreme good and thus find true happiness. Yet, in 399 B.C., Socrates was brought to trial, convicted, and executed on charges of corrupting the youth of the city and introducing new gods.

Socrates' student Plato (427–347 B.C.) carried on his master's search for truth. Unlike Socrates, Plato wrote down his thoughts and theories and founded a philosophical school, the Academy. Plato developed the theory that all visible, tangible things are unreal and temporary, copies of "forms" or "ideas" that are constant and indestructible. Only the mind – not the senses – can perceive the eternal forms. In Plato's view the highest form is the idea of good.

In *The Republic* Plato applied his theory of forms to politics in an effort to describe the ideal polis. His perfect polis is utopian; it aims at providing the greatest good and happiness to all its members. Plato thought that the ideal polis could exist only if its rulers were philosophers. He divided society into rulers, guardians of the polis, and workers. The role of people in each category is decided by the education, wisdom, and ability of the individual. In Plato's republic men and women are equal to one another, and women can become rulers. The utopian polis is a balance, with each individual doing what he or she can to support the state and with each receiving from the state his or her just due.

In a later work, *The Laws,* Plato discarded the ideal polis of *The Republic* in favor of a second-best state. The polis of *The Laws* is grimly reminiscent of the modern dictatorship. At its head is a young tyrant, who is just and good. He meets with a council that sits only at night, and together they maintain the spirit of the laws. Nearly everything about this state is coercive; the free will of the citizens counts for little. The laws speak to every aspect of life; their sole purpose is to make people happy.

Aristotle (384–322 B.C.) carried on the philosophical tradition of Socrates and Plato. A student of Plato, Aristotle went far beyond his teacher in his efforts to understand the universe. The very range of Aristotle's thought is staggering. Everything within human experience was fit subject for his inquiry. In his *Politics* Aristotle followed Plato's lead by writing about the ideal polis. Yet

Aristotle approached the question more realistically than Plato had, and he criticized *The Republic* and *The Laws* on many points. In the *Politics* and elsewhere, Aristotle stressed moderation and concluded that the balance of his ideal state depended on people of talent and education who could avoid extremes.

Not content to examine old questions, Aristotle opened up whole new fields of inquiry. He tried to understand the changes of nature – what caused them and where they led. In the *Physics* and *Metaphysics* he evolved a theory of nature in which he developed the notions of matter, form, and motion. He attempted to bridge the gap between abstract truth and concrete perception that Plato had created.

In *On the Heaven,* Aristotle took up the thread of Ionian speculation. His theory of cosmology added ether to air, fire, water, and earth as building-blocks of the universe. He concluded that the universe revolves and that it is spherical and eternal. He wrongly thought that the earth is the center of the universe, with the stars and other planets revolving around it. The Hellenistic scientist Aristarchus of Samos later realized that the earth revolves around the sun, but Aristotle's view was accepted until the time of the fifteenth-century astronomer Nicolaus Copernicus.

Aristotle's scientific interests also included zoology. In several works he describes various animals and makes observations on animal habits, animal anatomy, and how animals move. He also explored the process of reproduction. Intending to examine the entire animal kingdom, he assigned the world of plants to his follower Theophrastus (see Chapter 4).

Aristotle possessed one of the keenest and most curious philosophical minds of Western civilization. While rethinking the old topics

DEPARTING WARRIOR *Scenes like this were all too common from 431 to 338 B.C., as young men donned their armor and left for battle. This warrior and a young woman, probably his sister, pour a libation to the gods before he leaves for the war. (Museum of Fine Arts, Boston)*

explored by the Pre-Socratics, he also created whole new areas of study. In short, he tried to learn everything possible about the universe and everything in it. He did so in the belief that all knowledge could be synthesized to produce a simple explanation of the universe and of humanity.

## THE FINAL ACT (403–338 B.C.)

The end of the Peloponnesian War only punctuated a century of nearly constant war-

THE LION OF CHAERONEA    *Alone on his base, this stylized lion marks the mass grave of nearly 300 elite Theban soldiers who valiantly died fighting the Macedonians at the battle of Chaeronea. After the battle, when Philip viewed the bodies of these brave troops, he said to those around him: "May those who suppose that these men did or suffered anything dishonorable perish wretchedly." (Photo: Caroline Buckler)*

fare that lasted from 431 to 338 B.C. The events of the fourth century demonstrated that no single Greek state possessed enough power and resources to dominate the others. There nevertheless ensued an exhausting struggle for hegemony among the great powers, especially Sparta, Athens, and Thebes. Immediately after the Peloponnesian War, with Athens humbled, Sparta began striving for empire over the Greeks. The arrogance and imperialism of the Spartans turned their former allies against them. Even with Persian help Sparta could not maintain its hold on Greece. In 371 B.C. the Spartans met their match on the plain of Leuctra in Boeotia. A Theban army under the command of Epaminondas, one of Greece's most brilliant generals, destroyed the flower of the Spartan army on a single summer day. The victory at Leuctra left Thebes the most powerful state in Greece. Under Epaminondas the Thebans destroyed Sparta as a first-rank power and checked the ambitions of Athens, but they were unable to bring peace to Greece. In 362 B.C. Epaminondas was killed in battle, and a period of stalemate set in. The Greek states were virtually exhausted.

The man who turned the situation to his own advantage was Philip II, king of Macedonia (359–336 B.C.). Throughout most of Greek history Macedonia, which bordered Greece in the north, in modern Greece and Yugoslavia, had been a backward and disunited kingdom, but Philip's genius, courage, and drive turned it into a major power. One of the ablest statesmen of antiquity, Philip united his powerful kingdom behind him, built a redoubtable army, and pursued his ambition with drive and determination. His horizon was not limited to Macedonia, for he realized that he could turn the rivalry and exhaustion of the Greek states to his own purposes. By clever use of his wealth and superb army Philip won control of the northern Aegean and awakened fear in Athens, which had vital interests there. Demosthenes, an Athenian patriot and a fine orator, warned his fellow citizens against Philip:

*Most of all there is this to fear. This cunning and terrible man makes use of his accomplishments, yielding on points when he must, threatening (and he certainly appears to mean it) on others. He slanders us and our inactivity. He fosters and takes for himself anything of value.*[27]

Others too saw Philip as a threat. A comic playwright depicted one of Philip's ambassadors warning the Athenians:

*Do you know that your battle will be with men*
*Who dine on sharpened swords,*
*And gulp burning firebrands for wine?*
*Then immediately after dinner the slave*
*Brings us dessert – Cretan arrows*
*Or pieces of broken spears.*
*We have shields and breastplates for*
*Cushions and at our feet slings and arrows,*
*And we are crowned with catapults.*[28]

Finally the Athenians joined forces with Thebes, which also appreciated the Macedonian threat, to stop Philip. In 338 B.C. the combined Theban-Athenian army met Philip's veterans at the Boeotian city of Chaeronea. Philip's army won a hard-fought victory: he had conquered Greece and put an end to Greek freedom. Because the Greeks could not put aside their quarrels, they fell to an invader.

---

In a comparatively brief span of time the Greeks progressed from a primitive folk, backward and rude compared to their Near Eastern neighbors, to one of the most influential peoples of history. The originators of science and philosophy asked penetrating questions about the nature of life and society, and came up with deathless responses to many of their own questions. Greek achievements range from the development of sophisticated political institutions to the creation of a stunningly rich literature. Brilliant but quarrelsome, they were their own worst enemies. As the Roman historian Pompeius Trogus later said of their fall:

*The states of Greece, while each one wished to rule alone, all squandered sovereignty. Indeed, hastening without moderation to destroy one another in mutual ruin, they did not realize, until they were all crushed, that every one of them lost in the end.*[29]

Nonetheless, their achievement outlived their political squabbles to become the cornerstone of all later Western development.

---

## NOTES

1. K. J. Beloch, *Griechische Geschichte,* vol. I, pt. I, K. J. Trübner, Strassburg, 1912, p. 49.

2. Aristotle *Politics* 1253a3-4.

3. Herodotus *The Histories* 2.53.

4. Hesiod *Works and Days* 263-266.

5. Ibid., 511-514.

6. F. Lasserre, *Archiloque,* Société d'Edition "Les Belles Lettres," Paris, 1958, frag. 9, p. 4.

7. W. Barnstable, *Sappho,* Doubleday, Garden City, N.Y., 1965, frag. 24, p. 22.

8. Ibid., frag. 132, p. 106.

9. Ibid., frag. 23, p. 20.

10. J. M. Edmonds, *Greek Elegy and Iambus,* Harvard University Press, Cambridge, Mass., 1931, I.70, frag. 10.

11. Ibid., frag. 11, p. 72.

12. Edmonds, *Greek Elegy and Iambus,* frag. 4, p. 118.

13. R. Meiggs and D. Lewis, *A Selection of Greek Historical Inscriptions,* Clarendon Press, Oxford, 1969, no. 52, lines 21–32.

14. Ibid., no. 40, lines 9–11.

15. Thucydides *History of the Peloponnesian War* 1.23.

16. Ibid.

17. Herodotus *The Histories* 1.1.

18. Ibid., 7.102.

19. Thucydides *The Peloponnesian War* 1.1.

20. Plutarch *Life of Pericles* 13.5.

21. Mark Twain, *The Innocents Abroad,* Signet Classics, New York, 1966, p. 249.

22. K. J. Dover, *Greek Homosexuality,* Random House, New York, 1980, p.1.

23. G. Devereux, "Greek Pseudo-Homosexuality and the 'Greek Miracle'," *Symbolae Osloenses* (1968): 70.

24. S. B. Pomeroy, *Goddesses, Whores, Wives and Slaves,* Schocken, New York, 1975, p. 92.

25. E. Diels and W. Krantz, *Fragmente der Vorsokratiker,* 8th ed. Weidmannsche Verlagsbuchhandlung, Berlin, 1960, Anaximander frag. A30.

26. Ibid., Heraclitus frag. B30.

27. Demosthenes *First Olynthiac* 3.

28. J. M. Edmonds, *The Fragments of Attic Comedy,* E. J. Brill, Leiden, 2.366–369, Mnesimachos frag. 7.

29. Justin 8.1.1–2.

## SUGGESTED READING

Translations of the most important writings of the Greeks and Romans can be found in the volumes of the Loeb Classical Library, published by Harvard University Press. Paperback editions of the major Greek and Latin authors are available in the Penguin Classics. Recent translations of documents include those by N. Lewis, *Greek Historical Documents: The Fifth Century* B.C. (1971); J. Wickersham and G. Verbrugghe, *Greek Historical Documents: The Fourth Century* B.C. (1973); and C. Fornara, *Translated Documents of Greece and Rome,* vol. 1: *Archaic Times to the End of the Peloponnesian War* (1977).

Among the many general treatments of Greek history, H. D. F. Kitto, *The Greeks* (1951), is a delightful introduction. V. Ehrenberg in two works, *From Solon to Socrates,* 2nd. ed. (1973) and *The Greek State* (1960), covers major areas of Greek history.

For early Greece the most recent treatments include R. J. Hopper, *The Early Greeks* (1976), and L. H. Jeffery, *Archaic Greece* (1976). No finer introduction to the Lyric Age can be found than A. R. Burn's *The Lyric Age* (1960) and its sequel, *Persia and the Greeks* (1962). A good recent survey of work on Sparta is P. Oliva, *Sparta and Her Social Problems* (1971). Sound discussions of Athenian democracy are available in A. H. M. Jones, *Athenian Democracy* (1957), and C. Hignett, *History of the Athenian Constitution* (1952).

A. J. Graham, *Colony and Mother City in Ancient Greece* (1964), gives a good account of Greek colonization. Athens in the fifth century and the outbreak of the Peloponnesian War are covered in G. E. M. de Ste Croix, *The Origins of the Peloponnesian War* (1972), and R. Meiggs, *The Athenian Empire* (1972).

Several books on fourth-century history have recently appeared. D. M. Lewis' *Sparta and Persia* (1977) is rich in information on the administration of the Persian Empire, Spartan diplomacy, and much else. J. Buckler, *The Theban Hegemony, 371–362 B.C.* (1980) treats the period of Theban ascendancy. J. Cargill, *The Second Athenian League* (1981), a significant new study, traces Athenian policy during the century. J. R. Ellis, *Philip II and Macedonian Imperialism* (1976), and G. Cawkwell, *Philip of Macedon* (1978), analyze the career of the great conqueror.

Daily life, the family, women, and homosexuality receive treatment in Pomeroy's book cited in the Notes; T. B. L. Webster, *Life in Classical Greece* (1969); M. and C. H. B. Quennell, *Everyday Things in Ancient Greece* (1954); and a special issue of the Journal *Arethusa* 6 (1973).

For Greek literature, culture, and science, see A. Lesky, *A History of Greek Literature* (English trans., 1963); W. Jaeger, *Paideia,* 3 vols., (English trans., 1944–1945); H. C. Baldry, *The Greek Tragic Theater* (1971); J. Burnet, *Early Greek Philosophy,* 4th ed.

(1930), and *Greek Philosophy, Thales to Plato* (1914); M. Clagett, *Greek Science in Antiquity* (1971); and E. R. Dodds, *The Greeks and the Irrational* (1951).

The classic treatment of Greek architecture is W. B. Dinsmoor, *The Architecture of the Ancient Greeks,* 3rd ed. (1950). More recent (and perhaps more readable) is A. W. Lawrence, *Greek Architecture,* 3rd ed. (1973). J. Boardman, *Greek Art,* rev. ed. (1973), is both perceptive and sound, as is J. J. Pollitt, *Art and Experience in Classical Greece* (1972).

D. Haynes, *Greek Art and the Idea of Freedom* (1981), traces the evolving freedom of the human personality in Greek art.

J. Pinsent, *Greek Mythology* (1969), is a handy introduction. M. P. Nilsson, *Cults, Myths, Oracles and Politics in Ancient Greece* (1951), examines Greek religion and myth in the contemporary context. See also G. S. Kirk, *The Nature of Greek Myths* (1974).

# CHAPTER 4

## HELLENISTIC DIFFUSION

*TWO YEARS AFTER* his conquest of Greece, Philip of Macedon fell victim to an assassin's dagger. Philip's twenty-year-old son, known to history as Alexander the Great (336–323 B.C.) assumed the Macedonian throne. This young man, one of the most remarkable personalities of Western civilization, was to have a profound impact on history. "For in twelve years having conquered not a small part of Europe and nearly all of Asia, he was justly famous and his glory was equal to that of the heroes of old and of the demigods."[1]

By overthrowing the Persian Empire and by spreading Hellenism – Greek culture, language, thought and the Greek way of life – as far as India, Alexander was instrumental in creating a new era, traditionally called Hellenistic to distinguish it from the Hellenic. As a result of Alexander's exploits, the individualistic and energetic culture of the Greeks came into intimate contact with the venerable older cultures of the Near East.

What did the spread of Hellenism mean to the Greeks and the peoples of the Near East? What did the meeting of West and East hold for the development of philosophy, religion, science, medicine, and economics? These are the questions this chapter will explore.

## ALEXANDER AND THE GREAT CRUSADE

In 336 B.C., Alexander inherited not only Philip's crown but also his policies. After his victory at Chaeronea, Philip had organized the states of Greece into a huge league under his leadership, and announced to the Greeks his plan to lead them and his Macedonians against the Persian Empire. Fully intending to carry out Philip's designs, Alexander proclaimed to the Greek world that the invasion of Persia was to be a great crusade, a mighty act of revenge for the Persian invasion of Greece in 480 B.C.

Despite his youth, Alexander was well prepared to lead the attack. Philip had groomed his son to become king, and had given him the best education possible. In 343 B.C., Philip invited the philosopher Aristotle to tutor his son. From Aristotle Alexander learned to appreciate Greek culture and literature, and the teachings of the great philosopher left a lasting mark on him. Alexander must also have profited from Aristotle's practical knowledge, but he never accepted Aristotle's political theories. At the age of sixteen Alexander became regent of Macedonia, and two years later at the battle of Chaeronea he helped defeat the Greeks. By 336 B.C., Alexander had acquired both the theoretical and the practical knowledge to rule peoples and lead armies.

In 334 B.C., Alexander led an army of Macedonians and Greeks into Asia Minor. With him went a staff of philosophers and poets, scientists whose job was to map the country and to study strange animals and plants, and the historian Callisthenes, who was to write an account of the campaign. Alexander planned not only to conquer the Persians but to lead an expedition of discovery to open up the East to Greek knowledge.

In the next three years Alexander won three major battles at the Granicus River, Issus, and Gaugamela. As Map 4.1 shows, these battle sites stand almost as road signs marking his march to the East. After his victory at Gaugamela, Alexander captured the principal Persian capital of Persepolis, where he performed a symbolic act of retribution by burning the buildings of Xerxes, the invader of Greece. In 330 B.C., he took Ecbatana, the last Persian capital, and pursued the Persian king to his death.

The Persian Empire had fallen and the war of revenge was over, but Alexander had no intention of stopping. He dismissed his Greek troops, but permitted many of them to serve on as mercenaries. Alexander then began his personal odyssey. With his Macedonian soldiers and Greek mercenaries he set out to conquer the rest of Asia. He plunged deeper into the East, into lands completely unknown to the Greek world. Alexander's way was marked by bitter fighting and bloodshed. It took four more years to conquer Bactria and the easternmost parts of the now-defunct Persian Empire, but still Alexander was determined to march on.

In 326 B.C., Alexander crossed the Indus River and entered India. There too he saw hard fighting, and finally at the Hyphasis River his troops refused to go farther. Alexander was enraged by the mutiny, for he believed that he was near the end of the world. Nonetheless, the army stood firm, and Alexander had to relent. Still eager to explore the limits of the world, Alexander returned south to the Indian Ocean. Even though the tribes in the area did not oppose him, he waged a bloody, ruthless, and unnecessary war against them. After reaching the Indian Ocean and turning west, he led his army through the grim Gedrosian Desert, apparently to punish his troops for their mutiny at the Hyphasis. The army suffered fearfully, and many men died along the way, but in 324 B.C. Alexander reached his camp at Susa. The great crusade was over, and Alexander himself died the next year in Babylon.

## ALEXANDER'S LEGACY

Of Alexander the man history knows little: he too quickly became a figure of legend, a figure larger than life. Of Alexander's plans and intentions history likewise knows little. Although some scholars have seen him as a high-minded philosopher, his bloody and sav-

COIN OF ALEXANDER *The head on this coin is that of the demigod Heracles, whom Alexander admired and imitated. Alexander claimed that he was descended from Heracles, and on several occasions he even dressed like Heracles. (Courtesy, World Heritage Museum. Photo: Caroline Buckler)*

age campaigns in the East seem the work of a ruthless and callous conqueror. Yet for the Hellenistic period and for Western civilization in general, what Alexander intended was less important than what he actually did (see Map 4.1).

Alexander was instrumental in changing the face of politics in the eastern Mediterranean. His campaign swept away the Persian Empire, which had ruled the East for over two hundred years. In its place he established a Macedonian monarchy. More important in the long run was his foundation of new cities and military colonies, which scattered Greeks and Macedonians throughout the East. Thus the practical result of Alexander's campaign was to open the East to the tide of Hellenism.

### THE POLITICAL LEGACY

In 323 B.C., Alexander the Great died at the age of thirty-two. The main question at his death was whether his vast empire could be

MAP 4.1 ALEXANDER'S CONQUESTS This
map shows the course of Alexander's invasion of the
Persian Empire and the speed of his progress.

held together. The answer became obvious
immediately. Within a week of Alexander's
death began a round of fighting that was to
continue for forty years. No single Macedonian general was able to replace Alexander as
emperor of his entire domain. By 275 B.C., as
Map 4.2 shows, three of Alexander's officers
had divided it into large monarchies. Antig-
onus Gonatas became king of Macedonia and
established the Antigonid dynasty, which
ruled until the Roman conquest in 168 B.C.
Ptolemy Lagus made himself king of Egypt,
and his descendants, the Ptolemies, assumed
the powers and position of pharaohs. Se-

leucus, founder of the Seleucid dynasty, carved
out a kingdom that stretched from the coast
of Asia Minor to India. In 263 B.C., Eumenes,
the Greek ruler of Pergamum, a city in western Asia Minor, won his independence from
the Seleucids and created the Pergamene
monarchy. Though the Seleucid kings soon
lost control of their easternmost provinces,
Greek influence in this area did not wane. In
modern Turkestan and Afghanistan another
line of Greek kings established the kingdom
of Bactria, and even managed to spread their
power and culture into northern India.

The political face of Greece itself changed

*ALEXANDER AT THE BATTLE OF ISSOS    At the left, Alexander the Great, bareheaded and wearing a breastplate, charges King Darius, who is standing in a chariot. This moment marks the turning point of the battle, as Darius turns to flee from the attack. (Museo Nazionale, Naples. Alinari/Scala)*

during the Hellenistic period. The day of the polis was over, and in its place arose leagues of city-states. The two most powerful and most extensive were the Aetolian League in western and central Greece, and the Achaean League in the Peloponnesus. Once-powerful city-states like Athens and Sparta sank to the level of third-rate powers.

The political history of the Hellenistic period was dominated by the great monarchies and the Greek leagues. The political fragmentation and incessant warfare that marked the Hellenic period continued on an even wider and larger scale during the Hel-

lenistic period. Never did the Hellenistic world achieve political stability or lasting peace. Hellenistic kings never forgot the vision of Alexander's empire, spanning Europe and Asia, secure under the rule of one man. Try as they did, they were never able to recreate it. In this respect, Alexander's legacy fell not to his generals but to the Romans of a later era.

## THE CULTURAL LEGACY

As Alexander waded ever deeper into the East, distance alone presented him with a serious problem: how was he to retain contact with the Greek world behind him? Communications were vital, for he drew supplies and reinforcements from Greece and Macedonia. Alexander had to be sure that he was never cut off and stranded far from the Mediterranean world. His solution was to plant cities and military colonies in strategic places. In these settlements Alexander left Greek mercenaries and Macedonian veterans no longer up to active campaigning. Besides keeping the road open to the West, these settlements dominated the countryside around them.

Their military significance apart, Alexander's cities and colonies became powerful instruments in the spread of Hellenism throughout the East. Plutarch described Alexander's achievement in glowing terms: "Having founded over 70 cities among barbarian peoples and having planted Greek magistracies in Asia, Alexander overcame its wild and savage way of life."[2] Alexander had indeed opened the East to an enormous wave of immigration, and his successors continued his policy by inviting Greek colonists to settle in their realms. For seventy-five years after Alexander's death, Greek immigrants poured into the East. At least 250 new Hellenistic colonies were established. The Mediterranean world had seen no comparable movement of peoples since the days of Archilochus (see page 82), when wave after wave of Greeks had turned the Mediterranean basin into a Greek-speaking region.

The overall result of Alexander's settlements and those of his successors was the spread of Hellenism as far east as India. Throughout the Hellenistic period Greeks and Easterners became familiar with and adapted themselves to each other's customs, religions, and ways of life. Although Greek culture did not completely conquer the East, it gave the East a vehicle of expression that linked it to the West. Hellenism became a common bond among the East, peninsular Greece, and the western Mediterranean. This pre-existing cultural bond was later to prove supremely valuable to Rome — itself heavily influenced by Hellenism — in its efforts to impose a comparable political unity on the known world.

## THE SPREAD OF HELLENISM

When the Greeks and Macedonians entered Asia Minor, Egypt, and the more remote East, they encountered civilizations older than their own. In some ways the Eastern cultures were more advanced than the Greek, in others less so. Thus this third great tide of Greek migration differed from preceding waves, which had spread over land that was uninhabited or inhabited by less-developed peoples.

What did the Hellenistic monarchies offer Greek immigrants, both politically and materially? More broadly, how did Hellenism and the cultures of the East affect one another? What did the meeting of East and West entail for the history of the world?

### CITIES AND KINGDOMS

Although Alexander's generals created huge kingdoms, the concept of monarchy never replaced the ideal of the polis. Consequently, the monarchies never won the deep emotional loyalty that Greeks had once felt for the polis. Hellenistic kings needed large numbers of Greeks to run their kingdoms. Otherwise, royal business would grind to a halt, and the conquerors would soon be swallowed up by the far more numerous conquered population. Obviously, then, the kings had to encourage Greeks to immigrate and build new homes.

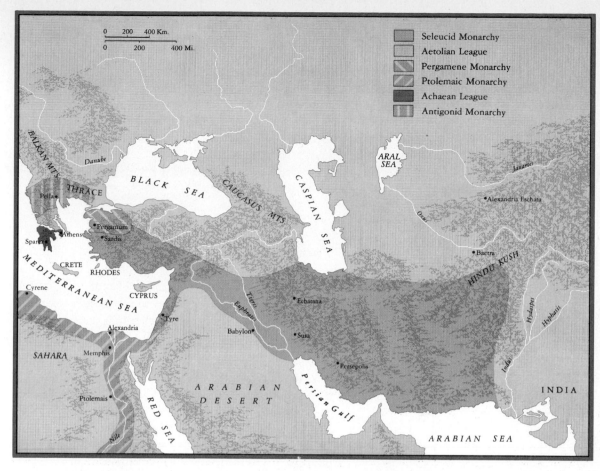

MAP 4.2 THE HELLENISTIC WORLD *After Alexander's death, no single commander could hold his vast conquests together, resulting in the empire's break-up into several kingdoms and leagues.*

To these Greeks monarchy was something out of the heroic past, something found in Homer's *Iliad* but not in daily life. The Hellenistic kings thus confronted the problem of making life in the new monarchies resemble the traditional Greek way of life. Since Greek civilization was urban, the kings continued Alexander's policy of establishing cities throughout their kingdoms in order to entice Greeks to immigrate. Yet the creation of these cities posed a serious problem, which the Hellenistic kings failed to solve.

To the Greeks civilized life was unthinkable without the polis, which was far more than a mere city. The Greek polis was by definition sovereign – an independent, autonomous state run by its citizens free from any outside power or restraint. Hellenistic kings, however, refused to grant sovereignty to their cities. In effect, these kings willingly built cities, but refused to build a polis. Instead they attempted a compromise that ultimately failed.

Hellenistic monarchs gave to their cities all the external trappings of a polis. Each had an assembly of citizens, a council to prepare legislation, and a board of magistrates to conduct the political business of the city. Yet however similar to the Greek city-state they appeared,

THE CITADEL OF PERGAMUM    *The shape of Hellenistic cities is obvious in this model of the citadel of Pergamum. The citadel, which is surrounded by a wall, was filled with temples to various gods, palaces, military buildings, and a magnificent theater. The kings of Pergamum used their city to proclaim to the world that they too were Greeks and that their city was a Greek polis. (Staatliche Museen zu Berlin)*

these cities could not engage in diplomatic dealings, make treaties, pursue their own foreign policy, or wage their own wars. None could govern its own affairs without interference from the king, who, even if he stood in the background, was the real sovereign. In the eyes of the king the cities were important parts of the kingdom, but the welfare of the kingdom as a whole came first. The cities had to follow royal orders, and the king often placed his own officials in the cities to see that his decrees were carried out.

A new Hellenistic city differed from a Greek polis in other ways as well. The Greek polis had enjoyed political and social unity even though it was normally composed of citizens, slaves, and resident aliens. The polis had one body of law and one set of customs. In the Hellenistic city the Greeks represented an elite citizen class. Natives and non-Greek foreigners who lived in Hellenistic cities

usually possessed lesser rights than those of the Greeks and often had their own laws. In some instances this disparity spurred natives to assimilate Greek culture in order to rise both politically and socially. Other peoples, such as the Jews, firmly resisted the essence of Hellenism. The Hellenistic city was not homogeneous, and it could not spark the intensity of feeling that marked the polis.

In many respects, the Hellenistic city resembled a modern city. It was a cultural center with theaters, temples, and libraries. It was a seat of learning, the home of poets, writers, scholars, teachers, and artists. It was the place where people could find amusement. The Hellenistic city was also an economic center that provided a ready market for the grain and produce raised in the surrounding countryside. The city was an emporium, the scene of trade and manufacturing. In short, the Hellenistic city offered cultural and economic opportunities, but did not foster a sense of united, integrated enterprise.

There were no constitutional links between the city and the king. The city was simply his possession. It and its citizens had no voice in how the kingdom was run. The city had no rights except for those the king granted, and even those he could summarily take away. Ambassadors from the city could entreat the king for favors and petition him on such matters as taxes, boundary disputes, and legal cases. But the city had no right to advise the king on royal policy, and it enjoyed no political function within the kingdom.

Hellenistic kings tried to make the kingdom the political focus of citizens' allegiance. If the king could secure the frontiers of his kingdom, he could give it a geographical identity. He could then hope that his subjects would direct their primary loyalty to the kingdom rather than a particular city. However, the kings' efforts to fix their borders led only to sustained warfare. Boundaries were determined by military power, and rule by force became the chief political principle of the Hellenistic world.

Border wars were frequent and exhausting. The Seleucids and the Ptolemies, for instance, waged five wars for the possession of southern Syria. Other kings refused to acknowledge any boundaries at all. These men followed the example of Alexander and waged wars to reunify his empire under their own authority. By the third century B.C., a weary balance of power was reached, but only as the result of stalemate. It was not maintained by any political principle.

The Hellenistic kings failed to create in their kingdoms a political unit to replace the polis. Even the Hellenistic city, despite its beauty and Hellenic trappings, failed to win the devotion and love that the Greeks had readily and enthusiastically given the polis.

Nor did the Hellenistic kings ever give the Greeks anything else to which to attach their political loyalty.

## THE GREEKS AND THE OPENING OF THE EAST

If the Hellenistic kings failed to satisfy the Greeks' political yearnings, they nonetheless succeeded in giving them unequaled economic and social opportunities. The ruling dynasties of the Hellenistic world were Macedonian, and Greeks filled all important political, military, and diplomatic positions. These people constituted an upper class that sustained Hellenism in the barbarian East. Besides building Greek cities, Hellenistic kings offered Greeks land and money as a lure to further immigration.

The more splendid, prestigious, and famous the kingdom, the easier it was to attract settlers. Each kingdom strove to be more philhellenic – more Greek-like and more appreciative of Greek culture – than the others. Each claimed the ability to provide Greeks with the necessities of Greek life. The burden of these policies fell upon the native population of the various kingdoms. Easterners paid for these enticements through heavy taxation.

The opening of the East offered ambitious Greeks opportunities for well-paying jobs and economic success. The Hellenistic monarchy, unlike the Greek polis, did not depend solely on its citizens to fulfill its political needs. Talented Greeks could expect to rise quickly within the governmental bureaucracy. Appointed by the king, these administrators did not have to stand for election each year, as had many of the officials of a Greek polis. Since they held their jobs year after year, they had ample time to evolve new administrative techniques. Naturally, they became more efficient than the amateur officials common in the Greek city-states of the Hellenic period. The needs of the Hellenistic monarchy and the opportunities it offered thus gave rise to a professional corps of Greek administrators.

Greeks and Macedonians also found ready employment in the armies and navies of the Hellenistic monarchies. Alexander had proved the Greco-Macedonian style of warfare to be far superior to that of the Easterners, and Alexander's successors, themselves experienced officers, realized the importance of trained Greek and Macedonian soldiers. Moreover, Hellenistic kings were extremely reluctant to arm the native population or to allow them to serve in the army, fearing military rebellions among their conquered subjects. The result of this situation was the emergence of professional armies and navies consisting entirely of Greeks and Macedonians.

Greeks were able to dominate other professions as well. In order to be really philhellenic, the kingdoms and their cities needed Greek writers and artists to create Greek literature, art, and culture on Asian soil. Architects, engineers, and skilled craftsmen found their services in great demand because of the building policies of the Hellenistic monarchs. If Hellenistic kingdoms were to have Greek cities, those cities needed Greek buildings – temples, porticoes, gymnasia, theaters, fountains, and houses. Architects and engineers were sometimes commissioned to design and build whole cities, which they laid out in checkerboard fashion and filled with typical Greek buildings. A truly enormous wave of construction took place during the Hellenistic period.

Despite the opportunities they offered, the Hellenistic monarchies were hampered by their artificial origins. Their failure to win the political loyalty of their Greek subjects and their policy of wooing Greeks with lucrative positions encouraged a feeling of uprootedness and self-serving individualism among Greek immigrants. Once a Greek had left home to take service with, for instance, the army or the bureaucracy of the Ptolemies, he had no incentive beyond his pay and the comforts of life in Egypt to keep him there. If the Seleucid king offered him more money or a promotion, he might well accept it and take his talents to Asia Minor. Why not? In the realm of the Seleucids he, a Greek, would find the same sort of life and environment that the kingdom of the Ptolemies had provided him. Thus professional Greek soldiers and administrators were highly mobile and prone to look to their own interests, not those of the kingdom they joined.

As long as Greeks continued to replenish their professional ranks, the kingdoms remained strong. In the process they drew an immense amount of talent from the Greek peninsula, draining the vitality of the Greek homeland. However, the Hellenistic monarchies could not keep recruiting Greeks forever, in spite of their wealth and willingness to spend lavishly to attract and keep the Greeks coming. In time, the huge surge of immigration slowed greatly. Even then the Hellenistic monarchs were reluctant to recruit Easterners to fill posts normally held by Greeks. The result was at first the stagnation of the Hellenistic world and finally, after 202 B.C., collapse in the face of the young and vigorous Roman Republic.

## GREEKS AND EASTERNERS

The Greeks in the East were a minority, and Hellenistic cities were islands of Greek culture in an Eastern sea. But Hellenistic monarchies were remarkably successful in at least partially hellenizing Easterners and spreading a uniform culture throughout the East, a culture to which Rome eventually fell heir. The prevailing institutions, laws, and language of the East became Greek. Indeed, the Near East had seen nothing comparable since the days when Mesopotamian culture had spread throughout the area.

Yet the spread of Greek culture was wider than it was deep. At best it was a veneer, thicker in some places than in others. Hellenistic kingdoms were never entirely unified in language, customs, and thought. Greek culture took firmest hold along the shores of the Mediterranean, but in the Far East, in Persia and Bactria, it eventually gave way to Eastern cultures.

The Ptolemies in Egypt made no effort to spread Greek culture, and unlike other Hellenistic kings they were not city builders. Indeed, they founded only the city of Ptolemais near Thebes. At first the native Egyptian population, the descendants of the pharaoh's people, retained their traditional language, outlook, religion, and way of life. Initially untouched by Hellenism, the natives continued to be the foundation of the state: they fed it by their labor in the fields, and they financed its operations by their taxes.

Under the pharaohs, talented Egyptians had been able to rise to high office, but during the third century B.C. the Ptolemies cut off this avenue of advancement. They tied the natives to the land ever more tightly, making it nearly impossible for them to leave their villages. The bureaucracy of the Ptolemies was ruthlessly efficient, and the native population was viciously and cruelly exploited. Even in times of hardship the king's taxes came first, though payment might mean starvation for the natives. The desperation of the native population was summed up by one Egyptian, who scrawled the warning: "We are worn out; we will run away."[3] To many Egyptians revolt or a life of brigandage was certainly preferable

to working the land under the harsh Ptolemies.

Throughout the third century B.C., the Greek upper class had little to do with the native population. Many Greek bureaucrats established homes in Alexandria and Ptolemais, where they managed finances, served as magistrates, and administered the law. Other Greeks settled in military colonies and supplied the monarchy with fighting men.

In the second century B.C., Greeks and native Egyptians began to intermarry and mingle their cultures. The language of the native population influenced Greek, and many Greeks adopted Egyptian religion and ways of life. Simultaneously, natives adopted Greek customs and language, and began to play a role in the administration of the kingdom and even to serve in the army. While many Greeks and Egyptians remained aloof from each other, the overall result was the evolution of a widespread Greco-Egyptian culture.

Meanwhile the Seleucid kings established many cities and military colonies in western Asia Minor and along the banks of the Tigris and Euphrates rivers in order to nurture a vigorous and numerous Greek population. Especially important to the Seleucids were the military colonies, for they depended on Greeks to defend the kingdom. The Seleucids had no elaborate plan for hellenizing the native population, but the arrival of so many Greeks was bound to have an impact. Seleucid military colonies were generally founded near native villages, thus exposing Easterners to all aspects of Greek life. Many Easterners found Greek political and cultural forms attractive, and imitated them. In Asia Minor and Syria, for instance, numerous native villages and towns developed along Greek lines, and some of them became hellenized cities. Farther East the Greek kings who replaced the Seleucids in the third century B.C. spread Greek culture to their neighbors and even into the Indian subcontinent.

For Easterners the prime advantage of Greek culture was its very pervasiveness. The Greek language became the common speech of the East. Indeed, a common dialect, called *koine,* even influenced the speech of peninsular Greece itself. Greek became the speech of the royal court, the bureaucracy, and the military. It was also the speech of commerce: any Easterner who wanted to compete in business had to learn Greek. As early as the third century B.C., some Greek cities were giving citizenship to hellenized natives.

The vast majority of hellenized Easterners, however, took only the externals of Greek culture while retaining the essentials of their own way of life. Though Greeks and Easterners adapted themselves to each others' ways, there was never a true fusion of cultures. Nonetheless, each found useful things in the civilization of the other, and the two fertilized each other. This fertilization, this mingling of Greek and Eastern elements, is what makes Hellenistic culture unique and distinctive.

*HELLENISM AND THE JEWS* A prime illustration of how the East took what it wanted from Hellenism while remaining true to itself is the impact of Greek culture on the Jews. At first Jews in Hellenistic cities were treated as resident aliens. As they grew more numerous, they received permission to form a political corporation, a *politeuma,* which gave them a great deal of autonomy. The *politeuma* allowed Jews to attend to their religious and internal affairs without interference from the Greek municipal government. The Jewish politeuma had its own officials, the leaders of the synagogue. In time the Jewish politeuma gained the special right to be judged by its own law and its own officials, thus becoming in effect a Jewish city within a Hellenistic city.

The Jewish politeuma, like the Hellenistic city, obeyed the commands of the king, but there was virtually no royal interference with the Jewish religion. Indeed, the Greeks were always very reluctant to tamper with anyone's religion. Only the Seleucid king Antiochus Epiphanes (175–ca 164 B.C.) tried to suppress the Jewish religion in Judaea. He did so not because he hated the Jews (who were a small part of his kingdom), but because he was trying to unify his realm culturally to meet the threat of Rome. To the Jews he extended the same policy that he applied to all of his subjects. Apart from this instance, Hellenistic Jews suffered no official religious persecution. Some Jews were given the right to become full citizens of Hellenistic cities, but few exercised that right. Citizenship would have allowed them to vote in the assembly and serve as magistrates, but it would also have obliged them to worship the gods of the city – a practice few Jews chose to follow.

Jews living in Hellenistic cities often embraced a good deal of Hellenism. So many Jews learned Greek, especially in Alexandria, that the Old Testament was translated into Greek, and services in the synagogue came to be conducted in Greek. Jews often took Greek names, used Greek political forms, adopted Greek practice by forming their own trade associations, put inscriptions on graves as the Greeks did, and much else. Yet no matter how much of Greek culture or its externals Jews borrowed, they normally remained true to their religion. Their ideas and those of the Greeks were different. The exceptions were some Jews in Asia Minor and Syria who incorporated Greek or local Eastern cults into their worship. To some degree this development was due not only to the strength and attraction of these cults but also to the growing belief among Greeks and Easterners that all peoples, despite differences in cult and ritual, actually worshiped the same gods.

Thus, in spite of their Hellenistic trappings, hellenized Jews remained Jews at heart. The value of Hellenism both to Jews and to other Easterners was its gift of a common cultural background and means of expression.

## THE ECONOMIC SCOPE OF THE HELLENISTIC WORLD

Alexander's conquest of the Persian Empire not only changed the political face of the ancient world, it also brought the East fully into the sphere of Greek economics. Yet the Hellenistic period did not see a revolution in the way people lived and worked. The material demands of Hellenistic society remained as simple as those of Athenian society in the fifth century B.C. Clothes and furniture were essentially unchanged, as were household goods, tools, and jewelry. The real achievement of Alexander and his successors was linking East and West in a broad commercial network. The spread of Greeks throughout the East created new markets and stimulated trade. The economic unity of the Hellenistic world, like its cultural bonds, would later prove valuable to the Romans.

### COMMERCE

Alexander's conquest of the Persian Empire had immediate effects on trade. In the Persian capitals Alexander had found vast sums of gold, silver, and other treasure. This wealth financed the creation of new cities, the building of roads, and the development of harbors.

Most of the great monarchies coined their money on the Attic standard, which meant that much of the money used in the Hellenistic kingdoms had the same value. Traders were less in need of moneychangers than in the days when each major power coined money on a different standard. As a result of Alexander's conquests, geographical knowledge of the East increased dramatically, making the East far better known to the Greeks than previously. The Greeks spread their law and methods of transacting business throughout the East. Whole new fields lay open to Greek merchants, and they eagerly took advantage of the new opportunities. Commerce itself was a leading area where Greeks and Easterners met on grounds of common interest. In bazaars, ports, and trading centers Greeks learned of Eastern customs and traditions, while spreading knowledge of their own culture.

The Seleucid and Ptolemaic dynasties traded as far afield as India, Arabia, and Africa. Overland trade with India and Arabia was conducted by caravan and was largely in the hands of Easterners. The caravan trade never dealt in bulk items or essential commodities, for only luxury goods could be transported in this very expensive fashion. Once the goods reached the Hellenistic monarchies, Greek merchants took a hand in the trade.

In the early Hellenistic period the Seleucids and Ptolemies ensured that the caravan trade proceeded efficiently. Later in the period — a time of increased war and confusion — they left the caravans unprotected. Taking advantage of this situation, Palmyra in the Syrian desert and Nabataean Petra in Arabia arose as caravan states. Such states protected the caravans from bandits and marauders, and served as dispersal areas of caravan goods.

The Ptolemies discovered how to use monsoon winds to establish direct contact with India. One hardy merchant has left a first-hand account of sailing this important maritime link:

*Hippalos, the pilot, observing the position of the ports and the conditions of the sea, first discovered how to sail across the ocean. Concerning the winds of the ocean in this region, when with us the Etesian winds begin, in India a wind between southwest and south, named for Hippalos, sets in from the open sea. From then until now some mariners set forth from Kanes and some from the Cape of Spices. Those sailing to Dimurikes [in southern India] throw the bow of the ship farther out to sea. Those bound for Barygaza and the realm of the Sakas [in northern India] hold to the land no more than three days; and if the wind remains favorable, they hold the same course through the outer sea, and they sail along past the previously mentioned gulfs.*[4]

Although this sea route never replaced overland caravan traffic, it kept alive direct relations with the East, stimulating the exchange of ideas as well as goods.

More economically important than this exotic trade were commercial dealings in essential commodities like raw materials, grain, and industrial products. The Hellenistic monarchies usually raised enough grain for their own needs as well as a surplus for export. For the cities of Greece and the Aegean this trade in grain was essential, because many of them could not grow enough of their own. Fortunately for them, abundant supplies of wheat were available nearby in Egypt and in the Crimea in southern Russia.

The large-scale wars of the Hellenistic period often interrupted both the production and distribution of grain. This was especially true when the successors of Alexander were trying to carve out their kingdoms. In addition, natural calamities, such as excessive rain or drought, frequently damaged harvests. Throughout the Hellenistic period famine or severe food shortage remained a grim possibility.

Most trade in bulk commodities was seaborne, and the Hellenistic merchant ship was the workhorse of the day. The merchant ship had a broad beam and relied on sails for propulsion. It was far more seaworthy than the contemporary warship, which was long, narrow, and built for speed. A small crew of experienced sailors could handle it easily. Maritime trade gave rise to other industries and trades: sailors and shipbuilders, dock workers, merchants, accountants, teamsters, and pirates. Piracy was always a factor in the Hellenistic world and remained so until Rome extended its power throughout the East.

The Greek cities paid for their grain by exporting olive oil and wine. When agriculture and oil production developed in Syria, Greek products began to encounter competition from the Seleucid monarchy. Later in the Hellenistic period Greek oil and wine found a lucrative market in Italy. Another significant commodity was fish, which for export was either salted, pickled, or dried. This trade was doubly important because fish provided poor people with an essential element of their diet. Salt too was often imported, and there was some very slight trade in salted meat, which was a luxury item. Far more important was the trade in honey, dried fruit, nuts, and vegetables. Among raw materials wood ranked high in demand, but there was little trade in manufactured goods.

Slaves were a staple of Hellenistic trade. The wars provided prisoners for the slave market, and to a lesser extent so did kidnapping and capture by pirates. The number of slaves involved cannot be estimated, but there

*HARBOR AND WAREHOUSES AT DELOS   During the Hellenistic period Delos became a thriving trading center. Shown here is the row of warehouses at water's edge. From Delos cargoes were shipped to virtually every part of the Mediterranean. (Photo: Caroline Buckler)*

is no doubt that slavery flourished. Both the old Greek states and the new Hellenistic kingdoms were ready markets for slaves, as was Rome when it emerged triumphant from the Second Punic War (Chapter 5). The war took a huge toll of Italian manpower, and Rome bought slaves in vast numbers to replace them in the fields.

Throughout the Mediterranean world, slaves were almost always in demand. Only the Ptolemies discouraged both the trade and slavery itself, and they did so only for economic reasons. Their system had no room for slaves, who would only have competed with free labor. Otherwise, slave labor was to be found in the cities and temples of the Hellenistic world, in the factories and fields, and in the homes of wealthier people. In Italy and some parts of the East, slaves performed the manual labor for large estates and worked the mines. They were vitally important to the Hellenistic economy.

SCENE FROM DAILY LIFE    *Art in the Hellenistic period often pursued two themes: increased realism and scenes from daily life. This statuette illustrates both themes. Either a peasant or a slave, the man carries a wine jar over his left shoulder and in his right hand a bag, perhaps his lunch. On his back is a basket. He is so heavily loaded that he is walking with difficulty. (Reproduced by Courtesy of the Trustees of the British Museum)*

Although demand for goods increased during the Hellenistic period, no new techniques of production appear to have developed. The discoveries of Hellenistic mathematicians and thinkers failed to produce any significant corresponding technological development. Manual labor, not machinery, continued to turn out the raw materials and few manufactured goods the Hellenistic world used. Human labor was so cheap and so abundant that kings had no incentive to encourage the invention and manufacture of laborsaving machinery.

Perhaps only one noteworthy technological innovation dates to the Hellenistic period — the introduction of the Archimedean screw for pumping water out of mines. At Thoricus in Attica miners dug ore by hand and hauled it from the mines for processing. This was grueling work, and invariably miners were slaves, criminals, or forced laborers. The conditions under which they worked were frightful. At Laurium, which provided silver ore for the processing plant at Thoricus, one can still crawl into the labyrinthine shafts. They are narrow and have very low ceilings. The miners dug out the ore on their hands and knees; never did they have a chance to stand upright. Once a miner passed the entrance of the mine and crawled inside, his only light came from the oil lamp that he carried. Ventilation was poor, and the air must have been foul and stifling.

The Ptolemies ran their gold mines along the same harsh lines. One historian gave a grim picture of the miners' lives:

*The kings of Egypt condemn [to the mines] those found guilty of wrong-doing and those taken prisoner in war, those who were victims of false accusations and were put into jail because of royal anger. . . . The condemned — and they are very many — all of them are put in chains, and they work persistently and continually, both by day and throughout the night, getting no rest, and carefully cut off from escape.*[5]

The Ptolemies even condemned women and children to work in the mines. The strongest men lived and died swinging iron sledgehammers to break up the gold-bearing quartz rock. Others worked underground following the seams of quartz, men who labored with lamps bound to their foreheads and who were whipped by overseers if they slacked off. Once the diggers had cut out blocks of quartz, young boys gathered up the blocks and carried them outside. All of them — men, women, and boys — worked until they died.

Apart from gold and silver, which were used primarily for coins and jewelry, iron was the most important metal, and saw the most varied use. Even so, the method of its production never became very sophisticated. The Hellenistic Greeks did manage to produce a low-grade steel by adding carbon to iron.

Pottery remained an important commodity, and most of it was made locally. The pottery used in the kitchen, the coarse ware, did not change at all. Indeed, it is impossible to tell whether specimens of this type of pottery are Hellenic or Hellenistic. Fancier pots and bowls, decorated with a shiny black glaze, came into use during the Hellenistic period. This ware originated in Athens, but potters in other places began to imitate its style, heavily cutting into the Athenian market. In the second century B.C., a red-glazed ware, often called Samian, burst upon the market and soon dominated it. Athens still held its own, however, in the production of fine pottery. Despite the change in pottery styles, the method of production of all pottery, whether plain or fine, remained essentially unchanged.

Although new techniques of production and wider use of machinery in industry did not occur, the volume of goods produced increased in the Hellenistic period. Such goods were mostly made locally. Small manufacturing establishments existed in nearly all parts of the Hellenistic world.

## AGRICULTURE

Hellenistic kings paid special attention to agriculture. Much of their revenue was derived from it: from the produce of royal lands, rents paid by the tenants of royal land, and taxation of agricultural land. Some Hellenistic kings even sought out and supported agricultural experts. The Ptolemies, for instance, sponsored experiments on seed grain, selecting seeds that seemed hardy and productive and trying to improve their characteristics. Hellenistic authors wrote handbooks that discussed how farms and large estates could be most profitably run. These handbooks described soil types, covered the proper times for planting and reaping, and discussed care of farm animals. Whether these efforts had any impact on the average farmer is difficult to determine.

The Ptolemies made the greatest strides in agriculture, but their success was largely political. Egypt had a strong tradition of central authority dating back to the pharaohs, which the Ptolemies inherited and tightened. They could decree what crops Egyptian farmers would plant and what animals would be raised, and they had the power to carry out their commands. The Ptolemies recognized the need for well-planned and constant irrigation, and much native labor went into the digging and maintenance of canals and ditches. The Ptolemies also reclaimed a great deal of land from the desert, including the Fayum, a dried lake bed.

The centralized authority of the Ptolemies

explains how agricultural advances occurred at the local level in Egypt. But such progress was not possible in any other Hellenistic monarchy. Despite royal interest in agriculture and a more studied approach to it in the Hellenistic period, there is no evidence that agricultural productivity increased. Whether Hellenistic agricultural methods had any influence on Eastern practices is unknown.

## RELIGION IN THE HELLENISTIC WORLD

In religion Hellenism gave Easterners far less than the East gave the Greeks. At first the Hellenistic period saw the spread of Greek religious cults throughout the East. When Hellenistic kings founded cities, they also built temples and established new cults and priesthoods for the old Olympian gods. The new cults enjoyed the prestige of being the religion of the conquerors, and they were supported by public money.

The most attractive aspects of the Greek cults were their rituals and festivities. Greek cults sponsored literary, musical, and athletic contests, which were staged in beautiful surroundings among impressive Greek buildings. In short, the cults offered bright and lively entertainment, both intellectual and physical. They fostered Greek culture and traditional sports, and thus were a splendid means of displaying Greek civilization in the East.

Despite various advantages, Greek cults suffered from some severe shortcomings. They were primarily concerned with ritual. Participation in the civic cults did not even involve belief. Greeks and others could observe the rituals without believing in the existence of the deities being worshiped. Nor did civic cults impose an ethical code of conduct. Greeks did not have to follow any particular

rule of life, practice certain virtues, or even live decent lives in order to participate in the cults. On the whole, the civic cults neither appealed to religious emotions nor embraced matters such as sin and redemption. Greek mystery religions helped fill this gap, but the centers of these religions were in old Greece. Although the new civic cults were lavish in pomp and display, they could not satisfy deep religious feelings or spiritual yearnings.

Even though the Greeks participated in the new cults for cultural reasons, they felt little genuine religious attachment to them. In comparison to the emotional and sometimes passionate religions of the East, the Greek cults seemed sterile. Greeks increasingly sought solace from other sources. Educated and thoughtful people turned to philosophy as a guide to life, while others turned to superstition, magic, or astrology. Still others might shrug and speak of *Tyche,* which meant Fate or Chance.

In view of the spiritual decline of Greek religion, it is surprising that Eastern religions did not make more immediate headway among the Greeks, but at first they did not. Although Hellenistic Greeks clung to their own cults as expressions of their Greekness rather than for any ethical principles, they did not rush to embrace native religions. Only in the second century B.C., after a century of exposure to Eastern religions, did Greeks begin to adopt them.

Nor did Hellenistic kings make any effort to spread Greek religion among their Eastern subjects. The Greeks always considered religion a matter best left to the individual. Greek cults were attractive only to those socially aspiring Easterners who adopted Greek culture for personal advancement. Otherwise, Easterners were little affected by Greek religion. Nor did native religions suffer from the arrival of the Greeks. Some Hellenistic kings limited the power of native priesthoods, but

RELIGIOUS SYNCRETISM  *This relief was found at the Greek outpost of Dura-Europus, located on the Euphrates. In the center sits Zeus Olympius-Baalshamin, a combination of a Greek and a Semitic god. The eastern priest at the left is burning incense on* *an altar, while the figure on the right in Macedonian dress crowns the god. Both the religious sentiments and the style of art show the meeting of East and West. (Yale University Art Gallery, Dura-Europos Collection)*

they also subsidized some Eastern cults with public money. Alexander the Great actually reinstated several Eastern cults that the Persians had suppressed.

The only significant junction of Greek and Eastern religious traditions was the growth and spread of new mystery religions, so called because they featured a body of ritual not to be divulged to anyone not initiated into the cult. The new mystery cults incorporated aspects of both Greek and Eastern religions, and had broad appeal for both Greeks and Easterners who yearned for personal immortality. Since the Greeks were already familiar with old mystery cults, such as the Eleusinian mys-

teries in Attica, the new cults did not strike them as alien or barbarian. Familiar too was the concept of preparation for an initiation. Devotees of the Eleusinian mysteries and other such cults had to prepare themselves mentally and physically before entering the presence of the gods. Thus the new mystery cults fit well with traditional Greek usage.

The new religions enjoyed one tremendous advantage over the old Greek mystery cults. Whereas old Greek mysteries were tied to particular places, such as Eleusis, the new religions spread throughout the Hellenistic world. People did not have to undertake long and expensive pilgrimages just to become

STATUE OF ISIS   *Though originally Egyptian, Isis became a Greek goddess during the Hellenistic period. Her cult spread throughout the Hellenistic world, and she became identified with many purely Greek goddesses. Still popular in the Roman period, her cult profoundly influenced the Christian cult of Mary, the mother of Jesus. (Museo Nazionale, Naples)*

members of the religion. In that sense, the new mystery religions came to the people, for temples of the new deities sprang up wherever Greeks lived.

The mystery religions all claimed to save their adherents from the worst that Tyche could do, and they promised life for the soul after death. They all had a single concept in common: the belief that by the rites of initiation the devotees became united with the god, who had himself died and risen from the dead. The sacrifice of the god and his victory over death saved the devotee from eternal death. Similarly, all mystery religions demanded a period of preparation in which the convert strove to become holy – that is, to live by the precepts taught by the religion. Once aspirants had prepared themselves, they went through an initiation in which they learned the secrets of the religion. The initiation was usually a ritual of great emotional intensity, a baptism into a new life.

The Eastern mystery religions that took the Hellenistic world by storm were the Egyptian cults of Serapis and Isis. Serapis, who was invented by King Ptolemy, combined elements of the Egyptian god Osiris with aspects of the Greek gods Zeus, Pluto the prince of the underworld, and Asclepius. Serapis was believed to be the judge of souls, who rewarded virtuous and righteous people with eternal life. Like Asclepius he was a god of healing. Serapis became an international god, and many Hellenistic Greeks thought of him as Zeus. Associated with Isis and Serapis was Anubis, the old Egyptian god who, like Charon in the Greek pantheon, guided the souls of initiates to the realm of eternal life.

The cult of Isis enjoyed even wider appeal than that of Serapis. Isis, the wife of Osiris, claimed to have conquered Tyche, and promised to save any mortal who came to her. She became the most important goddess of the

Hellenistic world, and her worship was very popular among women. Her priests claimed that she bestowed upon humanity the gift of civilization and that she founded law and literature. She was the goddess of marriage, conception, and childbirth, and like Serapis a deity who promised to save the souls of her believers.

There was neither conflict between Greek and Eastern religions nor wholesale acceptance of one or the other. Nonetheless, the Hellenistic world was slowly moving toward belief in a single god who ruled over all people. Greeks and Easterners noticed similarities among one another's deities and assumed that they were worshiping the same gods in different garb. These tendencies toward religious universalism and the desire for personal immortality would prove significant when the Hellenistic world came under the sway of Rome, for Hellenistic developments paved the way for the spread of Christianity.

## PHILOSOPHY AND THE COMMON MAN

Philosophy during the Hellenic period was the exclusive province of the wealthy, for only they had leisure enough to pursue philosophical studies. During the Hellenistic period, however, philosophy reached out to touch the lives of more men and women than ever before. The reasons for this development were several. Since the ideal of the polis had declined, politics no longer offered people an intellectual outlet. Moreover, much of Hellenistic life, especially in the new cities of the East, seemed unstable and without venerable traditions. Greeks were far more mobile than they had ever been before, but their very mobility left them feeling uprooted. Many people

in search of something permanent, something unchanging in a changing world, turned to philosophy. Another reason for the increased influence of philosophy was the decline of traditional religion and a growing belief in Tyche. Tyche was more than Fate — it was Chance and Doom, capricious and sometimes malevolent. To protect against the worst that Tyche could do, many Greeks looked to philosophy.

Philosophers themselves became much more numerous, and several new schools of philosophical thought emerged. The Cynics preached the joy of a simple life. The Epicureans taught that pleasure is the chief good. The Stoics emphasized the importance of deeds well done. There was a good deal of rivalry as philosophers tried to demonstrate the superiority of their views, but in spite of their differences the major branches of philosophy agreed on the necessity of making people self-sufficient. They all recognized the need to equip men and women to deal successfully with Tyche. The major schools of Hellenistic philosophy all taught that people could be truly happy only when they had turned their backs on the world around them and focused full attention on one enduring thing. They differed chiefly on what that enduring thing was.

### CYNICS

Undoubtedly the most unusual of the new philosophers were the Cynics, who urged a return to nature. They advised men and women to discard traditional customs and conventions (which were in decline anyway) and to live simply. The Cynics believed that by rejecting material things people become free, and that nature will provide all necessities.

The founder of the Cynics was Antisthenes

(b. ca 440 B.C.), but it was Diogenes of Sinope (ca 412–323 B.C.), one of the most colorful men of the period, who spread the philosophy. Diogenes came to Athens to study philosophy and soon evolved his own ideas on the ideal life. He hit upon the solution that happiness was possible only by living according to nature and forgoing luxuries. He attacked social conventions because he considered them contrary to nature. Throughout Greece he gained fame for the rigorous way in which he put his beliefs into practice.

Diogenes' disdain for luxury and social pretense also became legendary. Once when he was living at Corinth, he was supposedly visited by Alexander the Great: "While Diogenes was sunning himself . . . Alexander stood over him and said: 'Ask me whatever gift you like.' In answer Diogenes said to him: 'Get out of my sunlight.' "[6] The story underlines the essence of Diogenes' teachings: even a great, powerful, and wealthy conqueror like Alexander could give people nothing of any real value. Nature had already provided people with everything essential.

Diogenes did not establish a philosophical school in the manner of Plato and Aristotle. Instead, he and his followers took their teaching to the streets and marketplaces. They more than any other philosophical group tried to reach the common man. As part of their return to nature they often did without warm clothing, sufficient food, or adequate housing, which they considered unnecessary. The Cynics also tried to break down political barriers by declaring that people owed no allegiance to any city or monarchy. Rather, they said, all people are cosmopolitan – that is, citizens of the world. The Cynics reached across political boundaries to create a community of people, all sharing their humanity and living as close to nature as humanly possible. The Cynics set a striking example of

how people could turn away from materialism. Although comparatively few men and women could follow such rigorous precepts, the Cynics influenced all the other major schools of philosophy.

### EPICUREANS

Epicurus (340–270 B.C.), who founded his own school of philosophy at Athens, based his view of life on scientific theories. Accepting Democritus' theory that the universe is composed of indestructible particles, Epicurus put forth a naturalistic theory of the universe. Although he did not deny the existence of the gods, he taught that they had no effect on human life. The essence of Epicurus' belief was that the principal good of human life is pleasure, which he defined as the absence of pain. He was not advocating drunken revels or sensual dissipation, which he thought actually caused pain. Instead, Epicurus concluded that any violent emotion is undesirable. Drawing on the teachings of the Cynics, he advocated mild self-discipline. Even poverty he considered good, as long as people have enough food, clothing, and shelter. Epicurus also taught that individuals can most easily attain peace and serenity by ignoring the outside world and looking into their personal feelings and reactions. Thus Epicureanism led to quietism.

Epicureanism taught its followers to ignore politics and the issues of the day, for politics led to tumult, which would disturb the soul. Although the Epicureans thought that the state originated through a social contract among individuals, they did not care about the political structure of the state. They were content to live in a democracy, oligarchy, monarchy, or whatever, and they never speculated about the ideal state. Their very ideals stood outside all political forms.

Opposed to the passivity of the Epicureans, Zeno (335–262 B.C.), a Hellenized Phoenician, put forth a different concept of human beings and the universe. When Zeno first came to Athens, he listened avidly to the Cynics. Concluding, however, that the Cynics were extreme, he stayed in Athens to form his own school, the Stoa, named after the building where he preferred to teach.

Stoicism became the most popular philosophy of the Hellenistic world, and the one that later captured the mind of Rome. Zeno and his followers considered nature an expression of divine will, and in their view people could be happy only when they lived in accordance with nature. They stressed the unity of man and the universe, stating that all men were brothers and obliged to help one another. Stoicism's science was derived from Heraclitus, but its broad and warm humanity was the work of Zeno and his followers.

Unlike the Epicureans, the Stoics taught that people should participate in politics and worldly affairs. Yet this idea never led to the belief that individuals ought to try to change the order of things. Time and again the Stoics used the image of an actor in a play: the Stoic plays an assigned part and never tries to change the play. To the Stoics the important question was not whether they achieved anything, but whether they lived virtuous lives. In that way they could triumph over Tyche: for Tyche could destroy achievements but not the goodness and nobility of their lives.

Even though the Stoics evolved the concept of a world order, they thought of it strictly in terms of the individual. Like the Epicureans, they were indifferent to specific political forms. They believed that people should do their duty to the state in which they found themselves. The universal state they preached about was ethical, not political. The most significant practical achievement of the Stoics was the creation of the concept of natural law. The Stoics concluded that since all men were brothers, since all men partook of divine reason, and since all good men were in harmony with the universe, one law — a part of the natural order of life — governed them all.

The Stoic concept of a universal state governed by natural law is one of the finest heirlooms the Hellenistic world passed on to Rome. The Stoic concept of natural law, of one law for all people, became a valuable tool when the Romans began to deal with many different peoples with different laws. The ideal of the universal state gave the Romans a rationale for extending their empire to the farthest reaches of the world. The duty of individuals to their fellows served the citizens of the Roman Empire as the philosophical justification for doing their duty. In this respect, too, the real fruit of Hellenism was to ripen only under the cultivation of Rome.

## HELLENISTIC WOMEN

With the growth of monarchy in the Hellenistic period came a major new development: the importance of royal women, many of whom played an active part in political and diplomatic life. In the Hellenic period the polis had replaced kingship, except at Sparta, and queens were virtually unknown, apart from myth and legend. Even in Sparta queens did not participate in politics. Hellenistic queens, however, did exercise political power, either in their own right or by manipulating their husbands. Many Hellenistic queens were depicted as willful or ruthless, especially in power struggles over the throne, and in some cases those charges are accurate. Other Hel-

STATUE OF A PRIESTESS *Women in the Hellenistic period continued to play an important part in society and religion by serving as priestesses. Here the young priestess holds a tray, on which she carries the cult objects used in the god's ritual. (Museo Nazionale Romano)*

lenistic royal women, however, set an example of courage and nobility. This is especially true of Cratesiclea, mother of the king Cleomenes.

In 224 B.C., Cleomenes was trying to rebuild Sparta as a major power, but he needed money. King Ptolemy of Egypt promised to help the Spartans because doing so would further his own diplomatic ends. In return for his support Ptolemy demanded that Cleomenes give him his mother, Cratesiclea, as a hostage. Ptolemy's demand was an insult and a grave dishonor to the Spartan lady, yet Cleomenes' plans could not succeed without Ptolemy's money. Reluctant to agree to Ptolemy's terms, Cleomenes was also reluctant to mention the matter to his mother. Plutarch related her reaction:

*Finally, when Cleomenes worked up his courage to speak about the matter, Cratesiclea laughed aloud and said: "Is this what you often started to say but flinched from? Rather put me aboard a ship and send me away, wherever you think this body of mine will be most useful to Sparta, before sitting here it is destroyed by old age."*[7]

Cratesiclea's selflessness and love of her state became legendary. Other Hellenistic queens and women of royal blood demonstrated the same qualities of self-sacrifice and devotion to duty.

The example of the queens had a profound effect on Hellenistic attitudes toward women in general. In fact, the Hellenistic period saw a great expansion in social and economic opportunities for women. More women than ever before received educations that enabled them to enter the professions and medicine. As the American scholar Sarah Pomeroy has observed: "The serious pursuit of intellectual, artistic, or scientific goals, as an addition, or as a prelude, or even as an alternative to marriage, was a new phenomenon for Greek women."[8] Literacy among women increased dramatically, and their options expanded accordingly. Some won fame as poets, while others studied with philosophers and contributed to the intellectual life of the age. As a rule, however, these developments touched only wealthier women. Poor women, and probably the majority of women, were barely literate, if literate at all.

Women began to participate in politics on at least a limited basis. Often they served as priestesses, as they had in the Hellenic period, but they also began to serve in civil capacities. For their services to the state they received public acknowledgment. Women sometimes received honorary citizenship from foreign cities because of aid given in times of crisis. Few women achieved these honors, however, and those who did were from the upper classes.

This major development was not due to male enlightenment. Although Hellenistic philosophy addressed itself to many new questions, the position of women was not one of them. The Stoics, in spite of their theory of the brotherhood of man, thought of women as men's inferiors. Only the Cynics, who waged war on all accepted customs, treated women as men's equals. The Cynics were interested in women as individuals, not as members of a family or as citizens of the state. Their view did not make much headway. Like other aspects of Cynic philosophy, this attitude was more admired than followed.

The new prominence of women was largely due instead to their increased participation in economic affairs. During the Hellenistic period some women took part in commercial transactions. Nonetheless, they still lived under legal handicaps. In Egypt, for example, a Greek woman needed a male guardian to buy, sell, or lease land, to borrow money, and to represent her in other transactions. Yet often such a guardian was present only to fulfill the letter of the law. The woman was the real agent, and she handled the business being transacted. In Hellenistic Sparta women accumulated large fortunes and vast amounts of land. As early as the beginning of the Hellenistic period women owned two-fifths of the land of Laconia. Spartan women, however, were exceptional. In most other areas, even women who were very wealthy in their own right were at least formally under the protection of a male relative.

These changes do not amount to a social revolution. Women had begun to participate in business, politics, and legal activities. Yet such women were rare, and they labored under handicaps that men did not have. Even so, it was a start.

## HELLENISTIC SCIENCE

The area in which Hellenistic culture achieved its greatest triumphs was science. Here too the ancient Near East made contributions to Greek thought. The patient observations of the Babylonians, who for generations had scanned the skies, had provided the raw materials for Thales' speculations, which were the foundation of Hellenistic astronomy. The most notable of the Hellenistic astronomers was Aristarchus of Samos (ca. 310–230 B.C.), who was educated in Aristotle's school. Aristarchus concluded that the sun is far larger than the earth and that the stars are enormously distant from the earth. He argued against Aristotle's view that the earth is the center of the universe. Instead, Aristarchus propounded the heliocentric theory – that is, that the earth and the planets revolve around the sun. His work is all the more impressive because he lacked even a rudimentary telescope. Aristarchus had only the human eye and the human brain, but they were more than enough.

Unfortunately, Aristarchus' theories did not persuade the ancient world. In the second century A.D., Claudius Ptolemy, a mathematician and astronomer in Alexandria, accepted Aristotle's theory of the earth as the center of the universe, and their view prevailed for 1400 years. Aristarchus' heliocentric theory lay dormant until resurrected by the brilliant Polish astronomer Nicolaus Copernicus (1473–1543).

In geometry Hellenistic thinkers discovered little that was new, but Euclid (ca 300 B.C.), a mathematician who lived in Alexandria, compiled a valuable textbook of existing knowledge. His book, *The Elements of Geometry,* has exerted immense influence on Western civilization, for it rapidly became the standard introduction to geometry. Generations of students, from the Hellenistic period to the present day, have learned the essentials of geometry from it.

The greatest thinker of the Hellenistic period was Archimedes (ca 287–212 B.C.), who was a clever inventor as well. He lived in Syracuse in Sicily and watched Rome emerge as a power in the Mediterranean. When the Romans laid siege to Syracuse in the Second Punic War (see Chapter 5), Archimedes invented a number of machines to thwart the Roman army. His catapults threw rocks large enough to sink ships and disrupt battle lines. His grappling devices lifted warships out of the water. The Romans developed a healthy respect for Archimedes, as Plutarch reports: "At last the Romans were so terrified . . . that if a small piece of rope or a small timber was seen protruding from the walls, they bellowed

'There's the thing; Archimedes is unleashing some machine against us,' and turned around and fled."[9]

In the Hellenistic period the practical applications of the principles of mechanics were primarily military, for the building of artillery and siege engines. Archimedes built such machines out of necessity, but they were of little real interest to him. In a more peaceful vein, he invented the Archimedean screw, a device used to pump water into irrigation ditches and out of mines. He also invented the compound pulley. Plutarch described Archimedes' dramatic demonstration of how easily it could move huge weights with little effort:

*A three-masted merchant ship of the royal fleet had been hauled on land by hard work and many hands. Archimedes put aboard her many men and the usual freight. He sat far away from her; without haste, but gently working a compound pulley with his hand, he drew her towards him smoothly and without faltering, just as though she were running on the surface of the sea.*[10]

Archimedes was far more interested in pure mathematics than in practical inventions. His mathematical research, which covered many fields, was his greatest contribution to Western thought. In his book *On Plane Equilibriums* Archimedes dealt for the first time with the basic principles of mechanics, including the principle of the lever. He once said that if he were given a lever and a suitable place to stand, he could move the world. In his treatise *Sand-Counter* Archimedes devised a system to express large numbers, a difficult matter considering the deficiencies of Greek numerical notation. *Sand-Counter* also discussed the heliocentric theory of Aristarchus. With his treatise *On Floating Bodies* Archimedes founded the science of hydrostatics. He concluded that whenever a solid floats in a liquid, the weight of the solid is equal to the volume of liquid displaced. The way in which he made his discovery has become famous:

*When he was devoting his attention to this problem, he happened to go to a public bath. When he climbed down into the bathtub there, he noticed that water in the tub equal to the bulk of his body flowed out. Thus, when he observed this method of solving the problem, he did not wait. Instead, moved with joy, he sprang out of the tub, and rushing home naked he kept indicating in a loud voice that he had indeed discovered what he was seeking. For while running he was shouting repeatedly in Greek, "eureka, eureka" ("I have found it, I have found it").*[11]

Archimedes' other works include *On the Measurement of a Circle, On the Sphere and Cylinder, On Conoids and Spheroids,* and *On Spirals.*

Archimedes was willing to share his work, and one of those with whom he communicated was Eratosthenes (285–ca 204 B.C.), a man of almost universal interests. From his native Cyrene in North Africa, Eratosthenes traveled to Athens, where he studied philosophy and learned mathematics. He refused to join any of the philosophical schools, for he was interested in too many things to follow any particular dogma. Hence, his thought was eclectic: he took his doctrines from many schools of thought. For instance, in philosophy Eratosthenes was influenced by Zeno, but Stoicism could not satisfy his mathematical and geographical interests. Besides his scientific work, he devoted time to poetry, in which he showed genuine talent, and he wrote a book on Attic comedy.

Around 245 B.C., King Ptolemy invited Eratosthenes to Alexandria. The Ptolemies had done much to make Alexandria an intellectual, cultural, and scientific center. They had established a lavish library and museum, undoubtedly the greatest seat of learning in the Hellenistic world. At the crown's expense, the Ptolemies maintained a number of distinguished scholars and poets. Eratosthenes came to Alexandria to become the librarian of the royal library, a position of great prestige. While there he continued his mathematical work and by letter struck up a friendship with Archimedes. Eratosthenes solved the problem of how to double a cube, built a machine to illustrate his proof, and in a short poem dedicated his work to King Ptolemy.

Unlike his friend Archimedes, Eratosthenes did not devote his life entirely to mathematics, although he never lost interest in it. He used his mathematics to further the geographical studies for which he is most famous. He calculated the circumference of the earth geometrically, estimating it as about 24,675 miles. He was not wrong by much: the earth is actually 24,860 miles in circumference. Of this achievement Carl Sagan, the noted contemporary astronomer, has said:

*Eratosthenes' only tools were sticks, eyes, feet, and brains, plus a taste for experiment. With them he deduced the circumference of the earth with an error of only a few percent, a remarkable achievement for 2,200 years ago. He was the first person accurately to measure the size of a planet.*[12]

Eratosthenes also concluded that the earth is a spherical globe, that the landmass is roughly foursided, and that the land is surrounded by ocean. He discussed the shapes and sizes of land and ocean and the irregularities of the earth's surface. He drew a map of the earth and used his own system of explaining the divisions of the earth's landmass.

Using geographical information gained by Alexander the Great's scientists, Eratosthenes tried to fit the East into Greek geographical knowledge. Although for some reason he ignored the western Mediterranean and Europe, he declared that a ship could sail from Spain either around Africa to India or directly westward to India. Not until the great days of Western exploration did sailors such as Vasco da Gama and Magellan actually prove Eratosthenes' theories. Greek geographers like Eratosthenes also turned their attention southward to Africa. During this period the people of the Mediterranean learned of the climate and customs of Ethiopia, and gleaned some scant information about equatorial Africa.

In his life and work Eratosthenes exemplifies the range and vitality of Hellenistic science. His interests were varied and included the cultural and humanistic as well as the purely scientific. Although his chief interest was in the realm of speculative thought, he did not ignore the practical. He was quite willing to deal with old problems and to break new ground.

In the Hellenistic period the scientific study of botany had its origin. Aristotle's pupil Theophrastus (ca 372–288 B.C.), who became head of the Lyceum, the school established by Aristotle, studied the botanical information made available by Alexander's penetration of the East. Aristotle had devoted a good deal of his attention to zoology, and Theophrastus extended his work to plants. He wrote two books on the subject, *History of Plants* and *Causes of Plants*. He carefully observed phenomena and based his conclusions on what he had actually seen. Theophrastus classified plants and accurately described their parts. He detected the process of germination and realized the importance of climate and soil to plants. Some of Theophrastus' work found its way into agricultural handbooks, but for the most part Hellenistic science did not carry the study of botany any further.

## HELLENISTIC MEDICINE

The study of medicine flourished during the Hellenistic period, and Hellenistic physicians carried the work of Hippocrates into new areas. Herophilus, who lived in the first half of the third century B.C., worked at Alexandria and studied the writings of Hippocrates. He accepted Hippocrates' theory of the four humors, and approached the study of medicine in a systematic, scientific fashion. He dissected dead bodies and measured what he observed. He discovered the nervous system and concluded that two types of nerves, motor and sensory, exist. Herophilus also studied the brain, which he considered the center of intelligence, and discerned the cerebrum and cerebellum. His other work dealt with the liver, lungs, and uterus. His younger contemporary, Erasistratus, also conducted research on the brain and the nervous system, and he improved on Herophilus' work. He too followed in the tradition of Hippocrates and preferred to let the body heal itself by means of diet and air.

Both Herophilus and Erasistratus were members of the Dogmatic school of medicine at Alexandria. In this school speculation played an important part in research. So too did the study of anatomy. To learn more about human anatomy Herophilus and Erasistratus dissected corpses and even vivisected criminals whom King Ptolemy contributed for the purpose. Vivisection – cutting into the body of a living animal or person – was seen as a necessary cruelty: the Dogmatists argued that the knowledge gained from the suffering of a few evil men benefited many others. Nonetheless, the practice of vivisection seems to have been short-lived, although dissection continued. Better knowledge of anatomy led to improvements in surgery. These advances enabled the Dogmatists to invent new surgical instruments and new techniques.

In about 280 B.C., Philinus and Serapion, two pupils of Herophilus, led a reaction to the Dogmatists. Believing that the Dogmatists had become too speculative, they founded the Empiric school of medicine at Alexandria. Claiming that the Dogmatists' emphasis on anatomy and physiology was misplaced, they concentrated instead on the observation and cure of illnesses. They also laid heavier stress on the use of drugs and medicine to treat illnesses. Heraclides of Tarentum (perhaps first century B.C.) carried on the Empirical tradition and dedicated himself to observation and use of medicines. He discovered the benefits of opium and worked with other drugs that relieved pain. He also steadfastly rejected magic and sorcery as pertinent to the application of drugs and medicines.

Hellenistic medicine had its dark side, for many physicians were moneygrubbers, fools, and quacks. One of the angriest complaints comes from the days of the Roman Empire:

*Of all men only a physician can kill a man with total impunity. Oh no, on the contrary, censure goes to him who dies and* he *is guilty of excess, and furthermore* he *is blamed. . . . Let me not accuse their [physicians'] avarice, their greedy deals with those whose fate hangs in the balance, their setting a price on pain, and their demands for down payment in case of death, and their secret doctrines.*[13]

Abuses such as these existed already in the Hellenistic period. As is true today, many Hellenistic physicians did not take the Hippocratic oath very seriously.

Besides incompetent and greedy physicians, the Hellenistic world was plagued by people who claimed to cure illnesses through incantations and magic. Their potions included such concoctions as blood from the ear of an ass mixed with water to cure fever, or the liver of a cat, killed when the moon was waning, and preserved in salt. Broken bones could be cured by applying the ashes of a pig's jawbone to the break. The dung of a goat mixed with old wine was good for healing broken ribs. One charlatan claimed that he could cure epilepsy by making the patient drink, from the skull of a man who had been killed but not cremated, water drawn from a spring at night. These quacks even claimed that they could cure mental illness with their remedies. The treatment for a person suffering from melancholy was calf dung boiled in wine. No doubt the patient became too sick to be depressed.

Quacks who prescribed such treatments were very popular, but they did untold harm to the sick and injured. They and the greedy physicians also damaged the reputation of dedicated doctors who honestly and intelligently tried to heal and alleviate pain. The medical abuses that arose in the Hellenistic period were so flagrant that the Romans who later entered the Hellenistic world developed an intense dislike and distrust of physicians. The Romans considered the study of Hellenistic medicine beneath the dignity of a Roman, and even as late as the Roman Empire few Romans undertook the study of Greek medicine. Nonetheless, the work of men like Herophilus and Serapion made valuable contributions to the knowledge of medicine, and the fruits of their work were preserved and handed on to the West.

———◆———

The Hellenistic period fostered the spread of Hellenism throughout the East, disseminating the knowledge, customs, and laws of the Greeks and bringing East and West into intimate contact. Though often called degenerate and stagnant, the Hellenistic period could boast of numerous advances, especially in the sciences and medicine. Hellenistic thinkers created a golden age of scientific discovery and speculation, while Hellenistic philosophy reached out to touch the lives of rich and poor, princes and peasants.

The Hellenistic period also prepared the way for Rome. Although the Hellenistic monarchies, like the Greek city-states, fought to a standstill and seriously weakened each other, they made something new of the East. Greek and Easterner alike changed the East, and into this world Rome moved. Rome brought political stability and Roman law, but in doing so it built upon the society and culture created by Hellenistic men and women.

## NOTES

1. Diodorus 17.1.4.

2. Plutarch *Moralia* 328E.

3. Quoted in W. W. Tarn and G. T. Griffith, *Hellenistic Civilisation,* Meridian Books, Cleveland and New York, 1961, p. 199.

4. *Periplous of the Erythraian Sea* 57.

5. Diodorus 3.12.2–3.

6. Diogenes Laertius 6.38.

7. Plutarch *Lives of Agis and Cleomenes* 22.5.

8. S. B. Pomeroy, "Technikai kai Mousikai," *American Journal of Ancient History* 2 (1977): 51.

9. Plutarch *Life of Marcellus* 17.4.

10. Ibid., 14.13.

11. Vitruvius *On Architecture* 9 Preface, 10.

12. Carl Sagan, "The Measure of Eratosthenes," *Harvard Magazine* 83 (1980): 10.

13. Pliny the Elder *Natural History* 29.8.18, 21.

## SUGGESTED READING

General treatments of Hellenistic political, social, and economic history can be found in S. A. Cook, et al., *The Cambridge Ancient History,* vol. 7 (1928), and in the shorter and handier works of M. Cary, *A History of the Greek World 323–146 B.C.,* 2nd ed. (1951), and W. W. Tarn and G. T. Griffith, *Hellenistic Civilisation,* 3rd ed. (1951, 1961). M. M. Austin, *The Hellenistic World from Alexander to the Roman Conquest* (1981) is an excellent selection of primary sources in an accurate and readable translation. F. W. Walbank, *The Hellenistic World* (1981) is a fresh new appraisal by one of the foremost scholars of the period. The undisputed classic in this field is M. Rostovtzeff, *The Social and Economic History of the Hellenistic World,* 3 vols. (1941).

Each year brings a new crop of biographies of Alexander the Great. Still the best, however, is J. R. Hamilton, *Alexander the Great* (1973). Old but still useful is U. Wilcken, *Alexander the Great* (English translation, 1967), which has had a considerable impact on scholars and students alike. On the topic of Alexander's place in history, see A. R. Burn, *Alexander the Great and the Hellenistic World* (1947), a lively and sane treatment. Newer is C. B. Welles, *Alexander and the Hellenistic World* (1970). Recent political studies of the Hellenistic period include G. J. D. Aalders, *Political Theory in Hellenistic Times* (1975), and E. V. Hansen, *The Attalids of Pergamon,* 2nd ed. (1971).

On the spread of Hellenism throughout the Near East, see F. E. Peters, *The Harvest of Hellenism* (1970), and most recently, A. Momigliano, *Alien Wisdom: The Limits of Hellenization* (1975).

A. H. M. Jones, *The Greek City from Alexander to Justinian* (1940), deals with urban life during the Hellenistic, Roman, and early Byzantine periods. P. M. Fraser, *Ptolemaic Alexandria,* 3 vols. (1972), covers the life, history, and culture of the most flourishing and prominent of the Hellenistic cities. G. Downey, *A History of Antioch in Syria from Seleucus to the Arab Conquest* (1961), gives a good account of a major city in Asia Minor. Hellenistic Athens is described by C. Mossé, *Athens in Decline, 404–86 B.C.* (1973). G. M. Cohen, *The Seleucid Colo-*

*nies* (1978), treats all aspects of the Seleucid colonizing effort.

Two general studies of religion within the Hellenistic world are F. Grant, *Hellenistic Religion: The Age of Syncretism* (1953), and H. J. Rose, *Religion in Greece and Rome* (1959). For the effects of Hellenistic religious developments on Christianity, see A. D. Nock, *Early Gentile Christianity and Its Hellenistic Background* (1964). V. Tscherikover, *Hellenistic Civilization and the Jews* (1959) treats the impact of Hellenism on Judaism, and R. E. Witt, *Isis in the Graeco-Roman World* (1971), which is illustrated, studies the origins and growth of the Isis cult. The cult of her consort Osiris is the subject of J. G. Griffiths, *The Origins of Osiris and His Cult* (1980).

Hellenistic philosophy and science have attracted the attention of a number of scholars, and the various philosophical schools are especially well covered. A convenient survey of Hellenistic philosophy is A. A. Long, *Hellenistic Philosophy* (1974). F. Sayre, *The Greek Cynics* (1948), focuses on Diogenes' thought and manners, while C. Bailey, *Epicureans* (1926), although dated, is still a useful study of the origins and nature of Epicureanism. Two recent treatments of Stoicism are J. Rist, *Stoic Philosophy* (1969), and F. H. Sandbach, *The Stoics* (1975). A good survey of Hellenistic science is G. E. R. Lloyd, *Greek Science after Aristotle* (1963), and specific studies of major figures can be found in T. L. Heath's solid work, *Aristarchus of Samos* (1920), still unsurpassed, and E. J. Dijksterhuis, *Archimedes* (1956).

# CHAPTER 5

# THE RISE OF ROME

"*WHO IS SO THOUGHTLESS* and lazy that he does not want to know in what way and with what kind of government the Romans in less than 53 years conquered nearly the entire inhabited world and brought it under their rule – an achievement previously unheard of?"[1] This question was first asked by Polybius, a Greek historian who lived in the second century B.C. With keen awareness Polybius realized that the Romans were achieving something unique in world history.

What was that achievement? Was it simply the creation of a huge empire? Hardly. The Persians had done the same thing. For that matter, Alexander the Great had conquered vast territories in a shorter time. Was it the creation of a superior culture? Even the Romans admitted that in matters of art, literature, philosophy, and culture they learned from the Greeks. Rome's achievement lay in the ability of the Romans not only to conquer peoples but to incorporate them into the Roman system. Rome succeeded where the Greek polis had failed. Unlike the Greeks, who refused to share citizenship, the Romans extended their citizenship first to the Italians and later to the peoples of the provinces. With that citizenship went Roman government and Roman law. Rome created a world state that embraced the entire Mediterranean area.

Nor was Rome's achievement limited to the ancient world. Rome's law, language, and administrative practices were a precious heritage to medieval and modern Europe. London, Paris, Vienna, and many other modern European cities began as Roman colonies or military camps. When the Founding Fathers created the American Republic they looked to Rome as a model. On the darker side, Napoleon and Mussolini paid their own tribute to Rome by aping its forms. Whether Founding Father or modern autocrat, they were all ac-

MAP 5.1 *ITALY AND THE CITY OF ROME* *The geographical configuration of the Italian peninsula shows how Rome stood astride north-south communications and how the state that united Italy stood poised to move into Sicily and northern Africa.*

knowledging their admiration for the Roman achievement.

Roman history is usually divided into two periods: the Republic, the age in which Rome grew from a small city-state to ruler of an empire, and the Empire, the period when the republican constitution gave way to constitutional monarchy. How did Rome rise to greatness? What effects did the conquest of the Mediterranean have on the Romans themselves? Finally, why did the republic collapse? These are the questions this chapter will attempt to answer.

## THE LAND AND THE SEA

To the west of Greece the boot-shaped peninsula of Italy, with Sicily at its toe, occupies the center of the Mediterranean basin. As Map 5.1 shows, Italy and Sicily thrust southward toward Africa: the distance between southwestern Sicily and the northern African coast is at one point only about a hundred miles. Italy and Sicily literally divide the Mediterranean into two basins and form the focal point between the halves.

Like Greece and other Mediterranean lands, Italy enjoys a genial, almost subtropical climate. The winters are rainy, but the summer months are dry. Because of the climate the rivers of Italy usually carry little water during the summer, and some go entirely dry. The low water level of the Arno, one of the principal rivers of Italy, once led Mark Twain to describe it as "a great historical creek with four feet in the channel and some scows

ALPS

Po

Trebia

Trebia River ✕

A P P E N N I N E S

Arno

ETRURIA

L. Trasimene ✕

UMBRIA

PICENUM

Tiber

CORSICA

Veii

Rome

LATIUM

SAMNIUM

APULIA

Cannae ✕

CAMPANIA

Tarentum

CALABRIA

LUCANIA

A D R I A T I C   S E A

SARDINIA

T Y R R H E N I A N   S E A

BRUTTIUM

Messana

SICILY

Syracuse ✕

Carthage

Cape Bon

Zama ✕

- - - -  Roman boundary before the Punic wars
———  Roman boundary before Augustus
   ✕   Major battle
———  Major road

0      50      100      150 Km.
0      50      100      150 Mi.

ROME

0        500      1000 m.
0      1500      3000 Ft.

Field of Mars

Tiber

QUIRINAL

VIMINAL

CAPITOLINE

Senate House

Temple of Jupiter

Forum

Regia

ESQUILINE

JANICULUM

PALATINE

CAELIAN

Circus Maximus

AVENTINE

floating around. It would be a very plausible river if they would pump some water into it."[2] The Arno at least is navigable. Most of Italy's other rivers are not. Clearly, these small rivers were unsuitable for regular, large-scale shipping. Italian rivers, unlike Twain's beloved Mississippi, never became major thoroughfares for commerce and communications.

Geography discouraged maritime trade as well. Italy lacks the numerous good harbors that are such a prominent feature of the Greek landscape. Only in the south are there good harbors, and Greek colonists had early claimed those ports for themselves. Yet geography. gave rise to — and the rivers nourished — a bountiful agriculture that sustained a large population. The strength of Italy lay in the land and its produce.

Geography encouraged Italy to look to the Mediterranean. In the north Italy is protected by the Apennine Mountains, which break off from the Alps and form a natural barrier. The Apennines retarded but did not prevent peoples from penetrating Italy from the north. Throughout history, in modern times as well as ancient, various invaders have entered Italy by this route. From the north the Apennines run southward the entire length of the Italian boot; they virtually cut off access to the Adriatic Sea, which further induced Italy to look west to Spain and Carthage rather than east to Greece. Even though most of the land is mountainous, the hill country is not as inhospitable as are the Greek highlands. In antiquity the general fertility of the soil provided the basis for a large population. Nor did the mountains of Italy so carve up the land as to prevent the development of political unity. Geography proved kinder to Italy than to Greece.

In their southward course the Apennines leave two broad and fertile plains, those of Latium and Campania. These plains attracted settlers and invaders from the time when peoples began to move into Italy. Among these peoples were the Romans, who established their city on the Tiber River in Latium.

This site enjoyed several advantages. The Tiber provided Rome with a constant source of water. Located at an easy crossing-point on the Tiber, Rome thus stood astride the main avenue of communications between northern and southern Italy. The famous seven hills of Rome were defensible and safe from the floods of the Tiber. Rome was in an excellent position to develop the resources of Latium and maintain contact with the rest of Italy.

## THE ETRUSCANS AND ROME
### (750–509 B.C.)

In recent years archaeologists have found traces of numerous early peoples in Italy. The origins of these cultures and their precise relations with one another are not yet well understood. In fact, no clear account of the prehistory of Italy is yet possible. Of the period before the appearance of the Etruscans (1200–750 B.C.) one fundamental fact is indisputable: peoples speaking Indo-European languages were moving into Italy from the north, probably in small groups. They were part of the awesome but imperfectly understood movement of peoples that spread the Indo-European family of languages from Spain to India.

Only with the coming of the Greeks does Italy enter the light of history. A great wave of Greek immigration swept into southern Italy and Sicily during the eighth century B.C., as was described on pages 81–82. The Greeks brought urban life to these regions, spreading cultural influence far beyond the walls of their city-states.

In the north the Greeks encountered the Etruscans, one of the truly mysterious peoples of antiquity. Who the Etruscans were, where they came from, and what language they spoke are unknown. Nonetheless, this fascinating people was to leave an indelible mark on the Romans. Skillful metal workers, the Etruscans amassed extensive wealth by trading their manufactured goods in Italy and beyond. The strength of their political and military institutions enabled them to form a loosely organized league of cities whose dominion extended as far north as the Po valley and as far south as Latium and Campania (see Map 5.1). In Latium they founded cities and took over control of Rome. Like the Greeks, the Etruscans promoted urban life, and one of the places that benefited from Etruscan influence was Rome.

The Etruscans found the Romans settled on three of Rome's seven hills. The site of the future Forum Romanum, the famous public square and center of political life, was originally the cemetery of the small community. According to Roman legend, Romulus and Remus founded Rome in 753 B.C. Romulus built his settlement on the Palatine Hill, while Remus chose the Aventine (see inset, Map 5.1). Jealous of his brother's work, Remus ridiculed it by jumping over Romulus's unfinished wall. In a rage, Romulus killed his brother and vowed, "So will die whoever else shall leap over my walls." In this instance legend preserves some facts. Archaeological investigation has confirmed that the earliest settlement at Rome was situated on the Palatine and that it dates to the first half of the eighth century B.C. The legend also shows traces of Etruscan influence on Roman customs. The inviolability of Romulus's walls

*STATUETTE OF AN ETRUSCAN WARRIOR  The warrior shows the Etruscan military debt to Greece. He wears Greek armor and carries the spear of the Greek heavy infantryman. The artistic rendering of the warrior, however, shows that Italic artists were moving away from Greek models and were creating a style of their own. (Collection of the University Museum, The University of Pennsylvania)*

recalls the Etruscan concept of the *pomerium,* a sacred boundary intended to keep out anything evil or unclean.

During the years 753–509 B.C., the Romans picked up many Etruscan customs. They adopted the Etruscan alphabet, which the Etruscans themselves had adopted from the Greeks. The Romans later handed on this alphabet to medieval Europe and thence to the modern Western world. The Romans also adopted symbols of political authority from the Etruscans. The symbol of the Etruscan king's right to execute or scourge his subjects was a bundle of rods and an ax, called in Latin the *fasces,* which the king's retainer carried before him on official occasions. When the Romans expelled the Etruscan kings, they created special attendants called lictors to carry the fasces before their new magistrates, the consuls. Even the toga, the white woolen robe worn by citizens, came from the Etruscans. In engineering and architecture the Romans adopted from the Etruscans the vault and the arch. Above all, it was thanks to the Etruscans that the Romans truly became urban dwellers.

Etruscan power and influence at Rome were so strong that Roman traditions preserved the memory of Etruscan kings who ruled the city. Under the Etruscans, Rome enjoyed contacts with the larger Mediterranean world, and the city began to grow. In the years 575–550 B.C., temples and public buildings began to grace the city. The Capitoline Hill became the religious center of the city when the temple of Jupiter Optimus Maximus (Jupiter the Best and Greatest) was built there. The forum ceased to be a cemetery and began its history as a public meeting place, much like the agora of a Greek city. Metalwork became common, and the wealthier classes began to import large numbers of fine Greek vases. The Etruscans had found Rome a collection of villages and made of it a city.

## THE ROMAN CONQUEST OF ITALY
### (509–290 B.C.)

Early Roman history is an uneven mixture of fact and legend. Roman traditions often contain an important kernel of truth, but that does not make them history. In many cases they are significant because they illustrate the ethics, morals, and ideals that Roman society considered valuable. Rome's early history also presents the historian with another problem. Historical writing did not begin among the Romans until the third century B.C., hundreds of years after the founding of Rome. Much later still, around the time of Jesus, the historian Livy (59 B.C.–A.D. 17) gave final form to these legends.

How much genuine information about the early years did Romans like Livy have? Or did they simply take what they knew and try to make of it an intelligible story? Livy gave his own answer to these questions: "Events before Rome was born or thought of have come down to us in old tales with more of the charm of poetry than of sound historical record, and such traditions I propose neither to affirm nor refute."[3] Livy also admitted that these legends and tales depicted men and women not necessarily as they were, but as Romans should be. For him, the story of early Rome was an impressive moral tale. Today, historians would say that Livy took these legends and made of them a sweeping epic. But they would also admit that the epic preserved the broad outlines of the Roman conquest of Italy and the development of Rome's internal

THE ROMAN FORUM    *The forum was the center of Roman political life. From simple beginnings it developed into the very symbol of Rome's imperial majesty. (Italian Government Travel Office)*

affairs. Both parts of the epic – legend and fact – are worth examining for what they say about the Romans.

According to Roman tradition, the Romans expelled the Etruscan king Tarquin the Proud from Rome in 509 B.C. and founded the republic. In the years that followed, the Romans fought numerous wars with their neighbors on the Italian peninsula. They became soldiers, and the grim fighting bred tenacity, a prominent Roman trait. War also involved diplomacy, at which the Romans became masters. At an early date they learned the value of alliances and how to provide leadership for their allies. Alliances with the Latin towns around them provided them with a large reservoir of manpower. Their alliances also involved the Romans in still other wars and took them farther and farther afield in the Italian peninsula.

One of the earliest wars was with two nearby peoples, the Aequi and the Volsci, and from this contest arose the legend of Cincinnatus. At one point, when the Aequi had launched a serious invasion, the Romans called upon Cincinnatus to assume the office of dictator. In this period the Roman dictator, unlike modern dictators, was a legitimate magistrate given ultimate powers for a specified period of time. The Roman officials found Cincinnatus working his three-acre farm. Wiping the sweat from himself, he listened to the appeal of his countrymen and accepted the office. Fifteen days later, after he had defeated the Aequi, he returned to his farm. Cincinnatus personified the ideal of the Roman citizen – a man of simplicity, a man who put his duty to Rome before any consideration of personal interest or wealth.

Roman tradition tells of grand campaigns

and continuous Roman success in these wars. In reality, most campaigns were neither grand nor always victorious. A good idea of what the fighting was like comes from the legend of the Fabii, one of Rome's noblest families. On one occasion 306 members of the Fabii set out toward Etruscan territory on what was nothing more than a cattle raid. What could be more patriotic than to reduce the enemy's wealth while increasing your own? The Etruscans, however, ambushed the Fabii and surrounded them. One boy escaped from the fighting, but the rest of the Fabii died to the last man, as good Romans were supposed to do. The excessive losses belong to the realm of legend, but the Fabii's type of combat was no doubt typical of the hard-fought border skirmishes and raids, in which the Romans at times took a beating. Gradually, Roman tenacity and numbers exhausted the strength of the enemy. The conflicts also taught the Romans to bounce back from defeat and to modify their institutions to deal effectively with changing problems and situations.

The growth of Roman power was slow but steady. Not until roughly a century after the founding of the republic did the Romans try to drive the Etruscans entirely out of Latium. In 405 B.C. they laid siege to Veii, the last neighboring Etruscan city. Ten years later they captured it. The story of the siege of Veii is in some ways the Roman equivalent of the Greek siege of Troy. But once again tradition preserves a kernel of truth, confirmed now by archaeological exploration of Veii. This was an important Roman victory, for the land of Veii went to the Romans and provided additional resources for Rome's growing population. Rome's concentrated landholdings formed a strong, unified core in central Italy. After the destruction of Veii, Rome overshadowed its Latin allies and its enemies alike.

Although the Romans slowly but steadily advanced their power in central Italy, they suffered a major setback about 390 B.C. A new people, the Celts — or Gauls, as the Romans called them — had been spreading their culture throughout the regions of modern France, Belgium, and southern Germany. By about 550 B.C. the Gauls were trading with the Greek colony of Massilia (modern Marseilles) and with Etruscan cities in the Po valley. Lured by the wealth of northern Italy, bands of Gauls began to push into the Po valley. Around 390 B.C. one band struck as far south as Latium. The great German historian Eduard Meyer has vividly recaptured the terror of the event:

*With gloomy fear the sons of the Mediterranean looked upon these giants [the Gauls], with their long red hair and huge moustaches. They were a wild warrior folk who trampled down whatever stood in their way. With the severed heads of their enemies they bedecked their horses and their huts with skulls. Half naked they went into battle, their necks and arms adorned with thick gold rings and chains. Their many-colored mantles they threw aside; only shields covered their bodies. Their weapons were spears and mighty, but slender and wickedly-shaped, swords.*[4]

The Gauls swept aside a Roman army and sacked Rome. More intent on loot than land, they agreed to abandon Rome in return for a thousand pounds of gold. The decision to buy off the Gauls made a lasting impression on the Romans. According to Roman tradition, when the Gauls produced their own scale, the Romans howled with indignation. The Gallic chieftain then threw his sword on the scale, exclaiming "Vae victis" — "woe to the conquered." These words, though legendary, became a challenge to the Romans. Thereafter they made it their policy never to accept peace, much less to surrender, as long as the enemy were still in the field.

Although the Gauls left Rome in rubble — another fact confirmed by modern archaeology — they also inadvertently helped the Romans: on their way to central Italy they broke forever the power of the Etruscans. When the Gauls took their gold and returned to the Alps, they left the north open to Roman expansion.

During the century from 390 to 290 B.C., Romans rebuilt their city and recouped their losses. They also reorganized their army to create the mobile legion, a flexible unit capable of fighting on either broken or open terrain. The Romans finally brought Latium and their Latin allies fully under their control, and they conquered Etruria. In 343 B.C., they grappled with the Samnites in a series of bitter wars for the possession of Campania and southern Italy. The Samnites were a formidable enemy, and they inflicted some serious losses on the Romans. But the superior organization, institutions, and manpower of the Romans won out in the end. Although Rome had yet to subdue the whole peninsula, for the first time in history the city stood unchallenged in Italy.

Rome's success in diplomacy and politics was as important as its military victories. Unlike the Greeks, the Romans did not simply conquer and then dominate. Instead, they shared with other Italians both political power and degrees of Roman citizenship. The Romans did not start out to build a system. They were always a practical people — that was one of their greatest strengths. When they found a treaty or a political arrangement that worked, they used it wherever possible. When it did not, they turned to something else. Consequently, Rome had a network of alliances and treaties with other peoples and states.

With many of their oldest allies, such as the Italian cities, they shared full Roman citizenship. In other instances they granted citizenship without the franchise (*civitas sine suffragio*). Allies who held this status enjoyed all the rights of Roman citizenship except that they could not vote or hold Roman offices. They were subject to Roman taxes and calls for military service, but they ran their own local affairs. The Latin allies were able to acquire full Roman citizenship by moving to Rome.

By their willingness to extend their citizenship the Romans took Italy into partnership. Here the political genius of Rome triumphed where Greece had failed: Rome proved itself superior to the Greek polis because it both conquered and shared the fruits of conquest with the conquered. Rome could consolidate where Greece could only dominate. The unwillingness of the Greek polis to share its citizenship condemned it to a limited horizon. Not so with Rome. The extension of Roman citizenship strengthened the state, gave it additional manpower and wealth, and laid the foundations of the Roman Empire itself.

## THE ROMAN STATE

The Romans summed up their political existence in a single phrase: *senatus populusque Romanus,* the Roman senate and the people. The real genius of the Romans lay in the fields of politics and law. Unlike the Greeks, they did not often speculate on the ideal state or on political forms; instead, they realistically met actual challenges and created institutions, magistracies, and legal concepts to deal with practical problems. Change was consequently a commonplace feature of Roman political life, and the constitution of 509 B.C. was far simpler than that of 27 B.C. Nonetheless, the principal magistracies and political organs of the state can be briefly sketched.

In the early republic, social divisions determined the shape of politics. Political power was in the hands of the aristocracy – the patricians, who were wealthy landowners. Patrician families formed clans, as did aristocrats in early Greece. They dominated the affairs of state, provided military leadership in time of war, and monopolized knowledge of law and legal procedure. The common people of Rome, the plebeians, had few of the advantages of the patricians. Some plebeians formed clans of their own, and rivaled the patricians in wealth. Many plebeian merchants increased their wealth in the course of Roman expansion, but most plebeians were poor. They were the artisans, the small farmers, and the landless urban dwellers. The plebeians, rich and poor alike, were free citizens and had a voice in politics. Nonetheless, they were overshadowed by the patricians.

Perhaps the greatest institution of the republic was the senate, which had originated under the Etruscans as a council of noble elders who advised the king. During the republic the senate advised the consuls and the other magistrates. Because the senate sat year after year, while magistrates changed annually, it provided stability and continuity. It also served as a reservoir of experience and knowledge. Technically, the senate could not pass legislation; it could only offer its advice. But increasingly because of the senate's prestige its advice came to have the force of law.

The Romans created several assemblies through which the people elected magistrates and passed legislation. The earliest was the *comitia curiata,* which had religious, political, and military functions. According to Roman tradition, king Servius Tullius (578–535 B.C.), who reorganized the state into 193 centuries (military and political units) for military purposes, created the *comitia centuriata.* Since the patricians shouldered most of the burden of defense, they dominated the *comitia centuriata,* and could easily outvote the plebeians. In 471 B.C., the plebeians won the right to meet in an assembly of their own, the *concilium plebis,* and to pass ordinances. In 287 B.C., the bills passed in the concilium plebis were recognized as binding on the entire population, patrician and plebeian alike.

The chief magistrates of the republic were the two consuls, elected for one-year terms. At first the consulship was open only to the patricians. The consuls commanded the army in battle, administered state business, convened the comitia centuriata, and supervised financial affairs. In effect, they and the senate ran the state. The consuls appointed quaestors to assist them in their duties, and in 421 B.C. the quaestorship became an elective office open to the plebeians. The quaestors took charge of the public treasury and prosecuted criminals in the popular courts.

In 366 B.C., the Romans created a new office, that of praetor, and in 227 B.C. the number of praetors was increased to four. When the consuls were away from Rome, the praetor could act in their place. The praetor dealt primarily with the administration of justice. When he took office, the praetor issued a proclamation declaring the principles along which he would interpret the law. These proclamations became very important because they usually covered areas where the law was vague. Thus, they helped clarify the law.

The lowest officials were the aediles, four in number, who supervised streets and markets and presided over public festivals.

After the age of overseas conquest (pages 154–157), the Romans divided the Mediterranean area into provinces, which were governed by ex-consuls and ex-praetors. Because of their experience in Roman politics, they were well suited to administer the affairs of the provincials and to fit Roman law and custom into new contexts that they might encounter.

One of the most splendid achievements of the Romans was their development of law. Roman law began as a set of rules that regulated the lives and relations of citizens. This civil law, or *ius civile,* consisted of statutes, customs, and forms of procedure. Roman assemblies added to the body of law, and praetors interpreted it. The spirit of the law aimed at protecting the property, lives, and reputations of citizens, redressing wrongs, and giving satisfaction to the victims of injustice.

As the Romans came into more frequent contact with foreigners, they had to devise laws to deal with disputes between Romans and foreigners and between foreigners under Roman jurisdiction. In these instances, where there was no precedent to guide the Romans, the legal decisions of the praetors proved to be of immense importance. The praetors adopted aspects of other legal systems, and they resorted to the law of equity – what they thought was right and just to all parties. Thus, the praetors were in effect free to determine law, and they enjoyed a great deal of flexibility. This situation illustrates the practicality and the genius of the Romans. By addressing specific, actual circumstances the praetors developed a body of law, the *ius gentium,* that applied to Romans and foreigners and that laid the foundation for a universal conception of law. By the time of the late republic Roman jurists were reaching decisions on the basis of the Stoic concept of *ius naturale,* natural law, a universal law that could be applied to all societies.

## SOCIAL CONFLICT IN ROME

War was not the only aspect of Rome's early history. In Rome itself a great social conflict, usually known as the Struggle of the Orders, developed between the patricians and the plebeians. What the plebeians wanted was real political representation and safeguards against patrician domination. The efforts of the plebeians to obtain recognition of their rights is the crux of the Struggle of the Orders.

Rome's early wars gave the plebeians the leverage they needed: Rome's survival depended on the army, and the army needed the plebeians. The first showdown between the plebeians and the patricians came, according to tradition, in 494 B.C. To force the patricians to grant concessions, the plebeians seceded from the state; they literally walked out of Rome and refused to serve in the army. Livy tells how Menenius Agrippa, acting as spokesman for the senate, persuaded them to return by relating the story of the belly and the limbs.

Agrippa said that the limbs of the body once went on strike against the stomach because it did nothing but enjoy all the good things it received from the limbs. Yet the limbs found that by starving the stomach they also starved themselves. (In the same vein Benjamin Franklin once told the Founding Fathers that unless they all hung together they would all hang separately.) Livy's story is legend, but once again the legend preserves truth. The Struggle of the Orders was marked by hard bargaining, but also by compromise and concession. Throughout the conflict plebeian and patrician alike were sincerely concerned for the welfare of Rome. Only this true patriotism prevented the conflict from becoming civil war.

The general strike of the plebeians worked. Because of it the patricians made important concessions. They recognized the right of the plebeians to elect their own officials, the tribunes. The tribunes in turn had the right to protect the plebeians from the arbitrary conduct of patrician magistrates. The tribunes brought plebeian complaints and grievances to the senate for resolution. In 471 B.C., when the plebeians won the right to hold their own assembly, the concilium plebis, and to enact ordinances that concerned only themselves, the plebeians became a state within a state. This situation could have led to chaos, but Rome was not a house divided against itself. The plebeians were not bent on undermining the state. Rather, they used their gains only to win full equality under the law.

The law itself was the next target of the plebeians. Only the patricians knew what the law was, and only they could argue cases in court. All too often they had used the law for their own benefit. The plebeians wanted the law codified and published. The result of their agitation was the Law of the Twelve Tables, so called because the laws, which covered civil and criminal matters, were inscribed on large bronze plaques. Like Draco's law code, the Law of the Twelve Tables seems stiff and even harsh. For instance, Table IV commands, "A seriously deformed child should be quickly killed." Table VIII deals handily with slander: "If anyone has sung or composed a song which caused dishonor or disgrace to another, he should be beaten to death with clubs." But at least all Romans could learn their rights and guard against arbitrary judgments. Later still, the plebeians forced the patricians to publish legal procedures as well. They had broken the patricians' legal monopoly. Henceforth, they enjoyed full protection under the law.

The decisive plebeian victory came with the passage of the Licinian-Sextian rogations (or laws) in 367 B.C. Licinius and Sextus were two plebeian tribunes who led a ten-year fight for further reform. Rich plebeians, like Licinius and Sextus themselves, joined the poor to mount a sweeping assault on patrician privilege. Wealthy plebeians wanted the opportunity to provide political leadership for the state. They demanded that the patricians allow them access to all the magistracies of the state. If they could hold the consulship, they could also sit in the senate and advise the senate on policy. The two tribunes won approval from the senate for a law that stipulated that one of the two annual consuls had to be a plebeian.

Licinius and Sextus also protected the interests of the plebeian poor, those who owned little or no land and whose poverty had driven them into debt. These plebeians wanted access to public land so that they could make a new start. The two tribunes sponsored legislation that limited the amount of public land an individual could hold. This restriction struck hard at the patricians, many of whom had used large tracts of public land for their own profit. The new law allowed magistrates to parcel out land in small lots, which plebeians could claim and work for themselves.

The Struggle of the Orders resulted in a Rome stronger and better united than before. It could have led to anarchy, but again the Roman political genius triumphed. Resistance and confrontation never exploded into class warfare. Instead, both sides resorted to compromises to hammer out a realistic solution. Important too were Roman patience and tenacity – and a healthy sense of the practical. These qualities enabled both sides to keep working until they had resolved the crisis. The Struggle of the Orders ended in 367 B.C. with a new concept of Roman citizenship. All citizens shared equally under the law. Theoretically, all could aspire to the highest

# THE ROMAN REPUBLIC

| | |
|---|---|
| 509 B.C. | Expulsion of the Etruscan king and founding of the Roman republic |
| 471 B.C. | Plebians win official recognition of their assembly, the *concilium plebis* |
| ca 450 B.C. | Law of the Twelve Tables |
| 390 B.C. | The Gauls sack Rome |
| 390–290 B.C. | Rebuilding of Rome; reorganization of the army; Roman expansion in Italy |
| 367 B.C. | Licinian-Sextian rogations |
| 287 B.C. | Legislation of the *concilium plebis* made binding on entire population |
| 282–146 B.C. | The era of overseas conquest |
| 264–241 B.C. | First Punic War: Rome builds a navy, defeats Carthage, acquires Sicily |
| 218–202 B.C. | Second Punic War: Scipio defeats Hannibal; Rome dominates the western Mediterranean |
| 200–148 B.C. | Rome conquers the Hellenistic east |
| 149–146 B.C. | Third Punic War: savage destruction of Carthage |
| 133–121 B.C. | The Gracchi introduce land reform; murder of the Gracchi by some senators. |
| 107 B.C. | Marius becomes consul and begins the professionalization of the army. |
| 91–88 B.C. | War with Rome's Italian allies |
| 88 B.C. | Sulla marches on Rome and seizes dictatorship |
| 79 B.C. | Sulla abdicates |
| 78–27 B.C. | Era of civil war |
| 60–49 B.C. | First Triumvirate: Pompey, Crassus, Julius Caesar |
| 45 B.C. | Julius Caesar defeats Pompey's forces and becomes dictator |
| 44 B.C. | Assassination of Julius Caesar |
| 43–36 B.C. | Second Triumvirate: Marc Antony, Lepidus, Octavian |
| 31 B.C. | Octavian defeats Antony and Cleopatra at Actium |

political offices. Patrician or plebeian, rich or poor, Roman citizenship was equal for all.

## THE AGE OF OVERSEAS CONQUEST (282–146 B.C.)

In 282 B.C., Rome embarked on a series of wars that left it the ruler of the Mediterranean world. There was nothing ideological about these wars. Unlike Napoleon or Hitler, the Romans did not map out grandiose strategies for world conquest. In 282 B.C., they had no idea of what lay in store for them. If they could have looked into the future, they would have stood amazed. In many instances the Romans did not even initiate action; they simply responded to situations as they arose. Nineteenth-century Englishmen were fond of saying, "We got our empire in a fit of absence of mind." The Romans could not go quite that far. Even though they sometimes declared war reluctantly, they nonetheless felt the need to dominate, to eliminate any state that could threaten them.

Rome was imperialistic, and its imperialism took two forms. In the barbarian West, the home of fierce tribes, Rome resorted to bald aggression to conquer new territory. In areas like Spain, and later in Gaul, the fighting was fierce and savage, and gains came slowly. In the civilized East, the world of Hellenistic states, Rome tried to avoid annexing territory. The East was already heavily populated, and those people would have become Rome's responsibility. New responsibilities meant new problems, and such headaches the Romans shunned. In the East the Romans preferred to be patrons rather than masters. Only when that policy failed did they directly annex land. But in 282 B.C., all this lay in the future.

The Samnite wars had drawn the Romans into the political world of southern Italy. In 282 B.C., alarmed by the powerful newcomer, the Greek city of Tarentum in southern Italy called for help from Pyrrhus, king of Epirus in western Greece. A relative of Alexander the Great and an excellent general, Pyrrhus won two furious battles but suffered heavy casualties – thus the phrase "Pyrrhic victory" for a victory involving severe losses. Roman bravery and tenacity led him to comment: "If we win one more battle with the Romans, we'll be completely washed up." Against Pyrrhus's army the Romans threw new legions, and in the end Roman manpower proved decisive. In 275 B.C., the Romans drove Pyrrhus from Italy and extended their sway over southern Italy. Once they did, the island of Sicily became important to them.

Pyrrhus once described Sicily as a future "wrestling ground for the Carthaginians and Romans." The Phoenician city of Carthage, in North Africa (see Map 5.2), had for centuries dominated the western Mediterranean. Sicily had long been a Carthaginian target. Since Sicily is the steppingstone to Italy, the Romans could not let it fall to an enemy. In 264 B.C., Carthage and Rome came to blows over the city of Messina, which commanded the straits between Sicily and Italy. This conflict, the First Punic War, lasted for twenty-three years. The Romans quickly learned that they could not conquer Sicily unless they controlled the sea. Yet they lacked a fleet and hated the sea as fervently as cats hate water. Nevertheless, with grim resolution the Romans built a navy and challenged the Carthaginians at sea. The Romans fought seven major naval battles with the Carthaginians and won six. Twice their fleet went down in gales. But finally the Romans wore down the Carthaginians. In 241 B.C., the Romans de-

MODEL OF A ROMAN WARSHIP  *This rare ancient model was found off the southern coast of the Peloponnesus near Sparta. The bow of the warship is capped by a ram, behind which run the seats for the rowers. At the stern is the poop, the station of the officers and steersmen. (Photo: Caroline Buckler)*

feated them and took possession of Sicily, which became their first real province. Once again Rome's resources, manpower, and determination proved decisive.

The First Punic War was a beginning, not an end. Carthage was still a formidable enemy. After the First Punic War the Carthaginians expanded their power to Spain and turned the Iberian Peninsula into a rich field of operations. By 219 B.C., Carthage had found its avenger – Hannibal. In Spain, Hannibal learned how to lead armies and to wage war on a large scale. A brilliant general, he realized the advantages of swift mobile forces, and he was an innovator in tactics.

In 219 B.C., Hannibal defied the Romans by laying siege to the small city of Saguntum in Spain. When the Romans declared war the following year, he gathered his forces and led them on one of the most spectacular marches in ancient history. Hannibal carried the Second Punic War to the very gates of Rome. Starting in Spain, he led his troops – infantry,

cavalry, and elephants – over the Alps and into Italy on a march of more than a thousand miles. Once in Italy, he defeated one Roman army at the battle of Trebia and later another at the battle of Lake Trasimene in 217 B.C. At the battle of Cannae in 216 B.C. Hannibal inflicted some forty thousand casualties on the Romans. He spread devastation throughout Italy, but failed to crush Rome's iron circle of Latium, Etruria, and Samnium. The wisdom of Rome's political policy of extending rights and citizenship to its allies showed itself in these dark hours. Italy stood solidly with Rome against the invader. And Rome fought back.

The Roman general Scipio Africanus copied Hannibal's methods of mobile warfare. He streamlined the legions by making their components capable of independent action and by introducing new weapons. Scipio gave his new army combat experience in Spain, which he wrested from the Carthaginians. Meanwhile the Roman fleet dominated the western

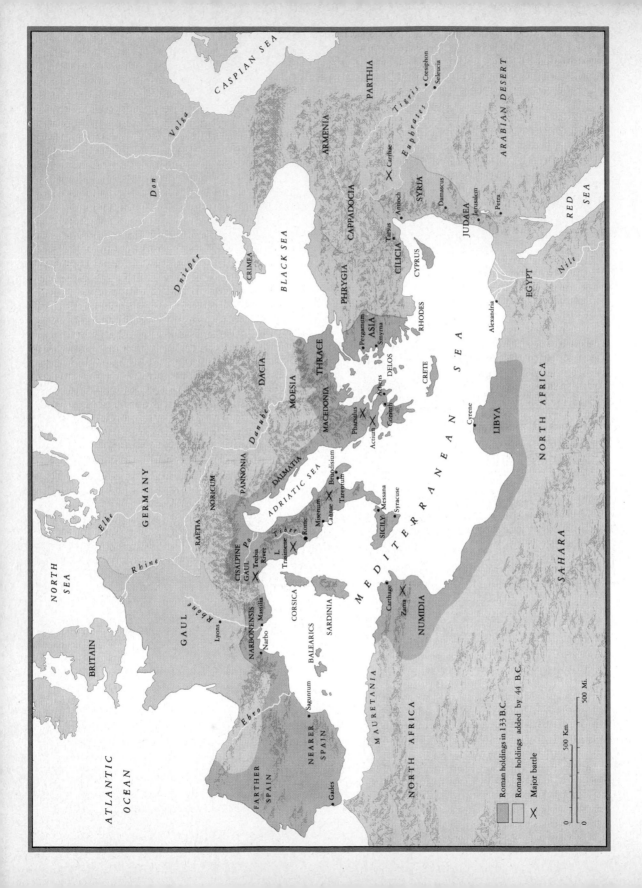

ATLANTIC OCEAN

NORTH SEA

BRITAIN

GERMANY

*Elbe*

*Rhine*

GAUL

*Rhone*

Lyons

RAETIA

NORICUM

PANNONIA

*Danube*

*Volga*

*Don*

*Dnieper*

CASPIAN SEA

CRIMEA

BLACK SEA

DACIA

MOESIA

THRACE

PARTHIA

ARMENIA

CAPPADOCIA

PHRYGIA

*Tigris*

*Euphrates*

Ctesiphon
Seleucia

ARABIAN DESERT

Carrhae ✕

SYRIA

Antioch

Damascus

Jerusalem
Petra

JUDAEA

RED SEA

CILICIA

Tarsus

CYPRUS

ASIA

Pergamum
Smyrna

RHODES

CRETE

DELOS

Athens

Corinth

Actium ✕

Pharsalus ✕

MACEDONIA

DALMATIA

ADRIATIC SEA

Brundisium ✕
Tarentum

EGYPT

*Nile*

Alexandria

Cyrene

LIBYA

NORTH AFRICA

MEDITERRANEAN SEA

SAHARA

CISALPINE
GAUL

*Po*

Trebia ✕
River

*Tiber*

Rome

L.
Trasimene

Cannae ✕

Misenum

SICILY

Messana
Syracuse

Carthage

Zama ✕

NUMIDIA

NORTH AFRICA

MAURETANIA

CORSICA

SARDINIA

BALEARICS

NARBONENSIS

Narbo

Massilia

*Ebro*

Saguntum

NEARER
SPAIN

FARTHER
SPAIN

Gades

Roman holdings in 133 B.C.

Roman holdings added by 44 B.C.

✕ Major battle

500 Km.

500 Mi.

0

0

MAP 5.2   ROMAN EXPANSION DURING THE
REPUBLIC   *The main spurt of Roman expansion occurred between 264 and 133 B.C., when most of the
Mediterranean fell to Rome, followed by the conquest
of Gaul and the eastern Mediterranean by 44 B.C.*

Mediterranean and interfered with Carthaginian attempts to reinforce Hannibal. In 204 B.C., the Roman fleet landed Scipio in Africa, which prompted the Carthaginians to recall Hannibal from Italy to defend the homeland.

In 202 B.C., near the town of Zama (see Map 5.2), Scipio Africanus defeated Hannibal in one of the world's truly decisive battles. Scipio's victory meant that the world of the western Mediterranean would henceforth be Roman. Roman language, law, and culture, fertilized by Greek influences, would in time permeate this entire region. The victory at Zama meant that Rome's heritage — not Carthage's — would be passed on to the Western world.

The Second Punic War contained the seeds of still other wars. Unabated fear of Carthage led to the Third Punic War, a needless, unjust, and savage conflict that ended in 146 B.C., when Scipio Aemilianus, grandson of Scipio Africanus, destroyed the old hated rival. As the Roman conqueror watched the death pangs of that great city, he turned to his friend Polybius with the words: "I fear and foresee that someday someone will give the same order about my fatherland." It would, however, be centuries before an invader would stand before the gates of Rome.

During the war with Hannibal the Romans had invaded Spain, a peninsula rich in material resources and the home of fierce warriors. When the Roman legions tried to reduce Spanish tribesmen, they met with bloody and determined resistance. Not until 133 B.C., after years of brutal and ruthless warfare, did Scipio Aemilianus finally conquer Spain.

When the Romans intervened in the Hellenistic East, they went from triumph to triumph. The Romans dealt with the Greeks in a civilized fashion. There were hard-fought battles in the East, but the bloodletting and carnage that marked the battles in the West were not repeated in the cultured East. Even so, the results were essentially the same. The kingdom of Macedonia fell to the Roman legions, as did Greece and the Seleucid monarchy. By 146 B.C., the Romans stood unchallenged in the eastern Mediterranean, and they had turned many states and kingdoms into provinces. In 133 B.C., the king of Pergamum in Asia Minor left his kingdom to the Romans in his will. The Ptolemies of Egypt meekly obeyed Roman wishes. The following years would bring the Romans new victories, and they would establish their system of provincial administration. But by 146 B.C., the work of conquest was largely done. The Romans had turned the entire Mediterranean basin into *mare nostrum* — "our sea."

## OLD VALUES AND GREEK CULTURE

Rome had conquered the Mediterranean world, but some Romans considered that victory a misfortune. The historian Sallust (86–34 B.C.), writing from hindsight, complained that the acquisition of an empire was the beginning of Rome's troubles:

*But when through labor and justice our Republic grew powerful, great kings defeated in war, fierce nations and mighty peoples subdued by force, when Carthage the rival of the Roman people was wiped out root and branch, all the seas and lands lay open, then fortune began to be harsh and to throw everything into confusion. The Romans had easily*

BATTLE BETWEEN THE ROMANS AND THE GAULS  All the brutality and fury of Rome's wars with the barbarians of western Europe come to life in this Roman sarcophagus of 225 B.C. Even the bravery and strength of the Gauls were no match for the steadiness and discipline of the Roman legions. (Alinari/ Scala)

*borne labor, danger, uncertainty, and hardship. To them leisure, riches — otherwise desirable — proved to be burdens and torments. So at first money, then desire for power grew great. These things were a sort of cause of all evils.*[5]

Sallust was not alone in his feelings. At the time, some senators had opposed the destruction of Carthage on the grounds that fear of their old rival would keep the Romans in check. Did Rome gain the whole world only to lose its soul? Sallust obviously thought so, and he could have made a good case. It is true that the new empire provided many Romans with golden opportunities to amass fortunes wrung from the conquered. It is true that numerous generals, provincial governors, and other magistrates oppressed the vanquished for their personal gain. But it is also true that Rome continued to produce patriotic, noble, and hard-working men and women, just as it had in the past. Rome did not suddenly become weak and evil, but Roman society was

undergoing a fundamental change. In the process, Rome's early period became sentimentalized as the "good old days," a golden age of virtue the early Romans themselves would never have recognized.

In the second century B.C., Romans learned that they could not return to what they fondly considered a simple life. They were world rulers. The responsibilities they faced were complex and awesome. They had to change their institutions, their social patterns, and their way of thinking to meet the new era. They were in fact building the foundations of a great imperial system. It was an awesome challenge, and there were failures along the way. Roman generals and politicians would destroy each other. Even the republican constitution would eventually be discarded. But in the end Rome triumphed here just as it had on the battlefield, for out of the turmoil would come the pax Romana — the Roman peace.

How did the Romans of the day meet these

challenges? How did they lead their lives and cope with these momentous changes? Obviously, there are as many answers to these questions as there were Romans. Yet two men can be taken to represent the major trends of the second century B.C. Cato the Elder shared the mentality of those who longed for the good old days and idealized the traditional agrarian way of life. Scipio Aemilianus led those who embraced the new urban life with its eager acceptance of Greek culture. Forty-nine years older than Scipio, Cato was a product of an earlier generation, one that confronted a rapidly changing world. Cato and Scipio were both aristocrats and neither of them was typical, even of the aristocracy. But they do exemplify opposing sets of attitudes that marked Roman society and politics in the age of conquest.

### CATO AND THE TRADITIONAL IDEAL

Marcus Cato was born a plebeian, but his talent and energy carried him to Rome's highest offices. He cherished the old virtues and consistently imitated the old ways. Cato had inherited an estate north of Rome and began his career as a man of moderate means. Near his estate were the fields and cottage of Manius Curius, the general who had driven Pyrrhus from Italy forty years before Cato was born. Curius had been another Cincinnatus; although Curius had held the consulship and commanded armies, he worked his small farm alone. He once refused a large bribe, saying that a man of his simple tastes did not need gold. It was the example of Curius that Cato constantly held before his eyes.

In Roman society ties within the family were very strong. In this sense Cato and his family were typical. Cato was *paterfamilias,* a term that meant far more than merely "father." The paterfamilias was the oldest

dominant male of the family. He held nearly absolute power over the lives of his wife and children so long as he lived. He could legally kill his wife for adultery or divorce her at will. He could kill his children or sell them into slavery. He could force them to marry against their will. Until the paterfamilias died, his sons could not legally own property. At his death, his wife and children inherited his property.

Despite his immense power, the paterfamilias did not necessarily act alone or arbitrarily. To deal with important family matters he usually called a council of the adult males. In this way the leading members of the family aired their views. They had the opportunity to give their support to the paterfamilias or to dissuade him from harsh decisions. In these councils the women of the family had no formal part, but it can safely be assumed that they played an important behind-the-scenes role. Although the possibility of serious conflicts between a paterfamilias and his grown sons is obvious, no one in ancient Rome ever complained about the institution. Perhaps in practice the paterfamilias preferred to be lenient rather than absolute.

Cato's wife (whose name is unknown) was the matron of the family, a position of authority and respect. The virtues expected of a Roman matron were those of Lucretia, a legendary figure from the early republic. According to Livy's account, the son of the last Etruscan king wanted to sleep with Lucretia. One night while her husband was away, the king's son slipped into her room and tried to seduce her. When she refused him, he threatened to kill her and then he raped her. When he had gone, Lucretia sent for her father and husband and told them the whole story. They tried to console her, telling her that she had been helpless and was free from any shame. Her answer was short: "Never shall Lucretia

ROMAN SCHOOL    Seated between two students with scrolls in their hands, the teacher discusses a point with the student on his left. To his far left, a tardy pupil arrives, lunchbox in hand. Roman education, even in the provinces, lasted well into late antiquity, and was a cultural legacy to the medieval world. (Landesmuseum Trier)

provide a precedent for unchaste women to escape what they deserve." She demanded vengeance, the death of the king's son. Then, innocent though she was, she drew a knife and killed herself. Clearly, Lucretia was the ideal, but numerous funerary inscriptions testify that the virtues of chastity and modesty were highly valued. The tribute of one husband to his wife is typical of many:

*Here is laid a woman dutiful, temperate, pure, chaste, Sempronia Moschis, to whom thanks are returned by her husband for her merits.*[6]

Like most Romans, Cato and his family began the day early in the morning. The Romans divided the period of daylight into twelve hours and the darkness into another twelve. The day might begin as early as half past four in summer, as late as half past seven in winter. Because Mediterranean summers are invariably hot, the farmer and his wife liked to take every advantage of the cool mornings. Cato and his family, like modern Italians, ordinarily started the morning with a light breakfast, usually nothing more than some bread and cheese. After breakfast the family went about its work.

Because of his political aspirations Cato often used the mornings to plead law cases. He walked to the marketplace of the nearby town and defended anyone who wished his help. He received no fees for these services, but did put his neighbors in his debt. In matters of law and politics Roman custom was very strong. It demanded that Cato's clients give him their political support or their votes in repayment whenever he asked for them. These clients knew and accepted their obligations to Cato for his help.

Cato's wife shared her husband's love for the old ways. While he was in town, she ran the household. She spent the morning spinning and weaving wool for the clothes they wore. She supervised the domestic slaves, planned the meals, and devoted a good deal of attention to her son. In wealthy homes during this period the matron had begun to employ a slave as a wet nurse. Cato's wife refused to delegate her maternal duties. Like most ordinary Roman women, she nursed her son herself. She also bathed and swaddled him daily. Later, the boy was allowed to play with toys and terra-cotta dolls. Roman children, like children everywhere, kept pets. Dogs were especially popular, and they were valuable as house guards. Children played all sorts of games, and games of chance were very popular. Until the age of seven the child was under the matron's care. During this time the mother began to educate her daughter in the management of the household. After the age of seven, the son — and in many wealthy households the daughter too — began formal education.

In the country, Romans like Cato continued to take their main meal at midday. This meal included either coarse bread made from the entire husk of wheat or porridge made with milk or water; it also included turnips, cabbage, olives, and beans. When Romans ate meat, they preferred pork. Unless they lived by the sea, the average farm family did not eat fish, which was an expensive delicacy. Cato once complained that Rome was a place where a fish could cost more than a cow. With the midday meal the family drank an ordinary wine mixed with water. Afterward any Roman who could took a nap. This was especially true in the summer, when the Mediterranean heat can be fierce. Slaves, artisans, and hired laborers, however, went about their work. In the evening the Romans ate a light meal and went to bed about nightfall.

The agricultural year followed the sun and the stars; they were the farmer's calendar. Like Hesiod in Boeotia, the Roman farmer looked to the sky to determine when to plant, weed, shear sheep, and perform other chores. Varro (116–27 B.C.), one of the most famous writers on agriculture, did everything by the sun and stars. He advised farmers in Italy to harvest their grain crops between the summer solstice and the rising of the Dog Star. He suggested that they sow at the setting of the Pleiades. Varro's book on agriculture owed much to Hellenistic Greek manuals, but it also reflected actual Roman practice. Besides, the farmer could not depend on the civil calendar. The lunar year is 354 days long, and the solar year is 365¼ days long. So the civil calendar had to be adjusted to both lunar and solar years. To make matters worse, politicans often tampered with the calendar. In 46 B.C., when Julius Caesar reformed the civil calendar, it was some 2½ months out of step with the solar year. Obviously, farmers had to depend on something more reliable than this. Their solution was the sun, moon, and stars.

Spring was the season for plowing. Roman farmers plowed their land at least twice and preferably three times. The third plowing was to cover the sown seed in ridges and to use the furrows to drain off excess water. The Romans used a variety of plows. Some had detachable shares. Some were heavy for thick soil, others light for thin, crumbly soil. Farmers used oxen and donkeys to pull the plow. They collected the dung of their animals for fertilizer. Besides spreading manure, some farmers fertilized their fields by planting lupines and beans; when they began to pod, farmers plowed them under. The main money crops, at least for rich soils, were wheat and flax. Forage crops included clover, vetch, and alfalfa. Prosperous farmers like Cato raised olive trees chiefly for the oil. They also raised grapevines for the production of wine. Cato and his neighbors harvested their cereal crops in summer and their grapes in autumn. Harvests varied depending on the soil, but farmers could usually expect yields of 5½ bushels of wheat or 10½ bushels of barley per acre.

*MANUMISSION OF SLAVES    During the Republic
some Roman masters began to free slaves in public
ceremonies. Here two slaves come before their master or
a magistrate, who is in the process of freeing the
kneeling slave by touching him with a manumission-
rod. The other slave shows his gratitude and his good
faith with a handshake. (Collection Waroque, Marie-
mont, Belgium. © A. C. L. Brussels)*

In the early republic the master of the
household worked the farm himself. By the
second century B.C., however, Cato was noticeably old-fashioned because he stripped to
the waist in summer and sweated alongside
his slaves and day laborers.

An influx of slaves resulted from Rome's
wars and conquests. Prisoners from Spain,
Africa, and the Hellenistic East, and even
some blacks from Hannibal's army, came to

Rome as the spoils of war. The Roman attitude toward slaves and slavery had little in
common with modern views. To the Romans
slavery was a misfortune that befell some
people. But slavery did not entail any racial
theories. Races were not enslaved because the
Romans thought them inferior. The black
African slave was treated no worse – and no
better – than the Spaniard. Indeed, some slaves
were valued because of their physical distinctiveness: black Africans and blond Germans were particular favorites. For the
talented slave, the Romans always held out
the hope of eventual freedom. Manumission
– the freeing of individual slaves by their
masters – became so common that it had to
be limited by law. Not even Christians questioned the institution of slavery. It was just a
fact of life.

Slaves were entirely the property of their
master, and they might be treated with great
cruelty. Many Romans were practical enough
to realize that they got more out of their
slaves by kindness than by severity. Yet in Sicily slave owners treated their slaves viciously.
They bought slaves in huge numbers, branded
them for identification, put them in irons, and
often made them go without food and clothing. In 135 B.C., these conditions gave rise to a
major slave revolt, during which many of the
most brutal masters died at the hands of their
slaves. Italy too had trouble with slave unrest,
but conditions there were generally better
than in Sicily.

Cato urged his countrymen to treat slaves
humanely. Varro suggested that masters
should control slaves with knowledge and not
with whips. Yet even Cato could be hard-
hearted. Although he worked and ate with his
slaves, he never forgot their money value.
When they grew too old to work, he sold
them to save the expense of feeding them.

Not all Romans were Catos, though. Between many slaves and masters there developed genuine bonds of affection. On numerous occasions slaves risked or gave their lives to protect kind masters.

Part of the reason for such good relations probably stems from the fact that many slaves came from the Hellenistic East. They were certainly not barbarians. Many of them were more cultured than their owners. Greek male slaves frequently became the tutors of the master's children. These men especially were likely to receive their freedom. Slaves who gained their freedom also became Roman citizens. Freedmen and freedwomen often continued to live with their previous owners. And it was not unusual for Romans to permit their ex-slaves to be buried with them.

For Cato and most other Romans, religion played an important part in life. Originally, the Romans thought of the gods as invisible and shapeless natural forces. Only through Etruscan and Greek influence did Roman deities take on human form. Jupiter, the sky god, and his wife Juno became equivalent to the Greek Zeus and Hera. Mars was the god of war, but he was also the god who guaranteed the fertility of the farm and protected it from danger. Cato habitually sacrificed a pig, a ram, and a bull to Mars to obtain his help and protection. Cato or one of his farmhands led the animals around the boundaries of the farm and then called upon Mars the Father

*that you hold back, repel, and turn away disease seen and unseen, blight and devastation; that you allow my crops, grain, vines, and thickets to increase and flourish; that you keep my shepherd and flocks safe; that you watch over and give good health and strength to me, my house, and household.*[7]

Cato then sacrificed the animals to Mars and offered the god small cakes. The Romans used a similar ritual, the Robigalia, to protect the grain crops from mildew. The Robigalia later gave rise to the Christian practice of purifying farms on Rogation Days, when the priest and his congregation marched in procession around the farms while calling upon Jesus and the saints for protection. Cato would have approved.

These two religious practices are illustrative of Roman religion in general. The gods of the Romans were not loving and personal. They were stern, powerful, and aloof. But as long as the Romans honored the cults of their gods, they could expect divine favor.

Along with the great gods the Romans believed in spirits who haunted fields, forests, crossroads, and even the home itself. Some of these deities were hostile, and only magic could ward them off. The spirits of the dead, like ghosts in modern horror films, frequented the places where they had lived. They too had to be placated, but they were ordinarily benign. As the poet Ovid (43 B.C.–A.D. 17) put it:

*The spirits of the dead ask for little.*
*They are more grateful for piety than for an expensive gift —*
*Not greedy are the gods who haunt the Styx below.*
*A rooftile covered with a sacrificial crown,*
*Scattered kernels, a few grains of salt,*
*Bread dipped in wine, and loose violets —*
*These are enough.*
*Put them in a potsherd and leave them in the middle of the road.*[8]

A good deal of Roman religion consisted of such rituals as those Ovid describes. These practices lived on long after the Romans had lost interest in the great gods. Even Christianity could not entirely wipe them out. Instead, Christianity was to incorporate many of these rituals into its own style of worship.

## SCIPIO: GREEK CULTURE AND URBAN LIFE

The old-fashioned ideals that Cato represented came into conflict with a new spirit of wealth and leisure. The conquest of the Mediterranean world and the spoils of war made Rome a great city. Some, like the historian Velleius Paterculus (first century A.D.), viewed these developments with distaste:

*Scipio Africanus opened the way for Roman power. Scipio Aemilianus opened the way for luxury. Indeed, when Rome was free of the fear of Carthage, and its rival in empire was removed, Rome fell, not gradually but in headlong course, from virtue towards vice. The old discipline was deserted and the new introduced. The state turned from vigilance to sleep, from military affairs to pleasures, from work to leisure.*[9]

Roman life, especially in the cities, *was* changing and becoming less austere. The spoils of war went to the building of baths, theaters, and other places of amusement. Romans and Italian townsmen began to spend more of their time in leisure pursuits. But simultaneously the new responsibilities of governing the world produced in Rome a sophisticated society. Romans developed new tastes and a liking for Greek culture and literature. They began to learn the Greek language. It became common for an educated Roman to speak both Latin and Greek. Hellenism dominated the cultural life of Rome. Even diehards like Cato found a knowledge of Greek essential for political and diplomatic affairs. The poet Horace (64–8 B.C.) summed it up well: "Captive Greece captured her rough conqueror and introduced the arts into rustic Latium."

One of the most avid devotees of Hellenism and the new was Scipio Aemilianus, the destroyer of Carthage. Scipio was also the man whom Velleius had accused of introducing luxury into Rome. Scipio realized that broad and worldly views had to replace the old Roman narrowness. The new situation called for new ways. Rome was no longer a small city on the Tiber; it was the capital of the world, and Romans had to adapt themselves to that fact. Scipio was ready to become an innovator both in politics and culture. He broke with the past in the conduct of his political career. He embraced Hellenism wholeheartedly. Perhaps more than anyone else of his day, Scipio represented the new Roman – imperial, cultured, and independent.

Scipio even dared to be independent in his political career, which differed from that of traditional politicians. He set out on a course of personal politics, determined to carve out a career for himself on the strength of his own merits. In doing so he set an example for future politicians. One of the most successful of Scipio's imitators would be Julius Caesar.

In his education and interests, too, Scipio broke with the past. As a boy, he had received the traditional Roman training, learning to read and write Latin and becoming acquainted with the law. He mastered the fundamentals of rhetoric and learned how to throw the javelin, fight in armor, and ride a horse. But later Scipio also learned Greek and became a fervent Hellenist. As a young man he formed a lasting friendship with the historian Polybius, who actively encouraged him in his study of Greek culture and in his intellectual pursuits. In later life Scipio's love of Greek learning, rhetoric, and philosophy became legendary. Scipio also promoted the spread of Hellenism in Roman society. He became the center of the Scipionic Circle, a small group of Greek and Roman artists, philosophers, historians, and poets. Conservatives like Cato tried to stem the rising tide of Hellenism, but men like Scipio carried the day and helped make the heritage of Greece an abiding factor in Roman life.

The new Hellenism profoundly stimulated the growth and development of Roman art and literature. The Roman conquest of the Hellenistic East resulted in wholesale confiscation of Greek paintings and sculpture to grace Roman temples, public buildings, and private homes. Roman artists copied many aspects of Greek art, but their emphasis on realistic portraiture carried on a native tradition.

Fabius Pictor (second half of the third century B.C.), a senator, wrote the first *History of Rome* in Greek. Other Romans translated Greek classics into Latin. Still others, like the poet Ennius (239-169 B.C.), the father of Latin poetry, studied Greek philosophy, wrote comedies in Latin, and adapted many of Euripides' tragedies for the Roman stage. Ennius also wrote a history of Rome in Latin verse. Plautus (ca 254-184 B.C.) specialized in rough humor. He too decked out Greek plays in Roman dress, but was no mere imitator. Indeed, his play *Amphitruo* was itself copied eighteen hundred years later by the French playwright Molière and the English poet John Dryden. The Roman dramatist Terence (ca 195-159 B.C.), a member of the Scipionic Circle, wrote comedies of refinement and grace that owed their essentials to Greek models. His plays lacked the energy and the slapstick of Plautus's rowdy plays. All of early Roman literature was derived from the Greeks, but it managed in time to speak in its own voice and to flourish because it had something of its own to say.

The conquest of the Mediterranean world brought the Romans leisure, and Hellenism influenced how they spent their free time. During the second century B.C., the Greek custom of bathing became a Roman passion and an important part of the day. In the early republic Romans had bathed infrequently, especially in the winter. Now large buildings containing pools and exercise rooms went up in great numbers, and the baths became an essential part of the Roman city. Architects built intricate systems of aqueducts to supply the bathing establishments with water. Conservatives railed at this Greek custom too, calling it a waste of time and an encouragement to idleness. The conservatives were correct in that bathing establishments were more than just places to take a bath. They included gymnasia, where men exercised and played ball. Women had places of their own to bathe, generally sections of the same baths used by men; for some reason, women's facilities lacked gymnasia. The baths contained hot-air rooms to induce a good sweat and pools of hot and cold water to finish the actual bathing. They also contained snack bars and halls where people chatted and read. The baths were socially important places where men and women went to see and be seen: social climbers tried to talk to "the right people" and wangle invitations to dinner; politicians took advantage of the occasion to discuss the affairs of the day. Despite the protests of conservatives and moralists, the baths at least provided people – rich and poor – with places for clean and healthy relaxation.

This period also saw a change in the eating habits of urban dwellers. The main meal of the day shifted from midday to evening. Dinner became a more elaborate meal and dinner parties became fashionable. Although Scipio Aemilianus detested fat people, more and more Romans began to eat excessively. Rich men and women displayed their wealth by serving exotic dishes and gourmet foods. After a course of vegetables and olives came the main course of meat, fish, or fowl. Pig was a favorite dish, and a whole suckling pig might be stuffed with sausage. A lucky guest might even dine on peacock and ostrich, each

*BATHS OF CARACALLA   Once introduced into the Roman world, social bathing became a passion. These baths, which date to the Roman Empire, are the ultimate development of sophistication and size. (Italian Government Travel Office)*

served with rich sauces. Dessert, as in Italy today, usually consisted of fruit. With the meal the Romans served wine, and during this period vintage wines became very popular. Household slaves sometimes read poetry or performed music during the meal. People of more vulgar tastes hired jesters. Dwarves were in great demand, and the evening's entertainment consisted of buffoonery and coarse jokes. After dinner the party drank wine and talked, often late into the night.

Although the wealthy gorged themselves whenever they could, poor artisans and workers could rarely afford rich meals. Their dinners resembled Cato's. Yet they too occasionally spent generously on food, especially during the major festivals. The Roman calendar was crowded with religious festivals, occasions not of dreary piety but of cheerful celebration. One such was the festival of Anna Perenna, a festival of fertility, longevity, and prosperity. It was an occasion for fun and exuberant but harmless excess. The poet Ovid caught all the joy and charm of the event in these lines:

*The ordinary people come [to the banks of the Tiber];*
*    And scattering themselves over the green grass,*
*They drink and lie down, each man with his woman.*
*Some remain under the open sky, a few put up tents,*
*    Others build leafy huts of twigs.*
*Some set up reeds instead of unbending columns,*
*    Over which they spread their togas.*
*Yet they grow warm with sun and wine, and pray*
*    For as many years as cups of wine they take, and they drink that many.*

· · · · · · · · · · · ·

*There also they sing the songs they have heard in*
*the theaters,*
*And they beat time to the words with lively*
*hands.*
*Putting down the bowl, they join in rough ring*
*dances,*
*And the trim girlfriend dances with her hair*
*flying.*
*As they return home, they stagger and are a spec-*
*tacle to the vulgar.*
*When meeting them, the crowd calls them*
*blessed.*
*The procession came my way recently (a worthy*
*sight in my opinion):*
*A drunk woman dragged along a drunk old*
*man.* [10]

Robust religious festivals and a decided love
of good food and drink were characteristics of
the average Roman, whether rich or poor.

Did Hellenism and the new social customs
corrupt the Romans? Perhaps the best answer
is simply this: the Roman state and the empire it ruled continued to exist for six more
centuries. Rome did not collapse; the state
continued to prosper. The golden age of literature was still before it. The high tide of its
prosperity still lay in the future. The Romans
did not like change, but they took it in stride.
That was part of their practical turn of mind
and part of their genius.

## THE LATE REPUBLIC (133–27 B.C)

The wars of conquest created serious problems for the Romans, some of the most
pressing of which were political. The republican constitution had suited the needs of a
simple city-state, but it was inadequate to
meet the requirements of Rome's new position in international affairs (see Map 5.2).

Sweeping changes and reforms were necessary
to make it serve the demands of empire. A
whole system of provincial administration
had to be established. Officials had to be
appointed to govern the provinces and to
administer the law. These officials and
administrative organs had to find places
within the constitution. Armies had to be
provided to defend the provinces, and a system of tax collection had to be created.

Other political problems were equally serious. During the wars Roman generals commanded huge numbers of troops for long
periods of time. Men such as Scipio Aemilianus were on the point of becoming too
mighty for the state to control. Although
Rome's Italian allies had borne much of the
burden of the fighting, they received fewer
rewards than did Roman officers and soldiers.
Italians began to agitate for full Roman citizenship and a voice in politics.

There were serious economic problems too.
Hannibal's operations and the warfare in Italy
had left the countryside a shambles. The
movements of numerous armies had disrupted
agriculture. The prolonged fighting had also
drawn untold numbers of Roman and Italian
men away from their farms for long periods.
The families of these soldiers could not keep
the land under full cultivation. The people
who defended Rome and conquered the world
for Rome became impoverished for having
done their duty.

These problems, complex and explosive,
largely account for the turmoil of the closing
years of the republic. The late republic was
one of the most dramatic eras in Roman history. It produced some of Rome's most
famous figures: Marius, Sulla, Cicero, Pompey, and Julius Caesar, among others. In one
way or another each of these men attempted
to solve Rome's problems.

When the legionaries returned to their

farms in Italy, they encountered an appalling situation. All too often their farms looked like the farms of people they had conquered. Two courses of action were open to them. They could rebuild as their forefathers had done. Or they could take advantage of an alternative not open to their ancestors: they could sell their holdings. The wars of conquest had made some men astoundingly rich. These men wanted to invest their wealth in land. They bought up small farms to create huge estates, which the Romans called latifundia.

The purchase offers of the rich landowners appealed to the veterans for a variety of reasons. Many veterans had seen service in the East, where they had tasted the rich city life of the Hellenistic states. They were reluctant to return home and settle down to a dull life on the farm. Often their farms were so badly damaged that rebuilding hardly seemed worth the effort. Besides, it was hard to make big profits from small farms. Nor could the veterans supplement their income by working on the latifundia. Although the owners of the latifundia occasionally hired free men as day laborers, they preferred to use slaves to work their land. Slaves could not strike, and they could not be drafted into the army. Confronted by these conditions, veterans and their families opted to sell their land. They took what they could get for their broken farms and tried their luck elsewhere.

Most veterans migrated to the cities, especially to Rome. Although some found work, most did not. Industry and small manufacturing were generally in the hands of slaves. Even when there was work, slave labor kept the wages of free men low. Instead of a new start, veterans and their families encountered slum conditions that matched those of modern American cities. Sanitation was virtually non-existent. Housing was frequently shabby and

structurally unsound, but expensive nonetheless. Fire and police protection were unknown. These conditions were especially prevalent in Rome and some larger cities. Within a brief period of time Rome became the home of a large body of urban poor.

This trend held ominous consequences for the strength of Rome's armies. The Romans had always believed that only landowners should serve in the army, for only they had something to fight for. Landless men, even if they were Romans and lived in Rome, could not be conscripted into the army. These landless men may have been veterans of major battles and numerous campaigns; they may have won distinction on the battlefield. But once they sold their land they became ineligible for further military service. A large pool of experienced manpower was going to waste. The landless ex-legionaries wanted a new start, and they were willing to support any leader who would provide it.

One man who recognized the plight of Rome's peasant farmers and urban poor was an aristocrat, Tiberius Gracchus (163–133 B.C.). Appalled by what he saw, Tiberius warned his countrymen that the legionaries were losing their land even while fighting Rome's wars:

*The wild beasts that roam over Italy have every one of them a cave or lair to lurk in. But the men who fight and die for Italy enjoy the common air and light, indeed, but nothing else. Houseless and homeless they wander about with their wives and children. And it is with lying lips that their generals exhort the soldiers in their battles to defend sepulchres and shrines from the enemy, for not a man of them has an hereditary altar, not one of all these many Romans an ancestral tomb, but they fight and die to support others in luxury, and though they are styled masters of the world, they have not a single clod of earth that is their own.*[11]

Until his death, Tiberius Gracchus sought a solution to the problems of the veterans and the urban poor.

After his election as tribune of the people, Tiberius in 133 B.C. proposed that public land be given to the poor in small lots. His was an easy and sensible plan, but it angered many wealthy and noble people who had usurped large tracts of public land for their own use. They had no desire to give any of it back, and they bitterly resisted Tiberius's efforts. Violence broke out in Rome when a large body of senators killed Tiberius in cold blood. It was a black day in Roman history. The very people who directed the affairs of state and administered the law had taken the law into their own hands. The death of Tiberius was the beginning of an era of political violence. In the end that violence would bring down the republic.

Although Tiberius was dead, his land bill became law. Furthermore, Tiberius's brother Gaius (153–121 B.C.) took up the cause of reform. Gaius was a veteran soldier with an enviable record, but this fiery orator made his mark in the political arena. Gaius also became tribune, and demanded even more extensive reform than had his brother. To help the urban poor Gaius pushed legislation to provide them with cheap grain for bread. He defended his brother's land law and suggested other measures for helping the landless. He proposed that Rome send many of its poor and propertyless people out to form colonies in southern Italy. The poor would have a new start and could lead productive lives. The city of Rome would immediately benefit because excess and nonproductive families would leave for new opportunities abroad. Rome would be less crowded, sordid, and dangerous.

Gaius went a step further and urged that all Italians be granted full rights of Roman citizenship. This measure provoked a storm of opposition, and it was not passed in Gaius's

*UNUSUAL ROMAN HELMET   Not standard issue, this metal helmet is a craftsman's masterpiece. The helmet itself is decorated with battle scenes and originally probably bore a crest. The molded face is actually a hinged visor. (Reproduced by Courtesy of the Trustees of the British Museum)*

lifetime. Yet in the long run he proved wiser than his opponents. In 91 B.C., many Italians revolted against Rome over the issue of full citizenship. After a brief but hard-fought war the senate gave Roman citizenship to all Italians. Had the senate listened to Gaius earlier, it could have prevented a great deal of bloodshed. Instead, reactionary senators rose against Gaius and murdered him and three thousand of his supporters. Once again the cause of reform had met with violence. Once again it was Rome's leading citizens who flouted the law.

More trouble for Rome came from an unexpected source. In 112 B.C., war broke out in North Africa, when a Numidian king named Jugurtha rebelled against Rome. The Roman legions made little headway against him until 107 B.C., when Gaius Marius, an Italian "new man" (a politician not from the traditional Roman aristocracy), became consul. Marius's values were those of the military camp. A man of fierce vigor and courage, Marius saw the army as the tool of his ambition. To prepare for the war with Jugurtha, Marius reformed the Roman army. He was the first Roman officer to recruit an army by permitting landless men to serve in the legions. Marius thus tapped Rome's vast reservoir of idle manpower. His volunteer army was a professional force, not a body of draftees. Marius also reorganized the Roman legion into smaller units, called cohorts, which made the legion more mobile and flexible. He rearmed the legion by making the sword and javelin the standard weapons of the legionaries.

There was, however, a disturbing side to Marius's reforms, one that would henceforth haunt the republic. To encourage enlistments, Marius promised land to his volunteers after the war. Poor and landless veterans flocked to him, and together they handily defeated Jugurtha. When Marius proposed a bill to grant land to his veterans, the senate refused to act, in effect turning its back on the soldiers of Rome. This was a disastrous mistake. Henceforth, the legionaries expected their commanders – not the senate or the state – to protect their interests. Through Marius's reforms the Roman army became a professional force, but it owed little allegiance to the state. By failing to reward the loyalty of Rome's troops, the senate set the stage for military rebellion and political anarchy.

Nor was trouble long in coming. The senate's refusal to honor Marius's promises to his soldiers, and the brief but bitter war between the Romans and their Italian allies (91–88 B.C.), set off serious political disturbances in Rome. In 88 B.C., the Roman general and conqueror Sulla marched on Rome with his army to put an end to the turmoil. Sulla made himself dictator – a far cry from Cincinnatus's dictatorship. He put his enemies to death and confiscated their land. The constitution thus disrupted was never effectively put back together.

In 79 B.C. Sulla voluntarily abdicated as dictator and permitted the republican constitution to function normally once again. Yet his dictatorship cast a long shadow over the late republic. Sulla the political reformer proved far less influential than Sulla the successful general and dictator. Civil war was to be the constant lot of Rome for the next fifty years, until the republican constitution gave way to the empire of Augustus in 27 B.C. The history of the late republic is the story of the power struggles of some of Rome's most famous figures: Julius Caesar and Pompey, Augustus and Marc Antony. One figure who stands apart is Cicero (106–43 B.C.), a practical politician whose greatest legacy to the Roman world and to Western civilization is his mass of political and oratorical writings.

Pompous, vain, and sometimes silly, Cicero was nonetheless one of the few men of the period to urge peace and public order. As consul in 63 B.C. he put down a conspiracy against the republic, but he refused to use force to win political power. Instead, he developed the idea of "concord of the orders," an idealistic and probably unattainable balance among the elements that constituted the Roman state. A truly brilliant master of Latin prose and undoubtedly Rome's finest orator, Cicero used his vast literary ability to promote political and social reforms and to explore the underlying principles of statecraft. Yet Cicero commanded no legions, and only legions commanded respect.

In the late republic the Romans were grappling with the simple and inescapable fact that their old city-state constitution was unequal to the demands of overseas possessions and the problems of governing provinces. Thus even Sulla's efforts to put the constitution back together again proved hollow. Once the senate and the other institutions of the Roman state had failed to come to grips with the needs of empire, once the authorities had lost control of their own generals and soldiers, and once the armies put their faith in their commanders instead of in Rome, the republic was doomed.

Sulla's real political heirs were Pompey and Julius Caesar, who realized that the days of the old republican constitution were numbered. Pompey, a man of boundless ambition, began his career as one of Sulla's lieutenants. After his army put down a rebellion in Spain, he himself threatened to rebel unless the senate allowed him to run for consul. He and another ambitious politician, Crassus, pooled their political resources and both won the consulship. They dominated Roman politics until the rise of Julius Caesar, who became consul in 59 B.C. Together the three concluded a political alliance, the First Triumvirate, in which they agreed to advance each other's interests.

The man who cast the longest shadow over these troubled years was Julius Caesar (100–44 B.C.). More than a mere soldier, Caesar was a cultivated man. Born of a noble family, he received an excellent education, which he furthered by studying in Greece with some of the most eminent teachers of the day. He had serious intellectual interests, and his literary ability was immense. Caesar was a superb orator, though second to Cicero, and his affable personality and wit made him popular. He was also a shrewd politician of unbridled ambition. Since military service was an effective stepping-stone to politics, Caesar launched his military career in Spain, where his courage won the respect and affection of his troops. Personally brave and tireless, Caesar was a military genius who knew how to win battles and how to turn victories into permanent gains.

In 58 B.C., Caesar became governor of Gaul, the region of modern France, a huge area he had conquered in the name of Rome. Caesar's account of his operations, his *Commentaries* on the Gallic wars, became a classic in Western literature and most schoolchildren's introduction to Latin. By 49 B.C., the First Triumvirate had fallen apart. Crassus had died in battle, and Caesar and Pompey, each suspecting the other of treachery, came to blows. The result was a long and bloody civil war, which raged from Spain across northern Africa to Egypt. Although Pompey enjoyed the official support of the government, Caesar finally defeated Pompey's forces in 45 B.C. He had overthrown the republic and made himself dictator.

Julius Caesar was not merely another victorious general. Politically brilliant, he was determined to make basic reforms, even at the expense of the old constitution. He took the first long step to break down the barriers between Italy and the provinces, extending citizenship to many of the provincials who had supported him. Caesar also took measures to cope with Rome's burgeoning population. By Caesar's day perhaps 750,000 people lived in Rome. Caesar drew up plans to send his veterans and some 80,000 of the poor and unemployed to colonies throughout the Mediterranean. He founded at least twenty colonies, most of which were located in Gaul,

Spain, and North Africa. These colonies were important agents in spreading Roman culture in the western Mediterranean. Caesar's work would eventually lead to a Roman empire composed of citizens, not subjects.

In 44 B.C., a group of conspirators assassinated Caesar and set off another round of civil war. Caesar had named his eighteen-year-old grandnephew, Octavian – or Augustus, as he is better known to history – as his heir. Augustus joined forces with two of Caesar's lieutenants, Marc Antony and Lepidus, in a pact known as the Second Triumvirate, and together they hunted down and defeated Caesar's murderers. In the process, however, Augustus and Antony came into conflict. Antony, "boastful, arrogant, and full of empty exultation and capricious ambition," proved to be the major threat to Augustus's designs.[12] In 33 B.C., Augustus branded Antony a traitor and a rebel. Augustus painted lurid pictures of Antony lingering in the eastern Mediterranean, a romantic and foolish captive of the seductive Cleopatra, queen of Egypt and bitter enemy of Rome. In 31 B.C., with the might of Rome at his back, Augustus met and defeated the army and navy of Antony and Cleopatra at the battle of Actium in Greece. Augustus's victory put an end to an age of civil war that had lasted since the days of Sulla.

———◆———

The final days of the republic, even though filled with war and chaos, should not obscure the fact that much of the Roman achievement survived the march of armies. The Romans had conquered the Mediterranean world only to find that conquest required them to change their way of life. Socially, they imbibed Greek culture and adjusted themselves to the superior civilization of the Hellenistic East. Politically, their city-state constitution broke down

and expired in the wars of the late republic. Even so, men like Caesar and later Augustus sought new solutions to the problems confronting Rome. The result, as Chapter 6 will describe, was a system of government capable of administering an empire with justice and fairness. Out of the failure of the republic arose the pax Romana of the empire.

## NOTES

1. Polybius *The Histories* 1.1.5.
2. Mark Twain, *The Innocents Abroad,* Signet Classics, New York, 1966, p. 176.
3. Livy *History of Rome* Preface 6.
4. E. Meyer, *Geschichte des Altertums,* 6th ed., vol 5, Wissenschaftliche Buchgesellschaft, Darmstadt, 1975, pp. 144–145.
5. Sallust *War with Catiline* 10.1–3.
6. *Corpus Inscriptionum Latinarum,* vol. 6, G. Reimer, Berlin, 1882, no. 26192.
7. Cato *On Agriculture* 141.2–3.
8. Ovid *Fasti* 2.535–539.
9. Velleius Paterculus *History of Rome* 2.1.1.
10. Ovid *Fasti* 3.525–542.
11. Plutarch *Life of Tiberius Gracchus* 9.5–6.
12. Plutarch *Life of Antony* 2.8.

## SUGGESTED READING

H. H. Scullard covers much of Roman history in a series of books: *The Etruscan Cities and Rome* (1967), *A History of the Roman World, 753–146 B.C.,* 3rd ed. (1961), and *From the Gracchi to Nero,* 4th ed. (1976). The Etruscans have inspired much new work, most notably L. Banti, *The Etruscan Cities and Their Culture* (English translation, 1973), M. Pallottino, *The Etruscans,* rev. ed. (1975), and R. M. Ogilvie, *Early Rome and the Etruscans* (1976), an excellent account of Rome's early relations with them.

Roman expansion is the subject of J. Heurgon, *The Rise of Rome to 264 B.C.* (English translation, 1973), R. M. Errington, *The Dawn of Empire* (1971), and W. V. Harris, *War and Imperialism in Republican Rome 327-70 B.C.* (1979). J. F. Lazenby, *Hannibal's War: A Military History of the Second Punic War* (1978), is a recent and detailed treatment of one of Rome's greatest struggles. More general and encompassing is E. Gabba, *Republican Rome, the Army, and the Allies* (English translation, 1976). One of the best studies of Rome's political evolution is the classic, A. N. Sherwin-White, *The Roman Citizenship,* 2nd ed. (1973), a work of enduring value.

The great figures and events of the late republic have been the object of much new work. E. S. Gruen, *The Last Generation of the Roman Republic* (1974), treats the period as a whole. Very important are the studies of E. Badian, *Roman Imperialism in the Late Republic* (1968) and *Publicans and Sinners* (1972). R. Syme, *The Roman Revolution,* revised ed. (1952) is a classic. Valuable also are P. A. Brunt, *Social Conflicts in the Roman Republic* (1971); A. J. Toynbee, *Hannibal's Legacy,* 2 vols. (1965); and A. W. Lintott, *Violence in the Roman Republic* (1968).

Many new works deal with individual Romans who left their mark on this period. H. C. Boren, *The Gracchi* (1968), treats the work of the two brothers, and B. Levick, *Tiberius the Politician* (1976), offers closer scrutiny of the elder of the brothers, as does A. Bernstein, *Tiberius Sempronius Gracchus, Tradition and Apostacy* (1978). A. E. Astin has produced two works that are far more extensive than their titles indicate: *Scipio Aemilianus* (1967) and *Cato the Censor* (1978). J. Leach, *Pompey the Great* (1978), surveys the career of this politician, and B. Rawson, *The Politics of Friendship, Pompey and Cicero* (1978), treats both figures in their political environment. M. Gelzer, *Caesar, Politician and Statesman* (English translation, 1968) is easily the best study of one of history's most significant figures. Those interested in learning more about Caesar and the importance of his writings in the late Republic should see the fine article by L. Raditsa, "Julius Caesar and His Writings," in *Aufstieg und Niedergang der römischen Welt,* vol. I, part 3 (1973), pp. 417-456. His one-time colleague Marcus Crassus is treated in B. A. Marshall, *Crassus: A Political Biography* (1976), and A. Ward, *Marcus Crassus and the Late Roman Republic* (1977).

K. D. White, *Roman Farming* (1970), deals with agriculture, and J. P. V. D. Balsdon covers social life in the republic and the empire in two works: *Life and Leisure in Ancient Rome* (1969) and *Roman Women,* revised ed. (1974). Greek cultural influence on Roman life is the subject of A. Wardman, *Rome's Debt to Greece* (1976). F. Schulz, *Classical Roman Law* (1951) is a useful introduction to an important topic. Lastly, H. H. Scullard, *Festivals and Ceremonies of the Roman Republic* (1981), gives a fresh look at religious practices.

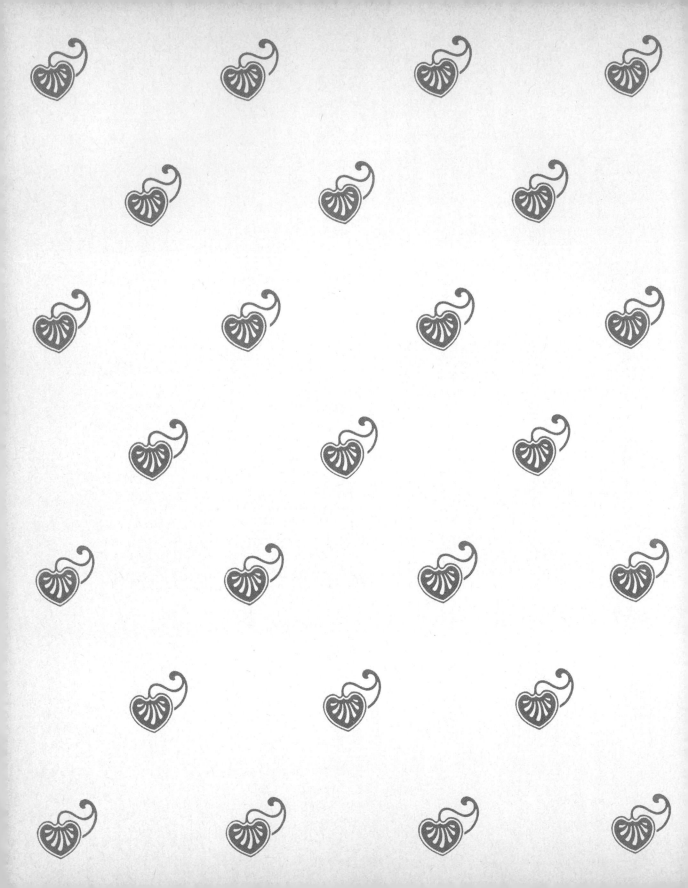

# CHAPTER 6

## THE PAX ROMANA

*HAD THE ROMANS* conquered the entire Mediterranean world only to turn it into their battlefield? Would they, like the Greeks before them, become their own worst enemies, destroying each other and wasting their strength until they perished? At Julius Caesar's death in 44 B.C. it must have seemed so to many. Yet finally, in 31 B.C., Augustus restored peace to a tortured world, and with peace came prosperity, new hope, and a new vision of Rome and Rome's destiny. The Roman poet Virgil expressed this vision most nobly:

*You, Roman, remember — these are your arts:*
*To rule nations, and to impose the ways of peace,*
*To spare the humble and to war down the proud.*[1]

In place of the republic, Augustus established a constitutional monarchy. He attempted to achieve a lasting cooperation in government and a balance among the people, the magistrates, the senate, and the army. His efforts were not always successful. His settlement of Roman affairs did not permanently end civil war. Yet he carried on Caesar's work. It was Augustus who created the structure that the modern world calls the Roman Empire. He did his work so well, and his successors so capably added to it, that Rome realized Virgil's hope. For the first and second centuries A.D. the lot of the Mediterranean world was peace — the *pax Romana,* a period of security, order, and harmony, of flourishing culture and expanding economy. It was a period that saw the wilds of Gaul, Spain, Germany, and eastern Europe introduced to Greco-Roman culture. By the third century A.D., when the empire gave way to the medieval world, the greatness of Rome and the blessings of Roman culture had left an indelible mark on the yet-unseen ages to come.

How did the Roman emperors govern the empire, and how did they spread Roman influence into northern Europe? What were the fruits of the pax Romana? Why did Christianity, originally a minor and local religion, sweep across the Roman world to change it fundamentally? Finally, how did the empire meet the grim challenge of barbarian invasion and economic decline? These are the main questions this chapter will consider.

## *AUGUSTUS'S SETTLEMENT (31 B.C.–A.D. 14)*

When Augustus put an end to the civil wars that had raged since 83 B.C., he faced monumental problems of reconstruction. Rome and the entire Mediterranean world were in his power, and the legions were obedient to his word. Sole ruler as no Roman had ever been, he had a rare opportunity to shape the future. But how was that to be accomplished?

Augustus could easily have declared himself dictator as Caesar had, but the thought was repugnant to him. Augustus was neither an autocrat nor a revolutionary. His solution was to restore the republic. But was that possible? Some eighteen years of anarchy and civil war had shattered the republican constitution. It could not be rebuilt in a day. Augustus recognized these problems, but did not let them stop him. From 29 to 23 B.C., he toiled to heal Rome's wounds. The first problem facing him was to rebuild the constitution and the organs of government. Next he had to demobilize the army and care for the welfare of the provinces. Then he had to meet the danger of barbarians at Rome's European frontiers. Augustus was highly successful in meeting these challenges; his gift of peace to a war-torn world sowed the seeds of a literary flowering that produced some of the finest fruits of the Roman mind.

### The Principate and the Restored Republic

Restoring the republic and creating a place for himself in it proved to be the biggest challenges to Augustus. Typically Roman, he preferred not to create anything new; he intended instead to modify republican forms and offices to meet new circumstances. Augustus planned for the senate to take upon itself a serious burden of duty and responsibility. He expected it to administer some of the provinces, to continue to be the chief deliberative body of the state, and to act as a court of law. Yet he did not give the senate enough power to become his partner in government. As a result, the senate failed to live up to its responsibilities, and increasingly its prerogatives shifted to Augustus by default.

Augustus's own position within the restored republic was something of an anomaly. He could not simply surrender the reins of power, for someone else would only have seized them. But how was he to fit into a republican constitution? Again Augustus had his own answer. He became *princeps civitatis,* "the First Citizen of the State." This prestigious title carried no power; it indicated only that Augustus was the most distinguished of all Roman citizens. In effect, it designated Augustus as the first among equals and a little more equal than anyone else in the state. His real power resided in the magistracies he held, the powers granted him by the senate, and his control of the army. Clearly, much of the principate, as the position of First Citizen is known, was a legal fiction. Yet that need not imply that Augustus, like a modern dictator, tried to clothe himself with constitutional legitimacy. In an inscription known as *Res Gestae (The Deeds of Augustus),* Augustus described his constitutional position in these terms:

COIN OF AUGUSTUS  *This portrait shows Augustus as a mature* princeps. *Like many of his coins, this one too has a propaganda value. On the reverse is his grandson Gaius. Augustus may have minted this coin to publicize Gaius's participation in Tiberius's campaign against the Germans. (Courtesy, World Heritage Museum. Photo: Caroline Buckler)*

*In my sixth and seventh consulships [28–27 B.C.], I had ended the civil war, having obtained through universal consent total control of affairs. I transferred the Republic from my power to the authority of the Roman people and the senate. . . . After that time I stood before all in rank, but I had power no greater than those who were my colleagues in any magistracy.*[2]

Augustus was not being a hypocrite. As consul he had no more constitutional and legal power than his fellow consul. Yet in addition to the consulship Augustus held many other magistracies, which his fellow consul did not. Constitutionally, his ascendancy within the state stemmed from the number of magistracies he held and the power granted him by the senate. At first he held the consulship annually, and then the senate voted him permanent proconsular power. The senate also voted him *tribunicia potestas* – the full power of the tribunes. Tribunician power gave Augustus the right to call the senate into session, present legislation to the people, and defend their rights. He held either high office or the powers of the chief magistrate year in and year out. No other magistrate could do the same. In 12 B.C., he became *pontifex maximus,* chief priest of the state. By assuming this position of great honor, Augustus became the chief religious official within the state.

The main source of Augustus's power was his position as commander of the Roman army. His title *imperator,* with which Rome customarily honored a general after a major victory, came to mean "emperor" in the modern sense of the term. Augustus governed the provinces where troops were needed for defense. The frontiers were his special concern. There Roman legionaries held the German barbarians at arm's length. The frontiers were also the areas where fighting could be expected to break out. Augustus made sure that Rome went to war only at his command. He controlled the deployment of the Roman army and paid its wages. He granted it bonuses and gave veterans retirement benefits. Thus, he avoided the problems with the army that the old senate had created for itself. Augustus never shared control of the army, and no Roman found it easy to defy him militarily.

The very size of the army was a special problem for Augustus. Rome's legions numbered thousands of men, far more than were necessary to maintain peace. What was Augustus to do with so many soldiers? This sort of problem had constantly plagued the late republic, whose leaders never found a solution to it. Augustus gave his own answer in the *Res Gestae:* "I founded colonies of soldiers in

Africa, Sicily, Macedonia, Spain, Achaea, Gaul, and Pisidia. Moreover, Italy has 28 colonies under my auspices."[3] At least forty new colonies arose, most of them in the western Mediterranean. Augustus's veterans took abroad with them their Roman language and culture. His colonies, like those of Julius Caesar, were a significant tool in the further spread of Roman culture throughout the West.

Roman colonies were very different from the Greek colonies of Archilochus's time (pages 81–82). Greek colonies were independent. Once founded, they went their own way. Roman colonies were part of a system – the Roman Empire – that linked East with West in a mighty political, social, and economic network. The glory of the Roman Empire was its great success in uniting the Mediterranean world and spreading Greco-Roman culture throughout it. Roman colonies played a crucial part in that process, and deservedly did Augustus boast of his foundations.

What is to be made of Augustus's constitutional settlement? Despite his claims to the contrary, Augustus had not restored the republic. In fact, he would probably have agreed with the words of John Stuart Mill, the nineteenth-century English philosopher: "When society requires to be rebuilt, there is no use in attempting to rebuild it on the old plan." Augustus had created a constitutional monarchy, something completely new in Roman history. The title *princeps,* "First Citizen," came to mean in Rome, as it does today, "prince" in the sense of a sovereign ruler.

Augustus also failed to solve a momentous problem. He never found a way to institutionalize his position with the army. The ties between the princeps and the army were always personal. The army was loyal to the princeps but not necessarily to the state. The

Augustan Principate worked well at first, but by the third century A.D. the army would make and break emperors at will. Nonetheless, it is a measure of Augustus's success that his settlement survived as long and as well as it did.

## AUGUSTUS'S ADMINISTRATION OF THE PROVINCES

To gain an accurate idea of the total population of the empire, Augustus ordered a census to be taken in 28 B.C. In Augustus's day the population of the Roman empire was between 70 and 100 million people, fully 75 percent of whom lived in the provinces. In the areas under his immediate jurisdiction Augustus put provincial administration on an ordered basis. He improved its functioning as well. Believing that the cities of the empire should look after their own affairs, he encouraged and fostered local self-government and urbanism. Augustus respected local customs and ordered his governors to do the same. The lengths he was willing to go to can be seen in Judaea.

Augustus wished to avoid antagonizing the Jews. As early as 40 B.C., long before he had put an end to the civil war, he and Antony had prevailed upon the senate to give the Jews their own king, Herod the Great, as a gesture of goodwill. Also, when the Roman legionaries stationed outside of Jerusalem entered the city, they left their standards behind in deference to the Jewish belief that the standards showed graven images. This was a magnanimous gesture, the equivalent of a modern army leaving its national flags behind. Augustus saw no reason to interfere with the customs, institutions, and traditions of cities as long as they functioned peacefully and effectively.

As a spiritual bond between the provinces and Rome, Augustus encouraged the cult of Roma, the goddess and guardian of the state. In the Hellenistic East, where king-worship was an established custom, the cult of Roma et Augustus grew up and spread rapidly. Augustus then introduced it in the West. By the time of his death in A.D. 14, nearly every province in the Empire could boast an altar or shrine to Roma et Augustus. In the West it was not the person of the emperor who was worshiped but his *genius* – his guardian spirit. In praying for the good health and welfare of the emperor Romans and provincials were praying for the empire itself. The cult became a symbol of Roman unity.

## ROMAN EXPANSION INTO NORTHERN AND WESTERN EUROPE

For the history of Western civilization one of the most momentous aspects of Augustus's reign was Roman expansion into the wilderness of northern and western Europe (see Map 6.1). In this Augustus was following in Julius Caesar's footsteps. Between 58 and 51 B.C., Caesar had subdued Gaul and unsuccessfully attacked Britain. Carrying on his work, Augustus pushed Rome's frontier into the region of modern Germany. The Germanic tribes were tough opponents, and the Roman legions saw much bitter fighting against them in the north.

For the common soldier this fighting must have been exceptionally grim. Forests were believed to be the haunts of evil spirits, places of dim light and unidentifiable sounds. As early as the third century B.C. Roman armies habitually skirted the forests of Etruria. The vast forests of central Germany, with their thick, impenetrable gloom, must have oppressed even veteran legionaries. The thought of coming suddenly onto a war party of tall bearded Germans was not particularly pleasing either. Even so, the Roman legionary was

CASPIAN SEA

PARTHIA

ARMENIA

*Volga*

*Don*

*Tigris*

Ctesiphon

Seleucia

*Dnieper*

BLACK SEA

CRIMEA

CAPPADOCIA

*Euphrates*

SYRIA

Antioch

Damascus

JUDAEA

Jerusalem

Petra

ARABIAN DESERT

RED SEA

PHRYGIA

CILICIA

Tarsus

CYPRUS

THRACE

Byzantium

ASIA

PISIDIA

Pergamum

Ephesus

RHODES

*Nile*

Alexandria

EGYPT

MOESIA

DACIA

*Danube*

MACEDONIA

Corinth

Athens

ACHAEA

CRETE

MEDITERRANEAN SEA

Cyrene

LIBYA

DALMATIA

PANNONIA

NORICUM

RAETIA

Ravenna

Brundisium

Capua

SICILY

Syracuse

NORTH AFRICA

GERMANY

Teutoberger Forest ✕

*Main*

*Rhine*

Cologne

CISALPINE GAUL

*Po*

Arretium

Rome

*Tiber*

SAHARA

JUTLAND

*Elbe*

BELGIUM

*Rhine*

Massilia

CORSICA

SARDINIA

Carthage

NUMIDIA

NORTH SEA

GAUL

Lyons

NARBONENSIS

BALEARICS

MAURETANIA

NORTH AFRICA

BRITAIN

ATLANTIC OCEAN

*Ebro*

NEARER SPAIN

FARTHER SPAIN

Gades

500 Mi.

500 Km.

250

250

0

0

✕  Major battle

Roman Empire under Augustus

Territory added by the time of Hadrian

stouthearted, and these obstacles did not stop Roman expansion.

Augustus began his work in the north by completing the conquest of Spain. In Gaul, apart from minor campaigns, most of his work was peaceful. He founded twelve new towns. The Roman road system linked new settlements with one another and with Italy. But the German frontier, along the Rhine River, was the scene of hard fighting. In 12 B.C., Augustus ordered a major invasion of Germany beyond the Rhine. Roman legions advanced to the Elbe River, and a Roman fleet explored the North Sea and Jutland. The area north of the Main River and west of the Elbe was on the point of becoming Roman. But in 9 B.C., Augustus's general Varus lost some twenty thousand troops at the battle of the Teutoburger Forest. Thereafter the Rhine remained the Roman frontier.

Meanwhile, more successful generals extended the Roman standards as far as the Danube. Roman legions penetrated the area of modern Austria and western Hungary. The regions of modern Serbia, Bulgaria, and Rumania fell to Roman troops. Within this area the legionaries built fortified camps. Roads linked these camps with one another, and settlements grew up around the camps. Traders began to frequent the frontier and to traffic with the barbarians. Thus Roman culture – the rough-and-ready kind found in military camps – gradually spread into the northern wilderness.

Augustus's achievements in the north were monumental. For the first time in history, Greco-Roman culture spread beyond the sunny Mediterranean into the heart of Europe.

Amid the vast expanse of forests, Roman towns, trade, language, and law began to exert a civilizing influence on the barbarians. The Roman way of life attracted the barbarians, who soon recognized the benefits of assimilating Roman culture. Military camps often became towns; many modern European cities owe their origins to the forts of the Roman army. For the first time, the barbarian north came into direct, immediate, and continuous contact with Mediterranean culture.

## LITERARY FLOWERING

The Augustan settlement's gift of peace inspired a literary flowering unparalleled in Roman history. With good reason this period is known as the golden age of Latin literature. Augustus and many of his friends actively encouraged poets and writers. As Virgil, Rome's greatest poet, summed up Augustus and his era:

*Here is the man, here is he whom you often hear promised to you,*
*Augustus Caesar, offspring of the deified [Julius Caesar], who will establish*
*Once more a golden age in Latium.*[4]

Virgil was not alone in this sentiment. The poet Horace felt the same:

*With Caesar* [Augustus] *the guardian of the state*
*Not civil rage nor violence shall drive out peace,*
*Nor wrath which forges swords*
*And turns unhappy cities against each other.*[5]

These lines are not empty flattery, despite Augustus's support of many contemporary Latin writers. To a generation that had known only vicious civil war, Augustus's settlement was an unbelievable blessing.

The tone and ideal of Roman literature, like that of the Greeks, was humanistic and

*ARA PACIS  This scene from the Ara Pacis, the Altar of Peace, celebrates Augustus's restoration of peace and the fruits of peace. Here Mother Earth is depicted with her children. The cow and the sheep under the goddess represent the prosperity brought by peace, especially the agricultural prosperity so highly cherished by Virgil. (Alinari/Scala)*

worldly. Roman poets and prose writers celebrated the dignity of humanity and the range of its accomplishments. They stressed the physical and emotional joys of a comfortable, peaceful life. Their works were highly polished, elegant in style, and intellectual in conception. Roman poets referred to the gods frequently and treated mythological themes, but always the core of their work was human, not divine.

Virgil (70–19 B.C.) celebrated the new age in the *Georgics,* four books of poems on agriculture. Virgil delighted in his own farm, and his poems sing of the pleasures of peaceful farm life. The *Georgics* are also a manual of agriculture written in meter. The poet tells how to keep bees, grow grapes and olives, plow, and manage a farm. Throughout the

*Georgics* Virgil wrote about things he himself had seen, rather than drawing his theme from the writings of others. For instance, he describes the worker bees returning to the hive at nightfall:

*The weary young bees come back late at night,*
*Their legs full of thyme. Far and wide they feed*
    *on arbutus and grey-green willows and red*
    *crocus*
*And rich linden and rust-colored hyacinth.*[6]

Virgil could be vivid and graphic as well as pastoral. Even a small event could be a drama for him. The death of a bull while plowing is hardly epic material; yet Virgil captures the sadness of the event in the image of the farmer unyoking the remaining animal:

*Look, the bull, shining under the rough plough,
   falls to the ground
and vomits from his mouth blood mixed with
   foam,
and releases his dying groan.
Sadly moves the ploughman, unharnessing the
   young steer grieving for the death of his brother
and leaves in the middle of the job
   the plough stuck fast.*[7]

Virgil's poetry is robust yet graceful. A sensitive man who delighted in simple things, Virgil left in his *Georgics* a charming picture of life in the Italian countryside in a period of peace.

Virgil's masterpiece is the *Aeneid,* an epic poem that is the Latin equivalent of the Greek *Iliad* and *Odyssey.* In the *Aeneid* Virgil expressed his admiration for Augustus's work by celebrating the shining ideal of a world blessed by the pax Romana. Virgil's account of the founding of Rome and the early years of the city gave final form to the legend of Aeneas, the Trojan hero who escaped to Italy at the fall of Troy. The principal Roman tradition held that Romulus was the founder of Rome, but the legend of Aeneas was also very old; it was known by the Etruscans as early as the fifth century B.C. Although Rome could not have had two founders, Virgil linked the legends of Aeneas and Romulus and kept them both. In so doing he also connected Rome with Greece's heroic past. Recounting the story of Aeneas and Dido, the queen of Carthage, Virgil made their ill-fated love affair the cause of the Punic wars. But above all, the *Aeneid* is the expression of Virgil's passionate belief in Rome's greatness. It is a vision of Rome as the protector of the good and noble against the forces of darkness and disruption.

In its own way Livy's history of Rome, entitled simply *Ab Urbe Condita (From the Founding of the City)*, is the prose counterpart of the *Aeneid.* Livy (59 B.C.–A.D. 17) received training in Greek and Latin literature, rhetoric, and philosophy. He even urged the future emperor Claudius to write history. Livy loved and admired the heroes and the great deeds of the republic, but he was also a friend of Augustus and a supporter of the principate. He especially approved of Augustus's efforts to restore the old republican virtues and morality.

Livy's history began with the legend of Aeneas and ended with the reign of Augustus. His theme of the greatness of the republic fitted admirably with Augustus's program of restoring the republic. Livy's history was colossal, consisting of 142 books of which only 25 percent still exists. Livy was a sensitive writer, and something of a moralist. Like Thucydides, he felt that history should be applied to the present. His history later became one of Rome's legacies to the modern world. During the Renaissance *Ab Urbe Condita* found a warm admirer in the poet Petrarch and left its mark on Machiavelli, who read it avidly.

The poet Horace (65–8 B.C.) rose from humble beginnings to friendship with Augustus. The son of an ex-slave and tax collector, Horace nonetheless received an excellent education. He loved Greek literature and finished his education in Athens. After Augustus's victory he returned to Rome and became Virgil's friend. Horace acquired a small farm north of Rome, which delighted him. He was as content as Virgil on his farm, and expressed his joy in a few lines:

*Strive to add nothing to the myrtle plant!
The myrtle befits both you, the servant,
And me the master, as I drink under the
Thick-leaved vine.*[8]

Horace happily turned his pen to celebrating Rome's newly won peace and prosperity. One of his finest odes commemorates Augustus's victory over Cleopatra at Actium in 31 B.C. Cleopatra is depicted as a frenzied queen, drunk with desire to destroy Rome. Horace saw in Augustus's victory the triumph of West over East, of simplicity over oriental excess. One of the truly moving aspects of Horace's poetry, like Virgil's, is his deep and abiding gratitude for the pax Romana.

For Rome, Augustus's age was one of hope and new beginnings. Augustus had put the empire on a new foundation. Constitutional monarchy was firmly established, and government was to all appearances a partnership between the princeps and the senate. The Augustan settlement was a delicate structure, and parts of it would in time be discarded. Nevertheless it worked, and by building on it later emperors would carry on Augustus's work.

The solidity of Augustus's work became obvious at his death in A.D. 14. Since the principate was not technically an office, Augustus could not legally hand it to a successor. Augustus had recognized this problem, and long before his death had found a way to solve it. He shared his consular and tribunician powers with his adopted son Tiberius, thus grooming him for the principate. In his will Augustus left most of his vast fortune to Tiberius, and the senate formally requested Tiberius to assume the burdens of the principate. All the formalities apart, Augustus had succeeded in creating a dynasty.

## JUDAISM AND THE RISE OF CHRISTIANITY

During the reign of the emperor Tiberius (A.D. 14–37), perhaps in A.D. 29, Pontius Pilate, prefect of Judaea, condemned Jesus of Nazareth to death. At the time a minor event, this has become one of the best-known moments in history. How did these two men come to their historic meeting? The question is not idle, for Rome was as important as Judaea to Christianity. Jesus was born in a troubled time, when Roman rule aroused hatred and unrest among the Jews. This climate of hostility affected the lives of all who lived in Judaea, Roman and Jew alike. It forms the backdrop of Jesus' life, and it had a fundamental impact on his ministry. Without an understanding of this age of anxiety in Judaea, Jesus and early Christianity cannot properly be appreciated.

The entry of Rome into Jewish affairs was anything but peaceful. The civil wars that destroyed the republic wasted the prosperity of Judaea and the entire eastern Mediterranean world. Jewish leaders took sides in the fighting, and Judaea suffered its share of ravages and military confiscations. Peace brought little satisfaction to the Jews. Although Augustus treated Judaea generously, the Romans won no popularity by making Herod king of Judaea. King Herod gave Judaea prosperity and security, but the Jews hated his acceptance of Greek culture. He was also a bloodthirsty prince, who murdered his own wife and sons. Upon his death, the Jews broke out in revolt. For the next ten years Herod's successor waged almost constant war against the rebels. Added to the horrors of civil war were years of crop failure, which caused famine and plague. Men who called themselves prophets proclaimed the approach of the end of the world and the coming of the Messiah, the savior of Israel.

At length the Romans intervened to restore order. Augustus put Judaea under the charge of a prefect answerable directly to the emperor. Religious matters and local affairs became the responsibility of the Sanhedrin, the highest Jewish judicial body. Although many prefects tried to perform their duties scrupulously and conscientiously, many others were rapacious and indifferent to Jewish culture. Often acting from fear rather than cruelty, some prefects fiercely stamped out any signs of popular discontent. Pontius Pilate, prefect in A.D. 26–36, is typical of such incompetent officials. Although eventually relieved of his duties in disgrace, Pilate brutally put down even innocent demonstrations. Especially hated were the Roman tax collectors, called publicans, many of whom pitilessly gouged the Jews. Publicans and sinners – the words became synonymous. Clashes between Roman troops and Jewish guerrillas inflamed the anger of both sides.

In A.D. 40 the emperor Caligula undid part of Augustus's good work by ordering his statue erected in the temple at Jerusalem. The order, though never carried out, further intensified Jewish resentment. Thus, the Jews became embittered by Roman rule because of taxes, sometimes unduly harsh enforcement of the law, and a misguided interference in their religion.

Among the Jews two movements spread. First was the rise of the Zealots, extremists who worked and fought to rid Judaea of the Romans. Resolute in their worship of Yahweh, they refused to pay any but the tax levied by the Jewish temple. Their battles with the Roman legionaries were marked by savagery on both sides. As usual, the innocent caught in the middle suffered grievously. As Roman policy grew tougher, even moderate Jews began to hate the conquerors. Judaea came more and more to resemble a tinderbox, ready to burst into flames at a single spark.

The second movement was the growth of militant apocalyptic sentiment – the belief that the coming of the Messiah was near. This belief was an old one among the Jews. But by the first century A.D. it had become more

widespread and fervent than ever before. Typical was the Apocalypse of Baruch, which foretold the destruction of the Roman Empire. First would come a period of great tribulation, misery, and injustice. At the worst of the suffering, the Messiah would appear. The Messiah would destroy the Roman legions and all the kingdoms that had ruled Israel. Then the Messiah would inaugurate a period of happiness and plenty.

This was no abstract notion among the Jews. As the ravages of war became ever more widespread and conditions worsened, more and more people prophesied the imminent coming of the Messiah. One such was John the Baptist, "the voice of one crying in the wilderness, prepare ye the way of the lord."[9] Many Jews did just that. The sect described in the Dead Sea Scrolls readied itself for the end of the world. Its members were probably Essenes, and their social organization closely resembled that of the early Christians. Members of this group shared their possessions, precisely as John the Baptist urged people to do. Yet this sect, unlike the Christians, also made military preparations for the day of the Messiah.

Into this climate of Roman severity, fanatical Zealotry, and Messianic hope came Jesus of Nazareth (ca 3 B.C.–A.D. 29). He was raised in Galilee, the stronghold of the Zealots. Yet Jesus himself was a man of peace. Jesus urged his listeners to love god as their father and each other as god's children. The kingdom that he proclaimed was no earthly one, but one of eternal happiness in a life after death. Jesus' teachings are strikingly similar to those of Hillel (30 B.C.–A.D. 9), a great rabbi and interpreter of the Scriptures. Hillel taught the Jews to love one another as they loved god. He taught them to treat others as they themselves wished to be treated. Jesus' preaching was in this same serene tradition.

Jesus' teachings were entirely and thoroughly Jewish. He declared that he would change not one jot or tittle of the Jewish law. His orthodoxy enabled him to preach in the synagogue and the temple. His only deviation from orthodoxy was his insistence that he taught in his own name, not in the name of Yahweh. Was he then the Messiah? A small band of followers thought so, and Jesus revealed himself to them as the Messiah. Yet Jesus had his own conception of the Messiah. Unlike the Messiah of the Apocalypse of Baruch, Jesus would not destroy the Roman Empire. He told his disciples flatly that they were to "render unto Caesar the things that are Caesar's." Jesus would establish a spiritual kingdom, not an earthly one. Repeatedly he told his disciples that his kingdom was "not of this world."

Of Jesus' life and teachings the prefect Pontius Pilate knew little and cared even less. All that concerned him was the maintenance of peace and order. The crowds following Jesus at the time of the Passover, a highly emotional time in the Jewish year, alarmed Pilate, who faced a volatile situation. Some Jews believed that Jesus was the long-awaited Messiah. Others were disappointed because he refused to preach rebellion against Rome. Still others who hated and feared Jesus wanted to be rid of him. The last thing that Pilate wanted was a riot on his hands. Christian tradition has made much of Pontius Pilate. In the medieval West he was considered a monster. In the Ethiopian church he is considered a saint. Neither monster nor saint, Pilate was simply a hard-bitten Roman official. He did his duty, at times harshly. In Judaea his duty was to enforce the law and to keep the peace. These were the problems on his mind when Jesus stood before him. Jesus as King of the Jews did not worry him. The popular agitation surrounding Jesus did. To avert a riot

and bloodshed Pilate condemned Jesus to death.

Once Pilate's soldiers had carried out the sentence, the entire matter seemed to be closed. There were rumors that Jesus had risen from the dead or that his disciples had stolen his body, but otherwise the tumult subsided. Jesus' followers lived quietly and peacefully, unmolested by Roman or Jew. Pilate had no quarrel with them, and Judaism already had many minor sects. Peter (d. A.D. 67?), the first of Jesus' followers, became the head of the sect, which continued to observe Jewish law and religious customs. Peter, a man of traditional Jewish beliefs, felt that Jesus' teachings were meant exclusively for the Jews. Only in their practices of baptism and the Lord's Supper did the sect differ from normal Jewish custom. Meanwhile, they awaited the return of Jesus.

Christianity might have remained a purely Jewish sect had it not been for Paul of Tarsus (A.D. 5?–67?). The conversion of Hellenized Jews and of Gentiles (non-Jews) to Christianity caused the sect grave problems. Were the Gentiles subject to the law of Moses? If not, was Christianity to have two sets of laws? The answer to these questions was Paul's momentous contribution to Christianity. Paul was unlike Jesus or Peter. Born in a thriving and busy city filled with Romans, Greeks, Jews, Syrians, and others, he was at home in the world of Greco-Roman culture. After his conversion to Christianity he taught that his native Judaism was the preparation for the Messiah, and that Jesus by his death and resurrection had fulfilled the prophesy of Judaism and initiated a new age. Paul taught that Jesus was the Son of God, the beginning of a new law, and he preached that Jesus' teachings were to be proclaimed to all people, whether Jew or Gentile. Paul thus made a significant break with Judaism, Christianity's parent religion, for Judaism was exclusive and did not seek converts.

Paul's influence was far greater than that of any other early Christian. He traveled the length and breadth of the eastern Roman world, spreading his doctrine and preaching of Jesus. To little assemblies of believers in cities as distant as Rome and Corinth he taught that Jesus had died to save all people. Paul's vision of Christianity won out over Peter's traditionalism. Christianity broke with Judaism and embarked on its own course.

What was Christianity's appeal to the Roman world? What did this obscure sect give people that other religions did not? Christianity possessed many different attractions. One of its appeals was its willingness to embrace both men and women, slaves and nobles. Many of the Eastern mystery religions with which Christianity competed were exclusive in one way or another. Mithraism, a mystery religion descended from Zoroastrianism, spread throughout the entire empire. Mithras the sun god embodied good and warred against evil. Like Christianity, Mithraism offered elaborate and moving rituals including a form of baptism, a code of moral conduct, and the promise of life after death. Unlike Christianity, however, Mithraism permitted only men to become devotees. Much the same was true of the ancient Eleusinian mysteries of Greece, which were open only to Greeks and Romans.

Christianity appealed to common people and to the poor. Its communal celebration of the Lord's Supper gave men and women a sense of belonging. Christianity also offered its adherents the promise of salvation. Christians believed that Jesus on the cross had defeated evil, and that he would reward his followers with eternal life after death. Christianity also offered the possibility of forgiveness. Human nature was weak, and even the

best Christians would fall into sin. But Jesus loved sinners and forgave those who repented. In its doctrine of salvation and forgiveness alone Christianity had a powerful ability to give solace and strength to those who believed.

Christianity was attractive to many because it gave the Roman world a cause. Hellenistic philosophy had attempted to make men and women self-sufficient: people who became indifferent to the outside world could no longer be hurt by it. That goal alone ruled out any cause except the attainment of serenity. The Romans, who were never innovators in philosophy, merely elaborated this lonely and austere message. Instead of passivity Christianity stressed the ideal of striving for a goal. Each and every Christian, no matter how poor or humble, worked to realize the triumph of Christianity on earth. This was God's will, a sacred duty for every Christian. By spreading the word of Christ, Christians played their part in God's plan. No matter how small a part each Christian played, that part was important. Since this duty was God's will, Christians believed that sooner or later the goal would be achieved. The Christian was not to be discouraged by temporary setbacks, believing Christianity to be invincible.

Christianity gave its devotees a sense of community. No Christian was alone. All members of the Christian community strived toward the same goal of fulfilling God's plan. Each individual community was in turn a member of a greater community. And that community, the Church General, was indestructible. After all, Jesus himself had promised, "Thou art Peter, and upon this rock I will build my church; and the gates of hell shall not prevail against it."[10]

So Christianity's attractions were many, from forgiveness of sin to an exalted purpose for each individual. Its insistence on the importance of the individual gave solace and encouragement, especially to the poor and meek. Its claim to divine protection fed hope in the eventual success of the Christian community. Christianity made participation in the universal possible for each and every person. The ultimate reward promised by Christianity was eternal bliss after death. Though at first the educated and wealthy scoffed at this message, they too succumbed to its charm. It was unlike anything the average man and woman had ever known.

## THE JULIO-CLAUDIANS AND THE FLAVIANS (27 B.C.–A.D. 96)

For fifty years after Augustus's death the dynasty that he established – known as the Julio-Claudians because they were all members of the Julian and Claudian clans – provided the emperors of Rome. Some of the Julio-Claudians, like Tiberius and Claudius, were sound rulers and able administrators. Others, like Caligula and Nero, were weak and frivolous men who exercised their power stupidly and brought misery to the empire. Writers such as the biting and brilliant historian Tacitus (ca A.D. 55–ca 116) and the gossipy Suetonius (ca A.D. 75–150) have left unforgettable – and generally hostile – portraits of these emperors that are literary masterpieces. Yet the venom of Tacitus and Suetonius cannot obscure the fact that Julio-Claudians were responsible for some notable achievements and that during their reigns the empire on the whole prospered.

One of the most momentous achievements of the Julio-Claudians was Claudius's creation of an imperial bureaucracy composed of professional administrators. Even the most energetic emperor could not run the empire alone.

The numerous duties and immense reponsibilities of the emperor prompted Claudius to delegate power. He began by giving the freedmen of his household official duties, especially in the field of finances. It was a simple, workable system. Claudius knew his ex-slaves well and could discipline them at will. The effect of Claudius's innovations was to enable the emperor to rule the empire more easily and efficiently.

One of the worst defects of Augustus's settlement – the army's ability to interfere in politics – became obvious during the Julio-Claudian period. Augustus had created a special standing force, the Praetorian Guard, as an imperial bodyguard. In A.D. 41 one of the praetorians murdered Caligula while others hailed Claudius as the emperor. Under the threat of violence the senate ratified the praetorians' choice. It was a story repeated frequently. During the first three centuries of the empire the Praetorian Guard all too often murdered emperors they were supposed to protect and saluted emperors of their own choosing.

In A.D. 69, Nero's inept rule led to an extensive military uprising that caused widespread disruption. No fewer than four men became emperor that year, known as the Year of the Four Emperors. Roman armies in Gaul, on the Rhine, and in the East marched on Rome to make their commanders emperor. The man who emerged triumphant was Vespasian, commander of the eastern armies, who entered Rome in 70 and restored order. Nonetheless, the Year of the Four Emperors proved that the Augustan settlement had failed to end civil war.

Not a brilliant politician, Vespasian did not institute reforms as had Augustus or tackle the problem of the army in politics. To prevent usurpers from claiming the throne Vespasian designated his sons Titus and Domitian as his successors. By establishing the Flavian (the name of Vespasian's clan) dynasty Vespasian turned the principate into an open and admitted monarchy. He also expanded the power of the emperor by increasing the size of the budding bureaucracy Claudius had created.

One of Vespasian's first tasks was to suppress rebellions that had erupted at the end of Nero's reign. The most famous had taken place in Judaea, which still seethed long after Jesus' crucifixion. Long-standing popular unrest and atrocities committed by Jews and Romans alike sparked a massive revolt in A.D. 66. Four years later a Roman army reconquered Judaea and reduced Jerusalem by siege. The Jewish survivors were enslaved, their state destroyed. The mismanagement of Judaea was one of the few — and worst — failures of Roman imperial administration.

The Flavians carried on Augustus's work on the frontiers. Domitian, the last of the Flavians, won additional territory in Germany and consolidated it in two new provinces. He defeated barbarian tribes on the Danube frontier and strengthened that area as well. Nonetheless, Domitian was one of the most hated of Roman emperors, and he fell victim to an assassin's dagger. Nevertheless, the Flavians had given the Roman world peace and had kept the legions in line. Their work paved the way for the era of the "Five Good Emperors," the golden age of the empire.

## THE AGE OF THE FIVE GOOD EMPERORS (A.D. 96–180)

*In the second century of the Christian era, the Empire of Rome comprehended the fairest part of the earth, and the most civilised portion of mankind. The frontiers of that extensive monarchy*

THE PRAETORIAN GUARD *Instituted by Augustus as the imperial bodyguard, the Praetorian Guard began making and breaking emperors as early as the Julio-Claudian period. For all of their power, they were not crack troops, but their access to the emperor gave them an influence far greater than their numerical strength or fighting ability. (Giraudon)*

*were guarded by ancient renown and disciplined valour. The gentle but powerful influence of laws and manners had gradually cemented the union of the provinces. Their peaceful inhabitants enjoyed and abused the advantages of wealth and luxury. The image of a free constitution was preserved with decent reverence: the Roman senate appeared to possess the sovereign authority, and devolved on the emperors all the executive powers of government. During a happy period (A.D. 98–180) of more than fourscore years, the public administration was conducted by the virtue and abilities of Nerva, Trajan, Hadrian, and the two Antonines.*[11]

Thus Edward Gibbon (1737–1794) began his monumental *History of the Decline and Fall of the Roman Empire.* Gibbon saw the era of Nerva, Trajan, Hadrian, Antoninus Pius, and Marcus Aurelius — the "five good emperors" — as the happiest period in human history, the last burst of summer before the autumn of failure and barbarism. Gibbon recognized a great truth: the age of the Antonines, as the "five good emperors" are often called, was one of almost unparalleled prosperity. Wars were minor and confined to the frontiers. Even the serenity of Augustus's day seemed to pale in comparison. These emperors were among the noblest, most dedicated, and ablest men in Roman history. Yet fundamental political and military changes had taken place since Augustus's day.

## THE ANTONINE MONARCHY

The age of the Antonines was the age of full-blown monarchy. Gibbon wrote:

*The obvious definition of a monarchy seems to be that of a state, in which a single person, by whatsoever name he may be distinguished, is entrusted with the execution of the laws, the management of the revenue, and the command of the army.*[12]

Augustus clearly fits Gibbon's definition of a monarch in all essentials. But there is a significant difference between Augustus's position and that of an emperor like Hadrian.

Augustus claimed that his influence arose from the collection of offices the senate had bestowed upon him. However, there was in law no such office as emperor. Augustus was merely the First Citizen. Under the Flavians the principate became a full-blown monarchy, and by the time of the Antonines the principate was an office with definite rights, powers, and prerogatives. In the years between Augustus and the Antonines the emperor had become an indispensable part of the imperial machinery. In short, without the emperor the empire would quickly fall to pieces. Augustus had been monarch in fact but not in theory; the Antonines were monarchs in both.

The Antonines were not power-hungry autocrats. The concentration of power was the result of empire, as the American historian M. Hammond has pointed out:

*Monarchy was indeed an inescapable result of the existence of the empire; the more efficient the imperial government became, the more it assumed new functions; and the more that increasing pressure made its task heavier, so much the more it became monarchical.*[13]

In short, the easiest and most efficient way to run the Roman Empire was to invest the emperor with vast powers. Furthermore, Roman emperors on the whole proved to be effective rulers and administrators. As capable and efficient emperors took on new tasks and functions, the hand of the emperor was felt in more and more areas of life and government. Increasingly, the emperors became the source of all authority and guidance within the empire. The five good emperors were benevolent and exercised their power intelligently, but they were absolute kings all the same. Lesser men would later throw off the façade of constitutionality and use this same power in a despotic fashion.

Typical of the five good emperors is the career of Hadrian, who became emperor in A.D. 117. He was born in Spain, a fact that illustrates the importance of the provinces in Roman politics. Hadrian received his education at Rome and became an ardent admirer of Greek culture. He caught the attention of his elder cousin Trajan — the future emperor — who started him on a military career. At age nineteen Hadrian served on the Danube frontier, where he learned the details of how the Roman army lived and fought and saw for himself the problems of defending the fron-

# ROMAN HISTORY AFTER AUGUSTUS

| PERIOD | IMPORTANT EMPERORS | SIGNIFICANT EVENTS |
|---|---|---|
| Julio-Claudians 27 B.C.–A.D. 68 | Augustus, 27 B.C.–A.D. 14<br>Tiberius, 14–37<br>Caligula, 37–41<br>Claudius, 41–54<br>Nero, 54–68 | Augustan settlement<br>Beginning of the principate<br>Birth and death of Jesus<br>Expansion into northern and western Europe<br>Creation of the imperial bureaucracy |
| Year of the Four Emperors, 68–69 | Nero<br>Galba<br>Otho<br>Vitellius | Civil war<br>Major breakdown of the concept of the principate |
| Flavians 69–96 | Vespasian, 69–79<br>Titus, 79–81<br>Domitian, 81–96 | Growing trend toward the concept of monarchy<br>Defense and further consolidation of the European frontiers |
| Antonines 96–192 | Nerva, 96–98<br>Trajan, 98–117<br>Hadrian, 117–138<br>Antoninus Pius, 138–161<br>Marcus Aurelius, 161–180<br>Commodus, 180–192 | The "golden age" – the era of the "five good emperors"<br>Economic prosperity<br>Trade and growth of cities in northern Europe<br>Beginning of barbarian menace on the frontiers |
| Severi 193–235 | Septimius Severus, 193–211<br>Caracalla, 211–217<br>Elagabalus, 218–222<br>Severus Alexander, 222–235 | Military monarchy<br>All free men within the empire given Roman citizenship |
| "Barracks Emperors" 235–284 | Twenty-two emperors in forty-nine years | Civil war<br>Breakdown of the Empire<br>Barbarian invasions<br>Severe economic decline |
| Tetrarchy 284–337 | Diocletian, 284–305<br>Constantine, 306–337 | Political recovery<br>Autocracy<br>Legalization of Christianity<br>Transition to the Middle Ages in the West<br>Birth of the Byzantine Empire in the East |

tiers. When Trajan became emperor in A.D. 98, he began giving Hadrian high military and administrative positions in which he learned how to defend and run the empire. At Trajan's death in 117, Hadrian assumed the reins of power.

Roman government had changed since Augustus's day. One of the most significant changes was the enormous growth of the imperial bureaucracy created by Claudius. Hadrian reformed this system by putting the bureaucracy on an organized, official basis. He established imperial administrative departments to handle the work formerly done by the imperial freedmen. Hadrian also separated civil service from military service. Men with little talent or taste for the army could instead serve the state as administrators. Hadrian's bureaucracy demanded professionalism from its members. Administrators made a career of the civil service. These innovations made for more efficient running of the empire, and increased the authority of the emperor, who was the ruling power of the bureaucracy.

### CHANGES IN THE ARMY

The Roman army had also changed since Augustus's time. The Roman legion had once been a mobile unit, but its duties under the empire no longer called for mobility. The successors of Augustus called a halt to further conquests. The army was expected to defend what had already been won. Under the Flavian emperors (A.D. 69–96) the frontiers became firmly fixed. Forts and watch stations guarded the borders. Behind the forts the Romans built a system of roads, which allowed the forts to be quickly supplied and reinforced in times of trouble. The army had evolved into a garrison force, with legions guarding specific areas for long periods.

The personnel of the legions was changing too. Italy could no longer supply all the recruits needed for the army. Increasingly, only the officers came from Italy and from the more Romanized provinces. The legionaries were mostly drawn from the less civilized provinces, especially the ones closest to the frontiers. A major trend was already obvious in Hadrian's day: fewer and fewer Roman soldiers were really Roman. In the third century A.D., the barbarization of the army would result in an army indifferent to Rome and its traditions. In the age of the Antonines, however, the army was still a source of economic stability and a Romanizing agent. Provincials and even barbarians joined the army to learn a trade and to gain Roman citizenship. Even so, the signs were ominous. Julius Caesar's veterans would hardly have recognized Hadrian's troops as Roman legionaries.

### LIFE IN THE GOLDEN AGE

*If a man were called to fix the period in the history of the world, during which the condition of the human race was most happy and prosperous, he would without hesitation, name that which elapsed from the death of Domitian to the accession of Commodus.* [14]

Thus, according to Gibbon, the age of the five good emperors was a golden age in human history. How does Gibbon's picture correspond to the popular image of Rome as a city of bread, brothels, and gladiatorial games? If the Romans were degenerates who spent their time carousing, who kept Rome and the empire running? Can life in Rome be taken as representative of life in other parts of the empire?

Truth and exaggeration are mixed both in Gibbon's view and in the popular image of Rome. Rome and the provinces must be treated separately. Rome no more resembled a provincial city like Cologne than New York resembles Keokuk, Iowa. Rome was unique and must be seen as such. Only then can one turn to the provinces to obtain a full and reasonable picture of the empire under the Antonines.

## IMPERIAL ROME

Rome was truly an extraordinary city, especially by ancient standards. It was also an enormous city, with a population somewhere between 500,000 and 750,000. Although Rome could boast of stately palaces, noble buildings, and beautiful residential areas, most people lived in jerrybuilt apartment houses. Fire and crime were perennial problems, even after Augustus created fire and urban police forces. Streets were narrow and drainage inadequate. During the republic sanitation had been a common problem. Numerous inscriptions record prohibitions against the dumping of human refuse and even cadavers within the grounds of sanctuaries and cemeteries. Under the empire this situation improved. By comparison with medieval and early modern European cities, Rome was a healthy enough place to live.

Rome was such a huge city that the surrounding countryside could not feed it. Because of the danger of starvation, the emperor, following republican practice, provided the citizen population with free grain for bread, and later included oil and wine. By feeding the citizenry the emperor prevented bread riots caused by shortages and high prices. For the rest of the urban population who did not enjoy the rights of citizenship,

COIN OF HADRIAN   *The emperor Hadrian not only energetically ruled the Roman Empire, he also helped to set a new fashion in Rome by sporting a full beard. Since Scipio Aemilianus's day, Romans had ordinarily been clean-shaven. (Courtesy, World Heritage Museum. Photo: Caroline Buckler)*

the emperor provided grain at low prices. This measure was designed to prevent speculators from forcing up the price of grain in times of crisis. By maintaining the grain supply the emperor kept the favor of the people and insured that Rome's poor and idle did not starve.

The emperor also entertained the Roman populace, often at vast expense. The most popular forms of public entertainment were gladiatorial contests and chariot racing. Gladiatorial fighting was originally an Etruscan funerary custom, a blood sacrifice for the dead. Even a humane man like Hadrian staged extravagant contests. In A.D. 126 he sponsored six days of such combats, during which 1,835

*APARTMENT HOUSES AT OSTIA    At heavily populated places such as Rome and Ostia, which was the port of Rome, apartment buildings housed urban dwellers. The brick construction of this building is a good example of solid Roman work. In Rome some apartment buildings were notoriously shoddy and unsafe. (Italian Government Travel Office)*

pairs of gladiators dueled, usually with swords and shields. Many gladiators were criminals, some of whom were sentenced to be slaughtered in the arena. These convicts were given no defensive weapons and stood little real chance of survival. Other criminals were sentenced to fight in the arena as fully armed gladiators. Some gladiators were the slaves of gladiatorial trainers; others were prisoners of war. Still others were free men who volunteered for the arena. Even women at times engaged in gladiatorial combat. What drove these men and women? Some obviously had no other choice. For a criminal condemned to death, the arena was preferable to the imperial mines, where convicts worked digging ore and died under wretched conditions. At least

in the arena the gladiator might fight well enough to win his or her freedom. Others no doubt fought for the love of danger and for fame. Although some Romans protested against gladiatorial fighting, most delighted in it – one of their least attractive sides. Not until the fifth century did Christianity put a stop to it.

The Romans were even more addicted to chariot racing than to gladiatorial shows. Under the empire four permanent teams competed against one another. Each team had its own color – red, white, green, or blue. Some Romans claimed that people cared more about their favorite team than about the race itself. Two-horse and four-horse chariots ran a course of seven laps, about five miles. A successful driver could be the hero of the hour. One charioteer, Gaius Appuleius Diocles, raced for twenty-four years. During that time he drove 4,257 starts and won 1,462 of them. His admirers honored him with an inscription that proclaimed him the champion of all charioteers.

But people like the charioteer Diocles were no more typical of the common Roman than Babe Ruth is of the average American. Ordinary Romans have left their mark in the inscriptions that grace their graves. These inscriptions offer a glimpse of Roman life. Ordinary Romans were proud of their work and accomplishments. They were affectionate toward their families and friends, and eager to be remembered after death. They did not spend their lives in idleness, watching gladiators or chariot races. They had to make a living. They dealt with everyday problems and rejoiced over small pleasures. An impression of them and their cares can be gained from their epitaphs. The funerary inscription of Paprius Vitalis to his wife is particularly engaging:

*If there is anything good in the lower regions — I, however, finish a poor life without you — be happy there too, sweetest Thalassia . . . married to me for 40 years.*[15]

As moving is the final tribute of a patron to his ex-slave:

*To Grania Clara, freedwoman of Aulus, a temperate freedwoman. She lived 23 years. She was never vexatious to me except when she died.*[16]

In another epitaph the wife of a merchant honored her husband for his honest dealings. Even the personal philosophies of typical Romans have come down from antiquity. Marcus Antonius Encolpus erected a funerary inscription to his wife that reads in part:

*Do not pass by my epitaph, traveler.*
*But having stopped, listen and learn, then go your way.*
*There is no boat in Hades, no ferryman Charon, no caretaker Aiakos, no dog Cerberus.*
*All we who are dead below*
*have become bones and ashes, but nothing else.*
*I have spoken to you honestly, go on, traveler, lest even while dead I seem loquacious to you.*[17]

Others put it more simply: "I was, I am not, I don't care." "To each his own tombstone." These Romans went about their lives much as people have always done. Though fond of brutal spectacles, they also had their loves and their dreams.

## THE PROVINCES

In the provinces and even on the frontiers many men and women would have agreed with Gibbon's opinion of the second century. The age of the Antonines was one of extensive prosperity, especially in western Europe. The Roman army had beaten back the barbarians and exposed them to the civilizing effects of Roman traders. The resulting peace and security opened Britain, Gaul, Germany, and the lands of the Danube to immigration. Agriculture flourished as large tracts of land came under cultivation. Most of this land was in the hands of free tenant farmers. From the time of Augustus slavery had declined in the empire, as had the growth of latifundia (see page 168). Augustus and his successors encouraged the rise of free farmers. Under the Antonines this trend continued, and the holders of small parcels of land thrived as never before. The Antonines provided loans on easy terms to farmers. These loans enabled them to rent land previously worked by slaves. It also permitted them to cultivate the

SCENE FROM TRAJAN'S COLUMN  *From 101 to 107 Trajan fought the barbarian tribes along the Danube. This scene depicts Roman soldiers unloading supplies at a frontier city, which forms the background. Not only did such walled cities serve as Roman strong points, they were also centers of Roman civilization, with their shops, homes, temples, and amphitheaters. (Alinari/Scala)*

new lands that were being opened up. Consequently, the small tenant farmer was becoming the backbone of Roman agriculture.

In continental Europe the army was largely responsible for the new burst of expansion. The areas where the legions were stationed readily became Romanized. When legionaries retired from the army, they often settled in the locality where they had served. Since they had usually learned a trade in the army, they brought essential skills to areas that badly needed trained men. These veterans took their retirement pay and used it to set themselves up in business.

Since the time of Augustus towns had gradually grown up around the camps and forts. The roads that linked the frontier with the rearward areas served as commercial lifelines for the new towns and villages. Part Roman, part barbarian, these towns were truly outposts of civilization, much like the raw towns of the American West. In the course of time many of them grew to be Romanized cities. As they did, emperors gave them the status of full Roman municipalities, with charters and constitutions. This development was very pronounced along the Rhine and Danube frontiers. Thus while defending the borders, the army also spread Roman culture. This process would go so far that in A.D. 212 the emperor Caracalla would grant Roman citizenship to every free man within the empire.

The eastern part of the empire also participated in the boom. The Roman navy had swept the sea of pirates, and Eastern merchants traded their wares throughout the Mediterranean. The flow of goods and produce in the East matched that of the West. Venerable cities like Corinth, Antioch, and Ephesus flourished as rarely before. The cities of the East built extensively, bedecking themselves with new amphitheaters, temples, fountains, and public buildings. For the East, the age of the Antonines was the heyday of the city. Urban life there grew ever richer and more comfortable.

Trade among the provinces increased dramatically. Britain and Belgium became prime producers of grain, much of their harvests going to the armies of the Rhine. Britain's famous wool industry probably got its start under the Romans. Italy and southern Gaul produced wine in huge quantities. The wines of Italy went principally to Rome and the Danube, while Gallic wines were shipped to Britain and the Rhineland. Roman colonists had introduced the olive to southern Spain and northern Africa, an experiment so successful that these regions produced most of the oil consumed in the western empire. In the East, Syrian farmers continued to cultivate the olive, and the production of oil reached an all-time high. Egypt was the prime grain producer of the East, and tons of Egyptian wheat went to feed the populace of Rome. The

Roman army in Mesopotamia consumed a high percentage of the raw materials and manufactured products of Syria and Asia Minor. The spread of trade meant the end of isolated and self-contained economies. By the time of the Antonines the empire had become an economic reality as well as a political one.

One of the most striking features of this period was the growth of industry in the provinces. Cities in Gaul and Germany eclipsed the old Mediterranean manufacturing centers. Italian cities were particularly hard-hit by this development. Cities like Arrentium and Capua had dominated the production of glass, pottery, and bronze ware. Yet in the second century A.D. Gaul and Germany took over the pottery market. Lyons in Gaul became the new center of the glassmaking industry. The technique of glass blowing spread to Britain and Germany, and later in the second century Cologne replaced Lyons in glass production. The cities of Gaul were nearly unrivaled in the manufacture of bronze and brass. Gallic craftsmen invented a new technique of tin-plating and decorated their work with Celtic designs. Their wares soon drove Italian products out of the northern European market. For the first time in history northern Europe was able to rival the Mediterranean as a producer of manufactured goods. Europe had entered fully into the economic and cultural life of the Mediterranean world.

The age of the Antonines was generally one of peace, progress, and prosperity. The work of the Romans in northern and western Europe was a permanent contribution to the history of Western society. The cities that grew up in Britain, Belgium, Gaul, Germany, Austria, and elsewhere survived the civil wars that racked the empire in the third century A.D. Likewise, they survived the barbarian invasions that destroyed the western empire, and handed on a precious heritage, both cultural and material, to the medieval world. The period of the Antonine monarchy was also one of consolidation. Roads and secure sea-lanes linked the empire in one vast web. The empire had become a commonwealth of cities, and urban life was the hallmark of this civilization.

## CIVIL WARS AND INVASION IN THE THIRD CENTURY

The age of the Antonines gave way to a period of chaos and stress. During the third century A.D., the empire was stunned by civil wars and barbarian invasions. By the time peace was restored, the economy was shattered, cities had shrunk in size, and agriculture was becoming manorial (see pages 203–204). In the disruption of the third century and the reconstruction of the fourth, the medieval world had its origins.

After the death of Marcus Aurelius, the last of the five good emperors, his son Commodus came to the throne, a man who was totally unsuited to govern the empire. His misrule led to his murder and a renewal of civil war. After a brief but intense spasm of fighting, the African general Septimius Severus defeated other rival commanders and established the Severan dynasty (A.D. 193–235). Although Septimius Severus was able to stabilize the empire, his successors proved incapable of disciplining the legions. When the last of the Severi was killed by one of his own soldiers, the empire plunged into still another grim, destructive, and this time prolonged round of civil war.

Over twenty different emperors ascended the throne in the forty-nine years between 235

and 284, and many rebels died in the attempt to seize power. At various times, parts of the empire were lost to rebel generals, one of whom, Postumus, set up his own empire in Gaul for about ten years (A.D. 259–269). Yet other men like the iron-willed Aurelian (A.D. 270–275) dedicated their energies to restoring order. So many military commanders seized rule that the middle of the third century has become known as the age of the "barracks emperors." The Augustan Principate had become a military monarchy, and that monarchy was nakedly autocratic.

The disruption caused by civil war opened the way for widespread barbarian invasions. Throughout the empire, barbarian invasions and civil war devastated towns, villages, and farms and caused a catastrophic economic depression. Indeed, the Roman Empire seemed on the point of collapse.

### BARBARIANS ON THE FRONTIERS

The first and most disastrous result of the civil wars was trouble on the frontiers. It was Rome's misfortune that this era of anarchy coincided with immense movements of barbarian peoples. Historians still dispute the precise reason for these migrations, though their immediate cause was pressure from tribes moving westward across Asia. In the sixth century A.D., Jordanes, a Christianized Goth, preserved the memory of innumerable wars among the barbarians in his *History of the Goths.* Goths fought Vandals, Huns fought Goths. Steadily, the defeated and displaced tribes moved toward the Roman frontiers. Finally, like "a swarm of bees" – to use Jordanes's image – the Goths burst into Europe in A.D. 258.

When the barbarians reached the Rhine and Danube frontiers, they often found huge gaps in the Roman defenses. Typical is the case of Decius, a general who guarded the Danube frontier in Dacia (modern Rumania). In A.D. 249, he revolted and invaded Italy in an effort to become emperor. Decius left the frontier deserted, and the Goths easily poured in looking for new homes. Through much of the third century A.D., bands of Goths devastated the Balkans as far south as Greece. They even penetrated Asia Minor. The Alamanni, a German people, swept across the Danube. At one point they entered Italy and reached Milan before they were beaten back. Meanwhile the Franks, still another German folk, hit the Rhine frontier. The Franks then invaded eastern and central Gaul and northeastern Spain. Saxons from Scandinavia entered the English Channel in search of loot. In the East the Sassanids, of Persian stock, overran Mesopotamia. If the army had been guarding the borders instead of creating and destroying emperors, none of these invasions would have been possible. The "barracks emperors" should be credited with one accomplishment, however: they fought barbarians when they were not fighting each other. Only that kept the empire from total ruin.

## TURMOIL IN FARM AND VILLAGE LIFE

How did the ordinary people cope with this period of iron and blood? What did it mean to the lives of men and women on farms and in villages? How did local officials continue to serve their emperor and their neighbors? Some people became outlaws. Others lived their lives more prosaically. Some voiced their grievances to the emperor, thereby leaving a record of the problems they faced. In a sur-

prising number of cases the barbarians were less of a problem than the lawlessness of soldiers, imperial officials, and local agents. For many ordinary people official corruption was the tangible and immediate result of the breakdown of central authority. In one instance some tenant farmers in Lydia (modern Turkey) complained to the emperor about arbitrary arrest and the killing of prisoners. They claimed that police agents had threatened them and prevented them from cultivating the land. Tenant farmers in Phrygia (modern Turkey) voiced similar complaints. They suffered extortion at the hands of public officials. Military commanders, soldiers, and imperial agents requisitioned their livestock and compelled the farmers to forced labor. The farmers were becoming impoverished, and many people deserted the land to seek safety elsewhere. The inhabitants of an entire village in Thrace (modern Bulgaria) complained that they were being driven from their homes. From imperial and local officials they suffered insolence and violence. Soldiers demanded to be quartered and given supplies. Many villagers had already abandoned their homes to escape. The remaining villagers warned the emperor that unless order was restored, they too would flee.

Local officials were sometimes unsympathetic or violent toward farmers and villagers because of their own plight. They were responsible for the collection of imperial revenues. If their area could not meet its tax quota, they paid the deficit from their own pockets. For instance, Aurelius Hermophilus complained that he could no longer perform public duties because he had gone bankrupt. When Aemilius Stephanus, a wealthy Roman in Egypt, learned that he had been nominated to the local council of his town, he surrendered all his property to the man who had nominated him. In one Egyptian municipality fistfights broke out among the officials. Finally the emperor had to forbid fighting in the council house. Because the local officials were so hard-pressed, they squeezed whatever they could from the villagers and farmers.

## RECONSTRUCTION UNDER DIOCLETIAN AND CONSTANTINE (A.D. 284–337)

At the close of the third century A.D., the emperor Diocletian (284–305) put an end to the period of turmoil. Repairing the damage done in the third century was the major work of the emperor Constantine (306–337) in the fourth. But the price was high.

Under Diocletian, Augustus's polite fiction of the emperor as "first among equals" gave way to the emperor as absolute autocrat. The princeps became *dominus* – lord. The emperor claimed that he was "the elect of god" – that he ruled because of god's favor. Constantine even claimed to be the equal of Jesus' first twelve followers. To underline the emperor's exalted position, Diocletian and Constantine adopted the gaudy court ceremonies and trappings of the Persian Empire. People entering the emperor's presence prostrated themselves before him and kissed the hem of his robes. Constantine went so far as to import Persian eunuchs to run the palace. The Roman emperor had become an oriental monarch.

No mere soldier, Diocletian gave serious thought to the ailments of the empire. He recognized that the empire and its difficulties had become too great for one man to handle. He also realized that during the third century provincial governors had frequently used their positions to foment or participate in rebellions. To solve the first of these problems

MAP 6.2 THE ROMAN WORLD DIVIDED *Under Diocletian, the Roman empire was first divided into a western and an eastern half, a development that foreshadowed the medieval division between the Latin West and the Byzantine East.*

Diocletian divided the empire into a western half and an eastern half (see Map 6.2). Diocletian assumed direct control of the eastern part; he gave the rule of the western part to a colleague, along with the title *augustus,* which had become synonymous with emperor. Diocletian and his fellow augustus further delegated power by appointing two men to assist them. Each man was given the title of *caesar* to indicate his exalted rank. Although this system is known as the Tetrarchy because four men ruled the empire, Diocletian was clearly the senior partner and the final source of authority.

Each half of the empire was further split into two prefectures, governed by a prefect responsible to an augustus. Diocletian reduced the power of the old provincial governors by dividing provinces into smaller units: he organized the prefectures into smaller administrative units called dioceses, which were in turn subdivided into small provinces. Provincial governors were also deprived of their military power, leaving them only civil and administrative duties.

Diocletian's division of the empire into two parts was a momentous step, for it became permanent. Constantine and later emperors tried hard to keep the empire together, but without success. Throughout the fourth century A.D., the East and the West drifted apart. In later centuries the western part witnessed the fall of Roman government and the rise of barbarian kingdoms, while the eastern empire evolved into the majestic Byzantine Empire.

The most serious immediate matters con-

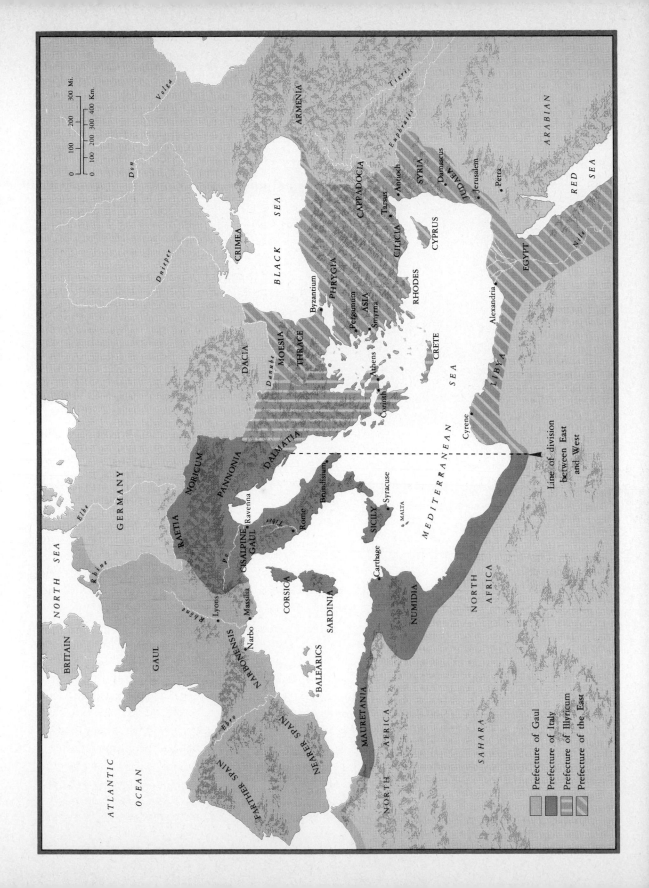

ARMENIA

ARABIAN

Don

Volga

Tigris

Dnieper

RED SEA

Nile

Euphrates

CRIMEA

BLACK SEA

CAPPADOCIA

SYRIA

Damascus

Antioch

JUDAEA

Jerusalem

Petra

Byzantium

PHRYGIA

CILICIA

Tarsus

CYPRUS

Pergamum

ASIA

Smyrna

RHODES

EGYPT

DACIA

Danube

MOESIA

THRACE

Athens

Corinth

CRETE

Alexandria

LIBYA

Cyrene

MEDITERRANEAN SEA

Line of division
between East
and West

NORICUM

PANNONIA

DALMATIA

RAETIA

CISALPINE
GAUL

Ravenna

Brundisium

Syracuse

Rome

SICILY

MALTA

Po

Tiber

GERMANY

Elbe

Rhine

Carthage

NUMIDIA

NORTH AFRICA

NORTH SEA

BRITAIN

GAUL

Rhône

Lyons

Massilia

Narbo

NARBONENSIS

CORSICA

SARDINIA

BALEARICS

SAHARA

ATLANTIC OCEAN

MAURETANIA

NORTH AFRICA

Ebro

FARTHER SPAIN

NEARER SPAIN

SPAIN

Prefecture of Gaul

Prefecture of Italy

Prefecture of Illyricum

Prefecture of the East

THE ARCH OF CONSTANTINE  *To celebrate the victory which made him emperor, Constantine built this triumphal arch at Rome. Rather than decorate the arch with the inferior work of his own day, Constantine plundered other Roman monuments, including those of Trajan and Marcus Aurelius. (Italian Government Travel Office)*

fronting Diocletian and Constantine were economic, social, and religious. They needed additional revenues to support the army and the imperial court. Yet the wars and the barbarian invasions had caused widespread destruction and poverty. The fighting had struck a serious blow to Roman agriculture, which the emperors tried to revive. Christianity had become too strong either to ignore or to crush. How Diocletian, Constantine, and their successors dealt with those problems helped create the economic and social patterns medieval Europe inherited.

## INFLATION AND TAXES

The barracks emperors had dealt with economic hardship by depreciating the currency: they cut the silver content of coins until money was virtually worthless. As a result the entire monetary system fell into ruin. In Egypt governors had to order bankers to accept imperial money. The immediate result was a crippling inflation throughout the empire.

The empire was less capable of recovery than in earlier times. Wars and invasions had disrupted normal commerce and the means of production. Mines were exhausted in the attempt to supply much-needed ores, especially gold and silver. War and invasion had hit the cities especially hard. Markets were disrupted, and travel became dangerous. Craftsmen, artisans, and traders rapidly left devastated regions. The prosperous industry and commerce of Gaul and the Rhineland declined markedly. Those who owed their prosperity to commerce and the needs of urban life likewise suffered. Cities were no longer places where trade and industry thrived. The devastation of the countryside increased the difficulty of feeding and supplying the cities. The destruction was so extensive that many wondered whether the ravages could be repaired at all.

The response of Diocletian and Constantine to these problems was marked by compulsion, rigidity, and loss of individual freedom. Diocletian's attempt to curb inflation illustrates the methods of absolute monarchy: in a move unprecedented in Roman history, he issued an edict that fixed maximum prices and wages throughout the empire. The measure failed because it was unrealistic and unenforceable.

The emperors dealt with the tax system just as strictly and inflexibly. As in the past, local officials bore the responsibility of collecting imperial taxes. Constantine made these officials into a hereditary class; son followed father whether he wanted to or not. In this period of severe depression, many localities could not pay their taxes. In such cases these local officials had to make up the difference from their own funds. This system soon wiped out a whole class of moderately wealthy people.

With the monetary system in ruins, most imperial taxes became payable in kind — that is, in goods or produce instead of money. The major drawback of payment in kind is its demands on transportation. Goods have to be moved from where they are grown or manufactured to where they are needed. Accordingly, the emperors locked into their occupations all those involved in the growing, preparation, and transportation of food and essential commodities. A baker or shipper could not go into any other business, and his son took up the trade upon his death. The late Roman Empire had a place for everyone, and everyone had a place.

## THE DECLINE OF SMALL FARMS

The late Roman heritage to the medieval world is most obvious in agriculture. Because of worsening conditions, free tenant farmers were reduced to serfdom. During the third century A.D., many were killed or fled the land to escape the barbarians, or abandoned farms ravaged in the fighting. Consequently, large tracts of land lay deserted. Great landlords with ample resources began at once to reclaim as much of this land as they could. The huge estates that resulted were the forerunners of medieval manors. Like manors, villas were self-sufficient. Since they often produced more than they consumed, they successfully competed with the declining cities by selling their surplus in the countryside. They became islands of stability in an unsettled world.

While the villas were growing, the small farmers who remained on the land barely held their own. They were too poor and powerless to stand against the tide of chaos. They were exposed to the raids of barbarians or brigands and to the tyranny of imperial officials. For relief they turned to the great landlords. After all, the landowners were men of considerable resources, lords in their own right. They were wealthy, and they had many people working

A LARGE ROMAN VILLA   During the third and fourth centuries, as the Roman Empire was breaking up, large villas such as this often became the focus of life. The villa was at once a fortress, as can be seen by the towers at the corner of the building, and the economic and social center of the neighborhood. (Courtesy, German Archeological Institute)

their land. They were independent and capable of defending themselves. If need be, they could — and at times did — field a small force of their own. Already influential, they stood up to imperial officials.

In return for the protection and security that landlords could offer, the small landholders gave over their lands. Free men and their families became clients of the landlords, and lost much of their freedom. To guarantee a steady supply of labor the landlords bound them to the soil. They could no longer decide to move elsewhere. Henceforth, they and their families worked the land of their patrons. Free men and women were in effect becoming serfs.

## THE LEGALIZATION OF CHRISTIANITY

In religious affairs Constantine took the decisive step of recognizing Christianity as a legitimate religion. No longer would Christians suffer persecution for their beliefs. Constantine himself died a Christian in 337. Constantine has been depicted both as a devout convert to Christianity and as a realistic opportunist who used the young religion to his own imperial ends. Certainly Constantine was realistic enough to recognize and appreciate Christianity's spread and hold on his subjects. He correctly gauged the strength of the Christian ecclesiastical organization, and realized that the new church could serve as a friend of his empire. Yet there is no solid reason to doubt the sincerity of his conversion to the Christian religion. In short, Constantine was a man personally inclined toward Christianity and an emperor who could bestow on it a legal and legitimate place within the Roman empire.

Why had the pagans – those who believed in the Greco-Roman gods – persecuted Christians in the first place? Polytheism is by nature tolerant of new gods and accommodating in religious matters. Why was Christianity singled out for violence? These questions are still matters of scholarly debate, but some broad answers can be given.

Even an educated and cultured man like the historian Tacitus opposed Christianity. He believed that Christians hated the whole human race. As a rule early Christians, like Jews, kept to themselves. Romans distrusted and feared their exclusiveness, which seemed unsociable and even subversive. Most pagans genuinely misunderstood Christian practices. They thought that the Lord's Supper, at which Christians said they ate and drank the body and blood of Jesus, was an act of cannibalism. Pagans thought that Christians indulged in immoral and indecent rituals. They considered Christianity one of the worst of the oriental mystery cults, for one of the hallmarks of many of those cults was disgusting rituals.

Even these feelings of distrust and revulsion do not entirely account for persecution. The main reason seems to have been sincere religious conviction on the part of the pagans. Time and again they accused Christians of atheism. Indeed, Christians either denied the existence of pagan gods or called them evil spirits. For this same reason many Romans hated the Jews. Tacitus no doubt expressed the common view when he said that Jews despised the gods. Christians went even further than Jews – they said that no one should worship pagan gods.

At first, some pagans were repelled by the fanaticism of these monotheists. No good could come from scorning the gods. The whole community might end up paying for the wickedness and blasphemy of the Christians. Besides – and this is important – pagans did not demand that Christians *believe* in pagan gods. Greek and Roman religion was never a matter of belief or ethics. It was purely a religion of ritual. One of the clearest statements of pagan theological attitudes comes from the Roman senator Symmachus:

*We watch the same stars; heaven is the same for us all; the same universe envelops us: what importance is it in what way anyone looks for truth? It is impossible to arrive by one route at such a great secret.*[18]

Yet Roman religion was inseparable from the state. An attack on one was an attack on the other. The Romans were being no more fanatical or intolerant than an eighteenth-century English judge who declared the Christian religion part of the law of the land. All the pagans expected was performance of the ritual act, a small token sacrifice. Any Christian who sacrificed went free, no matter what he or she personally believed. The earliest persecutions of the Christians were minor and limited. Even Nero's famous persecution was temporary and limited to Rome. Subsequent persecutions were sporadic and local.

As time went on, pagan hostility decreased.

Pagans gradually realized that Christians were not working to overthrow the state and that Jesus was no rival of Caesar. The emperor Trajan forbade his governors to hunt down Christians. Trajan admitted that he thought Christianity an abomination, but he preferred to leave Christians in peace.

The stress of the third century, however, seemed to some emperors the punishment of the gods. What else could account for such anarchy? With the empire threatened on every side, a few emperors thought that one way to appease the gods was by offering them the proper sacrifices. Such sacrifices would be a sign of loyalty to the empire, a show of Roman solidarity. Consequently, a new wave of persecutions began. Yet even they were never very widespread or long-lived; by the late third century, pagans had become used to Christianity. Although a few emperors, including Diocletian, vigorously persecuted Christians, most pagans left them alone. Nor were they very sympathetic to the new round of persecutions. Pagan and Christian alike must have been relieved when Constantine legalized Christianity.

In time the Christian triumph would be complete. In 380, the emperor Theodosius made Christianity the official religion of the Roman Empire. At that point Christians began to persecute the pagans for their beliefs. History had come full circle.

## THE CONSTRUCTION OF CONSTANTINOPLE

The triumph of Christianity was not the only event that made Constantine's reign a turning-point in Roman history. Constantine took the bold step of building a new capital for the empire. Constantinople, the New Rome, was constructed on the site of Byzantium, an old Greek city on the Bosporus. Throughout the third century, emperors had found Rome and

the West hard to defend. The eastern part of the empire was more easily defensible, and escaped the worst of the barbarian devastation. It was wealthy and its urban life still vibrant. Moreover, Christianity was more widespread in the East than in the West, and Constantinople was intended to be a Christian city.

## THE AWFUL REVOLUTION

On the evening of October 15, 1764, Edward Gibbon, a young Englishman, sat in Rome among the ruins of the Capitol listening to the chanting of some monks. As the voices of the Christian present echoed against the stones of the pagan past, Gibbon wondered how the Roman Empire had given way to the medieval world. His curiosity aroused, he dedicated himself to the study of what he considered the greatest problem in history.

Twelve years later, in 1776, Gibbon published *The History of the Decline and Fall of the Roman Empire,* one of the monuments of English literature, a brilliant work fashioned with wit, learning, humor, and elegance.

Gibbon's thesis is, as the title of his work indicates, that the Roman Empire, after the first two centuries of existence, declined in strength, vitality, and prosperity and then fell into ruin. His concept of Rome's "decline and fall," a process he called "the awful revolution," has dominated historical thought for two hundred years. Even those who disagree with Gibbon over details have usually accepted his concept of "decline and fall." What explanations did Gibbon give for the fate of the Roman Empire, and how have others responded to his views? Is Gibbon's concept valid, and is it the only way of looking at this problem?

## GIBBON'S RATIONALISTIC THEORIES

Gibbon was a true son of the Enlightenment, the eighteenth-century mode of thought that honored reason and despised faith. He regarded Christianity with contempt and as nothing more than vile superstition. In Gibbon's view the glory of the ancient world, with its learning, arts, manners, and philosophy, gleamed in comparison with the "Dark Ages" of the medieval period, when the church held Europe in the thrall of ignorance and sorcery. Christianity emphasized the virtues of humility, patience, and piety – qualities hardly masculine or imperial and totally inadequate for the maintenance of a proud and vigorous empire. Christianity praised chastity and the monastic life, which, in Gibbon's view, drained the empire of vitality and creativity. Nor did he admire the Germans who invaded and infiltrated the empire. Uncivilized and uncouth, they were, in Gibbon's eyes, even incapable of using reason. Although he acknowledged their hardiness and manly vigor, he scorned them as savages who ate horsemeat.

Despite the value of Gibbon's work, Christianity cannot reasonably be made the villain of the piece. True, many very able minds and forceful characters devoted their lives and energies to the Christian church and not to the empire. True, monasticism flourished and led to a passive and politically unproductive existence. Yet the numbers involved in these pursuits were small in proportion to the total population. Furthermore, the Byzantine Empire, which evolved from the eastern part of the Roman Empire, demonstrated that Christians could handle the sword and spear as well as the cross.

Gibbon also argued that the empire had grown so large that it fell of its own weight. In his words, "the decline of Rome was the natural and inevitable effect of immoderate greatness. . . . The story of its ruin is simple and obvious; and instead of inquiring *why* the Roman empire was destroyed, we should rather be surprised that it had subsisted so long."[19] In effect, Gibbon begs his own question, and instead chronicles the later history of the Roman world.

## PSEUDOSCIENTIFIC THEORIES: SCIENCE ABUSED

Gibbon is not alone in trying to explain Rome's fate. The question has absorbed the attention of many, some of whom have misused scientific techniques in their search. They have applied bits of scientific fact and method to a vast and imperfectly known historical development, ignoring the simple fact that the end of the Roman Empire, unlike the composition of DNA, cannot be scientifically determined.

A slightly altered form of Gibbon's view of natural decline has recently found supporters who look at historical developments in biological terms. According to them, states and empires develop like living organisms, progressing through periods of birth and growth to maturity and consolidation, followed by decrepitude, decline, and collapse. This argument is simply false analogy, unsupported by any scientific evidence.

Some twentieth-century writers have resorted to pseudoscientific theories blaming the "collapse" of the empire on racial corruption. As the physically strong, morally pure, and creatively intelligent Romans conquered inferior Asian and African peoples, so the explanation goes, they intermingled with them. The physical and intellectual traits of the less fit came to predominate. This "mongrelization" of the empire steadily sapped the physical and moral fiber of the Romans. When faced with a military crisis, Rome was too weak to cope. Even taken on its own terms, this theory is nonsense. The eastern half of the empire, the home of the "inferior" Asiatics, survived a thousand years longer than the "superior" western one.

Not all those who have used science to explain Rome's fate have been cranks. Some writers have tried to use statistical information and demographic arguments to explain Rome's fall. According to this view, a sharp decline in population diminishes a society's ability to defend itself and weakens its economy and ultimately the entire civilization. In 167 A.D., they argue, the bubonic plague swept the empire and apparently killed large numbers of people. Yet it is a serious error to conclude that the ravages of disease in the second century were responsible for later catastrophes. Economic historians have demonstrated that even severe epidemics have only a short-term economic effect, after which conditions quickly normalize themselves. There was ample time for the empire to recover from this plague.

Population did decline in the third and fourth centuries, for which the most likely explanation is losses due to war and devastation. Even so, the population of the Roman Empire outnumbered the invading barbarians, and there were more than enough people to defend the empire.

## THE SOCIOECONOMIC THEORIES OF FERDINAND LOT

The twentieth-century French scholar Ferdinand Lot relied on economics to explain "the awful revolution." He acknowledged that the causes of Rome's "decline" were many and interrelated, but maintained that the basic causes were socioeconomic. Lot pointed out that the Roman economy was badly adjusted;

in fact, according to him, it never really developed. Although the Romans had technological skill, Rome never industrialized. An almost limitless supply of slaves provided cheap labor and discouraged the development of labor-saving methods. Roman conquests brought a steady stream of slaves to the West. Slaves worked the land on the latifundia and produced what little was manufactured in the West. The Roman aristocracy lived on the revenues from their estates. The few people involved in trade and commerce served as middlemen, moneylenders, tax collectors, or civil bureaucrats. A commercial and industrial middle class failed to develop.

Western products — primarily, in Lot's view, raw materials — did not begin to equal the value of imports. Increasingly, the balance of trade within the empire worsened: the western part bought much more than it sold and paid for purchases with precious metals. The pressure of the German invasions made social and economic conditions worse. Once the West was cut off from sources of goods and without goods of its own to export, it reverted to an agrarian and isolated economy. The level of learning deteriorated and technical skills were lost. According to Lot, economic collapse accelerated political ruin. Moreover, great cities in the West drastically declined in population, and simultaneously trade and commerce slowed to a trickle. With the tax base gone, cultural movements and intellectual activities could not be maintained.

The force of Lot's argument is weakened by the fact that large-scale emancipation of slaves occurred during the empire. Roman emperors encouraged the growth of a prosperous class of small tenant farmers. Slavery also existed in the East, and did not prevent the West from industrializing. Cities in Gaul and Germany became centers of manufacturing, and even managed to dominate the production of glass, pottery, and bronze ware. Furthermore, these industries were usually manned by free labor, not slaves.

Lot's theories also make too little of political factors. The economic woes of the empire began during the civil wars and invasions of the middle of the third century — wars that left wide tracts of land desolate and manufacturing centers in shambles. Roman failure to create a stable form of government exposed the empire to serious disruption that could not fail to have dire economic effects. Though enlightening in many respects, Lot's theories are incapable of explaining the "decline and fall."

## POLITICAL EXPLANATIONS

Over the years political explanations have won the widest acceptance. The Roman imperial government never solved the problem of succession: it never devised a peaceful and regular way to pass on the imperial power when an emperor died. The legions enjoyed too much power, often creating and destroying civil governments at will, and in the process disrupting the state. The assassinations of emperors and frequent changes of government produced chronic instability, weakening the state's ability to solve its problems.

From the late third century onward, successive approaches to Rome's economic difficulties proved disastrous. Emperors depreciated the coinage. The middle classes carried an increasingly heavy burden of taxation, and all the while the imperial bureaucracy grew bigger, though not more efficient. These factors combined to destroy the ordinary citizen's confidence in the state. Consequently, according to the political explanation, with the economy and society undermined, the empire was destroyed by its internal difficulties.

There is no question that the Roman Empire suffered from severe political problems, which were never solved. Energy that could have been spent defending the frontiers or policing the sea-lanes was all too often squandered in bloody and costly civil war. The same fate had overtaken the republic, but at least then there were no land-hungry barbarian tribes ready to turn Roman weakness to their own advantage. Political explanations, too, have their defects, for emperors such as Diocletian showed how the empire could survive even fearful ravages. Nor do political theories adequately explain why the West "fell" while the East survived for another millennium.

## CONTINUITY AND CHANGE

Some writers have rejected the whole idea of decline. As early as 1744, before Gibbon had contemplated writing the *Decline and Fall of the Roman Empire,* the Frenchman Abbé Galliani wrote: "The fall of empires? What can that mean? Empires being neither up nor down do not fall. They change their appearance."[20] The concept of change and development, instead of decline, has much to recommend it, inasmuch as many aspects of the Roman world survived to influence the medieval and eventually the modern world. Roman law left its traces on the legal and political systems of most European countries. Roman roads, aqueducts, bridges, and buildings remained in use, standing as constant reminders of the Roman past and its link with the present. The Latin language, with its rich vocabulary and its strict but rational grammatical rules, facilitated communication over a wide area and allowed for precision of expression. For almost two thousand years Latin language and literature remained the core of all education in the West. Those who studied Latin came to some degree under the spell of

Rome, as Roman attitudes and patterns of thought fertilized the intellectual lives of generation after generation of Europeans. Slowly, almost imperceptibly, the Roman Empire gave way to the medieval world.

———◆———

Never before in Western history and not again until modern times did one state govern so many people over so much of the world for so long a span of time. The true heritage of Rome is its long tradition of law and freedom. Under Roman law and government the West enjoyed relative peace and security for extensive periods of time. Under the auspices of Rome northern Europe entered into the civilized world of the Mediterranean. Through Rome the best of ancient thought and culture was preserved to make its contribution to modern life. Perhaps no better epitaph for Rome can be found than the words of Virgil:

*While rivers shall run to the sea,*
*While shadows shall move across the valleys of*
    *mountains,*
*While the heavens shall nourish the stars,*
*Always shall your honor and your name and your*
    *fame endure.*[21]

## NOTES

1. Virgil *Aeneid* 6.851–853.
2. Augustus *Res Gestae* 6.34.
3. Ibid., 5.28.
4. Virgil *Aeneid* 6.791–794.
5. Horace *Odes* 4.15.
6. Virgil *Georgics* 4.180–183.
7. Ibid., 3.515–519.
8. Horace *Odes* 1.38.
9. Matthew 3:3.
10. Matthew 16:18.
11. Edward Gibbon, *The History of the Decline and Fall of the Roman Empire,* Modern Library, New York, n.d., 1.1.
12. Ibid., 1.52.
13. M. Hammond, *The Antonine Monarchy,* American Academy in Rome, Rome, 1959, p. x.
14. Gibbon, 1.70.
15. *Corpus Inscriptionum Latinarum,* vol. 6, G. Reimer, Berlin, 1882, no. 9792.
16. Ibid., vol. 10, no. 8192.
17. Ibid., vol. 6, no. 14672.
18. Symmachus *Relations* 3.10.
19. Gibbon, 2.438.
20. Quoted in F. W. Walbank, *The Awful Revolution,* University of Toronto Press, Toronto, 1969, p. 121.
21. Virgil *Aeneid* 1.607–609.

## SUGGESTED READING

Of the works cited in the Notes, that by Hammond is a classic in the field, and Gibbon's *Decline and Fall* is of course one of the masterpieces of English literature. Some good general treatments of the empire include B. Cunliffe, *Rome and Her Empire* (1978), which is profusely illustrated, and P. Petit, *Pax Romana* (English translation, 1976). The role of the emperor is superbly treated by F. Millar, *The Emperor in the Roman World* (1977), and the defense of the empire is brilliantly studied by E. N. Luttwak, *The Grand Strategy of the Roman Empire* (1976). The army that carried out that strategy is the subject of G. Webster, *The Roman Imperial Army* (1969).

Favorable to Augustus is M. Hammond, *The Augustan Principate* (1933), and G. W. Bowersock, *Augustus and the Greek World* (1965), is excellent intellectual history. C. M. Wells, *The German Policy of Augustus* (1972), uses archaeological findings to illustrate Roman expansion into northern Europe.

The commercial life of the empire is the subject of M. P. Charlesworth, *Trade Routes and Commerce of the Roman Empire,* 2nd ed. (1926). Newer, if briefer, is the stimulating article by L. Casson, "Rome's Trade with the East: The Sea Voyage to Africa and India," *Transactions of the American Philological Association* 110 (1980): 21–36. R. Duncan-Jones, *The Economy of the Roman Empire: Quantitative Studies,* 2nd ed. (1982), employs new techniques of historical inquiry. J. Percival, *The Roman Villa* (1976), is a lively study of an important institution. The classic treatment, which ranges across the empire, is M. Rostovtzeff, *The Economic and Social History of the Roman Empire* (1957).

Social aspects of the empire are the subject of R. Auguet, *Cruelty and Civilization: The Roman Games* (English translation, 1972); P. Garnsey, *Social Status and Legal Privilege in the Roman Empire* (1970); and A. N. Sherwin-White, *Racial Prejudice in Imperial Rome* (1967). A general treatment is R. MacMullen, *Roman Social Relations, 50 B.C. to A.D. 284* (1981). N. Kampen, *Image and Status: Roman Working Women in Ostia* (1981) is distinctive for its treatment of ordinary Roman women. An important feature of Roman history is treated by R. P. Saller, *Personal Patronage under the Early Empire* (1982).

Christianity, paganism, and Judaism receive treatment in E. M. Smallwood, *The Jews under Roman Rule* (corrected ed., 1981); R. A. Markus, *Christianity in the Roman World* (1975); and A. D. Momigliano, *The Conflict between Paganism and Christianity in the Fourth Century* (1963). Two important topics in the study of early Christianity are treated in W. H. C. Frend, *Martyrdom and Persecution in the Early Church* (1965); and M. Hengel, *Acts and the History of Earliest Christianity* (1979). The significance of the cult of Roma in the empire is well treated by R. Mellor, "The Goddess Roma", in *Aufstieg und Niedergang der römischen Welt,* vol. II, part 17 (1981), pp. 952–1030.

A convenient survey of Roman literature is J. W. Duff, *Literary History of Rome from the Origins to the Close of the Golden Age* (1953) and *Literary History of Rome in the Silver Age,* 3rd ed. (1964).

The fall of Rome continues to be a fertile field of investigation: A. H. M. Jones, *The Decline of the Ancient World* (1966); F. W. Walbank, *The Awful Revolution* (1969); and R. MacMullen's two books: *Soldier and Civilian in the Later Roman Empire* (1963) and *Enemies of the Roman Order: Treason, Unrest, and Alienation in the Empire* (1966).

# CHAPTER 7

# THE MAKING OF EUROPE

THE CENTURIES BETWEEN approximately 400 and 900 present the student with a paradox. These years witnessed the disintegration of the Roman Empire, which had been one of humanity's great political and cultural achievements. On the other hand, these five centuries were a creative and important period, during which Europeans laid the foundations for the development of medieval and modern Europe. It is not too much to say that this period saw the making of Europe.

The basic ingredients that went into the making of a distinctly European civilization were the cultural legacy of Greece and Rome, the customs and traditions of the Germanic peoples, and the Christian faith. The most important of these was Christianity, because it absorbed and assimilated the other two. It reinterpreted the classics in a Christian sense. It instructed the Germanic peoples and gave them new ideals of living and social behavior. Christianity became the cement that held European society together.

During this period the Byzantine Empire centered at Constantinople served as a protective buffer between Europe and savage peoples to the east. The Greeks preserved the philosophical and scientific texts of the ancient world, which later formed the basis for study in science and medicine; and they produced a great synthesis of Roman law, the Justinian Code. In the urbane and sophisticated life led at Constantinople, the Greeks set a standard far above the primitive existence of the West.

In the seventh and eighth centuries, Arabic culture spread around the southern fringes of Europe – to Spain, Sicily, and North Africa, and to Syria, Palestine, and Egypt. The Arabs translated the works of such Greek thinkers as Euclid, Hippocrates, and Galen, and made important contributions in mathematics, astronomy, and physics. In Arabic translation, Greek texts trickled to the West, and most later European scientific study rested on the Arabic work.

European civilization resulted from the fusion of Germanic traditions, the Greco-Roman heritage, and the Christian faith. How did these components act upon one another? How did they bring about the making of Europe? What influence did the Byzantine and Islamic cultures have on the making of European civilization? These are the questions discussed in this chapter.

## THE MIGRATION OF THE GERMANIC PEOPLES

The migration of peoples from one area to another has been a dominant and continuing feature of European history. Mass movements of Europeans occurred in the fourth through sixth centuries, in the ninth and tenth centuries, and in the twelfth and thirteenth centuries. From the sixteenth century to the present such movements have been almost continuous, and have involved not just the European continent but the entire world. The causes of these migrations varied, and they are not thoroughly understood by scholars. But there is no question that they profoundly affected both the regions to which peoples moved and the ones they left behind.

The *völkerwanderungen*, or migrations of the Germanic peoples, was an important factor in the decline of the Roman Empire. Many twentieth-century historians and sociologists have tried to explain who the Germans were and why they emigrated, but scholars have not had much success at answering these questions. The surviving evidence is primarily archaeological, scanty, and not yet adequately explored. Conclusions are still tentative.

*VANDAL LANDOWNER   The adoption of Roman dress — short tunic, cloak, and sandals — reflects the way the Germanic tribes accepted Roman lifestyles. Likewise both the mosaic art form and the man's stylized appearance show the Germans' assimilation of Roman influences. (Notice that the rider has a saddle but not stirrups.) (The British Museum)*

What answers do exist rest on archaeological evidence found later inside the borders of the Roman Empire: bone fossils, cooking utensils, jewelry, instruments of war, and other surviving artifacts. Like the Vikings, who first terrorized and then settled in many sections of Europe in the ninth and tenth centuries, the Germans came from eastern Germany and the areas of modern Denmark, Sweden, and Norway. Ethnically they were Scandinavians.

Since about 250, Germanic tribes had pressed along the Rhine-Danube frontier of the Roman Empire. Depending upon their closeness to that border, these tribes differed considerably from one another in level of civilization. Some tribes, such as the Visigoths and Ostrogoths, led a settled existence, engaged in agriculture and trade, and accepted an unorthodox form of Christianity called Arianism. Long acquaintance with Roman ways made them very civilized, and some had been welcomed into the empire and served as mercenaries in the imperial army. Tribes such as the Anglo-Saxons and the Huns, who lived far from the Roman frontiers, were not af-

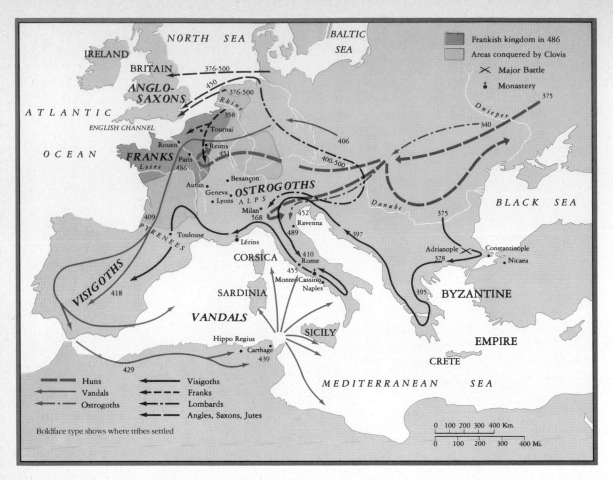

MAP 7.1. THE GERMANIC MIGRATIONS *The Germanic tribes infiltrated and settled in all parts of Western Europe. The Huns, who were not German ethnically, originated in central Asia.*

fected by the civilizing influences of Rome. They remained primitive, nomadic, even barbaric peoples.

Historians do not know exactly when the Mongolian tribe called the Huns began to move westward from China, but about 370 they pressured the Goths living along the Rhine-Danube frontier. The Huns easily defeated the Ostrogoths, and the frightened Visigoths petitioned the emperor to be allowed to settle within the empire. Once inside, however, they revolted. In 378, a Visigothic

army decisively defeated the emperor's army. This date marks the beginning of massive Germanic invasions; Germans flooded into the empire (see Map 7.1).

Why did the Germans emigrate? In the absence of literary evidence one can only speculate. Perhaps overpopulation and food shortages resulting from polygamy (the practice of having several wives simultaneously) caused migration. Perhaps victorious tribes forced the vanquished ones to move south. Perhaps tales of the luxurious lifestyle of the cities of the Roman Empire attracted settlers. Perhaps the Germans migrated for a combination of all these reasons.

Some tribes that settled within the borders of the Roman Empire numbered perhaps no more than ten thousand individuals. Others, such as the Ostrogoths and Visigoths, were about twenty or thirty times larger. Because they settled near and quickly intermingled with Romans and Romanized peoples, it is impossible to specify numbers of the original migrators. Dense forests, poor soil, and inadequate equipment probably kept food production low. This meant that the Germans could not increase very rapidly in their new locations.

Except for the Lombards, whose conquests of Italy persisted through the sixth and seventh centuries, the movements of Germanic peoples on the Continent ended about 600. Between 450 and 565, the Germans established a number of kingdoms, but none except the Frankish kingdom lasted very long. Since the German kingdoms were not states with definite geographical boundaries, their locations are approximate. The Visigoths overran much of southwestern Gaul. Establishing their headquarters at Toulouse, they exercised a weak domination over Spain until a great Muslim victory at Guadalete in 711 ended Visigothic rule. The Vandals, whose destructive ways are commemorated in the word *vandal,* settled in North Africa. In northern and western Europe in the sixth century, the Burgundians established rule over lands roughly circumscribed by the old Roman army camps at Lyons, Besançon, Geneva, and Autun.

In northern Italy, the sixth-century Ostrogothic king Theodoric pursued a policy of assimilation between Germans and Romans. He maintained close relations with the Roman emperor at Constantinople and drew Roman scholars and diplomats into the royal civil service. He was a crude German, however, and his reign was disliked by the pagan Roman aristocrats. Moreover, he was an Arian Christian, so Roman Catholics hated him as heretical. His royal administration fell apart during the reconquest of Italy by the Byzantine emperor Justinian in the sixth century. Weakness, war, and plague then made northern Italy ripe for the Lombard conquest in the seventh century.

The most enduring Germanic kingdom was established by the Frankish chieftain Clovis (481–511). Originally only a petty chieftain with headquarters in the region of Tournai in northwestern Gaul (modern Belgium), Clovis began to expand his territories in 486. His defeat of the Gallo-Roman general Syagrius extended his jurisdiction to the Loire. Clovis's conversion to orthodox Christianity in 496 won him the crucial support of the papacy and the bishops of Gaul. As the defender of Roman Catholicism against heretical German tribes, he went on to conquer the Visigoths, extending his domain as far as the Pyrenees and making Paris his headquarters. Because he was descended from the half-legendary chieftain Merovech, the dynasty Clovis founded has been called Merovingian. Clovis's sons subjugated the Burgundians in eastern Gaul and the Ostrogothic tribes living north of the Alps.

## GERMANIC SOCIETY

The Germans replaced the Romans as rulers of most of the European continent, and German customs and traditions formed the basis of European society for centuries. What pat-

THE BAPTISM OF CLOVIS *In this thirteenth-century representation, Remigius, Bishop of Rheims, blesses Clovis, a noble holds the crown symbolizing royal victory, while the Holy Spirit descends with holy oil. Clovis respected Remigius and supported his work of conversion; Remegius urged obedience to Clovis. (Biblothèque Nationale, Paris)*

terns of social and political life characterized the Germans? What kind of economy did they practice?

Scholars are hampered in answering these questions because the Germans could not write, and so kept no written records before their conversion to Christianity. The earliest information about them comes from moralistic accounts by such Romans as the historian Tacitus, who was acquainted only with the tribes living closest to the borders of the empire. Furthermore, Tacitus wrote his *Germania* at the end of the first century A.D., and by the fifth century German practices differed from those of Tacitus's time. Our knowledge of the Germans depends largely on information in

records written in the sixth and seventh centuries and projected backward.

### KINSHIP AND CUSTOM

The Germans had no notion of the state as we in the twentieth century use that concept; they thought in social, not political, terms. The basic social unit of the Germans was the tribe, or folk. Members of the folk believed they were all descended from a common ancestor. Blood united them. Kinship protected them. Law was custom — unwritten, preserved in the minds of the elders of the tribe, and handed down by word of mouth from generation to generation. Custom regulated everything. Every tribe had its customs, and every member of the tribe knew what they were. Members were subject to their tribe's customary law wherever they went, and friendly tribes respected one another's laws.

Germanic tribes were led by a king, or tribal chieftain. The chief was that member of the folk recognized as the strongest, the bravest in battle. He was elected from among the male members of the strongest family. He led the tribe in war, settled disputes among tribal members, conducted negotiations with outside powers, and offered sacrifices to the gods. Closely associated with the king was the *gesith,* or war band (known in Latin as the *comitatus*). The members of the war band were usually the bravest young men in the tribe. They swore loyalty to the chief and fought with him in battle. They were not supposed to leave the battlefield without him; to do so implied cowardice and disloyalty and brought terrible disgrace.

## *LAW*

As long as custom determined all behavior, the early Germans had no need for written law. Beginning in the late sixth century, however, German tribal chieftains began to collect, write, and publish lists of their customs. Why then? The Christian missionaries who were slowly converting the Germans to Christianity wanted to know the tribal customs, and they encouraged German rulers to set down their customs in written form. Churchmen wanted to read about German ways in order to assimilate the tribes to Christianity. Moreover, by the sixth century the German kings needed rules and regulations for the Romans living under their jurisdiction as well as for their own people.

Today if a person holds up a bank, American law maintains that the robber attacks both the bank and the state in which it exists. That is a sophisticated notion involving the abstract idea of the state. In early German law, all crimes were regarded as crimes against a person.

According to the code of the Salian Franks, every person had a particular monetary value to the tribe. This value was called the *wergeld,* which literally means man-money or "money to buy off the spear." Men of fighting age had the highest wergeld, then women of childbearing age, then children, and finally the aged. Everyone's value reflected his or her potential military worthiness. If a person accused of a crime agreed to pay the wergeld, and if the victim and his or her family accepted the payment, there was peace (hence the expression "money to buy off the spear"). If the accused refused to pay the wergeld, or if the victim's family refused to accept it, a blood feud ensued. Individuals depended on their kin for protection, and kinship served as a force of social control.

Historians and sociologists have difficulty applying the early law codes, partly because they are patchwork affairs studded with additions made in later centuries. For example, the Salic Law — the law code of the Salian Franks — was issued by Clovis in the late fifth century and amended first in the eighth and again in the ninth century. Thus it cannot be taken as an entirely accurate representation of conditions in the sixth century. Nevertheless, it does offer a general picture of Germanic life and problems in the early Middle Ages, and it is typical of the law codes of other tribes, such as the Visigoths, the Burgundians, the Lombards, and the Anglo-Saxons.

The Salic Law lists the money fines to be paid to the victim or the family for such injuries as theft, rape, assault, arson, and murder:

*If any person strike another on the head so that the*

*brain appears, and the three bones which lie above the brain shall project, he shall be sentenced to 1200 denars, which make 300 shillings.*

*But if it shall have been between the ribs or in the stomach, so that the wound appears and reaches to the entrails, he shall be sentenced to 1200 denars — which make 300 shillings — besides five shillings for the physician's pay.*

*If any one have hit a free woman who is pregnant, and she dies, he shall be sentenced to 2800 denars, which make 700 shillings.*

*If any one have killed a free woman after she has begun bearing children, he shall be sentenced to 2400 denars, which make 600 shillings.*

*If any one shall have drawn a harrow through another's harvest after it has sprouted, or shall have gone through it with a waggon where there was no road, he shall be sentenced to 120 denars, which make 30 shillings.*

*If any one shall have killed a free Frank, or a barbarian living under the Salic law, and it have been proved on him, he shall be sentenced to 8000 denars.*

*But if any one have slain a man who is in the service of the king, he shall be sentenced to 2400 denars, which make 600 shillings.*

*If any one have slain a Roman who eats in the king's palace, and it have been proved on him, he shall be sentenced to 1200 denars, which make 300 shillings.*[1]

This is not really a code of law at all, but a list of tariffs or fines for particular offenses. German law aimed at the prevention or reduction of violence. It was not concerned with justice.

At first Romans had been subject to Roman law, and Germans to Germanic custom. As German kings accepted Christianity, and as Romans and Germans increasingly intermarried, the distinction between the two laws blurred and, in the course of the seventh and eighth centuries, disappeared. The result

of the fusion would be the new feudal law, to which all people were subject.

## LIFE IN THE FORESTS

How did the Germans live? The dark, dense forests that dotted the continent of Europe were the most important physical and psychological factor in the lives of the Germanic peoples who were not quickly Romanized. Forests separated one tribe from another. The pagan Germans believed that gods and spirits inhabited the forests. Trees were holy, and to cut them down was an act of grave sacrilege. Thus the Germans cut no trees. They also feared building a mill or a bridge on a river, lest the river spirit be offended. This attitude prevented the clearing of land for farming and tended to keep the Germans isolated.

In the course of the sixth through eighth centuries, the Germans slowly adapted to Greco-Roman and Christian attitudes and patterns of behavior. Acceptance of Christianity and the end of animistic beliefs that spiritual forces live in natural objects had profound consequences. In fact, the decline of animistic beliefs marks a turning-point in the economic and intellectual progress of the West. A more settled and less nomadic way of life developed as people no longer feared to make use of natural resources such as rivers and forests. Once animistic beliefs were dispelled, the forests were opened to use, and all members of the community had common rights in them. Trees provided everyone with wood for building and for fuel; the forests served as the perfect place for grazing animals throughout the Middle Ages. The steady reduction of forest land between the sixth and thirteenth centuries was a major step in the agricultural development of Europe.

Within the forests the Germans clustered in small villages of a few families. Individual families lived in huts made of mud, wood, or wattle (poles intertwined with twigs or reeds) and thatched with straw. Recent archaeological excavations at Thetford in East Anglia in England uncovered a sixth-century village. Evidence from places on the Continent suggests that this English village was typical. It contained a number of one-room huts about twelve feet long, most without a fireplace. Uprights in the center of the gable supported the roof. These dwellings were scattered over a small cleared area, without alignment or evidence of town planning.

Each German family owned its plot of land and passed it on to the next generation. All members of the small community worked together to cultivate the clearing. Apparently, the land farmed was adjacent to the dwellings. Farmers helped one another to plow and harvest, and all had to agree on the uniform rotation of crops. It is difficult to generalize about agricultural methods. The German plow dug deeper than the Roman plow, but it was hard to turn around at the end of the furrow. The difficulty of this operation probably brought about the division of arable land into long narrow strips.

Bread was the basic food, and oats and rye the predominant grains in the fifth and sixth centuries. Later these cereals were held in low esteem, and wheat was raised everywhere it would grow. Peas and beans (a source of protein), turnips, onions, and cabbage supplemented the diet. Beside the field under cultivation, another stood fallow. Cattle grazed on it and fertilized it.

## ANGLO-SAXON ENGLAND

The island of Britain, conquered by Rome during the reign of Claudius, shared fully in the life of the Roman Empire during the first four centuries of the Christian era. A military

THE TARA BROOCH *Men and women of the Germanic tribes wore brooches to fasten their cloaks at the shoulder. This elaborately decorated brooch (a reproduction) was worn by a person of the warrior aristocracy. Ordinary people used a thorn. (Courtesy, World Heritage Museum. Photo: Caroline Buckler)*

aristocracy governed, and the official religion was the cult of the emperor. Towns were planned in the Roman fashion, with temples, public baths, theaters, and amphitheaters. In the countryside large manors controlled the surrounding lands. Roman merchants brought Eastern luxury goods and Eastern religions – including Christianity – into Britain. The native Britons, a gentle Celtic people, had become thoroughly Romanized. Their language was Latin. Their lifestyle was Roman.

But an event in the distant eastern province of Thrace changed all this. In 378, the Visigoths crossed the Danube and inflicted a severe defeat on the Roman emperor Valens at Adrianople. Even Britain felt the consequences. Rome was forced to retrench, and in 407 Roman troops were withdrawn from the island, leaving it unprotected. The savage Picts from Scotland continued to harass the

MAP 7.2. ANGLO-SAXON ENGLAND *Can you identify the seven kingdoms of the Heptarchy? Where is Bede's monastery Jarrow?*

north. Teutonic tribes from Scandinavia and modern-day Belgium – the Angles, Saxons, and Jutes – stepped up their assaults, attacking in a hit-and-run fashion. Their goal was plunder, and at first their invasions led to no permanent settlements. As more Germans arrived, however, they took over the best lands and humbled the Britons. Increasingly, the natives fled to the west and settled in Wales. These sporadic raids continued for over a century and led to Germanic control of most of Britain. Historians have labeled the period 500 to 1066 Anglo-Saxon.

Except for the Jutes, who probably came from Frisia (modern Belgium), the Teutonic tribes came from the least Romanized and least civilized parts of Europe. They destroyed Roman culture in Britain. Tribal custom superseded Roman law.

The beginnings of the Germanic kingdoms in Britain are very obscure, but scholars suspect they came into being in the seventh and eighth centuries. Writing in the eighth century, the scholar Bede (pages 266–267) described seven kingdoms: the Jutish kingdom of Kent; the Saxon kingdoms of the East Saxons (Essex), South Saxons (Sussex), and West Saxons (Wessex); and the kingdoms of the Angles, Mercians, and Northumbrians (see Map 7.2). The names imply that these peoples thought of themselves in tribal rather than geographical terms. They referred to the kingdom of the West Saxons, for example, rather than simply Wessex. Because of Bede's categorization, scholars refer to the Heptarchy, or seven kingdoms of Anglo-Saxon Britain. The suggestion of total Anglo-Saxon domination, however, is not entirely accurate. Germanic tribes never subdued Scotland, where the Picts remained strong, or Wales, where the Celts and native Britons continued to put up stubborn resistance.

Thus Anglo-Saxon England was divided along racial and political lines. The Teutonic kingdoms in the south, east, and center were opposed by the Britons in the west, who wanted to get rid of the invaders. The Anglo-Saxon kingdoms also fought among themselves, with the result that boundaries shifted constantly. Finally in the ninth century, under pressure of the Danish, or Viking, invasions, the Britons and the Germanic peoples were molded together under the leadership of King Alfred of Wessex (871–899).

## THE SURVIVAL AND GROWTH OF THE EARLY CHRISTIAN CHURCH

While many elements of the Roman Empire disintegrated, the Christian church survived and grew. Having gained the support of the fourth-century emperors, the church gradually adopted the Roman system of organization. Christianity had a dynamic missionary policy, and the church slowly succeeded in assimilating — that is, adapting — pagan peoples, both Germans and Romans, to Christian teaching. Moreover, the church possessed able administrators and leaders and highly literate and creative thinkers. These factors help to explain the survival and growth of the early Christian church in the face of repeated Germanic invasions.

## The Church and the Roman Emperors

The early church benefited considerably from the support of the emperors. In return, the emperors expected the support of the Christian church in the maintenance of order and unity. Constantine had legalized the practice of Christianity within the empire in 312. Although he himself was not baptized until he was on his deathbed, Constantine encouraged Christianity throughout his reign. He freed the clergy from imperial taxation. At the churchmen's request, he helped to settle theological disputes and thus to preserve doctrinal unity within the church. Constantine generously endowed the building of Christian churches, and one of his gifts — the Lateran Palace in Rome — remained the official residence of the popes until the fourteenth century. Constantine also declared Sunday a public holiday, a day of rest for the service of God. As the result of its favored position within the empire, Christianity slowly became the leading religion.

At the end of the fourth century, the emperor Theodosius went further than Constantine and made Christianity the official religion of the empire. Theodosius stripped Roman pagan temples of their statues, made the practice of the old Roman state religion a treasonable offense, and persecuted Christians who dissented from orthodox doctrine. Most significant, he allowed the church to establish its own courts. Church courts began to develop their own body of law, called canon law. These courts, not the Roman government, had jurisdiction over the clergy and ecclesiastical disputes. At the death of Theodosius, the Christian church was completely independent of the authority of the Roman state. The foundation for the power of the medieval church had been laid.

What was to be the church's relationship to secular powers? How was the Christian to render unto Caesar the things that were his while returning to God his due? This problem had troubled the earliest disciples of Christ. The toleration of Christianity and the coming to power of Christian emperors in the fourth century did not make it any easier. Striking a balance between responsibility to secular rulers and loyalty to spiritual duties was difficult.

In the fourth century, theological disputes arose within Christianity — primarily disagreements about the nature of Christ. Constantine, to whom religious disagreement meant civil disorder, intervened. In 325, Constantine summoned a council of church leaders to Nicaea in Asia Minor, and presided over it personally.

The council debated whether Christ was of a different substance from God, as Arius, a priest of Alexandria, maintained, or of the same substance, as Bishop Athanasius of Alexandria held. The council decided against the Arians and supported the doctrine that Christ was of the same substance as God. This became the orthodox position. Anxious to preserve the unity of the empire, Constantine insisted on its acceptance by all Christians. The participation of the emperor in a theological dispute within the church paved the way for later rulers to claim they could do the same.

So active was the emperor Theodosius's participation in church matters that he eventually came to loggerheads with Bishop Ambrose of Milan (339-397). Theodosius ordered Ambrose to hand over his cathedral church to the emperor. Ambrose's response had important consequences for the future:

*At length came the command, "Deliver up the Basilica"; I reply, "It is not lawful for us to deliver it up, nor for your Majesty to receive it. By no law can you violate the house of a private man, and do you think that the house of God may be taken away? It is asserted that all things are lawful to the Emperor, that all things are his. But do not burden your conscience with the thought that you have any right as Emperor over sacred things. Exalt not yourself, but if you would reign the longer, be subject to God. It is written, God's to God and Caesar's to Caesar. The palace is the Emperor's, the Churches are the Bishop's. To you is committed jurisdiction over public, not over sacred buildings."[2]*

Ambrose's statement was to serve as the cornerstone of the ecclesiastical theory of state-church relations throughout the Middle Ages. Ambrose insisted that the church was independent of the state's jurisdiction. The two powers were, he maintained, separate and autonomous. He insisted that in matters relating to the faith or the church, the bishops were to be the judges of emperors, not the other way around. In a Christian society, harmony and peace depended upon agreement between the bishop and the secular ruler. But if disagreement developed, the church was ultimately the superior power because the church was responsible for the salvation of all individuals (including the emperor).

Theodosius accepted Ambrose's argument and bowed to the church. In later centuries theologians, canonists, and propagandists repeatedly cited Ambrose's position as the basis of relations between the two powers. The precedent set by Theodosius was repeatedly recalled by church leaders in the Middle Ages as proof that secular power had to yield to ecclesiastical authority.

## INSPIRED LEADERSHIP

The early Christian church benefited from the brilliant administrative abilities of some church leaders and from identification of the authority and dignity of the bishop of Rome with the grand imperial traditions of the city. Some highly able Roman citizens accepted baptism and applied their intellectual powers and administrative skills to the service of the church rather than the empire. With the empire in decay, educated people joined and worked for the church in the belief that it was the one institution able to provide leadership. Bishop Ambrose, for example, was the son of the Roman prefect of Gaul, a trained lawyer and governor of a province. As bishop of Milan, he exercised considerable responsibility and influence in the temporal as well as ecclesiastical affairs of northern Italy.

During the reign of Diocletian (284-305), the Roman Empire had been divided for administrative purposes into geographical units called dioceses. Gradually the church made use of this organizational structure. Christian bishops – the leaders of early Christian communities, popularly elected by the Christian people – established their headquarters, or sees, in the urban centers of the old Roman dioceses. Their jurisdiction extended throughout all parts of the diocese. The center of the bishop's authority was his cathedral (the word derives from the Latin *cathedra,* meaning "chair"). Thus church leaders capitalized on the Roman imperial method of organization and adapted it to ecclesiastical purposes.

After the removal of the capital and the emperor to Constantinople (page 206), the bishop of Rome exercised vast influence in the West because he had no real competitor there. Bishops of Rome – known as popes from the Latin word *papa,* meaning "father" – began to identify their religious offices with the imperial traditions of the city. They stressed that Rome had been the capital of a worldwide empire, and they emphasized the special importance of Rome within the framework of that empire. Successive bishops of Rome reminded Christians in other parts of the world that Rome was the burial-place of Saint Peter and Saint Paul. Moreover, according to tradition Saint Peter, the chief of Christ's first twelve followers, had lived and been executed in Rome. No other city in the world could make such claims.

In the fifth century, the bishops of Rome began to stress their supremacy over other Christian communities and to urge other churches to appeal to Rome for the resolution of complicated doctrinal issues. Thus Pope Innocent I (401–417) wrote to the bishops of Africa:

[*We approve your action in following the principle*] *that nothing which was done even in the most remote and distant provinces should be taken as finally settled unless it came to the notice of this See, that any just pronouncement might be confirmed by all the authority of this See, and that the other churches might from thence gather what they should teach. . . .*[3]

The prestige of Rome and the church as a whole was also enhanced by the courage and leadership of the Roman bishops. According to tradition, Pope Leo I (440–461) met the advancing army of Attila the Hun in 452 and, through his power of persuasion, saved Rome from a terrible sacking. Three years later, Leo repeated this performance and secured concessions from the Vandal leader Gaiseric.

By the time Gregory I (590–604) became pope, there was no civic authority left to handle the problems pressing the city. Flood, famine, plague, and invasion by the Lombards made for an almost disastrous situation. Pope Gregory concluded a peace with the Lombards, organized relief services that provided water and food for the citizens, and established hospitals for the sick and dying. The fact that it was Christian leaders, rather than imperial administrators, who responded to the city's dire needs could not help but increase the prestige and influence of the church.

## MISSIONARY ACTIVITY

The word *catholic* derives from a Greek word meaning "general," "universal," or "worldwide." Early Christians believed that Christ's teaching was intended for all peoples, and they sought to make their faith catholic – that is, believed everywhere. This could be accomplished only through missionary activity. As Saint Paul had written to the Christian community at Colossae in Asia Minor:

*You have stripped off your old behavior with your old self, and you have put on a new self which will progress towards true knowledge the more it is renewed in the image of its creator; and in that image there is no room for distinction between Greek and Jew, between the circumcised or the uncircumcised, or between barbarian or Scythian, slave and free man. There is only Christ; he is everything and he is in everything.*[4]

Paul urged Christians to bring the "good news" of Christ to all peoples. The Mediterranean served as the highway over which Christianity spread to the cities of the empire.

During the Roman occupation, there were

also scattered and isolated Christian communities in Gaul, Britain, and Ireland. However, they had no wide impact on the populations of their countries, and the migration of the German tribes in the fourth and fifth centuries virtually destroyed Christianity in remote and isolated Britain. The Christianization of the Germans really began in 597, when Pope Gregory I sent a delegation of monks under the Roman Augustine to Britain to convert the Britons. Augustine's approach, adopted by all subsequent missionaries, was to concentrate on converting the king. When he succeeded in converting Ethelbert, king of Kent, the baptism of Ethelbert's people took place as a matter of course. Augustine established his headquarters, or cathedral seat, at Canterbury, the capital of Kent.

In the course of the seventh century, two Christian forces competed for the conversion of the pagan Anglo-Saxons: Roman-oriented missionaries traveling north from Canterbury, and Celtic monks from Ireland and northwestern Britain. Monasteries were established at Iona, Lindisfarne, Jarrow, Whitby, and York (see Map 7.2).

The Roman and Celtic traditions differed completely in their forms of church organization, types of monastic life, and methods of arriving at the date of the central feast of the Christian calendar, Easter. At the Synod (ecclesiastical council) of Whitby in 664, the Roman tradition was completely victorious. The conversion of the English, and the close attachment of the English church to Rome, had far-reaching consequences, because Britain later served as a base for the Christianization of the Continent.

Between the fifth and tenth centuries, the great majority of peoples living on the European continent and the nearby islands accepted the Christian religion — that is, they received baptism, though baptism in itself did not automatically transform people into Christians.

Religion influenced all aspects of tribal life. All members of the tribe participated in religious observances, because doing so was a social duty. Religion was not a private or individual matter; the religion of the chieftain or king determined the religion of the people. Thus missionaries concentrated their initial efforts not on the people but on kings or tribal chieftains. According to custom, tribal chiefs negotiated with all foreign powers, including the gods. Because the Christian missionaries represented a "foreign" power (the Christian God), the king dealt with them. If the ruler accepted Christian baptism, his people did so too. The result was mass baptism.

Once a ruler had marched his people to the waters of baptism, however, the work of Christianization had only begun. Baptism meant either sprinkling the head or immersing the body in water. Conversion meant mental and heartfelt acceptance of the beliefs of Christianity. What does it mean to be a Christian? This question has troubled sincere people from the time of Saint Paul to the present. The problem rests in part in the basic teaching of Jesus in the Gospel:

*Then fixing his eyes on his disciples he said:*
*"How happy are you who are poor: yours is the kingdom of God. Happy you who are hungry now: you shall be satisfied. Happy you who weep now: you shall laugh.*
*"Happy are you when people hate you, drive you out, abuse you, denounce your name as criminal, on account of the Son of man. Rejoice when that day comes and dance for joy, then your reward will be great in heaven. This was the way their ancestors treated the prophets."*

*THE CURSES*
*"But alas for you who are rich: you are having*

your consolation now. Alas for you who have your fill now: you shall go hungry. Alas for you who laugh now: you shall mourn and weep.

"Alas for you when the world speaks well of you: This was the way their ancestors treated the false prophets."

### LOVE OF ENEMIES

"But I say this to you who are listening: Love your enemies, do good to those who hate you, bless those who curse you, pray for those who treat you badly. To the man who slaps you on one cheek, present the other cheek too; to the man who takes your cloak from you, do not refuse your tunic. Give to everyone who asks you, and do not ask of your property back from the man who robs you. Treat others as you would like them to treat you."[5]

These ideas are among the most radical and revolutionary the world has heard, and it has proved very difficult to get people to live by them.

The German peoples were warriors who idealized the military virtues of physical strength, ferocity in battle, and loyalty to the leader. Victors in battle enjoyed the spoils of success and plundered the vanquished. The greater the fighter, the more trophies and material goods he collected. Thus the Germans had trouble accepting the Christian precepts of "love your enemies" and "turn the other cheek." How could a person be poor and happy at the same time, as Christians claimed?

The Germanic tribes found the Christian notions of sin and repentance virtually incomprehensible. Sin in Christian thought meant disobedience to the will of God as revealed in the Ten Commandments and the teachings of Christ. Good or "moral" behavior to the barbarians meant the observance of tribal customs and practices. Dishonorable behavior caused social ostracism. The inculcation of Christian ideals took a very long time.

## CONVERSION AND ASSIMILATION

In Christian theology, conversion involves a turning toward God — that is, a conscious effort to live according to the gospel message. How did missionaries and priests get masses of pagan and illiterate peoples to understand and live by Christian ideals and teachings? Through preaching, through assimilation, and through the penitential system. Preaching aimed at instruction and edification. Instruction presented the basic teachings of Christianity. Edification was intended to strengthen the newly baptized in their faith through stories about the lives of Christ and the saints. Deeply ingrained pagan customs and practices could not be stamped out by words alone, or even by imperial edicts. Christian missionaries often pursued a policy of assimilation, easing the conversion of pagan men and women by stressing similarities between their customs and beliefs and those of Christianity. A letter that Pope Gregory I wrote to Augustine of Canterbury beautifully illustrates this policy. The letter, carried to Augustine in Britain by one Mellitus in 601, expresses the pope's intention that pagan buildings and practices be given a Christian significance:

To our well beloved son Abbot Mellitus: Gregory servant of the servants of God. . . . Therefore, when by God's help you reach our most reverent brother, Bishop Augustine, we wish you to inform him that we have been giving careful thought to the affairs of the English, and have come to the conclusion that the temples of the idols among that people should on no account be destroyed. The idols are to be destroyed, but the temples themselves are to be aspersed with holy water, altars set up in them, and relics deposited there. For if these temples are well-built, they must be purified from the worship of demons and dedicated to the service of the true God. In this way, we hope that the people, seeing

THE PANTHEON (INTERIOR)    Originally a temple for the gods, the Pantheon later served as a Christian church. As such, it symbolizes the adaptation of pagan elements to Christian purposes. (Alinari/Scala)

that their temples are not destroyed, may abandon their error and, flocking more readily to their accustomed resorts, mav come to know and adore the true God. And since they have a custom of sacrificing many oxen to demons, let some other solemnity be substituted in its place, such as a day of Dedication or the Festivals of the holy martyrs whose relics are enshrined there. On such occasions they might well construct shelters of boughs for themselves around the churches that were once temples, and celebrate the solemnity wth devout feasting. . . . For it is certainly impossible to eradicate all errors from obstinate minds at one stroke, and whoever wishes to climb to a mountain top climbs gradually step by step, and not in one leap.[6]

How assimilation works is perhaps best

appreciated through the example of a festival familiar to all Americans, Saint Valentine's Day. There were two Romans named Valentine. Both were Christian priests, and both were martyred for their beliefs around the middle of February in the third century. Since about 150 B.C. the Romans had celebrated the festival of Lupercalia, at which they asked the gods for fertility for themselves, their fields, and their flocks. This celebration occurred in mid-February, shortly before the Roman New Year and the arrival of spring. Thus the early church "converted" the old festival of Lupercalia into Saint Valentine's Day. (Nothing in the lives of the two Christian martyrs connects them with lovers or the exchange of messages and gifts. That practice began in the

later Middle Ages.) February 14 was still celebrated as a festival, but it had taken on Christian meaning.

Assimilation is a slow process. Probably
more immediate in its impact on the uncon-
verted masses was the penitential system.
Penitentials were manuals for the examination
of conscience. Irish priests wrote the earliest
ones, which English missionaries then carried
to the Continent. The illiterate penitent knelt
beside the priest, who questioned the penitential about sins he or she might have committed. The recommended penance was then
imposed. Penance usually meant fasting for
three days each week on bread and water,
which served as a "medicine" for the soul.
Here is a section of the penitential prepared
by Archbishop Theodore of Canterbury (668–
690), which circulated widely at the time:

*If anyone commits fornication with a virgin he
shall do penance for one year. If with a married
woman, he shall do penance for four years, two of
these entire, and in the other two during the three
forty-day periods and three days a week.*

*A male who commits fornication with a male
shall do penance for three years.*

*If a woman practices vice with a woman, she
shall do penance for three years.*

*Whoever has often committed theft, seven years
is his penance, or such a sentence as his priest shall
determine, that is, according to what can be arranged with those whom he has wronged. And he
who used to steal, when he becomes penitent, ought
always to be reconciled to him against whom he
has offended and to make restitution according to
the wrong he has done to him; and [in such case]
he shall greatly shorten his penance.*

*If a layman slays another with malice afore-
thought, if he will not lay aside his arms, he shall
do penance for seven years; without flesh and wine,
three years.*

*If one slays a monk or a cleric, he shall lay
aside his arms and serve God, or he shall do penance for seven years.*

*He who defiles his neighbor's wife, deprived of
his own wife, shall fast for three years two days a
week and in the three forty-day periods.*

*If [the woman] is a virgin, he shall do penance
for one year without meat and wine and mead.*

*If he defiles a vowed virgin, he shall do penance
for three years, as we said above, whether a child is
born of her or not.*

*Women who commit abortion before [the fetus]
has life, shall do penance for one year or for the
three forty-day periods or for forty days, according
to the nature of the offense; and if later, that is,
more than forty days after conception, they shall do
penance as murderesses, that is for three years on
Wednesdays and Fridays and in the three forty-day
periods. This according to the canons is judged
[punishable by] ten years.*

*If a mother slays her child, if she commits
homicide, she shall do penance for fifteen years,
and never change except on Sunday.*

*If a poor woman slays her child, she shall do
penance for seven years. In the canon it is said that
if it is a case of homicide, she shall do penance for
ten years.*[7]

As this sample suggests, writers of penitentials were preoccupied with sexual transgressions. Penitentials are much more akin to
the Jewish law of the Old Testament than to
the spirit of the New Testament. They provide an enormous amount of information
about the ascetic ideals of early Christianity
and about the crime-ridden realities of Celtic
and Germanic societies. Penitentials also reveal the ecclesiastical foundations of some
modern attitudes toward sex, birth control,
and abortion. Most important, the penitential
system led to the growth of a different attitude toward religion: formerly public, corporate, and social, religious observances
became private, personal, and individual.[8]

## CHRISTIAN ATTITUDES TOWARD CLASSICAL CULTURE

Probably the major dilemma the early Christian church faced concerned Greco-Roman culture. The Roman Empire as a social, political, and economic force gradually disintegrated. Its culture, however, survived. In Greek philosophy, art, and architecture, in Roman law, literature, education, and engineering, the legacy of a great civilization continued. The Christian religion had begun and spread within this intellectual and psychological milieu. What was to be the attitude of Christians to the Greco-Roman world of ideas?

### HOSTILITY

Christians in the first and second centuries believed that the end of the world was near. Christ had promised to return, and Christians expected to witness that return. Therefore they considered knowledge useless and learning a waste of time. The important duty of the Christian was to prepare for the Second Coming of the Lord.

Early Christians harbored a strong hatred of pagan Roman culture – in fact, of all Roman civilization. Had not the Romans crucified Christ? Had not the Romans persecuted Christians and subjected them to the most horrible tortures? Did not the Book of Revelation in the New Testament call Rome the great whore of the world, filled with corruption, sin, and every kind of evil? Roman culture was sexual, sensual, and materialistic. The sensual poetry of Ovid, the pornographic descriptions of the satirist Petronius, the political poetry of Virgil, even the rhetorical brilliance of Cicero represented a threat, in the eyes of serious Christians, to the spiritual aims and ideals of Christianity. Good Christians who sought the Kingdom of Heaven through the imitation of Christ believed they had to disassociate themselves from the filth that Roman culture embodied.

As Saint Paul wrote, "The wisdom of the world is foolishness, we preach Christ crucified." Tertullian (ca 160–220), an influential African Christian writer, condemned all secular literature as foolishness in the eyes of God. He called the Greek philosophers, such as Aristotle, "hucksters of eloquence" and compared them to "animals of self-glorification." "What has Athens to do with Jerusalem," he demanded, "the Academy with the Church? We have no need for curiosity since Jesus Christ, nor for inquiry since the gospel." Tertullian insisted that Christians would find in the Bible all the wisdom they needed.

### COMPROMISE AND ADJUSTMENT

At the same time, Christianity encouraged adjustment to the ideas and institutions of the Roman world. Some Biblical texts clearly urged Christians to accept the existing social, economic, and political establishment. In a letter specifically addressed to Christians living among non-Christians in the hostile environment of Rome, Saint Peter had written about the obligations of Christians:

*TOWARDS PAGANS*
*Always behave honourably among pagans, so that they can see your good works for themselves and, when the day of reckoning comes, give thanks to God for the things which now make them denounce you as criminals.*

*TOWARDS CIVIL AUTHORITY*
*For the sake of the Lord, accept the authority of every social institution: the emperor, as the supreme authority, and the governors as commissioned by*

*him to punish criminals and praise good citizenship. God wants you to be good citizens. . . . Have respect for everyone and love for your community; fear God and honour the emperor.*[9]

Christians really had little choice. Greco-Roman culture was the only culture they knew. Only men received a formal education, and they went through the traditional curriculum of grammar and rhetoric. They learned to be effective speakers in the forum or law courts. No other system of education existed. Many early Christians had grown up as pagans, been educated as pagans, and were converted only as adults. Toward homosexuality, for example, Christians of the first three or four centuries simply imbibed the attitude of the world in which they lived. Many Romans indulged in homosexual activity, and contemporaries did not consider such behavior (or inclinations to it) immoral, bizarre, or harmful. Several emperors were openly homosexual, and homosexuals participated freely in all aspects of Roman life and culture. Early Christians too considered homosexuality a conventional expression of physical desire, and they were no more susceptible to anti-homosexual prejudices than pagans were. Some prominent Christians experienced loving same-gender relationships that probably had a sexual element. What eventually led to a change in public and Christian attitudes toward sexual behavior was the shift from the sophisticated urban culture of the Greco-Roman world to the rural culture of medieval Europe.[10]

Even had early Christians wanted to give up their classical ideas and patterns of thought, they would have had great difficulty doing so. Therefore, they had to adapt or adjust their Roman education to their Christian beliefs. Saint Paul himself believed there was a good deal of truth in pagan thought, as long

THE ANTIOCH CHALICE *This earliest surviving Christian chalice, which dates from the fourth century A.D., combines the typical Roman shape with Christian motifs. The chalice is decorated with figures of Christ and the apostles, leaves, and grapes, which represent the sacrament of the Eucharist. (The Metropolitan Museum of Art; the Cloisters Collection; purchase, 1950)*

as it was correctly interpreted and properly understood.

The result was a compromise. Christians gradually came to terms with Greco-Roman culture. Saint Jerome (340–419), a distinguished theologian and linguist, remains famous for his translation of the Old and New Testaments from the Hebrew and Greek into vernacular Latin. Called the Vulgate, his edition of the Bible served as the official translation until the sixteenth century, and even today scholars rely on it. Saint Jerome was also familiar with the writings of such classical authors as Cicero, Virgil, and Terence. He believed that Christians should study the best of ancient thought, because it would direct their minds to God. Jerome maintained that the best ancient literature should be interpreted in light of the Christian faith.

## SYNTHESIS: SAINT AUGUSTINE

The finest representative of the blending of classical and Christian ideas, and indeed one of the most brilliant thinkers in the history of the Western world, was Saint Augustine of Hippo (354–430). Aside from the scriptural writers, no one else has had a greater impact on Christian thought in succeeding centuries. Saint Augustine was born into an urban family in what is now Algeria in North Africa. His father was a pagan, his mother a devout Christian. Because his family was poor – his father was a minor civil servant – the only avenue to success in a highly competitive world was a classical education.

Augustine's mother believed that a good classical education, though pagan, would make her son a better Christian, so Augustine's father scraped together the money to educate him. The child received his basic education in the local school. By modern and even medieval standards, that education was extremely narrow: textual study of the writings of the poet Virgil, the orator-politician Cicero, the historian Sallust, and the playwright Terence. At that time, learning meant memorization. Education in the late Roman world aimed at appreciation of words, par-

ticularly those of renowned and eloquent orators.

At the age of seventeen, Augustine went to nearby Carthage to continue his education. There he took a mistress with whom he lived for fifteen years. At Carthage, Augustine entered a difficult psychological phase and began an intellectual and spiritual pilgrimage that led him through experiments with several philosophies and heretical Christian sects. In 383, he traveled to Rome, where he endured illness and disappointment in his teaching: his students fled when their bills were due.

Finally, in Milan in 387, through his friendship with Ambrose and the insights he gained from reading Saint Paul's Letter to the Romans, Augustine was converted and received Christian baptism. He later became bishop of the seacoast city of Hippo Regius in his native North Africa. He was a renowned preacher to Christians there, a vigorous defender of orthodox Christianity, and the author of over ninety-three books and treatises.

Augustine's autobiography, *The Confessions*, is a literary masterpiece and one of the most influential books in the history of Europe. Written in the form of a prayer to God, its language is often incredibly beautiful:

*Great are thou, O Lord, and exceedingly to be praised: great is thy power and of thy wisdom there is no reckoning. And man, indeed, one part of thy creation, has the will to praise thee: yea, man, though he bears his mortality about with him . . . even man, a small portion of thy creation, has the will to praise thee. Thou dost stir him up, that it may delight him to praise thee, for thou hast made us for thyself, and our hearts are restless till they find repose in thee.* [11]

*Too late have I loved thee, O beauty ever ancient and ever new, too late have I loved thee! And be-*

*hold! Thou wert within and I without, and it was without that I sought thee. Thou wert with me, and I was not with thee. Those creatures held me far from thee which, were they not in thee, were not at all. Thou didst call, thou didst cry, thou didst break in upon my deafness; thou didst gleam forth, thou didst shine out, thou didst banish my blindness; thou didst send forth thy fragrance, and I drew breath and yearned for thee; I tasted and still hunger and thirst; thou didst touch me, and I was on flame to find thy peace.*[12]

*The Confessions* describes Augustine's moral struggle, the conflict between his spiritual and intellectual aspirations and his sensual and material self. It tells the eternally human story of a man constantly tempted by sin but aware also of the providence of God. *The Confessions* reveals the change and development of a human mind and personality steeped in the philosophy and culture of the ancient world.

Greek and Roman philosophers had taught that knowledge and virtue are the same thing: a person who really knows what is right will do what is right. Augustine rejected this idea. He believed that a person may know what is right but fail to act righteously because of the innate weakness of the human will. People do not always act on the basis of rational knowledge. Here Augustine made a profound contribution to the understanding of human nature: he demonstrated that a very learned person can also be corrupt and evil. *The Confessions,* written in the rhetorical style and language of late Roman antiquity, marks the synthesis of Greco-Roman forms and Christian thought.

When the Visigothic chieftain Alaric conquered Rome in 410, horrified pagans blamed the disaster on the Christians. In response, Augustine wrote *City of God.* This profoundly original work contrasts Christianity with the secular society in which it existed. *City of God* presents a moral interpretation of the Roman government, and in fact of all history. Written in Latin and filled with references to ancient history and mythology, it is the best statement of the Christian philosophy of history.

According to Augustine, history is the account of God acting in time. Human history reveals that there are two kinds of people: those who live according to the flesh in the city of Babylon and those who live according to the spirit in the City of God. In other words, humanity is composed of individuals who live entirely according to their selfish inclinations and individuals who live according to the Word of God. The former will endure eternal hellfire, the latter eternal bliss.

Augustine maintained that states came into existence as the result of Adam's fall and people's inclination to sin. The state is a necessary evil, responsible only for providing the peace and order Christians need in order to pursue their pilgrimage to the City of God. The particular form of government – whether monarchy, aristocracy, or democracy – is basically irrelevant. Any civil government that fails to provide order, law, and justice is no more than a band of gangsters.

Since the state results from moral lapse, from sin, it follows that the church, which is concerned with salvation, is responsible for everyone, including Christian rulers. Churchmen in the Middle Ages used Augustine's theory to defend their belief in the ultimate superiority of the spiritual power over the temporal. This remained the dominant political theory until the late thirteenth century.

Augustine had no objection to drawing on pagan knowledge to support Christian thought. Augustine used Roman history as evidence to defend Christian theology. In doing so he assimilated Roman history, and indeed all of classical culture, into Christian teaching.

## MONASTICISM AND THE RULE OF SAINT BENEDICT

Christianity began and spread as a city religion. Since the first century, however, some especially pious Christians had felt that the only alternative to the decadence of urban life was complete separation from the world. All-consuming pursuit of material things, gross sexual promiscuity, and general political corruption disgusted them. They believed that the Christian life as set forth in the Gospel could not be lived in the midst of such immorality. They rejected the established values of Roman society and were the first real nonconformists in the church.

At first individuals and small groups left the cities and went to live in caves or rude shelters in the desert or the mountains. These people were called hermits, from the Greek word *eremos,* meaning "desert." There is no way of knowing how many hermits there were in the fourth and fifth centuries, partly because their conscious aim was a secret and hidden life known only to God.

Several factors worked against the eremitical variety of monasticism in western Europe. First was the climate. The cold, snow, ice, and fog that covered much of Europe for many months of the year discouraged isolated living. Dense forests filled with wild animals and wandering barbaric German tribes presented obvious dangers. Furthermore, church leaders did not really approve of the eremitical life. Hermits sometimes claimed to have mystical experiences, direct communications with God. No one could verify these experiences.

But if hermits could communicate directly with the Lord, what need had they for the priest and the institutional church? The church hierarchy, or leaders, encouraged coenobitic monasticism – that is, communal living in monasteries.

In the fifth and sixth centuries, many experiments in communal monasticism were made in Gaul, Italy, Spain, Anglo-Saxon England, and Ireland. John Cassian, after studying both eremitical and coenobitic mysticism in Egypt and Syria, established two monasteries near Marseilles in Gaul around 415. One of Cassian's books, *Conferences,* based on conversations he had had with holy men in the East, discussed the dangers of the isolated hermit's life. The abbey or monastery of Lérins on the Mediterranean Sea near Cannes (ca 410) also had significant contacts with monastic centers in the Middle East and North Africa. Lérins encouraged the severely penitential and extremely ascetic behavior common in the East, such as long hours of prayer, fasting, and self-flagellation. It was this tradition of harsh self-mortification that the Roman-British monk Saint Patrick carried from Lérins to Ireland in the fifth century. Church organization in Ireland became closely associated with the monasteries, and Irish monastic life followed the ascetic Eastern form.

Around 540, the Roman senator Cassiodorus retired from public service and established a monastery, the Vivarium, on his estate in Italy. Cassiodorus wanted the Vivarium to become an educational and cultural center, and enlisted highly educated and sophisticated men for it. He set the monks to copying both sacred and secular manuscripts, intending this to be their sole occupation. Cassiodorus started the association of monasticism with scholarship and learning. This developed into a great tradition in the medieval and modern worlds. But Cassiodorus's experiment did not become the most influential form of monasticism in European society. The fifth and sixth centuries witnessed the appearance of many other monastic lifestyles.

In 529 Benedict of Nursia (480–543), who had experimented with both the eremitical and the communal forms of monastic life, wrote a brief set of regulations, or rules, for the monks who had gathered around him at Monte Cassino between Rome and Naples. This guide for monastic life slowly replaced all others. *The Rule of Saint Benedict* has influenced all forms of organized religious life in the Roman church.

## THE RULE OF SAINT BENEDICT

Saint Benedict conceived of his *Rule* as a simple code for ordinary men. It outlined a monastic life of regularity, discipline, and moderation. Each monk had ample food and adequate sleep. Self-destructive acts of mortification were forbidden. In an atmosphere of silence, the monk spent part of the day in formal prayer, which Benedict called the Work of God. This consisted of chanting psalms and other prayers from the Bible in that part of the monastery church called the choir. The rest of the day was passed in study and manual labor. After a year of probation, the monk made three vows.

First, the monk vowed stability: he promised to live his entire life in the monastery of his profession. The vow of stability was Saint Benedict's major contribution to Western monasticism; his object was to prevent the wandering so common in his day. Second, the monk vowed conversion of manners — that is, to strive to improve himself and to come closer to God. Third, he promised obedience, the most difficult vow because it meant the complete surrender of his will to the abbot, or head of the monastery. The first sentence of

ST. BENEDICT *from Agnolo Gaddi,* Madonna Enthroned with Saints, *ca 1385. The first word of his Rule, which Benedict holds in his left hand, is "Listen." Listening was the posture of students, and St. Benedict called his monastery a "School of the Lord's Service," where the monks listened not only to their abbot but through the abbot to Christ himself. In his right hand, Benedict carries the rods of correction. (National Gallery of Art, Washington, Andrew W. Mellon Collection)*

the *Rule* urged the monk, by the labor of obedience, to return to God, from whom he had departed "by the sloth of disobedience."

*The Rule of Saint Benedict* expresses the assimilation of the Roman spirit into Western monasticism. It reveals the logical mind of its creator and the Roman concern for order, organization, and respect for law. Its spirit of moderation and flexibility is reflected in the patience, wisdom, and understanding with which the abbot is to govern, and, indeed, the entire life is to be led. The *Rule* could be used in vastly different physical and geographical circumstances, in damp and cold Germany as well as in warm and sunny Italy. The *Rule* was quickly adapted for women, and many convents of nuns were established in the early Middle Ages.

Saint Benedict's *Rule* implies that a person who wants to become a monk or nun need have no previous ascetic experience or even a particularly strong bent toward the religious life. Thus, it allowed for the admission of newcomers with different backgrounds and personalities. This flexibility helps to explain the attractiveness of Benedictine monasticism throughout the centuries. *The Rule of Saint Benedict* is a superior example of the way in which the Greco-Roman heritage and Roman patterns of thought were preserved.

At the same time, the *Rule* no more provides a picture of actual life within a Benedictine abbey of the seventh or eighth (or twentieth) century than the American Constitution of 1789 describes living conditions in the United States today. A code of laws cannot do that. Monasteries were composed of individuals, and human beings defy strict classification according to rules, laws, or statistics. *The Rule of Saint Benedict* had one fundamental purpose. The exercises of the monastic life were designed to draw the individual, slowly but steadily, away from attachment to the world and love of self and toward the love of God.

## The Success of Benedictine Monasticism

Why was the Benedictine form of monasticism so successful? Why did it eventually replace other forms of Western monasticism? The answer lies partly in its spirit of flexibility and moderation and partly in the balanced life it provided. Early Benedictine monks and nuns spent part of the day in prayer, part in

study or some other form of intellectual activity, and part in manual labor. The monastic life as conceived by Saint Benedict did not lean too heavily in any one direction; it struck a balance between asceticism and idleness. It thus provided opportunities for persons of entirely different abilities and talents – from mechanics to gardeners to literary scholars. Benedict's *Rule* contrasts sharply with Cassiodorus's narrow concept of the monastery as a place for aristocratic scholars and bibliophiles.

Benedictine monasticism also suited the social circumstances of early medieval society. The German invasions had fragmented European life: the self-sufficient rural estate replaced the city as the basic unit of civilization. A monastery too had to be economically self-sufficient. It was supposed to produce from its lands and properties all that was needed for food, clothing, buildings, and liturgical service of the altar. The monastery fitted in – indeed, represented – the trend toward localism.

Benedictine monasticism also succeeded partly because it was so materially successful. In the seventh and eighth centuries, monasteries pushed back forest and wasteland, drained swamps, and experimented with crop rotation. For example, the abbey of Saint Wandrille, founded in 645 near Rouen in northwestern Gaul, sent squads of monks to clear the forests that surrounded it. Within seventy-five years the abbey was immensely wealthy. The abbey of Jumièges, also in the diocese of Rouen, followed much the same pattern. Such Benedictine houses made a significant contribution to the agricultural development of Europe. The socialistic nature of their organization, whereby property was held in common and profits pooled and reinvested, made this contribution possible.

Finally, monasteries conducted schools for the education of the young people of the neighborhood. Some learned about prescriptions and herbal remedies for disease, and

JUSTINIAN AND HIS COURT   The Emperor Justinian (center) with ecclesiastical and court officials personifies the unity of the Byzantine state and the orthodox church in the person of the emperor. Just as the emperor was both king and priest, so all his Greek subjects belonged to the orthodox church. (Alinari/Scala)

went on to provide medical treatment for their localities. A few copied manuscripts and wrote books. This training did not go unappreciated in a society desperately in need of it. Local and royal governments drew upon the services of the literate men, the able administrators whom the monasteries produced. This was not what Saint Benedict had intended, but the effectiveness of the institution he designed made it perhaps inevitable.

## THE BYZANTINE EAST
### (CA 400–788)

Constantine (306–337) had tried to maintain the unity of the Roman Empire, but during the fifth and sixth centuries the western and eastern halves drifted apart. Later emperors worked to hold the empire together. Justinian (527–565) waged long and hard-fought wars against the Ostrogoths and temporarily regained Italy and North Africa. But his conquests had disastrous consequences. Justinian's wars exhausted the resources of the Byzantine state, destroyed Italy's economy, and killed a large part of its population. The wars paved the way for the easy conquest of Italy by another Germanic tribe, the Lombards, shortly after Justinian's death. In the late sixth century, the territory of the western Roman Empire came under Germanic sway, while in the East the Byzantine Empire continued the traditions and institutions of the caesars.

Latin Christian culture was only one legacy the Roman Empire bequeathed to the Western world. The Byzantine culture centered at Constantinople – Constantine's New Rome – was another. The Byzantine Empire maintained a high standard of living, and for centuries the Greeks were the most civilized people in the Western world. The Byzantine Empire held at bay, or at least hindered, barbarian peoples who could otherwise have wreaked additional devastation on western Europe, retarding its development. Most important, however, is the role of Byzantium as preserver of the wisdom of the ancient world. Throughout the long years when barbarians in western Europe trampled down the old and then painfully built something new, Byzantium protected and then handed on to the West the intellectual heritage of Greco-Roman civilization.

## BYZANTINE EAST AND GERMANIC WEST

As imperial authority disintegrated in the West during the fifth century, civic functions were performed first by church leaders and then by German chieftains. As we have seen, Pope Leo I negotiated with Attila the Hun and persuaded him to withdraw from Rome. There was no other authority in Rome to do so. The death of the Roman emperor Romulus Augustus in 476 signaled the end of the empire in the West. Thereafter, German chieftains held power.

Meanwhile in the East, the Byzantines preserved the forms and traditions of the old Roman Empire, and even called themselves Romans. Byzantine emperors traced their lines back past Constantine to Augustus. The senate that sat in Constantinople carried on the traditions and preserved the glory of the old Roman senate. The army that defended the empire was the direct descendant of the

old Roman legions. Even the chariot factions of the Roman Empire lived on under the Byzantines, who cheered their favorites as enthusiastically as had the Romans of Hadrian's day.

The position of the church differed considerably in the Byzantine East and the Germanic West. The fourth-century emperors Constantine and Theodosius had wanted the church to act as a unifying force within the empire, but the Germanic invasions made that impossible. The bishops of Rome repeatedly called upon the emperors at Constantinople for military support against the invaders, but rarely could the emperors send it. The church in the West steadily grew away from the empire and became involved in the social and political affairs of Italy and the West. Nevertheless, until the eighth century, the popes, who were selected by the clergy of Rome, continued to send announcements of their elections to the emperors at Constantinople – a sign that the Roman popes long thought of themselves as bishops of the Roman Empire.

The popes were preoccupied with conversion of the Germans, the Christian attitude toward classical culture, and relations with the German rulers. The church in the West concentrated on its missionary function. It took time for the clergy to be organized and for the papacy to get in touch with all clerics. Most of the theology of the church in the West came from the East, and the overwhelming majority of popes were themselves of Eastern origin.

Tensions occasionally developed between church officials and secular authorities in the West. The dispute between Bishop Ambrose of Milan and the emperor Theodosius is a good example. A century later, Pope Gelasius I (492–496) insisted that bishops, not civil authorities, were responsible for the administration of the church. Gelasius maintained that two powers governed the world, the sacred authority of the popes and the royal power of kings. Because priests have to answer to God even for kings, the sacred power was the greater.

Such an assertion was virtually unheard of in the East, where the emperor's jurisdiction over the church was fully acknowledged. The emperor in Constantinople nominated the patriarch, as the highest prelate of the church in the East was called. The emperor looked upon religion as a branch of the state. Religion was such a vital aspect of the social life of the people that the emperor devoted considerable attention to it. He considered it his duty to protect the faith, not only against heathen enemies but also against heretics within the empire. In case of doctrinal disputes, the emperor, following Constantine's example at Nicaea, summoned councils of bishops and theologians to settle problems.

In the East, Christianity was the established religion. All citizens of the Byzantine Empire were Christians; to be Byzantine meant to be Christian. The Greek church was an imperial state church subject to and guided by the emperor. The clergy were well organized. The level of theological debate was high. Fine points of Christian theology held the attention of the leaders of the Greek church.

The expansion of the Arabs in the Mediterranean in the seventh and eighth centuries furthered the separation of the churches by dividing the two parts of Christendom. Separation bred isolation. Isolation, combined with prejudice on both sides, bred hostility. Finally, in 1054, a theological disagreement led the bishop of Rome and the patriarch of Constantinople to excommunicate each other. The outcome was a permanent schism, or split, between the Roman Catholic and the Greek Orthodox churches.

In spite of religious differences, the Byzantine Empire served as a bulwark for the West, protecting it against invasions from the east. The Greeks stopped the Persians in the seventh century. They blunted – though they could not stop – Arab attacks in the seventh and eighth centuries, and they fought courageously against Turkish invaders until the fifteenth century, when they were finally overwhelmed. Byzantine Greeks slowed the impetus of the Slavic incursions in the Balkans and held the Russians at arm's length.

Turning from war to the arts of peace, the Byzantines set about civilizing the Slavs, both in the Balkans and in Russia. Byzantine missionaries spread the word of Christ, and one of their triumphs was the conversion of the Russians. The Byzantine missionary Cyril adapted the Greek alphabet to the Russian language, and this script (called the Cyrillic alphabet) is still in use today. Cyrillic script made possible the birth of Russian literature. Similarly, Byzantine art and architecture became the basis and inspiration of Russian forms. The Byzantines were so successful that the Russians claimed to be the successors of the Byzantine Empire. For a time Moscow was even known as "the Third Rome" (the second Rome being Constantinople).

## THE LAW CODE OF JUSTINIAN

One of the most splendid achievements of the Byzantine emperors was the preservation of Roman law for the medieval and modern worlds. Roman law had developed from many sources – decisions by judges, edicts of the emperors, legislation passed by the senate, and the opinions of jurists expert in the theory and practice of law. By the fourth century, Roman law had become a huge bewildering mass. Its sheer bulk made it almost unusable. Some laws had become outdated, some repeated others, and some contradicted others. Faced with this vast, complex, and confusing hodgepodge, the emperor Theodosius decided to clarify and codify the law. He explained the need to do so:

*When we consider the enormous multitude of books, the diverse modes of process and the difficulty of legal cases, and further the huge mass of imperial constitutions, which hidden as it were under a rampart of gross mist and darkness precludes men's intellects from gaining a knowledge of them, we feel that we have met a real need of our age, and dispelling the darkness have given light to the laws by a short compendium. . . . Thus having swept away the clouds of volumes, on which many wasted their lives and explained nothing in the end, we established a compendious knowledge of the Imperial constitutions since the time of the divine Constantine.*[13]

Theodosius's work was only a beginning. He left centuries of Roman law untouched.

A far more sweeping and systematic codification took place under the emperor Justinian. Justinian intended to simplify the law and to make it known to everyone. He appointed a committee of eminent jurists to sort through and organize the laws. In 529, Justinian published the *Code,* which distilled the legal genius of the Romans into a coherent whole, eliminated outmoded laws, eliminated contradictions, and clarified the law itself. Not content with the *Code,* Justinian set about bringing order to the equally huge body of Roman jurisprudence, the science or philosophy of law.

During the second and third centuries the foremost Roman jurists, at the request of the emperors, had expressed learned opinions on complex legal problems, but often these opinions differed from one another. To harmonize this body of knowledge, Justinian directed his jurists to clear up disputed points and to issue definitive rulings. Accordingly, in 533 his lawyers published the *Digest,* which codified Roman legal thought. Finally, Justinian's lawyers compiled a handbook of civil law, the *Institutes.*

These three works – the *Code, Digest,* and *Institutes* – are the backbone of the *corpus juris civilis,* the body of civil law, which is the foundation of law for nearly every modern European nation. Even England, which developed its own common law, has been influenced by it. The work of Justinian and his dedicated band of jurists still affects the life of the modern world nearly fifteen hundred years later.

## BYZANTINE INTELLECTUAL LIFE

Among the Byzantines education was highly prized, and because of them many masterpieces of ancient Greek literature survived to fertilize the intellectual life of the modern world. The literature of the Byzantine Empire was predominantly Greek, although Latin was long spoken among top politicians, scholars, and lawyers. Indeed, Justinian's *Code* was first written in Latin. Among the reading public, which was quite large, history was a favorite subject. Generations of Byzantines read the historical works of Herodotus, Thucydides, and others. Some Byzantine historians abbreviated long histories, such as those of Polybius, while others wrote detailed narratives of their own days.

The most remarkable Byzantine historian was Procopius (ca 500–ca 562), who left a rousing account of Justinian's reconquest of North Africa and Italy. Proof that the wit and venom of ancient writers like Archilochus and Aristophanes lived on in the Byzantine era can be found in Procopius's *Secret History,* a vicious and uproarious attack on Justinian and his wife, the empress Theodora. Although the

Byzantines are often depicted as dull and lifeless, such opinions are hard to defend in the face of Procopius's descriptions of Justinian's character:

*For he was at once villainous and amenable; as people say colloquially, a moron. He was never truthful with anyone, but always guileful in what he said and did, yet easily hoodwinked by any who wanted to deceive him. His nature was an unnatural mixture of folly and wickedness.*[14]

Procopius even accused Justinian of being a demon who possessed strange powers:

*And some of those who have been with Justinian at the palace late at night, men who were pure of spirit, have thought they saw a strange demonaic form taking his throne and walked about, and indeed he was never wont to remain sitting for long, and immediately Justinian's head vanished, while the rest of his body seemed to ebb and flow; whereat the beholder stood aghast and fearful, wondering if his eyes were deceiving him. But presently he perceived the vanished head filling out and joining the body again as strangely as it had left it.*[15]

The *Secret History* may not be great history, but it is robust literature.

Later Byzantine historians chronicled the victories of their emperors and the progress of their barbarian foes. Like Herodotus before them, they were curious about foreigners. They have left striking descriptions of the Turks, who eventually overwhelmed Byzantium. They painted unflattering pictures of the uncouth and grasping princes of France and England, who saw in the Crusades the perfect combination of faith and piety, bloodshed and profit.

In mathematics and geometry the Byzantines discovered nothing new. Yet they were exceptionally important as catalysts, for they passed Greco-Roman learning on to the

*LID—BYZANTINE BOX   Probably made in Alexandria, Egypt in the fifth century, this medicine box (15.2 cm. high and 8.9 cm. wide) was divided into six compartments intended to hold various medicines. The female figure on the lid carries a rudder in one hand, symbolizing Alexandria's maritime activities, and a cornucopia suggesting material prosperity or good health in the other. Alexandria was a great medical center until about 700 A.D., after which leadership in medical practice passed to Constantinople. (Dumbarton Oaks Center for Byzantine Studies, Trustees of Harvard University)*

Arabs, who assimilated it and made remarkable advances upon it. The Byzantines were equally uncreative in astronomy and natural science, but they at least faithfully learned what the ancients had to teach.

Only when science could be put to military use did the Byzantines make advances. The best-known Byzantine scientific discovery was chemical – "Greek fire," a combustible liquid that was the medieval equivalent of the flame thrower. In mechanics the Byzantines continued the work of Hellenistic and Roman inventors of artillery and seige machinery. Just as Archimedes had devised machines to stop the Romans, so Byzantine scientists improved and modified devices for defending their empire.

The Byzantines devoted a great deal of attention to medicine, and the general level of medical competence was far higher in the Byzantine Empire than it was in the medieval West. The Byzantines assimilated the discoveries of Hellenic and Hellenistic medicine but added very few of their own. The basis of their medical theory was Hippocrates' concept of the four humors of the body (page 101). Byzantine physicians emphasized the importance of diet and rest, and relied heavily on drugs made from herbs. Perhaps their chief weakness was their excessive use of bleeding and burning, which often succeeded only in further weakening an already feeble patient. Hospitals were a prominent feature of Byzantine life, and the army too had a medical corps.

## THE ARABS AND ISLAM

Around 610, in the obscure town of Mecca in what is now Saudi Arabia, a moderately successful merchant called Mohammed began to

*ISLAMIC RELIGIOUS HERITAGE In these two miniature paintings a Muslim artist acknowledges the Islamic debt to Judaism and to Christianity. Above, Samson destroys the temple of the Philistines (Judges 16: 28–30). Below, Christ at a window watches Mohammed's flight from Mecca. (Edinburgh University Library)*

have religious visions. By the time he died in 632, all Arabia had accepted his creed. A century later his followers controlled Syria, Palestine, Egypt, all of North Africa, Spain, and part of France. This Arabic expansion profoundly affected the development of European culture. Through centers at Salerno in southern Italy and Toledo in central Spain, Arabic and Greek learning reached the West. Arabic mathematicians not only preserved ancient learning but also made original contributions. Western knowledge, especially in medicine, mathematics, and engineering, rests heavily on Arabic achievements.

### THE ARABS

In Mohammed's time, Arabia was inhabited by Semitic tribes, most of whom were Bedouins. These primitive and warlike peoples grazed their goats and sheep on the sparse patches of grass that dotted the vast semi-arid peninsula. Other Arabs, called Hejaz, lived in the southern valleys and coastal towns along the Red Sea – in Yemen, Mecca, and Medina. The Hejaz led a more sophisticated life and supported themselves by agriculture and trade. Their caravan routes crisscrossed Arabia and carried goods to Byzantium, Persia, and Syria. The Hejaz had wide commercial dealings, but avoided cultural contacts with their Jewish, Christian, and Persian neighbors. The wealth produced by their business transactions led to luxurious and extravagant living in the towns.

Although the nomadic Bedouins condemned the urbanized lifestyle of the Hejaz as immoral and corrupt, Arabs of both types deeply respected each other's local tribal customs. They had no political unity beyond their tribal bonds. Tribal custom regulated their lives. Custom demanded the rigid observance of family obligations and the performance of religious rituals. Custom insisted that an Arab be proud, generous, and swift to take revenge. Custom required manly courage in public and avoidance of shameful behavior that could bring social disgrace.

Although the various tribes differed markedly, they did have certain religious rules in common. For example, all Arabs kept three months of the year as sacred, and during that time fighting stopped so that everyone could attend the holy ceremonies in peace. The city of Mecca was the religious center of the Arab world, and fighting was never tolerated there. All Arabs prayed at the Kaaba, the sanctuary in Mecca. Within the Kaaba was a sacred black stone that Arabs revered because they believed it had fallen from heaven.

What eventually molded the diverse Arab tribes into a powerful political and social unity was the religion founded by Mohammed.

### MOHAMMED AND THE FAITH OF ISLAM

Except for a few vague autobiographical remarks in the Koran, the sacred book of Islam, Mohammed (ca 571–632) left no account of his life. Arab tradition accepts as historically true some of the sacred legends that developed about him, but those legends were not written down until about a century after his death. Orphaned at the age of six, Mohammed was brought up by his grandfather. As a young man he became a merchant in the caravan trade. Later he entered the service of a wealthy widow, and their subsequent marriage brought him financial independence. The Koran reveals him as an extremely devout man, ascetic, self-disciplined, literate but not educated.

Since childhood Mohammed had had strange seizures, or fits, during which he completely lost consciousness and had visions. After 610, these attacks and the accompanying visions apparently became more frequent. Unsure for a time what he should do, Mohammed discovered his mission after a vision in which the angel Gabriel instructed him to preach. Mohammed described his visions in verse form and used these verses as his Qur'an (Koran) or prayer recitation. During his lifetime Mohammed's secretary, Zaid ibn Thabit, jotted down these revelations haphazardly. After Mohammed's death, scribes organized the revelations into chapters, and in 651 Mohammed's second successor as religious leader, Othman, published an official version of them known as the Koran.

The religion Mohammed founded is called Islam; a believer in that faith is called a Muslim. Mohammed's religion eventually attracted great numbers of people, partly because of the simplicity of its doctrines. The subtle and complex reasoning Christianity had acquired by the seventh century was absent from Islam. Nor did Islam emphasize study and learning, as did Judaism.

The strictly monotheistic theology outlined in the Koran has only a few tenets. Allah, the Muslim god, is all-powerful and all-knowing. Mohammed, Allah's prophet, preached his word and carried his message. Mohammed described himself as the successor both of the Jewish patriarch Abraham and of Christ, and claimed that his teachings replaced theirs. Mohammed invited and won converts from Judaism and Christianity.

Because Allah is all-powerful, believers

must submit themselves to him. ("Islam" literally means "submission to the word of God.") This Islamic belief is closely related to the central feature of Muslim doctrine, the coming Day of Judgment. Muslims need not be concerned about *when* judgment will occur, but they must believe with absolute and total conviction that the Day of Judgment *will* come. Consequently, all of a Muslim's thoughts and actions at every hour of every day should be oriented toward the Last Judgment.

The Islamic Day of Judgment will be very similar to the Christian one: on that day God will separate the saved and the damned. Mohammed described in lengthy detail the frightful tortures with which Allah will punish the damned: scourgings, beatings with iron clubs, burnings, and forced drinking of boiling water. The prophet's depiction of the heavenly rewards of the saved and the blessed are just as graphic but different in kind from those of Christian theology. The Muslim vision of heaven features lush green gardens surrounded by refreshing streams. There the saved, clothed in rich silks, lounge about on soft cushions and couches, nibbling ripe fruits, sipping delicious beverages served by handsome youths, and enjoying the companionship of plump black-eyed maidens. It is not difficult to understand how these particular sensual delights would appeal to a people living in or near the hot, dry desert.

In order to merit the rewards of heaven, Mohammed prescribed a strict code of morality and behavior. The Muslim must recite a profession of faith in Allah and in Mohammed as God's prophet: "There is no god but Allah and Mohammed is his prophet." The believer must pray five times a day, fast and pray during the sacred month of Ramadan, make a pilgrimage to the holy city of Mecca once during his or her lifetime, and

give alms to the poor. The Koran forbids alcoholic beverages and gambling. It condemns usury in business — that is, lending money at high interest rates or taking advantage of market demands for products by charging high prices for them. Some foods, such as pork, are forbidden, a dietary regulation adopted directly from the Mosaic law of the Jews.

By earlier Arab standards, the Koran sets forth an austere sexual morality. Muslim jurisprudence condemned licentious behavior on the part of men as well as women, and the status of women in Muslim society gradually improved. About marriage, illicit intercourse, and inheritance, the Koran states:

*(Of) . . . women who seem good in your eyes, marry but two, three, or four; and if ye still fear that ye shall not act equitably, then only one; or the slaves whom ye have acquired: this will make justice on your part easier.*
*The whore and the fornicator: whip each of them a hundred times. . . .*
*The fornicator shall not marry other than a whore; and the whore shall not marry other than a fornicator. . . .*
*They who defame virtuous women, and fail to bring four witnesses (to swear that they did not), are to be whipped eighty times. . . .*
*Men who die and leave wives behind shall bequeath to them a year's maintenance. . . .*
*And your wives shall have a fourth part of what you leave, if you have no issue; but if you have issue, then they shall have an eighth part. . . .*
*With regard to your children, God commands you to give the male the portion of two females; and if there be more than two females, then they shall have two-thirds of what their father leaves; but if there be one daughter only, she shall have the half. (The man who is shamed at the birth of a daughter) hides himself from the people because of the ill tidings: shall he keep it with disgrace or*

*bury it in the dust? Are not his judgments wrong? ... Kill not your children for fear of want: for them and for you will we provide. Verily, the killing of them is a great wickedness.*

By contrast, Western law has tended to punish prostitutes but not their clients. Westerners tend to think polygamy degrading to women, but in a military society where there are apt to be many widows, polygamy provided women a measure of security. The prohibition against killing unwanted female infants by burial obviously represents a more humane attitude. With respect to matters of property, Muslim women were more emancipated than Western women. For example, a Muslim woman retained complete jurisdiction over one-third of her property when she married, and she could dispose of it in any way she wished. A Western woman had no such power.[16]

The Muslim who faithfully observed the laws of the Koran could hope for salvation. The believer who suffered and died for his faith in battle was assured the sensual rewards of the Muslim heaven immediately. According to the Koran, salvation is by Allah's grace and choice alone. A Muslim will not "win" salvation as a reward for good behavior. Because Allah is all-knowing and all-powerful, he knows from the moment of a person's conception whether or not that person will be saved. Nevertheless, Mohammed maintained, predestination gave the believer the will and the courage to try to achieve the impossible. Devout Muslims came to believe that mechanical performance of the basic rules of the faith would automatically gain them salvation.

Historians and ecumenically minded theologians have pointed out many similarities among Islam, Christianity, and Judaism. All three religions are monotheistic. Like Jews,

Muslims are forbidden to eat pork. Like Christians, Muslims are urged to practice charity and to be generous to the poor and the weak. And like Christians, Muslims believe in the Last Judgment. Mohammed probably had a general familiarity with the Old and New Testaments, and he must have learned something about Jewish and Christian cultures on his commercial travels.

In the Koran, Mohammed gave his believers a holy book of revelation, moral principles, and history on a par with the Old and New Testaments. Like Jews and Christians, Muslims became people with a sacred book. But the Koran was not only a sacred book. It was written with great eloquence and poetic charm, qualities the Arabs of Mohammed's day especially valued.

### MUSLIM EXPANSION IN THE WEST

Mohammed's preaching at first did not appeal to many people. Legend has it that for the first three years he attracted only fourteen believers. One explanation for the slow acceptance of Islam is that Mohammed urged the destruction of the idols in the sanctuary at Mecca. This site drew thousands of devout Arabs annually and thus brought important revenue to the city. The townspeople turned against Mohammed, and he and his followers were forced to flee to Medina. This Hegira, or flight, occurred in 622, and Muslims subsequently dated the beginning of their era from that event. At Medina, Mohammed attracted increasing numbers of believers, and his teachings began to have an impact.

The social and political effects of Islam were massive. Mohammed destroyed the communal and tribal quality of Arab life. Individuals could perform the religious rituals, such as the five daily prayers, alone. Although

MAP 7.3. THE EXPANSION OF ISLAM TO 733 *Political weaknesses in the territories they conquered, as well as superior fighting skills, help explain the speed with which the Muslims expanded.*

Muslims customarily worshiped together at sundown on Fridays, no assembly or organized church was essential. Islam lacked the public and corporate aspects of tribal religion. Every Muslim hoped that by following the simple requirements of Islam he or she could achieve salvation. For the believer, the significance of the petty disputes and conflicts of tribal society paled before the simple teachings of Allah. On this basis Mohammed united the nomads of the desert and the merchants of the cities. The doctrines of Islam, instead of the ties of local custom, bound all Arabs.

The faith of Allah, having united the Arabs, redirected their warlike energies. Hostilities were launched outward. By the time

Mohammed died in 632, he had welded together all the Bedouin tribes. The crescent of Islam, the Muslim symbol, controlled the entire Arabian peninsula. In the following century, between 632 and 733, one rich province of the old Roman Empire after another came under Muslim domination – first Syria, then Egypt and Persia, and then all of North Africa (see Map 7.3). The governmental headquarters of this vast new empire was established at Damascus in Syria by the ruling Omayyad family. A contemporary proverb speaks of the Mediterranean as a Muslim lake.

In 711, a Muslim force crossed the Straits of Gibraltar and at Gaudalete easily defeated the weak Visigothic kingdom in Spain. The Muslims swept across Spain in seven years

DOME OF THE ROCK *Built in 691 by Mohammed's second successor, the Caliph Omar, this domed mosque was the first Islamic religious building in Jerusalem after the Arab conquest of Palestine. Because the* Koran *forbade representations of the human figure, geometrical designs decorate the walls. (Israel Government Tourist Administration)*

and, as one scholar has written, "What was lost in seven years, it took seven hundred to regain."[17] A few Christian princes supported by the Frankish rulers held out in northern mountain fortresses, but the Muslims controlled most of Spain until the twelfth century. The political history of Spain in the Middle Ages is the history of the *reconquista,* or Christian reconquest of that country.

In 719, the Arabs pushed beyond the Pyrenees into the kingdom of the Franks. At the battle of Tours in 733, the Frankish ruler Charles Martel defeated the Arabs and halted their further expansion. Ultimately Charlemagne expelled them from France.

Nor was Muslim expansion confined to northern Africa and southern Europe. From the Arabian peninsula, Muslims also carried their faith deep into Africa and across Asia all the way to India. In the West, however, Arab political influence was felt almost exclusively in Spain. A member of the Omayyad dynasty, Abdurrahman (756–788), established the Moorish kingdom of Spain with its capital at

Cordova. (The Spanish kingdom and Spanish culture were called Moorish after the dark-skinned Moors of North Africa, also known as Berber-Arabs, who had conquered the Iberian Peninsula.) Jewish people were generally well treated in Moorish Spain, and Christians were tolerated as long as they paid a small tax.

Toledo became an important center of learning through which Arab intellectual achievements entered and influenced western Europe. Arabic knowledge of science and mathematics, derived from the Chinese, Greeks, and Hindus, was highly sophisticated. The Muslim mathematician Al-Khwarizmi (d.830) wrote the important treatise *Algebra,* the first work in which the word *algebra* is used mathematically, to mean the transposing of negative terms in an equation to the opposite side. Al-Khwarizmi used Arabic numerals in *Algebra,* and applied mathematics to problems of physics and astronomy. Muslims also instructed Westerners in the use of the zero, which permitted the execution of complicated problems of multiplication and long division. Use of the zero represented an enormous advance over the clumsy Roman numerals.

Muslim medical knowledge was also far superior to that of Westerners. By the ninth century, Arab physicians had translated most of the treatises of Hippocrates and Galen. Unfortunately, these Greek treatises came to the West as translations from Greek to Arabic to Latin, and inevitably lost a great deal in translation. Nevertheless, in the ninth and tenth centuries, Arabic knowledge and experience in anatomy and pharmaceutical prescriptions much enriched Western knowledge. Later, Greek philosophical thought passed to the West by way of Arabic translation.

There is no question that Islam was a significant ingredient in the making of Europe.

Muslim expansion meant that Mediterranean civilization would be divided into three spheres of influence, the Byzantine, the Arabic, and the Western. Beginning in the ninth century, Arabic mathematics, medicine, philosophy, and science played a decisive role in the formation of European culture. A few of the words that came into English from Arabic suggest the extent of Arabic influence: alcohol, admiral, algebra, almanac, candy, cipher, coffee, damask, lemon, orange, sherbet, zero.[18]

———◆———

Saint Augustine died in 430 as the Vandals approached the coastal city of Hippo. Scholars have sometimes described Augustine as standing with one foot in the ancient world and one in the Middle Ages. Indeed, Augustine does represent the end of ancient culture and the birth of what has been called the Middle Ages. A new and different kind of society was gestating in the mid-fifth century.

The world of the Middle Ages combined Germanic practices and institutions, classical ideas and patterns of thought, Christianity, and a significant dash of Islam. Christianity, because it creatively and energetically fashioned the Germanic and the classical legacies, was the most powerful agent in the making of Europe. Saint Augustine of Hippo, dogmatic thinker and Christian bishop, embodies the coming world-view.

## NOTES

1. E. F. Henderson, ed., *Select Historical Documents of the Middle Ages,* G. Bell & Sons, London, 1912, pp. 176–189.
2. R. C. Petry, ed., *A History of Christianity: Read-*

*ings in the History of Early and Medieval Christianity,* Prentice-Hall, Englewood Cliffs, N.J., 1962, p. 70.

3. H. Bettenson, ed., *Documents of the Christian Church,* Oxford University Press, Oxford, 1947, p. 113.

4. Colossians 3:9–11 (*Jerusalem Bible*).

5. Luke 6:20–32 (*Jerusalem Bible*).

6. L. Sherley-Price, trans., *Bede: A History of the English Church and People,* Penguin Books, Baltimore, 1962, pp. 86–87.

7. J. T. McNeill and H. Gamer, trans., *Medieval Handbooks of Penance,* Octagon Books, New York, 1965, pp. 184–197.

8. L. White, "The Life of the Silent Majority," in *Life and Thought in the Early Middle Ages,* ed. R. S. Hoyt, University of Minnesota Press, Minneapolis, 1967, p. 100.

9. I Peter 2:11–20 (*Jerusalem Bible*).

10. See John Boswell, *Christianity, Social Tolerance, and Homosexuality: Gay People in Western Europe from the Beginning of the Christian Era to the Fourteenth Century,* University of Chicago Press, Chicago, 1980, chs. 3 and 5, esp. pp. 87, 127–131.

11. F. J. Sheed, trans., *The Confessions of St. Augustine,* Sheed & Ward, New York, 1953, book I, pt. 3.

12. Ibid., book 10, pt. 27, p. 236.

13. Quoted by J. B. Bury, *History of the Later Roman Empire,* vol. I, Dover Publications, New York, 1958, pp. 233–234.

14. R. Atwater, trans., *Procopius: The Secret History,* University of Michigan Press, Ann Arbor, 1963, book 8.

15. Ibid., book 12.

16. Julia O'Faolain and Lauro Martines, eds., *Not in God's Image: Women in History from the Greeks to the Victorians,* Harper & Row, New York, 1973, pp. 108–115.

17. J. H. Elliott, *Imperial Spain, 1496–1716,* St. Martin's Press, London, 1966, p. 26.

18. F. B. Artz, *The Mind of the Middle Ages,* Alfred A. Knopf, New York, 1967, p. 178.

## SUGGESTED READING

In addition to the studies listed in the Notes, this chapter leans on the following works, which students may consult for a broader treatment of the characteristics of the early Middle Ages.

P. Brown, *The World of Late Antiquity, A.D. 150–750* (1971), is a well-illustrated and lucidly written introduction to the entire period, with an emphasis on social and cultural change. B. Lyon, *The Origins of the Middle Ages: Pirenne's Challenge to Gibbon* (1972), is an excellent bibliographical essay with extensive references. For the Germans, see J. M. Wallace-Hadrill, *The Barbarian West, The Early Middle Ages A.D. 400–1000* (1962), and A. Lewis, *Emerging Europe, A.D. 400–1000* (1967), both of which describe German customs and society and the Germanic impact on the Roman Empire. F. Lot, *The End of the Ancient World* (1965), emphasizes the economic and social causes of Rome's decline.

There is a rich literature on the Christian church and its role in the transition between ancient and medieval civilizations. F. Oakley, *The Medieval Experience: Foundations of Western Cultural Singularity* (1974), stresses the Christian roots of Western cultural uniqueness. J. Danielou and H. Marrou, *The Christian Centuries,* vol. 1: *The First Six Hundred Years* (1964), is a clearly written and comprehensive history. G. Le Bras, "The Sociology of the Church in the Early Middle Ages," in S. L. Thrupp, ed., *Early Medieval Society* (1967), discusses the Christianization of the barbarians. Students interested in the synthesis of classical and Christian cultures should see C. N. Cochrane, *Christianity and Classical Culture* (1957), a deeply learned monograph. T. E. Mommsen, "Saint Augustine and the Christian Idea of Progress: The Background of the City of God," *Journal of the History of Ideas* 12 (1951):346–374, and G. B. Ladner, *The Idea of Reform* (1959), examine ideas of history and progress among the early fathers of the Christian church. The best biography of St. Augustine is

P. Brown, *Augustine of Hippo* (1967), which treats him as a symbol of change.

Monasticism has attracted the interest of Westerners from sixth-century Germans to twentieth-century hippies. L. Doyle, trans., *St. Benedict's Rule for Monasteries* (1957), presents the monastic guide in an accessible pocket-size form; a more scholarly edition is J. McCann, ed. and trans., *The Rule of Saint Benedict* (1952). Two beautifully illustrated syntheses by distinguished authorities are D. Knowles, *Christian Monasticism* (1969), which sketches monastic history through the middle of the twentieth century, and G. Zarnecki, *The Monastic Achievement* (1972), which focuses on the medieval centuries. L. J. Daly, *Benedictine Monasticism* (1965), stresses the day-to-day living of the monks, and H. B. Workman, *The Evolution of the Monastic Ideal* (1962), concentrates on monasticism as a spiritual and intellectual ideal.

For Byzantium and the Arabs, see J. Hussey, *The Byzantine World* (1961); A. A. Vasiliev, *History of the Byzantine Empire* (1968); S. Runciman, *Byzantine Civilization* (1956); B. Lewis, *The Arabs in History* (1966); T. Andrae, *Mohammed: The Man and His Faith* (1970); M. Rodinson, *Mohammed* (1974); and G. E. von Grunebaum, *Medieval Islam* (1961), which are all excellent treatments of the subject.

# CHAPTER 8

## THE CAROLINGIAN WORLD: EUROPE

## IN THE EARLY MIDDLE AGES

IN 733, the Frankish chieftain Charles Martel defeated the Muslim invaders at the battle of Tours in central France. At the time it was only another skirmish in the struggle between Christians and Muslims, but in retrospect it looms as one of the great battles of history: this Frankish victory halted Arab expansion in Europe. A century later, in 843, Charles Martel's three great-great-grandsons, after a bitter war, concluded the Treaty of Verdun, which divided the European continent among themselves.

Between 733 and 843, a society emerged that was distinctly European. A new kind of social and political organization, later called feudalism, appeared. And for the first time since the collapse of the Roman Empire, most of western Europe was united under one government. That government reached the peak of its development under Charles Martel's grandson, Charlemagne. Christian missionary activity among the Germanic peoples continued, and strong ties were forged with the Roman papacy. A revival of study and learning, sometimes styled the Carolingian Renaissance, occurred under Charlemagne.

This chapter will explore the following questions. What was feudalism? How did it come about? How did Charlemagne acquire and govern his vast empire? What was the significance of the relations between Carolingian rulers and the church? What was the Carolingian Renaissance? The culture of the Carolingian Empire has been described as "the first European civilization." What does this mean?

## THE EIGHTH CENTURY: END OF THE ANCIENT WORLD?

Scholars have traditionally designated the fifth century as the end of the ancient world. But an influential twentieth-century historian, the Belgian Henri Pirenne, has argued that the eighth century was the real turning-point in Western civilization.

Pirenne's thesis focuses on the Mediterranean Sea. The Roman Empire had controlled the Mediterranean from the Bosporus in the east to the Straits of Gibraltar in the west. Roman trade, Roman armies, and Greco-Roman ideas had travelled on the Mediterranean; it was the highway that united the empire. Although the German tribes had conquered the western provinces in the fifth and sixth centuries, they had perpetuated many Roman ways. The Germans gradually converted to Christianity, and with Christianization came Romanization. German rulers in the West continued trade and economic relations with the East, and the Germans shared in the economic and cultural unity the Mediterranean provided.

But the Muslim conquests of the seventh and eighth centuries ended all this. The Mediterranean, long the thoroughfare of the Greco-Roman world, became a Muslim lake. By the time of Charlemagne in the late eighth century, the Muslims controlled the Mediterranean and the land bordering three sides of it. According to Pirenne, their control meant the real end of the ancient world, which had centered on the Mediterranean. In the eighth century, western Europe, which had been relying on Eastern imports, was cut off from its sources of supply. An isolated and agrarian economy developed as a result. Charlemagne's capital at Aix-la-Chapelle was a sign of the shift of political and military power to the north, away from the Mediterranean. For the next five hundred years, northern Europe, rather than Rome and Italy, was to be the center of culture and civilization. Thus the imperial coronation of Charlemagne by Pope Leo III on Christmas Day in the year 800 can be seen as the symbolic end of the ancient world and the start of the medieval.

Pirenne's argument rests heavily on Mohammed; indeed, as Pirenne put it, "It is therefore strictly correct to say that without Mohammed, Charlemagne would have been inconceivable."[1] By this he meant that the entire empire of Charlemagne was centered in northern Europe and oriented to the West as the direct consequence of Muslim expansion. Pirenne's interpretation has provoked vigorous debate. Historians have questioned his facts and disputed his conclusions. For one thing, considerable evidence suggests that trade between the East and the West continued through the eighth and ninth centuries and was not shut off by Muslim control of the Mediterranean. As this debate vividly illustrates, the division of time spans into distinct periods is always subject to interpretation. Whatever the merits of Pirenne's thesis, the eighth century deserves attention as a great turning point.

EQUESTRIAN STATUE OF CHARLEMAGNE *A medieval king was expected to be fierce (and successful) in battle, to defend the church and the poor, and to give justice to all. This majestic and idealized figure of Charlemagne conveys these qualities. The horse is both the symbol and the means of his constant travels. (French Embassy Press and Information Division)*

## TOWARD A FEUDAL SOCIETY

In the period of the Germanic invasions the Roman imperial government had been compelled to retrench. Roman troops and Roman administrators were withdrawn from the provinces. Gallo-Romans in Gaul and Romanized natives in Britain were forced to cope as best they could. No authority was strong enough to provide peace over a wide area.

Men who could fight, or who owned horses, or who were wealthy and had the time to learn how to fight and ride could join a local band of warriors. But the vast defenseless majority, compelled to work the land for their livelihood, had little choice but to seek out some local strongman and ask that "lord"

for protection. Local lords replaced Roman administrators. Western Europe was governed by the simple law that he should take who has the power, and he should keep who can.

### FEUDALISM

Between the sixth and eighth centuries, European society evolved toward a condition that scholars later termed feudalism. Feudalism may be defined as a kind of social organization in which public political power resided in the private hands of a small military elite. The fundamental strength of the feudal elite rested on its military might. The ethos, the values — indeed, the entire culture of feudal society —

was military. Almost everything was determined by war or the preparation for war. Thus, loyalty was the highest virtue. It was the cement that held a warring society together.

In order to ensure the support of his fighters, a lord gave them land in exchange for their loyalty. Charles Martel got land to distribute to his men by confiscating church property. Lesser lords, as they defeated weaker neighbors and seized their property, divided it among their followers. Early feudalism resulted from a fusion of the Germanic custom of swearing allegiance to a warrior leader with the Roman practice of granting an estate or the booty of war to fighters or important servants. The mounted warrior became a vassal (from the Celtic word for "a well-born young man") of the lord. Though he was obliged to perform services in return for holding the land – his feud, or fief – the vassal lost nothing in social status.

The political power of the ruling class rested upon the ability to raise a contingent of fighting men, to hold courts, to coin money, and to conduct relations and make agreements with outside powers. These powers were held by many lords, both lay and ecclesiastical, and not just by monarchs. Many men became the vassals of several lords in order to acquire more land or money and thus improve their economic position. Feudal lords everywhere were out for themselves, and everywhere they tended to resist the centralizing ambitions of kings.

The ceremony by which a man became the vassal of another involved the use of religious objects, such as the Bible or relics of the saints, and the presence of a priest. The vassal knelt, placed his folded hands between those of the lord, and declared his intention to become the lord's man. By this he meant that he would fight for the lord or perform some

other kind of military service, such as castle-guard. The vassal then rose and swore his faith (or fidelity) on the Bible or the relics. Lord and vassal exchanged a kiss on the mouth, symbolizing peace between two social equals. The conclusion of the ceremony was marked by the lord's investing his new vassal with a symbol of his fief, such as a clump of earth.

Because feudal society was a military society, men held the dominant positions in it. A high premium was put on physical strength, fighting skill, and bravery. The legal and social position of women was not as insignificant as might be expected, however. Charters recording gifts to the church indicate that women held land in many areas. Women frequently endowed monasteries, churches, and other religious establishments. The possession of land obviously meant economic power. Moreover, women inherited fiefs. In southern France and Catalonia in Spain, women inherited feudal property as early as the tenth century. Other kinds of evidence attest to the status of women. In parts of northern France, children sometimes identified themselves in legal documents by their mother's name rather than their father's name, indicating that the mother's social position in the community was higher than the father's.

In a treatise he wrote in 822 on the organization of the royal household, Archbishop Hincmar of Reims placed the queen directly above the treasurer. She was responsible for giving the knights their annual salaries. She supervised the manorial accounts. Thus, in the management of large households, with many knights to oversee and complicated manorial records to supervise, the lady of the manor had highly important responsibilities. With such responsibility went power and influence.[2]

Feudalism concerned the rights, powers, and lifestyle of the military elite; manorialism involved the services and obligations of the peasant classes. The *economic* power of the warring class rested upon landed estates, which were worked by peasants. Hence feudalism and manorialism were inextricably linked. Peasants needed protection, and lords demanded something in return for that protection. Free peasants surrendered themselves and their lands to the lord's jurisdiction. The land was given back, but the peasants became tied to the land by various kinds of payments and services. In France, England, Germany, and Italy, local custom determined precisely what those services were, but certain practices became common everywhere. The serf was obliged to turn over to the lord a percentage of the annual harvest, usually in produce, sometimes in cash. The peasant paid a fee to marry someone from outside the lord's estate. He paid a fine, often his best beast, to inherit property. Above all, the peasant became part of the lord's permanent labor force. With vast stretches of uncultivated virgin land and a tiny labor population, lords encouraged population growth and immigration. The most profitable form of capital was not land but laborers. The small feudal class led lives devoted to war and leisure; toil was the usual fate of those who were not warriors or clerics.

In entering into a relationship with a feudal lord, the free farmer lost status. His position became servile, and he became a serf. That is, he was bound to the land and could not leave it without the lord's permission. He was also subject to the jurisdiction of the lord's court in any dispute over property or suspicion of criminal behavior.

The transition from freedom to serfdom was slow; its speed was closely related to the degree of political order in a given geographical region. Even in the late eighth century there were still many free men. And within the legal category of serfdom there were many economic levels, ranging from the highly prosperous to the desperately poor. Nevertheless, a social and legal revolution was taking place. Around the year 800, perhaps 60 percent of the population of Western Europe – completely free a century before – had been reduced to serfdom. The ninth-century Viking assaults on Europe created extremely unstable conditions and individual insecurity, leading to additional loss of personal freedom. Chapter 10 will look in detail at the lives of the peasants. As we shall see, although the later Middle Ages witnessed considerable upward social mobility, serfdom remained the condition of most Europeans, in fact if not in law, for almost a thousand years.

## THE RISE OF THE CAROLINGIAN DYNASTY

In the seventh century, the kingdom of the Franks steadily deteriorated. Weak and incompetent rulers lost power to local strongmen. Central authority collapsed in the face of brute force. The administrative agencies of the Merovingian kings slipped into the hands of local powers.

The rise of the Carolingian family – whose name derives from the Latin *Carolus,* for "Charles" – began with the efforts of Pippin I in the mid-seventh century. Pippin made himself mayor of the palace of Austrasia, which meant that he was head of the Frankish administration. His grandson Pippin II (d. 714) also gained the title of mayor of the palace, and from that position worked to reduce the power of the Frankish aristocracy.

It was Pippin's son Charles Martel (714–741) who defeated the Muslims at Tours and thus checked Arab expansion into Europe. Charles's wars against the Saxons, the Burgundians, and the Frisians broke those weakening forces. His victory over the infidels and his successful campaigns within the Frankish kingdom added to the prestige of his family the reputation of great military strength. Charles Martel held the real power in the Frankish kingdom; the Merovingians were king in name only.

The rise of the Carolingian dynasty rested partly on papal support. In the early eighth century, while Charles Martel and his son Pippin III were attempting to bring the various Germanic tribes under their jurisdiction, they gained the support of two Anglo-Saxon missionaries, Willibrord and Wynfrith. The Northumbrian monk Willibrord crossed the English Channel and preached to the pagans on the Frisian Islands and in the area of the modern Netherlands, Belgium, and Luxembourg. With enormous zeal Willibrord organized the church of Friesland, established the see of Utrecht, and acted as the first archbishop. He also founded the abbey of Echternach (in what is now Luxembourg), which subsequently became an important missionary center.

Even more spectacular were the achievements of Wynfrith, or Boniface (680–754), as he was later called. A native of Devonshire in England, Boniface preached in Bavaria and Hesse in southern Germany. There, assisted by other monks from Britain, his many conversions attracted the attention of both Charles Martel and Pope Gregory II. Boniface traveled to Rome several times and was made a bishop. He became an enthusiastic champion of ecclesiastical principles and of papal authority in the Frankish kingdom.

Given the semibarbarous peoples with whom he was dealing, Boniface's achievements were remarkable. He founded the see of Mainz, the chief see of Germany, and the abbey of Fulda, which became one of the great centers of Christian culture in the ninth century. He built churches. He established the *Rule of Saint Benedict* in all the monasteries he founded or reformed. With the full support of Pippin III, Boniface held several councils that reformed the Frankish church. He even succeeded in cutting down the famous Oak of Thor, the center of a pagan cult.

Saint Boniface preached throughout Germany against divorce, polygamous unions, and incest. On these matters German custom and ecclesiastical law completely disagreed. The Germans allowed divorce simply by the mutual consent of both parties. The Germanic peoples also practiced polygamy and incest – sexual relations between brothers and sisters or between parents and children – on a wide scale. (Incest, in fact, is a major theme of a seventh-century German legend about the twins Sigmund and Siglinda, whose tragic love and the life of their son Siegfried were immortalized in three operas by the nineteenth-century composer Richard Wagner.) Church councils in the sixth and seventh centuries repeatedly condemned incest, indicating that it was common. And theologians since Saint Augustine had stressed that marriage, validly entered into, could not be ended.

Boniface's preaching was not without impact, for in 802 Charlemagne prohibited incest, and decreed that a husband might separate from an adulterous wife. The woman could be punished, and the man could not remarry in her lifetime. Charlemagne also encouraged severe punishment for adulterous men. In so doing, he contributed to the dignity of marriage, the family, and women.

Saint Boniface, known as the Apostle of Germany, is one of the most important fig-

# THE CAROLINGIAN DYNASTY TO 877

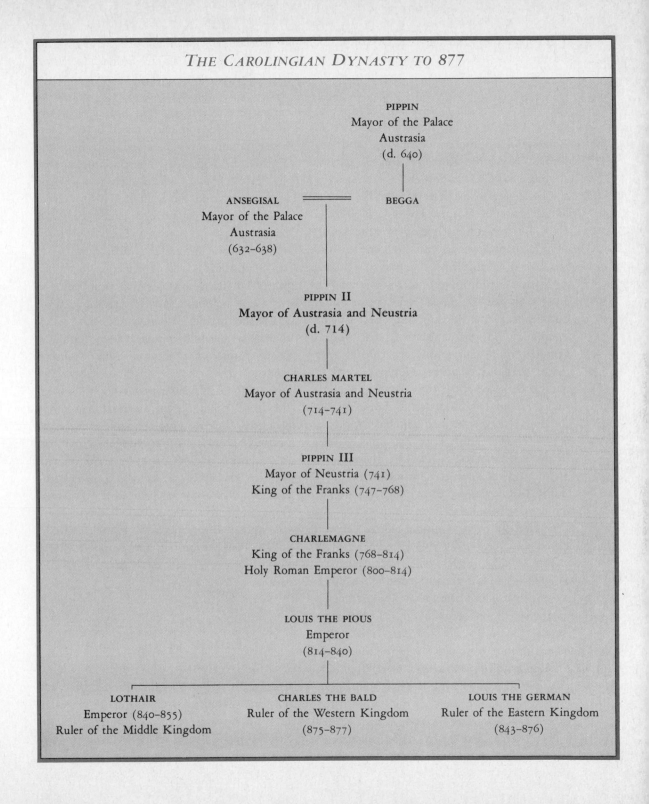

**PIPPIN**
Mayor of the Palace
Austrasia
(d. 640)

**ANSEGISAL** ══════ **BEGGA**
Mayor of the Palace
Austrasia
(632–638)

**PIPPIN II**
**Mayor of Austrasia and Neustria**
(d. 714)

**CHARLES MARTEL**
Mayor of Austrasia and Neustria
(714–741)

**PIPPIN III**
Mayor of Neustria (741)
King of the Franks (747–768)

**CHARLEMAGNE**
King of the Franks (768–814)
Holy Roman Emperor (800–814)

**LOUIS THE PIOUS**
Emperor
(814–840)

**LOTHAIR**
Emperor (840–855)
Ruler of the Middle Kingdom

**CHARLES THE BALD**
Ruler of the Western Kingdom
(875–877)

**LOUIS THE GERMAN**
Ruler of the Eastern Kingdom
(843–876)

ures in early European history. In all of his missionary activity he promoted peace and respect for legally established civil authorities. Charles Martel and Pippin III protected Boniface, and he preached Christian obedience to rulers. Because of his staunch adherence to Roman ideas, Roman traditions, and the Roman pope, the Romanization of Europe accompanied Christianization.

Charles Martel had been king of the Franks in fact but not in title. His son Pippin III (747–768) made himself king in title as well as in fact. In Germanic custom – and custom was law – the kingship had to pass to someone with royal blood. Pippin did not want to do away with the ineffectual Merovingian king, but he did want the kingship. Because the missionary activity of Boniface had spread Christian ideals and enhanced papal influence in the Frankish kingdom, Pippin decided to consult the pope about the kingship. Accordingly, Pippin sent Boniface to Rome to ask the pope whether the man who has the power is entitled to be king. Pope Zacharias, guided by the Augustinian principle that the real test of kingship is whether it provides for order and justice, responded in 751 that he who has the power should also have the title. This answer constituted recognition of the Carolingians.

Just as the emperors Constantine and Theodosius in the fourth century had taken actions that would later be cited as precedents in the relations between church and state (pages 223 and 224), so Pippin III in the eighth century took papal confirmation as official approval of his title. In 752, Pippin III was formally elected king of the Franks by the great lords, or magnates, of the Frankish territory. Two years later the pope – who needed Pippin's protection from the Lombards – came to Gaul and personally anointed Pippin king at Paris.

Thus an important alliance was struck between the papacy and the Frankish ruler. In 754, Pope Stephen gave Pippin the title of protector of the Roman church. Pippin in turn agreed to restore to the papacy territories in northern Italy recently seized by the Lombards; he promptly marched into Italy and defeated the Lombards. The Carolingian family had received official recognition and anointment from the leading spiritual power in Europe. The papacy had gained a military protector.

On a second successful campaign in Italy in 756, Pippin made a large donation to the papacy. The gift was estates in central Italy that technically belonged to the Byzantine emperor at Constantinople. Known as the Papal States, they existed over a thousand years, until the newly formed kingdom of Italy abolished them in 1870.

Because of his anointment, Pippin's kingship took on a special spiritual and moral character. Before Pippin, only priests and bishops had received anointment: Pippin became the first lay person to be anointed with the sacred oils. His person was considered sacred. He was acknowledged as *rex et sacerdos* (king and priest). Pippin also cleverly eliminated possible threats to the Frankish throne, and the pope promised him support in the future. When Pippin died, his son Charlemagne succeeded him.

## THE EMPIRE OF CHARLEMAGNE

Charles the Great (768–814) built on the military and diplomatic foundations of his ancestors. Charles's secretary and biographer, the Saxon Einhard, wrote a lengthy description of this warrior-ruler. It has serious flaws, partly because it is modeled directly on the Roman author Suetonius's *Life of the Emperor Augustus.* Still, it is the earliest medieval biography of a layman, and historians consider it generally accurate:

*Charles was large and strong, and of lofty stature, though not disproportionately tall . . . the upper part of his head was round, his eyes very large and animated, nose a little long, hair fair, and face laughing and merry. Thus his appearance was always stately and dignified . . . although his neck was thick and somewhat short, and his belly rather prominent; but the symmetry of the rest of his body concealed these defects. His gait was firm, his whole carriage manly, and his voice clear, but not so strong as his size led one to expect. His health was excellent, except during the four years preceding his death. . . . Even in those years he consulted rather his own inclinations than the advice of physicians, who were almost hateful to him, because they wanted him to give up roasts, to which he was accustomed, and to eat boiled meat instead. In accordance with the national custom, he took frequent exercise on horseback and in the chase, accomplishments in which scarcely any people in the world can equal the Franks. He enjoyed the exhalations from natural warm springs, and often practiced swimming, in which he was such an adept that none could surpass him; and hence it was that he built his palace at Aix-la-Chapelle, and lived there constantly during his latter years until his death. He used not only to invite his sons to his bath, but his nobles and friends, and now and then a troop of his retinue or bodyguard. . . .*

*He used to wear the national, that is to say, the Frank, dress — next his skin a linen shirt and linen breeches, and above these a tunic fringed with silk; while hose fastened by bands covered his lower limbs, and shoes his feet, and he protected his shoulder and chest in winter by a close-fitting coat of otter or marten skins. Over all he flung a blue cloak, and he always had a sword girt about him, usually one with a gold or silver hilt and belt; he*

*sometimes carried a jeweled sword, but only on great feastdays or at the reception of ambassadors from foreign nations.*[3]

Though crude and brutal, Charlemagne was a man of enormous intelligence. He appreciated good literature, such as Saint Augustine's *City of God,* and Einhard considered him an unusually effective speaker. On the other hand, he could not even write his own name.

For all Charles's concern for moderation in food and wine, he had three wives, one after the other, and after they died, three concubines simultaneously. The austere code of sexual morality he published for the empire reflects the attitude of the clerics who wrote it far more than the behavior of the warrior-king. The most striking feature of Charlemagne's character was his phenomenal energy, which helps to account for his great military achievements.

### TERRITORIAL EXPANSION

Continuing the expansionist policies of his ancestors, Charlemagne fought more than fifty campaigns and became the greatest warrior of the early Middle Ages. In what is now France, he subdued all of the north. In the south, the lords of the mountainous ranges of Aquitaine — what is now called Basque country — fought off his efforts at total conquest. The Muslims in northeastern Spain were checked by the establishment of strongly fortified areas known as marches.

Charlemagne's greatest successes were in what is today called Germany. There, his concerns were basically defensive. In the course of a thirty-year war against the semibarbaric Saxons, he added most of the northwestern German tribes to the Frankish kingdom. The story goes that because of their repeated rebellions, Charlemagne ordered more than four thousand Saxons slaughtered on one day.

To the south, he achieved spectacular results. In 773–774, the Lombards in northern Italy once again threatened the papacy. Charlemagne marched south, overran fortresses at Pavia and Spoleto, and incorporated Lombardy — including Venetia, Istria, and Dalmatia — into the Frankish kingdom. To his title as king of the Franks, he added king of the Lombards. This victory ended all serious attempts at the unification of Italy until the nineteenth century.

By around 805, the Frankish kingdom included all of continental Europe except Spain, Scandinavia, southern Italy, and the Slavic fringes of the east (see Map 8.1). Not since the third century A.D. had any ruler controlled so much of the Western world. Not until Napoleon Bonaparte in the early nineteenth century was the feat to be repeated.

## THE GOVERNMENT OF THE CAROLINGIAN EMPIRE

Charlemagne ruled a vast rural world dotted with isolated estates and characterized by constant petty violence. His empire was definitely not a state as people today understand that term; it was a collection of primitive peoples and semibarbarian tribes. Apart from a small class of warrior-aristocrats and clergy, almost everyone engaged in agriculture. Trade and commerce played only a small part in the economy. Cities served as the headquarters of bishops and as ecclesiastical centers.

By constant travel, personal appearances, and the sheer force of his personality, Charlemagne sought to awe his conquered peoples with his fierce presence and his terrible justice. By confiscating the estates of the great territorial magnates, he acquired land with which to gain the support of lesser lords.

Charles divided his kingdom into counties, which served as administrative units. Two or three hundred counts were appointed as the king's representatives. They had full military and judicial powers to maintain law and order and to dispense justice at the local level. They held their offices for life. As a link between local authorities and the central government of the emperor, Charles appointed officials called *missi dominici,* agents of the lord king. The empire was divided into visitorial districts. Each year, beginning in 802, two missi, usually a count and a bishop or abbot, visited assigned districts. They held courts and investigated the judicial, financial, and clerical activities of the district. They held commissions to regulate crime, moral conduct, the clergy, education, the poor, and many other matters. The missi checked up on the counts and worked to prevent the counts' positions from becoming hereditary: strong counts with hereditary estates would have weakened the power of the emperor.

In especially barbarous areas, such as the Spanish and Danish borders, Charles set up areas called marks. There, royal officials called margraves had extensive powers to govern their dangerous localities.

A modern state has institutions of government, such as a civil service, courts of law, financial agencies for the collection and apportionment of taxes, and police and military powers with which to maintain order internally and defend against foreign attack. These simply did not exist in Charlemagne's empire. What held society together were relationships of dependence cemented by oaths promising faith and loyalty.

Although the empire lacked viable institutions, some of the Carolingians involved in governing did have vigorous political ideas. The abbots and bishops who served as Charlemagne's advisers worked out what was for

IRELAND

NORTHUMBRIA
✝ Jarrow
• York

MERCIA

NORTH WALES

EAST ANGLIA

ESSEX

WEST WALES    WESSEX    KENT

SUSSEX

DANISH MARCH

SAXONY
804

• Fulda

Aix-la-Chapelle ⊙    AUSTRASIA

Echternach ⚑    • Mainz

• Rouen

Paris •

BRITTANY
811

NEUSTRIA

Tours •

BAVARIA
788

ALEMANNIA

BURGUNDY

AQUITAINE

Lyons •

Bordeaux •

VENETIA

• Milan

Pavia •

ISTRIA

DALMATIA

TRIBUTARY SLAVIC PEOPLES

Marseilles •

Roncevalles •

SPANISH MARCH
811

CORSICA

PAPAL STATES

• Spoleto

Rome •

⚑ Monte Cassino

DUCHY OF BENEVENTO

Salerno •

OMMAYAD  KINGDOM  OF  SPAIN

• Barcelona

• Toledo

SARDINIA

• Cordova

BYZANTINE EMPIRE

SICILY

⚑  Monasteries

□  Frankish Kingdom, 768
▨  Areas conquered by Charlemagne

□  Tributary peoples
▨  Byzantine Empire

0    100    200 Km.

0    100    200 Mi.

MAP 8.1.  THE CAROLINGIAN WORLD  *The extent of Charlemagne's nominal jurisdiction was extraordinary; it was not equalled until the nineteenth century.*

THE IMPERIAL CORONATION OF CHARLE-
MAGNE *Contemporary evidence for Charlemagne's
coronation by Pope Leo III is literary and contradictory. This fifteenth-century illustration supports the
ecclesiastical view that Charlemagne (kneeling) hum-*
*bly accepted the crown, which the papacy could grant
or withhold. The presence of two cardinals (in
broad-brimmed hats) and the dress of all show this is
a late medieval interpretation of the event. (Musée
Condé, Chantilly/Giraudon)*

their time a sophisticated political ideology.
In letters and treatises they set before the emperor high ideals of behavior and of government. They wrote that a ruler may hold
power from God, but he is responsible to the
law. Just as all subjects of the empire were
required to obey him, so he too was obliged
to respect the law. They envisioned a unified
Christian society presided over by a king who
was responsible for the maintenance of peace,
which would enable Christians to pursue their
pilgrimage to the City of God. They encouraged the emperor to maintain law and
order and to do justice, without which neither
the ruler nor the "state" has any justification.
These views derived largely from Saint Augustine's theories of kingship. Inevitably, they
could not be realized in an illiterate, half-
Christianized, and preindustrial society. But
they were the seeds from which medieval and
even modern ideas of government were to
develop.

## THE IMPERIAL CORONATION OF
## CHARLEMAGNE (800)

In the autumn of the year 800, Charlemagne
paid a momentous visit to Rome. Here are
two accounts of what happened.

According to the Frankish *Royal Annals,* a
year-by-year description of events:

*On the very day of the most holy nativity of the
Lord [Christmas], when the king at Mass had
risen from prayer before the tomb of Blessed Peter
the Apostle, Pope Leo placed the crown on his
head, and by all the people of Rome he was ac-*

*claimed: Long Life and Victory to the August Charles, the Great and Peace-Giving Emperor, crowned by God. And after the ovations, the pope did obeisance to him according to the custom observed before the ancient emperors, and the title of Patricius [Protector] being dropped, he was called Emperor and Augustus.*[4]

Charlemagne's secretary Einhard wrote:

*His last journey there [to Rome] was due to another factor, namely that the Romans, having inflicted many injuries on Pope Leo – plucking out his eyes and tearing out his tongue, he had been compelled to beg the assistance of the king. Accordingly, coming to Rome in order that he might set in order those things which had exceedingly disturbed the condition of the Church, he remained there the whole winter. It was at the time that he accepted the name of Emperor and Augustus. At first he was so much opposed to this that he insisted that although that day was a great [Christian] feast, he would not have entered the Church if he had known beforehand the pope's intention. But he bore very patiently the jealousy of the Roman Emperors [that is, the Byzantine rulers] who were indignant when he received these titles. He overcame their arrogant haughtiness with magnanimity, a virtue in which he was considerably superior to them, by sending frequent ambassadors to them and in his letters addressing them as brothers.*[5]

Charlemagne became *Holy* Roman emperor, adding the sacred authority of the Christian church to the universal authority of the Roman emperor. Einhard says that Charlemagne seldom used the imperial title. But the fact that he sometimes used it illustrates a significant point. Charlemagne governed most of continental Europe. He considered himself a Christian king ruling a Christian people. The title expressed his connection with the Rome of the caesars and the Rome of the popes. By using it, Charlemagne was consciously perpetuating the old Roman imperial

notions, while at the same time identifying with the new Rome of the Christian church. Charlemagne and his government represent a combination of German feudal practices and Christian ideals. These two elements were basic constituents of Europe in the early Middle Ages.

For centuries scholars have debated the significance of the imperial coronation of Charlemagne. Did Charles plan the coronation in St. Peter's on Christmas Day? What did he have to gain from the imperial title? Did Pope Leo III arrange the coronation in order to identify the Frankish monarchy with the papacy and papal policy? Did a coronation actually happen, or are accounts of it later inventions?

Although final answers will probably never be found, two things are certain. First, later German rulers were anxious to gain the imperial title and to associate themselves with the legend of Charlemagne and with ancient Rome. They wanted to use the ideology of imperial Rome to strengthen their own positions. Second, ecclesiastical authorities continually cited the event as proof that the dignity of the imperial crown could be granted only by the pope. The imperial coronation of Charlemagne, whether event or nonevent, was to have a profound effect on the course of German history and on the later history of Europe.

## THE CAROLINGIAN INTELLECTUAL REVIVAL

It is ironic that Charlemagne's most enduring legacy was the stimulus he gave to scholarship and learning. Barely literate himself, preoccupied with the control of vast territories, much more of a warrior than a thinker, he nevertheless set in motion a cultural revival that had "international" and long-lasting consequences. The revival of learning associated with Charlemagne and his court at Aix-la-Chapelle drew its greatest inspiration from seventh- and eighth-century intellectual developments in the Anglo-Saxon kingdom of Northumbria, situated on the northernmost tip of the old Roman world.

## NORTHUMBRIAN CULTURE

The victory of the Roman forms of Christian liturgy and monastic life at the Synod of Whitby in 664 marked the official end of the Celtic church in Britain (page 226). But Whitby did not end the Celtic influence on Christianity in Northumbria. Irish-Celtic culture – through such monasteries as Lindisfarne and York – permeated the Roman church in Britain and resulted in a flowering of artistic and scholarly activity.

Northumbrian creativity owes a great deal to the intellectual curiosity and collecting zeal of Saint Benet Biscop (ca 628–689). Descended from a noble Northumbrian family, Benet Biscop became a monk at Lérins, an island monastery in the Mediterranean that enjoyed valuable contacts with the Eastern monastic tradition of Syria and Egypt. He returned to Britain in the company of the Syrian archbishop of Canterbury, Theodore of Tarsus. Between 674 and 682, Benet Biscop founded the monasteries of Wearmouth and Jarrow. A strong supporter of Benedictine monasticism, he introduced the Roman form of ceremonial into the new religious houses and encouraged it in older ones. Benet Biscop made five dangerous trips to Italy, raided the libraries, and brought back to Northumbria manuscripts, relics, paintings, and other treasures. These books and manuscripts formed the libraries on which much later study was based.

Northumbrian monasteries produced scores of books: missals (used for the celebration of the mass), psalters (which contained the 150 psalms and other prayers used by the monks in their devotions), commentaries on the Scriptures, illuminated manuscripts, law codes, and collections of letters and sermons. The finest product of Northumbrian art is probably the Gospel book produced at Lindisfarne around 700. The incredible expense involved in the publication of such a book – for vellum, coloring, gold leaf – represents in part an aristocratic display of wealth. The script, called uncial, is a Celtic version of contemporary Greek and Roman handwriting. The illustrations have a strong Eastern quality. They combine the abstract style of the Christian Middle East and the narrative approach of classical Roman art. Likewise, the use of geometrical decorative designs shows the influence of Syrian art. Many scribes, artists, and illuminators must have participated in its preparation.

The finest representative of Northumbrian and indeed all Anglo-Saxon scholarship is the Venerable Bede (ca 673–735). The simplicity of Bede's life illustrates his greatness. Given by his parents when he was seven years old as an oblate or "offering" to Benet Biscop's monastery at Wearmouth, he was later sent to the new monastery at Jarrow five miles away. There, surrounded by the books Benet Biscop had brought from Italy, Bede spent the rest of his life.

Bede's scrupulous observance of the *Rule of Saint Benedict* expressed his deep piety. His days were punctuated only by the bells for choir and other religious duties. As a scholar, his patience and diligence reflected his deep love for learning. Contemporaries revered Bede for his learned commentaries on the Scriptures and for the special holiness of his life, which earned him the title "Venerable." He was the most widely read author in the entire Middle Ages.

Modern scholars praise Bede for his *Ecclesiastical History of the English Nation.* Broader in scope than the title suggests, it is the chief source of information about early Britain. Bede searched far and wide for his information, discussed the validity of his evidence, compared various sources, and exercised a rare critical judgment. For these reasons, he has been called "the first scientific intellect among the Germanic peoples of Europe."[6]

Bede was probably the greatest master of chronology of the Middle Ages. He began the system of dating events from the birth of Christ, rather than from the foundation of the city of Rome, as the Romans had done, or from the regnal years of kings, as the Germans did. Bede introduced the term *anno Domini,* "in the year of the Lord," abbreviated A.D. He fit the entire history of the world into this new dating method. (The reverse, or diminishing, dating system of B.C., before Christ, does not seem to have been widely used before 1700.) The Anglo-Saxon missionary Saint Boniface introduced this system of reckoning time throughout the Frankish empire of Charlemagne.

At the very time that monks at Lindisfarne were producing their Gospel book, and Bede at Jarrow was writing his *History,* another Northumbrian monk was at work on a nonreligious epic poem that provides considerable information about the society that produced it. The poem *Beowulf* is perhaps the finest expression of the secular literature of the eighth century. Though the tale is almost childish in its simplicity, scholars have hailed it as a masterpiece of Western heroic literature.

The great hall of the Danish king Hrothgar has been ravaged for twelve years by a half-human monster called Grendel. Hrothgar and his men cannot stop Grendel's attacks. Finally Beowulf, a relative of the Swedish royal house, hears of Grendel's murderous destruc-

*THE SCRIBE EZRA Monks at Bede's monastery at Jarrow made this copy of an early Christian manuscript showing the Jewish scribe Ezra writing his chronicle. The backless bench on which he works appears very uncomfortable. Books were stored against theft and climate in heavy chests or cabinets. (Scala/ Editorial Photocolor Archives)*

tion. With a bodyguard of fourteen trusted warriors, Beowulf sails to Denmark and in a brutal battle destroys Grendel. Hrothgar and his queen, Wealhtheow, give a great banquet for Beowulf and his followers. Afterward, Grendel's mother enters the hall and carries off one of Hrothgar's closest advisers to revenge her son's death. Beowulf ultimately catches and destroys her. This victory is followed by more feasting, and Beowulf returns home to Sweden laden with rich gifts.

Beowulf later becomes king of a Swedish tribe and rules them for fifty years. When his country is ravaged by a terrible dragon, the aged Beowulf challenges him. In the ensuing battle, Beowulf is overwhelmed by the dragon's fiery breath, and all but one of his followers flee. Beowulf defeats the dragon, but is mortally wounded and dies.[7]

The story resembles ordinary Norse legends, but it is actually permeated with classical, Germanic, and Christian elements. Though the poem was written in England, all the action takes place in Scandinavia. This reflects the "international" quality of the culture of the age, or at least the close ties between England and the Continent in the eighth century. (Britain exported wool to the settlements in Frisia that later became the flourishing commercial centers at Ypres and Bruges, which produced cloth.)

Beowulf's entire life was devoted to fighting and war. His values are military and aristocratic: the central institution in the poem is the *gesith,* or Germanic band of warriors united to fight with Beowulf. The highest virtue is loyalty to him, and loyalty is maintained by the giving of gifts. Yet the author was a Christian monk, and the basic theme of the poem is the conflict between good and evil. Beowulf, however, does not exhibit any Christian humility. Never one to hide his light under a bushel, he boasts of his exploits unashamedly. In this, he embodies the classical idea of fame, the notion that fame is the greatest achievement because it is all that a person leaves behind.

Pagan and Germanic symbols and practices suffuse Beowulf. Fighting, feasting, and drinking preoccupy its warrior heroes. There is no glimpse of those who raised and prepared the food they consume. The author did not think peasants deserved mention. In a famous scene Hrothgar's beautiful queen Wealhtheow enters the great hall, dispensing grace and gifts. The scene suggests that women of the upper class served a decorative function in aristocratic society. But Wealhtheow may have been handing out presents to the warriors because she had custody of and responsibility for her husband's treasure.

In another scene the body of a dead king, along with considerable treasure, is put on a ship and floated out to sea. That this was a typical method of burial for Scandinavian kings is known from the ship burial uncovered at Sutton Hoo in England in 1939. Such customs are a far cry from traditional Christian burial. A monk may have composed *Beowulf,* but the persistence of this practice indicates that conversion was still imperfect in much of Europe.

Reading *Beowulf,* one enters a world of darkness, cold, gloom, and pessimism, pierced by a weak ray of Christian hope. It is the foremost expression of the psychological complexities and spiritual contradictions of what has been called the heroic age of Scandinavia — the eighth and ninth centuries.

A less serious literary genre than the epic poem, highly popular in Anglo-Saxon England and Carolingian Europe, was the riddle. Riddles were more than a guessing game for children; in the riddle a poet took on the characteristics or personality of someone or something. Riddles were intended to instruct and to entertain:

*Swings by his thigh a thing most magical!*
*Below the belt, beneath the folds*
*of his clothes it hangs, a hole in its front end,*
*stiff-set & stout, but swivels about.*

*Levelling the head of this hanging instrument,*
*its wielder hoists his hem above the knee:*
*it is his will to fill a well-known hole*
*that it fits fully when at full length.*

*He has often filled it before. Now he fills it again.*[8]

The answer is a key. Riddling was a popular

game in monasteries, and the subjects were not always pious.

The physical circumstances of life in the seventh and eighth centuries make Northumbrian cultural achievements all the more remarkable. Learning was pursued under terribly primitive conditions. Monasteries such as Jarrow and Lindisfarne stood on the very fringes of the European world. The barbarian Picts, just an afternoon's walk from Jarrow, were likely to attack at any time.

Food was not the greatest problem. The North Sea and the nearby rivers, the Tweed and the Tyne, yielded abundant salmon and other fish, which could be salted or smoked for winter, a nutritious if monotonous diet. Climate was another matter. Winter could be extremely harsh. In 664, for example, deep snow was hardened by frost from early winter until mid-spring. When it melted away, many animals, trees, and plants were found dead. To make matters worse, disease and sickness could take terrible tolls. Bede described events in the year 664:

*In the same year of our Lord 664 there was an eclipse of the sun on the third day of May at about four o'clock in the afternoon. Also in that year a sudden pestilence first depopulated the southern parts of Britain and then attacked the kingdom of the Northumbrians as well. Raging far and wide for a long time with cruel devastation it struck down a great multitude of men. . . . This same plague oppressed the island of Ireland with equal destruction.*[9]

Damp cold with bitter winds blowing across the North Sea must have pierced everyone and everything, even the stone monasteries. Inside, only one room, the calefactory or warming room, had a fire. Scribes in the scriptorium, or writing room, had to stop frequently to rub the circulation back into their numb hands. These monk-artists and

BINDING OF THE LINDAU GOSPELS This splendid example of the Carolingian revival combines the geometric forms of Anglo-Irish art with the Roman portrait tradition. The strong face of Christ shows no suffering. The semiprecious stones around the border are raised to catch the light. (The Pierpont Morgan Library)

monk-writers paid a very high physical price for what they gave to posterity.

Had they remained entirely insular, Northumbrian cultural achievements would have been of slight significance. As it happened, an Englishman from Northumbria played a decisive role in the transmission of English learning to the Carolingian Empire and continental Europe.

## THE CAROLINGIAN RENAISSANCE

Charlemagne's empire disintegrated shortly after his death in 814. But the support he gave to education and learning preserved the writings of the ancients and laid the foundations for all subsequent medieval culture. Charlemagne promoted a revival that scholars have named the Carolingian Renaissance.

At his court at Aix-la-Chapelle, Charlemagne assembled learned men from all over Europe. From Visigothic Spain came Theodulf, the best writer of Latin verse of the day. From Pavia in Lombardy came the monk-historian Paul the Deacon, who later wrote the invaluable *History of the Lombards,* still the chief source for the history of the sixth and seventh centuries. From the abbey of Fulda came Einhard, who served as a royal administrator and Charlemagne's closest adviser and biographer.

The most important scholar and the leader of the palace school was the Northumbrian Alcuin. He was born about a year after Bede's death (ca 735) and educated at the cathedral school at York. On a visit to Italy in 781, Alcuin met Charlemagne, who invited him to his court. From then until his death in 804, Alcuin remained the emperor's major adviser on religious and educational matters.

Alcuin was an unusually prolific scholar. He prepared some of the emperor's official documents, and wrote many moral *exempla,* or models, which set high standards for royal behavior and constitute a treatise on kingship. Alcuin's letters to Charlemagne set forth political theories on the authority, power, and responsibilities of a Christian ruler.

What did the scholars at Charlemagne's court do? They copied books and manuscripts and built up libraries. They devised the beautifully clear handwriting known as Carolingian minuscule, from which modern Roman type is derived. (This script is called minuscule because it has lower-case letters; the Romans had only capitals.) They established schools all across Europe, attaching them to

monasteries and cathedrals. They placed great emphasis on the education of priests, trying to make all of them at least able to read, write, and do simple arithmetical calculations. The greatest contribution of the scholars at Aix-la-Chapelle was not so much the originality of their ideas as their hard work of salvaging and preserving the thought and writings of the ancients. Thus the Carolingian Renaissance was a rebirth of interest in, and the study and preservation of, the ideas and achievements of classical Greece and Rome.

Language has been called "the nourishing mother of history." It is the core, the center, of all culture and civilization. Without the ability to communicate ideas, grammatically and effectively, orally and in writing, an individual or a society is barbaric. The revival of learning inspired by Charlemagne and directed by the Northumbrian Alcuin halted the dangers of barbaric illiteracy on the European continent. Although hardly widespread by later standards, basic literacy was established among the clergy and even among some of the nobility. The small group of scholars at Aix-la-Chapelle preserved Greek and Latin culture from total extinction in the West.

Meanwhile, the common people spoke their local or vernacular languages. The Bretons, for example, retained their local dialect, and the Saxons and Bavarians could not understand each other (see Map 8.1). Communication among the diverse peoples of the Carolingian Empire was possible only through the medium of Latin.

Once basic literacy was established, monastic and other scholars went on to more difficult work. By the middle years of the ninth century there was a great outpouring of more sophisticated books. Collections of canon law, illustrated manuscripts, codes of Frankish law, commentaries on the Bible and on the church

N

HERBS

PHYSICIAN

INFIRMARY

LEECHING

CHAPEL

KITCHEN & BATH

NOVITIATE

KITCHEN & BATH

ORCHARD CEMETERY

GARDEN

GARDENER

GEESE

CARETAKERS OF FOWL

CHICKENS

PREPARATION OF SACRAMENTAL ELEMENTS

CHIMNEY

SCRIPTORIUM LIBRARY

SACRISTY VESTRY

LATRINA

BARN
THRESHING FLOOR

ABBOT'S HOUSE

CALEFACTORY
DORMITORY ABOVE

BATH

SHOPS

VISITING MONKS SCHOOL & GUEST MASTERS

CLOISTER

GARTH

REFECTORY

SCHOOL

BREW HOUSE

MONKS' BAKERY

MILL

PARLOUR

CELLAR

PRESS

GUEST HOUSE

HOSPICE MASTER

KITCHEN

KITCHEN BREW & BAKEHOUSE FOR GUESTS

ALMONRY

TURNERS, COOPERS

BREWERY GRAIN

KILN OR DRYING HOUSE

KITCHEN, BREW & BAKEHOUSE FOR ALMONRY

SERVITORS MARES

STABLE

SERVITORS BULLS

HOSTEL(?)

ENTRANCE WAY

SHEEP

GOATS

COWS

SERVITORS

PIGS

HORSES

PLAN FOR AN IDEAL MONASTERY   This is a ninth-century architectural design for a self-supporting monastic community of 270 members. The monks' lives centered around the church and the cloister (center). Note the herb garden close to the physician's quarters. The western entrance for visitors was surrounded by the hostel for poor guests and pens for farm animals — with all the inevitable smells. (Kenneth John Conant, Carolingian and Romanesque Architecture, 800–1200. Pelican History of Art, 2nd rev. ed. New York. 1978. p. 57) fathers flowed from monastic and cathedral scriptoria. Ecclesiastical writers, imbued with the legal ideas of ancient Rome and the theocratic ideals of Saint Augustine, instructed the semibarbarian rulers of the West. And it is no accident that medical study in the West began, at Salerno in southern Italy, in the late ninth century, *after* the Carolingian Renaissance.

Alcuin completed the work of his countryman Boniface — the Christianization of northern Europe. Latin Christian attitudes penetrated deeply into the consciousness of European peoples. By the tenth century, the patterns of thought and lifestyles of educated western Europeans were those of Rome and Latin Christianity. Even the violence and destruction of the great invasions of the late ninth and tenth centuries could not destroy the strong foundations laid by the Northumbrian Alcuin and his colleagues.

## HEALTH AND MEDICAL CARE IN THE EARLY MIDDLE AGES

Scholars' careful examination of medical treatises, prescription (or herbal) books, manuscript illustrations, and archaeological evidence has recently revealed a surprising amount of information about medical treatment in the early Middle Ages. In a society devoted to fighting, warriors and civilians alike stood a strong chance of wounds from sword, spear, battle-axe, or some blunt instrument. Trying to eke a living from poor soil with poor tools, perpetually involved in pushing back forest and wasteland, the farmer and his family daily ran the risk of accidents. Poor diet weakened everyone's resistance to disease. People bathed rarely. Low standards of personal hygiene increased the danger of

infection. This being the case, what medical or surgical attention was available to medieval people?

The Germanic peoples had no rational understanding of the causes of and cures for disease. They believed that sickness was due to one of three factors: elf-shot, in which elves hurled darts that produced disease and pain; wormlike creatures in the body; and the number 9. Treatment involved the use of charms, amulets, priestly incantations, and potions. Drinks prepared from mistletoe, for example, were thought to serve as an antidote to poison and to make women fertile.

Medical practice consisted primarily of drug and prescription therapy. Through the monks' efforts and through the recovery of Greek and Arabic manuscripts, a large body of the ancients' prescriptions was preserved and passed on. For almost any ailment, several recipes were likely to exist in the prescription lists. Balsam was recommended for coughs. For asthma an ointment combining chicken, wormwood, laurel berries, and oil of roses was to be rubbed on the chest. The scores of prescriptions to rid the body of lice, fleas, and other filth reflect the frightful standards of personal hygiene. The large number of prescriptions for eye troubles suggests that they too must have been very common. This is understandable, given the widespread practice of locating the fireplace in the center of the room. A lot of smoke and soot filtered into the room, rather than going up the chimney. One remedy calls for bathing the eyes in a solution of herbs mixed with honey, balsam, rainwater, saltwater, or wine.

Poor diet caused frequent stomach disorders and related ailments such as dysentery, constipation, and diarrhea. The value of dieting and avoiding greasy foods was recognized. For poor circulation, a potion of meadow wort, oak rind, and lustmock was recommended. Pregnant women were advised to abstain from eating the flesh of almost all male animals, because their meat might deform the child. Men with unusually strong sexual appetites were advised to fast and to drink at night the juice from agrimony (an herb of the rose family) boiled in ale. If a man suffered from a lack of drive, the same plant boiled in milk gave him "courage."

Physicians were not concerned with the treatment of specific diseases or illnesses. They did not examine patients. The physician, or leech, as he was known in Anglo-Saxon England, treated only what he could see or deduce from the patient's obvious symptoms. Treatment consisted of the application of herbal, animal, or superstitious remedies to these symptoms. The physician knew little about the pathology of disease or physiological functions. He knew little of internal medicine. He had no accurate standards of weights and measures. Prescriptions called for "a pinch of" or "a handful" or "an eggshell full."

Warfare and the dangers inherent in working the land made broken bones, wounds, and burns common. All wounds and open injuries invited infection, and infection invited gangrene. Several remedies were known for wounds. Physicians appreciated the antiseptic properties of honey, and prescriptions recommended that wounds be cleaned with it. When an area or limb had become gangrenous, a good technique of amputation existed. The physician was instructed to cut above the diseased flesh, that is, to cut away some healthy tissue and bone, in order to hasten cure. The juice of white poppy plants – the source of heroin – could be added to wine and drunk as an anesthetic. White poppies, however, grew only in southern Europe and North Africa. If a heavy slug of wine was not enough to dull the patient, he or she had to be held down forcibly while the physician

MEDICAL INSTRUMENTS *Medieval physicians invented hundreds of instruments for surgical operations. This page shows a number of knives and saws. The accompanying text explains which instrument to use for various operations. (Yale Medical Library)*

cut. Butter and egg whites, which have a soothing effect, were prescribed for burns.

Teeth survive long periods of burial and give reasonably good information about disease. Evidence from early medieval England shows that the incidence of tooth decay was very low. In the adult population, the rate of cavities was only one-sixth that of the present day. Cavities below the gum line, however, were very common, due to the prevalence of carbohydrates and starch in the diet. The result was abscesses of the gums. These and other forms of periodontal disease were widespread after the age of thirty.[10]

The spread of Christianity in the Carolingian era had a beneficial effect on medical knowledge and treatment. Several of the church fathers expressed serious interest in medicine. Some of them even knew something about it. The church was deeply concerned about human suffering, whether physical or mental. Christian teaching vigorously supported concern for the poor, sick, downtrodden, and miserable. Churchmen taught that while all knowledge came from God, he had supplied it so that people could use it for their own benefit.

In the period of the bloodiest violence, the sixth and seventh centuries, medical treatment was provided by the monasteries. No other places offered the calm and quiet atmosphere necessary for treatment and recuperation. Monks took care of the sick. They collected and translated the ancient medical treatises. They cultivated herb gardens from which medicines were prepared. Monks practiced medicine throughout the Middle Ages, as did lay people.

The foundation of a school at Salerno in southern Italy sometime in the ninth century gave a tremendous impetus to medical study by lay people. Its location attracted Arabic, Greek, and Jewish physicians from all over the Mediterranean region. Students flocked there from northern Europe. The Jewish physician Shabbathai Ben Abraham (931–982) left behind pharmacological notes that were widely studied in later centuries.

By the eleventh century, the medical school at Salerno enjoyed international fame. Its most distinguished professor then was Constantine the African. A native of Carthage, he had studied medicine throughout the Middle East and, because of his thorough knowledge of oriental languages, served as an important transmitter of Arabic culture to the West. Constantine taught and practiced medicine at Salerno for some years before becoming a monk at Monte Cassino.

Several women physicians also contributed to the celebrity of the school. Trotula, an authority on gynecological problems, wrote a book called *On Female Disorders.* Though not connected with the Salerno medical school, the abbess Hildegard (1098–1179) of Rupertsberg in Hesse, Germany, reputedly treated the emperor Frederick Barbarossa. Hildegard's treatise *On the Physical Elements* shows a remarkable degree of careful scientific observation.

How available was medical treatment? Most people lived on isolated rural estates, and had to take such advice and help as was available locally. Physicians were very few. They charged a fee, which only the rich could afford. Most illnesses, apparently, simply took their course. People had to develop a stoical attitude. Death came early. A person of forty was considered old. People's vulnerability to ailments for which there was no probable cure contributed to a fatalistic acceptance of death at an early age. Early medical literature shows that attempts to relieve pain and suffering were primitive and crude. Still, it is significant that serious attempts *were* made.

## DIVISION AND DISINTEGRATION OF THE CAROLINGIAN EMPIRE (814–887)

Charlemagne left his vast empire to his only surviving son, Louis the Pious (814–840), who had actually been crowned emperor in his father's lifetime. Deeply religious he was, and well educated, but Louis was no soldier. Thus he could not retain the respect and loyalty of the warrior-aristocracy on whom he depended for troops and for administration of his territories. Disintegration began almost at once.

The basic reason for the collapse of the Carolingian Empire is simply that it was too big. In Charlemagne's lifetime it was held together by the sheer force of his personality and driving energy. After his death, it began to fall apart. The empire lacked a bureaucracy like that of the Roman Empire — the administrative machinery necessary for strong and enduring government. It was a collection of tribes held together at the pleasure of warrior-aristocrats, men most interested in strengthening their own local positions and insuring that they could pass on to their sons the offices and estates they had amassed. Counts, abbots, bishops — both lay and ecclesiastical magnates needed estates to support themselves and reward their followers. In their localities, they simply assumed judicial, military, and financial functions. Why should they obey an unimpressive distant ruler who represented a centralizing power, a power that threatened their localistic interests? What counted was strength in one's own region and the preservation of family holdings.

Bad roads filled with thugs and rivers swarming with pirates made communication within the empire very difficult. Add to this the Frankish custom of dividing estates among all male heirs. Between 817 and his death in 840, Louis the Pious made several divisions of the empire. Dissatisfied with their portions and anxious to gain the imperial title, Louis's sons, Lothair, Louis the German, and Charles the Bald fought bitterly among themselves. Finally, in the Treaty of Verdun of 843, the brothers agreed to partition the empire (see Map 8.2).

MAP 8.2.   THE DIVISION OF THE CAROLINGIAN EMPIRES, 843   The treaty of Verdun (843), which divided the empire among Charlemagne's grandsons, is frequently taken as the start of the separate development of Germany, France, and Italy. The "Middle Kingdom" of Lothair, however, lacking defensive borders and any political or linguistic unity, soon broke up into several territories.

Lothair, the eldest, received the now-empty title of emperor and the "middle kingdom," which included Italy and the territories bordered by the Meuse, Saône, and Rhône rivers in the west and the Rhine in the east. Almost immediately this kingdom broke up into many petty principalities extending diagonally across Europe from Flanders to Lombardy. When the French and German monarchs were trying to build strong central governments in the twelfth and thirteenth centuries, this area was constantly contested between them. Even in modern times, the "middle kingdom" of Lothair has been blood-soaked.

The eastern and most Germanic part of the Carolingian Empire passed to Louis the German. The western kingdom went to Charles the Bald; it included the provinces of Aquitaine and Gascony and formed the basis of medieval and modern France. The descendants of Charles the Bald held on in the west until 987, when the leading magnates elected Hugh Capet as king. The heirs of Louis the German ruled the eastern kingdom until 911, but real power was in the hands of local chieftains. Everywhere in the tenth century, fratricidal warfare among the descendants of Charlemagne accelerated the spread of feudalism.

## GREAT INVASIONS OF THE NINTH CENTURY

After the Treaty of Verdun and the division of Charlemagne's empire among his grandsons, continental Europe presented an easy target for foreign invaders. All three kingdoms were torn by domestic dissension and disorder. No European political power was strong enough to put up effective resistance to external attacks. The frontier and coastal defenses erected by Charlemagne and maintained by Louis the Pious were completely neglected.

From the moors of Scotland to the mountains of Sicily there arose in the ninth century the Christian prayer "Save us, O God, from the violence of the Northmen." The Northmen, also known as Normans or Vikings, were Germanic peoples from Norway, Sweden, and Denmark who had remained beyond the sway of the Christianizing and civilizing influences of the Carolingian Empire. Some scholars believe that the name "Viking" derives from the Old Norse word *vik,* meaning creek. A Viking, then, was a pirate who waited in a creek or bay to attack passing vessels.

Charlemagne had established marches, fortresses, and watchtowers along his northern coasts to defend his territory against Viking raids. Their assaults began around 787, and by the mid-tenth century they had brought large chunks of continental Europe and Britain under their sway. In the east they pierced the rivers of Russia as far as the Black Sea. In the west they sailed as far as Greenland and even to the coast of North America, perhaps as far south as Boston.

The Vikings were superb seamen. Their advanced methods of boatbuilding gave them great speed and maneuverability. Propelled either by oars or sails, deckless, about sixty-five feet long, a Viking ship could carry between forty and sixty men — quite enough to harass an isolated monastery or village effectively. These boats, navigated by thoroughly experienced and utterly fearless sailors, moved through the most complicated rivers, estuaries, and waterways in Europe. They could move swiftly, attack, and get away before help could arrive.

Scholars disagree about the reasons for these migrations. Some maintain that because the Vikings practiced polygamy, their countries were vastly overpopulated. Since the property of a family passed to the oldest son, other sons had to emigrate. Others argue that climatic conditions and crop failures forced migration. Still others insist that the Northmen were looking for trade and new commercial contacts. What better targets of plunder, for example, than the mercantile centers of northern France and Frisia?

Plunder they did. Viking attacks were bitterly savage. At first they attacked and sailed off laden with booty. Later, they returned, settled down, and colonized the areas they had conquered. For example, the Vikings overran a large part of northwestern France and called

VIKING SHIP MODEL *The Norwegian original was built entirely of oak, weighed over twenty tons, and could carry a sizable contingent of men and horses. With fleets of these ships, the Vikings conducted piratical raids, territorial conquests, and colonizing ventures. (Courtesy, World Heritage Museum. Photo: Caroline Buckler)*

the territory Norsemanland, from which the word "Normandy" is derived.

Scarcely had the savagery of the Viking assaults begun to subside when Europe was hit from the east and south (see Map 8.3). Beginning around 862, Magyar, or Hungarian, tribes crossed the Danube and pushed steadily westward. They subdued northern Italy, compelled Bavaria and Saxony to pay tribute, and penetrated even into the Rhineland and Burgundy. These roving bandits attacked isolated villages and monasteries, taking prisoners and selling them in the Eastern slave markets. The Magyars were not colonizers; their sole object was booty and plunder.

The Magyars and Vikings depended upon fear. In their initial attacks on isolated settlements, every man, woman, and child was put to the sword. A few attractive women might be spared to satisfy the lusts of the conquerors or to be sold into slavery. The Hungarians and Scandinavians struck such terror in rural and defenseless peoples that they often gave up without a struggle. Many communities bought peace by paying tribute.

From the south the Muslims began new encroachments, concentrating on the two southern peninsulas, Italy and Spain. Their goal too was plunder. In Italy the monks of Monte Cassino were forced to flee. The Muslims drove northward and sacked Rome in 846. Most of Spain had remained under their

TO GREENLAND AND
NORTH AMERICA

ICELAND

874

FAEROES
800

SHETLANDS
700

*VIKINGS*

Novgorod 820

*Volga*

IRELAND
839

866-878

841-884

BRITAIN

*Vistula*

882

*Dnieper*

Rouen

Aix-la-Chapelle

*Elbe*

*Oder*

895

NORMANDY

*Seine*

*Rhine*

900

*MAGYARS*

Loire
896-911

883

843-882

917

*Rhône*

899

895

907

941

866

Santiago

Bordeaux

*Garonne*

Marseilles

CORSICA

*Danube*

Barcelona

Rome

Constantinople

*Tagus*

850-861

846

Monte
Cassino

0        200      400 Km.

Lisbon

BALEARICS

SARDINIA

0     200     400 Mi.

844

844

842

827
SICILY

840-896

*MUSLIMS*

Monastery

Vikings

Magyars

Muslims

MAP 8.3. THE GREAT INVASIONS OF THE
NINTH CENTURY    *Note the Viking penetration of
eastern Europe and their probable expeditions to
North America. What impact did their various invasions have on European society?*

domination since the sixth century (page 247). Expert seamen, they sailed around the Iberian peninsula, braved the notoriously dangerous shoals and winds of the Atlantic coast, and attacked the settlements along the coast of Provence. Muslim attacks on the European continent in the ninth and tenth centuries were less destructive, primarily because in comparison to the rich and sophisticated culture of the Arab capitals, northern Europe was primitive, backward, and offered little.

What was the effect of these invasions on the structure of European society? Viking, Magyar, and Muslim attacks accelerated the development of feudalism. Lords capable of rallying fighting men, supporting them, and putting up resistance to the invaders did so. They also assumed political power in their territories. Weak and defenseless people sought the protection of local strongmen. Free men sank to the level of serfs. Consequently, European society became further fragmented. Public power became increasingly decentralized.

## FEUDALISM AND HISTORY

The adjective *feudal* is often used disparagingly to describe something antiquated and barbaric. It is similarly commonplace to think of medieval feudalism as a system that let a small group of lazy military leaders exploit the producing class, the tillers of the soil. This is not a very useful approach. Preindustrial societies from ancient Greece to the American South before the Civil War to some twentieth-century Latin American countries have been characterized by sharp divisions between the "exploiters" and the "exploited." To call all such societies feudal strips the term of significant meaning and distorts our understanding of medieval feudalism. As many twentieth-century scholars have demonstrated, when feudalism developed it served the needs of medieval society.

The term *feudalism* was first coined in the late seventeenth century. The men who used it meant a type of government in which political power was treated as a private possession and divided among a large number of lords. Later, abolition of feudalism was among the main rallying-cries of the French Revolution and other eighteenth-century democratic revolutions. (What the revolutionaries really meant was manorialism and aristocratic privilege; by that time, feudalism had not existed in France for several hundred years.)

Scholars agree that feudalism was a persistent feature of medieval European culture. It was, however, far from uniform. The feudalism developing in Charlemagne's ninth-century Frankish kingdom was vastly different from the feudalism of thirteenth-century France under Louis IX. The feudalism of eleventh-century Normandy was considerably different from that of eleventh-century Anglo-Saxon England just twenty-six miles away. The word itself inaccurately implies the constancy of the feud, the land a lord gave to a vassal in return for his promise to fight or perform some other service. In fact, the giving of land was largely a tenth-century development. Eighth-century lords maintained their vassals in their own households, and even in the tenth century most vassals in France held no land. Some lords gave their vassals cash instead of land.

Feudalism is often characterized as a pyramid with weak men at the bottom, ever more important lords in the middle, and the king at the top. But lords and kings never arranged themselves so neatly. Many men became vassals of several lords in order to acquire more land or money. Medieval European feudalism frequently lacked organization, regularity, and rational connections. Feudal lords everywhere were out for themselves, and everywhere they tended to oppose the centralizing ambitions of kings.

The central point about medieval society is that economic and political power were in the hands of military leaders. Successful lords provided protection for the peasants who worked the land. They also exercised political and judicial authority over the dependent serfs. When the lord was a bishop or abbot, he had ecclesiastical as well as civil jurisdiction over his peasants. Because almost all communities were rural, isolated, and vulnerable to attack, the basic need of society was physical security. Consequently, the military virtues and values of the feudal nobility infused all aspects of the culture.

——————◆——————

The culture that emerged in Europe between 733 and 843 has justifiably been called the first European civilization. That civilization had definite characteristics: it was feudal, Christian, and infused with Latin ideas and models. A military elite controlled most forms of economic and political power. Almost all peoples were baptized Christians. Latin was the common language of educated people everywhere; what was written was written in Latin. In spite of the disasters of the ninth and tenth centuries, these features remained basic aspects of European culture for centuries to come.

The century and a half after the death of Charlemagne in 814 witnessed a degree of disintegration, destruction, and disorder unparalleled in Europe until the twentieth century. The Viking, Magyar, and Muslim invasions made a frightful situation absolutely disastrous. The Carolingian Empire was split into several parts, each tending to go its own way. No civil or religious authority could maintain stable government over a very wide area. Local strongmen provided what little security existed. Commerce and long-distance trade were drastically reduced. Leadership of the church became the political football of Roman aristocratic families. The rich became warriors; the poor sought protection. The result was that society underwent feudalization.

## NOTES

1. H. Pirenne, *Mohammed and Charlemagne,* Barnes & Noble, New York, 1955, pp. 234–235.

2. See D. Herlihy, "Land, Family, and Women in Continental Europe, 701–1200," in *Women in Medieval Society,* ed. S. M. Stuart, University of Pennsylvania Press, Philadelphia, 1976, pp. 13–45.

3. Einhard, *The Life of Charlemagne,* with a foreword by S. Painter, University of Michigan Press, Ann Arbor, 1960, pp. 50–51.

4. B. D. Hill, ed., *Church and State in the Middle Ages,* John Wiley & Sons, New York, 1970, p. 45.

5. Ibid., pp. 46–47.

6. R. W. Southern, *Medieval Humanism and Other Studies,* Basil Blackwell, Oxford, 1970, p. 3.

7. D. Wright, trans., *Beowulf,* Penguin Books, Baltimore, 1957, pp. 9–19.

8. M. Alexander, trans., *The Earliest English Poems,* Penguin Books, Baltimore, 1972, p. 99.

9. L. Sherley-Price, trans., *Bede: A History of the English Church and Peoples,* Penguin Books, Baltimore, 1962, book 3, chap. 27, p. 191.

10. See S. Rubin, *English Medieval Medicine,* Barnes & Noble, New York, 1974.

# Suggested Reading

In spite of centuries of war, violence, and destruction, a sizable literature survives from the period once inaccurately described as the Dark Ages. Scholars have devoted considerable attention to that literature because it was produced in such a crucial period, and the enterprising student who seeks further information about it may find the following works useful.

Chapters 4, 5, and 6 of J. B. Russell, *A History of Medieval Christianity: Prophecy and Order* (1968), describe the mind of the Christian church and show how it gradually made an impact on pagan Germanic peoples. C. Dawson, *Religion and the Rise of Western Culture* (1958), emphasizes the religious origins of Western culture. C. H. Talbot, ed., *The Anglo-Saxon Missionaries in Germany* (1954), gives a good picture, through biographies and correspondence, of eighth-century religious life.

Einhard's *Life of Charlemagne* is probably the best starting point for study of the great chieftain. There is no easily accessible and thorough treatment of the man and his government, but the advanced student with a knowledge of French should see L. Halphen, *Charlemagne et L'Empire Carolingien* (1949), the standard scholarly treatment. Recent research has been incorporated in E. Perroy, "Carolingian Administration," in S. Thrupp, ed., *Early Medieval Society* (1967). J. Brondsted, *The Vikings* (1960), is an excellently illustrated study of many facets of the culture of the Northmen.

In addition to the references to Bede, Beowulf, and Anglo-Saxon poetry in the Notes, D. L. Sayers, trans., *The Song of Roland* (1957), provides an excellent key, in epic form, to the values and lifestyles of the feudal classes. For the eighth-century revival of learning, see W. Levison, *England and the Continent in the Eighth Century* (1946); M. L. W. Laistner, *Thought and Letters in Western Europe, 500–900* (1931); and the beautifully written evocation by P. H. Blair, *Northumbria in the Days of Bede* (1976). E. S. Duckett, *Alcuin, Friend of Charlemagne* (1951),

makes light and enjoyable reading. L. Wallach, *Alcuin and Charlemagne,* rev. ed. (1968), is a technical study of Alcuin's treatises for the advanced student. The best treatment of the theological and political ideas of the period is probably K. F. Morrison, *The Two Kingdoms: Ecclesiology in Carolingian Political Thought* (1964), a difficult book.

Those interested in the role of women and children in early medieval society should see two articles: D. Herlihy, "Land, Family, and Women in Continental Europe, 701–1200," and E. Coleman, "Infanticide in the Early Middle Ages," both in S. M. Stuart, ed., *Women in Medieval Society* (1976).

For health and medical treatment, the curious student should consult S. Rubin, *Medieval English Medicine, A.D. 500–1300* (1974), especially pp. 97–149; W. H. McNeill, *Plagues and Peoples* (1976); A. Castiglioni, *A History of Medicine,* trans. E. B. Krumbhaar (1941); and the important article by J. M. Riddle, "Theory and Practice in Medieval Medicine," *Viator* 5 (1974): 157–184.

The literature on feudalism and manorialism is very rich. F. L. Ganshof, *Feudalism* (1961), and J. R. Strayer, "Feudalism in Western Europe," in *Feudalism in History,* ed. R. Coulborn (1956), are probably the best introductions. M. Bloch, *Feudal Society,* trans. L. A. Manyon (1961) remains the standard scholarly study. The more recent treatments of Perry Anderson, *Passages from Antiquity to Feudalism* (1978), and Georges Duby, *The Early Growth of the European Economy: Warriors and Peasants from the Seventh to the Twelfth Century* (1978), stress the evolution of social structures and mental attitudes. For the significance of the ceremony of vassalage, see Jacques Le Goff, "The Symbolic Ritual of Vassalage," in his *Time, Work, & Culture in the Middle Ages,* trans. Arthur Goldhammer (1982), a collection of provocative but difficult essays that includes his "The Peasants and the Rural World in the Literature of the Early Middle Ages." The best broad treatment of peasant life and conditions is Georges Duby, *Rural Economy and Country Life in the Medieval West,* trans. C. Postan (1968).

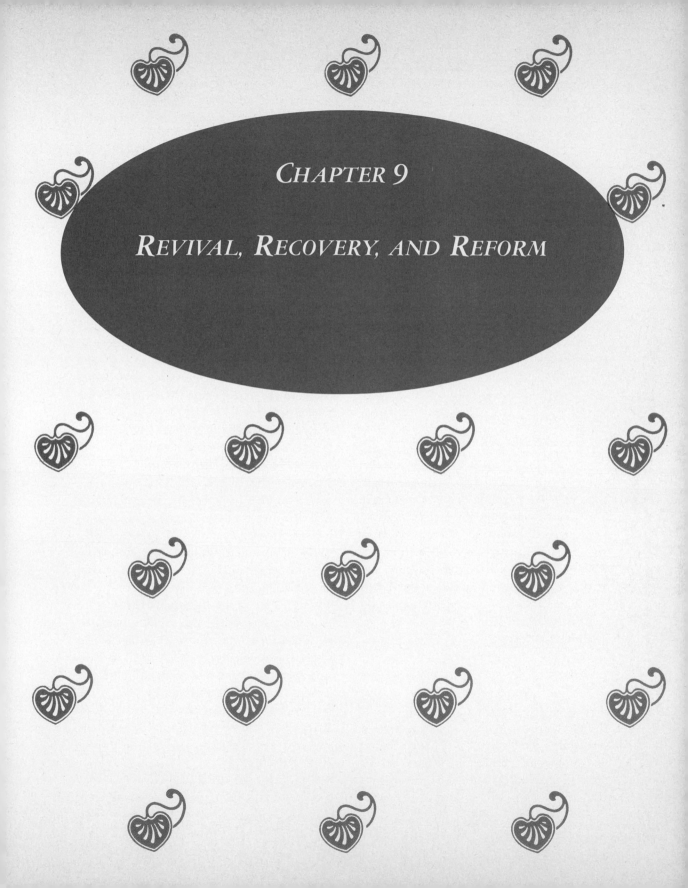

# CHAPTER 9

## REVIVAL, RECOVERY, AND REFORM

*By THE LAST QUARTER* of the tenth century, after a long and bitter winter of discontent, the first signs of European spring were appearing. The European springtime lasted from the early eleventh century to the end of the thirteenth century. This period from about 1050 to 1300 has often been called the High Middle Ages. The term designates a time of crucial growth and remarkable cultural achievement between two eras of economic, political, and social crisis.

What were the ingredients of revival? How did they come about? What was the social and economic impact of the recovery of Europe? How did reform of the Christian church affect relations between the church and civil authorities? These are the questions discussed in this chapter.

## POLITICAL REVIVAL

The eleventh century witnessed the beginnings of political stability in western Europe. Foreign invasions gradually declined, and domestic disorder subsided. This development gave people security in their persons and property. Security and political stability, supported by the peace movements of the church, contributed to a slow increase in population. Political order and stability paved the way for economic recovery.

### THE DECLINE OF INVASION AND CIVIL DISORDER

The most important factor in the revival of Europe after the disasters of the ninth century was the gradual decline in foreign invasions and the reduction of domestic violence. In 911 the Norwegian leader Rollo subdued large parts of what was later called Normandy. The West Frankish ruler Charles the Simple, unable to oust the Northmen, went along with that territorial conquest. He recognized Rollo as duke of Normandy on the condition that Rollo swear allegiance to him and hold the territory as a sort of barrier against future Viking assaults. This agreement, embodied in the treaty of Saint-Clair-sur-Epte, marks the beginning of the rise of Normandy.

Rollo kept his word. He exerted strong authority over Normandy and in troubled times supported the weak Frankish king. Rollo and his men were baptized as Christians. Although additional Viking settlers arrived, they were easily pacified. The tenth and eleventh centuries saw the steady assimilation of Normans and French. Major attacks on France had ended.

Rollo's descendant, Duke William I (1035–1087), made feudalism work as a system of government in Normandy. William attached specific quotas of military or knight service to the lands he distributed. Vassals who defaulted on their military obligations or refused attendance at the duke's court were ruthlessly executed. William forbade the construction of private castles, always the symbol of feudal independence. He limited private warfare and vigorously supported a peace movement sponsored by the church. He kept strict control over the coinage and maintained strong supervision over the church, actively participating in church councils and in the selection of abbots and bishops. By 1066 — the year William and the Normans invaded England — the duchy of Normandy was the strongest and the most peaceful territory in Western Europe.

Recovery followed a somewhat different pattern in England. Between 960 and 1040,

England was part of a vast Scandinavian empire that stretched from Normandy to Iceland and even to the eastern coast of North America. The Danish ruler Canute, king of England (1016–1035) and after 1030 king of Norway as well, made England the center of his empire. Canute promoted a policy of assimilation and reconciliation between Anglo-Saxons and Vikings.

Canute governed with the help of a *witan* – literally, a council of wise men – composed of Anglo-Saxons and Danes. He republished the laws of tenth-century Anglo-Saxon kings to show the continuity of his government with theirs. Canute and his followers accepted Christianity and Christian ideas about the responsibilities of a good and just king. Slowly the two peoples were molded together. The assimilation of Viking and Anglo-Saxon was personified by King Edward the Confessor (1042–1066), the son of an Anglo-Saxon father and a Norman mother who had taken Canute as her second husband.

In the East the German king Otto I (936–973) inflicted a crushing defeat on the Hungarians on the banks of the Lech River in 955. This battle halted the Magyars' westward expansion and threat to Germany, and made Otto a great hero to the Germans. It also signified the revival of the German monarchy and demonstrated that Otto was a worthy successor to Charlemagne.

When he was chosen king, Otto had selected Aix-la-Chapelle as the site of his coronation to symbolize his intention to continue the work and tradition of Charlemagne. The basis of his power was to be an alliance with, and control of, the church. Otto asserted the right to invest bishops and abbots with the symbols of their office – the ring, which symbolized the bishop's union with his dioceses, and the staff, which was the symbol of his pastoral authority. This assertion gave Otto effective control over ecclesiastical appointments. Before receiving religious consecration, bishops and abbots had to perform feudal homage for the lands that accompanied the church office. (This practice, later known as lay investiture, was to create a grave crisis in the eleventh century.)

Otto realized that he had to use the financial and military resources of the church to halt feudal anarchy. He used the higher clergy extensively in his administration, and the bulk of his army came from monastic and other church lands. Between 936 and 955, Otto succeeded in breaking the territorial power of the great German dukes.

In 962 Otto was crowned Holy Roman emperor by the pope. The imperial coronation had important results. It revived the Holy Roman Empire and its traditions, and it showed that Otto had the full support of the church in Germany and Italy. The uniting of the kingship with the imperial crown advanced German interests. Otto filled a power vacuum in northern Italy and brought about peace among the great aristocratic families. He established stable government there for the first time in over a century. Peace and political stability in turn promoted the revival of northern Italian cities, such as Venice.

By the start of the eleventh century, the Italian maritime cities were seeking a place in the rich Mediterranean trade. Pisa and Genoa fought to break Muslim control of the trade and shipping with the Byzantine Empire and the Orient. Once the Muslim fleets had been destroyed, the Italian cities of Venice, Genoa, and Pisa embarked on the road to prosperity. The eleventh century witnessed their steadily rising strength and wealth. Freedom from invasion and domestic security made economic growth possible all over western Europe.

## THE PEACE MOVEMENTS OF THE CHURCH

Meanwhile the church was working to end arson, rape, homicide, and wanton destruction. The knights were developing a consciousness of themselves as a class, and the social gap between knight and serf was widening. Local lords ignored all laws and restraints, and attacks on churches were common. Physical assaults on the peasants and the devastation of their fields caused terrible suffering.

In the last quarter of the tenth century, councils of bishops met in Burgundy. The place is significant, for Burgundy was the part of the Carolingian Empire where anarchy was worst and where the clergy and the poor had no defenders whatsoever. The bishops accordingly proclaimed the Peace of God. It placed certain persons — monks who lived in monasteries, clergy who lived in villages and cathedral cities, and the poor — and certain places — church buildings and peasant fields — under ecclesiastical protection. Those who attacked such persons and places were anathematized, which meant that they were to be totally excluded from contact with all Christians. The bishops convinced their relatives among the aristocracy to participate in trying to enforce the peace.

In 1027, a council published the Truce of God, which attempted to regulate the times of fighting. An agreement was sworn that "in order to enable every man to show respect for the Lord's Day," no one was to attack an enemy between Saturday evening and Monday morning. Before 1050, the number of restricted days was increased. Thursday, Friday, and Saturday were added as reminders of the Last Supper, the Crucifixion, and the Entombment. Gradually, some saints' days were added and then the seasons of Advent (the four weeks before Christmas) and Lent (the six weeks before Easter). Lords and knights were urged to form groups to preserve the peace. How effective they were is not known, but without strong and determined lay support they would not have been very successful.

The chief importance of the peace movements lies in their influence on secular rulers. Around 1050, Duke William of Normandy compelled his vassals to join the movement. His backing, and eventually that of other leaders, was an important element in the promotion of peace.

## INCREASING POPULATION AND MILD CLIMATE

A steady growth of population also contributed to the general recovery of Europe. The decline of foreign invasions and of internal civil disorder reduced the number of people killed and maimed. Feudal armies in the eleventh through thirteenth centuries continued their destruction, but they were very small by modern standards and fought few pitched battles. Most medieval warfare consisted of the besieging of castles or fortifications. As few as twelve men could defend a castle. With sufficient food and an adequate water supply, they could hold out for a long time. Monastic chroniclers, frequently bored and almost always writing from hearsay evidence, tended to romanticize medieval warfare (as long as it was not in their own neighborhoods). Most conflicts were petty skirmishes with slight loss of life. The survival of more young people, those most often involved in warring activities, and those usually the most sexually active meant a population rise.

Nor was there any "natural," or biological, hindrance to population expansion. Between the tenth and fourteenth centuries, Europe was not hit by any major plague or other medical scourge, though leprosy and malaria did strike down some people. Leprosy had entered Europe in the early Middle Ages. Although caused by a virus, the disease was not very contagious and, if contracted, worked slowly. Lepers presented a frightful appearance: the victim's arms and legs rotted away, and gangrenous sores emitted a horrible smell. Physicians had no cure. For these reasons, and because of the command in the thirteenth chapter of Leviticus that lepers be isolated, medieval lepers were segregated in hospitals called leprosaria.

Malaria, spread by protozoa-carrying mosquitoes that infested swampy areas, also caused problems. Malaria is characterized by alternate chills and fevers, and leaves the afflicted person extremely weak. Peter the Venerable, the ninth abbot of the monastery of Cluny (1122–1156), suffered for many of his later years from recurring bouts of malaria contracted on a youthful trip to Rome. Still, relatively few people caught malaria or leprosy. Crop failure and the ever-present danger of starvation were much more pressing threats.

The weather cooperated with the revival. Meteorologists believe that a slow but steady retreat of polar ice occurred between the ninth and the eleventh centuries. A significant warming trend occurred and continued until about 1200. The century between 1080 and 1180 witnessed exceptionally clement weather in England, France, and Germany, with mild winters and dry summers.

Good weather helps to explain advances in population growth, land reclamation, and agricultural yield. Increased agricultural output had a profound impact on society: it affected Europeans' health, commerce, trade, industry, and general lifestyle.

The greatest manifestation of the recovery of Europe was the rise of towns and the development of a new business and commercial class. This development was to lay the foundations for Europe's transformation, centuries later, from a rural and agricultural society into an industrial and urban society. This change, which had global implications, had its beginnings in the Middle Ages.

Why did these developments occur when they did? What sorts of people first populated the towns and where did they come from? What is known of town life in the High Middle Ages? What relevance did towns have for medieval culture? Part of the answer to at least one of these questions has already been given. Without increased agricultural output, there would not have been an adequate food supply for new town dwellers. Without a rise in population, there would have been no one to people the towns. Without a minimum of peace and political stability, merchants could not have transported and sold goods. (Merchants dislike nothing more than domestic disorder.)

### THE RISE OF TOWNS

Medieval society was traditional, agricultural, and rural. The emergence of a new class that was none of these constituted a social revolution. The new class — artisans and merchants — came from the peasantry. They were landless younger sons of large families, driven away by land shortage. Or they were forced by war and famine to seek new possibilities. Or they were unusually enterprising and adventurous, curious and willing to take a chance.

One of the most exciting aspects of the

THE CITY WALLS OF MANTUA *Town walls protected citizens from theft and physical attack. Up-keep of the walls was usually the town's heaviest expense. (The Granger Collection)*

study of history is that facts and evidence may be explained in a variety of ways. There is no final or definitive interpretation. Serious investigation of the origin of European towns began only in the twentieth century. Historians have proposed three basic theories. Some scholars believe towns began as boroughs — that is, as forts or fortifications erected during the ninth-century Viking invasions. According to this view, towns were at first places of

defense or security into which farmers from the surrounding countryside moved when their area was attacked. Later, merchants were attracted to the fortifications because they had something to sell and wanted to be where the potential customers were. But most residents of the early towns made their livings by farming outside the town.

The Belgian historian Henri Pirenne maintained that towns sprang up when merchants who engaged in long-distance trade gravitated toward attractive or favorable spots, such as near a fort. Usually traders settled just outside the walls, in the *faubourgs* or *suburbs* – both of which mean "outside," or "in the shelter of the walls." As their markets prospered and as their number outside the walls grew, the merchants built a new wall around themselves. Such construction might be necessary every century or so. According to Pirenne, a medieval town consisted architecturally of a number of concentric walls, and the chief economic pursuit of its residents was trade and commerce.

A third explanation focuses on the great cathedrals and monasteries. The large numbers of clergy attached to a cathedral or monastery represented a demand for goods and services. Cathedrals such as Notre Dame in Paris conducted schools, which drew students from far and wide. Consequently, traders and merchants settled near the religious establishments to cater to the residents' economic needs. Concentrations of people accumulated, and towns came into being.

All three theories have validity, though none of them explains the origins of *all* medieval towns. Few towns of the tenth and eleventh centuries were "new" in the sense that American towns and cities were new in the seventeenth and eighteenth centuries. They were not carved out of forest and wilderness. Some medieval towns that had become flourishing centers of trade by the mid-twelfth century had originally been Roman army camps: York in northern England, Bordeaux in west central France, and Cologne in west central Germany are good examples of ancient towns that underwent revitalization in the eleventh century. Some Italian seaport cities, such as Pisa and Genoa, had been centers of shipping and commerce in earlier times. Muslim attacks and domestic squabbles had cut their populations and drastically reduced the volume of their trade in the early Middle Ages, but trade with Constantinople and the Orient had never stopped entirely. The restoration of order and political stability promoted rebirth and new development. Pirenne's interpretation accurately describes the Flemish towns of Bruges and Ypres. It does not fit the course of development in the Italian cities or in such centers as London.

Whether evolving from a newly fortified place or an old Roman army camp, from a cathedral site or a river junction or a place where several overland routes met, all medieval towns had a few common characteristics. Walls enclosed the town. (The terms "burgher" and "bourgeois" derive from the Old English and Old German words *burg, burgh, borg,* and *borough* for a walled or fortified place. Thus, a burgher or bourgeois was originally a person who lived or worked inside the walls.) The town had a marketplace. It often had a mint for the coining of money and a court to settle disputes.

In each town many people inhabited a small, cramped area. Census records do not exist for most of Europe before the early eighteenth century, but tax returns reveal the populations of many English towns in 1377. The largest city, London, had 23,314 people. The second largest city, Bristol, had only 6,345 citizens. Some continental cities, such as Paris, were probably much bigger. Size was not important; the real strength of the medieval towns rested in their people (see Map 9.1).

By the late eleventh century many towns in Western Europe had small Jewish populations. Jews had emigrated in post-Roman times from the large cities of the Mediterranean region to France, the Rhineland, and Britain. During the Carolingian period Jews had the reputation of being richer and more

Over 80,000
Over 40,000
Over 20,000
Over 10,000

Dublin +
Lübeck
Magdeburg
London
Bruges
Ghent
Tournai
Cologne
Prague
Amiens
Rouen
Strasbourg
Augsburg
Vienna
Paris
Orléans
Tours
Dijon +
Bordeaux
Bergamo
Brescia
Vicenza
Padua
Milan
Cremona
Verona
Venice
Pavia
Mantua
Piacenza
Parma
Ravenna
Genoa
Bologna
Rimini
Lucca
Montpellier
Florence
Toulouse
Pisa
Arezzo
Narbonne
Sienna
Perugia
Orvieto
Valladolid
Rome
Barcelona
Naples
Lisbon
Toledo
Valencia
Messina
Cordoba
Palermo
Seville
Granada

0   100   200   300 Km.
0   100   200   300 Mi.

MAP 9.1   POPULATION OF EUROPEAN URBAN
AREAS, CA LATE THIRTEENTH CENTURY
*Although there were scores of urban centers in the*
*thirteenth century, the Italian and Flemish towns had*
*the largest concentrations of people. By modern stan-*
*dards, Paris was Europe's only real city.*

learned than the semibarbarian peoples among
whom they lived. They typically earned their
livelihoods in the lesser trades or by lending
money at interest, and Jews engaged in trade
had to be literate to keep records. The laws of
most countries forbade Jews to own land,
though they could hold land pledged to them
for debts. As townspeople they often possessed cultural eminence over their neighbors.
By the twelfth century many Jews were
usurers: they lent to consumers but primarily

to new or growing business enterprises. New
towns and underdeveloped areas where cash
was scarce welcomed Jewish settlers. Like
other businesspeople, the Jews preferred to
live near their work; they also settled close to
their synagogue or school. Thus originated
the Jews' street or quarter or ghetto. Such
neighborhoods gradually became legally defined sections where Jews were required to
live.

In their backgrounds and abilities, townspeople represented diversity and change. They constituted an entirely new element in medieval society. They fit into none of the traditional categories. Their occupations, their preoccupations, their very lives were different from those of the feudal nobility and the laboring peasantry. They were the "middle" class.

The aristocratic nobility glanced down with contempt and derision at the money-grubbing townspeople, but were not above borrowing from them. The rural peasantry peered up with suspicion and fear at the town dwellers. What was the point, the farmers wondered, of making money? Only land had real permanence.

Nor did the new commercial classes make much sense initially to churchmen. The immediate goal of the middle class was obviously not salvation. It was to be a good while before churchmen developed a theological justification for the new classes.

## TOWN LIBERTIES

In the words of the Greek poet Alcaeus, "Not houses finely roofed or well built walls, nor canals or dockyards make a city, but men able to use their opportunity."[1] Men and opportunity. That is fundamentally what medieval towns meant – concentrations of people and varieties of chances. No matter where groups of traders congregated, they settled on someone's land and had to secure from king or count, abbot or bishop, permission to live and trade. Aristocratic nobles and churchmen were suspicious of and hostile to the middle class. They soon realized, however, that profits and benefits flowed to them and their territories from the markets set up on their land.

The history of towns in the eleventh through thirteenth centuries consists largely of the efforts of merchants to acquire "liberties." In the Middle Ages, liberties meant special privileges. For the town dweller, liberties included the privilege of living and trading on the lord's land. The most important privilege a medieval townsperson could gain was freedom. It gradually developed that an individual who lived in a town for a year and a day was free of servile obligations and status. More than anything else, perhaps, the liberty of personal freedom that came with residence in a town contributed to the emancipation of the serfs in the High Middle Ages. Liberty meant citizenship, and citizenship in a town implied the right to buy and sell goods there. Unlike foreigners and outsiders of any kind, the full citizen did not have to pay taxes and tolls in the market. Obviously, this increased profits.

In the twelfth and thirteenth centuries towns fought for, and slowly gained, legal and political rights. Since the tenth century, some English boroughs had held courts with jurisdiction over members of the town in civil and criminal matters. In the twelfth century, such English towns as London and Norwich developed courts that applied a special kind of law, called law merchant. It dealt with commercial transactions, debt, bankruptcy, proof of sales, and contracts. Law merchant was especially suitable to the needs of the new bourgeoisie. Around 1116, the count of Flanders granted to the burgesses of Ypres the right to hold a municipal court that alone could judge members of the town. Gradually, other towns across Europe acquired the same right. In effect it gave them judicial independence.[2]

In the acquisition of full rights of self-government, the merchant guilds played a large role. Medieval men were long accustomed to communal enterprises. In the late tenth and early eleventh centuries, men who were engaged in foreign trade joined together in merchant guilds; united enterprise provided them greater security and less risk of losses than did individual action. At about the same time, the artisans and craftsmen of particular trades formed guilds of their own. These were the butchers, the bakers, and the candlestick makers. Members of the craft guilds determined the quality, quantity, and price of the goods produced and the number of apprentices and journeymen affiliated with the guild. Terrible conflicts were to arise between the craft guilds and the merchant guilds in the thirteenth and fourteenth centuries, but that is a later story.

Women engaged in every kind of urban commercial activity, both as helpmates to their husbands and independently. In many manufacturing trades women predominated, and in some places women were a large percentage of the labor force. In fourteenth-century Frankfurt, for example, about 33 percent of the crafts and trades were entirely female, about 40 percent wholly male, and the remaining crafts roughly divided between the sexes. Craft guilds provided greater opportunity for women than did merchant guilds. In late twelfth-century Cologne, women and men had equal rights in the turners' guild (those who made wooden objects on a lathe). Most members of the Paris silk and woolen trades were women, and some achieved the mastership. Widows frequently followed their late husbands' professions, but if they remarried outside the craft they lost the mastership. Between 1254 and 1271 the chief magistrate of Paris drew up the following regulations for the silk industry:

*Any woman who wishes to be a silk spinster (woman who spins) on large spindles in the city of Paris — i.e. reeling, spinning, doubling and re-*

*twisting — may freely do so, provided she observe the following customs and usages of the craft:*

*No spinster on large spindles may have more than three apprentices, unless they be her own or her husband's children born in true wedlock; nor may she contract with them for an apprenticeship of less than seven years or for a fee of less than 20 Parisian sols to be paid to her, their mistress. . . . If a working woman comes from outside Paris and wishes to practice the said craft in the city, she must swear before the guardians of the craft that she will practice it well and loyally and conform to its customs and usages. . . . No man of this craft who is without a wife may have more than one apprentice; . . if, however, both husband and wife practice the craft, they may have two apprentices and as many journeymen as they wish.*[3]

Guild records show that women received lower wages than men for the same work, on the grounds that they needed less income.

By the late eleventh century, especially in the towns of the Low Countries (present-day Belgium and Holland) and northern Italy, the leading men in the merchant guilds were quite rich and powerful. They constituted an oligarchy in their towns, controlling economic life and bargaining with kings and lords for political independence. Full rights of self-government included the right to hold a town court, the right to select the mayor and other municipal officials, and the right to tax and collect taxes. Kings often levied on their serfs and unfree townspeople arbitrary taxes called tallage, or the taille. Such taxes (also known as customs) called attention to the fact that men were not free. Citizens of a town much preferred to levy and collect their own taxes.

A charter that King Henry II of England granted to the merchants of Lincoln around

1157 nicely illustrates the town's rights. The emphasized passages clearly suggest that the merchant guild had been the governing body in the city for almost a century and that anyone who lived in Lincoln for a year and a day was considered free:

*Henry, by the grace of God, etc., to the bishop of Lincoln, and to the justices, sheriffs, barons, servants and all his liegemen, both French and English, of Lincoln, greeting. Know that I have granted to my citizens of Lincoln all their liberties and customs and laws which they had in the time of Edward* [King Edward the Confessor] *and William and Henry, kings of England.* And I have granted them their gild-merchant, comprising men of the city and other merchants of the shire, as well and freely as they had it in the time of our aforesaid predecessors, kings of England. *And all the men who live within the four divisions of the city and attend the market, shall stand in relation to gelds* [taxes] *and customs and the assizes* [ordinances or laws] *of the city as well as ever they stood in the time of Edward, William and Henry, kings of England. I also confirm to them that* if anyone has lived in Lincoln for a year and a day without dispute from any claimant, *and has paid the customs, and if the citizens can show by the laws and customs of the city that the claimant has remained in England during that period and has made no claim,* then let the defendant remain in peace in my city of Lincoln as my citizen, *without* [having to defend his] *right.*[4]

Kings and lords were reluctant to grant towns self-government, fearing loss of authority and revenue if they gave the merchant guilds full independence. But the lords discovered that towns attracted increasing numbers of people to an area — people whom the lords could tax. Moreover, when burghers bargained for a town's political independence, they offered sizable amounts of ready cash. Consequently, feudal lords ultimately agreed to self-government.

## TOWN LIFE

Protective walls surrounded almost all medieval towns and cities. The valuable goods inside a town were too much of a temptation to marauding bands for the town to be without the security of bricks and mortar. The walls were pierced by gates, and visitors waited at the gates to gain entrance to the town. When the gates were opened early in the morning, guards inspected the quantity and quality of the goods brought in and collected the customary taxes. Part of the taxes went to the king or lord on whose land the town stood, part to the town council for civic purposes. Constant repair of the walls was usually the town's greatest expense.

Peasants coming from the countryside and merchants traveling from afar set up their carts as stalls just inside the gates. The result was that the road nearest the gate was the widest thoroughfare. It was the ideal place for a market, because everyone coming in or going out used it. Most streets in a medieval town were marketplaces as much as passages for transit. They were narrow, just wide enough to transport goods through.

Medieval cities served, above all else, as markets. In some respects the entire city was a marketplace. The place where a product was made and sold was also typically the merchant's residence. Usually the ground floor was the scene of production. A window or door opened from the main workroom directly onto the street. The window displayed the finished product, and passersby could look in and see the goods being produced. The

MEDIEVAL STREET SCENE  *Merchants displayed their goods from shop windows on the ground floor: tailors, furriers, a barber, and a grocer. Merchants with shops on the street that linked the two main town* *gates naturally profited more than did those on side streets which were blocked by the town wall. (Bibliothèque Nationale, Paris)*

merchant and his family lived above the business on the second or third floor. As his business and his family expanded, he built additional stories on top of his house.

Because space within the walls of the town was limited, expansion occurred upward. Second and third stories were built jutting out over the ground floor and thus over the street. Neighbors on the opposite side of the road did the same. Since the streets were narrow to begin with, houses thus lacked fresh air and light. Initially, houses were made of wood and thatched with straw. Fire represented a con-

stant danger, and because houses were built so close together, fires spread rapidly. Municipal governments consequently urged construction in stone or brick.

Most medieval cities developed haphazardly. There was little town planning. As the population increased, space became more and more limited. Air and water pollution presented serious problems. Many families raised pigs for household consumption in sties next to the house. Horses and oxen, the chief means of transportation and power, dropped tons of dung on the streets every year. It was universal practice in the early towns to dump household waste, both animal and human, into the road in front of one's house. The stench must have been abominable. In 1298, the burgesses of the town of Boutham in Yorkshire, England, received the following order (one long, vivid sentence):

*To the bailiffs of the abbot of St. Mary's York, at Boutham. Whereas it is sufficiently evident that the pavement of the said town of Boutham is so very greatly broken up and that all the singular passing and going through that town sustain immoderate damages and grievances, and in addition the air is so corrupted and infected by the pigsties situated in the king's highways and in the lanes of that town and by the swine feeding and frequently wandering about in the streets and lanes and by dung and dunghills and many other foul things placed in the streets and lanes, that great repugnance overtakes the king's ministers staying in that town and also others there dwelling and passing through, the advantage of more wholesome air is impeded, the state of men is grievously injured, and other unbearable inconveniences and many other injuries are known to proceed from such corruption, to the nuisance of the king's ministers aforesaid and of others there dwelling and passing through, and to the peril of their lives, and to the manifest shame and reproach of the bailiffs and other the inhabitants of that town: the king, being unwilling longer to tolerate such great and unbearable defects there, orders the bailiffs to cause the pavement to be suitably repaired within their liberty before All Saints next, and to cause the pigsties, aforesaid streets and lanes to be cleansed from all dung and dunghills, and to cause them to be kept thus cleansed hereafter, and to cause proclamation to be made throughout their bailiwick forbidding any one, under pain of grievous forfeiture, to cause or permit their swine to feed or wander outside his house in the king's streets or the lanes aforesaid.*[5]

A great deal of traffic passed through Boutham in 1298 because of the movement of the English troops to battlefronts in Scotland. Conditions there were probably not typical. Still, this document suggests that problems of space, air pollution, and sanitation bedeviled urban people in medieval times just as they do today.

The church took a great interest in townspeople as Christians. Parish clergy catered to their spiritual needs. As the bourgeoisie gained in wealth, they expressed their continuing Christian faith by refurbishing old churches, constructing new ones, and giving stained-glass windows, statues, and carvings. The twelfth-century chronicler William of Newburgh, writing about 1170, could proudly boast that the city of London had 126 parish churches, in addition to 13 monastic churches and the great cathedral of St. Paul's.

Some literary descriptions of medieval cities survive, but they do not tell all that we would like to know. Most illustrations of walls, streets, and houses date only from the fifteenth century. Medieval cities, like modern ones, changed a great deal in the course of decades and, of course, centuries. A fifteenth-century picture is not a very accurate representation of twelfth-century conditions. William of Newburgh, however, left a detailed description of the city of London around 1175:

*Among the noble and celebrated cities of the world that of London, the capital of the kingdom of the English, is one which extends its glory farther than all the others and sends its wealth and merchandise more widely into distant lands. Higher than all the rest does it lift its head. . . .*

*It has on the east the Palatine castle [the Tower of London], very great and strong: the keep and walls rise from very deep foundations and are fixed with a mortar tempered by the blood of an-*

A FIFTEENTH-CENTURY HOUSE   *Medieval merchants conducted their business on the ground floor and lived with their families on the floors above. As additional stories were added on, they jutted out one over the other. Since this form of building was done on both sides of the street, streets received little light during the day and were dangerously dark at night. (Royal Commission on Historical Monuments, England)*

imals. On the west there are two castles very strongly fortified, and from these there runs a high and massive wall with seven double gates and with towers along the north at regular intervals. London was once also walled and turreted on the south, but the mighty Thames, so full of fish, has with the sea's ebb and flow washed against, loosened, and thrown down those walls in the course of time. Upstream to the west there is the royal palace [the Palace of Westminster]. . . .

Everywhere outside the houses of those living in the suburbs, and adjacent to them, are the spacious and beautiful gardens of the citizens, and these are planted with trees. Also there are on the north side pastures and pleasant meadow lands through which flow streams wherein the turning of mill-wheels makes a cheerful sound. Very near lies a great forest with woodland pastures in which there are the lairs of wild animals: stags, fallow deer, wild boars and bulls. . . .

Those engaged in business of various kinds, sellers of merchandise, hirers of labour, are distributed every morning into their several localities according to their trade. Besides, there is in London on the river bank among the wines for sale in ships and in the cellars of the vintners a public cook-shop. There daily you may find food according to the season, dishes of meat, roast, fried and boiled, large and small fish, coarser meats for the poor and more delicate for the rich, such as venison and big and small birds. If any of the citizens should unexpectedly receive visitors, weary from their journey, who would fain not wait until fresh food is bought and cooked, or until the servants have brought bread or water for washing, they hasten to the river bank and there find all they need. . . .

Immediately outside one of the gates there is a field [Smithfield] which is smooth both in fact and in name. On every sixth day of the week, unless it be a major feast-day, there takes place there a famous exhibition of fine horses for sale. Earls, barons and knights, who are in the town, and many citizens come out to see or to buy. It is pleasant to see the high-stepping palfreys with their gleaming coats, as they go through their paces, putting down their feet alternately on one side together. . . .

By themselves in another part of the field stand the goods of the countryfolk: implements of husbandry, swine with long flanks, cows with full udders, oxen of immense size, and woolly sheep. There also stand the mares fit for plough, some big with foal, and others with brisk young colts closely following them.

To this city from every nation under heaven merchants delight to bring their trade by sea. The Arabian sends gold; the Sabaean spice and incense. The Scythian brings arms, and from the rich, fat lands of Babylon comes oil of palms. The Nile sends precious stones; the men of Norway and Russia, furs and sables; nor is China absent with purple silk. The Gauls come with their wines. . . .

We now come to speak of the sports of the city, for it is not fitting that a city should be merely useful and serious-minded, unless it be also pleasant and cheerful. . . .

Furthermore, every year on the day called Carnival – to begin with the sports of boys (for we were all boys once) – scholars from the different schools bring fighting-cocks to their masters, and the whole morning is set apart to watch their cocks do battle in the schools, for the boys are given a holiday that day. After dinner all the young men of the town go out into the fields in the suburbs to play ball. The scholars of the various schools have their own ball, and almost all the followers of each occupation have theirs also. The seniors and the fathers and the wealthy magnates of the city come on horseback to watch the contests of the younger generation, and in their turn recover their lost youth: the motions of their natural heat seem to be stirred in them at the mere sight of such strenuous activity and by their participation in the joys of unbridled youth.

Every Sunday in Lent after dinner a fresh swarm of young men goes forth into the fields on war-horses, steeds foremost in the contest, each of which is skilled and schooled to run in circles. From the gates there sallies forth a host of laymen, sons of the citizens, equipped with lances and shields, the younger ones with spears forked at the top, but with the steel point removed. They make a pretence at war, carry out field-exercises and indulge in mimic combats. Thither too come many courtiers, when the king is in town, and from the households of bishops, earls and barons come youths and adolescents, not yet girt with the belt of knighthood, for the pleasure of engaging in combat with one another. Each is inflamed with the hope of victory. . . .

On feast-days throughout the summer the young men indulge in the sports of archery, running, jumping, wrestling, slinging the stone, hurling the javelin beyond a mark and fighting with sword and buckler. . . .

Others, more skilled at winter sports, put on their feet the shin-bones of animals, binding them firmly around their ankles, and, holding poles shod with iron in their hands, which they strike from time to time against the ice, they are propelled swift as a bird in flight or a bolt shot from an engine of war. . . . [6]

People wanted to get into medieval cities because they represented a means of economic advancement, social mobility, and improvement in legal status. For the adventurous, the ambitious, and the shrewd, cities offered tremendous opportunities.

## THE REVIVAL OF LONG-DISTANCE TRADE

The eleventh century witnessed a remarkable revival of trade as artisans and craftsmen manufactured goods for local and foreign consumption (see Map 9.2). Most trade centered in towns and was controlled by professional traders. Because long-distance trade was risky and required large investments of capital, it could be practiced only by professionals. The transportation of goods involved serious risks. Shipwrecks were common. Pirates infested the sea-lanes, and robbers and thieves roamed virtually all of the land routes. Since the risks were so great, merchants preferred to share them. A group of men would thus pool some of their capital to finance an expedition to a distant place. When the ship or caravan returned and the goods brought back were sold, the investors would share the profits. If disaster struck the caravan, an investor's loss was limited to the amount of his investment.

What goods were exchanged? What towns took the lead in medieval "international" trade? In the late eleventh century, the Italian cities, especially Venice, led the West in trade in general and completely dominated the oriental market. Ships carried salt from the Venetian lagoon, pepper and other spices from North Africa, and silks and purple textiles from the Orient to northern and western Europe. Venetian caravans brought slaves from the Crimea and Chinese silks from Mongolia to the town markets and regional fairs of France, Flanders, and England. (Fairs were periodic gatherings that attracted buyers, sellers, and goods from all over Europe.) Flanders controlled the cloth industry. The towns of Bruges, Ghent, and Ypres built up a vast industry in the manufacture of cloth. Italian merchants exchanged their products for Flemish tapestries, fine broadcloths, and various other textiles.

Two circumstances help to explain the lead Venice and the Flemish towns gained in long-distance trade. Both enjoyed a high degree of peace and political stability. Geographical factors were equally if not more important. Venice was ideally located at the northwestern end of the Adriatic Sea, with easy access to both the transalpine land routes and the Adriatic and Mediterranean sea-lanes. The markets of North Africa, Byzantium, and Russia and the great fairs of Ghent in Flanders and Champagne in France provided commercial opportunities that Venice quickly seized. The

MAP 9.2. *TRADE AND MANUFACTURING IN MEDIEVAL EUROPE* *Note the number of cities and the sources of silver, iron, copper, lead, paper, wool, carpets and rugs, and slaves.*

geographical situation of Flanders also offered unusual possibilities. Just across the Channel from England, Flanders had easy access to English wool. Indeed, Flanders and England developed a very close economic relationship.

Sheep had been raised for their wool in England since Roman times. The rocky soil and damp climate of Yorkshire and Lincolnshire, though poorly suited for agriculture, were excellent for sheep farming. Beginning in the early twelfth century, but especially after the arrival of Cistercian monks around 1130, the size of the English flocks doubled and then tripled. Scholars have estimated that by the end of the twelfth century roughly 6 million sheep grazed on the English moors and downs. They produced fifty thousand sacks of wool a year.[7] Originally, a "sack" of wool was the burden one packhorse could carry, an amount eventually fixed at 364 pounds; fifty thousand sacks, then, represented huge production.

Wool was the cornerstone of the English medieval economy. Population growth in the twelfth century and the success of the Flemish and Italian textile industries created foreign demand for English wool. The production of English wool stimulated Flemish manufacturing, and the expansion of the Flemish cloth industry in turn spurred the production of English wool. The availability of raw wool also encouraged the development of domestic cloth manufacture within England. The towns of Lincoln and York in the north, Leicester and Northampton in the central counties, Winchester in the south, and Exeter in the west became important cloth-producing

towns. The port cities of London, Hull, Boston, and Bristol thrived on the wool trade. In the thirteenth century commercial families in these towns grew fabulously rich.

The wool and cloth trades serve as a good barometer of the economic growth and decline of English towns. The supply of wool depended upon such natural factors as the amount of land devoted to grazing, the weather, and the prevalence of sheep disease or scab. The price of wool, unlike that of wheat or other foodstuffs, was determined not by supply but by demand. Changes in demand – often the result of political developments over which merchants had no control – could severely damage the wool trade. In the 1320s, for example, violent disorder exploded in the Flemish towns, causing a sharp drop in demand for English wool. When wool exports fell, the economies of London, Hull, and Southampton slumped. Then, during the Hundred Years War (pages 402–403), the English Crown laid increasingly high export taxes on raw wool, and again the wool trade hurt. On the other hand, the decline of wool exports encouraged the growth of cloth manufacturing in older centers such as Lincoln and in new ones such as Tiverton and Lavenham. In the fourteenth century these towns experienced some population growth and considerable prosperity – a prosperity directly linked to the cloth industry.

## THE COMMERCIAL REVOLUTION

A steadily expanding volume of international trade from the late eleventh through the thirteenth centuries was a sign of the great economic surge, but it was not the only one. In cities all across Europe trading and transportation firms opened branch offices. Credit was widely extended, considerably facilitating exchange. Merchants devised the letter of credit, which made unnecessary the slow and dangerous shipment of coin for payment.

A new capitalistic spirit developed. Professional merchants were always on the lookout for new markets and new opportunities. They invested their surplus capital in new enterprises to make more money. They diversified their interests and got involved in a wide variety of operations. The typical prosperous merchant in the later thirteenth century might well be involved in buying and selling, in shipping, in lending some capital at interest, and in other types of banking. Medieval merchants were fiercely competitive.

Some scholars consider capitalism a modern phenomenon, beginning in the fifteenth or sixteenth century. But in their use of capital to make more money, in their speculative pursuits and willingness to gamble, in their competitive spirit, and in the variety of their interests and operations, medieval businessmen displayed the essential traits of capitalists.

The ventures of the English cloth industry in the fourteenth century illustrate these impulses. Profits had steadily accumulated in the cloth-producing towns, where manufacturers often had close ties with wool dealers. With the Flemish cloth industry in trouble, English merchant-manufacturers invaded Flemish markets on the continent and invested their capital in a variety of enterprises. Cloth merchants began to deal in French wines, Flemish tapestries, Baltic fish, furs, and naval stores, and Italian silks. English businessmen established trading centers called factories with long-term residents at Antwerp, Bergen in Norway, Danzig on the Baltic, and Cologne on the Rhine; a single English company might have factories in all of these cities. The foreign commodities exchanged for finished cloth or raw wool were imported into England for domestic sale. These activities re-

*A Flemish Dock Scene* Flemish towns early developed commercial ties with neighboring countries. The Flemish purchased wool from England and manufactured excellent textiles, which they sold to merchants from all over Europe. This print shows bales of cloth being loaded at dockside for transport abroad. (Bodleian Library)

quired capital, willingness to take risks, and the aggressive pursuit of opportunities – the essential ingredients of capitalism. They also yielded fat profits.

These developments added up to what one modern scholar who knows the period well has called "a commercial revolution, . . probably the greatest turning point in the history of our civilization."[8] This is not a wildly extravagant statement. In the long run the commercial revolution of the High Middle Ages brought about radical change in European society and culture. One remarkable aspect of this change is that the commercial classes did not constitute a large part of the total population – never more than 10 percent. They exercised an influence far in excess of their actual numbers.

The commercial revolution created a great deal of new wealth. Wealth meant a higher standard of living. The new availability of something as simple as spices, for example, allowed for variety in food. Dietary habits gradually changed. Taste became more sophisticated. Contact with Eastern civilizations introduced Europeans to eating utensils such as forks. Table manners improved. People learned to eat with forks and knives, instead of tearing the meat from the roast with their hands. They began to use napkins, instead of wiping their greasy fingers on the dogs lying under the table.

The existence of wealth did not escape the attention of kings and other rulers. Wealth could be taxed, and through taxation kings could create strong and centralized states. In the years to come, alliances with the middle classes were to enable kings to defeat feudal powers and aristocratic interests and to build the states that came to be called modern.

The commercial revolution also provided the opportunity for thousands of serfs to improve their social position. The slow but steady transformation of European society from almost completely rural and isolated to relatively more sophisticated constituted the greatest effect of the commercial revolution that began in the eleventh century.

Even so, merchants and businesspeople did not run medieval communities, except in central and northern Italy and in the county of Flanders. Towns remained small: as late as the 1320s a town of 5000 people was considered sizable, and Paris with about 80,000 souls was Europe's greatest city. The castle, the manorial village, and the monastery dominated the landscape. The feudal nobility and churchmen determined the preponderant social attitudes, values, and patterns of thought and behavior. The commercial changes of the eleventh and twelfth centuries did, however, lay the economic foundations for the development of urban life and culture that occurred during the Renaissance.

## REVIVAL AND REFORM IN THE CHRISTIAN CHURCH

The eleventh century also witnessed the beginnings of a remarkable religious revival. Monasteries, always the leaders in ecclesiastical reform, remodeled themselves under the leadership of the Burgundian abbey of Cluny. Subsequently, new religious orders, such as the Cistercians, were founded and became a broad spiritual movement.

The papacy itself, after a century of corruption and decadence, was cleaned up. The popes worked to clarify church doctrine and to codify church law. They and their officials sought to communicate with all the clergy and peoples of Europe through a clearly defined and obedient hierarchy of bishops. The popes wanted the basic loyalty of all members of the clergy. Pope Gregory VII (1073–1085) tried to enforce an entirely new theory of Christian kingship, and his assertion of papal power caused profound changes and serious conflicts with secular authorities. The revival of the Christian church was manifested in the twelfth and thirteenth centuries by a flowering of popular piety, reflected in the building of magnificent cathedrals.

### MONASTIC REVIVAL

In the early Middle Ages the best Benedictine monasteries had been citadels of good Christian living and centers of education and learning. Between the seventh and ninth centuries,

MONT ST.-MICHEL *At the summit of a 250-foot cone of rock rising out of the sea and accessible only at low tide, Mont St.-Michel combined fortified castle and monastery. Thirteenth century monarchs considered it crucial to their power in northwestern France,* *and it played a decisive role in French defenses against the English during the Hundred Years War. The abbots so planned the architecture that monastic life went on undisturbed by military activity. (Mark Sheridan OSB)*

religious houses like Bobbio in northern Italy, Luxeuil in France, and Jarrow in England copied and preserved manuscripts, maintained schools, and set high standards of monastic observance. Charlemagne had encouraged and supported these monastic activities, and the collapse of the Carolingian Empire had disastrous effects.

The Viking and Muslim invaders attacked and ransacked many monasteries across Europe. Some communities fled and dispersed. In the period of political disorder that followed the disintegration of the Carolingian Empire, many religious houses fell under the control and domination of local feudal lords. Powerful laymen appointed themselves or their relatives as abbots, while keeping their wives or mistresses. They took for themselves the lands and goods of monasteries. They spent monastic revenues and sold monastic offices. Temporal powers all over Europe dominated the monasteries. The level of spiritual observance and intellectual activity declined.

In 909 William the Pious, duke of Aquitaine, established the abbey of Cluny near Mâcon in Burgundy. This was to be a very important event. In his charter of endowment Duke William declared that Cluny was to enjoy complete independence from all feudal or secular lordship. The new monastery was to be subordinate only to the authority of Saints Peter and Paul as represented by the pope. The duke then renounced his own possession of and influence over Cluny.

This monastery and its foundation charter came to exert vast religious influence. The first two abbots of Cluny, Berno (910-927) and Odo (927-942), set very high standards of religious behavior. They stressed strict observance of the *Rule of Saint Benedict,* the development of a personal spiritual life by the individual monk, and the importance of the liturgy. In the church as a whole, Cluny gradually came to stand for clerical celibacy and the suppression of simony (the sale of church offices). Within a generation neighboring monasteries sought Cluny's help and were reformed along Cluniac lines.

In the course of the eleventh century, Cluny was fortunate in having a series of extremely able abbots, who all ruled for a long time. They paid careful attention to sound economic management and to the principle of independence from lay influence. In the Holy Roman Empire, Cluniac reform had the strong and significant support of the emperor Henry III (1039-1056). He aided the religious houses in their struggle for independence from the lay aristocracy. Hundreds of monasteries across Europe, in France, Germany, Italy, Spain, and England, placed themselves under Cluny's jurisdiction. By the time of the sixty-year reign of Abbot Hugh (1049-1109), the Cluniac reforming spirit was felt everywhere.

Success for an institution, as for an individual, is measured by the degree to which it lives up to the goals it sets for itself. In religion nothing leads to failure like material success. By the last quarter of the eleventh century, some monasteries enjoyed wide reputations for the beauty and richness of their chant and the piety of the monks' lives. Deeply impressed laymen showered gifts upon them. Jewelry, rich vestments and elaborately carved sacred vessels, lands and properties poured into some houses. With this wealth came the influence of laymen. As the monasteries became richer, the lifestyle of the monks became luxurious. Monastic observance and spiritual fervor declined.

Once again the ideals of the pristine Benedictine life were threatened. Fresh demands for reform were heard, and the result was the founding of new religious orders in the late eleventh and early twelfth centuries. The best representatives of the new reforming spirit and monastic piety of the twelfth century were the Cistercians.

In 1098 a group of monks left the rich abbey of Molesmes in Burgundy and founded a new house in the swampy forest of Cîteaux. They had specific goals and high ideals. They planned to avoid all involvement with secular feudal society. They decided to accept only uncultivated lands far from regular habitation. They intended to refuse all gifts of mills, serfs, tithes, ovens – the traditional manorial sources of income. The early Cistercians determined to avoid elaborate liturgy and ceremony and to keep their chant simple. Finally, they refused to allow the presence of high and powerful laymen in their monasteries, because they knew that such influence was usually harmful to careful observance.

To the Cistercian reformers the older Benedictine monasteries represented power, wealth, and luxurious living, which violated the spirit of the *Rule of Saint Benedict*. The Cistercian life was to be a new kind of commune. It was to be simple, isolated, austere, and purified of all the economic and religious complexities found in the Benedictine houses.

These Cistercian goals coincided perfectly with the needs of twelfth-century society. The late eleventh and early twelfth centuries witnessed energetic agricultural expansion and land reclamation all across Europe. The early Cistercians wanted to farm only land that had previously been uncultivated, or swampland, or fenland, and that was exactly what needed to be done. They thus became the great pioneers of the twelfth century. Their churches had to be plain, and they wanted their daily lives to be simple. A pioneer existence in a commune where all had to work hard and all resources were pooled obviously had enormous economic and social possibilities. Unavoidably the success of the Cistercians' efforts brought wealth, and wealth brought power and influence.

The first monks at Citeaux experienced sickness, a dearth of recruits, and terrible privations. Their obvious sincerity and high idealism eventually attracted attention. In 1112, a twenty-three-year-old nobleman called Bernard joined the community at Citeaux, together with thirty of his aristocratic friends and companions. Thereafter, this reforming movement gained wide impetus. Citeaux founded hundreds of new monasteries in the course of the twelfth century, and its influence on European society was profound.

## REFORM OF THE PAPACY

Some scholars believe that the monastic revival spreading from Cluny influenced reform of the Roman papacy and eventually of the entire Christian church. Certainly, Abbot Odilo of Cluny (994–1048) was a close friend of the German emperor Henry III, who promoted reform throughout the empire. Pope Gregory VII, who carried the ideals of reform to extreme lengths, had spent some time at Cluny. And the man who consolidated the reform movement and strengthened the medieval papal monarchy, Pope Urban II (1088–1099), had been a monk and prior at Cluny. The precise degree of Cluny's impact on the reform movement cannot be measured. But the broad goals of the Cluniac movement and those of the Roman papacy were the same.

The papacy provided little leadership to the Christian peoples of western Europe in the tenth century. Factions in Rome sought to control the papacy for their own material gain. Popes were appointed to advance the political ambitions of their families – the great aristocratic families of the city – and not because of special spiritual qualifications. The office of pope, including its spiritual powers and influence, was frequently bought and sold, though this grave crime, called simony, had been condemned by Saint Peter. The licentiousness and debauchery of the papal court scandalized people. According to a contemporary chronicler, for example, Pope John XII (955–963), who had secured the papal office at the age of eighteen, wore himself out from sexual excesses before he was twenty-eight. Such conditions weakened the religious prestige and moral authority of the pope.

At the local parish level there were many married priests. Taking Christ as the model for the priestly life, the Roman church had always encouraged clerical celibacy, and it had been an obligation for ordination since the fourth century. But in the tenth and eleventh

POPE LEO IX *Called the "founder of the medieval papal monarchy," Leo IX stood for the ideal of the papacy as a moral force throughout Europe. A strong supporter of the Cluniac reform movement, Leo is portrayed here blessing an abbey church. (Burgerbibliothek, Bern. Cod. 292, fol. 73)*

centuries, probably a majority of the priests of Europe were married or living with a woman. Such priests were called Nicolaites from a reference in the Book of Revelation to early Christians who advocated a return to pagan sexual practices.

Several factors may account for the uncelibate state of the clergy. The explanation may lie in the basic need for warmth and human companionship. Perhaps village priests could not survive economically on their small salaries and needed the help of a mate. Perhaps the tradition of a married clergy was so deep-rooted by the tenth century that each generation simply followed the example of its predecessor. In any case, the disparity between the law and the reality shocked people in the lay community and bred disrespect for the clergy.

Serious efforts at reform began under Pope Leo IX (1049–1054). Not only was Leo related to Emperor Henry III but, as bishop of Toul and a German, he was also an outsider who owed nothing to any Roman faction. Leo traveled widely and held councils at Pavia, Reims, and Mainz that issued decrees against simony, Nicolaism, and violence. Leo's representatives held church councils across Europe, pressing for moral reform. They urged individuals who could not secure justice at home to appeal to the pope, the ultimate source of justice.

Leo himself was a man of deep humility and great pastoral zeal. By his character and his actions, he set high moral standards for the West. The reform of the papacy had legal as well as moral aspects. During Leo's pontificate a new collection of ecclesiastical law was prepared – the Collection of 74 Titles. Based on letters of popes and the decrees of councils, the Collection of 74 Titles laid great emphasis on papal authority. The substance of the Collection was to stress the rights, the legal position, and the supreme spiritual prerogatives of the bishop of Rome as the successor of Saint Peter.

Papal reform continued after Leo IX. In the short reign of Nicholas II (1058–1061), a council held in the ancient church of St. John Lateran in 1059 reached a momentous decision. A new method was devised for electing the pope. Since the eighth century the priests of the major churches in and around Rome had constituted a special group, called a college, that advised the pope when he summoned them to meetings. These chief priests were called cardinals from the Latin word *cardo,* meaning "hinge." The cardinals were the hinges on which the church turned. The Lateran Synod of 1059 decreed that the authority and power to elect the pope rested solely in this college of cardinals. The college retains that power today.

The object of the decree was to remove this crucial decision from the secular squabbling of Roman aristocratic factions. When the office of pope was vacant, the cardinals were responsible for the government of the church. (In the Middle Ages the college of cardinals numbered around twenty-five or thirty, most of them from Italy. In 1586, the figure was set at seventy. In the 1960s, Pope Paul VI virtually doubled that number, appointing men from the remotest parts of the globe to reflect the international character of the church.) By 1073, the progress of reform in the Christian church was well advanced. The election of Cardinal Hildebrand as Pope Gregory VII changed the direction of reform from a moral to a political one.

## THE GREGORIAN REVOLUTION

The papal reform movement of the eleventh century is frequently called the Gregorian reform movement, after Pope Gregory VII. The label is not accurate, in that reform began long before Gregory's pontificate and continued after it. Gregory's reign did, however, inaugurate a radical or revolutionary phase that had important political and social consequences.

In contrast to his predecessors and successors in the eleventh century, Cardinal Hildebrand – who took the name Gregory when he was elected pope – was not of aristocratic descent but the son of poor Tuscan peasants. Some historians have argued that his bitter clash with the German emperor Henry IV was the result of a lowborn upstart's desire to humble the chief secular power in Europe. This idea is intriguing, if not thoroughly convincing. Gregory's education probably had more influence on his mature attitudes than his social origins did. He received a good education at Rome and spent some time at Cluny, where his strict views of clerical life were strengthened. Hildebrand had served in the papal secretariat under Leo IX, and after 1065 was probably the chief influence there.

Hildebrand was dogmatic, inflexible, and unalterably convinced of the truth of his own views. He believed that the pope, as the successor of Saint Peter, was the Vicar of God on earth and that papal orders were the orders of God. His ideas of kingship were even more notorious – and threatening – to his contemporaries. In a Christian society, he believed, the king was responsible for providing peace and order so that Christians could pursue their pilgrimage to the City of God.

The king was obliged to act righteously. If he did not, he was a tyrant, to whom *no one* owed allegiance. Who was to decide if a ruler was a tyrant? The pope, as the Vicar of God, would make that decision and, Hildebrand maintained, could release subjects from their duty of obedience. This had been the Christian view of kingship since the time of Saint Augustine. But Hildebrand wanted to put the theory into practice, and in that respect he was very much a radical.

Once Hildebrand became pope, the reform of the papacy took on a new dimension. Its goal was not just the moral regeneration of the clergy and centralization of the church under papal authority. Gregory and his assistants began to insist upon "the freedom of the church." By this they meant the freedom of all churchmen to obey the newly codified canon law, and freedom from control and interference by laymen.

"Freedom of the church" pointed to the end of lay investiture – the selection and appointment of church officials by secular authority. Ecclesiastical opposition to lay investiture was not new in the eleventh century. It too had been part of church theory for centuries. But Gregory's attempt to put theory into practice was a radical departure from tradition. Since feudal monarchs depended upon churchmen for the operation of their governments, Gregory's program seemed to spell disaster for stable royal administration. It provoked a terrible crisis.

## THE CONTROVERSY OVER LAY INVESTITURE

In February 1075, Pope Gregory held a council at Rome. It published decrees not only against Nicolaism and simony but also, for the first time, against lay investiture:

*If anyone henceforth shall receive a bishopric or abbey from the hands of a lay person, he shall not be considered as among the number of bishops and abbots.... Likewise if any emperor, king ... or any one at all of the secular powers, shall presume to perform investiture with bishoprics or with any other ecclesiastical dignity ... he shall feel the divine displeasure as well with regard to his body as to his other belongings.*[9]

In short, clerics who accepted investiture from laymen were to be deposed, and laymen who invested clerics were to be excommunicated (cut off from contact with other Christians).

The church's penalty of excommunication relied for its effectiveness on public opinion. Since most Europeans favored Gregory's moral reforms, he believed that excommunication would compel rulers to abide by his changes. Immediately, however, Henry IV in the German Empire, William the Conqueror in England, and Philip I in France protested.

The strongest reaction came from Germany. Henry IV had strongly supported the moral aspects of church reform within the empire. In fact, they would not have achieved much success without his support. But of all the countries of Europe, the Holy Roman Empire most depended upon the services of churchmen. Governing a vast territory of half Christianized and half pagan peoples, the emperor relied heavily upon the assistance of churchmen. His fledgling bureaucracy could not survive without the literacy and administrative knowhow of bishops and abbots. Naturally, then, he had selected and invested most of them.

Over and beyond the subject of lay investiture, however, a more fundamental issue was at stake. Gregory's decree raised the question of the proper role of the monarch in a Christian society. Did a king have ultimate jurisdiction over all his subjects, including the clergy? For centuries tradition had answered this question in favor of the ruler; so it is no wonder that Henry vigorously protested the papal assertions about lay investiture. By implication they undermined imperial power and sought to make papal authority supreme.

An increasingly bitter exchange of letters ensued. Gregory accused Henry of lack of respect for the papacy and insisted that disobedience to the pope was disobedience to God. Henry protested in a now-famous letter beginning, "Henry King not by usurpation, but by the pious ordination of God, to Hildebrand, now not Pope, but false monk."

Within the empire, those who had most to gain from the dispute quickly took advantage of it. In January 1076, in the southwestern German city of Worms on the Rhine, the German bishops who had been invested by Henry withdrew their allegiance from the pope. Gregory replied by excommunicating them and the emperor. The lay nobility delighted in the bind the emperor had been placed in: with Henry IV excommunicated and cast outside the fold of the Christian faithful, they did not have to obey him and could advance their own interests. Gregory hastened to support them. The Christmas season of 1075 witnessed an ironic situation within Germany: the greater clergy supported the emperor, while the great nobility favored the pope.

Henry outwitted Gregory. Crossing the Alps in January, he approached the pope's residence at Canossa in northern Italy. According to legend, Henry stood for three days in the snow seeking forgiveness. As a priest, Pope Gregory was obliged to grant absolution and to readmit the emperor to the Christian community. Henry's going to Canossa is often described as the most dramatic incident in the High Middle Ages. Some historians claim that it marked the peak of papal power because the most powerful ruler in Europe, the Holy Roman emperor, had bowed before the pope. Actually, Henry scored a temporary victory. When the sentence of excommunication was lifted, Henry regained the kingship and his authority over his rebellious subjects. But in the long run, in Germany and elsewhere, secular rulers were reluctant to pose a

TWELFTH-CENTURY ROMANESQUE CROZIER *This ivory crozier or staff (a reproduction) shows Saint John baptizing Christ in the Jordan River, while the Holy Spirit in the form of a dove descends and God the Father blesses the event. Old Testament prophets with scrolls surround the head of the crozier. (Courtesy, World Heritage Museum. Photo: Caroline Buckler)*

serious challenge to the papacy for the next two hundred years.

For the German empire the incident at Canossa settled nothing. The controversy over lay investiture and the position of the king in Christian society continued. In 1080 Gregory VII again excommunicated and deposed the emperor, but this time it appeared to public opinion that Henry was being persecuted. The papal edicts had little effect. Moreover, Henry invaded Italy, captured Rome, and controlled the city when Gregory died in exile in 1085. But Henry won no lasting victory. Gregory's successors encouraged Henry's sons to revolt against their father. With lay investiture the ostensible issue, the conflict between the papacy and the successors of Henry IV continued into the twelfth century.

The kings of England and France were just as guilty of lay investiture as the German emperor. William the Conqueror (1066–1087) ignored papal decrees against the practice. He selected bishops and counted them among his most important tenants-in-chief. He presided over church councils and refused to allow papal letters or legates into England without his permission. He did, though, work to achieve in England the moral goals of reform. Under the Conqueror's sons William Rufus and Henry I, however, disagreement with the popes over lay investiture was long and violent.

Philip I (1060–1108) of France also quarreled with Gregory, but the subject of their dispute was more Philip's adulterous marriage than lay investiture. Philip enjoyed the profits he received from the sale of church offices. And he probably thought that a church independent of royal control would be a real threat to the French monarchy. Rome's conflict with the western rulers never reached the proportions of the dispute with the German emperor. Gregory VII and his successors had the diplomatic sense to avoid creating three enemies at once.

A long and exhausting propaganda campaign followed the confrontation at Canossa. Finally, in 1122, at a conference held at Worms, the issue was settled by compromise. The terms, as it happened, were the same as those agreed on by the papacy and the English king Henry I in 1107. Bishops were to be chosen according to canon law – that is, by the clergy – in the presence of the emperor or his delegate. The emperor surrendered the right of investing bishops with the ring and staff. But, since lay rulers were permitted to be present at ecclesiastical elections and to accept or refuse feudal homage from the new prelates, they still possessed an effective veto over ecclesiastical appointments. At the same time, the papacy achieved technical success, because rulers could no longer invest. Papal power was enhanced. Thus neither side won a clear victory. The real winners in Germany were the great princes and the lay aristocracy.

The long controversy had tremendous social and political consequences in Germany. For half a century, between 1075 and 1125, civil war was chronic within the empire. Preoccupied with Italy and the quarrel with the papacy, emperors could do little about it. To control their lands, great lords built castles, symbolizing their increased power and growing independence. (In no European country do more castles survive today.) The castles were both military strongholds and centers of administration for the surrounding territories. The German aristocracy subordinated the knights and reinforced their dependency with strong feudal ties. They reduced freemen and serfs to an extremely humble and servile position. Henry IV and Henry V were compelled to surrender rights and privileges to the nobility. Particularism, localism, and feudal independence characterized the Holy Roman Empire in the High Middle Ages. The investiture controversy had a catastrophic effect there, severely retarding the development of a strong centralized monarchy.

### THE PAPACY IN THE HIGH MIDDLE AGES

In the late eleventh century and throughout the twelfth, the papacy pressed Gregory's campaign for reform of the church. Pope

Urban II laid the real foundations for the papal monarchy by reorganizing the central government of the Roman church, the papal writing office (the chancery) and papal finances. He recognized the college of cardinals as a definite consultative body. These agencies, together with the papal chapel, constituted the papal court, or curia – the papacy's administrative bureaucracy and its court of law. The papal curia, although not fully developed until the mid-twelfth century, was the first well-organized institution of monarchial authority in medieval Europe.

The Roman curia had its greatest impact as a court of law. As the highest ecclesiastical tribunal, it formulated canon law for all of Christendom. It was the instrument with which the popes pressed the goals of reform and centralized the church. The curia sent legates to hold councils in various parts of Europe. Councils published decrees and sought to enforce the law. When individuals in any part of Christian Europe felt they were being denied justice in their local church courts, they could appeal to Rome. Slowly but surely, in the High Middle Ages the papal curia developed into the court of final appeal for all of Christian Europe.

In the course of the twelfth century, appeals to the curia steadily increased. The majority of cases related to disputes over church property or ecclesiastical elections and above all to questions of marriage and annulment. Significantly, most of the popes in the twelfth and thirteenth centuries were themselves canon lawyers. The most famous of them, the man whose pontificate represented the height of medieval papal power, was Innocent III (1198–1216).

Innocent judged a vast number of cases. He compelled King Philip Augustus of France to take back his wife, Ingeborg of Denmark. He arbitrated the rival claims of two disputants to the imperial crown of Germany. He forced King John of England to accept as archbishop of Canterbury a man whom John did not really want. Innocent exerted papal authority in the Iberian Peninsula, in Norway and Sweden, in the Balkans, and even in distant Cyprus and Armenia.

By the early thirteenth century, papal efforts at reform begun more than a century before had attained phenomenal success. The popes themselves were men of high principles and strict moral behavior. The frequency of clerical marriage had declined considerably. The level of violence had dropped sharply. Simony was much more the exception than the rule. The church enjoyed a huge success in most places and provided leadership for Christian Europe.

Yet the seeds of future difficulties were being planted. As the volume of appeals to Rome multiplied, so did the size of papal bureaucracy. As the number of lawyers increased, so did concern for legal niceties and technicalities, fees, and church offices. As early as the mid-twelfth century, John of Salisbury, an Englishman working in the papal curia, had written a blistering critique of the expanding curial bureaucracy. The people, he wrote, condemned the curia for its greed and indifference to human suffering. Nevertheless, the trend continued.

Thirteenth-century popes, a long series of canon lawyers, devoted their attention to the bureaucracy and to their conflicts with the German emperor Frederick II. Some, like Gregory IX (1227–1241), abused their prerogatives to such an extent that their moral impact was seriously weakened. Even worse, Innocent IV (1243–1254) used secular weapons, including military force, to maintain his leadership. These popes badly damaged papal prestige and influence. By the early fourteenth century, the seeds of disorder would grow into a vast and sprawling tree, and once again cries for reform would be heard.

———◆———

The end of the great invasions signaled the beginning of profound changes in European society – economic, social, political, and ecclesiastical. In the year 1000, having enough to eat was the rare privilege of a few noblemen, priests, and monks. In the course of the eleventh century, however, manorial communities slowly improved their agricultural equipment; this advance, aided by warmer weather, meant more food and increasing population. Surplus population on the land led to the growth of old towns and the foundation of new ones. Towns and cities represented an entirely new social class, new opportunities, and a more sophisticated way of life.

In the eleventh century, also, rulers and local authorities gradually imposed some degree of order within their territories. Peace and domestic security, vigorously pushed by the church, meant larger crops for the peasants and improved trading conditions for the townspeople. The church overthrew the domination of lay influences, and the spread of the Cluniac and the Cistercian orders marked the ascendancy of monasticism. Having put its own house in order, the Roman papacy in the twelfth and thirteenth centuries built the first strong governmental bureaucracy. In the High Middle Ages the church exercised general leadership of European society.

---

## NOTES

1. Quoted by R. S. Lopez, "Of Towns and Trade," in *Life and Thought in the Early Middle Ages,* ed. R. S. Hoyt, University of Minnesota Press, Minneapolis, 1967, p. 33.

2. H. Pirenne, *Economic and Social History of Medieval Europe,* Harcourt Brace, New York, 1956, p. 53.

3. Quoted by Julia O'Faolain and Lauro Martines, eds., *Not In God's Image: Women in History from the Greeks to the Victorians,* Harper & Row, New York, 1973, pp. 155–156.

4. D. Douglas and G. W. Greenaway, eds., *English Historical Documents,* Eyre & Spottiswoode, London, 1961, 2.969.

5. H. Rothwell, ed., *English Historical Documents,* Eyre & Spottiswoode, London, 1975, 3.854.

6. Douglas and Greenaway, 2.956–961.

7. M. M. Postan, *The Medieval Economy and Society: An Economic History of Britain in the Middle Ages,* Penguin Books, Baltimore, 1975, pp. 213–214.

8. R. S. Lopez, "The Trade of Medieval Europe: The South," in *The Cambridge Economic History of Europe,* ed. M. M. Postan and E. E. Rich, Cambridge University Press, Cambridge, 1952, 2.289.

9. B. D. Hill, ed., *Church and State in the Middle Ages,* John Wiley & Sons, New York, 1970, p. 68.

---

## SUGGESTED READING

In addition to the references in the Notes, the curious student will find a fuller treatment of many of the topics raised in this chapter in the following works.

Both C. D. Burns, *The First Europe* (1948), and G. Barraclough, *The Crucible of Europe: The Ninth and Tenth Centuries in European History* (1976), survey the entire period and emphasize the transformation from a time of anarchy to one of great creativity; Barraclough also stresses the importance of stable government. His *The Origins of Modern Germany* (1963) is essential for central and eastern Europe. For the social significance of the peace movements, see H. E. J. Cowdray, "The Peace and the Truce of God in the Eleventh Century," *Past and Present* 46 (1970): 42–67.

For economic and social history, see Gerald A. J.

Hodgett, *A Social and Economic History of Medieval Europe* (1974), a broad survey, and Carlo M. Cipolla, *Before the Industrial Revolution: European Society and Economy, 1000–1700* (1980), which draws on a wealth of recent research to treat demographic shifts, technological change, and business practices. The effect of climate on population and economic growth is discussed in the remarkable work of E. L. Ladurie, *Times of Feast, Times of Famine: A History of Climate since the Year 1000,* trans. B. Bray (1971). A masterful account of agricultural changes and their sociological implications is to be found in G. Duby, *The Early Growth of the European Economy: Warriors and Peasants from the Seventh to the Twelfth Centuries* (1978).

Students interested in the origins of medieval towns and cities will learn how historians use the evidence of coins, archeology, tax records, geography, and laws in J. F. Benton, ed., *Town Origins: The Evidence of Medieval England* (1968). H. Pirenne, *Medieval Cities* (1956), is an important and standard work, which concentrates on the Low Countries. H. Saalman, *Medieval Cities* (1968), gives a fresh description of the layouts of medieval cities, with an emphasis on Germany, and shows how they were places of production and exchange. Colin Platt's well-illustrated *The English Medieval Town* (1979) makes excellent use of archeological evidence and contains detailed information on the

wool and cloth trades. Richard Muir, *The English Village* (1980), offers a broad survey of many aspects of the daily lives of ordinary people. For readability, few works surpass J. and F. Gies, *Life in a Medieval City* (1973).

For the Christian church, the papacy, and ecclesiastical developments, G. Barraclough's richly illustrated *The Medieval Papacy* (1968) is a good general survey that emphasizes the development of administrative bureaucracy. The advanced student may tackle W. Ullmann, *A Short History of the Papacy in the Middle Ages* (1972). S. Williams, ed., *The Gregorian Epoch: Reformation, Revolution, Reaction?* (1964), contains significant interpretations of the eleventh-century reform movements. Ullmann's *The Growth of Papal Government in the Middle Ages,* rev. ed. (1970) traces the evolution of papal law and government. G. Tellenbach, *Church, State, and Christian Society at the Time of the Investiture Contest* (1959), emphasizes the revolutionary aspects of the Gregorian reform program. The relationship of the monks to the ecclesiastical crisis of the late eleventh century is discussed by N. F. Cantor, "The Crisis of Western Monasticism," *American Historical Review* 66 (1960), and by H. E. J. Cowdray, *The Cluniacs and the Gregorian Reform* (1970), an impressive but difficult study. J. B. Russell, *A History of Medieval Christianity: Prophecy and Order* (1968), is an important and sensitively written work.

# CHAPTER 10

## LIFE IN CHRISTIAN EUROPE IN THE

## HIGH MIDDLE AGES

THE REVIVAL OF TRADE and commerce in the eleventh century brought into being a new class of merchants and businessmen. However, traders and other city dwellers were not typical of medieval society. They may have represented the wave of the future, but in the twelfth century that future was far in the distance. Some historians, trying to show the links between medieval and modern urban society, have concentrated their attention on the medieval commercial classes. In doing so, they have presented a distorted and anachronistic picture of medieval society. Other scholars have painted medieval society as static and unchanging. This picture also is inaccurate, because there was a good deal of movement, change, and migration.

In his biography of the Anglo-Saxon king Alfred, the tenth-century monk Asser described Christian society as composed of those who pray (the monks), those who fight (the nobles), and those who work (the peasants). This description, which was widely accepted and frequently repeated by other writers in the High Middle Ages, set forth the basic social composition of the medieval world. It does not take into consideration the emerging commercial classes. But medieval people were usually contemptuous (at least officially) of profit-making activities, and long after the appearance of commercial and urban groups, the general medieval view of Christian society remained the one formulated by Asser in the tenth century.

The most representative figures of Christian society in the High Middle Ages were peasants, monks, and nobles. How did these people actually live? What were their preoccupations and lifestyles? To what extent was social mobility possible for them? These are some of the questions this chapter seeks to answer.

## THOSE WHO WORK

The largest and economically most productive group in medieval European society was the peasants. The men and women who worked the land in the twelfth and thirteenth centuries made up the overwhelming majority of the population, probably more than 90 percent. Yet it is difficult to form a coherent picture of them. The records that serve as historical sources were written by and for the aristocratic classes. Since farmers did not perform what were considered "noble" deeds, the aristocratic monks and clerics did not waste time or precious paper and ink on them. When peasants were mentioned, it was usually with contempt or in terms of the services and obligations they owed.

Usually – but not always. In the early twelfth century, Honorius, a monk and teacher at Autun who composed a popular handbook of sermons, wrote: "What do you say about the agricultural classes? Most of them will be saved because they live simply and feed God's people by means of their sweat."[1] This sentiment circulated widely. Honorius's comment suggests that peasant workers may have been appreciated and in a sense respected more than is generally believed.

In the last twenty-five years, historians have made remarkable advances in their knowledge of the medieval European peasantry. They have been able to do so by bringing fresh and different questions to old documents, by paying greater attention to such natural factors as geography and climate, and by studying demographic changes. Nevertheless, this new information raises additional questions, and a good deal remains unknown.

In 1932, a distinguished economic historian

THE THREE CLASSES *Medieval people believed that their society was divided among warriors, clerics, and workers, here represented by a monk, a knight, and a peasant. The new commercial class had no recognized place in the agrarian military world. (The British Museum)*

wrote, "The student of medieval social and economic history who commits himself to a generalization is digging a pit into which he will later assuredly fall and nowhere does the pit yawn deeper than in the realm of rural history."[2] This remark is virtually as true today as when it was written. It is, therefore, important to remember that peasants' conditions varied widely across Europe, that geographical and climatic features as much as human initiative and local custom determined the peculiar quality of rural life. The problems that faced the farmer in Yorkshire, England, where the soil was rocky and the climate rainy, were very different from those of the Italian peasant in the sun-drenched Po valley.

Another difficulty has been historians' tendency to group all peasants into one social class. That is a serious mistake. It is true that medieval theologians simply lumped everyone who worked the land into the category of "those who work." In actual fact, however, there were many gradations, classes, and levels of peasants, ranging all the way from complete slaves to free and very rich farmers. The period from 1050 to 1250 was one of considerable fluidity with no little social mobility. The status of the peasantry varied widely all across Europe.

### SLAVERY, SERFDOM, AND UPWARD MOBILITY

Slaves were found in western Europe in the High Middle Ages, but in steadily declining numbers. That the word *slave* derives from "Slav" attests to the widespread trade in men and women from the Slavic areas in the early Middle Ages. Around the year 1200, there were in aristocratic and upper-middle-class households in Provence, Catalonia, Italy, and Germany a few slaves – blond Slavs from the Baltic, olive-skinned Syrians, and blacks from Africa.

Since ancient times, it had been a universally accepted practice to reduce conquered peoples to slavery. The church had long taught that all baptized Christians were brothers in Christ and that all Christians belonged to one "international" community. Although the church never issued a blanket condemnation of slavery, it did vigorously oppose the enslaving of Christians. In attacking the enslavement of Christians and in criticizing the reduction of pagans and infidels to slavery, the church made a contribution to the development of human liberty.

In western Europe during the Middle Ages legal language differed considerably from place to place, and the distinction between slave and serf was not always clear. Both lacked freedom – the power to do as one wished – and were subject to the arbitrary will of one man, the lord. A serf, however,

could not be bought and sold like an animal or an inanimate object, as the slave could.

The serf was required to perform labor services on the lord's land. The number of workdays varied but it was usually three days a week, except in the planting or harvest seasons, when it would be more. Serfs frequently had to pay arbitrary taxes. When a man married, he had to pay his lord a fee. When he died, his son or heir had to pay an inheritance tax to inherit his parcels of land. The precise amounts of tax paid to the lord on these important occasions depended upon local custom and tradition. Every manor had its particular obligations. A free person had to do none of these things. For his or her landholding, rent had to be paid to the lord, and that was often the sole obligation. A free person could move and live as he or she wished.

Serfs were tied to the land, and serfdom was a hereditary condition. A person born a serf was likely to die a serf, though many did secure their freedom. About 1187, Glanvill, an official of King Henry II and an expert on English law, described how villeins (literally, inhabitants of small villages) – as English serfs were called – could be made free:

*A person of villein status can be made free in several ways. For example, his lord, wishing him to achieve freedom from the villeinage by which he is subject to him, may quit-claim him from himself and his heirs; or he may give or sell him to another with intent to free him. It should be noted, however, that no person of villein status can seek his freedom with his own money, for in such a case he could, according to the law and custom of the realm, be recalled to villeinage by his lord, because all the chattels of a villein are deemed to such an extent the property of his lord that he cannot redeem himself from villeinage with his own money, as against his lord. If, however, a third party pro-*

*vides the money and buys the villein in order to free him, then he can maintain himself for ever in a state of freedom as against his lord who sold him. . . . If any villein stays peaceably for a year and a day in a privileged town and is admitted as a citizen into their commune, that is to say, their gild, he is thereby freed from villeinage.*[3]

Many energetic and hardworking serfs acquired their freedom in the High Middle Ages. More than anything else, the economic revival that began in the eleventh century advanced the cause of individual liberty. The revival saw the rise of towns, increased land productivity, the growth of long-distance trade, and the development of a money economy. With the advent of a money economy, serfs could save money and buy their freedom.

Another opportunity for increased personal freedom, or at least for a reduction in traditional manorial obligations and dues, was provided by the reclamation of waste and forest land in the eleventh and twelfth centuries. Resettlement on newly cleared land offered unusual possibilities for younger sons and for those living in areas of acute land shortage or on overworked, exhausted soil. Historians still do not know very much about this movement: how the new frontier territory was advertised, how men were recruited, how they and their households were transported, and how the new lands were distributed. It is certain, however, that there was significant migration and that only a lord with considerable authority over a wide territory could sponsor such a movement. Great lords supported the fight against the marshes of northern and eastern Germany and against the sea in the Low Countries.

As land long considered poor was brought under cultivation, there was a steady nibbling away at the wasteland on the edges of old vil-lages. Clearings were made in forests. Marshes and fens were drained and slowly made arable. This type of agricultural advancement frequently improved the peasants' social and legal condition. A serf could clear a patch of fen or forest land, make it productive, and, through prudent saving, buy more land and eventually purchase his freedom. There were in the thirteenth century many free tenants on the lands of the bishop of Ely in eastern England, tenants who had moved into the area in the twelfth century and drained the fens. Likewise, settlers on the low lands of the abbey of Bourbourg in Flanders, who had erected dikes and extended the arable lands, possessed hereditary tenures by 1159. They secured personal liberty and owed their over-lord only small payments.

Peasants who remained in the villages of their birth often benefited because landlords, threatened with the loss of serfs, relaxed ancient obligations and duties. While it would be unwise to exaggerate the social impact of the settling of new territories, frontier lands in the Middle Ages did provide opportunities for upward mobility.

## THE MANOR

In the High Middle Ages, most European peasants, free and unfree, lived on estates called manors. The word *manor* derives from a Latin term meaning "dwelling," "residence," or "homestead." In the twelfth century it meant the estate of a lord and his dependent tenants.

The manor was the basic unit of medieval rural organization and the center of rural life. All other generalizations about manors and manorial life have to be limited by variations in the quality of the soil, local climatic conditions, and methods of cultivation. Some

Field 1: Planted

Field 2: Fallow

Field 3: Planted

Woodland

Wasteland

Manor house

Barn

Church

House of parish priest

Bake oven

Blacksmith

Orchard

Mill

Village

Meadow

Common pasture

Marsh

Land cultivated for the lord

*FIGURE 10.1    A MEDIEVAL MANOR    The basic unit of rural organization and the center of life for most people, the manor constituted the medieval peasants' world. Since manors had to be economically self-sufficient, life meant endless toil.*

manors were vast, covering several thousand acres of farmland; others were no larger than 120 acres. A manor might include several villages or none at all, but usually it contained a single village and was subject to one lord (see Figure 10.1).

The arable land of the manor was divided into two sections. The demesne, or home farm, was cultivated for the lord. The other part was held by the peasantry. Usually, the peasants' portion was larger, held on condition that they cultivate the lord's demesne. All the arable, both the lord's and the peasants',

was divided into strips, and the strips belonging to any given individual were scattered throughout the manor. All peasants cooperated in the cultivation of the land, working it as a group. This meant that all shared in any disaster as well as any large harvest.

A manor usually held pasture or meadowland for the grazing of cattle, sheep, and sometimes goats. Often the manor had some forest land as well. Forests had enormous economic importance: they were the source of wood for building and resin for lighting; ash for candles, and ash and lime for fertilizers and all sorts of sterilizing products; wood for fuel and bark for the manufacture of rope. From the forests came wood for the construction of barrels, vats, and all sorts of storage containers. Last but hardly least, the forests were used for the feeding of pigs, cattle, and domestic animals on nuts, roots, and wild berries. If the manor was intersected by a river, it had a welcome source of fish and eels.

## AGRICULTURAL METHODS

The fundamental objective of all medieval agriculture was the production of an adequate food supply. According to the method historians have called the open-field system, at any one time half the manorial land was under cultivation and the other half lay fallow; the length of the fallow period was usually one year. Every peasant farmer had strips scattered in both halves. One part of the land under cultivation was sown with winter cereals, such as wheat and rye, the other with spring crops, such as peas, beans, and barley. What was planted in a particular field varied each year when the crops were rotated.

Local needs, the fertility of the soil, and dietary customs determined what was planted and the method of crop rotation. Where one or several manors belonged to a great aristocratic establishment, such as the abbey of Cluny, which needed large quantities of oats for horses, more of the arable land would be planted in oats than in other cereals. Where the land was extremely fertile, such as the Alsace region of France, a biennial cycle was used: one crop of wheat was sown and harvested every other year, and in alternate years all the land lay fallow. The author of an English agricultural treatise advised his readers to stick to a two-field method of cultivation and insisted that a rich harvest every second year was preferable to two mediocre ones

every three years. Farmers everywhere obviously sought to use the land in the most productive way and to get the greatest output.

Nor were they ignorant of the value of animal fertilizers. Chicken manure, because of its high nitrogen content, was the richest but limited in quantity. Sheep manure was also valuable. Gifts to English Cistercian monasteries were frequently given on condition that the monks' sheep be allowed to graze at certain periods on the benefactor's demesne. Because cattle were fed on the common pasture and were rarely stabled, gathering their manure was laborious and time-consuming. Nevertheless, whenever possible, animal manure was gathered and thinly spread. So also was house garbage – eggshells, fruit cores, onion skins – that had disintegrated on a compost heap.

Tools and farm implements are often shown in medieval manuscripts. But accepting such representations at face value is misleading. Rather than going out into a field to look at a tool, medieval artists simply copied drawings from classical and other treatises. Thus a plow or harrow pictured in a book written in the Ile-de-France may actually have been used in England or Italy a half century before.

In the early twelfth century the production of iron increased greatly. There is considerable evidence for the manufacture of iron plowshares (the part of the plow that cuts the furrow into and grinds up the earth). In the thirteenth century the wooden plow continued to be the basic instrument of agricultural production, but its edge was strengthened with iron. Only after the start of the fourteenth century, when lists of manorial equipment began to be kept, is there evidence for pitchforks, spades, axes, and harrows. Harrows were used to smooth out the soil after it had been broken up. A crude harrow appears

God spede ye plouз, ⁊ seude us koꝛue ꝥ now

*LATE MEDIEVAL WHEELLESS PLOW   This plow has a sharp-pointed colter, which cut the earth while the attached mold-board lifted, turned, and pulverized the soil. As the man steers the plow, his wife prods the oxen. The caption reads, "God speed the plow, and send us corn (wheat) now." (Trinity College Library, Cambridge)*

in the illustration for the month of October in the *Très riches heures du duc de Berry,* completed in the mid-fifteenth century. The harrow is made of wood and weighted down with a large stone to force it to cut more deeply into the earth.

The harrow was drawn by horses. The use of horses rather than oxen in the agricultural economy increased in the later thirteenth century. Horses were a large investment, perhaps comparable to a modern tractor. They had to be shod (another indication of increased iron production) and the oats they ate were costly. But horses represented an important element in the improvement of the medieval agricul-

tural economy. Because of their greater strength, horses brought far greater efficiency to farming than oxen. Indeed, some scholars believe that the use of the horse in agriculture is one of the decisive ways in which western Europe advanced over the rest of the world. But horses were not universally adopted. The Mediterranean countries, for example, did not use horsepower. And, at the same time, tools remained pitifully primitive.

Agricultural yields varied widely from place to place and from year to year. Even with good iron tools, horsepower, and careful use of seed and fertilizer, medieval peasants were at the mercy of the weather. Even today, lack of rain or too much rain can cause terrible financial loss and extreme hardship. How much more vulnerable was the medieval peasant with his primitive tools! By twentieth-century standards medieval agricultural yields were very low. The inadequate preparation of the soil, the poor selection of seed, the lack of sufficient manure – all made this virtually inevitable.

Yet there was striking improvement over time. Between the ninth and early thirteenth centuries, it appears that yields of cereals approximately doubled, and that on the best-managed estates, for every bushel of seed planted, the farmer harvested five bushels of grain. This is a very tentative conclusion. Because of the great scarcity of manorial inventories before the thirteenth century, the student of medieval agriculture has great difficulty determining how much the land produced. The author of a treatise on land husbandry, Walter of Henley, who lived in the mid-thirteenth century, wrote that the land should yield three times its seed; that amount was necessary for sheer survival. The surplus would be sold to grain merchants in the nearest town. Townspeople were wholly dependent on the surrounding countryside for food, which could not be shipped a long distance. A poor harvest meant that both town and rural people suffered.

Grain yields were probably greatest on the large manorial estates, where there was more professional management. For example, the estates of Battle Abbey in Sussex, England, enjoyed a very high yield of wheat, rye, and oats in the century and a half between 1350 and 1499. This was due to heavy seeding, good crop rotation, and the use of manure from the monastery's sheep flocks. Battle Abbey's yields seem to have been double those of smaller, less efficiently run farms. A modern Illinois farmer expects to get 40 bushels of soybeans, 150 bushels of corn, and 50 bushels of wheat for every bushel of seeds planted. Of course, modern costs of production in labor, seed, and fertilizer are quite high, but this yield is at least ten times that of the farmer's medieval ancestor. The average manor probably got a yield of 5:1 in the thirteenth century.[4] As low as that may seem by current standards, it marked a rise in the level of productivity equal to that of the years just before the great agricultural revolution of the eighteenth century.

## LIFE ON THE MANOR

Life for most people in medieval Europe meant country life. A person's horizons were largely restricted to the manor on which he or she was born. People rarely traveled more than twenty-five miles beyond their villages. Everyone's world was small, narrow, and provincial in the original sense of the word: limited by the boundaries of the province. This way of life did not have entirely unfortunate results. A farmer had a strong sense of family and the certainty of its support and help in time of trouble. People knew what their life's work would be – the same as their mother's or father's. They had a sense of place, and pride in that place was reflected in adornment of the village church. Religion and the village gave people a sure sense of identity and with it psychological peace. Modern people – urban, isolated, industrialized, rootless, and thoroughly secular – have lost many of these reinforcements.

On the other hand, even aside from the unending physical labor, life on the manor was dull. Medieval men and women must have had a crushing sense of frustration. They lived lives of quiet desperation. Often they sought escape in heavy drinking. English judicial records of the thirteenth century reveal

SHEEPSHEARING *After the sheep was tied up, the farmer clipped the wool and bagged it. English wool was internationally famous for its fine quality, and the English and the Flemish economies depended upon the wool trade. (The British Museum)*

a surprisingly large number of "accidental" deaths. Strong, robust, and commonsensical farmers do not ordinarily fall down on their knives and stab themselves, or slip out of a boat and drown, or get lost in the woods on a winter's night, or fall from their horses and get trampled. They were probably drunk. Many of these accidents occurred, as the court records say, "coming from an ale." Brawls and violent fights were frequent at taverns. They reflect in part the drudgery of life and simple human frustration.

Women played a significant role in the agricultural life of medieval Europe. This obvious fact is often overlooked by historians. Women shared with their fathers and husbands the backbreaking labor in the fields, work that was probably all the more difficult

for them because of weaker muscular development and frequent pregnancies. The adage from the Book of Proverbs – "Houses and riches are the inheritances of fathers: but a prudent wife is from the Lord" – was seldom more true than in an age when the wife's prudent management was often all that separated a household from starvation in a year of crisis. And starvation was a very real danger to the peasantry until the eighteenth century.

Women managed the house. The size and quality of peasants' houses varied according to their relative prosperity, and that prosperity usually depended upon the amount of land held. Poorer peasants lived in windowless cottages built of wood and clay or wattle and thatched with straw. These cottages consisted of one large room that served as the kitchen and living quarters for all. Everyone slept there. The house had an earthen floor and a fireplace. The lack of windows meant that the room was very sooty. A trestle table, several stools, one or two beds, and a chest for storing clothes constituted the furniture. A shed attached to the house provided storage for tools and shelter for animals. Prosperous peasants added rooms and furniture as they could be afforded, and some wealthy peasants in the early fourteenth century had two-story houses with separate bedrooms for parents and children.

Every house had a small garden and an outbuilding. Onions, garlic, turnips, and carrots were grown and stored through the winter in the main room of the dwelling or in the shed attached to it. Cabbage was raised almost everywhere and, after being shredded, salted, and packed in vats in hot water, was turned into kraut. Peasants ate vegetables not because they appreciated their importance for good health but because there was usually little else. Some manors had fruit trees – apple, cherry, and pear in northern Europe; lemon, lime, and olive in the south. But because of the high price of sugar, when it was available, fruit could not be preserved. Preserving and storing other foods were the basic responsibility of the women and children.

Women also had to know the correct proportions of barley, water, yeast, and hops to make beer – the universal drink of the common people in northern Europe. By modern American standards the rate of beer consumption was heroic. Each monk of Abingdon Abbey in England in the twelfth century was allotted three gallons a day, and a man working in the fields for ten or twelve hours a day probably drank much more.

The mainstay of the diet for peasants everywhere – and for all other classes – was bread. It was a hard, black substance made of barley, millet, and oats, rarely of expensive wheat flour. The housewife usually baked the supply for the household once a week. Where sheep, cows, or goats were raised, she also made cheese. In places like the Bavarian Alps region of southern Germany, where hundreds of sheep grazed on the mountainsides, or at Cheddar in southwestern England, cheese was a staple of the diet.

The diet of those living in an area with access to a river, lake, or stream would be supplemented with fish, which could be preserved by salting. In many places there were severe laws against hunting and trapping in the forests. Deer, wild boars, and other game were strictly reserved for the king and nobility. These laws were flagrantly violated, however, and stolen rabbits and wild game often found their way to the peasants' tables. Woods and forests also provided nuts, which housewives and small children would gather in the fall.

Lists of peasant obligations and services to the lord, such as the following from a manor in Battle Abbey in England, commonly included the payment of chickens and eggs:

*John of Coyworth holds a house and thirty acres of land, and owes yearly 2 p at Easter and Michaelmas; and he owes a cock and two hens at Christmas, of the value of 4 d.*[5]

Chickens and eggs must have been highly valued in the prudently managed household. Except for the rare chicken or the illegally caught wild game, meat appeared on the table only on the great feast days of the Christian year: Christmas, Easter, and Pentecost. Then, the meat was likely to be pork from the pig that had been slaughtered in the fall and salted for the rest of the year. Some scholars believe that by the mid-thirteenth century there was a great increase in the consumption of meat generally. If so, this improvement in

*WORKING IN THE FIELDS  Women shared with men all the difficult agricultural work. These farm scenes show women hoeing, sowing seed, cutting and tying the grain, and carrying it to the mill. Although the sickles and the spade appear to have an iron tip, the hoe is entirely wooden. (Rheinisches Landesmuseum, Bonn)*

the diet is further evidence of a better standard of living.

Breakfast, eaten at dawn before the farmer departed for his work, might well consist of bread, an onion (easily stored through the winter months), and a piece of cheese, washed down with milk or beer. Farmers then as now ate their main meal around noon. This was often soup – a thick *potage* of boiled cabbage, onions, turnips, and peas, seasoned with a bone or perhaps a sliver of meat. The evening meal, taken at sunset, consisted of leftovers from the noon meal, perhaps with bread, cheese, milk, or beer.

Once children were able to walk, they helped their parents in the hundreds of chores that had to be done. Small children were set to collecting eggs, if the family possessed chickens, or gathering twigs and sticks for firewood. As they grew older, children had more responsible tasks, such as weeding the family vegetable garden, milking the cows, shearing the sheep, cutting wood for fires, helping with the planting or harvesting, and assisting their mothers in the endless tasks of baking, cooking, and preserving. Because of poor diet, terrible sanitation, and lack of medical care, the death rate among children was phenomenally high.

## POPULAR RELIGION

Apart from the land and the weather and the peculiar conditions that existed on each manor, the Christian religion had the greatest impact on the daily lives of ordinary people in the High Middle Ages. Religious practices varied widely from country to country and even from province to province. But nowhere was religion a one-hour-on-Sunday or High Holy Days affair. Christian practices and attitudes shaded and permeated virtually all aspects of everyday life.

In the ancient world participation in religious rituals was a public and social duty. As the Germanic and Celtic peoples were Christianized, their new religion became a fusion of Jewish, pagan, Roman, and Christian practices. By the High Middle Ages, religious rituals and practices represented a synthesis of many elements, and all people shared as a natural and public duty in the religious life of the community.

The village church was the center of manorial life — social, political, and economic as well as religious. Most of the important events in a person's life took place in or around the church. A person was baptized there, within hours of birth. Men and women confessed their sins to the village priest there and received, usually at Easter and Christmas, the sacrament of the Eucharist. In front of the

church, the bishop reached down from his horse and confirmed a person as a Christian by placing his hands over the candidate's head and making the sign of the cross on the forehead. (Bishops Thomas Becket of Canterbury and Hugh of Lincoln were considered especially holy men because they got down from their horses to confirm.) Young people courted in the churchyard and, so the sermons of the priests complained, made love in the church cemetery. They were married before the altar in the church.

The stone in the church altar contained relics of the saints, often a local saint to whom the church itself had been dedicated. In the church women and men could pray to the Virgin and the local saints. The saints had once lived on earth and thus could well understand human problems. They could be helpful intercessors with Christ or God the Father. According to official church doctrine, the center of the Christian religious life was the mass, the re-enactment of Christ's sacrifice on the cross. Every Sunday and on holy days, the villager stood at mass or squatted on the floor (there were no chairs), breaking the painful routine of work. Finally, people wanted to be buried in the church cemetery, close to the holy place and the saints believed to reside there.

The church was the center of village social life. The feasts that accompanied baptisms, weddings, funerals, and other celebrations were commonly held in the churchyard. Medieval drama originated within the church. Mystery plays, based on biblical episodes, were performed first in the sanctuary, then on the church porch, and finally in the village square, which was often in front of the west door.

From the church porch the priest read to his parishioners orders and messages from royal and ecclesiastical authorities. Royal judges traveling on circuit opened their courts on the church porch. The west front of the

THIRTEENTH-CENTURY CRUCIFIX *Christian teaching in the High Middle Ages stressed the humanity, compassion, and understanding of Christ, as the face of Christ on this richly enamelled crucifix suggests. (Courtesy, World Heritage Museum. Photo: Caroline Buckler)*

church, with its scenes of the Last Judgment, was the background against which the justices disposed of civil and criminal cases. Farmers from outlying districts pushed their carts to the marketplace in the village square near the west front. In busy mercantile centers such as London, business agreements and commercial exchanges were made in the aisles of the church itself, as at St. Paul's.

Popular religion consisted largely of rituals heavy with symbolism. Before slicing a loaf of

bread, the good wife tapped the sign of the cross on it with her knife. Before the planting, the village priest customarily went out and sprinkled the fields with water, symbolizing refreshment and life. Shortly after a woman had successfully delivered a child, she was "churched." This was a ceremony of thanksgiving, based on the Jewish rite of purification. When a child was baptized, a few grains of salt were dropped on its tongue. Salt had been the symbol of purity, strength, and incorruptibility for the ancient Hebrews, and the Romans had used it in their sacrifices. It was used in Christian baptism both to drive away demons and to strengthen the infant in its new faith.

The entire calendar was designed with reference to the great festivals of the Christian year — Easter, Christmas, and Pentecost. Saints' days were legion. Everyone participated in village processions. The colored vestments the priests wore at mass gave the villagers a sense of the changing seasons of the church's liturgical year. The signs and symbols of Christianity were visible everywhere.

Was popular religion entirely a matter of ritualistic formulas and ceremonies? What did the peasants actually *believe?* They accepted what family, customs, and the clergy ingrained in them. They learned the fundamental teachings of the church from the homilies of the village priests. The mass was in Latin, but the priest delivered homilies on the gospel in the vernacular. People grasped the meaning of biblical stories and church doctrines from the paintings on the village church wall. If their parish was wealthy, the scenes depicted in the church's stained-glass windows instructed them. Illiterate and uneducated, they certainly could not reason out the increasingly sophisticated propositions of clever theologians. Still, scriptural references and proverbs dotted everyone's language. Christianity was a basic element in the common people's culture; indeed, it was their culture.

Christians had long had special reverence and affection for the Virgin Mary, as the Mother of Christ. In the eleventh century theologians began to emphasize the depiction of Mary at the crucifixion in the Gospel of John:

*But standing by the cross of Jesus were his mother, and his mother's sister, Mary the wife of Clopas, and Mary Magdalene. When Jesus saw his mother and the disciple whom he loved standing near, he said to his mother, "Woman, behold, your son!" Then he said to the disciple, "Behold, your mother!"*[6]

Medieval scholars interpreted this passage as expressing Christ's compassionate concern for all humanity and Mary's spiritual motherhood of all Christians. The huge outpouring of popular devotions to Mary concentrated on her role as Queen of Heaven and, because of her special relationship to Christ, as all-powerful intercessor with Him. Masses on Saturdays specially commemorated her, sermons focused on her unique influence with Christ, and hymns and prayers to her multiplied. The most famous prayer, *Salve Regina*, perfectly expresses medieval people's attitude toward Mary:

*Hail, holy Queen, Mother of Mercy! Our life, our sweetness, and our hope. To thee we cry, poor banished children of Eve; to thee we send up our sighs, mourning and weeping in this valley of tears. Turn, then, most gracious advocate, thy merciful eyes upon us; and after this our exile show us the blessed fruit of thy womb, Jesus. O merciful, O loving, O sweet Virgin Mary!*

The prayer vividly and lovingly declares medieval people's confidence in Mary, to whom they recommend themselves as the exiled sons

BURIAL OF THE VIRGIN *Carved in a piece of ivory 5" × 2½", this detailed scene of Mary's burial reflects both the profound faith of the age and the incredible skill of medieval artists. (Courtesy, World Heritage Museum. Photo: Caroline Buckler)*

of Eve in this world, and in her power as advocate with Christ.

Peasants had a strong sense of the universal presence of God. They believed that God intervened directly in human affairs and could reward the virtuous and bring peace, health, and material prosperity. They believed, too, that God punished men and women for their sins with disease, poor harvests, and the destructions of war. Sin was caused by the Devil, who lurked everywhere. The Devil constantly incited people to evil deeds and sin, especially sins of the flesh. Sin frequently took place in the dark. Thus, evil and the Devil were connected in the peasant's mind with darkness or blackness. In medieval literature the Devil is often portrayed as a Negro, an identification that has had a profound and sorry impact on Western racial attitudes.

For peasants, life was not only hard but short. Few lived much beyond the age of forty. They had a great fear of nature: storms, thunder, and lightning terrified them. They had a terror of hell, whose geography and awful tortures they knew from sermons. And they certainly saw that the virtuous were not always rewarded but sometimes suffered considerably on earth. These things, which they could not explain, bred in them a deep pessimism.

No wonder, then, that pilgrimages to shrines of the saints were so popular. They offered hope in a world of gloom. They satisfied a strong emotional need. They meant change, adventure, excitement. The church granted indulgences to those who visited the shrines of great saints. Though indulgences only reduced the priest-imposed penalties for sin, people equated them with salvation. They generally believed that the indulgence received from a pilgrimage cut down the amount of time one would spend in hell. Thus pilgrimages "promised" salvation. Vast numbers embarked on pilgrimages to the shrines of St. James at Santiago de Compostella in Spain, Thomas Becket at Canterbury, St.-Gilles de Provence, and Saints Peter and Paul at Rome.

## THOSE WHO FIGHT

In the High Middle Ages members of the nobility were those who fought. Also from the nobility came the great majority of monks and clerics, as well as the opinions, attitudes, and behavior that, to a considerable extent, shaped the lives of other classes. How did the lifestyle and social status of the nobility in the twelfth and thirteenth centuries differ from what they had been in the tenth century? What political and economic role did the nobility play?

Nobility was a legal status that a person acquired automatically at birth or received from a king or ruler as a reward for outstanding fighting skill or unusual services. Nobles considered themselves aristocrats – the word *aristocrat* derives from a Greek term meaning "the best" – but only toward the end of the twelfth century did the European nobility begin to develop a definite class consciousness. Nobles had a way of life based on a chivalric code and the observance – at least among those they considered social equals – of ideals of courtesy, generosity, graciousness, and hospitality. Most monks came from noble families, and the opinions they expressed were aristocratic.

The aristocratic nobility, though a small fraction of the total population, strongly influenced all aspects of culture – political, economic, religious, educational, and artistic. For that reason European society in the twelfth and thirteenth centuries may be termed aristocratic. In spite of scientific, industrial, and political revolutions, the nobility continued to hold the real political and social power in Europe down to the nineteenth century. In order to account for this continuing influence in later centuries, it is important to understand its development in the High Middle Ages.

The noble was almost always a military man, and he frequently used the Latin title *miles,* or knight, to indicate his nobility. He possessed a horse and a sword. These, and the leisure time in which to learn how to use them in combat, were the visible signs of his nobility.

Members of the nobility enjoyed a special legal status. The noble was free personally and in his possessions. He had immunity from almost all outside authorities. He was limited only by his military obligation to king, duke, or prince. As the result of his liberty, he had certain rights and responsibilities. He raised troops and commanded them in the field. He held courts that dispensed a sort of justice. Sometimes he coined money for use within his territories. He conducted relations with outside powers. He was the political, military, and judicial lord of the people who settled on his lands. He made political decisions affecting them, he resolved disputes among them, and he protected them in time of attack. The liberty of the noble and the privileges that went with his liberty were inheritable; they were perpetuated by blood and not by wealth alone.

Women whose fathers or husbands were noble were considered noble too, but not in their own right. Noble ladies often performed the political and military obligations of the men of their class, but there is no evidence of a woman being raised to the nobility. The values of a society are largely determined by its needs, and in the High Middle Ages those needs were military. Fighting was usually done by men, and so men were given noble status.

In the course of the twelfth century, the aristocratic knights slowly evolved into a distinct and closely knit class with feelings of superiority and an attitude of exclusivity. They had a common culture based on consciousness of family, the veneration of ancestors, and a sense of their own worth. Those who were or aspired to be aristocrats wanted

CHAIN MAIL  *This long shirt of interlinked metal rings, though heavy and uncomfortable, was flexible and allowed movement. Knights wore it because before the manufacture of plate armor, chain mail provided a fair degree of protection. (Courtesy, World Heritage Museum. Photo: Caroline Buckler)*

to possess a castle, the symbol of feudal independence and of a military lifestyle. Nobles almost always married within their class.

## INFANCY AND CHILDHOOD

Some very exciting research has been done on childbirth in the Middle Ages. Most information comes from manuscript illuminations, which depict the birth process from the moment of coitus through pregnancy to delivery. An interesting thirteenth-century German miniature from Vienna shows a woman in labor. She is sitting on a chair or stool surrounded by four other women, who are pres-

*MIDWIVES HASTENING DELIVERY   Relatives or midwives assist the woman in childbirth by shaking her up and down. Significantly, no physician is present. With such treatment, the death-rate for both mothers and infants was high. (Bildarchiv der Österreichischen Nationalbibliothek)*

ent to help her in the delivery. They could be relatives or neighbors. If they are midwives, the woman in labor is probably noble or rich, since midwives charged a fee. Two midwives seem to be shaking the mother up and down to hasten delivery. One of the women is holding a coriander seed near the mother's vagina. Coriander is an herb of the carrot family, and its seeds were used for cleaning purposes. They were thought to be helpful for expelling gas from the alimentary canal — hence their value for speeding up delivery.

The rate of infant mortality in the High Middle Ages must have been staggering. Such practices as jolting the pregnant woman up and down and inserting a seed into her surely contributed to the death rate of both the newborn and the mother. Natural causes – disease and poor or insufficient food – also resulted in many deaths. Infanticide, however, which was common in the ancient world, seems to have declined in the High Middle Ages. Ecclesiastical pressure worked steadily against it. High mortality due to foreign invasions and the generally violent and unstable conditions of the ninth and tenth centuries also made unnecessary the deliberate killing of one's own children. On the other hand, English court records from the counties of Warwickshire, Staffordshire, and Gloucestershire for 1221 reveal a suspiciously large number of children dying from "accidental deaths" – drowning, falling from carts, disappearing into the woods, falling into the fire. Still, accidental deaths in rural conditions are more common than is usually thought. Until more research is done, we cannot be certain about the prevalence of infanticide in the High Middle Ages.

Noble women did not nurse their own children. They sent newborns out to wet nurses – women who had recently given birth and therefore had milk. When Richard Plantagenet was born to Henry II and Eleanor on September 8, 1157, his mother immediately gave him to a woman of St. Alban's to nurse. The wet nurse had also had a son on September 8. How long the infant Richard and other medieval children were nursed is not known.

Swaddling appears to have been common in the Middle Ages. Strips of cloth were wrapped tightly around the child's arms, legs, and entire body until it was immobile. The infant was often strapped to a board, which could be set down in a corner or hung up in an out-of-the-way spot. Swaddling depressed the bodily functions: the heartbeat slowed, the child slept more and cried less. Theoretically, this practice arose from adult fears that the child would harm itself if its limbs were free. Probably, too, swaddling was a convenience to the nurse or parent. A swaddled child could be ignored for hours.[7] Any number of unfortunate things could happen to the inert infant, not the least of which was lying for a long time in its own filth. Swaddling surely led to body rashes, disease, and death.

For children of aristocratic birth, the years from infancy to around the age of seven or eight were primarily years of play. Infants had their rattles, as the twelfth-century monk Guibert of Nogent reports, and young children their special toys. Of course, then as now, children would play with anything handy – balls, rings, pretty stones, horns, any small household object. Gerald of Wales, who later became a courtier of King Henry II, describes how as a child he built monasteries and churches in the sand while his brothers were making castles and palaces. Vincent of Beauvais, who composed a great encyclopedia around 1250, recommended that children be bathed twice a day, fed well, and given ample playtime.

Guibert of Nogent speaks in several places in his autobiography of "the tender years of childhood" – the years from six to twelve. Describing the severity of the tutor whom his mother assigned to him, Guibert wrote:

*Placed under him, I was taught with such purity and checked with such honesty from the vices which commonly spring up in youth that I was kept from ordinary games and never allowed to leave my master's company, or to eat anywhere else than at home, or to accept gifts from anyone without his leave; in everything I had to show self-control in word, look, and deed, so that he seemed to require of me the conduct of a monk rather than a clerk. While others of my age wandered everywhere at will and were unchecked in the indulgence of such inclinations as were natural at their age, I, hedged in with constant restraints and dressed in my clerical garb, would sit and look at the troops of players like a beast awaiting sacrifice. Even on Sundays and saints' days I had to submit to the severity of school exercises. At hardly any time, and never for a whole day, was I allowed to take a holiday; in fact, in every way and at all times I was driven to study. Moreover, he devoted himself exclusively to my education, since he was allowed to have no other pupil.*[8]

Guibert's mother had intended him for the church. Other boys and girls had more playtime and more freedom.

Aristocrats deliberately had large families in order to insure the continuation of the family. Although many women died in childbirth and many children died before the age of seven, the survival of four or five children was not uncommon. Parents decided upon the futures of their children as soon as they were born or when they were still toddlers. Sons were prepared for one of the two positions considered suitable to their birth and position. Careers for the youngest sons might well be found in the church; for the rest, a suitable position meant a military career. Likewise, parents determined early which daughters would be married – and to whom – and which would become nuns.

At about the age of seven a boy of the noble class who was not intended for the church was placed in the household of one of his father's friends or relatives. There he became a servant to the lord and received his formal training in arms. He was expected to serve the lord at the table, to assist him as a private valet when called upon to do so, and, as he gained experience, to care for the lord's

horses and equipment. The boy might have a great deal of work to do, depending upon the size of the household and the personality of the lord. The work children did, medieval people believed, gave them experience and preparation for later life.

Training was in the arts of war. The boy learned to ride and to manage a horse. He had to acquire skill in wielding a sword, which sometimes weighed as much as twenty-five pounds. He had to be able to hurl a lance, shoot with a bow and arrow, and care for armor and other equipment. In the eleventh and twelfth centuries, noble youths were rarely taught to read and write. On thousands of charters from that period nobles signed with a cross (+) or some other mark. Literacy for the nobility became a little more common in the thirteenth century. Formal training was concluded around the age of eighteen with the ceremony of knighthood.

By the twelfth century, all men who were legally and socially noble had been formally knighted and could use the titles *dominus* and *messire,* which mean "lord." The ceremony of knighthood was one of the most important in a man's life. Once knighted, a young man was supposed to be courteous, generous, and if possible handsome and rich. Above all, he was to be loyal to his lord and brave in battle. Loyalty was the greatest and most important virtue. In a society lacking strong institutions of government, loyalty was the cement that held aristocratic society together. That is why the greatest crime was called a felony, which meant treachery to one's lord.

### YOUTH

Knighthood, however, did not mean adulthood, power, and responsibility. Sons were completely dependent upon their fathers for support. Unless a young man's father was dead, he was still considered a youth. He remained a youth until he was in a financial position to marry — that is, until his father died. That might not happen until he was in his late thirties, and marriage at forty was not uncommon. A famous English soldier of fortune, William Marshal, had to wait until he was forty-five to take a wife. One factor — the inheritance of land and the division of properties — determined the lifestyle of the aristocratic nobility. The result was tension, frustration, and sometimes violence.

Once he had been knighted, the young man traveled. His father selected a group of friends to accompany, guide, and protect him. The band's chief pursuit was fighting. They meddled in local conflicts. Sometimes they departed on crusades. They did the tournament circuit. The tournament, in which a number of men competed from horseback (in contrast to the joust, which involved only two competitors), gave the bachelor knight experience in pitched battle. Since the horses and equipment of the vanquished were forfeited to the victors, the knight could also gain a reputation and a profit. The group hunted. They took great delight in spending money on horses, armor, gambling, drinking, and women. Everywhere these bands of youths went they stirred up trouble. It is no wonder that kings supported the Crusades. Those foreign excursions rid their countries of considerable violence caused by bands of footloose young knights.

The period of traveling lasted two or three years. Although some young men met violent death and others were maimed or injured, many returned home, still totally dependent upon their fathers for support. Serious trouble frequently developed at this stage, for the father was determined to preserve intact the properties of the lordship and to maintain his power and position within the family. Young men could not marry and set up a household on their own without the father's approval.

When fathers survived until advanced years, marriage and independence had to be long postponed.

Parents often wanted to settle their daughters' futures as soon as possible. Men, even older men, tended to prefer young brides. A woman in her late twenties or thirties would have fewer years of married fertility, limiting the number of children she could produce and thus threatening the survival of the family. Therefore, aristocratic girls in the High Middle Ages were married at around the age of sixteen.

The future of many young women was not enviable. For a girl of sixteen, marriage to a man in his thirties was not the most attractive prospect, and marriage to a widower in his forties and fifties would be even less so. If there were a large number of marriageable young girls in a particular locality, their market value was reduced. In the early Middle Ages it had been the custom for the groom to present a dowry to the bride and her family, but by the late twelfth century the process was reversed. Thereafter, the size of the marriage portions offered by brides and their families rose higher and higher.

Many girls of aristocratic families did not marry at all, although there were few professions a well-born lady could honorably enter. She certainly could not be apprenticed to a trader or artisan. Even less did her blood and dignity allow her to perform any manual labor. The sole alternative was the religious life. Benedictine abbeys for women provided "career opportunities" for some unmarriageable girls. Parents commonly decided upon this option, especially if there were several daughters in the family, when the child was under ten. If a girl felt no particular inclination toward becoming a nun, her mother changed her mind quickly enough. The girl of eleven or twelve years was taken to the childbed of a relative or neighbor to observe the pain and blood that was the lot of married women. It was an event she would not quickly forget. This traumatic experience made her willing to go along with her parent's wishes.

In England in the later Middle Ages there were 138 nunneries, whose residents were overwhelmingly women from the nobility and the upper middle classes. Most convents were small, however, and did not have places for everyone desiring entrance. The new religious orders of the thirteenth century, the Franciscan and the Dominican, provided some relief by establishing many convents for girls and women of the upper class.

Within noble families and within medieval society as a whole, paternal control of the family property and wealth led to serious difficulties. Because marriage was long delayed for men, a considerable age difference existed between husbands and wives and between fathers and their sons. Because of this generation gap, as one scholar has written, "the father became an older, distant, but still powerful figure. He could do favors for his sons, but his very presence, once his sons had reached maturity, blocked them in the attainment and enjoyment of property and in the possession of a wife."[9] Consequently, disputes between the generations were common in the twelfth and thirteenth centuries. Older men held on to property and power. Younger sons wanted a "piece of the action." This helps explain the conflicts and rebellions that occurred in the years 1173–1189 between Henry II of England and his sons Henry, Geoffrey, and John. Their case was quite typical.

The relationship between the mother and her sons was also affected. Closer in years to her children than her husband, she was perhaps better able to understand their needs and frustrations. She often served as a mediator between conflicting male generations. One authority, discussing the role of the mother in French epic poetry, has written, "In extreme need, the heroes betake themselves to their mother, with whom they always find love, counsel and help. She takes them under her protection, even against their father."[10]

When society included so many married young women and unmarried young men, sexual tensions also arose. The young male noble, unable to marry for a long time, could satisfy his lust with peasant girls or prostitutes. But what was a young woman unhappily married to a much older man to do? The literature of courtly love is filled with stories of young bachelors in love with young married women. How hopeless their love was is not known. The cuckolded husband is a stock figure in such masterpieces as *The Romance of Tristan and Isolde,* Chaucer's *The Merchant's Tale,* and Boccaccio's *Fiammetta's Tale.*

In the High Middle Ages, for economic reasons, a man might remain a bachelor knight – a "youth" – for a very long time. The identification of bachelorhood with youth has survived into modern times, and the social attitude persists that marriage makes a man mature – an adult. Marriage, however, is no guarantee of that.

## POWER AND RESPONSIBILITY

A member of the nobility became an adult when he came into the possession of his property. He then acquired vast authority over lands and people. With it went responsibility. The first obligation of the noble was to fight. He was supposed to be the protector and the defender of Christian society against its enemies. In the words of Honorius of Autun:

*Soldiers: You are the arm of the Church, because you should defend it against its enemies. Your duty*

FRENCH CASTLE UNDER SIEGE *Most medieval warfare consisted of small skirmishes and the besieging of castles. If surrounded by a moat and supplied with food and water, a few knights could hold a castle against large armies for a long time. Notice the use of engines to hurl missiles. (The British Museum)*

*is to aid the oppressed, to restrain yourself from rapine and fornication, to repress those who impugn the Church with evil acts, and to resist those who are rebels against priests. Performing such a service, you will obtain the most splendid of benefices from the greatest of Kings.*[11]

Nobles rarely lived up to this ideal, and there are countless examples of nobles attacking the church. In the early thirteenth century, Peter of Dreux, count of Brittany, spent so much of his time attacking the church that he was known as "the Scourge of the Clergy."

The nobles' conception of rewards and gratification did not involve the kind of postponement envisioned by the clergy. They wanted rewards immediately. Since by definition a military class is devoted to war, those rewards came through the pursuit of arms. When nobles were not involved in local squabbles with neighbors — usually disputes over property or over real or imagined slights — they participated in tournaments.

Complete jurisdiction over his properties allowed the noble, at long last, to gratify his desire for display and lavish living. Since his status in medieval society depended upon the size of his household, he would be anxious to increase the number of his household retainers. The elegance of his clothes, the variety and richness of his table, the number of his horses and followers, the freedom with which he spent money – all these things were public indications of his social standing. The aristocratic lifestyle was luxurious and extravagant. To maintain it, nobles often had to borrow from Jewish financiers or wealthy monasteries.

At the same time nobles had a great deal of work to do. The responsibilities of a noble in the High Middle Ages depended upon the size and extent of his estates, the number of his dependents, and his position in his territory relative to others of his class and to the king. As a vassal he was required to fight for his lord or for the king when called upon to do so. By the mid-twelfth century this service was limited in most parts of western Europe to forty days a year. He might have to perform guard duty at his lord's castle for a certain number of days a year. He was obliged to attend his lord's court on important occasions when the lord wanted to put on great displays, such as at Easter, Pentecost, and Christmas. When the lord knighted his eldest son or married off his eldest daughter, he called his vassals to his court. They were expected to attend and to present a contribution known as a gracious aid.

Throughout the year a noble had to look after his own estates. He had to appoint prudent and honest overseers and to make sure that they paid him the customary revenues and services. Since the estates of a great lord were usually widely scattered, he had to travel frequently.

Until the late thirteenth century, when royal authority intervened, a noble in France or England had great power over the knights and peasants on his estates. He maintained order among them and dispensed justice to them. Holding the manorial court, which punished criminal acts and settled disputes, was one of his gravest obligations. The quality of justice varied widely: some lords were vicious tyrants who exploited and persecuted their peasants; others were reasonable and evenhanded. In any case, the quality of life on the manor and its productivity were related in no small way to the temperament and decency of the lord – and his lady.

Women played a large and important role in the functioning of the estate. They were responsible for the practical management of the household's "inner economy" – cooking, brewing, spinning, weaving, overseeing servants, caring for yard animals. The lifestyle of the medieval warrior nobles required constant travel, both for purposes of war and for the supervision of distant properties. When the lord was away for long periods, the women frequently managed the herds, barns, granaries, and outlying fields as well.

Frequent pregnancies and the reluctance to expose women to hostile conditions kept the lady at home and therefore able to assume supervision over the family's fixed properties. When a husband went away on crusade – and his absence could last anywhere from two to five years, if he returned at all – his wife was often the sole manager of the family properties. When her husband went to the Holy Land between 1060 and 1080, the lady Hersendis was the sole manager of the family properties in the Vendômois region in northern France.

Nor were the activities of women confined to managing family households and estates in the absence of their husbands. Medieval warfare was largely a matter of brief skirmishes, and few men were killed in any single encounter. But altogether the number slain ran high, and there were many widows. Aristocratic widows frequently controlled family properties and fortunes and exercised great authority. Although the evidence is scattered and sketchy, there are indications that women performed many of the functions of men. In Spain, France and Germany they bought, sold, and otherwise transferred property. Gertrude, labeled "Saxony's almighty widow" by the chronicler Ekkehard of Aaura, took a leading role in the conspiracies against the emperor Henry V. Sophia, wife of Berthold of Zohringer, assisted her brother Henry the Proud with eight hundred knights at the siege of Falkenstein in 1129. And Eilika Billung, the widow of Count Otto of Ballenstedt, built a castle at Burgwerben on the Saale River and, as advocate of the monastery of Goseck, removed one abbot and selected his successor. From her castle at Bernburg, the countess Eilika was also reputed to ravage the countryside.

Throughout the High Middle Ages fighting remained the dominant feature of the noble lifestyle. The church's preachings and condemnations reduced but did not stop violence. Lateness of inheritance, depriving the nobility of constructive outlets for their energy, together with the military ethos of their culture, encouraged petty warfare and disorder. The nobility thus represented a constant source of trouble for monarchy. In the thirteenth century kings drew on the financial support of the middle classes to build the administrative machinery that gradually laid the foundations for strong royal government. The Crusades relieved the rulers of France, England, and the German Empire of some of their most dangerous elements. Complete royal control of the nobility, however, came only in modern times.

## THOSE WHO PRAY

According to Asser, monks performed the most important service to society. In the

MONKS IN CHOIR  *Seven times during the day and once during the night monks went to the church to chant the psalms and other prayers, performing what everyone believed to be a valuable service for the rest of society. (The British Museum)*

Middle Ages prayer was looked upon as a vital social service, one that was just as crucial as the agricultural labor of the farmers and the military might of the nobles. Just as the knights protected and defended society with the sword, and the peasants provided food and sustenance through their toil, so the monks with their prayers and chants worked to secure God's blessing for society.

Monasticism represented some of the finest aspirations of medieval civilization. The monasteries were devoted to prayer, and their standards of Christian behavior influenced the entire church. The monasteries produced the educated elite that was continually drawn into the administrative services of kings and great lords. Monks kept alive the remains of classical culture and experimented with new styles of architecture and art. They introduced new techniques of estate management and land reclamation. Although relatively few in number in the High Middle Ages, the monks played a significant role in medieval society.

## RECRUITMENT

Toward the end of his *Ecclesiastical History of England and Normandy,* when he was a man well into his sixties, Orderic Vitalis, a monk of the Norman abbey of St. Evroul, interrupted his narrative to explain movingly how he happened to become a monk:

*It was not thy will, O God, that I should serve thee longer in that place, for fear that I might be less attentive to thee among kinsfolk, who are often a burden and an impediment to thy servants, or might in any way be distracted from obeying the law through human affection for my family. And so, O glorious God, you didst inspire my father Odeleric to renounce me utterly and submit me in all things to thy goverance. So, weeping, he gave me, a weeping child, into the care of the monk Reginald, and sent me away into exile for love of thee, and never saw me again. And I, a mere boy, did not presume to oppose my father's wishes, but obeyed him in all things, for he promised me for his part that if I became a monk I should taste of the joys of Heaven with the Innocents after my death. . . . And so, a boy of ten, I crossed the English channel and came into Normandy as an exile, unknown to all, knowing no one. Like Joseph in Egypt I heard a language which I could not understand. But thou didst suffer me through thy grace to find nothing but kindness among strangers. I was received as an oblate in the abbey of St.*

*Evroul by the venerable abbot Mainier in the eleventh year of my life. . . . The name of Vitalis was given me in place of my English name, which sounded harsh to the Normans.*[12]

Orderic Vitalis (ca 1075– ca 1140) was one of the leading scholars of his times. As such, he is not a representative figure or even a typical monk. Intellectuals, those who earn their living or spend most of their time working with ideas, are never typical figures of their times. In one respect, however, Orderic was quite representative of the monks of the High Middle Ages: although he had no doubt that God wanted him to be a monk, the decision was actually made by his parents who gave him to a monastery as a child-oblate. Orderic was the third son of Odeleric, a knight who fought for William the Conqueror at the battle of Hastings (1066). For his participation in the Norman conquest of England, Odeleric was rewarded with lands in western England. Concern for the provision of his two older sons probably led him to give his youngest to the monastery.

Medieval monasteries were religious institutions whose organization and structure fulfilled the social needs of the feudal nobility. Between the tenth and thirteenth centuries, economic necessities compelled great families, or aspiring ones, to seek a life in the church for some members. There simply were not sufficient resources or career opportunities to provide suitable, honorable positions in life for all the children in aristocratic families. The monasteries provided these children an honorable and aristocratic life and opportunities for ecclesiastical careers.[13]

Until well into modern times, and certainly in the Middle Ages, almost everyone believed in and accepted the thorough subjection of children to their parents. This belief was the logical consequence of the fact that young noblemen were not expected to work and were therefore totally dependent on their fathers. Some men did become monks as adults, and apparently for a wide variety of reasons: belief in a direct call from God, disgust with the materialism and violence of the secular world, the encouragement and inspiration of others, economic failure or lack of opportunity, poverty, sickness, the fear of hell. However, most men who became monks, until about the early thirteenth century, seem to have been given as child-oblates by their parents.

In the thirteenth century, the older Benedictine and Cistercian orders had to compete with the new orders of friars – the Franciscans and the Dominicans. More and more monks had to be recruited from the middle class, that is, from small landholders or traders in the district near the abbey. As medieval society changed economically, and as European society ever so slowly developed middle-class traits, the monasteries almost inevitably drew their manpower, when they were able, from the middle classes. Until that time, they were preserves of the aristocratic nobility.

MONK HARVESTING GRAIN *Saint Benedict wrote, "they are truly monks when they live by the labor of their hands" (Rule, chapter 48). The isolated and localized nature of life in the early Middle Ages required that monasteries be entirely self-supporting. (Bibliothèque Publique de Dijon)*

## PRAYER AND OTHER WORK

The pattern of life within individual monasteries varied widely from house to house and from region to region. Each monastic community was shaped by the circumstances of its foundation and endowment, by tradition, by the interests of its abbots and members, and by local conditions. It would therefore be a mistake to think that Christian monasticism in the High Middle Ages was everywhere the same. One central activity, however – the work of God – was performed everywhere. Daily life centered around the liturgy.

Seven times a day and once during the night, the monks went to choir to chant the psalms and other prayers prescribed by Saint Benedict. Prayers were offered for peace, rain, good harvests, the civil authorities, the monks' families, and their benefactors. Monastic patrons in turn lavished gifts upon the monasteries, which often became very wealthy. Through their prayers the monks performed a valuable service for the rest of society.

Prayer justified the monks spending a large percentage of their income on splendid objects to enhance the liturgy; monks praised God, they believed, not only in prayer but in everything connected with prayer. They sought to accumulate priestly vestments of the finest silks, velvets, and embroideries; and sacred vessels – chalices, patens, and thuribles – of embossed silver and gold. Thuribles

*MONK INSTRUCTING ILLUMINATOR   All monks had to learn to read in order to perform the religious services. A few of the intellectually and artistically gifted were often taught to copy and to illuminate manuscripts. (The Pierpont Morgan Library)*

containing sweet-smelling incense brought at great expense from the Orient were used for the incensation of the altars, following ancient Jewish ritual. The pages of gospel books were richly decorated with gold leaf and the books' bindings were ornamented and bejewelled. Every monastery tried to acquire the relics of its patron saint, which necessitated the production of a beautiful reliquary to house the relics. The liturgy, then, inspired a great deal of art, and the monasteries became the crucibles of art in Western Christendom.

The monks fulfilled their social responsibility by praying. It was generally agreed that they could best carry out this duty if they were not distracted by worldly matters. Thus, great and lesser lords gave the monasteries lands that would supply the community with

necessities. Each manorial unit was responsible for provisioning the abbey for a definite period of time, and the expenses of each manor were supposed to equal its income.

The administration of the abbey's estates and properties consumed considerable time. The operation of a large establishment, such as Cluny in Burgundy or Bury St. Edmunds in England, which by 1150 had several hundred monks, involved planning, prudence and wise management. Although the abbot or prior had absolute authority in making assignments, common sense advised that tasks be allotted according to the ability and talents of individual monks.

The usual method of economic organization was the manor. Many monastic manors were small enough and close enough to the abbey to be supervised directly by the abbot. But if a monastery held and farmed vast estates, the properties were divided into administrative units under the supervision of one of the monks of the house. The lands of the German abbey of St. Emmeran at Regensburg, for example, were divided into thirty-three manorial centers.

Because the choir monks were aristocrats, they did not till the land themselves. In each house one monk, the cellarer or general financial manager, was responsible for supervising the peasants or lay brothers who did the actual agricultural labor. Lay brothers were vowed religious drawn from the servile classes, with simpler religious and intellectual obligations than those of the choir monks. The cellarer had to see to it that the estates of the monastery produced enough income to cover its expenses. Another monk, the almoner, was responsible for feeding and caring for the poor of the neighborhood. At the French abbey of St.-Requier in the eleventh century, 110 persons were fed every day. At Corbie, fifty loaves of bread were distributed daily to the poor.

The precentor, or cantor, was responsible for the library and the careful preservation of books. The sacristan of the abbey had in his charge all the materials and objects connected with the liturgy – vestments, candles, incense, sacred vessels, altar cloths, and hangings. The novice master was responsible for the training of recruits, instructing them in the *Rule,* the chant, the Scriptures, and the history and traditions of the house. For a few of the monks, work was some form of intellectual activity, such as the copying of books and manuscripts, the preparation of manuals, and the writing of letters.

Although the church forbade monks to study law and medicine, that rule was often ignored. In the twelfth and thirteenth cen-

turies, many monks gained considerable reputations for their knowledge and experience in the practice of both the canon law of the church and the civil law of their countries. For example, the Norman monk Lanfranc, because of his legal knowledge and administrative ability, became the chief adviser of William the Conqueror.

Although knowledge of medicine was primitive by twentieth-century standards, monastic practitioners were less ignorant than one would suspect. Long before 1066, a rich medical literature had been produced in England. The most important of these treatises was *The Leech Book of Bald* ("leech" means medical). This work exhibits a wide knowledge of herbal prescriptions, familiarity with ancient authorities, and evidence based on empirical practice. Bald discusses diseases of the lungs and stomach together with their remedies and demonstrates his acquaintance with surgery. *The Leech Book of Bald* was copied and circulated widely in the eleventh through thirteenth centuries, and many monastic libraries in England and on the Continent had a copy of it. Medical knowledge was sometimes rewarded. King Henry II of England made his medical adviser, the monk Robert de Veneys, abbot of Malmesbury.

The religious houses of medieval Europe usually took full advantage of whatever resources and opportunities their location offered. For example, the raising of horses could produce income in a world that depended on horses for travel and for warfare. Some monasteries, such as the Cistercian abbey of Jervaulx in Yorkshire, became famous for and quite wealthy from their production of prime breeds. In the eleventh and twelfth centuries, a period of considerable monastic expansion, large tracts of swamp, fen, forest, and wasteland were brought under cultivation – principally by the Cistercians.

The Cistercians, whose constitution insisted that they accept lands far from human habitation and forbade them to be involved in the traditional feudal-manorial structure, were ideally suited to the agricultural needs and trends of their times. In the Low Countries they built dikes to hold back the sea, and the reclaimed land was put to the production of cereals. In the eastern parts of the Holy Roman Empire – in Silesia, Mecklenburg, and Pomerania – they took the lead in draining swamps and cultivating wasteland. Because of a labor shortage, they advertised widely all across Europe for monks and brothers. Because of their efforts, the rich, rolling land of French Burgundy was turned into lush vineyards. In northern and central England, the rocky soil and damp downs of Lincolnshire, poorly suited to agriculture, were turned into sheep runs; by the third quarter of the twelfth century, the Cistercians were raising sheep and playing a very large role in the production of England's staple crop, wool.

Some monasteries got involved in iron and lead mining. In 1291, the Cistercian abbey of Furness operated at least forty forges. The German abbeys of Königsbronn, Waldsassen, and Saarbegen also mined iron in the thirteenth century. The monks entered this industry first to fill their own needs, but in an expanding economy they soon discovered a large market. Iron had hundreds of uses. Nails, hammers, plows, armor, spears, axes, stirrups, horseshoes, and many weapons of war were all made from this basic metal. When King Richard of England was preparing to depart on crusade in 1189, he wanted to take fifty thousand horseshoes with him. Lead also had a great variety of uses. It could be used for the roofing of buildings, and as alloy for strengthening the silver coinage, for framing pane-glass windows in parish, mon-astery, and cathedral churches, and even for lavatory drainpipes.

Whatever work particular monks did and whatever economic activities individual monasteries were involved in, monks also performed social services and exerted an influence for the good. Monasteries often ran schools that gave primary education to young boys. Abbeys like St. Albans, situated north of London on a busy thoroughfare, served as hotels and resting-places for travelers. Monasteries frequently operated "hospitals" and leprosaria, which provided care and attention to the sick, the aged, and the afflicted – primitive care, it is true, but often all that was available. In short, they performed a variety of social services in an age when there was no "state" and no conception of social welfare as a public responsibility.

## ECONOMIC DIFFICULTIES

In the twelfth century, expenses in the older Benedictine monastic houses increased more rapidly than did income, leading to a steadily worsening economic situation. Cluny is a good example. Life at Cluny was lavish and extravagant. There were large quantities of rich food. The monks' habits were made of the best cloth available. Cluny's abbots and priors traveled with sizable retinues, as great lords were required to do. The abbots worked to make the liturgy ever more magnificent, and large sums were spent on elaborate vestments and jeweled vessels. Abbot Hugh embarked on an extraordinarily expensive building program. He entirely rebuilt the abbey church, and when Pope Urban II consecrated it in 1095 it was the largest church in Christendom. The monks lived like lords, which in a sense they were.

Revenue came from the hundreds of monasteries scattered across France, Italy, Spain,

CLUNY, CA 1157  Begun in 1085 and supported by the generosity of kings and peasants, the church (right center) and monastery of Cluny was the administrative center of a vast monastic and feudal empire. Note the apse around the east end of the church and the large foreground complex, which served as monastic infirmary and guest hostel. (The Mediaeval Academy of America)

and England that Cluny had reformed in the eleventh century; each year they paid Cluny a cash sum. Novices were expected to make a gift of land or cash when they entered. For reasons of security, knights departing on crusade often placed their estates under Cluny's authority. Still, this income was not enough. The management of Cluny's manors all across Europe was entrusted to bailiffs or wardens who were not monks and who were given lifetime contracts. Frequently these bailiffs were poor managers and produced no profits. But they could not be removed and replaced. In order to meet expenses, Cluny had to rely on cash reserves. For example, Cluny's estates produced only a small percentage of needed food supplies; the rest had to be bought and paid for from cash reserves.

Cluny had two basic alternatives – improve management to cut costs or borrow money. The abbey could have placed the monastic manors under the jurisdiction of monks, rather than hiring bailiffs who would grow rich as middlemen. It could have awarded annual rather than lifetime contracts, supervised all revenues, and tried to cut costs within the monastery. Cluny chose the second alternative – borrowing. Consequently, the abbey spent hoarded reserves of cash and fell into debt.

In contrast to the abbot of Cluny, Suger (1122–1151), the superior of the royal abbey of St.-Denis near Paris, was a shrewd manager. Although he too spared no expense to enhance the beauty of his monastery and church, Suger kept an eye on costs and made sure that his properties were soundly managed. But the management of St.-Denis was unusual. Far more typical was the economic mismanagement at Cluny. By the later twelfth century, small and great monasteries were facing comparable financial difficulties.

———◆———

During the eleventh century the term *chevaliers,* meaning "horsemen" or "knights," gained widespread currency in France. Non-French peoples gradually adopted it to refer to the nobility, "who sat up high on their war-horses, looking down on the poor masses and terrorizing the monks."[14] By 1100 the knightly class was united in its ability to fight on horseback, its insistence that each member was descended from a valorous ancestor, its privileges, and its position at the top of the social hierarchy. The interests and activities of the nobility centered around warfare, but its economic power rested upon its ability to extract labor services and rents from the peasants. Generalizations about peasant life in the High Middle Ages must always be qualified by manorial customs, by the weather in a given year, and by the personalities of local lords. Everywhere, however, the performance of agricultural services and the payment of rents preoccupied peasants. Although they led hard lives, social mobility was possible through exceedingly hard work, luck, or flight to a town.

The monks exercised a profound influence on matters of the spirit. In their prayers the monks battled for the Lord, just as the chivalrous knights did on the battlefield. In their chant and rich ceremonial, in the Romanesque architecture of their buildings, and in the ex-ample of many monks' lives, the monasteries inspired Christian peoples to an incalculable degree. As the crucibles of sacred art, the monasteries became the cultural centers of Christian Europe.

## NOTES

1. Honorius of Autun, "Elucidarium sive Dialogus de Summa Totius Christianae Theologiae," in *Patrologia Latina,* ed. J. P. Migne, Garnier Bros., Paris, 1854, vol. 172, col. 1149.

2. E. Power, "Peasant Life and Rural Conditions," in J. R. Tanner et al., *The Cambridge Medieval History,* Cambridge University Press, Cambridge, 1958, 7.716.

3. Glanvill, "De Legibus Angliae," book 5, chap. 5, in *Social Life in Britain from the Conquest to the Reformation,* ed. G. G. Coulton, Cambridge University Press, London, 1956, pp. 338–339.

4. G. Duby, *Early Growth of the European Economy,* Cornell University Press, Ithaca, N.Y., 1977, pp. 213–219.

5. S. R. Scargill-Bird, ed., *Custumals of Battle Abbey in the Reign of Edward I and Edward II,* Camden Society, London, 1887, p. 19.

6. John 19: 25–27.

7. L. Demause, "The Evolution of Childhood," in *The History of Childhood,* ed. L. Demause, Psychohistory Press, New York, 1974, pp. 32–37.

8. J. F. Benton, ed. and trans., *Self and Society in Medieval France: The Memoirs of Abbot Guibert of Nogent,* Harper & Row, New York, 1970, p. 46.

9. D. Herlihy, "The Generation Gap in Medieval History," *Viator* 5 (1974): 360.

10. Cited in ibid., p. 361.

11. Honorius of Autun in *Patrologia Latina,* vol. 172, col. 1148.

12. M. Chibnall, ed. and trans., *The Ecclesiastical History of Orderic Vitalis,* Oxford University Press, Oxford, 1972, 2.xiii.

13. R. W. Southern, *Western Society and the Church in the Middle Ages,* Penguin Books, Baltimore, 1970, pp. 224–230, esp. p. 228.

14. G. Duby, *The Age of the Cathedrals: Art and Society, 980–1420,* trans. Eleanor Levieux and Barbara Thompson, University of Chicago Press, Chicago, 1981, p. 38.

## SUGGESTED READING

The best short introduction to the material of this chapter is C. Brooke, *The Structure of Medieval Society* (1971), a beautifully illustrated book. The student interested in aspects of medieval slavery, serfdom, or the peasantry should begin with M. Bloch, "How Ancient Slavery Came to an End" and "Personal Liberty and Servitude in the Middle Ages, Particularly in France," in *Slavery and Serfdom in the Middle Ages: Selected Essays,* trans. W. R. Beer (1975). There is an excellent discussion of these problems in the magisterial work of G. Duby, *Rural Economy and Country Life in the Medieval West,* trans. C. Postan (1968). G. C. Homans, *English Villagers of the Thirteenth Century* (1975), is a fine combination of sociological and historical scholarship, while the older study of H. S. Bennett, *Life on the English Manor: A Study of Peasant Conditions* (1960), contains much useful information presented in a highly readable fashion. Emmanuel LeRoy Ladurie, *Montaillou: Cathars and Catholics in a French Village, 1294–1324,* trans. Barbara Bray (1978), is a fascinating glimpse of village life. G. Duby, *The Early Growth of the European Economy: Warriors and Peasants from the Seventh to the Twelfth Century* (1977), is a superb synthesis by a leading authority. Advanced students should see the same author's *The Three Orders: Feudal Society Imagined* (1980), a brilliant but difficult book.

For the nobility, see L. Genicot, "The Nobility in Medieval Francia: Continuity, Break, or Evolution?"; A. Borst, "Knighthood in the High Middle Ages: Ideal and Reality"; and two studies by G. Duby, "The Nobility in Eleventh and Twelfth Century Maconnais" and "Northwestern France: The 'Youth' in Twelfth Century Aristocratic Society": all these articles appear in F. L. Cheyette, ed., *Lordship and Community in Medieval Europe: Selected Readings* (1968). Social mobility among both aristocracy and peasantry are discussed in T. Evergates, *Feudal Society in the Bailliage of Troyes under the Counts of Champagne, 1152–1284* (1976). M. Bloch, *Feudal Society* (1966), remains the standard.

E. Power, *Medieval Women* (1976), is a nicely illustrated sketch of the several classes of women. For women, marriage, and the family in the High Middle Ages, J. McNamara and S. F. Wemple, "Sanctity and Power: The Dual Pursuit of Medieval Women," in *Becoming Visible: Women in European History* (1977), ed. R. Bridenthal and C. Koonz; and E. R. Coleman, "Medieval Marriage Characteristics: A Neglected Factor in the History of Medieval Serfdom," in *The Family in History: Interdisciplinary Essays* (1973), ed. T. K. Rabb and R. I. Rotberg, make interesting reading.

There is no dearth of good material on the monks in medieval society. The titles listed in the Suggested Reading for Chapter 7 represent a useful starting point for study. Anne Boyd, *The Monks of Durham* (1975), is an excellently illustrated sketch of many facets of monastic culture in the High Middle Ages. L. J. Lekai, *The Cistercians: Ideals and Reality* (1977), is a broad scholarly survey of the White Monks. Georges Duby, *The Age of the Cathedrals,* cited in the Notes to this chapter, is especially strong on the monastic origins of medieval art. Both W. Braunfels, *Monasteries of Western Europe: the Architecture of the Orders* (1972), and C. Brooke, *The Monastic World* (1974), have splendidly illustrated texts and good bibliographies.

# CHAPTER 11

## THE CREATIVITY AND VITALITY OF

## THE HIGH MIDDLE AGES

THE HIGH MIDDLE AGES witnessed some of the most remarkable achievements in the entire history of Western society. Europeans displayed tremendous creativity and vitality in many realms of culture. Rulers tried to establish contact with all of their peoples, developed new legal and financial institutions, and slowly consolidated power in the hands of the monarchy. The kings of England and France succeeded in laying the foundations of the modern national state. The university, a uniquely Western contribution to civilization and a superb expression of medieval creativity, came into being at the same time. The Gothic cathedral manifested medieval peoples' deep Christian faith and their appreciation for the worlds of nature, man, and God. The Crusades, a series of holy wars to recover the Holy Land from the Muslims, also expressed European Christians' strong, even fanatical, religious faith.

This chapter will discuss the following questions. How did medieval rulers in England, France, and the Holy Roman Empire work to solve their problems of government? How did universities develop, and what needs of medieval society did they serve? What does the Gothic cathedral reveal about the ideals, attitudes, and interests of medieval people? What functions did the cathedral serve? Finally, what combination of motives inspired the Crusades, and what results did they have?

## MEDIEVAL ORIGINS OF THE MODERN STATE

Rome's great legacy to Western civilization had been the concepts of the state and the law, but for almost five hundred years after the disintegration of the Roman Empire in the West the state as a reality did not exist. Political authority was completely decentralized. Power was spread among many feudal lords, who gave their localities such protection and security as their strength allowed. The fiefdoms, kingdoms, and territories that covered the continent of Europe did not have the qualities or provide the services of a modern state. They did not have jurisdiction over many people, and their laws affected a relative few. In the mid-eleventh century, there existed many layers of authority — earls, counts, barons, knights — between a king and the ordinary people.

In these circumstances, medieval kings had common goals. The rulers of England, France, and the Holy Roman Empire wanted to strengthen and extend royal authority within their territories. They wanted to establish an effective means of communication with all peoples in order to increase public order. They wanted more revenue and efficient state bureaucracies. The solutions they found to these problems laid the foundations for modern national states.

The modern state is an organized territory with definite geographical boundaries that are recognized by other states. It has a body of law and institutions of government. If the state claims to govern according to law, it is guided in its actions by the law. The modern national state counts on the loyalty of its citizens, or at least a majority of them. It provides order so that citizens can go about their daily work and other activities. It protects its citizens in their persons and property. The state tries to prevent violence and to apprehend and punish those who commit it. It supplies a currency or medium of exchange that permits financial and commercial transactions. The state conducts relations with foreign governments. In order to accomplish even these minimal functions, the state must have officials, bureaucracies, laws and courts

DEDERVNT:HAROLDO: ORO NA: REGIS HIC RE SIDET:HAROLD REX:AN GLORVM: STIGANT ARCHIEPS

THE BAYEUX TAPESTRY Measuring 231' by 19½", the Bayeux Tapestry gives a narrative description of the events surrounding the Norman Conquest of England. The tapestry provides an important historical source for the clothing, armor, and lifestyles of the Norman and Anglo-Saxon warrior class. (Tapisserie de la Reine Mathilde, Ville de Bayeux)

of law, soldiers, information, and money. States with these attributes are relatively recent developments.

## UNIFICATION AND COMMUNICATION

ENGLAND Under the pressure of the Danish (or Viking) invasions of the ninth and tenth centuries, the seven kingdoms of Anglo-Saxon England united under one king. At the same period, for reasons historians still cannot fully explain, England was divided into local units called shires, or counties, each under the jurisdiction of a sheriff appointed by the king. The Danish king Canute (1016–1035) and his successor Edward the Confessor (1042–1066) exercised broader authority than any contemporary ruler on the Continent. All the English thegns, or local chieftains, recognized the central authority of the kingship.

The kingdom of England, therefore, had a political head start on the rest of Europe.

When Edward the Confessor died, his cousin Duke William of Normandy claimed the English throne and in 1066 defeated the Anglo-Saxon claimant on the battlefield of Hastings. As William subdued the rest of the country, he distributed lands to his Norman followers and assigned specific military quotas to each estate. He also required all feudal lords to swear an oath of allegiance to him as king.

William the Conqueror (1066–1087) preserved the Anglo-Saxon institution of sheriffs representing the king at the local level, but replaced Anglo-Saxon sheriffs with Normans. A sheriff, who always lived in the county where he worked, had heavy duties. He maintained order in the shire. He caught criminals and punished them in the shire court, over which he presided. He collected taxes and, when the king ordered him to do so, raised an army of foot soldiers. The sheriff also organized adult males in groups of ten, with each member liable for the good behavior of the others. The Conqueror thus made local people responsible for order in their communities. For all his efforts, the sheriff received no pay. This system, whereby unpaid officials governed the county, served as the basic pattern of English local government for many centuries. It cost the Crown nothing, but restricted opportunities for public service to the well-to-do.

William also retained another Anglo-Saxon device, the writ. This brief administrative order written in the vernacular (Anglo-Saxon) by a government clerk was the means by which the central government communicated with people at the local level. Sheriffs were empowered to issue writs relating to matters in their counties.

In 1086 the Conqueror introduced into England a major innovation, the Norman inquest. At his Christmas court in 1085, William discussed the state of the kingdom with his vassals and decided to conduct a systematic investigation of the entire country. The survey was to be made by means of inquests, or general inquiries, held throughout England. William wanted to determine how much wealth there was in his new kingdom, who held what land, and what lands had been disputed among his vassals since the conquest of 1066. In 1086 groups of royal officials or judges were sent to every part of the country. In every village and farm, the priest and six ordinary people were put under oath to answer the questions asked of them by the king's commissioners. Everybody and everything was counted and listed. In the words of a contemporary chronicler:

*He sent his men over all England into every shire and had them find out how many hundred hides there were in the shire, or what land and cattle the king himself had, or what dues he ought to have in twelve months from the shire. Also ... what or how much everybody had who was occupying land in England, in land or cattle, and how much money it was worth. So very narrowly did he have it investigated, that there was no single hide nor yard of land, nor indeed ... one ox nor one cow nor one pig was there left out, and not put down in his record: and all these records were brought to him afterwards.*[1]

The resulting record, called *Domesday Book* from the Anglo-Saxon word *doom* meaning "judgment," still survives. It is an invaluable source of social and economic information about medieval England.

The Conqueror's scribes compiled *Domesday Book* in less than a year, using the evidence given by local people. *Domesday Book* provided William and his descendants with information vital for the exploitation and government of the country. Knowing the amount of wealth every area possessed, the king could tax accordingly. Knowing the amount of land his vassals had, he could allot knight service fairly. *Domesday Book* was a unique document. Its inclusion of material about all of England helped enable English kings to think of their country as a single unit and to work to bind it together. Across the English Channel, state building took a different course.

*FRANCE* In the early twelfth century, France consisted of a number of virtually independent provinces. Each was governed by its local ruler; each had its own laws and customs; each had its own coinage; each had its own dialect. Unlike the king of England, the king of France had jurisdiction over a very small area. Chroniclers called King Louis VI (1108–1137) *roi de St.-Denis,* king of St.-Denis, because the territory he controlled was limited to Paris and the St.-Denis area surrounding the city. This region, called the Ile-de-France or royal domain, became the nucleus of the French state. The clear goal of the medieval French monarchy was to increase the royal domain and extend the power and authority of the king (see Map 11.1).

The work of unifying France began under Louis VI's grandson Philip II (1180–1223). Rigord, Philip's biographer, gave him the title "Augustus" (from a Latin word meaning "to increase") because he vastly enlarged the territory of the kingdom of France. By defeating a baronial plot against the Crown, Philip Augustus acquired the northern counties of Artois and Vermandois. When King John of England, who was Philip's vassal for the rich province of Normandy, defaulted on his feudal obligation to come to the French court, Philip declared Normandy forfeit to the French crown. He enforced this declaration militarily, and in 1204 Normandy fell to the French. Within two years Philip also gained the prosperous farmlands of Maine, Touraine, and Anjou. By the end of his reign Philip was effectively master of northern France.

In the thirteenth century Philip Augustus's descendants made important acquisitions in the south. Louis VIII (1223–1226) added the county of Poitou to the kingdom of France by war. Louis IX (1226–1270) gained Toulouse and a vital interest in the Mediterranean province of Provence through his marriage to Margaret of Provence. Louis' son Philip III (1270–1285) secured Languedoc through inheritance. By the end of the thirteenth century, most of the provinces of modern France had been added to the royal domain through diplomacy, marriage, war, and inheritance. The king of France was stronger than any group of antagonistic French nobles who might try to challenge his authority.

Philip Augustus devised a method of governing the provinces and providing for communication between the central government in Paris and local communities. Philip decided that each province would retain its own institutions and laws. But royal agents, called baillis in the north and seneschals in the south, were sent from Paris into the provinces as the king's official representatives with authority to act for him. Often middle-class lawyers, these men possessed full judicial, financial, and military jurisdiction in their districts. The baillis and seneschals were appointed by, paid by, and responsible to the king. Unlike the English sheriffs, they were never natives of the provinces to which they were assigned, and they could not own land there. This policy reflected the fundamental principle of French administration that royal interests superseded local interests.

While English governmental administration was based on the services of unpaid local officials, France was administered by a professional royal bureaucracy. Bureaucracy was the cornerstone of French royal government. As new territories came under royal control, the bureaucracy expanded. So great was the variety of customs, laws, and provincial institutions that any attempt to impose uniformity would have touched off a rebellion. The French system was characterized by diversity at the local level and centralization at the top. Although it sometimes fell into disrepair, the basic system that Philip Augustus created worked so well that it survived until the Revolution of 1789.

*THE HOLY ROMAN EMPIRE* The political problems of the Holy Roman Empire differed considerably from those of France and England. The eleventh-century investiture controversy between the German emperor and the Roman papacy had left the empire shattered and divided (pages 308–310). In the twelfth and thirteenth centuries, the Holy Roman Empire was split into hundreds of indepen-

ENGLAND

ENGLISH CHANNEL

Bruges
Ghent
Calais
Ypres
FLANDERS
ARTOIS
✕ Bouvines 1214
Meuse
Arras
VERMANDOIS
Amiens
Rouen
Soissons
Reims
NORMANDY
CHAMPAGNE
HOLY
Paris
Seine
ILE-DE-FRANCE
(ROYAL DOMAIN)
Troyes
Chartres
MAINE
BLOIS
Orléans
ROMAN
BRITTANY
Loire
BURGUNDY
Nantes
ANJOU
Tours
TOURAINE
Bourges
POITOU
BOURBON
Poitiers
Cluny
BAY
Clermont
EMPIRE
OF
Lyons
BISCAY
AQUITAINE
Bordeaux
Garonne
Rhône
Avignon
TOULOUSE
PROVENCE
GASCONY
Toulouse
Montpellier
Marseilles
MEDITERRANEAN   SEA

| | Crown lands in 1180 |
| | Added by Philip Augustus, 1180–1223 |
| | Added 1223–1270 |
| | Added 1270–1314 |
| | Royal fiefs |
| ✕ | Major battle |

0   50   100 Km.
0   50   100 Mi.

SPAIN

LANGUEDOC

MAP 11.1   THE GROWTH OF THE KINGDOM OF
FRANCE   *Some scholars believe that Philip II received the title "Augustus" (from a Latin word
meaning "to increase"), because he vastly expanded
the territories of the kingdom of France. In spite of
differences, what similarities among peoples made expansion from Paris likely?*

dent provinces, principalities, bishoprics, duchies, and free cities. Princes, dukes, and local rulers held power over small areas.

There were several barriers to the development of a strong central government. The German rulers lacked a strong royal domain, like that of the French kings, to use as a source of revenue and a base from which to expand royal power. No accepted principle of succession to the throne existed, and as a result the death of the emperor was often followed by disputes, civil war, and anarchy. Moreover, German rulers were continually attracted south by the wealth of the northern Italian cities or by dreams of restoring the imperial glory of Charlemagne. Time after time the German emperors got involved in Italian affairs, and in turn the papacy, fearful of a strong German power in northern Italy, interfered in German affairs. German princes took bribes from whichever authority — the emperor or the pope — best supported their own particular ambitions. Consequently, the centralization of authority in Germany, in contrast to that in France and England, occurred very slowly. In medieval Germany, power remained in the hands of numerous princes instead of the emperor.

Through most of the first half of the twelfth century, civil war wracked the Holy Roman Empire as the emperors tried to strengthen their position by playing off baronial factions against one another. When the emperor Conrad III died in 1152, the resulting anarchy was so terrible that the electors — the seven princes responsible for choosing the emperor — decided that the only alternative to continued chaos was the selection of a strong ruler. They chose Frederick Barbarossa of the house of Hohenstaufen.

Frederick Barbarossa (1152–1190) tried valiantly to unify the empire. Just as the French rulers branched out from their compact do-main in the Ile-de-France, Frederick tried to use his family duchy of Swabia in southwestern Germany as a power base (see Map 11.2). Just as William the Conqueror had done, Frederick required all vassals in Swabia to take an oath of allegiance to him as emperor, no matter who their immediate lord might be. He appointed officials called ministeriales, men of low social origin, to exercise the full imperial authority over administrative districts of Swabia. Ministeriales linked the emperor and local communities.

Outside of Swabia, Frederick tried to make feudalism work as a system of government. The princes throughout the empire exercised tremendous power, and Frederick tried to subordinate them to the authority of the royal government. He made alliances with the great lay princes in which they acknowledged that their lands were fiefs of the emperor, and he in turn recognized their military and political jurisdiction over their territories. Frederick also compelled the great churchmen to become his vassals, so that when they died he could control their estates. Frederick solved the problem of chronic violence by making the princes responsible for the establishment of peace within their territories. At a great assembly held at Roncaglia in 1158, private warfare was forbidden and severe penalties were laid down for violations of the peace.

Unfortunately Frederick Barbarossa did not concentrate his efforts and resources in one area. He too became embroiled in the affairs of Italy. He too wanted to restore the Holy Roman Empire, joining Germany and Italy. In the eleventh and twelfth centuries, the northern Italian cities had grown rich on trade, and Frederick believed that if he could gain the imperial crown, he could cash in on Italian wealth. Frederick saw that although the Italian cities were populous and militarily strong, they lacked stable governments and

HOLSTEIN
• Lübeck
POMERANIA
BRANDENBURG
• Bremen
• Brandenburg
FRISIA
SAXONY
LUSATIA
POLAND
• Goslar
• Cologne
THURINGIA
MEISSEN
LOWER
LORRAINE
• Aix-la-Chapelle
FRANCONIA
• Prague
BOHEMIA
• Trier
• Mainz
UPPER
• Worms
MORAVIA
LORRAINE
• Verdun
AUSTRIA
• Toul
BAVARIA
FRANCE
• Augsburg
SWABIA
• Salzburg
STYRIA
• Besançon
CARINTHIA
BURGUNDY—ARLES
HUNGARY
CARNIOLA
VERONA
LOMBARDY
✕ Legnano 1176
• Milan
• Venice
• Pavia
• Roncaglia
• Avignon
PROVENCE
• Florence
• Arles
PAPAL
REPUBLIC OF VENICE
• Marseilles
TUSCANY
STATES
• Rome
APULIA
KINGDOM OF SICILY
• Naples
• Salerno
• Messina
• Palermo
SICILY

✕ Major battle
Holy Roman Empire, ca 1200
Kingdom of Sicily
Republic of Venice

Scale:
0  100  200 Km.
0  100  200 Mi.

MAP 11.2 THE HOLY ROMAN EMPIRE,

were often involved in struggles with one another. The German emperor mistakenly believed that moneygrubbing infantrymen could not stand up against his tough aristocratic knights. He did not realize that the merchant oligarchs who ran the city governments of Milan, Venice, and Florence considered themselves just as noble as he; they prized their independence and were determined to fight for it. Frederick's desire to control the papacy and to end papal claims to suzerainty over the empire also attracted him southward. He did not know that the popes feared a strong German state in northern Italy even more than they feared the rich and (the popes suspected) slightly heretical Italian cities.

Between 1154 and 1188, Frederick made six expeditions into Italy. His scorched-earth policy was successful at first, making for significant conquests in the north. The brutality of his methods, however, provoked revolts, and the Italian cities formed an alliance with the papacy. In 1176, Frederick suffered a catastrophic defeat at Legnano (see Map 11.2). This battle marked the first time a feudal cavalry of armed knights was decisively defeated by bourgeois infantrymen. Frederick was forced to recognize the independence of the northern Italian cities. Germany and Italy remained separate countries and followed separate courses of development.

Frederick Barbarossa's Italian ventures contributed nothing to the unification of the German states. Because the empire lacked a stable bureaucratic system of government, his presence was essential for the maintenance of peace. In Frederick's absences, the fires of independence and disorder spread. The princes

and magnates consolidated their power, and the unsupervised royal ministeriales gained considerable independence. By 1187, Frederick had to accept again the reality of private warfare. The power of the princes grew at the expense of a centralized monarchy.

## FINANCE

As medieval rulers expanded their territories and extended their authority, they required more officials, larger armies, and more and more money. Officials and armies had to be paid, and kings had to find ways to raise revenue.

In England, William the Conqueror's son Henry I (1100–1135) established a bureau of finance called the Exchequer (for the checkered cloth at which his officials collected and audited royal accounts). Henry's income came from a variety of sources: from taxes paid by peasants living on the king's estates; from the Danegeld, an old tax originally levied to pay tribute to the Danes; from the *dona,* an annual gift from the church; from money paid to the Crown for settling disputes; and from fines paid by people found guilty of crimes. Henry also received income because of his position as feudal lord. If, for example, one of his vassals died and the son wished to inherit the father's properties, the heir had to pay Henry a relief tax. The sheriff in each county was responsible for collecting all these sums and for paying them twice a year to the king's Exchequer. Henry, like other medieval kings, made no distinction between his private income and state revenues.

An accurate record of expenditures and income is needed to insure a state's solvency. Henry assigned a few of the barons and bishops at his court to keep careful records of the monies paid into and out of the royal treasury. These financial officials, called barons of the Exchequer, gradually developed into a professional organization with its own rules, procedures, and esprit de corps. The Exchequer, which always sat in London, became the first institution of the governmental bureaucracy of England. Because of its work, an almost complete series of financial records for England dating back to 1130 survives; after 1154 the series is complete.

The development of royal financial agencies in most continental countries lagged behind the English Exchequer. Twelfth-century French rulers derived their income from their royal estates in the Ile-de-France. As Philip Augustus and his successors added provinces to the royal domain, the need for money became increasingly acute. Philip made the baillis and seneschals responsible for collecting taxes in their districts. This income came primarily from fines and confiscations imposed by the courts. Three times a year the baillis and seneschals reported to the king's court with the monies they had collected.

In the thirteenth century, French rulers found additional sources of revenue. They acquired some income from the church and some from people living in the towns. Townspeople paid tallage – a tax arbitrarily laid by the king. In all parts of the country feudal vassals owed military service to the king when he called for it. Louis IX converted this military obligation into a cash payment, called host tallage, and thus increased his revenues. Philip Augustus, Louis VIII, and Louis IX all taxed the Jews mercilessly.

Medieval people believed that a good king lived on the income of his own land and taxed only in time of a grave emergency – that is, a just war. Because the church, and not the state, performed what twentieth-century people call social services, such as education and care of the sick, the aged, and orphaned children, there was no ordinary need for the government to tax. Taxation meant war

financing. The French monarchy could not continually justify taxing the people on the grounds of the needs of war. Thus the French kings were slow to develop an efficient bureau of finance. French localism – in contrast to England's early unification – also retarded the growth of a central financial agency. Not until the fourteenth century, as a result of the demands of the Hundred Years' War, did a state financial bureau emerge – the Chamber of Accounts.

The one European government other than England that developed an efficient financial bureaucracy in the High Middle Ages was the kingdom of Sicily. Sicily is a good example of how strong government could be built on a feudal base by determined rulers.

Like England, Sicily had come under Norman domination. Between 1061 and 1091, a bold Norman knight, Roger de Hauteville, with a small band of mercenaries had defeated the Muslims and Greeks who controlled the island. Like William the Conqueror in England, Robert introduced Norman feudalism in Sicily and made it work as a system of government. Roger distributed scattered fiefs to his followers, so that no vassal had a centralized power base. He took an inquest of royal properties and rights, and he forbade private warfare. Roger adapted his Norman experience to Arabic and Greek governmental practices. Thus he retained the Muslims' main financial agency, the *diwan,* a sophisticated bureau for recordkeeping.

His son and heir, Count Roger II (1130–1154), continued the process of state building. He subdued the province of Apulia in southern Italy, united it with his Sicilian lands, and had himself crowned king of Sicily (1130–1154). Roger II organized the economy in the interests of the state; for example, the Crown secured a monopoly on the sale of salt and lumber. With the revenues thus acquired, Roger hired mercenary troops. His judiciary welcomed appeals from local communities. The army, the judiciary, and the *diwan* were staffed by Greeks and Muslims as well as Normans.

Under Frederick II Hohenstaufen (1212–1250), grandson of Roger II, Sicily underwent remarkable development. Frederick, also the grandson and heir of Frederick Barbarossa, was a brilliant legislator and administrator, and he constructed the most advanced bureaucratic state in medieval Europe. The institutions of the kingdom of Sicily were harnessed in the service of the state as represented by the king.

Frederick banned private warfare, and he placed all castles and towers under royal administration. Frederick also replaced town officials with royal governors. In 1231, he published the Constitutions of Melfi, a collection of laws that vastly enhanced royal authority. Both feudal and ecclesiastical courts were subordinated to the king's courts. Each year royal judges visited all parts of the kingdom, and the supreme court at Capua heard appeals from all lesser courts. Thus churchmen accused of crimes were tried in the royal courts. Royal control of the nobility, of the towns, and of the judicial system added up to great centralization, which required a professional bureaucracy and sound state financing.

In 1224, Frederick founded the University of Naples to train clerks and officials for his bureaucracy. University-educated administrators and lawyers emphasized the stiff principles of Roman law, such as the Justinian maxim that "what pleases the prince has the force of law." Frederick's financial experts regulated agriculture, public works, and even business. His customs service carefully supervised all imports and exports, collecting taxes for the Crown on all products. Royal revenues increased tremendously. Moreover, Frederick strictly regulated the currency and forbade the export of gold and silver bullion.

GERMAN BRONZE BIRD   *Dating from the twelfth or thirteenth century, this may possibly be the eagle that surmounted the staff of the Emperor Frederick II, or possibly a falcon representing Frederick's interest in falconry, on which he was a great authority. The eagle symbolizes the royal virtues of justice and generosity, whereas the falcon was the favorite aristocratic hunting bird. (Metropolitan Museum of Art, The Cloisters Collection, 1947)*

Finally, Frederick secured the tacit consent of his people to regular taxation. This was an incredible achievement in the Middle Ages, when most people believed that taxes should be levied only in time of grave emergency, the just war. Frederick defined emergency broadly. For much of his reign he was involved in a bitter dispute with the papacy. Churchmen hardly considered the emperor's wars with the popes as just, but Frederick's position was so strong that he could ignore criticism and levy taxes.

Frederick's contemporaries called him "The Transformer of the World." He certainly transformed the kingdom of Sicily, creating a state that was in many ways modern. But Frederick was highly ambitious: he wanted to control the entire peninsula of Italy. The popes, fearful of being encircled, waged a long conflict to prevent that. The kingdom of Sicily required constant attention, and Frederick's absences took their toll. Shortly after he died, the unsupervised bureaucracy he had built fell to pieces. The pope, claiming feudal suzerainty over Sicily, called in a French prince to rule.

Frederick showed little interest in Germany. He concentrated his attention on Sicily rather than the historic Hohenstaufen stronghold in Swabia, and the focus of imperial concerns shifted southward. When he visited the empire, in the expectation of securing German support for his Italian policy, he made sweeping concessions to the princes, bishops, duchies, and free cities. In 1220, for example, he exempted German churchmen from taxation and from the jurisdiction of imperial authorities. In 1231, he gave lay princes the same exemptions and even threw in the right to coin money. Frederick gave away so much that imperial authority was seriously weakened. In the later Middle Ages, lay and ecclesiastical princes held sway in the Holy Roman Empire. The centralizing efforts of Frederick Barbarossa were destroyed by his grandson Frederick II.

## LAW AND JUSTICE

Throughout Europe, the form and application of laws depended upon local and provincial custom and practice. In the twelfth and thirteenth centuries the law was a hodgepodge of Germanic customs, feudal rights, and provincial practices. Kings wanted to blend these elements into a uniform system of rules acceptable and applicable to all their peoples. In France and England kings successfully contributed to the development of national states through the administration of their laws. Legal developments in continental countries like France were strongly influenced by Roman law, while England slowly built up a unique unwritten common law.

The French king Louis IX was famous in his time for his concern for justice. Each French province, even after being made part of the kingdom of France, retained its unique laws and procedures, but Louis IX created a royal judicial system. He established the Parlement of Paris, a kind of supreme court that welcomed appeals from local administrators and from the courts of feudal lords throughout France. By the very act of appealing the decisions of feudal courts to the Parlement of Paris, French people in far-flung provinces were recognizing the superiority of royal justice. By reviewing the decisions of baronial courts, the Parlement of Paris dispensed the king's justice to all French people.

Louis sent royal judges to all parts of the country to check up on the work of the baillis and seneschals and to hear complaints of injustice. He was the first French monarch to publish laws for the entire kingdom. The Parlement of Paris registered (or announced) these laws, which forbade private warfare, judicial duels, gambling, blaspheming, and prostitution. Louis sought to identify justice with the kingship, and gradually royal justice touched all parts of the kingdom.

Under Henry II (1154–1189), England developed and extended a common law, a law common to and accepted by the entire country. No other country in medieval Europe did so. Henry I had occasionally sent out circuit judges (royal officials who traveled a given circuit or district) to hear civil and criminal cases. Henry II made this way of extending royal justice an annual practice. Every year royal judges left London and set up court in the counties. Wherever the king's judges sat, there sat the king's court. Slowly, the king's court gained jurisdiction over all property disputes and criminal actions.

Henry made an important innovation in civil or property law. Disputes over land and movable property had caused a great deal of violence. Henry established a procedure whereby a person who felt unjustly deprived of possessions could seek a remedy in the royal court. The aggrieved person applied to the sheriff for help. The sheriff summoned a jury of local people before the king's judges, and there in the royal court the jury answered questions about rightful possession. On the basis of the jury's verdict, the disputed property was awarded. Thus, rather than attempting to get property back by force, English people had recourse to the king's court.

Henry also improved procedure in criminal justice. In 1166, he instructed the sheriffs to summon local juries to conduct inquests and draw up lists of known or suspected criminals. These lists, sworn to by the juries, were to be presented to the royal judges when they arrived in the community. This accusing jury is the ancestor of the modern grand jury.

An accused person formally charged with a crime did *not* undergo trial by jury. He or she was tried by ordeal. The accused was tied hand and foot and dropped in a lake or river. People believed that water was a pure substance and would reject anything foul or unclean. Thus a person who sank was considered innocent, and a person who floated was considered guilty. Trial by ordeal was a ritual that appealed to the supernatural for judgment. God determined innocence or guilt, and thus a priest had to be present to bless the water.

Henry II and others considered this ancient Germanic method irrational and a poor way of determining results, but they knew no alternative. In 1215, the Fourth Lateran Council of the church forbade the presence of priests at trials by ordeal and thus effectively abolished them. Gradually, in the course of the thirteenth century, the king's judges adopted the practice of calling upon twelve people (other than the accusing jury) to consider the question of innocence or guilt. This became the jury of trial, but it was very slowly accepted because medieval people had more confidence in the judgment of God than in that of twelve ordinary people.

Henry's innovations in civil procedure, the use of the accusing jury, and regular visits by circuit judges marked a decisive step forward. As the judges advanced the notion that any serious crime belonged under the king's jurisdiction, crime was no longer considered a violent act against an individual to be avenged by the victim and his or her family. Criminal acts became deeds against the state, or against the king as the embodiment of the state.

One aspect of Henry's judicial reforms encountered stiff resistance from an unexpected source: a friend and former chief adviser whom Henry had made archbishop of Canterbury – Thomas Becket. Henry selected Becket as archbishop in 1162 because he believed he could depend on Becket's support. But when Henry wanted to bring all persons in the kingdom under the jurisdiction of the royal courts, Thomas Becket's opposition led to another dramatic conflict between temporal and spiritual powers.

In the 1160s, many literate people accused of crimes claimed "benefit of clergy," even though they were not clerics and often had no intention of being ordained. "Benefit of clergy" gave the accused the right to be tried in church courts, which meted out mild punishments. A person found guilty in the king's court might suffer mutilation – loss of a hand

THE MARTYRDOM OF THOMAS BECKET
*Becket's murder evoked many illustrations in the thirteenth century. This illumination faithfully follows the manuscript sources: while one knight held off the archbishop's defenders, the other three attacked. With a powerful stroke, the crown of his head was slashed off and his brains scattered on the cathedral floor. (Walters Art Gallery)*

or foot, or castration – or even death. Ecclesiastical punishments tended to be an obligation to say certain prayers or to make a pilgrimage. In 1164 Henry II insisted that everyone, including clerics, be subject to the royal courts.

Becket vigorously protested that church law required clerics to be subject to church courts. When he proceeded to excommunicate one of the king's vassals, the issue became more complicated. Because no one was supposed to have any contact with an excommunicated person, it appeared that the church could arbitrarily deprive the king of necessary military forces. The disagreement between Henry II and Becket dragged on for years. Becket maintained that as archbishop he had to defend the rights of the church. Henry insisted that the Crown should have full jurisdiction over all its subjects. The king grew increasingly bitter that his appointment of Becket had proved to be such a mistake. Late in December 1170, in a fit of rage, Henry expressed the wish that Becket be destroyed. Four knights took the king at his word, went to Canterbury, and killed the archbishop in his cathedral as he was leaving evening services.

What Thomas Becket could not achieve in life, he gained in death. The assassination of an archbishop in his own church during the Christmas season turned public opinion in England and throughout western Europe against the king. Within months miracles were recorded at Becket's tomb, and in a short time Canterbury Cathedral became a major pilgrimage and tourist site. Henry had to back down. He did public penance for the murder and gave up his attempts to bring clerics under the authority of the royal court.

Henry II's sons Richard I ("the Lion-Hearted") (1189-1199) and John (1199-1216) lacked their father's interest in the work of government. Handsome, athletic, and with an international reputation for military prowess, Richard looked upon England as a source of revenue for his military enterprises. Soon after his accession, he departed on crusade to the Holy Land. During his reign he spent only six months in England, and the government was run by ministers trained under Henry II.

Unlike Richard, King John was incompetent as a soldier and unnecessarily suspicious that the barons were plotting against him. His basic problems, however, were financial. King John inherited a heavy debt from his father and brother. The country had paid dearly for Richard's crusading zeal. Returning from the Holy Land, Richard had been captured, and England had paid an enormous ransom to secure his release. In 1204, John lost the rich province of Normandy to Philip Augustus of France and then spent the rest of his reign trying to get it back. To finance that war, he got in deeper and deeper trouble with his barons. John squeezed as much money as possible from his position as feudal lord. He took scutage, a tax paid by his vassals in lieu of performing knight service. Each time John collected it, he increased the amount due. He forced widows to pay exorbitant fines to avoid unwanted marriages. He sold young girls who were his feudal wards to the highest bidder. These actions antagonized the nobility.

John also alienated the church and the English townspeople. He rejected Pope Innocent III's nominee to the see of Canterbury. And he infuriated the burghers of the towns by extorting money from them and threatening to revoke their charters of self-government.

All the money John raised did not bring him success. In July 1214, John's coalition of Flemish, German, and English cavalry suffered a severe defeat at the hands of Philip Augustus of France at Bouvines in Flanders. This battle ended English hopes for the recovery of territories from France. The battle of Bouvines also strengthened the barons' opposition to John. On top of his heavy taxation, his ineptitude as a soldier in a society that idealized military glory was the final straw. Rebellion begun by a few hotheaded northern barons eventually grew to involve a large number of the English nobility, including the archbishop of Canterbury and the earl of Pembroke, the leading ecclesiastical and lay

peers. After lengthy negotiations in the spring of 1215, John met the barons at Runnymede, a meadow along the Thames River. There he was forced to sign the treaty called Magna Carta, which became the cornerstone of English justice and law.

Magna Carta signifies the principle that the king and the government shall be under the law, that everyone including the king must obey the law. It contains clauses to protect the rights and property of all English people. It defends the interests of widows, orphans, townspeople, and freemen. Some clauses contain the germ of the idea of due process of law and of the right to a fair and speedy trial. Every English king in the Middle Ages reissued Magna Carta as evidence of his promise to observe the law. Because it was reissued frequently, and because later generations appealed to Magna Carta as a written statement of English liberties, it acquired an almost sacred importance as a guarantee of law and justice.

In the thirteenth century, the judicial precedents set under Henry II slowly evolved into permanent institutions. The king's judges asserted the royal authority and applied the same principles everywhere in the country. English people found the king's justice more rational and more evenhanded than the justice meted out in the baronial courts. The royal courts gained popularity, and the baronial courts lost rights and business. Respect for the king's law and the king's courts promoted loyalty to the Crown. By the time of Henry's great-grandson, Edward I (1272–1307), one law, the common law, operated all over England.

In the later Middle Ages, the English common law developed features that differed strikingly from the system of Roman law operative in continental Europe. The common law relied on precedents: a decision in an important case served as an authority for deciding similar cases. By contrast, continental judges, trained in Roman law, used the fixed legal maxims of the Justinian Code (pages 239–240) to decide their cases. Thus the common-law system evolved according to the changing experience of the people, while the Roman-law tradition tended toward an absolutist approach. In countries influenced by the common law, such as Canada and the United States, the court is open to the public; in countries with Roman-law traditions, such as France and the Latin American nations, courts need not be public. Under the common law, the accused in criminal cases has a right to access to the evidence against him; under the other system, he need not. The common law requires that judges be strictly impartial; in the Roman-law system judges interfere freely in many activities in their court rooms. Finally, whereas torture is foreign to the common-law tradition, it was once widely used in the Roman legal system.

The extension of royal law and justice led to a phenomenal amount of legal codification all over Europe. Governments wanted the law written down in an orderly and systematic fashion. The English judge Henry of Bracton (d. 1268) wrote a *Treatise on the Laws and Customs of England,* the French jurist Philippe de Beaumanoir (1250–1296) produced the *Customs of Beauvais,* and an anonymous German scholar compiled the *Sachsenspiegel* (1253). Legal texts and encyclopedias exalted royal authority, consolidated royal power, and emphasized political and social uniformity. The pressure for social conformity in turn contributed to a rising hostility toward minorities, Jews, and homosexuals.

Early Christians, as we have seen (page 231), displayed no special prejudice against homosexuals. While some of the Church Fathers, such as St. John Chrysostom (347–407), preached against them, a general indifference to homosexual activity prevailed throughout the early Middle Ages. In the early twelfth century a large homosexual literature circulated. Publicly known homosexuals such as Ralph, archbishop of Tours (1087–1118), and King Richard the Lion-Hearted of England held high ecclesiastical and political positions.

Beginning in the late twelfth century, however, a profound change occurred in public attitudes toward homosexual behavior. Why, if prejudice against homosexuals cannot be traced to early Christianity? Scholars have only begun to investigate this question, and the root cause of intolerance rarely yields to easy analysis. In the thirteenth century a fear of foreigners, especially Muslims, became associated with the crusading movement. Heretics were the most despised minority in an age that stressed religious and social uniformity. The notion spread that both Muslims and heretics, the great foreign and domestic menaces to the security of Christian Europe, were inclined to homosexual relations. Finally, the systematization of law and the rising strength of the state made any religious or sexual distinctiveness increasingly unacceptable. Whatever the precise cause, "between 1250 and 1300 homosexual activity passed from being completely legal in most of Europe to incurring the death penalty in all but a few legal compilations."[2] Spain, France, England, Norway, and several Italian city-states adopted laws condemning homosexual acts. Most of these laws remained on statute books until the twentieth century.

## MEDIEVAL UNIVERSITIES

Just as the first strong secular states emerged in the thirteenth century, so did the first universities. This was no coincidence. The new bureaucratic states needed educated administrators, and universities were a response to this need. The word *university* derives from the Latin *universitas*, meaning "corporation" or "guild." Medieval universities were educational guilds that produced educated and trained individuals. They were also an expression of the tremendous vitality and creativity of the High Middle Ages. Their organization, methods of instruction, and goals continue to influence institutionalized learning in the Western world.

## ORIGINS

In the early Middle Ages, anyone who received any education got it from a priest. Priests instructed the clever boys on the manor in the Latin words of the mass, and taught them the rudiments of reading and writing. Few boys acquired elementary literacy, however, and girls did not even obtain that. The peasant who wished to send his son to school had to secure the permission of his lord, because the result of formal schooling tended to be a career in the church or some trade. If a young man were to pursue either profession, he had to leave the manor and gain free status. Because the lord stood to lose the services of educated peasants, he carefully limited the number of serfs who were sent to school.

Few schools were available anyway. Society was organized for war and defense and gave slight support to education. By the late eleventh century, however, social conditions had markedly improved. There was greater political stability, and favorable economic conditions had advanced many people beyond the level of bare subsistence. The curious and able felt the lack of schools and teachers.

Since the time of the Carolingian Empire, monasteries and cathedral schools had offered the only formal instruction available. The monasteries were geared to religious concerns, and the monastic curriculum consisted of studying the Scriptures and the writings of the church fathers. Monasteries wished to maintain an atmosphere of seclusion and silence and were unwilling to accept large numbers of noisy lay students. In contrast, schools attached to cathedrals and run by the bishop and his clergy were frequently situated in bustling cities, and in Italian cities like Bologna wealthy businessmen had established municipal schools. Cities inhabited by peoples of many backgrounds and "nationalities" stimulated the growth and exchange of ideas. In the course of the twelfth century, cathedral schools in France and municipal schools in Italy developed into universities (see Map 11.3).

The school at Chartres Cathedral in France became famous for its studies of the Latin classics and for the broad literary interests it fostered in its students. The most famous graduate of Chartres was the Englishman John of Salisbury (d. 1180), who wrote *The Statesman's Book,* an important treatise on the corrupting effects of political power. But Chartres, situated in the center of rich farmland remote from the currents of commercial traffic and intellectual ideas, did not develop into a university. The first European universities appeared in Italy, at Bologna in the north and Salerno in the south.

The growth of the University of Bologna coincided with a revival of interest in Roman law. The study of Roman law as embodied in the Justinian Code had never completely died out in the West, but this sudden burst of interest seems to have been inspired by Irnerius (d. 1125), a great teacher at Bologna. His fame attracted students from all over Europe. Irnerius not only explained the Roman law of the Justinian Code, he applied it to difficult practical situations. An important school of civil law was founded at Montpellier in

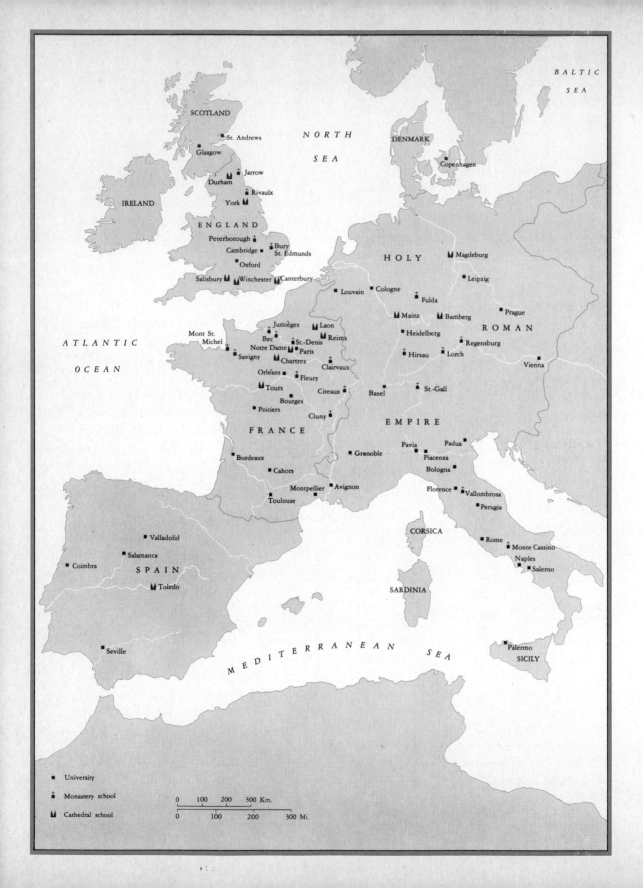

BALTIC
SEA

SCOTLAND
■ St. Andrews
Glasgow ■
NORTH
SEA
DENMARK
■ Copenhagen
Jarrow ✝
Durham ✝
■ Rivaulx
York ♜
IRELAND
ENGLAND
HOLY
♜ Magdeburg
Peterborough ✝
Cambridge ■
Bury ✝
St. Edmunds
■ Oxford
Leipzig
Louvain ■
Cologne ✝
Salisbury ♜ Winchester ♜
Canterbury ♜
Fulda ✝
Mainz ■
Bamberg ♜
Prague
Mont St.
Michel ✝
Jumièges ✝
Laon ■
ROMAN
Bec ■
St.-Denis ✝
Reims ✝
Heidelberg ■
Regensburg ✝
Notre Dame ♜
Paris ■
Hirsau ✝
Lorch ✝
Savigny ✝
Chartres ♜
Clairvaux ✝
Vienna ■
ATLANTIC
Orléans ■
Fleury ✝
OCEAN
Tours ♜
Cîteaux ✝
St.-Gall ✝
Bourges ■
Basel ■
Poitiers ■
Cluny ✝
EMPIRE
FRANCE
Pavia ■
Padua ■
Grenoble ■
Piacenza ■
Bordeaux ■
Cahors ■
Bologna ■
Florence ■
Vallombrosa ✝
Montpellier ■
Avignon ■
Toulouse ■
Perugia ■
CORSICA
Valladolid ■
Rome ■
Monte Cassino ✝
Salamanca ■
Naples ■
Coimbra ■
SPAIN
SARDINIA
Salerno ■
Toledo ♜
Seville ■
Palermo ■
SICILY
MEDITERRANEAN   SEA

■ University
✝ Monastery school
♜ Cathedral school

0   100   200   300 Km.
0   100   200   300 Mi.

MAP 11.3   INTELLECTUAL CENTERS OF MEDIE-
VAL EUROPE   *Universities obviously provided more
sophisticated instruction than did monastic and cathedral schools. What other factors distinguish the
three kinds of intellectual centers?*

southern France, but Bologna remained the greatest law school throughout the Middle Ages.

At Salerno, interest in medicine had persisted for centuries. Greek and Muslim physicians there had studied the use of herbs as cures for disease, and they had experimented with surgery. The twelfth century ushered in a new interest in Greek medical texts and in the work of Arab and Greek doctors. Students of medicine poured into Salerno, and their study soon attracted royal attention. In 1140, when King Roger II of Sicily took the practice of medicine under royal control, his ordinance stated:

*Who, from now on, wishes to practice medicine, has to present himself before our officials and examiners, in order to pass their judgment. Should he be bold enough to disregard this, he will be punished by imprisonment and confiscation of his entire property. In this way we are taking care that our subjects are not endangered by the inexperience of the physicians.*

*Nobody dare practice medicine unless he has been found fit by the convention of the Salernitan masters.*[3]

King Roger sought to protect the people of the kingdom of Sicily from incompetent doctors.

In the first decades of the twelfth century, students converged upon Paris. They crowded into the cathedral school of Notre Dame and spilled over into the area later called the Latin Quarter – whose name probably reflects the Italian origin of many of the students attracted to Paris by the surge of interest in the classics, logic, and theology. The cathedral

school's international reputation had already drawn to Paris scholars from all over Europe, one of the most famous of whom was Peter Abélard.

The son of a minor Breton knight, Peter Abélard (1079-1142) studied in Paris, quickly absorbed a large amount of material, and set himself up as a teacher. Abélard was fascinated by logic, which he believed could be used to solve most problems. He had a brilliant mind and, although orthodox in his philosophical teaching, appeared to challenge ecclesiastical authorities. His book *Sic et Non (Yes and No)* was a list of apparently contradictory propositions drawn from the Bible and the writings of the church fathers. One such proposition, for example, stated that sin is pleasing to God and is not pleasing to God. Abélard used a method of systematic doubting in his writing and teaching. As he put it in the preface to *Sic et Non,* "By doubting we come to questioning, and by questioning we perceive the truth." While other scholars merely asserted theological principles, Abélard discussed and analyzed them. Through reasoning he even tried to describe the attributes of the three persons of the Trinity, the central mystery of the Christian faith. Abélard was severely censured by a church council, but his cleverness, boldness, and imagination made him highly popular with students.

The influx of students eager for learning, together with dedicated and imaginative teachers, created the atmosphere in which universities grew. In northern Europe – at Paris and later at Oxford and Cambridge in England – associations or guilds of professors organized universities. They established the curriculum, set the length of time for study, and determined the form and content of examinations. In 1200, King Philip Augustus officially recognized the University of Paris, and in 1208 Pope Innocent III, who had studied there, designated the community of students and scholars a *universitas.*

## INSTRUCTION AND CURRICULUM

University faculties grouped themselves according to academic disciplines, called schools – law, medicine, philosophy, and theology. The professors, known as schoolmen or scholastics, developed a method of thinking, reasoning, and writing in which questions were raised and authorities cited on both sides of the question. The goal of the scholastic method was to arrive at definitive answers and to provide a rational explanation for what was believed on faith. Schoolmen held that reason and faith constitute two harmonious realms in which the truths of faith and reason complement each other. The scholastic approach rested upon the recovery of classical philosophical texts.

Ancient Greek and Arabic texts had entered Europe in the early twelfth century, primarily through Toledo in Muslim Spain. Thirteenth-century philosophers relied on Latin translations of these texts, especially those of Aristotle. Aristotle had stressed direct observation of nature, as well as the principles that theory must follow fact and that knowledge of a thing requires an explanation of its causes. The schoolmen reinterpreted Aristotelian texts in a Christian sense.

In exploration of the natural world, Aristotle's axioms were not precisely followed. Medieval scientists argued from authority, such as the Bible, the Justinian Code, or an ancient scientific treatise, rather than from direct observation and experimentation, as modern scientists do. Thus, the conclusions of medieval scientists were often wrong. Nevertheless, natural science gradually emerged as a discipline distinct from philosophy. Scholastics made important contributions to the advancement of knowledge. They preserved the Greek and Arabic texts that contained the body of ancient scientific knowledge, which would otherwise have been lost. And, in asking questions about nature and the universe, scholastics laid the foundations for later scientific work.

Many of the problems that scholastic philosophers raised dealt with theological issues. They addressed, for example, the question that interested all Christians, educated and uneducated: how is a person saved? St. Augustine's thesis – that, as the result of Adam's fall, human beings have a propensity to sin – had become a central feature of medieval church doctrine. The church taught that it possessed the means to forgive the sinful: through grace conveyed through the sacraments. However, although grace provided a predisposition to salvation, the scholastics held that one must also *decide* to use the grace received. In other words, a person must use his or her reason to advance to God.

Thirteenth-century scholastics devoted an enormous amount of time to collecting and organizing knowledge on all topics. These collections were published as *summa,* or reference books. There were summa on law, philosophy, vegetation, animal life, theology. Saint Thomas Aquinas (1225-1274), a professor of theology at Paris, produced the most famous collection, the *Summa Theologica,* which deals with a vast number of theological questions.

Aquinas drew an important distinction between faith and reason. He maintained that, although reason can demonstrate many basic Christian principles such as the existence of God, other fundamental teachings such as the Trinity and original sin cannot be proven by logic. That reason cannot establish them does not, however, mean they are contrary to reason. People can gain an understanding of such

# ART: A MIRROR OF SOCIETY

Art reveals the interests and values of society and frequently gives intimate and unique glimpses of how people actually lived. In portraits and statues, whether of saints, generals, philosophers, popes, poets, or merchants, it preserves the memory and fame of men and women who shaped society. In paintings, drawings, and carvings, it also shows how people worked, played, relaxed, suffered, and triumphed. Art, therefore, is extremely useful to the historian, especially for periods such as the ancient and medieval, when written records are scarce. Every work of art and every part of it has meaning and has something of its own to say.

Ancient and medieval art, apart from splendid public buildings, temples, cathedrals, and monasteries, was created by and for an aristocratic elite. It reflected the tastes and the interests of the aristocracy. Only a wealthy Greek could afford to buy a richly painted vase

or wine cup. Only a wealthy Roman family could decorate the floors of their house with dazzling mosaics. The Royal Standard of Ur, below, shows aspects of Sumerian society in peacetime. The upper band of the standard, a triangular box on a pole used on ceremonial occasions, depicts a royal banquet, with the king and his nobles drinking and listening to music. In the lower band herdsmen lead animals. (By courtesy of the British Museum.) Art was also created primarily for the aristocracy in the Middle Ages, when upper-class people commissioned mosaics, illuminated manuscripts, carved and jewelled objects, and miniatures and paintings. Furthermore, in the Middle Ages the primary function of art was to teach. Most medieval artists were clerics or monks, their subject matter was religious, and consequently religious themes pervade their art.

Art also manifests the changes and continuity of European life. Scenes of agricultural work and commerce were popular both in antiquity and in the Middle Ages. As values changed in Europe, so did major artistic themes. The religious art of the early Middle Ages replaced the sensuous pagan art of antiquity. In turn, the art of the later Middle Ages, a time which saw the emergence of a rich urban middle class, increasingly displayed secular interests. Europeans of the sixteenth and seventeenth centuries remained deeply religious but showed a new interest in the world around them: their middle-class attitudes and concerns were harbingers of developments to come.

*ATHENIAN WOMEN AT A FOUNTAIN HOUSE* (left) The Greeks often decorated their vases with scenes from daily life. Here five well-dressed Athenian women are seen filling their water jugs at a fountain house. They used the occasion to chat and exchange information. Scenes such as this one suggest that Athenian women were not so sheltered as they are often portrayed. (Courtesy, Museum of Fine Arts, Boston.)

*BLACKSMITH'S SHOP* (right) One blacksmith holds the heated metal in tongs while his husky companion wields a hammer. Hanging from the wall is one man's cloak, a water jug, and knives and axes that the smiths have made or repaired. In the winter the blacksmith's shop, kept warm by a constant fire, was a favorite place for the men to chat and to come in from the cold. (Courtesy, Museum of Fine Arts, Boston.)

*PALESTRINA MOSAIC* (below) Fish and birds abound as boatsmen steer among rocks and try their hand at spearing fish. The Nile was legendary for its fertility and the exotic animals that could be encountered along its course. Mosaics such as this were common in the ancient world and could be found in temples and the homes of the wealthy. (Scala/EPA.)

THE BURY ST. EDMUNDS' CROSS (above, left) Probably made for the English abbot Samson of Bury St. Edmunds' (1181–1211) and used in ceremonial processions, this walrus ivory cross, 2 ft. high and 14 in. across, contains 8 scenes, 108 figures, and 60 inscriptions from the Old and New Testaments. A superb example of late twelfth-century craftsmanship, piety, and, some inscriptions imply, anti-Semitic attitudes. (The Metropolitan Museum of Art; The Cloisters Collection, 1963.)

LES TRÈS RICHES HEURES DU JEAN, DUC DE BERRY (above, right) This illustrates March in a book of calendar miniatures produced for the duke of Berry, brother of the king of France. With exquisite detail the artists capture four scenes of agricultural life in the early fifteenth century. A shepherd with a dog guards a flock of sheep. Three peasants prune vines while another works in a different field. And an aged farmer guides a wheeled plow and oxen. Symbolically, the vast castle of Lusignan dominates the landscape. (Chantilly, Musée Condé/Giraudon.)

THE CAMPIN ALTARPIECE (ca 1425–1428), by Robert Campin (d. 1444). This 4-by 2-ft. painting in oil on wood was intended to hang behind the altar, facing the people. The Annunciation scene in the center panel occurs in the house of a Flemish burgher. Every detail has significance. For example, the serious, modestly dressed middle-class donors in the left panel are memorialized observing the mystery, the lilies on the table in the center panel represent the Virgin's chastity, and Joseph in the right panel carves a mousetrap, symbolizing Christ, the bait set to catch the devil. (The Metropolitan Museum of Art, The Cloisters Collection.)

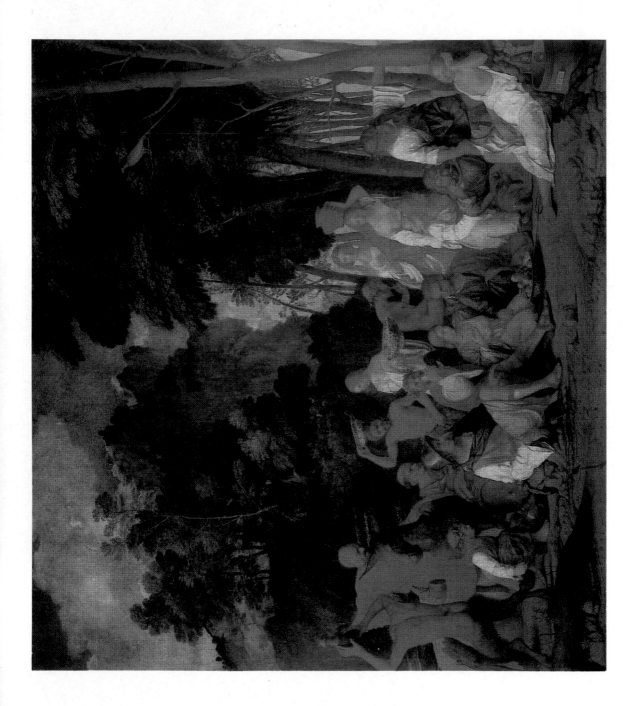

FEAST OF THE GODS (above) Giovanni Bellini (1430?-1516). In this pastoral scene based on a story of the Roman poet Ovid, Olympian gods picnic in a wooded grove as satyrs and nymphs serve them. The peacock in the tree symbolizes the gods' immortality. The pagan theme, the appreciation for perspective and nature, and the sensual atmosphere make this painting a fine example of Italian Renaissance classicism. (National Gallery of Art, Washington, D.C.)

A WOMAN PEELING APPLES (below left) Pieter de Hooch (1629-1677). Stability, seriousness, and thrift are idealized in this Dutch domestic scene. The light filtering through the window represents a technical achievement and the secular appreciation for the world of nature and of man. (Reproduced by permission of the Trustees of the Wallace Collection.)

GEORG GISZE (below, right) Hans Holbein (1497-1543). Born in Danzig, Gisze became a rich London merchant. Here he is portrayed with quill and ink, seal, scales, and business letters hung on racks behind him. The Caucasian rug covering the desk was probably woven in Asia Minor in the fifteenth century. (Gemäldegalerie, Berlin.)

COMBAT BETWEEN CARNIVAL AND LENT (above) Pieter Bruegel the Elder (ca 1525–1559). One of the most original Flemish painters of the sixteenth century, Bruegel concentrated on scenes of peasant life. He treated many subjects satirically. In this conflict be- tween gluttony and asceticism, a common Reformation theme, Bruegel suggests that neither side is a perfect model of Christian living. (Courtesy, Museum of Fine Arts, Boston.)

doctrines through revelation embodied in Scripture. Scripture cannot contradict reason, nor reason Scripture:

*The light of faith that is freely infused into us does not destroy the light of natural knowledge [reason] implanted in us naturally. For although the natural light of the human mind is insufficient to show us these things made manifest by faith, it is nevertheless impossible that these things which the divine principle gives us by faith are contrary to those implanted in us by nature [reason]. Indeed, were that the case, one or the other would have to be false, and, since both are given to us by God, God would have to be the author of untruth, which is impossible. . . . it is impossible that those things which are of philosophy can be contrary to those things which are of faith.*[4]

Aquinas also investigated the branch of philosophy called epistemology, which is concerned with how a person knows something. Aquinas stated that one knows, first, through sensory perception of the physical world — seeing, hearing, touching, and so on. He maintained that there can be nothing in the mind that is not first in the senses. Secondly, knowledge comes through reason, the mind exercising its natural abilities. Aquinas stressed the power of human reason to know, even to know God. Proofs of the existence of God exemplify the scholastic method of knowing.

Aquinas begins with the things of the natural world — earth, air, trees, water, birds. From these things, he inquires back to their original source or cause, the mover, creator, planner who started it all. Everything, Aquinas maintained, has an ultimate and essential explanation, a reason for existing. Here he was following Aristotle. Aquinas went further and identified the reason for existing, or first mover, with God. Thomas Aquinas and all medieval intellectuals held that the end

of both faith and reason was the knowledge of, and union with, God. His work later became the fundamental text of Roman Catholic doctrine.

At all universities, the standard method of teaching was the lecture — that is, a reading. The professor read a passage from the Bible, the Justinian Code, or one of Aristotle's treatises. He then explained and interpreted the passage; his interpretation was called a gloss. Students wrote down everything. Texts and glosses were sometimes collected and reproduced as textbooks. For example, the Italian Peter Lombard (d. 1160), a professor at Paris, wrote what became the standard textbook in theology, *Sententiae (The Sentences),* which was a compilation of basic theological principles.

Because books had to be copied by hand, they were extremely expensive and few students could afford them. Students therefore depended for study on their own or friends' notes accumulated over a period of years. The choice of subjects was narrow. The syllabus at all universities consisted of a core of ancient texts that everyone studied and, if they wanted to get ahead, mastered.

There were no examinations at the end of a series of lectures. Examinations were given after three, four, or five years of study, when the student applied for a degree. The professors determined the amount of material students had to know for each degree, and students frequently insisted that the professors specify precisely what that material was. When the candidate for a degree believed himself prepared, he presented himself to a committee of professors for examination.

Examinations were oral and very difficult. (Not only did paper and ink cost a great deal, the examination was designed to test the student's ability to think quickly on his feet and to express his thoughts effectively.) If the candidate passed, he was awarded the first, or

*A UNIVERSITY LECTURE Some students doze, some chat, and some are attentive to the lecturer. All students appear much older than undergraduates today. (Bildarchiv Preussischer Kulturbesitz)*

bachelor's, degree. Further study, about as long, arduous, and expensive as it is today, enabled the graduate to try for the master's and doctor's degrees. All degrees certified competence in a given subject, and degrees were technically licenses to teach. Most students, however, did not become teachers.

### STUDENT LIFE

The students and faculties of medieval universities were from the middling rungs of so-

ciety, very much like many of the students and teachers at American state universities today. Most students (all of whom were male) came from families of lesser knights, burgesses of the towns, merchants, and artisans – the group that today would be called middle-class. Undergraduates were usually in their twenties and thirties, poor, ambitious, and aggressively upwardly mobile. They wanted and received an education that was practical, utilitarian, and vocational.

Students wanted to acquire as quickly as

possible the knowledge necessary for a secure, well-paying job in the service of the church or secular government. Consequently, once the first degree had been attained, law was the subject most often pursued for an advanced degree. Students studied law because governments needed the expertise of lawyers. Philip Augustus of France employed law graduates as baillis and seneschals. Frederick II, when he established the University of Naples, had clearly stated in the university's charter that the school's purpose was to train men who would dispense the law throughout his kingdom.

Medieval students exercised more power in their universities than do students today. In the Middle Ages students often traveled long distances to work with great scholars. They arrived as foreigners in the countries where they studied, and, fearful of the natives, formed associations for mutual security. Some guilds were set up for sheer physical protection; others sought to defend students from the high rates charged by local boardinghouses and innkeepers. Student guilds, especially in southern Italy, hired the professors, paid their fees, and demanded that teachers cover the syllabus within an agreed-upon time. If they became dissatisfied with incompetent professors or the financial gouging of townspeople, students did not hesitate to boycott lectures or to leave the town entirely. Cambridge University, for example, began when students at Oxford got fed up with conditions there.

Municipal court records of towns like Paris, Oxford, and Cambridge reveal that in the thirteenth and fourteenth centuries student riots and rebellions were common. Townspeople resented what they considered the wasteful lives of students. Students protested the high costs of living in university towns or what they felt were the unfair deci-

sions of professors or university officials. Friction between students and townspeople or between students and university authorities was common. But the aim of medieval student movements was never to reform society as a whole. Medieval students had no interest in changing the basic social system. They wanted, instead, to get into the system; they wanted a piece of the action.

Medieval universities did not have luxurious dormitories, semiprofessional athletic teams, vast administrations, or even classrooms. The first professors lectured in rented halls. In the later thirteenth century, first at Paris and then at Oxford, noblemen and wealthy businessmen established colleges, or residence halls, and endowed scholarships for poor students. Most students lived in abject poverty, and before the sixteenth century they led a cold, uncomfortable, and hand-to-mouth existence. Nevertheless, in establishing the system of lectures, textbooks, faculties, examinations, and degrees, medieval universities laid the foundations for modern institutional learning.

## GOTHIC ART

Medieval churches stand as the most spectacular manifestations of the vitality and creativity of the High Middle Ages. It is difficult for twentieth-century people to appreciate the extraordinary amounts of energy, imagination, and money involved in building them. Between 1180 and 1270 in France alone, eighty cathedrals, about five hundred abbey churches, and tens of thousands of parish churches were constructed. This construction represents a remarkable investment for a country of scarcely 18 million people. More stone was quarried for churches in medieval France than

ROMANESQUE AND GOTHIC ARCHES *The round barrel vault characterizes the Romanesque style. Cross vaults built on arches and supported by buttresses typify the Gothic.*

had been mined in ancient Egypt, where the Great Pyramid alone consumed 40.5 million cubic feet of stone. All these churches displayed a new architectural style. Fourteenth-century critics called the new style "Gothic" because they mistakenly believed the Goths of the fifth century had invented it. The Gothic style actually developed partly in reaction to an earlier style named Romanesque, which supposedly resembled ancient Roman architecture.

Gothic cathedrals were built in towns, and they reflect both bourgeois wealth and enormous civic pride. The manner in which a society spends its wealth expresses its values. Cathedrals, abbeys, and village churches testify to the deep religious faith and piety of medieval people. If the dominant aspect of medieval culture had not been the Christian faith, the builder's imagination and the merchant's money would have been used in other ways.

## FROM ROMANESQUE GLOOM TO "UNINTERRUPTED LIGHT"

The relative political stability and increase of ecclesiastical wealth in the eleventh century encouraged the arts of peace. In the ninth and tenth centuries, the Vikings and Magyars had burned hundreds of wooden churches. In the eleventh century, abbots wanted to rebuild in a more permanent fashion, and after the year 1000 church building increased on a wide scale. Because fireproofing was essential, the ceiling had to be made of stone. Therefore, builders replaced wooden roofs with arched stone ceilings called vaults. The stone ceilings were heavy; only thick walls would support them. Because the walls were so thick, the windows were small, allowing little light into the interior of the church. The basic features of Romanesque architecture, as this style is called, are stone vaults in the ceiling, a rounded arch over the nave (the central part of the church), and thick, heavy walls. In northern Europe, twin bell towers often crowned the Romanesque churches, giving them a powerful, fortresslike appearance. Built primarily by the monasteries, Romanesque churches reflect the quasi-military, aristocratic, and pre-urban society that built them.

The inspiration for the Gothic style originated in the brain of one monk, Suger, abbot of St.-Denis (1122–1151), whose life is a remarkable medieval success story. Born of very poor parents, he was given as a child-oblate to the abbey of St.-Denis. St.-Denis was a royal abbey, closely associated with the French monarchy, the custodian of the royal insignia, and the burial place of the French kings. Suger became chief adviser to Louis VI and

Louis VII; and when Louis VII was away on crusade, he served as the regent of France. When Suger became abbot, he decided to reconstruct the old Carolingian abbey church at St.-Denis. Work began in 1137. On June 11, 1144, King Louis VII and a large crowd of bishops, dignitaries, and common people witnessed the solemn consecration of the first Gothic church in France.

The basic features of Gothic architecture — the pointed arch, the ribbed vault, and the flying buttress — were not unknown before 1137. What was without precedent was the interior lightness they made possible. Since the ceiling of a Gothic church weighed less, the walls could be thinner. Windows were cut into the stone, allowing the church to be flooded with light. Stained-glass windows crowned the Gothic style. The bright interior was astounding. Suger, describing his achievement, exulted:

*Moreover, it was cunningly provided that . . . the central nave of the old nave should be equalized, by means of geometrical and arithmetical instruments, with the central nave of the new addition; and, likewise, that the dimensions of the old side-aisles should be equalized with the dimensions of the new side-aisles, except for that elegant and praiseworthy extension, in [the form of] a circular string of chapels, by virtue of which the whole [church] would shine with the wonderful and uninterrupted light of most sacred windows, pervading the interior beauty.*[5]

Thirteenth-century people referred to Gothic architecture as "the new style," or "the Frankish work." Begun in the Ile-de-France, Gothic architecture spread throughout France with the expansion of royal power. French architects were soon invited to design and supervise the construction of churches in other parts of Europe. For example, William of Sens, an experienced architect, was commis-

FOURTEENTH-CENTURY FRENCH STAINED GLASS *Stained glass illuminated both the church and, in the stories told, the minds of the viewers. In the left lancet the prophet Isaiah holds a scroll predicting that a Virgin will bear a son; in the right Mary Magdalene weeps because she cannot find Christ. (Metropolitan Museum of Art, The Cloisters, New York)*

WEST FRONT OF NOTRE DAME CATHEDRAL
In this powerful vision of the Last Judgment, Christ sits in judgment surrounded by angels, the Virgin, and Saint John. Scenes of paradise fill the arches on Christ's right, scenes of hell on the left. In the lower lintel, the dead arise incorruptible, and in the upper lintel (below Christ's feet), the saved move off to heaven, while devils push the damned to hell. Below, the twelve apostles line the doorway. (Alinari/Scala)

sioned to rebuild Canterbury Cathedral after a disastrous fire in 1174. The distinguished scholar John of Salisbury was then in Canterbury and observed William's work. After John became bishop of Chartres, he wanted William of Sens to assist in the renovation of Chartres Cathedral. Through such contacts "the new style" traveled rapidly over Europe.

## THE CREATIVE OUTBURST

The construction of a Gothic cathedral represented a gigantic investment of time, money, and corporate effort. It was the bishop and the clergy of the cathedral who made the decision to build, but they depended on the support of all the social classes. Bishops raised revenue from contributions by people in their dioceses, and the clergy appealed to the king and the nobility. The French rulers were generous benefactors of many cathedrals. Louis IX endowed so many churches in the Ile-de-France – most notably Sainte Chapelle, a small chapel he built to house the crown of thorns – that scholars speak of a "court style" of Gothic. Noble families often gave in order to have their crests in the stained-glass windows. Above all, the church relied on the financial help of those with the greatest amount of ready cash, the commercial classes.

Money was not the only need. A great number of craftsmen had to be assembled: quarrymen, sculptors, stonecutters, masons, mortar makers, carpenters, blacksmiths, glassmakers, roofers. Each master craftsman had his own apprentices, and unskilled laborers had to be recruited for the heavy work. The construction of a large cathedral was rarely completed in one lifetime; many were never finished at all. Because generation after generation of craftsmen added to the building,

many Gothic churches show the architectural influences of two or even three centuries.

The surge of church building in the twelfth and thirteenth centuries is intimately associated with the growth of towns and the increase of commercial wealth. The medieval cathedrals are monuments to the interest and support of the business classes. Townspeople had secured their independence from feudal authorities, and they celebrated that freedom by building splendid cathedrals. A large and magnificent church also reflected the wealth and prosperity of the townspeople – and the cleverness and industry needed to acquire that wealth. What better way to display that wealth than in the house of God?

Since cathedrals were symbols of bourgeois civic pride, towns competed to build the largest and most splendid church. In northern France in the late twelfth and early thirteenth centuries, cathedrals grew progressively taller. In 1163, the citizens of Paris began Notre Dame cathedral, intending it to reach a height of 114 feet. Reconstruction on Chartres Cathedral was begun in 1194: it was to be 119 feet. The people of Beauvais exceeded everyone: their church, started in 1247, reached 157 feet; unfortunately, the weight imposed on the vaults was too great, and the building collapsed in 1284. Medieval people built cathedrals to glorify God – and if mortals were impressed, so much the better.[6]

Cathedrals served secular as well as religious purposes. The sanctuary containing the altar and the bishop's chair belonged to the clergy, but the rest of the church belonged to the people. In addition to marriages, baptisms, and funerals, there were scores of feast days on which the entire town gathered in the cathedral for festivities. Amiens Cathedral could hold the entire town of ten thousand people. Local guilds, which fulfilled the economic, fraternal, and charitable functions of

*CROUCHING BLACK MAN   From the north transept of Chartres Cathedral, ca 1230. The thousands of representations of blacks in medieval art show that Europeans were familiar with them — from commercial contacts with Muslim parts of Spain and Italy, the crusades, and the slave trade. Europeans' attitudes reflected a curious fascination with the social feeling, as here implied, that black people should occupy menial positions. The black man supports the Queen of Sheba, who symbolizes the pagan world in need of conversion. (Mark Sheridan OSB)*

modern labor unions, met in the cathedrals to arrange business deals and plan recreational events and the support of disabled members. Magistrates and municipal officials held political meetings there. Some towns never built town halls, because all civic functions took place in the cathedral. Pilgrims slept there, lovers courted there, traveling actors staged plays there. The cathedral belonged to all.

The structure of the Gothic cathedral mirrored the interests of all classes of medieval society. The clergy planned the design of the building along orderly theological principles, putting into practice the axiom of the fifth-century mystical writer Dennis the Areopagite, "Through the senses man may rise to the contemplation of the divine." The cathedral was intended to teach the people the doctrines of the Christian faith through visual images.

Architecture became the servant of theology. The main altar was at the east end, pointing toward Jerusalem, the city of peace. The west front of the cathedral faced the setting sun, and its wall was usually devoted to scenes of the Last Judgment. The north side, which received the least sunlight, displayed events from the Old Testament. The south side, washed in warm sunshine for much of the day, depicted scenes from the New Testament. This symbolism implied that the Jewish people of the Old Testament lived in darkness and that the gospel brought by Christ illuminated the world. Every piece of sculpture, furniture, and stained glass had some religious or social significance.

Stained glass beautifully reflects the creative energy of the High Middle Ages. It is both an integral part of Gothic architecture and a distinct form of painting. The glassmaker "painted" his picture with small fragments of glass held together with strips of lead. As Gothic churches became more skeletal and had more windows, stained glass replaced manuscript illumination as the leading kind of painting.

Contributors to the cathedral and the workmen left their imprint upon it. The stonecutter cut his mark on every block of stone, partly so that he would be paid, partly

*FIFTEENTH-CENTURY FLEMISH TAPESTRY
The weavers of Tournai (in present-day Belgium)
spent twenty-five years (1450–1475) producing this
magnificent tapestry, which is based on the Old Testament story of Jehu, Jezebel, and the sons of Ahab (2
Kings, 9–10). The elegant costumes show fifteenth-
century upper-class dress styles. (Isabella Stewart
Gardner Museum)*

too so that his work would be remembered.
At Chartres Cathedral the craft and merchant
guilds – drapers, furriers, haberdashers, tan-
ners, butchers, bakers, fishmongers, and wine
merchants – donated money and are memorialized in the stained-glass windows. The incredibly beautiful window of the wine
merchants depicts their business in three central medallions: a wine merchant and his cart;
a man pouring wine from a cask; and the
wine being used at the mass. Thousands of
scenes in the cathedral celebrate nature,

country life, and the activities of ordinary
people. All members of medieval society had a
place in the City of God, which the Gothic
cathedral represented. No one, from kings to
milkmaids, was excluded.

Tapestry making also came into its own in
the fourteenth century. Heavy woolen tapestries were first made in monasteries and convents as wall hangings for churches. Because
they could be moved and lent an atmosphere
of warmth, they subsequently replaced mural
paintings. Early tapestries depicted religious

scenes, but later hangings produced for the knightly class bore secular designs, especially romantic forests and hunting spectacles.

The drama, derived from the church's liturgy, emerged as a distinct art form during the same period. For centuries skits based on Christ's Resurrection and Nativity had been performed in monasteries and cathedrals. Beginning in the thirteenth century, plays based on these and other biblical themes and on the lives of the saints were performed in the towns. Guilds financed these "mystery plays," so called because they were based on the mysteries of the Christian faith; in a long production, each of a town's guilds was responsible for a different scene. Actors used very simple costumes and props, and comical or vulgar farces from the lives of ordinary people were interspersed with serious religious scenes. Performed first at the cathedral altar, then in the church square, and later in the town marketplace, mystery plays enjoyed great popularity. They allowed the common people to understand and identify with religious figures and the mysteries of their faith. While provoking the individual conscience to reform, mystery plays were also an artistic manifestation of local civic pride.

## THE CRUSADES

Crusades in the late eleventh and early twelfth centuries were holy wars sponsored by the papacy for the recovery of the Holy Land from the Muslim Arabs or the Turks. In the later twelfth and through the thirteenth century, crusades were also directed against Europe's domestic enemies, heretics. Between 1096 and 1270 there were at least eight campaigns to wrest the Holy Land from the in-

fidels. Throughout this period Christians alone and in groups left Europe in a steady trickle for the Middle East. Although people of all ages and classes participated in the Crusades, so many knights did so that crusading became a distinctive feature of the upper-class lifestyle. In an aristocratic military society men coveted a reputation as a Crusader; the Christian knight who had been to the Holy Land enjoyed great prestige. The Crusades manifested the religious and chivalric ideals – as well as the tremendous vitality – of medieval society.

The Crusades of the High Middle Ages grew out of earlier conflict between Christians and Muslims in Spain. The concept of a holy war originated in the Spanish peninsula and gradually influenced all parts of western Europe. In the eighth century, the Arabs had overrun the peninsula, and Christian lords had fled into the mountains in the north. In the tenth century, Christians started the *reconquista,* or holy war of reconquest. Christian warriors made slow progress – not until 1492 did Isabella and Ferdinand finally succeed in expelling the Arabs – but by about 1100 Christian kings had regained about a fourth of the peninsula. The *reconquista* dominates the history of medieval Spain.

The Roman papacy supported the holy war in Spain, and by the late eleventh century had strong reasons for wanting to launch an expedition against Muslim infidels in the Middle East as well. The papacy had been involved in a bitter struggle over investiture with the German emperors. If the pope could muster a large army against the enemies of Christianity, his claim to be the leader of Christian society in the West would be strengthened.

Moreover, in 1054 a serious theological disagreement had split the Greek church of Byzantium and the Roman church of the

West. The pope believed that a crusade would lead to strong Roman influence in Greek territories and eventually the reunion of the two churches. Then, in 1071 at Manzikert in eastern Anatolia, Turkish soldiers in the pay of the Arabs defeated a Greek army and occupied much of Asia Minor. The emperor at Constantinople appealed to the West for support. Shortly afterward, the holy city of Jerusalem, the scene of Christ's preaching and burial, fell to the Turks. Pilgrimages to holy places in the Middle East became very dangerous, and the papacy was outraged that the holy city was in the hands of infidels.

In 1095, Pope Urban II journeyed to Clermont in France and called for a great Christian holy war against the infidels. He stressed the sufferings and persecution of Christians in Jerusalem. He urged Christian knights who had been fighting one another to direct their energies against the true enemies of God, the Muslims. Urban proclaimed an indulgence, or remission of sin, to those who would fight for and regain the holy city of Jerusalem. Few speeches in history have had such a dramatic effect as Urban's call at Clermont for the First Crusade.

The response was fantastic. Godfrey of Bouillon, Geoffrey of Lorraine, and many other great lords from northern France immediately had the cross of the Crusader sewn on their tunics. Encouraged by popular preachers like Peter the Hermit, and by papal legates in Germany, Italy, and England, thousands of people of all classes joined the crusade. Although most of the Crusaders were French, pilgrims from all countries streamed southward from the Rhineland, through Germany and the Balkans. No development in the High Middle Ages better reveals Europeans' religious zeal and emotional fervor, and the influence of the reformed papacy, than the incredible outpouring of support for the First Crusade.

Religious convictions inspired many, but mundane motives were also involved. Except for wives, who had to remain at home to manage estates, many people expected to benefit from the crusade. For the curious and the adventurous, it offered foreign travel and excitement; it promised escape from the dullness of everyday life. The crusade provided kings, who were trying to establish order and to build states, the perfect opportunity to get rid of troublemaking knights. It gave land-hungry younger sons a chance to acquire fiefs in the Middle East. Even some members of the middle class who stayed at home profited from the crusade. Nobles often had to borrow money from the middle class to pay for their expeditions, and they put up part of their land as security. If a noble did not return home or could not pay the interest on the loan, the middle-class creditor took over the land.

The First Crusade was successful mostly because of the dynamic enthusiasm of the participants. The Crusaders had little more than religious zeal. They knew nothing about the geography or climate of the Middle East. Although among the host there were several counts with military experience, the Crusaders could never agree on a leader, and the entire expedition was marked by disputes among the great lords. Lines of supply were never set up. Starvation and disease wracked the army, and the Turks slaughtered hundreds of noncombatants. Nevertheless, convinced that "God wills it" – the war cry of the Crusaders – the army pressed on and in 1099 captured Jerusalem. Although the Crusaders fought bravely, Arab disunity was a chief reason for their victory. At Jerusalem, Edessa, Tripoli, and Antioch, Crusader kingdoms were founded on the Western feudal model (see Map 11.4).

**Legend:**
····► First Crusade, 1096-1099
——► Second Crusade, 1147-1149
– – ► Third Crusade, 1189-1192
——► Fourth Crusade, 1202-1204
� Crusader kingdoms in the East
✕ Major battle

0    250    500 Km.
0    250    500 Mi.

MAP 11.4  THE ROUTES OF THE CRUSADES
*The crusades led to a major cultural encounter be-
tween Muslim and Christian values. What significant
intellectual and economic effects resulted?*

Between 1096 and 1270, the crusading ideal
was expressed in eight papally approved expeditions to the East. In addition to those eight,
the papacy in 1208 proclaimed a crusade
against heretics in southern France. In the
same year, two expeditions of children set out
on a crusade to the Holy Land. One contingent turned back; the other was captured and
sold into slavery. And, in 1227 and 1239, the
pope launched a crusade against the emperor
Frederick II. None of the crusades against the
Muslims achieved very much. The third one
(1189-1192) was precipitated by the recapture
of Jerusalem by the sultan Saladin in 1187.
Frederick Barbarossa of the Holy Roman Empire, Richard the Lion-Hearted of England,
and Philip Augustus of France participated,
and the Third Crusade was better financed

than previous ones. But disputes among the
leaders and strategic problems prevented any
lasting results.

During the Fourth Crusade (1198-1204),
careless preparation and inadequate financing
had disastrous consequences for Byzantine-
Latin relations. Hoping to receive material
support from the Greeks, the leaders of the
crusade took the expedition to Constantinople
before advancing to Jerusalem. But once
there, they sacked the city and established the
Latin Empire of Constantinople. This assault
by one Christian people on another, when one
of the goals of the crusade was the reunion of
the Greek and Latin churches, helped to dis-
credit the entire crusading movement. Two
later crusades undertaken by King Louis IX
of France added to his prestige as a pious

ruler. Apart from that, the last of the official crusades accomplished nothing at all.

Crusades were also mounted against groups perceived as Christian Europe's social enemies. In 1208 Pope Innocent III proclaimed a crusade against the Albigensians, a heretical sect. The Albigensians, whose name derived from the southern French town of Albi where they were concentrated, rejected orthodox doctrine on the relationship of God and man, the sacraments, and the hierarchy. Believing the Albigensians a political threat, the French monarchy joined the crusade. Under Count Simon de Montfort the French inflicted a savage defeat on the Albigensians at Muret in 1213; the county of Toulouse passed to the authority of the French Crown. The popes in the mid-thirteenth century, fearful of encirclement by imperial territories, promoted crusades against Emperor Frederick II. This use of force against a Christian ruler backfired, damaging papal credibility as the sponsor of peace.

The Crusades brought few cultural changes to western Europe. By the late eleventh century, strong economic and intellectual ties with the East had already been made. The Crusades testify to the religious enthusiasm of the High Middle Ages. But, as Steven Runciman, a distinguished scholar of the Crusades, concluded in his three-volume history:

*The triumphs of the Crusade were the triumphs of faith. But faith without wisdom is a dangerous thing. . . . In the long sequence of interaction and fusion between Orient and Occident out of which our civilization has grown, the Crusades were a tragic and destructive episode. . . . There was so much courage and so little honour, so much devotion and so little understanding. High ideals were besmirched by cruelty and greed, enterprise and endurance by a blind and narrow self-righteousness; and the Holy War itself was nothing more than a long act of intolerance in the name of God, which is the sin against the Holy Ghost.*[7]

---

Societies, like individuals, cannot maintain a high level of energy indefinitely. In the later years of the thirteenth century, Europeans seemed to run out of steam. The crusading movement gradually fizzled out. No new cathedrals were constructed, and if a cathedral had not been completed by 1300, the chances were that it never would be. The strong rulers of France and England, building on the foundations of their predecessors, increased their authority and gained the loyalty of all their subjects. The vigor of those kings, however, did not pass to their immediate descendants. The church, which for two centuries had guided Christian society, began to face grave difficulties. A violent dispute between the papacy and the kings of France and England badly damaged papal prestige.

In 1296, Kind Edward I of England and Philip the Fair of France declared war upon each other. To finance this war both kings laid taxes on the clergy. Kings had been taxing the church for decades. Pope Boniface VIII (1294–1303), a staunch defender of papal supremacy, forbade churchmen to pay the taxes. But Edward and Philip refused to accept this decree, partly because it hurt royal finances, and partly because the papal order threatened royal authority within their countries. Edward immediately denied the clergy the protection of the law, which meant that they could be attacked with impunity. Philip halted the shipment of all ecclesiastical revenue to Rome. Boniface had to back down.

Philip the Fair and his ministers continued their attack on all powers in France outside royal authority. Philip arrested a French bishop who was also the papal legate. When

*THE CAPTURE OF JERUSALEM IN 1099   As engines hurl stones to breach the walls, crusaders enter on scaling ladders. Scenes from Christ's passion (above) identify the city as Jerusalem. (Bibliothèque Nationale, Paris)*

Boniface defended the ecclesiastical status and diplomatic immunity of the bishop, Philip replied with the trumped-up charge that the pope was a heretic. The papacy and the French monarchy waged a bitter war of propaganda. Finally in 1302, in a letter entitled *Unam Sanctam* (because its opening sentence spoke of one holy Catholic church), Boniface insisted that Philip, like everyone else, submit to papal authority. Philip's university-trained advisers responded with an argument drawn from Roman law: they maintained that the king of France was completely sovereign in his kingdom and responsible to God alone. French mercenary troops went to Italy and arrested the aged pope at Anagni. Although Boniface was soon freed, he died shortly afterward. The incident at Anagni marked a decisive turning point.

The French attack on the leadership of the church signaled the weakening of religious authority. The Christian church had been the strongest influence in medieval society, but now a new power, the national secular state, was emerging in western Europe. Boniface's successors not only retracted *Unam Sanctam* but apologized for it. The centralized power of the French monarchy, which had been growing for over a century, scored a victory over the papacy. The presence of King Philip the Fair at the coronation of Pope Clement V at Lyons in 1305 was symbolic: Clement was French, and he established the papal court at Avignon, within the borders of the Holy Roman Empire but very much a French city. For the next sixty years, the Roman papacy was strongly influenced by France. Anagni foreshadowed serious difficulties within the Christian church, but additional difficulties awaited Western society in the fourteenth century.

## NOTES

1. D. C. Douglas and G. E. Greenaway, eds., *English Historical Documents,* II, Eyre & Spottiswoode, London, 1961, p. 853.

2. This section leans heavily on John Boswell, *Christianity, Social Tolerance, and Homosexuality: Gay People in Western Europe from the Beginning of the Christian Era to the Fourteenth Century,* University of Chicago Press, Chicago, 1980, pp. 270–293; the quotation is from p. 293.

3. Quoted by H. E. Sigerist, *Civilization and Disease,* University of Chicago Press, Chicago, 1943, p. 102.

4. Quoted by John H. Mundy, *Europe in the High Middle Ages, 1150–1309,* Basic Books, New York, 1973, pp. 474–475.

5. E. Panofsky, trans., *Abbot Suger on the Abbey Church of St.-Denis and Its Art Treasures,* Princeton University Press, Princeton, 1946, p. 101.

6. See J. Gimpel, *The Cathedral Builders,* Grove Press, New York, 1961, pp. 42–49.

7. S. Runciman, *A History of the Crusades,* vol. 3, *The Kingdom of Acre,* Cambridge University Press, Cambridge, 1955, p. 480.

## SUGGESTED READING

The achievements of the High Middle Ages have attracted considerable scholarly attention, and the curious student will have no difficulty finding exciting material on the points raised in this chapter. Three general surveys of the period 1050–1300 are especially recommended: J. R. Strayer, *Western Europe in the Middle Ages* (1955), a masterful synthesis; J. W. Baldwin, *The Scholastic Culture of the Middle Ages* (1971), which stresses the intellectual features of medieval civilization; and F. Heer, *The Medieval World* (1963).

G. O. Sayles, *The Medieval Foundations of England* (1961), traces English conditions to the end of the thirteenth century, while R. Fawtier, *The Capetian Kings of France* (1962), shows how the French monarchy built a nation. G. Barraclough, *Origins of Modern Germany* (1963), provides the best explanation of the problems and peculiarities of the Holy Roman Empire; this is a fine example of a Marxist interpretation of medieval history. Tom Corfe, *Archbishop Thomas Becket and King Henry II* (1980), treats many aspects of the political and religious life of twelfth century England, as well as the conflict between those two persons, in a cleverly illustrated little study: this book is in the Cambridge History of Mankind series. J. R. Strayer, *On the Medieval Origins of the Modern State* (1972), is an excellent treatment of the political and bureaucratic development of European states, also with emphasis on France and England. The advanced student of French medieval administrative history should consult Joseph R. Strayer, *The Reign of Philip the Fair* (1980). Students interested in approaching the High Middle Ages through biographies of leading political figures will find D. C. Douglas, *William the Conqueror* (1964); W. L. Warren, *Henry II* (1974); and E. Kantorowicz, *Frederick II* (1931), interesting and thorough.

For the new currents of thought in the High Middle Ages, see C. Brooke, *The Twelfth Century Renaissance* (1970), a splendidly illustrated book with copious quotations from the sources; E. Gilson, *Héloise and Abélard* (1960) which treats the medieval origins of modern humanism against the background of Abélard the teacher; D. W. Robertson, Jr., *Abélard and Héloise* (1972), which is highly readable, commonsensical, and probably the best recent study of Abélard and the love affair he supposedly had; and C. W. Hollister, ed., *The Twelfth Century Renaissance* (1969), a well-constructed anthology with source materials on many aspects of twelfth-century culture. N. Orme, *English Schools in the Middle Ages* (1973), focuses on the significance of schools and literacy in English Medieval society, while J. Leclercq, *The Love of Learning and the Desire of God* (1974), discusses monastic literary culture.

On the medieval universities, C. H. Haskins, *The Rise of the Universities* (1959), is a good introduction, while H. Rashdall, *The Universities of Europe in the Middle Ages* (1936), is the standard scholarly work. G. Leff, *Paris and Oxford Universities in the Thirteenth and Fourteenth Centuries* (1968), gives a fascinating sketch and includes a useful bibliography.

Students will find a good general introduction to Romanesque and Gothic architecture in N. Pevsner, *An Outline of European Architecture* (1963), a standard work. D. Grivot and G. Zarnecki, *Gislebertus, Sculptor of Autun* (1961), is the finest appreciation of Romanesque architecture written in English. For the actual work of building, see D. Macaulay, *Cathedral: The Story of Its Construction* (1973), a prizewinning, simply written, and cleverly illustrated re-creation of the problems and duration of cathedral building. J. Gimpel, *The Cathedral Builders* (1961), explores the engineering problems involved in cathedral building and places the subject within its social context. Advanced students will enjoy E. Mâle, *The Gothic Image: Religious Art in France in the Thirteenth Century* (1958), which contains a wealth of fascinating and useful detail. For the most important cathedrals in France, architecturally and politically, see A. Temko, *Notre Dame of Paris, the Biography of a Cathedral* (1968); G. Henderson, *Chartres* (1968); and A. Katzenellenbogen, *The Sculptural Programs of Chartres Cathedral* (1959), by a distinguished art historian. E. Panofsky, *Abbot Suger on the Abbey Church of St.-Denis and Its Art Treasures* (1946), provides a contemporary background account of the first Gothic building. E. G. Holt, ed., *A Documentary History of Art* (1957), contains source materials useful for writing papers. J. Gimpel, *The Medieval Machine: The Industrial Revolution of the Middle Ages* (1977), discusses the mechanical and scientific problems involved in the earlier industrial revolution and shows how construction affected the medieval environment; this is an extremely useful book.

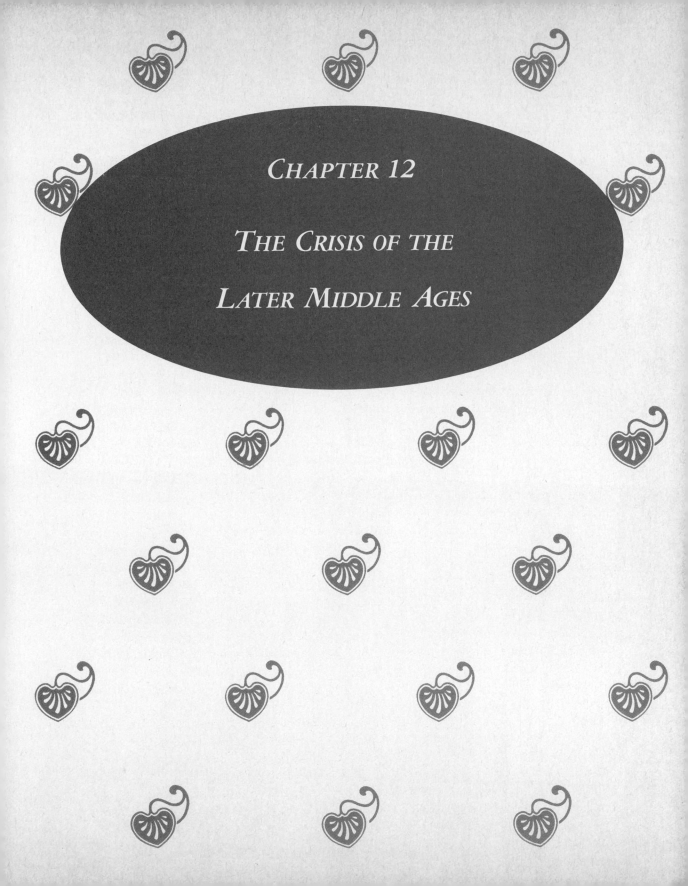

# CHAPTER 12

# THE CRISIS OF THE

# LATER MIDDLE AGES

*IN THE LATER MIDDLE AGES,* the last book of the New Testament, the Book of Revelation, inspired thousands of sermons and hundreds of religious tracts. The Book of Revelation deals with visions of the end of the world, with disease, war, famine, and death. It is no wonder this part of the Bible was so popular. Between 1300 and 1450, Europeans experienced a frightful series of shocks: economic dislocation, plague, war, social upheaval, and increased crime and violence. Death and preoccupation with death make the fourteenth century one of the gloomiest periods in Western civilization.

The miseries and disasters of the later Middle Ages bring to mind a number of questions. What were the social and psychological effects of repeated attacks of plague and disease? Some scholars maintain that war is often the catalyst for political, economic, and social change. Does this theory have validity for the fourteenth century? Finally, what provoked the division of the church in the fourteenth century? What other ecclesiastical difficulties was the schism a sign of, and what impact did it have on the faith of the common people? This chapter seeks to answer these questions.

## PRELUDE TO DISASTER

The fourteenth century began with serious economic problems. In the first decade, the countries of northern Europe experienced a considerable price inflation. The costs of grain, livestock, and dairy products rose sharply. Bad weather made a serious situation worse. An unusual number of storms brought torrential rains. Almost everywhere, heavy rains ruined the wheat, oats, and hay crops on which people and animals depended. Since long-distance transportation of food was ex-

pensive and difficult, most urban areas depended for bread and meat on areas no more than a day's journey away. Poor harvests — and one in four was likely to be poor — led to scarcity and starvation. Almost all of northern Europe suffered a terrible famine in the years 1315-1317.

Hardly had western Europe begun to recover from this disaster when another struck. An epidemic of typhoid fever carried away thousands. In 1316, 10 percent of the population of the city of Ypres in Belgium may have died between May and October alone. Then in 1318 disease hit cattle and sheep, drastically reducing the herds and flocks. Another bad harvest in 1321 brought famine, starvation, and death.

The large province of Languedoc in southern France presents a classic example of agrarian crisis. For over 150 years, Languedoc had enjoyed continual land reclamation, steady agricultural expansion, and enormous population growth. Then the fourteenth century opened with four years of bad harvests, 1302 through 1305. Torrential rains in 1310 ruined the harvest and brought on terrible famine. Harvests failed again in 1322 and 1329. In 1332, desperate peasants survived the winter on raw herbs. In the half-century from 1302 to 1348, poor harvests occurred twenty times. The undernourished population was ripe for the Grim Reaper, who appeared in 1348 in the form of the Black Death.

These catastrophes had inevitable social consequences. Poor harvests meant that marriages had to be postponed. Later marriages and the deaths caused by famine and disease meant a further reduction in population. Thus, after the steady population growth of the twelfth and thirteenth centuries, western Europe suffered a gradual decline in the first third of the fourteenth century. Meanwhile, the international character of trade and commerce meant that a disaster in one country had serious implications elsewhere. For example, the infection that attacked English sheep in 1318 caused a sharp decline in wool exports in the following years. Without wool, Flemish weavers could not work, and thousands were laid off. Without woolen cloth, the businesses of Flemish, French, and English merchants suffered. Unemployment encouraged many men to turn to crime.

To none of these problems did governments have any solutions. In fact, they even lacked policies. After the death of Edward I in 1307, England was governed by the incompetent and weak Edward II (1307–1327), whose reign was dominated by a series of baronial conflicts. In France the three sons of Philip the Fair who followed their father to the French throne between 1314 and 1328 took no interest in the increasing economic difficulties. In the Holy Roman Empire power drifted into the hands of local rulers. The only actions the governments took tended to be in response to the demands of the upper classes. Economic and social problems were aggravated by the appearance in western Europe of a frightful disease.

---

## THE BLACK DEATH

Around 1331, the bubonic plague broke out in China. In the course of the next fifteen years, merchants, traders, and soldiers carried the disease across the Asian caravan routes until, in 1346, it reached the Crimea in southern Russia. From there the plague had easy access to the Mediterranean lands and western Europe.

In 1291, Genoese sailors had opened the Straits of Gibraltar to Italian shipping by defeating the Moroccans. Then, shortly after

1300, important advances were made in the design of Italian merchant ships. A square rig was added to the mainmast, and ships began to carry three masts instead of just one. Additional sails better utilized wind power to propel the ship. The improved design permitted year-round shipping for the first time, and Venetian and Genoese merchant ships could sail the dangerous Atlantic coast even in the winter months. With ships continually at sea, the rats that bore the disease spread rapidly beyond the Mediterranean to Atlantic and North Sea ports.

In October 1347, Genoese ships brought the plague to Messina, from which it spread to Sicily. Venice and Genoa were hit in January 1348, and from the port of Pisa the disease spread south to Rome and north to Florence and all Tuscany. By late spring southern Germany was attacked. Frightened French authorities chased a galley bearing the disease from the port of Marseilles, but not before plague had infected the city, from which it spread to Languedoc and Spain. In June 1348, two ships entered the Bristol Channel and introduced it into England. All Europe felt the scourge of this horrible disease (See Map 12.1).

### PATHOLOGY

Modern understanding of the bubonic plague rests on the research of two bacteriologists, one French and one Japanese, who in 1894 independently identified *Pasteurella pestis,* the bacillus that causes the plague (so labeled after the French scientist's teacher, Louis Pasteur). The bacillus liked to live in the bloodstream of an animal or, ideally, in the stomach of a flea. The flea in turn resided in the hair of a rodent, sometimes a squirrel but preferably the hardy, nimble, and vagabond black rat. Why the host black rat moved so much, sci-

MAP 12.1 THE COURSE OF THE BLACK DEATH
IN FOURTEENTH-CENTURY EUROPE *Note the
routes that the bubonic plague took across Europe.
How do you account for the fact that several regions
were spared the "dreadful death"?*

entists still do not know, but it often traveled
by ship. There the black rat could feast for
months on a cargo of grain or live snugly
among bales of cloth. Fleas bearing the bacillus also had no trouble nesting in saddlebags.[1]
Comfortable, well fed, and often having
greatly multiplied, the black rats ended their
ocean voyage and descended upon the great
cities of Europe.

Although by the fourteenth century urban
authorities from London to Paris to Rome
had begun to try to achieve a primitive level
of sanitation, urban conditions remained ideal
for the spread of disease. Narrow streets filled

with mud, refuse, and human excrement were
as much cesspools as thoroughfares. Dead animals and sore-covered beggars greeted the
traveler. Houses whose upper stories projected over the lower ones eliminated light
and air. And extreme overcrowding was commonplace. When all members of an aristocratic family lived and slept in one room, it
should not be surprising that six or eight
persons in a middle-class or poor household
slept in one bed — if they had one. Closeness,
after all, provided warmth. Houses were beginning to be constructed of brick, but many
remained of wood, clay, and mud. A deter-

mined rat had little trouble entering such a house.

Standards of personal hygiene remained frightfully low. Since water was considered dangerous, partly for good reasons, people rarely bathed. Skin infections, consequently, were common. Lack of personal cleanliness, combined with any number of temporary ailments such as diarrhea and the common cold, naturally weakened the body's resistance to serious disease. Fleas and body lice were universal afflictions: everyone from peasants to archbishops had them. One more bite did not cause much alarm. But if that nibble came from a bacillus-bearing flea, an entire household or area was doomed.

The symptoms of the bubonic plague started with a growth the size of a nut or an apple in the armpit, the groin, or on the neck. This was the boil, or *buba,* that gave the disease its name and caused agonizing pain. If the *buba* was lanced and the pus thoroughly drained, the victim had a chance of recovery. The secondary stage was the appearance of black spots or blotches caused by bleeding under the skin. (This syndrome did not give the disease its common name; contemporaries did not call the plague the Black Death. Sometime in the fifteenth century the Latin phrase *atra mors,* meaning "dreadful death" was translated "black death," and the phrase stuck.) Finally, the victim began to cough violently and spit blood. This stage, indicating the presence of thousands of bacilli in the bloodstream, signaled the end, and death followed in two or three days. Rather than evoking compassion for the victim, a French scientist has written, everything about the bubonic plague provoked horror and disgust: "All the matter which exuded from their bodies let off an unbearable stench; sweat, excrement, spittle, breath, so fetid as to be overpowering; urine turbid, thick, black or red."[2]

THE PLAGUE-STRICKEN  *Even as the dead were wrapped in shrouds and collected in carts for mass burial, the disease struck others. The man collapsing has the symptomatic buba on his neck. As Saint Sebastian pleads for mercy (above), a winged devil, bearer of the plague, attacks an angel. (Walters Art Gallery)*

Medieval people had no rational explanation for the disease nor any effective medical treatment for it. Fourteenth-century medical literature indicates that physicians could sometimes ease the pain, but they had no cure. Most people — lay, scholarly, and medical — believed that the Black Death was caused by some "vicious property in the air" that carried the disease from place to place. All authorities assumed that some corruption of the atmosphere caused the disease.

PROCESSION OF FLAGELLANTS  *The horrors of the Black Death provoked terrible excesses. People believed that the disease was God's punishment for humanity's sins, which could be atoned for only through severe penances. In this procession of robed and hooded flagellants, two of the men flog those ahead of them. (Bibliothèque Royale Albert I, Brussels)*

The Italian writer Giovanni Boccaccio (1313–1375), describing the course of the disease in Florence in the preface to his book of tales, *The Decameron,* pinpointed the cause of the spread:

*Moreover, the virulence of the pest was the greater by reason that intercourse was apt to convey it from the sick to the whole, just as fire devours things dry or greasy when they are brought close to it. Nay, the evil went yet further, for not merely by speech or association with the sick was the malady communicated to the healthy with consequent peril of common death, but any that touched the clothes of the sick or aught else that had been touched or used by them, seemed thereby to contract the disease.[3]*

The highly infectious nature of the plague was recognized by a few sophisticated Arabs.

When the disease struck the town of Salé in Morocco, Ibu Abu Madyan shut in his household with sufficient food and water and allowed no one to enter or leave until the plague had passed. Madyan was entirely successful. In European cities, those who could afford it fled to the countryside, which generally suffered less. Few were so wise or lucky, however, and the plague took a staggering toll.

The mortality rate cannot be specified, because population figures for the period before the arrival of the plague do not exist for most countries and cities. The largest amount of material survives for England, but it is difficult to use and, after enormous scholarly controversy, only educated guesses can be made. Of a total population of perhaps 4.2 million, probably 1.4 million died of the Black Death in its several visits.[4] Densely populated Italian cities endured incredible losses. Florence lost between half and two-thirds of its 1347 population of 85,000 when the plague visited in 1348. In general, rural areas suffered much less than urban ones. The disease recurred intermittently in the 1360s and 1370s and reappeared several times down to 1700. There have been twentieth-century outbreaks in such places as Hong Kong, Bombay, and Uganda.

## SOCIAL AND PSYCHOLOGICAL CONSEQUENCES

Predictably, the poor died more rapidly than the rich, because the rich enjoyed better health to begin with; but the powerful were not unaffected. In England two archbishops of Canterbury fell victim to the plague in 1349, King Edward III's daughter Joan died, and many leading members of the London guilds followed her to the grave.

It is noteworthy that in an age of mounting criticism of clerical wealth and luxury, the behavior of the clergy during the plague was often exemplary. Priests, monks, and nuns cared for the sick and buried the dead. In places like Venice, where even physicians ran away, priests remained to give what ministrations they could. Consequently, their mortality rate was phenomenally high. The German clergy, especially, suffered a severe decline in personnel in the years after 1350. With the ablest killed off, the wealth of the German church fell into the hands of the incompetent and weak. The situation was already ripe for reform.

The plague accelerated the economic decline that had begun in the early part of the fourteenth century. In many parts of Europe there had not been enough work for the people to do. The Black Death was a grim remedy to this problem. Population decline, however, led to an increased demand for labor and to considerable mobility among the peasant and working classes. Wages rose sharply. The shortage of labor and steady requests for higher wages put landlords on the defensive. They retaliated with such measures as the English Statute of Laborers (1351), which attempted to freeze salaries and wages at pre-1347 levels. The statute could not be enforced and therefore the move was largely unsuccessful.

Even more frightening than the social effects were the psychological consequences. The knowledge that the disease meant almost certain death provoked the most profound pessimism. Imagine an entire society in the grip of the belief that it was at the mercy of a frightful affliction about which nothing could be done, a disgusting disease from which family and friends would flee, leaving one to die alone and in agony. It is not surprising that some sought release in orgies and gross sensuality while others turned to the severest forms of asceticism and frenzied religious fervor. Some extremists joined groups of flagellants, who collectively whipped and scourged themselves as penance for their and society's sins in the belief that the Black Death was God's punishment for humanity's wickedness.

The literature and art of the fourteenth century reveal a terribly morbid concern with death. One highly popular artistic motif, the Dance of Death, depicted a dancing skeleton leading away a living person. No wonder survivors experienced a sort of shell shock and a terrible crisis of faith. Lack of confidence in the leaders of society, lack of hope for the future, defeatism, and malaise wreaked enormous anguish and contributed to the decline of the Middle Ages. A long international war added further misery to the frightful disasters of the plague.

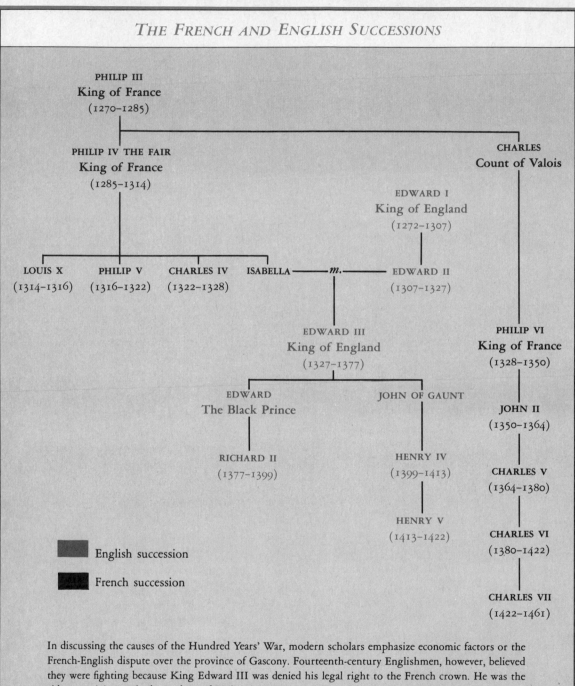

## THE FRENCH AND ENGLISH SUCCESSIONS

**PHILIP III**
King of France
(1270–1285)

**PHILIP IV THE FAIR**
King of France
(1285–1314)

**CHARLES**
Count of Valois

**EDWARD I**
King of England
(1272–1307)

**LOUIS X**
(1314–1316)

**PHILIP V**
(1316–1322)

**CHARLES IV**
(1322–1328)

**ISABELLA** —— *m.* —— **EDWARD II**
(1307–1327)

**PHILIP VI**
King of France
(1328–1350)

**EDWARD III**
King of England
(1327–1377)

**EDWARD**
The Black Prince

**JOHN OF GAUNT**

**JOHN II**
(1350–1364)

**RICHARD II**
(1377–1399)

**HENRY IV**
(1399–1413)

**CHARLES V**
(1364–1380)

**HENRY V**
(1413–1422)

**CHARLES VI**
(1380–1422)

**CHARLES VII**
(1422–1461)

English succession

French succession

In discussing the causes of the Hundred Years' War, modern scholars emphasize economic factors or the French-English dispute over the province of Gascony. Fourteenth-century Englishmen, however, believed they were fighting because King Edward III was denied his legal right to the French crown. He was the eldest surviving male descendant of Philip the Fair.

## THE HUNDRED YEARS' WAR
### (CA 1337–1453)

In January 1327, Queen Isabella of England, her lover Mortimer, and a group of barons, having deposed and murdered Isabella's incompetent husband King Edward II, proclaimed his fifteen-year-old son king as Edward III. A year later Charles IV of France, the last surviving son of the French king Philip the Fair, died childless. With him ended the Capetian dynasty. An assembly of French barons, intending to exclude Isabella – who was Charles's sister and daughter of Philip the Fair – and her son Edward III from the French throne, proclaimed that "no woman nor her son could succeed to the [French] monarchy." The barons passed the crown to Philip VI of Valois (1328–1350), a nephew of Philip the Fair. In these actions lie the origins of another phase of the centuries-old struggle between the English and the French monarchies, one that was fought intermittently from 1337 to 1453.

### CAUSES

Edward III of England, as the eldest surviving direct male descendant of Philip the Fair of France, believed he was entitled to the French throne. God had given him the French kingdom, he maintained, and it was his special duty to claim it. Edward was also duke of Aquitaine, in France (see Map 12.2), and in 1329 he did homage to Philip VI for the duchy. Thus Edward was a vassal of the French ruler, though their interests were diametrically opposed. Moreover, the dynastic argument had feudal implications: in order to increase their independent power, French vassals of Philip VI used the excuse that they had to transfer their loyalty to a more legitimate overlord, Edward III. This position resulted in widespread conflicts.

Economic factors involving the wool trade, the ancient dispute over Aquitaine, control of the Flemish towns – for centuries these had served as justifications for war between France and England. The causes of the conflicts known as the Hundred Years' War were dynastic, feudal, political, and economic. Recent historians have stressed the economic factors. The wool trade between England and Flanders served as the cornerstone of the economies of both countries; they were closely interdependent. Flanders was a fief of the French crown, and the Flemish aristocracy was highly sympathetic to the monarchy in Paris. But the wealth of the Flemish merchants and cloth manufacturers depended on English wool, and the Flemish burghers strongly supported the claims of Edward III. The disruption of their commerce with England threatened their prosperity.

It is impossible to measure the precise influence of the Flemings on the cause and course of the war. Certainly, Edward could not ignore their influence, because it represented money he needed to carry on the war. Although the war's impact on commerce fluctuated, over the long run it badly hurt the wool trade and the cloth industry.

Why did the struggle last so long? One historian has written in jest that if Edward III had been locked away in a castle with a pile of toy knights and archers to play with, he would have done far less damage.[5] The same might be said of Philip VI. Both rulers glorified war and saw it as the perfect arena for the realization of their chivalric ideals. Neither king possessed any sort of policy for dealing with his kingdom's social, economic, or political ills. Both sought military adventure as a means of diverting attention from domestic problems.

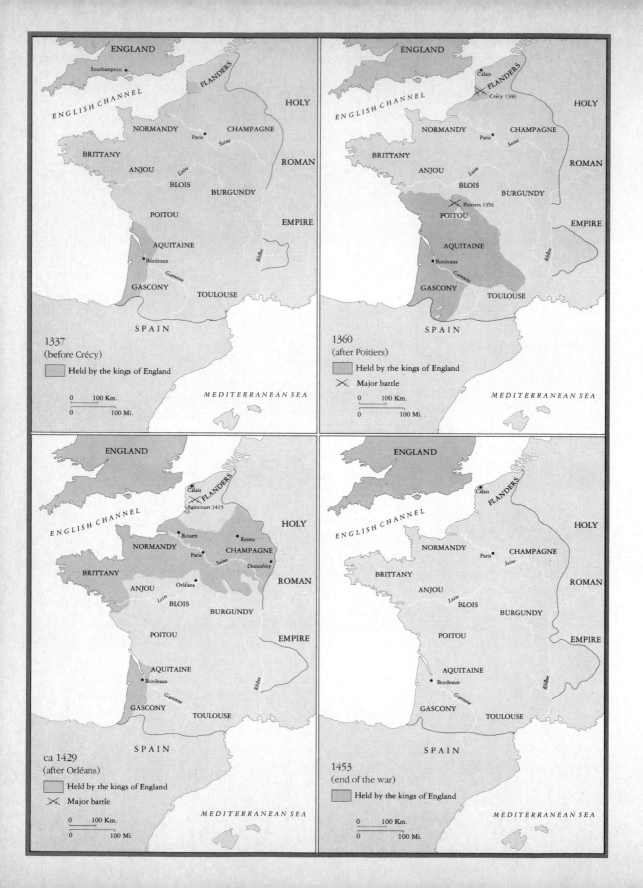

**1337**
(before Crécy)

Held by the kings of England

| 0 | 100 Km. |
| 0 | 100 Mi. |

**1360**
(after Poitiers)

Held by the kings of England

✕ Major battle

| 0 | 100 Km. |
| 0 | 100 Mi. |

**ca 1429**
(after Orléans)

Held by the kings of England

✕ Major battle

| 0 | 100 Km. |
| 0 | 100 Mi. |

**1453**
(end of the war)

Held by the kings of England

| 0 | 100 Km. |
| 0 | 100 Mi. |

MAP 12.2  ENGLISH HOLDINGS IN FRANCE DURING THE HUNDRED YEARS WAR  *The year 1429 marked the greatest extent of English holdings in France. Why was it unlikely that England could have held these territories permanently?*

## THE POPULAR RESPONSE

The governments of both England and France manipulated public opinion to support the war. Whatever significance modern students ascribe to the economic factor, public opinion in fourteenth-century England held that the war was waged for one reason: to secure for King Edward the French crown he had been denied.[6] Edward III issued letters to the sheriffs describing in graphic terms the evil deeds of the French and listing the royal needs. Royal letters instructed the clergy to deliver sermons filled with patriotic sentiment. Frequent assemblies of Parliament – which theoretically represented the entire nation – spread royal propaganda for the war. The royal courts sensationalized the wickedness of the other side and stressed the great fortunes to be made from the war. Philip VI sent agents to warn communities about the dangers of invasion and to stress the French Crown's revenue needs to meet the attack.

The royal campaign to rally public opinion was highly successful, at least in the early stage of the war. Edward III gained widespread support in the 1340s and 1350s. The English developed a deep hatred of the French and feared that King Philip intended "to have seized and slaughtered the entire realm of England." As England was successful in the field, pride in the country's military proficiency increased.

Most important of all, the war was popular because it presented unusual opportunities for wealth and advancement. Poor and unemployed knights were promised regular wages.

Criminals who enlisted were granted pardons. The great nobles expected to be rewarded with estates. Royal exhortations to the troops before battles repeatedly stressed that, if victorious, the men might keep whatever they seized. The French chronicler Jean Froissart wrote that at the time of Edward III's expedition of 1359, men of all ranks flocked to the king's banner. Some came to acquire honor, but many came in order "to loot and pillage the fair and plenteous land of France."[7]

## THE INDIAN SUMMER OF MEDIEVAL CHIVALRY

The period of the Hundred Years' War witnessed the final flowering of the aristocratic code of medieval chivalry. Indeed, the enthusiastic participation of the nobility in both France and England was in response primarily to the opportunity the war provided to display chivalric behavior. Chivalry was a code of conduct originally devised by the clergy to improve the crude and brutal behavior of the knightly class. A knight was supposed to be brave, anxious to win praise, courteous, loyal to his commander, gracious, and generous. What better place to display these qualities than on the field of battle?

War was considered an ennobling experience; there was something elevating, manly, fine, and beautiful about it. When Shakespeare in the sixteenth century wrote of "the pomp and circumstance of glorious war," he was echoing the fourteenth- and fifteenth-century chroniclers who had glorified the trappings of war. Describing the French army before the battle of Poitiers (1356), a contemporary said, "Then you might see banners and pennons unfurled to the wind, whereon fine gold and azure shone, purple, gules and ermine. Trumpets, horns and clarions – you might hear sounding through the camp; the Dauphin's great battle made the earth ring."[8]

The chronicler Froissart repeatedly speaks of the beauty of an army assembled for battle. Writing of the French army before the battle of Bergues in 1383, Froissart reflected the attitudes of the aristocratic classes: it was "a great beauty to see the banners, pennons, and basinets glittering against the sun, and such a great multitude of men-at-arms that the eye of man could not take them in, and it seemed that they bore a veritable forest of lances." At Poitiers, it was marvelous and terrifying to hear the thundering of the horses' hooves, the cries of the wounded, the sound of the trumpets and clarions, and the shouting of war cries. The tumult was heard at a distance of more than three leagues. And it was a great grief to see and behold the flower of all the nobility and chivalry of the world go thus to destruction, to death, and to martyrdom on both sides.

This romantic and "marvelous" view of war holds little appeal for modern men and women, who are more conscious of the slaughter, brutality, dirt, and blood that war inevitably involves. Also, modern thinkers are usually conscious of the broad mass of people, while the chivalric code applied only to the aristocratic military elite. Chivalry had no reference to those outside the knightly class.

The knight was supposed to show courtesy, graciousness, and generosity to his social equals, but certainly not to his social inferiors. When English knights fought French ones, they were social equals fighting according to a mutually accepted code of behavior. The infantry troops were looked upon as inferior beings. When a peasant force at Longueil destroyed a contingent of English knights, their comrades mourned them because "it was too much that so many good fighters had been killed by mere peasants."[9]

Armies in the field were commanded by rulers themselves, by princes of the blood such as Edward III's son Edward, the Black Prince — so-called because of the color of his armor — or by great aristocrats. Knights formed the cavalry; the despised peasantry served as infantrymen, pikemen, and archers. Edward III set up recruiting boards in the counties to enlist the strongest peasants. Perhaps 10 percent of the adult population of England was involved in the actual fighting or in supplying and supporting the troops. The French contingents were even larger. By medieval standards, the force was astronomically large, especially considering the difficulty of transporting men, weapons, and horses across the English Channel. The costs of these armies stretched French and English resources to the breaking point.

The war was fought almost entirely in France and the Low Countries. It consisted mainly of a series of random sieges and cavalry raids. In 1335 the French began supporting Scottish incursions into northern England, ravaging the countryside in Aquitaine, and sacking and burning English coastal towns, such as Southampton. Naturally, such tactics lent weight to Edward III's propaganda campaign. In fact, royal propaganda on both sides fostered a kind of early nationalism.

In the early stages of the war, England was highly successful. At Crécy in northern France in 1346, English longbowmen scored a great victory over French knights and crossbowmen. Although the fire of the longbow was not very accurate, it allowed for rapid reloading, and the English archers could send off three arrows to the French crossbowmen's one. The result was a blinding shower of arrows that unhorsed the French knights and caused mass confusion. The firing of cannon —

THE BATTLE OF CRÉCY, 1346 *Pitched battles were unusual in the Hundred Years' War. At Crécy, however, the English (on the right with lions on their royal standard) scored a spectacular victory. The longbow proved a more effective weapon than the French crossbow, and the low-born English archers withstood a charge of the aristocratic French knights. (Photo: Larousse)*

probably the first use of artillery in the West — created further panic. Thereupon the English horsemen charged and butchered the French.

This was not war according to the chivalric rules that Edward III would have preferred. The English victory at Crécy rests on the skill and swiftness of the despised peasant archers, who had nothing at all to do with the chi- valric ideals for which the war was being fought. Ten years later Edward the Black Prince, using the same tactics as at Crécy, smashed the French at Poitiers, captured the French king, and held him for ransom. Again at Agincourt near Arras in 1415, the chivalric English soldier-king Henry V (1413–1422) gained the field over vastly superior numbers. Henry followed up his triumph at Agincourt

**FIFTEENTH-CENTURY ARMOR** *This kind of expensive plate armor was worn by the aristocratic nobility in the fifteenth and sixteenth centuries. The use of gunpowder gradually made armor outmoded. (Courtesy, World Heritage Museum. Photo: Caroline Buckler)*

with the reconquest of Normandy. By 1419, the English had advanced to the walls of Paris (see Map 12.2).

But the French cause was not lost. Though England had won the initial victories, France won the war.

### JOAN OF ARC AND FRANCE'S VICTORY

The ultimate French success rests heavily on the actions of an obscure French peasant girl, Joan of Arc, whose vision and work revived French fortunes and led to victory. A great deal of pious and popular legend surrounds Joan the Maid, because of her peculiar appearance on the scene, her astonishing success, her martyrdom, and her canonization by the Catholic church. The historical fact is that she saved the French monarchy, which was the embodiment of France.

Born in 1412 in the village of Domrémy in Champagne to well-to-do peasants, Joan of Arc grew up in a religious household. During adolescence she began to hear voices, which she later said belonged to Saint Michael, Saint Catherine, and Saint Margaret. In 1428, these voices spoke to her with great urgency, telling her that the dauphin (the uncrowned King Charles VII) had to be crowned and the English expelled from France. Joan went to the French court, persuaded the king to reject the rumor that he was illegitimate, and secured his support for her relief of the besieged city of Orléans.

The astonishing thing is not that Joan the Maid overcame serious obstacles to see the dauphin, not even that Charles and his advisers listened to her. What is amazing is the swiftness with which they were convinced. French fortunes had been so low for so long that the court believed only a miracle could save the country. Because Joan cut her hair short and dressed like a man, she scandalized the court. But hoping she would provide the necessary miracle, Charles allowed her to accompany the army that was preparing to raise the English siege of Orléans.

In the meantime Joan, herself illiterate, dictated the following letter calling upon the English to withdraw:

*JHESUS MARIA*

*King of England, and you Duke of Bedford, calling yourself regent of France, you William Pole, Count of Suffolk John Talbot, and you Thomas Lord Scales, calling yourselves Lieutenants of the said Duke of Bedford, do right in the King of Heaven's sight. Surrender to* The Maid *sent hither by God the King of Heaven, the keys of all the good towns you have taken and laid waste in France. She comes in God's name to establish the Blood Royal, ready to make peace if you agree to abandon France and repay what you have taken. And you, archers, comrades in arms, gentles and others, who are before the town of Orléans, retire in God's name to your own country. If you do not, expect to hear tidings from* The Maid *who will shortly come upon you to your very great hurt. And to you, King of England, if you do not thus, I am a chieftain of war, and whenever I meet your followers in France, I will drive them out; if they will not obey, I will put them all to death. I am sent here in God's name, the King of Heaven, to drive you body for body out of all France.*[10]

Joan apparently thought of herself as an agent of God.

Joan arrived before Orléans on April 28, 1429. Seventeen years old, she knew little of warfare and believed that if she could keep the French troops from swearing and frequenting whorehouses, victory would be theirs. On May 8, the English, weakened by disease and lack of supplies, withdrew from Orléans. Ten days later, Charles VII was crowned king at Reims. These two events marked the turning point in the war.

JOAN OF ARC *Later considered the symbol of the French state in its struggle against the English, Joan of Arc here carries a sword in one hand and a banner with the royal symbol of fleur-de-lis in the other. Her face, which scholars believe to be a good resemblance, shows inner strength and calm determination. (Archives Nationales, Paris/Giraudon)*

In 1430 England's allies, the Burgundians, captured Joan and sold her to the English. When the English handed her over to the ecclesiastical authorities for trial, the French court did not intervene. While the English wanted Joan eliminated for obvious political reasons, sorcery (witchcraft) was the ostensible charge at her trial. Witch persecution was increasing in the fifteenth century and Joan's wearing of men's clothes appeared not only aberrant but indicative of contact with the devil. Asked why she did so, Joan replied, "It is a little thing and of small importance. I did not don it by the advice of men of this world. I donned it only by the command of God and the angels."[11]

Joan of Arc's political impact on the course of the Hundred Years' War and on the development of the kingdom of France has led scholars to examine her character and behavior very closely. Besides being an excellent athlete and a superb rider, she usually dressed like a rich and elegant young nobleman. Some students maintain that Joan's manner of dress suggests uncertainty about her own sexual identity. She did not menstruate – very rare in a healthy girl of eighteen – though she was female in every external respect: many men, including several dukes, admired her beautiful breasts. Perhaps, as Joan said, wearing men's clothes meant nothing at all. On the other hand, as some writers believe, she may have wanted to assume a completely new identity. Joan always insisted that God had specially chosen her for her mission. The richness and masculinity of her clothes, therefore, emphasized her uniqueness and made her highly conspicuous.[12] In 1431 the court condemned her as a heretic – her claim of direct inspiration from God, thereby denying the authority of church officials, constituted heresy – and burned her at the stake in the marketplace in Rouen. A fresh trial in 1456 rehabilitated her name. In 1902 she was canonized and declared a holy maiden, and today she is revered as the second patron saint of France. The nineteenth-century French historian Jules Michelet extolled Joan of Arc as a symbol of the vitality and strength of the French peasant classes.

The relief of Orléans stimulated French pride and rallied French resources. In England, as the war dragged on, loss of life mounted, and money appeared to be flowing into a bottomless pit, demands for an end increased. The clergy and the intellectuals pressed for peace. Parliamentary opposition to additional war grants stiffened. Slowly the

French reconquered Normandy and, finally, ejected the English from Aquitaine. At the end of the war, in 1453, only the town of Calais remained in English hands.

## COSTS AND CONSEQUENCES

For both France and England, the war proved a disaster. In France, the English had slaughtered thousands of soldiers and civilians. In the years after the sweep of the Black Death, this additional killing meant a grave loss of population. The English had laid waste to hundreds of thousands of acres of rich farmland, leaving the rural economy of many parts of France in a shambles. The war had disrupted trade and the great fairs, resulting in the drastic reduction of French participation in international commerce. Defeat in battle and heavy taxation contributed to widespread dissatisfaction and aggravated peasant grievances.

In England, only the southern coastal ports experienced much destruction; yet England fared little better than France. The costs of war were tremendous: England spent over £5 million in the war effort, a huge sum in the fourteenth and fifteenth centuries. The worst loss was in manpower. Between 10 and 15 percent of the adult male population between the ages of fifteen and forty-five fought in the army or navy. In the decades after the plague, when the country was already suffering a severe manpower shortage, war losses made a bad situation frightful. Peasants serving in France as archers and pikemen were desperately needed to till the fields. The knights who ordinarily handled the work of local government as sheriffs, coroners, jurymen, and justices of the peace were abroad, and their absence contributed to the breakdown of order at the local level. The English government attempted to finance the war effort by raising taxes on the wool crop. Because of steadily increasing costs, the Flemish and Italian buyers could not afford English wool. Consequently, wool exports slumped drastically between 1350 and 1450.

Many men of all social classes had volunteered for service in France in the hope of acquiring booty and becoming rich. The chronicler Walsingham, describing the period of Crécy, tells of the tremendous prosperity and abundance resulting from the spoils of war: "For the woman was of no account who did not possess something from the spoils of . . . cities overseas in clothing, furs, quilts, and utensils . . . tablecloths and jewels, bowls of murra [semiprecious stone] and silver, linen and linen cloths."[13] Walsingham is referring to 1348, in the first generation of war. As time went on, most fortunes seem to have been squandered as fast as they were made.

If English troops returned with cash, they did not invest it in land. In the fifteenth century, returning soldiers were commonly described as beggars and vagabonds, roaming about making mischief. Even the large sums of money received from the ransom of the great – such as the £250,000 paid to Edward III for the freedom of King John of France – and the monies paid as indemnities by captured towns and castles did not begin to equal the £5 million-plus spent. England suffered a serious net loss.[14]

The long war also had a profound impact on the political and cultural lives of the two countries. Most notably, it stimulated the development of the English Parliament. Edward III's constant need for money to pay for the war compelled him to summon not only the great barons and bishops but knights of the shires and burgesses from the towns as well. Between the outbreak of the war in 1337 and the king's death in 1377, parliamentary assemblies met twenty-seven times. Parliament met in thirty-seven of the fifty years of Edward's reign.

The frequency of the meetings is significant. Representative assemblies were becoming a habit, a tradition. Knights and burgesses – or the Commons, as they came to be called – recognized their mutual interests and began to meet apart from the great lords. The Commons gradually realized that they held the country's purse strings, and a parliamentary statute of 1341 required that all nonfeudal levies have parliamentary approval. When Edward III signed the law, he acknowledged that the king of England could not tax without Parliament's consent. Increasingly, during the course of the war, money grants were tied to royal redress of grievances: if the government was to raise money, it had to correct the wrongs its subjects protested.

As the Commons met in a separate chamber – the House of Commons – it also developed its own organization. The speaker came to preside over debates in the House of Commons and to represent the Commons before the House of Lords and the king. Clerks kept a record of what transpired during discussions in the Commons.

In England theoretical consent to taxation and legislation was given in one assembly for the entire country. France had no such single assembly; instead, there were many regional or provincial assemblies. Why did a national representative assembly fail to develop in France? The initiative for convening assemblies rested with the king, who needed revenue almost as much as the English ruler. But the French monarchy found the idea of representative assemblies thoroughly distasteful. The advice of a counselor to King Charles VI (1380–1422), "above all things be sure that no great assemblies of nobles or of *communes* take place in your kingdom,"[15] was accepted. Charles VII (1422–1461) even threatened to punish those proposing a national assembly.

The English Parliament was above all else a court of law, a place where justice was done and grievances remedied. No French assembly (except that of Brittany) had such competence. The national assembly in England met frequently. In France general assemblies were so rare that they never got the opportunity to develop precise procedures or to exercise judicial functions.

No one in France wanted a national assembly. Linguistic, geographic, economic, legal, and political differences were very strong. People tended to think of themselves as Breton, Norman, Burgundian, or whatever, rather than as French. Through much of the fourteenth and early fifteenth centuries, weak monarchs lacked the power to call a national assembly. Provincial assemblies, highly jealous of their independence, did not want a national assembly. The costs of sending delegates to it would be high, and the result was likely to be increased taxation. Finally, the Hundred Year's War itself hindered the growth of a representative body. Violence on dangerous roads discouraged travel. As the fifteenth-century English jurist Sir John Fortescue wrote, "Englishmen made such war in France that the three Estates dared not come together."[16]

In both countries, however, the war did promote the growth of nationalism – the feeling of unity and identity that binds together a people who speak the same language, have a common ancestry and customs, and live in the same area. In the fourteenth century, nationalism largely took the form of hostility to foreigners. Both Philip VI and Edward III drummed up support for the war by portraying the enemy as an alien, evil people. Edward III linked his personal dynastic quarrel with England's national interests. As the Parliament Roll of 1348 states:

*The Knights of the shires and the others of the Commons were told that they should withdraw together and take good counsel as to how, for with-standing* the malice of the said enemy *and for the salvation of our said lord the King and his Kingdom of England . . . the King could be aided.*[17]

After victories, each country experienced a surge of pride in its military strength. Just as English patriotism ran strong after Crécy and Poitiers, so French national confidence rose after Orléans. French national feeling demanded the expulsion of the enemy not merely from Normandy and Aquitaine but from French soil. Perhaps no one expressed this national consciousness better than Joan of Arc, when she exulted that the enemy had been "driven out of *France.*"

## VERNACULAR LITERATURE

Few developments expressed the emergence of national consciousness more vividly than the emergence of national literatures. Across Europe people spoke the language and dialect of their particular locality and class. In England, for example, the common people spoke regional English dialects, while the upper classes conversed in French. Official documents and works of literature were written in Latin or French. Beginning in the fourteenth century, however, national languages – the vernacular – came into use not only in verbal communication but in literature as well. Three masterpieces of European culture, Dante's *Divine Comedy* (1321), Chaucer's *Canterbury Tales* (1387–1400), and Villon's *Grand Testament* (1461) brilliantly manifest this new national pride.

Dante Aligheri (1265–1321) descended from an aristocratic family in Florence, where he held several positions in the city government. Dante called his work a comedy because

DANTE   *In this sixteenth-century allegorical tribute to the most famous of all Florentines, the crowned poet laureate broods over the eternal conflict between the spiritual and the temporal. His right hand protects his* beloved Florence, *while his left hand holds the* Divine Comedy *open to paradise, which is seen in the distance surrounded by light. (National Gallery of Art, Washington, D.C. Samual H. Kress Collection 1961)*

he wrote it in Italian and in a different style from the "tragic" Latin; a later generation added the adjective "divine," referring both to its sacred subject and to Dante's artistry. The *Divine Comedy* is an allegorical trilogy of one hundred cantos (verses) whose three equal parts (1+33+33+33) each describe one of the realms of the next world, Hell, Purgatory, and Paradise. Dante recounts his imaginary journey through these regions toward God. The Roman poet Virgil, representing reason, leads Dante through Hell where he observes the torments of the damned and denounces the disorders of his own time, especially ec-

clesiastical ambition and corruption. Passing up into Purgatory, Virgil shows the poet how souls are purified of their disordered inclinations. In Paradise, home of the angels and saints, St. Bernard – representing mystic contemplation – leads Dante to the Virgin Mary. Through her intercession he at last attains a vision of God.

The *Divine Comedy* portrays contemporary and historical figures, comments on secular and ecclesiastical affairs, and draws on scholastic philosophy. Within the framework of a symbolic pilgrimage to the City of God, the *Divine Comedy* embodies the psychological tensions of the age. A profoundly Christian poem, it also contains bitter criticism of some church authorities. In its symmetrical structure and use of figures from the ancient world, such as Virgil, the poem perpetuates the classical tradition, but as the first major work of literature in the Italian vernacular it is distinctly modern.

Geoffrey Chaucer (1340–1400), the son of a London wine merchant, was an official in the administrations of the English kings Edward III and Richard II who wrote poetry as an avocation. Chaucer's *Canterbury Tales* is a collection of stories in a lengthy rhymed narrative. On a pilgrimage to the shrine of St. Thomas Becket at Canterbury (see page 362), thirty people of various social backgrounds each tell a tale. The Prologue sets the scene and describes the pilgrims, whose characters are further revealed in the story each person tells. For example, the gentle Christian Knight relates a chivalric romance; the gross Miller tells a vulgar story about a deceived husband; the earthy Wife of Bath, who earns her living as a weaver and has buried five husbands, sketches a fable about the selection of a spouse; and the elegant Prioress, who violates her vows by wearing jewelry, delivers a homily on the Virgin. In depicting the interests and behavior of all types of people, Chaucer presents a rich panorama of English social life in the fourteenth century. Like the *Divine Comedy,* the *Canterbury Tales* reflects the cultural tensions of the times. Ostensibly Christian, many of the pilgrims are also materialistic, sensual, and worldly, suggesting the ambivalence of the broader society's concern for the next world and frank enjoyment of this one.

Our knowledge of François Villon (1413–1463), probably the greatest poet of late medieval France, derives from Paris police records and his own poetry. Born to desper-ately poor parents in the year of Joan of Arc's execution, Villon was sent by his guardian to the University of Paris where he earned the Master of Arts degree. A rowdy and free-spirited student, he disliked the stuffiness of academic life. In 1455 Villon killed a man in a street brawl; banished from Paris, he joined one of the bands of wandering thieves that harassed the countryside after the Hundred Years' War. For his fellow bandits he composed ballads in thieves' jargon.

Villon's *Lais* (1456), a pun on the word *legs* (meaning "legacy"), is a series of farcical bequests to his friends and enemies. *Ballade des Pendus* (Ballad of the Hanged) was written while contemplating that fate in prison. (His execution was commuted.) Villon's greatest and most self-revealing work, the *Grand Testament,* contains another string of bequests, including a legacy to a prostitute, and describes his unshakeable faith in the beauty of life here on earth. The *Grand Testament* possesses elements of social rebellion, bawdy humor, and rare emotional depth. While the themes of Dante's and Chaucer's poetry are distinctly medieval, Villon's celebration of the human condition here on earth brands him as definitely modern. While he used medieval forms of versification, Villon's language was the despised vernacular of the poor and the criminal.

## THE DECLINE OF THE CHURCH'S PRESTIGE

In times of crisis or disaster, people of all faiths have sought the consolation of religion. In the fourteenth century, however, the official Christian church offered very little solace. In fact, the leaders of the church added to the sorrow and misery of the times.

From 1309 to 1372, the popes lived in the city of Avignon in southeastern France. In order to control the church and its policies, Philip the Fair of France pressured Pope Clement V to settle in Avignon (page 383). Clement, critically ill with cancer, lacked the will to resist Philip. This period in church history is often called the Babylonian Captivity (referring to the seventy years the ancient Hebrews were held captive in Mesopotamian Babylon).

The Babylonian Captivity badly damaged papal prestige. The Avignon papacy reformed its financial administration and centralized its government. But the seven popes at Avignon concentrated on bureaucratic matters to the exclusion of spiritual objectives. Although some of the popes led austere lives at Avignon, the general atmosphere was one of luxury, splendor, and extravagance. The leadership of the church was cut off from its historic roots and the source of its ancient authority, the city of Rome. In the absence of the papacy, the Papal States in Italy lacked stability and good government. The economy of Rome had long been based on the presence of the papal court and the rich tourist trade the papacy attracted. The Babylonian Captivity left Rome poverty-stricken. As long as the French crown dominated papal policy, papal influence in England (with whom France was intermittently at war) and in Germany declined.

Many devout Christians urged the popes to return to Rome. The Dominican mystic Catherine of Siena, for example, made a special trip to Avignon to plead with the pope to return. In 1377, Pope Gregory XI brought the papal court back to Rome. Unfortunately, he died shortly after the return. At Gregory's death, Roman citizens demanded an Italian pope who would remain in Rome. Determined to influence the papal conclave (the assembly of cardinals who choose the new pope) to elect an Italian, a Roman mob surrounded St. Peter's Basilica, blocked the roads leading out of the city, and seized all boats on the Tiber River. Between the time of Gregory's death and the opening of the conclave, great pressure was put on the cardinals to elect an Italian. At the time, none of them protested this pressure.

Sixteen cardinals – eleven Frenchmen, four Italians, and one Spaniard – entered the conclave on April 7, 1378. After two ballots they unanimously chose a distinguished administrator, the archbishop of Bari, Bartolomeo Prignano, who took the name Urban VI. Each of the cardinals swore that Urban had been elected "sincerely, freely, genuinely, and canonically."

Urban VI (1378–1389) had excellent intentions for church reform: he wanted to abolish simony, pluralism (holding several church offices at the same time), absenteeism, clerical extravagance, and ostentation. These were the very abuses being increasingly criticized by Christian peoples across Europe. Unfortunately, Pope Urban went about the work of reform in a tactless, arrogant, and bullheaded manner. The day after his coronation he delivered a blistering attack on cardinals who lived in Rome while drawing their income from benefices elsewhere. His criticism was well-founded but ill-timed, and provoked opposition among the hierarchy before Urban had consolidated his authority.

In the weeks that followed Urban stepped up attacks on clerical luxury, denouncing individual cardinals by name. He threatened to strike the cardinal archbishop of Amiens. Urban even threatened to excommunicate certain cardinals, and when he was advised that such excommunications would not be lawful unless the guilty had been warned three times, he shouted, "I can do anything, if it be my will and judgment."[18] Urban's quick temper and irrational behavior have led scholars to question his sanity. Whether he was medically insane or just drunk with power is a moot point. In any case, Urban's actions brought on disaster.

In groups of two and three, the cardinals slipped away from Rome and met at Anagni. They declared Urban's election invalid because it had come about under threats from the Roman mob, and they asserted that Urban himself was excommunicated. The cardinals then proceeded to the city of Fondi between Rome and Naples and elected Cardinal Robert of Geneva, the brother of King Charles V of France, as pope. Cardinal Robert took the name Clement VII. There were thus two popes – Urban at Rome and the anti-pope Clement VII (1378–1394), who set himself up at Avignon in opposition to the legally elected Urban. So began the Great Schism, which divided Western Christendom until 1417.

## THE GREAT SCHISM

The powers of Europe aligned themselves with Urban or Clement along strictly political lines. France naturally recognized the French anti-pope, Clement. England, France's historic enemy, recognized Pope Urban. Scotland, whose attacks on England were subsidized by France, followed the French and supported Clement. Aragon, Castile, and Portugal hesitated before deciding for Clement at Avignon. The German emperor, who enjoyed the title of king of the Romans and bore ancient hostility to France, recognized Urban VI. At first the Italian city-states recognized Urban; when he alienated them, they opted for Clement.

John of Spoleto, a professor at the law school at Bologna, eloquently summed up intellectual opinion of the schism:

*The longer this schism lasts, the more it appears to be costing, and the more harm it does: scandal, massacres, ruination, agitations, troubles and disturbances . . . this dissention is the root of everything: divers tumults, quarrels between kings, seditions, extortions, assassinations, acts of violence, wars, rising tyranny, decreasing freedom, the impunity of villains, grudges, error, disgrace, the madness of steel and of fire given license.*[19]

The scandal of competing popes "rent the seamless garment of Christ," as the church was called, and provoked horror and vigorous cries for reform. The common people, wracked by inflation, wars, and plague, were thoroughly confused about which pope was legitimate. The schism weakened the religious faith of many Christians and gave rise to instability and religious excesses. It brought the leadership of the church into serious disrepute. At a time when ordinary Christians needed the consolation of religion and confidence in their religious leaders, church officials were fighting among themselves for power.

## THE CONCILIAR MOVEMENT

Calls for reform of the church were not new. A half-century before the Great Schism, in 1324, Marsiglio of Padua, then rector of the University of Paris, had published *Defensor Pacis* (*The Defender of the Peace*). Dealing as it did with the authority of the state and the church, *Defensor Pacis* proved to be one of the most controversial works written in the Middle Ages.

Marsiglio argued that the state was the great unifying power in society and that the church was subordinate to the state. He put forth the revolutionary ideas that the church had no inherent jurisdiction and should own no property. Authority in the Christian church, according to Marsiglio, should rest in a general council, made up of laymen as well as priests and superior to the pope. These ideas directly contradicted the medieval notion of a society governed by the church and the state, with the church ultimately supreme.

*Defensor Pacis* was condemned by the pope and Marsiglio was excommunicated. But the idea that a general council representing all of the church had a higher authority than the pope was repeated by John Gerson (1363–1429), a later chancellor of the University of Paris and influential theologian.

Even more earthshaking than the theories of Marsiglio of Padua were the ideas of the English scholar and theologian John Wyclif (1329-1384). Wyclif wrote that papal claims of temporal power had no foundation in the Scriptures, and that the Scriptures alone should be the standard of Christian belief and practice. He urged the abolition of such practices as the veneration of saints, pilgrimages, pluralism, and absenteeism. Every sincere Christian, according to Wyclif, should read the Bible for himself. Wyclif's views had broad social and economic significance. He urged that the church be stripped of its property. His idea that every Christian free of mortal sin possessed lordship was seized upon by peasants in England during a revolt in 1381 and used to justify their goals.

In advancing these views, Wyclif struck at the roots of medieval church structure and religious practices. Consequently, he has been hailed as the precursor of the Reformation of the sixteenth century. Although Wyclif's ideas were vigorously condemned by ecclesiastical authorities, they were widely disseminated by humble clerics and enjoyed great popularity in the early fifteenth century. Wyclif's followers were called Lollards. The term, meaning mumblers of prayers and psalms, refers to what they criticized. After the Czech king Wenceslaus's sister Anne married Richard II of England, members of Queen Anne's household carried Lollard principles back to Bohemia, where they were spread by John Hus, rector of the University of Prague.

While John Wyclif's ideas were being spread, two German scholars at the University of Paris, Henry of Langenstein and Conrad of Gelnhausen, produced treatises urging the summoning of a general council. Conrad wrote that the church, as the congregation of all the faithful, was superior to the pope. Although canon law held that only a pope might call a council, a higher law existed, the common good. The common good of Christendom required the convocation of a council.

In response to continued Europe-wide calls for a council, the two colleges of cardinals — one at Rome, the other at Avignon — summoned a council at Pisa in Italy in 1409. A distinguished gathering of prelates and theologians deposed both popes and selected another. Neither the Avignon pope nor the Roman pope would resign, however, and the appalling result was a threefold schism.

Finally, due to the pressure of the German emperor Sigismund, a great council met at Constance in Switzerland (1414-1418). It had three objectives: to end the schism, to reform the church "in head and members" (from top to bottom), and to wipe out heresy. The council condemned the Lollard ideas of John Hus, and he was burned at the stake. The council eventually deposed both the Roman pope and the successor of the pope chosen at Pisa, and it isolated the Avignonese anti-pope. A conclave elected a new leader, the Roman Cardinal Colonna, who took the name Martin V (1417-1431).

Martin proceeded to dissolve the council. Nothing was done about reform. The schism was over, and the conciliar movement in effect ended. For a time thereafter, the papacy concentrated on Italian problems to the exclusion of universal Christian interests. But the schism and the conciliar movement had exposed the crying need for ecclesiastical reform, thus laying the foundations for the great reform efforts of the sixteenth century.

## THE LIFE OF THE PEOPLE

In the fourteenth century, economic and political difficulties, disease, and war profoundly affected the lives of European peoples. Decades of slaughter and destruction, punctuated by the decimating visits of the Black Death, made a grave economic situation virtually disastrous. In many parts of France and the Low Countries fields lay in ruin or untilled for lack of manpower. In England, as taxes increased, criticism of government policy and mismanagement multiplied. Crime, always a factor in social history, aggravated economic troubles, and throughout Europe the frustrations of the common people erupted into widespread revolts. For most people, marriage and the local parish church continued to be the center of their lives.

### FUR-COLLAR CRIME

The Hundred Years' War had provided employment and opportunity for thousands of idle and fortune-seeking knights. But during periods of truce and after the war finally ended, many nobles once again had little to do. Inflation also hurt them. Although many were living on fixed incomes, their chivalric code demanded lavish generosity and an aristocratic lifestyle. Many nobles turned to crime as a way of raising money. The fourteenth and fifteenth centuries witnessed a great deal of "fur-collar crime," so-called for the miniver fur the nobility alone were allowed to wear on their collars. England provides a good case study of upper-class crime.

Fur-collar crime rarely involved such felonies as homicide, robbery, rape, and arson. Instead, nobles used their superior social status to rob and extort from the weak and then to corrupt the judicial process. Groups of noble brigands roamed the English countryside stealing from both rich and poor. Sir John de Colseby and Sir William Bussy led a gang of thirty-eight knights who stole goods worth £3,000 in various robberies. Operating exactly like modern urban racketeers, knightly gangs demanded that peasants pay "protection money" or else have their hovels burned and their fields destroyed. Members of the household of a certain Lord Robert of Payn beat up a victim and then demanded money for protection from future attack.

Attacks on the rich often took the form of kidnaping and extortion. Individuals were grabbed in their homes, and wealthy travelers were seized on the highways and held for ransom. In northern England a gang of gentry led by Sir Gilbert de Middleton abducted Sir Henry Beaumont and his brother, the bishop-elect of Durham, and two Roman cardinals in England on a peacemaking visit. Only after a ransom was paid were the victims released.[20]

Fur-collar criminals were terrorists, but like some twentieth-century white-collar criminals who commit nonviolent crimes, medieval aristocratic criminals got away with their outrages. When accused of wrongdoing, fur-collar criminals intimidated witnesses. They threatened jurors. They used "pull" or influence or cash to bribe judges. As a fourteenth-century English judge wrote to a young nobleman, "For the love of your father I have hindered charges being brought against you and have prevented execution of indictment actually made."[21]

The ballads of Robin Hood, a collection of folk legends from late medieval England, describe the adventures of the outlaw hero and his band of followers, who lived in Sherwood Forest and attacked and punished those who violated the social system and the law. Most of the villains in these simple tales are fur-collar criminals — grasping landlords, wicked sheriffs such as the famous sheriff of Nottingham, and mercenary churchmen. Robin and his merry men performed a sort of retributive justice. Robin Hood was a popular figure, because he symbolized the deep resentment of aristocratic corruption and abuse; he represented the struggle against tyranny and oppression.

Criminal activity by nobles continued decade after decade because governments were not strong enough to stop it. Then, too, much of the crime was directed against a lord's own serfs, and the line between a noble's legal jurisdiction over his peasants and criminal behavior was a very fine one indeed. Persecution by lords, coming on top of war, disease, and natural disasters, eventually drove long-suffering peasants all across Europe to revolt.

## PEASANT REVOLTS

Peasant revolts occurred often in the Middle Ages. Early in the thirteenth century, the French preacher Jacques de Vitry asked rhetorically, "How many serfs have killed their lords or burnt their castles?"[22] Social and economic conditions in the fourteenth and fifteenth centuries caused a great increase in peasant uprisings.

In 1358, when French taxation for the Hundred Years' War fell heavily on the poor, the frustrations of the French peasantry exploded in a massive uprising called the *Jacquerie,* after the nickname of a supposedly happy agricultural laborer, Jacques Bonhomme (Good Fellow). Peasants in Picardy and Champagne went on the rampage.

Crowds swept through the countryside slashing the throats of nobles, burning their castles, raping their wives and daughters, killing or maiming their horses and cattle. Peasants blamed the nobility for oppressive taxes, for the criminal brigandage of the countryside, for defeat in war, and for the general misery. Artisans, small merchants, and parish priests joined the peasants. Urban and rural groups committed terrible destruction, and for several weeks the nobles were on the defensive. Then the upper class united to repress the revolt with savage and merciless ferocity. Thousands of the "Jacques," innocent as well as guilty, were cut down.

This forcible supppression of social rebellion, without some effort to alleviate its underlying causes, could only serve as a stopgap measure and drive protest underground. Between 1363 and 1484, serious peasant revolts swept the Auvergne; in 1380, uprisings occurred in the Midi; and in 1420, they erupted in the Lyonnais region of France.

The Peasants' Revolt in England in 1381, involving perhaps a hundred thousand people, was probably the largest single uprising of the entire Middle Ages. The causes were complex and varied from place to place. In general, though, the thirteenth century had witnessed the steady commutation of labor services for cash rents, and the Black Death had drastically cut the labor supply. As a result, peasants demanded higher wages and fewer manorial obligations. The parliamentary Statute of Laborers of 1351 (see page 393) declared:

*Whereas to curb the malice of servants who after the pestilence were idle and unwilling to serve without securing excessive wages, it was recently ordained . . . that such servants, both men and women, shall be bound to serve in return for salaries and wages that were customary . . . five or six years earlier.*[23]

THE JACQUERIE   *Because social revolt on the part of war-weary, frustrated poor seemed to threaten the natural order of Christian society, the upper classes everywhere exacted terrible vengeance on peasants and* artisans. In this scene some jacques *are cut down, some beheaded, and others drowned. (Bibliothèque Nationale, Paris)*

This statute was an attempt by landlords to freeze wages and social mobility.

The statute could not be enforced. As a matter of fact, the condition of the English peasantry steadily improved in the course of the fourteenth century. Some scholars believe that the peasantry in most places was better off in the period 1350–1450 than it had been for centuries before or was to be for four centuries after.

Why then was the outburst in 1381 so serious? It was provoked by a crisis of rising expectations. The relative prosperity of the laboring classes led to demands that the upper classes were unwilling to grant. Unable to climb higher, the peasants' frustration found release in revolt. Economic grievances combined with other factors. Decades of aristocratic violence, much of it perpetrated against the weak peasantry, had bred hostility and bitterness. In France frustration over the lack of permanent victory increased. In England the social and religious agitation of the popular preacher John Ball fanned the embers of discontent. Such sayings as Ball's famous couplet

*When Adam delved and Eve span*
*Who was then the gentleman?*

reflect real revolutionary sentiment. But the lords of England believed that God had permanently fixed the hierarchical order of society and that nothing man could do would change that order. Moreover, the south of England, where the revolt broke out, had been subjected to frequent and destructive French raids. The English government did little to protect the south, and villages grew increasingly scared and insecure. Fear erupted into violence.

The straw that broke the camel's back in England was a head tax on all adult males. Although it met widespread opposition in 1380, the royal council ordered the sheriffs to collect it again in 1381 on penalty of a huge fine. Beginning with assaults on the tax collectors, the uprising in England followed much the same course as had the Jacquerie in France. Castles and manors were sacked; manorial records were destroyed. Many nobles, including the archbishop of Canterbury, who had ordered the collection of the tax, were murdered.

Although the center of the revolt was the highly populated and economically advanced south and east, sections of the north and the Midlands also witnessed rebellions. Violence took different forms in different places. The townspeople of Cambridge expressed their hostility to the university by sacking one of the colleges and building a bonfire of academic property. In towns containing skilled Flemish craftsmen, fear of competition led to their attack and murder. Urban discontent merged with rural violence. Apprentices and journeymen, frustrated because the highest positions in the guilds were closed to them, rioted.

The boy-king Richard II (1377–1399) met the leaders of the revolt, agreed to charters insuring peasants' freedom, tricked them with false promises, and then proceeded to crush the uprising with terrible ferocity. Although the nobility tried to restore ancient duties of serfdom, virtually a century of freedom had elapsed, and the commutation of manorial services continued. Rural serfdom had disappeared in England by 1550.

Conditions in England and France were not unique. In Florence in 1378, the *ciompi,* the poorest workmen, revolted. Serious social trouble occurred in Lübeck, Brunswick, and other cities of the Holy Roman Empire. In Spain in 1391, aristocratic attempts to impose new forms of serfdom combined with demands for tax relief led to massive working-class and peasant uprisings in Seville and Barcelona. These took the form of vicious attacks on Jewish communities. Rebellions and uprisings everywhere reveal deep peasant and working-class frustration and the general socioeconomic crisis of the times.

## MARRIAGE

Marriage and the family provided such peace and satisfaction as most people attained. In fact, life for those who were not clerics or nuns meant marriage. Apart from sexual and emotional urgency, the community expected people to marry. For a girl, childhood was a preparation for marriage. In addition to the thousands of chores involved in running a household, girls learned obedience, or at least subordination. Adulthood meant living as a wife or widow. However, sweeping statements about marriage in the Middle Ages have limited validity. Most peasants were illiterate and left slight record of their feelings toward their spouses or about marriage as an institution. The gentry, however, often could write, and the letters exchanged between

Margaret and John Paston, upper-middle-class people who lived in Norfolk, England, in the fifteenth century, provide important evidence of the experience of one couple.

John and Margaret Paston were married about 1439, after an arrangement concluded entirely by their parents. John spent most of his time in London fighting through the law courts to increase his family properties and business interests; Margaret remained in Norfolk to supervise the family lands. Her enormous responsibilities involved managing the Paston estates, hiring workers, collecting rents, ordering supplies for the large household, hearing complaints and settling disputes among tenants, and marketing her crops. In these duties she proved herself a remarkably shrewd businessperson. Moreover, when an army of over a thousand men led by the aristocratic thug Lord Moleyns attacked her house, she successfully withstood the siege. When the Black Death entered her area, Margaret moved her family to safety.

Margaret Paston did all this on top of raising eight children (there were probably other children who did not survive childhood). Her husband died before she was forty-three, and she later conducted the negotiations for the children's marriages. Her children's futures, like her estate management, were planned with an eye toward economic and social advancement. When one daughter secretly married the estate bailiff, an alliance considered beneath her, the girl was cut off from the family as if she were dead.[24]

The many letters surviving between Margaret and John reveal slight tenderness toward their children. They seem to have reserved their love for each other, and during many of his frequent absences they wrote to express mutual affection and devotion. How typical the Paston relationship was, modern historians cannot say, but the marriage of John and Margaret, although completely arranged by their parents, was based on respect, responsibility, and love.[25]

In the later Middle Ages, as earlier – indeed, until the late nineteenth century – economic factors, rather than romantic love or physical attraction, determined whom and when a person married. The young agricultural laborer on the manor had to wait until he had sufficient land. Thus most men had to wait until their fathers died or yielded the holding. The age of marriage was late, which in turn affected the number of children a couple had. The journeyman craftsman in the urban guild faced the same material difficulties. Prudent young men selected (or their parents selected for them) girls who would bring the most land or money to the union. Once a couple married, the union ended only with the death of one partner.

Divorce – the complete dissolution of the contract between a woman and man lawfully married – did not exist in the Middle Ages. The church held that a marriage validly entered into could not be dissolved. A valid marriage consisted of the oral consent or promise of the two parties made to each other. Church theologians of the day urged that the marriage be publicized by banns, or announcements made in the parish church, and that the couple's union be celebrated and witnessed in a church ceremony and blessed by a priest.

A great number of couples did not observe the church's regulations. Some treated marriage as a private act – they made the promise and spoke the words of marriage to each other without witnesses and then proceeded to enjoy the sexual pleasures of marriage. This practice led to a great number of disputes, because one or the other of the two parties could later deny having made a marriage agreement. The records of the ecclesiastical courts reveal many cases arising from privately made contracts. Here is a typical case heard by the ecclesiastical court at York in England in 1372:

*[The witness says that] one year ago on the feast day of the apostles Philip and James just past, he was present in the house of William Burton, tanner of York. . . . when and where John Beke, saddler . . . called the said Marjory to him and said to her, "Sit with me." Acquiescing in this, she sat down. John said to her, "Marjory, do you wish to be my wife?" And she replied, "I will if you wish." And taking at once the said Marjory's right hand, John said, "Marjory, here I take you as my wife, for better or worse, to have and to hold until the end of my life; and of this I give you my faith." The said Marjory replied to him, "Here I take you John as my husband, to have and to hold until the end of my life, and of this I give you my faith." And then the said John kissed the said Marjory. . . .*[26]

This was a private arrangement, made in secret and without the presence of the clergy. Evidence survives of marriages contracted in a garden, in a blacksmith's shop, at a tavern, and, predictably, in a bed. Church courts heard a great number of similar cases. The records of those courts that relate to marriage reveal that rather than suits for divorce, the great majority of petitions asked the court to enforce the marriage contract that one of the parties believed she or he had validly made. Annulments were granted in extraordinary circumstances, such as male impotence, on the grounds that a lawful marriage had never existed.

## LIFE IN THE PARISH

In the later Middle Ages, the land and the parish remained the focus of life for the European peasantry. Work on the land continued to be performed collectively. All men, for example, cooperated in the annual tasks of planting and harvesting. The close association

of the cycle of agriculture and the liturgy of the Christian calendar endured. The parish priest blessed the fields before the annual planting, offering prayers on behalf of the people for a good crop. If the harvest was a rich one, the priest led the processions and celebrations of thanksgiving.

How did the common people feel about their work? Since the vast majority were illiterate and inarticulate, it is difficult to say. It is known that the peasants hated the ancient services and obligations on the lords' lands and tried to get them commuted for money rents. When lords attempted to reimpose service duties, the peasants revolted.

In the thirteenth century, the craft guilds provided the small minority of men living in towns and cities with the psychological satisfaction of involvement in the manufacture of a superior product. The guild member also had economic security. The craft guilds set high standards for their merchandise. The guilds looked after the sick, the poor, the widowed, and the orphaned. Masters and journeymen worked side by side.

In the fourteenth century, those ideal conditions began to change. The fundamental objective of the craft guild was to maintain a monopoly on its product, and to do so recruitment and promotion were carefully restricted. Some guilds required a high entrance fee for apprentices; others admitted only the sons or relatives of members. Apprenticeship increasingly lasted a long time, seven years. Even after a young man had satisfied all the tests for full membership in the guild and had attained the rank of master, other hurdles had to be crossed, such as finding the funds to open his own business or special connections just to get in a guild. Restrictions limited the number of apprentices and journeymen to the anticipated openings for masters. The larger a particular business was, the greater was the likelihood that the master did not know his employees. The separation of master and journeyman and the decreasing number of openings for master craftsmen created serious frustrations. Strikes and riots occurred in the Flemish towns, in France, and in England.

The recreation of all classes reflected the fact that late medieval society was organized for war and that violence was common. The aristocracy engaged in tournaments or jousts; archery and wrestling had great popularity among ordinary people. Everyone enjoyed the cruel sports of bullbaiting and bearbaiting. As the great French scholar Marc Bloch wrote, "Violence was an element in manners. Medieval men had little control over their immediate impulses; they were emotionally insensitive to the spectacle of pain, and they had small regard for human life . . ."[27] Thus, the

hangings and mutilations of criminals were exciting and well-attended events, with all the festivity of a university town before a Saturday football game. Chronicles exulted in describing executions, murders, and massacres. Here a monk gleefully describes the gory execution of William Wallace in 1305:

*Wilielmus Waleis, a robber given to sacrilege, arson and homicide . . . was condemned to most cruel but justly deserved death. He was drawn through the streets of London at the tails of horses, until he reached a gallows of unusual height, there he was suspended by a halter; but taken down while yet alive, he was mutilated, his bowels torn out and burned in a fire, his head then cut off, his body divided into four, and his quarters transmitted to four principal parts of Scotland.*

*Behold the end of the merciless man, who himself perished without mercy.*[28]

Violence was as English as roast beef and plum pudding, as French as bread, cheese, and *potage.*

Alcohol, primarily beer or ale, provided solace to the poor, and the frequency of drunkenness reflects their terrible frustrations.

In the fourteenth and fifteenth centuries, the laity began to exercise increasing influence and control over the affairs of the parish. Churchmen were criticized. The constant quarrels of the mendicant orders (the Franciscans and Dominicans), the mercenary and grasping attitude of the parish clergy, the scandal of the Great Schism and a divided Christendom – all these did much to weaken the spiritual mystique of the clergy in the popular mind. The laity steadily took responsibility for the management of parish lands. Laymen and laywomen organized associations to vote on and purchase furnishings for the church. And ordinary lay people secured jurisdiction over the structure of the church building, its vestments, books, and furnishings. These new responsibilities of the laity reflect the increased dignity of the parishioners in the late Middle Ages.[29]

———◆———

Late medieval preachers likened the crises of their times to the Four Horsemen of the Apocalypse in the Book of Revelation, who brought famine, war, disease, and death. The crises of the fourteenth and fifteenth centuries were acids that burned deeply into the fabric of traditional medieval European society. Bad weather brought poor harvests, which contributed to the international economic depression. Disease, over which people also had little control, fostered widespread psychological depression and dissatisfaction. Population losses caused by the Black Death and the Hundred Years' War encouraged the working classes to try to profit from the labor shortage by selling their services higher: they wanted to move up the economic ladder. The socialistic ideas of thinkers like John Wyclif, John Hus, and John Ball fanned the flames of social discontent. When peasant frustrations exploded in uprisings, the frightened nobility and upper middle class crushed the revolts and condemned heretical preachers as agitators of social rebellion. But the war had heightened social consciousness among the poor.

The Hundred Years' War served as a catalyst for the development of representative government in England. The royal policy of financing the war through Parliament-approved taxation gave the middle classes an increased sense of their economic power. They would pay taxes in return for some influence in shaping royal policies.

In France, on the other hand, the war stiffened opposition to national assemblies. The disasters that wracked France decade after decade led the French people to believe that the best solutions to complicated problems lay not in an assembly but in the hands of a strong monarch. France became the model for continental countries in the evolution toward royal absolutism.

The war also stimulated technological experimentation, especially with artillery. After about 1350, the cannon, although highly inaccurate, was commonly used all over Europe.

Religion remained the cement that held society together. European culture was a Christian culture. But the Great Schism weakened the prestige of the church and people's faith in papal authority. The conciliar movement, by denying the church's universal sovereignty, strengthened the claims of secular governments to jurisdiction over all their peoples. The later Middle Ages witnessed a steady shift of basic loyalty from the Christian church to the emerging national states.

*ALBRECHT DÜRER: THE FOUR HORSEMEN OF THE APOCALYPSE* *From right to left, representatives of war, strife, famine, and death gallop across Christian society leaving thousands dead or in misery. The horrors of the age made this subject extremely popular in art, literature, and sermons. (Courtesy, Museum of Fine Arts, Boston)*

# NOTES

1. W. H. McNeill, *Plagues and Peoples,* Doubleday, New York, 1976, pp. 151–168.

2. Quoted by P. Ziegler, *The Black Death,* Pelican Books, Harmondsworth, England, 1969, p. 20.

3. J. M. Rigg, trans., *The Decameron of Giovanni Boccaccio,* J. M. Dent & Sons, London, 1903, p. 6.

4. Ziegler, pp. 232–239.

5. N. F. Cantor, *The English: A History of Politics and Society to 1760,* Simon & Schuster, New York, 1967, p. 260.

6. J. Barnie, *War in Medieval English Society: Social Values and the Hundred Years' War,* Cornell University Press, Ithaca, N.Y., 1974, p. 6.

7. Quoted by Barnie, p. 34.

8. Ibid., p. 73.

9. Ibid., pp. 72–73.

10. W. P. Barrett, trans., *The Trial of Jeanne d'Arc,* George Routledge, London, 1931, pp. 165–166.

11. Quoted by Edward A. Lucie-Smith, *Joan of Arc,* W. W. Norton, New York, 1977, p. 32.

12. Ibid., pp. 32–35.

13. Quoted by Barnie, pp. 36–37.

14. M. M. Postan, "The Costs of the Hundred Years' War," *Past and Present* 27 (April 1964):34–53.

15. Quoted by P. S. Lewis, "The Failure of the Medieval French Estates," *Past and Present* 23 (November 1962):6.

16. Ibid., p. 10.

17. C. Stephenson and G. F. Marcham, eds., *Sources of English Constitutional History,* rev. ed., Harper & Row, New York, 1972, p. 217.

18. Quoted by J. H. Smith, *The Great Schism 1378: The Disintegration of the Papacy,* Weybright & Talley, New York, 1970, p. 141.

19. Ibid., p. 15.

20. B. A. Hanawalt, "Fur Collar Crime: The Pattern of Crime Among the Fourteenth-Century English Nobility," *Journal of Social History* 8 (Spring 1975):1–14.

21. Ibid., p. 7.

22. Quoted by M. Bloch, *French Rural History,* trans. Janet Sondheimer, University of California Press, Berkeley, 1966, p. 169.

23. Stephenson and Marcham, p. 225.

24. A. S. Haskell, "The Paston Women on Marriage in Fifteenth Century England," *Viator* 4 (1973):459–469.

25. Ibid., p. 471.

26. Quoted by R. H. Helmholz, *Marriage Litigation in Medieval England,* Cambridge University Press, Cambridge, 1974, pp. 28–29.

27. M. Bloch, *Feudal Society,* trans. L. A. Manyon, Routledge & Kegan Paul, London, 1961, p. 411.

28. A. F. Scott, ed., *Everyone a Witness: The Plantagenet Age,* Thomas Y. Crowell, New York, 1976, p. 263.

29. See E. Mason, "The Role of the English Parishioner, 1000–1500," *Journal of Ecclesiastical History* 27:1 (January 1976):17–29.

## SUGGESTED READING

Students who wish further elaboration of the topics covered in this chapter should consult the following studies, on which the chapter leans extensively. For the Black Death and health generally, see W. H. McNeill, *Plagues and Peoples* (1976), a fresh, challenging, and comprehensive study; F. F. Cartwright, *Disease and History* (1972), which contains an interesting section on the Black Death; P. Ziegler, *The Black Death* (1969), a fascinating and highly readable book; and H. E. Sigerist, *Civilization and Disease* (1970), which presents a worthwhile treatment of the many social implications of disease.

The standard study of the long military conflicts of the fourteenth and fifteenth centuries remains that of E. Perroy, *The Hundred Years' War* (1959). J. Henneman, *Royal Taxation in Fourteenth Century France: The Development of War Financing, 1322–1356* (1971), is an important technical work by a distinguished historian. J. Barnie's *War in Medieval English Society: Social Values and the Hundred Years' War* (1974), treats the attitude of patriots, intellectuals, and the general public. Desmond Seward, *The Hundred Years' War: The English in France, 1337–1453* (1981), tells an exciting story, and John Keegan, *The Face of Battle* (1977), Chapter 2, "Agincourt," describes what war meant to the ordinary soldier. Barbara Tuchman, *A Distant Mirror: The Calamitous 14th Century* (1980), gives a vivid picture of many facets of fourteenth-century life, while concentrating on the war. The best treatment of the financial costs of the war is probably M. M. Postan, "The Costs of the Hundred Years' War," *Past and Present* 27 (April 1964):34–53. E. Searle and R. Burghart, "The Defense of England and the Peasants' Revolt," *Viator* 3 (1972), is a fascinating study of the peasants' changing social attitudes.

For political and social conditions in the fourteenth and fifteenth centuries, the following studies are all useful: P. S. Lewis, *Later Medieval France: The Polity* (1968), and "The Failure of the French Medieval Estates," *Past and Present* 23 (November 1962); L. Romier, *A History of France* (1962); G. O. Sayles, *The King's Parliament of England* (1974); M. Bloch, *French Rural History* (1966); I. Kershaw, "The Great Famine and Agrarian Crisis in England, 1315–1322," *Past and Present* 59 (May 1973); B. A. Hanawalt, "Fur Collar Crime: The Pattern of Crime Among the Fourteenth-Century English Nobility," *Journal of Social History* 8 (Spring 1975): 1–17, a fascinating discussion; K. Thomas, "Work and Leisure in Pre-Industrial Society," *Past and Present* 29 (December 1964); M. Keen, *The Outlaws of Medieval Legend* (1961) and "Robin Hood – Peasant or Gentleman?," *Past and Present* 19 (April 1961):7–18; P. Wolff, "The 1391 Pogrom in Spain, Social Crisis or Not?," *Past and Present* 50 (February 1971):4–18; and R. H. Helmholz, *Marriage Litigation in Medieval England* (1974). Students are especially encouraged to consult the brilliant achievement of E. L. Ladurie, *The Peasants of Languedoc,* trans. John Day (1976).

The poetry of Dante, Chaucer, and Villon may be read in the following editions: Dorothy Sayers, trans., *Dante: The Divine Comedy,* 3 vols. (1963); Nevil Coghill, trans., *Chaucer's Canterbury Tales* (1977); Peter Dale, trans., *The Poems of Villon* (1973). The social setting of Chaucer's *Canterbury Tales* is brilliantly evoked in D. W. Robertson, Jr., *Chaucer's London* (1968).

Many of the preceding titles treat the religious history of the period. In addition, the following contain interesting and valuable information: G. Barraclough, *The Medieval Papacy* (1968), which is splendidly illustrated; W. Ullmann, *A Short History of the Papacy in the Middle Ages* (1972); E. Mason, "The Role of the English Parishioner, 1000–1500," *Journal of Ecclesiastical History* 27 (January 1976):17–29; and J. H. Smith, *The Great Schism 1378: The Disintegration of the Medieval Papacy* (1970).

# CHAPTER 13

# EUROPEAN SOCIETY IN THE AGE OF THE RENAISSANCE

*WHILE THE FOUR HORSEMEN* of the Apocalypse carried war, plague, famine, and death across the Continent, a new culture was emerging in southern Europe. The fourteenth century witnessed the beginnings of remarkable changes in many aspects of Italian society. In the fifteenth century, these phenomena spread beyond Italy and gradually influenced society in northern Europe. These cultural changes have been collectively labeled the Renaissance. What does the term *Renaissance* mean? How did the Renaissance manifest itself in politics, government, and social organization? What developments occurred in the evolution of the nation state? Did the Renaissance involve shifts in religious attitudes? This chapter explores these questions.

## THE IDEA OF THE RENAISSANCE

The Renaissance was an intellectual movement that began in Italy in the fourteenth century. It was characterized by hostility to the culture of the Middle Ages and fascination with the ancient world. Writers and artists of the Renaissance displayed great concern for individualism, a serious interest in human nature based on the study of the Greek and Latin classics, and a new excitement about life in this world. The cultural movement scholars have called the Renaissance was limited to a small, self-conscious, educated elite; it never directly involved the masses of people.

The realization that something new and unique was happening first came to men of letters of the fourteenth century, especially to the poet and humanist Francesco Petrarch (1304–1374). Petrarch thought that he was living at the start of a new age, a period of light following a long night of Gothic gloom. He believed that the first and second centuries

of the Roman Empire represented the peak in the development of human civilization. The Germanic invasions had caused a sharp cultural break with the glories of Rome and inaugurated what Petrarch called "the Dark Ages." Medieval people had believed that they were continuing the glories that had been ancient Rome, and had recognized no cultural division between the world of the emperors and their own times. But for Petrarch and many of his contemporaries, the thousand-year period between the fourth and the fourteenth centuries constituted a barbarian, or Gothic, or middle age. The sculptors, painters, and writers of the Renaissance spoke contemptuously of their medieval predecessors and identified themselves with the thinkers and artists of Greco-Roman civilization. Petrarch believed he was witnessing a new golden age of intellectual achievement – a rebirth or, to use the French word that came into English, a renaissance. The division of historical time into periods is often arbitrary and done for the convenience of historians. In terms of the way most people lived and thought, no sharp division exists between the Middle Ages and the Renaissance. Nevertheless, Petrarch's categorization of time periods has had great influence. Most scholars use the word *Renaissance* to mean the artistic and cultural developments in western Europe that began in the fourteenth century and lasted into the seventeenth.

## ITALIAN ORIGINS OF THE RENAISSANCE

The Renaissance began in Italy. Why did a brilliant flowering of artistic and intellectual creativity occur in Italy in the fourteenth through sixteenth centuries? This question has troubled scholars for a long time, and they still have not arrived at a definite answer. Some have offered economic explanations for Italy's cultural flowering, emphasizing the material prosperity without which the arts cannot flourish.

By the middle of the fourteenth century, the commercial classes of Florence and other Italian cities had acquired enough money that they could finance non-moneymaking activities. The cornerstone of northern Italian economic activity was international trade, commerce, and banking. The northern Italian cities had led the way in the commercial revival of the eleventh century. By the middle of the twelfth century, Venice, Genoa, Florence, and Milan were enjoying a great volume of trade with the Middle East and with northern Europe. These Italian cities fully exploited their geographical position as natural crossroads for exchange between the East and the West. Venice had profited tremendously from the Fourth Crusade. In the early fourteenth century, furthermore, Genoa and Venice made important strides in shipbuilding, allowing their ships for the first time to sail all year long. Improvements in the construction of cargo ships enabled the Venetians and Genoese to carry more bulk and to navigate the dangerous Atlantic Ocean. Most goods were purchased directly from the producers and sold a good distance away. For example, Italian merchants bought fine English wool directly from the Cistercian abbeys of Yorkshire in northern England. The wool was transported to the bazaars of North Africa either overland or by ship through the Straits of Gibraltar. The risks in such an operation were great, but the profits were enormous. These profits were continually reinvested to earn more.

It is generally agreed that the first manifestations of the Italian Renaissance – in art, ar-

*BUSINESS ACTIVITIES IN A FLORENTINE BANK The Florentines early developed new banking devices. One man (left) presents a letter of credit or a bill of exchange, forerunners of the modern check, which allowed credit in distant places. A foreign merchant (right) exchanges one kind of currency for another. The bank profited from the fees it charged for these services. (Prints Division; New York Public Library; Astor, Lenox and Tilden Foundation)*

chitecture, and literary creativity – appeared in Florence, and Florence possessed enormous wealth. Geography had not helped Florence; it was an inland city without easy access to water transportation. But toward the end of the thirteenth century, Florentine merchants and bankers acquired control of papal banking. From their position as tax collectors for the papacy, Florentine mercantile families began to dominate European banking on both sides of the Alps. These families had offices in Paris and London, Barcelona and Marseilles, Tunis and the North African ports, and, of course, Naples and Rome. The profits from loans, investments, and money exchanges that poured back to Florence were pumped into urban industries. Such profits contributed to the city's economic vitality.

The Florentine wool industry, however, was the major factor in the city's financial expansion and population increase. Florence purchased the best-quality wool from England and Spain, developed remarkable techniques for its manufacture, and employed thousands of workers to turn it into cloth. Florentine weavers produced immense quantities of superb woolen cloth, which brought the highest prices in the fairs, markets, and bazaars of Europe, Asia, and Africa.

By the first quarter of the fourteenth century, the economic foundations of Florence were so strong that even two severe crises could not destroy the city. In 1344, King Edward III of England repudiated his huge debts to Florentine bankers and forced some of them into bankruptcy. Florence also suffered frightfully from the Black Death, losing perhaps half its population. Still, the basic Florentine economic structure remained stable. Driving enterprise, technical know-how, and competitive spirit saw Florence through the difficult economic period of the late fourteenth century.[1]

One inconsistency in this economic explanation of the origins of the Renaissance lies in the fact that in the middle of the fourteenth century the Florentine wool and banking industries experienced a serious depression. Trade declined, affected by the Black Death and the international business slump. Moreover, such cities as Genoa, which had at one time enjoyed considerable prosperity, made no profound contribution to the Renaissance. It may be, however, that Florentine businessmen who found foreign markets closed invested instead in art, expecting a financial return from art works that increased in value.

A leading interpretation of the Italian Renaissance traces its origins to the development of civic humanism, or public pride, in Florence. In the 1380s, Florence was severely threatened by the conquests of Gian Galeazzo Visconti, duke of Milan. The Florentines put up a heroic and successful resistance, and in so doing came to appreciate the special virtues of their republican form of government – in contrast to the tyranny represented by Visconti. Awareness of their unique political heritage, which they traced back to the time of the Roman Empire, led the Florentines to take great pride in their city. Civic humanism took the form of public respect for Florence's achievements, whether in trade or architecture, education or the arts. They embarked upon a policy of beautification. This civic self-consciousness eventually spread to the other city-states of Italy.

Unlike the countries of northern Europe, Italy had never been heavily feudalized. Italian feudal lords rarely exercised the vast independent powers held by the barons of France, England, and the Holy Roman Empire. Although the volume of urban trade and the size of urban populations severely declined in the early Middle Ages, cities survived as commercial centers. In the twelfth and thirteenth centuries, northern Italian cities like Venice and Milan gained control of their surrounding territories. The wealth they steadily gained was used to acquire and solidify their independence; the Holy Roman emperors never fully exploited the wealth of the cities.

Italian society in the fourteenth century meant urban society, and this fundamental fact helps to account for the Italian origin of the Renaissance. The cities of Milan, Venice, Florence, Genoa, and Pisa were visited by traders and businessmen from all parts of the Western world. Foreigners brought with them their own customs, traditions, and values, and considerable social interchange inevitably took place. The merchant Francesco Datini, for example, was involved in commercial transactions with two hundred cities,

THE WEDDING FEAST *This picture was one of a series Botticelli produced illustrating a story in Boccaccio's Decameron. The classical architecture with its vision of nature beyond, the pomp with which the meal is served, and the philosophical discussion at the tables — all represent the tastes and ideals of the Florentine aristocracy under the Medici. (Courtesy of Christie's)*

from Alexandria and Beirut in the south to Stockholm in the north. Italians gained an awareness of different parts of the world. They grew more refined, more sophisticated in their tastes and lifestyles, more worldly and urbane. Although Italians remained devoted sons and daughters of the church, they grew more secular in their outlook and behavior. Class distinctions remained strong in Renaissance Italy, but those distinctions were based on wealth rather than birth. And enterprise, imagination, and hard work could lead to wealth in the urban environment.

Moreover, the wealthy burghers of the cities began to strike military and marital contracts with the rural nobility of northern Italy. These alliances enabled the nobles to maintain a high standard of living in a rising money economy and gave the cities military support and protection. When the rich merchants united with the rural nobility, two significant developments occurred: the possession of land gradually came into the hands of bankers and merchants, and as a result the cities obtained political as well as economic jurisdiction over the surrounding countryside. In no other part of Europe did cities acquire such political power, primarily because the aristocratic ethos forbade feudal barons to unite with the moneygrubbing bourgeoisie. Nor did cities elsewhere have the commercial and financial strength of the Italian towns.

A foreign element also played a significant role. Beginning in the late fourteenth century, a steady stream of educated Greek refugees came from Byzantium to Italy to escape Turkish domination. Greek scholars like Manuel

Chrysoloras, John Bessarion, and Jonus Lascaris taught the Greek language and translated important Greek literary classics into Latin. Venice became the center of Greek scholarship, but Florence and Rome also gained an international reputation for Greek learning. Greek emigration to Italy broadened the intellectual horizon and enriched Italian Renaissance culture.

Finally, the Renaissance started in Italy because Italian poets, sculptors, painters, and philosophers of the fifteenth and sixteenth centuries considered themselves the natural heirs of the ancient Romans. Italy still possessed the literary manuscripts, the architectural monuments, the roads that constituted the heritage of Roman civilization. The national past of Italy was visible everywhere. Above all, Italians retained the historical memory of Roman power and imperial grandeur, and looked back on Roman antiquity as the golden age, as an ideal to be restored and reborn.

Increased wealth afforded more leisure time. Wealth in itself is usually not sufficient to satisfy the human psyche. When the physical and material needs of life are fulfilled and there is a surplus, then the spirit can be enriched by esthetic and intellectual interests.

The Renaissance, then, was an artistic and intellectual movement that began in the Italian cities and was supported and sustained by urban wealth.

## HALLMARKS OF THE RENAISSANCE

The Renaissance was characterized, as we have seen, by the self-conscious awareness among fourteenth- and fifteenth-century Italians that they were living in a new era. The Renaissance also manifested itself in a new attitude toward men and women and the world – an attitude that may be described as individualism. A humanism characterized by a deep interest in the Latin classics and the deliberate attempt to revive antique lifestyles emerged, as did a bold new secular spirit.

### INDIVIDUALISM

In the Middle Ages individuals thought of themselves as part of a group – as a member of a guild, as a resident of a particular area. The very few people who considered themselves so unusual that they indulged in autobiography – Saint Augustine in the fifth century and Guibert of Nogent in the twelfth, for example – were unique for that very reason. Christian humility and the concept of Western society as an organic entity encouraged people to define themselves in terms of a larger religious, economic, or social group.

This organic view of society eroded during the fourteenth and fifteenth centuries in Italy. The Renaissance witnessed the emergence of many distinctive personalities who gloried in their uniqueness. Italians of unusual abilities were self-consciously aware of their singularity, and unafraid to be unlike their neighbors; they had enormous confidence in their ability to achieve great things. Leon Battista Alberti (1404–1474), a writer, architect, and mathematician, remarked, "Men can do all things if they will."[2] Completely lacking in modesty, real or false, talented people of the Renaissance were proud of their abilities and eager for everyone to know about them. The Florentine goldsmith and sculptor Benvenuto Cellini (1500–1574) prefaced his *Autobiography* with a sonnet that declares:

*My cruel fate hath warr'd with me in vain:*
*Life, glory, worth, and all unmeasur'd skill,*
*Beauty and grace, themselves in me fulfill*
*That many I surpass, and to the best attain.*[3]

Cellini, certain of his genius, wrote so that the whole world might appreciate it.

Individualism stressed personality, genius, uniqueness, and the fullest development of capabilities and talents. Artist, athlete, painter, scholar, sculptor, whatever – a person's potential should be stretched until fully realized. Thirst for fame, a driving ambition, a burning desire for success drove such people to the complete achievement of their potential. The quest for glory was central to Renaissance individualism.

## THE REVIVAL OF ANTIQUITY

In the cities of Italy, and especially in Rome, civic leaders and the wealthy populace showed phenomenal archaeological zeal for the recovery of manuscripts, statues, and monuments. Pope Nicholas V (1447-1455), a distinguished scholar, planned the Vatican Library for the nine thousand manuscripts he had collected. Pope Sixtus IV (1471-1484) built that library, which remains one of the richest repositories of ancient and medieval documents.

Patrician Italians consciously copied the lifestyle of the ancients and even searched out pedigrees dating back to ancient Rome. Aeneas Silvius Piccolomini, a native of Siena who became Pope Pius II (1458-1464), once pretentiously declared, "Rome is as much my home as Siena, for my House, the Piccolomini, came in early times from the capital to Siena, as is proved by the constant use of the names Aeneas and Silvius in my family."[4]

The revival of antiquity also took the form of profound interest in and study of the Latin classics. This feature of the Renaissance became known as the "new learning," or simply "humanism," the term of the Florentine rhetorician and historian Leonardo Bruni (1370-1444). The words *humanism* and *humanist* derive ultimately from the Latin *humanitas,* which Cicero used to mean the literary culture needed by anyone who would be considered educated and civilized. Humanists studied the Latin classics to learn what they reveal about human nature. Humanism emphasized human beings, their achievements, interests, and capabilities. Although churchmen supported the new learning, Italian humanism was a preponderantly lay phenomenon.

Appreciation for the literary culture of the Romans had never died completely in the West. Bede, Alcuin, and Einhard in the eighth century, and Ailred of Rievaulx, Bernard of Clairvaux, and John of Salisbury in the twelfth century had all studied and imitated the writings of the ancients. Medieval writers, however, had studied the ancients in order to come to know God. Medieval thinkers held that human beings are the noblest of god's creatures, and that though they have fallen, they are still capable of regeneration and thus deserving of respect. Medieval scholars interpreted the classics in a Christian sense and invested the ancients' poems and histories with Christian meaning.

Renaissance philosophers and poets also emphasized human dignity, but usually not in a Christian context. In a remarkable essay, "On the Dignity of Man," the Florentine writer Pico della Mirandola maintained that man's place in the universe may be somewhere between the beasts and the angels but that there are no limits to what he can accomplish.

Humanists tried to approach the classical texts with an open mind, to learn what the ancients had thought. They rejected the religious interpretations and systematic and formal scholastic works of the Middle Ages. They hated scholasticism because they believed it denied humanity and destroyed style.

The fourteenth- and fifteenth-century humanists loved the language of the classics and considered it superior to the corrupt Latin of the medieval schoolmen. Renaissance writers were very excited by the purity of ancient Latin. They eventually became concerned more about form than content, more about the way an idea was expressed than about the significance and validity of the idea. Literary humanists of the fourteenth century wrote each other highly stylized letters imitating ancient authors, and they held witty philosophical dialogues in conscious imitation of the Platonic Academy of the fifth century B.C. Wherever they could, Renaissance humanists heaped scorn on the "barbaric" Latin style of the medievalists. The leading humanists of the early Renaissance were rhetoricians, seeking effective and eloquent communication, both oral and written.

## SECULAR SPIRIT

Secularism involves a basic concern with the material world instead of eternal and spiritual interests. A secular way of thinking tends to find the ultimate explanation of everything and the final end of human beings within the limits of what the senses can discover. In a religious society, such as the medieval, the focus is on the other-worldly, on life after death. In a secular society, attention is concentrated on the here and now, often on the acquisition of material things. The fourteenth and fifteenth centuries witnessed the slow but steady growth of secularism in Italy.

The economic changes and rising prosperity of the Italian cities in the thirteenth century worked a fundamental change in social and intellectual attitudes and values. In the Middle Ages the feudal nobility and the higher clergy had determined the dominant patterns of culture. The medieval aristocracy expressed disdain for moneymaking. Christian ideas and values infused literature, art, politics, and all other aspects of culture. In the Renaissance, by contrast, the business concerns of the urban bourgeoisie required constant and rational attention.

Worries about shifting rates of interest, shipping routes, personnel costs, and employee relations did not leave much time for thoughts about penance and purgatory. The busy bankers and merchants of the Italian cities calculated ways of making and increasing their money. Money allowed greater material pleasures, a more comfortable life, the leisure time to appreciate and patronize the arts. Money could buy many sensual gratifications, and the rich, social-climbing patricians of Venice, Florence, Genoa, and Rome came to see life more as an opportunity to be enjoyed than as a painful pilgrimage to the City of God.

In *On Pleasure,* the humanist Lorenzo Valla (1406–1457) defended the pleasures of the senses as the highest good. Scholars praise Valla as the father of modern historical criticism. His study *On the False Donation of Constantine* (1444) demonstrated by careful textual examination that an anonymous eighth-century document supposedly giving the papacy jurisdiction over vast territories in western Europe was a forgery. Medieval people had accepted the Donation of Constantine as a reality, and the proof that it was an invention seriously weakened the foundations of papal claims to temporal authority. Lorenzo Valla's work exemplifies the application of critical scholarship to old and almost sacred writings, as well as the new secular spirit of the Renaissance. The tales in the *Decameron* by the Florentine Boccaccio (1313–1375), which describe ambitious merchants, lecherous friars, and cuckolded husbands, portray a frankly acquisitive, sensual, and secular society. The "contempt of the world" theme, so pervasive in medieval literature, had disappeared. Renaissance writers justified the accumulation and enjoyment of wealth with references to ancient authors.

Nor did church leaders do much to combat the new secular spirit or set high moral standards. In the fifteenth and early sixteenth centuries, the papal court and the households of the cardinals were just as worldly as those of great urban patricians. Of course, most of the popes and higher church officials had come from the bourgeois aristocracy. The Medici pope Leo X (1513–1521), for example, supported artists and men of letters because patronage was an activity he had learned in the household of his father, Lorenzo the Magnificent. Renaissance popes beautified the city of Rome and patronized the arts. They expended enormous enthusiasm and huge sums of money on the re-embellishment of the city. A new papal chancellery, begun in 1483 and finished in 1511, stands as one of the architectural masterpieces of the High Renaissance (roughly the period 1500–1530). Pope Julius II (1503–1513) tore down the old St. Peter's Basilica and began work on the present structure in 1506. Michelangelo's dome for St. Peter's is still considered his greatest work. Papal interests, far removed from spiritual concerns, fostered rather than discouraged the new worldly attitude.

But the broad mass of the people and even the intellectuals and leaders of society remained faithful to the Christian church. Few people questioned the basic tenets of the Christian religion. Italian humanists and their aristocratic patrons were antiascetic, antischolastic, and anticlerical, but they were not agnostics or skeptics. The thousands of pious paintings, sculptures, processions, and pilgrimages of the Renaissance period prove that strong religious feeling persisted.

## ART AND THE ARTIST

No feature of the Renaissance evokes greater admiration than its artistic masterpieces. The 1400s (quattrocento) and 1500s (cinquecento) witnessed a dazzling creativity in painting, architecture, and sculpture. In all the arts, the city of Florence consistently led the way. According to the Renaissance art historian Giorgio Vasari (1511–1574), the painter Perugino once asked why it was in Florence and not elsewhere that men achieved perfection in the arts. The first answer he received was, "There were so many good critics there, for the air of the city makes men quick and perceptive and impatient of mediocrity."[5]

Some historians and art critics have maintained that the Renaissance "rediscovered" the world of nature and of human beings. This is nonsense, as a quick glance at a Gothic cathedral reveals. The enormous detail applied to the depiction of animals' bodies, the careful carving of leaves, flowers, and all kinds of vegetation, the fine sensitivity frequently shown in human faces – these clearly show medieval and ancient people's appreciation for nature in all its manifestations. Saint Francis of Assisi (1181–1226) encouraged throughout his entire life an awareness of nature. No historical period has a monopoly on the appreciation of nature or beauty.

### ART AND SOCIETY

Significant changes in the realm of art did occur in the fourteenth century. Art served

BOTTICELLI: ADORATION OF THE MAGI *The Florentine artist, biographer, and Medici courtier Giorgio Vasari (1511–1574) says that this painting contains the most faithful likenesses of Cosimo (kneel-* *ing before the Christ child) and Lorenzo (far left). Although the subject is Christian, the painting has a secular spirit, introduces individual portraits, and serves to glorify the Medici family. (Alinari/Scala)*

the newly rich middle class as well as the institutional church. The patrons of Renaissance art were more frequently laypeople than ecclesiastics. Patrician merchants and bankers supported the arts as a means of self-glorification and self-perpetuation. Art may also have been a form of financial investment. Great families, such as the Medicis in Florence, used works of art as a means of gaining and maintaining public support for their rule. A magnificent style of living, enriched by works of art, seemed to prove the greatness of the rulers.

As the fifteenth century advanced, the subject matter of art became steadily more secular. The study of classical texts and manuscripts brought deeper understanding of ancient ideas. Classical themes and motifs, such as the lives and loves of pagan gods and goddesses, figured increasingly in painting and sculpture. Religious topics, such as the Annunciation of the Virgin and the Nativity, remained popular among both patrons and artists, but frequently the patron had himself and his family portrayed in the picture. In Botticelli's *Adoration of the Magi,* for example,

Cosimo de' Medici appears as one of the Magi kneeling before the Christ child. People were conscious of their physical uniqueness, and they wanted their individuality immortalized. Paintings cost money and thus were also means of displaying wealth. Although many Renaissance paintings have classical or Christian themes, the appearance of the patron reflects the new spirit of individualism and secularism.

The style of Renaissance art was decidedly different from that of the Middle Ages. The individual portrait emerged as a distinct artistic genre. In the fifteenth century members of the newly-rich middle class often had themselves painted in a scene of romantic chivalry or in courtly society. Rather than reflecting a spiritual ideal, as medieval painting and sculpture tended to do, Renaissance portraits mirrored reality. The Florentine painter Giotto (1276-1337) led the way in the depiction of realism; his treatment of the human body and face replaced the formal stiffness and artificiality that had for so long characterized the representation of the human body. The sculptor Donatello (1386-1466) probably exerted the greatest influence of any Florentine artist before Michelangelo. His many statues express an appreciation of the incredible variety of human nature. While medieval artists had depicted the nude human body only in a spiritualized and moralizing context, Donatello revived the classical figure with its balance and self-awareness. The short-lived Florentine Masaccio (1401-1428), sometimes called the father of modern painting, inspired a new style characterized by great realism, narrative power, and remarkably effective use of light and dark.

Narrative artists depicted the body in a more scientific and natural manner. The female figure is voluptuous and sensual. The male body, as in Michelangelo's *David* and *The Last Judgment,* is strong and heroic. Renaissance glorification of the human body reveals the secular spirit of the age. Filippo Brunelleschi (1377-1446), together with Piero della Francesca (1420-1492), seems to have pioneered perspective in painting, the linear representation of distance and space on a flat surface. *The Last Supper* of Leonardo da Vinci (1452-1519), with its stress on the tension between Christ and the disciples, is an incredibly subtle psychological interpretation.

## THE STATUS OF THE ARTIST

In the Renaissance the social status of the artist improved. The lower-middle-class medieval master mason had been viewed in the same light as a mechanic. The artist in the Renaissance was considered an independent intellectual worker. Some artists and architects achieved not only economic security but very great wealth. All aspiring artists received a practical (not theoretical) education in a recognized master's workshop. For example, Michelangelo (1475-1564) was apprenticed at age thirteen to the artist Ghirlandaio (1449-1494), although he later denied the fact to make it appear he never had any formal training. The more famous the artist, the more he attracted assistants or apprentices. Lorenzo Ghiberti (1378-1455) had twenty assistants during the period he was working on the bronze doors of the Baptistery in Florence, his most famous achievement.

Ghiberti's salary of two hundred florins a year compared very favorably with that of the head of the city government, who earned five hundred florins. Moreover, at a time when a man could live in a princely fashion on three hundred ducats a year, Leonardo da Vinci was making two thousand annually. Michelangelo was paid three thousand ducats for painting

HANS MEMLING: MARIA AND TOMMASO POR-
TINARI *A Florentine citizen, Tommaso Portinari
earned a fortune as representative of the Medici banking interests in Bruges, Flanders. Husband and wife
are dressed in a rich but durable black broadcloth;*

*Maria's necklace displays their wealth. Although both
faces show a sharp intelligence, there is a melancholy
sadness about them, suggestive of the pessimism of
northern religious piety. (The Metropolitan Museum
of Art: Bequest of Benjamin Altman, 1913)*

the ceiling of the Sistine Chapel. When he
agreed to work on St. Peter's Basilica, he refused a salary; he was already a wealthy man.[6]

Renaissance society respected and rewarded
the distinguished artist. In 1537, the prolific
letter writer, humanist, and satirizer of
princes Pietro Aretino (1492–1556), wrote to
Michelangelo while he was painting the Sistine Chapel:

*TO THE DIVINE MICHELANGELO:*
*Sir, just as it is disgraceful and sinful to be un-
mindful of God so it is reprehensible and dishon-
ourable for any man of discerning judgement not
to honour you as a brilliant and venerable artist
whom the very stars use as a target at which to
shoot the rival arrows of their favour. You are so
accomplished, therefore, that hidden in your hands*

*lives the idea of a new king of creation, whereby
the most challenging and subtle problem of all in
the art of painting, namely that of outlines, has
been so mastered by you that in the contours of the
human body you express and contain the purpose of
art.... And it is surely my duty to honour you
with this salutation, since the world has many
kings but only one Michelangelo.[7]*

When the Holy Roman emperor Charles V
(1519–1556) visited the workshop of the
great Titian (1477–1576) and stooped to pick
up the artist's dropped paintbrush, the emperor was demonstrating that the patron
himself was honored in the act of honoring
the artist. The social status of the artist of
genius was immortally secured.

Renaissance artists were not only aware of

their creative power; they boasted about it. The architect Brunelleschi had his life written, and Ghiberti and Cellini wrote their autobiographies. Many medieval sculptors and painters had signed their own works; Renaissance artists almost universally did so, and many of them incorporated self-portraits, usually as bystanders, in their paintings. These actions reflect an acute consciousness of creative genius.

The Renaissance, in fact, witnessed the birth of the concept of the artist as genius. In the Middle Ages people believed that only God created, albeit through individuals; the medieval conception recognized no particular value in artistic originality. Renaissance artists and humanists came to think that a work of art was the deliberate creation of a unique personality, of an individual who goes beyond traditions, rules, and theories. A genius has a peculiar gift, which ordinary laws should not inhibit. Cosimo de'Medici described a painter, because of his genius, as "divine," implying that the artist shared in the powers of God. The word *divine* was widely applied to Michelangelo. The Renaissance thus bequeathed the idea of genius to the modern world.

The student must guard against interpreting Italian Renaissance culture in twentieth-century democratic terms. The culture of the Renaissance was that of a small mercantile elite, a business patriciate with aristocratic pretensions. Renaissance culture did not directly affect the broad middle classes, let alone the vast urban proletariat. The typical small tradesman or craftsman could not read the sophisticated Latin essays of the humanists, even if he had the time to do so. He could not afford to buy the art works of the great masters. A small, highly educated minority of literary humanists and artists created the culture of and for an exclusive elite. They cared little

for ordinary people. Castiglione, Machiavelli, and Vergerio, for example, thoroughly despised the masses. Renaissance humanists were a smaller and narrower group than the medieval clergy had ever been. High churchmen had commissioned the construction of the Gothic cathedrals, but, once finished, the buildings were for all to enjoy. The modern visitor can still see the deep ruts in the stone floors of Chartres and Canterbury where the poor pilgrims slept at night. Nothing comparable was built in the Renaissance. Insecure, social-climbing merchant princes were hardly egalitarian.[8] The Renaissance ushered in a gulf between the learned minority and the uneducated multitude that has survived for many centuries.

## SOCIAL CHANGE

The Renaissance changed many aspects of Italian, and subsequently European, society. The new developments brought about real breaks with the medieval past. What impact did the Renaissance have on educational theory and practice, on political thought? How did printing, the era's most stunning technological discovery, affect fifteenth- and sixteenth-century society? Did women have a Renaissance?

### EDUCATION AND POLITICAL THOUGHT

One of the central preoccupations of the humanists was education and moral behavior. Humanists poured out treatises, often in the form of letters, on the structure and goals of education and the training of rulers. In one of the earliest systematic programs for the young, Peter Paul Vergerio (1370-1444) wrote Ubertinus, the ruler of Carrara:

SCHOOL OF LUCA DELLA ROBBIA: VIRGIN AND
CHILD *In the late fifteenth century, della Robbia's
invention of the process of making polychrome-glazed
terracottas led contemporaries to consider him a great
artistic innovator. The warm humanity of this roun-
del (circular panel) is characteristic of della Robbia's
art. (Marion Gray. By permission of St. Anselm's
Abbey, Washington, D.C.)*

*The lives of men of position are passed, as it were, in public view; and are fairly expected to serve as witness to personal merit and capacity on the part of those who occupy such exceptional place amongst their fellow men. You therefore, Ubertinus, . . . the representative of a house for many generations sovereign in our ancient and most learned city of Padua, are peculiarly concerned in attaining this excellence in learning of which we speak. . . . Progress in learning . . . as in character, depends largely on ourselves.*

*For the education of children is a matter of more than private interest; it concerns the State, which indeed regards the right training of the young as, in certain aspects, within its proper sphere. . . . In order to maintain a high standard of purity all enticements of dancing, or suggestive spectacles, should be kept at a distance: and the society of women as a rule carefully avoided. A bad companion may wreck the character. Idleness, of mind and body, is a common source of temptation to indulgence, and unsociable, solitary temper must be disciplined, and on no account encouraged. Tutors and comrades alike should be chosen from amongst those likely to bring out the best qualities, to attract by good example, and to repress the first signs of evil. . . . Above all, respect for Divine ordinances is of the deepest importance; it should be inculcated from the earliest years. Reverence towards elders and parents is an obligation closely akin. In this, antiquity offers us a beautiful illustration. For the youth of Rome used to escort the Senators, the Fathers of the City, to the Senate House: and awaiting them at the entrance, accompany them at the close of their deliberations on their return to their homes. In this the Romans saw an admirable training in endurance and in patience. This same quality of reverence will imply courtesy towards guests, suitable greeting to elders, to friends and to inferiors. . . .*

*We call those studies liberal which are worthy of a free man; those studies by which we attain and practise virtue and wisdom; that education*

*which calls forth, trains and develops those highest gifts of body and of mind which ennoble men, and which are rightly judged to rank next in dignity to virtue only. . . .*[9]

Part of Vergerio's treatise specifies subjects for the instruction of young men in public life: history teaches virtue by examples from the past; ethics focuses on virtue itself; and rhetoric or public speaking trains for eloquence.

No book on education achieved wider fame or broader influence than Baldassare Castiglione's *The Courtier* (1528). This treatise sought to train, discipline, and fashion the young man into the courtly ideal, the gentleman. According to Castiglione, the educated man of the upper class should have a broad background in many academic subjects, and his spiritual and physical, as well as intellectual, capabilities should be trained. The courtier should have easy familiarity with dance, music, and the arts. Castiglione envisioned a man who could compose a sonnet, wrestle, sing a song and accompany himself on an instrument, ride expertly, solve difficult mathematical problems, and, above all, speak and write eloquently. With these accomplishments, he would be the perfect Renaissance man. Whereas the medieval chivalric ideal stressed the military virtues of bravery and loyalty, the Renaissance man had to develop his artistic and intellectual potential as well as his fighting skills.

In contrast to the pattern of medieval education, the Renaissance courtier had the aristocrat's hostility to specialization and professionalism. Medieval higher education, as offered by the universities, had aimed at providing a practical grounding in preparation for a career. After exposure to the rudiments of grammar and rhetoric, which the medieval student learned mainly through memorization, he was trained for a profession

– usually law – in the government of the state or the church. Education was very functional and, by later standards, middle class.

In manner and behavior, the Renaissance courtier had traits his medieval predecessor probably had not had time to acquire. The gentleman was supposed to be relaxed, controlled, always composed and cool, elegant but not ostentatious, doing everything with a casual and seemingly effortless grace. In the sixteenth and seventeenth centuries, *The Courtier* was widely read. It influenced the social mores and patterns of conduct of elite groups in Renaissance and early modern Europe. The courtier became the model of the European gentleman.

No Renaissance book on any topic, however, has been more widely read and studied in all the centuries since its publication than the short political treatise *The Prince,* by Niccolò Machiavelli (1469-1527). Some political scientists maintain that Machiavelli was describing the actual competitive framework of the Italian states with which he was familiar. Other thinkers praise *The Prince* because it revolutionized political theory and destroyed medieval views of the nature of the state. Still other scholars consider this work a classic because it deals with eternal problems of government and society.

Born to a modestly wealthy Tuscan family, Machiavelli received a good education in the Latin classics. He entered the civil service of the Florentine government and served on thirty diplomatic missions. When the exiled Medicis returned to power in the city in 1512, they expelled Machiavelli from his position as officer of the city government. In exile he wrote *The Prince.*

The subject of *The Prince* is political power: how the ruler should gain, maintain, and increase his power. In this, Machiavelli implicitly addresses the question of the citizen's relationship to the state. As a good humanist, he explores the problems of human nature and concludes that human beings are selfish, corrupt, and out to advance their own interests. This pessimistic view leads him to maintain that the prince should manipulate the people in any way he finds necessary:

*The manner in which men live is so different from the way in which they ought to live, that he who leaves the common course for that which he ought to follow will find that it leads him to ruin rather than to safety. For a man who, in all respects, will carry out only his professions of good, will be apt to be ruined amongst so many who are evil. A prince therefore who desires to maintain himself must learn to be not always good, but to be so or not as necessity may require.*[10]

The prince should combine the cunning of a fox with the ferocity of a lion to achieve his goals. Asking rhetorically whether it is better for a ruler to be loved or feared, Machiavelli wrote:

*A prince, therefore, should not mind the ill repute of cruelty, when he can thereby keep his subjects united and loyal; for a few displays of severity will really be more merciful than to allow, by an excess of clemency, disorders to occur, which are apt to result in rapine and murder; for these injure a whole community, whilst the executions ordered by the prince fall only upon a few individuals. And, above all others, the new prince will find it almost impossible to avoid the reputation of cruelty, because new states are generally exposed to many dangers. . . .*

*. . . This, then, gives rise to the question "whether it be better to be loved than feared, or to be feared than be loved." It will naturally be answered that it would be desirable to be both the one and the other; but as it is difficult to be both at the same time, it is much more safe to be feared than to be loved, when you have to choose between the*

*two. For it may be said of men in general that they are ungrateful and fickle, dissemblers, avoiders of danger, and greedy of gain. So long as you shower benefits upon them, they are all yours. . . . And the prince who relies upon their words, without having otherwise provided for his security, is ruined; for friendships that are won by rewards, and not by greatness and nobility of soul, although deserved, yet are not real, and cannot be depended upon in time of adversity.*[11]

Medieval political theory derived ultimately from Saint Augustine's view that the state arose as a consequence of Adam's fall and people's propensity to sin. The test of good government was whether it provided justice, law and order. Political theorists and theologians from Alcuin to Marsiglio of Padua had stressed the way government ought to be; they set high moral and Christian standards for the ruler's conduct.

Machiavelli divorced government from moral and ethical considerations. He was concerned not with the way things ought to be but with the way they actually are. Consequently, the sole test of a "good" government was whether it was effective, whether the ruler increased his power. The state Machiavelli envisioned was a dynamic, amoral force.

Scholars have debated whether Machiavelli was writing a satire, trying to ingratiate himself with the Medicis, objectively describing contemporary Italian events, or advocating a fierce Italian nationalism that would achieve the unification of the peninsula. In any case, the word *Machiavellian* entered English as a synonym for devious, crafty, and corrupt politics in which the end justifies any means.

## THE PRINTED WORD

Sometime in the thirteenth century, paper money and playing cards from China reached the West. They were block printed — that is, Chinese characters or pictures were carved into a wooden block, inked, and the words or illustrations put on paper. Since each word, phrase, or picture was on a separate block, this method of reproduction was extraordinarily expensive and time-consuming.

Around 1455, probably through the combined efforts of three men — Johan Gutenberg, Johan Fust, and Peter Schoffer, all experimenting at Mainz — movable type came into being. The mirror image of each letter (rather than entire words or phrases) was carved in relief on a small block. Individual letters, easily movable, were put together to form words; words separated by blank spaces formed lines of type; and lines of type were brought together to make up a page. Once the printer had placed wooden pegs around the type for a border, and locked the whole in a frame, the page was ready for printing. Since letters could be arranged into any format, an infinite variety of texts could be printed by reusing and rearranging pieces of type.

By the middle of the fifteenth century, paper was no problem. The technologically advanced but extremely isolated Chinese knew how to manufacture paper as early as the first century A.D. This knowledge reached the West in the twelfth century, when the Arabs introduced the process into Spain. Europeans quickly learned that old rags could be shredded, mixed with water, placed in a mold, squeezed, and dried to make a durable paper, far less expensive than the vellum (calfskin) and parchment (sheepskin) on which medieval scribes had relied for centuries.

The effects of the invention of movable-type printing were not felt overnight. Nevertheless, within a half-century of the publication of Gutenberg's Bible in 1456, movable type brought about radical changes. The costs of reproducing books were drasti-

THE PRINT SHOP  *Sixteenth-century printing involved a division of labor. Two persons (left) at separate benches set the pieces of type. Another (center, rear) inks the chase (or locked plate containing the set type). Another (right) operates the press which prints the sheets. The boy removes the printed pages and sets them to dry. Meanwhile, a man carries in fresh paper on his head. (BBC Hulton Picture Library)*

cally reduced. It took less time and money to print a book by machine than to make copies by hand. The press also reduced the chances of error. If the type had been accurately set, all the copies would be correct no matter how many were reproduced. The greater the number of pages a scribe copied, the greater the chances for human error.

Printing stimulated the literacy of the laity. Although most of the earliest books dealt with religious subjects, students, businessmen, and upper- and middle-class people sought books on all kinds of subjects. Thus, intellectual interests were considerably broadened. International communication was enormously facilitated. The invention of printing

permitted writers and scholars of different countries to learn about one another's ideas and discoveries quickly. Intellectuals working in related fields got in touch with each other and cooperated in the advancement of knowledge.

Within the past twenty-five years, two inventions have revolutionized life for most Americans, television and the computer. By the late 1960s, the tired business executive or mechanic could return home in the evening, flip on "the tube," and while eating dinner watch battles in Vietnam or Israel that had occurred only a few hours before. The American tourist in Copenhagen or Florence or Tokyo who suddenly needs to draw on a bank account in New Orleans or Portland can have the account checked by computer in a matter of minutes. The impact of these relatively recent developments has been absolutely phenomenal. The invention of movable type likewise transformed European society in the fifteenth century.

The process of learning was made much easier by printing. In the past, students had had to memorize everything because only the cathedral, monastery, or professor possessed the book. The greater availability of books meant that students could begin to buy their own. If information was not at the tip of the tongue, it was at the tip of the fingers. The number of students all across Europe multiplied. It is not entirely accidental that between 1450 and 1517 seven new universities were established in Spain, three in France, nine in Germany, and six new colleges were set up at Oxford in England.

Printing also meant that ideas critical of the established order in state or church could be more rapidly disseminated. In the early sixteenth century, for example, the publication of Erasmus's *The Praise of Folly* helped pave the way for the Reformation. After 1517, the printing press played no small role in the spread of Martin Luther's political and social views. Cartoons and satirical engravings of all kinds proliferated. They also provoked state censorship, which had been very rare in the Middle Ages. The printed word eventually influenced every aspect of European culture: educational, economic, religious, political, and social.

## WOMEN

The status of upper-class women declined during the Renaissance. If women in the High Middle Ages are compared with those of fifteenth- and sixteenth-century Italy with respect to the education they received, the kind of work they performed, their access to property and political power, and the role they played in shaping the outlook of their society, it is clear that ladies in the Renaissance ruling classes generally had less power than comparable ladies of the feudal age.

In the cities of Renaissance Italy, girls received the same education as boys. Young ladies learned their letters and studied the classics. Many read Greek as well as Latin, knew the poetry of Ovid and Virgil, and could speak one or two "modern" languages, such as French or Spanish. In this respect, Renaissance humanism represented a real educational advance for women. Girls also received some training in painting, music, and dance. What were they to do with this training? They were to be gracious, affable, charming – in short, decorative. Renaissance women were better educated than their medieval counterparts. But whereas education trained a young man to rule and to participate in the public affairs of the city, it prepared a woman for the social functions of the home. An educated lady was supposed to know how to attract artists and literati to her husband's court; she was to grace her husband's household.

A striking difference also exists between the medieval literature of courtly love, the etiquette books and romances, and the widely studied Renaissance manual on courtesy and good behavior, Castiglione's *The Courtier.* In the medieval books manners shaped the man to please the lady; in *The Courtier* the lady was to make herself pleasing to the man. With respect to love and sex, the Renaissance witnessed a downward shift in women's status. In contrast to the medieval tradition of relative sexual equality, Renaissance humanists laid the foundations for the bourgeois double standard. Men, and men alone, operated in the public sphere; women belonged in the home. Castiglione, the foremost spokesman of Renaissance love and manners, completely separated love from sexuality. For women, sex was restricted entirely to marriage. Ladies were bound to chastity, to the roles of wife and mother in a politically arranged marriage. Men, however, could pursue sensual indulgence outside marriage. The Italian Renaissance courts accepted a dual sexual standard, as the medieval courts had not. Although some noble ladies were highly educated and some exercised considerable political power, Renaissance culture did little to advance the dignity of women. They usually served as decorative objects in a male society.[12]

Popular attitudes toward rape provide another index of the status of women in the Renaissance. A careful study of the legal evidence from Venice in the years 1338–1358 is informative. The Venetian shipping and merchant elite held economic and political power and made the laws. Those laws reveal that rape was not considered a particularly serious crime against either the victim or society. Noble youths committed a higher percentage of rapes than their small numbers in Venetian society would imply, despite government-regulated prostitution. The rape of a young girl of marriageable age or a child under twelve was considered a graver crime than the rape of a married woman. Still, the punishment for rape of a noble marriageable girl was only a fine or about six months' imprisonment. In an age when theft and robbery were punished by mutilation, and forgery and sodomy by burning, this penalty was very mild indeed. When a youth of the upper class was convicted of the rape of a nonnoble girl, his punishment was even lighter.

By contrast, the sexual assault on a noblewoman by a man of working-class origin, which was extraordinarily rare, resulted in severe penalization because the crime had social and political overtones.

In the eleventh century, William the Conqueror had decreed that rapists should be castrated, thus implicitly according women protection and a modicum of respect. But in the early Renaissance, rape was treated as a minor offense. Venetian laws and their enforcement show that the populace believed that rape damaged, but only slightly, men's property – women.[13]

Evidence from Florence in the fifteenth century also sheds light on infanticide, which historians are only now beginning to study in the Middle Ages and the Renaissance. Early medieval penitentials and church councils had legislated against abortion and infanticide, though it is known that Pope Innocent III (1198–1216) was moved to establish an orphanage "because so many women were throwing their children into the Tiber."[14] In the fourteenth and early fifteenth centuries, a considerable number of children died in Florence under suspicious circumstances. Some were simply abandoned outdoors. Some were said to have been crushed to death while sleeping in the same bed with their parents. Some died from "crib death" or suffocation. These deaths occurred too frequently to have all been accidental. And far more girls than boys died thus, reflecting societal discrimination against girl children as inferior and less useful than boys. The dire poverty of parents led them to do away with unwanted children.

The gravity of the problem of infanticide, which violated both the canon law of the church and the civil law of the state, forced the Florentine government to build the Foundling Hospital. Supporters of the institution maintained that without public responsibility, "many children would soon be found dead in the rivers, sewers, and ditches, unbaptized."[15] The city fathers commissioned

TITIAN: THE RAPE OF EUROPA *According to Greek myth, the Phoenician princess Europa was carried off to Crete by the god Zeus disguised as a white bull. The story was highly popular in the Renaissance with its interests in the classics. In this masterpiece, the erotic and voluptuous female figure reveals the new interest in the human form and the secular element in Renaissance art. (Isabella Stewart Gardner Museum)*

Filippo Brunelleschi, who had recently completed the dome over the Cathedral of Florence, to design the building. (Interestingly enough, the Foundling Hospital – completed in 1445 – is the very first building to use the revitalized Roman classic design that characterizes Renaissance architecture.) The unusually large size of the hospital suggests that great numbers of children were abandoned.

## BLACKS IN RENAISSANCE SOCIETY

Ever since the time of the Roman republic, a few black people had lived in Western Europe. They had come, along with white slaves, as the spoils of war. Even after the collapse of the Roman Empire, Muslim and Christian merchants continued to import them. The evidence of medieval art attests to the presence of Africans in the West and Eu-

BALDUNG: ADORATION OF THE MAGI  Early
sixteenth-century German artists produced thousands
of adoration scenes depicting a black man as one of the
three kings: these paintings were based on direct observation, reflecting the increased presence of blacks in
Europe. The elaborate costumes, jewelry, and landscape expressed royal dignity, Christian devotion, and
oriental luxury. (Gemälde galerie. Staatliche Museen
Preussischer Kulturbesitz, Berlin [West])

ropeans' awareness of them. In the twelfth and thirteenth centuries a large cult surrounded St. Maurice, martyred in the fourth century for refusing to renounce his Christian faith, who was portrayed as a black knight. St. Maurice received the special veneration of the nobility. The numbers of blacks, though, had always been small.

Beginning in the fifteenth century, however, hordes of black slaves entered Europe. Portuguese explorers imported perhaps a thousand a year and sold them at the markets of Seville, Barcelona, Marseilles, and Genoa. The Venetians specialized in the import of white slaves, but blacks were so greatly in demand at the Renaissance courts of northern Italy that the Venetians defied papal threats of excommunication to secure them. What roles did blacks play in Renaissance society? What image did Europeans have of Africans?

The medieval interest in curiosities, the exotic, and the marvelous continued into the Renaissance. Because of their rarity, black servants were highly prized and much sought after. In the late fifteenth century Isabella, the wife of Gian Galeazzo Sforza, took pride in the fact that she had ten blacks, seven of them females; a black lady's maid was both a curiosity and a symbol of wealth. In 1491 Isabella of Este, Duchess of Mantua, instructed her agent to secure a black girl between four and eight years old, "shapely and as black as possible." The duchess saw the child as a source of entertainment: "we shall make her very happy and shall have great fun with her." She hoped that the little girl would become "the best buffoon in the world."[16] The cruel ancient tradition of a noble household retaining a professional "fool" for the family's amusement persisted through the Renaissance – and even down to the twentieth century.

Adult black slaves filled a variety of positions. Many served as maids, valets, domestic servants; Italian aristocrats such as the Marchesa Elena Grimaldi had their portraits painted with their black page boys to indicate their wealth. The Venetians employed blacks – slave and free – as gondoliers and stevedores on the docks. Tradition, stretching back at least as far as the thirteenth century, connected blacks with music and dance. In Renaissance Spain and Italy blacks performed as dancers, as actors and actresses in courtly dramas, and as musicians, sometimes composing full orchestras.[17]

Before the sixteenth-century "discoveries" of the non-European world, Europeans had little interest in Africans and African culture. Consequently, Europeans knew little about them beyond biblical accounts. The European attitude toward Africans was ambivalent. On the one hand, Europeans perceived Africa as a remote place, the home of strange people isolated by heresy and Islam from superior European civilization. Africans' contact even as slaves with Christian Europeans could only "improve" the blacks. Most Europeans' knowledge of the black as a racial type was based entirely on theological speculation. Theologians taught that God is light. Blackness, the opposite of light, therefore represented the hostile forces of the underworld: evil, sin, and the devil. Thus the devil was commonly represented as a black man in medieval and early Renaissance art. Blackness, however, also possessed certain positive qualities. It symbolized the emptiness of worldly goods, the humility of the monastic way of life. Black clothes permitted a conservative and discreet display of wealth. Black vestments and funeral trappings indicated grief, and Christ had said that those who mourn are blessed. Until the exploration and observation of the sixteenth, seventeenth, and nineteenth centuries allowed, ever so slowly, for the development of more scientific knowledge, the Western conception of Africa and black people remained bound up with religious notions.[18]

## THE ENVIRONMENT

Historians and natural scientists are only today beginning to study the attitude of peoples in earlier centuries toward their natural environment. An enormous amount of exciting research, which could improve ecological knowledge and aid in the solution of present-day problems, waits to be done. The measures the city of Florence took against water pollution in the fifteenth century provide some interesting information.

In 1450, the Florentine governing body expressed concern that fishermen and others several miles southeast of the city were using toxic substances to harvest more fish from the Arno River, which flowed through the city and was the source of much of Florence's fish. Fewer fresh fish reached the city markets. Ecclesiastical law required Christians to abstain from meat during the Fridays of the year and during the seasons of Advent and Lent. Fish was an obvious substitute, and the fishing industry was large and influential. The law of 1450 states:

*Whereas it often happens, especially in parts of the Casentino and areas near there, that poisons and toxic substances are put and inserted into the neighboring rivers and waters to capture and angle fish more easily and in greater number . . .*

*This is done where those fish are procreated and made which are called Trout, and truly noble and impressive fish they are. The result is that the said fish are destroyed and wasted.*

*And certainly if this were not so, our city and also other neighboring areas would continually and far more abound in the said fish. So that, therefore, the said genus of fish is preserved, and*

*our city and the other said areas have a copious and abundant supply of such fish, the magnificent . . . lords priors . . . ordain . . .[19]*

The citizens of Florence apparently did not understand the ecological problem and were not concerned about conservation. While they appreciated the beauty of the "noble trout," their concern was only that if upstream waters were polluted and the fish there killed, there would be fewer fish caught and brought to market in Florence. Government officials did not object to the damage to the river as a source of beauty, pleasure, and drinking water. Variations of the law of 1450 were put on the statute books in 1455, 1460, 1471, and 1477,[20] suggesting that these early conservation measures could not be enforced.

## THE RENAISSANCE IN THE NORTH

In the last quarter of the fifteenth century, Renaissance thought and ideals penetrated northern Europe. Students from the Low Countries, France, Germany, and England flocked to Italy, imbibed the "new learning," and carried it back to their countries. Northern humanists interpreted Italian ideas about and attitudes toward classical antiquity, individualism, and humanism in terms of their own traditions. The cultural traditions of northern Europe tended to remain more distinctly Christian, or at least pietistic, than those of Italy. Thus while the Renaissance in Italy was characterized by a secular and pagan spirit and focused on Greco-Roman motifs and scholarship, north of the Alps the Renaissance had a religious character and emphasized biblical and early Christian themes. Scholars have termed the northern Renaissance "Christian humanism."

Christian humanists were interested in the development of an ethical way of life. To achieve it they believed that the best elements of classical and Christian cultures should be combined. For example, the classical ideals of calmness, stoical patience, and broad-mindedness should be joined in human conduct with the Christian virtues of love, faith, and hope. Northern humanists also stressed the use of reason, rather than acceptance of dogma, as the foundation for an ethical way of life. Like the Italians, they were extremely impatient with scholastic philosophy. Christian humanists had a profound faith in the power of the human intellect to bring about moral and institutional reform. They believed that although human nature had been corrupted by sin it was fundamentally good and capable of improvement through education, which would lead to piety and an ethical way of life.

This optimistic viewpoint found expression in scores of lectures, treatises, and collections of precepts. Treatises such as Erasmus's *The Education of a Christian Prince* express the naive notion that peace, harmony among nations, and a truly ethical society will result from a new system of education. This hope has been advanced repeatedly in Western history — by the ancient Greeks, by the sixteenth-century Christian humanists, by the eighteenth-century philosophers of the Enlightenment, and by nineteenth-century advocates of progress. The proposition remains highly debatable, but each time the theory has reappeared education has been further democratized.

The work of the French priest Jacques Lefèvre d'Etaples (ca 1455-1536) is one of the early attempts to apply humanistic learning to religious problems. A brilliant thinker and able scholar, he believed that more accurate texts of the Bible would lead people to live better lives. According to Lefèvre, a solid ed-ucation in the Scriptures would increase piety and raise the level of behavior in Christian society. Lefèvre produced an edition of the Psalms and a commentary on Saint Paul's Epistles. In 1516, when Martin Luther lectured to his students at Wittenberg on Paul's Letter to the Romans, he relied on Lefèvre's texts.

Lefèvre's English contemporary John Colet (1466-1519) also published lectures on Saint Paul's Epistles, approaching them in the new critical spirit. Unlike the medieval theologians, who studied the Bible for allegorical meanings, Colet, who was a priest, interpreted the Pauline letters historically — that is, within the social and political context of the times when they were written. Both Colet and Lefèvre d'Etaples were later suspected of heresy, as humanistic scholarship got entangled with the issues of the Reformation.

Colet's friend and countryman Thomas More (1472-1535) towers above other figures in sixteenth-century English social and intellectual history. More's political stance at the time of the Reformation (page 492), a position that in part flowed from his humanist beliefs, got him into serious trouble with King Henry VIII and has tended to obscure his contribution to Christian humanism.

The early career of Thomas More presents a number of paradoxes that reveal the marvelous complexity of the man. Trained as a lawyer, More lived as a student in the London Charterhouse, a Carthusian monastery. He subsequently married and practiced law, but became deeply interested in the classics, and his household served as a model of warm Christian family life and a mecca for foreign and English humanists. Following the career pattern of such Italian humanists as Petrarch, he entered government service under Henry VIII and was sent as ambassador to Flanders. There More found the time to write *Utopia*

# THE LATER MIDDLE AGES, RENAISSANCE, AND PROTESTANT AND CATHOLIC REFORMATIONS, 1300–1600

As is evident in this chronology, early manifestations of the Renaissance and Protestant Reformation coincided in time with major events of the Later Middle Ages.

| | |
|---|---|
| 1300–1321 | Dante, *The Divine Comedy* |
| 1304–1374 | Petrarch |
| 1309–1372 | Babylonian Captivity of the papacy |
| 1337–1453 | Hundred Years' War |
| 1347–1351 | The Black Death |
| ca 1350 | Boccaccio, *The Decameron* |
| 1356 | Golden Bull: transforms the Holy Roman Empire into an aristocratic federation |
| 1358 | The Jacquerie |
| ca 1376 | John Wyclif publishes *Civil Dominion* attacking the church's temporal power and asserting the supremacy of Scripture |
| 1377–1417 | The Great Schism |
| 1378 | Laborers' revolt in Florence |
| 1381 | Peasants' Revolt |
| 1385–1400 | Chaucer, *Canterbury Tales* |
| 1414–1418 | Council of Constance: ends the schism, postpones reform, executes John Hus |
| 1431 | Joan of Arc is burned at the stake |
| 1434 | Medici domination of Florence begins |
| 1438 | Pragmatic Sanction of Bourges: declares autonomy of the French church from papal jurisdiction |
| 1453 | Capture of Constantinople by the Ottoman Turks, ending the Byzantine Empire |
| 1453–1471 | Wars of the Roses in England |
| 1456 | Gutenberg Bible |
| 1492 | Columbus reaches the Americas |
| | Unification of Spain under Ferdinand and Isabella; expulsion of Jews from Spain |
| 1494 | France invades Italy, inaugurating sixty years of war on Italian soil |
| | Florence expels the Medici and restores republican government |

| | |
|---|---|
| 1509 | Erasmus, *The Praise of Folly* |
| 1512 | Restoration of the Medici in Florence |
| 1512–1517 | Lateran Council undertakes reform of clerical abuses |
| 1513 | Balboa discovers the Pacific |
| | Macchiavelli, *The Prince* |
| 1516 | Concordat of Bologna between France and the papacy: rescinds the Pragmatic Sanction of 1438, strengthens French monarchy, establishes Catholicism as the national religion |
| | Thomas More, *Utopia* |
| 1517 | Martin Luther proclaims the 95 Theses |
| 1519–1522 | Magellan's crew circumnavigates the earth |
| 1523 | Luther's translation of the New Testament into German |
| 1524 | Peasants' Revolt in Germany |
| 1527 | Sack of Rome by mercenaries of Holy Roman Emperor Charles |
| 1528 | Castiglione, *The Courtier* |
| 1530 | Confession of Augsburg, official formulation of Lutheran theology |
| 1534 | Act of Supremacy inaugurates the English Reformation |
| 1534–1541 | Michelangelo, *The Last Judgment* |
| 1535 | Execution of Thomas More for treason |
| 1536 | John Calvin, *Institutes of the Christian Religion* |
| 1540 | Loyola founds the Society of Jesus (Jesuits) |
| 1541 | Calvin establishes a theocracy in Geneva |
| 1543 | Copernicus, *On the Revolutions of the Heavenly Spheres* |
| 1545–1563 | Council of Trent |
| 1555 | Peace of Augsburg: German princes determine the religion of their territories; no privileges for Calvinism |
| 1572 | St. Bartholemew's Day Massacre |
| 1588 | Spanish Armada |
| 1598 | Edict of Nantes grants French Protestants freedom of worship in certain towns |
| 1603 | Shakespeare, *Hamlet* |
| 1605 | Sir Francis Bacon, *The Advancement of Learning* |

(1516), which presented a revolutionary view of society.

*Utopia,* which literally means "nowhere," describes an ideal socialistic community on a South Sea island. All its children receive a good education, primarily in the Greco-Roman classics, and learning does not cease with maturity, for the goal of all education is to develop rational faculties. Adults divide their days equally between manual labor or business pursuits (the Utopians were thoroughly familiar with advanced Flemish business practices) and various intellectual activities.

Because the profits from business and property are held strictly in common, there is absolute social equality. The Utopians use gold and silver to make chamber pots or to prevent wars by buying off their enemies. By this casual use of precious metals, More meant to suggest that the basic problems in society were caused by greed. Utopian law exalts mercy above justice. Citizens of Utopia lead an ideal and nearly perfect existence because they live by reason; their institutions are perfect.

More's ideas were profoundly original in the sixteenth century. Contrary to the long-prevailing view that vice and violence exist because women and men are basically corrupt, More maintained that *society's* flawed institutions are responsible for corruption and war. Today most people take this view so much for granted that it is difficult to appreciate how radical it was in the sixteenth century. According to More, the key to improvement and reform of the individual was reform of the social institutions that mold the individual.

Better known by his contemporaries than Thomas More was the Dutch humanist Desiderius Erasmus of Rotterdam (1469?–1536). Orphaned as a small boy, Erasmus was forced to enter a monastery. Although he intensely disliked the religious life, he developed there an excellent knowledge of the Latin language and a deep appreciation for the Latin classics. During a visit to England in 1499, Erasmus met John Colet, who decisively influenced his life's work: the application of the best humanistic learning to the study and explanation of the Bible. As a mature scholar with an international reputation stretching from Krakow to London, Erasmus could boast with truth, "I brought it about that humanism, which among the Italians ... savored of nothing but pure paganism, began nobly to celebrate Christ."[21]

Erasmus's long list of publications includes *The Adages* (1500), a list of Greek and Latin precepts on ethical behavior; *The Education of a Christian Prince* (1504), which combines idealistic and practical suggestions for the formation of a ruler's character through the careful study of Plutarch, Aristotle, Cicero, and Plato; *The Praise of Folly* (1509), a satire on monasticism and a plea for the simple and spontaneous Christian faith of children; and, most important of all, a critical edition of the Greek New Testament (1516). In the preface to the New Testament Erasmus explained the purpose of his great work:

*Only bring a pious and open heart, imbued above all things with a pure and simple faith.... For I utterly dissent from those who are unwilling that the sacred Scriptures should be read by the unlearned translated into their vulgar tongue, as though Christ had taught such subtleties that they can scarcely be understood even by a few theologians.... Christ wished his mysteries to be published as openly as possible. I wish that even the weakest woman should read the Gospel — should read the epistles of Paul. And I wish these were translated into all languages, so that they might be read and understood, not only by Scots and Irishmen, but also by Turks and Saracens. To make them understood is surely the first step. It may be that they might be ridiculed by many, but some would take them to heart. I long that the husbandman should sing portions of them to himself as he follows the plough, that the weaver should hum them to the tune of his shuttle, that the traveller should beguile with their stories the tedium of his journey. . . .*

*Why do we prefer to study the wisdom of Christ in men's writings rather than in the writing of Christ himself?*[22]

Two fundamental themes run through all of Erasmus's scholarly work. First, education was the means to reform, the key to moral and intellectual improvement. The core of education ought to be study of the Bible and the classics. Second, the essence of Erasmus's thought is, in his own phrase, "the philosophy of Christ." By this Erasmus meant that Christianity is an inner attitude of the heart or spirit. Christianity is not formalism, special ceremonies, law; Christianity is Christ – his life and what he said and did, not what theologians and commentators have written about him. The Sermon on the Mount, for Erasmus, expressed the heart of the Christian message.

While the writings of Colet, Erasmus, and More have strong Christian themes and have drawn the attention primarily of scholars, the stories of the French humanist François Rabelais (1490?–1553) possess a distinctly secular flavor and have attracted broad readership among the literate public. Rabelais' *Gargantua* and *Pantagruel* (serialized between 1532 and 1552) belong among the great comic masterpieces of world literature. These stories' gross and robust humor introduced the adjective *Rabelasian* into the language.

*Gargantua* and *Pantagruel* can be read on several levels: as comic romances about the adventures of the giant Gargantua and his son Pantagruel; as a spoof on contemporary French society; as a program for educational reform; or as illustrations of Rabelais' prodigious learning. The reader enters a world of Renaissance vitality, ribald joviality, and intellectual curiosity. On his travels Gargantua meets various absurd characters, and within their hilarious exchanges there occur serious discussions on religion, politics, philosophy, and education. Rabelais had received an excellent humanistic education in a monastery, and Gargantua discusses the disorders of contemporary religious and secular life. Like More and Erasmus, Rabelais did not denounce institutions directly. Like Erasmus, Rabelais satirized hypocritical monks, pedantic academics, and pompous lawyers. But where Erasmus employed intellectual cleverness and sophisticated wit, Rabelais applied wild and gross humor. Like Thomas More, Rabelais believed that institutions molded individuals and that education was the key to a moral and healthy life. While the middle-class inhabitants of More's *Utopia* lived lives of restrained moderation, the aristocratic residents of Rabelais' Thélème lived for the full gratification of their physical instincts and rational curiosity.

Thélème, the abbey Gargantua establishes, parodies traditional religion and other social institutions. Thélème, whose motto is "Do as Thou Wilt," admits women *and* men, allows all to eat, drink, sleep, and work when they choose, provides excellent facilities for swimming, tennis, and football, and encourages sexual experimentation and marriage. Rabelais believed profoundly in the basic goodness of human beings and the rightness of instinct.

The most roguishly entertaining Renaissance writer, Rabelais was convinced that "laughter is the essence of manhood." A convinced believer in the Roman Catholic faith, he included in Gargantua's education an appreciation for simple and reasonable prayer.

*JEROME BOSCH: DEATH AND THE MISER  Netherlandish painters frequently used symbolism, and Bosch (ca 1450–1516) is considered the master-artist of symbolism and fantasy. Here, rats, which because of their destructiveness symbolize evil, control the miser's gold. Bosch's imagery appealed strongly to twentieth-century surrealist painters. (National Gallery of Art, Washington, D.C., Samual H. Kress Collection)*

Rabelais combined the Renaissance zest for life and enjoyment of pleasure with a classical insistence on the cultivation of the body and the mind.

The distinctly religious orientation of the literary works of the Renaissance in the north also characterized northern art and architecture. Some Flemish painters, notably Jan van Eyck (1366–1441), were the equals of Italian painters. One of the earliest artists successfully to use oil on wood panels, van Eyck, in paintings such as the *Ghent Altarpiece* and the portrait of *Giovanni Arnolfini and His Bride,* shows the Flemish love for detail; the effect is great realism. Van Eyck's paintings also demonstrate remarkable attention to human personality, as do those of Hans Memling (d. 1494) in his studies of *Tommaso Portinari and His Wife.* Typical of northern piety, the Portinari are depicted in an attitude of prayer (see p. 432).

Another Flemish painter, Jerome Bosch (c. 1450–1516) frequently used religious themes, but in combination with grotesque fantasies, colorful imagery, and peasant folk legends. Many of Bosch's paintings reflect the confusion and anguish often associated with the end of the Middle Ages. In *Death and the Miser,* Bosch's dramatic treatment of the Dance of Death theme, the miser's gold, increased by usury, is ultimately controlled by diabolical rats and toads, while his guardian angel urges him to choose the crucifix.

A quasi-spiritual aura likewise infuses architectural monuments in the north. The city halls of wealthy Flemish towns like Bruges, Brussels, Louvain, and Ghent strike the viewer more as shrines to house the bones of saints than as settings for the mundane decisions of politicians and businessmen. Northern architecture was little influenced by the classical revival so obvious in Renaissance Rome and Florence.

## POLITICS AND THE STATE IN THE RENAISSANCE (CA 1450-1521)

The High Middle Ages had witnessed the origins of many of the basic institutions of the modern national state. Sheriffs, inquests, juries, circuit judges, bureaucracies, and representative assemblies all trace their origins to the twelfth and thirteenth centuries (pages (351-364). The linchpin for the development of states, however, was strong monarchy, and during the period of the Hundred Years' War no ruler in western Europe was able to provide effective leadership. The resurgent power of feudal nobilities weakened the centralizing work begun earlier.

Beginning in the fifteenth century, rulers utilized the aggressive methods implied by Renaissance political ideas to rebuild their governments. First in Italy, then in France, England, and Spain, rulers began the work of reducing violence, curbing unruly nobles and troublesome elements, and establishing domestic order. Within the Holy Roman Empire of Germany, the lack of centralization helps to account for the later German distrust of the Roman papacy. Divided into scores of independent principalities, Germany could not deal with the Roman church as an equal.

The dictators and oligarchs of the Italian city-states, however, together with Louis XI of France, Henry VII of England, and Ferdinand of Spain, were tough, cynical, and calculating rulers. In their ruthless push for power and strong governments, they subordinated morality and considerations of right and wrong to the achievement of hard results. They preferred to be secure, if feared, rather than loved. Whether or not they actually read Machiavelli's *The Prince,* they acted as if they had.

Some historians have called Louis XI (1461-1483), Henry VII (1485-1509), and Ferdinand and Isabella of Spain (1474-1516) "new monarchs." The term is only partly appropriate. These monarchs were new in that they invested kingship with a strong sense of royal authority and national purpose. They stressed that monarchy was the one institution that linked all classes and peoples within definite territorial boundaries. Rulers emphasized the "royal majesty" and royal sovereignty and insisted that all must respect and be loyal to them. They ruthlessly suppressed opposition and rebellion, especially from the nobility. They loved the business of kingship and worked hard at it.

In other respects, however, the methods of these rulers, which varied from country to country, were not so new. They reasserted long-standing ideas and practices of strong monarchs in the Middle Ages. The Holy Roman emperor Frederick Barbarossa, the English Edward I, and the French King Philip the Fair had all applied ideas drawn from Roman law in the High Middle Ages. Renaissance princes also did so. They seized upon the maxim of the Justinian Code, "What pleases the prince has the force of law," to advance their authority. Some medieval rulers, such as Henry I of England, had depended heavily upon middle-class officials. Renaissance rulers too tended to rely on civil servants of middle-class background. With tax revenues, medieval rulers had built armies to crush feudal anarchy. Renaissance townspeople with commercial and business interests naturally wanted a reduction of violence and usually were willing to be taxed in order to achieve domestic order.

Scholars have often described the fifteenth-century "new monarchs" as crafty, devious, and thoroughly Machiavellian in their methods. Yet contemporaries of the Capetian Philip the Fair considered him every bit as devious and crafty as his Valois descendants, Louis XI and Francis I, were considered in the fifteenth and sixteenth centuries. Machiavellian politics were not new in the age of the Renaissance. What was new was a marked acceleration of politics, whose sole rationalization was the acquisition and expansion of power. Renaissance rulers spent precious little time seeking a religious justification for their actions. With these qualifications of the term "new monarchs" in mind, let us consider the development of national states in Italy, France, England, and Spain in the period 1450 to 1521.

## THE ITALIAN·CITY-STATES

In the fourteenth century, the Holy Roman emperors had made several efforts to impose imperial authority in Italy and continue the tradition begun by Charlemagne. But the German emperors, economically and militarily weak, could not defeat the powerful, though separate, city-states. The Italian city-states were thus entirely independent of the Holy Roman Empire.

In the fifteenth century, five powers dominated the Italian peninsula – Venice, Milan, Florence, the Papal States, and the kingdom of Naples (see Map 13.1). The rulers of the city-states – whether despots in Milan, patrician elitists in Florence, or oligarchs in Venice – governed as monarchs. They crushed proletarian revolts, levied taxes, killed their enemies, and used massive building programs to employ, and the arts to overawe, the masses.

Venice, with enormous trade and a vast colonial empire, ranked as an international power. Although Venice had a sophisticated constitution and was a republic in name, an oligarchy of merchant-aristocrats actually ran

the city. Milan was also called a republic, but despots of the Sforza family ruled harshly and dominated the smaller cities of the north. Likewise in Florence the form of government was republican, with authority vested in several councils of state. In reality, between 1434 and 1494, power in Florence was held by the great Medici banking family. Although they did not hold public office, Cosimo (1434–1464) and Lorenzo (1469–1492) ruled from behind the scenes.

A republic is a state in which political power resides in the people and is exercised by them or their chosen representatives. The Renaissance nostalgia for the Roman form of republican government, combined with a calculating shrewdness, prompted leaders of Venice, Milan, and Florence to preserve the old forms: the people could be deceived into thinking they still possessed the decisive voice.

Central Italy consisted mainly of the Papal States, which during the Babylonian Captivity had come under the sway of important Roman families. Pope Alexander VI (1492–1503), aided militarily and politically by his son Cesare Borgia, reasserted papal authority in the papal lands. Cesare Borgia became the hero of Machiavelli's *The Prince* because he began the work of uniting the peninsula by ruthlessly conquering and exacting total obedience from the principalities making up the Papal States.

South of the Papal States was the kingdom of Naples, consisting of virtually all of southern Italy and, at times, Sicily. The kingdom of Naples had long been disputed by the Aragonese and by the French. In 1435, it passed to Aragon.

The major Italian city-states controlled the smaller ones, such as Siena, Mantua, Ferrara, and Modena, and competed furiously among themselves for territory. The large cities used

HOLY ROMAN EMPIRE

DUCHY OF SAVOY

Turin

SALUZZO

DUCHY OF MILAN

Milan
Pavia
Lodi
Po

M. OF MANTUA

Padua

REPUBLIC OF VENICE

Venice

D. OF FERRARA

D. OF MODENA

Bologna

Ravenna

REP. OF GENOA

Genoa

REP. OF LUCCA

Pisa

Arno

REP. OF FLORENCE

Florence

Urbino

PAPAL STATES

Assisi

Siena

REP. OF SIENA

Tiber

Rome

OTTOMAN EMPIRE

DALMATIA

ADRIATIC SEA

CORSICA
(to Genoa)

SARDINIA

Naples
Salerno

KINGDOM OF NAPLES

Bari

MEDITERRANEAN SEA

Palermo

KINGDOM OF SICILY

0    50    100 Km.

0    50    100 Mi.

MAP 13.1 THE ITALIAN CITY-STATES, CA
1494  In the fifteenth century the Italian city-states
represented great wealth and cultural sophistication.
The political divisions of the peninsula invited foreign
intervention.

UCELLO: BATTLE OF SAN ROMANO   *The Medici commissioned this painting ca 1460 to commemorate a lucky Florentine victory over the Sienese in 1432, a victory which contributed to the rise of the Medici dynasty. Although mainly interested in perspective,* *Ucello in this unrealistic and decorative painting seems most concerned with the pageantry of war. (The National Gallery, London. Reproduced by courtesy of the Trustees.)*

diplomacy, spies, paid informers, and any other means to get information that could be used to advance their ambitions. While the states of northern Europe were moving toward centralization and consolidation, the world of Italian politics resembled a jungle where the powerful dominated the weak.

In one significant respect, however, the Italian city-states anticipated future relations among competing European states after 1500. Whenever one Italian state appeared to gain a predominant position within the peninsula, other states combined to establish a balance of power against the major threat. In 1450, for example, Venice went to war against Milan in protest against Francesco Sforza's acquisition of the title of duke of Milan. Cosimo de' Medici of Florence, a long-time supporter of a Florentine-Venetian alliance, switched his po-

sition and aided Milan. Florence and Naples combined with Milan against powerful Venice and the papacy. In the peace treaty signed at Lodi in 1454, Venice received territories in return for recognizing Sforza's right to the duchy. This pattern of shifting alliances continued until 1494.

At the end of the fifteenth century, Venice, Florence, Milan, and the papacy possessed great wealth and represented high cultural achievement. Their imperialistic ambitions at each other's expense, however, and their inability to form a common alliance against potential foreign enemies, made Italy an inviting target for invasion. When Florence and Naples entered into an agreement to acquire Milanese territories, Milan called upon France for support.

At Florence the French invasion had been

predicted by the Dominican friar Girolamo Savonarola (1452–1498). In a number of fiery sermons between 1481 and 1494, Savonarola attacked what he considered the paganism and moral vice of the city, the undemocratic government of Lorenzo de' Medici, and the corruption of Pope Alexander VI. For a time Savonarola enjoyed wide popular support among the ordinary people; he became the religious leader of Florence and as such contributed to the fall of the Medici. Eventually, however, people wearied of his moral denunciations, and he was excommunicated and executed. As an enemy of secularism, Savonarola stands as proof that the common people did not share the worldly outlook of the commercial and intellectual elite. His career also illustrates the internal instability of Italian cities such as Florence, an instability that invited foreign invasion.

The invasion of Italy in 1494 by the French king Charles VIII (1483–1498) inaugurated a new period in Italian and European power politics. Italy became the focus of international ambitions and the battleground of foreign armies. Charles swept down the peninsula with little opposition, and Florence, Rome, and Naples soon bowed before him. When Piero de' Medici, Lorenzo's son, went to the French camp seeking peace, the Florentines exiled the Medicis and restored republican government.

Charles's success simply whetted French appetites. In 1508, his son Louis XII formed the League of Cambrai with the pope and the German emperor Maximilian for the purpose of stripping rich Venice of its mainland possessions. Pope Leo X soon found the French a dangerous friend, and in a new alliance called upon the Spanish and Germans to expel the French from Italy. This anti-French combination was temporarily successful. But the French returned in 1522, and after Charles V

succeeded his grandfather Maximilian as Holy Roman emperor, there began the series of conflicts called the Habsburg-Valois wars (named for the German and French dynasties), whose battlefield was Italy.

In the sixteenth century, the political and social life of Italy was upset by the relentless competition for dominance between France and the empire. The Italian cities suffered severely from the continual warfare, especially in the frightful sack of Rome in 1527 by imperial forces under Charles V. Thus the failure of the city-states to form some federal system, or to consolidate, or at least to establish a common foreign policy, led to the continuation of the centuries-old subjection of the peninsula by outside invaders. Italy was not to achieve unification until 1870.

## FRANCE

The Hundred Years' War left France badly divided, drastically depopulated, commercially ruined, and agriculturally weak. Nonetheless, the ruler whom Joan of Arc had seen crowned at Reims, Charles VII (1422–1461), revived the monarchy and France. He seemed an unlikely person to do so. Frail, ugly, feeble, hypochondriacal, mistrustful, called "the son of a madman and a loose woman," Charles VII began France's long recovery.

Charles reconciled the Burgundians and Armagnacs, who had been waging civil war for thirty years. By 1453, French armies had expelled the English from French soil except in Calais. Charles reorganized the royal council, giving increased influence to the middle-class men, and he strengthened royal finances through such taxes as the gabelle (on salt) and the taille (a land tax). These taxes remained the Crown's chief sources of state income until the Revolution of 1789.

Charles also reformed the justice system

*FRENCH TRADESMEN A bootmaker, a cloth mer-
chant (with bolts of material on shelves), and a dealer
in gold plate and silver share a stall. Through sales
taxes, the French crown received a share of the profits.
(Bibliothèque Municipale, Rouen/Giraudon)*

and remodeled the army. By establishing regular companies of cavalry and archers — recruited, paid, and inspected by the state —
Charles created the first permanent royal
army. In 1438, Charles published the Pragmatic Sanction of Bourges, asserting the superiority of a general council over the papacy,
giving the French crown control over the appointment of bishops, and depriving the pope
of French ecclesiastical revenues. The Pragmatic Sanction established the Gallican (or
French) liberties, because it affirmed the autonomy of the French church from the
Roman papacy. Greater control over the
church, the army, and justice helped to consolidate the authority of the French crown.

Charles's son Louis XI, called "the Spider King" by his subjects because of his treacherous and cruel character, was very much a Renaissance prince. Facing the perpetual French problems of unification of the realm and reduction of feudal disorder, he saw money as the answer. Louis promoted new industries, such as silk weaving at Lyons and Tours. He welcomed tradesmen and foreign craftsmen, and he entered into commercial treaties with England, Portugal, and the towns of the Hanseatic League, a group of cities that played an important role in the development of towns and commercial life in northern Germany. The revenues raised through these economic activities and severe taxation were used to improve the army. With the army Louis stopped aristocratic brigandage and slowly cut into urban independence.

Luck favored his goal of expanding royal authority and unifying the kingdom. On the timely death of Charles the Bold, duke of Burgundy, in 1477 Louis invaded Burgundy and gained some territories. Three years later, the extinction of the house of Anjou brought Louis the counties of Anjou, Bar, Maine, and Provence.

Some scholars have credited Louis XI with laying the foundations for later French royal absolutism. Louis summoned only one meeting of the Estates General, and the delegates requested that they not be summoned in the future. Thereafter the king would decide. Building on the system begun by his father, Louis XI worked tirelessly to remodel the government following the debacle of the fourteenth and fifteenth centuries. In his reliance on finances supplied by the middle classes to fight the feudal nobility, Louis is typical of the new monarchs.

Two further developments strengthened the French monarchy. The marriage of Louis XII and Anne of Brittany added the large western duchy of Brittany to the state. Then, the French king Francis I and Pope Leo X reached a mutually satisfactory agreement in 1516. The new treaty, the Concordat of Bologna, rescinded the Pragmatic Sanction's assertion of the superiority of a general council over the papacy and approved the pope's right to receive the first year's income of new bishops and abbots. In return, Leo X recognized the French ruler's right to select French bishops and abbots. French kings thereafter effectively controlled the appointment and thus the policies of church officials within the kingdom.

## ENGLAND

English society suffered severely from the disorders of the fifteenth century. The aristocracy dominated the government of Henry IV (1399–1413) and indulged in mischievous violence at the local level. Population, decimated by the Black Death, continued to decline. While Henry V (1413–1422) gained chivalric prestige for his military exploits in France, he was totally dependent upon the feudal magnates who controlled the royal council and Parliament. Henry V's death, leaving a nine-month-old son, the future Henry VI (1422–1461), gave the barons a perfect opportunity to entrench their power. Between 1455 and 1471, adherents of the ducal houses of York and Lancaster waged civil war, commonly called the Wars of the Roses because the symbol of the Yorkists was a white rose and that of the Lancastrians a red one. Although only a small minority of the nobility participated, the chronic disorder hurt trade, agriculture, and domestic industry. Under the pious but spineless Henry VI, the authority of the monarchy sank lower than it had been in centuries.

Edward IV (1461–1483) began establishing domestic tranquility. He succeeded in defeating the Lancastrian forces and after 1471 began to reconstruct the monarchy and consolidate royal power. Edward, his brother Richard III (1483–1485), and Henry VII of the Welsh house of Tudor worked to restore royal prestige, to crush the power of the nobility, and to establish order and law at the local level. All three rulers used methods Machiavelli would have praised – ruthlessness, efficiency, and secrecy.

The Hundred Years' War had cost the nation dearly, and the money to finance it had been raised by Parliament. Dominated by various baronial factions, Parliament had been the arena where the nobility exerted its power. As long as the monarchy was dependent on the lords and the commons for revenue, the king had to call Parliament. Thus Edward IV revived the medieval ideal that he would "live of his own," meaning on his own financial resources. He reluctantly established a policy the monarchy was to follow with rare exceptions down to 1603. Edward, and subsequently the Tudors, conducted foreign policy on the basis of diplomacy, avoiding expensive wars. Thus the English monarchy did not depend on Parliament for money, and the Crown undercut that source of aristocratic influence.

Henry VII did, however, summon several meetings of Parliament in the early years of his reign. He used these assemblies primarily to confirm laws. Parliament remained the highest court in the land, and a statute registered (approved) there by the lords, bishops, and commons gave the appearance of broad national support plus thorough judicial authority.

The center of royal authority was the royal council, which governed at the national level. There too Henry VII revealed his distrust of the nobility: although they were not completely excluded, very few great lords were among the king's closest advisers. Regular representatives on the council numbered between twelve and fifteen men, and while many gained high ecclesiastical rank (the means, as it happened, by which the Crown paid them), their origins were the lesser landowning class and their education was in law. They were in a sense middle class.

The royal council handled any business the king put before it – executive, legislative, judicial. For example, the council conducted negotiations with foreign governments and secured international recognition of the Tudor dynasty through the marriage in 1501 of Henry VII's eldest son Arthur to Catherine of Aragon, the daughter of Ferdinand and Isabella of Spain. The council prepared laws for parliamentary ratification. The council dealt with real or potential aristocratic threats through a judicial offshoot, the court of Star Chamber, so-called because of the stars painted on the ceiling of the room.

The court of Star Chamber applied principles of Roman law, and its methods were terrifying: the accused was not entitled to see evidence against him; sessions were secret; torture could be applied to extract confessions; and juries were not called. These procedures ran directly counter to English common-law precedents, but they effectively reduced aristocratic troublemaking.

Unlike the continental countries of Spain and France, England had no standing army or professional civil-service bureaucracy. The Tudors relied upon the support of unpaid local officials, the justices of the peace. These influential landowners in the shires handled all the work of local government. They apprehended and punished criminals, enforced parliamentary statutes, supervised conditions of service, fixed wages and prices, maintained proper standards of weights and measures, and even checked up on moral behavior. Justices of the peace were appointed and supervised by the council. From the royal point of view, they were an inexpensive method of government.

The Tudors won the support of the influential upper middle class because the Crown linked government policy with their interests. A commercial or agricultural upper class fears and dislikes few things more than disorder and violence. If the Wars of the Roses served any useful purpose, it was killing off dangerous nobles and thus making the Tudors' work easier. The Tudors promoted peace and social order, and the gentry did not object to arbitrary methods like the court of Star Chamber, because the government had halted the long period of anarchy.

Grave, secretive, cautious, and always thrifty, Henry VII rebuilt the monarchy. He encouraged the cloth industry and built up the English merchant marine. Both English exports of wool and the royal export tax on that wool steadily increased. Henry crushed an invasion from Ireland and secured peace with Scotland through the marriage of his daughter Margaret to the Scottish king. When Henry VII died in 1509, he left a country at peace both domestically and internationally, a fat treasury, and the dignity of the royal majesty much enhanced.

## SPAIN

Political development in Spain followed a pattern different from that of France and England. The central theme in the history of medieval Spain – or, more accurately, of the separate kingdoms Spain comprised – was disunity and plurality. The various peoples who lived in the Iberian Peninsula lacked a common cultural tradition. Different languages, different laws, and different religious communities made for a rich diversity. Complementing the legacy of Hispanic, Roman, and Visigothic peoples, Muslims and Jews had made significant contributions to Spanish society.

The centuries-long *reconquista* – the attempts of the northern Christian kingdoms to control the entire peninsula – had both military and religious objectives: expulsion or conversion of the Arabs and Jews and political control of the south. By the middle of the fifteenth century, the kingdoms of Castile and Aragon dominated the weaker Navarre, Granada, and Portugal, and, with the exception of Granada, the Iberian Peninsula had been won for Christianity. The wedding in 1469 of the dynamic and aggressive Isabella, heiress of Castile, and the crafty and persistent Ferdinand, heir of Aragon, was the final major step in the unification and Christianization of Spain. This marriage, however, constituted a dynastic union of two royal houses, not the political union of two peoples. Although Ferdinand and Isabella pursued a common foreign policy, Spain under their rule remained a loose confederation of separate states. Each kingdom continued to maintain its own cortes (parliament), laws, courts, bureaucracies, and systems of coinage and taxation.

Isabella and Ferdinand determined to strengthen royal authority. In order to curb the rebellious and warring aristocracy, they revived an old medieval institution. Popular groups in the towns called *hermandades,* or brotherhoods, were given the authority to act both as local police forces and as judicial tribunals. Local communities were made responsible for raising troops and apprehending and punishing criminals. The *hermandades* repressed violence with such savage punishments that by 1498 they could be disbanded.

The second step Ferdinand and Isabella

took to curb aristocratic power was the restructuring of the royal council. Aristocrats and great territorial magnates were rigorously excluded; thus the influence of the nobility on state policy was greatly reduced. Ferdinand and Isabella intended the council to be the cornerstone of their governmental system, with full executive, judicial, and legislative power under the monarchy. The council was also to be responsible for the supervision of local authorities. The king and queen, therefore, appointed to the council only people of middle-class background. The council and various government boards recruited men trained in Roman law, a system that exalted the power of the Crown as the embodiment of the state.

In the extension of royal authority and the consolidation of the territories of Spain, the church was the linchpin. The church possessed vast power and wealth, and churchmen enjoyed exemption from taxation. Most of the higher clergy were descended from great aristocratic families, controlled armies and strategic fortresses, and fully shared the military ethos of their families.

The major issue confronting Isabella and Ferdinand was the appointment of bishops. If the Spanish crown could select the higher clergy, then the monarchy could influence ecclesiastical policy, wealth, and military resources. Through a diplomatic alliance with the papacy, especially with the Spanish pope Alexander VI, the Spanish monarchs secured the right to appoint bishops in Spain and in the Hispanic territories in America. This power enabled the "Catholic Kings of Spain," a title granted Ferdinand and Isabella by the papacy, to establish, in effect, a national church.[23]

The Spanish rulers used their power to reform the church, and they used some of its wealth for national purposes. For example,

they appointed a learned and zealous churchman, Cardinal Jiménez (1436–1517), to reform the monastic and secular clergy. Jiménez proved effective in this task, and established the University of Alcalá in 1499 for the education of the clergy, although instruction did not actually begin until 1508. A highly astute statesman, Jiménez twice served as regent of Castile.

Revenues from ecclesiastical estates provided the means to raise an army to continue the *reconquista*. The victorious entry of Ferdinand and Isabella into Granada on January 6, 1492, signaled the culmination of eight centuries of Spanish struggle against the Arabs in southern Spain and the conclusion of the *reconquista* (see Map 13.2). Granada in the south was incorporated into the Spanish kingdom, and in 1512 Ferdinand conquered Navarre in the north.

Although the Arabs had been defeated, there still remained a sizable and, in the view of the Catholic sovereigns, potentially dangerous minority, the Jews. Since ancient times, governments had never tolerated religious pluralism; religious faiths that differed from the official state religion were considered politically dangerous. Medieval writers quoted the fourth-century Byzantine theologian Saint John Chrysostom, who had asked rhetorically, "Why are the Jews degenerate? Because of their odious assassination of Christ." John Chrysostom and his admirers in the Middle Ages chose to ignore two facts: that it was the Romans who had killed Christ (because they considered him a *political* troublemaker), and that Christ had forgiven his executioners from the cross. France and England had expelled their Jewish populations in the Middle Ages, but in Spain Jews had been tolerated. In fact, Jews had played a decisive role in the economic and intellectual life of the several Spanish kingdoms.

MAP 13.2  THE CHRISTIANIZATION AND UNI-
FICATION OF SPAIN  *The political unification of
Spain was inextricably tied up with conversion or ex-
pulsion of the Muslims and the Jews. Why?*

Anti-Semitic riots and pogroms in the late fourteenth century had led many Jews to convert; they were called *conversos*. By the middle of the fifteenth century, many conversos held high positions in Spanish society as financiers, physicians, merchants, tax collectors, and even officials of the church hierarchy. Numbering perhaps 200,000 in a total population of about 7.5 million, Jews exercised an influence quite disproportionate to their numbers. Aristocratic grandees who borrowed heavily from Jews resented their financial dependence, and churchmen questioned the sincerity of Jewish conversions. At first, Isabella and Ferdinand continued the policy of royal toleration — Ferdinand himself had inherited Jewish blood from his mother. But many conversos apparently reverted to the faith of their ancestors, prompting Ferdinand and Isabella to secure Rome's permission to revive the In-

quisition, a medieval judicial procedure for the punishment of heretics.

Although the Inquisition was a religious institution established to insure the Catholic faith, it was controlled only by the Crown and served primarily as a politically unifying force in Spain. Because the Spanish Inquisition commonly applied torture to extract confessions, first from lapsed conversos, then from Muslims, and later from Protestants, it gained a notorious reputation. Thus, the word *inquisition,* meaning "any judicial inquiry conducted with ruthless severity," came into the English language. The methods of the Spanish Inquisition were cruel, though not as cruel as the investigative methods of some twentieth-century governments. In 1478 the deeply pious Ferdinand and Isabella introduced the Inquisition into their kingdoms to handle the problem of backsliding conversos. They solved the problem in a dire and drastic manner. Shortly after the reduction of the Moorish stronghold at Granada in 1492, Isabella and Ferdinand issued an edict expelling all practicing Jews from Spain. Of the community of perhaps 200,000 Jews, 150,000 fled. (Efforts were made through last-minute conversions to retain good Jewish physicians.) Absolute religious orthodoxy served as the foundation of the Spanish national state.

The diplomacy of the Catholic rulers of Spain achieved a success they never anticipated. Partly out of hatred for the French and partly to gain international recognition for their new dynasty, Ferdinand and Isabella in 1496 married their second daughter, Joanna, heiress to Castile, to the archduke Philip, heir through his mother to the Burgundian Netherlands and through his father to the Holy Roman Empire. Philip and Joanna's son, Charles V (1519-1556), thus succeeded to a vast patrimony on two continents. When Charles's son Philip II united Portugal to the Spanish crown in 1580, the Iberian Peninsula was at last politically united.

———◆———

Fourteenth-century Italy witnessed the rebirth of a strong interest in the ancient world, a Renaissance whose classicizing influences affected law and literature, government, education, religion, and art. Expanding outside Italy, this movement affected the entire culture of Europe. The chief features of the Renaissance were a secular attitude toward life, a belief in individual potential, and a serious interest in the Latin classics. The printing press revolutionized communication. Meanwhile the status of women in society declined, and black people entered Europe in sizable numbers for the first time since the collapse of the Roman Empire.

These changes rested upon important economic developments. The growth of Venetian and Genoese shipping and long-distance trade, Florentine banking and manufactures, Milanese and Pisan manufactures – these activities brought into being wealthy urban classes. As commercial oligarchies, they governed their city-states. In northern Europe city merchants and rural gentry allied with rising monarchies. With taxes provided by businesspeople, kings provided a greater degree of domestic peace and order, conditions essential for trade. In Spain, France, and England, rulers also emphasized royal dignity and authority, and they utilized Machiavellian ideas to insure the preservation and continuation of their governments. Feudal monarchies gradually evolved in the direction of nation states.

## NOTES

1. A. Brucker, *Renaissance Florence,* John Wiley & Sons, New York, 1969, chap. 2.

2. Quoted by J. Burckhardt, *The Civilization of the Renaissance in Italy,* Phaidon Books, London, 1951, p. 89.

3. *Memoirs of Benvenuto Cellini; A Florentine Artist; Written by Himself,* Everyman's Library, J. M. Dent & Sons, London, 1927, p. 2.

4. Quoted by Burckhardt, p. 111.

5. B. Burroughs, ed., *Vasari's Lives of the Artists,* Simon & Schuster, New York, 1946, pp. 164-165.

6. See chap. 3, "The Social Status of the Artist," in A. Hauser, *The Social History of Art,* vol. 2, Vintage Books, New York, 1959, esp. pp. 60, 68.

7. G. Bull, trans., *Aretino: Selected Letters,* Penguin Books, New York, 1976, p. 109.

8. Hauser, pp. 48-49.

9. Quoted by W. H. Woodward, *Vittorino da Feltre and Other Humanist Educators,* Cambridge University Press, Cambridge, 1897, pp. 96-97.

10. C. E. Detmold, trans., *The Historical, Political*

and *Diplomatic Writings of Niccolò Machiavelli,* J. R. Osgood & Co., Boston, 1882, pp. 51–52.

11. Ibid., pp. 54–55.

12. This account rests on the excellent study of J. Kelly-Gadol, "Did Women Have a Renaissance?" in R. Bridenthal and C. Koonz, eds., *Becoming Visible: Women in European History,* Houghton Mifflin, Boston, 1977, pp. 137–161, esp. p. 161.

13. G. Ruggiero, "Sexual Criminality in the Early Renaissance: Venice 1338–1358," *Journal of Social History* 8 (Spring 1975):18–31.

14. Quoted by R. C. Trexler, "Infanticide in Florence: New Sources and First Results," *History of Childhood Quarterly* 1:1 (Summer 1973): 99.

15. Ibid., p. 100.

16. See Jean Devisse and Michel Mollat, *The Image of the Black in Western Art,* vol. II, part 2, trans. William Granger Ryan, William Morrow and Company, New York, 1979, pp. 187–188.

17. Ibid., pp. 190–194.

18. Ibid., pp. 255–258.

19. Quoted by R. C. Trexler, "Measures against Water Pollution in Fifteenth-Century Florence," *Viator* 5 (1974):463.

20. Ibid., pp. 464–467.

21. Quoted by E. H. Harbison, *The Christian Scholar and His Calling in the Age of the Reformation,* Charles Scribner's Sons, New York, 1956, p. 109.

22. Quoted by F. Seebohm, *The Oxford Reformers,* Everyman's Library, J. M. Dent & Sons, London, 1867, p. 256.

23. See J. H. Elliott, *Imperial Spain 1469–1716,* Mentor Books, New York, 1963, esp. pp. 97–108 and p. 75.

## SUGGESTED READING

There are scores of exciting studies available on virtually all aspects of the Renaissance. In addition to the titles given in the Notes, the curious student interested in a broad synthesis should see J. H. Plumb, *The Italian Renaissance* (1965), a superbly written book based on deep knowledge and understanding; this book is probably the best starting point. J. R. Hale, *Renaissance Europe: The Individual and Society, 1480–1520* (1978), is an excellent treatment of individualism by a distinguished authority. F. H. New, *The Renaissance and Reformation: A Short History* (1977), gives a concise, balanced, and up-to-date account. M. P. Gilmore, *The World of Humanism* (1962), is an older but sound study that recent scholarship has not superseded on many subjects. Students interested in the problems the Renaissance has raised for historians should see K. H. Dannenfeld, ed., *The Renaissance: Medieval or Modern* (1959), an anthology with a variety of interpretations, and W. K. Ferguson, *The Renaissance in Historical Thought* (1948), a valuable but difficult book. For the city where much of it originated, G. A. Brucker, *Renaissance Florence* (1969), gives a good description of Florentine economic, political, social, and cultural history.

J. R. Hale, *Machiavelli and Renaissance Italy* (1966), is the best short biography of Machiavelli and broader in scope than the title would imply. G. Bull, trans., *Machiavelli: The Prince* (1959), is a readable and easily accessible edition of the political thinker's major work. C. Singleton, trans., *The Courtier* (1959), presents an excellent picture of Renaissance court life.

The best introduction to the Renaissance in northern Europe and a book that has greatly influenced twentieth-century scholarship is J. Huizinga, *The Waning of the Middle Ages: A Study of the Forms of Life, Thought, and Art in France and the Netherlands in the Dawn of the Renaissance* (1954). The leading northern humanist is sensitively treated in M. M. Philips, *Erasmus and the Northern Renaissance* (1965), and in J. Huizinga, *Erasmus of Rotterdam* (1952), probably the best biography. The standard biography of *Thomas More* remains that of R. W. Chambers (1935), but see also E. E. Reynolds, *Thomas More* (1962). Jacques LeClercq, trans., *The Complete Works of Rabelais* (1963), is easily available.

Renaissance art has understandably inspired vast researches. In addition to Vasari's volume of biographical sketches on the great masters referred to in the Notes, A. Martindale, *The Rise of the Artist in the Middle Ages and Early Renaissance* (1972), is a splendidly illustrated introduction. B. Berenson, *Italian Painters of the Renaissance* (1957), the work of an American expatriate who was an internationally famous art historian, has become a classic. W. Sypher, *Four Stages of Renaissance Style* (1956), relates drama and poetry to the visual arts of painting and sculpture. One of the finest appreciations of Renaissance art, written by one of the greatest art historians of this century, is E. Panofsky, *Meaning in the Visual Arts* (1955). Both Italian and northern painting are treated in the brilliant study of M. Meiss, *The Painter's Choice: Problems in the Interpretation of Renaissance Art* (1976), a collection of essays dealing with Renaissance style, form, and meaning. The splendidly illustrated work of Mary McCarthy, *The Stones of Florence* (1959), celebrates the energy and creativity of the greatest Renaissance city.

The student who wishes to study blacks in medieval and early modern European society should see the rich and original achievement of Jean Devisse and Michel Mollat, *The Image of the Black in Western Art,* vol. II: Part 1, *From the Demonic Threat to the Incarnation of Sainthood,* and Part 2, *Africans in the Christian Ordinance of the World: Fourteenth to Sixteenth Century,* trans. William Granger Ryan, William Morrow & Co., New York, 1979.

The following works are not only useful for the political and economic history of the age of the Renaissance but also contain valuable bibliographical information: A. J. Slavin, ed., *The "New Monarchies" and Representative Assemblies* (1965), a collection of interpretations; R. Lockyer, *Henry VII* (1972), a biography with documents illustrative of the king's reign; J. H. Elliott, *Imperial Spain: 1469–1716* (1966), with a balanced treatment of Isabella and Ferdinand; and I. Origo, *The Merchant of Prato* (1957), a perceptive and detailed account of one busy Florentine businessman.

# CHAPTER 14

## REFORM AND RENEWAL IN THE CHRISTIAN CHURCH

THE IDEA OF REFORM is as old as Christianity itself. In his letter to the Christians of Rome, Saint Paul exhorted: "Do not model yourselves on the behavior of the world around you, but let your behavior change, reformed by your new mind. That is the only way to discover the will of God and know what is good, what it is that God wants, what is the perfect thing to do."[1] In the early fifth century, Saint Augustine of Hippo, describing the final stage of world history, wrote, "In the sixth age of the world our reformation becomes manifest, in newness of mind, according to the image of Him who created us." In the middle of the twelfth century, Saint Bernard of Clairvaux complained about the church of his day: "There is as much difference between us and the men of the primitive Church as there is between muck and gold."

The need for reform of the individual Christian and of the institutional church is central to the Christian faith. The Christian humanists of the late fifteenth and early sixteenth centuries – More, Erasmus, Lefèvre d'Etaples, and Jiménez – urged reform of the church on the pattern of the early church primarily through educational and social change. Men and women of every period believed the early Christian church represented a golden age, and critics in every period called for reform.

Sixteenth-century cries, therefore, were hardly new. Why then did sixteenth-century demands for reform lead to revolution in the Christian church and to lasting divisions in Christian society? What role did social and political factors play in the several reformations? What were the consequences of religious division? To resolve these questions, the related issue of the condition of the church within European society must first be explored.

## THE CONDITION OF THE CHURCH (CA 1400–1517)

The papal conflict with the German emperor Frederick II in the thirteenth century, followed by the Babylonian Captivity and then by the Great Schism, badly damaged the prestige of church leaders. In the fourteenth and fifteenth centuries, conciliarists reflected educated public opinion when they called for the reform of the church "in head and members." The secular humanists of Italy and the Christian humanists of the north denounced corruption in the church. As Machiavelli put it, "We Italians are irreligious and corrupt above others, because the Church and her representatives set us the worst example."[2] In *The Praise of Folly,* Erasmus condemned the absurd superstitions of the parish clergy and the excessive rituals of the monks. The records of episcopal visitations of parishes, civil court records, and even such literary masterpieces as Chaucer's *Canterbury Tales* and Boccaccio's *Decameron* tend to confirm the sarcasms of the humanists.

Concrete evidence of disorder is spotty and scattered. Since a great deal of corruption may have gone unreported, the moral situation may have been worse than the evidence suggests. On the other hand, bishops' registers and public court records mention the exceptional, not the typical. The thousands of priests who quietly and conscientiously went about their duties and did not warrant correction received no mention in the documents.

The religious life of most people in early sixteenth-century Europe took place at the village or local level. Any assessment of the moral condition of the parish clergy must take into account one fundamental fact: parish priests were peasants, and they were poor. All too frequently the spiritual quality of their lives was not much better than that of the people to whom they ministered. The clergy identified religion with life; that is, they injected religious symbols and practices into everyday living. Some historians, therefore, have accused the clergy of vulgarizing religion. But if the level of belief and practice was vulgarized, still the lives of rural, isolated, and semipagan people were spiritualized.

## SIGNS OF DISORDER

In the early sixteenth century, critics of the church concentrated their attacks on three disorders: clerical immorality, clerical ignorance, and clerical pluralism with the related problem of absenteeism. There was little pressure for doctrinal change; the emphasis was on moral and administrative reform.

Since the fourth century, church law had required that candidates for the priesthood accept absolute celibacy. It had always been difficult to enforce. Many priests, especially those ministering to country people, had concubines, and reports of neglect of the rule of celibacy were common. Immorality, of course, included more than sexual transgressions. Clerical drunkenness, gambling, and indulgence in fancy dress were frequent charges. There is no way of knowing how many priests were guilty of such behavior. But because such conduct was so much at odds with the church's rules and moral standards, it scandalized the educated faithful.

The bishops enforced regulations regarding the education of priests very casually. As a result, standards for ordination were shockingly low. Many priests could barely read and write, and critics laughed at the illiterate priest mumbling the Latin words of the mass, which he could not understand. Predictably, this was

the disorder the Christian humanists, with their concern for learning, particularly condemned.

Absenteeism and pluralism constituted the third major abuse. Many clerics, especially higher ecclesiastics, held several benefices (or offices) simultaneously but seldom visited their benefices, let alone performed the spiritual responsibilities those offices entailed. Instead, they collected revenues from all of them and paid a poor priest a fraction of the income to fulfill the spiritual duties of a particular local church.

Many Italian officials in the papal curia held benefices in England, Spain, and Germany. Revenues from those countries paid the Italian priests' salaries, provoking not only charges of absenteeism but nationalistic resentment. King Henry VIII's chancellor Thomas Wolsey was archbishop of York for fifteen years before he set foot in his diocese. The French king Louis XII's famous diplomat Antoine du Prat is perhaps the most notorious example of absenteeism: as archbishop of Sens, the first time he entered his cathedral was in his own funeral procession. Critics condemned pluralism, absenteeism, and the way money seemed to change hands when a bishop entered into his office.

Although royal governments strengthened their positions and consolidated their territories in the fifteenth and sixteenth centuries, rulers lacked sufficient revenues to pay and reward able civil servants. The Christian church, with its dioceses and abbeys, possessed a large proportion of the wealth of the countries of Europe. What better way to reward government officials than with high church offices? After all, the practice was sanctioned by centuries of tradition. Thus in Spain, France, England, and the Holy Roman Empire — in fact, all over Europe — because

THE CHURCH CONTRASTED *Satirical woodcuts as well as the printed word attacked conditions in the church. Here the mercenary spirit of the sixteenth-century papacy is contrasted with the attitude of Christ toward money changers: Christ drove them from the temple, but the pope kept careful records of revenues owed to the church. (Photos: Caroline Buckler)*

church officials served their monarchs, those officials were allowed to govern the church.

The broad mass of the people, in supporting the church, supported everything that churchmen did. Bishops and abbots did a lot of work for secular governments. Churchmen served as royal councilors, diplomats, treasury officials, chancellors, viceroys, and judges. These positions had nothing whatsoever to do with spiritual matters. Bishops worked for their respective states as well as for the church, and they were paid by the church for their services to the state. It is astonishing that so many conscientiously tried to carry out their religious duties on top of their public burdens.

The prodigious wealth of the church inevitably stimulated criticism. For centuries devout laymen and laywomen had bequeathed land, money, rights, and privileges to religious institutions. By the sixteenth century, these gifts and shrewd investments had resulted in vast treasure. Some was spent in the service of civil governments. Much of it was used to alleviate the wretched condition of the poor. But some also provided a luxurious lifestyle for the church hierarchy.

In most countries except England, members of nobility occupied the highest positions in the church. The sixteenth century was definitely not a democratic age. The spectacle of proud, aristocratic prelates living in magnificent splendor contrasted very unfavorably with the simple fishermen who were Christ's first disciples. Nor did the popes of the period 1450–1550 set much of an example. They lived like secular Renaissance princes. Pius II (1458–1464), although deeply learned and a tireless worker, enjoyed a reputation as a clever writer of love stories and witty Latin poetry. Sixtus IV (1471–1484) beautified the city of Rome, built the famous Sistine Chapel, and generously supported several artists. Innocent VIII (1484–1492) made the papal court a model of luxury and scandal. All three popes used papal power and papal wealth to advance the material interests of their own families.

The court of the Spanish pope Rodrigo Borgia, Alexander VI (1492–1503), who publicly acknowledged his mistress and children, reached new heights of impropriety. Because of the prevalence of intrigue, sexual promiscuity, and supposed poisonings, the name Borgia became a synonym for moral corruption. Julius II (1503–1513), the nephew of Sixtus IV, donned military armor and personally led papal troops against the French invaders of Italy in 1506. After him, Giovanni de' Medici, the son of Lorenzo the Magnificent, carried on as Pope Leo X (1513–1521) the Medicean tradition of being a great patron of the arts.

Through the centuries, papal prestige and influence had rested heavily on the moral quality of the popes' lives — that is, on their strong fidelity to Christian teaching as revealed in the Gospel. The lives of Renaissance popes revealed little of this Gospel message.

## SIGNS OF VITALITY

Calls for reform testify to the spiritual vitality of the church as well as to its problems. Before a patient can be cured of sickness, he or she must acknowledge that a problem exists. In the late fifteenth and early sixteenth centuries, both individuals and groups within the church were working actively for reform. In Spain, Cardinal Francisco Jiménez visited religious houses, encouraged the monks and friars to keep their rules and constitutions, and set high standards for the training of the diocesan clergy. Jiménez founded the University of Alcalá (1499) partly for the education of priests.

Lefèvre d'Etaples in France and John Colet in England called for a return to the austere Christianity of the early church. Both men stressed the importance of sound preaching of the Scriptures.

In Holland, beginning in the late fourteenth century, a group of pious laymen and laywomen called the Brethren of the Common Life lived in stark simplicity while daily carrying out the Gospel teaching of feeding the hungry, clothing the naked, and visiting the sick. The Brethren also established schools for the education of the young, their most famous pupil being Erasmus of Rotterdam. The spirituality of the Brethren of the Common Life found its finest expression in the classic *The Imitation of Christ* by Thomas à Kempis. As its title suggests, *The Imitation of Christ* urges ordinary Christians to take Christ as their model and to seek perfection in a simple way of life. The movement, which spread to Germany, France, and Italy, was a real religious revival.

So too were the activities of the Oratories of Divine Love in Italy. The oratories were groups of priests living in communities who worked to revive the church through prayer and preaching. They did not withdraw from the world as medieval monks had done, but devoted themselves to pastoral and charitable activities such as founding hospitals and orphanages. Oratorians served God in an active ministry.

If external religious observances are a measure of depth of heartfelt conviction, Europeans in the early sixteenth century remained deeply pious and loyal to the Roman Catholic church. Villagers participated in processions honoring the local saints. Middle-class people made pilgrimages to the great national shrines, as the enormous wealth of Saint Thomas Becket's tomb at Canterbury in England and the shrine of Saint James de Compostella in Spain testify. The upper classes continued to remember the church in their wills. In England, for example, between 1480 and 1490 almost £30,000, a prodigious sum in those days, was bequeathed to religious foundations. People of all social classes devoted an enormous amount of their time and

GRUNEWALD: CRUCIFIXION *The bloodless hands, tortured face, and lacerated body reveal profound sorrow for Christ's physical agony and suggest the intense piety of northern Europe. Grunewald, court painter to Albert of Brandenburg, shows in this painting (ca 1510) his strong attraction to Luther's ideas. (National Gallery of Art, Washington, D.C. Samual H. Kress Collection)*

income to religious causes and foundations. Sixteenth-century society remained deeply religious; all across Europe people sincerely yearned for salvation.

The papacy also expressed concern for reform. Pope Julius II summoned an ecumenical (universal) council, which met in the church of St. John Lateran in Rome from 1512 to 1517. Since most of the bishops were Italian and did not represent a broad cross-section of international opinion, the term *ecumenical* is not appropriate. Nevertheless, the bishops and theologians present strove earnestly to reform the church. They criticized the ignorance of priests, lamenting that only 2 percent of the clergy could understand the Latin of the liturgical books. The Lateran Council also condemned superstitions believed by many of the laity. The council recommended higher standards for education of the clergy and instruction of the common people. The bishops placed the responsibility for eliminating bureaucratic corruption squarely on the papacy and suggested significant doctrinal reforms. But many obstacles stood in the way of ecclesiastical change. Nor did the actions of an obscure German friar immediately force the issue.

## MARTIN LUTHER AND THE BIRTH OF PROTESTANTISM

As the result of a personal religious struggle, a German Augustinian friar, Martin Luther (1483–1546), launched the Protestant Reformation of the sixteenth century. Luther was not a typical person of his time; miners' sons who become professors of theology are never typical. But Luther is representative of his time in the sense that he articulated the widespread desire for reform of the Christian church and the deep yearning for salvation. In the sense that concern for salvation motivated Luther and other reformers, the sixteenth-century Reformation was in part a continuation of the medieval religious search.

### LUTHER'S EARLY YEARS

Martin Luther was born at Eisleben in Saxony, the second son of a hardworking and ambitious copper miner. At considerable sacrifice, his father sent him to school and then to the University of Erfurt, where Martin earned a master's degree with distinction at the young age of twenty-one. Hans Luther intended his son to proceed to the study of law and a legal career, which had since Roman times been the steppingstone to public office and material success. Badly frightened during a thunderstorm, however, Martin Luther vowed to become a friar. Without consulting his father, he entered the monastery of the Augustinian friars at Erfurt in 1505. Luther was ordained a priest in 1507, and after additional study earned the doctorate of theology. From 1511 until his death in 1546, he served as professor of Scripture at the new University of Wittenberg.

Martin Luther was exceedingly scrupulous in his monastic observances and devoted to prayer, penances, and fasting; nevertheless, the young friar's conscience troubled him constantly. The doubts and conflicts felt by any sensitive young person who has just taken a grave step were especially intense in young Luther. He had terrible anxieties about sin and worried continually about his salvation. Luther intensified his monastic observances but still found no peace of mind.

A recent psychological interpretation of Luther's early life suggests that he underwent a severe inner crisis in the years 1505–1515. Luther had disobeyed his father, thus viola-

**YOUNG LUTHER** *Lucas Cranach, court painter to Elector Frederick of Saxony and a friend of Luther's, captured the piety, the strength, and the intense struggle of the young friar. (Photo: Caroline Buckler)*

ting one of the Ten Commandments, and serious conflict persisted between them. The religious life seemed to provide no answers to his mental and spiritual difficulties. Three fits that he suffered in the monastic choir during those years may have been outward signs of his struggle.[3] Luther was grappling, as had thousands of medieval people before him, with the problem of salvation and thus the meaning of life. He was also searching for his life's work.

Luther's wise and kindly confessor, Staupitz, directed him to the study of Saint Paul's letters. Gradually, Luther arrived at a new understanding of the Pauline letters and of all Christian doctrine. He came to believe that salvation comes not through external observances and penances but through a simple faith in Christ. Faith is the means by which God sends humanity his grace, and faith is a free gift that cannot be earned. Thus Martin Luther discovered himself, God's work for him, and the centrality of faith in the Christian life.

## THE NINETY-FIVE THESES

An incident illustrative of the condition of the church in the early sixteenth century propelled Martin Luther onto the stage of history and brought about the Reformation in Germany. The University of Wittenberg lay within the ecclesiastical jurisdiction of the archdiocese of Magdeburg. The twenty-seven-year-old archbishop of Magdeburg, Albert, was also administrator of the see of Halberstadt and had been appointed archbishop of Mainz. To hold all three offices simultaneously — blatant pluralism — required papal dispensation. At that moment Pope Leo X was anxious to continue the construction of St. Peter's Basilica, but was hard pressed for funds. Archbishop Albert borrowed money from the Fuggers, a wealthy banking family of Augsburg, to pay for the papal dispensation allowing him to hold the several episcopal benefices. Only a few powerful financiers and churchmen knew the details of the arrangement, but Leo X authorized Archbishop Albert to sell indulgences, or pardons, in Germany. With the proceeds the archbishop could repay the Fuggers.

Wittenberg was in the political jurisdiction of Frederick of Saxony, one of the seven electors of the Holy Roman Empire. When Frederick forbade the sale of indulgences within his duchy, people of Wittenberg, including some of Professor Luther's students, streamed across the border from Saxony into Jüteborg in Thuringia to buy indulgences.

What was an indulgence? According to Catholic theology, individuals who sin alienate themselves from God and his love. In order to be reconciled to God, the sinner must confess his or her sins to a priest and do the penance assigned. For example, the man who steals must first return the stolen goods and then perform the penance given by the priest, usually certain prayers or good works. This is known as the temporal (or earthly) penance, since no one knows what penance God will ultimately require.

The doctrine of indulgence rested on three principles. First, God is merciful, but he is also just. Second, Christ and the saints, through their infinite virtue, established a "treasury of merits," which the church, through its special relationship with Christ and the saints, can draw upon. Third, the church has the authority to grant to sinners the spiritual benefits of those merits. Originally, an indulgence was a remission of the temporal (priest-imposed) penalties for sin. Beginning in the twelfth century, the papacy and bishops had given Crusaders such indulgences. By the later Middle Ages people widely believed that an indulgence secured total remission of penalties for sin – on earth or in purgatory – and assured swift entry into heaven.

Archbishop Albert hired the Dominican friar John Tetzel to sell the indulgences. Tetzel mounted a blitz advertising campaign. One of his slogans – "As soon as coin in coffer rings, the soul from purgatory springs" – brought phenomenal success. Men and women could buy indulgences not only for themselves but for deceased parents, relatives, or friends. Tetzel even drew up a chart with specific prices for the forgiveness of particular sins. The

massive amounts of junk that "sophisticated" Americans buy today should make one cautious in condemning the gullibility of sixteenth-century German peasants. Who wouldn't want a spiritual insurance policy?

Luther was severely troubled that ignorant people believed that they had no further need for repentance once they had purchased an indulgence. Accordingly, in the academic tradition of the times, on the eve of All Saints' Day (October 31) 1517, he attached to the door of the church at Wittenberg castle a list of ninety-five theses (or propositions) on indulgences. By this act Luther intended only to start a theological discussion of the subject and to defend the theses publicly.

Some of the theses challenged the pope's power to grant indulgences, and others criticized papal wealth: "Why does not the Pope, whose riches are at this day more ample than those of the wealthiest of the wealthy, build the one Basilica of St. Peter's with his own money, rather than with that of poor believers . . . ?"[4] Luther at first insisted that the pope had not known about the traffic in indulgences, for if he had known, he would have put a stop to it.

The theses were soon printed and read by Germans all over the empire. Immediately, broad theological issues were raised. When questioned, Luther insisted that Scripture persuaded him of the invalidity of indulgences. He rested his fundamental argument on the principle that there was no biblical basis for indulgences. But, replied Luther's opponents, to deny the legality of indulgences was to deny the authority of the pope who had authorized them. The issue was drawn: where did authority lie in the Christian church?

Through 1518 and 1519, Luther studied the history of the papacy. Gradually, he gained the conviction, like Marsiglio and Hus before him (pages 408–409), that ultimate authority in the church belonged not to the papacy but to a general council. Then, in 1519, in a large public disputation with the Catholic debater John Eck at Leipzig, Luther denied both the authority of the pope and the infallibility of a general council. The Council of Constance, he said, had erred when it condemned John Hus in 1415.

The papacy responded with a letter condemning some of Luther's propositions, ordering that his books be burned, and giving him two months to recant or be excommunicated. Luther retaliated by publicly burning the letter. Shortly afterward – January 3, 1521 – his excommunication became final. By this time the controversy involved more than theological issues. The papal legate wrote, "All Germany is in revolution. Nine-tenths shout 'Luther' as their war-cry; and the other tenth cares nothing about Luther, and cries 'Death to the court of Rome.' "[5]

In this highly charged atmosphere the twenty-one-year-old emperor Charles V held his first diet (assembly of the Estates of the empire) at Worms and summoned Luther to appear before it. When ordered to recant, Luther replied in language that rang all over Europe:

*Unless I am convinced by the evidence of Scripture or by plain reason – for I do not accept the authority of the Pope or the councils alone, since it is established that they have often erred and contradicted themselves – I am bound by the Scriptures I have cited and my conscience is captive to the Word of God. I cannot and will not recant anything, for it is neither safe nor right to go against conscience. God help me. Amen.*[6]

Luther was declared an outlaw of the empire, which meant that he was denied legal protection.

Between 1520 and 1530, Luther worked out the basic theological tenets that became the articles of faith for his new church and subsequently for all Protestant groups. The word *Protestant* derives from the protest drawn up by a small group of reforming German princes at the Diet of Speyer in 1529. The princes "protested" the decisions of the Catholic majority. At first Protestant meant Lutheran, but with the appearance of many protesting sects it became a general term applied to all non-Catholic Christians. Lutheran Protestant thought was officially formulated in the Confession of Augsburg in 1530.

Ernst Troeltsch, a German student of the sociology of religion, has defined Protestantism as a "modification of Catholicism, in which the Catholic formulation of questions was retained, while a different answer was given to them." Luther provided new answers to four old, basic theological issues.

First, how is a person to be saved? Traditional Catholic teaching held that salvation was achieved by both faith *and* good works. Luther held that salvation comes by *faith alone*. Women and men are saved, said Luther, by the arbitrary decision of God, irrespective of good works or the sacraments.

Second, where does religious authority reside? Christian doctrine had long maintained that authority rests both in the Bible and in the traditional teaching of the church. Luther maintained that authority rests in the Word of God as revealed in the Bible alone and as interpreted by an individual's conscience. He urged that each person read and reflect upon the Scriptures.

Third, what is the church? Luther reemphasized the Catholic teaching that the church consists of the entire community of

Christian believers. The medieval church had tended to identify the church with the clergy. Luther insisted upon the priesthood of all believers.

Finally, what is the highest form of Christian life? The medieval church had stressed the superiority of the monastic and religious life over the secular. Luther argued that all vocations have equal merit, whether ecclesiastical or secular, and that every person should serve God in his or her individual calling.[7] Protestantism, in sum, represented a reformulation of the Christian heritage.

## THE SOCIAL IMPACT OF LUTHER'S BELIEFS

In the sixteenth century, religion infused many aspects of life, and theological issues had broad social implications. The Lutheran movement started a religious revolution, which soon led to social revolt. As early as 1521, Luther had a vast following. Every encounter with ecclesiastical or political authorities attracted attention to him. Pulpits and printing presses spread his message all over Germany. By the time of his death, people of all social classes had become "Lutheran."

What was the immense appeal of Luther's religious ideas? Historians have puzzled over this question for centuries. It is always difficult to distinguish between spiritual and altruistic motives and materialistic, self-serving ones. The attraction of the German peasants to Lutheran beliefs was logical and almost predictable. Luther himself came from a peasant background, and he knew their ceaseless toil. The peasants must have admired Luther's defiance of the authority of the church. Moreover, they thrilled to the words Luther used in his treatise *On Christian Liberty* (1520): "A Christian man is the most free lord of all and

subject to none." Taken by themselves, these words easily contributed to social unrest.

In the early sixteenth century, the economic condition of the peasantry varied from place to place, but was generally worse than it had been in the fifteenth century and was continuing to deteriorate. Although the lords did not attempt to reimpose or increase servile obligations that had been set aside after the Black Death, nevertheless rising prices hurt people living on fixed incomes. A huge number of beggars swelled the populations of the towns. At Hamburg, for example, perhaps 20 percent of the people were paupers.

The upper classes viewed the peasants and their wretched conditions with contempt. Nobles looked upon peasants as little more than animals, "the ox without horns." Luther's fellow professor and colleague in reform at Wittenberg, Philip Melanchthon, enjoyed a great reputation as a Christian humanist, yet dismissed the peasants with the words "the ass *will* have blows and the people *will* be ruled by force."

In June 1524, a massive revolt broke out near the Swiss frontier and swept into the Rhineland, Swabia, Franconia, and Saxony. As many townspeople as farm laborers participated. Urban proletariat and agricultural laborers poured their grievances into the *Twelve Articles,* published in 1525. The peasants wanted complete abolition of serfdom, an end to oppressive taxes and tithes, reform of the clergy, confiscation of church property, and such basic privileges as the right to cut wood in the lords' forests. The slogans of the crowds that swept across Germany came directly from Luther's writings. "God's righteousness" and "the Word of God" were invoked in the effort to secure social and economic justice.[8]

The poor who expected Luther's support

THE PEASANTS' REVOLT *The peasants were attracted to Luther's faith because it seemed to give religious support to their economic grievances. Carrying the banner of the Peasants' League and armed with pitchforks and axes, a group of peasants surround a knight. (Photo: Caroline Buckler)*

were soon disillusioned. Background, education, and monastic observance all inclined him toward obedience to political authority and respect for social superiors. Luther had written of the "freedom" of the Christian, but he had meant the freedom to obey the Word of God, for in sin men and women lose their freedom and break their relationship with God. Freedom for Luther meant independence from the authority of the Roman church; it did *not* mean opposition to legally established secular powers. Accordingly he tossed off a tract, *Against the Murderous, Thieving Hordes of the Peasants,* calling upon the nobility to

put down the unlawful revolt. The German nobility crushed it with ferocity. Historians have estimated that as many as a hundred thousand peasants were slaughtered.

Luther took literally these words of Saint Paul's letter to the Romans: "Let every soul be subject to the higher powers. For there is no power but of God: the powers that be are established by God. Whosoever resists the power, resists the ordinance of God: and they that resist shall receive to themselves damnation."[9] As it developed, Lutheran theology exalted the state, subordinated the church to the state, and everywhere championed "the powers that be." The consequences for German society were profound and have redounded into the twentieth century. After the revolt, the condition of the working classes worsened, and their religion taught complete obedience to divinely appointed authority, the state.

Scholars in many disciplines have attributed Luther's fame and success to the new invention of the printing press, which rapidly reproduced and made known his ideas. Equally important is Luther's incredible skill with language. Some thinkers have lavished praise on the Wittenberg reformer; others have bitterly condemned him. But, in the words of psychologist Erik Erikson:

*The one matter on which professor and priest, psychiatrist and sociologist, agree is Luther's immense gift for language: his receptivity for the written word; his memory for the significant phrase; and his range of verbal expression (lyrical, biblical, satirical, and vulgar) which in English is paralleled only by Shakespeare.*[10]

Language proved to be the weapon with which this peasant's son changed the world.

Educated people and humanists, like the peasants, were much attracted by Luther's words. He advocated a simpler, personalized religion based on faith, a return to the spirit of the early church, the centrality of the Scriptures in the liturgy and in the Christian life, the abolition of elaborate ceremonial — precisely the reforms the nothern Christian humanists had been calling for. Ulrich Zwingli (1483–1531), for example, a humanist of Zurich, was strongly influenced by Luther's writings; they stimulated Zwingli's reforms in that Swiss city. The nobleman Ulrich von Hutton (1488–1523), who had published several humanistic tracts, in 1519 dedicated his life to the advancement of Luther's reformation. And as we shall see, the Frenchman John Calvin (1509–1564), often called the organizer of Protestantism, owed a great deal to Luther's thought.

The publication of Luther's German translation of the New Testament in 1523 democratized religion. His insistence that everyone should read and reflect upon the Scriptures attracted the literate and thoughtful middle classes partly because Luther appealed to their intelligence. Moreover, the business classes, preoccupied with making money, envied the church's wealth, disapproved of the luxurious lifestyle of some churchmen, and resented tithes and ecclesiastical taxation. Luther's doctrines of salvation by faith and the priesthood of all believers not only raised the religious status of the commercial classes but protected their pocketbooks as well.

Martin Luther's attitude toward women became the standard for German and Protestant women for centuries. Luther believed that marriage was a woman's career. A student recorded Luther as saying, early in his public ministry, "Let them bear children until they are dead of it; that is what they are for." A happy marriage to the ex-nun Katharine von Bora mellowed him, and another student later quoted him as saying, "Next to God's Word there is no more precious treasure than holy matrimony. God's highest gift on earth is a pious, cheerful, God-fearing, home-keeping wife, with whom you may live peacefully, to whom you may entrust your goods, and body and life."[11] Although Luther deeply loved his "dear Katie," he believed that women's concerns revolved exclusively around the children, the kitchen, and the church. A happy woman was a patient wife, an efficient manager, and a good mother.

Luther's viewpoint reflected contemporary values: German women were no more oppressed than Italian, Spanish, or even French ones. But few men considered women intelligent enough to handle a profession outside the home.

## GERMANY AND THE PROTESTANT REFORMATION

The history of the Holy Roman Empire in the later Middle Ages is a story of dissension, disintegration, and debility. Unlike Spain, France, and England, the empire lacked a strong central power. The Golden Bull of 1356 created government by an aristocratic federation. Each of seven electors – the archbishops of Mainz, Trier, and Cologne, the margrave of Brandenburg, the duke of Saxony, the count palatine of the Rhine, and the king of Bohemia – gained virtual sovereignty in his own territory. The agreement ended disputed elections in the empire; it also reduced the central authority of the emperor. Thereafter, Germany was characterized by weak borders, localism, and chronic disorder. The nobility strengthened their territories, while imperial power declined.

Against this background of decentralization and strong local power, Martin Luther had launched a movement to reform the church. Two years after Luther posted the Ninety-Five Theses, the electors chose as emperor a nineteen-year-old Habsburg prince, who ruled as Charles V. How did the goals and interests of the emperor influence the course of the Reformation in Germany? What impact did the upheaval in the Christian church have on the political condition in Germany?

### THE RISE OF THE HABSBURG DYNASTY

The marriage in 1477 of Maximilian I of the house of Habsburg and Mary of Burgundy was a decisive event in early modern European history. Through this union with the rich and powerful duchy of Burgundy, the Austrian house of Habsburg became the strongest ruling family within the empire. Its fortunes became permanently linked to those of the empire.

In the fifteenth and sixteenth centuries, as in the Middle Ages, relations among states continued to be greatly affected by the connections of royal families. Marriage often determined the diplomatic status of states. The Habsburg-Burgundian marriage angered the French, who considered Burgundy part of French territory. Louis XI of France repeatedly ravaged parts of the Burgundian Netherlands until he was able to force Maximilian to accept French terms: the Treaty of Arras (1482) emphatically declared Burgundy a part of the kingdom of France. The Habsburgs, however, never really renounced their claim to Burgundy, and intermittent warfare over it continued between France and Maximilian. Within the empire, German principalities that resented Austria's pre-eminence began to see that they shared interests with France. The marriage of Maximilian and Mary was to inaugurate two centuries of conflict between the Austrian house of Habsburg and the Valois kings of France. And Germany was to be the chief arena of the struggle.

"Other nations wage war; you, Austria, marry." Historians dispute the origins of the adage, but no one questions its accuracy. The heir of Mary and Maximilian, Philip of Burgundy, married Joanna of Castile, daughter of Ferdinand and Isabella of Spain. Philip and Joanna's son Charles V (1500–1558) fell heir to a vast conglomeration of territories. Through a series of accidents and unexpected deaths, Charles inherited Spain from his mother, together with her possessions in the New World and the Spanish dominions in

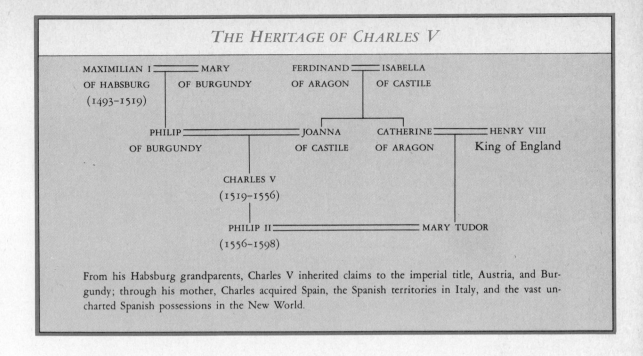

## THE HERITAGE OF CHARLES V

```
MAXIMILIAN I ═══════ MARY          FERDINAND ═══════ ISABELLA
OF HABSBURG        OF BURGUNDY      OF ARAGON        OF CASTILE
(1493-1519)
```

```
          PHILIP ═══════════════ JOANNA      CATHERINE ═══════════ HENRY VIII
          OF BURGUNDY            OF CASTILE   OF ARAGON             King of England
```

```
                CHARLES V
                (1519-1556)
```

```
                PHILIP II ═══════════════════════════════ MARY TUDOR
                (1556-1598)
```

From his Habsburg grandparents, Charles V inherited claims to the imperial title, Austria, and Burgundy; through his mother, Charles acquired Spain, the Spanish territories in Italy, and the vast uncharted Spanish possessions in the New World.

Italy, Sicily, Sardinia, and Naples. From his father he inherited the Habsburg lands in Austria, southern Germany, the Low Countries, and Franche-Comté in east central France.

Charles's inheritance was an incredibly diverse collection of states and peoples, each governed in a different manner and held together only by the person of the emperor. Charles's Italian adviser, the grand chancellor Gattinara, told the young ruler: "God has set you on the path towards world monarchy." Charles not only believed this; he was convinced that it was his duty to maintain the political and religious unity of Western Christendom. In this respect Charles V was the last medieval emperor.

Charles needed and in 1519 secured the imperial title. Forward-thinking Germans proposed governmental reforms. They urged placing the administration in the hands of an imperial council whose president, the emperor's appointee, would have ultimate executive power. Reforms of the imperial finances, the army, and the judiciary were also recommended. Such ideas did not interest the young emperor at all. When he finally arrived in Germany from Spain and opened his first diet at Worms in January 1521, he naively announced that "the empire from of old has had not many masters, but one, and it is our intention to be that one." Charles went on to say that he was to be treated as of greater account than his predecessors because he was more powerful than they had been. In view of the long history of aristocratic power, Charles's notions were pure fantasy.

Charles continued the Burgundian policy of his grandfather Maximilian. That is, German revenues and German troops were subordinated to the needs of other parts of the empire, first Burgundy and then Spain. Habs-

EMPEROR CHARLES V  *Sometimes called a second Charlemagne, Charles V unsuccessfully tried to unite millions of people divided by geography, custom, language, and centuries of historical development under his family rule. The full beard partially conceals the long jutting jaw, a Habsburg family trait. (Photo: Caroline Buckler)*

burg international interests came before the need for reform in Germany.

### THE POLITICAL IMPACT OF LUTHER'S BELIEFS

In the sixteenth century, the practice of religion remained a public matter. Everyone par-

ticipated in the religious life of the community, just as almost everyone shared in the local agricultural work. Whatever spiritual convictions individuals held in the privacy of their consciences, the emperor, king, prince, magistrate, or other civil authority determined the official form of religious practice within his jurisdiction. Religion had too many social implications to be left to individual judgment. Almost everyone believed that the presence of a faith different from that of the majority represented a political threat to the security of the state. Only a tiny minority, and certainly none of the princes, believed in religious liberty.

Against this background, the religious storm launched by Martin Luther swept across northern and central Germany. Several elements in his religious reformation stirred patriotic feelings. Anti-Roman sentiment ran high. Humanists lent eloquent intellectual support. And Luther's translation of the New Testament into German evoked national pride. Lutheranism contributed to the development of German nationalism.

For decades devout laymen and churchmen had called on the German princes to reform the church. In 1520, Luther took up the cry in his *Appeal to the Christian Nobility of the German Nation.* Unless the princes destroyed papal power in Germany, Luther argued, reform was impossible. He urged the princes to confiscate ecclesiastical wealth and to abolish indulgences, dispensations, pardons, and clerical celibacy. He told them that it was their public duty to bring about the moral reform of the church. Luther based his argument in part on the papacy's financial exploitation of Germany:

*Now that Italy is sucked dry, they come into Germany, and begin, oh so gently. But let us beware, or Germany will soon become like Italy. Already we have some cardinals; what the Romans seek by that the "drunken Germans" are not to understand until we have not a bishopric, a monastery, a living, a benefice, a mite or a penny left. . . . They skim the cream off the bishoprics, monasteries, and benefices, and because they do not yet venture to turn them all to shameful use, as they have done in Italy, they only practice for the present the sa-* *cred trickery of coupling together ten or twenty prelacies and taking a yearly portion from each of them so as to make a tidy sum after all. The priory of Würzburg yields a thousand gulden; that of Bamberg, something; Mainz, Trier, and the others, something more; and so . . . that a cardinal might live at Rome like a rich king.*

*How comes it that we Germans must put up with such robbery and such extortion of our property at the hands of the pope? If the Kingdom of France has prevented it, why do we Germans let them make such fools and apes of us? It would all be more bearable if in this way they only stole our property; but they lay waste the churches and rob Christ's sheep of their pious shepherds, and destroy the worship and the Word of God. Even if there were not a single cardinal, the Church would not go under. As it is they do nothing for the good of Christendom; they only wrangle about the incomes of bishoprics and prelacies, and that any robber could do. . . .*

*Since we here come to the heart of the matter, we will pause a little, and let it be seen that the Germans are not quite such gross fools as not to note or understand the sharp practices of the Romans. I do not now complain that at Rome God's command and Christian law are despised; for such is the state of Christendom, and particularly of Rome, that we may not now complain of such high matters. Nor do I complain that natural or temporal law and reason count for nothing. The case is worse even than that. I complain that they do not keep their own self-devised canon law, though it is, to be sure, mere tyranny, avarice, and temporal splendor, rather than law. . . .*[12]

These words fell on welcome ears and itchy fingers. Luther's appeal to German patriotism gained him strong support, and national feeling influenced many princes otherwise confused by or indifferent to the complexities of the religious issues.

The church in Germany possessed great

wealth. And, unlike other countries, Germany had no strong central government to check the flow of gold to Rome. Rejection of Roman Catholicism and adoption of Protestantism would mean the legal confiscation of lush farmlands, rich monasteries, and wealthy shrines. Some German princes, such as the prince-archbishop of Cologne, Hermann von Wied, were sincerely attracted to Lutheranism, but many civil authorities realized that they had a great deal to gain by embracing the new faith. A steady stream of duchies, margraviates, free cities, and bishoprics secularized church property, accepted Lutheran theological doctrines, and adopted simpler services conducted in German. The decision reached at Worms in 1521 to condemn Luther and his teaching was not enforced because the German princes did not want to enforce it.

Charles V was a vigorous defender of Catholicism, and contemporary social and political theory denied the possibility of two religions coexisting peacefully in one territory. Thus, many princes used the religious issue to extend their financial and political independence. When doctrinal differences became linked to political ambitions and financial receipts, the results proved unfortunate for the improvement of German government. The Protestant movement ultimately proved a political disaster for Germany.

Charles V must share blame with the German princes for the disintegration of imperial authority in the empire. He neither understood nor took an interest in the constitutional problems of Germany, and he lacked the material resources to oppose Protestantism effectively there. Throughout his reign he was preoccupied with his Flemish, Spanish, Italian, and American territories.

Five times between 1521 and 1555, Charles V went to war with the Valois kings of France. The issue each time was the Habsburg lands acquired by the marriage of Maximilian and Mary of Burgundy. Much of the fighting occurred in Germany. The cornerstone of French foreign policy in the sixteenth and seventeenth centuries was the desire to keep the German states divided. Thus Europe witnessed the paradox of the Catholic king of France supporting the Lutheran princes in their challenge to his fellow Catholic, Charles V. French policy was successful. The long dynastic struggle commonly called the Habsburg-Valois wars advanced the cause of Protestantism and promoted the political fragmentation of the German empire.

Charles's efforts to crush the Lutheran states were unsuccessful. Finally in 1555 he agreed to the Peace of Augsburg, which, in accepting the status quo, officially recognized Protestantism. Each prince was permitted to determine the religion of his territory. Most of northern and central Germany became Lutheran, while the south remained Roman Catholic. There was no freedom of religion, however. Princes or town councils established state churches to which all subjects of the area had to belong. Dissidents, whether Lutheran or Catholic, had to convert or leave. The political difficulties Germany inherited from the Middle Ages had been compounded by the religious crisis of the sixteenth century.

## THE GROWTH OF THE PROTESTANT REFORMATION

The printing press publicized Luther's defiance of the Roman church and spread his theological ideas all over Europe. Working people discovered in Luther's ideas the economic theories they wanted to find. Christian humanists believed initially that Luther supported their own educational and intellectual goals. Princes steadily read in Luther's theories an expansion of state power and authority. What began as one man's religious search in a small corner of Germany soon became associated with many groups' interests and aspirations.

By 1555, much of northern Europe had broken with the Roman Catholic church. All of Scandinavia, England, Scotland, and such self-governing cities as Geneva and Zurich in Switzerland and Strasbourg in eastern France had rejected the religious authority of Rome and adopted new faiths. In that a common religious faith had been the one element uniting all of Europe for almost a thousand years, the fragmentation of belief led to profound changes in European life and society. The most significant new form of Protestantism was Calvinism, of which the Peace of Augsburg had made no mention at all.

## CALVINISM

In 1509, while Luther was studying for the doctorate at Wittenberg, John Calvin (1509–1564) was born in Noyon in northwestern France. Luther inadvertently launched the Protestant Reformation. Calvin, however, had the greater impact on future generations. His theological writings profoundly influenced the social thought and attitudes of Europeans and English-speaking peoples all over the world, especially in Canada and the United States. Although he had originally intended to have an ecclesiastical career, Calvin studied law, which had a decisive impact on his mind and later thought. In 1533, he experienced a religious crisis, as a result of which he converted to Protestantism.

JOHN CALVIN *The lean, ascetic face with the strong jaw reflects the iron will and determination of the organizer of Protestantism. The fur collar represents his training in law. (Photo: Caroline Buckler)*

Calvin believed that God had delegated him to reform the church. Accordingly, he accepted an invitation to assist in the reformation of the Swiss city of Geneva. There, beginning in 1541, Calvin established a theocracy, which was, according to contemporary theory, a society ruled by God through reformed ministers and civil magistrates. Geneva, "a city that was a Church," became the model of a Christian community for sixteenth-century Protestant reformers.

To understand Calvin's Geneva, it is necessary to understand Calvin's ideas. These he embodied in *The Institutes of the Christian Re-*

*ligion,* first published in 1536 and definitively issued in 1559. The cornerstone of Calvin's theology was his belief in the absolute sovereignty and omnipotence of God and the total weakness of humanity. Before the infinite power of God, he asserted, men and women are as insignificant as grains of sand:

*Our souls are but faint flickerings over against the infinite brilliance which is God. We are created, he is without beginning. We are subject to ignorance and shame. God in his infinite majesty is the summation of all virtues. Whenever we think of him we should be ravished with adoration and astonishment. . . . The chief end of man is to enjoy the fellowship of God and the chief duty of man is to glorify God. . . .* [13]

Calvin did not grant free will to human beings, because that would detract from the sovereignty of God. Men and women cannot actively work to achieve salvation; rather, God in his infinite wisdom decided at the beginning of time who would be saved and who damned. This viewpoint constitutes the theological principle called predestination:

*Predestination we call the eternal decree of God, by which he has determined in himself, what he would have become of every individual of mankind. For they are not all created with a similar destiny; but eternal life is foreordained for some, and eternal damnation for others. . . .*

*In conformity, therefore, to the clear doctrine of the Scripture, we assert, that by an eternal and immutable counsel, God has once for all determined, both whom he would admit to salvation, and whom he would condemn to destruction. We affirm that this counsel, as far as concerns the elect, is founded on his gratuitous mercy, totally irrespective of human merit; but that to those whom he devotes to condemnation, the gate of life*

*is closed by a just and irreprehensible, but incomprehensible, judgment.*

*How exceedingly presumptuous it is only to inquire into the causes of the Divine will; which is in fact, and is justly entitled to be, the cause of everything that exists. . . . For the will of God is the highest justice; so that what he wills must be considered just, for this very reason, because he wills it.* [14]

Many people have found this a pessimistic view of the nature of God, who revealed himself in the Old and New Testaments as merciful as well as just. Calvin's response was that although individuals cannot know whether they will be saved — and the probability is that they will be damned — still, good works are a "sign" of election. In any case, people should concentrate on worshiping God and doing his work and not waste time worrying about salvation.

While Luther subordinated the church to the state, Calvin made the state subordinate to the church, and he succeeded in arousing Genevans to a high standard of public and private behavior. For Calvin, God was perpetually active, vigilant, and busy, and he selected certain individuals to do his work. Calvin, convinced that he was one of those individuals, worked tirelessly to transform Geneva into the perfect Christian community. Those who denied predestination were banished.

Austere living, religious instruction for all, public fasting, and evening curfew became the order of the day. Dancing, card playing, fashionable clothes, and heavy drinking were absolutely prohibited. The ministers investigated the private morals of citizens but were unwilling to punish the town prostitutes as severely as Calvin would have preferred.

Calvin reserved his harshest condemnation for religious dissenters. He declared:

*If anybody slanders a mortal man he is punished and shall we permit a blasphemer of the living God to go unscathed? If a prince is injured, death appears to be insufficient for vengeance. And now when God, the sovereign Emperor, is reviled by a word, is nothing to be done? God's glory and our salvation are so conjoined that a traitor to God is also an enemy to the human race and worse than a murderer because he brings souls to perdition. Some object that since the offense consists only in words, there is no need for severity. But we muzzle dogs, and shall we leave men free to open their mouths as they please? Those who object are dogs and swine. They murmur that they will go to America where nobody will bother them.*

*God makes plain that the false prophet is to be stoned without mercy. We are to crush beneath our heel all affections of nature when His honor is concerned. The father should not spare his child, nor brother his brother, nor husband his own wife or the friend who is dearer to him than life. No human relationship is more than animal unless it be grounded in God*[15]

Calvin translated his words into action. In the 1550s, the Spanish humanist Michael Servetus had gained international notoriety for his publications denying the Christian dogma of the Trinity, which holds that God is three divine persons, Father, Son, and Holy Spirit. Servetus had been arrested by the Spanish Inquisition, but escaped to Geneva, where he hoped for support. He was promptly rearrested. At his trial he not only held to his belief that there is no scriptural basis for the Trinity but rejected child baptism and insisted that a person under twenty cannot commit a mortal sin. The city fathers considered this last idea dangerous to public morality, "especially in these days when the young are so corrupted." Although Servetus begged that he be punished by banishment, Calvin and the

town council maintained that the denial of child baptism and the Trinity amounted to a threat to all society. Whispering "Jesus, Son of the eternal God, have pity on me," Servetus was burned at the stake.

To many sixteenth-century Europeans, Calvin's Geneva seemed "the most perfect school of Christ since the days of the Apostles." Religious refugees from France, England, Spain, Scotland, and Italy poured into the city. Subsequently, Calvin's church served as the model for the Presbyterian church in Scotland, the Huguenot church in France, and Puritan churches in England and New England.

Calvinism became the compelling force in international Protestantism. The Calvinist ethic of the "calling" dignified all work with a religious aspect. Hard work, well done, was pleasing to God. This doctrine encouraged an aggressive, vigorous social activism. In the *Institutes* Calvin provided a systematic theology for Protestantism. The reformed church of Calvin had a strong and well-organized machinery of government. These factors, together with the social and economic applications of Calvin's theology, made Calvinism the most dynamic force in sixteenth- and seventeenth-century Protestantism.

## THE ANABAPTISTS

The name *Anabaptist* derives from a Greek word meaning "to baptize again." The Anabaptists, sometimes described as "the left wing of the Reformation," believed that only adults could make a free choice about religious faith, baptism, and entry into the Christian community. Thus they considered the practice of baptizing infants and children preposterous and claimed there was no scriptural basis for it. They wanted to rebaptize believers who had been baptized as children.

Anabaptists took the Gospel and, at first, Luther's teachings absolutely literally and favored a return to the kind of church that had existed among the earliest Christians — a voluntary association of believers who had experienced an inner light.

Anabaptists maintained that only a few people would receive the inner light. This position meant that the Christian community and the Christian state were not identical. In other words, Anabaptists believed in the separation of church and state and in religious tolerance. They almost never tried to force their values on others. In an age that believed in the necessity of state-established churches, Anabaptist views on religious liberty were far ahead of their time.

Each Anabaptist community or church was entirely independent; it selected its own ministers and ran its own affairs. In 1534 the community at Münster in Germany, for example, established a legal code that decreed the death penalty for insubordinate wives. Moreover, the Münster community also practiced polygamy and forced all women under a certain age to marry or face expulsion or execution.

Anabaptist attitudes toward women were sexist and discriminatory, although Anabaptists admitted women to the priesthood. They shared goods as the early Christians had done, refused all public offices, and would not serve in the armed forces. In fact, they laid great stress on pacifism. A favorite Anabaptist scriptural quotation was "By their fruits you shall know them," meaning that if Christianity was a religion of peace, the Christian should not fight. Good deeds were the sign of Christian faith, and to be a Christian meant to imitate the meekness and mercy of Christ. With such beliefs Anabaptists were inevitably a minority. Anabaptism attracted the poor, the unemployed, the uneducated. Geographically, Anabaptists drew their members from depressed urban areas — from among the followers of Zwingli in Zurich, and from Basel, Augsburg, and Nuremberg.

Ideas such as absolute pacifism and the distinction between the Christian community and the state brought down upon these unfortunate people fanatical hatred and bitter persecution. Zwingli, Luther, Calvin, and Catholics all saw — quite correctly — the separation of church and state as leading ultimately to the complete secularization of society. The powerful rulers of Swiss and German society immediately saw the connection between religious heresy and economic dislocation. Civil authorities feared that the combination of religious differences and economic grievances would lead to civil disturbances. In Saxony, in Strasbourg, and in the Swiss cities, Anabaptists were either banished or cruelly executed by burning, beating, or drowning. Their ideas, however, survived.

Later, the Quakers with their gentle pacifism; the Baptists with their emphasis on an inner spiritual light, the Congregationalists with their democratic church organization; and, in 1789, the authors of the United States Constitution with their concern for the separation of church and state — all these trace their origins in part to the Anabaptists of the sixteenth century.

## THE ENGLISH REFORMATION

As on the Continent, the Reformation in England had social and economic causes as well as religious ones. As elsewhere, too, Christian humanists had for decades been calling for the purification of the church. When the political matter of the divorce of King Henry VIII (1509-1547) became enmeshed with other issues, a complete break with Rome resulted.

Demands for ecclesiastical reform dated back to the fourteenth century. The Lollards (pages 409–410) had been driven underground in the fifteenth century, but survived in parts of London, East Anglia, west Kent, and southern England. Working-class people, especially cloth workers, were attracted to their ideas. The Lollards stressed the individual's reading and interpretation of the Bible, which they considered the only standard of Christian faith and holiness. Consequently, they put no stock in the value of the sacraments and were vigorously anticlerical. Lollards opposed ecclesiastical wealth, the veneration of the saints, prayers for the dead, and all war. Although they had no notion of justification by faith, like Luther they insisted upon the individual soul's direct responsibility to God.

The work of the English humanist William Tyndale (ca 1494–1536) stimulated cries for reform. Tyndale visited Luther at Wittenberg in 1524, and a year later at Antwerp he began printing an English translation of the New Testament. From Antwerp merchants carried the New Testament into England, where it was distributed by Lollards. Fortified with copies of Tyndale's English Bible and some of Luther's ideas, the Lollards represented the ideal of "a personal, scriptural, non-sacramental, and lay-dominated religion."[16] Thus, in this manner, doctrines that would later be called Protestant flourished underground in England before any official or state-approved changes.

In the early sixteenth century the ignorance of much of the parish clergy, and the sexual misbehavior of some, compared unfavorably with the education and piety of lay people. In 1510 Dr. William Melton, an official of York Cathedral, exhorted the newly ordained priests of the diocese:

*. . . from this darkness of ignorance . . . arises that great and deplorable evil throughout the whole Church of God, that everywhere throughout town and countryside there exists a crop of oafish and boorish priests, some of whom are engaged in ignoble and servile tasks, while others abandon themselves to tavern haunting, swilling and drunkenness. Some cannot get along without their wenches; others pursue their amusement in dice and gambling and other such trifling all day long. . . . This is inevitable, for since they are completely ignorant of good literature, how can they obtain improvement or enjoyment in reading and study. Nay rather, they throw aside their books in contempt and everywhere they return to the wretched and unlovely life I have mentioned. . . . We must avoid and keep far from ourselves that grasping, deadly plague of avarice for which practically every priest is accused and held in disrepute before the people, when it is said that we are greedy for rich promotions, or harsh and grasping in retaining and amassing money. . . .[17]*

Even more than the ignorance and lechery of the lower clergy, the wealth of the English church fostered resentment and anticlericalism. The church controlled perhaps 20 percent of the land, and also received an annual tithe of the produce of lay people's estates. Since the church had jurisdiction over wills, the clergy also received mortuary fees, revenues paid by the deceased's relatives. Mortuary fees led to frequent lawsuits, since the common lawyers nursed a deep jealousy of the ecclesiastical courts.

The career of Thomas Wolsey (1474?–1530) provides an extreme example of pluralism in the English church in the early sixteenth century. The son of a butcher, Wolsey became a priest and in 1507 secured an

*HENRY VIII'S "VICTORY"* This cartoon shows Henry VIII, assisted by Cromwell and Cranmer, triumphing over Pope Clement VII. Although completely removed from the historical facts, such illustrations were effectively used to promote antipapal feeling in late sixteenth-century England. (Photo: Caroline Buckler)

appointment as chaplain to Henry VII. In 1509 Henry VIII made Wolsey a privy councillor, where his remarkable ability and energy won him rapid advancement. In 1515 he became a cardinal and lord chancellor, and in 1518 papal legate. As chancellor, Wolsey dominated domestic and foreign policy, prosecuted the rich in the royal courts, and attacked the nobility in Parliament. As papal legate he ruled the English church, with final authority in all matters relating to marriage, wills, the clergy, and ecclesiastical appointments. Wolsey had more power than any previous royal minister, and he used that power to amass a large number of church offices, including the archbishopric of York, the rich bishoprics of Winchester and Lincoln, and the abbacy of St. Albans. He displayed the vast wealth these positions brought him with ostentation and arrogance, which in turn fanned the embers of anticlericalism. The divorce of Henry VIII ignited all these glowing coals.

Having fallen in love with Anne Boleyn, sister of his cast-off mistress Mary Boleyn, Henry wanted to divorce his wife Catherine of Aragon. Legal, diplomatic, and theological problems stood in his way, however. Catherine had first been married to Henry's brother Arthur. Contemporaries doubted that Arthur's union with Catherine had been consumated during the short time Arthur lived, and theologians therefore believed that no true marriage existed between them. When Henry married Catherine in 1509, he boasted that she was a virgin. According to custom, and in order to eliminate all doubts and legal technicalities about Catherine's marriage to Arthur, Henry secured a dispensation from Pope Julius II. For eighteen years Catherine and Henry lived together in what contemporaries thought a happy marriage. Catherine produced six children, but only the princess Mary survived childhood.

Precisely when Henry lost interest in his wife as a woman is unknown, but around 1527 he began to quote from a passage in the Old Testament Book of Leviticus: "You must not uncover the nakedness of your brother's wife; for it is your brother's nakedness. . . . The man who takes to wife the wife of his brother: that is impurity; he has uncovered his brother's nakedness, and they shall be childless."[18] Henry insisted that God was denying him a male heir to punish him for marrying his brother's widow. Henry claimed that he wanted to spare England the dangers of a disputed succession. The anarchy and disorders of the Wars of the Roses would surely be repeated if a woman, the princess Mary, inherited the throne. Although Henry contended that the succession was the paramount issue in his mind, his behavior suggests otherwise.

Henry went about the business of insuring a peaceful succession in a most extraordinary manner. He petitioned Pope Clement VII for an annulment of his marriage to Catherine. Henry wanted the pope to declare that a legal marriage with Catherine had never existed, in which case Princess Mary was illegitimate and thus ineligible to succeed to the throne. The pope was an indecisive man whose attention at the time was focused on the Lutheran revolt in Germany and the Habsburg-Valois struggle for control of Italy. Clement delayed acting on Henry's request. The capture and sack of Rome in 1527 by the emperor Charles V, Queen Catherine's nephew, thoroughly tied the pope's hands. Charles could hardly allow the pope to grant the annulment, thereby acknowledging that Charles's aunt, the queen of England, was a loose woman who had lived in sin with Henry VIII.

Accordingly, Henry determined to get his divorce in England. The convenient death of the archbishop of Canterbury allowed Henry to appoint a new archbishop, Thomas Cranmer (1489–1556). Cranmer heard the case in his archiepiscopal court, granted the annulment, and thereby paved the way for Henry's marriage to Anne Boleyn. English public opinion was against this marriage and strongly favored Queen Catherine as a woman much wronged. By rejecting Catherine, Henry ran serious political risks, and all for a woman whom contemporaries found neither very intelligent nor very attractive. The only distinguishing feature they noticed was a sixth finger on her right hand. The marriage between Henry and Anne was publicly announced on May 28, 1533. In September the princess Elizabeth was born.

Since Rome had refused to support Henry's matrimonial plans, he decided to remove the English church from papal jurisdiction. Henry used Parliament to legalize the Reformation in England. The Act in Restraint of Appeals (1533) declared that:

*Where, by divers sundry old authentic histories and chronicles, it is manifestly declared and expressed that this realm of England is an empire, and so hath been accepted in the world, governed by one supreme head and king having the dignity and royal estate of the imperial crown of the same (he being also institute and furnished by the goodness and sufferance of Almighty God with plenary, whole, and entire power, pre-eminence, authority, prerogative, and jurisdiction to render and yield justice and final determination to all manner of folk residents or subjects within this his realm, in all causes, matters, debates, and contentions happening to occur, insurge, or begin within the limits thereof, without restraint or provocation to any foreign princes or potentates of the world. . . .).* [19]

The act went on to forbid all judicial appeals to the papacy, thus establishing the Crown as the highest legal authority in the land. In effect, the Act in Restraint of Appeals placed sovereign power in the king. The Act for the Submission of the Clergy (1534) required churchmen to submit to the king and forbade the publication of all ecclesiastical laws without royal permission. The Supremacy Act of 1534 declared the king the supreme head of the Church of England.

Englishmen had long criticized ecclesiastical abuses. Sentiment for reform was strong, and a minority of people held distinctly Protestant doctrinal views. Still, it is difficult to gauge the degree of popular support for Henry's break with Rome. Scholars have pointed out that the king had to bribe, threaten, and intimidate the House of Commons to get his legislation passed. Some op-

posed the king. John Fisher, the bishop of Rochester, a distinguished scholar and humanist who had preached the oration at the funeral of Henry VII, lashed the clergy with scorn for their cowardice. Another humanist, Thomas More, resigned the chancellorship to protest the passage of the Act for the Submission of the Clergy and would not take an oath recognizing Anne's heir. Fisher, More, and other dissenters were beheaded.

When Anne Boleyn failed in her second attempt to produce a male child, Henry VIII charged her with adulterous incest and in 1536 had her beheaded. Parliament promptly proclaimed the princess Elizabeth illegitimate and, with the royal succession thoroughly confused, left the throne to whomever Henry chose. His third wife, Jane Seymour, gave Henry the desired son, Edward, and then died in childbirth. Henry went on to three more wives. Before he passed to his reward in 1547, he got Parliament to reverse the decision of 1536, relegitimating Mary and Elizabeth and fixing the succession first in his son and then in his daughters.

Between 1535 and 1539, under the influence of his chief minister, Thomas Cromwell, Henry decided to dissolve the English monasteries because, he charged, they were economically mismanaged and morally corrupt. Actually, he wanted their wealth. Justices of the peace and other local officials who visited religious houses throughout the land found the contrary. Ignoring their reports, the king ended nine hundred years of English monastic life, dispersed the monks and nuns, and confiscated their lands. Hundreds of properties were later sold to the middle and upper classes and the proceeds spent on war. The dissolution of the monasteries did not achieve a more equitable distribution of land and wealth or advance the cause of social justice. Rather, the "bare ruined choirs where late the

HOLBEIN: SIR THOMAS MORE  *This powerful portrait (1527), revealing More's strong character and humane sensitivity, shows Holbein's complete* *mastery of detail—down to the stubble on More's chin. The chain was an emblem of More's service to Henry VIII. (© The Frick Collection, New York)*

sweet birds sang" – as Shakespeare described the desolate religious houses – testified to the loss of a valuable esthetic and cultural force in English life.

The English Reformation under Henry VIII was primarily a matter of political, social, and economic issues, rather than religious ones. In fact, the Henrician Reformation retained such traditional Catholic practices and doctrines as confession to a priest, clerical celibacy, and transubstantiation (the doctrine of the real presence of Christ in the bread and wine of the Eucharist). On the other hand, Protestant literature circulated, Protestant doctrines captured increasing numbers of people, and Henry approved the selection of men with known Protestant sympathies as tutors for his son. Until late in the century the religious situation remained fluid.

The nationalization of the church and the dissolution of the monasteries led to important changes in governmental administration. Vast tracts of land came temporarily under the Crown's jurisdiction, and new bureaucratic machinery had to be developed to manage those properties. New departments had to be coordinated with old ones. Medieval government had been household government: all branches of the state were associated with the person and personality of the monarch. In finances, for example, no distinction was made between the king's personal income and state revenues. Each branch of government was supported with funds from a specific source; if the source had a bad year, that agency suffered while other branches of government were well in the black. Massive confusion and overlapping of responsibilities existed.

Thomas Cromwell reformed and centralized the king's household, the council, the secretariats, and the Exchequer. New departments of state were set up. Surplus funds from all departments went into a liquid fund to be applied to areas where there were deficits. This balancing resulted in greater efficiency and economy. In Henry VIII's reign can be seen the growth of the modern centralized bureaucratic state.

For several decades after Henry's death in 1547, the English church shifted left and right. In the short reign of Henry's sickly son Edward VI (1547–1553), the strongly Protestant ideas of Archbishop Thomas Cranmer exerted a significant influence on the religious life of the country. Cranmer drastically simplified the liturgy, invited Protestant theologians to England, and prepared the first *Book of Common Prayer* (1549). In stately and dignified English, the *Book of Common Prayer* included, together with the Psalter, the order for all services of the Church of England.

The equally brief reign of Mary Tudor (1553–1558) witnessed a sharp move back to Catholicism. The devoutly Catholic daughter of Catherine of Aragon, Mary rescinded the Reformation legislation of her father's reign and fully restored Roman Catholicism. Mary's marriage to her cousin Philip of Spain, son of the emperor Charles V, proved highly unpopular in England, and her persecution and execution of several hundred Protestants further alienated her subjects. During her reign many Protestants fled to the Continent. Mary's death raised to the throne her sister Elizabeth (1558–1603) and inaugurated the beginnings of religious stability.

For a long time, Elizabeth's position as queen was insecure. Although the populace cheered her accession, many questioned her legitimacy. On the one hand, Catholics wanted a Roman Catholic ruler. On the other hand, a vocal number of returned English exiles wanted all Catholic elements in the Church of England destroyed. The latter, because they wanted to "purify" the church, were called Puritans.

Elizabeth had been raised a Protestant, but if she had genuine religious convictions she kept them to herself. Probably one of the shrewdest politicians in English history, Elizabeth chose a middle course between Catholic and Puritan extremes. She insisted upon dignity in church services and political order in the land. She did not care what people believed as long as they kept quiet about it. Avoiding precise doctrinal definitions, Elizabeth had herself styled "Supreme Governor of the Church of England, Etc.," and left it to her subjects to decide what the "Etc." meant.

The parliamentary legislation of the early years of Elizabeth's reign — laws sometimes labeled the "Elizabethan Settlement" — required outward conformity to the Church of England and uniformity in all ceremonies. Everyone had to attend Church of England services; those who refused were fined. In 1563, a convocation of bishops approved the Thirty-Nine Articles, a summary in thirty-nine short statements of the basic tenets of the Church of England. During Elizabeth's reign, the Anglican church (for the Latin *Ecclesia Anglicana*), as the Church of England was called, moved in a moderately Protestant direction. Services were conducted in English, monasteries were not re-established, and the clergy were allowed to marry. But the bishops remained as church officials, and apart from language, the services were quite traditional.

## The Establishment of the Church of Scotland

Reform of the church in Scotland did not follow the English model. In the early sixteenth century, the church in Scotland presented an extreme case of clerical abuse and corruption, and Lutheranism initially attracted sympathetic support. In Scotland as elsewhere, political authority was the decisive influence in reform. The monarchy was very weak, and factions of virtually independent nobles competed for power. King James V and his daughter Mary, Queen of Scots (1560–1567), staunch Catholics and close allies of Catholic France, opposed reform. The Scottish nobles supported it. One man, John Knox (1505?–1572) dominated the movement for reform in Scotland.

In 1559, Knox, a dour, narrow-minded, and fearless man with a reputation as a passionate preacher, set to work reforming the church. He had studied and worked with Calvin in Geneva, and was determined to structure the Scottish church after the model of Calvin's Geneva. In 1560, Knox persuaded the Scottish parliament, which was dominated by reform-minded barons, to enact legislation ending papal authority. The mass was abolished and attendance at it forbidden under penalty of death. Knox then established the Presbyterian Church of Scotland, so named because presbyters, or ministers — not bishops — governed it. The Church of Scotland was strictly Calvinist in doctrine, adopted a simple and dignified service of worship, and laid great emphasis on preaching. Knox's *Book of Common Order* (1564) became the liturgical directory for the church. The Presbyterian Church of Scotland was a national, or state, church, and many of its members maintained close relations with English Puritans.

## Protestantism in Ireland

To the ancient Irish hatred of English political and commercial exploitation, the Reformation added the bitter antagonism of religion. Henry VIII wanted to "reduce that realm to the knowledge of God and obedience to us." English rulers in the sixteenth century regarded the Irish as barbarians, and a policy of complete extermination was rejected only because "to enterprise [attempt] the whole extirpation and total destruction of all the Irishmen in the land would be a marvelous sumptious charge and great difficulty."[20] In other words, it would have cost too much.

In 1536, on orders from London, the Irish parliament, which represented only the English landlords and the people of the Pale (the area around Dublin), approved the English laws severing the church from Rome and making the English king sovereign over ecclesiastical organization and practice. The Church of Ireland was established on the English pattern, and the (English) ruling class adopted the new reformed faith. Most of the Irish, probably for political reasons, defiantly remained Roman Catholic. Monasteries were secularized. Catholic property was confiscated and sold, and the profits shipped to England. With the Roman church driven underground, the Catholic clergy acted as national as well as religious leaders.

### LUTHERANISM IN SWEDEN, NORWAY, AND DENMARK

In Sweden, Norway, and Denmark the monarchy took the initiative in the religious reformation. The resulting institutions were Lutheran state churches. Since the late fourteenth century, the Danish kings had ruled Sweden and Norway as well as Denmark. In 1520, the Swedish nobleman Gustavus Vasa led a successful revolt against Denmark, and Sweden became independent. As king, Gustavus Vasa seized church lands and required the bishops' loyalty to the Swedish crown. The Wittenberg-educated Swedish reformer Olaus Petri (1493–1552) translated the New Testament into Swedish and, with the full support of Gustavus Vasa, organized the church along strict Lutheran lines. This consolidation of the Swedish monarchy in the

MAP 14.1  THE PROTESTANT AND THE CATHOLIC REFORMATIONS  *The reformations shattered the religious unity of Western Christendom. What common cultural traits predominated in regions where a particular branch of the Christian faith was maintained or took root?*

sixteenth century was to have a profound effect on Germany in the seventeenth century.

In Denmark, King Christian III (1534–1559) secularized church property and set up a Lutheran church. Norway, which was governed by Denmark until 1814, became Lutheran under Danish influence.

## THE CATHOLIC AND THE COUNTER REFORMATIONS

Between 1517 and 1547, the reformed versions of Christianity known as Protestantism made remarkable advances. All of England, Scotland, Scandinavia, half of Germany, and sizable parts of France and Switzerland adopted the creeds of Luther, Calvin, and other reformers. Still, the Roman Catholic church made a significant comeback. After about 1540, no new large areas of Europe, except for the Netherlands, accepted Protestant beliefs (see Map. 14.1).

Historians distinguish between two types of reform within the Catholic church in the sixteenth and seventeenth centuries. The Catholic Reformation began before 1517 and sought renewal basically through the stimulation of a new spiritual fervor. The Counter Reformation started in the 1530s as a reaction to the rise and spread of Protestantism. The Counter Reformation involved Catholic efforts to convince dissidents or heretics to return to the church lest they corrupt the entire community of Catholic believers. Fear of the "infection" of all Christian society by the religious dissident was a standard sixteenth-

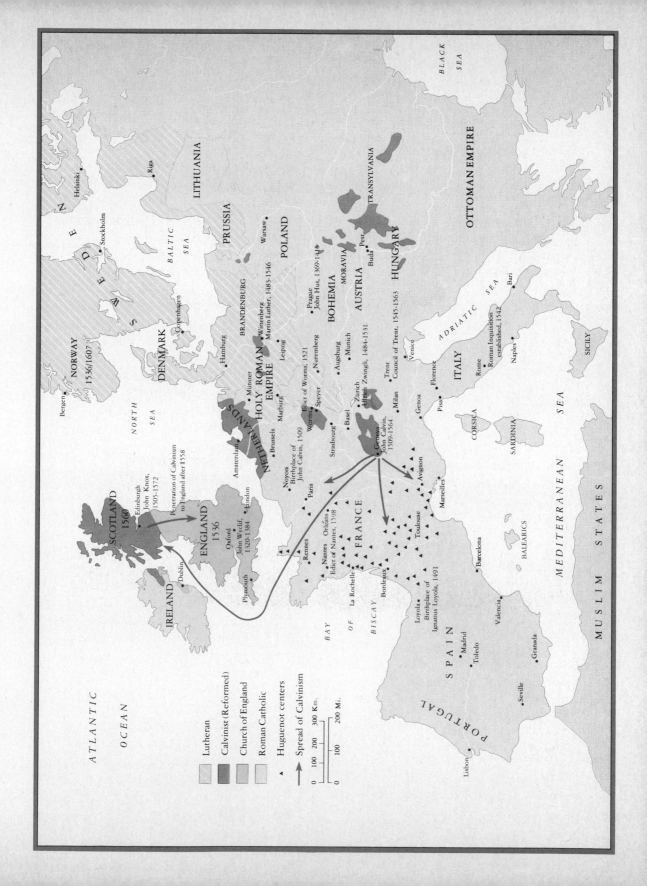

BLACK
SEA

LITHUANIA

NORWAY
1536/1607

SWEDEN

Helsinki

Riga

Stockholm

PRUSSIA

BALTIC
SEA

POLAND

TRANSYLVANIA

OTTOMAN EMPIRE

Bergen

DENMARK

Copenhagen

BRANDENBURG

Warsaw

HUNGARY

NORTH
SEA

Hamburg

Münster

HOLY ROMAN
EMPIRE

Wittenberg
Martin Luther, 1483-1546

Leipzig

BOHEMIA

Prague
John Hus, 1369-1415

MORAVIA

AUSTRIA

Pest

Buda

ADRIATIC SEA

Roman Inquisition
established, 1542

SICILY

Brussels

Marburg

NETHERLANDS

Worms

Edict of Worms, 1521

Speyer

Nuremberg

Augsburg

Munich

Zurich
Ulrich Zwingli, 1484-1531

Trent
Council of Trent, 1545-1563

Venice

Bari

ITALY

Amsterdam

Birthplace of
John Calvin, 1509

Strasbourg

Basel

Geneva
John Calvin, 1509-1564

Milan

Genoa

Rome

Naples

SCOTLAND
1560

Edinburgh
John Knox, 1505-1572

Penetration of Calvinism
to England after 1558

Noyon

Paris

FRANCE

Avignon

Marseilles

Florence

Pisa

CORSICA

SARDINIA

MEDITERRANEAN

IRELAND

Dublin

ENGLAND
1536

Oxford

London

John Wyclif,
1320-1384

Orléans

Nantes
Edict of Nantes, 1598

Rennes

Toulouse

Barcelona

BALEARICS

MUSLIM STATES

Plymouth

La Rochelle

Bordeaux

Loyola
Birthplace of
Ignatius Loyola, 1491

Valencia

SEA

ATLANTIC

BAY    OF    BISCAY

SPAIN

Madrid

OCEAN

PORTUGAL

Toledo

Granada

Seville

Lisbon

Lutheran

Calvinist (Reformed)

Church of England

Roman Catholic

▲ Huguenot centers

→ Spread of Calvinism

0   100   200   300 Km.

0       100       200 Mi.

century attitude. If the heretic could not be persuaded to reconvert, counter-reformers believed it necessary to call upon temporal authorities to defend Christian society by expelling or eliminating the dissident. The Catholic Reformation and the Counter Reformation were not mutually exclusive; in fact, after about 1540 they progressed simultaneously.

What factors influenced the attitudes and policies of the papacy? Why did church leaders wait so long before dealing with the issues of schism and reform? How did the Catholic church succeed in reforming itself and in stemming the tide of Protestantism?

## THE SLOWNESS OF INSTITUTIONAL REFORM

The Renaissance princes who sat on the throne of Saint Peter were not blind to the evils that existed. Modest reform efforts had begun with the Lateran Council called in 1512 by Pope Julius II. The Dutch pope Adrian VI (1522–1523) had instructed his legate in Germany to

*say that we frankly confess that God permits this [Lutheran] persecution of his church on account of the sins of men, especially those of the priests and prelates. . . . We know that in this Holy See now for some years there have been many abominations, abuses in spiritual things, excesses in things commanded, in short that all has become perverted. . . . We have all turned aside in our ways, nor was there, for a long time, any who did right — no, not one.*[21]

Why did the popes, spiritual leaders of the Western church, move so slowly? The answers lie in the personalities of the popes themselves, their preoccupation with political affairs in Italy, and the awesome difficulty of reforming so complicated a bureaucracy as the Roman curia.

Pope Leo X (1513–1521), who opened his pontificate with the words "Now that God has given us the papacy, let us enjoy it," typified the attitude of the Renaissance papacy. Leo concerned himself with artistic beauty and sensual pleasures. He first dismissed the Lutheran revolution as "a monkish quarrel," and by the time he finally acted with a letter condemning Luther, much of northern Germany had already rallied around the sincere Augustinian.

Adrian VI tried desperately to reform the church and to check the spread of Protestantism. His reign lasted only thirteen months, however, and the austerity of his life and his Dutch nationality provoked the hostility of pleasure-loving Italian curial bureaucrats.

Clement VII, a true Medicean, was far more interested in elegant tapestries and Michelangelo's painting of the Last Judgment than in theological disputes in barbaric Germany. Indecisive and vacillating, Pope Clement must bear much of the responsibility for the great spread of Protestantism. While Emperor Charles V and the French king Francis I competed for the domination of divided Italy, the papacy worried about the security of the Papal States. Clement tried to follow a middle course, backing first the emperor and then the French ruler. At the battle of Pavia in 1525, Francis I suffered a severe defeat and was captured. In a reshuffling of diplomatic alliances, the pope switched from Charles and the Spaniards to Francis I. The emperor was victorious once again, however, and in 1527 his Spanish and German mercenaries sacked and looted Rome and captured the pope. Obviously, papal concern about Italian affairs and the Papal States diverted attention from reform.

The idea of reform was closely linked to the idea of a general council representing the entire church. Early in the sixteenth century, Ferdinand of Spain appointed a committee of Spanish bishops to draft materials for conciliar reform of the church. In France, the University of Paris also pressed for a council. (French monarchs subsequently used this academic demand to support their military intervention in Italy.) The emperor Charles V, increasingly disturbed by the Lutheran threat, called for "a free Christian council in German lands." German Catholic bishops drew up lists of "oppressive disorders" that needed reform. A strong contingent of countries from beyond the Alps – from Spain, Germany, and France – wanted to reform the vast bureaucracy of Latin officials, reducing offices, men, and revenues.

Popes from Julius II to Clement VII, remembering fifteenth-century conciliar attempts to limit papal authority, resisted calls for a council. The papal bureaucrats who were the popes' intimates warned the popes against a council, fearing loss of power and prestige. Five centuries before, Saint Bernard of Clairvaux had anticipated the situation: "The most grievous danger of any Pope lies in the fact that, encompassed as he is by flatterers, he never hears the truth about his own person and ends by not wishing to hear it."[22]

## THE COUNCIL OF TRENT

In the papal conclave that followed the death of Clement VII, Cardinal Alexander Farnese promised two German cardinals that if he were elected pope he would summon a council. He won the election and ruled as Pope Paul III (1534–1549). This Roman aristocrat, humanist, and astrologer, who immediately made his teenage grandsons cardinals, seemed an unlikely person to undertake serious reform. Yet Paul III appointed as cardinals several learned churchmen, such as Caraffa (later Pope Paul IV), established the Inquisition in the Papal States and – true to his word – called a council, which finally met at Trent in northern Italy.

The Council of Trent met intermittently from 1545 to 1563. It was called not only to reform the church but to secure reconciliation with the Protestants. Lutherans and Calvinists were invited to participate, but their insistence that the Scriptures be the sole basis for discussion made reconciliation impossible. Other problems bedeviled all the sessions of the council. International politics repeatedly cast a shadow over the theological debates. Charles V opposed discussions on any matter that might further alienate his Lutheran subjects, fearing the loss of additional imperial territory to Lutheran princes. Meanwhile, the French kings worked against the reconciliation of Roman Catholicism and Lutheranism: as long as religious issues divided the German states, the empire would be weakened, and a weak and divided empire meant a stronger France.

Trent had been selected as the site for the council because of its proximity to Germany. The city's climate, small size, and poor accommodations, the advanced age of many bishops, the difficulties of travel in the sixteenth century, and the refusal of Charles V and Henry II of France to allow their national bishops to attend certain sessions – these factors drastically reduced attendance. Portugal, Poland, Hungary, and Ireland sent representatives, but very few German bishops attended.

Another problem was the persistence of the conciliar theory of church government. Some bishops wanted a concrete statement asserting the supremacy of a church council over the

THE COUNCIL OF TRENT *This seventeenth-century engraving depicts one of the early and sparsely attended sessions of the Council of Trent. The tridentine sessions of 1562–63 drew many more bishops and laymen, but there were never many representatives from northern Europe. (Photo: Caroline Buckler)*

papacy. The adoption of the conciliar principle could have led to a divided church. The bishops had a provincial and national outlook; only the papacy possessed an international perspective. Fortunately, the centralizing tenet was established that all acts of the council required papal approval.

In spite of the obstacles, the achievements of the Council of Trent are impressive. It dealt with both doctrinal and disciplinary matters. The council gave equal validity to the Scriptures and to tradition as sources of religious truth and authority in the church. It reaffirmed the seven sacraments and the traditional Catholic teaching on transubstantiation – the belief in the conversion of the bread and wine used in the Mass into the actual body and blood of Christ. Thus, Lutheran and Calvinist positions were rejected.

The council tackled the problems arising from ancient abuses by strengthening ecclesiastical discipline. Tridentine (from *Tridentum,* the Latin word for Trent) decrees required bishops to reside in their own dioceses, suppressed pluralism and simony, and forbade the sale of indulgences. Clerics who kept concubines were to be warned to give them up and, if they refused, stripped of all ecclesiastical income. The jurisdiction of bishops over all the clergy of their dioceses was made almost absolute, and bishops were ordered to visit every religious house within the diocese at least once every two years. In a highly original canon, the council required every diocese to establish a seminary for the education and training of the clergy; the council even prescribed the curriculum and insisted that preference for admission be given to sons of the poor. Finally, great emphasis was laid on preaching and instructing the laity, especially the uneducated.

The Council of Trent did not meet everyone's expectations. Reconciliation with Prot-estantism was not achieved, nor was reform brought about immediately. Nevertheless, the Tridentine decrees laid a solid basis for the spiritual renewal of the church and for the enforcement of correction. For four centuries the doctrinal and disciplinary legislation of Trent served as the basis for Roman Catholic faith, organization, and practice.

## NEW RELIGIOUS ORDERS

The establishment of new religious orders within the church reveals a central feature of the Catholic Reformation. These new orders developed in response to one crying need: to raise the moral and intellectual level of the clergy. Education was a major goal of them all.

The Ursuline order of nuns founded by Angela Merici (1474-1540) attained enormous prestige for the education of women. The daughter of a country gentleman, Angela Merici worked for many years among the poor, sick, and uneducated around her native Brescia in northern Italy. In 1535 she established the Ursuline order to combat heresy through Christian education. The first religious order concentrating exclusively on teaching young girls, the Ursulines sought to re-Christianize society by training future wives and mothers. Approved as a religious community by Paul III in 1544, the Ursulines rapidly grew and spread to France and the New World. Their schools in North America, stretching from Quebec to New Orleans, provided superior education for young women and inculcated the spiritual ideals of the Catholic Reformation.

The Society of Jesus, founded by Ignatius Loyola (1491-1556), a former Spanish soldier, played a powerful international role in resisting the spread of Protestantism, converting Asians and Latin American Indians to Catholicism, and spreading Christian education all over Europe. While recuperating from a severe battle wound in his legs, Loyola studied a life of Christ and other religious books and decided to give up his military career and become a soldier of Christ. During a year spent in seclusion, prayer, and personal mortification, he gained the religious insights that went into his great classic, *Spiritual Exercises.* This work, intended for study during a four-week period of retreat, directed the individual imagination and will to the reform of life and a new spiritual piety.

Loyola was apparently a man of considerable personal magnetism. After study at the universities in Salamanca and Paris, he gathered a group of six companions and in 1540 secured papal approval of the new Society of Jesus, whose members were called Jesuits. Their goals were the reform of the church primarily through education, preaching the Gospel to pagan peoples, and fighting Protestant heresy. Within a short time, the Jesuits had attracted many recruits.

The Society of Jesus was a highly centralized, tightly knit organization. Candidates underwent a two-year novitiate, in contrast to the usual one-year probation. Although new members took the traditional vows of poverty, chastity, and obedience, the emphasis was on obedience. Carefully selected members made a fourth vow of obedience to the pope and the governing members of the society. As faith was the cornerstone of Luther's life, so obedience became the bedrock of the Jesuit tradition.

The Jesuits had a modern, quasi-military quality; a sort of ecclesiastical Green Berets, they achieved phenomenal success for the papacy and the reformed church. Jesuit schools adopted modern teaching methods, and while they first concentrated on the children of the poor, they were soon educating the sons of the nobility. As confessors and spiritual directors to kings, Jesuits exerted great political influence. Operating on the principle that the end sometimes justifies the means, they were not above spying. Indifferent to physical comfort and personal safety, they carried Christianity to the Moluccan Islands, Ceylon, and Japan before 1550, to Brazil and the Congo in the seventeenth century. Within Europe, the Jesuits brought southern Germany and much of eastern Europe back to Catholicism.

## THE SACRED CONGREGATION OF THE HOLY OFFICE

In 1542, Pope Paul III established the Sacred Congregation of the Holy Office with jurisdiction over the Roman Inquisition, which became a powerful instrument of the Counter Reformation. The Inquisition was a committee of six cardinals with judicial authority over all Catholics and with the power to arrest, imprison, and execute. Under the direction of the fanatical Cardinal Caraffa, it vigorously attacked heresy.

The Roman Inquisition operated under the principles of Roman law. It accepted hearsay evidence, was not obliged to inform accused people of the charges against them, and sometimes applied torture. Echoing one of Calvin's remarks about heresy, Cardinal Caraffa wrote, "No man is to lower himself by showing toleration towards any sort of heretic, least of all a Calvinist."[23] The Holy Office published the *Index of Prohibited Books,* a catalog of forbidden reading that included the publications of many printers.

Within the Papal States in central Italy, the Inquisition effectively destroyed heresy (and many heretics). Outside the papal territories, however, its influence was slight. Governments had their own judicial systems for the suppression of treasonable activities, as religious heresy was then considered. The republic of Venice is a good case in point.

In the sixteenth century, Venice was one of the great publishing centers of Europe. The Inquisition and the Index could have badly damaged the Venetian book trade. Authorities there cooperated with the Holy Office only when heresy became a great threat to the security of the republic. The Index had no influence on scholarly research in nonreligious areas, such as law, classical literature, and mathematics. Venetians and Italians, as a result of the Inquisition, were not cut off from the main currents of European learning.[24]

———◆———

The age of the Reformation presents very real paradoxes. The break with Rome and the rise of Lutheran, Anglican, Calvinist, and other faiths destroyed the unity of Europe as an organic Christian society. Saint Paul's exhortation, "There should be no schism in the body [of the church]. . . . You are all one in Christ,"[25] was gradually ignored. On the other hand, religious belief remained tremendously strong. In fact, the strength of religious convictions caused political fragmentation. In the later sixteenth century and through most of the seventeenth, religion and religious issues continued to play a major role in the lives of individuals and in the policies and actions of governments. Religion, whether Protestant or Catholic, decisively influenced the growth of national states.

For almost a thousand years, the church had taught Europeans "to believe in order that you may know." In the seventh through ninth centuries, European peoples had been led in massive numbers to the waters of Christian baptism. The Christian faith and Christian practices, however, meant little to the pagan barbarians of the early Middle Ages.

Many centuries passed before the church had a significantly Christianizing impact on those peoples. Therein lies another paradox. At the moment when literature, sermons, and especially art were expressing the widespread desire for individual and emotional experience within a common spiritual framework, the schism brought confusion, divisiveness, and destruction. The Reformation was, ironically, a tribute to the successful educational work of the medieval church.

Finally, scholars have maintained that the sixteenth century witnessed the beginnings of the modern world. They are both right and wrong. The sixteenth-century revolt from the church paved the way for the eighteenth-century revolt from the Christian God, one of the strongest supports of life in Western culture. In this respect, the Reformation marked the beginning of the modern world, with its secularism and rootlessness. At the same time, it can equally be argued that the sixteenth century represented the culmination of the Middle Ages. Martin Luther's anxieties about salvation show him to be very much a medieval man. His concerns had deeply troubled serious individuals since the time of Saint Augustine. Modern people tend to be less troubled by this issue. The sixteenth century was a definite watershed.

---

## NOTES

1. Romans 12:2-3.

2. Quoted by J. Burckhardt, *The Civilization of the Renaissance in Italy,* Phaidon Books, London, 1951, p. 262.

3. See E. Erickson, *Young Man Luther: A Study in Psychoanalysis and History,* W. W. Norton, New York, 1962, passim.

4. T. C. Mendenhall et al., eds., *Ideas and Institu-*

*tions in European History: 800–1715*, Henry Holt, New York, 1948, p. 220.

5. Quoted by O. Chadwick, *The Reformation*, Penguin Books, Baltimore, 1976, p. 55.

6. Quoted by E. H. Harbison, *The Age of Reformation*, Cornell University Press, Ithaca, N.Y., 1963, p. 52.

7. I have leaned heavily here on Harbison, pp. 52–55.

8. H. Hillerbrand, *Men and Ideas in the Sixteenth Century*, Rand McNally, Chicago, 1969, p. 28.

9. Romans 13:1–2.

10. Erickson, p. 47.

11. Quoted by J. Atkinson, *Martin Luther and the Birth of Protestantism*, Penguin Books, Baltimore, 1968, pp. 247–248.

12. *Martin Luther: Three Treatises*, Muhlenberg Press, Philadelphia, 1947, pp. 28–31.

13. Quoted by R. Bainton, *The Travail of Religious Liberty*, Harper & Brothers, New York, 1958, p. 65.

14. J. Allen, trans., *John Calvin: The Institutes of the Christian Religion*, Westminster Press, Philadelphia, 1930, book 3, chap. 21, paras. 5, 7.

15. Quoted by Bainton, pp. 69–70.

16. A. G. Dickens, *The English Reformation*, Schocken Books, New York, 1964, p. 36.

17. A. G. Dickens and Dorothy Carr, eds., *The Reformation in England to the Accession of Elizabeth I*, Edward Arnold, London, 1969, pp. 15–16.

18. Leviticus 18:16, 20, 21.

19. C. Stephenson and G. F. Marcham, *Sources of English Constitutional History*, Harper & Row, New York, 1937, p. 304.

20. Quoted by P. Smith, *The Age of the Reformation*, rev. ed., Henry Holt, New York, 1951, p. 346.

21. Ibid., p. 84.

22. Quoted by H. Jedin, *A History of the Council of Trent*, Nelson & Sons, London, 1957, 1.126.

23. Quoted by Chadwick, p. 270.

24. See P. Grendler, *The Roman Inquisition and the Venetian Press, 1540–1605*, Princeton University Press, Princeton, N.J., 1977.

25. I Corinthians 1:25, 27.

## SUGGESTED READING

There are many lucidly written and easily accessible studies of the religious reformations of the sixteenth century. O. Chadwick, *The Reformation* (1976); E. H. Harbison, *The Age of Reformation* (1963); R. Bainton, *The Reformation of the Sixteenth Century* (1961); and H. Hillerbrand, *Men and Ideas in the Sixteenth Century* (1969), are all good general introductions. P. Smith's *The Age of the Reformation*, rev. ed. (1951) is an older but comprehensive and often amusing treatment. The recent work of Steven Ozment, *The Age of Reform, 1250–1550: An Intellectual and Religious History of Late Medieval and Reformation Europe* (1980), provides a sophisticated survey of the ideas of the period.

Students who wish to explore aspects of Luther's life and work in greater detail should see, in addition to the titles in the Notes, R. Bainton, *Here I Stand* (1960); J. Atkinson, *Martin Luther and the Birth of Protestantism* (1968); and the sensitively scholarly work of H. Boehmer, *Martin Luther: Road to Reformation* (1960), a well-balanced book by a distinguished Protestant theologian. The perceptive study of H. G. Haile, *Luther: An Experiment in Biography* (1980), focuses on the character of the mature and aging reformer. The pioneering work of Gerald Strauss, *Luther's House of Learning: The Indoctrination of the Young in the German Reformation* (1978), describes how plain people were imbued with Reformation ideas and behavior. The best biography of the central political figure in the period of the German Reformation remains K. Brandi, *Charles V* (1954), while G. Barraclough, *The Origins of Modern Germany* (1952), gives a closet Marxist treatment.

The best introduction to Calvin as a man and theologian is probably the balanced account of F. Wendel, *Calvin: The Origins and Development of His Thought*, trans. P. Mairet (1963). J. T. McNeill, *History and Character of Calvinism* (1954), presents useful and previously inaccessible information. W. E. Monter, *Calvin's Geneva* (1967), is an excellent account of the impact of Calvinism on the social and economic life of that Swiss city. R. T. Kendall,

*Calvinism and English Calvinism to 1649* (1981), treats English conditions, while Robert M. Mitchell, *Calvin and the Puritan's View of the Protestant Ethic* (1979), provides a good interpretation of the socioeconomic implications of Calvin's thought. Students interested in the left wing of the Reformation should see the profound work of G. H. Williams, *The Radical Reformers* (1962).

For England, in addition to the fundamental works by Dickens cited in the Notes, see S. T. Bindoff, *Tudor England* (1959), a good short synthesis. The marital trials of Henry VIII are treated in both the sympathetic study of G. Mattingly, *Catherine of Aragon* (1949), and H. A. Kelly, *The Matrimonial Trials of Henry VIII* (1975). A persuasive treatment of Henry VIII's possible syphilis and its effects on his children is given in F. S. Cartwright, *Disease and History* (1972). The legal implications of Henry VIII's divorces have been thoroughly analyzed by J. J. Scarisbrick, *Henry VIII* (1968), an almost definitive biography. On the dissolution of the English monasteries, see D. Knowles, *The Religious Orders in England,* vol. 3 (1959), one of the finest examples of historical prose in English written in the twentieth century. Knowles's *Bare Ruined Choirs* (1976) is an attractively illustrated abridgement of *Religious Orders.* G. R. Elton, *The Tudor Revolution in Government* (1959), discusses the modernization of English government under Thomas Cromwell.

P. Janelle, *The Catholic Reformation* (1951), is a fine comprehensive treatment of the Catholic reformation from a Catholic point of view, and A. G. Dickens, *The Counter Reformation* (1969), gives the Protestant standpoint in a beautifully illustrated book. The definitive study of the Council of Trent was written by H. Jedin, *A History of the Council of Trent,* 3 vols. (1957–1961).

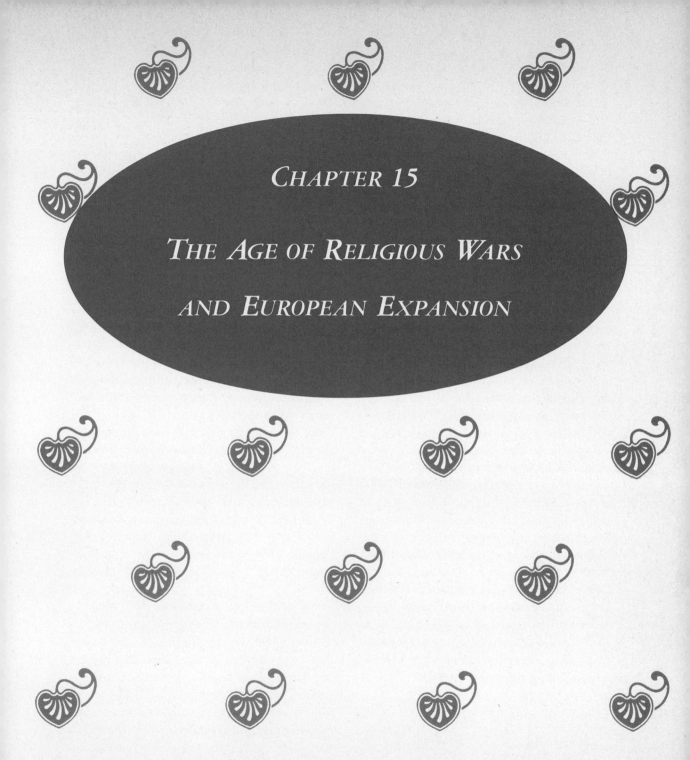

# CHAPTER 15

# THE AGE OF RELIGIOUS WARS
# AND EUROPEAN EXPANSION

THE RENAISSANCE and the reformations of the fifteenth and sixteenth centuries drastically altered intellectual, political, religious, and social life in Europe. But even before Martin Luther initiated the movement to reform the church, European peoples had been involved in overseas activities that had profound consequences for the domestic life of Europe and for the rest of the world. In the middle of the fifteenth century, Europeans began to confront ancient civilizations in Africa, Asia, and the Americas. These confrontations led first to conquest, then to exploitation, and finally to significant changes in both Europe and the conquered territories. European expansion took place amidst domestic and international conflict.

For much of the period 1560–1648, war and religious issues dominated the politics of European states. Wars were fought for power and territorial expansion, although religion was commonly used to rationalize those wars. Meanwhile Europeans carried their political, religious, and social attitudes to the new continents they subdued. This chapter seeks to explore the following questions. Why, in the sixteenth and seventeenth centuries, did European peoples expand overseas? How were a relatively small number of people living on the edge of the Eurasian landmass able to gain control of the major sea-lanes of the world and establish economic and political hegemony on distant continents far from home? What effect did overseas expansion have on Europe and on conquered societies?

## DISCOVERY, RECONNAISSANCE, AND EXPANSION

Historians have variously called the period 1450–1650 "The Age of Discovery," "The

*WORLD MAP OF VESCONTE MAGGIOLI, 1511 Renaissance geographers still accepted the Greco-Egyptian Ptolemy's theory (second century A.D.) that the earth was one continuous land mass. Cartographers could not subscribe to the idea of a new, separate continent. Thus, this map, inaccurate when it was drawn, shows America as an extension of Asia. (John Carter Brown Library, Brown University, Providence)*

Age of Reconnaissance," and "The Age of Expansion." All three labels are appropriate. "The Age of Discovery" refers to the era's phenomenal advances in geographical knowledge and in technology, often achieved through trial and error. In 1350, it took as long to sail from the eastern end of the Mediterranean to the western end as it had taken a thousand years earlier, in 350. Even in the fifteenth century, Europeans knew little more about the earth's surface than the Romans had known. By 1650, however, Europeans had made an extensive reconnaissance – or preliminary exploration – and had sketched fairly accurately the physical outline of the whole earth. Much of the geographical information they had gathered was tentative and not fully understood – hence the appropriateness of the term "The Age of Reconaissance."

The designation of the era as "The Age of Expansion" refers to the migration of Europeans to other parts of the world. This colonization resulted in political control of much of South America and North America, coastal regions of Africa, India, China, Japan, and many Pacific islands. Political hegemony was accompanied by economic exploitation, religious domination, and the introduction of European patterns of social and intellectual life. The sixteenth-century expansion of European society launched a new age in world history.

## OVERSEAS EXPLORATION AND CONQUEST

The outward expansion of Europe began with the Viking voyages across the Atlantic in the tenth and eleventh centuries. Under Eric the Red and Leif Ericson, the Vikings discovered Greenland and the eastern coast of North America. They may even have traveled down the New England coast as far south as Boston. The Crusades of the eleventh through thirteenth centuries were another phase in Europe's attempt to explore, Christianize, and exploit territories and peoples on the periphery of the Continent. But these early thrusts outward resulted in no permanent settlements. The Vikings made only quick raids in search of booty. Lacking stable political institutions in Scandinavia, they had no workable forms of government to impose on distant continents. In the twelfth and thirteenth centuries, the lack of a strong territorial base, weak support from the West, and sheer misrule combined to make the medieval Crusader kingdoms short-lived. Even in the mid-fifteenth century, Europe seemed ill-prepared for international ventures. By 1450, a grave new threat had appeared in the East — the Ottoman Turks.

Combining excellent military strategy with efficient administration of their conquered territories, the Turks had subdued most of Asia Minor and begun to settle on the Western side of the Bosporus. The Ottoman Turks under Sultan Mohammed II (1451–1481) captured Constantinople in 1453, pressed southwest into the Balkans, and by the early sixteenth century controlled the eastern Mediterranean. The Turkish menace badly frightened Europeans. In France in the fifteenth and sixteenth centuries, twice as many books were printed about the Turkish threat as about the American discoveries. The Turks imposed a military blockade on eastern Europe, thus forcing Europeans' attention westward. Yet the fifteenth and sixteenth centuries witnessed a fantastic continuation, on a global scale, of European expansion: great discoveries led to overseas empires.

Political centralization in Spain, France, and England helps to explain those countries' outward push. In the fifteenth century, Isabella and Ferdinand had consolidated their several kingdoms to achieve a united Spain. The Catholic rulers slashed the powers of the nobility, revamped the Spanish bureaucracy, and humbled dissident elements, notably the Muslims and the Jews. The Spanish monarchy was stronger than ever before, and in a position to support foreign ventures; it could bear the costs and dangers of exploration. But Portugal, situated on the extreme southwestern edge of the European continent, got the start on the rest of Europe.

Portugal's taking of Ceuta, an Arab city in northern Morocco, in 1415 marked the beginning of European exploration and control of overseas territory. The objectives of Portuguese policy included the historic Iberian crusade to Christianize Muslims, and the search for gold, for an overseas route to the spice markets of India, and for the mythical Christian ruler of Ethiopia, Prester John.

In the early phases of Portuguese exploration, Prince Henry (1394–1460), called "the Navigator" because of the annual expeditions he sent down the western coast of Africa, played the leading role. In the fifteenth century, most of the gold that reached Europe came from the Sudan in West Africa and from Ashanti blacks living near the gold coast. Muslim caravans brought the gold from the African cities of Niani and Timbuktu and carried it north across the Sahara to Mediterranean ports. Then the Portuguese muscled in on this commerce in gold. Prince Henry's carefully planned expeditions succeeded in reaching Guinea, and under King John II (1481–1495), the Portuguese established trading posts and forts on the Guinea coast and penetrated into the continent all the way to Timbuktu (see Map 15.1). Portuguese ships transported gold to Lisbon, and by 1500 Portugal controlled the flow of gold to Europe. The golden century of Portuguese prosperity had begun.

Still the Portuguese pushed farther south down the west coast of Africa. In 1487, Bartholomew Diaz rounded the Cape of Good Hope at the southern tip, but storms and a threatened mutiny forced him to turn back. On a second expedition (1497–1499), the Portuguese mariner Vasco da Gama reached India and returned to Lisbon loaded with samples of Indian wares (see Map 15.1). King Manuel (1495–1521) promptly dispatched thirteen ships under the command of Pedro Alvares Cabral, assisted by Diaz, to set up trading posts in India. On April 22, 1500, the coast of Brazil in South America was sighted and claimed for the crown of Portugal. Cabral then proceeded south and east around the Cape of Good Hope and reached India. Half the fleet was lost on the return voyage, but the six spice-laden vessels that dropped anchor in Lisbon harbor in July 1501 more than paid for the entire expedition. Thereafter, convoys were sent out every March. Lisbon became the entrance port for Asian goods into Europe – but not without a fight.

For centuries the Muslims had controlled the rich spice trade of the Indian Ocean, and they did not surrender it willingly. Portuguese commercial activities were accompanied by the destruction or seizure of strategic Muslim coastal forts, which later served Portugal as both trading posts and military bases.

Alfonso de Albuquerque, whom the Portuguese crown appointed as governor of India (1509–1515), decided that these bases and not inland territories should control the Indian Ocean. Accordingly, his cannon blasted open the ports of Calicut, Ormuz, Goa, and Malacca, the vital centers of Arab domination of south Asian trade. This bombardment laid the foundation for Portuguese imperialism in the sixteenth and seventeenth centuries: a strange way to bring Christianity to "those who were in darkness." As one scholar wrote about the opening of China to the West, "while Buddha came to China on white elephants, Christ was borne on cannon balls."[1]

In March 1493, between the first and second voyages of Vasco da Gama, Spanish ships entered Lisbon harbor bearing a triumphant Italian explorer in the service of the Spanish monarchy. Christopher Columbus (1451–1506), a Genose mariner, had secured Spanish support for an expedition to the East. He sailed from Palos, Spain, to the Canary Islands and crossed the Atlantic to the Bahamas, landing in October 1492 on an island that he named San Salvador and believed to be the coast of India.

Columbus explained the motives for his expedition in the journal of his voyage, entitled *Book of the First Navigation and Discovery of the Indies:*

*And Your Highnesses, as Catholic Christians and Princes devoted to the Holy Christian Faith and the propagators thereof, and enemies of the sect of Mahomet and of all idolatries and heresies, resolved to send me Christopher Columbus to the said regions of India, to see the said princes and peoples and lands and [to observe] the disposition of them and of all, and the manner in which may be undertaken their conversion to our Holy Faith, and ordained that I should not go by land (the usual*

JAPAN 1542

KYUSHU

PHILIPPINES

1521

NEW GUINEA 1511

AUSTRALIA

ASIA

CHINA

Canton 1513
Macao 1517

Malacca 1509
BORNEO

MOLUCCAS 1511

1522

JAVA

SUMATRA

CEYLON 1505

INDIA

Calicut 1498

Goa 1510

Ormuz 1507

PERSIA

Muscat

ARABIA

Aden 1513

1498

INDIAN

OCEAN

MADAGASCAR 1500

Mombasa 1498

Mozambique

Magellan and crew

Columbus

Da Gama

Other

Spanish holdings

Portuguese holdings

Constantinople

EUROPE

Amsterdam
Antwerp

SAHARA

AFRICA

Lisbon
Seville

Ceuta 1415

Timbuktu

CAPE VERDE 1444

Niani

GUINEA

GOLD COAST

1497

1522

CAPE OF GOOD HOPE

ATLANTIC

OCEAN

NEWFOUNDLAND 1497

AZORES

CANARY IS.

1492

1493

CAPE VERDE IS. 1456

1519

St. Augustine 1565

CUBA

SAN SALVADOR 1492

PUERTO RICO

JAMAICA

HONDURAS

HISPANIOLA 1492

TRINIDAD 1498

SPANISH MAIN

Vera Cruz 1519

Cartagena

Panama

Quito 1534

PERU

Lima 1535

NEW SPAIN

Zacatecas
Guanajuato

Mexico City 1519

NORTH

AMERICA

SOUTH

AMERICA

BRAZIL

Rio de Janeiro 1516

Potosí

Buenos Aires 1535

Santiago

STRAITS OF MAGELLAN

CAPE HORN

1520

PACIFIC

OCEAN

MAP 15.1 OVERSEAS EXPLORATION AND CONQUEST, FIFTEENTH AND SIXTEENTH CENTURIES *The voyages of discovery marked another phase in the centuries-old migrations of European peoples. Consider the major contemporary significance of each of the three voyages depicted on the map.*

*way) to the Orient, but by the route of the Occident, by which no one to this day knows for sure that anyone has gone.*[2]

Like most people of his day, Christopher Columbus was a deeply religious man. The crew of his flagship, *Santa Maria,* recited vespers every night and sang a hymn to the Virgin, the "Salve Regina," before going to bed. Nevertheless, the Spanish fleet, sailing westward to find the East, sought wealth as well as souls to convert to Christianity.

Between 1492 and 1502, Columbus made four voyages to America, discovering all the major islands of the Caribbean – Haiti (which he called Dominica and the Spanish named Hispaniola), San Salvador, Puerto Rico, Jamaica, Cuba, Trinidad – and Honduras in Central America. Columbus believed until he died that the islands he found were off the coast of India. In fact, he had opened up for the rulers of Spain a whole new world. The Caribbean islands – the West Indies – represented to Spanish missionary zeal millions of Indian natives for conversion to Christianity. Hispaniola, Cuba, and Puerto Rico also offered gold.

Forced labor, disease, and starvation in the Spaniards' gold mines rapidly killed off the Indians of Hispaniola. When Columbus arrived in 1493, the population had been approximately 100,000; in 1570, 300 people survived. Indian slaves from the Bahamas and black Africans from Guinea were then imported to do the mining.

The search for precious metals determined the direction of Spanish exploration and expansion into South America. When it became apparent that placer mining in the Caribbean islands was slow and the rewards slim, new routes to the East and new sources of gold and silver were sought.

In 1519, the Spanish ruler Charles V commissioned Ferdinand Magellan (1480-1521) to find a direct route to the Moluccan Islands off the southeast coast of Asia. Magellan sailed southwest across the Atlantic to Brazil, and proceeded south around Cape Horn into the Pacific Ocean (see Map 15.1). He crossed the Pacific, sailing west, to the Malay Archipelago, which he called the Western Isles. (These islands were conquered in the 1560s and named the Philippines for Philip II of Spain.)

Although Magellan was killed, the expedition continued, returning to Spain in 1522 from the east by way of the Indian Ocean, the Cape of Good Hope, and the Atlantic. Terrible storms, mutiny, starvation, and disease haunted this voyage. Nevertheless, it verified Columbus's theory that the earth was round and brought information about the vastness of the Pacific. Magellan also proved that the earth was much larger than Columbus and others had believed.

In the West Indies, the slow recovery of gold, the shortage of a healthy labor force, and sheer restlessness speeded up Spain's search for wealth. In 1519, the year Magellan departed on his worldwide expedition, a brash and determined Spanish adventurer Hernando Cortez (1485-1547), crossed from Hispaniola to mainland Mexico with six hundred men, seventeen horses, and ten canon. Within three years, Cortez had conquered the fabulously rich Aztec empire, taken captive the Aztec emperor Montezuma, and founded Mexico City as the capital of New Spain. The subjugation of northern Mexico took longer, but between 1531 and 1550 the Spanish gained

*COLUMBUS LANDS ON SAN SALVADOR The printed page and illustrations, such as this German woodcut, spread reports of Columbus's voyage all over Europe. According to Columbus, a group of naked Indians greeted the Spaniards' arrival. Pictures of the Indians as "primitive" and "uncivilized" instilled prejudices which centuries have not erased. (Photo: Caroline Buckler)*

control of Zacatecas and Guanajuato, where rich silver veins were soon tapped.

Another Spanish conquistador, Francisco Pizzaro (1470–1541), repeated Cortez's feat in Peru. Between 1531 and 1536, with even fewer resources, Pizzaro crushed the Inca empire in northern South America and established the Spanish viceroyalty of Peru with its center at Lima. In 1545, Pizzaro opened at Potosí in the Peruvian highlands what became the richest silver mines in the New World.

Between 1525 and 1575, the riches of the Americas poured into the Spanish port of Seville and the Portuguese capital of Lisbon. For all their new wealth, however, Lisbon and Seville did not become important trading centers. It was the Flemish city of Antwerp, although controlled by the Spanish Habsburgs, that developed into the great entrepôt for overseas bullion and Portuguese spices and served as the commercial and financial capital of the entire European world.

Since the time of the great medieval fairs, cities of the Low Countries – so called because much of the land lies below sea level – had been important sites for the exchange of products from the Baltic and Italy. Antwerp, ideally situated on the Scheldt River at the intersection of many trading routes, steadily expanded as the chief intermediary for international commerce and finance. English woolens, Baltic wheat, fur, and timber, Portuguese spices, German iron and copper, Spanish fruit, French wines and dyestuffs, Italian silks, marbles, and mirrors, together with vast amounts of cash, were exchanged at Antwerp. The city's harbor could dock 2,500 vessels at once, and 5,000 merchants from many nations gathered daily in the bourse (or exchange). Spanish silver was drained to the Netherlands to pay for food and luxury goods. Even so, the desire for complete economic independence from Spain was to play a major role in the Netherlands' revolt in the late sixteenth century.

By the end of the century, Amsterdam had overtaken Antwerp as the financial capital of Europe. The Dutch had also embarked on foreign exploration and conquest. The Dutch East India Company, founded in 1602, became the major organ of Dutch imperialism and within a few decades expelled the Portuguese from Ceylon and other East Indian islands. By 1650, the Dutch West India Company had successfully horned in on the Spanish possessions in America and gained control of much of the African and American trade.

English and French explorations lacked the immediate and sensational results of the Spanish and Portuguese. In 1497 John Cabot, a Genoese merchant living in London, sailed for Brazil but discovered Newfoundland. The next year he returned and explored the New England coast and perhaps as far south as Delaware. Since these expeditions found no spices or gold, the English king Henry VII lost interest in exploration. Between 1534 and 1541, the Frenchman Jacques Cartier made several voyages and explored the St. Lawrence region of Canada, but the first permanent French settlement, at Quebec, was not founded until 1608.

## COLONIAL ADMINISTRATION

Columbus, Cortez, and Pizarro claimed the lands they had "discovered" for the crown of Spain. How were they to be governed? According to the Spanish theory of absolutism, the Crown was entitled to exercise full authority over all imperial lands. In the sixteenth century the Crown divided its New World territories into four viceroyalties or administrative divisions: New Spain, which consisted of Mexico, Central America, and present-day California, Arizona, New Mexico, and Texas, with the capital at Mexico City; Peru, originally all the lands in continental South America, later reduced to the territory of modern Peru, Chile, Bolivia, and Equador, with the viceregal seat at Lima; New Granada, including present-day Venezuela, Colombia, Panama, and after 1739 Ecuador, with Bogata as its administrative center; and La Plata, consisting of Argentina, Uruguay, and Paraguay,

with Buenos Aires as the capital. Within each territory, the viceroy or imperial governor exercised broad military and civil authority as the direct representative of the sovereign in Madrid. The viceroy presided over the *audiencia,* a board of twelve to fifteen judges, which served as his advisory council and the highest judicial body. The enlightened Spanish king Charles III (1716-1788) introduced the system of intendants. These royal officials possessed broad military, administrative, and financial authority within their intendancy, and were responsible not to the viceroy but to the Crown in Madrid.

From the early sixteenth century to the beginning of the nineteenth, the Spanish monarchy acted on the mercantilist principle that the colonies existed for the financial benefit of the mother country. The mining of gold and silver was always the most important industry in the colonies. The Crown claimed the *quinto,* one-fifth of all precious metals mined in South America. Gold and silver yielded the Spanish monarchy 25 percent of its total income. In return, it shipped manufactured goods to America and discouraged the development of native industries.

The Portuguese governed their colony of Brazil in a similar manner. After the union of the crowns of Portugal and Spain in 1580, Spanish administrative forms were introduced. Local officials called *corregidores* held judicial and military powers. Mercantilist policies placed severe restrictions on Brazilian industries that might compete with those of Portugal. In the seventeenth century the use of black slave labor made possible the cultivation of coffee and cotton, and in the eighteenth century Brazil led the world in the production of sugar. The unique feature of colonial Brazil's culture and society was its thoroughgoing intermixture of Indians, whites, and blacks.

## The Economic Effects of Spain's Discoveries in the New World

The sixteenth century has often been called the golden century of Spain. The influence of Spanish armies, Spanish Catholicism, and Spanish wealth was felt all over Europe. This greatness rested largely upon the influx of precious metals from the New World.

The mines at Zacatecas and Guanajuato in Mexico and Potosí in Peru poured out huge quantities of precious metals. To protect this treasure from French and English pirates, armed convoys transported it each year to Spain. Between 1503 and 1650, 16 million kilograms of silver and 185,000 kilograms of gold entered the port of Seville. Scholars have long debated the impact of all this bullion on the economies of Spain and Europe as a whole. Spanish predominance, however, proved temporary.

In the sixteenth century, Spain experienced a steady population increase, creating a sharp rise in the demand for food and goods. Spanish colonies in the Americas also represented a demand for products – olive oil, wine, wool, steel cutlery, and a variety of luxury goods. Since Spain had expelled some of the best farmers and businessmen, the Muslims and the conversos, in the fifteenth century, the Spanish economy was already suffering and could not meet the new demands. Prices rose. Because the costs of manufacturing cloth and other goods increased, Spanish products could not compete in the international market with cheaper products made elsewhere. The textile industry was badly hurt. Prices spiraled upward, faster than the government could levy taxes to dampen the economy. (Higher taxes would have cut the public's buying power; with fewer goods sold, prices would have come down.)

Several times between 1557 and 1647, Philip II and his successors were forced to repudiate the state debt, which in turn undermined confidence in the government. The enormous flow of silver and gold from the Americas thus contributed to the destruction of Spanish agriculture and industry. When the flow declined in the seventeenth century, the economy was in a shambles.

As Philip II paid his armies and foreign debts with silver bullion, the Spanish inflation was transmitted to the rest of Europe. Between 1560 and 1600, much of Europe experienced large price increases. Prices doubled and in some cases quadrupled. Spain suffered most severely, but all European countries were affected. People who lived on fixed incomes, such as the continental nobles, were badly hurt because their money bought less. Those who owed fixed sums of money, such as the middle class, prospered: in a time of rising prices, debts had less value each year. Food costs rose most sharply, and the poor fared worst of all.

## Technological Stimuli to Exploration

Technological developments were the key to Europe's remarkable outreach. By 1350, cannon – iron or bronze guns that fired iron or stone balls – had been fully developed in western Europe. These pieces of artillery emitted frightening noises and great flashes of fire and could batter down fortresses and even city walls. Sultan Mohammed II's siege of Constantinople in 1453 provides a classic illustration of the effectiveness of cannon fire.

Constantinople had the strongest walled fortifications in the West. The sultan secured the services of a Western technician who built fifty-six small cannon and a gigantic gun that could hurl stone balls weighing about eight hundred pounds. The gun could be moved only by several hundred oxen, and loaded and fired only by about a hundred men working together. Reloading took two hours. This awkward but powerful weapon breached the walls of Constantinople before it cracked on the second day of the bombardment. Lesser cannon finished the job.

Early cannon posed serious technical difficulties. Iron cannon were cheaper than bronze to construct, but they were difficult to cast effectively and were liable to crack and injure the artillerymen. Bronze guns, made of copper and tin, were less subject than iron to corrosion, but they were very expensive. All cannon were extraordinarily difficult to move, required considerable time for reloading, and were highly inaccurate. They thus proved inefficient for land warfare. However, they could be used at sea.

The mounting of cannon on ships and improved techniques of shipbuilding gave impetus to European expansion.[3] Since ancient times, most seagoing vessels had been narrow open boats called galleys, propelled by manpower. Slaves or convicts who had been sentenced to the galleys manned the oars of the ships that sailed the Mediterranean, and both cargo and warships carried soldiers for defense. Although well suited to the placid and thoroughly explored waters of the Mediterranean, galleys could not withstand the rough winds and uncharted shoals of the Atlantic. The need for sturdier craft, as well as population losses caused by the Black Death, forced the development of a new style of ship that would not require soldiers for defense.

In the course of the fifteenth century, the Portuguese developed the caravel, a small, light, three-masted sailing ship. Although somewhat slower than the galley, the caravel held more cargo and was highly maneuverable. When fitted with cannon, it could dominate larger vessels, such as the round ships commonly used as merchantmen. The substitution of windpower for manpower, and artillery fire for soldiers, signaled a great technological advance and gave Europeans navigational and fighting ascendancy over the rest of the world.[4]

Other fifteenth-century developments in navigation helped make possible the conquest of the Atlantic. The magnetic compass enabled sailors to determine their direction and position at sea. The astrolabe, an instrument used to determine the altitude of the sun and other celestial bodies, permitted mariners to plot their latitude, or position north or south of the equator. Steadily improved maps and sea charts provided information about distance, sea depths, and general geography.

## THE EXPLORERS' MOTIVES

The expansion of Europe was not motivated by demographic pressures. The Black Death had caused serious population losses from which Europe had not recovered in 1500. Few Europeans emigrated to North or South America in the sixteenth century. Half of those who did sail to begin a new life in America died en route; half of those who reached the New World eventually returned to their homeland. Why, then, did explorers brave the Atlantic and Pacific oceans, risking their lives to discover new continents and spread European culture?

The reasons are varied and complex. People of the sixteenth century were still basically medieval, in the sense that their attitudes and values were shaped by religion and expressed in religious terms. In the late fifteenth century, crusading fervor remained a basic part of the Portuguese and Spanish national ideal. The desire to Christianize Muslims and pagan peoples played a central role in European expansion. Queen Isabella of Spain, for example, showed a fanatical zeal for converting the Muslims to Christianity, but she concentrated her efforts on the Arabs in Granada. After the abortive crusading attempts of the thirteenth century, Isabella and other rulers realized full well that they lacked the material resources to mount the full-scale assault on Islam necessary for victory. Crusading impulses thus shifted from the Muslims to the pagan peoples of Africa and the Americas.

Government sponsorship and encouragement of exploration also help to account for the results of the various voyages. Mariners and explorers could not afford, as private individuals, the massive sums needed to explore mysterious oceans and to control remote continents. The strong financial support of Prince Henry the Navigator led to Portugal's phenomenal success in the spice trade. Even the grudging and modest assistance of Isabella and Ferdinand eventually brought untold riches – and complicated problems – to Spain. The Dutch in the seventeenth century, through such government-sponsored trading companies as the Dutch East India Company, reaped enormous wealth, and although the Netherlands was a small country in size, it dominated the European economy in 1650. In England, by contrast, Henry VII's lack of interest in exploration delayed English expansion for a century.

Scholars have frequently described the European discoveries as a manifestation of Renaissance curiosity about the physical universe, the desire to know more about the geography and peoples of the world. There is truth to this explanation. Cosmography, natural history, and geography aroused enormous interest among educated people in the fifteenth and sixteenth centuries. Just as science fiction and speculation about life on other planets excite readers today, quasi-scientific literature about Africa, Asia, and the Americas captured the imaginations of literate Europeans. Oviedo's *General History of the Indies,* a detailed eyewitness account of plants, animals, and peoples, was widely read.

Spices were another important incentive to undertake voyages of discovery. Introduced into western Europe by the Crusaders in the twelfth century, nutmeg, mace, ginger, cinnamon, and pepper added flavor and variety to the monotonous diet of Europeans. Spices were also used in the preparation of medicinal drugs and in the manufacture of incense for religious ceremonies. In the late thirteenth century, the Venetian Marco Polo (1254?–1324?), the greatest of the medieval travelers, had visited the court of the Chinese emperor. The widely publicized account of his travels in the *Book of Various Experiences* stimulated a rich trade in spices between Asia and Italy. The Venetians came to hold a monopoly of the spice trade in western Europe.

Spices were grown in India and China, shipped across the Indian Ocean to ports on the Persian Gulf, and then transported by Arabs across the Arabian Desert to Mediterranean ports. But the rise of the Ming dynasty in China in the late fourteenth century resulted in the expulsion of foreigners. And the steady penetration of the Ottoman Turks into the eastern Mediterranean and of hostile Muslims across North Africa forced Europeans to seek a new route to the Asian spice markets.

The basic reason for European exploration and expansion, however, was the quest for material profit. Mariners and explorers frankly admitted this. As Bartholomew Diaz put it, his motives were "to serve God and His Majesty, to give light to those who were in darkness and to grow rich as all men desire to do." When Vasco da Gama reached the port of Calicut, India, in 1498, a native asked what the Portuguese wanted. Da Gama replied, "Christians and spices."[5] The bluntest of the Spanish conquistadors, Hernando Cortez, announced as he prepared to conquer Mexico, "I have come to win gold, not to plow the fields like a peasant."[6]

Spanish and Portuguese explorers carried the fervent Catholicism and missionary zeal of the Iberian Peninsula to the New World, and once in America they urged home governments to send clerics "to bring light to those who were in darkness." At bottom, however, wealth was the driving motivation. A sixteenth-century diplomat, Ogier Gheselin de Busbecq, summed up this paradoxical attitude well: in expeditions to the Indies and the Antipodes, he said, "religion supplies the pretext and gold the motive."[7] The mariners, explorers, and conquistadors were religious and "medieval" in justifying their actions, materialistic and "modern" in their behavior.

## POLITICS, RELIGION, AND WAR

In 1559, France and Spain signed the Treaty of Cateau-Cambrésis, which ended the long conflict known as the Habsburg-Valois wars. This event marks a decisive watershed in early modern European history. Spain was the victor. France, exhausted by the struggle, had to acknowledge Spanish dominance in Italy, where much of the war had been fought. Spanish governors ruled in Sicily, Naples, and Milan, and Spanish influence was strong in the Papal States and Tuscany.

The emperor Charles V had divided his attention between the Holy Roman Empire and Spain. Under his son Philip II (1556–1598), however, the center of the Habsburg empire and the political center of gravity for all of Europe shifted westward to Spain. Before 1559, Spain and France had fought bitterly for control of Italy; after 1559, the two Catholic powers aimed their guns at Protestantism. The Treaty of Cateau-Cambrésis ended an era of dynastic wars and initiated a period of conflicts in which religion played a dominant role.

Because a variety of issues were stewing, it is not easy to generalize about the wars of the late sixteenth century. Some were continuations of struggles between the centralizing goals of monarchies and the feudal reactions of nobilities. Some were crusading battles between Catholics and Protestants. Some were struggles for national independence or for international expansion.

These wars differed considerably from earlier wars. Sixteenth- and seventeenth-century armies were bigger than medieval ones; some forces numbered as many as fifty thousand men. Because large armies were expensive, governments had to reorganize their administrations to finance them. The use of gunpowder altered both the nature of war and popular attitudes toward it. Guns and cannon killed and wounded from a distance, indiscriminately. Writers scorned gunpowder as a coward's weapon that allowed a common soldier to kill a gentleman. The Italian poet Ariosto lamented:

*Through thee is martial glory lost, through*
*Thee the trade of arms becomes a worthless art:*
*And at such ebb are worth and chivalry that*
*The base often plays the better part.*[8]

Gunpowder destroyed the notion, common during the Hundred Years' War, that warfare was an ennobling experience. Governments had to utilize propaganda, pulpits, and the printing press to arouse public opinion to support war.[9]

Late-sixteenth-century conflicts fundamentally tested the medieval ideal of a unified Christian society governed by one political ruler, the emperor, to whom all rulers were theoretically subordinate, and one church, to which all people belonged. The Protestant Reformation had killed this ideal, but few people recognized it as dead. Catholics continued to believe that Calvinists and Lutherans could be reconverted; Protestants persisted in thinking that the Roman church should be destroyed. Catholics and Protestants alike feared people of the other faith living in their midst. The settlement finally achieved in 1648, known as the Peace of Westphalia, signaled the end of the medieval ideal.

## THE ORIGINS OF DIFFICULTIES IN FRANCE (1515–1559)

In the first half of the sixteenth century, France continued the recovery begun under Louis XI (page 457). The population losses caused by the plague and the disorders accompanying the Hundred Years' War had created such a labor shortage that serfdom virtually disappeared. Cash rents replaced feudal rents and servile obligations. This development clearly benefited the peasantry. Meanwhile, the declining buying power of money hurt the nobility. The steadily increasing French population brought new lands under cultivation, but the division of property among sons meant that most peasant holdings were very small. Domestic and foreign trade picked up; mercantile centers such as Rouen and Lyons expanded; and in 1517 a new port city was founded at Le Havre.

*ROSSO AND PRIMATICCIO: THE GALLERY OF FRANCES I  Flat paintings alternating with rich sculpture provide a rhythm that directs the eye down the long gallery at Fontainebleau, the construction of which occupied much of Francis I's attention from 1530 to 1540. He sought to re-create in France the elegant Renaissance lifestyle he had discovered in Italy. (Giraudon)*

The charming and cultivated Francis I (1515–1547) and his athletic, emotional son Henry II (1547–1559) governed through a small, efficient council. Great nobles held titular authority in the provinces as governors, but Paris-appointed officials, the baillis and seneschals, continued to exercise actual fiscal and judicial responsibility (pages 353–354). In 1539, Francis issued an ordinance that placed all France under the jurisdiction of the royal law courts and made French the language of those courts. This act had a powerful centralizing impact. The taille, a tax on land, provided such strength as the monarchy had and supported a strong standing army. Unfortunately, the tax base was too narrow for France's extravagant promotion of the arts and ambitious foreign policy.

Deliberately imitating the Italian Renaissance princes, the Valois monarchs lavished money on a magnificent court and vast building program, and on Italian artists. Francis I commissioned the Paris architect Pierre Lescot to rebuild the palace of the Louvre. Francis secured the services of Michelangelo's star pupil, Il Rosso, who decorated the wing of the Fontainebleau chateau, subsequently called the Gallery Francis I, with rich scenes of classical and mythological literature. After acquiring Leonardo da Vinci's Mona Lisa, Francis brought Leonardo himself to France, where he soon died. Henry II built a castle at Dreux for his mistress, Diana de Poitiers, and a palace in Paris, the Tuileries, for his wife, Catherine de' Medici. Art historians credit

Francis I and Henry II with importing Italian Renaissance art and architecture to France. Whatever praise these monarchs deserve for their cultural achievement, they spent far more than they could afford.

The Habsburg-Valois wars, waged intermittently through the first half of the sixteenth century, also cost more than the government could afford. Financing the war posed problems. In addition to the time-honored practices of increasing taxes and heavy borrowing, Francis I tried two new devices to raise revenue: the sale of public offices and a treaty with the papacy. The former proved to be only a temporary source of money. The offices sold tended to become hereditary within a family, and once a man bought an office he and his heirs were tax-exempt. The sale of public offices thus created a tax-exempt class called the nobility of the robe, which held positions beyond the jurisdiction of the Crown.

The treaty with the papacy was the Concordat of Bologna (page 457), in which Francis agreed to recognize the supremacy of the papacy over a universal council. In return, the French crown gained the right to appoint all French bishops and abbots. This understanding gave the monarchy a rich supplement of money and offices and a power over the church that lasted until the Revolution of 1789. The Concordat of Bologna helps to explain why France did not later become Protestant: it in effect established Catholicism as the national religion. Because they possessed control over appointments and had a vested financial interest in Catholicism, French rulers had no need to revolt from Rome.

However, the Concordat of Bologna perpetuated disorders within the French church. Ecclesiastical offices were used primarily to pay and reward civil servants. Churchmen in France, as elsewhere, were promoted to the hierarchy not for any special spiritual qualifications but because of their services to the state. Such bishops were unlikely to work to elevate the intellectual and moral standards of the parish clergy. Few of the many priests in France devoted scrupulous attention to the needs of their parishioners. The teachings of Luther and Calvin, as the presses disseminated them, found a receptive audience.

Luther's tracts first appeared in France in 1518, and his ideas attracted some attention. After the publication of Calvin's *Institutes* in 1536, sizable numbers of French people were attracted to the "reformed religion," as Calvinism was called. Because Calvin wrote in French, rather than Latin, his ideas gained wide circulation. Initially, Calvinism drew converts from among reform-minded members of the Catholic clergy, the industrious middle classes, and from artisan groups. Most Calvinists lived in major cities, such as Paris, Lyons, Meaux, and Grenoble.

In spite of condemnation by the universities, government bans, and massive burnings at the stake, the numbers of Protestants grew steadily. When Henry II died in 1559, there were 40 well-organized and 2,150 mission churches in France. Perhaps one-sixth of the population had become Calvinist.

## RELIGIOUS RIOTS AND CIVIL WAR IN FRANCE (1559–1589)

For thirty years, from 1559 to 1589, violence and civil war divided and shattered France. The feebleness of the monarchy was the seed from which the weeds of civil violence germinated. The three weak sons of Henry II who occupied the throne could not provide the necessary leadership. Francis II (1559–1560) died after seventeen months. Charles IX (1560–1574) succeeded at the age of ten and was thoroughly dominated by his opportunis-

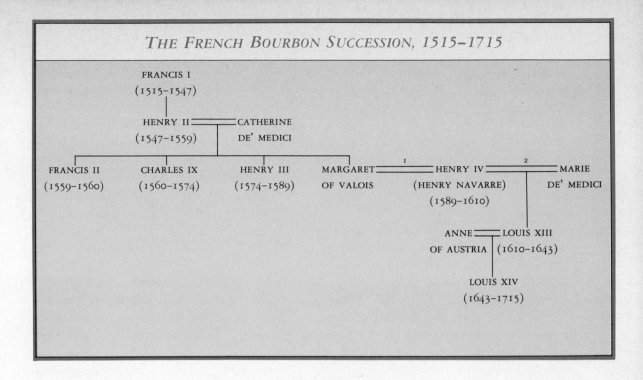

## THE FRENCH BOURBON SUCCESSION, 1515–1715

```
                        FRANCIS I
                       (1515–1547)

                    HENRY II ════════ CATHERINE
                   (1547–1559)         DE' MEDICI

   FRANCIS II      CHARLES IX      HENRY III     MARGARET ═══1═══ HENRY IV ═══2═══ MARIE
  (1559–1560)     (1560–1574)    (1574–1589)    OF VALOIS       (HENRY NAVARRE)    DE' MEDICI
                                                                 (1589–1610)

                                                          ANNE ════ LOUIS XIII
                                                        OF AUSTRIA  (1610–1643)

                                                             LOUIS XIV
                                                            (1643–1715)
```

tic mother, Catherine de' Medici, who would support any party or position to maintain her influence. The intelligent and cultivated Henry III (1574–1589) divided his attention between debaucheries with his male lovers and frantic acts of repentance.

The French nobility took advantage of this monarchial weakness. In the second half of the sixteenth century, between two-fifths and half of the nobility at one time or another became Calvinist. Just as German princes in the Holy Roman Empire had adopted Lutheranism as a means of opposition to the emperor Charles V, so French nobles frequently adopted the "reformed religion" as a religious cloak for their independence. No one believed that peoples of different faiths could coexist peacefully within the same territory. The Reformation thus led to a resurgence of feudal disorder. Armed clashes between Catholic royalist lords and Calvinist antimonarchial lords occurred in many parts of France.

Among the upper classes the Catholic-Calvinist conflict was the surface issue, but the fundamental object of the struggle was power. Working-class crowds composed of skilled craftsmen and the poor wreaked terrible violence on people and property. Both Calvinists and Catholics believed that the others' books, services, and ministers polluted the community. Preachers incited violence, and ceremonies like baptisms, marriages, and funerals triggered it. Protestant pastors encouraged their followers to destroy statues and liturgical objects in Catholic churches. Catholic priests urged their flocks to shed the blood of the Calvinist heretics.

In 1561 in the Paris church of St.-Médard, a Protestant crowd cornered a baker guarding a box containing the consecrated Eucharistic bread. Taunting "Does your God of paste protect you now from the pains of death?"[10] the mob proceeded to kill the poor man. Calvinists believed that the Catholic emphasis on symbols in their ritual desecrated what was truly sacred and promoted the worship of images. In scores of attacks on Catholic churches religious statues were knocked down, stained-glass windows smashed, and sacred vestments, vessels, and Eucharistic elements defiled. In 1561, a Catholic crowd charged a group of just-released Protestant prisoners, killed them, and burned their bodies in the street. Hundreds of Huguenots, as French Calvinists were called, were tortured, had their tongues or throats slit, were maimed or murdered.

In the fourteenth and fifteenth centuries, crowd action – attacks on great nobles and rich prelates – had expressed economic grievances. Religious rioters of the sixteenth century believed that they could assume the power of public magistrates and rid the community of corruption. Municipal officials criticized the crowds' actions, but the participation of pastors and priests in these demonstrations lent riots a sort of legitimacy.[11]

A savage Catholic attack on Calvinists in Paris on August 24, 1572 (Saint Bartholomew's Day) followed the usual pattern. The occasion was a religious ceremony, the marriage of the king's sister Margaret of Valois to the Protestant Henry of Navarre. Among the many Calvinists present for the wedding festivies was the admiral de Coligny, head of one of the great noble families of France and leader of the Huguenot party. Coligny had recently replaced Catherine in influence over the young king Charles IX. When, the night before the wedding, the leader of the Catholic aristocracy, Henry of Guise, had Coligny murdered, rioting and slaughter followed. The Huguenot gentry in Paris were massacred, and religious violence spread to the provinces. Between August 25 and October 3, perhaps twelve thousand Huguenots perished at

Meaux, Lyons, Orléans, and Paris. The contradictory orders of the unstable Charles IX worsened the situation.

The Saint Bartholomew's Day massacre launched the War of the Three Henrys, a civil conflict among factions led by the Catholic Henry of Guise, the Protestant Henry of Navarre, and King Henry III, who succeeded the tubercular Charles IX in 1574. Although he remained Catholic, King Henry realized that the Catholic Guise group represented his greatest danger. The Guises wanted, through an alliance of Catholic nobles called the Holy League, not only to destroy Calvinism but also to replace Henry III as king with a member of the Guise family. Violence continued. France suffered fifteen more years of religious rioting and domestic anarchy. Agriculture in many areas was destroyed; commercial life declined severely; starvation and death haunted the land.

What ultimately saved France was a small group of Catholic moderates called *politiques* who believed that only the restoration of strong monarchy could reverse the trend toward collapse. No religious creed was worth the incessant disorder and destruction. Therefore the *politiques* supported religious toleration. The death of Catherine de' Medici, followed by the assassinations of Henry of Guise and King Henry III, paved the way for the accession of Henry of Navarre, who became Henry IV (1589–1610).

This glamorous prince, "who knew how to fight, to make love and to drink," as a contemporary remarked, wanted above all a strong and united France. He knew too that the majority of the French were Roman Catholics. Declaring "Paris is worth a mass," Henry knelt before the archbishop of Bourges and was received into the Roman Catholic church. Henry's willingness to sacrifice religious principles to political necessity saved France. The Edict of Nantes, which Henry published in 1598, granted to Huguenots liberty of conscience and liberty of worship in certain specified towns, such as La Rochelle. The reign of Henry IV and the Edict of Nantes prepared the way for French absolutism in the seventeenth century by helping to restore internal peace in France.

## THE NETHERLANDS UNDER CHARLES V

In the last quarter of the sixteenth century, the political stability of England, the international prestige of Spain, and the moral influence of the Roman papacy all became mixed up with the religious crisis in the Low Countries. The Netherlands was the pivot around which European money, diplomacy, and war revolved. What began as a movement for the reformation of the church developed into a struggle for Dutch independence.

The emperor Charles V (1519-1556) had inherited the seventeen provinces that compose present-day Belgium and Holland (pages 480-481). Ideally situated for commerce between the Rhine and Scheldt rivers, the great towns of Bruges, Ghent, Brussels, Arras, and Amsterdam made their living by trade and industry. The French-speaking southern towns produced fine linens and woolens, while the wealth of the Dutch-speaking northern cities rested on fishing, shipping, and international banking. The city of Antwerp was the largest port and the greatest money market in Europe. In the cities of the Low Countries trade and commerce had produced a vibrant cosmopolitan atmosphere, which was well personified by the urbane Erasmus of Rotterdam.

Each of the seventeen provinces of the Netherlands possessed historic liberties: each was self-governing and enjoyed the right to make its own laws and collect its own taxes. Only the recognition of a common ruler in the person of the emperor Charles V united the provinces. Delegates from each province met together in the Estates General, but important decisions had to be referred back to each province for approval. In the middle of the sixteenth century, the seventeen provinces had a limited sense of federation.

In the Low Countries as elsewhere, corruption in the Roman church and the critical spirit of the Renaissance provoked pressure for reform. Lutheran tracts and Dutch translations of the Bible flooded the seventeen provinces in the 1520s and 1530s, attracting many people to Protestantism. Charles V's government responded with condemnation and mild repression. This policy was not particularly effective, however, because ideas circulated freely in the cosmopolitan atmosphere of the commercial centers. But Charles's personality checked the spread of Lutheranism. Charles had been born in Ghent and raised in the Netherlands; he was Flemish in language and culture. He identified with the Flemish and they with him.

In 1556, however, Charles V abdicated, dividing his territories between his brother Ferdinand, who received Austria and the Holy Roman Empire, and his son Philip, who inherited Spain, the Low Countries, and the Spanish possessions in America. Charles delivered his abdication speech before the Estates General at Brussels. The emperor was then fifty-five years old, white-haired, and so crippled in the legs that he had to lean for support on the young Prince William of Orange. According to one account:

*His under lip, a Burgundian inheritance, as faithfully transmitted as the duchy and county, was heavy and hanging, the lower jaw protruding so far beyond the upper that it was impossible for him to bring together the few fragments of teeth which still remained, or to speak a whole sentence in an intelligible voice.*[12]

Charles spoke in Flemish. His small, shy, and sepulchral son Philip responded in Spanish; he could speak neither French nor Flemish. The Netherlanders had always felt Charles one of themselves. They were never to forget that Philip was a Spaniard.

## THE REVOLT OF THE NETHERLANDS (1556–1587)

By the 1560s, there was a strong, militant minority of Calvinists in most of the cities of the Netherlands. The seventeen provinces possessed a large middle-class population, and the "reformed religion," as a contemporary remarked, had a powerful appeal "to those who had grown rich by trade and were therefore ready for revolution."[13] Calvinism appealed to the middle classes because of its intellectual seriousness, moral gravity, and emphasis on any form of labor well done. It took deep root among the merchants and financiers in Amsterdam and the northern provinces. Working-class people were also converted, partly because their employers would hire only fellow Calvinists. Well-organized and with the backing of rich merchants, Calvinists quickly gained a wide following. Lutherans taught respect for the powers that be; the "reformed religion," however, tended to encourage opposition to "illegal" civil authorities.

In 1559, Philip II appointed his half-sister Margaret as regent of the Netherlands (1559–1567). A proud, energetic, and strong-willed woman who once had Ignatius Loyola as her confessor, Margaret pushed Philip's orders to wipe out Protestantism. She introduced the Inquisition. Her more immediate problem, however, was revenue to finance the government of the provinces. Charles V had steadily increased taxes in the Low Countries. When Margaret appealed to the Estates General, they claimed that the Low Countries were more heavily taxed than Spain. Nevertheless, Margaret raised taxes. In so doing, she quickly succeeded in uniting the opposition to the government's fiscal policy with the opposition to official repression of Calvinism.

In August 1566, fanatical Calvinists, primarily of the poorest classes, embarked upon a rampage of frightful destruction. As in France, Calvinist destruction in the Low Countries was incited by popular preaching, and attacks were aimed at religious images as symbols of false doctrines, not at people. The Cathedral of Notre Dame at Antwerp was the first target. Begun in 1124 and finished only in 1518, this church stood as a monument to the commercial prosperity of Flanders, the piety of the business classes, and the artistic genius of centuries. On six successive summer evenings, crowds swept through the nave. While the town harlots held tapers to the greatest concentration of art works in northern Europe, people armed with axes and sledgehammers smashed altars, statues, paintings, books, tombs, ecclesiastical vestments, missals, manuscripts, ornaments, stained-glass windows, and sculptures. Before the havoc was over, thirty more churches had been sacked and irreplaceable libraries burned. From Antwerp the destruction spread to Brussels and Ghent and north to the provinces of Holland and Zeeland.

From Madrid, Philip II sent twenty thousand Spanish troops under the duke of Alva to pacify the Low Countries. Alva interpreted

TO PURIFY THE CHURCH  *The destruction of pictures and statues representing biblical events, Christian doctrine, or sacred figures was a central feature of the Protestant Reformation. Here Dutch Protestant soldiers destroy what they consider idols in the belief that they are purifying the church. (Fotomas Index)*

"pacification" to mean the ruthless extermination of religious and political dissidents. On top of the Inquisition he opened his own tribunal, soon called the Council of Blood. On March 3, 1568, fifteen hundred men were executed. Even Margaret was sickened and resigned her regency. Alva resolved the financial crisis by levying a 10 percent sales tax on every transaction, which in a commercial society

caused widespread hardship and confusion.

For ten years, between 1568 and 1578, civil war raged in the Netherlands between Catholics and Protestants and between the seventeen provinces and Spain. A series of Spanish generals could not halt the fighting. In 1576, the seventeen provinces united under the leadership of Prince William of Orange, called "the Silent" because of his remarkable discretion. In 1578, Philip II sent his nephew Alexander Farnese, duke of Parma, to crush the revolt once and for all. A general with a superb sense of timing, an excellent knowledge of the geography of the Low Countries, and a perfect plan, Farnese arrived with an army of German mercenaries. Avoiding pitched battles, he fought by patient sieges. One by one the cities of the south fell — Maastricht, Tournai, Bruges, Ghent, and finally the financial capital of northern Europe, Antwerp. Calvinism was forbidden in these territories, and Protestants were compelled to convert or leave. The collapse of Antwerp marked the farthest extent of Spanish jurisdiction and the political division of the Netherlands.

The ten southern provinces, the Spanish Netherlands (the future Belgium), remained under the control of the Spanish Habsburgs. The seven northern provinces, led by Holland, formed the Union of Utrecht, and in 1581 declared their independence from Spain. Thus was born the United Provinces of the Netherlands (see Map 15.2).

Geography, language and sociopolitical structure differentiated the two countries. The northern provinces were ribboned with sluices and canals and therefore were highly defensible. Several times the Dutch had broken the dikes and flooded the countryside to halt the advancing Farnese. In the southern provinces the Ardennes mountains interrupt the otherwise flat terrain. The Dutch spoken in the north was akin to German, while the Flemish spoken in the south was close to French. In the north the commercial aristocracy possessed the predominant power; in the south the landed nobility had the greater influence. The north was Protestant; the south remained Catholic.

Philip II and Alexander Farnese did not accept this geographical division, and the struggle continued after 1581. The United Provinces repeatedly begged the Protestant Queen Elizabeth of England for assistance.

The crown on the head of Elizabeth I (pages 494-495) did not rest easily. She had steered a moderately Protestant course between the Puritans, who sought the total elimination of Roman Catholic elements in the English church, and the Roman Catholics, who wanted full restoration of the old religion. Elizabeth survived a massive uprising by the Catholic north in 1569-1570. She survived two serious plots against her life. In the 1570s, the presence in England of Mary, Queen of Scots, a Roman Catholic and the legal heir to the English throne, produced a very embarrassing situation. Mary was the rallying point of all opposition to Elizabeth, yet the English sovereign hesitated to set the terrible example of regicide by ordering Mary executed.

Elizabeth faced a grave dilemma. If she responded favorably to Dutch pleas for military support against the Spanish, she would antagonize Philip II. The Spanish king had the steady flow of silver from the Americas at his disposal, and Elizabeth, lacking such treasure, wanted to avoid war. But if she did not help the Protestant Netherlands and they were crushed by Farnese, the likelihood was that the Spanish would invade England.

Three developments forced Elizabeth's hand. First, the wars in the Low Countries — the chief market for English woolens — badly hurt the English economy. When wool was not exported, the Crown lost valuable customs revenues. Second, the murder of William the Silent in July 1584 eliminated not only a great Protestant leader but the chief military check on the Farnese advance. Third, the collapse of Antwerp appeared to signal a

Catholic sweep throughout the Netherlands. The next step, the English feared, would be a Spanish invasion of their island. For these reasons, Elizabeth pumped £250,000 and two thousand troops into the Protestant cause in the Low Countries between 1585 and 1587. Increasingly fearful of the plots of Mary, Queen of Scots, Elizabeth finally signed her death warrant. Mary was beheaded on February 18, 1587. Sometime between March 24 and 30, the news of Mary's death reached Philip II.

## PHILIP II AND THE SPANISH ARMADA

Philip pondered the Dutch and English developments at the Escorial northwest of Madrid. Begun in 1563 and completed under the king's personal supervision in 1584, the Monastery of Saint Lawrence of the Escorial served as a monastery for Jeromite monks, a tomb for the king's Habsburg ancestors, and a royal palace for Philip and his family. The vast buildings resemble a gridiron, the instrument on which Saint Lawrence (d. 258) had supposedly been roasted alive. The royal apartments were in the center of the Italian Renaissance building complex. King Philip's tiny bedchamber possessed a concealed sliding window that opened directly onto the high altar of the monastery church so he could watch the services and pray along with the monks. In this somber atmosphere, surrounded by a community of monks and close to the bones of his ancestors, the Catholic ruler of Spain and of much of the globe passed his days.

Philip of Spain considered himself the international defender of Catholicism and the heir to the medieval imperial power. Hoping to keep England within the Catholic church when his wife Mary Tudor died, Philip had asked Elizabeth to marry him; she had em-

MAP 15.2  THE NETHERLANDS, 1578–1609
*Although small in geographical size, the Netherlands held a strategic position in the religious struggles of the sixteenth century. Why?*

phatically refused. Several popes had urged him to move against England. When Pope Sixtus V (1585–1590) heard of the death of the queen of Scots, he promised to pay Philip 1 million gold ducats the moment Spanish troops landed in England. Alexander Farnese had repeatedly warned that to subdue the Dutch, he would have to conquer England and cut off the source of Dutch support. Philip worried that the vast amounts of South American silver he was pouring into the conquest of the Netherlands seemed to be going down a bottomless pit. Two plans for an expedition were considered. Philip's naval adviser recommended that a fleet of 150 ships sail from Lisbon, attack the English navy in the Channel, and invade England. In Antwerp, Farnese urged Philip to assemble a collection of barges and troops in Flanders to stage a cross-Channel assault. With the "inevitable" support of English Catholics, Spain would achieve a great victory.

Philip compromised. He prepared a vast armada to sail from Lisbon to Flanders, fight off Elizabeth's navy *if* it attacked, rendezvous with Farnese, and escort his barges across the English Channel. The expedition's purpose was to transport the Flemish army.

On May 9, 1588, *la felicissima armada* – "the most fortunate fleet," as it was ironically called in official documents – sailed from Lisbon harbor on the last medieval crusade. The Spanish fleet of 130 vessels carried 123,790 cannon balls and perhaps 30,000 men, every one of whom had confessed his sins and received the Eucharist. An English fleet of about 150 ships met the Spanish in the Channel. It was composed of smaller, faster, more maneuverable ships, many of which had greater firing power. A combination of storms and squalls, spoiled food and rank water, inadequate Spanish ammunition, and, to a lesser extent, English fire ships that caused the Spanish to panic and scatter, gave England the victory. Many Spanish ships went to the bottom of the ocean; perhaps 65 managed to crawl home by way of the North Sea.

The battle in the Channel has frequently been described as one of the decisive battles in the history of the world. In fact, it had mixed consequences. Spain soon rebuilt its navy, and after 1588 the quality of the Spanish fleet improved. The destruction of the Armada did not halt the flow of silver from the New World. More silver reached Spain between 1588 and 1603 than in any other fifteen-year period. The war between England and Spain dragged on for years.

The defeat of the Spanish Armada was decisive, however, in the sense that it prevented Philip II from reimposing unity on western Europe by force. He did not conquer England, and Elizabeth continued her financial and military support of the Dutch. In the Netherlands, however, neither side gained significant territory. The borders of 1581 tended to become permanent. In 1609, Philip III of Spain (1598–1621) agreed to a truce, in effect recognizing the independence of the United Provinces.

## THE THIRTY YEARS' WAR (1618–1648)

While Philip II dreamed of building a second armada and Henry IV began the reconstruction of France, the political-religious situation in central Europe deteriorated. An uneasy truce had prevailed in the Holy Roman Empire since the Peace of Augsburg of 1555 (page 484). The Augsburg settlement, in recognizing the independent power of the German princes, had destroyed the authority of the central government. The Habsburg ruler in Vienna enjoyed the title of emperor but had no power.

According to the Augsburg settlement, the faith of the prince determined the religion of his subjects. Later in the century, though, Catholics grew alarmed because Lutherans, in violation of the Peace of Augsburg, were steadily acquiring north German bishoprics. The spread of Calvinism further confused the issue. The Augsburg settlement had pertained only to Lutheranism and Catholicism, but Calvinists ignored it and converted several princes. Lutherans feared that the Augsburg principles would be totally undermined by

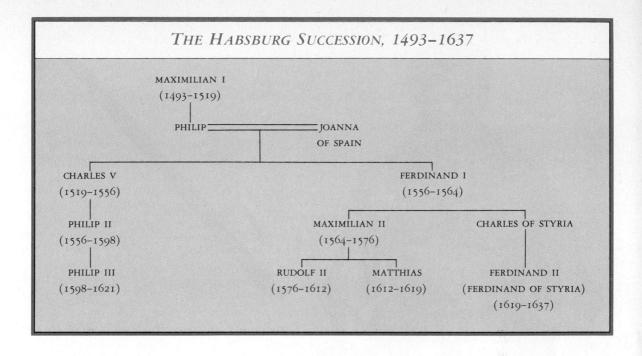

MAXIMILIAN I
(1493–1519)

PHILIP ══════════════ JOANNA
OF SPAIN

CHARLES V                                    FERDINAND I
(1519–1556)                                  (1556–1564)

PHILIP II              MAXIMILIAN II          CHARLES OF STYRIA
(1556–1598)            (1564–1576)

PHILIP III        RUDOLF II      MATTHIAS      FERDINAND II
(1598–1621)       (1576–1612)    (1612–1619)   (FERDINAND OF STYRIA)
                                               (1619–1637)

Catholic and Calvinist gains. Also, the militantly active Jesuits had reconverted several Lutheran princes to Catholicism. In an increasingly tense situation, Lutheran princes formed the Protestant Union (1608) and Catholics retaliated with the Catholic League (1609). Each alliance was determined that the other should make no religious (that is, territorial) advance. The empire was composed of two armed camps.

Dynastic interests were also involved in the German situation. When Charles V abdicated in 1556, he had divided his possessions between his son Philip II and his brother Ferdinand I. This partition began the Austrian and Spanish branches of the Habsburg family. Ferdinand inherited the imperial title and the Habsburg lands in central Europe, including Austria, Bohemia, and Hungary. Ferdinand's

grandson, Matthias, had no direct heirs and promoted the candidacy of his fanatically Catholic cousin, Ferdinand of Styria. The Spanish Habsburgs strongly supported the goals of their Austrian relatives: the unity of the empire and the preservation of Catholicism within it.

In 1617, Ferdinand of Styria secured election as king of Bohemia, a title that gave him jurisdiction over Silesia and Moravia as well as Bohemia. The Bohemians were Czech and German in nationality, and Lutheran, Calvinist, Catholic, and Hussite in religion; all these faiths enjoyed a fair degree of religious freedom. When Ferdinand proceeded to close some Protestant churches, the heavily Protestant Estates of Bohemia protested. On May 23, 1618, Protestants hurled two of Ferdinand's officials from a castle window in

*Sixteenth-Century German Battle Hammer*   *Held in the hand with the leather thong secured around the wrist, a powerful blow from this battle hammer could instantly crush a skull or smash a rib cage. (Photo: Caroline Buckler)*

*Seventeenth-Century Battle Armor*   *Armor remained a symbol of the noble's high social status and military profession, although armor gave much less protection after the invention of gun powder. The maker had a sense of humor. (Photo: Caroline Buckler)*

Prague. They fell seventy feet but survived: Catholics claimed that angels had caught them; Protestants said the officials fell on a heap of soft horse manure. Called "the defenestration of Prague," this event marked the beginning of the Thirty Years' War.

Historians traditionally divide the war into four phases. The first or Bohemian phase (1618-1625) was characterized by civil war in Bohemia between the Catholic League, led by Ferdinand, and the Protestant Union, headed by Prince Frederick of the Palatinate. The Bohemians fought for religious liberty and independence from Habsburg rule. In 1618, the Bohemian Estates deposed Ferdinand and gave the crown of Bohemia to Frederick, thus uniting the interests of German Protestants with those of the international enemies of the Habsburgs. Frederick wore his crown only a few months. In 1620, he was totally defeated by Catholic forces at the battle of the White Mountain. Ferdinand, who had recently been elected Holy Roman emperor as Ferdinand II, followed up his victories by wiping out Protestantism in Bohemia through forcible conversions and the activities of militant Jesuit missionaries. Within ten years, Bohemia was completely Catholic.

The second or Danish phase of the war (1625-1629) – so called because of the participation of King Christian IV of Denmark (1588-1648), the ineffective leader of the Protestant cause – witnessed additional Catholic victories. The Catholic imperial army led by Albert of Wallenstein scored smashing victories. It swept through Silesia, north through Schleswig and Jutland to the Baltic, and east into Pomerania. Wallenstein had made himself indispensable to the emperor Ferdinand, but he was an unscrupulous opportunist who used his vast riches to build an army loyal only to himself. The general seemed interested more in carving out an empire for himself than in aiding the Catholic cause. He quarreled with the Catholic League, and soon the Catholic forces were badly divided. Religion was eclipsed as a basic issue of the war.

The year 1629 marked the peak of Habsburg power. The Jesuits persuaded the emperor to issue the Edict of Restitution, whereby all Catholic properties lost to Protestantism since 1552 were to be restored and only Catholics and Lutherans (*not* Calvinists, Hussites, or other sects) were to be allowed to practice their faiths. Ferdinand appeared to be embarked on a policy to unify the empire. When Wallenstein began ruthless enforcement of the edict, Protestants throughout Europe feared a complete collapse of the balance of power in north central Europe.

The third or Swedish phase of the war (1630-1635) began with the arrival in Germany of the Swedish king Gustavus Adolphus (1594-1632). The ablest administrator of his day and a devout Lutheran, Gustavus Adolphus intervened to support the oppressed Protestants within the empire and to assist his relatives, the exiled dukes of Mecklenburg. Cardinal Richelieu, the chief minister of King Louis XIII of France (1610-1643) subsidized the Swedes, hoping to weaken Habsburg power in Europe. In 1631, with a small but well-disciplined army equipped with superior muskets and warm uniforms, Gustavus Adolphus won a brilliant victory at Breitenfeld. Again in 1632, he was victorious at Lützen, although he was fatally wounded in the battle.

The participation of the Swedes in the Thirty Years' War proved decisive for the future of Protestantism and of later German history. When Gustavus Adolphus landed on German soil, he had already brought Denmark, Poland, Finland, and the smaller Baltic states under Swedish influence. The Swedish victories ended the Habsburg ambition of uniting all the German states under imperial authority.

The death of Gustavus Adolphus, followed by the defeat of the Swedes at the battle of Nördlingen in 1634, prompted the French to enter the war on the side of the Protestants. Thus began the French, or international, phase of the Thirty Years' War (1635–1648). For almost a century French foreign policy had been based on opposition to the Habsburgs, because a weak empire divided into scores of independent principalities enhanced France's international stature. In 1622, when the Dutch had resumed the war against Spain, the French had supported Holland. Now, in 1635, Cardinal Richelieu declared war on Spain and again sent financial and military assistance to the Swedes and the German Protestant princes. The war dragged on. French, Dutch, and Swedes, supported by Scots, Finns, and German mercenaries, burned, looted, and destroyed German agriculture and commerce. The Thirty Years' War lasted so long because neither side had the resources to win a quick, decisive victory. Finally, in October 1648, peace was achieved.

The treaties signed at Münster and Osnabrück, commonly called the Peace of Westphalia, mark a turning point in European political, religious, and social history. The treaties recognized the sovereign independent authority of the German princes. Each ruler could govern his particular territory and make war and peace as well. With power in the hands of more than three hundred princes, with no central government, courts, or means of controlling unruly rulers, the Holy Roman Empire as a real state was effectively destroyed (see Map 15.3).

The independence of the United Provinces of the Netherlands was acknowledged. The

MAP 15.3 EUROPE IN 1648 *Which country emerged from the Thirty Years War as the strongest European power? What dynastic house was that country's major rival in the early modern period?*

international stature of France and Sweden was also greatly improved by the Peace of Westphalia. The political divisions within the empire, the weak German frontiers, and the acquisition of the province of Alsace increased France's size and prestige. The treaties allowed France to intervene at will in German affairs. Sweden received a large cash indemnity and jurisdiction over German territories along the Baltic Sea. The powerful Swedish presence in northeastern Germany subsequently posed a major threat to the future kingdom of Brandenburg-Prussia. The treaties also denied the papacy the right to participate in German religious affairs – a restriction symbolizing the reduced role of the Roman Catholic church in European politics.

In religion the Westphalian treaties stipulated that the Augsburg agreement of 1555 should stand permanently. The sole modification was that Calvinism, along with Catholicism and Lutheranism, would become a legally permissible creed. In practice the north German states remained Protestant, the south German states Catholic. The war settled little. Both sides had wanted peace, and with remarkable illogic they fought for thirty years to get it.

## GERMANY AFTER THE THIRTY YEARS' WAR

The Thirty Years' War was a disaster for the German economy and society, probably the most destructive event in German history before the twentieth century. Population losses were frightful. Perhaps one-third of the urban residents and two-fifths of the inhabitants of

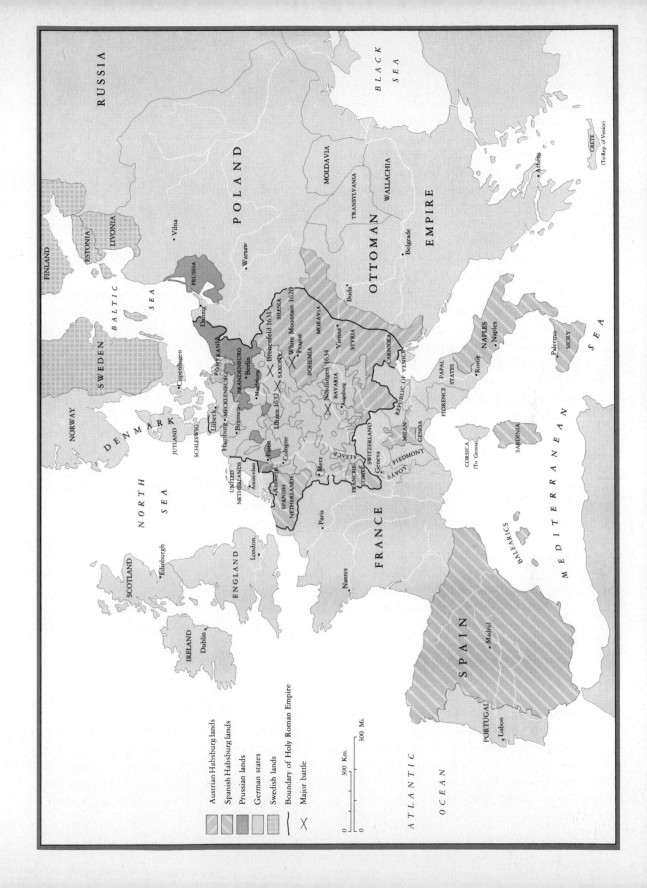

RUSSIA

*BLACK*

*SEA*

FINLAND

ESTONIA

LIVONIA

POLAND

•Vilna

MOLDAVIA

TRANSYLVANIA

WALLACHIA

•Warsaw

OTTOMAN

•Belgrade

EMPIRE

*B A L T I C*

*S E A*

PRUSSIA

•Danzig

SWEDEN

CRETE

(To Rep. of Venice)

•Athens

Breitenfeld 1631

SILESIA

White Mountain 1620

MORAVIA

•Buda

•Copenhagen

POMERANIA

BRANDENBURG

•Berlin

SAXONY

BOHEMIA

•Prague

Vienna•

STYRIA

NORWAY

MECKLENBURG

•Magdeburg

Lützen 1632

Nördlingen 1634

BAVARIA

•Augsburg

CARNIOLA

DENMARK

JUTLAND

SCHLESWIG

•Lübeck

Hamburg•

•Bremen

REPUBLIC OF VENICE

*N O R T H*

*S E A*

UNITED
NETHERLANDS

•Amsterdam

•Essen

Cologne•

SWITZERLAND

•Geneva

MILAN

GENOA

PIEDMONT

SAVOY

FLORENCE

PAPAL
STATES

•Rome

NAPLES

•Naples

•Palermo

SICILY

*M E D I T E R R A N E A N*

*S E A*

SPANISH
NETHERLANDS

•Antwerp

•Metz

ALSACE

FRANCHE-
COMTÉ

•Paris

CORSICA

(To Genoa)

SARDINIA

SCOTLAND

•Edinburgh

ENGLAND

London•

•Nantes

FRANCE

BALEARICS

IRELAND

Dublin•

SPAIN

•Madrid

PORTUGAL

Lisbon•

*A T L A N T I C*

*O C E A N*

Austrian Habsburg lands
Spanish Habsburg lands
Prussian lands
German states
Swedish lands
Boundary of Holy Roman Empire
Major battle

300 Mi.

300 Km.

0

0

rural areas died. Entire areas of Germany were depopulated, partly by military actions, partly by disease – typhus, dysentery, bubonic plague, and syphilis accompanied the movements of armies – and partly by the thousands of refugees who fled to safer areas.

In the late sixteenth and early seventeenth centuries, all Europe experienced an economic crisis primarily caused by the influx of silver from South America. Because the Thirty Years' War was fought on German soil, these economic difficulties were badly aggravated in the empire. Scholars still cannot estimate the value of losses in agricultural land and livestock, in trade and commerce. The trade of southern cities like Augsburg, already hard hit by the shift in transportation routes from the Mediterranean to the Atlantic, was virtually destroyed by the fighting in the south. Meanwhile, towns like Lübeck, Hamburg, and Bremen in the north and Essen in the Ruhr actually prospered because of the many refugees they attracted. The destruction of land and foodstuffs, compounded by the flood of Spanish silver, brought on a severe price rise. During and after the war, inflation was worse in Germany than anywhere else in Europe.

Agricultural areas suffered catastrophically. The population decline caused a rise in the value of the labor, and owners of great estates had to pay more for agricultural workers. Farmers who needed only small amounts of capital to restore their lands started over again. Many small farmers, however, lacked the revenue to rework their holdings and had to become day laborers. Nobles and landlords bought up many small holdings and acquired great estates. In some parts of Germany, especially east of the Elbe in areas like Mecklenburg and Pomerania, peasants' loss of land led to the rise of a new serfdom.[14] Thus the Thirty Years' War contributed to the legal and economic decline of the largest segment of German society.

## THE GREAT EUROPEAN WITCH-HUNT

The period of the religious wars witnessed a startling increase in the phenomenon of witch-hunting, whose prior history was long but sporadic. "A witch," according to Chief Justice Coke of England, "was a person who hath conference with the Devil to consult with him or to do some act." This definition by the highest legal authority in England demonstrates that educated people, as well as the ignorant, believed in witches. Belief in witches – individuals who could mysteriously injure other people, for instance by causing them to become blind or impotent, and who could harm animals, for example by preventing cows from giving milk – dates back to the dawn of time. For centuries tales had circulated about old women who made nocturnal travels on greased broomsticks to "sabbats," or assemblies of witches, where they participated in sexual orgies and feasted on the flesh of infants. In the popular imagination witches had definite characteristics: the vast majority were married women or widows between fifty and seventy years old, crippled or bent with age, with pockmarked skin; they often practiced midwifery or folk medicine, and most had sharp tongues and were quick to scold.

In the sixteenth century religious reformers' extreme notions of the devil's powers, and the insecurity created by the religious wars, contributed to the growth of belief in witches. The idea developed that witches made pacts with the devil in return for the power to work mischief on their enemies. Since pacts with the devil meant the renunciation of God, witchcraft was considered heresy, and all religions persecuted it.

Fear of witches took a terrible toll of innocent lives in parts of Europe. In southwestern Germany 3,229 witches were executed between 1561 and 1670, most by burning. The communities of the Swiss Confederation tried 8,888 persons between 1470 and 1700 and executed 5,417 of them as witches. In all the centuries before 1500 witches in England had been suspected of causing perhaps "three deaths, a broken leg, several destructive storms and some bewitched genitals." Yet between 1559 and 1736 witches were thought to have caused thousands of deaths, and in that period almost 1,000 witches were executed in England.[15]

Historians and anthropologists have offered a variety of explanations for the great European witch-hunt. Some scholars maintain that charges of witchcraft were a means of accounting for inexplicable misfortunes. Just as the English in the fifteenth century had blamed their military failures in France on Joan of Arc's sorcery, so in the seventeenth century the English Royal College of Physicians attributed undiagnosable illnesses to witchcraft. Some scholars hold that in small communities, which typically insisted on strict social conformity, charges of witchcraft were a means of attacking and eliminating the nonconformist; witches, in other words, served the collective need for scapegoats. The evidence of witches' trials, some writers suggest, shows that women were not accused because they harmed or threatened their neighbors; rather, their communities believed such women worshiped the devil, engaged in wild sexual activities with him, and ate infants. Other scholars argue the exact opposite:

that people were tried and executed as witches because their neighbors feared their evil powers. Finally, there is the theory that the unbridled sexuality of which witches were accused was a psychological projection on the part of their accusers, resulting from Christianity's repression of sexuality. The reasons for the persecution of witches probably varied from place to place. Perhaps witches, symbolizing unacceptable ideas or practices, were "victims of society's constant pressure towards intellectual conformity."[16]

## SEXISM, RACISM, AND SKEPTICISM

The age of religious wars revealed extreme and violent contrasts. It was a deeply religious period in which men fought passionately for their beliefs; seventy percent of the books printed dealt with religious subjects. Yet the times saw the beginnings of religious skepticism. Europeans explored new continents, partly with the missionary aim of Christianizing the peoples they encountered. Yet the Spanish, Portuguese, Dutch, and English proceeded to enslave the Indians and blacks they encountered. While Europeans indulged in gross sensuality, the social status of women declined. Sexism, racism, and skepticism had all originated in ancient times. But late in the sixteenth century they began to take on their familiar modern forms.

### THE STATUS OF WOMEN

The decades between 1560 and 1648 witnessed another decline in the status of women in European society. The Reformation did not help women. The early reformers had urged study of the Bible as the means of improving human conduct. Scriptural study, however, tended to revive Saint Paul's notion that women are the source of sin and vice in the world. Also, the violence and upheaval of the religious wars was followed by a period of reaction and retrenchment. While early humanists such as Erasmus and Zwingli had allowed divorce on grounds of insanity and extreme cruelty, by 1600 all faiths firmly opposed divorce on any grounds. In England, for example, only an act of Parliament could dissolve a marriage.

Although private opinions and public laws relating to the social position of women varied widely, the weight of evidence from the sixteenth and seventeenth centuries indicates that women were considered to be decidedly inferior beings. Their social value rested on their ability to produce heirs. A few women, of course, had power and influence. Margaret of Austria, Charles V's aunt, and Louise of Savoy, Francis I's mother – they cannot be identified apart from their male relatives – conducted the diplomatic negotiations that in 1529 led to the Peace of Cambrai and the end of the second phase of the Habsburg-Valois wars. Jeanne d'Albret, the mother of Henry of Navarre (later Henry IV of France), legalized Calvinism in her domain and aided its spread through France; she was known as "the Saint of the Reform." Likewise, Mary Tudor reestablished Catholicism in England. All these women, however, were of royal blood.

The great majority of women were treated either as grown-up children to be teasingly indulged or as hopelessly irrational. The attitude of John Knox, the Calvinist reformer of the Scottish church, was not atypical: "Nature doth paint them forth to be weak, frail, impatient, feeble and foolish, and experience hath declared them to be unconstant, variable, cruel, and void of the spirit of council and regiment." (Knox had in mind the Catholic

*VERONESE: MARS AND VENUS UNITED BY LOVE  Taking a theme from classical mythology, the Venetian painter Veronese celebrates in clothing, architecture, and landscape the luxurious wealth of the aristocracy (painted ca 1580). The lush and curvaceous Venus and the muscular and powerfully built Mars suggest the anticipated pleasures of sexual activity and the frank sensuality of the age. (Metropolitan Museum of Art, New York, Kennedy Fund, 1910)*

Mary, Queen of Scots, whom he had good political reasons for fearing.) In 1595, the professors at Wittenberg University solemnly debated whether or not women are human beings. Humanists repeated the ancient story of woman the temptress and cause of sin in the world.

Artists' drawings of plump, voluptuous women and massive, muscular men reveal the contemporary standards of physical beauty. It was a sensual age that gloried in the delights of the flesh. Some people, such as the humanist-poet Aretino, found sexual satisfaction with both sexes. Reformers and public officials simultaneously condemned and condoned sexual "sins." The oldest profession had many practitioners, and when in 1566 Pope Pius IV expelled all the prostitutes from Rome, so many people left and the city suffered such a loss of revenue that in less than a month the pope was forced to rescind the order. Scholars debated Saint Augustine's notion that whores serve a useful social function by preventing worse sins. Prostitution was common, because desperate poverty forced women and young men into it. The general public took it for granted. Consequently, civil authorities in both Catholic and Protestant countries licensed houses of public prostitution. These establishments were intended for the convenience of single men, and some Protestant cities, such as Geneva and Zurich, installed officials in the brothels with the ex-

*WOMAN IN LABOR   The production of male heirs was women's major social responsibility. Long into modern times a sitting or squatting position for the delivery of babies was common, because it allowed the mother to push. The calm and wistful look on the mother's face suggests a remarkably easy delivery; it is the artist's misconception of the process. (Photo: Caroline Buckler)*

press purpose of preventing married men from patronizing them.

Marriage for all social classes remained a serious business, entered into primarily to advance the economic interests of the parties. There are some remarkable success stories. Elizabeth Hardwick, the orphaned daughter of an obscure English country squire, made four careful marriages, each of which brought her more property and carried her higher up the social ladder. She managed her estates, amounting to more than a hundred thousand acres, with a degree of business sense rare in any age. The two great mansions she built, Chatsworth and Hardwick, stand today as monuments to her acumen. As countess of Shrewsbury, "Bess of Hardwick" so thoroughly enjoyed the trust of Queen Elizabeth that Elizabeth appointed her jailer of Mary, Queen of Scots. Having established several aristocratic dynasties, the countess of Shrewsbury died in 1608, past her eightieth year, one of the richest people in England.[17]

While the Catholic church held up the ideal of celibacy and the religious life as the highest form of Christian life, Protestantism exalted the dignity of marriage. Luther insisted that absolute celibacy was impossible. In the Middle Ages, and later in Catholic countries, the religious life provided a career option for women who did not choose or could not afford to marry. For Protestant women, marriage became the only professional possibility. Protestant marriages took on the form of a contract, whereby each partner promised the other support, understanding, and sharing of material goods. Within marriage many women certainly controlled their own destinies, but there was no question of social or legal equality: wives were subordinate to their husbands.

If some nuns in the later Middle Ages

lacked a religious vocation, and if some religious houses witnessed moral laxness and financial mismanagement, nevertheless convents provided the only scope for the literary, artistic, and administrative talents of unmarried women. In abolishing the religious houses, Protestantism threw out the baby with the bathwater. Marriage became virtually the only occupation for Protestant women, which helps to explain why Anglicans, Calvinists, and Lutherans established communities of religious women in the eighteenth and nineteenth centuries.

Many sixteenth-century reformers, including Luther, Erasmus, and several popes, believed polygamy less of an evil than divorce. (By polygamy they meant a man having several wives at the same time, not a woman having more than one husband.) Theologians found scriptural justification for their position on polygamy. Except among the Anabaptists, however, polygamy was rarely practiced.

If the partners to a monogamous marriage found themselves unsuited, there was virtually no socially acceptable way out. In Catholic countries as well as Protestant ones, a woman could not secure a divorce on grounds of extreme cruelty, desertion, adultery, or complete incompatibility. Women's social and legal position became steadily more confined, and, apart from the upper classes, that position would not change much before the nineteenth century. Death alone dissolved a legitimate marriage. When a spouse died, the great majority of survivors remarried.[18]

### ORIGINS OF NORTH AMERICAN RACISM: THE AFRICAN SLAVE TRADE

The Age of Discovery opened up vast new continents for European exploration and exploitation. Once across the Atlantic, the major problem European settlers faced was a shortage of labor. As early as 1495, the Spanish solved the problem by enslaving the native Indians. In the sixteenth and seventeenth centuries, the Portuguese, the Dutch, and the English followed suit.

Unaccustomed to any form of manual labor, and certainly to panning gold for more than twelve hours a day in the broiling sun, the Indians died "like fish in a bucket," as one Spanish settler reported.[19] In 1515, a Spanish missionary, Bartholomé de Las Casas (1474-1566), who had seen the evils of Indian slavery, urged Emperor Charles V to end Indian slavery in his American dominions. Las Casas recommended the importation of blacks from Africa, both because church law did not strictly forbid black slavery and because blacks could better survive under South American conditions. The emperor agreed, and in 1518 the African slave trade began.

Several European nations participated in the African slave trade. Spain brought the first slaves to Brazil; by 1600, 44,000 were being imported annually. Between 1619 and 1623, the Dutch West India Company, with the full support of the government of the United Provinces, transported 15,430 Africans to Brazil. Only in the late seventeenth century, with the chartering of the Royal African Company, did the English get involved. Thereafter, large numbers of African blacks poured into the North American colonies. In 1790, there were 757,181 Negroes in a total United States population of 3,929,625. When the first census was taken in Brazil in 1798, Negroes numbered about 2 million in a total population of 3.25 million.

Almost all peoples in the world have engaged in slavery at some time in their histories. Since ancient times, victors in battle had enslaved conquered peoples. European slavers found slavery widespread in Africa when they arrived in the sixteenth and seventeenth centuries, and they had no difficulty finding Africans willing to sell their captured tribal enemies for cloth, jewelry, guns and whiskey. In seeking slaves in Africa, Europeans encouraged more slave hunting.

Almost as soon as the institution of black slavery was introduced into the New World, controversy arose about it. Las Casas and others soon became disgusted with the Spanish treatment of blacks, and criticized black slavery on the same grounds as Indian slavery: it was inhumane. By the late seventeenth century, abolitionist movements existed in both South and North America.

European settlers brought to the New World the racial attitudes they had absorbed in Europe. North American attitudes derive basically from England. On the eve of the Age of Discovery, the English were overwhelmingly a rural people. Tough, sober, accustomed to unending hard work relieved by few physical comforts, a quarrelsome but rarely violent people, they accepted life with stoical patience. The age was cruel, and the English were not compassionate. The public execution of criminals and the stoning of wretches tied up in the village stocks were major occasions for public entertainment. When a good workman fell from a ladder and was permanently disabled, his community was more concerned that he would become a public charge than about his misfortune.[20]

Early Christian writers in the fourth and fifth centuries had identified blackness with sin and corruption. This notion had become deep-rooted over the centuries. Thus in 1550, when the first black Africans appeared on the streets of London, the concept of blackness was already loaded with emotional meaning. Black meant "deeply stained with dirt, soiled,

*THE SPANISH IN AMERICA   The Spanish used barbaric methods to frighten and subdue the Indians. Based on the eyewitness accounts of the Spanish missionary Bartholomew de las Casas, illustrations of Spanish cruelties satisfied Europeans' curiosity about the New World, gratified appetites for bizarre tortures, and promoted anti-Spanish and anti-Catholic feelings. (Photo: Caroline Buckler)*

dirty, foul ... malignant, having dark or deadly purposes."[21] White, on the other hand, connoted purity and virginity, goodness and cleanliness. Physical beauty to the English meant an almost alabaster white skin tinged with pink. The Negro's black skin, "disfigured" facial features, and curled hair seemed the exact opposite of the physical ideal.

Art and literature had already given English people some acquaintance with "Ethiopians," as black Africans had been called since Roman times. In the sixteenth and seventeenth centuries, the English were still extremely curious about Africans' lives and customs, and slavers' accounts were extraordinarily popular. Travel literature depicted Africans as savages because of their eating habits, morals, clothing, and social customs; as barbarians because of their language and methods of war; and as heathens because they were not Christian. English people saw similarities between apes and Africans; thus, the terms "bestial" and "beastly" were frequently applied to Africans. Africans were believed to possess a potent sexuality and to be extremely lustful. One seventeenth-century observer considered Africans "very lustful and impudent, .. (for a Negroes hiding his members, their extraordinary greatness) is a token of their lust." African women were considered sexually aggressive and "possessed of a temper hot and lascivious."[22]

The English used the heathenism of the Africans as a justification for enslaving them.

Africans appeared to suit the agricultural needs of the underpopulated continent of North America. Unlike the North American Indians, who were armed, however primitively, and had the psychological support of their tribes, the Africans, stripped of their languages and tribal cultures, were powerless in the New World. Moreover, in spite of the dangers of the trade in Africa and the frightful loss of life among both traders and slaves, the profits in slavery were enormous.

In the seventeenth and eighteenth centuries, English colonists in North America continued to believe in these supposed social characteristics of Africans. Gradually they became part of the American mental furniture. The myths of black savagery, barbarism, and lechery became the classic stereotypes of modern American racial attitudes.

### THE ORIGIN OF MODERN SKEPTICISM: MICHEL DE MONTAIGNE

The decades of religious fanaticism, bringing in their wake death, famine, and civil anarchy, caused both Catholics and Protestants to doubt that any one faith contained absolute truth. The late sixteenth and early seventeenth centuries witnessed the beginnings of modern skepticism. Skepticism is a school of thought founded on doubt that total certainty or definitive knowledge is ever attainable. The skeptic is cautious and critical, and suspends judgment. Perhaps the finest representative of early modern skepticism is the Frenchman Michel de Montaigne (1533-1592).

Montaigne came from a bourgeois family that had made a fortune selling salted herring and in 1477 had purchased the title and property of Montaigne in Gascony. Montaigne received a classical education before studying law and securing a judicial appointment in 1554. Although a member of the nobility, in

embarking on a judicial career he identified with the new nobility of the robe. He condemned the ancient nobility of the sword for being more concerned with war and sports than with the cultivation of the mind.

At the age of thirty-eight, Montaigne resigned his judicial post, retired to his estate, and devoted the rest of his life to study, contemplation, and the effort to understand himself. Like the Greeks, he believed that the object of life was to "know thyself," for self-knowledge teaches men and women how to live in accordance with nature and God. Montaigne developed a new literary genre, the essay – from the French *essayer,* meaning to test or try – to express his thoughts and ideas.

Montaigne's *Essays* provide insight into the mind of a remarkably humane, tolerant, and civilized man. He was a humanist; he loved the Greek and Roman writers and was always eager to learn from them. In his essay "On Solitude," he quoted the Roman poet Horace:

*Reason and sense remove anxiety,*
*Not villas that look out upon the sea*

*Ambition, avarice, irresolution, fear, and lust do not leave us when we change our country.*

*Some said to Socrates that a certain man had grown no better by his travels. "I should think not," he said; "he took himself along with him...."*

*We should have wife, children, goods, and above all health, if we can; but we must not bind ourselves to them so strongly that our happiness depends on them. We must reserve a back shop all our own, entirely free, in which to establish our real liberty and our principal retreat and solitude....*[23]

From the ancient authors, especially the Roman stoic Seneca, Montaigne acquired a sense of calm, inner peace, and patience. The ancient authors also inculcated in him a tolerance and broad-mindedness. Montaigne had grown up during the French civil wars, perhaps the worst kind of war. Religious ideology had set family against family, even brother against brother. He wrote:

*In this controversy . . . France is at present agitated by civil wars, the best and soundest side is undoubtedly that which maintains both the old religion and the old government of the country. However, among the good men who follow that side (for I speak not of those who use it as a pretext either to wreak their private vengeances, or to supply their avarice, or to pursue the favor of princes; but of those who follow it out of true zeal toward their religion and a holy concern for maintaining the peace and the status of their fatherland) — of these, I say, we see many whom passion drives outside the bounds of reason, and makes them sometimes adopt unjust, violent, and even reckless courses. . . .*[24]

Although he remained a Catholic, Montaigne possessed a detachment, an independence, an openness of mind, and a willingness to look at all sides of a question. As he wrote, "I listen with attention to the judgment of all men; but so far as I can remember, I have followed none but my own. Though I set little value upon my own opinion, I set no more on the opinions of others."

In a violent and cruel age, Montaigne was a gentle and sensitive man. In his famous essay "On Cruelty," he said:

*Among other vices, I cruelly hate cruelty, both by nature and by judgment, as the extreme of all vices. . . .*

*I live in a time when we abound in incredible examples of this vice, through the license of our civil wars; and we see in the ancient histories nothing more extreme than what we experience of*

*this every day. But that has not reconciled me to it at all.*[25]

In the book-lined tower where Montaigne passed his days, he became a deeply learned man. Yet he was not ignorant of the world of affairs, and he criticized scholars and bookworms who ignored the life around them. Montaigne's essay "On Cannibals" reflects the impact of overseas discoveries on Europeans' consciousness. His tolerant mind rejected the notion that one culture is superior to another:

*I long had a man in my house that lived ten or twelve years in the New World, discovered in these latter days, and in that part of it where Villegaignon landed [Brazil]. . . .*

*I find that there is nothing barbarous and savage in [that] nation, by anything that I can gather, excepting, that every one gives the title of barbarism to everything that is not in use in his own country. As, indeed, we have no other level of truth and reason, than the example and idea of the opinions and customs of the place wherein we live: there is always the perfect religion, there is perfect government, there the most exact and accomplished usage of all things. . . .*[26]

In his belief in the nobility of human beings in the state of nature, uncorrupted by organized society, and in his cosmopolitan attitude toward different civilizations, Montaigne anticipated many eighteenth-century thinkers.

The thought of Michel de Montaigne marks a sharp break with the past. Faith and religious certainty had characterized the intellectual attitudes of Western society for a millennium. Montaigne's rejection of any kind of dogmatism, his secularism, and his skepticism thus represent a basic change. In his own time, and throughout the seventeenth century, few would have agreed with him. The publication of his ideas, however, anticipated a basic shift in attitudes. Montaigne inaugurated an era of doubt. "Wonder," he said, "is the foundation of all philosophy, research is the means of all learning, and ignorance is the end."[27]

## ELIZABETHAN AND JACOBEAN LITERATURE

The age of the religious wars and European expansion also experienced an extraordinary degree of intellectual ferment. In addition to the development of the essay as a distinct literary genre, the late sixteenth and early seventeenth centuries fostered remarkable creativity in other branches of literature. England, especially, in the latter part of Elizabeth's reign and the first years of her successor James I (1603–1625), witnessed unparalleled brilliance. The terms *Elizabethan* and *Jacobean* (referring to the reign of James) are used to designate the English music, poetry, prose, and drama of this period. The poetry of Sir Philip Sidney (1554–1586), such as *Astrophel and Stella,* strongly influenced later poetic writing. *The Faerie Queene* of Edmund Spenser (1552–1599) endures as one of the greatest moral epics in any language. The rare poetic beauty of the plays of Christopher Marlowe (1564–1593), such as *Tamburlaine* and *The Jew of Malta,* paved the way for the work of Shakespeare. Above all, the immortal dramas of Shakespeare and the stately prose of the Authorized or King James Bible mark the Elizabethan and Jacobean periods as the golden age of English literature.

William Shakespeare (1564–1616), the son of a successful glove manufacturer who rose to the highest municipal office in the Warwickshire town of Stratford-on-Avon, chose a career on the London stage. By 1592 he had gained recognition as an actor and playwright.

Between 1599 and 1603 Shakespeare performed in the Lord Chamberlain's Company and became co-owner of the Globe Theater, which after 1603 presented his plays.

Shakespeare's genius lies in the originality of his characterizations, the diversity of his plots, his understanding of human psychology, and his unexcelled gift for language. Shakespeare was a Renaissance man in his deep appreciation for classical culture, individualism, and humanism. Such plays as *Julius Caesar, Pericles,* and *Antony and Cleopatra* deal with classical subjects and figures. Several of his comedies have Italian Renaissance settings. The nine history plays, including *Richard II, Richard III,* and *Henry IV,* enjoyed the greatest popularity among Shakespeare's contemporaries. Written during the decade after the defeat of the Spanish Armada, the history plays express English national consciousness; lines such as these from *Richard II* reflect this sense of national greatness with unparalleled eloquence:

*This royal Throne of Kings, this scepter'd Isle,*
*This earth of Majesty, this seat of Mars,*
*This other Eden, demi-paradise,*
*This fortress built by Nature for herself,*
*Against infection and the hand of war:*
*This happy breed of men, this little world,*
*This precious stone, set in the silver sea,*
*Which serves it in the office of a wall,*
*Or as a moat defensive to a house,*
*Against the envy of less happier Lands,*
*This blessed plot, this earth, this Realm, this*
    *England. . .*

Shakespeare's later plays, above all the tragedies *Hamlet, Othello,* and *Macbeth,* explore an enormous range of human problems and are capable of an almost infinite variety of interpretations. *Othello,* which the nineteenth-century historian Thomas Macaulay called "perhaps the greatest work in the world,"

*A* ROYAL PICNIC   *The English court imitated the Italian Renaissance devotion to nature. (See Bellini's* Feast of the Gods — *in first color section.) In this pastoral atmosphere suggestive of classical mythology, Queen Elizabeth interrupts the day's hunt for a picnic in the forest. The meal seems to consist of fowl, bread, wine, and perhaps pastries. (The Huntington Library, San Marino, California)*

portrays an honorable man destroyed by a flaw in his own character and the satanic evil of his supposed friend Iago. *Macbeth's* central theme is exorbitant ambition. Shakespeare analyzes the psychology of sin in the figures of Macbeth and Lady Macbeth whose mutual love under the pressure of ambition leads to their destruction. The central figure in *Hamlet,* a play suffused with individuality, wrestles with moral problems connected with revenge and with man's relationship to life and death. The soliloquy in which Hamlet debates suicide is perhaps the most widely quoted passage in English literature:

*To be, or not to be: that is the question:*
*Whether 'tis nobler in the mind to suffer*
*The slings and arrows of outrageous fortune,*
*Or to take arms against a sea of troubles,*
*And by opposing end them? To die: to sleep;*
*No more; and by a sleep to say we end*
*The heart-ache and the thousand natural shocks*
*That flesh is heir to, 'tis a consummation*
*Devoutly to be wish'd.*

Hamlet's sad cry, "There is nothing either good or bad but thinking makes it so," expresses the anguish and uncertainty of modern man. *Hamlet* has always enjoyed great popularity, because in his many-faceted personality people have seen an aspect of themselves.

Shakespeare's dynamic language bespeaks his extreme sensitivity to the sounds and meanings of words. Perhaps no phrase better summarizes the reason for his immortality than this line, slightly modified, from *Antony and Cleopatra:* "Age cannot wither [him], nor custom stale/[his] infinite variety."

The other great masterpiece of the Jacobean period was the *Authorized Bible.* At a theological conference in 1604, a group of Puritans urged James I to support a new translation of the Bible. The king in turn assigned the task to a committee of scholars, who published their efforts in 1611. Based on the best scriptural research of the time and divided into chapters and verses, the Authorized Version is actually a revision of earlier Bibles more than an original work. Yet it provides a superb expression of the mature English vernacular in the early seventeenth century. Thus, Psalm 37:

*Fret not thy selfe because of evill doers, neither bee thou envious against the workers of iniquitie.*
*For they shall soone be cut downe like the grasse; and wither as the greene herbe.*
*Trust in the Lord, and do good, so shalt thou dwell in the land, and verely thou shalt be fed.*
*Delight thy selfe also in the Lord; and he shall give thee the desires of thine heart.*
*Commit thy way unto the Lord: trust also in him, and he shall bring it to passe.*
*And he shall bring forth thy righteousness as the light, and thy judgement as the noone day.*

The Authorized Version, so-called because it was produced under royal sponsorship – it had no official ecclesiastical endorsement – represented the Anglican and Puritan desire to encourage lay people to read the Scriptures. It quickly achieved great popularity and displaced all earlier versions. British settlers carried this Bible to the North American colonies, where it became known as the *King*

*James Bible.* For centuries the *King James Bible* has had a profound influence on the language and lives of English-speaking peoples.

———◆———

In the sixteenth and seventeenth centuries, Europeans explored and for the first time gained access to large parts of the globe. European peoples had the intellectual curiosity, the driving ambition, and the scientific technology to attempt feats that were as difficult and expensive then as is going to the moon in our own time. Exploration and exploitation contributed to a more sophisticated standard of living, in the form of spices and Asian luxury goods, and to a terrible international inflation resulting from the influx of South American silver and gold. Governments, the upper classes, and the peasantry were badly hurt by the inflation. Meanwhile the middle class of bankers, shippers, financiers, and manufacturers prospered for much of the seventeenth century.

European expansion and colonization took place against a background of religious conflict and budding national consciousness. The seventeenth century was by no means a secular period. Although the medieval religious framework had broken down, people still thought largely in religious terms. Europeans explained what they did politically and economically in terms of religious doctrine. Religious ideology served as a justification for a variety of goals: the French nobles' opposition to the Crown, the Dutch struggle for political and economic independence from Spain. In Germany religious pluralism and foreign ambitions added to political difficulties. After 1648, the divisions between Protestant and Catholic tended to become permanent. Religious skepticism and racial attitudes were harbingers of developments to come.

## NOTES

1. Quoted by C. M. Cipolla, *Guns, Sails, and Empires: Technological Innovation and the Early Phases of European Expansion, 1400-1700,* Minerva Press, New York, 1965, pp. 115-116.

2. Quoted by S. E. Morison, *Admiral of the Ocean Sea: A Life of Christopher Columbus,* Little, Brown, Boston, 1946, p. 154.

3. Cipolla, pp. 90-131.

4. J. H. Parry, *The Age of Reconnaissance,* Mentor Books, New York, 1963, chaps. 3 and 5.

5. Quoted by Cipolla, p. 132.

6. Quoted by F. H. Littell, *The Macmillan Atlas History of Christianity,* Macmillan, New York, 1976, p. 75.

7. Quoted by Cipolla, p. 133.

8. Quoted by J. Hale, "War and Public Opinion in the Fifteenth and Sixteenth Centuries," *Past and Present* 22 (July 1962):29.

9. See ibid., pp. 18-32.

10. Quoted by N. Z. Davis, "The Rites of Violence: Religious Riot in Sixteenth Century France," *Past and Present* 59 (May 1973):59.

11. See ibid., pp. 51-91.

12. Quoted by J. L. Motley, *The Rise of the Dutch Republic,* David McKay, Philadelphia, 1898, 1.109.

13. Quoted by P. Smith, *The Age of the Reformation,* Henry Holt, New York, 1951, p. 248.

14. H. Kamen, "The Economic and Social Consequences of the Thirty Years' War," *Past and Present* 39 (April 1968):44-61.

15. Norman Cohn, *Europe's Inner Demons: An Enquiry Inspired by the Great Witch-Hunt,* Basic Books, New York, 1975, pp. 253-254; Keith Thomas, *Religion and the Decline of Magic,* Charles Scribner's Sons, New York, 1971, pp. 450-455.

16. See Keith Thomas, op. cit., pp. 435-446; Cohn, op. cit., pp. 258-263.

17. See D. Durant, *Bess of Hardwick: Portrait of an Elizabethan Dynast,* Weidenfeld & Nicolson, London, 1977.

18. S. M. Wyntjes, "Women in the Reformation Era," in *Becoming Visible: Women in European History,* ed. R. Bridenthal and C. Koonz, Houghton Mifflin, Boston, 1977, p. 187.

19. Quoted by D. P. Mannix, *Black Cargoes: A History of the Atlantic Slave Trade,* Viking, New York, 1968, p. 5.

20. W. Notestein, *The English People on the Eve of Colonization,* Harper & Brothers, New York, 1954, p. 14.

21. Quoted by W. D. Jordan, *The White Man's Burden: Historical Origins of Racism in the United States,* Oxford University Press, New York, 1974, p. 6.

22. Ibid., p. 19.

23. Quoted by D. M. Frame, trans., *The Complete Works of Montaigne,* Stanford University Press, Stanford, Calif., 1958, pp. 175-176.

24. Ibid., p. 177.

25. Ibid., p. 306.

26. Quoted by C. Cotton, trans., *The Essays of Michel de Montaigne,* A. L. Burt, New York, 1893, pp. 207, 210.

27. Ibid., p. 523.

## SUGGESTED READING

Perhaps the best starting point for the study of European society in the age of exploration is J. H. Parry, *The Age of Reconnaissance* (1963), which treats the causes and consequences of the voyages of discovery. Parry's splendidly illustrated *The Discovery of South America* (1979) examines Europeans' reactions to the maritime discoveries and treats the entire concept of new *discoveries.* The urbane studies of C. M. Cipolla present fascinating material on technological and sociological developments written in a lucid style: *Guns, Sails, and Empires: Technological Innovation and the Early Phases of European Expansion, 1400-1700* (1965); *Clocks and Culture, 1300-1700* (1967); *Cristofano and the Plague: A Study in the History of Public Health in the Age of* *Galileo* (1973); and *Public Health and the Medical Profession in the Renaissance* (1976). S. E. Morison, *Admiral of the Ocean Sea: A Life of Christopher Columbus* (1946), is the standard biography of the great discoverer.

For the religious wars, in addition to the references in the Suggested Reading for Chapter 14 and in the Notes to this chapter, see J. H. M. Salmon, *Society in Crisis: France in the Sixteenth Century* (1975), which traces the fate of French institutions during the civil wars. A. N. Galpern, *The Religions of the People in Sixteenth-Century Champagne* (1976), is a useful case study in religious anthropology, and William A. Christian, Jr., *Local Religion in Sixteenth Century Spain* (1981) traces the attitudes and practices of ordinary people.

A beautifully illustrated introduction to Holland is K. H. D. Kaley, *The Dutch in the Seventeenth Century* (1972). The best comprehensive treatment of the religious strife and civil wars in the Low Countries remains that of J. L. Motley, *The Rise of the Dutch Republic,* 3 vols. (1898). The student who reads French will find a wealth of material in H. Hauser, *La prépondérance espagnole, 1559-1660* (1948).

Of the many biographies of Elizabeth of England, Wallace T. MacCaffrey, *Queen Elizabeth and the Making of Policy, 1572-1588* (1981), examines the problems posed by the Reformation and how Elizabeth solved them. J. E. Neale, *Queen Elizabeth I* (1957), remains valuable, and L. B. Smith, *The Elizabethan Epic* (1966), is a splendid evocation of the age of Shakespeare with Elizabeth at the center.

Nineteenth- and early twentieth-century historians described the defeat of the Spanish Armada as a great victory for Protestantism, democracy, and capitalism, which those scholars tended to link together. Recent historians have treated the event in terms of its contemporary significance. G. Mattingly, *The Armada* (1959), combines superb readability with the highest scholarly standards: this is history at its best. M. Lewis, *The Spanish Armada* (1972), tells a good story from the English perspective; David Howarth, *The Voyage of the Armada: the Spanish Story* (1981), presents the other side in an exciting narrative. C. V. Wedgwood, *The*

*Thirty Years' War* (1961), must be qualified in light of recent research on the social and economic effects of the war, but it is still a good (if detailed) starting point on a difficult period. A variety of opinions on the causes and results of the war are given in T. K. Rabb's anthology, *The Thirty Years' War* (1981). The following articles, all of which appear in the scholarly journal *Past and Present,* provide some of the latest important findings: H. Kamen, "The Economic and Social Consequences of the Thirty Years' War," no. 39 (1968); J. Hale, "War and Public Opinion in the Fifteenth and Sixteenth Centuries," no. 22 (1962); J. V. Polišenský, "The Thirty Years' War and the Crises and Revolutions of Sixteenth Century Europe," no. 39 (1968); and for the overall significance of Sweden, M. Roberts, "Queen Christina and the General Crisis of the Seventeenth Century," no. 22 (1962).

As background to the intellectual changes instigated by the Reformation, D. C. Wilcox, ed., *In Search of God and Self: Renaissance and Reformation Thought* (1975), contains perceptive articles, and T. Ashton, ed., *Crisis in Europe, 1560–1660* (1967), is fundamental. On witches and witchcraft, see, in addition to the titles by Norman Cohn and Keith Thomas in the Notes, Jeffrey B. Russell, *Witchcraft in the Middle Ages* (1976); Montague Summers, *The History of Witchcraft and Demonology* (1973); and H. R. Trevor-Roper, *The European Witch-Craze of the Sixteenth and Seventeenth Centuries* (1967), a brilliant collection of essays. Among the fascinating studies on North American racism, the interested student should consult W. D. Jordan, *The White Man's Burden: Historical Origins of Racism in the United States* (1974), and D. P. Mannix in collaboration with M. Cowley, *Black Cargoes: A History of the Atlantic Slave Trade* (1968), a hideously fascinating account. South American conditions may be contrasted in C. R. Boxer, *Four Centuries of Portuguese Expansion* (1969). The leading authority on Montaigne is D. M. Frame. See his *Montaigne's Discovery of Man* (1955), and his translation, *The Complete Works of Montaigne* (1958).

# CHAPTER 16

# ABSOLUTISM AND CONSTITUTIONALISM IN WESTERN EUROPE (CA 1589–1715)

THE SEVENTEENTH CENTURY was a period of revolutionary transformation. Some of its most profound developments were political: the seventeenth century has been called the century when government became modern. The sixteenth century had witnessed the emergence of the nation-state. The long series of wars fought in the name of religion – but actually contests between royal authority and aristocratic power – brought social dislocation and agricultural and commercial disaster. Increasingly, strong national monarchy seemed the only solution. Spanish and French monarchs gained control of the major competing institution in their domains, the Roman Catholic church. In England and some of the German principalities, where rulers could not completely regulate the church, they set up national churches. In the German Empire the Treaty of Westphalia placed territorial sovereignty in the hands of the princes. The kings of France, England, and Spain claimed the basic loyalty of their subjects. Monarchs made laws, to which everyone within their borders was subject. These powers added up to something close to sovereignty.

A nation may be termed sovereign when it possesses a monopoly over the instruments of justice and the use of force within clearly defined boundaries. In a sovereign state no system of courts, such as ecclesiastical tribunals, competes with state courts in the dispensation of justice; and private armies, such as those of feudal lords, present no threat to royal authority because the national army is stronger. Royal law touches all persons within the country. Sovereignty had been evolving in the late sixteenth century. Seventeenth-century governments now faced the problem of *which* authority within the state would possess sovereignty – the Crown or the nobility.

In the period between roughly 1589 and 1715, two basic patterns of government emerged in Europe: absolute monarchy and the constitutional state. Almost all subsequent governments have been modeled on one or the other of these patterns. How were these forms of government "modern"? How did they differ from the feudal and dynastic monarchies of earlier centuries? Which countries best represent the new patterns of political organization? This chapter will be concerned with these political questions.

## ABSOLUTISM

In the absolutist state, sovereignty is embodied in the person of the ruler. The ruler is not restrained by any legal authority. Absolute kings claimed to rule by divine right, meaning that they were responsible to God alone. (Medieval kings had governed "by the grace of God," but invariably they acknowledged that they had to respect and obey the law.) Absolute monarchs in the seventeenth and eighteenth centuries were not checked by national assemblies. Estates general and parliaments met at the wish and in response to the needs of kings. Because these meetings provided opportunities for opposition to the Crown to coalesce, absolute monarchs eventually stopped summoning them.

Absolute rulers effectively controlled all competing jurisdictions, all institutions or interest groups within their territories. They regulated religious sects. They abolished the liberties (privileges) long held by certain areas, groups, or provinces. Absolute kings also secured mastery over the one class that historically had posed the greatest threat to monarchy, the nobility. Medieval governments had been able to do none of these things. They had been restrained by the church, by the feudal nobility, and by their own financial limitations.

In some respects the key to the power and success of absolute monarchs lay in how they solved their financial problems. The solution was the creation of new state bureaucracies, which directed the economic life of the country in the interests of the king, raising ever higher taxes or devising other methods of raising revenue.

Bureaucracies were composed of career officials, appointed by and solely accountable to the king. The backgrounds of these civil servants varied. Absolute monarchs sometimes drew on the middle class, as in France, or utilized members of the nobility, as in Spain and eastern Europe. Where there was no middle class or an insignificant one, as in Austria, Prussia, Spain, and Russia, the government of the absolutist state consisted of an interlocking elite of monarchy, aristocracy, and bureaucracy.

Royal agents in medieval kingdoms had used their public offices and positions to benefit themselves and their families. In England, for example, Crown servants from Thomas Becket to Thomas Wolsey had treated their high offices as their personal private property, and reaped considerable profit from the positions they held. The most striking difference between seventeenth-century bureaucracies and their medieval predecessors was that seventeenth-century civil servants served the state as represented by the king. Bureaucrats recognized that the offices they held were public, or state, positions. The state paid them salaries to handle revenues that belonged to the Crown, and they were not supposed to use their official positions for private gain. Bureaucrats gradually came to distinguish between public duties and private property.

Absolute monarchs also maintained permanent standing armies. Medieval armies had been raised by feudal lords for particular wars or campaigns, after which the troops were disbanded. In the seventeenth century, monarchs alone recruited and maintained armies – in peacetime as well as during war. Kings deployed their troops both inside and outside the country in the interests of the monarchy. Armies became basic features of absolutist, and modern, states. Absolute rulers also invented new methods of compulsion. They concerned themselves with the private lives of potentially troublesome subjects, often through the use of secret police.

Thus rule of absolute monarchs was not all-embracing because they lacked the financial and military resources and the technology to make it so. Thus the absolutist state was not the same as a totalitarian state. Totalitarianism is a twentieth-century phenomenon; it seeks to direct all facets of a state's culture – art, education, religion, the economy, and politics – in the interests of the state. By definition totalitarian rule is *total* regulation. By twentieth-century standards, the ambitions of an absolute monarch were quite limited: he sought the exaltation of himself as the embodiment of the state. When King Louis XIV of France declared, "L'état, c'est moi!" ("I am the state!"), he meant that he personally was the incarnation of France. Yet the absolutist state did foreshadow recent totalitarian regimes in two fundamental respects: in the glorification of the state over all other aspects of the national culture, and in the use of war and an expansionist foreign policy to divert attention from domestic ills.

All of this is best illustrated by the experience of France, aptly known as the model of absolute monarchy.

### THE FOUNDATIONS OF ABSOLUTISM IN FRANCE: HENRY IV AND SULLY

The ingenious Huguenot-turned-Catholic, Henry IV (pages 524–525), ended the French religious wars with the Edict of Nantes. The first of the Bourbon dynasty, and probably the first French ruler since Louis IX in the thirteenth century genuinely to care about the French people, Henry IV and his great minister Sully (1560–1641) laid the foundations of later French absolutism. Henry denied influence on the royal council to the nobility, which had harassed the countryside for half a century. Maintaining that "if we are without compassion for the people, they must succumb and we all perish with them," Henry also lowered the severe taxes on the overburdened peasantry.

Sully proved himself a financial genius. He not only reduced the crushing royal debt but began to build up the treasury. He levied an annual tax, the *paulette,* on people who had purchased financial and judicial offices and had consequently been exempt from royal taxation. One of the first French officials to appreciate the significance of overseas trade, Sully subsidized the Company for Trade with the Indies. He started a countrywide highway system and even dreamed of an international organization for the maintenance of peace.

In twelve short years Henry IV and Sully restored public order in France and laid the foundations for economic prosperity. By late-sixteenth-century standards, Henry IV's government was both progressive and promising. His murder in 1610 by a crazed fanatic plunged the country into civil war and threatened to undo his work.

### THE CORNERSTONE OF FRENCH ABSOLUTISM: LOUIS XIII AND RICHELIEU

After the death of Henry IV, the queen-regent Marie de' Medici led the government for the child-king Louis XIII (1610–1643), but in fact feudal nobles and princes of the blood dominated the political scene. In 1624, Marie de' Medici secured the appointment of Armand Jean du Plessis – Cardinal Richelieu (1585–1642) – to the council of ministers. It was a remarkable appointment. The next year Richelieu became president of the council, and after 1628 he was first minister of the French crown and the actual ruler of France. Richelieu used his strong influence over King Louis XIII to exalt the French monarchy as the embodiment of the French state. One of the greatest servants of the French state, Richelieu set in place the cornerstone of French absolutism, and his work served as the basis for France's cultural domination of Europe in the later seventeenth century.

Richelieu's policy was the total subordination of all groups and institutions to the French monarchy. The French nobility, with its selfish and independent interests, had long constituted the foremost threat to the centralizing goals of the Crown and to a strong national state. Therefore, Richelieu broke the power of the nobility. He leveled castles, long the symbol of feudal independence. He crushed aristocratic conspiracies with quick executions. For example, when the duke de Montmorency, the first peer of France and the godson of Henry IV, became involved in a revolt in 1632, he was summarily put to death. Richelieu abolished the great medieval military dignities that had exalted the prestige and local power of some great nobles. He banned dueling. He prevented the great lords from sitting in the king's council.

The constructive genius of Cardinal Richelieu is best reflected in the administrative system he established. He extended the use of royal commissioners called intendants. France was divided into thirty-two *généralités* (districts), in each of which a royal intendant had complete responsibility for justice, police, and finances. The intendants were authorized "to decide, order and execute all that they see good to do." Usually members of the upper middle class or minor nobility, the intendants were appointed directly by the monarch, to whom they were solely responsible. They had complete power in their districts and were to use that power for two related purposes: to enforce royal orders in the *généralités* of their jurisdiction and to weaken the power and influence of the regional nobility. The system of government by intendants derived from Philip Augustus's baillis and seneschals, and ultimately from Charlemagne's *missi dominici*. As the intendants' power grew during Richelieu's administration, so did the power of the centralized state.

Although Richelieu succeeded in building a rational and centralized political machine in the intendant system, he was not the effective financial administrator Sully had been. France lacked a sound system of taxation, a method of raising sufficient revenue to meet the needs of the state. Richelieu reverted to the old device of selling offices. He increased the number of sinecures, tax exemptions, and benefices that were purchasable and inheritable. In 1624, this device brought in almost 40 percent of royal revenues.

The rising cost of foreign and domestic policies led to the auctioning of tax farms, the system whereby a man bought the right to collect taxes. Tax farmers kept a very large part of the receipts they collected. The sale of offices and this antiquated system of tax collection were improvisations that promoted confusion and corruption. Even worse, state offices, once purchased, were passed on to heirs, which meant that a family that held a state office was eternally exempt from taxation. Richelieu's inadequate and temporary solutions created grave financial problems for the future.

The cardinal perceived that Protestantism all too often served as a cloak for the political intrigues of ambitious lords. When the Huguenots revolted in 1625, under the duke de Rohan, Richelieu personally supervised the siege of their walled city, La Rochelle, and forced it to surrender. Thereafter, fortified places of security were abolished. Huguenots were allowed to practice their faith, but they no longer possessed armed strongholds or the means to be an independent party in the state. Another aristocratic prop was knocked down.

French foreign policy under Richelieu was aimed at the destruction of the fence of Habsburg territories that surrounded France. Consequently, Richelieu supported the Habsburgs' enemies. In 1631, he signed a treaty with the Lutheran king Gustavus Adolphus promising French support against the Catholic Habsburgs in what has been called the Swedish phase of the Thirty Years' War (page 533). French influence became an important factor in the political future of the German empire. Richelieu added Alsace in the east (1639) and Arras in the north (1640) to French territory.

Richelieu's efforts at centralization extended even to literature. In 1635 he gave official recognition to a group of philologists who were interested in grammar and rhetoric. Thus was born the French Academy. With Richelieu's encouragement, the Academy began the preparation of a *dictionary* to standardize the French language; it was completed in 1694. The French Academy survives as a prestigious learned society, whose membership has been broadened to include people outside the field of literature.

Richelieu personified the increasingly secular spirit of the seventeenth century. Although a bishop of the Roman Catholic church, he gave his first loyalty to the French state. Although a Roman Catholic cardinal, he gave strong support to the Protestant Lutherans of Germany. The portrait of Richelieu by Philippe de Champaigne – with its penetrating eyes, expression of haughty and imperturbable cynicism, and dramatic sweep of rich red robes – reveals the authority, grandeur, and power the cardinal wanted to convey as first minister of France. Just before Richelieu died in 1642, worn out with work and ulcers, the curé of St.-Eustache asked him to forgive his enemies. Richelieu replied, characteristically, that he had no enemies save those of the king and the state.

Richelieu had persuaded Louis XIII to appoint his protegé Jules Mazarin (1602-1661) as his successor. An Italian diplomat of great charm, Mazarin served on the Council of State under Richelieu, acquiring considerable political experience. He became a cardinal in 1641 and a French citizen in 1643. When Louis XIII followed Richelieu to the grave in 1643 and a regency headed by Queen Anne of Austria governed for the child-king Louis XIV, Mazarin became the dominant power in the government. He continued the antifeudal and centralizing policies of Richelieu, but his attempts to increase royal revenues led to the civil wars known as the Fronde.

The word *fronde* means slingshot or catapult, and a *frondeur* was originally a street urchin who threw mud at the passing carriages of the rich. The term came to be used for anyone who opposed the policies of the government. Richelieu had stirred up the bitter resentment of the aristocracy, who felt its constitutional status and ancient privileges threatened. He also bequeathed to the Crown a staggering debt, and when Mazarin tried to impose financial reforms the monarchy incurred the enmity of the middle classes. Both groups plotted against Anne and Mazarin. Most historians see the Fronde as the last serious effort by the French nobility to oppose the monarchy by force. When in 1648 Mazarin proposed new methods for raising income, bitter civil war ensued between the monarchy on the one side and the frondeurs

(the nobility and the upper-middle classes) on the other. Riots and public turmoil wracked Paris and the nation. The violence continued intermittently for almost twelve years. Factional disputes among the nobles led to their ultimate defeat.

The conflicts of the Fronde had two significant results for the future: a badly disruptive effect on the French economy and a traumatic impact on the young Louis XIV. The king and his mother were frequently threatened and sometimes treated as prisoners by aristocratic factions. On one occasion a mob broke into the royal bedchamber to make sure the king was actually there; it succeeded in giving him a bad fright. Louis never forgot such humiliations. The period of the Fronde formed the cornerstone of his political education and of his unalterable conviction that the sole alternative to anarchy was absolute monarchy.

## THE ABSOLUTE MONARCHY OF LOUIS XIV

According to the court theologian Bossuet, the clergy at the coronation of Louis XIV in Reims Cathedral asked God to cause the splendors of the French court to fill all who beheld it with awe. God subsequently granted that prayer. In the reign of Louis XIV (1643–1715), the longest in European history, the French monarchy reached the peak of absolutist development. In the magnificence of his court, in his absolute power, in the brilliance of the culture over which he presided and which permeated all of Europe, and in his remarkably long life, Louis XIV dominated his age. No wonder scholars have characterized the second half of the seventeenth century as "The Grand Century," "The Age of Magnificence," and, echoing the eighteenth-century philosopher Voltaire, "The Age of Louis XIV."

Who was this phenomenon of whom it was said that when Louis sneezed, all Europe caught cold? Born in 1638, king at the age of five, he entered into personal, or independent, rule in 1661. One of his first recorded remarks reveals the astonishing sense of self that was to awe French people and foreigners alike. Taken as a child to his father's deathbed, he identified himself as "Louis Quatorze" ("Louis the fourteenth").

In old age Louis claimed that he had grown up learning very little, and many historians have agreed. He knew little Latin and only the rudiments of arithmetic, and was thus by Renaissance standards not well educated. On the other hand, he learned to speak Italian and Spanish fluently; he knew some French history, and more European geography than the ambassadors accredited to his court. He imbibed the devout Catholicism of his mother Anne of Austria, and throughout his long life scrupulously performed his religious duties. Religion, Anne, and Mazarin all taught Louis that God had established kings as His rulers on earth. The royal coronation consecrated him to God's service, and he was certain – to use Shakespeare's phrase – that there was a divinity that doth hedge a king. Although kings were a race apart, they could not do as they pleased: they must obey God's laws and rule for the good of the people.

Louis's education was more practical than formal. Under Mazarin's instruction he studied state papers as they arrived, and he attended council meetings and sessions at which French ambassadors were dispatched abroad and foreign ambassadors received. He learned by direct experience and gained professional training in the work of government. Above all, the misery he suffered during the Fronde gave Louis an eternal distrust of the nobility and a profound sense of his own isolation. Accordingly, silence, caution, and secrecy be-

came political tools for the achievement of his goals. His characteristic answer to requests of all kinds became the enigmatic "Je verrai" ("I shall see").

Louis grew up with an absolute sense of his royal dignity. Tall and distinguished in appearance, he was inclined to fatness because of the gargantuan meals in which he indulged. Seduced by one of his mother's maids when he was sixteen, the king matured into a highly sensual man easily aroused by an attractive female face and figure. It is to his credit, however, that neither his wife, Queen Maria Theresa, whom he married as the result of a diplomatic agreement with Spain, nor his mistresses ever possessed any political influence. Extraordinarily selfish, Louis doted on flattery, which he interpreted as glory.

Whatever his negative qualities, Louis XIV worked extremely hard and succeeded in being "every moment and every inch a king." Because he so thoroughly relished the role of king, historians have had difficulty distinguishing the man from the monarch. Louis XIV was a consummate actor, and his "terrifying majesty" awed all who saw him.

The reign of Louis XIV witnessed great innovations in style but few in substance; Louis extended and intensified earlier practices and trends. The most significant development was his acquisition of absolute control over the French nobility. Indeed, it is often said that Louis achieved the complete "domestication" of the nobility.

Louis XIV turned the royal court into a fixed institution. In the past the king of France and the royal court had traveled constantly, visiting the king's properties, the great noblemen, and his *bonnes villes* or good towns. Since the time of Louis IX, or even Charlemagne, rulers had traveled to maintain order in distant parts of the realm, to impress humbler subjects with the royal dignity and

*AERIAL VIEW OF VERSAILLES Awe-inspiring, monumental, and over a quarter of a mile long, Versailles is the supreme example of classical baroque architecture in the service of absolute monarchy. The vast formal gardens with their geometric regularity pro-* *vided the outdoor setting for Louis XIV's festivities, while the three avenues radiating from the palace symbolize the king as source of all power. (French Government Tourist Office)*

magnificence, and in so doing to bind the country together through loyalty to the king. Since the early Middle Ages, the king's court had consisted of his family, trusted advisers and councilors, a few favorites, and servants. Except for the very highest officials of the state, members of the council had changed constantly.

Louis XIV installed the court at Versailles, a small town ten miles from Paris. He required all the great nobility of France, at the peril of social, political, and sometimes economic disaster, to come live at Versailles for at least part of the year. Today, Versailles stands as the best surviving museum of a vanished society on earth. In the seventeenth century, it became a model of rational order, the center of France and thus the center of Western civilization, the perfect symbol of the king's absolute power.

Louis XIII had begun Versailles as a hunting lodge, a retreat from a queen he did not

HALL OF MIRRORS AT VERSAILLES *This long and magnificently impressive room takes up much of the central block of Versailles. The hundreds of mirrors, which give the illusion of width, reflected the court spectacles and the king's glory. The splendor of* *this hall and many other adjacent palace rooms was a far cry, however, from the cramped conditions that many nobles were forced to live with at the royal court. (French Government Tourist Office)*

like. His son's architects, Le Nôtre and Le Vau, turned what Saint-Simon called "the most dismal and thankless of sights" into a veritable paradise. Wings were added to the original building to make the palace U-shaped. Everywhere at Versailles the viewer has a sense of grandeur, vastness, and incredible elegance. Enormous state rooms became display galleries for inlaid tables, Italian marble statuary, Gobelin tapestries woven at the state factory in Paris, silver ewers, and beauti-

ful (if uncomfortable) furniture. If genius means attention to detail, Louis XIV and his designers had it: the décor was perfected down to the last doorknob and keyhole. In the gigantic Hall of Mirrors, which was later to reflect so much of German as well as French history, hundreds of candles illuminated the domed ceiling, where allegorical paintings celebrated the king's victories.

The Ambassador's Staircase is of brilliantly colored marble, with part of the railing gold-plated. The staircase is dominated by a great bust of the king, which when completed so overwhelmed a courtier that he exclaimed to the sculptor Bernini, "Don't do anything more to it, it's so good I'm afraid you might spoil it." The statue, like the staircase – and the entire palace – succeeded from the start in its purpose: it awed.

The formal, carefully ordered, and perfectly landscaped gardens at Versailles express at a glance the spirit of the age of Louis XIV. Every tree, every bush, every foot of grass, every fountain, pool, and piece of statuary within three miles is perfectly laid out. The vista is of the world made rational and absolutely controlled. Nature itself was subdued to enhance the greatness of the king.

Under the vast terrace stands one of the great architectural splendors of France, the Orangerie. Designed to house the king's twelve hundred potted palms and orange trees, the Orangerie is a huge vaulted space, so large that when it was completed in 1686 several operas could be performed there simultaneously without inconvenience. The Siamese ambassador is reputed to have said that the magnificence of Louis XIV must indeed be great, since he had raised so superb a palace simply for his orange trees.

Against this background of magnificent splendor, as the great aristocrat Saint-Simon describes, Louis XIV

*reduced everyone to subjection, and brought to his court those very persons he cared least about. Whoever was old enough to serve did not dare demur. It was still another device to ruin the nobles by accustoming them to equality and forcing them to mingle with everyone indiscriminately....*

*... To keep everyone assiduous and attentive, the King personally named the guests for each festivity, each stroll through Versailles, and each trip. These were his rewards and punishments. He*

*knew there was little else he could distribute to keep everyone in line. He substituted idle rewards for real ones and these operated through jealousy, the petty preferences he showed many times a day, and his artfulness in showing them. No one was more ingenious than him in nourishing the hopes and satisfactions to which these petty preferences and distinctions gave birth....*

*... Upon rising, at bedtime, during meals, in his apartments, in the gardens of Versailles, everywhere the courtiers had a right to follow, he would glance right and left to see who was there; he saw and noted everyone; he missed no one, even those who were hoping they would not be seen.... For the most distinguished persons, it was a demerit not to put in a regular appearance at court. It was just as bad for those of lesser rank to come but rarely, and certain disgrace for those who never, or almost never, came....*

*... Louis XIV took great pains to inform himself on what was happening everywhere, in public places, private homes, and even on the international scene.... Spies and informers of all kinds were numberless....*

*... But the King's most vicious method of securing information was opening letters....*[1]

Through ritual and ceremony the king turned the proud and ancient nobility into a pack of trained seals. He destroyed their ancient right to advise and counsel the monarch. Operas, fetes, and balls occupied the nobles' time and attention. They become solely instruments of the king's pleasure. Louis XIV may have had limited native intelligence, but through painstaking attention to detail and precisely calculated showmanship, he emasculated the major threat to his absolute power. He separated power from grandeur: the nobility enjoyed the grandeur in which they lived; the king alone enjoyed the power.

The art and architecture of Versailles served as fundamental tools of state policy under

Louis XIV. Architecture was the device the king used to overawe his subjects and foreign visitors. Versailles was seen as a reflection of French genius. Thus the Russian czar Peter the Great imitated Versailles in the construction of his palace, Peterhof, as did the Prussian emperor Frederick the Great in his palace at Potsdam outside Berlin.

As in architecture, so too in language. Beginning in the reign of Louis XIV, French became the language of polite society and the vehicle of diplomatic exchange. French also gradually replaced Latin as the language of international scholarship and learning. The wish of other kings to ape the courtly style of Louis XIV and the imitation of French intellectuals and artists spread the French language all over Europe. The royal courts of Sweden, Russia, Poland, and Germany all spoke French. In the eighteenth century, the great Russian aristocrats were more fluent in French than in Russian. In England the First Hanoverian king, George I, spoke French but no English. France inspired a cosmopolitan European culture in the late seventeenth century, and that culture was inspired by the king. That is what Voltaire meant when he called the period "The Age of Louis XIV."

Louis dominated the court, and the court was the center of France. In the king's scheme of things, the court was more significant than the government. Louix XIV made no innovations in the government of France. He continued the system of the intendants, appointing them entirely from the middle class. By curbing the power of the local aristocracy and gentry, the intendants advanced royal sovereignty in the provinces. Members of the royal councils — such as the Council of State, which dealt with diplomacy, war, and peace — were drawn from the class Saint-Simon called "the bookkeepers," the middle class.

Louis feared and distrusted the nobility, and so he eliminated them from government. Throughout his long reign, and in spite of increasing financial problems, he never called the French nobility together in a meeting of the Estates General. The nobility, therefore, had no means of united expression or action. Nor did Louis have a first minister, freeing him from worry about the inordinate power of a Richelieu. Louis's use of terror — a secret police force, a system of informers, and the practice of opening private letters — foreshadowed some of the devices of the modern state. French government remained highly structured, bureaucratic, centered in Paris, and responsible to Louis XIV.

## ECONOMIC MANAGEMENT UNDER LOUIS XIV: COLBERT AND MERCANTILISM

As controller-general of finances, the king named Jean Baptiste Colbert. The son of a draper of Reims, Colbert (1619–1683) came to manage the entire royal administration and proved himself a financial genius. Colbert's central principle was that the economy and the wealth of France should serve the state. He did not invent the economic system or program called mercantilism, but he rigorously applied it to France.

Mercantilism is a system for the regulation of economic activities, especially commercial activities, by and for the state. In seventeenth- and eighteenth-century economic theory, a nation's international power was thought to be based on its wealth, specifically its gold supply. To accumulate gold, a country should always sell abroad more than it bought. Colbert believed that a successful economic policy meant more than a favorable balance of trade. He insisted that the French sell abroad and buy *nothing* back. France should be self-sufficient, able to produce within its borders everything the subjects of the French king needed. Consequently, the outflow of gold would be halted and the power and prestige of the state enhanced.

Colbert attempted to accomplish self-sufficiency through state support for both old industries and newly created ones. He subsidized the established cloth industries at Abbeville, St.-Quentin, and Carcassonne. He granted special royal privileges to the rug and tapestry industries at Paris, Gobelin, and Beauvais. New factories at St.-Antoine in Paris manufactured mirrors to replace Venetian imports. Looms at Chantilly and Alençon competed with English lacemaking, and foundries at St.-Etienne made steel and firearms that cut Swedish imports. To insure a high-quality finished product, Colbert set up a system of state inspection and regulation. To insure order within every industry he compelled all craftsmen to organize into guilds, and within every guild he gave the masters absolute power over their workers. Colbert encouraged skilled foreign craftsmen and manufacturers to immigrate to France, and he gave them special privileges. To protect French products, Colbert enacted high tariffs, which prevented foreign goods from competing with French ones.

Colbert's most important work was the creation of a powerful merchant marine to transport French goods. He gave bonuses to French shipowners and builders, and established a method of maritime conscription, arsenals, and academies for the training of sailors. In 1661, France possessed 18 unseaworthy vessels; by 1681, France had 276 frigates, galleys, and ships of the line. Colbert tried to organize and regulate the entire French economy for the glory of the French state as embodied in the king.

Colbert hoped to make Canada — rich in untapped minerals and some of the best agricultural land in the world — part of a vast French empire. He gathered four thousand peasants from western France and shipped them to Canada, where they peopled the province of Quebec. (In 1608, one year after the English arrived at Jamestown, Virginia, Sully had established the city of Quebec, which became the capital of French Canada.) Subsequently, the Jesuit Marquette and the merchant Joliet sailed down the Mississippi River and took possession of the land on both sides as far south as present-day Arkansas. In 1684, the French explorer La Salle continued down the Mississippi to its mouth and claimed vast territories and the rich delta for Louis XIV. The area was called, naturally, Louisiana.

Nothing did more to destroy Colbert's system of commercial and colonial regulation than the revocation of the Edict of Nantes — an event that, on the surface at least, had little to do with economic life. For almost a century the edict had granted equal political and some religious rights to the Huguenots of France. Scholars have debated at length the reasons for Louis XIV's revocation of it in 1685. Was the revocation due to the powerful influence of the king's Catholic wife, Madame de Maintenon? Was it the result of pressure from Catholic business interests who resented the competition of the clever Huguenots? Did Louis abolish freedom of religion because of his pride and religious intolerance, which could not countenance the existence in France of a sizable group with a faith different from his own? Or was it sheer ignorance of the large numbers of his Calvinist subjects and their social and economic importance to the state, an ignorance attributable to the isolation of the court? Whatever the exact causes of the revocation, its consequences proved disastrous.

Perhaps 300,000 French citizens chose to emigrate rather than convert. Some of the best craftsmen, businessmen, soldiers, and sailors fled to England, Holland, and Prussia. They left their goods behind but carried their skills and hatred of Louis XIV with them. The loss of so many experts and the taxes they represented — on top of Louis's chronic need for money — severely aggravated the national financial situation. After 1685, the French government had to resort again to the expediency of creating offices and selling them on a broad scale. This stopgap measure paid for the present by mortgaging the future, since officeholders and their descendants paid no taxes.

Most catastrophic of all, the revocation of the Edict of Nantes provoked domestic turmoil within France and fear and hatred abroad. Calvinist peasants in Languedoc revolted, for example, and Louis was ultimately forced to back down. The Protestant states of northern Europe — Holland, Brandenburg, and Sweden — united against Louis XIV, and from 1688 until his death France was almost continually at war. With some justification, historians have called the revocation of the Edict of Nantes the greatest error the Bourbon dynasty committed.

## FRENCH CLASSICISM

Scholars characterize the art and literature of the age of Louis XIV as French Classicism. By this they mean that the artists and writers of the late seventeenth century deliberately imitated the subject matter and style of classical antiquity; that their work resembles that of Renaissance Italy; and that French art possessed the classical qualities of discipline, balance, and restraint. Classicism was the official style of Louis's court. In painting, however, French classicism had already reached its peak before 1661, the beginning of the king's personal government.

Nicholas Poussin (1593-1665) is generally considered the finest example of French classicist painting. Poussin spent all but eighteen months of his creative life in Rome because he found the atmosphere in Paris uncongenial. Deeply attached to classical antiquity, he believed that the highest aim of painting was to represent noble actions in a logical and orderly, but not realistic, way. His masterpiece, "The Rape of the Sabine Women," exhibits these qualities. Its subject is an incident in Roman history; the figures of people and horses are ideal representations, and the emotions expressed are studied, not spontaneous. Even the buildings are exact architectural models of ancient Roman structures.

While Poussin selected grand and "noble" themes, Louis Le Nain (1593-1648) painted genre scenes of peasant life. At a time when artists favored Biblical and classical allegories, Le Nain's paintings are unique for their depiction of peasants. The highly realistic group assembled in "The Peasant Family" have great human dignity. The painting itself is reminiscent of portrayals of peasants by seventeenth-century Dutch painters.

Le Nain and Poussin, whose paintings still had individualistic features, did their work before 1661. After Louis's accession to power, the principles of absolutism molded the ideals of French classicism. Individualism was not allowed, and artists' efforts were directed to the glorification of the state as personified by the king. Precise rules governed all aspects of culture, with the goal of formal and restrained perfection.

Contemporaries said that Louis XIV never

ceased playing the role of grand monarch on the stage of his court. If the king never fully relaxed from the pressures and intrigues of government, he did enjoy music and theater and used them as a backdrop for court ceremonial. Louis favored Jean-Baptiste Lully (1632–1687), whose orchestral works combine lively animation with the restrained austerity typical of French classicism. Lully also composed court ballets, and his operatic productions achieved a powerful influence throughout Europe. Louis supported Francois Couperin (1668–1733), whose harpsicord and organ works possess the regal grandeur the king loved, and Marc-Antoine Charpentier (1634–1704), whose solemn religious music entertained him at meals. Charpentier received a pension for the *Te Deums,* hymns of thanksgiving he composed to celebrate French military victories.

Louis XIV loved the stage, and in the plays of Molière and Racine his court witnessed the finest achievements in the history of the French theater. When Jean-Baptiste Poquelin (1622–1673), the son of a prosperous tapestry maker, refused to join his father's business and entered the theater, he took the stage name Molière. As playwright, stage manager, director, and actor, Molière produced comedies that exposed the hypocrisies and follies of society though brilliant caricature. *Tartuffe* satirized the religious hypocrite, *Le Bourgeois Gentilhomme (The Would-Be Gentleman)* attacked the social parvenu, and *Les Femmes savantes (The Learned Women)* mocked the fashionable pseudo-intellectuals of the day. In structure Molière's plays followed classical models, but they were based on careful social observation. Molière made the bourgeoisie the butt of his ridicule; he stopped short of criticizing the nobility, thus reflecting the policy of his royal patron.

While Molière dissected social mores, his

*POUSSIN: THE RAPE OF THE SABINE WOMEN Considered the greatest French painter of the seventeenth century, Poussin in this dramatic work (ca 1636) shows his complete devotion to the ideals of classicism. The heroic figures are superb physical specimens, but hardly life-like. (Metropolitan Museum of Art, New York [Dick Fund, 1946])*

contemporary Jean Racine (1639–1699) analyzed the power of love. Racine based his tragic dramas on Greek and Roman legends, and his persistent theme is the conflict of good and evil. Several plays – *Andromache, Berenice, Iphigenie,* and *Phedre* – bear the names of women and deal with the power of passion in women. Louis preferred *Mithridates* and *Brittanicus* because of the "grandeur" of their themes. For simplicity of language, symmetrical structure, and calm restraint, the plays of Racine represent the finest examples of French classicism. His tragedies and Molière's comedies are still produced today.

## LOUIS XIV'S WARS

Just as the architecture and court life at Versailles served to reflect the king's glory, and as the economy of the state under Colbert was managed to advance the king's prestige, so did Louis XIV use war to exalt himself above the other rulers and nations of Europe. He visualized himself as a great military hero. "The character of a conqueror," he remarked, "is regarded as the noblest and highest of titles." Military glory was his aim. In 1666, Louis appointed François le Tellier (later Marquis de Louvois) as secretary of war. Louvois created a professional army, which was modern in the sense that the French state, rather than private nobles, employed the soldiers.

Because of the justifiable fear that an army of native French soldiers would turn on their oppressors, the army of Louis XIV was re-

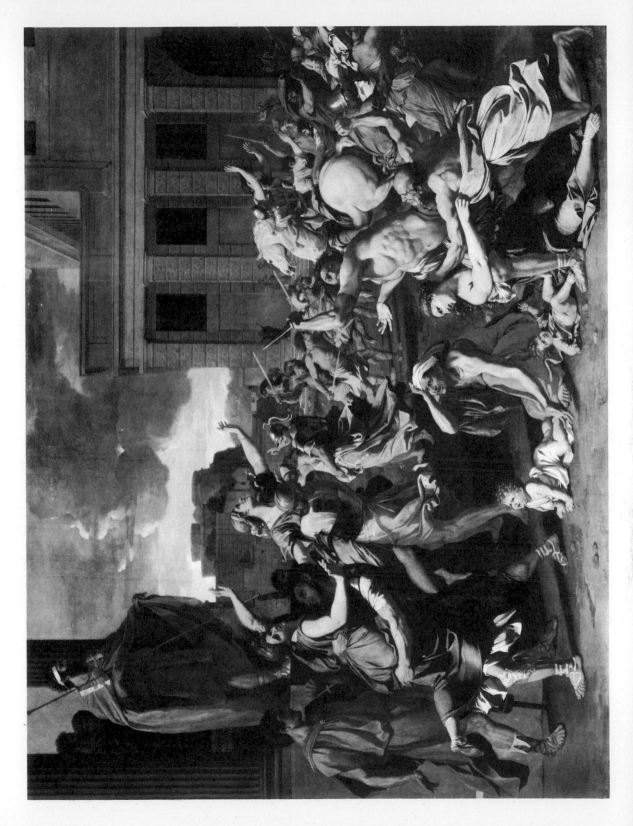

cruited heavily from Swiss, German, and Irish mercenaries. Officers were French, the ranks largely foreign. A foreign mercenary army could more easily be employed against rebellious peasants whose language they did not speak. It is one of the ironies of Louis' wars that a French army of Protestant Swiss and German troops was sent against the Protestant Dutch.

A commissariat was established to feed the troops, in place of the ancient practice of living off the countryside. An ambulance corps was designed to look after the wounded. Uniforms and weapons were standardized. Finally, a rational system of recruitment, training, discipline, and promotion was imposed. With this new military machine, for the first time in Europe's history one national state, France, was able to dominate the politics of Europe.

Louis continued on a broader scale the expansionist policy begun by Cardinal Richelieu. In 1667, using a dynastic excuse, he invaded Flanders, part of the Spanish Netherlands, and Franche-Comté in the east. In consequence he acquired twelve towns, including the important commercial centers of Lille and Tournai (see Map 16.1). Five years later, Louis personally led an army of over a hundred thousand men into Holland, and the Dutch ultimately saved themselves only by opening the dikes and flooding the countryside. This war, which lasted six years and eventually involved the German empire and Spain, was concluded by the Treaty of Nijmegen (1678). Louis gained additional Flemish towns and the whole of Franche-Comté.

Encouraged by his successes, by the weakness of the German empire, and by divisions among the other European powers, Louis continued his aggression. In 1684 he seized the city of Trier, and the province of Lorraine was permanently occupied by France. At that moment, the king seemed invincible.

In fact, Louis had reached the limit of his expansion at Nijmegen. The wars of the 1680s and 1690s brought him no additional territories. In 1689, the Dutch prince William of Orange, a bitter foe of Louis XIV, became king of England. William joined the League of Augsburg — which included the German emperor, the kings of Spain and Sweden, and the electors of Bavaria, Saxony, and the Palatinate — adding British resources and men to the alliance. Neither the French nor the league won any decisive victories. The alliance served instead as preparation for the long-expected conflict known as the War of the Spanish Succession.

This struggle (1701–1713), provoked by the territorial disputes of the past century, also involved the dynastic question of the succession to the Spanish throne. It was an open secret in Europe that the king of Spain, Charles II (1665–1700), was mentally defective and sexually impotent. In his will Charles left his territories to his grandnephew, Philip of Anjou, who was also Louis XIV's grandson. When Charles died on November 1, 1700, the line of the Spanish Habsburgs ended. Immediately, Louis claimed the Spanish throne on behalf of his grandson.

The union of the French and Spanish crowns would have totally upset the European balance of power, and Louis's declaration that "the Pyrenees no longer exist" provoked the long-anticipated crisis. In May 1702 England, Holland, and the Holy Roman Empire declared war on France. They claimed that they were fighting to prevent France from becoming too strong in Europe, but during the previous half-century overseas maritime rivalry among France, Holland, and England had created serious international tension. The secondary motive of the Allied Powers was to check France's expanding commercial power in North America, Asia, and Africa. In the

MAP 16.1  THE ACQUISITIONS OF LOUIS XIV,
1668–1713  *The desire for glory and the weakness
of his German neighbors encouraged Louis' expansionist policy. But he paid a high price for his acquisitions.*

ensuing series of conflicts, two great soldiers
dominated the alliance against France: Eugene, prince of Savoy, representing the Holy
Roman Empire, and the Englishman John
Churchill, subsequently duke of Marlborough. Eugene and Churchill inflicted a
crushing defeat on Louis in 1704 at Blenheim
in Bavaria. Marlborough followed with another victory at Romilles near Namur in Bra-
bant.

The war was finally concluded at Utrecht in
1713, where the principle of partition was applied. Louis's grandson Philip became the first
Bourbon king of Spain on the understanding

that the French and Spanish crowns would
never be united. France surrendered Newfoundland, Nova Scotia, and the Hudson Bay
territory to England, which also acquired
Gibraltar, Minorca, and the *asiento,* or control
of the African slave trade from Spain. The
Dutch received little because the former
Spanish Netherlands was given to Austria.

The Peace of Utrecht had important international consequences. It represented the
balance-of-power principle in operation, setting limits on the extent to which any one
power, in this case France, could expand. The
treaty completed the decline of Spain as a

great power. It vastly expanded the British Empire. Finally, Utrecht gave European powers experience in international cooperation and thus prepared them for the great alliances against France at the end of the eighteenth century.

For Louis XIV, Utrecht was a severe defeat. He had waged his wars in the quest for glory. He had gained little (see Map 16.1). Utrecht marked the end of French expansion. To raise revenue for the wars, forty thousand additional offices had been sold, thus increasing the number of families exempt from future taxation. Constant war had disrupted trade, which meant the state could not tax the profits of trade. Widespread starvation in the provinces provoked peasant revolts, especially in Brittany. In 1714, France hovered on the brink of financial bankruptcy. Louis had exhausted the country without much compensation. It is no wonder that when he died on September 1, 1715, Saint-Simon wrote, "Those . . . wearied by the heavy and oppressive rule of the King and his ministers, felt a delighted freedom. . . . Paris . . . found relief in the hope of liberation. . . . The provinces . . . quivered with delight . . . [and] the people, ruined, abused, despairing, now thanked God for a deliverance which answered their most ardent desires."[2]

## THE DECLINE OF ABSOLUTIST SPAIN IN THE SEVENTEENTH CENTURY

Spanish absolutism and greatness had preceded that of the French. In the sixteenth century, Spain had developed the standard features of absolute monarchy: a permanent bureaucracy staffed by professionals employed in the various councils of state, a standing army, and national taxes, the *servicios*, which fell most heavily on the poor.

France depended upon financial and admin-

*VELAZQUEZ: THE MAIDS OF HONOR   The Infanta Margarita painted in 1656 with her maids and playmates has invaded the artist's studio, while her parents' image is reflected in the mirror on the back wall. Velazquez (extreme left), who powerfully influenced nineteenth-century impressionist painters, imbued all of his subjects, including the pathetic dwarf (right, in black) with a sense of dignity. (Giraudon)*

istrative unification within its national borders; Spain had developed an international absolutism on the basis of silver bullion from Peru. Spanish gold and silver, Spanish armies, and Spanish glory had dominated the continent of Europe for most of the sixteenth century, but by the 1590s the seeds of disaster were sprouting. While France in the seventeenth century represented the classic model of the modern absolute state, Spain was experiencing steady decline and decay. Fiscal disorder, political incompetence, population decline, intellectual isolation, and psychological malaise – all combined to reduce Spain, by 1715, to the rank of a second-rate power.

The fabulous and seemingly inexhaustible flow of silver from Mexico and Peru had led Philip II (page 529) to assume the role of defender of Roman Catholicism in Europe. In order to humble the Protestant Dutch and to control the Spanish Netherlands, Philip believed that England, the Netherlands' greatest supporter, had to be crushed. He poured millions of Spanish ducats and all of Spanish hopes into the vast fleet that sailed in 1588. When the "Invincible Armada" went down in the North Sea, a century of Spanish pride and power went with it. After 1590, a spirit of defeatism and disillusionment crippled almost all efforts at reform.

Philip II's Catholic crusade had been financed by the revenues of the Spanish-Atlantic economy. These included, in addition to silver and gold bullion, the sale of cloth,

grain, oil, and wine to the colonies. In the early seventeenth century, the Dutch and English began to trade with the Spanish colonies, cutting into the revenues that had gone to Spain. Mexico and Peru themselves developed local industries, further lessening their need to buy from Spain. Between 1610 and 1650, Spanish trade with the colonies fell 60 percent.

At the same time the native Indians and African slaves, who worked the South American silver mines under conditions that would have disgraced the ancient Egyptian pharaohs, suffered frightful epidemics of disease. Moreover, the lodes started to run dry. Consequently, the quantity of metal produced for Spain steadily declined. Nevertheless, in Madrid royal expenditures constantly exceeded income. The remedies applied in the face of a mountainous state debt and declining revenues were devaluation of the coinage and declarations of bankruptcy. In 1596, 1607, 1627, 1647, and 1680 Spanish kings found no solution to the problem of an empty treasury other than cancellation of the national debt. Naturally, public confidence in the state deteriorated.

Spain, in contrast to the other countries of western Europe, had only a tiny middle class. Disdain for money, in a century of increasing commercialism and bourgeois attitudes, reveals a significant facet of the Spanish national character. Public opinion, taking its cue from the aristocracy, condemned moneymaking as vulgar and undignified. Those with influence or connections sought titles of nobility and social prestige. Thousands entered economically unproductive professions and became priests, monks, and nuns: there were said to be nine thousand monasteries in the province of Castile alone. The flood of gold and silver had produced severe inflation, pushing the costs of production in the textile industry higher and higher, to the point that Castilian cloth could not compete in colonial and international markets. Many manufacturers and businessmen found so many obstacles in the way of profitable enterprise that they simply gave up.[3]

Spanish aristocrats, attempting to maintain an extravagant lifestyle they could no longer afford, increased the rents on their estates. High rents and heavy taxes in turn drove the peasants from the land. Agricultural production suffered and the peasants departed for the large cities, where they swelled the ranks of unemployed beggars.

Their most Catholic majesties, the kings of Spain, had no solutions to these dire problems. The portraits of Philip III (1598–1622), Philip IV (1622–1665), and Charles II hanging in the Prado, the Spanish national museum in Madrid, reflect the increasing weakness of the dynasty. Their faces — the small beady eyes, the long noses, the jutting Habsburg jaws, the constipated and pathetically stupid expressions — tell a story of excessive inbreeding and decaying monarchy. These Spanish kings all lacked force of character. Philip III, a pallid, melancholy, and deeply pious man "whose only virtue appeared to reside in a total absence of vice," handed the government over to the lazy duke of Lerma, who used it to advance his personal and familial wealth. Philip IV left the management of his several kingdoms to Count Olivares.

Olivares was an able administrator. He did not lack energy and ideas; he devised new sources of revenue. But he clung to the grandiose belief that the solution to Spain's difficulties rested in a return to the imperial tradition. Unfortunately, the imperial tradition demanded the revival of war with the Dutch at the expiration of a twelve-year truce in 1622 and a long war with France over Mantua (1628–1659). These conflicts on top of an empty treasury brought disaster.

In 1640, Spain faced serious revolts in Naples and Portugal, and in 1643 the French inflicted a crushing defeat on a Spanish army in Belgium. By the Treaty of the Pyrenees of 1659, which ended the French-Spanish wars, Spain was compelled to surrender extensive territories to France. This treaty marked the end of Spain as a great power.

Seventeenth-century Spain was the victim of its past. It could not forget the grandeur of the sixteenth century and look to the future. The bureaucratic councils of state continued to function as symbols of the absolute Spanish monarchy. But because those councils were staffed by aristocrats, it was the aristocracy that held the real power. Spanish absolutism had been built largely on slave-produced gold and silver. When the supply of bullion decreased, the power and standing of the Spanish state declined.

The most cherished Spanish ideals were military glory and strong Roman Catholic faith. In the seventeenth century, Spain lacked the finances and the manpower to fight the expensive wars in which it foolishly got involved. Spain also ignored the new mercantile ideas and scientific methods, because they came from heretical nations, Holland and England. The incredible wealth of South America destroyed the tiny Spanish middle class and created contempt for business and manual labor.

The decadence of the Habsburg dynasty and the lack of effective royal councilors also contributed to Spanish failure. Spanish leaders seemed to lack the will to reform. Pessimism and fatalism permeated national life. In the reign of Philip IV, a royal council was appointed to plan the construction of a canal linking the Tagus and Manzanares rivers in Spain. After interminable debate, the committee decided that "if God had intended the rivers to be navigable, He would have made them so."

In the novel *Don Quixote,* the Spanish writer Cervantes (1547–1616) produced one of the great masterpieces of world literature. The main character, Don Quixote, lives in a world of dreams, traveling about the countryside seeking military glory. From the title of this book English has borrowed the word *quixotic.* Meaning idealistic but impractical, it characterizes seventeenth-century Spain.

## CONSTITUTIONALISM

The seventeenth century, which witnessed the development of absolute monarchy, also saw the appearance of the constitutional state. While France and later Prussia, Russia, and Austria solved the question of sovereignty with the absolutist state, England and Holland evolved toward the constitutional state. What is constitutionalism? Is it the same as democracy?

Constitutionalism is the limitation of government by law. Constitutionalism also implies a balance between the authority and power of the government on the one hand, and the rights and liberties of the subjects on the other. The balance is often very delicate.

A nation's constitution may be written or unwritten. In may be embodied in one basic document, occasionally revised by amendment or judicial decision, like the Constitution of the United States. Or a constitution may be partly written and partly unwritten and include parliamentary statutes, judicial decisions, and a body of traditional procedures and practices, like the English and Canadian constitutions. Whether written or unwritten, a constitution gets its binding force from the government's acknowledgment that it must respect that constitution — that is, that the state must govern according to the laws. Likewise, in a constitutional state, the people look upon the law and the constitution as the protectors of their rights, liberties, and property.

Modern constitutional governments may take either a republican or a monarchial form. In a constitutional republic, the sovereign power resides in the electorate and is exercised by the electorate's representatives. In a constitutional monarchy, a king or queen serves as the head of state and possesses some residual political authority, but again the ultimate or sovereign power rests in the electorate.

A constitutional government is not, however, quite the same as a democratic government. In a complete democracy, *all* the people have the right to participate either directly, or indirectly through their elected representatives, in the government of the state. Democratic government, therefore, is intimately tied up with the franchise (the vote). Most men could not vote until the late nineteenth century. Even then, women — probably the majority in Western societies — lacked the franchise; they gained the right to vote only in the twentieth century. Consequently, although constitutionalism developed in the seventeenth century, full democracy was achieved only in very recent times.

### THE DECLINE OF ROYAL ABSOLUTISM IN ENGLAND (1603–1649)

In the late sixteenth century the French monarchy was powerless; a century later the king's power was absolute. In 1588, Queen Elizabeth I of England exercised very great personal power; by 1689, the English monarchy was severely circumscribed and limited. Change in England was anything but orderly: England in the seventeenth century displayed as much political stability as some African states in the twentieth. They executed one king, experienced a bloody civil war, experimented with military dictatorship, then restored the son of the murdered king, and finally, after a bloodless revolution, established a constitutional monarchy. Political stability came only in the 1690s. How do we account for the fact that after such a violent and tumultuous century, England laid the foundations for a constitutional monarchy? What combination of political, socioeconomic, and religious factors brought on first a civil war in 1642–1649 and then the constitutional settlement of 1688–1689?

The extraordinary success of Elizabeth I had rested on her political shrewdness and flexibility, her careful management of finances, her wise selection of ministers, her clever manipulation of Parliament, and her sense of royal dignity and devotion to hard work. The aging queen had always refused to discuss the succession. After her Scottish cousin James Stuart succeeded her as James I (1603–1625), Elizabeth's strengths seemed even greater than they actually had been. The Stuarts lacked every quality Elizabeth had possessed.

King James was well educated and learned but lacking in common sense — he was once called "the wisest fool in Christendom." He also lacked the common touch. Urged to wave at the crowds who waited to greet their new ruler, James complained that he was tired, and threatened to drop his breeches "so they can cheer at my arse." Having left barbarous and violent Scotland for rich and prosperous England, James believed he had entered "the Promised Land." As soon as he got to London, the new English king went to see the Crown jewels.

Abysmally ignorant of English law and of the English Parliament, but sublimely arrogant, James was devoted to the theory of the divine right of kings. He expressed his ideas about divine right in his essay "The Trew Law of Free Monarchy." According to James I, a monarch has a divine (or God-given) right to his authority, and is responsible only to God. Rebellion is the worst of political crimes. If a king orders something evil, the subject should respond with passive disobedience but should be prepared to accept any penalty for non-compliance.

James substituted political theorizing and talk for real work. He lectured the House of Commons: "There are no privileges and immunities which can stand against a divinely appointed King." This notion, implying total royal jurisdiction over the liberties, persons, and properties of English men and women, formed the basis of the Stuart concept of absolutism. Such a view ran directly counter to the long-standing English idea that a person's property could not be taken away without due process of law. James's expression of such views before the English House of Commons constituted a grave political mistake.

The House of Commons guarded the pocketbook of the nation, and James and later Stuart kings badly needed to open that pocketbook. Elizabeth had bequeathed to James a sizable royal debt. Through prudent management the debt could have been gradually reduced, but James I looked upon all revenues as a happy windfall to be squandered on a lavish court and favorite courtiers. In fact, the extravagance and licentiousness of James' court, and the public flaunting of his male lovers, weakened respect for the monarchy.

Elizabeth had also left to her Stuart successors a House of Commons that appreciated its

THE
LAMENTABLE
COMPLAINTS
OF
NICK FROTH the Tapſter, and
RVLEROST the Cooke.
Concerning the reſtraint lately ſet forth,
againſt drinking, potting, and piping on the Sab-
bath day, and againſt ſelling meate.

Printed in the yeare, 1641.

*PURITAN IDEALS OPPOSED The Puritans preached sober living and abstention from alcoholic drink, rich food, and dancing. This pamphlet reflects the common man's hostility to such restraints. "Potting" refers to tankards of beer; "piping" means making music. (The British Museum)*

own financial strength and intended to use that strength to acquire a greater say in the government of the state. The knights and burgesses who sat at Westminster in the early seventeenth century wanted to discuss royal expenditures, religious reform, and foreign affairs. In short, the Commons wanted what amounted to sovereignty.

Profound social changes had occurred since the sixteenth century. The English House of Commons during the reigns of James I and his son Charles I (1625-1649) was very different from the assembly Henry VIII had terrorized into passing his Reformation legislation. A social revolution had brought about the change. The dissolution of the monasteries and the sale of monastic land had enriched many people. Agricultural techniques like the draining of wasteland and the application of fertilizers improved the land and its yield. Old manorial common land had been enclosed and turned into sheep runs; breeding was carefully supervised, and the size of the flocks increased. In these activities, as well as in renting and leasing parcels of land, precise accounts were kept.

Many men invested in commercial ventures at home, such as the expanding cloth industry, and in partnerships and joint stock companies engaged in foreign enterprises. They made prudent marriages. All these developments led to a great deal of social mobility. Both in commerce and in agriculture, the English in the late sixteenth and early seventeenth centuries were capitalists, investing their profits to make more money. Although the international inflation of the period hit everywhere, in England commercial and agricultural income rose faster than prices. Wealthy country gentry, rich city merchants, and financiers invested abroad.

The typical pattern was for the commercially successfully to set themselves up as country gentry, thus creating an elite group that possessed a far greater proportion of land and of the national wealth in 1640 than had been the case in 1540. Small wonder that in 1640 someone could declare in the House of Commons, probably accurately, "We could buy the House of Lords three times over." Increased wealth had also produced a better-educated and more articulate House of Commons. Many members had acquired at least a

smattering of legal knowledge, and they used that knowledge to search for medieval precedents from which to argue against the king. The class that dominated the Commons wanted political power corresponding to its economic strength.

In England, unlike France, there was no social stigma attached to paying taxes. Members of the House of Commons were willing to tax themselves provided they had some say in the expenditure of those taxes and in the formulation of state policies. The Stuart kings, however, considered such ambitions intolerable presumption and a threat to their divine-right prerogative. Consequently, at every Parliament between 1603 and 1640 bitter squabbles erupted between the Crown and the wealthy, articulate, and legal-minded Commons. Charles I's attempt to govern without Parliament (1629-1640), and to finance his government by arbitrary nonparliamentary levies, brought the country to a crisis.

An issue graver than royal extravagance and Parliament's desire to make the law also disturbed the English and embittered relations between the king and the House of Commons. That problem was religion. In the early seventeenth century, increasing numbers of English men and women felt dissatisfied with the Church of England established by Henry VIII and reformed by Elizabeth. Many believed the Reformation had not gone far enough. They wanted to "purify" the Anglican church of Roman Catholic elements — elaborate vestments and ceremonial, the position of the altar at the east end of the church, even the giving and wearing of wedding rings. These people were called Puritans.

It is very difficult to establish what proportion of the English population was Puritan. It is clear, however, that many English men and women were attracted by the socioeconomic implications of John Calvin's theology. Calvinism emphasized hard work, sobriety, thrift, competition, and postponement of pleasure, and tended to link sin and poverty with weakness and moral corruption. These attitudes fit in precisely with the economic approaches and practices of many (successful) businessmen and farmers. These values have frequently been called the Protestant, or middle-class, or capitalist, ethic. While it is hazardous to identify capitalism and progress with Protestantism – there were many successful Catholic capitalists – the "Protestant virtues" represented the prevailing values of the great majority of members of the House of Commons.

James I and Charles I both gave the impression of being highly sympathetic to Roman Catholicism. Charles supported the policies of William Laud, archbishop of Canterbury (1573–1645), who tried to impose elaborate ritual and rich ceremonial on all churches. Laud insisted on complete uniformity of church services, and enforced that uniformity through an ecclesiastical court called High Commission. People believed the country was being led back to Roman Catholicism. When in 1639 Laud attempted to impose a new prayer book, modeled on the Anglican Book of Common Prayer, on the Presbyterian Scots, the Scots revolted. In order to finance an army to put down the Scots, King Charles was compelled to summon Parliament in November 1640.

For eleven years Charles I had ruled without Parliament, financing his government through extraordinary stopgap levies, considered illegal by most English people. For example, the king revived a medieval law requiring coastal districts to help pay the cost of ships for defense, but levied the tax, called ship money, on inland as well as coastal counties. When the issue was tested in the courts, the judges, having been suborned, decided in the king's favor.

Most members of Parliament believed that such taxation without consent amounted to arbitrary and absolute despotism. Consequently, they were not willing to trust the king with an army. Accordingly, this Parliament, commonly called the Long Parliament because it sat from 1640 to 1660, proceeded to enact legislation that limited the power of the monarch and made arbitrary government impossible.

In 1641, the Commons passed the Triennial Act, which compelled the king to summon Parliament every three years. The Commons impeached Archbishop Laud and abolished the House of Lords and the Court of High Commission. It went further and threatened to abolish the institution of episcopacy. King Charles, fearful of a Scottish invasion – the original reason for summoning Parliament – accepted these measures. Understanding and peace were not achieved, however, partly because radical members of the Commons pushed increasingly revolutionary propositions, partly because Charles maneuvered to rescind those he had already approved. An uprising in Ireland precipitated civil war.

Ever since Henry II had conquered Ireland in 1171, English governors had mercilessly ruled the Irish, and English landlords had ruthlessly exploited them. The English Reformation had made a bad situation worse: because the Irish remained Catholic, religious differences became united with economic and political oppression. Without an army, Charles I could neither come to terms with the Scots nor put down the Irish rebellion, and the Long Parliament remained unwilling to place an army under a king it did not trust.

Charles thus instigated military action against parliamentary forces. He recruited an army drawn from the nobility and their cavalry staff, the rural gentry, and mercenaries. The Parliamentary army was composed of the militia of the City of London, country squires with business connections, and men with a firm belief in the spiritual duty of serving.

The English Civil War (1642-1646) tested whether sovereignty in England was to reside in the king or in Parliament. The Civil War did not resolve that problem, although it ended in 1649 with the execution of King Charles on the charge of high treason – a severe blow to royal power. The period between 1649 and 1660, called the Interregnum because it separated two monarchial periods, saw England's one experience of military dictatorship.

*PURITANICAL ABSOLUTISM IN ENGLAND: CROMWELL AND THE PROTECTORATE*

The problem of sovereignty was vigorously debated in the middle years of the seventeenth century. In *Leviathan,* the English philosopher and political theorist Thomas Hobbes (1588-1679) maintained that sovereignty is ultimately derived from the people, who transfer it to the monarchy by implicit contract. The power of the ruler is absolute, but kings do not hold their power by divine right. This view pleased no one in the seventeenth century.

When Charles I was beheaded on January 30, 1649, the kingship was abolished. A commonwealth, or republican form of government, was proclaimed. Theoretically, legislative power rested in the surviving members of Parliament and executive power in a council of state. In fact, the army that had defeated the royal forces controlled the government, and Oliver Cromwell controlled the army.

Although called the Protectorate, the rule of Cromwell (1653-1658) constituted military dictatorship.

Oliver Cromwell (1599-1658) came from the country gentry, the class that dominated the House of Commons in the early seventeenth century. He himself had sat in the Long Parliament. Cromwell rose in the parliamentary army, and achieved nationwide fame by infusing the army with his Puritan convictions and molding it into the highly effective military machine, called the New Model Army, that defeated the royalist forces.

Parliament had written a constitution, the Instrument of Government (1653), that invested executive power in a lord protector (Cromwell) and a council of state. The Instrument provided for triennial parliaments and gave Parliament the sole power to raise taxes. But after repeated disputes Cromwell tore the document up. He continued the standing army and proclaimed quasi-martial law. He divided England into twelve military districts, each governed by a major general. On the issue of religion Cromwell favored broad toleration, and the Instrument of Government gave all Christians, except Roman Catholics, the right to practice their faith. Toleration meant state protection of many different Protestant sects, and most English people had no enthusiasm for such a notion; the idea was far ahead of its time. Cromwell identified Irish Catholicism with sedition. In 1649 he crushed rebellion there with merciless savagery, leaving a legacy of Irish hatred for England that has not yet subsided. The state rigorously censored the press, forbade sports, and kept the theaters closed.

Cromwell's regulation of the nation's economy had features typical of seventeenth-century absolutism. The lord protector's policies were mercantilist, similar to those Colbert established in France. Cromwell enforced a navigation act requiring that English goods be transported on English ships. The navigation act was a great boost to the development of an English merchant marine, and brought about a short but successful war with the commercially threatened Dutch. Cromwell also welcomed the immigration of Jews, because of their skills, and they began to return to England in larger numbers after four centuries of absence.

Absolute government collapsed when Cromwell died in 1658. Absolutism failed because the English got fed up with military rule. They longed for a return to civilian government, restoration of the common law, and social stability. Moreover, the strain of creating a community of puritanical saints proved too psychologically exhausting. Government by military dictatorship was an unfortunate experiment that English men and women never forgot and never repeated. By 1660, they were ready to restore the monarchy.

### THE RESTORATION OF THE ENGLISH MONARCHY

The Restoration of 1660 re-established the monarchy in the person of Charles II (1660–1685), eldest son of Charles I. At the same time both houses of Parliament were restored, together with the established Anglican church, the courts of law, and the system of local government through justices of the peace. The Restoration failed to resolve two serious problems. What was to be the attitude of the state toward Puritans, Catholics, and dissenters from the established church? And what was to be the constitutional position of the king – that is, what was to be relationship between the king and Parliament?

About the first of these issues, Charles II, a relaxed, easygoing, and sensual man, was basically indifferent. He was not interested in

THE HOUSE OF COMMONS   This seal of the Commonwealth shows the small House of Commons in session with the speaker presiding; the legend "in the third year of freedom" refers to 1651, three years after the abolition of the monarchy. In 1653, however, Cromwell abolished this "Rump Parliament" — so-called because it consisted of the few surviving members elected before the Civil War — and he and the army governed the land. (The British Museum)

doctrinal issues. Parliamentarians were, and they proceeded to enact a body of laws that sought to compel religious uniformity. Those who refused to receive the sacrament of the Church of England could not vote, hold public office, preach, teach, attend the universities, or even assemble for meetings, according to the Test Act of 1673. These restrictions could not be enforced. When the Quaker William Penn held a meeting of his friends and was arrested, the jury refused to convict him.

In politics, Charles II was determined "not to set out in his travels again," which meant that he intended to get along with Parliament. Charles II's solution to the problem of the relationship between the king and the House of Commons had profound importance for later constitutional development. Generally good rapport existed between the king and the strongly royalist Parliament that had restored him. This rapport was due largely to the king's appointment of a council of five men who served both as his major advisers and as members of Parliament, thus acting as liaison agents between the executive and the legislature. This body — known as the Cabal from the names of its five members (Clifford, Arlington, Buckingham, Ashley-Cooper and Lauderdale) — was an ancestor of the later cabinet system. It gradually came to be accepted that the Cabal was answerable in Parliament for the decisions of the king. This development gave rise to the concept of ministerial responsibility: royal ministers must answer to the Commons.

Harmony between the Crown and Parliament rested on the understanding that Charles would summon frequent parliaments and that Parliament would vote him sufficient revenues. However, although Parliament believed Charles had a virtual divine right to govern, it did not grant him an adequate income. Accordingly, Charles entered into a secret agreement with Louis XIV. The French king would give Charles £200,000 annually, and in return Charles would relax the laws against Catholics, gradually re-Catholicize England, and support French policy against the Dutch.

When the details of this secret treaty leaked out, a great wave of anti-Catholic fear swept England. This fear was compounded by a crucial fact: although Charles had produced several bastards, he had no legitimate children. It therefore appeared that his brother and heir, James, Duke of York, who had publicly acknowledged his Catholicism, would inaugurate a Catholic dynasty. The combination of hatred for the French absolutism embodied in Louis XIV, hostility to Roman Catholicism, and fear of a permanent Catholic dynasty produced virtual hysteria. The Commons passed an exclusion bill denying the succession to a Roman Catholic, but Charles quickly dissolved Parliament and the bill never became law.

James II (1685–1688) did succeed his brother, and almost at once the worst English anti-Catholic fears were realized. In direct violation of the Test Act, James appointed Roman Catholics to positions in the army, the universities, and local government. When these actions were tested in the courts, the judges, whom James had appointed, decided for the king. The king was suspending the law at will, and appeared to be reviving the absolutism of his father and grandfather. He went further. Attempting to broaden his base of support with Protestant dissenters and nonconformists, James issued a declaration of indulgence granting religious freedom to all.

Two events gave the signals for revolution. First, seven bishops of the Church of England petitioned the king that they not be forced to read the declaration of indulgence because of their belief it was an illegal act. They were imprisoned in the Tower of London but subsequently acquitted amid great public enthusiasm. Second, in June 1688, James's queen produced a male heir. A Catholic dynasty seemed assured. The fear of a Roman Catholic monarchy, supported by France and ruling outside the law, prompted a group of eminent persons to offer the English throne to James's Protestant daughter Mary and her Dutch husband, Prince William of Orange. In November 1688, James II, his queen, and infant son fled to France and became pensioners of Louis XIV.

The English call the events of 1688 the Glorious Revolution. The revolution was indeed glorious in the sense that it replaced one king with another with a minimum of bloodshed. It also represented the destruction, once and for all, of the idea of divine-right monarchy. William and Mary accepted the English throne from Parliament, and in so doing explicitly recognized the supremacy of Parliament. The revolution of 1688 established the principle that sovereignty, the ultimate power in the state, rested in Parliament, and that the king ruled with the consent of the governed.

The men who had brought about the revolution quickly framed their intentions in the Bill of Rights, which is the cornerstone of the modern British constitution. The basic principles of the Bill of Rights were formulated in direct response to Stuart absolutism. Law was to be made in Parliament; once made, the law could not be suspended by the Crown. Parliament had to be called at least every three years. Both elections to and debate in Parliament were to be free in the sense that the Crown was not to interfere in them; this aspect of the Bill was widely disregarded in the eighteenth century. Judges would hold their offices "during good behavior," which assured the independence of the judiciary. No longer could the Crown get the judicial decisions it wanted by threats of removal. There was to be no standing army in peacetime – a limitation designed to prevent the repetition of either Stuart or Cromwellian military government. The Bill of Rights granted "that the subjects which are Protestants may have arms for their defense suitable to their conditions and as al-

lowed by law,"[4] meaning that Catholics could not possess firearms because the Protestant majority feared them. Additional parliamentary legislation granted freedom of worship to Protestant dissenters and nonconformists and required that the English monarch always be Protestant in faith.

The Glorious Revolution found its best defense in the political philosopher John Locke's "Second Treatise on Civil Government" (1690). A spokesman for the great land-owning class that had brought about the revolution, Locke (1632-1704) maintained that men set up civil governments in order to defend property. Thus the purpose of government is to protect life, liberty, and property. Locke's ideas, though not profound, had great influence throughout the eighteenth century.

However glorious, the events of 1688-1690 did not constitute a *democratic* revolution. The revolution placed sovereignty in Parliament, and Parliament represented the upper classes. The great majority of English people acquired no say in their government. The English revolution established a constitutional monarchy; it also inaugurated an age of aristocratic government, which lasted at least until 1832 and probably until 1914.

In the course of the eighteenth century, the cabinet system of government evolved. The term *cabinet* refers to the small private room in which English rulers consulted their chief ministers. In a cabinet system the leading ministers, who must have seats in and the support of a majority of the House of Commons, formulate common policy and conduct the business of the country. During the administration of one royal minister, Sir Robert Walpole (1721-1742), the idea developed that the cabinet was responsible to the House of Commons. The king normally presided at cabinet meetings, but because the Hanoverian king George I (1714–1727) did not understand enough English to follow the discussions, he stopped attending cabinet sessions. George II (1727–1760) followed that precedent. The influence of the Crown in decision making accordingly declined. Walpole enjoyed the favor of the monarchy and of the House of Commons, and came to be called the king's first, or prime, minister. In the English cabinet system both legislative and executive power are held by the leading ministers, who form the government.

## THE DUTCH REPUBLIC IN THE SEVENTEENTH CENTURY

The seventeenth century witnessed an unparalleled flowering of Dutch scientific, artistic, and literary achievement. In this period, often called "the golden age of the Netherlands," Dutch ideas and attitudes played a profound role in shaping a new and modern worldview. At the same time the Republic of the United Provinces of the Netherlands represents another model of the development of the modern state.

In the late sixteenth century, the seven northern provinces of the Netherlands, of which Holland and Zeeland were the most prosperous, succeeded in throwing off Spanish domination. This success was based on their geographical lines of defense, the wealth of the cities, the brilliant military strategy of William the Silent, the preoccupation of Philip II of Spain with so many other concerns, and the northern provinces' vigorous Calvinism. In 1581 the seven provinces of the Union of Utrecht had formed the United Provinces (page 528). Philip II continued to try to crush the Dutch with the Armada but in 1609 his son Philip III agreed to a truce that implicitly recognized the independence of the United Provinces. At the time neither side

expected the peace to be permanent. The Peace of Westphalia in 1648, however, confirmed the Dutch republic's independence.

Within each province an oligarchy of wealthy merchants called regents handled domestic affairs in the local Estates. The provincial Estates held virtually all the power. A federal assembly, or States General, handled matters of foreign affairs, such as war. But the States General did not possess sovereign authority, since all issues had to be referred back to the local Estates for approval. The States General appointed a representative, the stadholder, in each province. As the highest executive there, the stadholder carried out ceremonial functions and was responsible for defense and good order. The sons of William the Silent, Maurice and William Louis, held the office of stadholder in all seven provinces. The regents in each province jealously guarded local independence and resisted efforts at centralization. Nevertheless, Holland, which had the largest navy and the most wealth, dominated the republic and the States General. Significantly, the Estates assembled at Holland's capital, The Hague.

The government of the United Provinces fits none of the standard categories of seventeenth-century political organization. The Dutch were not monarchial, but fiercely republican. The government was controlled by wealthy merchants and financiers. Although rich, their values were not aristocratic but strongly middle-class, emphasizing thrift, hard work, and simplicity in living. The Dutch republic was not a strong federation but a confederation – that is, a weak union of strong provinces. The provinces were a temptation to powerful neighbors, yet the Dutch resisted the long Spanish effort at reconquest and withstood both French and English attacks in the second half of the century. Louis XIV's hatred of the Dutch was proverbial. They

MODEL OF A SEVENTEENTH-CENTURY FLUYT
The Dutch surpassed all nations in the design of fast-sailing ships. The fluyt or fluteship was cheap to construct, carried a large cargo, and required only a small crew. It gave the Dutch a great advantage, resulting in their notable commercial success. (Photo: Caroline Buckler)

represented all that he despised – middle-class values, religious toleration, and political independence.

The political success of the Dutch rested on the phenomenal commercial prosperity of the Netherlands. The moral and ethical bases of that commercial wealth were thrift, frugality, and religious toleration. John Calvin had written, "From where do the merchant's profits come except from his own diligence and industry"; this attitude undoubtedly encouraged a sturdy people who had waged a centuries-old struggle against the sea.

Alone of all European peoples in the seventeenth century, the Dutch practiced religious toleration. Peoples of all faiths were welcome within their borders. It is a striking testimony to the urbanity of Dutch society that in a century when patriotism was closely identified with religious uniformity, the Calvinist province of Holland allowed its highest official, Jan van Oldenbarneveldt, to continue to practice his Roman Catholic faith. As long as a businessman conducted his religion in private, the government did not interfere with him.

Toleration also paid off: it attracted a great deal of foreign capital and investment. Deposits at the Bank of Amsterdam were guaranteed by the city council, and in the middle years of the century the bank became Europe's best source of cheap credit and commercial intelligence, and the main clearinghouse for bills of exchange. Men of all races and creeds traded in Amsterdam, at whose docks on the Amstel River five thousand ships, half the merchant marine of the United Provinces, were berthed. Joost van den Vondel, the poet of Dutch imperialism, exulted:

*God, God, the Lord of Amstel cried, hold every*
*   conscience free;*
*And Liberty ride, on Holland's tide, with billow-*
*   ing sails to sea,*
*And run our Amstel out and in; let freedom gird*
*   the bold,*
*And merchant in his counting house stand elbow*
*   deep in gold.*⁵

The fishing industry was the cornerstone of the Dutch economy. For half the year, from June to December, fishing fleets combed the dangerous English coast and the North Sea, raking in tiny herring. Profits from herring stimulated shipbuilding, and even before 1600 the Dutch were offering the lowest shipping rates in Europe. Although Dutch cities became famous for their exports – diamonds, linen from Haarlem, pottery from Delft – Dutch wealth depended less on exports than on transport. The merchant marine was the largest in Europe.

In 1602, a group of the regents of Holland formed the Dutch East India Company, a joint stock company. Each investor received a percentage of the profits proportional to the amount of money he had put in. Within half a century, the Dutch East India Company had cut heavily into Portuguese trading in the Far East. The Dutch seized the Cape of Good

*VERMEER: WOMEN WEIGHING GOLD  Vermeer painted pictures of middle-class women involved in ordinary activities in the quiet interiors of their homes. Unrivaled among Dutch masters for his superb control of light, in this painting (ca 1657) Vermeer illuminates the pregnant woman weighing gold on her scales, as Christ in the painting on the wall weighs the saved and the damned. (National Gallery of Art, Washington, D.C. Widener Collection)*

Hope, Ceylon, and Malacca, and established trading posts in each place. In the 1630s, the Dutch East India Company was paying its investors about 35 percent return annually on their investments. The Dutch West India Company, founded in 1621, traded extensively with Latin America and Africa.

Although the initial purpose of both companies was commercial – the import of spices and silks to Europe – the Dutch found themselves involved in the imperialistic exploitation of large parts of the Pacific and Latin America. Amsterdam, the center of a worldwide Dutch empire, became the commercial and financial capital of Europe. During the seventeenth century the Dutch translated their commercial acumen and flexibility into political and imperialist terms with striking success. But war with France and England in the 1670s hurt the United Provinces. The long War of the Spanish Succession, in which the Dutch supported England against France, was a costly drain on Dutch manpower and financial resources. The peace signed in 1715 to end the war marked the beginning of Dutch economic decline.

———◆———

According to Thomas Hobbes, the central drive in every man is "a perpetual and restless desire of Power, after Power, that ceaseth only in Death." The seventeenth century solved the problem of *sovereign power* in two fundamental

ways, absolutism and constitutionalism. The France of Louis XIV witnessed the emergence of the fully absolutist state. The king commanded all the powers of the state: judicial, military, political, and to a great extent ecclesiastical. France developed a centralized bureaucracy, a professional army, a state-directed economy, all of which Louis personally supervised. For the first time in history all the institutions and powers of the national state were effectively controlled by a single person. The king saw himself as the representative of God on earth, and it has been said that "to the seventeenth century imagination God was a sort of image of Louis XIV."[6]

As Louis XIV personifies absolutism, so Stuart England exemplifies the evolution of the first modern constitutional state. The conflicts between Parliament and the first two Stuart rulers, James I and Charles I, tested where sovereign power would rest in the state. The resulting Civil War did not solve the problem. The Instrument of Government, the document produced in 1653 by the victorious parliamentary army, provided for a balance of governmental authority and recognition of popular rights; as such, the Instrument has been called the first modern constitution. Unfortunately, it lacked public support. James II's absolutist tendencies brought on the Revolution of 1688, and the people who made that revolution settled three basic issues. Sovereign power was divided between king and parliament, with parliament enjoying the greater share. Government was to be based on the rule of law. And the liberties of English people were made explicit in written form, in the Bill of Rights. The framers of the English constitution left to later generations the task of making constitutional government work.

The models of governmental power established by seventeenth-century England and France strongly influenced other states then and ever since. As the Mississippi novelist William Faulkner wrote, "The past isn't dead; it's not even past."

## NOTES

1. S. de Gramont, ed., *The Age of Magnificence: Memoirs of the Court of Louis XIV by the Duc de Saint-Simon,* Capricorn Books, New York, 1964, pp. 141–145.

2. Ibid., p. 183.

3. S. H. Elliott, *Imperial Spain, 1469–1716,* Mentor Books, New York, 1963, pp. 306–308.

4. C. Stephenson and G. F. Marcham, *Sources of English Constitutional History,* Harper & Row, New York, 1937, p. 601.

5. Quoted by D. Maland, *Europe in the Seventeenth Century,* Macmillan, New York, 1967, pp. 198–199.

6. Quoted by Carl J. Friedrich and Charles Blitzer, *The Age of Power,* Cornell University Press, Ithaca, New York, 1957, p. 112.

## SUGGESTED READING

Students who wish to explore the problems presented in this chapter in greater depth will easily find a rich and exciting literature with many titles available in paperback editions. Geoffrey Parker, *Europe in Crisis, 1598–1618* (1980), provides a readable introduction to the religious, social, and economic tensions of the period. C. Friedrich, *The Age of the Baroque, 1610–1660* (1962), is a good survey. Perhaps the best recent study of absolutism is P. Anderson, *Lineages of the Absolutist State* (1974), a Marxist interpretation of absolutism in western and eastern Europe. The short study of M. Beloff, *The Age of Absolutism* (1967), concentrates on the social forces that underlay administrative change. H. Rosenberg, "Absolute Monarchy and Its Legacy," in *Early Modern Europe, 1450–1650* (1967), ed. N. F. Cantor and S. Werthman, is a seminal study. T. Aston, ed., *Crisis in Europe, 1560–1660* (1967), contains stimulating essays by leading authorities. The classic treatment of constitutionalism remains that of C. H. McIlwain, *Constitutionalism: Ancient and Modern* (1940), written by a great scholar during the rise of German fascism. S. B. Crimes, *English Constitutional History* (1967), is an excellent survey with valuable chapters on the sixteenth through eighteenth centuries.

Louis XIV and his age have seduced the attention of many scholars. The best contemporary biography is J. Wolf, *Louis XIV* (1968), which stresses Louis' contribution to the development of the modern bureaucratic state. For a variety of opinions about Louis, see William F. Church, ed., *Louis XIV in Historical Thought* (1978). Two works of W. H. Lewis, *The Splendid Century* (1957) and *The Sunset of the Splendid Century* (1963), make delightful reading and contain useful material on social history. R. Hatton, *Europe in the Age of Louis XIV* (1979), is a splendidly illustrated survey of many aspects of European culture in the seventeenth century. O. Ranum, *Paris in the Age of Absolutism* (1968), describes the geographical, political, economic, and architectural significance of the cultural capital of Europe. R. Mousnier, *Peasant Uprisings in Seventeenth-Century France, Russia, and China* (1970), an important study in comparative history, treats agrarian relationships and social stratification. V. L. Tapie, *The Age of Grandeur: Baroque Art and Architecture* (1960), is a magnificently illustrated book that emphasizes the relationship between art and politics. Part 4 of L. Romier, *A History of France,* trans. A. L. Rowse (1962), offers an intelligible and nationalistic narrative. For Spain, J. H. Elliott, *Imperial Spain, 1469–1716,* rev. ed. (1977), is a sensitively written and authoritative study.

G. M. Trevelyan, *England Under the Stuarts* (1960), is a good starting point for English social and political history. Brief accounts of many facets of English culture are contained in M. Ashley, *England in the Seventeenth Century* (1961), and J. H. Plumb, *England in the Eighteenth Century* (1961). M. Weber, *The Protestant Ethic and the Spirit of Capitalism* (1958), traces the relationship between Protestantism and socioeconomic developments. W. Haller, *The Rise of Puritanism* (1957), is the best treatment of English Puritanism, but it is for the advanced student. For the background to the Civil War and the war itself, see C. V. Wedgwood, *The King's Peace* (1969) and *The King's War* (1959), both highly readable; the old but scholarly biography of Cromwell by C. Firth, *Oliver Cromwell* (1956); and the recent popular study by A. Fraser, *Cromwell* (1975). C. Brinton, *The Anatomy of Revolution* (1952), contains an interesting analysis of the English Civil War and contrasts it with the French and Russian revolutions. L. Stone, *The Crisis of the Aristocracy, 1558–1641* (1967), is broader in scope than the title implies and in fact treats many aspects of English social history. Stone is a leading authority on English family history.

On Holland, the best introduction to the relationship between commercial development and the growth of democratic ideas and institutions remains Henri Pirenne, *Early Democracies in the Low Countries* (1963), especially chapters X and XI. C. R. Boxer, *The Dutch Seaborne Empire* (1980), and the appropriate chapters of D. Maland, *Europe in the Seventeenth Century* (1967), are useful for Dutch overseas expansion and the reasons for Dutch prosperity. K. H. D. Haley, *The Dutch in the Seventeenth Century* (1972), is a splendidly illustrated appreciation of Dutch commercial and artistic achievements. No recent work has replaced the well-written, thorough narrative of J. L. Motley, *The Rise of the Dutch Republic,* 3 vols., (1898).

# CHAPTER 17

## ABSOLUTISM IN EASTERN EUROPE

### TO 1740

THE SEVENTEENTH CENTURY witnessed a struggle between constitutionalism and absolutism in eastern Europe. With the notable exception of the kingdom of Poland, monarchial absolutism was everywhere triumphant in eastern Europe; constitutionalism was decisively defeated. Absolute monarchies emerged in Austria, Prussia, and Russia. This was a development of great significance: these three monarchies exercised enormous influence until 1918, and they created a strong authoritarian tradition that is still dominant in eastern Europe.

Although the monarchs of eastern Europe were greatly impressed by Louis XIV and his model of royal absolutism, their states differed in several important ways from their French counterpart. Louis XIV built French absolutism on the heritage of a well-developed medieval monarchy and a strong royal bureaucracy. And when Louis XIV came to the throne the powers of the nobility were already somewhat limited, the French middle class was relatively strong, and the peasants were generally free from serfdom. Eastern absolutism rested upon a very different social reality: a powerful nobility, a weak middle class, and an oppressed peasantry condemned to serfdom.

These differences in social conditions raise three major questions. First, why did the basic structure of society in eastern Europe move away from that of western Europe in the early modern period? Second, how and why, in their different social environments, did the rulers of Austria, Prussia, and Russia manage to build powerful absolute monarchies, which proved more durable than that of Louis XIV? Finally, how did the absolute monarchs' interaction with artists and architects contribute to the splendid achievements of baroque culture? These are the questions this chapter seeks to answer.

## LORDS AND PEASANTS IN EASTERN EUROPE

When absolute monarchy took shape in eastern Europe in the seventeenth century, it built on social and economic foundations laid between roughly 1400 and 1650. In those years the princes and the landed nobility of eastern Europe rolled back the gains made by the peasantry during the High Middle Ages and reimposed a harsh serfdom on the rural masses. The nobility also reduced the importance of the towns and the middle classes. This process differed profoundly from developments in western Europe at the same time. In the west peasants won greater freedom and the urban capitalistic middle class continued its rise. Thus, the east that emerged contrasted sharply with the west – another aspect of the shattered unity of medieval Latin Christendom.

### THE MEDIEVAL BACKGROUND

Between roughly 1400 and 1650, nobles and rulers re-established serfdom in the eastern lands of Bohemia, Silesia, Hungary, eastern Germany, Poland, Lithuania, and Russia. The east – the land east of the Elbe River in Germany, which historians often call "East Elbia" – gained a certain social and economic unity in the process. But eastern peasants lost their rights and freedoms. They became bound first to the land they worked and then, by degrading obligations, to the lords they served.

This development was a tragic reversal of trends in the High Middle Ages. The period from roughly 1050 to 1300 had been a time of general economic expansion characterized by the growth of trade, towns, and population. Expansion also meant clearing the forests and colonizing the frontier beyond the Elbe River. Anxious to attract German settlers to their sparsely populated lands, the rulers and nobles of eastern Europe had offered potential new-comers attractive economic and legal incentives. Large numbers of incoming settlers obtained land on excellent terms and gained much greater personal freedom. These benefits were also gradually extended to the local Slavic populations, even those of central Russia. Thus by 1300 there had occurred a very general improvement in peasant conditions in eastern Europe. Serfdom all but disappeared. Peasants bargained freely with their landlords and moved about as they pleased. Opportunities and improvements east of the Elbe had a positive impact on western Europe, where the weight of serfdom was also reduced between 1100 and 1300.

After about 1300, however, as Europe's population and economy both declined grievously, mainly because of the Black Death, the east and the west went in different directions. In both east and west there occurred a many-sided landlord reaction, as lords sought to solve their tough economic problems by more heavily exploiting the peasantry. Yet this reaction generally failed in the west. In many western areas by 1500 almost all of the peasants were completely free, and in the rest of western Europe serf obligations had declined greatly. East of the Elbe, however, the landlords won. By 1500, eastern peasants were well on their way to becoming serfs again.

Throughout eastern Europe, as in western Europe, the drop in population and prices in the fourteenth and fifteenth centuries caused severe labor shortages and hard times for the nobles. Yet rather than offer better economic and legal terms to keep old peasants and attract new ones, eastern landlords used their political and police power to turn the tables on the peasants. They did this in two ways.

First, the lords made their kings and princes issue laws that restricted or eliminated the peasants' precious, time-honored right of free movement. Thus, a peasant could no longer leave to take advantage of better opportunities elsewhere without the lord's permission, and the lord had no reason to make such concessions. In Prussian territories by 1500, the law required that runaway peasants be hunted down and returned to their lords; a runaway servant was to be nailed to a post by one ear and given a knife to cut himself loose. Until the middle of the fifteenth century, medieval Russian peasants had been free to move wherever they wished and seek the best landlord. Thereafter this freedom was gradually curtailed, so that by 1497 a Russian peasant had the right to move only during a two-week period after the fall harvest. Eastern peasants were losing their status as free and independent men and women.

Second, lords steadily took more and more of their peasants' land and imposed heavier and heavier labor obligations. Instead of being independent farmers paying reasonable, freely negotiated rents, peasants tended to become forced laborers on the lords' estates. By the early 1500s, lords in many territories could command their peasants to work for them without pay as many as six days a week. A German writer of the mid-sixteenth century described peasants in eastern Prussia who "do not possess the heritage of their holdings and have to serve their master whenever he wants them."[1]

The gradual erosion of the peasantry's economic position was bound up with manipulation of the oppressive legal system. The local lord was also the local prosecutor, judge, and jailer. As a matter of course, he ruled in his own favor in disputes with his peasants. There were no independent royal officials to provide justice or uphold the common law.

## THE CONSOLIDATION OF SERFDOM

Between 1500 and 1650, the social, legal, and economic conditions of peasants in eastern Europe continued to decline. Free peasants lost their freedom and became serfs. In Poland, for example, nobles gained complete control over their peasants in 1574, after which they could legally inflict the death penalty on their serfs whenever they wished. In Prussia a long series of oppressive measures reached their culmination in 1653. Not only were all the old privileges of the lords reaffirmed, but peasants were assumed to be in "hereditary subjugation" to their lords unless they could prove the contrary in the lords' courts, which was practically impossible. Prussian peasants were serfs tied to their lords as well as to the land.

In Russia the right of peasants to move from a given estate was "temporarily" suspended in the 1590s and permanently abolished in 1603. In 1649, a new law code completed the process. At the insistence of the lower nobility, the Russian tsar lifted the nine-year time limit on the recovery of runaways. Henceforth, runaway peasants were to be returned to their lords whenever they were caught, as long as they lived. The last small hope of escaping serfdom was gone. Control of serfs was strictly the lords' own business, for the new law code set no limits on the lords' authority over their peasants. Although the political development of the various eastern states differed, the legal re-establishment of permanent hereditary serfdom was the common fate of peasants in the east by the middle of the seventeenth century.

The consolidation of serfdom between 1500 and 1650 was accompanied by the growth of estate agriculture, particularly in Poland and eastern Germany. In the sixteenth century European economic expansion and population growth resumed after the great declines of the late Middle Ages. Prices for agricultural commodities also rose sharply as gold and silver flowed in from the New World. Thus, Polish and German lords had powerful economic incentives to increase the production of their estates. And they did.

Lords seized more and more peasant land for their own estates and then demanded and received ever more unpaid serf labor on those enlarged estates. Even when the estates were inefficient and technically backward, as they generally were, the great Polish nobles and middle-rank German lords squeezed sizable, cheap, and thus very profitable surpluses out of their impoverished peasants. These surpluses in wheat and timber were easily sold to big foreign merchants, who exported them to the growing cities of the west. The poor east helped feed the much wealthier west.

The re-emergence of serfdom in eastern Europe in the early modern period was clearly a momentous human development, and historians have advanced a variety of explanations for it. As always, some scholars have stressed the economic interpretation. Agricultural depression and population decline in the fourteenth and fifteenth centuries led to a severe labor shortage, they have argued, and thus eastern landlords naturally tied their precious peasants to the land. With the return of prosperity and the development of export markets in the sixteenth century, the landlords finished the job, grabbing the peasants' land and making them work as unpaid serfs on the enlarged estates. This argument by itself is not very convincing, for almost identical economic developments "caused" the opposite result in the west. Indeed, some historians have maintained that labor shortage and subsequent renewed expansion were key factors in the virtual disappearance of serfdom in western Europe.

PUNISHING SERFS  *This seventeenth-century illustration from Olearius's famous* Travels to Moscovy *suggests what eastern serfdom really meant. The scene* *is eastern Poland. There, according to Olearius, a common command of the lord was, "Beat him till the skin falls from the flesh." (Photo: Caroline Buckler)*

It seems fairly clear, therefore, that political rather than economic factors were crucial in the simultaneous rise of serfdom in the east and decline of serfdom in the west. Specifically, eastern lords enjoyed much greater political power than their western counterparts. In the late Middle Ages, when much of eastern Europe experienced innumerable wars and general political chaos, the noble landlord class greatly increased its political power at the expense of the ruling monarchs. There were, for example, many disputed royal successions, so that weak kings were forced to grant political favors to win the support of the nobility. Thus while strong "new monarchs" were rising in Spain, France, and

England and providing effective central government, kings were generally losing power in the east. Such weak kings could not resist the demands of the lords regarding their peasants.

Moreover, most eastern monarchs did not want to resist even if they could. The typical king was only "first among equals" in the noble class. He too thought mainly in "private" rather than "public" terms. He too wanted to squeeze as much as he could out of *his* peasants and enlarge *his* estates. The western concept and reality of sovereignty, as embodied in a king who protected the interests of all his people, was not well developed in eastern Europe before 1650.

The political power of the peasants was also weaker in eastern Europe, and declined steadily after about 1400. Although there were occasional bloody peasant uprisings against the oppression of the landlords, they never succeeded. Nor did eastern peasants effectively resist day-by-day infringements on their liberties by their landlords. Part of the reason was that the lords, rather than the kings, ran the courts – one of the important concessions nobles extorted from weak monarchs. It has also been suggested that peasant solidarity was weaker in the east, possibly reflecting the lack of long-established village communities on the eastern frontier.

Finally, with the approval of weak kings, the landlords systematically undermined the medieval privileges of the towns and the power of the urban classes. Instead of selling their products to local merchants in the towns, as required in the Middle Ages, the landlords sold directly to big foreign capitalists. For example, Dutch ships sailed up the rivers of Poland and eastern Germany to the loading docks of the great estates, completely short-circuiting the local towns. Moreover, "town air" no longer "made people free," for the eastern towns lost their medieval right of refuge and were compelled to return runaways to their lords. The population of the towns and the importance of the urban middle classes declined greatly. This development both reflected and promoted the supremacy of noble landlords in most of eastern Europe in the sixteenth century.

---

## THE RISE OF AUSTRIA AND PRUSSIA

In spite of the strength of the nobility and the weakness of many monarchs before 1600,

strong kings did begin to emerge in many lands in the course of the seventeenth century. War and the threat of war aided rulers greatly in their attempts to build absolute monarchies. There was an endless struggle for power, as eastern rulers not only fought each other but also battled with hordes of Asiatic invaders. In this atmosphere of continuous wartime emergency, monarchs reduced the political power of the landlord nobility. Cautiously leaving the nobles the unchallenged masters of their peasants, the absolutist monarchs of eastern Europe gradually gained and monopolized political power in three key areas. They imposed and collected permanent taxes without consent. They maintained permanent standing armies, which policed their subjects in addition to fighting abroad. And they conducted relations with other states as they pleased.

As with all general historical developments, there were important variations on the absolutist theme in eastern Europe. The royal absolutism created in Prussia was stronger and more effective than that established in Austria. This advantage gave Prussia a thin edge over Austria in the struggle for power in east-central Europe in the eighteenth century. That edge had enormous long-term political significance, for it was a rising Prussia that unified the German people in the nineteenth century and imposed upon them a fateful Prussian stamp.

### AUSTRIA AND THE OTTOMAN TURKS

Like all the peoples and rulers of central Europe, the Habsburgs of Austria emerged from the Thirty Years' War (pages 530–536) impoverished and exhausted. The effort to root out Protestantism in the German lands had failed utterly, and the authority of the Holy Roman Empire and its Habsburg em-

THE OTTOMAN SLAVE TAX  *This contemporary drawing shows Ottoman officials rounding up male Christian children in the Balkans. The children became part of a special slave corps, which served the* *sultan for life as soldiers and administrators. The slave tax and the slave corps were of great importance to the Ottoman Turks in the struggle with Austria. (The British Museum)*

perors had declined almost to the vanishing point. Yet defeat in central Europe also opened new vistas. The Habsburg monarchs were forced to turn inward and eastward in the attempt to fuse their diverse holdings into a strong unified state.

An important step in this direction had actually been taken in Bohemia during the Thirty Years' War. Protestantism had been strong among the Czechs of Bohemia, and in 1618 the Czech nobles who controlled the Bohemian Estates – the semiparliamentary body of Bohemia – had risen up against their Habsburg king. Not only was this revolt crushed, but the old Czech nobility was wiped out as well. Those Czech nobles who did not die in 1620 at the battle of the White Mountain (page 533), a momentous turning point in Czech history, had their estates confiscated. The Habsburg king, Ferdinand II (1619–1637), then redistributed the Czech lands to a motley band of aristocratic soldiers of fortune from all over Europe.

In fact, after 1650, 80 to 90 percent of the Bohemian nobility was of recent foreign origin and owed everything to the Habsburgs.

MAP 17.1   THE GROWTH OF AUSTRIA AND
BRANDENBURG-PRUSSIA TO 1748   *Austria expanded to the southwest into Hungary and Transylvania at the expense of the Ottoman Empire. But it
was unable to hold the rich German province of Silesia, which was conquered by Brandenburg-Prussia.*

With the help of this new nobility, the Habsburgs established strong direct rule over reconquered Bohemia. The condition of the
enserfed peasantry worsened: three days per
week of unpaid labor – the *robot* – became
the norm, and a quarter of the serfs worked
for their lords every day but Sundays and
religious holidays. Serfs also paid the taxes,
which further strengthened the alliance between the Habsburg monarch and the Bohemian nobility. Protestantism was also stamped
out, in the course of which a growing unity
of religion was brought about. The reorgani-

zation of Bohemia was a giant step toward
absolutism.

After the Thirty Years' War, Ferdinand III
centralized the government in the old hereditary provinces of Austria proper, the second
part of the Habsburg holdings (see Map
17.1). For the first time he created a permanent standing army, which stood ready to put
down any internal opposition. The Habsburg
monarchy was then ready to turn toward the
vast plains of Hungary, which it claimed as
the third and largest part of its dominion, in
opposition to the Ottoman Turks.

The Ottomans came out of the Anatolia, in present-day Turkey, and they created one of history's greatest military empires. At their peak in the middle of the sixteenth century under Suleiman the Magnificent (1520–1566), they ruled the most powerful empire in the world, bar none. Their possessions stretched from western Persia across North Africa and up into the heart of central Europe. Apostles of Islam, the Ottoman Turks were old and determined foes of the Catholic Habsburgs. Their armies had almost captured Vienna in 1529, and for more than 150 years thereafter they ruled all of the Balkans, almost all of Hungary, and part of southern Russia.

The Ottoman Empire was originally built on a fascinating and very non-European conception of state and society. There was an almost complete absence of private landed property. All the agricultural land of the empire was the personal hereditary property of the sultan, who exploited the land as he saw fit according to Ottoman political theory. There was, therefore, no security of landholding and no hereditary nobility. Everyone was dependent upon the sultan and virtually his slave.

Indeed, the top ranks of the bureaucracy were staffed by the sultan's slave corps. Every year the sultan levied a "tax" of one to three thousand male children upon the conquered Christian populations in the Balkans. These and other slaves were raised in Turkey as Muslims, and trained to fight and to administer. The most talented slaves rose to the top of the bureaucracy; the less fortunate formed the brave and skillful core of the sultan's army, the so-called janissary corps.

As long as the Ottoman Empire expanded, the system worked well. As the sultan won more territory, he could impose his slave tax on larger populations. Moreover, he could amply reward loyal and effective servants by letting them draw a carefully defined income from conquered Christian peasants on a strictly temporary basis. For a long time Christian peasants in eastern Europe were economically exploited less by the Muslim Turks than by Christian nobles, and they were not forced to convert to Islam. After about 1570, however, the powerful, centralized Ottoman system slowly began to disintegrate as the Turks' western advance was stopped. Temporary landholders became hard-to-control permanent oppressors. Weak sultans left the glory of the battlefield for the delights of the harem, and the army lost its dedication and failed to keep up with European military advances.

Yet in the late seventeenth century, under vigorous reforming leadership, the Ottoman Empire succeeded in marshaling its forces for one last mighty blow at Christian Europe. After wresting territory from Poland, fighting a long inconclusive war with Russia, and establishing an alliance with Louis XIV of France, the Turks turned again on Austria. A huge Turkish army surrounded Vienna and laid siege to it in 1683. But after holding out against great odds for two months, the city was relieved by a mixed force of Habsburg, Saxon, Bavarian, and Polish troops, and the Ottomans were forced to retreat. Soon the retreat became a rout. As their Russian and Venetian allies attacked on other fronts, the Habsburgs conquered all of Hungary and Transylvania (part of present-day Rumania) by 1699.

The Turkish wars and this great expansion strengthened the Habsburg army and promoted some sense of unity in the Habsburg lands. The Habsburgs moved to centralize their power and make it as absolute as possible. These efforts to create a fully developed, highly centralized, absolutist state were only partly successful.

The Habsburg state was composed of three separate and distinct territories – the old "hereditary provinces" of Austria, the kingdom of Bohemia, and the kingdom of Hungary. These three parts were tied together primarily by their common ruler – the Habsburg monarch. Each part had its own laws and political life, for the three noble-dominated Estates continued to exist, though with reduced powers. The Habsburgs themselves were well aware of the fragility of the union they had forged. In 1713, Charles VI (1711–1740) proclaimed the so-called Pragmatic Sanction, which stated that the Habsburg possessions were never to be divided and were always to be passed intact to a single heir, who might be female since Charles had no sons. Charles spent much of his reign trying to get this principle accepted by the various branches of the Habsburg family, by the three different Estates of the realm, and by the states of Europe. His fears turned out to be well founded.

The Hungarian nobility, despite its reduced strength, effectively thwarted the full development of Habsburg absolutism. Time and again throughout the seventeenth century, Hungarian nobles – the most numerous in Europe, making up from 5 to 7 percent of the Hungarian population – rose in revolt against the attempts of Vienna to impose absolute rule. They never triumphed decisively, but neither were they ever crushed and replaced as the Czech nobility had been in 1620.

Hungarians resisted because many of them were Protestants, especially in the area long ruled by the more tolerant Turks, and they hated the heavy-handed attempts of the conquering Habsburgs to re-Catholicize everyone. Moreover, the lords of Hungary often found a powerful military ally in Turkey. Finally, the Hungarian nobility, and even part of the peasantry, had become attached to a national ideal long before most of the peoples of Europe. They were determined to maintain as much independence and local control as possible. Thus when the Habsburgs were bogged down in the War of the Spanish Succession (page 570), the Hungarians rose in one last patriotic rebellion under Prince Francis Rakoczy in 1703. Rakoczy and his forces were eventually defeated, but this time the Habsburgs had to accept a definitive compromise. Charles VI restored many of the traditional privileges of the Hungarian aristocracy in return for Hungarian acceptance of hereditary Habsburg rule. Thus Hungary, unlike Austria or Bohemia, never came close to being fully integrated into a centralized, absolute Habsburg state.

## PRUSSIA IN THE SEVENTEENTH CENTURY

After 1400, the status of east German peasants declined steadily; their serfdom was formally spelled out in the early seventeenth century. While the local princes lost political power and influence, a revitalized landed nobility became the undisputed ruling class. The Hohenzollern family, which ruled through its senior and junior branches as the electors of Brandenburg and the dukes of Prussia, had little real princely power. The Hohenzollern rulers were nothing more than the "first among equals," the largest landowners in a landlord society.

Nothing suggested that the Hohenzollerns and their territories would ever play an important role in European or even German affairs. The elector of Brandenburg's right to help choose the Holy Roman emperor with six other electors was of little practical value, and the elector had no military strength whatsoever. The territory of his cousin, the duke of Prussia, was actually part of the kingdom of Poland. Moreover, geography conspired against the Hohenzollerns. Brandenburg, their power base, was completely cut off from the sea (see Map 17.1). A tiny part of the vast north European plain that stretches from France to Russia, Brandenburg lacked natural frontiers and lay open to attack from all directions. The land was poor, a combination of sand and swamp. Contemporaries contemptuously called Brandenburg "the sand-box of the Holy Roman Empire."[2]

Brandenburg was a helpless spectator in the Thirty Years' War, its territory alternately ravaged by Swedish and by Habsburg armies. Population fell drastically, and many villages disappeared. The power of the Hohenzollerns reached its lowest point. Yet the devastation of the country prepared the way for Hohenzollern absolutism, because foreign armies dramatically weakened the political power of the Estates – the representative assemblies of the realm. This weakening of the Estates helped the very talented young elector Frederick William (1640–1688), later known as the Great Elector, to ride roughshod over traditional parliamentary liberties and to take a giant step toward royal absolutism. This constitutional struggle, often unjustly neglected by historians, was the most crucial in Prussian history for hundreds of years, until that of the 1860s.

When he came to power in 1640, the twenty-year-old Great Elector was determined to unify his three quite separate provinces and to add to them by diplomacy and war. These provinces were historic Brandenburg, the area around Berlin; Prussia, inherited in 1618 when the junior branch of the Hohenzollern family died out; and completely separate, scattered holdings along the Rhine in western Germany, inherited in 1614 (see Map 17.1). Each of the three provinces was inhabited by Germans; but each had its own Estates, whose power had increased until about 1600 as the power of the rulers declined. Although the Estates had not met regularly during the chaotic Thirty Years' War, they still had the power of the purse in their respective provinces. Taxes could not be levied without their consent. The Estates of Brandenburg and Prussia were dominated by the nobility and the landowning classes, known as the Junkers. But it must be remembered that this was also true of the English Parliament before and after the Civil War. Had the Estates successfully resisted the absolutist demands of the Great Elector, they too might have evolved toward more broadly based constitutionalism.

The struggle between the Great Elector and the provincial Estates was long, complicated, and intense. After the Thirty Years' War, the representatives of the nobility zealously reasserted the right of the Estates to vote taxes, a right the Swedish armies of occupation had simply ignored. Yet first in Brandenburg in 1653, and then in Prussia between 1661 and 1663, the Great Elector eventually had his way.

To pay for the permanent standing army he first established in 1660, Frederick William forced the Estates to accept the introduction of permanent taxation without consent. Moreover, the soldiers doubled as tax collectors and policemen, becoming the core of the rapidly expanding state bureaucracy. The power of the Estates declined rapidly thereafter, for the Great Elector had both financial independence and superior force. He turned the screws of taxation: the state's total revenue tripled during his reign. The size of the army leaped about tenfold. In 1688, a population of one million was supporting a peacetime standing army of thirty thousand. Many of the soldiers were French Huguenot immigrants, whom the Great Elector welcomed as the talented, hardworking citizens they were.

In accounting for the Great Elector's fateful triumph, two factors appear central. As in the formation of every absolutist state, war was a decisive factor. The ongoing struggle between Sweden and Poland for control of the

Baltic after 1648 and the wars of Louis XIV in western Europe created an atmosphere of permanent crisis. The wild Tartars of southern Russia swept through Prussia in the winter of 1656–1657, killing and carrying off as slaves more than fifty thousand people, according to an old estimate. This invasion softened up the Estates and strengthened the urgency of the elector's demands for more money for more soldiers. It was no accident that, except for commercially minded Holland, constitutionalism won out only in England, the only major country to escape devastating foreign invasions in the seventeenth century.

Second, the nobility had long dominated the government through the Estates, but only for its own narrow self-interest. When the crunch came, the Prussian nobles proved unwilling to join the representatives of the towns in a consistent common front against royal pretensions. The nobility was all too concerned with its own rights and privileges, especially its freedom from taxation and its unlimited control over the peasants. When, therefore, the Great Elector reconfirmed these privileges in 1653 and after, even while reducing the political power of the Estates, the nobility growled but did not bite. It accepted a compromise whereby the bulk of the new taxes fell upon towns, and royal authority stopped at the landlords' gates. The elector could and did use naked force to break the liberties of the towns. The main leader of the urban opposition in the key city of Königsberg, for example, was simply arrested and imprisoned for life without trial.

### THE CONSOLIDATION OF PRUSSIAN ABSOLUTISM

By the time of his death in 1688, the Great Elector had created a single state out of scattered principalities. But his new creation was still small and fragile. All the leading states of Europe had many more people – France with 20 million was fully twenty times as populous – and strong monarchy was still a novelty. Moreover, the Great Elector's successor, Elector Frederick III, "the Ostentatious" (1688–1713), was weak of body and mind.

Like so many of the small princes of Germany and Italy at the time, Frederick III imitated Louis XIV in every possible way. He built his own very expensive version of Versailles. He surrounded himself with cultivated artists and musicians and basked in the praise of toadies and sycophants. His only real political accomplishment was to gain the title of king from the Holy Roman emperor, a Habsburg, in return for military aid in the War of the Spanish Succession, and in 1701 he was crowned King Frederick I.

This tendency toward luxury-loving, happy, and harmless petty tyranny was completely reversed by Frederick William I (1713–1740), "the Soldiers' King." A crude, dangerous psychoneurotic, Frederick William I was nevertheless the most talented reformer ever produced by the Hohenzollern family. It was he who truly established Prussian absolutism and gave it its unique character. It was he who created the best army in Europe, for its size, and who infused military values into a whole society. In the words of a leading historian of Prussia:

*For a whole generation, the Hohenzollern subjects were victimized by a royal bully, imbued with an obsessive bent for military organization and military scales of value. This left a deep mark upon the institutions of Prussiandom and upon the molding of the "Prussian spirit."*[3]

Frederick William's passion for the army and military life was intensely emotional. He had, for example, a bizarre, almost pathological love for tall soldiers, whom he credited

THE "TOBACCO PARLIAMENT" *In absolutist Prussia the informal discussion of politics by the king and his friends over a pipe after dinner was the only parliament. (Historical Picture Service, Chicago)*

with superior strength and endurance. Austere and always faithful to his wife, he confided to the French ambassador: "The most beautiful girl or woman in the world would be a matter of indifference to me, but tall soldiers — they are my weakness." Like some fanatical modern-day basketball coach in search of a championship team, he sent his agents throughout both Prussia and all of Europe, tricking, buying, and kidnapping top recruits. Neighboring princes sent him their giants as gifts to win his gratitude. Prussian mothers told their sons: "Stop growing or the recruiting agents will get you."[4]

Profoundly military in temperament, Frederick William always wore an army uniform, and he lived the highly disciplined life of the professional soldier. He began his work by five or six in the morning; at ten he almost always went to the parade ground to drill or inspect his troops. A man of violent temper, Frederick William personally punished the

MOLDING THE PRUSSIAN SPIRIT   *Discipline was
strict and punishment brutal in the Prussian army.
This scene, intended to instruct school children, shows
one soldier being flogged while another is being beaten
with canes as he walks between rows of troops. (Photo:
Caroline Buckler)*

most minor infractions on the spot: a missing
button off a soldier's coat quickly provoked a
savage beating with his heavy walking stick.

Frederick William's love of the army was
also based on a hardheaded conception of the
struggle for power and a dog-eat-dog view of
international politics. Even before ascending
the throne he bitterly criticized his father's
ministers: "They say that they will obtain
land and power for the king with the pen; but
I say it can be done only with the sword."
Years later he summed up his life's philosophy in his instructions to his son: "A formidable army and a war chest large enough to
make this army mobile in times of need can
create great respect for you in the world, so
that you can speak a word like the other
powers."[5] This unshakable belief that the welfare of king and state depended upon the
army above all else reinforced Frederick William's personal passion for playing soldier.

The cult of military power provided the rationale for a great expansion of royal absolutism. As the king himself put it with his

characteristic ruthlessness: "I must be served with life and limb, with house and wealth, with honour and conscience, everything must be committed except eternal salvation – that belongs to God, but all else is mine."[6] To make good these extraordinary demands, Frederick William created a strong centralized bureaucracy. More commoners probably rose to top positions in the civil government than at any other time in Prussia's history. The last traces of the parliamentary Estates and local self-government vanished.

The king's grab for power brought him into considerable conflict with the noble landowners, the Junkers. In his early years, he even threatened to destroy them; yet, in the end, the Prussian nobility was not destroyed but enlisted – into the army. Responding to a combination of threats and opportunities, the Junkers became the officer caste. By 1739, all but 5 of 245 officers with the rank of major or above were aristocrats, and most of them were native Prussians. A new compromise had been worked out, whereby the proud nobility imperiously commanded the peasantry in the army as well as on its estates.

Coarse and crude, penny-pinching and hardworking, Frederick William achieved results. Above all, he built a first-rate army on the basis of third-rate resources. The standing army increased from 38,000 to 83,000 during his reign. Prussia, twelfth in Europe in population, had the fourth largest army by 1740. Only the much more populous states of France, Russia, and Austria had larger forces, and even France's army was only twice as large as Prussia's. Moreover, soldier for soldier, the Prussian army became the best in Europe, astonishing foreign observers with its precision, skill, and discipline. For the next two hundred years, Prussia and then Prussianized Germany would almost always win the crucial military battles.

Frederick William and his ministers also built an exceptionally honest and conscientious bureaucracy, which not only administered the country but tried with some success to develop it economically. Finally, like the miser he was, living very frugally off the income of his own landholdings, the king loved his "blue boys" so much that he hated to "spend" them. This most militaristic of kings was, paradoxically, almost always at peace.

Nevertheless, the Prussian people paid a heavy and lasting price for the obsessions of the royal drillmaster. Civil society became rigid and highly disciplined. Prussia became "the Sparta of the North"; unquestioning obedience was the highest virtue. As a Prussian minister later summed it up, "To keep quiet is the first civic duty."[7] Thus, the policies of Frederick William I combined with harsh peasant bondage and Junker tyranny to lay the foundations for what later evolved into probably the most militaristic country of modern times.

Frederick II (1740–1786), also known as Frederick the Great, built masterfully upon his father's work. This was somewhat surprising, for like many children with tyrannical (or kindly) parents, he rebelled against his parents' wishes in his early years. Rejecting the crude life of the barracks, Frederick embraced culture and literature, even writing poetry and fine prose in French, a language his father detested. He threw off his father's dour Calvinism and dabbled with atheism. After trying, unsuccessfully, to run away at age eighteen in 1730, he was virtually imprisoned and even compelled to watch his companion in flight beheaded at his father's command. Yet, like many other rebellious youths, Frederick eventually reached a reconciliation with his father, and by the time he came to the throne ten years later he was determined to follow in his father's footsteps.

When, therefore, the emperor of Austria, Charles VI, also died in 1740 and his young and beautiful daughter, Maria Theresa, became queen of the Habsburg dominions, Frederick suddenly and without warning invaded her rich all-German province of Silesia. This action defied solemn Prussian promises to respect the Pragmatic Sanction, which guaranteed Maria Theresa's succession, but no matter. For Frederick, it was the opportunity of a lifetime to expand the size and power of Prussia. Although Maria Theresa succeeded in dramatically rallying the normally quarrelsome Hungarian nobility, her multinational army was no match for Prussian precision. In 1742, as other greedy powers were falling upon her lands in the general European War of the Austrian Succession (1740–1748), she was forced to cede all of Silesia to Prussia. In one stroke Prussia doubled its population to 6 million people. Now Prussia unquestionably towered above all the other German states and stood as a European Great Power.

Frederick had to spend much of his reign fighting against great odds not only to hold onto his initial gains but to save Prussia from total destruction. In the end he succeeded, worthy heir of "the Soldiers' King" he sought to please. In 1760, at the very height of his struggle against invading armies on all sides, Frederick recounted a dream in which he met his father with his favorite general at the palace. "Have I done well?" he asked. "Very well," Frederick William replied. "That pleases me greatly," said Frederick. "Your approval means more to me than that of the whole world."[8]

## THE DEVELOPMENT OF RUSSIA

One of the favorite parlor games of nineteenth-century Russian (and non-Russian) in-

tellectuals was debating whether Russia was a part of western European civilization or was a "nonwestern," "Asiatic" civilization. This question was particularly fascinating because it was unanswerable. A good case could be made for either position. To this day Russia differs fundamentally from the West in some basic ways, though Russian history has paralleled that of the West in other ways. Thus the hypnotic attraction of Russian history.

The differences between Russia and the West were particularly striking before 1700, when Russia's overall development began to draw progressively closer to that of its western neighbors. These early differences and Russia's long isolation from Europe explain why little has so far been said here about Russia. Yet it is impossible to understand how Russia has increasingly influenced and been influenced by western European civilization since roughly the late seventeenth century without looking at the course of early Russian history. Such a brief survey will also help explain how, when absolute monarchy finally and decisively triumphed under the rough guidance of Peter the Great in the early eighteenth century, it was a quite different type of absolute monarchy from that of France or even Prussia.

### THE VIKINGS AND THE KIEVAN PRINCIPALITY

In antiquity the Slavs lived as a single people in central Europe. With the start of the mass migrations of the late Roman Empire, the Slavs moved in different directions and split into three groups. Between the fifth and ninth centuries the eastern Slavs, from whom the Ukrainians, the Russians, and the White Russians descend, moved into the vast and practically uninhabited area of present-day European Russia (see Map 17.2).

This enormous area consisted of an immense virgin forest to the north, where most of the eastern Slavs settled, and an endless prairie grassland to the south. Probably organized as tribal communities, the eastern Slavs, like many North American pioneers much later, lived off the great abundance of wild game and a crude "slash and burn" agriculture. After clearing a piece of the forest to build log cabins, they burned the stumps and brush. The ashes left a rich deposit of potash and lime, and the land gave several good crops before it was exhausted. The people then moved on to another untouched area and repeated the process.

In the ninth century the Vikings, those fearless warriors from Scandinavia, appeared in the lands of the eastern Slavs. Called Varangians in the old Russian chronicles, the Vikings were interested primarily in international trade, and the opportunities were good, since the Muslim conquests of the eighth century had greatly reduced Christian trade in the Mediterranean. Moving up and down the rivers, the Vikings soon linked Scandinavia and northern Europe with the Black Sea and the Byzantine Empire with its capital at Constantinople. They built a few strategic forts along the rivers, from which they raided the neighboring Slavic tribes and collected tribute. Slaves were the most important article of tribute, and the word *Slav* even became the word for slave in several European languages.

In order to increase and protect their international commerce, the Vikings declared themselves the rulers of the eastern Slavs. According to tradition, the semilegendary chieftain Ruirik founded the princely dynasty about 860. In any event, the Varangian ruler Oleg (878–912) established his residence at Kiev. He and his successors ruled over a loosely united confederation of Slavic territories – the Kievan state – until 1054. The Viking prince and his clansmen quickly became assimilated into the Slavic population, taking local wives and emerging as the noble class.

Assimilation and loss of Scandinavian ethnic identity was speeded up by the conversion of the Vikings to Eastern Orthodox Christianity by missionaries from the Byzantine Empire. The written language of these missionaries, Slavic – Church Slavonic – was subsequently used in all religious and nonreligious documents in the Kievan principality. Thus the rapidly Slavified Vikings left two important legacies for the future. They created a loose unification of Slavic territories under a single ruling prince and a single ruling dynasty. And they imposed a basic religious unity by accepting Orthodox Christianity, as opposed to Roman Catholicism, for themselves and the eastern Slavs.

Even at its height under Great Prince Iaroslav the Wise (1019–1054), the unity of the Kievan principality was extremely tenuous. Trade, rather than government, was the main concern of the rulers. Moreover, the Slavified Vikings failed to find a way of peacefully transferring power from one generation to the next. In medieval western Europe this fundamental problem of government was increasingly resolved by resort to the principle of primogeniture: the king's eldest son received the crown as his rightful inheritance when his father died. Civil war was thus averted; order was preserved. In early Kiev, however, there were apparently no fixed rules and much strife accompanied each succession.

Possibly to avoid such chaos, before his death in 1054 Great Prince Iaroslav divided the Kievan principality among his five sons, who in turn divided their properties when they died. Between 1054 and 1237, Kiev disintegrated into more and more competing units, each ruled by a prince claiming to be a descendant of Ruirik. Even when only one prince was claiming to be the great prince, the whole situation was very unsettled.

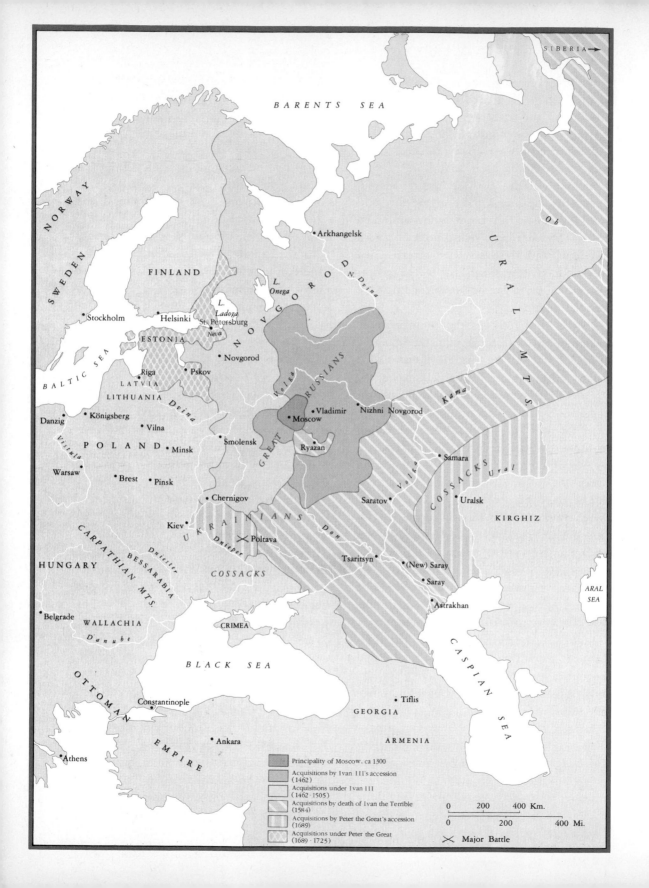

SIBERIA →

BARENTS SEA

NORWAY

SWEDEN

FINLAND

• Arkhangelsk

• Stockholm

• Helsinki

L. Ladoga

St. Petersburg

Neva

L. Onega

N. Dvina

Ob

URAL MTS.

ESTONIA

• Novgorod

NOVGOROD

• Riga

LATVIA

• Pskov

LITHUANIA

Dvina

Danzig

• Königsberg

• Vilna

POLAND

• Minsk

• Smolensk

Volga

GREAT RUSSIANS

• Moscow

• Vladimir

• Nizhni Novgorod

Kama

Warsaw

• Brest

• Pinsk

• Ryazan

Vistula

• Chernigov

Kiev

UKRAINIANS

Dniester

Dnieper

✕ Poltava

Don

Volga

• Saratov

• Samara

• Uralsk

Ural

COSSACKS

KIRGHIZ

CARPATHIAN MTS.

BESSARABIA

HUNGARY

COSSACKS

• Tsaritsyn

• (New) Saray

• Saray

• Belgrade

WALLACHIA

Danube

CRIMEA

• Astrakhan

ARAL SEA

OTTOMAN EMPIRE

• Constantinople

BLACK SEA

CASPIAN SEA

• Athens

• Ankara

• Tiflis

GEORGIA

ARMENIA

Principality of Moscow, ca 1300

Acquisitions by Ivan III's accession (1462)

Acquisitions under Ivan III (1462-1505)

Acquisitions by death of Ivan the Terrible (1584)

Acquisitions by Peter the Great's accession (1689)

Acquisitions under Peter the Great (1689-1725)

0        200        400 Km.

0        200        400 Mi.

✕ Major Battle

The princes divided their land like private property because they thought of it as private property. A given prince owned a certain number of farms or landed estates, and had them worked directly by his people, mainly slaves, called *kholops* in Russian. Outside of these estates, which constituted the princely domain, the prince exercised only very limited authority in his principality. Excluding the clergy, two kinds of people lived there: the noble boyars and the commoner peasants.

The boyars were the descendants of the original Viking warriors, and they also held their lands as free and clear private property. And although the boyars normally fought in princely armies, the customary law declared they could serve any prince they wished. The ordinary peasants were also truly free. The peasants could move at will wherever opportunities were greatest. In the touching phrase of the times, theirs was "a clean road, without boundaries."[9] In short, fragmented princely power, private property, and personal freedom all went together.

## THE MONGOL YOKE AND THE RISE OF MOSCOW

The eastern Slavs, like the Germans and the Italians, might have emerged from the Middle Ages weak and politically divided, had it not been for a development of extraordinary importance – the Mongol conquest of the Kievan state. Wild nomadic tribes from present-day Mongolia, the Mongols were temporarily unified in the thirteenth century by Jenghiz Khan (1162–1227), one of history's greatest conquerors. In five years his armies subdued all of China. His successors then wheeled westward, smashing everything in their path and reaching the plains of Hungary victoriously before they pulled back in 1242. The Mongol army – the Golden Horde – was savage in the extreme, often slaughtering the entire population of cities before burning them to the ground. On route to Mongolia, Archbishop John of Plano Carpini, the famous papal ambassador to Mongolia, passed through Kiev in southern Russia in 1245–1246 and wrote an unforgettable eyewitness account:

*The Mongols went against Russia and enacted a great massacre in the Russian land. They destroyed towns and fortresses and killed people. They besieged Kiev which had been the capital of Russia, and after a long siege they took it and killed the inhabitants of the city. For this reason, when we passed through that land, we found lying in the field countless heads and bones of dead people; for this city had been extremely large and very populous, whereas now it has been reduced to nothing: barely two hundred houses stand there, and those people are held in the harshest slavery.*[10]

Having devastated and conquered, the Mongols ruled the eastern Slavs for more than two hundred years. They built their capital of Saray on the lower Volga (see Map 17.2). They forced all the bickering Slavic princes to submit to their rule and to give them tribute and slaves. If the conquered peoples rebelled, the Mongols were quick to punish with death and destruction. Thus, the Mongols unified the eastern Slavs, for the Mongol khan was acknowledged by all as the supreme ruler.

The Mongol unification completely changed the internal political situation. Although the Mongols conquered, they were quite willing to use local princes as their obedient servants and tax collectors. Therefore they did not abolish the title of great prince, bestowing it instead upon the prince who served them best and paid them most handsomely.

Beginning with Alexander Nevsky in 1252, the previously insignificant princes of Moscow became particularly adept at serving the Mongols. They loyally put down popular uprisings and collected the khan's harsh taxes. By way of reward the princes of Moscow emerged as hereditary great princes. Eventually the Muscovite princes were able to destroy their princely rivals and even to replace the khan as supreme ruler. In this complex process, two princes of Moscow after Alexander Nevsky – Ivan I and Ivan III – were especially noteworthy.

Ivan I (1328–1341) was popularly known as Ivan the Moneybag. A bit like Frederick William of Prussia, he was extremely stingy and built up a large personal fortune. This enabled him to buy more property and to increase his influence by loaning money to less frugal princes to pay their Mongol taxes. Ivan's most serious rival was the prince of Tver, whom the Mongols at one point appointed as great prince.

In 1327, the population of Tver revolted against Mongol oppression, and the prince of Tver joined his people. Ivan immediately went to the Mongol capital of Saray, where he was appointed commander of a large Russian-Mongol army, which then laid waste to Tver and its lands. For this proof of devotion, the Mongols made Ivan the general tax collector for all the Slavic lands they had subjugated and named him great prince. Ivan also convinced the metropolitan of Kiev, the leading churchman of all eastern Slavs, to settle in Moscow; Ivan I thus gained greater prestige, while the church gained a powerful advocate before the khan.

In the next hundred-odd years, in the course of innumerable wars and intrigues, the great princes of Moscow significantly in-

creased their holdings. Then, in the reign of Ivan III (1462–1505), the long process was largely completed. After purchasing Rostov, Ivan conquered and annexed other principalities, of which Novgorod with its lands extending as far as the Baltic Sea was most crucial (see Map 17.2). Thus, more than four hundred years after Iaroslav the Wise had divided the embryonic Kievan state, the princes of Moscow defeated all the rival branches of the house of Ruirik and became the unique holder of princely power.

Another dimension to princely power developed. Not only were the princes of Moscow the *unique* rulers, they were the *absolute* rulers, the autocrat, the *tsar* – the Slavic contraction for caesar, with all its connotations. This imperious conception of absolute power is expressed in a famous letter from the aging Ivan III to the Holy Roman emperor Frederick III (1440–1493). Frederick had offered Ivan the title of king in conjunction with the marriage of his daughter to Ivan's nephew. Ivan proudly refused:

*We by the grace of God have been sovereigns over our domains from the beginning, from our first forebears, and our right we hold from God, as did our forebears.... As in the past we have never needed appointment from anyone, so now do we not desire it.*[11]

The Muscovite idea of absolute authority was powerfully reinforced by two developments. First, about 1480 Ivan III stopped acknowledging the khan as his supreme ruler. There is good evidence to suggest that Ivan and his successors saw themselves as khans. Certainly they assimilated the Mongol concept of kingship as the exercise of unrestrained and unpredictable power.

Second, after the fall of Constantinople to the Turks in 1453, the tsars saw themselves as the heirs of both the caesars and Orthodox Christianity, the one true faith. All the other kings of Europe were heretics: only the tsars were rightful and holy rulers. This idea was promoted by Orthodox churchmen, who spoke of "holy Russia" and "the Third Rome." As the metropolitan Zosima stated in 1492: "Two Romes have fallen, the third Rome will be Moscow and a fourth is not to be."[12] Ivan's marriage to Sofia, the daughter of the last Byzantine emperor, further enhanced the aura of an eastern imperial inheritance for Moscow. Worthy successor to the mighty khan and the true Christian emperor, the Muscovite tsar was a king above all others.

### TSAR AND PEOPLE TO 1689

By 1505, the great prince of Moscow – the tsar – had emerged as the single hereditary ruler of "all the Russias" – of all the lands of the eastern Slavs – and he was claiming unrestricted power as his God-given right. In effect, the tsar was demanding the same kind of total authority over all his subjects that the princely descendants of Ruirik had long exercised over their slaves on their own landed estates. This was an extremely radical demand.

While peasants had begun losing their freedom of movement in the fifteenth century, so had the noble boyars begun to lose power and influence. Ivan III pioneered in this regard, as in so many others. When Ivan conquered the principality of Novgorod in the 1480s, he confiscated fully 80 percent of the land, executing the previous owners or resettling them nearer Moscow. He then kept more than half of the confiscated land for himself, and distributed the remainder to members of a new emerging service nobility. The boyars had previously held their land as hereditary private property and been free to serve the prince of their choosing. The new service nobility held the tsar's land on the explicit condition that they serve in the tsar's

ST. BASIL'S CATHEDRAL in Moscow, with its steeply sloping roofs and proliferation of multicolored onion-shaped domes, was a striking example of powerful Byzantine influences on Russian culture. According to tradition, an enchanted Ivan the Terrible blinded the cathedral's architects, to insure they would never duplicate their fantastic achievement. (The New York Public Library)

army. Moreover, Ivan III began to require boyars outside of Novgorod to serve him if they wished to retain their lands. Since there were no competing princes left to turn to, the boyars had to yield.

The rise of the new service nobility accelerated under Ivan IV (1533–1584), the famous Ivan the Terrible. Having ascended the throne at age three, Ivan had suffered insults and neglect at the hands of the haughty boyars after his mother mysteriously died, possibly poisoned, when he was just eight. At age sixteen he suddenly pushed aside his hated boyar advisers. In an awe-inspiring ceremony complete with gold coins pouring down upon his head, he majestically crowned himself and officially took the august title of tsar for the first time.

Selecting the beautiful and kind Anastasia of the popular Romanov family for his wife and queen, the young tsar soon declared war on the remnants of Mongol power. He defeated the faltering khanates of Kazan and Astrakhan between 1552 and 1556, adding vast new territories to Russia. In the course of these wars Ivan virtually abolished the old distinction between hereditary boyar private property and land granted temporarily for service. All nobles, old and new, had to serve the tsar in order to hold any land.

The process of transforming the entire nobility into a service nobility was completed in the second part of Ivan the Terrible's reign. In 1557, Ivan turned westward, and for the next twenty-five years Muscovy waged an exhausting, unsuccessful war primarily with the large Polish-Lithuanian state, which controlled not only Poland but much of the Ukraine in the sixteenth century. Quarreling with the boyars over the war and blaming them for the sudden death of his beloved Anastasia in 1560, the increasingly cruel and demented Ivan turned to strike down all who stood in his way.

Above all, he struck down the ancient Muscovite boyars with a reign of terror. Leading boyars, their relatives, and even their peasants and servants were executed en masse by a special corps of unquestioning servants. Dressed in black and riding black horses, they were the forerunners of the modern dictator's secret police. Large estates were confiscated, broken up, and reapportioned to the lower service nobility. The great boyar families were severely reduced. The newer, poorer, more nearly equal service nobility, which was still less than .5 percent of the total population, was totally dependent upon the autocrat.

Ivan also took giant strides toward making all commoners servants of the tsar. His endless wars and demonic purges left much of central Russia depopulated. It grew increasingly difficult for the lower service nobility to squeeze a living for themselves out of the peasants left on their landholdings. As the service nobles demanded more from the remaining peasants, more and more peasants fled toward the wild, recently conquered territories to the east and south. There they formed free groups and outlaw armies known as Cossacks. The Cossacks maintained a precarious independence beyond the reach of the oppressive landholders and the tsar's hated officials. The solution to this problem was to complete the tying of the peasants to the land, to make them serfs perpetually bound to serve the noble landholders, who were bound in turn to serve the tsar.

In the time of Ivan the Terrible urban traders and artisans were also bound to their towns and jobs, so that the tsar could tax them more heavily. Ivan assumed that the tsar owned Russia's trade and industry, just as he owned all the land. In the course of the sixteenth and seventeenth centuries, the tsars therefore took over the mines and industries and monopolized the country's important commercial activities. The urban classes had no security in their work or property, and even the wealthiest merchants were basically dependent agents of the tsar. If a new commercial activity became profitable, it was often taken over by the tsar and made a royal monopoly. This royal monopolization was in sharp contrast to developments in western Europe, where the capitalist middle classes were gaining strength and security in their private property. The tsar's service obligations checked the growth of the Russian middle classes, just as they led to the decline of the boyars, the rise of the lower nobility, and the final enserfment of the peasants.

Ivan the Terrible's system of autocracy and compulsory service struck foreign observers forcibly. Sigismund Herberstein, a German traveler to Russia, wrote in 1571: "All the people consider themselves to be *kholops,* that is slaves of their Prince." At the same time Jean Bodin, the French thinker who did so much to develop the modern concept of sovereignty, concluded that Russia's political system was fundamentally different from those of all other European monarchies and comparable only to that of the Turkish empire. In both Turkey and Russia, as in other parts of Asia and Africa, "the prince is become lord of the goods and persons of his subjects . . . governing them as a master of a family does his slaves."[13] The Mongol inheritance weighed heavily upon Russia.

As has so often been the case in Russian history, the death of an iron-fisted tyrant — in this case Ivan the Terrible in 1584 — ushered in an era of confusion and violent struggles for power. Events were particularly chaotic after Ivan's son Theodore died in 1598 without an heir. The years from 1598 to 1613 are aptly called the Time of Troubles.

The close relatives of the deceased tsar intrigued against and murdered each other, alternately fighting and welcoming the invading Swedes and Poles, who even occupied Moscow. Most serious for the cause of autocracy, there was a great social upheaval as Cossack bands marched northward, rallying peasants and slaughtering nobles and officials. The mass of Cossacks and peasants called for the "true tsar," who would restore their freedom of movement and allow them to farm for whomever they pleased, who would reduce their heavy taxes and lighten the yoke imposed by the landlords.

This social explosion from below, which combined with a belated surge of patriotic opposition to Polish invaders, brought the nobles, big and small, to their senses. In 1613, they elected Ivan's sixteen-year-old grand-nephew, Michael Romanov, the new hereditary tsar. Then they rallied around him in the face of common internal and external threats. Michael's election was a real restoration, and his reign saw the gradual re-establishment of tsarist autocracy. Michael was understandably more kindly disposed toward the supportive nobility than toward the sullen peasants. Thus while peasants were completely enserfed in 1649, Ivan's heavy military obligations upon the nobility were relaxed considerably. In the long reign of Michael's successor, the pious Alexis (1645–1676), this asymmetry of obligations was accentuated. The nobility gained more exemptions from military service, while the peasants were further ground down.

The result was a second round of mass upheaval and protest. In the later seventeenth century the unity of the Russian Orthodox church was torn apart by a great split. The surface question was the religious reforms introduced in 1652 by the patriarch Nikon, a dogmatic purist who wished to bring "corrupted" Russian practices of worship into line with the Greek Orthodox model. The self-serving church hierarchy quickly went along, but the intensely religious common people resisted. They saw Nikon as the anti-Christ, who was stripping them of the only thing they had — the true religion of "holy Russia."

Great numbers left the church and formed illegal communities of Old Believers, who were hunted down and persecuted. As many as twenty thousand people burned themselves alive, singing the "halleluyah" in their chants three times rather than twice as Nikon had demanded and crossing themselves in the old style, with two rather than three fingers, as they went down in flames. After the great split the Russian masses were alienated from the established church, which became totally dependent upon the state for its authority.

Again the Cossacks revolted against the state, which was doggedly trying to catch up with them on the frontiers and reduce them to serfdom. Under Stenka Razin they moved up the Volga River in 1670–1671, attracting a great undisciplined army of peasants, murdering landlords and high church officials, and proclaiming freedom from oppression. This rebellion to overthrow the established order was finally defeated by the government. In response the thoroughly scared upper classes tightened the screws of serfdom even further. Holding down the peasants, and thereby maintaining the tsar, became almost the principal obligation of the nobility until 1689.

## THE REFORMS OF PETER THE GREAT

It is now possible to understand the reforms of Peter the Great (1689–1725) and his kind of monarchial absolutism. Contrary to some historians' assertions, Peter was interested primarily in military power and not in some grandiose westernization plan. A gigantic, seven-foot-tall man of enormous energy and will power, Peter was determined to redress the defeats the tsar's armies had occasionally suffered in their wars with Poland and Sweden since the time of Ivan the Terrible.

To be sure, these western foes had never seriously threatened the existence of the tsar's vast kingdom, except perhaps when they had added to the confusion of civil war and domestic social upheaval in the Time of Troubles. Russia had even gained a large mass of the Ukraine from the kingdom of Poland in 1667 (see Map 17.2). And tsarist forces had completed the conquest of the primitive tribes of all Siberia in the seventeenth century. Muscovy, which had been as large as all the rest

of Europe combined in 1600, was three times as large as the rest of Europe in 1689 and by far the largest kingdom on earth. But territorial expansion was the soul of tsardom, and it was natural that Peter would seek further gains. The thirty-six years of his reign knew only one year of peace.

When Peter came to the throne, the heart of his army still consisted of cavalry made up of boyars and service nobility. Foot soldiers played a secondary role, and the whole army served on a part-time basis. The Russian army was lagging behind the professional standing armies being formed in Europe in the seventeenth century. The core of such armies was a highly disciplined infantry – an infantry that fired and refired rifles as it fearlessly advanced, until it charged with bayonets fixed. Such a large permanent army was enormously expensive and could be created only at the cost of great sacrifice. Given the desire to conquer more territory, Peter's military problem was serious.

Peter's solution was, in essence, to tighten up Muscovy's old service system and really make it work. He put the nobility back in harness, with a vengeance. Every nobleman, great or small, was once again required to serve in the army or in the civil administration – for life. Since a more modern army and government required skilled technicians and experts, Peter created schools and even universities. One of his most hated reforms required five years of compulsory education away from home for every young nobleman. Peter established an interlocking military-civilian bureaucracy with fourteen ranks, and he decreed that all must start at the bottom and work toward the top. More people of nonnoble origins rose to high positions in the embryonic meritocracy. Peter searched out talented foreigners – twice in his reign he went abroad to study and observe – and placed them in his service. These measures combined to make the army and government more powerful and more efficient.

Peter also greatly increased the service requirements of the commoners. He established a regular standing army of more than 200,000 soldiers, made up mainly of peasants commanded by officers from the nobility. In addition, special forces of Cossacks and foreigners numbered more than 100,000. The departure of a drafted peasant boy was celebrated by his family and village almost like a funeral, as indeed it was, since the recruit was drafted for life. The peasantry also served with its taxes, which increased threefold during Peter's reign, as people – "souls" – replaced land as the primary unit of taxation. Serfs were also arbitrarily assigned to work in the growing number of factories and mines. Most of these industrial enterprises were directly or indirectly owned by the state, and they were worked almost exclusively for the military. In general, Russian serfdom became more oppressive under the reforming tsar.

The constant warfare of Peter's reign consumed 80 or 85 percent of all revenues but brought only modest territorial expansion. Yet the Great Northern War with Sweden, which lasted from 1700 to 1721, was crowned in the end by Russian victory. After initial losses, Peter's new war machine crushed the smaller army of Sweden's Charles XII in southern Russia at Poltava in 1709, one of the most significant battles in Russian history. Sweden never really regained the offensive, and Russia eventually annexed Estonia and much of present-day Latvia (see Map 17.2), lands that had never before been under Russian rule. Russia became the dominant power on the Baltic Sea and very much a European Great Power. If victory or defeat is the ultimate criterion for historical judgment, Peter's reforms were a success.

REFORMING THE NOBILITY    *After a military revolt in 1698 Peter took revenge by decreeing that all nobles adopt Western manners and dress. This contemporary cartoon shows a gigantic Peter personally cutting off the long beard of a noble, thereby humiliating him and symbolically imposing more modern values. (The New York Public Library)*

There were other important consequences of Peter's reign. Because of his feverish desire to use modern technology to strengthen the army, many westerners and western ideas flowed into Russia for the first time. A new class of educated Russians began to emerge. At the same time vast numbers of Russians, especially among the poor and weak, hated Peter's massive changes. The split between the enserfed peasantry and the educated nobility thus widened, even though all were caught up in the endless demands of the sovereign.

A new idea of state interest, as distinct from the tsar's personal interests, began to take hold. Peter himself fostered this conception of the public interest by claiming time and again to be serving the common good. For the first time a Russian tsar attached explanations to his decrees in an attempt to gain the confidence and more enthusiastic support of the populace. Yet, as before, the tsar alone decided what the common good was. Here was a source of future tension between tsar and people.

In sum, Peter built on the service obligations of old Muscovy. His monarchial absolutism was truly the culmination of the long development of a unique Russian civilization. Yet the creation of a more modern army and state introduced much that was new and western to that civilization. This development paved the way for Russia to move much closer to the European mainstream in its thought and institutions during the Enlightenment, especially under that famous administrative and sexual lioness, Catherine the Great.

## ABSOLUTISM AND THE BAROQUE

The rise of royal absolutism in eastern Europe had many consequences. Nobles served their powerful rulers in new ways while the great inferiority of the urban middle classes and the peasants was reconfirmed. Armies became larger and more professional, while taxes rose and authoritarian traditions were strengthened. Nor was this all. Royal absolutism also interacted with baroque culture and art, baroque music and literature. Inspired in part by Louis XIV of France, the great and not-so-great rulers called upon the artistic talent of the age to glorify their power and magnifi-

cence. This exaltation of despotic rule was particularly striking in architecture, whose lavish masterpieces reflected and reinforced the spirit of absolutism.

### BAROQUE ART AND MUSIC

Throughout European history, the cultural tastes of one age have often seemed quite unsatisfactory to the next. So it was with the baroque. The term *baroque* itself may have come from the Portuguese word for an "odd-shaped, imperfect pearl," and was commonly used by late-eighteenth-century art critics as an expression of scorn for what they considered an overblown, unbalanced style. The hostility of these critics, who also scorned the Gothic style of medieval cathedrals in favor of a classicism inspired by antiquity and the Renaissance, has long since passed. Specialists agree that the triumphs of the baroque marked one of the high points in the entire history of Western culture.

The early development of the baroque is complex, but most scholars stress the influence of Rome and the revitalized Catholic church of the later sixteenth century. The papacy and the Jesuits encouraged the growth of an intensely emotional, exuberant art. These patrons wanted artists to go beyond the Renaissance focus on pleasing a small, wealthy cultural elite. They wanted artists to appeal to the senses, and thereby touch the souls and kindle the faith of ordinary churchgoers, while proclaiming the power and confidence of the reformed Catholic church. In addition to this underlying religious emotionalism, the baroque drew its sense of drama, motion, and ceaseless striving from the Catholic Reformation. The interior of the famous Jesuit Church of Jesus in Rome – the Gesù – combined all these characteristics in its lavish, shimmering, wildly active decorations and frescoes.

Taking definite shape in Italy after 1600, the baroque style in the visual arts developed with exceptional vigor in Catholic countries – in Spain and Latin America, Austria, southern Germany, and Poland. Yet baroque art was more than just "Catholic art" in the seventeenth century and the first half of the eighteenth. True, neither Protestant England nor the Netherlands ever came fully under the spell of the baroque, but neither did Catholic France. And Protestants accounted for some of the finest examples of baroque style, especially in music. The baroque style spread partly because its tension and bombast spoke to an agitated age, which was experiencing great violence and controversy in politics and religion.

In painting, the baroque reached maturity early with Peter Paul Rubens (1577–1640), the most outstanding and representative of baroque painters. Studying in his native Flanders and in Italy, where he was influenced by the masters of the High Renaissance such as Michelangelo, Rubens developed his own rich, sensuous, colorful style, which was characterized by animated figures, melodramatic contrasts, and monumental size. Although Rubens excelled in glorifying monarchs, like queen mother Marie de' Medici of France, he was also a devout Catholic. Nearly half of his pictures treat Christian subjects. Yet one of Rubens' trademarks was fleshy, sensual nudes, who populate his canvasses as Roman goddesses, water nymphs, and remarkably voluptuous saints and angels.

Rubens was enormously successful. To meet the demand for his work, he established a large studio and hired many assistants to execute his rough sketches and gigantic murals. Sometimes the master artist added only the finishing touches. Rubens' wealth and position – on occasion he was given special diplomatic assignments by the Habsburgs – attest that distinguished artists continued to enjoy the high social status they had won in the Renaissance.

In music the baroque style reached its culminating point almost a century later in the dynamic, searching, soaring lines of the endlessly inventive Johann Sebastian Bach (1685–1750), one of the greatest composers the Western world has ever produced. Organist and choirmaster of several Lutheran churches across Germany, Bach was equally at home writing secular concertos and sublime religious cantatas. Bach's organ music, the greatest ever written, combined with unsurpassed mastery the baroque spirit of invention, tension, and emotion in an unforgettable striving toward the infinite. Unlike Rubens, Bach was not fully appreciated in his lifetime, but since the early nineteenth century his reputation has grown steadily.

## PALACES AND POWER

As soaring Gothic cathedrals expressed the idealized spirit of the High Middle Ages, so dramatic baroque palaces symbolized the age of absolutist power. By 1700, palace building had become a veritable obsession with the rulers of central and eastern Europe. These baroque palaces were clearly intended to overawe the people with the monarch's strength. The great palaces were also visual declarations of equality with Louis XIV, Europe's most awesome ruler, and were therefore modeled after Versailles to a greater or lesser extent. One such palace was Schönbrunn, an enormous Viennese Versailles, begun in 1695 by Emperor Leopold to celebrate Austrian military victories and Habsburg might. Charles XI of Sweden, having reduced the power of the aristocracy, ordered the construction in 1693 of his Royal Palace, which dominates the center of Stockholm to this day. Frederick I of Prussia began his imposing new royal residence in Berlin in 1701, a year after he attained the title of king.

Petty princes also contributed mightily to the palace-building mania. Frederick the Great of Prussia noted that every descendant of a princely family "imagines himself to be something like Louis XIV. He builds his Versailles, has his mistresses, and maintains his army."[14] The not very important elector-archbishop of Mainz, the ruling prince of that city, confessed apologetically that "building is a craze which costs much, but every fool likes his own hat."[15] The archbishop of Mainz's own "hat" was an architectural gem, like that of another churchly ruler, the prince-bishop of Würzburg. So too was the Zwinger palace of Dresden, built by Augustus the Strong of Saxony, who managed to get himself elected king of Poland and unsuccessfully challenged Prussia for leadership among the German states.

In central and eastern Europe the favorite noble servants of royalty became extremely rich and powerful, and they too built grandiose palaces in the capital cities. These palaces were in part an extension of the monarch, for they surpassed the buildings of less favored nobles and showed all with eyes to see the high road to fame and fortune. Take, for example, the palaces of Prince Eugene of Savoy. A French nobleman by birth and education, Prince Eugene entered the service of Leopold I with the relief of besieged Vienna in 1683, and he became Austria's most outstanding military hero. It was he who reorganized the Austrian army, smashed the Turks, fought Louis XIV to a standstill, and generally guided the triumph of absolutism in Austria. Rewarded with great wealth by his grateful royal employer, Eugene called upon the leading architects of the day, J. B. Fischer von Erlach and Johann Lukas von Hildebrandt, to consecrate his glory in stone and fresco. Fischer built Eugene's Winter (or Town) Palace in Vienna, and he and Hildebrandt collaborated on the prince's Summer Palace on the city's outskirts.

The Summer Palace was actually two enormous buildings, the Lower Belvedere and the Upper Belvedere, completed in 1713 and 1722 respectively, and joined by one of the most exquisite gardens in Europe. The Upper Belvedere, Hildebrandt's masterpiece, stood gracefully, even playfully, behind a great sheet of water. One entered through magnificent iron gates into a fantastic hall where sculptured giants crouched as pillars, and then moved on to a great staircase of dazzling whiteness and luscious ornamentation. Even today the emotional impact of this building is great: here, indeed, art and beauty create a sense of immense power and wealth.

Palaces like the Upper Belvedere were magnificent examples of the baroque style. They expressed the baroque delight in bold, sweeping statements, which were intended to provide a dramatic emotional experience. To create this experience baroque masters dissolved the traditional artistic frontiers: the architect permitted the painter and the artisan to cover his undulating surfaces with wildly colorful paintings, graceful sculptures, and fanciful carvings. Space was used in a highly original way, to blend everything together in a total environment. These techniques shone in all their glory in the churches of southern Germany and in the colossal entrance halls of palaces like that of the prince-bishop of Würzburg. Artistic achievement and political statement reinforced each other.

## ROYAL CITIES

Absolute monarchs and baroque architects were not content with fashioning ostentatious

THE WÜRZBURG RESIDENCE *This palace was a masterpiece of German baroque architecture. Here, in the Hall of the Kaiser, painter, sculptor, and architect have combined to create a dramatic visual experience. (AMA/Adelmann/EPA)*

palaces. They remodeled existing capital cities, or even built new ones, to reflect royal magnificence and the centralization of political power. Karlsruhe, founded in 1715 as the capital city of a small German principality, is only an extreme example. There, broad, straight avenues radiated out from the palace, so that all roads – like all power – were fo-

cused upon the ruler. More typically, the monarch's architects added new urban areas alongside the old city; these areas then became the real heart of the expanding capital.

The distinctive features of these new additions were their broad avenues, their imposing government buildings, and their rigorous mathematical layout. Along these major thoroughfares the nobles built elaborate baroque townhouses; stables and servants' quarters were built on the alleys behind. Wide avenues also facilitated the rapid movement of soldiers through the city to quell any disturbance (the king's planners had the needs of the military constantly in mind). Under the arcades along the avenues appeared smart and very expensive shops, the first department stores, with plateglass windows and fancy displays.

The new avenues brought reckless speed to the European city. Whereas everyone had walked through the narrow, twisting streets of the medieval town, the high and mighty raced down the broad boulevards in their elegant carriages. A social gap opened up between the wealthy riders and the ordinary, gaping, dodging pedestrians. "Mind the carriages!" wrote one eighteenth-century observer in Paris:

*Here comes the black-coated physician in his chariot, the dancing master in his coach, the fencing master in his surrey — and the Prince behind six horses at the gallop as if he were in the open country.... The threatening wheels of the overbearing rich drive as rapidly as ever over stones stained with the blood of their unhappy victims.*[16]

Speeding carriages on broad avenues, an endless parade of power and position: here was the symbol and substance of the baroque city.

## THE GROWTH OF ST. PETERSBURG

No city illustrated better than St. Petersburg the close ties among politics, architecture, and urban development in this period. In 1700, when the Great Northern War between Russia and Sweden began, the city did not exist. There was only a small Swedish fortress on one of the water-logged islands at the mouth of the Neva River, where it flows into the Baltic Sea. In 1702, Peter the Great's armies

seized this desolate outpost. Within a year the reforming tsar had decided to build a new city there and to make it, rather than ancient Moscow, his capital.

Since the first step was to secure the Baltic coast, military construction was the main concern for the next eight years. A mighty fortress was built on Peter Island, and a port and shipyards were built across the river on the mainland, as a Russian navy came into being. The land was swampy and uninhabited, the climate damp and unpleasant. But Peter cared not at all: for him, the inhospitable northern marshland was a future metropolis, gloriously bearing his name.

After the decisive Russian victory at Poltava in 1709 greatly reduced the threat of Swedish armies, Peter moved into high gear. In one imperious decree after another, he ordered his people to build a city that would equal any in the world. Such a city had to be western and baroque, just as Peter's army had to be western and permanent. From such a new city, his "window on Europe," Peter also believed it would be easier to reform the country militarily and administratively. The hand of tradition would rest lightly on the banks of the Neva.

These general political goals matched Peter's architectural ideas, which had been influenced by his travels in western Europe. First, Peter wanted a comfortable, "modern" city. Modernity meant broad, straight, stone-paved avenues, houses built in a uniform line and not haphazardly set back from the street, large parks, canals for drainage, stone bridges, and street lighting. Second, all building had to conform strictly to detailed architectural regulations set down by the government. Finally, each social group — the nobility, the merchants, the artisans, and so on — was to live in a certain section of town. In short, the city and its population were to conform to a

ST. PETERSBURG, CA 1760 *Rastrelli's remodeled Winter Palace is on the left and the Navy Office with its famous spire is on the right. Russia became a naval power and St. Petersburg became a great port. (From G. H. Hamilton,* Art and Architecture in Russia, *Penguin Books, 1954)*

carefully defined urban plan of the baroque type.

Peter used the traditional but reinforced methods of Russian autocracy to build his modern capital. The creation of St. Petersburg was just one of the heavy obligations he dictatorially imposed on all social groups in Russia. The peasants bore the heaviest burdens. Just as the government drafted peasants for the army, it also drafted twenty-five to forty thousand men each summer to labor in St. Petersburg for three months, without pay. Every ten to fifteen peasant households had to furnish one such worker each summer, and then pay a special tax in order to feed that worker in St. Petersburg.

Peasants hated this forced labor in the capital, and each year a fourth to a third of those sent risked brutal punishments and ran away. Many peasant construction workers died each summer from hunger, sickness, and accidents. Many also died because peasant villages tended to elect old men or young boys to labor in St. Petersburg, since strong and able-bodied men were desperately needed on the farm in the busy summer months. Thus beautiful St. Petersburg was built on the shoveling, carting, and paving of a mass of conscripted serfs.

Peter also drafted more privileged groups to his city, but on a permanent basis. Nobles were summarily ordered to build costly stone houses and palaces in St. Petersburg and to live in them most of the year. The more serfs a noble possessed, the bigger his dwelling had to be. Merchants and artisans were also commanded to settle and build in St. Petersburg. These nobles and merchants were then required to pay for the city's avenues, parks, canals, embankments, pilings, and bridges, all of which were very costly in terms of both money and lives because they were built upon a swamp. The building of St. Petersburg was, in truth, an enormous direct tax levied on the wealthy, who in turn forced the peasantry to do most of the work. The only real beneficiaries were the indispensable foreign architects and urban planners, whose often-princely salaries added to the tax burden. No wonder so many Russians hated Peter's new city.

Yet the tsar had his way. By the time of his death in 1725 there were at least six thousand houses and numerous impressive government buildings in St. Petersburg. Under the remarkable women who ruled Russia throughout most of the eighteenth century, St. Petersburg blossomed fully as a majestic and well-organized city, at least in its wealthy showpiece sections. Peter's youngest daughter, the quick-witted, sensual beauty Elizabeth (1741–1762), named as her chief architect Bartolomeo Rastrelli, who had come to Russia from Italy as a boy of fifteen in 1715. Combining Italian and Russian traditions into a unique, wildly colorful St. Petersburg style, Rastrelli built many palaces for the nobility and all the larger government buildings erected during Elizabeth's reign. He also rebuilt the Winter Palace as an enormous,

aqua-colored royal residence, now the Hermitage Museum. There Elizabeth established a flashy, luxury-loving, and slightly crude court, which Catherine in turn made truly imperial. All the while St. Petersburg grew rapidly, and its almost 300,000 inhabitants in 1782 made it one of the world's largest cities. Peter and his successors had created out of nothing a magnificent and harmonious royal city, which unmistakably proclaimed the power and grandeur of Russia's rulers.

———◆———

From about 1400 to 1650 social and economic developments in eastern Europe increasingly diverged from those in western Europe. In the east peasants and townspeople lost precious freedoms, while the nobility increased its power and prestige. It was within this framework of resurgent serfdom and entrenched nobility that Austrian and Prussian monarchs fashioned absolutist states in the seventeenth and early eighteenth centuries. Thus monarchs won absolutist control over standing armies, permanent taxes, and legislative bodies. But they did not question the underlying social and economic relationships. Indeed, they enhanced the privileges of the nobility, which furnished the leading servitors for enlarged armies and growing state bureaucracies.

In Russia the social and economic trends were similar but the timing of political absolutism was different. Mongol conquest and rule was a crucial experience, and a harsh indigenous tsarist autocracy was firmly in place by the reign of Ivan the Terrible in the sixteenth century. More than a century later Peter the Great succeeded in tightening up Russia's traditional absolutism and modernizing it by reforming the army, the bureaucracy, and the defense industry. In Russia and throughout eastern Europe, war and the needs of war weighed heavily in the triumph of absolutism.

Triumphant absolutism interacted spectacularly with the arts. Baroque art, which had grown out of the Catholic Reformation's desire to move the faithful and exalt the true faith, admirably suited the secular aspirations of eastern rulers. They built grandiose baroque palaces, monumental public squares, and even whole cities to glorify their power and majesty. Thus baroque art attained magnificent heights in eastern Europe, symbolizing the ideal and harmonizing with the reality of imperious royal absolutism.

## NOTES

1. Quoted by F. L. Carsten, *The Origins of Prussia,* Clarendon Press, Oxford, 1954, p. 152.

2. Ibid., p. 175.

3. H. Rosenberg, *Bureaucracy, Aristocracy, and Autocracy: The Prussian Experience, 1660–1815,* Beacon Press, Boston, 1966, p. 38.

4. Quoted by R. Ergang, *The Potsdam Führer: Frederick William I, Father of Prussian Militarism,* Octagon Books, New York, 1972, pp. 85, 87.

5. Ibid. pp. 6–7, 43.

6. Quoted by R. A. Dorwart, *The Administrative Reforms of Frederick William I of Prussia,* Harvard University Press, Cambridge, Mass., 1953, p. 226.

7. Quoted by Rosenberg, p. 40.

8. Quoted by Ergang, p. 253.

9. Quoted by R. Pipes, *Russia Under the Old Regime,* Charles Scribner's Sons, New York, 1974, p. 48.

10. Quoted by N. V. Riasanovsky, *A History of Russia,* Oxford University Press, New York, 1963, p. 79.

11. Quoted by I. Grey, *Ivan III and the Unification of Russia,* Collier Books, New York, 1967, p. 39.

12. Quoted by R. Mousnier, *Peasant Uprisings in Seventeenth-Century France, Russia, and China,* Harper & Row, New York, 1970, p. 154.

13. Both quoted by Pipes, pp. 65, 85.

14. Quoted by Ergang, p. 13.

15. Quoted by J. Summerson, in *The Eighteenth Century: Europe in the Age of Enlightenment,* ed. A. Cobban, McGraw-Hill, New York, 1969, p. 80.

16. Quoted by L. Mumford, *The Culture of Cities,* Harcourt Brace Jovanovich, New York, 1938, p. 97.

## SUGGESTED READING

All of the books cited in the Notes are highly recommended. F. L. Carsten's *The Origins of Prussia* (1954) is the best study on early Prussian history, and H. Rosenberg, *Bureaucracy, Aristocracy, and Autocracy: The Prussian Experience, 1660–1815* (1966), is a masterful analysis of the social context of Prussian absolutism. In addition to R. Ergang's exciting and critical biography of ramrod Frederick William I, *The Potsdam Führer* (1972), there is G. Ritter, *Frederick the Great* (1968), a more sympathetic study of the talented son by one of Germany's leading conservative historians. G. Craig, *The Politics of the Prussian Army, 1640–1945* (1964), expertly traces the great influence of the military on the Prussian state over three hundred years. R. J. Evans, *The Making of the Habsburg Empire, 1550–1770* (1979), and R. A. Kahn, *A History of the Habsburg Empire, 1526–1918* (1974), analyze the development of absolutism in Austria, as does A. Wandruszka, *The House of Habsburg* (1964). J. Stoye, *The Siege of Vienna* (1964), is a fascinating account of the last great Ottoman offensive, which is also treated in the interesting study by P. Coles, *The Ottoman Impact on Europe, 1350–1699* (1968). The Austro-Ottoman conflict is also a theme of L. S. Stavrianos, *The Balkans Since 1453* (1958), and D. McKay's fine biography, *Prince Eugene of Savoy* (1978).

On eastern peasants and serfdom, J. Blum, "The Rise of Serfdom in Eastern Europe," *American His-*

torical Review 62 (July 1957):807–836, is a good point of departure, while R. Mousnier, *Peasant Uprisings in Seventeenth-Century France, Russia, and China* (1970), is an engrossing comparative study. J. Blum, *Lord and Peasant in Russia from the Ninth to the Nineteenth Century* (1961), provides a good look at conditions in rural Russia, and P. Avrich, *Russian Rebels, 1600–1800* (1972), treats some of the violent peasant upheavals those conditions produced. R. Hellie, *Enserfment and Military Change in Muscovy,* (1971), is outstanding, as is Alexander Yanov's provocative *Origins of Autocracy: Ivan the Terrible in Russian History* (1981). In addition to the fine surveys by Pipes and Riasanovsky cited in the Notes, J. Billington, *The Icon and the Axe* (1970), is a stimulating history of early Russian intellectual and cultural developments, such as the great split in the church. M. Raeff, *Origins of the Russian Intelligentsia* (1966), skillfully probes the mind of the Russian nobility in the eighteenth century. B. H. Sumner, *Peter the Great and the Emergence of Russia* (1962), is a fine brief introduction, which may be compared with the brilliant biography by Russia's greatest prerevolutionary historian, Vasili Klyuchevsky, *Peter the Great* (trans. 1958), and with R. Massie, *Peter the Great* (1980). G. Vernadsky and R. Fisher, eds., *A Source Book for Russian History from Early Times to 1917,* 3 vols. (1972), is an invaluable, highly recommended collection of documents and contemporary writings.

Three good books on art and architecture are E. Hempel, *Baroque Art and Architecture in Central Europe* (1965); G. Hamilton, *The Art and Architecture of Russia* (1954); and N. Pevsner, *An Outline of European Architecture,* 6th ed. (1960). Bach, Handel, and other composers are discussed intelligently by M. Bufkozer, *Music in the Baroque Era* (1947).

# CHAPTER 18

# TOWARD A NEW WORLD-VIEW

*MOST PEOPLE* are not philosophers, but nevertheless they have certain ideas and assumptions about the world in which they live. These ideas and assumptions add up to a basic outlook on life, a more or less coherent world-view. At the risk of oversimplification, one may say that the world-view of medieval and early modern Europe was primarily religious and theological. Not only did Christian or Jewish teachings form the core of people's spiritual and philosophical beliefs, but religious teachings also permeated all the rest of human thought and activity. Political theory relied on the divine right of kings, for example, and activities ranging from marriage and divorce to eating habits and hours of business were regulated by churches and religious doctrines.

In the course of the eighteenth century, this religious and theological world-view of the educated classes of western Europe underwent a fundamental transformation. Many educated people came to see the world primarily in secular and scientific terms. And while few abandoned religious beliefs altogether, many became openly hostile to established Christianity. The role of churches and religious thinking in earthly affairs and in the pursuit of knowledge was substantially reduced. Among many in the upper and middle classes a new critical, scientific, and very "modern" world-view took shape. Why did this momentous change occur? How did this new outlook on life affect society and politics? This chapter seeks to answer these questions.

## THE SCIENTIFIC REVOLUTION

The foremost cause of the change in world-view was the scientific revolution. Modern science – precise knowledge of the physical world based upon the union of experimental observations with sophisticated mathematics – crystallized in the seventeenth century. Whereas science had been secondary and subordinate in medieval intellectual life, it became independent and even primary for many educated people.

The emergence of modern science was a development of tremendous long-term significance. A noted historian has even said that the scientific revolution of the late sixteenth and seventeenth centuries "outshines everything since the rise of Christianity and reduces the Renaissance and Reformation to the rank of mere episodes, mere internal displacements, within the system of medieval Christendom." The scientific revolution was "the real origin both of the modern world and the modern mentality."[1] This statement is an exaggeration, but not much of one. Of all the great civilizations, only that of the West developed modern science. It was with the scientific revolution that Western society began to acquire its most distinctive traits.

Although historians agree that the scientific revolution was enormously important, they approach it in quite different ways. Some scholars believe that the history of scientific achievement in this period had its own basic "internal" logic and that "nonscientific" factors had quite limited significance. These scholars write brilliant, often highly technical, intellectual studies, but they neglect the broader historical context. Other historians stress "external" economic, social, and religious factors, brushing over the scientific developments themselves. Historians of science now realize that these two approaches need to be brought together, but they are only beginning to do so. It is best, therefore, to examine the milestones on the fateful march toward modern science first and then to search for nonscientific influences along the route.

## SCIENTIFIC THOUGHT IN 1500

Since developments in astronomy and physics were at the heart of the scientific revolution, one must begin with the traditional European conception of the universe and movement in it. In the early 1500s, traditional European ideas about the universe were still based primarily upon the ideas of Aristotle, the great Greek philosopher of the fourth century B.C. These ideas had gradually been recovered during the Middle Ages and then brought into harmony with Christian doctrines by medieval theologians. According to this revised Aristotelian view, a motionless earth was fixed at the center of the universe. Around it moved ten separate, transparent, crystal spheres. In the first eight spheres were embedded, in turn, the moon, the sun, the five known planets, and the fixed stars. Then followed two spheres added during the Middle Ages to account for slight changes in the positions of the stars over the centuries. Beyond the tenth sphere was heaven, with the throne of God and the souls of the saved. Angels kept the spheres moving in perfect circles.

Aristotle's views, suitably revised by medieval philosophers, also dominated thinking about physics and motion on earth. Aristotle had distinguished sharply between the world of the celestial spheres and that of the earth – the sublunar world. The spheres consisted of a perfect, incorruptible "quintescence," or fifth essence. The sublunar world, however, was made up of four imperfect, changeable elements. The "light" elements – air and fire – naturally moved upward, while the "heavy" elements – water and earth – naturally moved downward. The natural directions of motion did not always prevail, however, for elements were often mixed together, and could be affected by an outside force such as a human being. Aristotle and his followers also believed that a uniform force moved an object at a constant speed and that the object would stop as soon as that force was removed.

Aristotle's ideas about astronomy and physics were accepted with minor revisions for two thousand years, and with good reason. First, they offered an understandable common-sense explanation for what the eye actually saw. Second, Aristotle's science, as interpreted by Christian theologians, fit neatly with Christian doctrines. It established a home for God and a place for Christian souls. It put human beings at the center of the universe, and made them the critical link in a "great chain of being" that stretched from the throne of God to the most lowly insect on earth. Thus science was primarily a branch of theology, and it reinforced religious thought. At the same time, medieval "scientists" were already providing closely reasoned explanations of the universe, explanations they felt were worthy of God's perfect creation.

## THE COPERNICAN HYPOTHESIS

The desire to explain and thereby glorify God's handiwork led to the first great departure from the medieval system. This departure was the work of the Polish clergyman and astronomer Nicolaus Copernicus (1473–1543). As a young man Copernicus studied church law and astronomy in various European universities. He saw how professional astronomers were still dependent for their most accurate calculations on the work of Ptolemy, the last great ancient astronomer, who had lived in Alexandria in the second century A.D. Ptolemy's achievement had been to work out complicated rules to explain the minor irregularities in the movement of the planets. These rules enabled stargazers and astrologers to track the planets with greater precision. Many people then (and now) believed that the changing relationships between planets and stars influenced and even determined an individual's future.

The young Copernicus was uninterested in astrology, and felt that Ptolemy's cumbersome and occasionally inaccurate rules detracted from the majesty of a perfect Creator. He hit upon an old Greek idea being discussed in Renaissance Italy: the idea that the sun rather than the earth was at the center of the universe. Finishing his university studies and returning to a church position in east Prussia, Copernicus worked on his hypothesis from 1506 to 1530. Never questioning the Aristotelian belief in crystal spheres or the idea that circular motion was most perfect and divine, Copernicus theorized that the stars and planets, including the earth, revolve around a fixed sun. Yet Copernicus was a cautious man. Fearing the ridicule of other astronomers, he did not publish his *On the Revolutions of the Heavenly Spheres* until 1543, the year of his death.

Copernicus's theory had enormous scientific and religious implications, many of which the conservative Copernicus was unaware of. First, it put the stars at rest, their apparent nightly movement simply a result of the earth's rotation. Thus it destroyed the main reason for believing in crystal spheres capable of moving the stars around the earth. Second, Copernicus's theory suggested a universe of staggering size. If in the course of a year the earth moved around the sun and yet the stars appeared to remain in the same place, then the universe was unthinkably large or even infinite. Finally, by characterizing the earth as just another planet, Copernicus destroyed the basic idea of Aristotelian physics – the idea that the earthly world was quite different from the heavenly one. Where, then, was the realm of perfection? Where was heaven and the throne of God?

The Copernican theory quickly brought sharp attacks from religious leaders, especially Protestant leaders. Hearing of Copernicus's work even before it was published, Martin Luther spoke of Copernicus as "the new astrologer who wants to prove that the earth moves and goes round. . . . The fool wants to turn the whole art of astronomy upside down." Luther did, however, note that "as the Holy Scripture tells us, so did Joshua bid the sun stand still and not the earth." Calvin also condemned Copernicus, citing as evidence the first verse of Psalm 93: "The world also is established that it cannot be moved." "Who," asked Calvin, "will venture to place the authority of Copernicus above that of the Holy Spirit?"[2] Catholic reaction was milder at first. The Catholic church had never been hypnotized by literal interpretations of the Bible, and not until 1616 did it officially declare the Copernican theory false.

This slow reaction also reflected the slow progress of Copernicus's theory for many years. Other events were almost as influential in creating doubts about traditional astronomical ideas. In 1572, a new star appeared and shone very brightly for almost two years. The new star, which was actually a distant exploding star, made an enormous impression

upon people. It seemed to contradict the idea that the heavenly spheres were unchanging and therefore perfect. In 1577, a new comet suddenly moved through the sky, cutting a straight path across the supposedly impenetrable crystal spheres. It was time, as a typical scientific writer put it, for "the radical renovation of astronomy."[3]

## FROM TYCHO BRAHE TO GALILEO

One astronomer who agreed was Tycho Brahe (1546–1601). Born into a leading Danish noble family and earmarked for a career in government, Brahe was at an early age tremendously impressed by a partial eclipse of the sun. It seemed to him "something divine that men could know the motions of the stars so accurately that they were able a long time beforehand to predict their places and relative positions."[4] Completing his studies abroad and returning to Denmark, Brahe established himself as Europe's leading astronomer with his detailed observations of the new star of 1572. Aided by generous grants from the king of Denmark, which made him one of the richest men in the country, Brahe built the most sophisticated observatory of his day. For twenty years he meticulously observed the stars and planets with the naked eye. An imposing man who had lost a piece of his nose in a duel and replaced it with a special bridge of gold and silver alloy, a noble who exploited his peasants arrogantly and approached the heavens humbly, Brahe's great contribution was his mass of data. His limited understanding of mathematics prevented him, however, from making much sense out of his data. Part Ptolemaic, part Copernican, he believed that all the planets revolved around the sun and that the entire group of sun and planets revolved in turn around the earth-moon system.

TYCHO BRAHE'S MAIN OBSERVATORY *Lavishly financed by the king of Denmark, Brahe built his magnificent observatory at Uraniborg between 1576 and 1580. For twenty years he studied the heavens and accumulated a mass of precise but undigested data. (The British Library)*

It was left to Brahe's brilliant young assistant, Johannes Kepler (1571–1630), to go much farther. Kepler was a medieval figure in many ways. Coming from a minor German noble family and trained for the Lutheran ministry, he long believed that the universe was built on mystical mathematical relationships and a musical harmony of the heavenly bodies. Working and reworking Brahe's

mountain of observations in a staggering sustained effort after the Dane's death, this brilliant mathematician eventually went beyond mystical intuitions.

Kepler formulated three famous laws of planetary motion. First, building upon Copernican theory, he demonstrated in 1609 that the orbits of the planets around the sun are elliptical rather than circular. Second, he demonstrated that the planets do not move at a uniform speed in their orbits. Third, in 1619 he showed that the time a planet takes to make its complete orbit is precisely related to its distance from the sun. Kepler's contribution was monumental. Whereas Copernicus had speculated, Kepler proved mathematically the precise relations of a sun-centered (solar) system. His work demolished the old system of Aristotle and Ptolemy, and in his third law he came close to formulating the idea of universal gravitation.

While Kepler was unraveling planetary motion, a young Florentine name Galileo Galilei (1564–1642) was challenging all the old ideas about motion. Like so many early scientists, Galileo was a poor nobleman first marked for a religious career. However, he soon became fascinated by mathematics. A brilliant student, Galileo became a professor of mathematics in 1589 at age twenty-five. He proceeded to examine motion and mechanics in a new way. Indeed, his great achievement was the elaboration and consolidation of the modern experimental method. Rather than speculate about what might or should happen, Galileo conducted controlled experiments to find out what actually *did* happen.

In his famous "acceleration experiment," he showed that a uniform force – in this case gravity – produced a uniform acceleration. Here is how Galileo described his pathbreaking method and conclusion in his *Two New Sciences*:

*A piece of wooden moulding . . . was taken; on its edge was cut a channel a little more than one finger in breadth. Having made this groove very straight, smooth and polished, and having lined it with parchment, also as smooth and polished as possible, we rolled along it a hard, smooth and very round bronze ball. . . . Noting . . . the time required to make the descent . . . we now rolled the ball only one-quarter the length of the channel; and having measured the time of its descent, we found it precisely one-half of the former. . . . In such experiments [over many distances], repeated a full hundred times, we always found that the spaces traversed were to each other as the squares of the times, and that this was true for all inclinations of the plane.*[5]

With this and other experiments, Galileo also formulated the law of inertia. That is, rather than "rest" being the natural state of objects, an object continues in motion forever unless stopped by some external force. Aristotelian physics was in a shambles.

In the tradition of Brahe, Galileo also applied the experimental method to astronomy. His astronomical discoveries had a very great impact on scientific development. On hearing that the telescope had just been invented in Holland, Galileo made one for himself and trained it on the heavens. He quickly discovered the first four moons of Jupiter, which clearly suggested that Jupiter could not possibly be embedded in any impenetrable crystal sphere. This discovery provided new evidence for the Copernican theory, in which Galileo already believed.

Galileo then pointed his telescope at the moon. He wrote in 1610 in *Siderus Nuncius:*

*I feel sure that the moon is not perfectly smooth, free from inequalities, and exactly spherical, as a large school of philosophers considers with regard to the moon and the other heavenly bodies. On the contrary, it is full of inequalities, uneven, full of hollows and protuberances, just like the surface of the earth itself, which is varied everywhere by lofty mountains and deep valleys. . . . The next object which I have observed is the essence or substance of the Milky Way. By the aid of a telescope anyone may behold this in a manner which so distinctly appeals to the senses that all the disputes which have tormented philosophers through so many ages are exploded by the irrefutable evidence of our eyes, and we are freed from wordy disputes upon the subject. For the galaxy is nothing else but a mass of innumerable stars planted together in clusters. Upon whatever part of it you direct the telescope straightway a vast crowd of stars presents itself to view; many of them are tolerably large and extremely bright, but the number of small ones is quite beyond determination.*[6]

Reading these famous lines, one feels that a crucial corner in Western civilization is being turned. The traditional religious and theological world-view, which rested on determining and then accepting the proper established authority, is beginning to give way in certain fields to a critical, "scientific" method. This new method of learning and investigating was the greatest accomplishment of the entire scientific revolution, for it has proved capable of enormous extension. A historian critically investigating the documents of the past, for example, is not much different from a Galileo investigating stars and rolling balls.

Galileo was employed in Florence by the Medici grand dukes of Tuscany, and his work eventually aroused the ire of some theologians. The issue was presented in 1624 to Pope Urban VII, who permitted Galileo to write about different possible systems of the world, as long as he did not presume to judge which one actually existed. After the publication in Italian of his widely read *Dialogue on the Two Chief Systems of the World* in 1632, which too openly lampooned the traditional views of Aristotle and Ptolemy and defended those of Copernicus, Galileo was tried for heresy by the papal Inquisition. Imprisoned and threatened with torture, the aging Galileo recanted, "renouncing and cursing" his Copernican errors. Of minor importance in the development of science, Galileo's trial later became for some writers the perfect symbol of the inevitable conflict between religious belief and scientific knowledge.

## NEWTON'S SYNTHESIS

The accomplishments of Kepler, Galileo, and other scientists had had their effect by about 1640. The old astronomy and physics were in ruins, and several fundamental breakthroughs had been made. The new findings had not, however, been fused together in a new synthesis, a synthesis that would provide a single set of explanations for motion both on earth and in the skies. That synthesis, which prevailed until the twentieth century, was the work of Isaac Newton (1642–1727).

Newton was born into the lower English gentry, and attended Cambridge University. He was a very complex individual. A great genius who spectacularly united the experimental and theoretical-mathematical sides of modern science, Newton was also fascinated by alchemy. He sought the elixir of life and a way to change base metals into gold and silver. Not without reason did the twentieth-century economist John Maynard Keynes call Newton "the last of the magicians." Newton was intensely religious. He had a highly suspicious nature, lacked all interest in women and sex, and in 1693 had a nervous breakdown from which he later recovered. He was far from being the perfect rationalist so endlessly eulogized by writers in the eighteenth and nineteenth centuries.

Of his intellectual genius and incredible powers of concentration there can be no doubt, however. Arriving at some of his most basic ideas about physics in 1666 at age twenty-four, but unable to prove these theories mathematically, he attained a professorship and studied optics for many years. In 1684, Newton returned to physics for eighteen extraordinarily intensive months. For weeks on end he seldom left his room except to read his lectures. His meals were sent up but he usually forgot to eat them, his mind fastened like a vise on the laws of the universe. Thus did Newton open the third book of his immortal *Mathematical Principles of Natural Philosophy,* published in Latin in 1687 and generally known as the *Principia,* with these lines:

*In the preceding books I have laid down the principles of philosophy [that is, science]. . . . These principles are the laws of certain motions, and powers or forces, which chiefly have respect to philosophy. . . . It remains that from the same principles I now demonstrate the frame of the System of the World.*

Newton made good his grandiose claim. His towering accomplishment was to integrate in a single explanatory system the astronomy of Copernicus, as corrected by Kepler's laws, with the physics of Galileo and his predecessors. Newton did this by means of a set of mathematical laws that explain motion and mechanics. These laws of dynamics are complex, and it took scientists and engineers two hundred years to work out all their implications. Nevertheless, the key feature of the Newtonian synthesis was the law of universal gravitation. According to this law, every body in the universe attracts every other body in the universe in a precise mathematical relationship, whereby the force of attraction is proportional to the quantity of matter of the objects and inversely proportional to the square of the distance between them. The whole universe – from Kepler's elliptical orbits to Galileo's rolling balls – was unified in one majestic system.

## CAUSES OF THE SCIENTIFIC REVOLUTION

With a charming combination of modesty and self-congratulation, Newton once wrote: "If I have seen further [than others], it is by standing on the shoulders of Giants."[7] Surely the path from Copernicus to Newton confirms the "internal" view of the scientific revolution as, first of all, a product of towering individual genius. The problems of science were inherently exciting, and solution of those problems was its own reward for inquisitive, high-powered minds. Yet there were certainly broader causes as well.

The long-term contribution of medieval intellectual life and medieval universities to the scientific revolution was much more considerable than historians unsympathetic to the Middle Ages once believed. By the thirteenth century, permanent universities with professors and large student bodies – six thousand in Paris in 1300, for example – had been established in western Europe. The universities were supported by society because they trained the lawyers, doctors, and church leaders society required. By 1300, philosophy had taken its place alongside law, medicine, and theology. Medieval philosophers developed a limited but real independence from theologians and a sense of free inquiry. They nobly pursued a body of knowledge and tried to arrange it meaningfully by means of abstract theories.

Within this framework, science was able to emerge as a minor but distinct branch of philosophy. In the fourteenth and fifteenth centuries, first in Italy and then elsewhere in Europe, leading universities established new professorships of mathematics, astronomy, and physics (natural philosophy) within their faculties of philosophy. The prestige of the new fields was still low among both professors and students. Nevertheless, this pattern of academic science, which grew out of the medieval commitment to philosophy and did not change substantially until the late eighteenth century, undoubtedly promoted scientific development. Rational, critical thinking was applied to scientific problems by a permanent community of scholars. And an outlet existed for the talents of a Galileo or a Newton: all of the great pathbreakers just considered either studied or taught at universities.

The Renaissance also stimulated scientific progress. One of the great deficiencies of medieval science was its rather rudimentary mathematics. The recovery of the finest works of Greek mathematics – a by-product of Renaissance humanism's ceaseless search for the knowledge of antiquity – greatly improved European mathematics well into the early seventeenth century. The recovery of more texts also showed that classical mathematicians had had their differences, and Europeans were forced to try to resolve these ancient controversies by means of their own efforts. Finally, the Renaissance pattern of patronage, especially in Italy, was often scientific as well as artistic and humanistic. Various rulers and wealthy businessmen supported scientific investigations, just as the Medicis of Florence supported those of Galileo.

The navigational problems of long sea voyages in the age of overseas expansion were a third factor in the scientific revolution. Ship captains on distant shores needed to be able to chart their positions as accurately as possible, so that reliable maps could be drawn and the risks of international trade reduced. As early as 1484, the king of Portugal appointed a commission of mathematicians to perfect tables to help seamen find their latitude. This resulted in the first European navigation manual.

The problem of fixing longitude was much more difficult. In England, the government and the great capitalistic trading companies turned to science and scientific education in an attempt to solve this pressing practical problem. When the famous Elizabethan financier Sir Thomas Gresham left a large amount of money to establish Gresham College in London, he stipulated that three of the college's seven professors had to concern themselves exclusively with scientific subjects. The professor of astronomy was directed to teach courses on the science of navigation. A seventeenth-century popular ballad took note of the new college's calling:

*This college will the whole world measure*
*Which most impossible conclude,*
*And navigation make a pleasure*
*By finding out the longitude.*[8]

At Gresham College scientists had, for the first time in history, an important, honored role in society. They enjoyed close ties with the top officials of the Royal Navy and with the leading merchants and shipbuilders. Gresham College became the main center of scientific activity in England in the first half of the seventeenth century. The close tie between practical men and scientists also led to the establishment in 1662 of the Royal Society of London, which published scientific papers and sponsored scientific meetings.

Navigational problems were also critical in the development of many new scientific instruments, such as the telescope, the barometer, the thermometer, the pendulum clock, the microscope, and the air pump. Better instruments, which permitted more accurate observations, often led to very important new

knowledge almost automatically. Galileo with his telescope was by no means unique.

Better instruments were part of the fourth factor, the development of better ways of obtaining knowledge about the world. Two important thinkers, Francis Bacon (1561–1626) and René Descartes (1596–1650), represented key aspects of this improvement in scientific methodology.

The English politician and writer Francis Bacon was the greatest early propagandist for the new experimental method, as Galileo was its greatest early practitioner. Rejecting the Aristotelian and medieval method of using speculative reasoning to build general theories, Bacon argued that new knowledge had to be pursued through empirical, experimental research. That is, the researcher who wants to learn more about leaves or rocks should not speculate about the subject, but rather collect a multitude of specimens and then compare and analyze them. Thus freed from sterile "medieval" speculation, the facts will speak for themselves and knowledge will increase. Bacon's contribution was to formalize the empirical method, which had already been used by scientists like Brahe and Galileo, into a general theory of deductive reasoning, which we call empiricism.

Bacon claimed that the empirical method would result not only in more knowledge, but in highly practical, extremely useful knowledge. According to Bacon, scientific discoveries, like those so avidly sought at Gresham College, would bring about much greater control over the physical environment and make people rich and nations powerful. Thus Bacon helped provide a radically new, highly effective justification for private and public support of scientists and scientific inquiry.

The French philosopher René Descartes was a true genius who made his first great discovery in mathematics. As a young, twenty-three-year-old soldier serving in the Thirty Years' War, he experienced on a single night in 1619 a life-changing intellectual vision. What Descartes saw was that there was a perfect correspondence between geometry and algebra, and that geometrical, spatial figures could be expressed as algebraic equations and vice-versa. A great step forward in the history of mathematics, Descartes' discovery of analytic geometry provided scientists with an important new tool. Descartes also made contributions to the science of optics, but his greatest achievement was to develop his initial vision into a whole philosophy of knowledge and science.

Like Bacon, Descartes scorned traditional science and had great faith in the powers of the human mind. Yet Descartes was much more systematic and mathematical than Bacon. He decided it was necessary to doubt everything that could reasonably be doubted and then, as in geometry, to use deductive reasoning from self-evident principles to ascertain scientific laws. Descartes' reasoning ultimately reduced all substances to *matter* and *mind* – that is, to the physical and the spiritual. His view of the world as consisting of two fundamental entities is known as Cartesian dualism. Descartes was a profoundly original and extremely influential thinker.

It is important to realize that the modern scientific method, which began to crystallize in the late seventeenth century, has combined Bacon's inductive experimentalism and Descartes' deductive, mathematical rationalism. Neither of these extreme approaches was sufficient by itself. Bacon's inability to appreciate the importance of mathematics and his obsession with practical results clearly showed the limitations of antitheoretical empiricism. Likewise, some of Descartes' positions – he believed, for example, that it was possible to deduce the whole science of medicine from

first principles – aptly demonstrated the inadequacy of rigid, dogmatic rationalism. Significantly, Bacon faulted Galileo for his use of abstract formulas, while Descartes criticized the great Italian for being too experimental and insufficiently theoretical. Thus the modern scientific method has typically combined Bacon and Descartes. It has joined precise observations and experimentalism with the search for general laws that may be expressed in rigorously logical, mathematical language.

Finally, there is the question of science and religion. Just as some historians have argued that Protestantism led to the rise of capitalism, others have concluded that Protestantism was a fundamental factor in the rise of modern science. Protestantism, particularly in its Calvinist varieties, supposedly made scientific inquiry a question of individual conscience and not religious doctrine. The Catholic church, on the other hand, supposedly suppressed scientific theories that conflicted with its teachings and thus discouraged scientific progress.

The truth of the matter is more complicated. *All* religious authorities – Catholic, Protestant, and Jewish – opposed the Copernican system to a greater or lesser extent until about 1630, by which time the scientific revolution was definitely in progress. The Catholic church was initially less hostile than Protestant and Jewish religious leaders. This early Catholic toleration and the scientific interests of Renaissance Italy help account for the undeniable fact that Italian scientists played a crucial role in scientific progress right up to the trial of Galileo in 1633. Thereafter the Counter Reformation church became more hostile to science, which helps account for the decline of science in Italy (but not in Catholic France) after 1640. At the same time some Protestant countries became quite "pro-science," especially if the country lacked a strong religious authority capable of imposing religious orthodoxy on scientific questions.

This was the case with England after 1630. English religious conflicts became so intense that it was impossible for the authorities to impose religious unity on anything, including science. It is significant that the forerunners of the Royal Society agreed to discuss only "neutral" scientific questions, so as not to come to blows over closely related religious and political disputes. The work of Bacon and his many followers during Cromwell's Commonwealth helped solidify the neutrality and independence of science. Bacon advocated the experimental approach precisely because it was open-minded and independent of any preconceived religious or philosophical ideas. Neutral and useful, science became an accepted part of life and developed rapidly in England after about 1640.

## SOME CONSEQUENCES OF THE SCIENTIFIC REVOLUTION

The rise of modern science had many consequences, some of which are still unfolding. First, it went hand in hand with the rise of a new and expanding social group – the scientific community. Members of this community were linked together by learned societies, common interests, and shared values. Expansion of knowledge was the primary goal of this community, and scientists' material and psychological rewards depended on their success in this endeavor. Thus science became quite competitive, and ever more scientific advance was inevitable.

Second, the scientific revolution introduced not only new knowledge about nature but also a new and revolutionary way of obtaining such knowledge – the modern scientific method. In addition to being both theoretical and experimental, this method was highly critical, and it differed profoundly from the old way of getting knowledge about nature. It refused to base its conclusions on tradition and established sources, on ancient authorities and sacred texts.

The scientific revolution had few consequences for economic life and the living standards of the masses until the late eighteenth century at the very earliest. True, improvements in the techniques of navigation facilitated overseas trade and helped enrich leading merchants. But science had relatively few practical economic applications, and the hopes of the early Baconians were frustrated. The close link between theoretical, or pure, science and applied technology, which we take for granted today, simply did not exist before the nineteenth century. Thus, the scientific revolution of the seventeenth century was first and foremost an intellectual revolution. It is not surprising that for more than a hundred years its greatest impact was on how people thought and believed.

## THE ENLIGHTENMENT

The scientific revolution was the single most important factor in the creation of the new world-view of the eighteenth-century Enlightenment. This world-view, which has played a very large role in shaping the modern mind, was made up of a rich mix of ideas, sometimes conflicting, for intellectuals delight in playing with ideas as athletes delight in playing games. In this rich diversity, three central concepts stand out.

The most important and original idea of the Enlightenment was that the methods of natural science could and should be used to examine and understand all aspects of life. This was what intellectuals meant by *reason,* a favorite word of Enlightenment thinkers. Nothing was to be accepted on faith. Everything was to be submitted to the rational, critical, "scientific" way of thinking. This approach brought the Enlightenment into a head-on conflict with the established churches, which rested their beliefs on the special authority of the Bible and Christian theology. A second important Enlightenment concept was that the scientific method was capable of discovering the laws of human society as well as those of nature. Thus was "social science" born. Its birth led to the third key idea, the idea of progress. Armed with the proper method of discovering the laws of human existence, Enlightenment thinkers be-

lieved it was at least possible to create better societies and better people. Their belief was strengthened by some genuine improvements in economic and social life during the eighteenth century, as we shall see in the next two chapters.

The Enlightenment was, therefore, profoundly secular. It revived and expanded the Renaissance concentration on worldly explanations. In the course of the eighteenth century, the Enlightenment had a profound impact on the thought and culture of the urban middle and upper classes. It did not have much appeal for the poor and the peasants.

### THE EMERGENCE OF THE ENLIGHTENMENT

The Enlightenment reached its maturity about 1750, when a brilliant band of French thinkers known as the philosophes effectively propagandized the new world-view across Europe. Yet it was the generation that came of age between the publication of Newton's masterpiece in 1687 and the death of Louis XIV in 1715 that tied the crucial knot between the scientific revolution and a new outlook on life.

Talented writers of that generation popularized the hard-to-understand scientific achievements for the educated elite. The most famous and influential popularizer was a very versatile French man of letters, Bernard de Fontenelle (1657–1757). Fontenelle practically invented the technique of making highly complicated scientific findings understandable to a broad nonscientific audience. He set out to make science witty and entertaining, as easy to read as a novel. This was a tall order, but Fontenelle largely succeeded.

His most famous work, *Conversations on the Plurality of Worlds* of 1686, begins with two elegant figures walking in the gathering shadows of a large park. One is a woman, a so-

POPULARIZING SCIENCE *The frontpiece illustration of Fontenelle's* Conversations on the Plurality of Worlds *invites the reader to share the pleasures of astronomy with an elegant lady and an entertaining teacher. (Photo: Caroline Buckler)*

*There came on the scene a certain German, one Copernicus, who made short work of all those various circles, all those solid skies, which the ancients had pictured to themselves. The former he abolished; the latter he broke in pieces. Fired with the noble zeal of a true astronomer, he took the earth and spun it very far away from the center of the universe, where it had been installed, and in that center he put the sun, which had a far better title to the honor.*[9]

Rather than tremble in despair in the face of these revelations, Fontenelle's lady rejoices in the advance of knowledge. Fontenelle thus went beyond entertainment to instruction, suggesting that the human mind was capable of making great progress.

This idea of progress was essentially a new idea of the later seventeenth century. Medieval and Reformation thinkers had been concerned primarily with sin and salvation. The humanists of the Renaissance had emphasized worldly matters, but they had been backward-looking. They had believed it might be possible to equal the magnificent accomplishments of the ancients, but they did not ask for more. Fontenelle and like-minded writers had come to believe that, at least in science and mathematics, their era had gone far *beyond* antiquity. Progress, at least intellectual progress, was clearly possible. During the eighteenth century, this idea would sink deeply into the consciousness of the European elite.

Fontenelle and other literary figures of his generation were also instrumental in bringing science into conflict with religion. Contrary to what is often assumed, many seventeenth-century scientists, both Catholic and Protestant, believed that their work exalted God. They did not draw antireligious implications from their scientific findings. The greatest scientist of them all, Isaac Newton, was a devout if unorthodox Christian who saw all of his studies as directed toward explaining God's

phisticated aristocrat, and the other is her friend, perhaps even her lover. They gaze at the stars, and their talk turns to a passionate discussion of . . . astronomy! He confides that "each star may well be a different world." She is intrigued by his novel idea: "Teach me about these stars of yours." And he does, gently but persistently stressing how error is giving way to truth. At one point he explains:

message. Newton devoted far more of his time to angels and biblical prophecies than to universal gravitation, and he was convinced that all of his inquiries were equally "scientific."

Fontenelle, on the other hand, was skeptical about absolute truth and cynical about the claims of organized religion. Since such views could not be stated openly in Louis XIV's France, Fontenelle made his point through subtle editorializing about science. His depiction of the cautious Copernicus as a self-conscious revolutionary was typical. In his *Eulogies of Scientists* Fontenelle exploited with endless variations the basic theme of rational, progressive scientists versus prejudiced, reactionary priests. Time and time again Fontenelle's fledgling scientists attended church and studied theology; then, at some crucial moment, each was converted from the obscurity of religion to the clarity of science.

The progressive and antireligious implications that writers like Fontenelle drew from the scientific revolution reflected a very real crisis in European thought at the end of the seventeenth century. This crisis had its roots in several intellectual uncertainties and dissatisfactions, of which the demolition of Aristotelian-medieval science was only one.

A second uncertainty involved the whole question of religious truth. The destructive wars of religion had been fought, in part, because religious freedom was an intolerable idea in the early seventeenth century. Both Catholics and Protestants had believed that religious truth was absolute and therefore worth fighting and dying for. It was also generally believed that a strong state required unity in religious faith. Yet the disastrous results of the many attempts to impose such religious unity, such as Louis XIV's expulsion of the French Protestants in 1685, led some people to ask if ideological conformity in re-

ligious matters was really necessary. Others skeptically asked if religious truth could ever be known with absolute certainty, and concluded that it could not.

The most famous of these skeptics was Pierre Bayle (1647–1706), a French Huguenot who took refuge in Holland. A teacher by profession and a crusading journalist by inclination, Bayle critically examined the religious beliefs and persecutions of the past in his *Historical and Critical Dictionary,* published in 1697. Demonstrating that human beliefs had been extremely varied and very often mistaken, Bayle concluded that nothing can ever be known beyond all doubt. In religion as in philosophy, humanity's best hope was open-minded toleration. Bayle's skeptical views were very influential. Many eighteenth-century writers mined his inexhaustible vein of critical skepticism for ammunition for their attacks on superstition and Christian theology. Bayle's four-volume *Dictionary* was more frequently found in the private libraries of eighteenth-century France than any other book.

The rapidly growing travel literature on non-European lands and cultures was a third cause of uncertainty. In the wake of the great discoveries, Europeans were learning that the peoples of China, India, Africa and the Americas all had their own very different beliefs and customs. Europeans shaved their faces and let their hair grow. The Turks shaved their heads and let their beards grow. In Europe a man bowed before a woman to show respect. In Siam a man turned his back on a woman when he met her, because it was disrespectful to look directly at her. Countless similar examples discussed in the travel accounts helped change the perspective of educated Europeans. They began to look at truth and morality in relative rather than absolute terms. Anything was possible, and who could say what was right or wrong? As one Frenchman wrote: "There is nothing that opinion, prejudice, custom, hope, and a sense of honor cannot do." Another wrote disapprovingly of religious skeptics who were corrupted "by extensive travel and lose whatever shreds of religion that remained with them. Every day they see a new religion, new customs, new rites."[10]

A fourth cause and manifestation of European intellectual turmoil was John Locke's epoch-making *Essay Concerning Human Understanding*. Published in 1690 – the same year Locke published his famous *Second Treatise on Civil Government* – Locke's essay brilliantly set forth a new theory about how human beings learn and form their ideas. In doing so he rejected the prevailing view of Descartes, who had held that all people are born with certain basic ideas and ways of thinking. Locke insisted that all ideas are derived from experience. The human mind is like a blank tablet at birth, a tablet on which environment writes the individual's understanding and beliefs. Human development is, therefore, determined by education and social institutions, for good or for evil. Locke's *Essay Concerning Human Understanding* passed through many editions and translations. It was, along with Newton's *Principia,* one of the dominant intellectual inspirations of the Enlightenment.

## THE PHILOSOPHES AND THEIR IDEAS

By the death of Louis XIV in 1715, many of the ideas that would soon coalesce into the new world-view had been assembled. Yet Christian Europe was still strongly attached to its traditional beliefs, as witnessed by the powerful revival of religious orthodoxy in the first half of the eighteenth century. By the outbreak of the American Revolution in 1775, however, a large portion of western Europe's educated elite had embraced many of the new ideas. This acceptance was the work of one of history's most influential groups of intellectuals, the philosophes. It was the philosophes who proudly and effectively proclaimed that they, at long last, were bringing the light of knowledge to their ignorant fellow creatures in a great Age of Enlightenment.

*Philosophe* is the French word for philosopher, and it was in France that the Enlightenment reached its highest development. The French philosophes were indeed philosophers. They asked fundamental philosophical questions about the meaning of life, about God, human nature, good and evil, and cause and effect. But, in the tradition of Bayle and Fontenelle, they were not content with abstract arguments or ivory-tower speculations among a tiny minority of scholars and professors. They wanted to influence and convince a broad audience.

The philosophes were intensely committed to reforming society and humanity, yet they were not free to write as they wished, since it was illegal in France to criticize openly either church or state. Their most radical works had to circulate in France in manuscript form, very much as critical works are passed from hand to hand in unpublished form in dictatorships today. Knowing that direct attacks would probably be banned or burned, the philosophes wrote novels and plays, histories and philosophies, dictionaries and encyclopedias, all filled with satire and double meanings to spread the message.

One of the greatest philosophes, the baron de Montesquieu (1689–1755), brilliantly pioneered this approach in *The Persian Letters,* an extremely influential social satire published in 1721. Montesquieu's work consisted of amusing letters supposedly written by Persian travelers, who see European customs in "strange ways" and thereby cleverly criticize existing practices and beliefs. Having shown wit to be a powerful weapon against the cruelty and superstition he despised, Montesquieu turned to political theory and as we shall see in Chapter 21, contributed greatly to the development of liberalism.

The most famous and in many ways most representative philosophe was François Marie Arouet, who was known by the pen name of Voltaire (1694-1778). In his long career this son of a comfortable middle-class family wrote over seventy witty volumes, hobnobbed with kings and queens, and died a millionaire because of shrewd business speculations. His early career, however, was turbulent. In 1717, Voltaire was imprisoned for eleven months in the Bastille in Paris for insulting the regent of France. In 1726, a barb from his sharp tongue led a great French nobleman to have him beaten and arrested. This experience made a deep impression upon Voltaire. All his life he struggled against legal injustice and class inequalities before the law.

Released from prison after promising to leave the country, Voltaire lived in England for three years. He then wrote various works praising English institutions and popularizing English scientific progress. Newton, he wrote, was history's greatest man, for he had used his genius for the benefit of humanity. "It is," wrote Voltaire, "the man who sways our minds by the prevalence of reason and the native force of truth, not they who reduce mankind to a state of slavery by force and downright violence . . . that claims our reverence and admiration."[11] In the true style of the Enlightenment, Voltaire mixed the glorification of science and reason with an appeal for better people and institutions.

Yet, like almost all of the philosophes, Voltaire was a reformer and not a revolutionary in social and political matters. Returning to France, he was eventually appointed royal historian in 1743, and his *Age of Louis XIV* portrayed Louis as the dignified leader of his age. Voltaire also began a long correspon-

VOLTAIRE *was a prodigious worker. This painting shows him dictating from the very moment he hops out of bed. (Bulloz)*

dence with Frederick the Great, and he accepted Frederick's flattering invitation to come brighten up the Prussian court in Berlin. The two men later quarreled, but Voltaire always admired Frederick as a freethinker and an enlightened monarch.

Voltaire pessimistically concluded that the best one could hope for in the way of government was an enlightened monarch, since human beings "are very rarely worthy to govern themselves." Nor did he believe in social equality in human affairs. The idea of making servants equal to their masters was "absurd and impossible." The only realizable equality Voltaire thought was that "by which the citizen only depends on the laws which protect the freedom of the feeble against the ambitions of the strong."[12]

Voltaire's philosophical and religious positions were much more radical. In the tradition of Bayle, his voluminous writings challenged – often indirectly – the Catholic church and Christian theology at almost every point. Although he was considered by many devout Christians to be a shallow blasphemer, Voltaire's religious views were influential and quite typical of the mature Enlightenment. The essay on religion from his widely read *Philosophical Dictionary* sums up many of his criticisms and beliefs:

*I meditated last night; I was absorbed in the contemplation of nature; I admired the immensity, the course, the harmony of these infinite globes which the vulgar do not know how to admire.*

*I admired still more the intelligence which directs these vast forces. I said to myself: "One must be blind not to be dazzled by this spectacle; one must be stupid not to recognize its author; one must be mad not to worship the Supreme Being."*

*I was deep in these ideas when one of those genii who fill the intermundane spaces came down to me ... and transported me into a desert all covered with piles of bones.... He began with the first pile. "These," he said, "are the twenty-three thousand Jews who danced before a calf, with the twenty-four thousand who were killed while lying with Midianitish women. The number of those massacred for such errors and offences amounts to nearly three hundred thousand.*

*"In the other piles are the bones of the Christians slaughtered by each other because of metaphysical disputes...."*

*"What!" I cried, "brothers have treated their brothers like this, and I have the misfortune to be of this brotherhood!... Why assemble here all these abominable monuments to barbarism and fanaticism?"*

*"To instruct you.... Follow me now."...*

*I saw a man with a gentle, simple face, who seemed to me to be about thirty-five years old. From afar he looked with compassion upon those piles of* whitened bones, through which I had been led to reach the sage's dwelling place. I was astonished to find his feet swollen and bleeding, his hands likewise, his side pierced, and his ribs laid bare by the cut of the lash. "Good God!" I said to him, "is it possible for a just man, a sage, to be in this state?... Was it ... by priests and judges that you were so cruelly assassinated?"

*With great courtesy he answered, "Yes."*

*"And who were these monsters?"*

*"They were hypocrites."*

*"Ah! that says everything; I understand by that one word that they would have condemned you to the cruelest punishment. Had you then proved to them, as Socrates did, that the Moon was not a goddess, and that Mercury was not a god?"*

*"No, it was not a question of planets. My countrymen did not even know what a planet was; they were all arrant ignoramuses. Their superstitions were quite different from those of the Greeks."*

*"Then you wanted to teach them a new religion?"*

*"Not at all; I told them simply: 'Love God with all your heart and your neighbor as yourself, for that is the whole of mankind's duty.' Judge yourself if this precept is not as old as the universe; judge yourself if I brought them a new religion."...*

*"Did you not say once that you were come not to bring peace, but a sword?"*

*"It was a scribe's error; I told them that I brought peace and not a sword. I never wrote anything; what I said can have been changed without evil intention."*

*"You did not then contribute in any way by your teaching, either badly reported or badly interpreted, to those frightful piles of bones which I saw on my way to consult with you?"*

*"I have only looked with horror upon those who have made themselves guilty of all these murders."*

*...[Finally] I asked him to tell me in what true religion consisted.*

*"Have I not already told you? Love God and your neighbor as yourself."*

*"What! Can we love God and still eat meat on Friday?"*

*"I always ate what was given me; for I was too poor to give dinner to anyone."*

*"Must I take sides for either the Greek or the Latin church?"*

*"When I was in the world I never made any distinction between the Jew and the Samaritan."*

*"Well, if that is so, I take you for my only master." Then he made me a sign with his head which filled me with consolation. The vision disappeared, and a clear conscience stayed with me.*[13]

This passage requires careful study, for it suggests many Enlightenment themes of religion and philosophy. As the opening paragraphs show, Voltaire clearly believed in a God. But the God of Voltaire and most philosophes was a distant, deistic God, a great Clockmaker who built an orderly universe and then stepped aside and let it run. Finally, the philosophes hated all forms of religious intolerance. They believed that people had to be wary of dogmatic certainty and religious disputes, which often led to fanaticism and savage, inhuman action. Simple piety and human kindness – the love of God and the golden rule – were religion enough, even Christianity enough, as Voltaire's interpretation of Christ suggests.

The ultimate strength of the philosophes lay, however, in their numbers, dedication, and organization. The philosophes felt keenly that they were engaged in a common undertaking that transcended individuals. Their greatest and most representative intellectual achievement was, quite fittingly, a group effort – the seventeen-volume *Encyclopedia: The Rational Dictionary of the Sciences, the Arts, and the Crafts,* edited by Denis Diderot (1713–1774) and Jean le Rond d'Alembert (1717–1783). Diderot and d'Alembert made a curious pair. Diderot began his career as a hack writer, first attracting attention with a skeptical tract on religion that was quickly burned by the judges of Paris. D'Alembert was one of Europe's leading scientists and mathematicians, the orphaned and illegitimate son of celebrated aristocrats. Moving in different circles and with different interests, the two men set out to find coauthors who would examine the whole of rapidly expanding human knowledge. Even more fundamentally, they set out to teach people how to think critically and objectively about all matters. As Diderot said, he wanted the *Encyclopedia* to "change the general way of thinking."[14]

The editors of the *Encyclopedia* had to conquer innumerable obstacles. After the appearance in 1751 of the first volume, which dealt with such controversial subjects as atheism, the soul, and blind people – all words beginning with *a* in French – the government temporarily banned publication. The pope later placed it on the Index and pronounced excommunication on all who read or bought it. The timid publisher mutilated some of the articles in the last ten volumes without the editors' consent in an attempt to appease the authorities. Yet Diderot's unwavering belief in the importance of his mission held the encyclopedists together for fifteen years, and the enormous work was completed in 1765. Hundreds of thousands of articles by leading scientists and famous writers, skilled workers and progressive priests, treated every aspect of life and knowledge.

Not every article was daring or original, but the overall effect was little short of revolutionary. Science and the industrial arts were exalted, religion and immortality questioned. Intolerance, legal injustice, and out-of-date social institutions were openly criticized. More generally, the writers of the *Encyclopedia* showed that human beings could use the proc-

CANAL WITH LOCKS  *The articles on science and the industrial arts in the* Encyclopedia *carried lavish explanatory illustrations. This typical engraving from* *the section on water and its uses shows advances in canal building and reflects the encyclopedists' faith in technical progress. (Photo: Caroline Buckler)*

ess of reasoning to expand human knowledge. Encyclopedists were convinced that greater knowledge would result in greater human happiness, for knowledge was useful and made possible economic, social, and political progress. The *Encyclopedia* was extremely influential in France and throughout western Europe as well. It summed up the new world-view of the Enlightenment.

## THE LATER ENLIGHTENMENT

After about 1770, the harmonious unity of the philosophes and their thought began to break down. As the new world-view became increasingly accepted by the educated public, some thinkers sought originality by exaggerating certain ideas of the Enlightenment to the exclusion of others. These latter-day philosophes built rigid, dogmatic systems.

In his *System of Nature* (1770) and other works, the aristocratic Baron Paul d'Holbach (1723–1789) argued that human beings were machines completely determined by outside forces. Free will, God, and immortality of the soul were foolish myths. D'Holbach's rabid atheism and determinism, which were coupled with extreme hostility toward Christianity and all other religions, dealt the Enlightenment movement a severe blow. Deists like Voltaire, who believed in God but not in established churches, found d'Holbach's inflexible atheism repulsive. They saw in him the same dogmatic intolerance they had been fighting all their lives.

Another aristocrat, the marquis Marie-Jean

de Condorcet (1743–1794), transformed the Enlightenment belief in gradual, hard-won progress into fanciful utopianism. In his *Progress of the Human Mind,* written in 1793 during the French Revolution, Condorcet traced the nine stages of human progress that had already occurred and predicted that the tenth would bring perfection. Ironically, Condorcet wrote this work while fleeing for his life. Caught and condemned by revolutionary extremists, he preferred death by his own hand to the blade of the guillotine.

Other thinkers and writers after about 1770 began to attack the Enlightenment's faith in reason, progress, and moderation. The most famous of these was the Swiss Jean-Jacques Rousseau (1712–1778), a brilliant but difficult thinker, an appealing but neurotic individual. Born into a poor family of watchmakers in Geneva, Rousseau went to Paris and was greatly influenced by Diderot and Voltaire. Always extraordinarily sensitive and suspicious, Rousseau came to believe his philosophe friends were plotting against him. In the mid-1750s he broke with them personally and intellectually, living thereafter as a lonely outsider with his uneducated common-law wife and going in his own highly original direction.

Like other Enlightenment thinkers, Rousseau was passionately committed to individual freedom. Unlike them, however, he attacked rationalism and civilization as destroying rather than liberating the individual. Warm, spontaneous feeling had to complement and correct the cold intellect. Moreover, the individual's basic goodness had to be protected from the cruel refinements of civilization. As we shall see in Chapter 23, these ideas greatly influenced the early romantic movement, which rebelled against the culture of the Enlightenment in the late eighteenth century.

Applying his heartfelt ideas to children,

Rousseau had a powerful impact upon the development of modern education. In his famous novel *Emile* (1762) he argued that education must shield the naturally unspoiled child from the corrupting influences of civilization and too many books. According to Rousseau, children must develop naturally and spontaneously, at their own speed and in their own way. It is eloquent testimony to Rousseau's troubled life and complicated personality that he placed all five of his own children in orphanages.

Rousseau also made an important contribution to political theory in the *Social Contract* (1762). His fundamental ideas were the general will and popular sovereignty. According to Rousseau, the general will is sacred and absolute, reflecting the common interests of the people, who have displaced the monarch as the holder of the sovereign power. The general will is not necessarily the will of the majority, however, although minorities have to subordinate themselves to it without question. Little noticed before the French Revolution, Rousseau's dogmatic concept of the general will appealed greatly to democrats and nationalists after 1789. The concept has also been used since 1789 by many dictators, who have claimed that they, rather than some momentary majority of the voters, represent the general will and thus the true interests of the sovereign masses.

## THE SOCIAL SETTING OF THE ENLIGHTENMENT

The philosophes were splendid talkers as well as effective writers. Indeed, sparkling conversation in private homes spread Enlightenment ideas to Europe's upper middle class and aristocracy. Paris set the example, and other French cities and European capitals followed. In Paris a number of talented and often rich women presided over regular social gatherings of the great and near-great in their elegant drawing rooms, or salons. There, a d'Alembert and a Fontenelle could exchange witty, uncensored observations on literature, science, and philosophy with great aristocrats, wealthy middle-class financiers, high-ranking officials, and noteworthy foreigners. These intellectual salons practiced the equality the philosophes preached. They were open to all men and women with good manners, provided only that they were famous or talented, rich or important. More generally, the philosophes championed greater rights and expanded education for women, arguing that the subordination of females was an unreasonable prejudice and the sign of a barbaric society.

One of the most famous salons was that of Madame Geoffrin, the unofficial godmother of the *Encyclopedia*. Having lost her parents at an early age, the future Madame Geoffrin was married at fifteen by her well-meaning grandmother to a rich and boring businessman of forty-eight. It was the classic marriage of convenience – the poor young girl and the rich old man – and neither side ever pretended that love was a consideration. After dutifully raising her children, Madame Geoffrin sought to break out of her gilded cage as she entered middle age. The very proper businessman's wife became friendly with a neighbor, the marquise de Tencin. In her youth the marquise had been rather infamous as the mistress of the regent of France, but she had settled down to run a salon that counted Fontenelle and the philosopher Montesquieu among its regular guests.

When the marquise died in 1749, Madame Geoffrin tactfully transferred these luminaries to her spacious mansion for regular dinners. At first Madame Geoffrin's husband loudly protested the arrival of this horde of "para-sites." But his wife's will was much stronger than his, and he soon opened his purse and even appeared at the twice-weekly dinners. "Who was that old man at the end of the table who never said anything?" an innocent newcomer asked one evening. "That," replied Madame Geoffrin without the slightest emotion, "was my husband. He's dead."[15]

When M. Geoffrin's death became official, Madame Geoffrin put the large fortune and spacious mansion she inherited to good use. She welcomed the encyclopedists – Diderot, d'Alembert, Fontenelle, and a host of others. She gave them generous financial aid and helped to save their enterprise from collapse, especially after the first eight volumes were burned by the authorities in 1759. She also corresponded with the king of Sweden and Catherine the Great of Russia. Madame Geoffrin was, however, her own woman. She remained a practicing Christian, and would not tolerate attacks on the church in her house. It was said that distinguished foreigners felt they had not seen Paris unless they had been invited to one of her dinners. The plain and long-neglected Madame Geoffrin managed to become the most renowned hostess of the eighteenth century.

There were many other hostesses, but Madame Geoffrin's greatest rival, Madame du Deffand, was one of the most interesting. While Madame Geoffrin was middle-class, pious, and chaste, Madame du Deffand was a skeptic from the nobility who lived fast and easy, at least in her early years. Another difference was that women – mostly highly intelligent, worldly members of the nobility – were fully the equal of men in Madame du Deffand's intellectual salon. Forever pursuing fulfillment in love and life, Madame du Deffand was an accomplished and liberated woman. An exceptionally fine letter writer, she carried on a vast correspondence with

*MADAME GEOFFRIN'S SALON  In this stylized group portrait a famous actor reads to a gathering of leading philosophes and aristocrats in 1755. Third from the right presiding over her gathering, is Ma-*
*dame Geoffrin, next to the sleepy ninety-eight-year-old Bernard de Fontenelle. (Malmaison Chateau/ Giraudon)*

leading men and women all across Europe. Voltaire was her most enduring friend.

Madame du Deffand's closest female friend was Julie de Lespinasse, a beautiful, talented young woman whom she befriended and made her protégée. The never-acknowledged illegitimate daughter of noble parents, Julie de Lespinasse had a hard youth, but she flowered in Madame du Deffand's drawing room – so much so that she was eventually dismissed by her jealous patroness.

Once again Julie de Lespinasse triumphed.

Her friends gave her money so that she could form her own salon. Her highly informal gatherings – she was not rich enough to supply more than tea and cake – attracted the keenest minds in France and Europe. As one philosophe marveled, "Nowhere was the conversation more brilliant nor better supervised. . . . She could toss out an idea for debate, make her contribution with clarity and sometimes with eloquence, and direct the conversation with the skill of a fairy." Another philosophe wrote:

*She could unite the different types, even the most antagonistic, sustaining the conversation by a well-aimed phrase, animating and guiding it at will. . . . Politics, religion, philosophy, news: nothing was excluded. Her circle met daily from five to nine. There one found men of all ranks in the State, the Church, and the Court, soldiers and foreigners, and the leading writers of the day.*[16]

Thus in France the ideas of the Enlightenment thrived in a social setting that graciously united members of the intellectual, economic, and social elites. Never before and never again would social and intellectual life be so closely and so pleasantly joined. In such an atmosphere the philosophes and the French nobility and upper middle class increasingly influenced one another. Critical thinking became fashionable, and flourished alongside hopes for human progress through greater knowledge.

## ENLIGHTENED ABSOLUTISM

How did the Enlightenment influence political developments? To this important question there is no easy answer. On the one hand, the philosophes were primarily interested in converting people to critical "scientific" thinking and were not particularly concerned with politics. On the other hand, such thinking naturally led to political criticism and interest in political reform. Educated people, who belonged mainly to the nobility and middle class, came to regard political change as both possible and desirable.

Until the American Revolution, however, most Enlightenment thinkers believed that political change should come from above — from the ruler — rather than from below, especially in central and eastern Europe. There were several reasons for this essentially moderate belief. First, royal absolutism was a fact

of life, and the kings and queens of Europe's leading states clearly had no intention of giving up their great powers. Second, the philosophes generally believed that a benevolent absolutism offered the best opportunities for improving society. Critical thinking was turning the art of good government into an exact science. Therefore, it was necessary only to educate and "enlighten" the monarch, who could then swiftly and successfully make good laws and promote human happiness. Third, the philosophes turned toward the rulers because the rulers seemed to be listening. Just as the philosophes and the increasingly receptive upper middle class and nobility influenced one another, so did the philosophes and the "enlightened monarchs" come to form a mutual admiration society. Finally, although the philosophes did not dwell on this fact, they distrusted the masses. Known simply as "the people" in the eighteenth century, the peasant masses and the urban poor were, according to the philosophes, still enchained by the superstitions of the priests. Moreover, violent passions rather than logical thinking guided the people's actions. No doubt the people were maturing, but they were still children in need of firm parental guidance.

Encouraged and instructed by the philosophes, several absolutist rulers of the later eighteenth century tried, to the best of their abilities, to govern in an enlightened manner. The actual programs of these rulers varied greatly. Let us, therefore, examine these monarchs at close range before trying to form any overall judgment regarding the success or failure of enlightened absolutism.

### THE "GREATS": FREDERICK OF PRUSSIA AND CATHERINE OF RUSSIA

Just as the French absolutism of Louis XIV had been the model for European rulers in the late seventeenth century, the enlightened absolutism of the French philosophes inspired European monarchs in the second half of the eighteenth century. French was the international language of the educated classes, and the education of future kings and queens across Europe lay in the hands of French tutors espousing Enlightenment ideas. France's cultural leadership was reinforced by the fact that it was still the wealthiest and most populous country in Europe. Thus, absolutist monarchs in several west German and Italian states, as well as in Spain and Portugal, proclaimed themselves more enlightened. By far the most influential of the new-style monarchs were Frederick II of Prussia and Catherine II of Russia, both styled "the Great."

*FREDERICK THE GREAT*  Frederick II, as we have seen (pages 605–606), carried on most of the stern military traditions he inherited from his father. His unprovoked attack on Maria Theresa's Austria in 1740 in order to seize Silesia helped contribute to a generation of warfare and almost resulted in the destruction of Prussia in the Seven Years' War (1756–1763). Yet in spite of his aggression and the philosophes' hatred of war, Frederick II was universally acknowledged as an "enlightened" absolute monarch, for two basic reasons.

First of all, Frederick adopted the cultural outlook of the Enlightenment. He wrote verse in French, delighted in witty conversation, and openly made fun of Christian doctrines. Yet he tolerantly allowed his subjects to believe as they wished in religious and philosophical matters. He also promoted the advancement of knowledge, improving his country's schools and universities.

Second, Frederick tried to improve the lives of his subjects. As he wrote his friend Voltaire: "I must enlighten my people, cultivate their manners and morals, and make them as happy as human beings can be, or as happy as the means at my disposal permit." The legal

system and the bureaucracy were Frederick's primary tools. Prussia's laws were simplified, and judges decided cases quickly and impartially. Prussian officials became famous for their hard work and honesty. After the Seven Years' War ended in 1763, Frederick's government also energetically promoted the reconstruction of agriculture and industry in his war-torn country. In all this Frederick set a good example. He worked hard and lived modestly, claiming that he was "only the first servant of the state." Thus, Frederick justified monarchy in terms of practical results and said nothing of the divine right of kings.

Frederick's dedication to high-minded principles went only so far, however. He never tried to change Prussia's existing social structure. True, he condemned serfdom in the abstract, but he accepted it in practice and did not even free the serfs on his own estates. He accepted the old privileges of the nobility and extended new ones as well. It became practically impossible for a middle-class person to gain a top position in the government. The Junker nobility remained the backbone of the army and the entire Prussian state.

*CATHERINE THE GREAT*  Catherine the Great of Russia (1762–1796) was one of the most remarkable rulers who ever lived, and the philosophes adored her. Catherine was a German princess from Anhalt-Zerbst, a totally insignificant principality sandwiched between Prussia and Saxony. Her father commanded a regiment of the Prussian army, but her mother was related to the Romanovs of Russia, and that proved to be her chance.

Peter the Great had abolished the hereditary succession of tsars so that he could name his successor and thus preserve his policies. This move opened a period of palace intrigue and a rapid turnover of rulers until Peter's youngest daughter Elizabeth came to the Russian throne in 1741. A crude, shrewd woman noted for her hard drinking and hard loving – one of her official lovers was an illiterate shepherd boy – Elizabeth named her nephew Peter heir to the throne and chose Catherine to be his wife in 1744. It was a mismatch from the beginning. The fifteen-year-old Catherine was intelligent and attractive; her husband was stupid and ugly, his face badly scarred by smallpox. Ignored by her childish husband, Catherine carefully studied Russian, endlessly read writers like Bayle and Voltaire, and made friends at court. Soon she knew what she wanted. "I did not care about Peter," she wrote in her *Memoirs,* "but I did care about the crown."[17]

As the old empress Elizabeth approached death, Catherine plotted against her unpopular husband. A dynamic, sensuous woman, Catherine used her powerful sexual desire to good political advantage. She selected as her new lover a tall, dashing young officer named Gregory Orlov, who with his four officer brothers commanded considerable support among the soldiers stationed in St. Petersburg. When Peter came to the throne in 1762, his first act was to withdraw Russian troops from the coalition against the hard-pressed Frederick of Prussia, whom he greatly admired. This decision saved Prussia from certain destruction, but it further alienated the army. Nor did Peter III's attempt to gain support from the Russian nobility by freeing it from compulsory state service succeed. At the end of six months Catherine and the military conspirators deposed Peter III in a palace revolution. Then the Orlov brothers murdered him. The German princess became empress of Russia.

Catherine had drunk deeply at the Enlightenment well. Never questioning the common assumption that absolute monarchy was the best form of government, she set out to rule in an enlightened manner. One of her most enduring goals was to bring the sophisticated culture of western Europe to backward Russia. To do so, she imported Western architects, sculptors, musicians, and intellectuals. She bought masterpieces of Western art in wholesale lots and created one of the best collections in all Europe. Throughout her reign Catherine patronized the philosophes. An enthusiastic letter writer, she corresponded extensively with Voltaire and praised him as "the champion of the human race." When the French government banned the *Encyclopedia,* she offered to publish it in St. Petersburg. She discussed reform with Diderot in St. Petersburg; and when Diderot needed money, she purchased his library for a small fortune but allowed him to keep it during his lifetime. With these and countless similar actions, Catherine skillfully won a good press for herself and for her country in the West. Moreover, this intellectual ruler, who wrote plays and articles and loved good talk, set the tone for the entire Russian nobility. Peter the Great westernized Russian armies, but it was Cahterine who westernized the thinking of the Russian nobility.

Catherine's second goal was domestic reform, and she began her reign with sincere and ambitious projects. Better laws were a major concern. In 1767, she drew up enlightened instructions for the special legislative commission she appointed to prepare a new law code. No new unified code was ever produced, but Catherine did restrict the practice of torture and allowed limited religious toleration. She also tried to improve education and strengthen local government. The philosophes applauded these measures and hoped more would follow.

Such was not the case. In 1773, a simple Cossack soldier named Emelian Pugachev sparked a gigantic uprising of serfs, very much as Stenka Razin had done a century earlier (page 614). Proclaiming himself the true tsar, Pugachev issued "decrees" abolishing serfdom, taxes, and army service. Thousands joined his cause, slaughtering landlords and officials over a vast area of southwestern Russia. Pugachev's hordes eventually proved no match for Catherine's noble-led regular army. Betrayed by his own men, Pugachev was captured and savagely executed.

Pugachev's rebellion was a decisive turning point in Catherine's domestic policy. On coming to the throne she had condemned serfdom in theory, but she was smart enough to realize that any changes would have to be very gradual or else she would quickly follow her departed husband. Pugachev's rebellion put an end to any illusions she might have had about reforming serfdom. The peasants were clearly dangerous, and her empire rested on the support of the nobility. After 1775, Catherine gave the nobles absolute control of their serfs. She extended serfdom into new areas, such as the Ukraine. In 1785, she formalized the nobility's privileged position, freeing them forever from taxes and state service. She also confiscated the lands of the Russian Orthodox church and gave them to favorite officials. Under Catherine the Russian nobility attained its most exalted position, and serfdom entered its most oppressive phase.

Catherine's third goal was territorial expansion, and in this respect she was extremely successful. Her armies subjugated the last descendants of the Mongols, the Crimean Tartars, and began the conquest of the Caucasus.

Her greatest coup by far was the partitioning of Poland. Poland had failed to build a strong absolutist state. For decades all important decisions had required the unanimous agreement of every Polish noble, which meant that nothing could ever be done. When be-

CATHERINE THE GREAT *Intelligent, pleasure-loving, and vain, Catherine succeeded in bringing Russia closer to western Europe than ever before. (John R. Freeman)*

tween 1768 and 1772 Catherine's armies scored unprecedented victories against the Turks and thereby threatened to disturb the balance of power between Russia and Austria in eastern Europe, Frederick of Prussia obligingly came forward with a deal. He proposed that Turkey be let off easily, and that Prussia, Austria, and Russia each "compensate" itself by taking a gigantic slice of Polish territory. Catherine jumped at the chance. The first partition of Poland took place in 1772. Two more partitions, in 1793 and 1795, gave all three powers more Polish territory, and the kingdom of Poland simply vanished from the map (see Map 18.1).

Expansion helped Catherine keep the nobility happy, for it provided her vast new lands to give to her faithful servants. Expansion also helped Catherine reward her lovers, of whom twenty-one have been definitely identified. Upon all these royal favorites she lavished large estates with many serfs, as if to make sure there were no hard feelings when her interest cooled. Until the end this remarkably talented woman – who always believed that, in spite of her domestic setbacks, she was slowly civilizing Russia – kept her zest for life. Fascinated by a new twenty-two-year-old flame when she was a roly-poly grandmother in her sixties, she happily reported her good fortune to a favorite former lover: "I have come back to life like a frozen fly; I am gay and well."[18]

## ABSOLUTISM IN FRANCE AND AUSTRIA

*LOUIS XV OF FRANCE*   In building French absolutism, Louis XIV successfully drew on the middle class to curb the powers of the nobility. As long as the Grand Monarch lived, the nobility could only grumble and, like the duke of Saint-Simon in his *Memoirs,* scornfully lament the rise of "the vile bourgeoisie." But when Louis XIV finally died in 1715, to be succeeded by his five-year-old great-grandson Louis XV (1715–1774), the nobility staged a rapid comeback. The duke of Orléans, who governed as regent until 1723, favored the high nobility.

The duke restored to the high court of Paris – the Parlement – the right to "register" and thereby approve the king's decrees. This was a fateful step. By the eighteenth century, the judges of the Parlement of Paris were mostly nobles. Moreover, they actually owned their seats on the bench and passed them as private property from father to son. They could not be replaced by the king. By establishing the right of this intensely aristocratic group to register the king's laws, the duke of Orléans practically destroyed French absolutism.

This result became clear when the heavy expenses of the War of the Austrian Succession (page 606) plunged France into a financial crisis. In 1748, Louis XV appointed a finance minister who decreed a 5 percent income tax on every individual regardless of social status. Exemption from taxation had been one of the most hallowed privileges of the nobility. The nobility immediately exploded in angry indignation, and the Parlement of Paris refused to ratify the new tax. All the other groups that had over time bought or extracted special privileges in taxation – the clergy, the large towns, certain wealthy bourgeoisie – added their voices to the protest. The monarchy retreated; the new tax was dropped. Following the disastrously expensive Seven Years' War the same drama was re-enacted. The government tried to maintain emergency taxes after the war ended. The nobility, effectively led by the Parlement of Paris, protested violently. The government caved in and withdrew the wartime measures in 1764. Indolent and sensual by nature, more inter-

MAP 18.1  THE PARTITION OF POLAND AND
RUSSIA'S EXPANSION, 1772–1795   *Although all
three of the great eastern absolutist states profited from
the division of large but weak Poland, Catherine's
Russia gained the most.*

ested in his many mistresses than in affairs of state, Louis XV finally roused himself for a determined attempt to salvage his absolutist inheritance. "The magistrates," he angrily told the Parlement of Paris in a famous face-to-face confrontation, "are my officers. . . . In my person only does the sovereign power rest."[19] In 1768, Louis appointed a tough career official named René de Maupeou as chancellor and ordered him to end the usurpations of the Paris judges.

Maupeou abolished the Parlement of Paris and exiled its members. He created a new and docile parlement of royal officials and began once again to tax the privileged groups. Most of the philosophes applauded these measures: the sovereign was using his power to introduce badly needed reforms for the common good. And in spite of the predictable cries from the nobility and their privileged allies, Louis XV might have prevailed – if he had lived to a very ripe old age.

But Louis XV died in 1774. The new king, Louis XVI (1774–1792), was a shy twenty-year-old with good intentions. Taking the throne, he is reported to have said: "What I should like most is to be loved."[20] The eager-to-please monarch immediately collapsed before the noble-led opposition, dismissing Maupeou and repudiating the great minister's work. The old Parlement of Paris was reinstated and the old ways were once again embraced. Royal absolutism, enlightened or otherwise, no longer existed in France. The country was drifting toward renewed financial crisis and political upheaval.

*JOSEPH II OF AUSTRIA*  In some ways Joseph II (1780–1790) of Austria was the most spectacular enlightened absolutist of all. Named co-regent with his mother, the empress Maria Theresa, in 1765 but able to exercise little influence on her policies of gradual reform, Joseph sought to make up for lost time after her death. Determined to improve the life of the people, he saw the nobility and the clergy as the chief obstacles to this goal.

In a series of revolutionary decrees Joseph attacked the privileged groups head-on. He abolished serfdom and gave the peasants secure tenure of their land. He taxed all groups equally. Establishing complete religious toleration even for atheists, Joseph took education out of the hands of the Catholic church. He granted equal civil rights to Protestants and Jews. To accomplish this revolution from above, Joseph strengthened the central state and tried to erase the old provincial differences. Although guided to a considerable extent by very personal beliefs, Joseph demonstrated that Enlightenment ideas had revolutionary social and political implications if pushed to their logical extreme.

Joseph II was a heroic but colossal failure. He encountered opposition from all the privileged groups. His top officials and local bureaucrats, who were of necessity drawn largely from the nobility since the middle class was small and weak, subverted his program at every turn. Hungary and other parts of the empire rose up in open revolt. Joseph died prematurely at forty-nine, a broken and disillusioned man. His brother Leopold (1790–1792) came to the throne and was forced to cancel almost all of Joseph's revolutionary edicts in order to re-establish order. The nobles won back most of their traditional privileges, and the peasants lost most of their gains. Once again peasants were required to do forced labor for their lords. After Leopold's death in 1792, the reaction born of the French Revolution swept away the rest of Joseph's progressive measures.

## AN OVERALL EVALUATION

In spite of their differences, the leading monarchs of the later eighteenth century all clearly believed that they were acting on the principles of the Enlightenment. The philosophes generally agreed with this assessment and cheered them onward. It is now possible to evaluate the enlightened absolutists and understand what they did and did not do.

The enlightened monarchs, especially Catherine and Frederick, encouraged and spread the cultural values of the Enlightenment. Perhaps this was their greatest achievement. Skeptical in religion and intensely secular in basic orientation, they unabashedly accepted the here-and-now and sought their happiness in the enjoyment of it. At the same time they were proud of their intellectual accomplishments and good taste, and they supported knowledge, education, and the arts. No wonder the philosophes felt the monarchs were kindred spirits.

The enlightened absolutists also tried to make life better for their subjects by enacting needed reforms. They had some successes, notably in Prussia and in the general area of the law and religious toleration. Yet cautious Frederick, ambitious Catherine, lazy Louis XV, and radical Joseph II all ended up with modest results. The life of the masses remained very hard in the eighteenth century. Everywhere the gap between the privileged nobility and the heavily burdened people remained as great as ever.

Some historians have concluded that the enlightened absolutists were not really sincere in their reform efforts. This interpretation, however, fits only in some instances. It probably applies to Catherine after Pugachev's rebellion, but it does not explain the failure of the fanatically committed Joseph II. It ignores Frederick's genuine concern for his subjects. It overlooks Louis XV's all-out effort to curb the Parlement of Paris and tax the nobility during Maupeou's administration. For a better explanation of the limited accomplishments of enlightened absolutism, one must look beyond motives to the structure of political and social power.

Chapters 16 and 17 have described how European monarchs dramatically strengthened their authority in the later seventeenth and early eighteenth centuries. With the striking exceptions of England, Holland, and Poland, European rulers created absolutist states. Arbitrarily and without consent, they raised standing armies, waged war, and imposed new taxes. In doing so, absolutist monarchs like Louis XIV and the Great Elector of Prussia reduced some of the power of the nobility, the only group besides themselves that really mattered politically.

Yet royal absolutism went only so far. It never touched the social and economic privileges of the nobility in any fundamental way. Indeed, nobles in eastern Europe often succeeded in working out very advantageous compromises: in return for accepting the monarch's greater control over the state, they won greater control over their peasants and the towns. The power of even the most absolute monarch was still balanced and restrained by the social and economic power of the nobles. Thus, the social and economic reforms of enlightened absolutists were of necessity limited and superficial: powerful nobilities simply would not permit radical measures to succeed.

More fundamentally, monarchs as a group were partners with the nobility and could not seriously support antinoble reforms for very long. Monarchy and nobility were like the husband and wife in an old-fashioned marriage. They loved and quarreled, cooperated

ENLIGHTENMENT CULTURE was elegant, intellectual, and international. This painting shows the seven-year-old Austrian child prodigy, Wolfgang Amadeus Mozart (1756–1791), playing his own composition while his older sister sings and his father plays the violin. The elder Mozart displayed his children in the houses of leading aristocrats all across Europe. (Musée Condé de Chantilly/Giraudon)

and changed; but they always knew they were joined together forever for better or worse. European monarchs and nobles were privileged groups in a society that used hierarchy and inequality as its basic organizing principles. Both appealed primarily to tradition to justify their inherited position, and the great privileges of one could hardly be secure without those of the other. No wonder that when monarchs built their absolutist states they normally turned to nobles to lead their armies and expanded bureaucracies. And if Louis XIV quite exceptionally preferred middle-class officials, Louis XV and Louis XVI did not: between 1714 and 1789, all but three of France's ministers were titled nobles.

The great eighteenth-century philosophe and aristocrat Montesquieu summed it all up in one famous line: "No monarchy, no nobility; no nobility, no monarchy."[21] Montesquieu was right: for centuries monarchy and nobility flourished together in Europe, and together they later declined and have almost disappeared.

———◆———

This chapter has focused on the complex development of a new world-view in Western civilization. This new view of the world was essentially critical and secular, drawing its inspiration from the Scientific Revolution and crystallizing in the Enlightenment.

The decisive breakthroughs in astronomy and physics in the seventeenth century, which demolished the imposing medieval synthesis of Aristotelian philosophy and Christian theology, had only limited practical consequences despite the expectations of scientific enthusiasts like Bacon. Yet the impact of new scientific knowledge on intellectual life became great. Interpreting scientific findings and Newtonian laws in an antitraditional, antireligious manner, the French philosophes of the Enlightenment extolled the superiority of rational, critical thinking. This new method, they believed, promised not just increased knowledge but even the discovery of the fundamental laws of human society, which could then be implemented by enlightened rulers for the general good. Although social and political realities frustrated these fond hopes, the philosophes succeeded in spreading their radically new world-view. That was a momentous accomplishment.

## NOTES

1. H. Butterfield, *The Origins of Modern Science,* Macmillan, New York, 1951, p. viii.

2. Quoted by A. G. R. Smith, *Science and Society in the Sixteenth and Seventeenth Centuries,* Harcourt Brace Jovanovich, New York, 1972, p. 97.

3. Quoted by Butterfield, p. 47.

4. Quoted by Smith, p. 100.

5. Ibid. pp. 115–116.

6. Ibid. p. 120.

7. A. R. Hall, *From Galileo to Newton, 1630–1720,* Harper & Row, New York, 1963, p. 290.

8. Quoted by R. K. Merton, *Science, Technology and Society in Seventeenth-Century England,* rev. ed., Harper & Row, New York, 1970, p. 164.

9. Quoted by P. Hazard, *The European Mind, 1680–1715,* Meridian Books, Cleveland, 1963, pp. 304–305.

10. Ibid., pp. 11–12.

11. Quoted by L. M. Marsak, ed., *The Enlightenment,* John Wiley & Sons, New York, 1972, p. 56.

12. Quoted by G. L. Mosse et al., eds., *Europe in Review,* Rand McNally, Chicago, 1964, p. 156.

13. M. F. Arouet de Voltaire, *Oeuvres complètes,* Firmin-Didot Frères, Fils et Cie, Paris, 1875, VIII, 188–90.

14. Quoted by P. Gay, "The Unity of the Enlightenment," *History* 3 (1960):25.

15. Quoted by G. P. Gooch, *Catherine the Great and Other Studies,* Archon Books, Hamden, Conn., 1966, p. 112.

16. Ibid., p. 149.

17. Ibid., p. 15.

18. Ibid., p. 53.

19. Quoted by R. R. Palmer, *The Age of Democratic Revolution,* Princeton University Press, Princeton, 1959, 1.95–96.

20. Quoted by G. Wright, *France in Modern Times,* Rand McNally, Chicago, 1960, p. 42.

21. Quoted by P. Anderson, *Lineages of the Absolutist State,* LLB, London, 1974, p. 298.

# SUGGESTED READING

The first three authors cited in the Notes – H. Butterfield (rev. ed. 1966), A. G. R. Smith, and A. R. Hall – have written excellent general interpretations of the scientific revolution. Another good study is M. Boas, *The Scientific Renaissance, 1450–1630* (1966), which is especially insightful on the influence of magic on science and on Galileo's trial. T. Kuhn, *The Copernican Revolution* (1957), is the best treatment of the subject; his *The Structure of Scientific Revolutions* (1962) is a challenging, much-discussed attempt to understand major breakthroughs in scientific thought over time. Two stimulating books on the ties between science and society in history are B. Merton, *Science, Technology and Society in Seventeenth-Century England,* rev. ed. (1970), and J. Ben-David, *The Scientist's Role in Society* (1971). E. Andrade, *Sir Isaac Newton* (1958), is a good, short biography, which may be compared with F. Manuel, *The Religion of Isaac Newton* (1974).

P. Hazard, *The European Mind, 1680–1715* (1963), is a classic study of the formative years of Enlightenment thought, and his *European Thought in the Eighteenth Century* (1954) is also recommended. A famous, controversial interpretation of the Enlightenment is that of C. Becker, *The Heavenly City of the Eighteenth Century Philosophes* (1932), which maintains that the world-view of medieval Christianity continued to influence the philosophes greatly. Becker's ideas are discussed interestingly in R. O. Rockwood, ed., *Carl Becker's Heavenly City Revisited* (1958). P. Gay has written several major studies on the Enlightenment: *Voltaire's Politics* (1959) and *The Party of Humanity* (1971) are two of the best. I. Wade, *The Structure and Form of the French Enlightenment* (1977), is a recent major synthesis. F. Baumer's *Religion and the Rise of Skepticism* (1969), H. Payne's *The Philosophes and the People* (1976), K. Rogers's *Feminism in Eighteenth-Century England* (1982), and J. B. Bury's old but still exciting *The Idea of Progress* (1932) are stimulating studies of important aspects of Enlightenment thought. Above all, one should read some of the philosophes and let them speak for themselves. Two good anthologies are C. Brinton, ed., *The Portable Age of Reason* (1956), and F. Manuel, ed., *The Enlightenment* (1951). Voltaire's most famous and very amusing novel, *Candide,* is highly recommended, as are S. Gendzier, ed., *Denis Diderot: The Encyclopedia: Selections* (1967) and A. Wilson's biography, *Diderot* (1972).

In addition to the works mentioned in the Suggested Reading for Chapters 16 and 17, the monarchies of Europe are carefully analyzed in Charles Tilly, ed., *The Formation of National States in Western Europe* (1975), and ably discussed in J. Gagliardo, *Enlightened Despotism* (1967), both of which have useful bibliographies. Other recommended studies on the struggle for power and reform in different countries are: F. Ford, *Robe and Sword* (1953), which traces the resurgence of the French nobility after the death of Louis XIV; R. Herr, *The Eighteenth-Century Revolution in Spain* (1958), on the impact of Enlightenment thought in Spain; and P. Bernard, *Joseph II* (1968). In addition to I. de Madariaga's masterful *Russia in the Age of Catherine the Great* (1981) and D. Ransel's solid *Politics of Catherinean Russia* (1975), the ambitious reader should look at A. N. Radishchev, *A Journey From St. Petersburg to Moscow* (trans. 1958), a famous 1790 attack on Russian serfdom and an appeal to Catherine the Great to free the serfs, for which Radishchev was exiled to Serbia.

The culture of the time may be approached through A. Cobban, ed., *The Eighteenth Century,* (1969), a richly illustrated work with excellent essays, and C. B. Behrens, *The Ancien Régime* (1967). C. Rosen, *The Classical Style: Haydn, Mozart, Beethoven* (1972), brilliantly synthesizes music and society, as did Mozart himself in his great opera *The Marriage of Figaro,* where the count is the buffoon and his servant the hero.

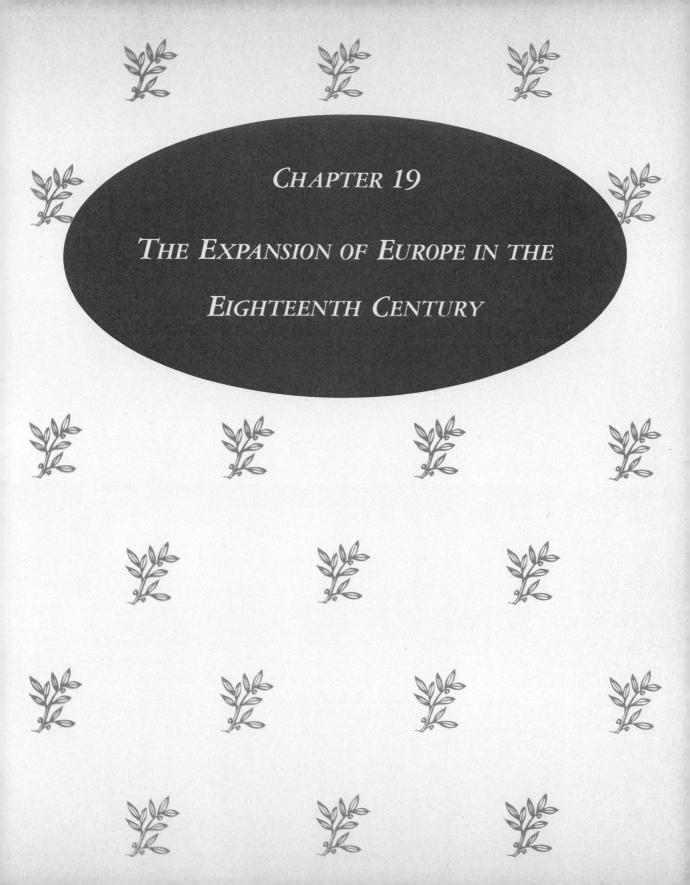

# CHAPTER 19

## THE EXPANSION OF EUROPE IN THE EIGHTEENTH CENTURY

THE WORLD OF ABSOLUTISM and aristocracy, a combination of raw power and elegant refinement, was a world apart from that of ordinary men and women. For the overwhelming majority of the population in the eighteenth century, life remained a struggle with poverty and uncertainty, with the landlord and the tax collector. In 1700, peasants on the land and artisans in their shops lived little better than had their ancestors in the Middle Ages. Only in science and thought, and there only among a few intellectual leaders, had Western society succeeded in going beyond the great achievements of the High Middle Ages, achievements that in turn owed so much to Greece and Rome.

Everyday life was a struggle because the men and women of European societies, despite their best efforts, still could not produce very much by modern standards. Ordinary people might work like their beasts in the fields, and they often did, but there was seldom enough good food, warm clothing, and decent housing. Life went on; history went on. The wars of religion ravaged Germany in the seventeenth century; Russia rose to become a Great Power; the kingdom of Poland simply disappeared; monarchs and nobles continuously jockeyed for power and wealth. In 1700 or even 1750, the idea of progress — the idea that the lives of great numbers of people could improve substantially here on earth — was still only the dream of a small elite in their fashionable salons.

Yet the economic basis of European life was beginning to change. In the course of the eighteenth century, the European economy emerged from the long crisis of the seventeenth century, responded to challenges, and began to expand once again. Some areas were more fortunate than others. The rising Atlantic powers — Holland, France, and above all England — and their colonies led the way.

Agriculture and industry, trade and population, began a surge comparable to that of the eleventh- and twelfth-century springtime of European civilization. Only this time development was not cut short. This time the response to new challenges led toward one of the most influential developments in human history, the Industrial Revolution, which we shall consider in Chapter 22. What were the causes of this renewed surge? Why were the fundamental economic underpinnings of European society beginning to change, and what were the dimensions of those changes? How did these changes affect people and their work? These are the questions this chapter will try to answer.

## AGRICULTURE AND THE LAND

At the end of the seventeenth century the economy of Europe was agrarian, as it had been for several hundred years. With the possible exception of Holland, at least 80 percent of the people of all western European countries drew their livelihoods from agriculture. In eastern Europe the percentage was considerably higher.

Men and women lavished their attention on the land, plowing fields and sowing seed, reaping harvests and storing grain. The land repaid these efforts, year after year yielding up the food and most of the raw materials for industry that made life possible. Yet the land was stingy. Even in a rich agricultural region like the Po valley in northern Italy, every bushel of wheat sown yielded on average only five or six bushels of grain at harvest during the seventeenth century. The average French yield in the same period was somewhat less. Such yields were barely more than those attained in fertile, well-watered areas in the

FARMING THE LAND *Agricultural methods in Europe changed very slowly from the Middle Ages to the early eighteenth century. This realistic picture from Diderot's* Encyclopedia *has striking similarities with agricultural scenes found in medieval manuscripts. (Photo: Caroline Buckler)*

thirteenth century or in ancient Greece. By modern standards output was distressingly low. (For each bushel of wheat seed sown today on fertile land with good rainfall, an American or French farmer can expect roughly forty bushels of produce.) In 1700, European agriculture was much more ancient and medieval than modern.

If the land was stingy, it was also capricious. In most regions of Europe in the six-

teenth and seventeenth centuries, harvests were poor, or even failed completely, every eight or nine years. The vast majority of the population who lived off the land might survive a single bad harvest by eating less and drawing on their reserves of grain. But when the land combined with persistent bad weather – too much rain rotting the seed, or drought withering the young stalks – the result was catastrophic. Meager grain reserves were soon exhausted, and the price of grain soared. Provisions from other areas with better harvests were hard to obtain.

In such crisis years, which periodically stalked Europe in the seventeenth and even into the eighteenth century, a terrible tightening knot in the belly forced people to tragic substitutes – the "famine foods" of a desperate population. People gathered chestnuts and stripped bark in the forests; they cut dandelions and grass; and they ate these substitutes to escape starvation. In one community in Norway in the early 1740s people were forced to wash dung from the straw in old manure piles in order to bake a pathetic substitute for bread. Even cannibalism occurred in the seventeenth century.

Such unbalanced and inadequate food in famine years made people weak and extremely susceptible to illness and epidemics. The eating of rough material like bark or grass – really unfit for human consumption – resulted in dysentery and intestinal ailments of every kind. Influenza and smallpox preyed with particular savagery upon populations weakened by famine. In famine years the number of deaths soared far above normal. A third of a village's population might disappear in a year or two. The 1690s were as dismal as many of the worst periods of earlier times. One county in Finland, which was probably typical of the entire country, lost fully 28 percent of its inhabitants in 1696 and 1697. Certain well-studied villages in the Beauvais region of northern France suffered a similar fate. In preindustrial Europe the harvest was the real king, and the king was seldom generous and often cruel.

To understand why Europeans produced barely enough food in good years and occasionally agonized through years of famine throughout the later seventeenth century, one must follow the plowman, his wife, and his children into the fields to observe their battle for food and life. There the ingenious pattern of farming that Europe had developed in the Middle Ages, a pattern that allowed fairly large numbers of people to survive but could never produce material abundance, was still dominant.

## THE OPEN-FIELD SYSTEM

The greatest accomplishment of medieval agriculture was the open-field system of village agriculture developed by European peasants (page 321). That system divided the land to be cultivated by the peasants into a few large fields, which were in turn cut up into long narrow strips. The fields were open and the strips were not enclosed into small plots by fences or hedges. An individual peasant family – if it were fortunate – held a number of strips scattered throughout the various large fields. The land of those who owned but did not till, primarily the nobility, the clergy, and wealthy townsmen, was also in scattered strips. The peasant community farmed each large field as a community, with each family following the same pattern of plowing, sowing, and harvesting in accordance with tradition and the village leaders.

The ever-present problem was exhaustion of soil. If the community planted wheat year after year in a field, the nitrogen in the soil was soon depleted and crop failure was certain. Since the supply of manure for fertilizer was limited, the only way for the land to recover its life-giving fertility was for a field to lie fallow for a period of time. In the early Middle Ages a year of fallow was alternated with a year of cropping, so that half the land stood idle in a given year. With time three-year rotations were introduced, especially on more fertile lands. This system permitted a year of wheat or rye to be followed by a year

MILLET: THE GLEANERS *Poor French peasant women search for grains and stalks the harvesters (in the background) have missed. The open-field system seen here could still be found in parts of Europe in 1857, when this picture was painted. Millet is known for his great paintings expressing social themes. (Cliché des Musées Nationaux, Paris)*

of oats or beans, and only then by a year of fallow. Even so, only awareness of the tragic consequences of continuous cropping forced undernourished populations to let a third (or a half) of their land lie constantly idle, especially when the fallow had to be plowed two or three times a year to keep down the weeds.

Traditional rights reinforced the traditional pattern of farming. In addition to rotating the field crops in a uniform way, villages maintained open meadows for hay and natural pasture. These lands were "common" lands, set aside primarily for the draft horses and oxen so necessary in the fields, but open to the cows and pigs of the village community as well. After the harvest, the people of the village also pastured their animals on the wheat or rye stubble. In many places such pasturing followed a brief period, also established by tradition, for the gleaning of grain. Poor women would go through the fields picking up the few single grains that had fallen to the ground in the course of the harvest. The subject of a great nineteenth-century painting, *The Gleaners* by Jean François Millet, this backbreaking work by hardworking but impoverished women meant quite literally the slender margin of survival for some people in the winter months.

In the age of absolutism and nobility, state and landlord continued to levy heavy taxes and high rents as a matter of course. In so doing they stripped the peasants of much of their meager earnings. The level of exploitation varied. Conditions for the rural population were very different in different areas.

Generally speaking, the peasants of eastern Europe were worst off. As we have seen in Chapter 17, they were still serfs, bound to their lords in hereditary service. Though serfdom in eastern Europe in the eighteenth century had much in common with medieval serfdom in central and western Europe, it was, if anything, harsher and more oppressive. In much of eastern Europe there were no real limitations on the amount of forced labor the lord could require, and five or six days of unpaid work per week on the lord's land was not uncommon. Well into the nineteenth century individual Russian serfs and serf families were regularly sold with and without land. Serfdom was often very close to slavery. The only compensating factor in much of eastern Europe was that, as with slavery, differences in well-being among serfs were slight. In Russia, for example, the land available to the serfs for their own crops was divided among them almost equally.

Social conditions were considerably better in western Europe. Peasants were generally free from serfdom. In France and western Germany they owned land and could pass it on to their children. Yet life in the village was unquestionably hard, and poverty was the great reality for most people. For the Beauvais region of France at the beginning of the eighteenth century, it has been carefully estimated that in good years and bad only a tenth of the peasants could live satisfactorily off the fruits of their landholdings. Owning less than half of the land, the peasants had to pay heavy royal taxes, the church's tithe, and dues to the lord, as well as set aside seed for the next season. Left with only half of their crop for their own use, they had to toil and till for others and seek work far afield in a constant scramble for a meager living. And this was in a country where peasants were comparatively well off. The privileges of the ruling elites weighed heavily upon the people of the land.

## AGRICULTURAL REVOLUTION

The social conditions of the countryside were well entrenched. The great need was for new farming methods that would enable Europeans to produce more and eat more. The idle fields were the heart of the matter. If peasants could replace the fallow with crops, they could increase the land under cultivation by 50 percent. So remarkable were the possibilities and the results that historians have often spoken of the progressive elimination of the fallow, which occurred slowly throughout Europe from the late seventeenth century onward, as an Agricultural Revolution.

This agricultural revolution, which took longer than historians used to believe, was a great milestone in human development. The famous French scholar Marc Bloch, who gave his life in the resistance to the Nazis in World War Two, summed it up well: "The history of the conquest of the fallow by new crops, a fresh triumph of man over the earth that is just as moving as the great land clearing of the Middle Ages, [is] one of the noblest stories that can be told."[1]

Because grain crops exhaust the soil and make fallowing necessary, the secret to eliminating the fallow lies in alternating grain with certain nitrogen-storing crops. Such crops not only rejuvenate the soil even better than fallowing, but give more produce as well. The most important of these land-reviving crops are peas and beans, root crops such as turnips and potatoes, and clovers and grasses. In the eighteenth century, peas and beans were old standbys; turnips, potatoes, and clover were newcomers to the fields. As time went on, the number of crops that were systematically rotated grew, and farmers developed increasingly sophisticated patterns of rotation to suit different kinds of soils. For example, farmers in French Flanders near Lille in the late eighteenth century used a ten-year rotation, alternating a number of grain, root, and hay crops on a ten-year schedule. Continuous experimentation resulted in more scientific farming.

Improvements in farming had multiple effects. The new crops made ideal feed for animals. Because peasants and larger farmers had more fodder – hay and root crops – for the winter months, they could build up their small herds of cattle and sheep. More animals meant more meat and better diets for the people. More animals also meant more manure for fertilizer, and therefore more grain for bread and porridge. The vicious cycle in which few animals meant inadequate manure, which meant little grain and less fodder, which led to fewer animals, and so on, could be broken. The cycle became positive: more animals meant more manure, which meant more grain and more fodder, which meant more animals.

Technical progress had its price, though. The new rotations were scarcely possible within the traditional framework of open fields and common rights. A farmer who wanted to experiment with new methods would have to control the village's pattern of rotation. To wait for the entire village to agree might mean waiting forever. The improving, innovating agriculturalist needed to enclose and consolidate his scattered holdings into a compact fenced-in field. In doing so, he would also seek to enclose his share of the natural pasture, the "common." Yet the common rights were precious to many rural people. Thus when the small landholders and the poor could effectively oppose the enclosure of the open fields, they did so. Only powerful social and political pressures could overcome the traditionalism of rural communities.

The old system of unenclosed open fields and the new system of continuous rotation coexisted in Europe for a very long time. In large parts of central Russia, for example, the old system did not disappear until after the Communist Revolution in 1917. It could also be found in much of France and Germany in the early years of the nineteenth century. Indeed, until the end of the eighteenth century the promise of the new system was extensively realized only in the Low Countries – present-day Holland, Belgium, and French Flanders – and in England.

## THE LEADERSHIP OF THE LOW COUNTRIES AND ENGLAND

The new methods of the agricultural revolution originated in the Low Countries. The vibrant, dynamic middle-class society of seventeenth-century republican Holland was the most advanced in Europe in many areas of human endeavor. In shipbuilding and navigation, in commerce and banking, in drainage and agriculture, the people of the Low Countries, especially the Dutch, provided models the jealous English and French sought to copy or to cripple.

By the middle of the seventeenth century, intensive farming was well established throughout much of the Low Countries. Enclosed fields, continuous rotation, heavy manuring, and a wide variety of crops: all these innovations were present. Agriculture was highly specialized and commercialized. The same skills that grew turnips produced flax to be spun into linen for clothes and tulip bulbs to lighten the heart with their beauty. The fat cattle of Holland, so beloved by Dutch painters, gave the most milk in Europe. Dutch cheeses were already world-renowned.

The reasons for early Dutch leadership in farming were basically threefold. In the first place, since the end of the Middle Ages the Low Countries had been one of the most densely populated areas in Europe. Thus, in order to feed themselves and provide employment, the Dutch were forced at an early date to seek maximum yields from their land, and to increase it through the steady draining of marshes and swamps. Even so, they had to import wheat from Poland and eastern Germany.

The pressure of population was connected with the second cause, the growth of towns and cities in the Low Countries. Stimulated by commerce and overseas trade, Amsterdam grew from 30,000 to 200,000 in its golden seventeenth century. The growth of urban population provided Dutch peasants with good markets for all they could produce and allowed each region to specialize efficiently in what it did best.

Finally, there was the quality of the people. Oppressed neither by grasping nobles nor warminded monarchs, the Dutch could develop their potential in a free and capitalistic society. The Low Countries became "the Mecca of foreign agricultural experts who came . . . to see Flemish agriculture with their own eyes, to write about it and to propagate its methods in their home lands."[2]

The English were the best students. Indeed, they were such good students that it is often forgotten that they had teachers at all. Drainage and water control was one subject in which they received instruction. Large parts of seventeenth-century Holland had once been sea and sea marsh, and the efforts of centuries had made the Dutch the world's leaders in the skills of drainage. In the first half of the seventeenth century, Dutch experts made a great contribution to draining the extensive marshes, or fens, of wet and rainy England.

The most famous of these Dutch engineers, Cornelius Vermuyden, directed one large drainage project in Yorkshire and another in Cambridgeshire. The project in Yorkshire was supported by Charles I and financed by a group of Dutch capitalists, who were to receive one-third of all land reclaimed in return for their investment. Despite local opposition, Vermuyden drained the land by means of a large canal – his so-called Dutch river – and settlers cultivated the new fields in the Dutch fashion. In the Cambridge fens, Vermuyden and his Dutch workers eventually reclaimed forty thousand acres, which were then farmed intensively in the Dutch manner. Although all these efforts were disrupted in the turbulent 1640s by the English Civil War, Vermuyden and his countrymen largely succeeded. A swampy wilderness was converted into thousands of acres of some of the best land in England. On such new land, where traditions and common rights were not established, farmers introduced new crops and new rotations fairly easily.

Dutch experience was also important to Viscount Charles Townsend (1674-1738), one of the pioneers of English agricultural improvement. This lord from the upper reaches of the English aristocracy learned about turnips and clover while serving as English ambassador to Holland. In the 1710s, he was using these crops in the sandy soil of his large

*SELECTIVE BREEDING meant bigger livestock and more meat on English tables. This gigantic champion, one of the new improved shorthorn breed, was known as the Newbus Ox. Such great fat beasts were pictured in the press and praised by poets. (Institute of Agricultural History and Museum of English Rural Life, University of Reading)*

estates in Norfolk in eastern England, already one of the most innovative agricultural areas in the country. When Lord Charles retired from politics in 1730 and returned to Norfolk, it was said that he spoke of turnips, turnips, and nothing but turnips. This led some wit to nickname his lordship "Turnip" Townsend. But Townsend had the last laugh. Draining extensively, manuring heavily, and sowing crops in regular rotation without fallowing, the farmers who leased Townsend's lands produced larger crops. They and he earned higher incomes. Those who had scoffed reconsidered. By 1740, agricultural improvement in various forms had become something of a craze among the English aristocracy.

Jethro Tull (1674–1741), part crank and part genius, was another important English innovator. A true son of the early Enlightenment, Tull constantly tested accepted ideas about farming in an effort to develop better methods through empirical research. He was especially enthusiastic about horses, in preference to slower-moving oxen. He also advocated sowing seed with drilling equipment, rather than scattering it by hand. Drilling distributed seed evenly and at the proper depth. There were also improvements in livestock, inspired in part by the earlier successes of English country gentlemen in breeding ever-faster horses for the races and fox hunts that were their passions. Selective breeding of ordinary livestock was a marked improvement over the old pattern, which has been graphically described as little more than "the haphazard union of nobody's son with everybody's daughter."

By the mid-eighteenth century, English agriculture was in the process of a radical and desirable transformation. The eventual result was that by 1870 English farmers produced 300 percent more food than they had produced in 1700, although the number of people working the land had increased by only 14 percent. This great surge of agricultural production provided food for England's rapidly growing urban population. It was a tremendous achievement.

## THE DEBATE OVER ENCLOSURE

To what extent was technical progress a product of social injustice? There are sharp differences of opinion among historians. The oldest and still widely accepted view is that the powerful ruling class, the English landowning aristocracy, enclosed the open fields and divided up the common pasture in such a way that poor people lost their small landholdings and were pushed off the land. The large landowners controlled Parliament, which made the laws. They had Parliament pass hundreds of "enclosure acts," each of which authorized the fencing of open fields in a given district and abolished common rights there. Small farmers who had little land and cottagers who had only common rights could no longer make a living. They lost position and security and had to work for a large landowner for wages or else move to town in search of work. This view, popularized by Karl Marx in

the nineteenth century, has remained dear to many historians to this day.

There is some validity to this idea, but more recent studies have shown that the harmful consequences of enclosure in the eighteenth century have often been exaggerated. In the first place, as much as half of English farmland was already enclosed by 1750. A great wave of enclosure of English open fields into sheep pastures had already occurred in the sixteenth and early seventeenth centuries, in order to produce wool for the thriving textile industry. In the later seventeenth and early eighteenth centuries, many open fields were enclosed fairly harmoniously by mutual agreement among all classes of landowners in English villages. Thus, parliamentary enclosure, the great bulk of which occurred after 1760 and particularly during the Napoleonic wars early in the nineteenth century, only completed a process that was in full swing. Nor did an army of landless farm laborers appear only in the last years of the eighteenth century. Much earlier, and certainly by 1700, there were perhaps two landless agricultural workers in England for every self-sufficient farmer. In 1830, after the enclosures were complete, the proportion of landless laborers on the land was not much greater.

Indeed, by 1700 a highly distinctive pattern of landownership existed in England. At one extreme were a few large landowners, at the other a large mass of laborers who held little land and worked for wages. In between stood two other groups: small self-sufficient farmers who owned their own land, and substantial tenant farmers who rented land from the big landowners and hired wage laborers. Yet the small independent English farmers were already declining in number by 1700, and they continued to do so in the eighteenth century.

They could not compete with the profit-minded, market-oriented tenant farmers.

The tenant farmers, many of whom had formerly been independent owners, were the key to mastering the new methods of farming. Well financed by the large landowners, the tenant farmers fenced fields, built drains, and improved the soil with fertilizers. Such improvements actually increased employment opportunities for wage workers in the countryside. So did new methods of farming, for land was farmed more intensively without the fallow, and new crops like turnips required more care and effort. Thus, enclosure did not force people off the land by eliminating jobs. By the early nineteenth century, rural poverty was often greatest in those areas of England where the new farming techniques had not been adopted.

## THE BEGINNING OF THE POPULATION EXPLOSION

There was another factor that affected the existing order of life and forced economic changes in the eighteenth century. This was the remarkable growth of European population, the beginning of the "population explosion." This population explosion continued in Europe until the twentieth century, by which time it was affecting non-Western areas of the globe. What caused the growth of population, and what did the challenge of more mouths to feed and more hands to employ do to the European economy?

### LIMITATIONS ON POPULATION GROWTH

Many commonly held ideas about population in the past are wrong. One such mistaken idea

FIGURE 19.1   THE GROWTH OF POPULATION IN ENGLAND 1000–1800.   England is a good example of both the uneven increase of European population before 1700 and the third great surge of growth, which began in the eighteenth century. (Source: E. A. Wrigley, Population and History, McGraw-Hill, New York, 1969)

is that people always married young and had large families. A related error is the belief that past societies were so ignorant that they could do nothing to control their numbers and that population was always growing too fast. On the contrary, until 1700 the total population of Europe grew slowly much of the time, and by no means constantly (see Figure 19.1). There were very few occurrences of the frightening increases so common in many poor countries today.

In seventeenth-century Europe, births and deaths, fertility and mortality, were in a crude but effective balance. The birthrate – annual births as a proportion of the population – was fairly high, but far lower than it would have been if all women between ages fifteen and forty-five had been having as many children as biologically possible. The death rate in normal years was also high, though somewhat lower than the birthrate. As a result, the population grew modestly in normal years at a rate of perhaps .5 to 1 percent, or enough to double the population in 70 to 140 years. This is, of course, a generalization encompassing many different patterns. In areas like Russia and colonial New England, where there was a great deal of frontier to be settled, the annual rate of increase might well exceed 1 percent. In a country like France, where the land had long been densely settled, the rate of increase might be less than .5 percent.

Although population growth of even 1 percent per year is fairly modest by the standards of many African and Latin American countries today – some of which are growing at about 3 percent annually – it will produce a very large increase over a long period. An annual increase of even 1 percent will result in sixteen times as many people in three hundred years. Such gigantic increases simply did not occur in agrarian Europe before the eighteenth century. In certain abnormal years and tragic periods, many more people died than were born. Total population fell sharply, even catastrophically. A number of years of modest growth would then be necessary to make up for those who had died in such an abnormal year. Such savage increases in deaths helped check total numbers and kept the population from growing rapidly for long periods.

The grim reapers of demographic crisis were famine, epidemic disease, and war. Famine, the inevitable result of poor farming methods and periodic crop failures, was particularly murderous because it was accompanied by disease. With a brutal one-two punch, famine stunned and weakened a population and disease finished it off. Disease could also ravage independently, even in years of adequate harvests. Bubonic plague returned again and again to Europe for more than three hundred years after the ravages of the Black Death in the fourteenth century. Not until the late 1500s did most countries have as many people as in the early 1300s. Epidemics of dysentery and smallpox also operated independently of famine.

War was another scourge. The indirect effects were more harmful than the organized killing. War spread disease. Soldiers and camp followers passed venereal disease through the countryside to scar and kill. Armies requisitioned scarce food supplies for their own use and disrupted the agricultural cycle. The Thirty Years' War (pages 530–536) witnessed all possible combinations of distress. In the German states, the number of inhabitants declined by more than *two-thirds* in some large areas and by at least one-third almost everywhere. The Thirty Years' War reduced total German population by no less than 40 percent. But numbers inadequately convey the dimensions of such human tragedy. One needs the vision of the artist. The great sixteenth-century artist, Albrecht Dürer, captured the horror of demographic crisis in his chilling woodcut *The Four Horsemen of the Apocalypse*. Death, accompanied by his trusty companions War, Famine, and Disease, takes his merciless ride of destruction. The narrow victory of life over death that prevails in normal times is being undone.

### THE NEW PATTERN OF THE EIGHTEENTH CENTURY

In the eighteenth century, the population of Europe began to grow markedly. This increase in numbers occurred in all areas of Europe – western and eastern, northern and southern, dynamic and stagnant. Growth was especially dramatic after about 1750, as Figure 19.2 shows.

Although it is certain that Europe's population grew greatly, it is less clear why. Recent painstaking and innovative research in population history has shown that, because population grew everywhere, it is best to look for general factors and not those limited to individual countries or areas. What, then, caused fewer people to die or, possibly, more babies to be born? In some kinds of families women may have had more babies than before. Yet the basic cause was a decline in mortality – fewer deaths.

The bubonic plague mysteriously disappeared. Following the Black Death in the fourteenth century, plagues remained a part of the European experience, striking again and again with savage force, particularly in towns. As a German writer of the early sixteenth century noted, "It is remarkable and astonishing that the plague should never wholly cease, but it should appear every year here and there, making its way from one place to another. Having subsided at one time, it returns within a few years by a circuitous route."[3]

As late as 1720, a ship from Syria and the Levant, where plague was ever-present, brought the monstrous disease to Marseilles. In a few weeks, forty thousand of the city's ninety thousand inhabitants died. The epidemic swept southern France, killing a third, a half, even three-fourths of those in the larger towns. Once again an awful fear swept across Europe. But the epidemic passed, and that was the last time plague fell upon western and central Europe. The final disappearance of plague was due in part to stricter measures of quarantine in Mediterranean ports and along the Austrian border with Turkey. Human carriers of plague were carefully isolated. Chance and plain good luck were more important, however.

It is now understood that bubonic plague is, above all, a disease of rats. The epidemic spreads among humans only after they are bitten by fleas that have fed on diseased rats. More precisely, it is the black rat that spreads major epidemics, for the black rat's flea is the principal carrier of the plague bacillus. After 1600, for reasons unknown, a new rat of Asiatic origin – the brown, or wander, rat –

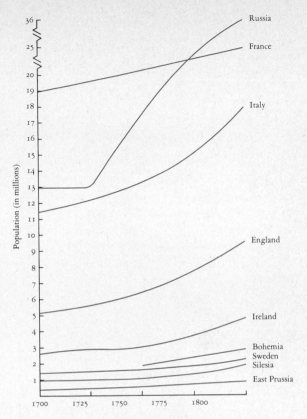

FIGURE 19.2 THE INCREASE OF POPULATION IN EUROPE IN THE EIGHTEENTH CENTURY *The number of people grew substantially all across Europe. France's large population continued to support French political and intellectual leadership, but Russia emerged as Europe's most populous state.*

began to drive out and eventually eliminate its black competitor. In the words of a noted authority, "This revolution in the animal kingdom must have gone far to break the lethal link between rat and man."[4] Although the brown rat also contracts the plague, another kind of flea is its main parasite. That flea carries the plague poorly and, for good measure, has little taste for human blood.

*Doctor in Protective Clothing* *Most doctors believed, incorrectly, that poisonous smells carried the plague. This doctor has placed strong-smelling salts in his "beak" to protect himself against deadly plague vapors. (Germanisches Nationalmuseum, Nuremberg)*

Advances in medical knowledge did not contribute much to reducing the death rate in the eighteenth century. The most important advance in preventive medicine in this period was inoculation against smallpox. Yet this great improvement was long confined mainly to England and probably did little to reduce deaths throughout Europe until the later part of the century. Improvements in the water supply and sewerage promoted somewhat better public health and helped reduce such diseases as typhoid and typhus in some urban areas of western Europe. Yet those early public-health measures had only limited general significance. In fact, changes in the rat population helped millions of human beings in their struggle against untimely death much more than did doctors and medical science in the eighteenth century.

Human beings were more successful in their efforts to safeguard the supply of food and protect against famine. The eighteenth century was a time of considerable canal and road building in western Europe. These advances in transportation, which were among the more positive aspects of enlightened absolutism, lessened the impact of local crop failure and famine. Emergency supplies could be brought in. The age-old spectacle of localized starvation became less frequent. Wars became more gentlemanly and less destructive than in the seventeenth century and spread fewer epidemics. New foods, particularly the potato, were introduced. Potatoes served as an important alternative source of vitamins A and C for the poor, especially when the grain crops were skimpy or failed. In short, population grew in the eighteenth century primarily because years of abnormal death rates were less catastrophic. Famines, epidemics, and wars continued to occur, but their severity moderated.

The growth of population in the eighteenth century cannot be interpreted as a sign of human progress. Plague faded from memory, transport improved, people learned to eat potatoes; yet for the common people life was still a great struggle. Indeed, for many it was more of a struggle than ever, for in many areas increasing numbers led to overpopulation. A serious imbalance between the number of people and the economic opportunities available to them developed. There was only so much land available, and tradition slowed the adoption of better farming methods. Therefore, agriculture could not provide enough work for the rapidly growing labor force. Everyone might work steadily during planting and harvesting, when many hands were needed, but at other times rural people were often unemployed or underemployed.

Growing numbers increased the challenge of poverty, especially the severe poverty of the rural poor. People in the countryside had to look for new ways to make a living. Even if work outside of farming paid poorly, small wages were better than none. Thus, in the eighteenth century growing numbers of people and acute poverty were even more influential than new farming methods as forces for profound changes in agrarian Europe.

## THE GROWTH OF COTTAGE INDUSTRY

The growth of population contributed to the development of industry in rural areas. The poor in the countryside were eager to supplement their earnings from agriculture with other types of work, and capitalists from the city were eager to employ them, often at lower wages than urban workers commanded.

Manufacturing with hand tools in peasant cottages grew markedly in the eighteenth century. Rural industry became a crucial feature of the European economy.

To be sure, peasant communities had always made some clothing, processed some food, and constructed some housing for their own use. But in the High Middle Ages peasants did not produce manufactured goods on a large scale for sale in a market; they were not handicraft workers as well as farmers and field laborers. Industry in the Middle Ages was dominated and organized by urban craft guilds and urban merchants, who jealously regulated handicraft production and sought to maintain it as an urban monopoly. By the eighteenth century, however, the pressures of rural poverty and the need for employment in the countryside had proved too great, and a new system was expanding lustily. The new system had many names. Sometimes referred to as cottage industry or domestic industry, it has often been called "the putting-out system."

### THE PUTTING-OUT SYSTEM

The two main participants in the putting-out system were the merchant-capitalist and the rural worker. The merchant lent or put out raw materials – raw wool, for example – to several cottage workers. Those workers processed the raw material in their own homes, spinning and weaving the wool into cloth in this case, and returned the cloth to the merchant. The merchant paid the outworkers for their work by the piece and proceeded to sell the finished product. There were endless variations on this basic relationship. Sometimes rural workers would buy their own materials and work as independent producers before they sold to the merchant. The relative im-

*RURAL INDUSTRY IN ACTION This French engraving suggests just how many things could be made in the countryside with simple hand tools. These men are making inexpensive but long-lasting wooden shoes, which were widely worn by the poor. (Photo: Caroline Buckler)*

portance of earnings from the land and from industry varied greatly for handicraft workers. In all cases, however, the putting-out system was a kind of capitalism. Merchants needed large amounts of capital, which they held in the form of goods being worked up and sold in distant markets. They sought to make profits and increase their capital in their businesses.

The putting-out system was not perfect, but it had definite advantages. It increased employment in the countryside and provided the poor with additional income. Since pro-

duction in the countryside was unregulated, workers and merchants could change procedures and experiment as they saw fit. Because they did not need to meet rigid guild standards, which maintained quality but discouraged the development of new methods, cottage industry became capable of producing many kinds of goods. Textiles, all manner of knives, forks, and housewares, buttons and gloves, clocks and musical instruments could be produced quite satisfactorily in the countryside. Luxury goods for the rich, such as exquisite tapestries and fine porcelain, de-

WOMEN WORKING  *This mother and her daughters may well be knitting, lace-making, and spinning
for some merchant capitalist. The close ties between
cottage industry and agriculture are well illustrated
in this summer scene. (Photo: Caroline Buckler)*

manded special training, close supervision,
and centralized workshops. Yet such goods
were as exceptional as those who used them.
The skills of rural industry were sufficient for
everyday articles.

Rural manufacturing did not spread across
Europe at an even rate. It appeared first in
England and developed most successfully
there, particularly for the spinning and weaving of woolen cloth. By 1500, half of England's textiles were being produced in the
countryside. By 1700, English industry was
generally more rural than urban and heavily

reliant on the putting-out system. Continental
countries developed rural industry more
slowly.

In France at the time of Louis XIV, Colbert
had revived the urban guilds and used them as
a means to control the cities and collect taxes
(page 565). But the pressure of rural poverty
proved too great. In 1762 the special privileges of urban manufacturing were abolished
in France, and the already-developing rural industries were given free rein from then on.
The royal government in France had come to
believe that the best way to help the poor

THE WOOLEN INDUSTRY    *Many steps went into the production of woolen cloth. This illustration suggests schematically how cottage workers combed out the fleece of the sheep and made raw wool ready for spinning.*

peasants was to encourage the growth of cottage manufacturing. Thus in France, as in Germany and other areas, the later part of the eighteenth century witnessed a remarkable expansion of rural industry in certain densely populated regions. The pattern established in England was spreading to the Continent.

### THE TEXTILE INDUSTRY

Throughout most of history, until at least the nineteenth century, the industry that has always employed the most people has been textiles. The making of linen, woolen, and eventually cotton cloth was the typical activity of cottage workers engaged in the putting-out system. A look inside the cottage of the English rural textile worker illustrates a way of life as well as an economic system.

The rural worker lived in a small cottage, with tiny windows and little space. Indeed, the worker's cottage was often a single room that served as workshop, kitchen, and bedroom. There were only a few pieces of furni-

ture, of which the weaver's loom was by far the largest and most important. That loom had changed somewhat in the early eighteenth century, when John Kay's invention of the flying shuttle enabled the weaver to throw the shuttle back and forth between the threads with one hand. Aside from that improvement, however, the loom was as it had been for much of history. In the cottage there were also spinning wheels, tubs for dyeing cloth and washing raw wool, and carding pieces to comb and prepare the raw material.

These different pieces of equipment were necessary because cottage industry was first and foremost a family enterprise. All the members of the family helped in the work, so that "every person from seven to eighty (who retained their sight and who could move their hands) could earn their bread," as one eighteenth-century English observer put it.[5] While the women and children prepared the raw material and spun the thread, the man of the house wove the cloth. There was work for everyone, even the youngest. After the dirt was beaten out of the raw cotton, it had to be thoroughly cleaned with strong soap in a tub, where tiny feet took the place of the agitator in a washing machine. George Crompton, the son of Samuel Crompton, who in 1784 invented the mule for cotton spinning, recalled that "soon after I was able to walk I was employed in the cotton manufacture.... My mother tucked up my petticoats about my waist, and put me into the tub to tread upon the cotton at the bottom."[6] Slightly older children and aged relatives carded and combed the cotton or wool, so the woman and the older daughter she had taught could spin it into thread. Each member had a task. The very young and very old worked in the family unit as a matter of course.

There was always a serious imbalance in this family enterprise: the work of four or five spinners was needed to keep one weaver steadily employed. Therefore, the wife and the husband had constantly to try to find more thread and more spinners. Widows and unmarried women – those "spinsters" who spun for their living – were recruited by the wife. Or perhaps the weaver's son went off on horseback to seek thread. The need for more thread might even lead the weaver and his wife to become small capitalist employers. At the end of the week, when they received the raw wool or cotton from the merchant-manufacturer, they would put out some of this raw material to other cottages. The following week they would return to pick up the thread and pay for the spinning – spinning that would help keep the weaver busy for a week until the merchant came for the finished cloth.

Relations between workers and employers were not always harmonious. In fact, there was continuous conflict. An English popular song written about 1700, called "The Cloth-ier's Delight, or the Rich Men's Joy and The Poor Men's Sorrow," has the merchant boasting of his countless tricks used to "beat down wages":

*We heapeth up riches and treasure great store*
*Which we get by griping and grinding the poor.*
*  And this is a way for to fill up our purse*
*  Although we do get it with many a curse.*[7]

There were constant disputes over weights of materials and the quality of the cloth. Merchants accused workers of stealing raw materials, and weavers complained that merchants delivered underweight bales. Both were right; each tried to cheat the other, even if only in self-defense.

There was another problem, at least from the merchant-capitalist's point of view. Rural labor was cheap, scattered, and poorly organized. For these reasons it was hard to control. Cottage workers tended to work in spurts. After they got paid on Saturday afternoon, the men in particular tended to drink and carouse for two or three days. Indeed, Monday was called "holy Monday" because inactivity was so religiously observed. By the end of the week the weaver was probably working feverishly to make his quota. But if he did not succeed, there was little the merchant could do. When times were good and the merchant could easily sell everything produced, the weaver and his family did fairly well and were particularly inclined to loaf, to the dismay of the capitalist. Thus, in spite of its virtues, the putting-out system in the textile industry had definite shortcomings. There was an imbalance between spinning and weaving. Labor relations were often poor, and the merchant was unable to control the quality of the cloth or the schedule of the workers. The merchant-capitalist's search for new methods of production became intense.

## BUILDING THE ATLANTIC ECONOMY

In addition to agricultural improvement, population pressure, and expanding cottage industry, the expansion of Europe in the eighteenth century was characterized by the growth of world trade. Spain and Portugal revitalized their empires and began drawing more wealth from renewed development. Yet, once again, the countries of northwestern Europe – the Netherlands, France, and above all Great Britain – benefited most. Great Britain (formed in 1707 by the union of England and Scotland in a single kingdom), became the leading maritime power. In the eighteenth century, British ships and merchants succeeded in dominating long-distance trade, particularly the fast-growing intercontinental trade across the Atlantic Ocean. The British played the critical role in building a fairly unified Atlantic economy, which offered remarkable opportunities for them and their colonists.

### MERCANTILISM AND COLONIAL WARS

Britain's commercial leadership in the eighteenth century had its origins in the mercantilism of the seventeenth century (page 565). European mercantilism was a system of economic regulations aimed at increasing the power of the state. As practiced by a leading advocate like Colbert under Louis XIV, mercantilism aimed particularly at creating a favorable balance of foreign trade in order to increase a country's stock of gold. A country's gold holdings served as an all-important treasure chest, to be opened periodically to pay for war in a violent age.

Early English mercantilists shared these views. As Thomas Mun, a leading merchant and early mercantilist, wrote in *England's Treasure by Foreign Trade* (1630, published 1664): "The ordinary means therefore to increase our wealth and treasure is by foreign trade wherein we must observe this rule; to sell more to strangers yearly than we consume of theirs in value." What distinguished English mercantilism was the unusual idea that governmental economic regulations could and should serve the private interests of individuals and groups as well as the public needs of the state. As Josiah Child, a very wealthy brewer and director of the East India Company, put it, in the ideal economy "Profit and Power ought jointly to be considered."[8]

In France and other continental countries, by contrast, seventeenth-century mercantilists generally put the needs of the state far above those of businessmen and workers. And they seldom saw a possible harmony of public and private interests for a common good.

The result of the English desire to increase both its military power and private wealth was the mercantile system of the Navigation Acts. Oliver Cromwell established the first of these laws in 1651, and the restored monarchy of Charles II extended them further in 1660 and 1663; the Navigation Acts of the seventeenth century were not seriously modified until 1786. The acts required that most goods imported from Europe into England and Scotland be carried on British-owned ships with British crews, or on ships of the country producing the article. Moreover, these laws gave British merchants and shipowners a virtual monopoly on trade with the colonies. The colonists were required to ship their products – sugar, tobacco, and cotton – on British ships, and to buy almost all of their European goods from the mother country. It was believed that these economic regulations would provide British merchants and workers with profits and employment, and colonial

*THE PORT OF DIEPPE IN 1754  This painting by Joseph Vernet (1714–1789) was one of fourteen in a famous series of port scenes commissioned by Louis XV. Vernet's work admirably captures the spirit and excitement of French maritime expansion. (Louvre. Photo: Bulloz)*

plantation owners and farmers with a guaranteed market for their products. And the state would develop a shipping industry with a large number of tough, experienced deepwater seamen, who could be drafted when necessary into the Royal Navy to protect the island nation.

The Navigation Acts were a form of economic warfare. Their initial target was the Dutch, who were far ahead of the English in shipping and foreign trade in the mid-seventeenth century. The Navigation Acts, in conjunction with three Anglo-Dutch wars between 1652 and 1674, did seriously damage Dutch shipping and commerce. The thriving Dutch colony of New Amsterdam was seized in 1664 and rechristened New York. By the later seventeenth century, when the Dutch and the English became allies to stop the expansion of France's Louis XIV, the Netherlands was falling behind England in shipping, trade, and colonies.

As the Netherlands followed Spain into relative decline, France emerged as a far more serious rival. Rich in natural resources and endowed with a population three or four times that of England, France too was intent upon building a powerful fleet and a worldwide system of rigidly monopolized colonial trade. And France, aware that Great Britain coveted large parts of Spain's American empire, was determined to revitalize its Spanish ally. Thus, from 1701 to 1763, Britain and France were locked in a series of wars to decide, in part, which nation would become the leading maritime power and claim a lion's share of the profits of Europe's overseas expansion (see Map 19.1).

The first round was the War of the Spanish Succession (page 570), which started when Louis XIV declared his willingness to accept the Spanish crown willed to his grandson. Besides upsetting the continental balance of power, a union of France and Spain threatened to destroy the British colonies in North America. The thin ribbon of British settlements along the Atlantic seaboard from Massachusetts to the Carolinas would be surrounded by a great arc of Franco-Spanish power stretching south and west from French Canada to Florida and the Gulf of Mexico (see Map 19.1). Defeated by a great coalition of states after twelve years of fighting, Louis XIV was forced in the Peace of Utrecht (1713) to cede Newfoundland and Nova Scotia to Britain. Spain was compelled to give Britain control of the lucrative West African slave trade – the so-called *asiento* – and to let Britain send one ship of merchandise into the Spanish colonies annually, through Porto Bello on the Isthmus of Panama.

France was still a mighty competitor. The War of the Austrian Succession (1740–1748), which started when Frederick the Great of Prussia seized Silesia from Austria's Maria Theresa, became a world war, including Anglo-French conflicts in India and North America. Indeed, it was the seizure of French territory in Canada by New England colonists that forced France to sue for peace in 1748, and to accept gladly a return to the territorial situation existing in North America at the beginning of the war. France's Bourbon ally, Spain, defended itself surprisingly well and Spain's empire remained intact.

MAP 19.1   THE ECONOMY OF THE ATLANTIC BASIN IN 1701   *The growth of trade encouraged both economic development and military conflict in the Atlantic Basin.*

This inclusive stand-off helped set the stage for the Seven Years' War (1756–1763). In central Europe, Austria's Maria Theresa sought to win back Silesia and crush Prussia, thereby re-establishing the Habsburgs' traditional leadership in German affairs. She almost succeeded, skillfully winning France – the Habsburgs' long-standing enemy – and Russia to her cause. Yet the Prussian state survived, saved by its army and the sudden decision of the newly crowned Peter III of Russia to withdraw from the war in 1762.

Outside of Europe, the Seven Years' War was the decisive round in the Franco-British competition for colonial empire. Led by William Pitt (1708–1788), whose grandfather had made a fortune as a trader in India, the British concentrated on using superior sea power to destroy the French fleet and choke off French commerce around the world. Capturing Quebec in 1759 and winning a great naval victory at Quiberon Bay, the British also strangled France's valuable sugar trade with its Caribbean islands and smashed French forts in India. After Spain entered the war on France's side in 1761, the surging British temporarily occupied Havana in Cuba, and Manila in the Philippines. With the Treaty of Paris (1763), France lost all its possessions on the mainland of North America. French Canada as well as French territory east of the Mississippi River passed to Britain, and France ceded Louisiana to Spain as compensation for Spain's loss of Florida to Britain. France also gave up most of its holdings in India, opening the way to British dominance on the subcontinent. By 1763, British naval power, built in large part upon the rapid growth of the British shipping

Great Britain
France
Portugal
Spain

HUDSON'S
BAY

LOUISIANA

MEXICO

NEW FRANCE

Mississippi

QUEBEC

Ohio

NEWFOUNDLAND
(To Gr. Br., 1713)

GREAT BRITAIN

ACADIA
(NOVA SCOTIA)
(To Gr. Br., 1713)

*Furs*

FLORIDA

*Tobacco*

NETH.

AUSTRIA

*Silver*

*Colonial products*

FRANCE

*Manufactured goods*

CUBA

*Sugar*

JAMAICA
(ENGLAND, 1670)

SANTO DOMINGO
(FRANCE, 1697)

PORTUGAL

SPAIN

Porto Bello

*Asiento*
(Spain; to Gr. Br.,
1713)

LESSER
ANTILLES
(English and
French since
about 1630)

ATLANTIC

OCEAN

CANARY IS.
(SPAIN)

NEW GRANADA

GUIANA

*Sugar*

(DUTCH)

(FRENCH)

CAPE VERDE IS.
(PORT.)

AFRICA

PERU

European forts and trading stations

*Slaves*

BRAZIL

ANGOLA

industry after the passage of the Navigation Acts, had triumphed decisively. Britain had realized its goal of monopolizing a vast trading and colonial empire for its exclusive benefit.

## LAND AND WEALTH IN NORTH AMERICA

Of all Britain's colonies, those on the North American mainland proved most valuable in the long run. The settlements along the Atlantic coast provided an important outlet for surplus population, so that migration abroad limited poverty in England, Scotland, and northern Ireland. The settlers also benefited. In the mainland colonies, they had privileged access to virtually free and unlimited land. The availability of farms was a precious asset in preindustrial Europe, where agriculture was the main source of income and prestige.

The possibility of having one's own farm was particularly attractive to ordinary men and women from the British Isles. Land in England was already highly concentrated in the hands of the nobility and gentry in 1700, and became more so with agricultural improvement in the eighteenth century. White settlers who came to the colonies as free men and women, or as indentured servants pledged to work seven years for their passage, or as prisoners and convicts, could obtain their own farms on easy terms as soon as they had their personal freedom. Many poor white farmers also came to the mainland from the British West Indies, crowded out of those islands by the growth of big sugar plantations using black slave labor. To be sure, life in the mainland colonies was hard and rough, especially on the frontier. Yet the settlers succeeded in paying little or no rent to grasping landlords, and taxes were very low. Unlike the great majority of European peasants, who had to accept high rents and taxes as part of the order of things, American farmers could keep most of what they managed to produce.

The availability of land made labor expensive in the colonies. This basic fact, rather than any repressive aspects of the Navigation Acts, limited the growth of industry in the colonies. As the Governor of New York put it in 1767:

*The price of labor is so great in this part of the world that it will always prove the greatest obstacle to any manufacturers attempting to set up here, and the genius of the people in a country where everyone can have land to work upon leads them so naturally into agriculture that it prevails over every other occupation.*[9]

The advantage for colonists was in farming, and farm they did.

Cheap land and scarce labor were also critical factors in the growth of slavery in the southern colonies. By 1700 British indentured servants were carefully avoiding the Virginia lowlands, where black slavery was spreading, and by 1730 the large plantations there had gone over completely to black slaves. Slave labor permitted an astonishing tenfold increase in tobacco production between 1700 and 1774, and created a wealthy aristocratic planter class in Maryland and Virginia.

In the course of the eighteenth century, the farmers of New England and, particularly, the middle colonies of Pennsylvania and New Jersey began to produce more food than they needed. They exported ever more food stuffs, primarily to the West Indies. There the owners of the sugar plantations came to depend on the mainland colonies for grain and dried fish to feed their slaves. The plantation owners, whether they grew tobacco in Virginia and Maryland or sugar in the West Indies, had the exclusive privilege of supplying the British Isles with their products. Eng-

## COLONIAL COMPETITION AND WAR, 1651–1763

| | |
|---|---|
| 1651–1663 | British Navigation Acts create the mercantile system, which is not seriously modified until 1786 |
| 1652–1674 | Three Anglo-Dutch wars damage Dutch shipping and commerce |
| 1664 | New Amsterdam is seized and renamed New York |
| 1701–1714 | War of the Spanish Succession |
| 1713 | Peace of Utrecht: Britain wins parts of Canada from France and control of the west African slave trade from Spain |
| 1740–1748 | War of the Austrian Succession, resulting in no change in territorial holdings in North America |
| 1756–1763 | Seven Years' War (known in North America as the French and Indian War), a decisive victory for Britain |
| 1763 | Treaty of Paris: Britain receives all French territory on the North American mainland and achieves dominance in India |

lishmen could not buy cheaper sugar from Brazil, nor were they allowed to grow tobacco in the home islands. Thus the colonists too had their place in the protective mercantile system of the Navigation Acts. The American shipping industry grew rapidly in the eighteenth century, for example, because colonial shippers enjoyed the same advantages as their fellow British citizens in the mother country.

The abundance of almost free land resulted in a rapid increase in the colonial population in the eighteenth century. In a mere three-quarters of a century after 1700, the white population of the mainland colonies multiplied a staggering ten times as immigrants arrived and colonial couples raised large families. In 1774, 2.2 million whites and 330,000 blacks inhabited what would soon become the independent United States.

Rapid population growth did not reduce the settlers to poverty. On the contrary, agricultural development resulted in fairly high standards of living for mainland colonists, in eighteenth-century terms. There was also an unusual degree of economic equality, by the standards of Europe. Few people were extremely rich and few were extremely poor. Most remarkable of all, on the eve of the American Revolution, the *average* white man or woman in the mainland British colonies probably had the highest income and standard of living in the world. It has been estimated that between 1715 and 1775 the real income of the average American was increasing about 1 percent per year per person, almost two-thirds as fast as it increased with massive industrialization between 1840 and 1959. When one considers that between 1775 and 1840 Americans experienced no improvement in their standard of living, it is clear just how

*TOBACCO was a key commodity in the Atlantic trade. This engraving from 1775 shows a merchant and his slaves preparing a cargo for sail. (The British Museum)*

much the colonists benefited from hard work and the mercantile system created by the Navigation Acts.[10]

### THE GROWTH OF FOREIGN TRADE

England also profited greatly from the mercantile system. Above all, the rapidly growing and increasingly wealthy agricultural populations of the mainland colonies provided an expanding market for English manufactured goods. This situation was extremely fortunate, for England in the eighteenth century was gradually losing, or only slowly expanding, its sales to many of its traditional European markets. However, rising demand for manufactured goods from North America, as well as from the West Indies, Africa, and Latin America, allowed English cottage industry to continue to grow and diversify. Merchant-capitalists and manufacturers found new and exciting opportunities for profit and wealth.

Since the late Middle Ages, England had relied very heavily on the sale of woolen cloth in foreign markets. Indeed, as late as 1700 woolen cloth was the only important manufactured good exported from England, and fully 90 percent of it was sold to Europeans. In the course of the eighteenth century, the states of continental Europe were trying to develop their own cottage textile industries in an effort to deal with rural poverty and overpopulation. Like England earlier, these states adopted protectionist, mercantilist policies. They tried by means of tariffs and other measures to exclude competing goods from abroad, whether English woolens or the cheap but beautiful cotton calicos the English East India Company brought from India and sold in Europe.

France had already closed its markets to the

English in the seventeenth century. In the eighteenth century, German states purchased much less woolen cloth from England and encouraged cottage production of coarse, cheap linens, which became a feared competitor in all of central and southern Europe. By 1773, England was selling only about two-thirds as much woolen cloth to northern and western Europe as it had in 1700. The decline of sales to the Continent meant that the English economy badly needed new markets and new products in order to develop and prosper.

Protected colonial markets came to the rescue. More than offsetting stagnating trade with Europe, they provided a great stimulus for many branches of English manufacturing. The markets of the Atlantic economy led the way, as may be seen in Figure 19.3. English exports of manufactured goods to continental Europe increased very modestly, from roughly £2.9 million in 1700 to only £3.3 million in 1773. Meanwhile, sales of manufactured products to the Atlantic economy – primarily the mainland colonies of North America and the West Indian sugar islands, with an important assist from West Africa and Latin America – soared from £500,000 to £3.9 million. Sales to other "colonies" – Ireland and India – also rose substantially in the eighteenth century.

English exports became much more balanced and diversified. To America and Africa went large quantities of metal items – axes to frontiersmen, firearms, chains for slaveowners. There were also clocks and coaches, buttons and saddles, china and furniture, musical instruments and scientific equipment, and a host of other things. By 1750, half the nails made in England were going to the colonies. Foreign trade became the bread-and-butter of some industries.

Thus, the mercantile system formed in the seventeenth century to attack the Dutch and

Note: Data exclude English re-exports.

FIGURE 19.3 EXPORTS OF ENGLISH MANU-FACTURED GOODS 1700–1774 *While trade with Europe stagnated after 1700, English exports to Africa and the Americas boomed and greatly stimulated English economic development. (Source: R. Davis, "English Foreign Trade, 1700–1774,"* Economic History Review, *2d series, 15 (1962); 302–303)*

win power and profit for England continued to shape trade in the eighteenth century. The English concentrated in their hands much of the demand for manufactured goods from the growing Atlantic economy. The pressure of demand from three continents upon the cottage industry of one medium-sized country heightened the efforts of English merchant-capitalists to find new and improved ways to produce more goods. By the 1770s, England stood on the threshold of radical industrial change, as we shall see in Chapter 22.

## REVIVAL IN COLONIAL LATIN AMERICA

When the last Spanish Habsburg, the feeble-minded Charles II, died in 1700 (page 570), Spain was "little less cadaverous than its defunct master."[11] Its vast empire lay before

Europe awaiting dismemberment. Yet, in one of those striking reversals with which history is replete, Spain revived. The empire held together and even prospered, while a European-oriented landowning aristocracy enhanced its position in colonial society.

Spain recovered in part because of better leadership. Louis XIV's grandson, who took the throne as Philip V (1700–1746), brought new men and fresh ideas with him from France, and rallied the Spanish people to his Bourbon dynasty in the long War of the Spanish Succession. When peace was restored, a series of reforming ministers reasserted royal authority, overhauling state finances and strengthening defense. To protect the colonies, they restored Spain's navy to a respectable third place in Europe behind Great Britain and France. Philip's ministers also promoted the economy with vigorous measures that included a gradual relaxation of the state monopoly on colonial trade. The able Charles III (1759–1788), a truly enlightened monarch, further extended economic and administrative reform.

Revitalization in Madrid had positive results in the colonies. The colonies succeeded in defending themselves from numerous British attacks and even increased in size. Spain received Louisiana from France in 1763, and missionaries and ranchers extended Spanish influence all the way to northern California.

Political success was matched by economic improvement. After declining markedly in the seventeenth century, silver mining recovered in Mexico and Peru. Output quadrupled between 1700 and 1800, when Spanish America accounted for half of world silver production. Ever a risky long shot at sudden riches, silver mining encouraged a gambler's attitude toward wealth and work. The big profits of the lucky usually went into land. Silver min-

ing also encouraged food production for large mining camps and gave the creoles – people of Spanish blood born in the Americas – the means to purchase more and more European luxuries and manufactured goods. A class of wealthy merchants arose to handle this flourishing trade, which often relied on smuggled goods from Great Britain. As in British North America, industry remained weak, although workshops employing forced Indian labor made Mexican and Peruvian wool into coarse fabrics for the Latin American masses. Spain's colonies were an important part of the Atlantic economy.

Economic development strengthened the creole elite, which came to rival the top government officials dispatched from Spain. As in most preindustrial societies, land was the main source of wealth. In contrast to British America but like Spain and eastern Europe, creole estate owners controlled much of the land. Small independent farmers were rare.

The Spanish crown had given large holdings to the conquering pioneers and their followers, and beginning in the late sixteenth century many big tracts of state land were sold to favored settlers. Thus, although the Crown decreed that Indian communities were to retain the use of their tribal lands, a class of big landholders grew up in sparsely settled regions and in the midst of the defeated Indian populations.

The Spanish settlers strove to become a genuine European aristocracy, and they largely succeeded. As good aristocrats, they believed that work in the fields was the proper occupation of a depressed, impoverished peasantry. The defenseless Indians suited their needs. As the Indian population recovered in numbers, slavery and periodic forced labor gave way to widespread debt peonage from 1600 onward. Under this system, a planter or rancher would keep his Christianized, increasingly Hispanicized Indians in perpetual debt bondage by periodically advancing food, shelter, and a little money. Debt peonage subjugated the Indians and was a form of agricultural serfdom.

The landowning class practiced primogeniture, passing everything from eldest son to eldest son to prevent fragmentation of land and influence. Also like European nobles, wealthy creoles built ornate townhouses, contributing to the development of a lavish colonial baroque style that may still be seen in Lima, Peru, and Mexico City. The creole elite followed European cultural and intellectual trends. Enlightenment ideas spread to colonial salons and universities, encouraging a questioning attitude and preparing the way for the creoles' rise to political power with the independence movements of the early nineteenth century.

There were also creoles of modest means, especially in the cities, since estate agriculture discouraged small white farmers. (Chile was an exception: since it had few docile Indians to exploit, white settlers had to work their small farms to survive.) The large middle group in Spanish colonies consisted of racially mixed *mestizos,* the offspring of Spanish men and Indian women. The most talented mestizos realistically aspired to join the creoles, for enough wealth and power could make one white. This ambition siphoned off the most energetic mestizos and lessened the build-up of any lower-class discontent. Thus, by the end of the colonial era roughly 20 percent of the population was classified as white and about 30 percent as mestizo. Pure-blooded Indians accounted for most of the remainder, for only on the sugar plantations of Cuba and Puerto Rico did black slavery ever take firm root in Spanish America.

The situation was quite the opposite in Portuguese Brazil. As in the West Indies, enormous numbers of blacks were brought in chains to work the sugar plantations. About half the population of Brazil was of African origin in the early nineteenth century. Even more than in the Spanish territories, the people of Brazil intermingled sexually and culturally. In contrast to North America, where racial lines were hard and fast, at least in theory, colonial Brazil made a virtue of miscegenation and the population grew to include every color in the racial rainbow.

———◆———

While some European intellectual elites were developing a new view of the world in the eighteenth century, Europe as a whole was experiencing a gradual but far-reaching expansion. As agriculture showed signs of modest improvement across the continent, first the Low Countries and then England succeeded in launching the epoch-making Agricultural Revolution. Plague disappeared and the populations of all countries grew significantly, encouraging the progress of cottage industry and merchant capitalism.

Europeans also continued their overseas expansion, fighting for empire and profit and consolidating their hold on the Americas in particular. A revived Spain and its Latin American colonies participated fully in this expansion. As in agriculture and cottage industry, however, England and its empire proved most successful. The English concentrated much of the growing Atlantic trade in their hands, which challenged and enriched English industry and intensified the search for new methods of production. Thus, by the 1770s, England was on the verge of an economic breakthrough fully as significant as the great political upheaval destined to develop shortly in neighboring France.

## NOTES

1. M. Bloch, *Les caractères originaux de l'histoire rurale française,* Librarie Armand Colin, Paris 1960, 1.244–245.

2. B. H. Slicher van Bath, *The Agrarian History of Western Europe,* A.D. *500–1850,* St. Martin's Press, New York, 1963, p. 240.

3. Quoted in E. E. Rich and C. H. Wilson, eds., *Cambridge Economic History of Europe,* Cambridge University Press, Cambridge, England, 4.74.

4. Ibid., p. 85.

5. Quoted by I. Pinchbeck, *Women Workers and the Industrial Revolution, 1750–1850,* F. S. Crofts, New York, 1930, p. 113.

6. Quoted by S. Chapman, *The Lancashire Cotton Industry,* Manchester University Press, Manchester, 1903, p. 13.

7. Quoted by P. Mantoux, *The Industrial Revolution in the Eighteenth Century,* Harper & Row, New York, 1961, p. 75.

8. Quoted by C. Wilson, *England's Apprenticeship, 1603–1763,* Longmans, Green, London, 1965, p. 169.

9. Quoted by D. Dillard, *Economic Development of the North Atlantic Community,* Prentice-Hall, Englewood Cliffs, N.J., 1967, p. 192.

10. G. Taylor, "America's Growth Before 1840," *Journal of Economic History* 24 (December 1970):427–444.

11. J. Rippy, *Latin America: A Modern History,* rev. ed., University of Michigan Press, Ann Arbor, 1968, p. 97.

## SUGGESTED READING

B. H. Slicher van Bath, *The Agrarian History of Western Europe,* A.D. *500–1850* (1963), is a wide-ranging general introduction to the gradual transformation of European agriculture, as is M. Bloch's great classic, cited in the Notes, which has been translated as *French Rural History* (1966). J. Blum, *The End of the Old Order in Rural Europe* (1978), is an impressive comparative study. J. de Vries, *The Dutch Rural Economy in the Golden Age, 1500–1700* (1974), skillfully examines the causes of early Dutch leadership in farming, and E. L. Jones, *Agriculture and Economic Growth in England, 1650–1815* (1967), shows the importance of the agricultural revolution for England. Two recommended and complementary studies on landowning nobilities are R. Forster, *The Nobility of Toulouse in the Eighteenth Century* (1960), and G. E. Mingay, *English Landed Society in the Eighteenth Century* (1963). A. Goodwin, ed., *The European Nobility in the Eighteenth Century* (1967), is an exciting group of essays on aristocrats in different countries. R. and E. Forster, eds., *European Society in the Eighteenth Century* (1969), assembles a rich collection of contemporary writing on a variety of economic and social topics. E. L. Ladurie, *The Peasants of Languedoc* (1976), a brilliant and challenging study of rural life in southern France for several centuries, complements J. Goody et al., eds., *Family and Inheritance: Rural Society in Western Europe, 1200–1800* (1976). Life in small-town preindustrial France comes alive in P. Higonnet, *Pont-de-Montvert: Social Structure and Politics in a French Village, 1700–1914* (1971), while O. Hufton deals vividly and sympathetically with rural migration, work, women, and much more in *The Poor in Eighteenth-Century France* (1974). P. Mantoux, *The Industrial Revolution in the Eighteenth Century* (1928), and D. Landes, *The Unbound Prometheus* (1969), provide excellent discussions of the development of cottage industry.

Two excellent multivolume series, *The Cambridge Economic History of Europe,* and C. Cipolla, ed., *The Fontana Economic History of Europe,* cover the sweep of economic developments from the Middle Ages to the present and have extensive bibliographies. In the area of trade and colonial competition, V. Barbour, *Capitalism in Amsterdam* (1963), and C. R. Boxer, *The Dutch Seaborne Empire* (1970), are very interesting on Holland. C. Wilson, *Profit and Power: A Study of England and the Dutch Wars* (1957), is exciting scholarship, as are W. Dorn, *The*

*Competition for Empire, 1740–1763* (1963), D. K. Fieldhouse, *The Colonial Empires* (1971), and R. Davies, *The Rise of Atlantic Economies* (1973). R. Pares, *Yankees and Creoles* (1956), is a short, lively work on trade between the mainland colonies and the West Indies. E. Williams, *Capitalism and Slavery* (1966), provocatively argues that slavery provided the wealth necessary for England's industrial development. Another exciting work is J. Nef, *War and Human Progress* (1968), which examines the impact of war on economic and industrial development in European history between about 1500 and 1800 and may be compared with M. Gutmann, *War and Rural Life in the Early Modern Low Countries* (1980). J. Fagg's *Latin America* (1969) provides a good introduction to the colonial period and has a useful bibliography, while C. Haring, *The Spanish in America* (1947), is a fundamental modern study.

Three very fine books on the growth of population are C. Cipolla's short and lively *The Economic History of World Population* (1962); E. A. Wrigley's more demanding *Population and History* (1969); and T. McKeown's scholarly *The Modern Rise of Population* (1977). In addition to works on England cited in the Suggested Reading for Chapter 22, D. George, *England in Transition* (1953), and C. Wilson, *England's Apprenticeship, 1603–1763* (1965), are highly recommended. The greatest novel of eighteenth-century English society is Henry Fielding's unforgettable *Tom Jones,* although Jane Austen's novels about country society, *Emma* and *Pride and Prejudice* are not far behind.

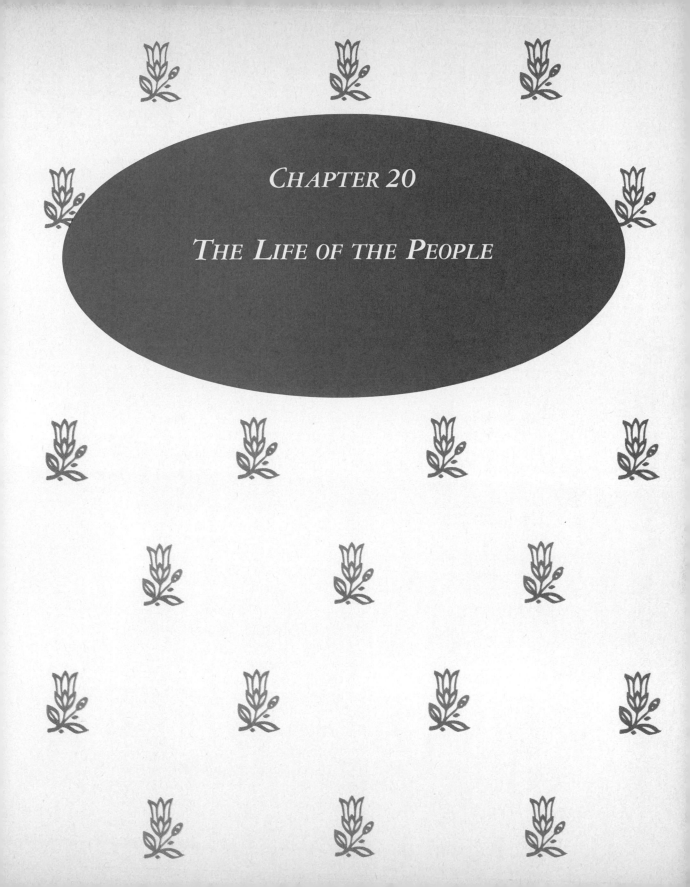

# CHAPTER 20

# THE LIFE OF THE PEOPLE

THE DISCUSSION OF AGRICULTURE and industry in the last chapter showed the ordinary man and woman at work, straining to make ends meet and earn a living. Yet work is only part of human experience. What about the rest? What about such basic things as marriage and childhood, food and drink, diet and medicine? How, in short, did "the people" — the peasant masses and the urban poor — really live in western Europe before the age of revolution began at the end of the eighteenth century? This is the simple but profound question that the economic and social developments naturally raise.

## MARRIAGE AND THE FAMILY

The basic unit of social organization is the family. It is within the structure of the family that human beings love, mate, and reproduce themselves. It is primarily the family that teaches the child, imparting values and customs that condition an individual's behavior for a lifetime. The family is also an institution woven into the web of history. It evolves and changes, and it has taken different forms in different times and places.

### EXTENDED AND NUCLEAR FAMILIES

In many traditional Asian and African societies, the typical family has often been an extended family. A newly married couple, instead of establishing their own home, will go to live with either the bride's or the groom's family. The couple raises their children while living under the same roof with their own brothers and sisters, who may also be married. The family is a big three- or four-generation clan, headed by a patriarch or perhaps a matriarch, and encompassing everyone from the youngest infant to the oldest grandparent.

Extended families, it is often said, provide security for adults and children in traditional agrarian peasant economies. Everyone has a place within the extended family, from cradle to grave. Sociologists frequently assume that the extended family gives way to the conjugal, or "nuclear," family with the advent of industrialization and urbanization. Couples establish their own households and their own family identities when they marry. They live with the children they raise, apart from their parents. Something like this is indeed happening in much of Asia and Africa today. And since Europe was once agrarian and preindustrial, it has often been believed that the extended family must also have prevailed in Europe before it was destroyed by the Industrial Revolution.

In fact, the situation was quite different in western and central European societies. By 1700, the extended three-generational family was a great rarity in western and central Europe. Indeed, the extended family may never have been common in Europe, although it is hard to know about the Middle Ages because there are fewer records for the historian to study. When young European couples married, they normally established their own households and lived apart from their parents. When a three-generation household came into existence, it was usually a parent who moved in with a married child, rather than a newly married couple moving in with either set of parents. The married couple, and the children that were sure to follow, were on their own from the beginning.

Perhaps because European couples set up separate households when they married, people did not marry young in the seventeenth and early eighteenth centuries. By the standards of today the average person, who was neither rich nor aristocratic, married suprisingly late, many years after reaching adulthood and many more after beginning to work. In one well-studied typical English village, both men and women married for the first time at an average age of twenty-seven or older in the seventeenth and eighteenth centuries. For one long period, the average age for women at first marriage was thirty years. In early eighteenth-century France the average man and woman marrying for the first time were in their late twenties. Moreover, a substantial portion of men and women never married at all.

Between two-fifths and three-fifths of European women capable of bearing children – that is, women between fifteen and forty-four – were unmarried at any given time. The contrast with traditional non-Western societies is once again striking. In those societies the pattern has very often been almost universal and very early marriage. The union of a teenage bride and her teenage groom has been the general rule.

The custom of late marriage and nuclear family was a distinctive characteristic of European society. The consequences have been tremendous, though still only partially explored. It seems likely that the dynamism and creativity that have characterized European society were due in large part to the pattern of marriage and family. This pattern fostered and required self-reliance and independence. In preindustrial western Europe in the sixteenth through eighteenth centuries, marriage normally joined a mature man and a mature woman – two adults who had already experienced a great deal of life and could transmit self-reliance and real skills to the next generation.

Why was marriage delayed? The main reason was that couples normally could not marry until they could support themselves economically. The land was the main source of income. The peasant son often needed to wait until his father's death to inherit the family farm and marry his sweetheart. Similarly, the peasant daughter and her family needed to accumulate a small dowry to help her boy friend buy land or build a house.

There were also laws and regulations to temper impetuous love and physical attraction. In some areas couples needed the legal permission or tacit approval of the local lord or landowner in order to marry. In Austria and Germany there were legal restrictions on marriage, and well into the nineteenth century poor couples had particular difficulty securing the approval of local officials. These officials believed that freedom to marry for the lower classes would mean more paupers, more abandoned children, and more money for welfare. Thus prudence, custom, and law combined to postpone the march to the altar. This pattern helped society maintain some kind of balance between the number of people and the available economic resources.

## WORK AWAY FROM HOME

Many young people worked within their families until they could start their own households. Boys plowed and wove; girls spun and tended the cows. Many others left home to work elsewhere. In the towns a lad might be apprenticed to a craftsman for seven or fourteen years to learn a trade. During that time he would not be permitted to marry. In most trades he earned little and worked hard, but if he were lucky he might eventually be admitted to a guild and establish his economic independence. More often, the young man would drift from one tough job to another: hired hand for a small farmer, laborer on a new road, carrier of water in a nearby town. He was always subject to economic fluctua-

THE CHIMNEY SWEEP  *Some boys and girls found work as chimney sweeps, especially if they were small. Climbing up into chimneys was dirty, dangerous work. Hot stones could set the sweep's clothing on fire. (Photo: Caroline Buckler)*

tions, and unemployment was a constant threat.

Girls also left their families to work, at an early age and in large numbers. The range of opportunities open to them was more limited, however. Service in another family's household was by far the most common job. Even middle-class families often sent their daughters into service (as they sent their sons to workshops and counting houses) and hired others as servants in return. Thus, a few years

away from home as a servant was a normal part of growing up. If all went well, the girl (or boy) would work hard and save some money for parents and marriage. At the least, there would be one less mouth to feed at home.

The legions of young servant girls worked hard but had little real independence. Sometimes the employer paid the girl's wages directly to her parents. Constantly under the eye of her mistress, her tasks were many – cleaning, shopping, cooking, caring for the baby – and often endless, for there were no laws to limit her exploitation. Few girls were so brutalized that they snapped under the strain, like the Russian servant girl Varka in Chekhov's chilling story, "Sleepy," who, driven beyond exhaustion, finally quieted her mistress's screaming child by strangling it in its cradle. But court records are full of complaints by servant girls of physical mistreatment by their mistresses. There were many others like the fifteen-year-old English girl in the early eighteenth century who told the judge that her mistress had not only called her "very opprobrious names, as Bitch, Whore and the like," but also "beat her without provocation and beyond measure."[1]

There was also the pressure of seducers and sexual attack. In theory, domestic service offered protection and security for a young girl leaving home. The girl had food, lodging, and a new family. She did not drift in a strange and often dangerous environment. But in practice, she was often the easy prey of a lecherous master, or his sons, or his friends. Indeed, "the evidence suggests that in all European countries, from Britain to Russia, the upper classes felt perfectly free to exploit sexually girls who were at their mercy."[2] If the girl became pregnant, she was quickly fired and thrown out in disgrace to make her own way. Prostitution and petty thievery were often the harsh alternatives that lay ahead. "What are we?" exclaimed a bitter Paris prostitute during the French Revolution. "Most of us are unfortunate women, without origins, without education, servants and maids for the most part."[3]

## PREMARITAL SEX AND BIRTH-CONTROL PRACTICES

Did the plight of some ex-servant girls mean that late marriage in preindustrial Europe went hand in hand with premarital sex and many illegitimate children? For most of western and central Europe, until at least 1750, the answer seems to be no. English parish registers, in which the clergy recorded the births and deaths of the population, seldom list more than one bastard out of every twenty children baptized. Some French parishes in the seventeenth century had extraordinarily low rates of illegitimacy, with less than one percent of the babies born out of wedlock. Illegitimate babies were apparently a rarity, at least as far as the official church records are concerned.

At the same time premarital sex was clearly commonplace. In one well-studied English village one-third of all first children were conceived before the couple was married, and many were born within three months of the marriage ceremony. No doubt many of these couples were already betrothed, or at least "going steady," before they entered into an intimate relationship. But the very low rates of illegitimate birth also reflect the powerful social controls of the traditional village, particularly the open-field village with its pattern of cooperation and common action. Irate parents and village elders, indignant priests and authoritative landlords, all combined to

pressure any young people who wavered about marriage in the face of unexpected pregnancy. These controls meant that premarital sex was not entered into lightly. In the countryside it was generally limited to those contemplating marriage.

Once a woman was married, she generally had several children. This does not mean that birth control within marriage was unknown in western and central Europe before the nineteenth century. But it was primitive and quite undependable. The most common method was coitus interruptus – withdrawal by the male before ejaculation. The French, who were apparently early leaders in contraception, were using this method extensively to limit family size by the end of the eighteenth century. The same technique was apparently used in some English communities and no doubt elsewhere, since awareness of this way to prevent conception was widespread. Withdrawal as a method of birth control was in keeping with the European pattern of nuclear family, in which the father bore the direct responsibility of supporting his children. Withdrawal – a male technique – was one way to meet that responsibility.

Mechanical and other means of contraception were not unknown in the eighteenth century, but they appear to have been used mainly by certain sectors of the urban population. The "fast set" of London used the "sheath" regularly, although primarily to protect against venereal disease, not pregnancy. Prostitutes used various contraceptive techniques to prevent pregnancy, and such information was probably available to anyone who really sought it. The second part of an indictment for adultery against a late-sixteenth-century English vicar charged that the wayward minister was "also an instructor of young folks [in] how to commit the sin of adultery or fornication and not to beget or bring forth children."[4]

## NEW PATTERNS OF MARRIAGE AND ILLEGITIMACY

In the second half of the eighteenth century, the pattern of late marriage and few illegitimate children began to break down. It is hard to say why. Certainly, changes in the economy had a gradual but profound impact. The growth of cottage industry created new opportunities for earning a living, opportunities not tied to limited and hard-to-get land. Because a scrap of ground for a garden and a cottage for the loom and spinning wheel could be quite enough for a modest living, young people had greater independence and did not need to wait for a good-sized farm. A contemporary observer of an area of rapidly growing cottage industry in Switzerland at the end of the eighteenth century described these changes: "The increased and sure income offered by the combination of cottage manufacture with farming hastened and multiplied marriages and encouraged the division of landholdings, while enhancing their value; it also promoted the expansion and embellishment of houses and villages."[5]

As a result cottage workers not only married earlier, but for different reasons. Nothing could be so businesslike, so calculating, as a peasant marriage, which was often dictated by the needs of the couple's families. After 1750, however, courtship became more extensive and freer as cottage industry grew. It was easier to yield to the attraction of the opposite sex and fall in love. The older generation was often shocked by the lack of responsibility they saw in the early marriages of the poor, the union of "people with only two spinning wheels and not even a bed." But the laws and regulations they imposed, especially in Germany, were often disregarded. Unions based on love rather than economic considerations were increasingly the pattern for cottage workers. Factory workers, numbers of whom first began to appear in England after about 1780, followed the path blazed by cottage workers.

Changes in the timing and motivation of marriage went hand in hand with a rapid increase in illegitimate births between about 1750 and 1850. Some historians even speak of an "illegitimacy explosion," a phrase that is no exaggeration in many instances. In Frankfurt, Germany, for example, only about 2 percent of all births were illegitimate in the early 1700s. This figure rose to 5 percent in about 1760, to about 10 percent in 1800, and peaked at about 25 percent around 1850. In Bordeaux, France, illegitimate births rose steadily until by 1840 fully one out of every three babies was born out of wedlock. Small towns and villages less frequently experienced such startlingly high illegitimacy rates, but increases from a range of 1 to 3 percent initially to 10 to 20 percent between 1750 and 1850 were commonplace. A profound sexual and cultural transformation was taking place. Fewer girls were abstaining from premarital intercourse, and fewer boys were marrying the girls they got pregnant.

It is hard to know exactly why this change occurred and what it meant. The old idea of a safe, late, economically secure marriage did not reflect economic and social realities. The growing freedom of thought in the turbulent years beginning with the French Revolution in 1789 influenced sexual and marital behavior. And illegitimate births, particularly in Germany, were also the result of open rebellion against class laws limiting the right of the poor to marry. Unable to show a solid financial position and thereby obtain a marriage license, couples asserted their independence and lived together anyway. Children were the natural and desired result of "true love" and greater freedom. Eventually, when the stuffy old-fashioned propertied classes gave in and repealed their laws against "imprudent marriage," poor couples once again went to the altar, often accompanied by their children, and the number of illegitimate children declined.

More fundamentally, the need to seek work outside farming and the village made young people more mobile. Mobility in turn encouraged new sexual and marital relationships, which were less subject to parental pressure and village tradition. As in the case of young servant girls who became pregnant and were then forced to fend for themselves, some of these relationships promoted loose living or prostitution. This resulted in more illegitimate births and strengthened an urban subculture of habitual illegitimacy.

### EARLY SEXUAL EMANCIPATION?

It has been suggested that the increase in illegitimate births represented a stage in the emancipation of women. According to this view, new economic opportunities outside the home, in the city and later in the factory, revolutionized women's attitudes about themselves. Young working women became individualistic and rebelled against old restrictions like late marriage. They sought fulfillment in the pleasure of sexuality. Since there was little birth control, freer sex for single women meant more illegitimate babies.

No doubt single working women in towns and cities were of necessity more independent and self-reliant. Yet, until at least the late nineteenth century, it seems unlikely that such young women were motivated primarily by visions of emancipation and sexual liberation. Most women were servants or textile workers. These jobs paid poorly, and the possibility of a truly independent "liberated" life was correspondingly limited. Most women in the city probably looked to marriage and family life as an escape from hard, poorly paid work and as the foundation of a satisfying life.

Hopes and promises of marriage from men of the working girl's own class led naturally enough to sex.[6] In one medium-sized French city in 1787–1788 the great majority of unwed mothers stated that sexual intimacy had followed promises of marriage. Many soldiers, day laborers, and male servants were no doubt sincere in their proposals. But their lives were insecure, and many hesitated to take on the heavy economic burdens of wife and child. Nor were their backbones any longer stiffened by the traditional pressures of the village.

In a growing number of cases, therefore, the intended marriage did not take place. The romantic yet practical dreams and aspirations of many young working women and men were frustrated by low wages, inequality, and changing economic and social conditions. Old patterns of marriage and family were breaking down among the common people. Only in the late nineteenth century would more stable patterns reappear.

## WOMEN AND CHILDREN

In the traditional framework of preindustrial Europe women married late, but then began bearing children rapidly. If a woman married before she was thirty, and if both she and her husband lived to forty-five, the chances were roughly one in two that she would give birth to six or more children. The newborn child entered a dangerous world. Infant mortality – the number of babies who would die

THE FACE OF POVERTY  *A poor Italian peasant woman nurses her infant and stoically begs for her children in this realistic painting by Ceruti. Begging was quite common in the eighteenth century. (Collection G. Testori, Novate)*

before their first birthday – was high. One in five was sure to die, and one in three was quite likely to in the poorer areas. Newborn children are very likely to catch infectious diseases of the stomach and chest. Not until the late nineteenth century were these diseases and their treatment understood. Thus little could be done for an ailing child, even in rich families. Childhood itself was dangerous. Parents in preindustrial Europe could count themselves fortunate if half their children lived to adulthood.

### CHILD CARE AND NURSING

Women of the lower classes generally breastfed their infants, and for much longer periods than is customary today. Breast-feeding de-

creases the likelihood of pregnancy for the average woman by delaying the resumption of ovulation. Although women may have been only vaguely aware of the link between nursing and not getting pregnant, they were spacing their children – from two and a half to three or more years apart in many communities – and limiting their fertility by nursing their babies. If a newborn baby died, nursing stopped and a new life could be created. Nursing also saved lives: the breast-fed infant was more likely to survive on its mother's milk than on any artificial foods. In many areas of Russia, where common practice was to give a new child a sweetened (and germ-ladened) rag to suck on for its subsistence, half the babies did not survive for the first year.

In contrast to the laboring poor, the women of the aristocracy and upper middle class seldom nursed their own children. The upper-class woman felt that breast-feeding was crude and common, and well beneath her dignity. Instead she hired a wet nurse – a nursing mother from the poor – to suckle her child. The mother of more modest means – the wife of a shopkeeper or artisan – also commonly used a wet nurse, sending her baby to some poor woman in the country as soon as possible.

Wet-nursing was a very widespread and flourishing business in the eighteenth century, a dismal business within the framework of the putting-out system. The traffic was in babies rather than in wool and cloth, and two or three years often passed before the wet-nurse worker finished her task. The great French historian Jules Michelet described with compassion the plight of the wet nurse, who was still going to the homes of the rich in the early nineteenth century in France:
*People do not know how much these poor women are exploited and abused, first by the vehicles*

*which transport them (often barely out of their confinement), and afterward by the employment of-fices which place them. Taken as nurses on the spot, they must send their own child away, and conse-quently it often dies. They have no contact with the family that hires them, and they may be dis-missed at the first caprice of the mother or doctor. If the change of air and place should dry up their milk, they are discharged without any compensa-tion. If they stay there [in the city] they pick up the habits of the easy life, and they suffer enor-mously when they are forced to return to their life of [rural] poverty. A good number become servants in order to stay in the town. They never rejoin their husbands, and the family is broken.*[7]

Other observers noted the flaws of wet nurses. It was a common belief that a nurse passed her bad traits to the baby with her milk. When a child turned out poorly, it was assumed that "the nurse changed it." Many observers charged that nurses were often neg-ligent and greedy. They claimed that there were large numbers of "killing nurses" with whom no child ever survived. The nurse let the child die quickly, so that she could take another child and another fee. No matter how the adults fared in the wet-nurse business, the child was a certain loser.

## FOUNDLINGS AND INFANTICIDE

In the ancient world and in Asian societies it was not uncommon to allow or force new-born babies, particularly girl babies, to die when there were too many mouths to feed. To its great and eternal credit the early medieval church, strongly influenced by Jewish law, de-nounced infanticide as a pagan practice and insisted that every human life was sacred. The willful destruction of newborn children be-came a crime punishable by death. And yet, as the reference to "killing nurses" suggests, direct and indirect methods of eliminating

unwanted babies did not disappear. There were, for example, many cases of "overlay-ing" – parents rolling over and suffocating the child placed between them in their bed. Such parents claimed they were drunk and had acted unintentionally. In Austria in 1784, suspicious authorities made it illegal for parents to take children under five into bed with them. Severe poverty on the one hand, and increasing illegitimacy on the other, con-spired to force the very poor to thin their own ranks.

The young girl – very likely a servant – who could not provide for her child had few choices. If she would not stoop to abortion or the services of a killing nurse, she could bun-dle up her baby and leave it on the doorstep of a church. In the late seventeenth century Saint Vincent de Paul was so distressed by the number of babies brought to the steps of Notre Dame in Paris that he established a home for foundlings. Others followed his ex-ample. In England the government acted on a petition calling for a foundling hospital "to prevent the frequent murders of poor, misera-ble infants at birth" and "to suppress the in-human custom of exposing newborn children to perish in the streets."

In much of Europe in the eighteenth cen-tury, foundling homes became a favorite charity of the rich and powerful. Great sums were spent on them. The foundling home in St. Petersburg, perhaps the most elaborate and lavish of its kind, occupied the former palaces of two members of the high nobility. In the early nineteenth century it had 25,000 chil-dren in its care and was receiving 5,000 new babies a year. At their best, the foundling homes of the eighteenth century were a good example of Christian charity and social con-cern in an age of great poverty and inequality.

Yet the foundling home was no panacea. By the 1770s, one-third of all babies born in

ABANDONED CHILDREN *At this Italian found-lings' home a frightened, secretive mother could discreetly deposit her baby. (Bettmann Archive)*

Paris were immediately abandoned to the foundling home by their mothers. Fully a third of all those foundlings were abandoned by married couples, a powerful commentary on the standard of living among the working poor, for whom an additional mouth to feed often meant tragedy. In London competition for space in the foundling home soon became so great that it led "to the disgraceful scene of women scrambling and fighting to get to the door, that they might be of the fortunate few to reap the benefit of the Asylum."[8]

Furthermore, great numbers of babies entered, but few left. Even in the best of these homes half the babies normally died within a year. In the worst, fully 90 percent did not survive! They succumbed to long journeys over rough roads, the intentional and unintentional neglect of their wet nurses, and the customary childhood illnesses. So great was the carnage that some contemporaries called the foundling hospitals "legalized infanticide."

Certainly, some parents and officials looked upon the hospitals as a dump for unwanted babies. In the early 1760s, when the London Foundling Hospital was obliged to accept all babies offered, it was deluged with babies from the countryside. Many parish officers placed with the foundling home the abandoned children in their care, just as others apprenticed five-year-old children to work in factories. Both practices reduced the cost of welfare at the local level. Throughout the eighteenth century, millions of children of the poor continued to exit after the briefest of appearances upon the earthly stage. True, they died after being properly baptized, an important consideration in still-Christian Europe. Yet those people who would dream of an idyllic past should do well to ponder the foundling's fate.

## ATTITUDES TOWARD CHILDREN

What were the more typical circumstances of children's lives? Did the treatment of foundlings reflect the attitudes of normal parents? Harsh as it may sound, the young child was very often of little concern to its parents and to society in the eighteenth century. This indifference toward children was found in all classes; rich children were by no means exempt. The practice of using wet nurses, who were casually selected and often negligent, is one example of how even the rich and the prosperous put the child out of sight and out of mind. One French moralist, writing in 1756 about how to improve humanity, observed that "one blushes to think of loving one's children." It has been said that the English gentleman of the period "had more interest in the diseases of his horses than of his children."[9]

Parents believed that the world of the child was an uninteresting one. When parents did stop to notice their offspring, they often treated them as dolls or playthings – little puppies to fondle and cuddle in a moment of relaxation. The psychological distance between parent and child remained vast.

Much of the indifference was due to the terrible frequency, the terrible banality, of death among children of all classes. Parents simply could not afford to become too emotionally involved with their children, who were so unlikely to survive. The great eighteenth-century English historian Edward Gibbon (1737–1794) wrote that "the death of a new born child before that of its parents may seem unnatural but it is a strictly probable event, since of any given number the greater part are extinguished before the ninth year, before they possess the faculties of the mind and the body." Gibbon's father named all his boys Edward, hoping that at least one of them would survive to carry his name. His prudence was not misplaced. Edward the future historian and eldest survived. Five brothers and sisters who followed him all died in infancy.

Doctors were seldom interested in the care of children. One contemporary observer quoted a famous doctor as saying that "he never wished to be called to a young child because he was really at a loss to know what to offer for it." There were "physicians of note who make no scruple to assert that there is nothing to be done for children when they are ill." Children were caught in a vicious circle: they were neglected because they were very likely to die, and they were likely to die because they were neglected.

Indifference toward children often shaded off into brutality. When parents and other adults did turn toward children, it was normally to discipline and control them. The novelist Daniel Defoe (1660?–1731), always delighted when he saw very young children working hard in cottage industry, coined the axiom "Spare the rod and spoil the child." He meant it. So did Susannah Wesley, mother of John Wesley (1703–1791), the founder of Methodism. According to her, the first task of a parent toward her children was "to conquer the will, and bring them to an obedient temper." She reported that her babies were "taught to fear the rod, and to cry softly; by which means they escaped the abundance of correction they might otherwise have had, and that most odious noise of the crying of children was rarely heard in the house, but the family lived in as much quietness as if there had not been a child among them."[10]

It was hardly surprising – indeed, it was quite predictable – that when English parish officials dumped their paupers into the first

THE FIVE SENSES    *Published in 1774, J. B. Base-*
*dow's* Elementary Reader *helped spread new atti-*
*tudes toward child development and education.*
*Drawing heavily upon the theories of Locke and*
*Rousseau, the German educator advocated nature*
*study and contact with everyday life. In this illustra-*
*tion for Basedow's reader, gentle teachers allow un-*
*corrupted children to learn about the five senses*
*through direct experience. (Photo: Caroline Buckler)*

factories late in the eighteenth century, the
children were beaten and brutalized, as we
shall see. That was part of the childrearing
pattern – widespread indifference on the one
hand and strict physical discipline on the
other – that prevailed through most of the
eighteenth century.

Late in the century this pattern came under
attack. Critics like Jean-Jacques Rousseau
called for greater love, tenderness, and understanding toward children. In addition to supporting foundling homes to discourage
infanticide and urging wealthy women to

nurse their own babies, these new voices ridiculed the practice of swaddling. Wrapping
youngsters in tight-fitting clothes and blankets
was generally believed to form babies properly
by "straightening them out." By the end of
the century small children were often dressed
in simpler, more comfortable clothing, allowing much greater freedom of movement.
More parents expressed a delight in the love
and intimacy of the child and found real pleasure in raising their offspring. These changes
were part of the general growth of humanitarianism and optimism about human poten-

tial that characterized the eighteenth-century Enlightenment.

## SCHOOLS AND EDUCATION

The role of formal education outside the home, in those special institutions called schools, was growing more important. The aristocracy and the rich had led the way in the sixteenth century with special colleges, often run by the Jesuits. But "little schools," charged with elementary education of the children of the masses, did not appear until the seventeenth century. Unlike medieval schools, which mingled all age groups, the little schools specialized in boys and girls from seven to twelve, who were instructed in basic literacy and religion.

Although large numbers of common people got no education at all in the eighteenth century, the beginnings of popular education were recognizable. France made a start in 1682 with the establishment of Christian schools, which taught the catechism and prayers as well as reading and writing. The Church of England and the dissenting congregations established "charity schools" to instruct the children of the poor. As early as 1717, Prussia made attendance at elementary schools compulsory. Inspired by the old Protestant idea that every believer should be able to read and study the Bible in the quest for personal salvation, and by the new idea of a population capable of effectively serving the state, Prussia led the way in the development of universal education. Religious motives were also extremely important elsewhere. From the middle of the seventeenth century, Presbyterian Scotland was convinced that the path to salvation lay in careful study of the Scriptures, and this belief led to an effective network of parish schools for rich and poor alike. The Enlightenment commitment to greater knowledge through critical thinking reinforced interest in education in the eighteenth century.

The result of these efforts was a remarkable growth of basic literacy between 1600 and 1800, especially after 1700. Whereas in 1600 only one male in six was barely literate in France and Scotland, and one in four in England, by 1800 almost 90 percent of the Scottish male population was literate. At the same time two out of three males were literate in France, and in advanced areas such as Normandy literacy approached 90 percent. More than half of English males were literate by 1800. In all three countries the bulk of the jump occurred in the eighteenth century. Women were also increasingly literate, although they probably lagged behind men somewhat in most countries. (For example, in England in 1840 – the first date for which there is complete census evidence – two-thirds of newly married men and half of newly married women were literate.) Some elementary education was becoming a reality for European peoples, and schools were of growing significance in everyday life.

## THE EUROPEAN'S FOOD

Plague, starvation, and economic crisis, which recurred often in the seventeenth century, gradually disappeared in the eighteenth century. This phenomenon probably accounts in large part for the rapid growth in the total number of Europeans and for their longer lives. The increase in the average life span, allowing for regional variations, was remarkable. In 1700, the average European could expect at birth to live only twenty-five years. A century later, a newborn European could expect to live fully ten years longer, to age thirty-five. The doubling of the adult life span meant that there was more time to produce and create, and more reason for parents to stress learning and preparation for adulthood.

People also lived longer because ordinary years were progressively less deadly. People ate better and somewhat more wisely. Doctors and hospitals probably saved a few more lives than they had in the past. How and why did health and life expectancy improve, and how much did they improve? And what were the differences between rich and poor? To answer these questions, it is necessary first to follow the eighteenth-century family to the table, and then to see what contribution doctors made.

## DIETS AND NUTRITION

Although the accomplishments of doctors and hospitals are constantly in the limelight today, the greater if less spectacular part of medicine is preventive medicine. The great breakthrough of the second half of the nineteenth century was the development of public health techniques – proper sanitation and mass vaccinations – to prevent outbreaks of communicable diseases. Even before the nineteenth century, when medical knowledge was slight and doctors were of limited value, prevention was the key to longer life. Good clothing, warm dry housing, and plentiful food make for healthier populations, much more capable of battling off disease. Clothing and housing for the masses probably improved only modestly in the eighteenth century, but the new agricultural methods and increased agricultural output had a beneficial effect. The average European ate more and better food and was healthier as a result in 1800 than in 1700. This pattern is apparent if we look at the fare of the laboring poor.

At the beginning of the eighteenth century, ordinary men and women depended on grain as fully as they had in the past. Bread was quite literally the staff of life. Peasants in the Beauvais region of France ate two pounds of bread a day, washing it down with water, green wine, beer, or (if they were lucky) a little skimmed milk. Their dark bread was made from a mixture of rough-ground wheat and rye – the standard flour of the poor. The poor also ate grains in soup and gruel. In rocky northern Scotland, for example, people depended on oatmeal, which they often ate half-cooked so it would swell in their stomachs and make them feel full. No wonder, then, that the supply of grain and the price of bread were always critical questions for most of the population.

The poor, rural and urban, also ate a fair quantity of vegetables. Indeed, vegetables were considered "poor people's food." Peas and beans were probably the most common; grown as field crops in much of Europe since the Middle Ages, they were eaten fresh in late spring and summer. Dried, they became the basic ingredients in the soups and stews of the long winter months. In most regions other vegetables appeared on the tables of the poor in season, primarily cabbages, carrots, and wild greens. Fruit was uncommon and limited to the summer months.

The European poor loved meat and eggs, but even in England – the wealthiest country in Europe in 1700 – they seldom ate their fill. Meat was too expensive. When the poor did eat meat – on a religious holiday or at a wedding or other special occasion – it was most likely lamb or mutton. Sheep could survive on rocky soils and did not compete directly with humans for the slender resources of grain.

Milk was rarely drunk. It was widely believed that milk caused sore eyes, headaches, and a variety of ills, except among the very young and very old. Milk was used primarily to make cheese and butter, which the poor liked but could afford only occasionally. Medical and popular opinion considered whey, the watery liquid left after milk was churned, "an excellent temperate drink."

The diet of the rich – aristocrats, officials, and the comfortable bourgeoisie – was traditionally quite different from that of the poor. The men and women of the upper classes were rapacious carnivores, gorging on meat, meat, and more meat. To a large extent a person's standard of living and economic well-being was judged by the amount of meat eaten. A truly elegant dinner among the great and the powerful consisted of one rich meat after another – a chicken pie, a leg of lamb, a grilled steak, for example. Three separate meat courses might be followed by three fish courses, laced with piquant sauces and complemented with sweets, cheeses, and nuts of all kinds. Fruits and vegetables were not often found on the tables of the rich. The long-standing dominance of meat and fish in the diet of the upper classes continued throughout the eighteenth century. There was extravagant living, and undoubtedly great overeating and gluttony, not only among the aristocracy but among the prosperous business and professional classes as well.

There was also an enormous amount of drunkenness and overdrinking among the rich. The English squire, for example, who loved to ride with his hounds, loved drink with a similar passion. He became famous as the "four-bottle man." With his dinner he drank red wine from France or white wine from the Rhineland, and with his dessert he took sweet but strong port or Madeira from Portugal. Sometimes he ended the evening under the table in a drunken stupor, but very often he did not. The wine and the meat were consumed together in long hours of sustained excess, permitting the "gentleman" and his guests to drink enormous quantities.

The diet of small traders, master craftsmen, minor bureaucrats – the people of the towns and cities – was probably less monotonous than that of the peasantry. The markets, stocked by market gardens in the outskirts, provided a substantial variety of meats, vegetables, and fruits, although bread and beans still formed the bulk of the poor family's diet.

There were also regional dietary differences in 1700. Generally speaking, northern, Atlantic Europe ate better than southern Mediterranean Europe. The poor of England probably ate best of all. Contemporaries on both sides of the Channel often contrasted the Englishman's consumption of meat with the French peasant's greater dependence on bread and vegetables. The Dutch were also considerably better fed than the average European, in large part because of their advanced agriculture and diversified gardens.

### THE IMPACT OF DIET ON HEALTH

How were the poor and the rich served by their quite different diets? Good nutrition depends on a balanced supply of food, as well as on an adequate number of calories. Modern research has shown that the chief determinant of nutritional balance is the relationship between carbohydrates (sugar and starch) and proteins. A diet consisting primarily of carbohydrates is seriously incomplete.

At first glance the diet of the laboring poor, relying as it did on carbohydrates, seems unsatisfactory. Even when a peasant got his daily two or three pounds of bread, his supply of protein and essential vitamins would seem too low. A closer look reveals a brighter picture. Most bread was "brown" or "black," made from wheat or rye. Flour was quite different from that used in the mushy white bread of an American supermarket. The flour of the eighteenth century was a whole-meal flour, produced by stone grinding. It contained most of the bran – the ground-up husk – and the all-important wheat germ. The bran and germ contain higher proportions of some minerals, vitamins, and good-quality proteins than does the rest of the grain. Only when they are removed does bread become a foodstuff providing relatively more starch and less of the essential nutrients.

In addition, the field peas and beans eaten by poor people since Carolingian days contained protein that complemented the proteins in whole-meal bread. The proteins in whey, cheese, and eggs, which the poor ate at least occasionally, also supplemented the value of the protein in the bread and vegetables. Indeed, a leading authority concludes that if a pint of milk and some cheese and whey were eaten each day, the balance of the poor people's diet "was excellent, far better indeed than in many of our modern diets."[11]

The basic bread-and-vegetables diet of the poor *in normal times* was satisfactory. It protected effectively against most of the disorders associated with a deficiency of the vitamin-B complex, for example. The lack of sugar meant that teeth were not so plagued by cavities. Constipation was almost unknown to peasants and laborers living on coarse cereal breads, which provided the roughage modern diets lack. The common diet of the poor also generally warded off anemia, although anemia among infants was not uncommon.

The key dietary problem was probably getting enough green vegetables (or milk), particularly in the late winter and early spring, to insure adequate supplies of vitamins A and C. A severe deficiency of vitamin C produces scurvy, an awful disease that leads to loose

teeth and rotting, stinking gums, swelling of the limbs, and great weakness. Before the season's first vegetables, many people had used up their bodily reserves of vitamin C and were suffering from mild cases of scurvy. Sailors on long voyages suffered most. By the end of the sixteenth century the exceptional antiscurvy properties of lemons and limes led to the practice of supplying some crews with a daily ration of lemon juice, which had highly beneficial effects. English sailors came to be known as "limeys" because of their habit of sucking on limes. "Scurvy grass" – a kind of watercress – also guarded against scurvy, and this disease was increasingly controlled on even the longest voyages.

The practice of gorging on meat, sweets, and spirits caused the rich their own nutritional problems. They too were very often deficient in vitamins A and C, because of their great disdain for fresh vegetables. Gout was a common affliction of the overfed and underexercised rich. No wonder they were often caricatured dragging their flabby limbs and bulging bellies to the table, to stuff their swollen cheeks and poison their livers. People of moderate means, who could afford some meat and dairy products with fair regularity but who had not abandoned the bread and vegetables of the poor, were probably best off from a nutritional standpoint.

## NEW FOODS AND NEW KNOWLEDGE

In nutrition and food consumption, Europe in the early eighteenth century had not gone

beyond its medieval accomplishments. This situation began to change markedly as the century progressed. Although the introduction of new methods of farming was confined largely to the Low Countries and England, a new food – the potato – came to the aid of the poor everywhere.

Introduced into Europe from the Americas, along with corn, squash, tomatoes, chocolate, and many other useful plants, the humble potato is an excellent food. It contains a good supply of carbohydrates and calories. More important, it is rich in vitamins A and C, especially if the skin is eaten and it is not overcooked. The lack of green vegetables that could lead to scurvy was one of the biggest deficiencies in the poor person's winter and early spring diet. The potato, which gave a much higher caloric yield than grain for a given piece of land, provided the needed vitamins and supplemented the bread-based diet. Doctors, increasingly aware of the dietary benefits of potatoes, prescribed them for the general public and in institutions such as schools and prisons.

For some poor people, especially desperately poor peasants who needed to get every possible calorie from a tiny plot of land, the potato replaced grain as the primary food in the eighteenth century. This happened first in Ireland, where in the seventeenth century Irish rebellion had led to English repression and the perfection of a system of exploitation worthy of the most savage Eastern tyrant. The foreign (and Protestant) English landlords took the best land, forcing large numbers of poor (and Catholic) peasants to live off tiny scraps of rented ground. By 1700, the poor in Ireland lived almost exclusively on the bountiful fruits of the potato plot. And since intensive cultivation gave so much good food from so little land, ever more people were able to eke out a meager existence.

Elsewhere in Europe the potato took hold more slowly. Potatoes were first fed to pigs and livestock, and there was considerable debate over whether they were fit for humans. In Germany the severe famines caused by the Seven Years' War (page 651) settled the matter: potatoes were edible and no "famine food." By the end of the century the potato was an important dietary supplement in much of Europe.

There was also a general growth of market gardening and a greater variety of vegetables in towns and cities. Potatoes, cabbages, peas, beans, radishes, spinach, asparagus, lettuce, parsnips, carrots, and other vegetables were much more common. They were sold in central markets and streets, from "moveable shops that run upon wheels, attended by ill looking fellows," according to one London observer. In the course of the eighteenth century the large towns and cities of maritime Europe began to receive semitropical fruit, such as oranges, lemons, and limes, from Portugal and the West Indies, although they were not cheap.

The growing variety of food was matched by some improvement in knowledge about diet and nutrition. For the poor, such improvement was limited primarily to the insight that the potato and other root crops improved health in the winter and helped to prevent scurvy. The rich began to be aware of the harmful effects of their meat-ladened, wine-drowned meals.

The waning influence of Galen's medical teachings was another aspect of progress. Galen's Roman synthesis of ancient medical doctrines held that the four basic elements – air, fire, water, and earth – combine to produce in each person a complexion and a corresponding temperament. Foods were grouped into four categories appropriate for each complexion. Galen's notions dominated the dietary thinking of the seventeenth-century medical profession: "Galen said that the flesh of a hare preventeth fatness, causeth sleep and cleanseth the blood," and so on for a thousand things.

Conventional wisdom had also held, quite erroneously, that vegetables and fruits caused poor health. Vegetables were seen as "windy" and tending to cause fevers, and fruits were considered dangerous except in very small amounts. Similarly, butter, an excellent food rich in vitamin A, which the poor used on bread whenever they could, was regarded with great suspicion by the rich and the medical profession. It was believed bad for children because, according to typical opinion, it choked the "glands and capillaries" and made children "weakly, corpulent, big-belly'd, very subject to breakings-out, and to breed lice."

The growth of scientific experimentation in the seventeenth century led to a generally beneficial questioning of the old views. Haphazardly, by trial and error, and influenced by advances in chemistry, saner ideas developed. Experiments with salts led to the belief that foods were by nature either acid (all fruits and most vegetables) or alkaline (all meats). Doctors and early nutritionists came to believe that one key to good health was a *balance* of the two types.

An English doctor writing at the end of the century as the "Soldier's Friend" on "the means of preserving the health of military men" stated categorically that "ripe fruits, in moderate quantity, are wholesome; and, contrary to the vulgar prejudice, tend rather to prevent than to induce bowel complaints."[12] Excessive consumption of meat was identified by some medical men as a dangerous practice. Gout, the class hazard of the rich, was linked with overeating and lack of exercise. Thus, the eighteenth century saw increased understanding of the importance of a balanced diet

for proper health. Such awareness – and the potato – were no doubt important factors in the rise in life expectancy and the growth of Europe's population.

Not all changes in the eighteenth century were for the better. Bread began to change, most noticeably in England. Rising incomes and new tastes led to a shift from whole-meal black or brown bread to white bread made from finely ground and sifted flour. On the Continent such white bread was generally limited to the well-to-do. To the extent that the preferred wheaten flour was stone-ground and sifted for coarse particles only, white bread remained satisfactory. But the desire for "bread as white as snow" was already leading to a decline in nutritional value.

The coarser bran, which is necessary for roughage, and at least some of the germ, which darkened the bread but contained the grain's nutrients, were already being sifted out to some extent. Bakers in English cities added the chemical alum to their white loaves to make them smoother, whiter, and larger. In the nineteenth century, "improvements" in milling were to lead to the removal of almost all the bran and germ from the flour, leaving it perfectly white and perfectly reduced in nutritional value. The only saving grace in the sad deterioration of bread was that people began to eat less of it and therefore depended on it less.

Another sign of nutritional decline was the growing consumption of sweets in general and sugar in particular. Initially a luxury, sugar dropped rapidly in price, as slave-based production increased in the Americas, and it was much more widely used in the eighteenth century. This development probably led to an increase in cavities and to other ailments as well. Overconsumption of refined sugar can produce, paradoxically, low blood sugar (hypoglycemia) and, for some individuals at least, a variety of physical and mental ailments. Of course the greater or lesser poverty of the laboring poor saved most of them from the problems of the rich and well-to-do.

## MEDICAL SCIENCE AND THE SICK

Advances in medical science played a very small part in improving the health and lengthening the lives of people in the eighteenth century. Such seventeenth-century advances as William Harvey's discovery of the circulation of blood were not soon translated into better treatment. The sick had to await the medical revolution of the later nineteenth century for much help from doctors.

Yet developments in medicine reflected the general thrust of the Enlightenment. The prevailing focus on discovering the laws of nature and on human problems, rather than on God and the heavens, gave rise to a great deal of research and experimentation. The century saw a remarkable rise in the number of doctors, and a high value was placed on their services. Thus when the great breakthroughs in knowledge came in the nineteenth century, they could be rapidly diffused and applied. Eighteenth-century medicine, in short, gave promise of a better human existence, but most of the realization lay far in the future.

### THE MEDICAL PROFESSIONALS

Care of the sick was the domain of several competing groups – faith healers, apothecaries, surgeons, and physicians. Since the great majority of common ailments have a tendency to cure themselves, each group could point to successes and win adherents. When the doctor's treatment made the patient worse, as it

often did, the original medical problem could always be blamed.

Faith healers, who had been one of the most important kinds of physicians in medieval Europe, remained active. They and their patients believed that demons and evil spirits caused disease by lodging in people and that the proper treatment was to exorcise or drive out the offending devil. Good Christians became exorcists: had not Jesus himself cured by casting out devils? The men and women who cast out devils had to be careful to keep their mouths closed, for the devil could jump from the patient's mouth into their own. By the eighteenth century, this demonic view of disease was still common among the poor, especially in the countryside, as was faith in the healing power of religious relics, prayer, and the laying on of hands. Faith healing was particularly effective in the treatment of mental disorders like hysteria and depression, where the link between attitude and illness is most direct.

Apothecaries, or pharmacists, sold a vast number of herbs, drugs, and patent medicines for every conceivable "temperament and distemper." Early pharmacists were seldom regulated, and they frequently diagnosed as freely as the doctors whose prescriptions they filled. Their prescriptions were incredibly complex – a hundred or more drugs might be included in a single prescription – and often very expensive. Some of the drugs undoubtedly worked: strong laxatives were given to the rich for their constipated bowels. The apothecary regularly and profitably administered enemas for the same purpose. Indeed, the medical profession continued to believe that regular "purging" of the bowels was essential for good health and the treatment of illness. Much purging was harmful, however, and only bloodletting for the treatment of disease was more effective in speeding patients to their graves.

Drugs were prescribed and concocted in a helter-skelter way. With so many different drugs being combined, it was impossible to isolate cause and effect. Nor was there any standardization. A complicated prescription filled by ten different pharmacists would result in ten different preparations with different medical properties.

Surgeons competed vigorously with barbers and "bone benders," the forerunners of chiropractors. The eighteenth-century surgeon (and patient) labored in the face of incredible difficulties. Almost all operations were performed without any pain killer, for anesthesia was believed too dangerous. The terrible screams of people whose limbs were being sawed off shattered hospitals and battlefields. Such operations were common, because a surgeon faced with an extensive wound sought to obtain a plain surface that he could cauterize with fire. Thus, if a person broke an arm or a leg and the bone stuck out, off came the limb. Many patients died from the agony and shock of such operations.

Surgery was also performed in the midst of filth and dirt. There simply was no knowledge of bacteriology and the nature of infection. The simplest wound treated by a surgeon festered, often fatally. In fact, surgeons encouraged wounds to fester in the belief — a remnant of Galen's theory — that the pus was beneficially removing the base portions of the body.

Physicians, the fourth major group, were trained like surgeons. They were apprenticed in their teens to a practicing physician for several years of on-the-job training. This training was then rounded out with hospital work or some university courses. To their credit, physicians in the eighteenth century

KNIVES FOR BLOODLETTING   *In the eighteenth century doctors continued to use these diabolical instruments to treat almost every illness, with disastrous results. (Courtesy, World Heritage Museum. Photo: Caroline Buckler)*

were increasingly willing to experiment with new methods, but the hand of Galen lay heavily upon them. Bloodletting was still considered a medical cure-all. It was the way "bad blood," the cause of illness, was removed and the balance of humors necessary for good health restored.

According to a physician practicing medicine in Philadelphia in 1799, "No operation of surgery is so frequently necessary as bleeding.... But though practiced by midwives, gardeners, blacksmiths, etc., very few know when it is proper." The good doctor went on to explain that bleeding was proper at the onset of all inflammatory fevers, in all inflammations, and for "asthma, sciatic pains, coughs, head-aches, rheumatisms, the apoplexy, epilepsy, and bloody fluxes." It was also necessary after all falls, blows, and bruises. The doctor warned against bleeding children with leeches, the common practice. With leeches, it was impossible to know the quantity of blood taken, and "the bleeding is often very difficult to stop, and the wounds are not easily healed."[13] With a little care, he advised, a child could be bled with a knife as easily as an adult.

Physicians, like apothecaries, laid great stress on purging. They also generally believed that disease was caused by bad odors, and for this reason they carried canes whose heads contained ammonia salts. As they made their rounds in the filthy, stinking hospitals, physicians held their canes to their noses to protect themselves from illness.

While ordinary physicians were bleeding, apothecaries purging, surgeons sawing, and faith healters praying, the leading medical thinkers were attempting to pull together and assimilate all the information and misinformation they had been accumulating. The attempt was ambitious: to systematize medicine around simple, basic principles, as Newton had done in physics. But the schools of thought resulting from such speculation and theorizing did little to improve medical care. Proponents of animism explained life and disease in terms of *anima,* the "sensitive soul," which they believed was present throughout the body and prevented its decay and self-destruction. Another school, vitalism, stressed "the vital principle," which inhabited all parts of the body. Vitalists tried to classify diseases systematically.

More interesting was the homeopathic system of Samuel Hahnemann of Leipzig. Hahnemann believed that very small doses of drugs that produce certain symptoms in a healthy person will cure a sick person with those symptoms. This theory was probably preferable to most eighteenth-century treatments, in that it was a harmless alternative to the extravagant and often fatal practices of bleeding, purging, drug taking, and induced vomiting. The patient gained confidence, and the body had at least a fighting chance of recovering. Hahnemann engaged in bitter debate with the apothecaries, whom he accused of incompetence and greed with their expensive treatments.

## HOSPITALS

Hospitals were terrible throughout most of the eighteenth century. There was no isolation of patients. Operations were performed in the patient's bed. The nurses were old, ignorant, greedy, and often drunk women. Fresh air was considered harmful, and infections of every kind were rampant. Diderot's article in the *Encyclopedia* on the Hôtel-Dieu in Paris, the "richest and most terrifying of all French hospitals," vividly describes normal conditions of the 1770s:

*Imagine a long series of communicating wards filled with sufferers of every kind of disease who are sometimes packed three, four, five or even six into a bed, the living alongside the dead and dying, the air polluted by this mass of unhealthy bodies, passing pestilential germs of their afflictions from one to the other, and the spectacle of suffering and agony on every hand. That is the Hôtel-Dieu.*

*The result is that many of these poor wretches come out with diseases they did not have when they went in, and often pass them on to the people they go back to live with. Others are half-cured and*

HOSPITAL LIFE *Patients crowded into hospitals like this one in Hamburg in 1746 had little chance of recovery. A priest by the window administers last rites, while in the center a surgeon coolly saws off the leg of a man who has received no anesthesia. (Germanisches Nationalmuseum, Nuremberg)*

*spend the rest of their days in an invalidism as hard to bear as the illness itself; and the rest perish, except for the fortunate few whose strong constitutions enable them to survive.*[14]

No wonder the poor of Paris hated hospitals and often saw confinement there as a plot to kill paupers.

In the last years of the century, the humanitarian concern already reflected in Diderot's description of the Hôtel-Dieu led to a movement for hospital reform through western Europe. Efforts were made to improve ventilation and eliminate filth, on the grounds that bad air caused disease. The theory was wrong, but the results were beneficial, since the spread of infection was somewhat reduced.

### MENTAL ILLNESS

Mental hospitals too were incredibly savage institutions. The customary treatment for mental illness was bleeding and cold water, administered more to maintain discipline than to effect a cure. Violent persons were chained to the wall and forgotten. A breakthrough of sorts occurred in the 1790s, when William Tuke founded the first humane sanatorium in

England. In Paris an innovative warden, Philippe Pinel, took the chains off the mentally disturbed in 1793 and tried to treat them as patients rather than prisoners.

In the eighteenth century, there were all sorts of wildly erroneous ideas about mental illness. One was that moonlight caused madness, a belief reflected in the word *lunatic* – someone harmed by lunar light. Another mid-eighteenth-century theory, which lasted until at least 1914, was that masturbation caused madness, not to mention acne, epilepsy, and premature ejaculation.

The initial form of this theory was the work of a Swiss doctor, Samuel Tissot. In 1758, Tissot argued that semen was

*the Essential Oil of the animal liquors . . . the dissipation whereof leaves the other humors weak. . . . The seminal liquor has so great an influence upon the corporeal powers that . . . the physicians of all ages have been unanimously of the opinion that the loss of an ounce of this humor would weaken more than that of forty ounces of blood.*[15]

This being the case, parents, religious institutions, and schools waged relentless war on masturbation by males, although they were curiously uninterested in female masturbation. In the nineteenth century this misguided idea was to reach its greatest height, resulting in increasingly drastic medical treatment. Doctors ordered their "patients" to wear mittens, fitted them with wooden braces between the knees, or simply tied them up in straitjackets.

## MEDICAL EXPERIMENTS AND RESEARCH

In the second half of the eighteenth century, medicine in general turned in a more practical and experimental direction. Some of the experimentation was creative quackery involving the recently discovered phenomenon of electricity. One magnificent quack, James Graham of London, opened a great hall filled with the walking sticks, crutches, eyeglasses, and ear trumpets of supposedly cured patients, which he kept as symbols of his victory over disease. Great glass globes, mysterious sphinxes, and the rich perfumes of burning incense awaited all who entered. Graham's principal treatment involved his Celestial Bed, which stood on forty pillars of rich glass and was decorated with magnets and electrical devices. Graham claimed that by sleeping in it youths would keep their good looks, their elders would be rejuvenated, and couples would have beautiful, healthy children. The fee for a single night in the Medico-Magnetico-Musico-Electrical Bed was £100 – a great sum of money.

The rich could buy expensive treatments, but the prevalence of quacks and the general lack of knowledge meant they often got little for their money. Because so many treatments were harmful, the poor were probably much less deprived by their almost total lack of access to medical care than one might think.

Renewed experimentation and the intensified search for solutions to human problems also led to some real advances in medicine after 1750, although most were still modest compared to the advances of the nineteenth and twentieth centuries. The eighteenth century's greatest medical triumph was the conquest of smallpox.

With the progressive decline of bubonic plague, smallpox became the most terrible of the infectious diseases. In the words of the historian Thomas Macaulay, "smallpox was always present, filling the churchyard with corpses, tormenting with constant fears all whom it had not stricken." In the seventeenth century, one in every four deaths in the British Isles was due to smallpox, and it is estimated that 60 million Europeans died of it in the eighteenth century. Fully 80 percent of the population was stricken at some point in life, and 25 percent of the total population was left permanently scarred. If ever a human problem cried out for a humane solution, it was smallpox.

The first step in the conquest of this killer came in the early eighteenth century. An English aristocrat whose great beauty had been marred by the pox, Lady Mary Wortley Montague, learned about the practice of inoculation in the Ottoman Empire while her husband was serving as British ambassador

there. She had her own son successfully inoculated in Constantinople, and was instrumental in spreading the practice in England after her return in 1722.

Inoculation against smallpox had long been practiced in the Middle East. The skin was deliberately broken, and a small amount of matter taken from the pustule of a smallpox victim was applied. The person thus contracted a mild case of smallpox that gave lasting protection against further attack. Inoculation was risky. Some of the very first to undergo it in England were felons sentenced to death, who were granted a pardon in return for inoculation. All these unsung heroes recovered and escaped hanging. Generally, about one person in fifty died from inoculation. Soon it was discovered that people who had been inoculated were just as infectious as those who had caught the disease by chance. Inoculated people thus spread the disease, and the practice of inoculation against smallpox was widely condemned in the 1730s.

Success in overcoming this problem in British colonies led the British College of Physicians in 1754 to strongly advocate inoculation. The procedure became complicated, however, involving elaborate and expensive preparatory treatment with bleeding, purging, blisters, and so on. Doctors reaped fine fees and large fortunes, and only people of substantial means could afford inoculation.

A successful search for cheaper methods led to something approaching mass inoculation in England in the 1760s. One specialist treated seventeen thousand patients and only five died. Both the danger and the cost had been reduced, and deadly smallpox struck all classes less frequently. On the Continent, the well-to-do were also inoculated, beginning with royal families like those of Maria Theresa and Catherine the Great. The practice then spread to the middle classes. Smallpox inoculation played some part in the decline of the death rate at the end of the century and the increase in population.

The final breakthrough against smallpox came at the end of the century. Edward Jenner (1749–1823), a talented country doctor, noted that in the English countryside there was a longstanding belief that dairy maids who had contracted cowpox did not get smallpox. Cowpox produces sores on the cow's udder and on the hands of the milker. The sores resemble those of smallpox, but the disease is mild and not contagious.

For eighteen years Jenner practiced a kind of Baconian science, carefully collecting data on protection against smallpox by cowpox. Finally, in 1796, he performed his first vaccination on a young boy, using matter taken from a milkmaid with cowpox. Two months later he inoculated the boy with smallpox pus, but the disease did not take. In the next two years twenty-three successful vaccinations were performed, and in 1798 Jenner published his findings. There was some skepticism and hostility, but after Austrian medical authorities replicated Jenner's results, the new method of treatment spread rapidly. Smallpox soon declined to the point of disappearance in Europe and then throughout the world. Jenner eventually received prizes of £30,000 from the British government for his great discovery, a fitting recompense for a man who gave an enormous gift to humanity and helped lay the foundation for the rise of the science of immunology in the nineteenth century. The struggle against fate and death, against the unknown but not unknowable, had won a great victory.

In recent years imaginative research has greatly increased the specialist's understanding of ordinary life and social patterns in the past. The human experience, as recounted by historians, has become richer and more meaningful, and many mistaken ideas have fallen. This has been particularly true of eighteenth-century, preindustrial Europe. The intimacies of family life, the contours of women's history and of childhood, and vital problems of medicine and nutrition are emerging from obscurity. Nor is this all. A deeper, truer understanding of the life of common people can shed light on the great economic and political developments of longstanding concern, as we shall see in the next chapter.

1. Quoted by J. M. Beattie, "The Criminality of Women in Eighteenth-Century England," *Journal of Social History* 8 (Summer 1975):86.

2. W. L. Langer, "Infanticide: A Historical Survey," *History of Childhood Quarterly* 1 (Winter 1974):357.

3. Quoted by R. Cobb, *The Police and the People: French Popular Protest, 1789–1820,* Clarendon Press, Oxford, 1970, p. 238.

4. Quoted by E. A. Wrigley, *Population and History,* McGraw-Hill, New York, 1969, p. 127.

5. Quoted in D. S. Landes, ed., *The Rise of Capitalism,* Macmillan, New York, 1966, pp. 56–57.

6. See L. A. Tilly, J. W. Scott, and M. Cohen, "Women's Work and European Fertility Patterns," *Journal of Interdisciplinary History* 6 (Winter 1976):447–476.

7. J. Michelet, *The People,* trans. with an introduction by J. P. McKay, University of Illinois Press, Urbana, 1973 (original publication, 1846), pp. 38–39.

8. J. Brownlow, *The History and Design of the Foundling Hospital,* London, 1868, p. 7.

9. Quoted by B. W. Lorence, "Parents and Children in Eighteenth-Century Europe," *History of Childhood Quarterly* 2 (Summer 1974):1–2.

10. Ibid., pp. 13, 16.

11. J. C. Drummond and A. Wilbraham, *The Englishman's Food: A History of Five Centuries of English Diet,* 2nd ed., Jonathan Cape, London, 1958, p. 75.

12. Ibid., p. 235.

13. Quoted by L. S. King, *The Medical World of the Eighteenth Century,* University of Chicago Press, Chicago, 1958, p. 320.

14. Quoted by R. Sand, *The Advance to Social Medicine,* Staples Press, London, 1952, pp. 86–87.

15. Quoted by R. P. Neuman, "Masturbation, Madness, and the Modern Concepts of Childhood and Adolescence," *Journal of Social History* 8 (Spring 1975):2.

Although often ignored in many general histories of the Western world, social topics of the kind considered in this chapter flourish in specialized journals today. The articles cited in the Notes are typical of the exciting work being done, and the reader is strongly advised to take time to look through recent volumes of some leading journals: *Journal of Social History, Past and Present, History of Childhood Quarterly,* and *Journal of Interdisciplinary History.* In addition, the number of book-length studies has begun to expand rapidly.

Among general introductions to the history of the family, women, and children, E. A. Wrigley, *Population and History* (1969), is excellent. P. Laslett, *The World We Have Lost* (1965), is an exciting pioneering investigation of England before the Industrial Revolution, though some of his conclusions have been weakened by further research. Lawrence Stone, *The Family, Sex and Marriage in England, 1500–1800* (1977), is a brilliant general interpretation, and L. Tilly and J. Scott, *Women, Work and Family* (1978), is excellent. P. Ariès, *Centuries of Childhood: A Social History of Family Life* (1962), is another stimulating study. E. Shorter, *The Making of the Modern Family* (1975), is an all-too-lively and rather controversial interpretation. All four works are highly recommended. T. Rabb and R. I. Rothberg, eds., *The Family in History* (1973), is a good collection of articles dealing with both Europe and the United States. A. MacFarlane, *The Family Life of Ralph Josselin* (1970), is a brilliant re-creation of the intimate family circle of a seventeenth-century English clergyman who kept a detailed diary; MacFarlane's *Origins of English Individualism: The Family, Property and Social Transition* (1978) is a major work. I. Pinchbeck and M. Hewitt, *Children in English Society* (1973), is a good introduction. E. Flexner has written a fine biography on the early feminist Mary Wollstonecraft (1972). Various aspects of sexual relationships are treated imaginatively by M. Foucault, *The History of Sexuality* (1981), and R. Wheaton and T. Hareven, eds., *Family and Sexuality in French History* (1980).

J. Burnett, *A History of the Cost of Living* (1969), has a great deal of interesting information about what people spent their money on in the past and complements the fascinating work of J. C. Drummond and A. Wilbraham, *The Englishman's Food: A History of Five Centuries of English Diet* (1958). J. Knyveton, *Diary of a Surgeon in the Year 1751–1752* (1937), gives a contemporary's unforgettable picture of both eighteenth-century medicine and social customs. Good introductions to the evolution of medical practices are B. Ingles, *History of Medicine* (1965); O. Bettmann, *A Pictorial History of Medicine* (1956); and H. Haggard's old but interesting *Devils, Drugs, and Doctors* (1929). W. Boyd, *History of Western Education* (1966), is a standard survey, which may be usefully supplemented by an important article by L. Stone, "Literacy and Education in England, 1640–1900," *Past and Present* 42

(February 1969):69–139. M. D. George, *London Life in the Eighteenth Century* (1965), is a delightfully written book, while L. Chevalier, *Labouring Classes and Dangerous Classes* (1973), is a keen analysis of the poor people of Paris in a slightly later period. G. Rudé, *The Crowd in History, 1730–1848* (1964), is an innovative effort to see politics and popular protest from below. An important series edited by Robert Forster and Orest Ranuum considers neglected social questions such as diet, abandoned children, and deviants, as does Peter Burke's excellent study, *Popular Culture in Early Modern Europe* (1978). Finally, J. Howard, *State of the Prisons,* first published in 1777 and reissued in 1929, takes one on an exhaustive tour of European jails in the eighteenth century and shows the beginning of concern for humanitarian reform of unbelievably harsh penal conditions.

# CHAPTER 21

# THE REVOLUTION IN POLITICS,

# 1775–1814

THE LAST YEARS of the eighteenth century were a time of great upheaval. A series of revolutions and revolutionary wars challenged the old order of kings and aristocrats. The ideas of freedom and equality, ideas that have not stopped shaping the world since that era, flourished and spread. The revolution began in North America in 1775. Then in 1789 France, the largest and most influential country in Europe, became the leading revolutionary nation. It established first a constitutional monarchy, then a radical republic, and finally a new empire under Napoleon. The armies of France also joined forces with patriots and radicals abroad in an effort to establish new governments based on new principles throughout much of Europe. The world of modern domestic and international politics was born.

What caused this era of revolution? What were the ideas and objectives of the men and women who rose up violently to undo the established system? What were the gains and losses for privileged groups and for ordinary people in a generation of war and upheaval? These are the questions this chapter will seek to answer in an examination of the French and American revolutions.

## LIBERTY AND EQUALITY

Two ideas fueled the revolutionary period in both America and Europe: liberty and equality. What did eighteenth-century politicians and other people mean by liberty and equality, and why were those ideas so radical and revolutionary in their day?

The call for liberty was first of all a call for individual human rights. Even the most enlightened monarchs customarily claimed that it was their duty to regulate what people wrote and believed. Liberals of the revolutionary era protested such controls from on high. They demanded freedom to worship according to the dictates of their consciences instead of according to the politics of their prince. They demanded the end of censorship and the right to express their beliefs freely in print and at public meetings. They demanded freedom from arbitrary laws and from judges who simply obeyed orders from the government.

These demands for basic personal freedoms, which were incorporated into the American Bill of Rights and other liberal constitutions, were very far-reaching. Indeed, eighteenth-century revolutionaries demanded more freedom than most governments today believe it is desirable to grant. The Declaration of the Rights of Man, issued at the beginning of the French Revolution, proclaimed, "Liberty consists in being able to do anything that does not harm another person." A citizen's rights had, therefore, "no limits except those which assure to the other members of society the enjoyment of these same rights." Liberals called for the freedom of the individual to develop and to create to the fullest possible extent. In the context of aristocratic and monarchial forms of government that then dominated Europe, this was a truly radical idea.

The call for liberty was also a call for a new kind of government. The revolutionary liberals believed that the people were sovereign — that is, that the people alone had the authority to make laws limiting the individual's freedom of action. In practice, this system of government meant choosing legislators who represented the people and who were accountable to them. Moreover, liberals of the revolutionary era believed that every people —

every ethnic group – had this right of self-determination, and thus the right to form a free nation.

By equality, eighteenth-century liberals meant that all citizens were to have identical rights and civil liberties. Above all, the nobility had no right to special privileges based on the accident of birth.

Liberals did not define equality as meaning that everyone should be equal economically. Quite the contrary. As Thomas Jefferson wrote in an early draft of the American Declaration of Independence, before changing "property" to the more noble-sounding "happiness," everyone was equal in "the pursuit of property." Jefferson and other liberals certainly did not expect equal success in that pursuit. Great differences in wealth and income between rich and poor were perfectly acceptable to liberals. The essential point was that everyone should legally have an equal chance. French liberals and revolutionaries said they wanted "careers opened to talent." They wanted employment in government, in business, and in the professions to be based on ability, not on family background or legal status.

Equality of opportunity was a very revolutionary idea in eighteenth-century Europe. Legal inequality between classes and groups was the rule, not the exception. Society was still legally divided into groups with special privileges, such as the nobility and the clergy, and groups with special burdens, like the peasantry. In many countries, various middle-class groups – professionals, businessmen, townspeople, and craftsmen – enjoyed privileges that allowed them to monopolize all sorts of economic activity. It was this kind of economic inequality, an inequality based on artificial legal distinctions, against which liberals protested.

The ideas of liberty and equality – the central ideas of classical liberalism – have deep roots in Western history. The ancient Greeks and the Judeo-Christian tradition had affirmed for hundreds of years the sanctity and value of the individual human being. The Judeo-Christian tradition, reinforced by the Reformation, had long stressed personal responsibility on the part of both common folk and exalted rulers, thereby promoting the self-discipline without which liberty becomes anarchy. The hounded and persecuted Protestant radicals of the later sixteenth century had died for the revolutionary idea that individuals were entitled to their own religious beliefs.

Although the liberal creed had roots deep in the Western tradition, classical liberalism first crystallized at the end of the seventeenth century and during the Enlightenment of the eighteenth century.

Liberal ideas reflected the Enlightenment's stress on human dignity and human happiness on earth. They shared the Enlightenment's general faith in science, rationality, and progress: the adoption of liberal principles meant better government and a better society for all. Almost all the writers of the Enlightenment were passionately committed to greater personal liberty. They preached religious toleration, freedom of press and speech, and fair and equal treatment before the law. Yet many of the French philosophers – Voltaire was typical – believed that these liberties could be realized through the enlightened absolutism of a wise king or queen. A minority of eighteenth-century thinkers thought otherwise. It was these thinkers who were mainly responsible for wedding the liberal concept of self-government to the Enlightenment's concern with personal freedom and legal equality.

Almost all the great proponents of the liberal theory of self-government came from England and France. Two of them were particularly influential. John Locke, who was so influential in giving the Enlightenment new ideas about how human beings learn (page 641), turned to English history as a basis for his political theory. England's long political tradition rested, according to Locke, on "the rights of Englishmen" and on representative government through Parliament. Thus in the controversy over excluding the strong-minded James, Duke of York, from the English throne, Locke argued for strict limitations on monarchy in order to preserve liberty. An admirer of the great Whig noblemen who subsequently made the bloodless revolution of 1688 (pages 582–583), Locke maintained that a government that oversteps its proper function – protecting the natural rights of life, liberty, and private property – becomes a tyranny. In such extreme cases the people have the natural right of rebellion. Locke thought such drastic action could usually be avoided, if the government respected the rights of its citizens and the people were zealous in the defense of their liberty. Thus Locke helped to revive the powerful idea, inherited from ancient Greece and Rome (page 131), that there are natural or universal rights that are equally valid for all peoples and societies.

It is important to note that Locke's strong defense of economic liberty and private property was linked to his love of political freedom. Locke prophetically saw that there was a close relationship between economic freedom and political freedom. If a significant number of citizens, such as the large English landowners, were not economically independent, there would be no basis for independent political opposition. Locke's ideas, as well as those of other English thinkers who lauded liberty and denounced the danger of tyranny, were particularly popular in colonial America.

Few of the French philosophes were particularly interested in political theorizing, but the baron de Montesquieu (1689–1755) was a towering exception. Having made his name as a social satirist, he turned to liberal political philosophy in the course of the eighteenth century. Montesquieu was a great noble, and he was dismayed by the triumph of absolute government in France under Louis XIV. Inspired by the example of the physical sciences, Montesquieu set out to apply the critical method to the problem of government in *The Spirit of Laws* (1748). The result was a comparative study of republics, monarchies, and despotisms – a great pioneering inquiry in the emerging social sciences.

Fearful of the tyrannical possibility of an unrestrained state, as was Locke, Montesquieu developed the idea that despotism would be avoided if political power were divided – among legislative, executive, and judicial branches of government. Each branch would check the tendency of the other to usurp power and curtail liberty. Montesquieu especially admired England and the English balance of power among the king, the Parliament, and the independent courts. Montesquieu's theory of separation of powers had great impact: the constitutions of the young United States in 1789 and of France in 1791 were based in large part on this theory.

## THE ATTRACTION OF LIBERALISM

Locke and Montesquieu were spokesmen for liberal ideals. Were they also, as is often said, spokesmen for "a rising middle class," a class impatient with the pretensions of monarchy and the privileges of aristocracy? To some extent, they were. Equality before the law and equality of opportunity were ideals particularly dear to ambitious and educated bourgeois. Yet liberal ideas about individual rights and political freedom also appealed to much of the aristocracy, at least in western Europe and as formulated by Montesquieu. Representative government did not mean democracy, which liberal thinkers tended to equate with mob rule. Rather, they envisioned voting for representatives as being restricted to those who owned property, those with "a stake in society." England had shown the way. After 1688, it had combined a parliamentary system and considerable individual liberty with a restricted franchise and unquestionable aristocratic pre-eminence.

Eighteenth-century liberalism, then, appealed not only to the middle class, but also to some aristocrats. It found broad support among the educated elite and the substantial classes in western Europe. What it lacked from the beginning was strong mass support. For comfortable liberals, the really important questions were theoretical and political. They had no need to worry about their stomachs and the price of bread. For the much more numerous laboring poor, the great questions were immediate and economic. Getting enough to eat was the crucial challenge. These differences in outlook and well-being were to lead to many misunderstandings and disappointments for both groups in the revolutionary era.

## THE AMERICAN REVOLUTION, 1775–1789

The era of liberal revolution began in the New World. The thirteen mainland colonies of British North America revolted against their mother country and then succeeded in establishing a new unified government.

Americans have long debated the meaning of their revolution. Some have even questioned whether or not it was a real revolution, as opposed to a war for independence. According to some scholars, the revolution was conservative and defensive in that its demands were for the traditional liberties of Englishmen; Americans were united against the British, but otherwise they were a satisfied people and not torn by internal conflict. Other scholars have argued that, on the contrary, the American Revolution was quite radical. It split families between patriots and Loyalists and divided the country. It achieved goals that were fully as advanced as those obtained by the French in their great revolution a few years later.

How does one reconcile these positions? Both contain large elements of truth. The American revolutionaries did believe they were demanding only the traditional rights of English men and women. But those traditional rights were liberal rights, and in the American context they had very strong democratic and popular overtones. Thus, the American Revolution was fought in the name of established ideals that were still quite radical in the context of the times. And in founding a government firmly based on liberal principles, the Americans set an example that had a forceful impact on Europe and speeded up political development there.

### THE ORIGINS OF THE REVOLUTION

The American Revolution had its immediate origins in a squabble over increased taxes. The British government had fought and decisively won the Seven Years' War (page 682) on the strength of its professional army and navy.

*THE BOSTON TEA PARTY   In this 1789 engraving men disguised as Indians dump East India Company tea into the harbor. The large crowd on shore indicates widespread support. (Library of Congress)*

The American colonists had furnished little real aid. The high cost of the war to the British, however, had led to a doubling of the British national debt. Anticipating further expense defending its recently conquered western lands from Indian uprisings like that of Pontiac, the British government in London set about reorganizing the empire with a series of bold, largely unprecedented measures. Breaking with tradition, the British decided to maintain a large army in North America after peace was restored in 1763. Moreover, they sought to exercise strict control over their newly conquered western lands and to tax the colonies directly. In 1765, the government pushed through Parliament the Stamp Act, which levied taxes on a long list of commercial and legal documents, diplomas, pamphlets, newspapers, almanacs, dice, and playing cards. A stamp glued to each article indicated the tax had been paid.

The effort to increase taxes as part of tightening up the empire seemed perfectly reasonable to the British. Heavier stamp taxes had been collected in Great Britain for two generations, and Americans were being asked only to pay a share of their own defense. Moreover, Americans had been paying only very low local taxes. The Stamp Act would have doubled taxes to about two shillings per person. No other people in the world (except the Poles) paid so little. The British, meanwhile, paid the world's highest taxes in about 1765 – twenty-six shillings per person. It is not surprising that taxes per person in the newly independent American nation were much higher in 1785 than in 1765, when the British no longer subsidized American defense. The colonists protested the Stamp Act vigorously and violently, however, and after rioting and boycotts against British goods, Parliament reluctantly repealed the new tax.

As the fury of the Stamp Act controversy revealed, much more was involved than taxes. The key question was political. To what extent could the home government refashion the empire and reassert its power while limiting the authority of colonial legislatures and their elected representatives? Accordingly, who should represent the colonies, and who had the right to make laws for Americans? While a troubled majority of Americans searched hard for a compromise, some radicals began to proclaim that "taxation without representation is tyranny." The British government replied that Americans were represented in Parliament, albeit indirectly (like most Englishmen themselves), and that the absolute supremacy of Parliament throughout the empire could not be questioned. Many Americans felt otherwise. As John Adams put it, "A Parliament of Great Britain can have no more rights to tax the colonies than a Parliament of Paris." Thus imperial reorganization and Parliamentary supremacy came to appear as grave threats to Americans' existing liberties and time-honored institutions.

Americans had long exercised a great deal of independence and gone their own way. In British North America, unlike England and Europe, there was no powerful established church, and personal freedom in questions of religion was taken for granted. The colonial assemblies made the important laws, which were seldom overturned by the home govern-ment. The right to vote was much more widespread than in England. In many parts of colonial Massachusetts, for example, as many as 95 percent of the adult males could vote.

Moreover, greater political equality was matched by greater social and economic equality. Neither a hereditary nobility nor a hereditary serf population existed, although the slavery of the Americas consigned blacks to a legally oppressed caste. Independent farmers were the largest group in the country and set much of its tone. In short, the colonial experience had slowly formed a people who felt themselves separate and distinct from the home country. The controversies over taxation intensified those feelings of distinctiveness and separation and brought them to the fore.

In 1773, the dispute over taxes and representation flared up again. The British government had permitted the financially hard-pressed East India Company to ship its tea from China directly to its agents in the colonies, rather than through London middlemen who then sold to independent merchants in the colonies. Thus, the company secured a virtual monopoly on the tea trade, and colonial merchants were suddenly excluded from a highly profitable business. The colonists were quick to protest.

In Boston, men disguised as Indians had a rowdy "tea party," and threw the company's tea into the harbor. This led to extreme measures. The so-called Coercive Acts closed the port of Boston, curtailed local elections and town meetings, and greatly expanded the royal governor's power. County conventions in Massachusetts protested vehemently and urged that the acts be "rejected as the attempts of a wicked administration to enslave America." Other colonial assemblies joined in the denunciations. In September 1774, the First Continental Congress met in Philadelphia, where the more radical members argued successfully against concessions to the Crown. Compromise was also rejected by the British Parliament and in April 1775 fighting began at Lexington and Concord.

## INDEPENDENCE

The fighting spread, and the colonists moved slowly but inevitably toward open rebellion and a declaration of independence. The uncompromising attitude of the British government and its use of German mercenaries went a long way toward dissolving long-standing loyalties to the home country and rivalries among the separate colonies. *Common Sense* (1775), a brilliant attack by the recently arrived English radical Thomas Paine, also mobilized public opinion in favor of independence. A runaway best seller with sales of 120,000 copies in a few months, Paine's tract ridiculed the idea of a small island ruling a great continent. In his call for freedom and republican government, Paine expressed Americans' growing sense of separateness and moral superiority.

On July 4, 1776, the Second Continental Congress adopted the Declaration of Independence. Written by Thomas Jefferson, the Declaration of Independence boldly listed the tyrannical acts committed by George III (1760–1820) and confidently proclaimed the natural rights of man and the sovereignty of the American states. Sometimes called the world's greatest political editorial, the Declaration of Independence in effect universalized the traditional rights of Englishmen and made them the rights of all mankind. It stated that "all men are created equal . . . they are endowed by their Creator with certain unalienable rights . . . among these are life, liberty, and the pursuit of happiness." No other American political document has ever caused

*THE DECLARATION OF INDEPENDENCE The famous document, principally authored by Thomas Jefferson, bears many well-known signatures. (National Archives, Washington, D.C.)*

such excitement, both at home and abroad.

Many American families remained loyal to Britain; many others divided bitterly. After the Declaration of Independence, the conflict often took the form of a civil war pitting patriot against Loyalist. The Loyalists tended to be wealthy and politically moderate. Many patriots too were wealthy – individuals such as John Hancock and George Washington – but willingly allied themselves with farmers and artisans in a broad coalition. This coalition harassed the Loyalists and confiscated their property to help pay for the American war effort. The broad social base of the revolutionaries tended to make the liberal revolution democratic. State governments extended the right to vote to many more people in the course of the war and re-established themselves as republics.

On the international scene, the French were sympathetic to the rebels from the beginning. They wanted revenge for the humiliating defeats of the Seven Years' War. Officially neutral until 1776, they supplied the great bulk of guns and gunpowder used by the American revolutionaries, very much as neutral Great Powers supply weapons for "wars of national liberation" today. In 1778, the French offered the Americans a formal alliance, and in 1779 and 1780 the Spanish and Dutch declared war on Britain. Catherine the Great of Russia helped organize a League of Armed Neutrality in order to protect neutral shipping rights, which Britain refused to recognize.

Thus by 1780, Great Britain was engaged in an imperial war against most of Europe as well as the thirteen colonies. In these circum-

# In CONGRESS. July 4, 1776.

## The unanimous Declaration of the thirteen united States of America,

When in the Course of human events, it becomes necessary for one people to dissolve the political bands which have connected them with another, and to assume among the powers of the earth, the separate and equal station to which the Laws of Nature and of Nature's God entitle them, a decent respect to the opinions of mankind requires that they should declare the causes which impel them to the separation. — We hold these truths to be self-evident, that all men are created equal, that they are endowed by their Creator with certain unalienable Rights, that among these are Life, Liberty and the pursuit of Happiness. — That to secure these rights, Governments are instituted among Men, deriving their just powers from the consent of the governed, — That whenever any Form of Government becomes destructive of these ends, it is the Right of the People to alter or to abolish it, and to institute new Government, laying its foundation on such principles and organizing its powers in such form, as to them shall seem most likely to effect their Safety and Happiness. Prudence, indeed, will dictate that Governments long established should not be changed for light and transient causes; and accordingly all experience hath shewn, that mankind are more disposed to suffer, while evils are sufferable, than to right themselves by abolishing the forms to which they are accustomed. But when a long train of abuses and usurpations, pursuing invariably the same Object evinces a design to reduce them under absolute Despotism, it is their right, it is their duty, to throw off such Government, and to provide new Guards for their future security. — Such has been the patient sufferance of these Colonies; and such is now the necessity which constrains them to alter their former Systems of Government. The history of the present King of Great Britain is a history of repeated injuries and usurpations, all having in direct object the establishment of an absolute Tyranny over these States. To prove this, let Facts be submitted to a candid world. — He has refused his Assent to Laws, the most wholesome and necessary for the public good. — He has forbidden his Governors to pass Laws of immediate and pressing importance, unless suspended in their operation till his Assent should be obtained; and when so suspended, he has utterly neglected to attend to them. — He has refused to pass other Laws for the accommodation of large districts of people, unless those people would relinquish the right of Representation in the Legislature, a right inestimable to them and formidable to tyrants only. — He has called together legislative bodies at places unusual, uncomfortable, and distant from the depository of their public Records, for the sole purpose of fatiguing them into compliance with his measures. — He has dissolved Representative Houses repeatedly, for opposing with manly firmness his invasions on the rights of the people. — He has refused for a long time, after such dissolutions, to cause others to be elected; whereby the Legislative powers, incapable of Annihilation, have returned to the People at large for their exercise; the State remaining in the mean time exposed to all the dangers of invasion from without, and convulsions within. — He has endeavoured to prevent the population of these States; for that purpose obstructing the Laws for Naturalization of Foreigners; refusing to pass others to encourage their migrations hither, and raising the conditions of new Appropriations of Lands. — He has obstructed the Administration of Justice, by refusing his Assent to Laws for establishing Judiciary powers. — He has made Judges dependent on his Will alone, for the tenure of their offices, and the amount and payment of their salaries. — He has erected a multitude of New Offices, and sent hither swarms of Officers to harrass our people, and eat out their substance. — He has kept among us, in times of peace, Standing Armies without the Consent of our legislatures. — He has affected to render the Military independent of and superior to the Civil power. — He has combined with others to subject us to a jurisdiction foreign to our constitution, and unacknowledged by our laws; giving his Assent to their Acts of pretended Legislation: — For Quartering large bodies of armed troops among us: — For protecting them, by a mock Trial, from punishment for any Murders which they should commit on the Inhabitants of these States: — For cutting off our Trade with all parts of the world: — For imposing Taxes on us without our Consent: — For depriving us in many cases, of the benefits of Trial by jury: — For transporting us beyond Seas to be tried for pretended offences: — For abolishing the free System of English Laws in a neighbouring Province, establishing therein an Arbitrary government, and enlarging its Boundaries so as to render it at once an example and fit instrument for introducing the same absolute rule into these Colonies: — For taking away our Charters, abolishing our most valuable Laws, and altering fundamentally the Forms of our Governments: — For suspending our own Legislatures, and declaring themselves invested with power to legislate for us in all cases whatsoever. — He has abdicated Government here, by declaring us out of his Protection and waging War against us. — He has plundered our seas, ravaged our Coasts, burnt our towns, and destroyed the lives of our people. — He is at this time transporting large Armies of foreign Mercenaries to compleat the works of death, desolation and tyranny, already begun with circumstances of Cruelty & perfidy scarcely paralleled in the most barbarous ages, and totally unworthy the Head of a civilized nation. — He has constrained our fellow Citizens taken Captive on the high Seas to bear Arms against their Country, to become the executioners of their friends and Brethren, or to fall themselves by their Hands. — He has excited domestic insurrections amongst us, and has endeavoured to bring on the inhabitants of our frontiers, the merciless Indian Savages, whose known rule of warfare, is an undistinguished destruction of all ages, sexes and conditions. — In every stage of these Oppressions We have Petitioned for Redress in the most humble terms: Our repeated Petitions have been answered only by repeated injury. A Prince, whose character is thus marked by every act which may define a Tyrant, is unfit to be the ruler of a free people. Nor have We been wanting in attentions to our British brethren. We have warned them from time to time of attempts by their legislature to extend an unwarrantable jurisdiction over us. We have reminded them of the circumstances of our emigration and settlement here. We have appealed to their native justice and magnanimity, and we have conjured them by the ties of our common kindred to disavow these usurpations, which, would inevitably interrupt our connections and correspondence. They too have been deaf to the voice of justice and of consanguinity. We must, therefore, acquiesce in the necessity, which denounces our Separation, and hold them, as we hold the rest of mankind, Enemies in War, in Peace Friends. —

We, therefore, the Representatives of the united States of America, in General Congress, Assembled, appealing to the Supreme Judge of the world for the rectitude of our intentions, do, in the Name, and by Authority of the good People of these Colonies, solemnly publish and declare, That these United Colonies are, and of Right ought to be Free and Independent States; that they are Absolved from all Allegiance to the British Crown, and that all political connection between them and the State of Great Britain, is and ought to be totally dissolved; and that as Free and Independent States, they have full Power to levy War, conclude Peace, contract Alliances, establish Commerce, and to do all other Acts and Things which Independent States may of right do. — And for the support of this Declaration, with a firm reliance on the protection of Divine Providence, we mutually pledge to each other our Lives, our Fortunes and our sacred Honor.

John Hancock

Button Gwinnett
Lyman Hall
Geo Walton

Wm Hooper
Joseph Hewes
John Penn

Edward Rutledge
Thos Heyward Junr
Thomas Lynch Junr
Arthur Middleton

Samuel Chase
Wm Paca
Thos Stone
Charles Carroll of Carrollton
George Wythe
Richard Henry Lee
Th Jefferson
Benja Harrison
Thos Nelson jr
Francis Lightfoot Lee
Carter Braxton

Robt Morris
Benjamin Rush
Benja Franklin
John Morton
Geo Clymer
Jas Smith
Geo Taylor
James Wilson
Geo Ross
Caesar Rodney
Geo Read
Tho M:Kean

Wm Floyd
Phil Livingston
Frans Lewis
Lewis Morris
Richd Stockton
Jno Witherspoon
Fras Hopkinson
John Hart
Abra Clark

Josiah Bartlett
Wm Whipple
Saml Adams
John Adams
Robt Treat Paine
Elbridge Gerry
Step Hopkins
William Ellery
Roger Sherman
Saml Huntington
Wm Williams
Oliver Wolcott
Matthew Thornton

stances, and in the face of severe reverses in India, the West Indies, and at Yorktown in Virginia, a new British government decided to cut its losses. American negotiators in Paris were receptive. They feared that France wanted a treaty that would bottle up the new United States east of the Alleghenies and give British holdings west of the Alleghenies to France's ally, Spain. Thus the American negotiators ditched the French and accepted the extraordinarily favorable terms Britain offered.

By the Treaty of Paris of 1783, Britain ceded all its territory between the Appalachians and the Mississippi River to the Americans and recognized the independence of the thirteen colonies. Out of the no-win rivalries of the Old World, the Americans snatched dominion over half a continent.

## FRAMING THE CONSTITUTION

The liberal program of the American Revolution was consolidated by the federal Constitution, the Bill of Rights and the creation of a national republic. Assembling in Philadelphia in the summer of 1787, the delegates to the Constitutional Convention were determined to end the period of economic depression, social uncertainty, and very weak central government that had followed independence. The delegates decided, therefore, to grant the federal, or central, government important powers: regulation of domestic and foreign trade, the right to levy taxes, and the means to enforce its laws.

Strong rule was placed squarely in the context of representative self-government. Senators and congressmen would be the lawmaking delegates of the voters, and the president of the republic would be an elected official. The central government was to operate in a Lockean framework of checks and balances. The executive, legislative, and judicial branches would systematically balance each other. The power of the federal government would in turn be checked by the powers of the individual states.

When the results of the secret deliberation of the Constitutional Convention were presented to the states for ratification, a great public debate began. The opponents of the proposed constitution – the Anti-Federalists – charged that the framers of the new document had taken too much power from the individual states and made the federal government too strong. Moreover, many Anti-Federalists feared for the personal liberties and individual freedoms for which they had just fought. In order to overcome these objections, the Federalists solemnly promised to spell out these basic freedoms as soon as the new constitution was adopted. The result was the first ten amendments to the Constitution, which the first Congress passed shortly after it met in New York in March 1789. These amendments formed an effective bill of rights to safeguard the individual. Most of them – trial by jury, due process of law, right to assembly, freedom from unreasonable search – had their origins in English law and the English Bill of Rights of 1689. Others – the freedoms of speech, the press, and religion – reflected natural-law theory and the American experience.

The American Constitution and the Bill of Rights exemplified the great strengths and the limits of what came to be called classical liberalism. Liberty meant individual freedoms and political safeguards. Liberty also meant representative government, but did not necessarily mean democracy with its principle of the one man, one vote.

Equality – slaves excepted – meant equality

before the law, not equality of political participation or economic well-being. Indeed, economic inequality was resolutely defended by the elite who framed the Constitution. The right to own property was guaranteed by the Fifth Amendment, and if the government took private property the owner was to receive "just compensation." The radicalism of liberal revolution in America was primarily legal and political, not economic or social.

## THE REVOLUTION'S IMPACT ON EUROPE

Hundreds of books, pamphlets, and articles analyzed and romanticized the American upheaval. Thoughtful Europeans noted, first of all, its enormous long-term implications for international politics. A secret report by the Venetian ambassador to Paris in 1783 stated what many felt: "If only the union of the Provinces is preserved, it is reasonable to expect that, with the favorable effects of time, and of European arts and sciences, it will become the most formidable power in the world."[1] More generally, American independence fired the imaginations of those few aristocrats who were uneasy with their privileges and of those commoners who yearned for greater equality. Many Europeans believed that the world was moving now and that America was leading the way. As one French writer put it in 1789: "This vast continent which the seas surround will soon change Europe and the universe."

Europeans who dreamed of a new era were fascinated by the political lessons of the American Revolution. The Americans had begun with a revolutionary defense against tyrannical oppression, and they had been victorious. They had then shown how rational beings could assemble together to consolidate their gains in a permanent written constitu-

tion – a new social contract. All this gave greater reality to the concepts of individual liberty and representative government. It reinforced one of the primary ideas of the Enlightenment, the idea that a better world here on earth was possible.

## THE FRENCH REVOLUTION, 1789–1791

No country felt the consequences of the American Revolution more directly than France. Hundreds of French officers served in America and were inspired by the experience. The most famous of these, the young and impressionable Marquis de Lafayette (1757–1834), left home wanting only to fight France's traditional foe, England. He returned with a love of liberty and firm republican convictions. French intellectuals and publicists engaged in passionate analysis of the federal Constitution, as well as the constitutions of the various states of the new United States. The American Revolution undeniably hastened upheaval in France.

Yet the French Revolution did not mirror the American example. It was more violent and more complex, more influential and more controversial, more loved and more hated. For Europeans and most of the rest of the world, it was *the* great revolution of the eighteenth century, the revolution that opened the modern era in politics.

### THE CRISIS OF THE OLD ORDER

Like the American Revolution, the French Revolution had its immediate origins in the financial difficulties of the government. War with England had greatly increased France's

LOUIS XVI  *Louis was a handsome, well-meaning youth when he came to the throne in 1774. This stunning portrait by Duplessis idealizes him as a majestic, self-confident ruler, worthy heir of Louis XIV and French absolutism. Actually, Louis XVI was shy, indecisive, and somewhat stupid. (Chateau de Versailles / Giraudon)*

national debt; bankruptcy or a sharp rise in taxes became inevitable. The government's yearly income from taxation and other sources was, quite simply, less than it spent. For a long time the government had been living with the problem by means of haphazard deficit financing, borrowing ever more money from bankers and the well-to-do. By 1788, fully half of France's annual budget went for ever-increasing interest payments on the ever-increasing debt. Another quarter went to maintain the military, while 6 percent was absorbed by the costly and extravagant king and his court at Versailles. Less than one-fifth of the entire national budget was available for the productive functions of the state, such as transportation and general administration. It was an impossible financial situation.

One way out would have been for the government to declare partial bankruptcy, forcing its creditors to accept greatly reduced payments on the debt. Following widespread medieval practice, the powerful Spanish monarchy had regularly repudiated large portions of its debt in the late sixteenth and seventeenth centuries. France had done likewise in the early eighteenth century, after an attempt by John Law, a Scottish adventurer, to establish a French national bank ended in financial disaster in 1720. Yet by the 1780s the French debt was held by an army of aristocratic and bourgeois creditors, and the French monarchy, though absolute in theory, had become far too weak for such a drastic and unpopular action.

Nor could the king and his ministers, unlike modern governments, print money and create inflation to cover their deficits. Unlike England and Holland, which had far larger national debts relative to their populations, France after John Law's unsuccessful experiment had no central bank, no paper currency, and no means of creating credit. French money was good gold coin. Even in times of severe economic crisis the government could not create credit and paper money. It could only beg, unsuccessfully, for new gold loans from its frightened and hard-pressed population. Bound up in the straitjacket of a primitive banking system, the monarchy had no alternative but to try to increase taxes.

## TAXES AND PRIVILEGES

France's system of taxation was unfair and out of date. Increased taxes were possible only in conjunction with developing new sources of revenue, and such tax reform opened a Pandora's box of social and political demands. Taxes were based on the inequality of a society still legally divided into the medieval orders or "estates" – the clergy, the nobility, and everyone else – and were apportioned among the estates very unequally.

Constituting only about 100,000 of France's 24 million inhabitants, the clergy had important privileges. It owned about 10 percent of the land in France and was lightly taxed. Moreover, it levied on the crops of the peasantry an oppressive tax (the tithe) that averaged somewhat less than 10 percent. The clergy's top jobs, soft and overpaid, were jealously monopolized by nobles, to the intense dissatisfaction of the poor parish priests of lower-class origin.

The second estate consisted of some 400,000 noblemen and noblewomen, whose privileges were not only great but growing. Fully in keeping with the general European compromise of bureaucratic absolutism, the French nobility in the late eighteenth century had come to hold almost all the top positions in the government. The nobles also owned fully 25 percent of all the land in the country and were very lightly taxed by the government. Like the clergy, they taxed the peasantry for their own profit. This was done by means of exclusive rights to hunt and fish, village monopolies on baking bread and pressing grapes for wine, fees for justice, and a host of other privileges. Thus in France, as in most of Europe, the wealthiest group in the country – the nobility – systematically exploited the poorest – the peasantry. Long accustomed to a sumptuous banquet of privilege, the appetite of the French nobility had only increased with eating. Ironically, in view of all that followed, it was the pretensions of the nobility that turned a financial crisis into a revolution.

Everyone else was a commoner, a member of the third estate. A few commoners were extremely rich businessmen or highly successful doctors and lawyers. Many more were urban artisans and unskilled day laborers. The vast majority of the third estate consisted of the peasants and agricultural workers in the countryside. Thus, the third estate was a conglomeration of vastly different social groups, united only by their shared legal status as distinct from the privileged nobility and clergy.

## FORMATION OF THE NATIONAL ASSEMBLY

The Revolution was under way by 1787, though no one could have realized what was to follow. That year Louis XVI's minister of finance dusted off old proposals to impose a general tax on all landed property, and he convinced the king to call an Assembly of Notables to gain support for the idea. The assembled notables, who were mainly important noblemen and high-ranking clergy of noble birth, were not in favor of it. In return for their support they demanded control over all government spending and decision making through provincial assemblies, which they expected to control. Denouncing arbitrary taxation by the king, the nobility sought in the name of liberty to assure its own domination of the state. The king tried to reassert his authority. A great wave of protest swept the country. Finlly, in July 1788, a beaten Louis XVI called for a spring session of the Estates General, the old representative body of all three estates that had not met since 1614. Absolute monarchy was falling.

What would replace it? Throughout the winter of 1788-1789, that question excited France. The Estates General of 1614 had sat as three separate houses – clergy, nobility, and commoners. Any action had required the agreement of all three branches, a requirement that had guaranteed control by the privileged orders. The nobility expected that history would repeat itself. The noble judges of the Parlement of Paris – a kind of supreme court in the eighteenth century – did their part. Accustomed to thundering against the rule of despotism, they ruled that the Estates should sit separately.

This ruling infuriated middle-class intellectuals. They wanted the three estates to meet as a single house, so that commoners from the third estate would have the dominant voice and be able to prevent aristocratic control. This issue and many others were thoroughly discussed in pamphlets and in the drafting of grievance petitions at the local level. There was great popular participation. Almost all male commoners twenty-five years or older had the right to vote for their representatives to the Estates General. However, the voting for the representatives required two, three, or even four stages, which meant that most of the representatives finally selected by the third estate were well-educated and prosperous members of the middle class. Most of them were not businessmen, but lawyers and government officials. Social status and prestige were matters of great concern to this economic elite. There were hardly any representatives from the great mass of laboring poor – the peasants, the artisans, and the day laborers.

In May 1789, the twelve hundred delegates of the three estates paraded in medieval pageantry through the streets of Versailles to an opening session clothed in feudal magnificence. The estates were almost immediately deadlocked. Delegates of the third estate refused to transact any business until the king ordered the privileged orders to sit with them in a single body. Finally, after a six-week war of nerves, a few parish priests began to go over to the third estate, which on June 17 voted to call itself the National Assembly. On June 20, excluded from their hall because of "repairs," they moved to a large indoor tennis court. There they swore the famous Oath of the Tennis Court, pledging never to disband until they had written a new constitution.

The king's actions were then somewhat contradictory. On June 23 he made a conciliatory speech to a joint session, urging reforms, and then ordered the three estates to meet together. At the same time he apparently followed the advice of the nobles, who saw things working out quite differently than they had expected and urged the king to dissolve the Estates General. The king called an army of eighteen thousand troops toward Versailles, and on July 11 he dismissed his finance minister and his more liberal ministers. Faced first with aristocratic and then with bourgeois revolt, Louis XVI had resigned himself to bankruptcy. Now he sought again to reassert his divine and historic right to rule. The middle-class delegates had done their best, but they were resigned to being disbanded at the point of bayonets. One third-estate delegate reassured a worried colleague: "You won't hang – you'll only have to go back home."[2]

### THE REVOLT OF THE POOR AND THE OPPRESSED

While the third estate struggled at Versailles for symbolic equality with the nobility and clergy in a single legislative body, economic hardship gripped the masses of France in a tightening vise. Grain was the basis of the diet of ordinary people, and in 1788 the harvest had been extremely poor. The price of bread, which had been rising gradually since 1785, began to soar. By July 1789, the price of bread in the provinces climbed as high as eight sous per pound. In Paris, where bread was subsidized by the government in an attempt to prevent popular unrest, the price rose to four sous. The poor could scarcely afford to pay two sous per pound, for even at that price a laborer with a wife and three children had to spend half of his wages to buy the family's bread.

Harvest failure and high bread prices unleashed a classic economic depression of the preindustrial age. With food so expensive and with so much uncertainty, the demand for manufactured goods collapsed. Thousands of artisans and small traders were thrown out of work. By the end of 1789, almost half of the French people would be in need of relief. One person in eight was a pauper, living in extreme want. In Paris, the situation was desperate in July 1789: perhaps 150,000 of the city's 600,000 people were without work.

Against this background of dire poverty and desperation, the people of Paris entered decisively onto the revolutionary stage. They believed in a general though ill-defined way that their economic distress had human causes. They believed that they should have steady work and enough bread to survive. Specifically, they feared that the dismissal of the king's moderate finance minister would throw them at the mercy of aristocratic landowners and grain speculators. Stories, like that quoting the wealthy financier Joseph François Foulon as saying that the poor "should eat grass, like my horses," and rumors that the king's troops would sack the city, began to fill the air. Angry crowds formed and passionate voices urged action. On July 13, the people began to seize arms for the defense of the city, and on July 14, several

STORMING THE BASTILLE This contemporary drawing conveys the fury and determination of the revolutionary crowd on July 14, 1789. This successful popular action had enormous symbolic significance, and July 14 has long been France's most important national holiday. (Photo: Flammarion)

hundred of the most determined people marched to the Bastille to search for gunpowder.

An old medieval fortress with walls ten feet thick and eight great towers each a hundred feet high, the Bastille had long been used as a prison. It was guarded by eighty retired soldiers and thirty Swiss guards. The governor of the fortress-prison refused to hand over the powder, panicked, and ordered his men to fire, killing ninety-eight people attempting to enter. Cannon were brought to batter the main gate, and fighting continued until the governor of the prison surrendered. While he was being taken under guard to city hall, a band of men broke through and hacked him to death. His head and that of the mayor of Paris, who had been slow to give the crowd arms, were stuck on pikes and paraded through the streets. The next day a committee of citizens appointed Lafayette commander of the city's armed forces. Paris was lost to the king, who was forced to recall the finance minister and to disperse his troops. The uprising of the masses of Paris had saved the National Assembly.

As the delegates resumed their long-winded and inconclusive debates at Versailles, the people in the countryside sent them a radical and unmistakable message. All across France peasants began to rise in spontaneous, violent, and effective insurrection against their lords. Neither middle-class landowners, who often owned manors and village monopolies, nor the larger, more prosperous farmers, were spared. In some areas the nobles and bourgeoisie combined forces and organized patrols to protect their property. Yet the peasant insurrection went on. Recent enclosures were undone; old common lands were reoccupied; and the forests were seized. Taxes went unpaid. Fear of vagabonds and outlaws – the so-called Great Fear – seized the countryside and fanned the flames of rebellion. The long-suffering peasants were doing their best to free themselves from aristocratic privilege and exploitation.

Faced with chaos and fearful of calling on the king to restore order, the more liberal aristocrats and bourgeois at Versailles responded to peasant demands with a surprise maneuver on the night of August 4, 1789. The duke of Aiguillon, one of the greatest landowners in France, declared that

*in several provinces the whole people forms a kind of league for the destruction of the manor houses, the ravaging of the lands, and especially for the seizure of the archives where the title deeds to feudal properties are kept. It seeks to throw off at last a yoke that has for many centuries weighted it down.*[3]

He urged equality in taxation and the elimination of feudal dues. In the end, all the old exactions were abolished, generally without compensation: serfdom where it still existed, exclusive hunting rights for nobles, fees for justice, village monopolies, the right to make peasants work on the roads, and a host of others. The church's tithe was also abolished. Thus the French peasantry, which already owned about 30 percent of all the land, quickly achieved a great and unprecedented victory. Henceforth, the French peasants would seek mainly to consolidate their triumph. As the Great Fear subsided, they became a force for order and stability.

## A LIMITED MONARCHY

The National Assembly moved forward. On August 27, 1789, it issued the Declaration of the Rights of Man. This great liberal document had a very American flavor, and Lafayette even discussed his draft in detail with the American ambassador in Paris, Thomas Jefferson, the author of the American Declaration of Independence. According to the French declaration, "men are born and remain free and equal in rights." Mankind's natural rights are "liberty, property, security, and resistance to oppression." Also, "every man is presumed innocent until he is proven guilty." As for law, "it is an expression of the general will; all citizens have the right to concur personally or through their representatives in its formation.... Free expression of thoughts and opinions is one of the most precious rights of mankind: every citizen may therefore speak, write, and publish freely." In short, this clarion call of the liberal revolutionary ideal guaranteed equality before the law, representative government for a sovereign people, and individual freedom. This revolutionary credo, only two pages long, was propagandized throughout France and Europe and around the world.

Moving beyond general principles to draft a constitution proved difficult. The questions of how much power the king should retain

*"To Versailles"* This print is one of many commemorating the women's march on Versailles. Notice on the left that the fashionable lady from the well-to-do is a most reluctant revolutionary. (Photo: Flammarion)

and whether he could permanently veto legislation led to another deadlock. Once again the decisive answer came from the poor, in this instance the poor women of Paris.

To understand what happened one must remember that the work and wages of women and children were essential in the family economy of the laboring poor. In Paris great numbers of women worked, particularly within the putting-out system in the garment industry — making lace, fancy dresses, embroidery, ribbons, bonnets, corsets, and so on. Most of these goods were beautiful luxury items, destined for an aristocratic and international clientele.[4] Immediately after the fall of the Bastille, many of France's greatest nobles

began to leave for foreign courts, so that demand for luxuries began to plummet. International markets also declined, and the church was no longer able to give its traditional grants of food and money to the poor. Unemployment and hunger increased further, and the result was another popular explosion.

On October 5, some seven thousand desperate women marched the twelve miles from Paris to Versailles to demand action. A middle-class deputy looking out from the assembly saw "multitudes arriving from Paris including fishwives and bullies from the market, and these people wanted nothing but bread." This great crowd invaded the assembly, "armed with scythes, sticks and pikes."

One coarse, tough old woman directing a large group of younger women defiantly shouted into the debate: "Who's that talking down there? Make the chatterbox shut up. That's not the point: the point is that we want bread."[5] Hers was the genuine voice of the people, without which any understanding of the French Revolution is hopelessly incomplete.

The women invaded the royal apartments, slaughtered some of the royal bodyguards, and furiously searched for the despised queen, Marie Antoinette. "We are going to cut off her head, tear out her heart, fry her liver, and that won't be the end of it," they shouted, surging through the palace in a frenzy. It seems likely that only the intervention of Lafayette and the National Guard saved the royal family. But the only way to calm the disorder was for the king to go and live in Paris, as the crowd demanded.

The next day the king, the queen, and their son left for Paris in the midst of a strange procession. The heads of two aristocrats, stuck on pikes, led the way. They were followed by the remaining members of the royal bodyguard, unarmed and surrounded and mocked by fierce men holding sabers and pikes. A mixed and victorious multitude surrounded the king's carriage, hurling crude insults at the queen. There was drinking and eating among the women. "We are bringing the baker, Mrs. Baker, and the baker's boy," they joyfully sang. The National Assembly followed the king to Paris. Reflecting the more radical environment, it adopted a constitution that gave the virtually imprisoned "baker" only a temporary veto in the lawmaking process. And, for a time, he and the government made sure that the masses of Paris did not lack bread.

The next two years until September 1791 saw the consolidation of the constructive phase of the Revolution. The National Assembly established a constitutional monarchy, which Louis XVI reluctantly accepted in July 1790. The king remained the head of state, but all lawmaking power was placed in the hands of the National Assembly, elected by the economic upper half of French males. Counties or departments of approximately equal size replaced the complicated old patchwork of provinces with their many historic differences. The jumble of weights and measures that varied from province to province was abolished and replaced by the simple, rational metric system. The National Assembly promoted economic freedom. Monopolies and guilds were prohibited, and barriers to trade within France were abolished in the name of economic liberty. Thus, the National Assembly applied the critical spirit of the Enlightenment to reform France's laws and institutions completely.

The assembly also seized the property of nobles who had left France, and it nationalized the property of the church. The government used former church property as collateral to guarantee a new paper currency, the so-called assignats, and then sold these properties in an attempt to put the state's finances on a solid footing. Although the church's land was sold in large blocks, a procedure that favored nimble speculators and the rich, peasants eventually purchased much of it as it was subdivided. These purchases strengthened their attachment to the revolutionary state.

The most unfortunate aspect of the reorganization of France was that it brought the new government into conflict with the Catholic church. Many middle-class delegates to the National Assembly, imbued with the rationalism and skepticism of the eighteenth-century philosophes, harbored a deep distrust of "superstitious religion." They were interested in the church only to the extent they could seize its land and use the church to strengthen the new state. In the Civil Constitution of the Clergy of 1790 they established a national church. In the face of resistance, the National Assembly required the clergy to take a loyalty oath to the new government. The clergy became just so many more employees of the state. The pope formally condemned this attempt to subjugate the church. Against such a backdrop, it is not surprising that only half the priests of France took the oath of allegiance. The result was a deep division within the country on the religious question, and confusion and hostility among French Catholics were pervasive. The attempted reorganization and subjugation of the Catholic church was the revolutionary government's first great failure.

## WORLD WAR AND REPUBLICAN FRANCE, 1791–1799

When Louis XVI accepted the final version of the completed constitution in September 1791, a young and still obscure provincial lawyer and member of the National Assembly named Maximilien Robespierre (1758–1794) evaluated the work of two years and concluded "The Revolution is over." Robespierre was both right and wrong. He was right in the sense that most of the constructive and lasting reforms were in place. Nothing substantial in the way of liberty and equality would be added in the next generation, though much would be lost. He was wrong in the sense that the most tormented and most radical stages lay ahead. New heroes and new myths were to emerge in revolutionary wars and international conflict.

### THE BEGINNING OF WAR

The outbreak and progress of revolution in France produced great excitement and a sharp division of opinion in Europe and the United States. Liberals and radicals such as the English scientist Joseph Priestley (1733–1804) and the American patriot Tom Paine (1739–1809) saw a mighty triumph of liberty over despotism. Conservative spirits like Edmund Burke (1729–1797) were deeply troubled. In 1790, Burke published *Reflections on the Revolution in France,* one of the great intellectual defenses of European conservatism. He defended inherited privileges in general and those of the English monarchy and aristocracy in particular. He predicted that unlimited reform would lead only to chaos and renewed tyranny. By 1791, fear was growing outside France that the great hopes raised by the revolution might be tragically dashed. The moderate German writer Friederich von Gentz was apprehensive that if moderate and intelligent revolution failed in France, all the old evils would be ten times worse: "It would be felt that men could be happy only as slaves, and every tyrant, great or small, would use this confession to seek revenge for the fright that the awakening of the French nation had given him."[6]

The kings and nobles of Europe, who had at first welcomed the revolution in France as weakening a competing power, began to feel threatened themselves. At their courts they listened to the French aristocrats who had fled France and were urging intervention in France's affairs. When Louis XVI and Marie Antoinette were arrested and returned to Paris after trying unsuccessfully to slip out of France in June 1791, the kings of Austria and Prussia issued the Declaration of Pillnitz. This carefully worded statement declared their willingness to intervene in France, but only with the unanimous agreement of all the Great Powers, which they did not expect to receive. Austria and Prussia expected their threat to have a sobering effect on revolutionary France without causing war.

The crowned heads of Europe misjudged the revolutionary spirit in France. When the National Assembly had disbanded, it had sought popular support by decreeing that none of its members would be eligible for election to the new Legislative Assembly. This meant that when the new representative body was duly elected and convened in October 1791, it had a different character. The great majority were still prosperous, well-educated, and middle class, but they were younger and more reckless than their predecessors. Loosely allied as Jacobins, so named after their political club, the new representatives were passionately committed to liberal revolution.

The Jacobins were full of hatred toward aristocrats and despotic monarchs, and easily whipped themselves into a patriotic fury with bombastic oratory. So the courts of Europe were attempting to incite a war of kings against France; well then, "we will incite a war of people against kings. . . . Ten million Frenchmen, kindled by the fire of liberty, armed with the sword, with reason, with eloquence would be able to change the face of the world and make the tyrants tremble on their thrones."[7] Only Robespierre and a very few others argued that people do not welcome liberation at the point of a gun. Such warnings were brushed aside. France would "rise to the full height of her mission," as one deputy urged. In April 1792, France declared war on the king of Austria.

France's crusade against tyranny went poorly at first. Prussia joined Austria in the Austrian Netherlands (present-day Belgium),

and French forces broke and fled at their first encounter with armies of this First Coalition. The road to Paris lay open, and it is possible that only conflict between the eastern monarchs over the division of Poland saved France from defeat.

Military reversals and Austro-Prussian threats caused a wave of patriotic fervor to sweep France. The Legislative Assembly declared the country in danger. Volunteer armies from the provinces streamed through Paris, fraternizing with the people and singing patriotic songs like the stirring *Marseillaise,* later the French national anthem.

In this supercharged wartime atmosphere, rumors of treason by the king and queen spread in Paris. Once again, as in the storming of the Bastille, the common people of Paris acted decisively. On August 10, 1792, a revolutionary mob attacked the royal palace at the Tuileries, capturing it after heavy fighting with the Swiss Guards. The king and his family fled for their lives to the nearby Legislative Assembly, which suspended the king from all his functions, imprisoned him, and called for a new National Convention to be elected by universal male suffrage. Monarchy in France was on its deathbed, mortally wounded by war and popular revolt.

## THE SECOND REVOLUTION

The fall of the monarchy marked a rapid radicalization of the Revolution, which historians often call "the second revolution." Louis's imprisonment was followed by the September Massacres, which disgraced the Revolution in the eyes of most of its remaining foreign supporters. Wild stories seized the city that imprisoned counter-revolutionary aristocrats and priests were plotting with the allied invaders. As a result, frenzied crowds invaded the pris-

THE END OF LOUIS XVI *Some cheered and others wept at the sight of Louis's severed head. The execution of the king was a victory for the radicals, but it horrified Europe's monarchs and conservatives. (Photo: Flammarion)*

ons of Paris and summarily slaughtered half the men and women they found. In late September 1792, the new, popularly elected National Convention proclaimed France a republic. The republic adopted a new revolutionary calendar, and citizens were expected to address each other with the friendly "thou" of the people, rather than with the formal "you" of the rich and powerful.

All of the members of the National Convention were Jacobins and republicans, and the great majority continued to come from the well-educated middle class. But the convention was increasingly divided into two well-defined, bitterly competitive groups –

the Girondists and the Mountain, so called because its members, led by Danton and Robespierre, sat on the uppermost left-hand rows of the assembly hall. Many indecisive members seated in "the Plain" below floated back and forth between the rival factions.

The division was clearly apparent after the National Convention overwhelmingly convicted Louis XVI of treason. By a single vote, 361 of the 720 members of the convention then unconditionally sentenced him to death in January 1793. Louis died with tranquil dignity on the newly invented guillotine. One of his last sentences was, "I am innocent and shall die without fear. I would that my death might bring happiness to the French, and ward off the dangers which I foresee."[8]

Both the Girondists and the Mountain were determined to continue the "war against tyranny." The Prussians had been stopped at the indecisive battle of Valmy on September 20, 1792, one day before the republic was proclaimed. Republican armies then successfully invaded Savoy and captured Nice. A second army corps invaded the German Rhineland and took the city of Frankfurt. To the north the revolutionary armies won their first major battle at Jemappes and occupied the entire Austrian Netherlands by November 1792. Everywhere they went, French armies of occupation chased the princes, "abolished feudalism," and found support among some peasants and middle-class people.

But the French armies also lived off the land, requisitioning food and supplies and plundering local treasures. The liberators looked increasingly like foreign invaders. International tensions mounted. In February 1793 the National Convention, at war with Austria and Prussia, declared war on Britain, Holland, and Spain as well. Republican France was now at war with almost all of Europe, a great war that would last almost without interruption until 1815.

As the forces of the First Coalition drove the French from the Austrian Netherlands, peasants in western France revolted against being drafted into the army. They were supported and encouraged by devout Catholics, royalists, and foreign agents.

In Paris, the quarrelsome convention found itself locked in a life-and-death political struggle between the Girondists and the Mountain. The two groups were in general agreement on questions of policy. Sincere republicans, they hated privilege and wanted to temper economic liberalism with social concern. Yet personal hatreds ran deep. The Girondists feared a bloody dictatorship by the Mountain, and the Mountain was no less convinced that the more moderate Girondists would turn to conservatives and even royalists in order to retain power. With the middle-class delegates so bitterly divided, the laboring poor of Paris emerged as the decisive political factor.

The great mass of the Parisian laboring poor always constituted – along with the peasantry in the summer of 1789 – the elemental force that drove the Revolution forward. It was the artisans, shopkeepers, and day laborers who had stormed the Bastille, marched on Versailles, driven the king from the Tuileries, and carried out the September Massacres. The laboring poor were often known as the *sans-culottes,* "without breeches," because they wore trousers instead of the knee breeches of the aristocracy and the solid middle class. The immediate interests of the sans-culottes were mainly economic, and in the spring of 1793 the economic situation was as bad as the military situation. Rapid inflation, unemployment, and food shortages were again weighing heavily on the poor.

Moreover, by the spring of 1793 the sans-culottes were keenly interested in politics. Encouraged by the so-called "angry men," such as the passionate young ex-priest and journalist Jacques Roux, the sans-culottes were demanding radical political action to guarantee them their daily bread. At first the Mountain joined the Girondists in violently rejecting these demands. But in the face of military defeat, peasant revolt, and hatred of the Girondists, the Mountain and especially Robespierre became more sympathetic. The Mountain joined with sans-culottes activists in the city government to engineer a popular uprising, which forced the convention to arrest thirty-one Girondist deputies for treason on June 2. All power passed to the Mountain.

## THE FRENCH REVOLUTION

| | |
|---|---|
| May 5, 1789 | Estates General convene at Versailles |
| June 17, 1789 | Third Estate declares itself the National Assembly |
| June 20, 1789 | Oath of the Tennis Court |
| July 14, 1789 | Storming of the Bastille |
| July–August 1789 | The Great Fear in the countryside |
| August 4, 1789 | National Assembly abolishes feudal privileges |
| August 27, 1789 | National Assembly issues Declaration of the Rights of Man |
| October 5, 1789 | Parisian women march on Versailles and force royal family to return to Paris |
| November 1789 | National Assembly confiscates church lands |
| July 1790 | Civil Constitution of the Clergy establishes a national church |
| | Louis XVI reluctantly agrees to accept a constitutional monarchy |
| June 1791 | Arrest of the royal family while attempting to flee France |
| August 1791 | Declaration of Pillnitz by Austria and Prussia |
| April 1792 | France declares war on Austria |
| August 1792 | Parisian mob attacks palace and takes Louis XVI prisoner |
| September 1792 | September Massacres |
| | National Convention declares France a republic and abolishes monarchy |

Robespierre and others from the Mountain joined the recently formed Committee of Public Safety, to which the Convention had given dictatorial power to deal with the national emergency. These developments in Paris triggered revolt in leading provincial cities, such as Lyons and Marseilles, where moderates denounced Paris and demanded a decentralized government. The peasant revolt spread and the republic's armies were driven back on all fronts. By July 1793, only the areas around Paris and on the eastern frontier were firmly controlled by the central government. Defeat appeared imminent.

## TOTAL WAR AND THE TERROR

A year later, in July 1794, the Austrian Netherlands and the Rhineland were once again in the hands of conquering French armies, and the First Coalition was falling apart. This remarkable change of fortune was due to the revolutionary government's success in harnessing, for perhaps the first time in history, the explosive forces of a planned economy, revolutionary terror, and modern nationalism in a total war effort.

Robespierre and the Committee of Public Safety advanced with implacable resolution on

| The French Revolution (continued) | |
|---|---|
| January 1793 | Execution of Louis XVI |
| February 1793 | France declares war on Britain, Holland, and Spain |
| | Revolts in provincial cities |
| March 1793 | Bitter struggle in the National Convention between Girondists and the Mountain |
| April–June 1793 | Robespierre and the Mountain organize the Committee of Public Safety and arrest Girondist leaders |
| September 1793 | Price controls to aid the sans-culottes and mobilize war effort |
| 1793–1794 | Reign of Terror in Paris and the provinces |
| Spring 1794 | French armies victorious on all fronts |
| July 1794 | Execution of Robespierre |
| | Thermidorean Reaction begins |
| 1795–1799 | The Directory |
| 1795 | End of economic controls and suppresion of the sans-culottes |
| 1797 | Napoleon defeats Austrian armies in Italy and returns triumphant to Paris |
| 1798 | Austria, Great Britain, and Russia form the Second Coalition against France |
| 1799 | Napoleon overthrows the Directory and seizes power |

several fronts in 1793–1794. In an effort to save revolutionary France, they collaborated with the fiercely patriotic and democratic sans-culottes. They established, as best they could, a planned economy with egalitarian social overtones. Rather than let prices be determined by supply and demand, the government decreed the maximum allowable prices, fixed in paper assignats, for a host of key products. Although the state was too weak to enforce all its price regulations, it did fix the price of bread in Paris at levels the poor could afford. Rationing and ration cards were introduced to make sure that the limited supplies of bread were shared fairly. Quality was also controlled. Bakers were permitted to make only the "bread of equality" – a brown bread made of a mixture of all available flours. White bread and pastries were outlawed as frivolous luxuries. The poor of Paris may not have eaten well, but they ate.

They also worked, mainly to produce arms and munitions for the war effort. Craftsmen and small manufacturers were told what to produce and when to deliver. The government nationalized many small workshops and requisitioned raw materials and grain from the peasants. Sometimes planning and control did

THE REIGN OF TERROR *A man, woman, and child accused of political crimes are brought before a special revolutionary committee for trial. The Terror's iron dictatorship crushed individual rights as well as treason and opposition. (Photo: Flammarion)*

not go beyond orders to meet the latest emergency: "Ten thousand soldiers lack shoes. You will take the shoes of all the aristocrats in Strasbourg and deliver them ready for transport to headquarters at 10 A.M. tomorrow." Failures to control and coordinate were failures of means and not of desire: seldom if ever before had a government attempted to manage an economy so thoroughly. The second revolution and the ascendancy of the sans-culottes had produced an embryonic emergency socialism, which was to have great influence on the subsequent development of socialist ideology.

While radical economic measures supplied the poor with bread and the armies with weapons, a Reign of Terror (1793–1794) was solidifying the home front. Special revolutionary courts, responsible only to Robespierre's Committee of Public Safety, tried rebels and "enemies of the nation" for political crimes. Drawing on popular, sans-culottes support centered in the local Jacobin clubs, these local courts ignored normal legal procedures and judged severely. Forty thousand French men and women were executed. Another 300,000 suspects crowded the prisons and often brushed close to death in a revolutionary court.

Robespierre's Reign of Terror was one of the most controversial phases of the French Revolution. Most historians now believe that the Terror was not directed against any single class. Rather, it was a political weapon directed impartially against all who might oppose the revolutionary government. For many Europeans of the time, however, the Reign of Terror represented a terrible perversion of the generous ideals of 1789. It strengthened the belief that France had foolishly replaced a weak king with a bloody dictatorship.

The third and perhaps decisive element in the French republic's victory over the First Coalition was its ability to continue drawing on the explosive power of patriotic dedication to a national state and a national mission. This is the essence of modern nationalism. With a common language and a common tradition, newly reinforced by the idea of popular sovereignty, the French people were stirred by a common loyalty. The shared danger of foreign foes and internal rebels unified all classes in a heroic defense of the nation.

In such circumstances war was no longer the gentlemanly game of the eighteenth century, but a life-and-death struggle between good and evil. Everyone had to participate in the national effort. According to a famous decree of August 1793:

*The young men shall go to battle and the married men shall forge arms. The women shall make tents and clothes, and shall serve in the hospitals; children shall tear rags into lint. The old men will be guided to the public places of the cities to kindle the courage of the young warriors and to preach the unity of the Republic and the hatred of kings.*

Like the wars of religion, war in 1793 was a crusade; this war, though, was fought for a secular rather than a religious ideology.

As all unmarried young men were subject to the draft, the French armed forces swelled to 1 million men in fourteen armies. A force of this size was unprecedented in the history of European warfare. The soldiers were led by young, impetuous generals, who had often risen rapidly from the ranks and personified the opportunities the Revolution seemed to offer gifted sons of the people. These generals used mass attacks at bayonet point by their highly motivated forces to overwhelm the enemy. By the spring of 1794, French armies were victorious on all fronts. The republic was saved.

## THE THERMIDORIAN REACTION AND THE DIRECTORY, 1794-1799

The success of the French armies led Robespierre and the Committee of Public Safety to relax the emergency economic controls, but they extended the political Reign of Terror. Their lofty goal was increasingly an ideal democratic republic, where justice would reign and there would be neither rich nor poor. Their lowly means were unrestrained despotism and the guillotine, which struck down any who might seriously question the new order. In March 1794, to the horror of many sans-culottes, Robespierre's Terror wiped out many of the "angry men," led by the radical social democrat Jacques Hébert. Two weeks later, several of Robespierre's long-standing collaborators, led by the famous orator Danton, marched up the steps to the guillotine. Knowing that they might be next, a strange assortment of radicals and moderates in the convention organized a conspiracy. They howled down Robespierre when he tried to speak to the convention on 9 Thermidor (July 27, 1794). On the following day it was Robespierre's turn to be shaved by the revolutionary razor.

As Robespierre's closest supporters followed their leader, France unexpectedly experienced a thorough reaction to the despotism of the Reign of Terror. In a general way this "Thermidorian reaction" recalled the early days of the Revolution. The respectable middle-class lawyers and professionals who had led the liberal Revolution of 1789 reasserted their authority. Drawing support from their own class, the provincial cities, and the better-off peasants, the convention abolished many economic controls, printed more paper currency, and let prices rise sharply. It severely restricted the local political organizations where the sans-culottes had their strength. And all the while, the wealthy bankers and new-rich speculators celebrated the sudden end of the Terror with an orgy of self-indulgence and ostentatious luxury.

The collapse of economic controls coupled with runaway inflation hit the working poor very hard. The gaudy extravagance of the rich wounded their pride. The sans-culottes accepted private property, but they believed passionately in small business and the right of all to earn a decent living. Increasingly disorganized after Robespierre purged their radical spokesmen, the common people of Paris finally revolted against the emerging new order in early 1795. The convention quickly used the army to suppress these insurrections. For the first time since the fall of the Bastille, bread riots and uprisings by Parisians living on the edge of starvation were effectively put down by a government that made no concessions to the poor.

In the face of all these catastrophes the revolutionary fervor of the laboring poor finally subsided. As far as politics was concerned, their interest and influence would remain very limited until 1830. There arose, especially from the women, a great cry for peace and a turning toward religion. As the government looked the other way, the women brought back the Catholic church and the worship of God. In one French town women fought with each other over which of their children should be baptized first. After six tumultuous years the women of the poor concluded that the Revolution was a failure.

As for the middle-class members of the convention, they wrote yet another constitution, which they believed would guarantee their political supremacy. The mass of the population could vote only for "electors," who would be men of means. The electors then elected the members of a reorganized assembly, as well as important officials throughout France. The assembly also chose the five-man executive – the Directory.

The men of the Directory continued to support French military expansion abroad. War was no longer so much a crusade as a means to meet the ever-present, ever-unsolved economic problem. Large, victorious French armies reduced unemployment at home, and they were able to live off the territories they conquered and plundered.

The unprincipled action of the Directory reinforced widespread disgust with war and starvation. This general dissatisfaction revealed itself clearly in the national elections of 1797, which returned a large number of conservative and even monarchial deputies who favored peace at almost any price. Fearing for their skins, the members of the Directory used the army to nullify the elections and began to govern dictatorially. Two years later, Napoleon Bonaparte ended the Directory in a coup d'état and substituted a strong dictatorship for a weak one. The Revolution was over.

## THE NAPOLEONIC ERA, 1799–1814

For almost fifteen years, from 1799 to 1814, France was in the hands of a keen-minded military dictator masquerading first as a Roman consul and then as an emperor. Napoleon Bonaparte was clever enough to end the civil strife in France, in order to consolidate his rule. Had he stopped there, his achievement would have been considerable. But he did not, for the military dictator was also a military adventurer. Peace was boring; the dream of universal empire was irresistible. Napoleon pushed onward with wars of aggression, steadfastly rejecting compromises with his foes until, at last, he destroyed himself.

## NAPOLEON'S RULE OF FRANCE

In 1799, when he seized power, young General Napoleon was a national hero. Born in Corsica into an impoverished noble family in 1769, Napoleon left home to become a lieutenant in the French artillery in 1785. Ever the opportunist, he went back to Corsica to fight for the island's independence in 1789. When that adventure failed miserably after about four years, he returned to France as a French patriot and a dedicated revolutionary. Rising rapidly in the new army, Napoleon was placed in command of French forces in Italy and won brilliant victories there in 1796 and 1797. His next campaign, in Egypt, was a failure, but Napoleon succeeded in abandoning his army and returning to France before the fiasco was generally known.

Napoleon soon learned that some prominent members of the assembly were plotting against the Directory. The dissatisfaction of these plotters stemmed not so much from the fact that the Directory was a dictatorship, but that it was a weak dictatorship. Ten years of upheaval and gore had made firm rule much more appealing than liberty and popular politics to these disillusioned revolutionaries. The abbé Sieyès personified this evolution in thinking. In 1789 he had written in his famous pamphlet *What Is the Third Estate?* that the nobility was useless and that the entire people should rule the French nation.

*"EMPEROR NAPOLEON" Napoleon soon minted new gold coins like this one. In doing so, he ended a decade of financial upheaval and gained support from the middle class. (Courtesy of the American Numismatic Society, New York)*

Now Sieyès' motto was "confidence from below, authority from above."

Like the other members of his group, Sieyès wanted a strong military ruler. The flamboyant thirty-year-old Napoleon was ideal. Thus the conspirators and Napoleon organized a takeover. On November 9, 1799, soldiers disbanded the assembly at bayonet point. Napoleon was named first consul of the republic, and a new constitution consolidating his position was overwhelmingly approved in a plebiscite in December 1799. Republican appearances were maintained for the moment, but Napoleon was the virtual dictator of France.

The essence of Napoleon's domestic policy was to use dictatorial powers to maintain order and put an end to civil strife. He did so by working out unwritten agreements with powerful groups in France, whereby these groups received favors in return for obedient service. Napoleon's bargain with the solid middle class was codified in the famous civil code of 1800, which reasserted two of the fundamental principles of this class and of their moderate revolution of 1789: equality of all citizens before the law, and absolute security of wealth and private property. Napoleon and the leading bankers of Paris established a privately owned Bank of France, which loyally served the interests of both the state and the financial oligarchy. Napoleon's devotion to the economic status quo also appealed to the peasants, who had bought some of the lands confiscated from the church and nobility. Thus, Napoleon accepted the gains of the peasantry and reassured the middle class, which had lost its revolutionary illusions in the face of social upheaval.

At the same time Napoleon accepted and strengthened the position of the French bureaucracy. France became a thoroughly centralized state. A network of prefects, subprefects, and centrally appointed mayors depended on Napoleon and served him well. Nor were members of the old nobility slighted. In 1800 and again in 1802 Napoleon granted amnesty to a hundred thousand émigrés on the condition that they return to France and take a loyalty oath. Members of this returning elite soon ably occupied many high posts in the expanding centralized state. Only a thousand diehard monarchists were exempted and remained abroad. Napoleon also created a new, ostentatious imperial nobility in order to reward his most talented generals and officials.

Napoleon's policy of buying off important groups in return for their support is illustrated by his treatment of the Catholic church in France. In 1800, the French clergy was still divided into two groups: those who had taken an oath of allegiance to the revolutionary government, and those in exile or hiding who had refused to do so. Personally uninterested in religion, Napoleon wanted to heal the religious division so that a united Catholic church in France could serve as one of the pillars of his regime. After long and arduous negotiations, Napoleon and Pope Pius VII (1800–1823) signed the Concordat of 1801. The pope gained for French Catholics the precious right to practice their religion freely, but Napoleon gained the most politically. His government now nominated bishops, paid the clergy, and exerted great influence over the church in France. Thus was Napoleon successful in using religion to strengthen his rule.

Napoleon's autocratic and supposedly efficient reorganization of France's church, bureaucracy, laws, and finances has led some historians to call him "the last of the enlightened despots." This discription is flattering, for it neglects Napoleon's endless foreign aggression and insatiable power drive, which might better earn him the epithet "the first of the modern madmen." Be that as it may, the characterization of Napoleon as an enlightened despot is at least half accurate: he was thoroughly despotic. Free speech and freedom of the press – fundamental rights of the liberal revolution, enshrined in the Declaration of the Rights of Man – were constantly and cynically violated. Shortly after seizing power, Napoleon reduced the number of newspapers in Paris from seventy-three to thirteen. By 1811, only four were left, and they were rigorously censored – little more than organs of government propaganda.

In 1802, Napoleon tried and failed to restore the black slavery the Revolution had abolished in France's former colony of Haiti; on the French islands of Martinique and Gua-

## THE NAPOLEONIC ERA

| | |
|---|---|
| November 1799 | Napoleon overthrows the Directory |
| December 1799 | French voters overwhelmingly approve Napoleon's new constitution |
| 1800 | Napoleon founds the Bank of France |
| 1801 | France defeats Austria and acquires Italian and German territories in the Treaty of Lunéville |
| | Napoleon signs a concordat with the pope |
| 1802 | Treaty of Amiens with Britain |
| March 1804 | Execution of the Duke of Engheim |
| December 1804 | Napoleon crowns himself emperor |
| October 1805 | Battle of Trafalgar: Britain defeats the French and Spanish fleets |
| December 1805 | Battle of Austerlitz: Napoleon defeats Austria and Prussia |
| 1807 | Treaties of Tilsit: Napoleon redraws the map of Europe |
| 1810 | Height of the Grand Empire |
| June 1812 | Napoleon invades Russia with 600,000 men |
| Winter 1812 | Disastrous retreat from Russia |
| March 1814 | Russia, Prussia, Austria, and Britain form the Quadruple Alliance to defeat France |
| April 1814 | Napoleon abdicates and is exiled to Elba |

deloupe, he succeeded. Here as elsewhere, the military dictator betrayed the revolutionary ideals of freedom and liberty.

Napoleon could honestly boast that his government was based on three forces: "My policemen, my officials, and my priests." The occasional elections were a farce. Later laws prescribed harsh penalties for political offenses. Whereas the Revolution had established that a person was presumed innocent until proven guilty, Napoleon's penal code placed the burden of proving one's innocence upon the defendant.

These changes in the law were part of the creation of a police state in France. Since Napoleon was usually busy making war, this task was largely left to Joseph Fouché, an unscrupulous opportunist who had earned a reputation for brutality during the Reign of Terror. As minister of police – a kind of super police chief at the national level – Fouché organized a ruthlessly efficient spy system, which kept thousands of citizens under continuous police surveillance. People even suspected of subversive thoughts were arbitrarily detained, placed under house arrest, or – shades of modern totalitarian states – consigned to insane asylums. After 1810 political suspects were held in state prisons, as they had been during the Terror. There were about 2,500 such political prisoners in 1814.

## NAPOLEON'S WARS AND FOREIGN POLICY

Napoleon was above all a military man, and a great one. After coming to power in 1799, he sent peace feelers to Austria and Great Britain, the two remaining members of the Second Coalition, which had been formed against France in 1798. When these overtures were rejected, French armies led by Napoleon decisively defeated the Austrians. In the Treaty of Lunéville (1801) Austria accepted the loss of its Italian possessions, and German territory on the west bank of the Rhine was incorporated into France. Once more, as in 1797, the British were alone, and war-weary, like the French.

Still seeking to consolidate his regime domestically, Napoleon concluded the Treaty of Amiens with Great Britain in 1802. Britain agreed to return Trinidad and the Caribbean islands, which it had seized from France since 1792. The treaty said very little about Europe, though. France remained in control of Holland, the Austrian Netherlands, the west bank of the Rhine, and most of the Italian peninsula. Napoleon was free to reshape the German states as he wished. To the dismay of British businessmen, the Treaty of Amiens did not provide for expansion of the commerce between Britain and the Continent. It was clearly a diplomatic triumph for Napoleon, and peace with honor and profit increased his popularity at home.

In 1802, Napoleon was secure but unsatisfied. Always more of a romantic gambler than an enlightened administrator, he could not contain his power drive. Aggressively redraw-

ing the map of Germany so as to weaken Austria and attract the secondary states of southwestern Germany toward France, Napoleon was also almost entirely responsible for renewed war with Great Britain. Regarding war with Britain as inevitable, he threatened British interests in the eastern Mediterranean and tried to restrict British trade with all of Europe. Britain had technically violated the Treaty of Amiens by failing to evacuate the island of Malta, but it was Napoleon's decision to renew war. Like Hitler in 1940, he concentrated his armies in the French ports on the Channel in the fall of 1803 and began making preparations to invade England. Yet Great Britain remained mistress of the seas. When Napoleon tried to bring his Mediterranean fleet around Gibraltar to northern France, a combined French and Spanish fleet was, after a series of mishaps, virtually annihilated by Lord Nelson at the battle of Trafalgar on October 21, 1805. Invasion of England was henceforth impossible.

Renewed fighting had its advantages, however, for the cunning first consul used the wartime atmosphere to have himself proclaimed emperor. He secretly supplied money to French royalists in England, who were organizing a conspiracy to restore the Bourbons, and then fell upon the émigrés caught in his trap when they got to France in early 1804. Unable to find any clear tie between the captured émigrés and any of the Bourbons, Napoleon nonetheless seized a Bourbon prince, the duke of Enghein, in the neutral German state of Baden in March 1804. Subsequently, aware that his widely publicized charges against the duke of Enghein were in fact false, Napoleon nevertheless had the duke executed immediately after his arrival in Paris. On the basis of these plots and lies, Napoleon then asked the people to make him emperor. He needed more power to save the nation

*WAR IN SPAIN   This drawing from Goya's* Disasters of War *shows French soldiers about to kill Spanish guerrillas. The patriotic Goya has captured the savagery of the struggle in Spain after 1808. (Courtesy of the Hispanic Society of America)*

from the Bourbons! It worked, and France accepted a restored monarchy.

Austria, Russia, and Sweden joined with Britain to form the Third Coalition against France shortly before the battle of Trafalgar. Actions like the execution of the duke of Enghein and Napoleon's decision to make himself king of Italy had convinced both Alexander I of Russia and Francis II of Austria that Napoleon had to be checked. Yet the Austrians and the Russians were no match for Napoleon, who scored a brilliant victory over

them at the battle of Austerlitz in December 1805. Alexander I decided to pull back, and Austria accepted large territorial losses in return for peace as the Third Coalition collapsed.

Victorious at Austerlitz, Napoleon proceeded to reorganize the German states to his liking. In 1806, he abolished many of the tiny German states as well as the ancient Holy Roman Empire, whose emperor had traditionally been the king of Austria. Napoleon established by decree a German Confederation of the Rhine, a union of fifteen German states minus Austria, Prussia, and Saxony. Naming himself "protector" of the confederation, Napoleon controlled western Germany with an iron hand. In 1806, for example, a Nuremberg bookseller named Johann Philipp Palm distributed a short work entitled *Germany in Her Deepest Humiliation.* Palm's pamphlet appealed to the kings of Saxony and Prussia to free the German people from Napoleon's destruction. Napoleon ordered Palm executed for this relatively minor offense.

Napoleon's actions in Germany alarmed the Prussians, who had been at peace with France for more than a decade. Expecting help from his ally Russia, Frederick William III of Prussia mobilized his armies. Napoleon attacked and won two more brilliant victories in October 1806 at Jena and Auerstadt, where the Prussians were outnumbered two to one. The war with Prussia and Russia continued into the following spring, and after Napoleon's larger armies won another victory Alexander decided to seek peace.

For several days in June 1807, the young tsar and the French emperor negotiated face-to-face on a raft anchored in the middle of the Niemen River. All the while, the helpless Frederick William rode back and forth on the shore, anxiously awaiting the results. As the German poet Heinrich Heine said later, Napoleon had but to whistle and Prussia would have ceased to exist. In the subsequent treaties of Tilsit, Prussia lost half of its population, while Russia accepted Napoleon's reorganization of western and central Europe, and Napoleon promised Alexander help against the Turks. A secret clause called upon Alexander I to declare war on Britain if Napoleon could not make peace on favorable terms with his island enemy.

After the victory of Austerlitz and even

MAP 21.1 NAPOLEONIC EUROPE IN 1810

more after the treaties of Tilsit, Napoleon saw himself as the emperor of Europe and not just of France. The so-called Grand Empire he built had three parts. The core was an ever-expanding France, which by 1810 included Belgium, Holland, parts of northern Italy, and much German territory on the east bank of the Rhine. Beyond French borders Napoleon established a number of dependent satellite kingdoms, upon the thrones of which he placed (and replaced) the members of his large family. Third, there were the independent but allied states of Austria, Prussia, and Russia. Both satellites and allies were expected after 1806 to support Napoleon's continental system, and thus to cease all trade with Britain.

The impact of the Grand Empire on the peoples of Europe was considerable. In the areas incorporated into France and in the satellites (see Map 21.1) Napoleon introduced many French laws, abolishing feudal dues and serfdom where French revolutionary armies had not already done so. Some of the peasants and middle-class benefited from these reforms. These benefits were purchased, however, at the price of heavy taxes in money and men for Napoleon's armies. Napoleon came to be regarded much more as a conquering tyrant than an enlightened liberator.

The first great revolt occurred in Spain. In 1808 a coalition of Catholics, monarchists, and patriots rebelled against Napoleon's attempts to make Spain a French satellite with a Bonaparte as its king. French armies occupied Madrid, but the foes of Napoleon fled to the hills and waged uncompromising guerrilla warfare. Spain was a clear warning. It was time to stop.

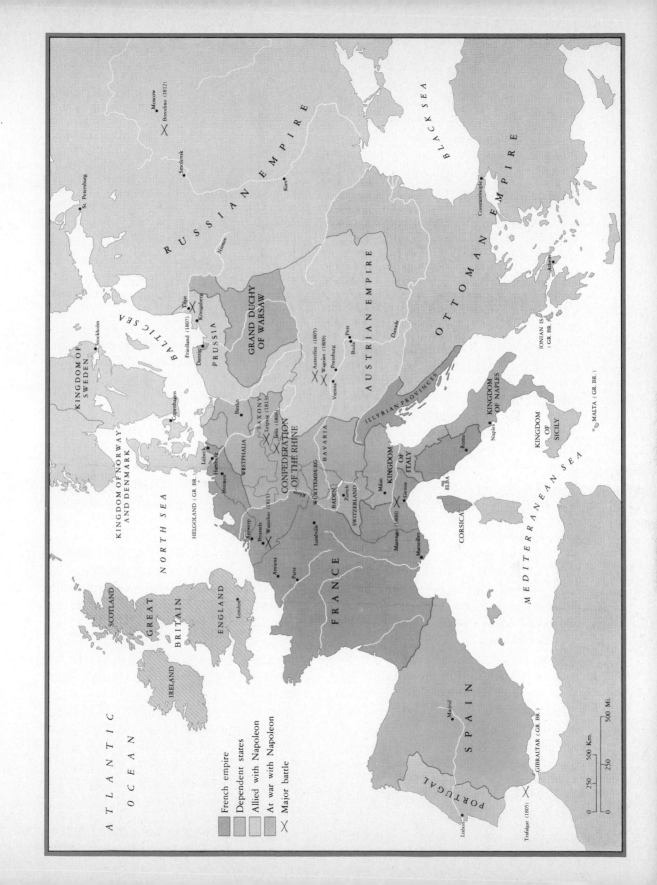

ATLANTIC
OCEAN

BLACK SEA

RUSSIAN EMPIRE

Moscow
Borodino (1812)

Smolensk

St. Petersburg

Kiev

OTTOMAN EMPIRE

Constantinople

Stockholm

KINGDOM OF SWEDEN

BALTIC SEA

Tilsit (1807)
Königsberg
Friedland (1807)
Danzig
PRUSSIA

GRAND DUCHY OF WARSAW

Danzig

Austerlitz (1805)
Wagram (1809)
Pest
Buda
Pressburg
AUSTRIAN EMPIRE
Vienna

IONIAN IS.
( GR. BR. )

Athens

Copenhagen

KINGDOM OF NORWAY
AND DENMARK

Berlin

SAXONY
Leipzig (1813)
Jena (1806)

CONFEDERATION
OF THE RHINE

ILLYRIAN PROVINCES

MALTA ( GR. BR. )

HELGOLAND ( GR. BR. )

NORTH
SEA

Lübeck
Hamburg
Bremen

WESTPHALIA

Rhine

WÜRTTEMBERG

BAVARIA

Milan

KINGDOM
OF
ITALY

Rome

KINGDOM
OF NAPLES

Naples

KINGDOM
OF
SICILY

MEDITERRANEAN SEA

SCOTLAND

GREAT
BRITAIN

ENGLAND

London

Antwerp
Brussels
Waterloo (1815)

Amiens
Paris

Lunéville

BADEN
Zürich
SWITZERLAND

ELBA

Genoa
Marengo (1800)
Marseilles

CORSICA

IRELAND

FRANCE

SPAIN

Madrid

PORTUGAL

Lisbon

GIBRALTAR ( GR. BR. )

Trafalgar (1805)

French empire
Dependent states
Allied with Napoleon
At war with Napoleon
Major battle

500 Km.
500 Mi.
250
250
0
0

Yet Napoleon would not, could not. In 1810, when the Grand Empire was at its height, Britain still remained at war with France, helping the guerrillas in Spain and Portugal (see Map 21.1). The continental system, organized to exclude British goods from the Continent and force that "nation of shopkeepers" to its knees, was a failure. Instead, it was France that suffered from Britain's counterblockade, which created hard times for Napoleon's strongest supporters – the French middle class. Perhaps looking for a scapegoat, Napoleon turned upon Alexander I of Russia, who had been fully supporting Napoleon's war of prohibitions against British goods.

Napoleon's invasion of Russia began in June 1812 with a force that eventually numbered 600,000, probably the largest force yet assembled in a single army. Only one-third of this force was French, however; nationals of all the satellites and allies were drafted into the operation. Originally planning to winter in the Russian city of Smolensk if Alexander did not sue for peace, Napoleon reached Smolensk and recklessly pressed on. The great battle of Borodino that followed was a draw, and the Russians retreated in good order. Alexander ordered the evacuation of Moscow, which then burned, and he refused to negotiate. Finally, after five weeks in the burned-out city, Napoleon ordered a retreat. That retreat was one of the great military disasters in history. The Russian army and the Russian winter cut Napoleon's army to pieces. Only 100,000 men returned to their homelands.

As before in Egypt, Napoleon deserted his troops and fled to Paris to raise yet another army. He might still have had peace and saved his throne if he had been willing to accept a France reduced to its historic size. This was what Austria's foreign minister Metternich proposed. But Napoleon refused. Austria and Prussia deserted Napoleon and joined Russia and Great Britain in the Fourth Coalition. All across Europe patriots called for a "war of liberation" against Napoleon's oppression, and the well-disciplined regular armies of Napoleon's enemies closed in for the kill. This time the coalition held together, cemented by the Treaty of Chaumont, which created a Quadruple Alliance to last for twenty years. Less than a month later, on April 4, 1814, a defeated, abandoned Napoleon abdicated his throne. An era had ended. Peace in Europe was possible.

———◆———

The revolution that began in America and spread to France was a liberal revolution. Inspired by English history, especially the Glorious Revolution, and some of the teachings of the Enlightenment, revolutionaries on both sides of the Atlantic sought to establish civil liberties and equality before the law within the framework of representative government. Success in America was subsequently matched by success in France, thanks to the decisive action of the poor and the oppressed – the sans-culottes and the peasants. The government and society established by the Declaration of the Rights of Man and the French constitution of 1791 were remarkably similar to those created in America by the federal Constitution and the Bill of Rights. All classes except the nobility benefited from this great step forward in human history, though the prosperous middle class may have profited most.

Yet the revolution in France did not end with the liberal victory of 1789–1791. As Robespierre led the determined French people in a total effort against foreign foes, it became more democratic, radical, and violent. This effort succeeded, but at the price of dictatorship, first by Robespierre himself and then by the Directory and Napoleon. Some historians blame the excesses of the French revolutionaries for the emergence of dictatorship, while others hold the conservative monarchs of Europe responsible. In any case, historians have often concluded that the French Revolution ended in failure.

This conclusion is highly debatable, though. After the fall of Robespierre the solid middle class with its liberal philosophy and Enlightenment world-view reasserted itself. Under the Directory it salvaged a good portion of the social and political gains that it and the peasantry had made between 1789 and 1791. In so doing, the middle-class leaders repudiated the radical social and economic measures associated with Robespierre, but they never reestablished the old order of privileged nobility and absolute monarchs. And although napoleon drastically curtailed thought and speech, his dictatorship used rather than weakened the middle class nd the peasantry. Careers were open to talent, and private wealth remained secure. In spite of a generation of war and upheaval, a very substantial part of the liberal triumph of 1789–1791 survived in France in 1814. Old Europe would never be the same.

## NOTES

1. Quoted by R. R. Palmer, *The Age of Democratic Revolution,* Princeton University Press, Princeton, N.J., 1959, 1.239.

2. G. Lefebvre, *The Coming of the French Revolution,* Vintage Books, New York, 1947, p. 81.

3. P. H. Beck, ed., *The French Revolution,* Walker, New York, 1970, p. 89.

4. O. Hufton, "Women in Revolution," *Past and Present* 53 (November 1971): 91–95.

5. G. Pernoud and S. Flaisser, eds., *The French Revolution,* Fawcett Publications, Greenwich, Conn., 1960, p. 61.

6. L. Gershoy, *The Era of the French Revolution, 1789–1799,* Van Nostrand, New York, 1957, p. 135.

7. Ibid., p. 150.

8. Pernoud and Flaisser, pp. 193–194.

## SUGGESTED READING

In addition to the fascinating eyewitness reports on the French Revolution in P. Beck, *The French Revolution,* and G. Pernoud and S. Flaisser, eds., *The French Revolution* (1960), A. Young's *Travels in France During the Years 1787, 1788 and 1789* (1969) offers an engrossing contemporary description of France and Paris on the eve of revolution. Edmund Burke, *Reflections on the Revolution in France,* first published in 1790, is the classic conservative indictment. The intense passions the French Revolution has generated may be seen in the nineteenth-century French historians, notably the enthusiastic Jules Michelet, *History of the French Revolution;* the hostile Hippolyte Taine; and the judicious Alexis de Tocqueville, whose masterpiece, *The Old Regime and the French Revolution,* was first published in 1856. Important recent general studies on the entire period are R. R. Palmer, *The Age of Democratic Revolution* (1959, 1964), which paints a comparative international picture; E. J. Hobsbawm, *The Age of Revolution, 1789–1848* (1962); C. Breunig, *The Age of Revolution and Reaction, 1789–1850* (1970); O. Connelly, *French Revolution – Napoleonic Era* (1979); and L. Dehio, *The Precarious Balance: Four Centuries of the European Power Struggle* (1962). C. Brinton's older but delightfully written *A Decade of Revolution, 1789–1799* (1934) complements his stimulating *Anatomy of Revolution* (1938), an ambitious comparative approach to revolution in England, America, France, and Russia. A. Cobban, *The Social Interpretation of the French Revolution* (1964), is an exciting reassessment of many well-worn ideas, to be compared with W. Doyle, *Origins of the French Revolution* (1981); G. Lefebvre, *The Coming of the French Revolution* (1947); and N. Hampson, *A Social History of the French Revolution* (1963). G. Rudé makes the men and women of the great days of upheaval come alive in his *The Crowd in the French Revolution* (1959). R. R. Palmer studies sympathetically the leaders of the Terror in *Twelve Who Ruled* (1941). Two other particularly interesting detailed works are C. L. R. James, *The Black Jacobins* (1938), on black slave revolt in Haiti, and J. C. Herold, *Mistress to an Age* (1955), on the remarkable Madame de Staël. On revolution in America, E. Morgan, *The Birth of the Republic, 1763–89,* and B. Bailyn, *The Ideological Origins of the American Revolution* (1967), are noteworthy. Three important recent studies on aspects of revolutionary France are D. Jourdan's vivid *The King's Trial: Louis XVI vs. the French Revolution* (1979); W. Sewell, Jr.'s imaginative *Work and Revolution in France: The Language of Labor from the Old Regime to 1848* (1980); and R. Phillips' *Family Breakdown in Late Eighteenth-Century France: Divorces in Rouen, 1792–1803* (1980).

P. Geyl, *Napoleon, For and Against* (1949), is a delightful discussion of changing historical interpretations of Napoleon. Good biographies are J. M. Thompson, *Napoleon Bonaparte: His Rise and Fall* (1952); F. H. M. Markham, *Napoleon* (1964); and E. Ludwig's popular novel *Napoleon* (1915). Other wonderful novels inspired by this period are Raphael Sabatini, *Scaramouche,* a swashbuckler of revolutionary intrigue with accurate historical details; Charles Dickens's classic *Tale of Two Cities;* and Leo Tolstoy's monumental saga of Napoleon's invasion of Russia (and much more), *War and Peace.*

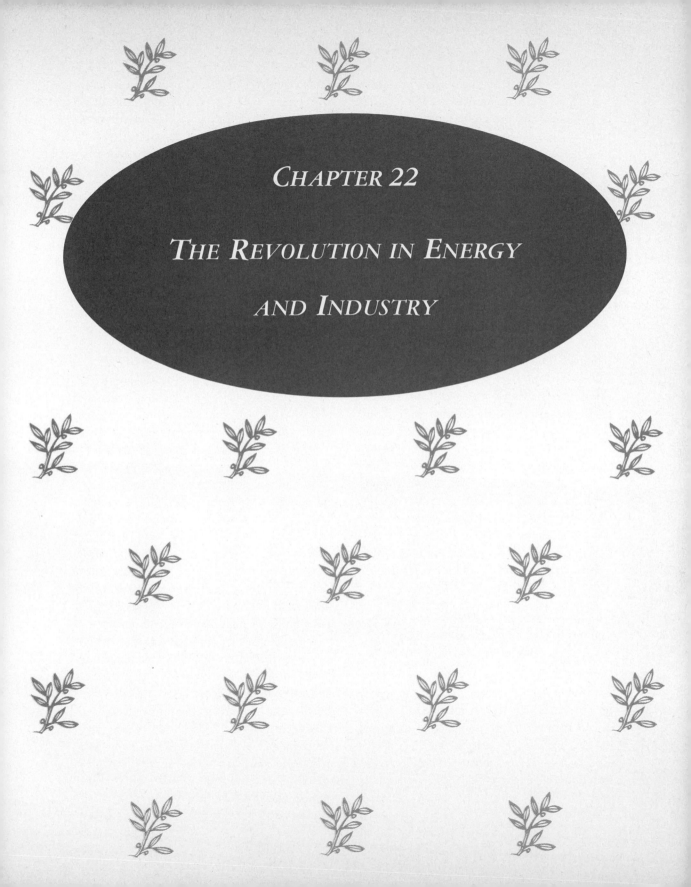

# CHAPTER 22

# THE REVOLUTION IN ENERGY

# AND INDUSTRY

*AT ABOUT THE TIME* the French Revolution was opening a new political era, another revolution was transforming economic and social life. This was the Industrial Revolution, which began in England in the 1780s and spread after 1815 to continental Europe and then around the world. Because the Industrial Revolution was less dramatic than the French Revolution, some historians see industrial development as basically moderate and evolutionary. In the long perspective, however, it was rapid and brought about radical changes. Perhaps only the development of agriculture in Neolithic times had a similar impact and significance.

The Industrial Revolution profoundly modified much of human experience. It changed patterns of work, transformed the social class structure, and eventually even altered the international balance of political power. It may quite possibly have saved Europe from the poverty of severe overpopulation and even from famine. How did this happen? How and why did drastic changes occur in industry, and how did these changes affect people and society? These are the questions this chapter will seek to answer. Chapter 24 will examine in detail the emergence of accompanying changes in urban civilization.

## THE INDUSTRIAL REVOLUTION IN ENGLAND

The Industrial Revolution began in England. It was something new in history, and it was quite unplanned. With no models to copy and no idea of what to expect, England had to pioneer not only in industrial technology but also in social relations and urban living. Between 1793 and 1815, these formidable tasks were complicated by almost constant war with France. As the trailblazer in economic development, as France was in political changes, England must command special attention.

### EIGHTEENTH-CENTURY ORIGINS

The Industrial Revolution grew out of the expanding Atlantic economy of the eighteenth century, which served mercantilist England remarkably well. England's colonial empire, augmented by a strong position in Latin America and in the African slave trade, provided a growing market for English manufactured goods. So did England itself. In an age when it was much cheaper to ship goods by water than by land, no part of England was more than twenty miles from navigable water. Beginning in the 1770s, a canal-building boom greatly enhanced this natural advantage (see Map 22.1). Nor were there any tariffs within the country to hinder trade, as there were in France before 1789 and in politically fragmented Germany.

Agriculture played a central role in bringing about the Industrial Revolution in England. English farmers were second only to the Dutch in productivity in 1700, and they were continuously adopting new methods of farming as the century went on. The result, especially before 1760, was a period of bountiful crops and low food prices. The ordinary English family did not have to spend almost everything it earned just to buy bread. It could spend more on other items, on manufactured goods – leather shoes or a razor for the man, a bonnet or a shawl for the woman, toy soldiers for the son, and a doll for the daughter. Thus, demand for goods within the country complemented the demand from the colonies.

England had other assets that helped give rise to the Industrial Revolution. Unlike eighteenth-century France, England had an effective central bank and well-developed credit markets. The monarchy and the aristocratic oligarchy, which had jointly ruled the country since 1688, provided stable and predictable government. At the same time the government let the domestic economy operate fairly freely and with few controls, encouraging personal initiative, technical change, and a free market. Finally, England had long had a large class of hired agricultural laborers, whose numbers were further increased by the enclosure movement of the late eighteenth century. These rural wage earners were relatively mobile – compared to village-bound peasants in France and western Germany, for example – and along with cottage workers they formed a potential industrial labor force for capitalist entrepreneurs.

All these factors combined to initiate the Industrial Revolution, which began in the 1780s – after the American war for independence and just before the French Revolution. Thus the great economic and political revolutions that have shaped the modern world occurred almost simultaneously, though they began in different countries. The Industrial Revolution was, however, a longer process. It was not complete in England until 1830 at the earliest, and it had no real impact on continental countries until after the Congress of Vienna ended the era of revolutionary wars in 1815.

### THE FIRST FACTORIES

The pressure to produce more goods for a growing market was directly related to the first decisive breakthrough of the Industrial Revolution – the creation of the world's first large factories in the English cotton textile industry. Technological innovations in the manufacture of cloth led to a whole new system of production and social relationships. Since no other industry experienced such a

MAP 22.1  COTTAGE INDUSTRY AND TRANS-PORTATION IN EIGHTEENTH-CENTURY ENG-LAND  *England had an unusually good system of navigable waterways even before river-linking canals made it better.*

rapid or complete transformation before 1830, these trail-blazing developments deserve special consideration.

Although the putting-out system of merchant capitalism (page 675) was expanding all across Europe in the eighteenth century, this pattern of rural industry was most fully developed in England. Thus it was in England, under the pressure of growing demand, that the system's shortcomings first began to outweigh its advantages. This was especially true in the textile industry after about 1760.

The constant shortage of thread in the textile industry focused attention on ways of improving spinning. Many a tinkering worker knew that a better spinning wheel promised rich rewards. Spinning of the traditional raw materials – wool and flax – proved hard to change, but cotton was different. Cotton textiles had first been imported into England from India by the East India Company, and by 1760 there was a tiny domestic industry in northern England. After many experiments over a generation, a gifted carpenter and jack-of-all trades, James Hargreaves, invented his cotton spinning jenny about 1765. At almost the same moment a barber-turned-manufacturer named Richard Arkwright invented (or possibly pirated) another kind of spinning machine, the water frame. These breakthroughs produced an explosion in the infant industry. By 1790, the new machines produced ten times as much cotton yarn as had been made in 1770. By 1800, the production of cotton thread was England's most important industry.

Hargreaves' jenny was simple and inexpensive. It was also hand-operated. In early models, from six to twenty-four spindles were mounted on a sliding carriage, and each spindle spun a fine slender thread. The woman moved the carriage back and forth with one hand and turned a wheel to supply power with the other. Now it was the weaver who could not keep up with his vastly more efficient wife.

Arkwright's water frame employed a different principle. It quickly acquired a capacity of several hundred spindles, and required much more power – water power. The water frame thus required large specialized mills, factories that employed as many as a thousand workers from the very beginning. The water frame could spin only coarse strong thread, which was then put out for respinning on in-

numerable hand-powered cottage jennies. Around 1790 Samuel Crompton's innovation, the "mule," began to require more power than the human arm could supply. (Crompton's invention was called the mule because it united the best aspects of the jenny and the water frame, as a mule combines the traits of its mother the horse and its father the donkey.) After that time, all cotton spinning was gradually concentrated in factories.

The first consequences of these revolutionary developments were much more beneficial than is usually believed. Cotton goods became much cheaper, and they were bought and treasured by all classes. In the past only the wealthy could afford the comfort and cleanliness of underwear, which was called body linen because it was made from expensive linen cloth. Now millions of poor people could afford to wear cotton slips and underpants, who had earlier worn nothing underneath their coarse, filthy outer garments.

The family was freed from its constant search for adequate yarn from scattered, part-time spinners, since all the thread needed could be spun in the cottage on the jenny or obtained from a nearby factory. The wages of weavers, now hard pressed to keep up with the spinners, rose markedly until about 1792. Weavers were among the best-paid workers in England. They were known to walk proudly through the streets with £5 notes stuck in their hatbands, and they dressed like the middle class.

One result of this unprecedented prosperity was that large numbers of agricultural laborers became weavers. Meanwhile, however, mechanics and capitalists were seeking to invent a power loom to save on labor costs. This Edmund Cartwright achieved in 1785. But the power looms of the factories worked poorly at first, and handloom weavers continued to receive good wages until at least 1800.

*HARGREAVES SPINNING JENNY This early model was rapidly improved. By 1783 one woman could easily spin by hand a hundred threads of cotton at a time. (Photo: Caroline Buckler)*

Working conditions in the early factories were less satisfactory than those of cottage weavers and spinners. But until the late 1780s most English factories were in rural areas, where they had access to water power. These factories employed a relatively small percentage of all cotton textile workers. People were reluctant to work in them, partly because they resembled the poorhouses where destitute inmates had to labor for very little pay. Therefore, factory owners turned to young children as a source of labor. More precisely, they turned to children who had been abandoned by their parents and put in the care of local parishes. The parish officers often "apprenticed" such unfortunate orphans to factory owners. The parish thus saved money and the factory owners gained workers over whom they exercised almost the authority of slave-owners. The hours were terrible, the conditions appalling. But only the nakedness of this exploitation was new. These children, and the women who came to work beside them in the next generation, were simply doing in the factory, under different conditions, the same kind of work they had long done in their cottages. It is some consolation that such exploitation of small children was at this point more nearly ending than beginning.

The creation of the world's first modern factories in the English cotton textile industry in the 1770s and 1780s, which grew out of the putting-out system of cottage production, was a momentous development. Both symbolically and in substance, the big new cotton mills marked the beginning of the Industrial Revo-

MAKING CHARCOAL    *After wood was carefully cut and stacked, iron masters slowly burned it to produce charcoal. Before the Industrial Revolution, a country's iron industry depended in large part on the size of its forests. (Photo: Caroline Buckler)*

lution in England in the 1780s and the acceleration of English industrial development.

## THE PROBLEM OF ENERGY

The growth of the cotton textile industry might have been stunted or cut short, however, if water from rivers and streams had remained the primary source of power for the new factories. But this did not occur. Instead, an epoch-making solution was found to the age-old problem of energy and power. It was this solution to the energy problem — a problem once again very much before us today — that permitted continued rapid development in cotton textiles, the gradual generalization of the factory system, and the triumph of the Industrial Revolution.

Human beings, like all living organisms, require energy. Adult men and women need from 2,000 to 4,000 calories (calories are units of energy) daily simply to fuel their bodies, work, and survive. Energy comes from a variety of sources; energy also takes different forms and one form may be converted into another. Plants have been converting solar energy into caloric matter for eons. And human beings have used their toolmaking abilities to construct machines that convert one form of energy into another for their own benefit.

Prehistoric people relied on plants and plant-eating animals as their sources of energy. With the development of agriculture, the early civilizations were able to increase the number of "useful" plants and thus the supply of energy. Some plants could be fed to domesticated animals, like the horse. Stronger than human beings, these animals converted the energy in the plants into useful work. In the medieval period people began to develop water mills to grind their grain and windmills to pump water and drain swamps. More efficient use of water and wind in the sixteenth and seventeenth centuries enabled human beings to accomplish more; intercontinental sailing ships are a prime example. Nevertheless, even into the eighteenth century society continued to rely for energy mainly on plants, and human beings and animals continued to perform most useful work. This dependence meant that Western civilization remained poor in energy and power.

Lack of power lay at the heart of the poverty that afflicted the large majority of people. The man behind the plow and the woman at the spinning wheel could employ only horsepower and human muscle in their labor. No matter how hard they worked, they could not produce very much. What people needed were new sources of energy and more power at their disposal. Then they would be able to work more efficiently, produce more, and live better.

Where was more energy to be found? Almost all energy came directly or indirectly from plants, and therefore from the land: grain for people, hay for animals, and wood for heat. The land was also the principal source of raw materials needed for industrial production: wool and flax for clothing, leather for shoes, wood for housing, tools, and ironmaking. And although swamps could be drained and marshes reclaimed from the sea, it was difficult to expand greatly the amount of land available. True, its yield could be increased, such as by the elimination of fallow; yet there were definite limits to such improvements.

The shortage of energy was becoming particularly severe in England by the eighteenth century. Because of the growth of population, most of the great forests of medieval England had long ago been replaced by fields of grain and hay. Wood was in ever shorter supply; yet it remained tremendously important. It was the primary source of heat for all homes and industries. It was also the key to transportation, since ships and wagons were made of wood. Moreover, wood was, along with iron ore, the basic raw material of the iron industry. Processed wood (charcoal) was the fuel mixed with iron ore in the blast furnace to produce pig iron. The iron industry's appetite for wood was enormous, and even very modest and constant levels of iron production had gone far toward laying bare the forests of England, as well as parts of Europe. By 1740, the English iron industry was stagnating. Vast forests enabled Russia in the eighteenth century to become the world's leading producer of iron, much of which was exported to England. But Russia's potential for growth was limited too, and in a few decades Russia would reach the barrier of inadequate energy that was already holding England back.

## "STEAM IS AN ENGLISHMAN"

As this early energy crisis grew worse, England looked toward its abundant and widely scattered reserves of coal as an alternative to its vanishing wood. Coal was first used in England in the late Middle Ages as a source of heat. By 1640, most homes in London were heated with it, and it also provided heat for making beer, glass, soap, and other products. Coal was not used, however, to produce mechanical energy or to power machinery. It was there that coal's potential was enormous, as a simple example shows.

One pound of good bituminous coal contains about 3,500 calories of heat energy. A miner who eats 3,500 calories of food can dig out 500 pounds of coal a day, using hand tools. Even an extremely inefficient converter, which transforms only 1 percent of the heat energy in coal into mechanical energy, will produce 27 horsepower-hours of work from the 500 pounds of coal the miner cut out of the earth. (The miner, by contrast, produces only about 1 horsepower-hour in the course of a day.) Much more energy is consumed by the converter, but much more work can be done.

Early steam engines were just such inefficient converters. As more coal was produced, mines were dug deeper and deeper and were constantly filling with water. Mechanical pumps, usually powered by animals walking in circles at the surface, had to be installed. At one mine, fully 500 horses were used in pumping. Such power was expensive and bothersome. In an attempt to overcome these disadvantages, Thomas Savery in 1698 and Thomas Newcomen in 1705 invented the first primitive steam engines.

Both of these engines were extremely inefficient. Both burned coal to produce steam, which was then injected into a cylinder or reservoir. In Newcomen's engine the steam in the cylinder was cooled, creating a partial vacuum in the cylinder. This vacuum allowed the pressure of the earth's atmosphere to push the piston in the cylinder down and operate a pump. By the 1770s, many Savery engines and hundreds of Newcomen engines were working successfully, though inefficiently, in English mines.

In the early 1760s, a gifted young Scot named James Watt (1736–1819) was drawn to a critical study of the steam engine. Watt was employed at the time by the University of Glasgow as a skilled craftsman making scientific instruments. The Scottish universities were pioneers in practical technical education, and in 1763 Watt was called on to repair a Newcomen engine being used in a physics course. After a series of observations, Watt saw why the Newcomen engine wasted so much energy: the cylinder was being heated and cooled for every single stroke of the piston. To remedy this problem Watt added a separate condenser, where the steam could be condensed without cooling the cylinder. This splendid invention greatly increased the efficiency of the steam engine.

To invent something in a laboratory is one thing; to make it a practical success is quite another. Watt needed skilled workers, precision parts, and capital, and the relatively advanced nature of the English economy proved crucial. A partnership with a wealthy, progressive toymaker, Matthew Boulton of Birmingham, provided risk capital and a manufacturing plant. In the craft tradition of locksmiths, tinsmiths, and millwrights Watt found skilled mechanics who could install,

*The ENGINE for Raising Water (with a power made) by Fire*

THE NEWCOMEN ENGINE *The enormous steam-filled cylinder (C) was cooled by injecting cold water from the tank above (G) by means of a pipe (M). Atmospheric pressure then pushed the piston down, raised the beam, and pumped water from the mine. (Science Museum, London)*

regulate, and repair his sophisticated engines. From ingenious manufacturers like the cannonmaker John Wilkinson, who learned to bore cylinders with a fair degree of accuracy, Watt was gradually able to purchase precision parts. This support allowed him to create an effective vacuum and regulate a complex engine. In more than twenty years of constant effort Watt made many further improvements. By the late 1780s, the steam engine was a practical and commercial success in England.

As a nineteenth-century saying put it, "Steam is an Englishman."

The steam engine of Watt and his followers was the Industrial Revolution's most fundamental advance in technology. For the first time in history humanity had, at least for a few generations, almost unlimited power at its disposal. For the first time inventors and engineers could devise and implement all kinds of power equipment to aid people in their work. For the first time abundance was at least a possibility for ordinary men and women.

The steam engine was quickly put to use in many industries in England. It made possible the production of ever more coal, to feed steam engines elsewhere. The steam-power plant began to replace water power in the cotton spinning mills during the 1780s, contributing greatly to that industry's phenomenal ascension. Steam also took the place of water power in flour mills, in the malt mills used in breweries, in the flint mills supplying the china industry, and in the mills exported to the West Indies to crush sugar cane.

Steam power promoted important breakthroughs in other industries. The English iron industry was radically transformed. The use of powerful steam-driven bellows in the blast furnaces helped ironmakers switch over rapidly from limited charcoal to unlimited coke (which is made from coal) in the smelting of pig iron after 1770. In the 1780s, Henry Cort developed the puddling furnace, which allowed pig iron to be refined in turn with coke. Strong, skilled ironworkers – the puddlers – "cooked" molten pig iron in a great vat, raking off globs of refined iron for further processing. Cort also developed heavy-duty steam-powered rolling mills, which were capable of spewing out finished iron in every shape and form.

The economic consequence of these technical innovations was a great boom in the English iron industry. In 1740, annual British iron production was only 17,000 tons. With the spread of coke smelting and the first impact of Cort's inventions, production reached 68,000 tons in 1788, 125,000 tons in 1796, and 260,000 tons in 1806. In 1844, Britain produced 3 million tons of iron. This was truly phenomenal expansion. Once scarce and expensive, iron became the cheap, basic building-block of the economy.

## THE COMING OF THE RAILROADS

Sailing ships had improved noticeably since the age of discoveries, and the second half of the eighteenth century saw extensive construction of hard and relatively smooth roads, particularly in France before the Revolution. Yet it was passenger traffic that benefited most from this construction. Overland shipment of freight, relying as it did solely on horsepower, was still quite limited and frightfully expensive; shippers relied on rivers and canals for heavy freight whenever possible. It was logical therefore that inventors would try to use steam power to improve inland transportation.

As early as 1800, an American ran a "steamer on wheels" through city streets. Other experiments followed. In the 1820s, English engineers perfected steam cars capable of carrying fourteen passengers at ten miles an hour – as fast as the mail coach. But the noisy, heavy steam automobiles frightened passing horses and damaged themselves as well as the roads with their vibrations. For the rest of the century horses continued to reign on highways and city streets.

The coal industry had long been using plank roads and rails to move coal wagons within mines and at the surface. Rails reduced friction and allowed a horse or a human being to pull a heavier load. Thus once a rail capable of supporting a heavy locomotive was developed in 1816, all sorts of experiments with steam engines on rails went forward. In 1825, after ten years of work, George Stephenson built an effective locomotive. In 1830, his *Rocket* sped down the track of the just-completed Liverpool and Manchester Railway at sixteen miles per hour. This was the world's first important railroad, fittingly steaming in the heart of industrial England.

The line from Liverpool to Manchester was

THE THIRD-CLASS CARRIAGE    *The French comic artist Honoré Daumier (1808–1879) was fascinated by the railroad and its human significance. This great painting focuses on the peasant grandmother, old and weary, absorbed in memories. The nursing mother is love and creativity, while the sleeping boy represents childhood innocence. (The Metropolitan Museum of Art. Bequest of Mrs. H. O. Havemeyer, 1929. The H. O. Havemeyer Collection)*

a financial as well as a technical success, and many private companies were quickly organized to build more rail lines. These companies had to get permission for their projects from Parliament and pay for the rights of way they needed; otherwise, their freedom was great. Within twenty years they had completed the main trunk lines of Great Britain. Other countries followed quickly with their own railway construction.

The significance of the railroad was tremendous. The railroad dramatically reduced the cost and uncertainty of shipping freight overland. This advance had many economic consequences. Previously, markets had tended to be small and local; as the barrier of high transportation costs was lowered, they became larger and even nationwide. Larger markets encouraged larger factories with more sophisticated machinery. Such factories could make goods cheaper, enabling people to pay less for them. They also tended to drive most cottage workers, many urban artisans, and some other manufacturers out of business.

In all countries the construction of railroads contributed to the growth of a class of urban workers. Cottage workers, farm laborers, and small peasants did not generally leave their jobs and homes to go directly to work in factories. However, the building of railroads created a strong demand for labor, especially unskilled labor, throughout a country. Like farm work, hard work on construction gangs was done in the open air with animals and hand tools. Many farm laborers and poor peasants, long accustomed to leaving their villages for temporary employment, went to build railroads. By the time the work was finished, life back home in the village often seemed dull and unappealing, and many men drifted to towns in search of work – with the railroad companies, in construction, in factories. By the time they sent for their wives and sweethearts to join them, they had become urban workers.

The railroad changed the outlook and values of the entire society. The last and culminating invention of the Industrial Revolution, the railroad dramatically revealed the power and increased the speed of the new age. Racing down a track at sixteen miles per hour or, by 1850, at a phenomenal fifty miles per hour was a new and awesome experience. As the noted French economist Michel Chevalier put it after a ride on the Liverpool and Manchester in 1833, "There are certain impressions that one cannot put into words!"

Some great painters like J. M. W. Turner (1775–1851) and Claude Monet (1840–1926) succeeded in expressing this sense of power and awe. So did the massive new train stations, the cathedrals of the industrial age. The leading railway engineers, like Isambard Kingdom Brunel and Thomas Brassey, whose tunnels pierced mountains and whose bridges spanned valleys, became the idols of the public – the astronauts of their day. Everyday speech absorbed the images of railroading.

After you got up a "full head of steam," you "highballed" along. And if you didn't "go off the track," you might "toot your own whistle." The railroad fired the imagination.

## BRITAIN AT MIDCENTURY

In 1851, London was the site of a famous industrial fair. This exposition was held in the newly built Crystal Palace, an architectural masterpiece made entirely of glass and iron, both of which were now cheap and abundant. For the hundreds of thousands who visited, one fact stood out. The little island of Britain – England, Wales, and Scotland – was "the workshop of the world." It alone produced two-thirds of the world's coal and more than half of its iron and cotton cloth. Britain was the first industrial nation (see Map 22.2).

Britain had unlocked and developed a new source of energy. With practically unlimited power, the British economy had enormously increased its production of manufactured goods. Between 1780 and 1800, Britain doubled its production of industrial goods. Between 1801 and 1851, the gross national product – the GNP that present-day newspapers and politicians are always talking about – rose three and a half times at constant prices. In other words, the British increased enormously their wealth and their national income. At the same time the population of Great Britain boomed, growing from about 9 million in 1780 to almost 21 million in 1851.

Since the economy grew much faster than the number of people, average real income per person grew markedly. (Real income is what people's money wages really buy after adjusting for the effects of inflation or deflation.) In fact, average real income per person in Britain just about *doubled* between 1801 and 1851, from £13 per person to £24 per person. Put very simply, and all other things being equal, the woman or man of 1851 could buy twice as much as the woman or man of 1801. Considering the poverty of the eighteenth century, poverty that all the drama and excitement of the French Revolution did little or nothing to reduce, this would appear to be a monumental achievement.

But perhaps all other things were not equal. Perhaps workers, farmers, and ordinary people did not share in the new wealth. Perhaps only the rich got richer, while the poor got poorer or made no progress. We shall turn to this great issue after looking at the spread of the Industrial Revolution to continental countries.

## THE SPREAD OF THE INDUSTRIAL REVOLUTION

The new methods of the Industrial Revolution spread rather slowly at first. Whereas Britain's economy began to speed up about 1780 and had created an industrial urban society by 1850, the economies of continental Europe began to follow only after 1815 and particularly after about 1830. First Belgium took up the challenge; then between about 1840 and 1860, France and the various states of Germany began developing rapidly, as did the United States. After 1870 Sweden, Russia, and Japan joined in and during the twentieth century many more countries have done so.

### THE CHALLENGE OF INDUSTRIALIZATION

If poverty was so widespread in Europe and if industrial development created so much more wealth per person in Great Britain, why did

MAP 22.2   THE INDUSTRIAL REVOLUTION IN ENGLAND, CA 1850   *Industry concentrated in the rapidly growing cities of the north and the midlands, where rich coal and iron deposits were in close proximity.*

continental countries wait years and even decades before they followed the British example? The eighteenth century was certainly an era of agricultural improvement, population increase, expanding foreign trade, and growing cottage industry. England led in these developments, but other countries participated in the general trend. Thus, when the pace of English industry began to accelerate in the 1780s, countries like France began to copy the new methods. English industry enjoyed clear superiority, but the Continent was not very far behind.

By 1815, however, the situation was quite different. In spite of wartime difficulties, English industry maintained the momentum of the 1780s and continued to grow and improve rapidly between 1789 and 1815. On the Continent the unending political and economic upheavals that began with the French Revolution had another effect. They disrupted trade, created runaway inflation, and fostered social anxiety. War severed normal communications between England and the Continent, severely handicapping continental efforts to use new British machinery and technology. Moreover, the years from 1789 to 1815 were, even for the privileged French economy, a time of "national catastrophe" – in the graphic words of a recent French scholar.[1] Thus, whatever the French Revolution and the Napoleonic era meant politically, economically and industrially they meant that France and the rest of Europe were much farther behind Britain in 1815 than in 1789.

This widening gap made it more difficult for other countries to follow the British example in energy and industry after 1815. British goods were being produced very economically, and they had come to dominate world markets completely while the continental states were absorbed in war between 1792 and 1815. In addition, British technology had become so advanced and complicated that very few engineers or skilled technicians outside England understood it. Moreover, the technology of steam power had grown much more expensive. It involved large investments in the iron and coal industries and, after 1830, required the existence of railroads, which were very costly. Continental businessmen had great difficulty finding the large sums of money the new methods demanded, and there was a shortage of laborers accustomed to

working in factories. Landowners and government officials were often so suspicious of the new form of industry and the changes it brought that they did little at first to encourage it. All these disadvantages slowed the spread of modern industry (see Map 22.3).

After 1815, however, when continental countries began to industrialize seriously, they had at least two important advantages. First, they did not need to develop, ever so slowly and expensively, their own advanced technology. Instead, they could simply "borrow" the new methods developed in Great Britain, as well as engineers and some of the financial resources they lacked. European countries like France and Russia had a second asset that many non-Western areas lacked in the nineteenth century. They had strong independent governments, which did not fall under foreign political control. These governments could fashion economic policies to serve their own interests, and they did. They could, eventually, use the power of the state to promote the growth of industry.

### AGENTS OF INDUSTRIALIZATION

To understand better the spread of modern industry, let us look at the fascinating careers of a few of the businessmen, workers, and apostles of industrialization who were involved. For economic life is as much the product of particular human efforts as of vast impersonal forces.

The British realized the great value of their technical discoveries and tried to keep knowledge of them to themselves. Until 1825 it was illegal for artisans and skilled mechanics to leave Britain; until 1843 the export of textile machinery and other equipment was forbidden. Many talented, ambitious workers, however, slipped out of the country illegally and introduced the new methods abroad.

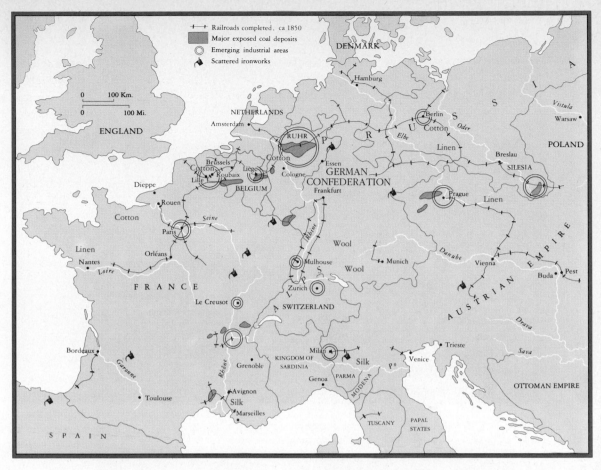

MAP 22.3 CONTINENTAL INDUSTRIALIZA-
TION, CA 1850 *Although continental countries
were beginning to make progress by 1850, they still
lagged far behind England. For example, continental*
*railroad building was still in an early stage, whereas
the English rail system was essentially complete (see
page 775).*

One such man was William Cockerill, a
Lancashire carpenter. He and his sons began
building cotton-spinning equipment in
French-occupied Belgium in 1799. In 1817,
the most famous son, John Cockerill, purchased the old summer palace of the deposed
bishops of Liège in southern Belgium. Cockerill converted the palace into a large industrial enterprise, which produced machinery,
steam engines, and then railway locomotives.
He also established modern ironworks and
coal mines at Liège, as well as other operations throughout western Europe.

Cockerill's plant at Seraing became an in-

dustrial nerve center, continually gathering
new information and transmitting it across
Europe. Many skilled British workmen came,
illegally, to work for Cockerill, and some
went on to found their own companies
throughout Europe. Newcomers brought the
latest plans and secrets, so that Cockerill
could boast that ten days after an industrial
advance occurred in Britain he knew all about
it in Belgium. Thus, British technicians and
skilled workers were a powerful force in the
spread of early industrialization.

Another instructive career is that of Fritz
Harkort, a pioneer in the German machinery

*COCKERILL'S WORKS  light up the night and display the awesome power of the new industrial technology in this lithograph of 1852. (The British Museum)*

industry. Harkort came from an old commercial family in Westphalia. He studied engineering developments in England while serving there as a Prussian army officer during the Napoleonic wars. Impressed and enchanted with what he saw, Harkort concluded that Germany had to match all these English achievements as quickly as possible. Setting up shop in an abandoned castle in the still-tranquil Ruhr Valley, Harkort felt an almost religious calling to build steam engines and become "the Watt of Germany."

Harkort's basic idea was simple, but it was enormously difficult to carry out. Steam engines had been greatly improved in the course

of thirty years, and the new models Harkort was trying to copy required much accuracy and know-how. Lacking skilled laborers to do the job, Harkort turned to England for experienced, though expensive, mechanics. He could not be choosy. As he later reminisced, "I had to cut several of my English workers down from the gallows, so to speak, if only in order to get some of them."[2] He longed for the day he could replace the haughty foreigners with his own countrymen.

Getting materials posed a great problem as well. German ironsmiths could not supply the thick iron boilers Harkort needed, and he had to import them from England at great cost and with frequent damage. There was a modest market for Harkort's engines, for the German coal industry was beginning to expand. But German roads were so bad – Harkort denounced them as death traps for man and beast – that steam engines had to be built at the works, completely dismantled and shipped piece by piece to the buyer, and then reassembled by Harkort's technicians. No wonder Harkort was a very early promoter of railroads, which, he predicted in 1829, "will bring countless revolutions to the world."

In spite of all these problems, Harkort built engines, sold them throughout Germany and the rest of Europe, and won fame and praise. His ambitious efforts also resulted in large financial losses for himself and his partners. These proved fatal, for Harkort's enterprise, like almost all the others of the day, was a private, capitalistic undertaking. It could not lose money indefinitely. In 1832, after sixteen years of activity and accomplishment, Harkort was forced out of his company by his financial backers, who cut back operations to reduce losses. In one sense, then, his career was a failure; yet Harkort was a pioneering visionary, the most creative German businessman of his era. His career illustrates both the great efforts of a few key business leaders to copy the British achievement and the extreme difficulty of the task.

Support from the government often helped businessmen in continental countries overcome some of their difficulties. Tariff protection was one such support. For example, after Napoleon's wars ended in 1815, France was suddenly flooded with cheaper and better English goods. The French government responded by laying high tariffs on many English imports, in order to protect the French economy. After 1815, continental governments bore the cost of building roads and canals to improve transportation, and they also bore much of the cost of building railroads.

The career of the German journalist and thinker Friedrich List (1789-1846) reflects government's greater role in the Industrial Revolution on the Continent than in England. List considered the growth of modern industry of the utmost importance because manufacturing was a primary means of increasing people's well-being and relieving their poverty. Moreover, List was a dedicated nationalist. He wrote that "the wider the gap between the backward and advanced nations becomes, the more dangerous it is to remain behind," for an agricultural nation was not only poor but weak, increasingly unable to defend itself and maintain its political independence. To promote industry was to defend the nation.

The practical policy List focused on in articles and in his *National System of Political Economy* (1841) was the tariff. He supported the formation of a customs union, or Zollverein, among the separate German states. Such a tariff union came into being in 1834. It allowed goods to move between the German member states without tariffs, and a single uniform tariff was erected against all other nations. List wanted a high protective tariff, which would encourage "infant industries," allowing them to develop and eventually to hold their own against their more advanced British counterparts. List denounced the English doctrine of free trade as little more than England's attempt "to make the rest of the world, like the Hindus, its serfs in all industrial and commercial relations." By the 1840s, List's ideas were increasingly popular in Germany and elsewhere.

Banks, like governments, also played a larger and more creative role on the Continent than in England. Previously, almost all banks in Europe had been private, organized as secretive partnerships. Such banks were content to deal with a few rich clients and a few big merchants. They avoided industry. In the 1830s, two Belgian banks pioneered in a new direction. The General Society of Belgium and the Bank of Belgium were big corporations with many stockholders, large and small. Thus their financial resources were large. The banks were able to use that money to develop industrial companies. They became in short, industrial banks.

Similar banks became important in France and Germany in the 1850s. They established and developed many railroads and many companies working in heavy industry. The most famous such bank was the Crédit Mobilier of Paris, founded by Isaac and Emile Pereire, two young Jewish journalists from Bordeaux. The Crédit Mobilier advertised extensively. It used the savings of thousands of small investors, as well as the resources of big ones. The activities of the bank were far-reaching; it built railroads all over France and Europe. As Emile Pereire had said in 1835, "It is not enough to outline gigantic programs on paper. I must write my ideas on the earth."

Industrial banks like the Crédit Mobilier mobilized the savings of thousands of small investors and invested those savings in industry and transportation, particularly in the 1850s. In doing so, the directors of these banks helped their countries find the capital needed for industrialization. They also often made themselves very wealthy.

## CAPITAL AND LABOR

Industrial development brought new social relations and problems between capital and labor. A new group of factory owners and big industrial capitalists arose. These men strengthened the wealth and size of the middle class, which had previously been made up mainly of merchants and professional people. The nineteenth century became the golden age of the middle class. Modern industry also created a much larger group – the factory workers. For the first time large numbers of men and women came together under one roof to work with complicated machinery for big capitalists and big companies. What was the nature of relations between these two new groups – between capital and labor? Did the new industrial middle class ruthlessly exploit the workers, as Karl Marx and others have charged?

### THE NEW CLASS OF FACTORY OWNERS

Early industrialists operated in a highly competitive economic system. As the careers of Watt and Harkort illustrate, there were countless problems of production, and success and large profits were by no means certain. Manufacturers, therefore, waged a constant battle to cut their costs of production and stay afloat. Most profit had to go back into the business for new and better machinery. "Dragged on by the frenzy of this terrible life," according to one of his dismayed critics, the struggling manufacturer had "no time for niceties. He must conquer or die, make a fortune or drown himself."[3]

The early industrialists came from a variety of backgrounds. Many, like Harkort, were from well-established merchant families, which provided capital and contacts. Others, like Watt and Cockerill, were of very modest means, especially in the early days. Artisans and skilled workmen of exceptional ability had unparalleled opportunities. The ethnic and religious groups that had been discrimin-

LARGE-SCALE INDUSTRY   *This fascinating drawing shows the main composing room of the central railroad printing shop in Paris in the 1870s. Most appropriately, the millions of tickets, timetables, and* *notices are being printed in a building of iron and glass, while France's cultural heroes look down approvingly. (Photo: Caroline Buckler)*

ated against in the traditional occupations controlled by the landed aristocracy jumped at the new chances. Quakers and Scots were tremendously important in England; Protestants and Jews dominated banking in Catholic France. Many of the industrialists were newly rich, and they were very proud and self-satisfied.

As factories grew larger, opportunities declined, at least in well-developed industries. It became considerably harder for a gifted but poor young mechanic to end up as a wealthy manufacturer. Formal education became more important as a means of advancement, and formal education at the advanced level was expensive. In England by 1830 and in France and Germany by 1860, leading industrialists

were more likely to have inherited their well-established enterprises, and they were financially much more secure than their fathers and grandfathers. They were also aware of a greater gap between themselves and their workers.

## THE NEW FACTORY WORKERS

The social consequences of the Industrial Revolution have long been hotly debated. Since any honest observer will see that some conditions got better and others got worse, vigorous debate is likely to continue. (Also, industry promoted rapid urbanization with its own great problems, as we shall see in Chapter 24.) Nevertheless, for workers and ordinary families, the Industrial Revolution brought a great transformation, which was, on balance, desirable. It marked a great step forward from the pattern of preindustrial life for the poor and the oppressed.

The condition of English workers in the Industrial Revolution has always generated the most controversy among historians, because England was the first country to industrialize and because the social consequences seem harshest there. Before 1850, other countries had not proceeded very far with industrialization, and almost everyone agrees that the economic conditions of European workers improved after 1850. The countries that followed England were able to benefit from English experience in social as well as technical matters. Thus, the early English Industrial Revolution provides the strongest case for the harmful social consequences of modern industrial development, at least prior to 1914, and it is fitting to focus on it.

From the beginning the Industrial Revolution in England had its critics. Among the first were the romantic poets. William Blake (1757–1827) called the early factories "satanic mills" and protested against the hard life of the London poor. William Wordsworth (1770–1850) lamented the destruction of the rural way of life and the pollution of the land and water. Doctors and reformers wrote eloquently of problems in the factories and new towns. Some handicraft workers, notably the Luddites who attacked whole factories in northern England in 1812 and after, smashed the new machines, which they believed were putting them out of work.

Another early critic was Friedrich Engels (1820–1895), the future revolutionary and colleague of Karl Marx. After studying conditions in northern England, this young middle-class German published *The Condition of the Working Class in England* in 1844. Engels

cast the problem of industrial life in class terms. "At the bar of world opinion," he wrote, "I charge the English middle classes with mass murder, wholesale robbery, and all the other crimes in the calendar."[4] Engels's charge of middle-class exploitation and increasing worker poverty was embellished by Marx and later socialists. It was extremely influential.

Meanwhile other observers believed that conditions were improving for the working class. Andrew Ure wrote in 1835 in his study of the cotton industry that conditions in most factories were not harsh and were even quite good. Edwin Chadwick, a great and conscientious government official well acquainted with the problems of the working class, concluded that "the whole mass of the laboring community" was increasingly able "to buy more of the necessities and minor luxuries of life."[5] Other observers were equally optimistic.

If all the contemporary indictments of observers like Engels and all the defenses of those like Ure were counted up, those who thought conditions were getting worse for working people would probably be the majority. Yet it is clear that opinions differed greatly. In an attempt to go deeper into the problem, historians must look at different kinds of sources.

Statistical evidence is one such source. It should help resolve the conflicting opinions of contemporary and often biased observers. If working people suffered a great decline, as Engels and later socialists asserted, then they must have bought less and less food, clothing, and other necessities as time went on. The purchasing power of the working person's wages must have declined drastically.

At the end of the nineteenth century, dispassionate British statisticians tried to pull together all the evidence on wages and prices and thereby measure what working-class peo-

COTTON MILL WORKERS *Family members often worked side by side in industry. Here women and children are combing raw cotton and drawing it into loose strands called rovings, which will then be spun into fine thread. (The Mansell Collection)*

ple could or could not have bought. Such an approach was only partially successful. England was not in a prestatistical age during its Industrial Revolution, but there were many gaps and shortcomings in the available numbers. Nevertheless, this approach does offer important insights.

During the period from about 1750 to 1790, when cottage industry was still dominant, the purchasing power of the average British laborer's wages seems to have risen somewhat. The workers – primarily cottage workers, artisans, and farm hands – could buy more goods, like food and clothing, over the years. Wages in industry were substantially higher than in agriculture, and all kinds of

wages rose faster in the industrializing areas of the north than in the purely agricultural counties of the south. The cautious conclusion must be that from 1750 to 1790 the growth of industry made for a more abundant life for working people, in terms of material goods.

The years from 1792 to 1815, a period of constant war against revolutionary and Napoleonic France, brought very different circumstances. Wages rose, but they did not keep up with inflation. Food prices rose most, as the price of wheat approximately doubled from 1790 to 1810. The condition of the working poor declined.

Between 1815 and 1850, the purchasing

power of workers' wages increased again. Money wages remained steady or fell somewhat, but prices fell more. The fullest studies show that the real wages of the average worker – agricultural and industrial – increased 25 percent between 1800 and 1825 and another 40 percent between 1825 and 1850.[6] The trend was definitely upward but the course was erratic. Between 1820 and 1840, real wages increased by only 5 to 10 percent. However, the wages of unskilled workers in British industry were again, as before 1790, about twice as high as those of unskilled workers in British agriculture. In short, throughout the Industrial Revolution, with the exception of the wartime period, there was apparently substantial economic improvement for British workers.

This important conclusion must be qualified, though. Increased purchasing power meant more goods, but it did not necessarily mean greater happiness. People do not live by bread alone. Also, these figures do not say anything about how the level of unemployment may have risen, for the simple reason that there are no good unemployment statistics from this period. Furthermore, the hours in the average workweek increased; to an unknown extent, workers earned more simply because they worked more. Finally, the wartime decline was of great importance. The war years were formative years for the new factory labor force. They were also some of the hardest. They colored the early experience of modern industrial life in somber tones.

Another way to consider the workers' standard of living is to look at the goods they purchased. Again, the evidence is somewhat contradictory. Speaking generally, workers ate somewhat more and better as the Industrial Revolution progressed, except in wartime. Diets became more varied; people ate more

potatoes and dairy products and more fruits and vegetables.

Clothing improved, but housing for working people did not. In short, per capita use of specific goods supports the position that the standard of living of the working classes rose, at least moderately, during the Industrial Revolution. The rich did get richer. So did the poor to some extent, especially if they worked in industry.

## CONDITIONS OF WORK

What about working conditions? Did workers earn more only at the cost of working longer and harder? Were workers exploited harshly by the new factory owners?

The first factories were cotton mills, which began functioning along rivers and streams in the 1770s. Cottage workers, accustomed to the putting-out system, were reluctant to work in factories even when they received relatively good wages, because factory work was different from what they were used to and unappealing. In the factory, workers had to keep up with the machine and follow its tempo. They had to show up every day and work long, monotonous hours. Factory workers had to adjust their daily lives to the shrill call of the factory whistle.

Cottage workers were not used to that kind of life and discipline. All members of the family worked hard and long but in spurts, setting their own pace. They could interrupt their work when they wanted to. Women and children could break up their long hours of spinning with other tasks. On Saturday afternoon the head of the family delivered the week's work to the merchant-manufacturer and got paid. Saturday night was a time of relaxation and drinking, especially for the

COTTON MILL NEAR MANCHESTER *The simple rural scene in the foreground of this 1834 engraving contrasts vividly with the massive brick factory building dominating the landscape. (Photo: Caroline Buckler)*

men. Recovering from his hangover on Tuesday, the weaver bent to his task on Wednesday and then worked like crazy to meet his deadline on Saturday. Like some students today, he might "pull an all-nighter" on Thursday or Friday, in order to get his work in.

Also, early factories resembled English poorhouses, where totally destitute people went to live on welfare. Some poorhouses were industrial prisons, where the inmates had to work in order to receive their food and lodging. The similarity between large brick factories and large stone poor-houses increased the cottage workers' fear of factories and their hatred of factory discipline.

It was cottage workers' reluctance to work in factories that prompted the early cotton-mill owners to turn to abandoned and pauper children for their labor. As we have seen, they contracted with local officials to employ large numbers of these children, who had no say in the matter. Pauper children were often badly treated and terribly overworked in the mills, as they were when they were apprenticed as chimney sweeps, market girls, shoemakers, and so forth. In the eighteenth century, semi-forced child labor seemed necessary and was socially accepted. From our modern point of view, it was cruel exploitation and a blot on the record of the new industrial system.

*GIRL DRAGGING COAL TUBS    Published by reformers in Parliament in 1842, this picture shocked public opinion and contributed to the Mines Act of 1842. Such work for children was not new, but with rapid industrialization it touched more people. (The British Museum)*

By 1790, the early pattern was rapidly changing. The use of pauper apprentices was in decline, and in 1802 it was forbidden by Parliament. Many more factories were being built, mainly in urban areas, where they could use steam rather than water power and attract a work force more easily than in the countryside. The need for workers was great. And, indeed, people came from near and far to work in the cities, both as factory workers and as laborers, builders, and domestic servants. Yet as they took these new jobs, working people did not simply give in to a system of labor that had formerly repelled them. Rather, they helped modify the system by carrying over old, familiar working traditions.

For one thing, they came to the mills and the mines as family units. This was how they had worked on farms and in the putting-out system. The mill or mine owner bargained with the head of the family and paid him or her for the work of the whole family. In the cotton mills children worked for their mothers or fathers, collecting wastes and "piecing" broken threads together. In the mines children sorted coal and worked the ventilation equipment. Their mothers hauled coal in the narrow tunnels below the surface, while their fathers hewed with pick and shovel at the face of the seam.

The preservation of the family as an economic unit in the factories from the 1790s on made the new surroundings more tolerable, both in Great Britain and in other countries during the early stages of industrialization. Parents disciplined their children, making firm measures socially acceptable, and directed their upbringing. The presence of the whole family meant that children and adults worked the same long hours (twelve-hour shifts were normal in cotton mills in 1800). In the early years, some very young children were employed solely to keep the family together. Jedediah Strutt, for example, believed children should be at least ten years old to work in his mills, but he reluctantly employed seven-year-olds to satisfy their parents. Adult workers were not particularly interested in limiting the minimum working age or hours of their children, as long as they worked side by side. Only when technical changes threatened to place control and discipline in the hands of impersonal managers and foremen did they protest against inhuman conditions in the name of their children.

But some enlightened employers and social reformers in Parliament definitely felt otherwise. "In an age of rising standards of humanitarianism the few were determined to impose higher standards on the many; and were able to exploit developing means of mass communication to do it."[7] These reformers had important successes.

Their first major accomplishment was the Factory Act of 1833. It limited the work day for children between nine and thirteen to eight hours and that of adolescents between fourteen and eighteen to twelve hours. The law also prohibited the employment of children under nine; they were to be enrolled in the elementary schools factory owners were required to establish. Since efficiency required standardized shifts for all workers, the Factory Act shattered the pattern of whole families working together in the factory. The employment of children declined rapidly. Similarly, the Mines Act of 1842 prohibited women and boys under ten from working underground.

Ties of blood and kinship remained important in other ways in England in the formative years between about 1790 and 1840. Many manufacturers and builders hired workers not directly but through subcontractors. They paid the subcontractors on the basis of what the subcontractors and their crews pro-

duced – for smelting so many tons of pig iron or moving so much dirt or gravel for a canal or roadbed. Subcontractors in turn hired and fired their own workers, many of whom were friends and relations. The subcontractor might be as harsh as the greediest capitalist, but the relationship between subcontractor and work crew was close and personal. This kind of traditional relationship was more acceptable to workers than impersonal factory discipline. This system also provided people an easy way to find a job. Even today, a friend or cousin who is a foreman is often worth a hundred formal application forms.

Ties of kinship were particularly important for newcomers, who often travelled considerable distances to find work. Many urban workers in Great Britain were from Ireland. Forced out of rural Ireland by population growth and deteriorating economic conditions from 1817 on, Irish in search of jobs could not be choosy; they took what they could get. As early as 1824 most of the workers in the Glasgow cotton mills were Irish; in 1851 one-sixth of the population of the great port of Liverpool was Irish. Even when Irish workers were not related directly by blood, they were held together by ethnic and religious ties. Like other immigrant groups elsewhere, they worked together, formed their own neighborhoods, and not only survived but thrived.

## A MATURE WORKING CLASS

By about 1850, the working people of urban Britain had, like British industry, gone a long way toward attaining maturity. Family employment in the factory had given way to the employment of adults, for whom the discipline of the clock and the regularity of the machine were familiar taskmasters. Gone were violent demonstrations against industrialization. In their place were increasing acceptance of the emerging industrial system and an ongoing effort to make that system serve workers better.

In Great Britain, and in other countries later on, workers slowly created a labor movement to serve their needs. In 1799, partly in panicked reaction to the French Revolution, Parliament had passed the Combination Acts outlawing unions and strikes. These acts were widely disregarded by workers. Societies of skilled factory workers organized unions, as printers, papermakers, carpenters, and other such craftsmen had long since done. The unions sought to control the number of skilled workers, limit apprenticeship to members' own children, and bargain with owners over wages. They were not afraid to strike; there was, for example, a general strike of adult cotton spinners in Manchester in 1810. In the face of widespread union activity, Parliament repealed the Combination Acts in 1824, and unions were tolerated though not fully accepted after 1825.

The next stage in the development of the British trade-union movement was the attempt to create a single large national union. This effort was led not so much by working people as by social reformers like Robert Owen (1771–1858). Owen, a self-made cotton manufacturer, had pioneered in industrial relations by combining firm discipline with concern for the health, safety, and hours of his workers. After 1815, he experimented with cooperative and socialist communities, including one at New Harmony, Indiana. Then, in 1834, Owen organized one of the largest and most visionary of the early national unions, the Grand National Consolidated Trades Union. When this and other grandiose schemes collapsed, the British labor movement moved once again after 1851 in the direction of bread-and-butter craft unions. The most famous of these "new model" unions was the Amalgamated Society of Engineers. These craft unions won real benefits for their members by fairly conservative means and thus helped make unions an accepted part of the industrial scene.

The maturity of British workers was also expressed in direct political activity in defense of their own interests. After the collapse of Owen's national trade union, a great deal of the energy of working people went into the Chartist movement, whose goal was political democracy. The key Chartist demand – that all men be given the right to vote – became the great hope of millions of aroused people. Workers were also active in campaigns to limit the workday in the factories to ten hours and to permit duty-free importation of wheat into Great Britain to secure cheap bread. Thus working people played an active role in shaping the new industrial system. Clearly, they were neither helpless victims nor passive beneficiaries.

## THE ALTERNATIVE TO INDUSTRIALIZATION

What was the alternative to the Industrial Revolution and the new urban society? What would have been the likely course of events – the likely alternative for Europe – if industrialization had not occurred? It is impossible to know exactly, yet a look at general developments and at the case of Ireland, which did not industrialize, may shed some light on this question.

### THE GROWTH OF POPULATION

The drama of industrialization must be viewed alongside the drama of rapid population growth. As we have seen, Europe's population began growing after 1720 (pages 672–675), leading to severe pressures on available resources and overpopulation in many areas. Large numbers of people had serious difficulty growing or buying the food they needed. There was widespread underemployment, acute poverty, and constant migration in search of work.

All these forces operated during and after the era of the French Revolution. Europe had roughly 140 million people in 1750, 188 million in 1800, and 266 million in 1850 – an increase of almost 40 percent in each half-century. Overpopulation worsened between 1800 and 1850 on much of the Continent, most noticeably in Flanders, parts of Scandinavia, and southwestern Germany. One result was migration from the countryside to nearby cities and towns, where unskilled laborers were already irregularly employed and poorly paid. Another result was that growing numbers of peasants liquidated their small and inadequate landholdings and went abroad. Thus in the early nineteenth century, particularly in the hungry 1840s, many German and Swedish settlers tried their luck and skill on prairie lands of the American Midwest.

The pressure of increasing numbers and rural poverty was most severe in Ireland. Although Ireland supplied many workers for factories in Britain, Ireland itself did not industrialize in the nineteenth century. Therefore, although Ireland was a particularly oppressed and exploited nation, its fate could have been that of much of Europe if not for the Industrial Revolution.

## THE POTATO FAMINE IN IRELAND

Late-eighteenth-century Ireland was a conquered country. The great mass of the population (outside the northern counties of Ulster which were partly Presbyterian) were Irish Catholic peasants, who rented their land from a tiny minority of Church of England Protestants, many of whom lived in England (page 710). These Protestant landlords lacked the improving zeal of their English counterparts. They knew they were perched on top of a volcano that erupted periodically, but they were quite content to use their powers to grab as much as possible, as quickly as possible.

The result was that the condition of the Irish peasantry around 1800 was abominable. The typical peasant family lived in a wretched cottage made of mud and could afford neither shoes nor stockings. Hundreds of shocking accounts describe hopeless poverty. Sir Walter Scott wrote:

*The poverty of the Irish peasantry is on the extreme verge of human misery; their cottages would scarce serve for pig styes even in Scotland; and their rags seem the very refuse of a sheep, and are spread over their bodies with such an ingenious variety of wretchedness that you would think nothing but some sort of perverted taste could have assembled so many shreds together.*

For a French traveler, Ireland was "pure misery, naked and hungry.... I saw the American Indian in his forests and the black slave in his chains, and I believed that I was seeing in their pitiful condition the most extreme form of human misery; but that was before I knew the lot of poor Ireland."[8] Yet in spite of these terrible conditions, population growth sped onward. The 3 million of 1725 reached 4 million in 1780, and doubled to 8 million in 1840. Between 1780 and 1840, 1.75 million men and women left Ireland for Britain and America.

The population of Ireland grew so quickly for three reasons: extensive cultivation of the potato, early marriage, and hideous exploitation of peasants by landlords. The potato, first

IRISH EMIGRANTS   *The potato famine forced hundreds of thousands of desperate Irish peasants, like these waiting to sail from Cork in 1850, to leave their native land. (Bettmann Archive)*

introduced into Ireland in the late sixteenth century, was the principal food of the Irish peasantry by the last years of the eighteenth century. The reason for dependence on the potato was originally the pressure of numbers, which forced the peasants to wring as many calories as they could out of a given piece of land. But once peasants began to live almost exclusively on potatoes, many more people could exist. A single acre of land spaded and planted with potatoes could feed a family of six for a year, whereas it would take at least two and probably four acres of grain and pasture to feed the same number. Moreover, the

potato was not choosy and could thrive on boggy wastelands.

Needing only a potato patch of an acre or two for survival, Irish boys and girls married much earlier than did their counterparts in rural England and France by the end of the eighteenth century. Setting up housekeeping was easy, for a cabin of mud and stone could be slapped together in a few days with the willing assistance of the young couple's neighbors and relatives. A mat for a bed, a chair or two, a table, and an iron pot to boil potatoes were easily acquired. To be sure, the young couple was accepting the life of extreme poverty that travelers and people of good conscience lamented. They would literally live on potatoes – ten pounds a day every day all year long for the average male – moistened with a cup of milk if they were lucky.

Nonetheless, the decision to marry early and have large families was quite reasonable, given Irish conditions. The landlords, not the peasants, owned and controlled the land. Because land was leased only for short periods on uncertain terms, peasants had no incentive to make permanent improvements. Any increase in profits went to the landlord, and anything beyond what preserved the peasants from absolute starvation was extorted from them. Poverty thus being inescapable in rural Ireland, it was better shared with a wife or husband. Children were a precious asset, as in many poor countries today, for there was no welfare or social security system, and an infirm or aged person's best hope of escaping starvation was a dutiful son or a loving daughter.

As the population continued to grow, conditions became increasingly precarious. The peasantry depended on a single crop, the size of which varied substantially from year to year. Potato failures cannot be detected in time to plant other crops, nor can potatoes be stored for more than a year. Furthermore, a potato economy is a subsistence economy. It lacks a well-developed network of roads and trade capable of distributing other foods in time of disaster. From 1820 onward, deficiencies in the potato crop became increasingly serious. Disease in the potato crop was becoming more common, and the accompanying fever epidemics that struck the population were growing more frequent. Some great catastrophe in the near future was almost completely inevitable.

In 1845 and 1846, and again in 1848 and 1851, the potato crop failed in Ireland and throughout much of Europe. The general result was high food prices, widespread suffering, and social unrest. In Ireland, which was farthest down the road to rural overpopulation and dependence on a disease-prone plant, the result was unmitigated disaster – the Great Famine. Blight attacked the young plants, the leaves withered, and the tubes rotted. Widespread starvation and mass fever epidemics followed. Cannibalism occurred, although starving people generally lived on the carcasses of diseased cattle, dogs, and horses, and on herbs of the field. In some places dead people were found with grass in their mouths.

Total losses were staggering. The population of Ireland was roughly 8 million in 1845, and without the famine it would have reached 9 million in 1851. But that year Ireland's population was only 6.5 million. Fully a million emigrants fled the famine between 1845 and 1851 (2 million left between 1840 and 1855), going primarily to the United States and Great Britain. Thus at least 1.5 million people died or went unborn because of the disaster. The British government's efforts at famine relief were too little and too late. Moreover, the government continued to collect its taxes and the landlords continued to demand their rents. Tenants who could not pay were evicted and their homes broken up or burned. Famine or no, Ireland was still the conquered jewel of foreign landowners.

The Great Famine shattered and reversed the pattern of Irish population growth. Alone among the nations of Europe, Ireland's numbers declined in the nineteenth century, to 4.4 million in 1911. Ireland remained a land of continuous out-migration. It also became a land of late marriage and widespread celibacy, as the landowning classes discouraged potato farming and converted much of the country into pasture for cattle and sheep. After great population decline and untold suffering, Ireland found a new demographic equilibrium within the framework of a poor pastoral economy.

———◆———

The fate of Ireland has real relevance for an understanding of the Industrial Revolution. The rapid population growth without industrialization that occurred in Ireland between 1780 and 1845 occurred elsewhere too – in central Russia, in western Germany, and in southern Italy, to name only three crucial regions. In these areas there were indications of acute poverty and overpopulation, and the potato played a crucial role as it had done in Ireland. In Prussia, for example, annual potato production grew from 1 to 11 million tons from 1815 to 1860. By 1850 in some parts of Europe bread was a luxury; workers and peasants were subsisting almost entirely on potatoes. In 1500 the average German had eaten about 200 pounds of meat a year; in 1850 his counterpart ate about 40 pounds.[9] The standard of living was declining. Other Irelands were in the making.

Population growth threatened to produce a morass of rural poverty, a demographic catastrophe, or both. In this connection, the historian T. S. Ashton once argued that the Industrial Revolution was the salvation rather than the curse of England and of the parts of Europe fortunate enough to follow England's lead. He may have overstated the case, but Ashton was surely closer to the truth than those who persist in arguing the contrary. The alternative to the revolution in energy and industry would probably have been, sooner or later, disaster.

## NOTES

1. M. Lévy-Leboyer, *Les banques européennes et l'industrialisation dans la première moitié du XIXe siècle,* Presses Universitaires de France, Paris, 1964, p. 29.

2. Quoted by D. S. Landes, *The Unbound Prometheus: Technological Change and Industrial Development in Western Europe from 1750 to the Present,* Cambridge University Press, Cambridge, 1969, p. 150.

3. J. Michelet, *The People,* University of Illinois Press, Urbana, 1973 (originally published, 1846), p. 64.

4. F. Engels, *The Condition of the Working Class in England,* trans. and ed. W. O. Henderson and W. H. Chaloner, Stanford University Press, Stanford, 1968, p. xxiii.

5. Quoted in W. A. Hayek, ed., *Capitalism and the Historians,* University of Chicago Press, Chicago, 1954, p. 126.

6. P. Deane and W. A. Cole, *British Economic Growth, 1688-1959,* Cambridge University Press, Cambridge, 1964, p. 25.

7. P. Mathias, *The First Industrial Nation: An Economic History of Britain, 1700-1914,* Charles Scribner's Sons, New York, 1969, p. 205.

8. Quoted by G. O'Brien, *The Economic History of Ireland from the Union to the Famine,* Longmans, Green, London, 1921, pp. 21-24.

9. W. L. Langer, *Political and Social Upheaval, 1832-1852,* Harper & Row, New York, 1969, p. 188.

## SUGGESTED READING

There is a vast and exciting literature on the Industrial Revolution. D. Landes's *The Unbound Prometheus* (1969), cited in the Notes, and S. Pollard, *Peaceful Conquest: The Industrialization of Europe* (1981), are the best general treatments of European industrial growth since 1750. P. Mathias, *The First Industrial Nation: An Economic History of Britain, 1700–1914* (1969); P. Deane, *The First Industrial Revolution* (1966); and P. Mantoux, *The Industrial Revolution in the Eighteenth Century* (1961), admirably discuss the various aspects of the English breakthrough and offer good bibliographies. (See also the Suggested Reading for Chapter 23.) W. Rostow, *The Stages of Economic Growth: A Non-Communist Manifesto* (1960), is a popular, provocative study. R. Cameron brilliantly traces the spread of railroads and industry across Europe in *France and the Economic Development of Europe, 1800–1914* (1961). The recent works of A. S. Milward and S. B. Saul, *The Economic Development of Continental Europe, 1780–1870* (1973), and *The Development of the Economies of Continental Europe, 1850–1914* (1977), may be compared with J. Clapham's old-fashioned classic, *Economic Development of France and Germany* (1963). C. Kindleberger, *Economic Growth in France and Britain, 1851–1950* (1964), is a stimulating study, especially for those with some background in economics. Other important works in recent years on industrial developments are C. Tilly and E. Shorter, *Strikes in France, 1830–1848* (1974); D. Ringrose, *Transportation and Economic Stagnation in Spain, 1750–1850* (1970); L. Schofer, *The Formation of a Modern Labor Force* (1975), which focuses on the Silesian part of Germany; and W. Blackwell, *The Industrialization of Russia,* 2nd ed. (1982).

The debate between "optimists" and "pessimists" about the consequences of industrialization in England goes on. P. Taylor, ed., *The Industrial Revolution: Triumph or Disaster?* (1970), is a useful introduction to different viewpoints, while W. A. Hayek, ed., *Capitalism and the Historians* (1954), is a

good collection of essays stressing positive aspects. It is also fascinating to compare Friedrich Engels's classic condemnation, *The Condition of the Working Class in England,* with Andrew Ure's optimistic defense, *The Philosophy of Manufactures,* first published in 1835 and reprinted recently. E. P. Thompson continues and enriches the Engels tradition in *The Making of the English Working Class* (1963), an exciting book rich in detail and early working-class lore. An unorthodox but moving account of a doomed group is D. Bythell, *The Handloom Weavers* (1969). F. Klingender, *Art and the Industrial Revolution,* rev. ed. (1968), is justly famous, and M. Ignatieff, *A Just Measure of Pain* (1980), is an engrossing study of prisons during English industrialization.

Among general studies, many of which are cited in the Suggested Reading for Chapter 23, G. S. R. Kitson Clark, *The Making of Victorian England* (1967), is particularly imaginative. A. Briggs, *Victorian People* (1955), provides an engrossing series of brief biographies. H. Ausubel discusses a major reformer in his work, *John Bright* (1966), and B. Harrison skillfully illuminates the problem of heavy drinking in *Drink and the Victorians* (1971). On poverty and politics in Ireland, K. H. Connell, *The Population of Ireland, 1750–1850* (1950), and S. Cronin, *Irish Nationalism: A History of Its Roots and Ideology* (1981), are excellent points of departure. The most famous contemporary novel dealing with the new industrial society is Charles Dickens's *Hard Times,* an entertaining but exaggerated story. *Mary Barton* and *North and South* by Elizabeth Gaskill are more realistic portrayals and both are highly recommended, as is Emile Zola's *Germinal,* a grim, powerful story of love and hate during a violent strike by French coal miners.

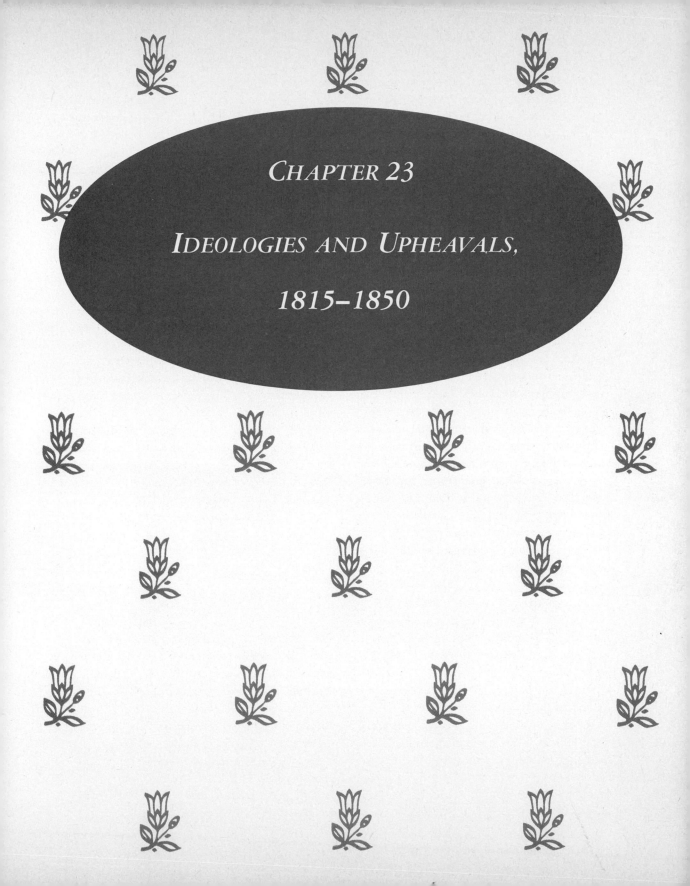

# CHAPTER 23

# IDEOLOGIES AND UPHEAVALS,

# 1815–1850

THE MOMENTOUS ECONOMIC and political transformation of modern times began in the late eighteenth century with the Industrial Revolution in England and then the French Revolution. Until about 1815, these revolutions were separate, involving different countries and activities and proceeding at very different paces. The Industrial Revolution created the factory system and new groups of capitalists and industrial workers in northern England, but almost continuous warfare with France checked its spread to continental Europe. Meanwhile, England's ruling aristocracy suppressed all forms of political radicalism at home and joined with crowned heads abroad to oppose and eventually defeat revolutionary and Napoleonic France. The economic and political revolutions worked at cross-purposes and even neutralized each other.

After peace returned in 1815, the situation changed. Economic and political changes tended to fuse, reinforcing each other and bringing about what the historian Eric Hobsbawm has incisively called "the dual revolution." For instance, the growth of the industrial middle class encouraged the drive for representative government, while the demands of the French sans-culottes in 1793–1794 inspired many socialist thinkers. Gathering strength and threatening almost every aspect of the existing political and social framework, the dual revolution rushed on to alter completely first Europe and then the world. Much of world history in the last two centuries can be seen as the progressive unfolding of the dual revolution.

Yet three qualifications must be kept firmly in mind. In Europe in the nineteenth century, as in Asia and Africa in more recent times, the dual revolution was not some inexorable mechanical monster grinding peoples and cultures into a homogenized mass. The economic and political transformation it wrought was built on complicated histories, strong traditions, and highly diverse cultures. Radical change was eventually a constant, but the particular results varied enormously.

Nor should the strength of the old forces be underestimated. In Europe especially, the traditional elites – the monarchs, noble landowners, and bureaucrats – long proved capable of defending their privileges and even of rerouting the dual revolution to serve their interests.

Finally, the dual revolution posed a tremendous intellectual challenge. The meanings of the economic, political, and social changes that were occurring, as well as the ways they could be shaped by human action, were anything but clear. These questions fascinated observers and stimulated new ideas and ideologies.

How then did the political revolution, derailed by class antagonisms in France and resisted by European monarchs, break out again in the era of early industrialization? And what ideas did thinkers develop to describe and shape the transformation going on before their eyes?

## THE PEACE SETTLEMENT

The eventual triumph of revolutionary economic and political forces was by no means certain in 1814. Quite the contrary. The conservative, aristocratic monarchies with their preindustrial armies and economies (Great Britain excepted) appeared firmly in the driver's seat once again. France had been decisively defeated by the off-again, on-again alliance of Russia, Prussia, Austria, and Great Britain. That alliance had been strengthened and reaffirmed in March 1814, when the allies pledged not only to defeat France but to hold it in line for twenty years thereafter. This goal was the basis of the Quadruple Alliance. Allied armies had then entered Paris, and Napoleon had abdicated his throne.

Most people felt an intense and profound longing for peace. The great challenge for statesmen in 1814 was to construct a peace settlement that would last and not sow the seeds of another war. Their efforts were largely successful and contributed to a century unmarred by destructive, generalized war (see Map 23.1).

## GOALS AND PRINCIPLES

The allied powers were concerned first and foremost with the defeated enemy, France. Uncertain and somewhat divided about the future government of France, they agreed to the restoration of the Bourbon dynasty, in part because demonstrations led by a few dedicated French monarchists indicated some support among the French people for that course of action. This support was temporarily consolidated when the new monarch, Louis XVIII (1814-1824), issued the Constitutional Charter which accepted many of France's revolutionary changes and established a fairly liberal regime. The allies signed the first Peace of Paris with the restored Bourbon monarchy on May 30, 1814.

The allies were quite lenient toward France. France was given the boundaries it possessed in 1792, which were larger than those of 1789. France lost only the territories it had conquered in Italy, Germany, and the Low Countries, in addition to a few colonial possessions. Although there was some sentiment for levying a fine on France to pay for the war, the allies did not press the matter when Louis XVIII stated firmly that his government would not pay any reparations. France was

even allowed to keep the art treasures Napoleon's agents had looted from the museums of Europe. Thus, the victorious powers did not punish harshly, and they did not foment a spirit of injustice and revenge in the defeated country.

At the same time a number of barriers were raised against renewed French aggression. The Low Countries – Belgium and Holland – were united under an enlarged Dutch monarchy capable of opposing France more effectively. Moreover, Prussia received considerably more territory on France's eastern border, so as to stand as the "sentinel on the Rhine" against France. In these ways the Quadruple Alliance combined leniency toward France with strong defensive measures. They held out a carrot with one hand and picked up a bigger stick with the other.

## THE BALANCE OF POWER

In their moderation toward France the allies were motivated by self-interest and traditional ideas about the balance of power. To Metternich and Castlereagh, the foreign ministers of Austria and Great Britain, as well as their French counterpart Talleyrand, the balance of power meant an international equilibrium of political and military forces, which would preserve the freedom and independence of each of the Great Powers. Such a balance would discourage aggression by any combination of states or, worse, the domination of Europe by any single state. As they saw it, the task of the powers was thus twofold. They had to make sure that France would not dominate Europe again, and they also had to arrange international relations so that none of the victors would be tempted to strive for domination in its turn. Such a balance involved many considerations and all of Europe. The Great Powers, assisted in a minor way by

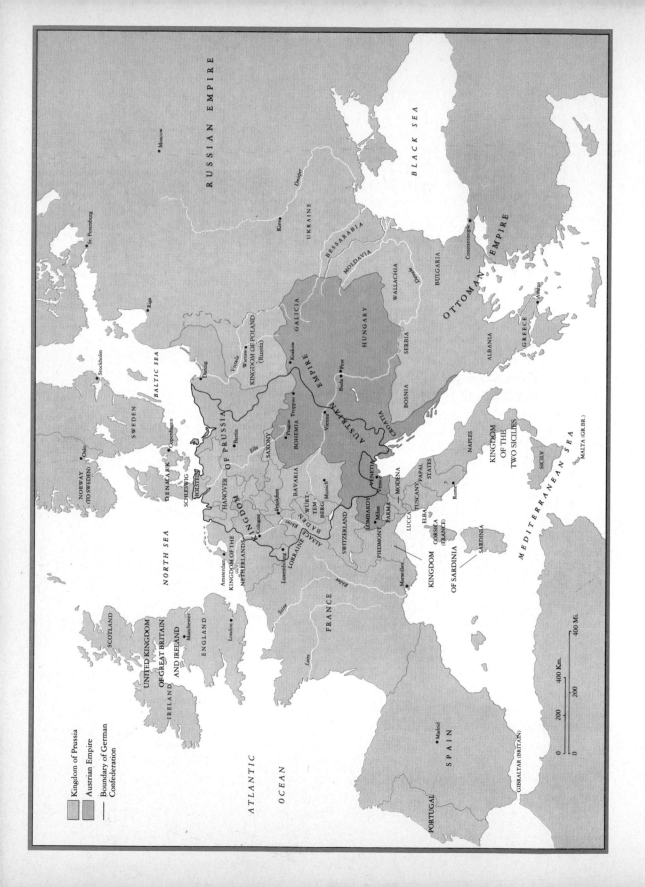

RUSSIAN EMPIRE

Moscow

St. Petersburg

BLACK SEA

UKRAINE

Kiev

Dnieper

BESSARABIA

MOLDAVIA

WALLACHIA

Danube

BULGARIA

SERBIA

OTTOMAN EMPIRE

Constantinople

ALBANIA

GREECE

Athens

MALTA (GR. BR.)

GALICIA

HUNGARY

Krakow

Buda • Pest

BOSNIA

CROATIA

AUSTRIAN EMPIRE

Vienna

VENETIA

Venice

Danzig

Vistula

Warsaw

KINGDOM OF POLAND
(Russia)

Riga

BALTIC SEA

Stockholm

SWEDEN

NORWAY
(TO SWEDEN)

Oslo

Copenhagen

DENMARK

SCHLESWIG

HOLSTEIN

KINGDOM

OF

PRUSSIA

Berlin

Elbe

SAXONY

Prague

BOHEMIA

Troppau

HANOVER

Rhine

Munich

BAVARIA

WÜRT-
TEM-
BERG

BADEN

Frankfurt

Cologne

KINGDOM OF THE

NETHERLANDS

Amsterdam

Luxembourg

LORRAINE

ALSACE

SWITZERLAND

PIEDMONT

LOMBARDY

Milan

PARMA

MODENA

LUCCA

TUSCANY

PAPAL
STATES

Rome

ELBA

CORSICA
(FRANCE)

SARDINIA

KINGDOM

OF SARDINIA

NAPLES

KINGDOM

OF THE

TWO SICILIES

SICILY

MEDITERRANEAN SEA

FRANCE

Marseilles

Rhône

Loire

Seine

NORTH SEA

ATLANTIC

OCEAN

UNITED KINGDOM

OF GREAT BRITAIN

AND IRELAND

SCOTLAND

IRELAND

ENGLAND

Manchester

London

SPAIN

Madrid

PORTUGAL

GIBRALTAR (BRITAIN)

NAPLES

Kingdom of Prussia

Austrian Empire

Boundary of German
Confederation

400 Km.

400 Mi.

200

200

0

0

the smaller European states, began a series of negotiations in Vienna in October 1814 to resolve these challenges.

The balance of power was the mechanism used by the Great Powers – Austria, Britain, Prussia, Russia, and France – to settle their own disputes, which became quite dangerous. There was general agreement among the victors that each of them should receive compensation in the form of territory for their successful struggle against the French. Great Britain had already won colonies and strategic outposts during the long wars, and these it retained. Metternich's Austria gave up territories in Belgium and southern Germany but expanded greatly elsewhere, taking the rich provinces of Venetia and Lombardy in northern Italy as well as its former Polish possessions and new lands on the eastern coast of the Adriatic (see Map 23.1). There was also agreement that Prussia and Russia should be compensated. But where, and to what extent? That was the ticklish question that almost led to renewed war in January 1815.

The vaguely progressive, impetuous Alexander I of Russia had already taken Finland and Bessarabia on his northern and southern borders. Yet he burned with ambition to restore the ancient kingdom of Poland, on which he expected to bestow the benefits of his autocratic rule. The Prussians were willing to go along and give up their Polish territories, provided they could swallow up the large and wealthy kingdom of Saxony, their German neighbor to the south.

These demands were too much for Castlereagh and Metternich, who feared an unbalancing of forces in central Europe. In an as-

tonishing about-face, they turned for diplomatic support to the wily Talleyrand and the defeated France he represented. On January 3, 1815, Great Britain, Austria, and France signed a secret alliance directed against Russia and Prussia. As Castlereagh concluded somberly, it appeared that "the peace we have so dearly purchased will be of short duration."[1]

The outcome, however, was compromise rather than war. When rumors of the alliance were intentionally leaked, the threat of war caused the rulers of Russia and Prussia to moderate their demands. They accepted Metternich's proposal: Russia established a small Polish kingdom, and Prussia received two-fifths rather than all of Saxony (see Map 23.1). This compromise was very much within the framework of balance-of-power ideology and eighteenth-century diplomacy: Great Powers became greater, but not too much greater. In addition, France had been able to intervene and tip the scales in favor of the side seeking to prevent undue expansion of Russia and Prussia. In so doing France regained its Great Power status and was no longer isolated, as Talleyrand gleefully reported to Louis XVIII.

As the final touches were being put on the peace settlement, Napoleon suddenly reappeared on the scene. After his unconditional abdication, the victorious allies had granted Napoleon the island of Elba off the coast of Italy as his own tiny state. Napoleon was allowed to keep his imperial title, and France was required to pay him a large yearly income of 2 million francs. But Napoleon was Napoleon, and he soon tired of his "comic kingdom." Hearing of diplomatic tensions in Vienna and political unrest in France, he escaped from Elba in February 1815. Landing in France, Napoleon issued appeals for support and marched on Paris with a small band. French officers and soldiers who had fought

*ADJUSTING THE BALANCE   The Englishman on the left uses his money to counterbalance the people that the Prussian and the fat Metternich are gaining in Saxony and Italy. Alexander I sits happily on his prize, Poland. The cartoon captures the essence of balance-of-power diplomacy in 1814. (Bibliothèque Nationale, Paris)*

so long with Napoleon joined with him. Louis XVIII fled, and once more Napoleon took command. But his wild gamble was doomed, for the allies were united against him. At the end of a frantic hundred days they crushed his forces at Waterloo and imprisoned him on the rocky island of St. Helena, far off the western coast of Africa.

Once again, Napoleon had done much harm and little good. Even so, the resulting peace – the second Peace of Paris – was still relatively moderate toward France. Fat old Louis XVIII was restored to his throne. France lost some territory, had to pay an indemnity of 700 million francs, and had to support a large army of occupation for five years. The rest of the settlement already concluded at Vienna was left intact. The allies did, however, agree to meet periodically to discuss their "common interests" and to consider appropriate measures for the "maintenance of peace in Europe." This agreement marked the beginning of the European "congress system," which lasted long into the nineteenth century and settled international crises by means of diplomatic conferences.

## INTERVENTION AND REPRESSION

There was also a domestic political side to the re-establishment of peace. Within their own countries the leaders of the victorious states were much less flexible. In 1815, under Metternich's leadership, Austria, Prussia, and Russia embarked on a crusade against the ideas and politics of the dual revolution. The crusade lasted until 1848.

The first step was the Holy Alliance, formed by Austria, Prussia, and Russia in September 1815. First proposed by Russia's Alexander I, the alliance proclaimed the intention of the three eastern monarchs to rule exclusively on the basis of Christian principles and to work together to maintain peace and justice on all occasions. Castlereagh refused to sign, characterizing the vague statement of principle as "a piece of sublime mysticism and nonsense." Yet it soon became a practical instrument for the repression of liberal and revolutionary movements all over Europe.

In 1820, revolutionaries succeeded in forcing the monarchs of Spain and the southern Italian kingdom of the Two Sicilies to grant liberal constitutions against their wills. Metternich was horrified: revolution was rising once again. Calling a conference at Troppau in Austria, he and Alexander I proclaimed the principle of active intervention to maintain all autocratic regimes, whenever they were threatened. Austrian forces then marched into Naples and restored Ferdinand I to the throne of the Two Sicilies. The French armies of Louis XVIII likewise restored the Spanish regime – after the Congress of Troppau had rejected Alexander's offer to send his Cossacks riding across Europe to teach the Spanish an unforgettable lesson.

Great Britain remained aloof, arguing that intervention in the domestic politics of foreign states was not an object of British diplomacy. In particular, Great Britain opposed any attempts by the restored Spanish monarchy to reconquer its former Latin American possessions, which had gained their independence during and after the Napoleonic wars. Encouraged by the British position, the young United States proclaimed its celebrated Monroe Doctrine in 1823. This bold document declared that European powers were to keep their hands off the New World and in no way attempt to re-establish their political system there. In the United States constitutional liberalism, an ongoing challenge to the conservatism of continental Europe, retained its cutting edge.

In the years following the crushing of liberal revolution in southern Italy in 1821 and in Spain in 1823, Metternich continued to battle against liberal political change. Sometimes he could do little, as in the case of the new Latin American republics. Nor could he undo the dynastic changes of 1830 in western Europe. Yet until 1848 his system was quite effective in central Europe, where his power was greatest.

Metternich's policies dominated not only Austria and the Italian peninsula but the entire German Confederation, which the peace settlement of Vienna had called into being. The confederation was composed of thirty-eight independent German states, including Prussia and Austria. (The Hungarian half of the Austrian Empire was not a member.) These states met in complicated assemblies dominated by Austria, with Prussia a willing junior partner in the planning and execution of repressive measures.

It was through the German Confederation that Metternich had the infamous Carlsbad Decrees issued in 1819. The decrees required the thirty-eight German member states to root out subversive ideas in their universities and newspapers. They also established a permanent committee with spies and informers to investigate and punish any liberal or radical organizations. Metternich's ruthless imposition of repressive internal policies on the governments of central Europe contrasted with the intelligent moderation he had displayed in the general peace settlement in 1815.

## METTERNICH AND CONSERVATISM

Metternich's determined defense of the status quo made him a villain in the eyes of most progressive, optimistic historians of the nineteenth century. Yet rather than denounce the man, it is more useful to try to understand him and the general conservatism he represented.

Born into the middle ranks of the landed nobility of the Rhineland, Prince Klemens von Metternich (1773–1859) was an internationally oriented aristocrat. In 1795 his splendid marriage to Eleonora von Kaunitz, granddaughter of Austria's famous statesman and heiress to vast estates, opened the door to the highest court circles and a brilliant diplomatic career. Austrian ambassador to Napoleon's court in 1806 and Austrian foreign minister from 1809 to 1848, the cosmopolitan Metternich always remained loyal to his class and jealously defended its rights and privileges to the day he died. Like most other conservatives of his time, he did so with a clear conscience. The nobility was one of Europe's most ancient institutions, and conservatives regarded tradition as the basic source of human institutions. In their view, the proper state and society remained that of pre-1789 Europe, which rested on a judicious blend of monarchy, bureaucracy, and aristocracy.

Metternich's commitment to conservatism was coupled with a passionate hatred of liberalism. He firmly believed that liberalism, as embodied in revolutionary America and France, had been responsible for a generation of war with untold bloodshed and suffering. Liberal demands for representative government and civil liberties had unfortunately captured the imaginations of some middle-class lawyers, businessmen, and intellectuals. Metternich thought that these groups had been and still were engaged in a vast conspiracy to impose their beliefs on society and destroy the existing order. Like many conservatives then and since, Metternich blamed liberal revolutionaries for stirring up the lower classes, whom he believed to be indifferent or hostile to liberal ideals, desiring nothing more than peace and quiet.

The threat of liberalism appeared doubly dangerous to Metternich because it generally went with national aspirations. Liberals, especially liberals in central Europe, believed that each people, each national group, had a right to establish its own independent government and seek to fulfill its own destiny. The idea of national self-determination was repellent to Metternich. It not only threatened the existence of the aristocracy, it also threatened to destroy the Austrian Empire and revolutionize central Europe.

The vast Austrian Empire of the Habsburgs was a great dynastic state. Formed over centuries by war, marriage, and luck, it was made up of many peoples speaking many languages (see Map 23.2). The Germans, long the dominant element, had supported and profited by the long-term territorial expansion of Austria; yet they accounted for only a quarter of the population. The Magyars (Hungarians), a substantially smaller group, dominated the kingdom of Hungary – which was part of the Austrian Empire – though they did not account for a majority of the population even there.

The Czechs, the third major group, were concentrated in Bohemia and Moravia. There were also large numbers of Italians, Poles, and Ukrainians, as well as smaller groups of Slovenes, Croats, Serbs, Ruthenians, and Rumanians. The various Slavic peoples represented a widely scattered and completely divided ma-

METTERNICH *This portrait by Sir Thomas Lawrence reveals much of Metternich the man. Handsome, refined, and intelligent, Metternich was a great aristocrat passionately devoted to the defense of his class and its interests. (Bettmann Archive)*

jority in an empire dominated by Germans and Hungarians. Different ethnic groups often lived in the same provinces and even the same villages. Thus, the different parts and provinces of the empire differed in languages, customs, and institutions. They were held to-gether primarily by their ties to the Habsburg emperor.

The multinational state Metternich served was both strong and weak. It was strong because of its large population and vast terri-tories; it was weak because of its many and

RUSSIA

POLAND

GALICIA

SILESIA

MORAVIA

BOHEMIA

• Prague

SWITZERLAND

GERMAN

STATES

BAVARIA

SALZBURG

TYROL

AUSTRIA

Vienna •

STYRIA

CORINTHIA

VENETIA

Venice •

LOMBARDY

Milan •

Po

ITALIAN

STATES

Danube

Tisza

HUNGARY

Budapest •

TRANSYLVANIA

RUMANIA

OTTOMAN EMPIRE

Danube

SERBIA

CROATIA—SLAVONIA

BOSNIA

ILLYRIA

ADRIATIC SEA

Germans

Hungarians

Italians

Rumanians

Poles

Czechs

Carpatho-Ukrainians (Ruthenians)

Serbs and Croats

Slovaks

Slovenes

—— Habsburg Monarchy boundaries

100 Mi.

100 Km.

50

50

0

0

MAP 23.2   PEOPLES OF THE HABSBURG MON-
ARCHY, 1815   *The old dynastic state was a patchwork of nationalities. Note the widely scattered pockets
of Germans and Hungarians.*

potentially dissatisfied nationalities. In these
circumstances Metternich virtually had to oppose liberalism and nationalism, for Austria
was simply unable to accommodate those ideologies of the dual revolution. Other conservatives supported Austria because they could
imagine no better fate for the jumble of small
nationalities wedged precariously between
masses of Germans and hordes of Russians in
east central Europe. Castlereagh even went so
far as to say that Austria was "the great hinge
upon which the fate of Europe must ultimately depend." Metternich's repressive conservatism may not appeal to many people
today, but it had understandable roots in the
dilemma of a multinational state in an age of
rising nationalism.

## RADICAL IDEAS AND EARLY SOCIALISM

The years following the peace settlement of
1815 were years of profound intellectual activity. Intellectuals and social observers were
seeking to understand the revolutionary
changes that had occurred and were still taking place. These efforts led to ideas that still
motivate the world.

Almost all of these basic ideas were radical.
In one way or another they opposed the old
deeply felt conservatism that Metternich exemplified so well. That revived conservatism,
with its stress on tradition, a hereditary monarchy, a strong and privileged landowning aristocracy, and an official church, was rejected
by radicals. Instead, radicals developed and re-

fined alternative visions – alternative ideologies – and tried to convince society to act on
them. With time, they were very successful.

### LIBERALISM

The ideas of liberalism – liberty and equality – were by no means defeated in 1815. First
realized successfully in the American Revolution and then achieved in part in the French
Revolution, this political and social philosophy continued to pose a radical challenge to
revived conservatism. Liberalism demanded
representative government as opposed to autocratic monarchy, equality before the law as
opposed to legally separate classes. Liberty
also continued to mean specific individual
freedoms: freedom of the press, freedom of
speech, freedom of assembly, and freedom
from arbitrary arrest. In Europe, only France
with Louis XVIII's Constitutional Charter
and Great Britain with its Parliament and
historic rights of English men and women
had realized much but by no means all of the
liberal program in 1815. Elsewhere, liberal
demands were still a call for revolutionary
change.

Yet although "classical" liberalism still had
its cutting edge, it was not as sharp a tool as
it had been. This was especially true of liberal
economic principles, which called for unrestricted private enterprise and no government
interference in the economy. This philosophy
was popularly known as the doctrine of laissez-faire.

The idea of a free economy had first been
persuasively formulated by a Scottish professor of philosophy, Adam Smith (1723-1790).
Smith, whose *Inquiry into the Nature and
Causes of the Wealth of Nations* (1776) founded
modern economics, was highly critical of
eighteenth-century mercantilism. Mercantilism, he said, meant stifling government regu-

lations as well as unjust privileges for private monopolies and government favorites. Far preferable was free competition, which would give all citizens a fair and equal opportunity to do what they did best. Smith argued effectively that freely competitive private enterprise would result in greater income for everyone, not just the rich.

Unlike some of his contemporaries, Smith applauded the modest rise in real wages of British workers in the eighteenth century and went so far as to say, "No society can surely be flourishing and happy, of which the far greater part of the members are poor and miserable." Smith also believed that greater competition meant higher wages for workers, since manufacturers and "masters are always and everywhere in a sort of tacit, but constant and uniform, combination, not to raise the wages of laborers above their actual rate." In short, Adam Smith was a spokesman for general economic development, not narrow business interests.

In the early nineteenth century, the British economy was progressively liberalized, as old restrictions on trade and industry were relaxed or eliminated. This liberalization promoted continued rapid economic growth in the Industrial Revolution. At the same time, however, economic liberalism and laissez-faire economic thought were tending to become a doctrine serving business interests. Businessmen used the doctrine to defend their right to do exactly as they wished in their factories. Labor unions were outlawed because they supposedly restricted free competition and the individual's "right to work."

The teachings of a kindly parson, Thomas Malthus (1766–1834), helped make economic liberalism an ideology of business interests in many people's minds. In his *Essay on the Principle of Population* (1798) Malthus argued that population would always tend to grow faster than the supply of food. In Malthus's opinion, the only hope of warding off such "positive checks" to population growth as war, famine, and disease was "prudential restraint." That is, young men and women had to limit the growth of population by the old tried-and-true means of marrying late in life. But Malthus was not optimistic about this possibility. The powerful attraction of the sexes would cause most people to marry early and have many children.

The wealthy English stockbroker and economist David Ricardo (1772–1823) was even less optimistic. His depressing "iron law of wages" posited that, because of the pressure of population growth, wages would always sink to the subsistence level. That is, wages would be just high enough to keep the workers from starving. Malthus and Ricardo thought of themselves as objective social scientists. Yet their teachings were often used by industrial and middle-class interests in England, the Continent, and the United States to justify opposing any kind of government intervention to protect workers and improve the lot of common people: if workers were poor, it was their own fault, the result of their breeding like rabbits.

In the early nineteenth century, liberal political ideals also became more closely associated with narrow class interests. Early nineteenth-century liberals favored representative government, but they generally wanted property qualifications attached to the right to vote. In practice, this meant limiting the vote to well-to-do aristocratic landowners, substantial businessmen, and successful members of the professions. Workers and peasants as well as the lower middle class of shopkeepers, clerks, and artisans did not own the necessary property and thus could not vote.

As liberalism became increasingly middle-class after 1815, some intellectuals and foes of conservatism felt that it did not go nearly far enough. Inspired by memories of the French Revolution and the contemporary example of exuberant Jacksonian democracy in the young American republic, they called for universal voting rights, at least for males. Giving all men the vote, they believed, would allow the masses to participate in government and would lead to democracy.

Many people who believed in democracy also believed in the republican form of government. They detested the power of the monarchy, the privileges of the aristocracy, and the great wealth of the upper middle class. These democrats and republicans were more radical than the liberals. Taking for granted much of the liberal program, they sought to go beyond it. Democrats and republicans were also more willing than most liberals to endorse violent upheaval to achieve goals. All of which meant that liberals and radical, democratic republicans could join forces against conservatives only up to a point.

GIUSEPPE MAZZINI *First imprisoned for revolutionary agitation in 1830 and spending much of his life in exile, Mazzini ceaselessly preached the doctrine of Italian rebirth in a free, democratic, and united Italy. (The Mansell Collection)*

## NATIONALISM

Between 1815 and 1850, most people who believed in either liberalism or radical, democratic republicanism also believed in nationalism. Conversely, many early nineteenth-century nationalists, like the Italian patriot Giuseppe Mazzini and the French historian Jules Michelet, were just as committed to liberty as they were to nationalism. Many governments, however, have been very nationalistic without favoring liberty and democracy. Why then was love of liberty almost synonymous with love of nation in the early nineteenth century?

A common faith in the creativity and nobility of the people was perhaps the single most important reason for people's linking these two concepts. Liberals and especially democrats saw the people as the ultimate source of all government. The people (or some of them) elected their officials and governed themselves within a framework of personal liberty. Yet such self-government would be possible only if the people were united by common traditions and common loyalties. In practice, common loyalties rested, first of all, on a common language. A shared language forged the basic unity of a people, a unity that transcended local or provincial interests and was not weakened by close contact with other ethnic groups.

Early nationalists usually believed that every nation, like every citizen, has the right to exist in freedom and to develop its character and spirit. They were confident that the independence and freedom of other nations, as in the case of other citizens within a nation, would not lessen the freedom of their own country. Rather, the symphony of nations would promote the harmony and ultimate unity of all peoples. As the historian Jules Michelet put it in *The People* in 1846, each citizen "learns to recognize his country . . . as a note in the grand concert; through it he himself participates and loves the world." Similarly, Mazzini believed that "in laboring according to the true principles of our country we are laboring for Humanity." Thus, the liberty of the individual and the love of a free nation overlapped greatly in the early nineteenth century.

Nationalism also had a negative side. Even as they talked of serving the cause of humanity, early nationalists stressed the differences between peoples. The German pastor and philosopher Johann Herder (1744-1803) had argued that every people has its own particular spirit and genius, which it expresses through its culture and language. Yet Herder (and others after him) could not define the uniqueness of the French, German, and Slavic peoples without comparing and contrasting one people with another. Thus, even early nationalism developed a strong sense of "we" and "they."

"They" were often the enemy. The leader of the Czech cultural revival, the passionate democrat and nationalist historian Francis Palacký, is a good example of this tendency. In his histories he lauded the achievements of the Czech people, which he characterized as a long struggle against brutal German domina-tion. To this "we-they" outlook, it was all too easy for nationalists to add two other highly volatile ingredients: a sense of national mission and a sense of national superiority. As Mazzini characteristically wrote, "Peoples never stop before they have achieved the ultimate aim of their existence, before having fulfilled their mission." Even Michelet, so alive to the aspirations of other peoples, could not help speaking in 1846 of the "superiority of France"; the principles espoused in the French Revolution had made France the "salvation of mankind."

German and Spanish nationalists had a very different opinion of France. To them the French often seemed as oppressive as the Germans seemed to the Czechs, as hateful as the Russians seemed to the Poles. The despised enemy's mission might seem as oppressive as the American national mission – as the American journalist and strident nationalist John Louis O'Sullivan sketched it in 1845 after the annexation of Texas – seemed to the Mexicans. O'Sullivan wrote that taking land from an "imbecile and distracted Mexico" was a laudable step in the "fulfillment of our manifest destiny to overspread the continent allotted by Providence for the free development of our yearly multiplying millions."[2]

Early nationalism was thus ambiguous. Its main thrust was liberal and democratic. But below the surface lurked ideas of national superiority and national mission, which could lead to aggressive crusades and countercrusades, as had happened in the French Revolution and in the "wars of liberation" against Napoleon.

## FRENCH UTOPIAN SOCIALISM

To understand the rise of socialism, one must begin with France. Despite the fact that France lagged far behind Great Britain in developing modern industry, almost all the early socialists were French. Although they differed on many specific points, these French thinkers were acutely aware that the political revolution in France and the rise of modern industry in England had begun a transformation of society. Yet they were disturbed by what they saw. Liberal practices in politics and economics appeared to be fomenting selfish individualism and splitting the community into isolated fragments. There was, they believed, an urgent need for a further reorganization of society to establish cooperation and a new sense of community. Starting from this shared outlook, individual French thinkers went in many different directions. They searched the past, analyzed existing conditions, and fashioned luxurious utopias. Yet certain ideas tied their critiques and visions together.

Early French socialists believed in economic planning. Inspired by the emergency measures of 1793 and 1794 in France, they argued that the government should rationally organize the economy and not depend on destructive competition to do the job. Early socialists also shared an intense desire to help the poor and to protect them from the rich. With passionate moral fervor they preached that the rich and the poor should be more nearly equal economically. Finally, socialists believed that private property should be abolished and replaced by state or community ownership. Planning, greater economic equality, and state ownership of property: these were the key ideas of early French socialism and of all socialism since.

One of the most influential of these thinkers was a nobleman, Count Henri de Saint-Simon (1760–1825). A curious combination of radical thinker and successful land speculator, Saint-Simon optimistically proclaimed the tremendous possibilities of industrial development: "The age of gold is before us!" The key to progress was proper social organization. Such an arrangement of society required the "parasites" – the court, the aristocracy, lawyers, churchmen – to give way, once and for all, to the "doers" – the leading scientists, engineers, and industrialists. The doers would carefully plan the economy and guide it forward by undertaking vast public-works projects and investment banks. Saint-Simon also stressed in highly moralistic terms that every social institution ought to have as its main goal improved conditions for the poor. Saint-Simon's stress on industry and science inspired middle-class industrialists and bankers, like the Pereire brothers, founders of the Crédit Mobilier.

After 1830, the socialist critique of capitalism became sharper. Charles Fourier (1772–1837), a lonely, saintly man with a tenuous hold on reality, described a socialist utopia in lavish mathematical detail. Hating the urban wage system, Fourier envisaged self-sufficient communities of 1,620 people living communally on 5,000 acres devoted to a combination of agriculture and industry. Fourier was also an early proponent of the total emancipation of women, abolition of marriage, and complete sexual freedom. Although Fourier waited in vain each day at noon in his apartment for a wealthy philanthrophist to endow his visionary schemes, he was very influential. Several utopian communities were founded along the lines he prescribed, mainly in the United States.

Louis Blanc (1811–1882), a sharp-eyed, intelligent journalist, was much more practical. In his *Organization of Work* (1839) he urged workers to agitate for universal voting rights and to take control of the state peacefully. Blanc believed that the full power of the state should be directed at setting up government-backed workshops and factories to guarantee full employment. The "right to work" had to become as sacred as any other right. Finally, there was Pierre Joseph Proudhon (1809–1865), a self-educated printer, who wrote a pamphlet in 1840 entitled *What Is Property?* His answer was that it was nothing but theft. Property was profit that was stolen from the worker, who was the source of all wealth. Unlike most socialists, Proudhon feared the power of the state and thus was often considered an anarchist.

Thus, a variety of French thinkers blazed the way with utopian socialism in the 1830s and 1840s. Their ideas were very influential, particularly in Paris, where poverty-stricken workers with a revolutionary tradition were attentive students. Yet the economic arguments of the French utopians were weak, and their specific programs usually seemed too fanciful to be taken seriously. To Karl Marx was left the task of establishing firm foundations for modern socialism.

## MARXIAN SOCIALISM

In 1848, the thirty-year-old Karl Marx and the twenty-eight-year-old Friedrich Engels published the *Communist Manifesto,* the Bible of socialism. The son of a Jewish lawyer who had converted to Christianity, the atheistic young Marx had studied philosophy at the University of Berlin before turning to journalism and economics. He read widely in French socialist thought and was developing his own socialist ideas by the time he was twenty-five.

Early French socialists often appealed to the middle class and the state to help the poor. Marx argued that the interests of the middle class and those of the industrial working class are inevitably opposed to each other. Indeed, according to the *Manifesto,* "the history of all previously existing society is the history of class struggles." In Marx's view, one class had

always exploited the other, and with the advent of modern industry, society was split more clearly than ever before: split between the middle class – the bourgeoisie – and the modern working class – the proletariat. Moreover, the bourgeoisie had reduced everything to a matter of money and "naked self-interest." "In a word, for exploitation, veiled by religious and political illusions, the bourgeoisie had substituted naked, shameless, direct brutal exploitation."

Just as the bourgeoisie had triumphed over the feudal aristocracy, Marx predicted, the proletariat was destined to conquer the bourgeoisie in a violent revolution. While a tiny minority owned the means of production and grew richer, the ever-poorer proletariat was constantly growing in size and in class consciousness. In this process the proletariat was aided, according to Marx, by a portion of the bourgeoisie who had gone over to the proletariat and who (like Marx and Engels) "had raised themselves to the level of comprehending theoretically the historical moment." And the critical moment was very near. "Let the ruling classes tremble at a Communist revolution. The proletarians have nothing to lose but their chains. They have a world to win. WORKING MEN OF ALL COUNTRIES, UNITE!" So ends the *Communist Manifesto.*

In brief outline, Marx's ideas may seem to differ only slightly from the wild and improbable ideas of the utopians of his day. Yet whatever one may think of the validity of Marx's analysis, he must be taken seriously. He united sociology, economics, and all human history in a vast and imposing edifice. He synthesized in his socialism not only French utopian schemes but English classical economics and German philosophy – the major intellectual currents of his day.

Marx's debt to England was great. He was

the last of the classical economists. Following David Ricardo, who had taught that labor was the source of all value, Marx went on to argue that profits were really wages stolen from the workers. Moreover, Marx incorporated Engels's charges of terrible oppression of the new class of factory workers in England; thus his doctrines seemed to be based on hard facts.

Marx's theory of historical evolution was built on the philosophy of the German Georg Hegel (1770–1831). Hegel believed that history is "ideas in motion": each age is characterized by a dominant set of ideas, which produces opposing ideas and eventually a new synthesis. The idea of being had been dominant initially, for example, and it had produced its antithesis, the idea of nonbeing. This idea in turn had resulted in the synthesis of becoming. History has, therefore, pattern and purpose.

Marx retained Hegel's view of history as a dialectic process of change, but made economic relationships between classes the driving force. This dialectic explained the decline of agrarian feudalism and the rise of industrial capitalism. And Marx stressed again and again that "the bourgeoisie, historically, has played a most revolutionary part. . . . During its rule of scarcely one hundred years the bourgeoisie has created more massive and more colossal productive forces than have all preceding generations together." Here was a convincing explanation for people trying to make sense of the dual revolution. Marx's next idea, that it was now the bourgeoisie's turn to give way to the socialism of revolutionary workers, appeared to many the irrefutable capstone of a brilliant interpretation of humanity's long development. Thus, Marx pulled together powerful ideas and insights to create one of the great secular religions out of the intellectual ferment of the early nineteenth century.

KARL MARX  *In 1849 the exiled Marx settled in London. There he laboriously wrote* Capital, *the weighty exposition of his socialist theories, and played a leading role in the successful organization of the First International of socialists in 1864. (The Mansell Collection)*

## THE ROMANTIC MOVEMENT

Developing radical concepts of politics and society were accompanied by comparable changes in literature and other arts during the dual revolution. The early nineteenth century marked the acme of the romantic movement, which profoundly influenced the arts and enriched European culture immeasurably.

The romantic movement was in part a revolt against classicism and the Enlightenment. Classicism was essentially a set of artistic rules and standards that went hand in glove with the Enlightenment's belief in rationality, order, and restraint. The classicists believed that the ancient Greeks and Romans had discovered eternally valid esthetic rules long ago and that playwrights and painters should continue to follow them. Classicists could enforce these rules in the eighteenth century because they dominated the courts and academies for which artists worked.

Forerunners of the romantic movement appeared from about 1750 on. Of these, Rousseau (pages 647–648) – the passionate advocate of feeling, freedom, and natural goodness – was most influential. Romanticism then crystallized fully in the 1790s, primarily in England and Germany. The French Revolution kindled the belief that radical reconstruction was also possible in cultural and artistic life (even though many early English and German romantics became disillusioned with events in France and turned from liberalism to conservatism in politics). Romanticism gained strength until the 1840s, when realism began to challenge it seriously.

## ROMANTICISM

Romanticism was characterized by a belief in emotional exuberance, unrestrained imagination, and spontaneity in both art and personal life. In Germany early romantics of the 1770s and 1780s called themselves the Storm and Stress *(Sturm und Drang)* group, and many romantic artists of the early nineteenth century lived lives of tremendous emotional intensity. Suicide, duels to the death, madness, and strange illnesses were not uncommon among leading romantics. Romantic artists typically led bohemian lives, wearing their

*DELACROIX: LIBERTY LEADING THE PEOPLE This great romantic painting idealistically glorifies the July Revolution in Paris in 1830. Raising the revolutionary tricolor on high, pure and beautiful Liberty unites the worker, the bourgeois, and the street child in a righteous crusade against privilege and oppression. (Louvre, Paris / Giraudon)*

hair long and uncombed in preference to powdered wigs, and living in cold garrets rather than frequenting stiff drawing rooms. They rejected materialism and sought to escape to lofty spiritual heights through their art. Great individualists, the romantics believed the full development of one's unique human potential to be the supreme purpose in life. The romantics were driven by a sense of an unlimited universe and by a yearning for the unattained, the unknown, the unknowable.

Nowhere was the break with classicism more apparent than in romanticism's general conception of nature. Classicism was not particularly interested in nature. In the words of the eighteenth-century English author Samuel Johnson, "A blade of grass is always a blade of grass; men and women are my subjects of inquiry." Nature was portrayed by classicists as beautiful and chaste, like an eighteenth-century formal garden. The romantics, on the other hand, were enchanted by nature. Sometimes they found it awesome and tempestuous, as in Théodore Géricault's painting *The Raft of the Medusa,* which shows the survivors of a shipwreck adrift in a turbulent sea. Others saw nature as a source of spiritual inspiration. As the great English landscape artist John Constable (1776–1837) declared, "Nature is Spirit visible."

Most romantics saw the growth of modern industry as an ugly, brutal attack on their beloved nature and on the human personality. They sought escape – in the unspoiled "Lake

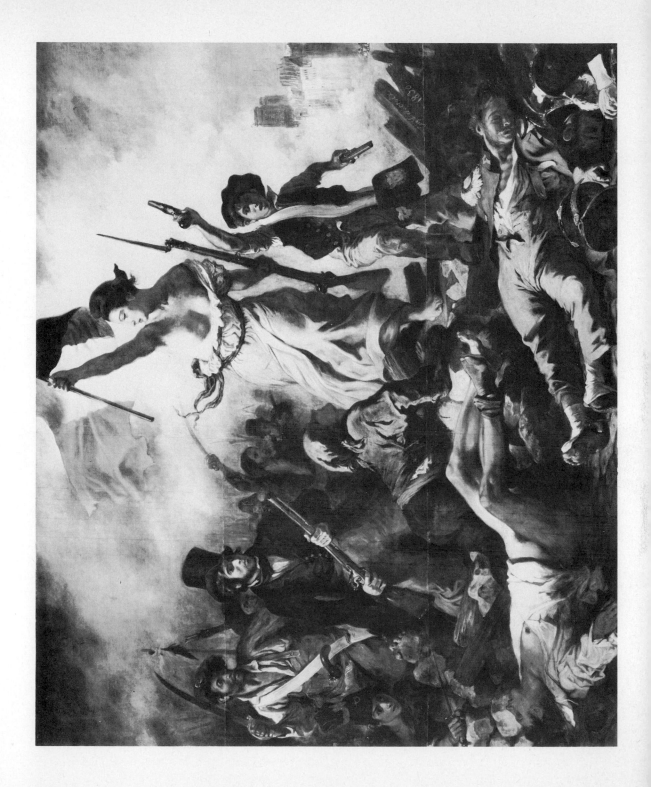

District" of northern England, in exotic North Africa, in an idealized Middle Ages. Yet some romantics found a vast, awesome, terribly moving power in the new industrial landscape. In ironworks and cotton mills they saw the flames of Hell and the evil genius of Satan himself. One of John Martin's last and greatest paintings, *The Great Day of His Wrath* (1850), vividly depicts the last judgment foretold in Revelations VI, "when the sun became black as sackcloth of hair, and the moon became as blood; and the stars of heaven fell unto the earth. . . ." Martin's romantic masterpiece was inspired directly by a journey through the Black country of the industrial Midlands in the dead of night. According to Martin's son:

*The glow of the furnaces, the red blaze of light, together with the liquid fire, seemed to him truly sublime and awful. He could not imagine anything more terrible even in the regions of everlasting punishment. All he had done or attempted in ideal painting fell far short, very far short, of the fearful sublimity.*[3]

Fascinated by color and diversity, the romantic imagination turned toward the study and writing of history with a passion. For romantics, history was not a minor branch of philosophy from which philosophers picked suitable examples to illustrate their teachings. History was beautiful, exciting, and important in its own right. It was the art of change over time – the key to a universe that was now perceived to be organic and dynamic, no longer mechanical and static as it had appeared to the philosophes of the eighteenth-century Enlightenment.

Historical studies supported the development of national aspirations and encouraged entire peoples to seek in the past their special destinies. This trend was especially strong in Germany and eastern Europe. As the famous English historian Lord Acton put it, the growth of historical thinking associated with the romantic movement was a most fateful step in the story of European thought.

## LITERATURE

Britain was the first country where romanticism flowered fully in poetry and prose, and the British romantic writers were among the most prominent in Europe. Wordsworth, Coleridge, and Scott were all active by 1800, to be followed shortly by Byron, Shelley, and Keats. All were poets: romanticism found its distinctive voice in poetry as the Enlightenment had in prose.

A towering leader of English romanticism, William Wordsworth (1770–1850) traveled in France after his graduation from Cambridge. There he fell passionately in love with a French woman named Annette Vallon, who bore him a daughter. He was deeply influenced by the philosophy of Rousseau and the spirit of the early French Revolution. Back in England, prevented by war and the Terror from returning to France, Wordsworth settled in the countryside with his sister Dorothy and Samuel Taylor Coleridge (1772–1834).

In 1798, the two poets published their *Lyrical Ballads,* one of the most influential literary works in the history of the English language. In defiance of classical rules, Wordsworth and Coleridge abandoned flowery poetic conventions for the language of ordinary speech, while simultaneously endowing simple subjects with the loftiest majesty. This twofold rejection of classical practice was at first ignored and then harshly criticized, but by 1830 Wordsworth had triumphed.

One of the best examples of Wordsworth's romantic credo and genius is "Daffodils":

*I wandered lonely as a cloud*
*That floats on high o'er vales and hills,*
*When all at once I saw a crowd,*
*A host, of golden daffodils;*
*Beside the lake, beneath the trees,*
*Fluttering and dancing in the breeze.*

*Continuous as the stars that shine*
*And twinkle on the Milky Way,*
*They stretched in never-ending line*
*Along the margin of a bay:*
*Ten thousand saw I at a glance,*
*Tossing their heads in sprightly dance.*

*The waves beside them danced, but they*
*Out-did the sparkling waves in glee:*
*A poet could not but be gay,*
*In such a jocund company:*
*I gazed – and gazed – but little thought*
*What wealth the show to me had brought:*

*For oft, when on my couch I lie*
*In vacant or in pensive mood,*
*They flash upon that inward eye*
*Which is the bliss of solitude;*
*And then my heart with pleasure fills,*
*And dances with the daffodils.*

Here indeed is simplicity and love of nature in commonplace forms. Here too is Wordsworth's romantic conviction that nature has the power to elevate and instruct, especially when interpreted by a high-minded poetic genius. Wordsworth's conception of poetry as "the spontaneous overflow of powerful feeling recollected in tranquillity" is well illustrated by the last stanza.

Born in Edinburgh, Walter Scott (1771–1832) personified the romantic movement's fascination with history. Raised on his grandfather's farm, Scott fell under the spell of the old ballads and tales of the Scottish border. He was also deeply influenced by German romanticism, and particularly by the immortal poet and dramatist Johann Wolfgang von Goethe (1749–1832). Scott translated Goethe's famous play about a sixteenth-century knight who revolted against centralized authority and championed individual freedom – at least in Goethe's romantic drama. A natural storyteller, Scott then composed long narrative poems and a series of historical novels. Scott excelled in faithfully recreating the spirit of bygone ages and great historical events, especially those of Scotland.

At first the strength of classicism in France inhibited the growth of romanticism there. Then, between 1820 and 1850, the romantic impulse broke through in the poetry and prose of Lamartine, Alfred de Vigny, Victor Hugo, Alexander Dumas, and George Sand. Of these, Victor Hugo (1802–1885) was the greatest in both poetry and prose.

Son of a Napoleonic general, Hugo achieved an amazing range of rhythm, language, and image in his lyric poetry. His powerful novels exemplified the romantic fascination with fantastic characters, strange settings, and human emotions. The hero of Hugo's famous *Hunchback of Notre Dame* (1831) is the great cathedral's deformed bellringer, a "human gargoyle" overlooking the teeming life of fifteenth-century Paris. A great admirer of Shakespeare, whom classical critics had derided as undisciplined and excessive, Hugo also championed romanticism in drama. His play *Hernani* (1830) consciously broke all the old rules, as Hugo renounced his early conservatism and equated freedom in literature with liberty in politics and society. Hugo's political evolution was thus exactly the opposite of Wordsworth's, in whom youthful radicalism gave way to middle-aged caution. As the contrast between the two artists suggests, romanticism was a cultural movement compatible with many political beliefs.

George Sand (1804–1876), a strong-willed and gifted woman, defied the narrow conventions of her time in an unending search for self-fulfillment. After eight years of unhappy marriage in the provinces, she abandoned her dullard of a husband and took her two children to Paris to pursue a career as a writer. There she soon achieved fame and wealth, eventually writing over eighty novels on a variety of romantic and social themes. All were shot through with a typically romantic love of nature and moral idealism. George Sand's striking originality and individualism went far beyond her flamboyant preference for men's clothing and taste for cigars and her notorious affairs with the poet Alfred Musset and the composer Frédéric Chopin, among others. Her semi-autobiographical novel *Lélia* was shockingly modern, delving deeply into her tortuous quest for sexual and personal freedom.

In central and eastern Europe literary romanticism and early nationalism often reinforced each other. Seeking a unique greatness in every people, well-educated romantics plumbed their own histories and cultures. Like modern anthropologists, they turned their attention to peasant life and transcribed the folk songs, tales, and proverbs that the cosmopolitan Enlightenment had disdained. The brothers Jacob and Wilhelm Grimm were particularly successful at rescuing German fairy tales from oblivion. In the Slavic lands, romantics played a decisive role in converting spoken peasant languages into modern written languages. The greatest of all Russian poets, Alexander Pushkin (1799–1837), rejecting eighteenth-century attempts to force Russian poetry into a classical strait-

jacket, used his lyric genius to mold the modern literary language.

## ART AND MUSIC

The greatest and most moving romantic painter in France was Eugène Delacroix (1798–1863), probably the illegitimate son of the French foreign minister Talleyrand. Delacroix was a master of dramatic, colorful scenes that stir the emotions. He was fascinated with remote and exotic subjects, whether lion hunts in Morocco or the languishing, sensuous women of a sultan's harem. Yet he was also a passionate spokesman for freedom. His masterpiece, *Liberty Leading the People,* celebrated the nobility of popular revolution in general and revolution in France in particular.

In England the most outstanding romantic painters were J. M. W. Turner (1775–1851) and John Constable (1776–1837). Both were fascinated by nature but their interpretations of it contrasted sharply, aptly symbolizing the tremendous emotional range of the romantic movement. Turner depicted nature's power and terror; wild storms and sinking ships were favorite subjects. Constable painted gentle Wordsworthian landscapes in which human beings are at one with their environment, the comforting countryside of unspoiled rural England.

It was in music that romanticism realized most fully and permanently its goals of free expression and emotional intensity. Whereas the composers of the eighteenth century had remained true to well-defined structures, like the classical symphony, the great romantics used a great range of forms to paint a thousand landscapes and evoke a host of powerful emotions. Romantic composers also transformed the small classical orchestra, tripling its size by adding wind instruments, percus-

HEROES OF ROMANTICISM    *Liszt plays for a gathering of friends. From left to right sit Alexander Dumas, George Sand (characteristically wearing men's clothing), and Marie d'Agoult, Liszt's mistress.* *Standing from left to right are Victor Hugo, Paganini, and Rossini. A portrait of Byron and a bust of Beethoven look down. (Bildarchiv Preussischer Kulturbisitz)*

sion, and more brass and strings. The crashing chords evoking the surge of the masses in Chopin's "Revolutionary" etude, the bottomless despair of the funeral march in Beethoven's Third Symphony, the solemn majesty of a great religious event in Schumann's Rhenish Symphony: such were the modern orchestra's musical paintings that plumbed the depth of human feeling.

This range and intensity gave music and musicians much greater prestige and importance than in the past. Music no longer simply complemented a church service or helped a nobleman digest his dinner. Music became a sublime end in itself. It became for many the greatest of the arts, precisely because it achieved the most ecstatic effect and most perfectly realized the endless yearning of the soul. It was worthy of great concert halls and the most dedicated sacrifice. The unbelievable one-in-a-million performer – the great virtuoso who could transport the listener to ecstasy and hysteria – became a cultural hero. The composer Franz Liszt (1811–1886) vowed to do for the piano what Paganini had done for the violin, and he was lionized as the greatest pianist of his age. People swooned for Liszt as they scream for rock idols today.

Though romanticism dominated music until late in the nineteenth century, no composer ever surpassed its first great master, Ludwig van Beethoven (1770–1827). Extending and breaking open classical forms, Beethoven used contrasting themes and tones to produce dramatic conflict and inspiring resolutions. As the contemporary German novelist Ernst Hoffmann (1776–1822) wrote, "Beethoven's music sets in motion the lever of fear, of awe, of horror, of suffering, and awakens just that infinite longing which is the essence of Romanticism." Beethoven's range was tremendous; has output included symphonies, chamber music, sonatas for violin and piano, masses, an opera, and a great many songs.

At the peak of his fame, in constant demand as a composer and recognized as the leading concert pianist of his day, Beethoven began to lose his hearing. He considered suicide, but eventually overcame despair: "I will take fate by the throat; it will not bend me completely to its will."[4] Beethoven continued to pour out immortal music. Among other achievements, he fully exploited for the first time the richness and beauty of the piano. Beethoven never heard much of his later work, including the unforgettable choral finale to the Ninth Symphony, for his last years were silent, spent in total deafness.

## REFORMS AND REVOLUTIONS

While the romantic movement was developing, liberal, national, and socialist forces battered against the conservatism of 1815. In some countries change occurred gradually and peacefully. Elsewhere pressure built up like steam in a pressure cooker without a safety valve, and eventually caused an explosion in 1848. Three important countries – Greece, Great Britain, and France – experienced variations on this basic theme.

### NATIONAL LIBERATION IN GREECE

National, liberal revolution, frustrated in Italy and Spain by conservative statesmen, succeeded first after 1815 in Greece. Since the fifteenth century, the Greeks had been living under the domination of the Ottoman Turks. In spite of centuries of foreign rule the Greeks had survived as a people, united by their language and the Greek Orthodox religion. It was perfectly natural that the general growth of national aspirations and a desire for independence would inspire some Greeks in the early nineteenth century. This rising national movement led to the formation of secret societies and then to revolt in 1821, led by Alexander Ypsilanti, a Greek patriot and a general in the Russian army.

The Great Powers, and particularly Metternich, were opposed to all revolution, even revolution against the Islamic Turks. They refused to back Ypsilanti and supported the Ottoman Empire. Yet for many Europeans the Greek cause became a holy cause. Educated Americans and Europeans were in love with the culture of classical Greece; Russians were stirred by the piety of their Orthodox brethren. Writers and artists, moved by the romantic impulse, responded enthusiastically to the Greek struggle. The flamboyant, radical poet Lord Byron went to Greece and died there in the struggle "that Greece might still be free." Turkish atrocities toward the rebels fanned the fires of European outrage and Greek determination. One of Delacroix's romantic masterpieces memorialized the massa-

| | |
|---|---|
| March 1814 | Russia, Prussia, Austria, and Britain form the Quadruple Alliance to defeat France |
| April 1814 | Napoleon abdicates |
| May–June 1814 | Restoration of the Bourbon monarchy; Louis XVIII issues Constitutional Charter accepting civil liberties and representative government |
| 1814 | First Peace of Paris: allies combine leniency with defensive posture toward France |
| October 1814–June 1815 | Congress of Vienna peace settlement: establishes balance-of-power principle and creates the German Confederation |
| February 1815 | Napoleon escapes from Elba and marches on Paris |
| June 1815 | Battle of Waterloo |
| September 1815 | Austria, Prussia, and Russia form the Holy Alliance to repress liberal and revolutionary movements |
| November 1815 | Second Peace of Paris and renewal of Quadruple Alliance: punishes France and establishes the European "congress system" |
| 1818 *France Louis— becomes Quintuple alliance* | |
| 1819 | Carlsbad Decrees: Metternich imposes repressive measures throughout the German Confederation |
| 1820 | Revolution in Spain and the Kingdom of the Two Sicilies |
| | Congress of Troppau: Metternich and Alexander I of Russia proclaim principle of intervention to maintain autocratic regimes |
| 1821 | Austria crushes liberal revolution in Naples and restores the Sicilian autocracy |
| | Greek revolt against the Ottoman Turks |
| 1823 | French armies restore the Spanish regime |
| | United States proclaims the Monroe Doctrine |
| 1824 | Reactionary Charles X succeeds Louis XVIII in France |
| 1830 | Charles X repudiates the Constitutional Charter; insurrection and government collapse; Louis Philippe succeeds to the throne and maintains a narrowly liberal regime to 1848 |
| | Greece wins independence from the Ottoman Empire |
| 1832 | Reform Bill expands British electorate and encourages the middle class |
| 1839 | Louis Blanc, *Organization of Work* |
| 1840 | Pierre Joseph Proudhon, *What Is Property?* |
| 1846 | Jules Michelet, *The People* |
| 1848 | Karl Marx and Friedrich Engels, *The Communist Manifesto* |

cre at Chios, where the Turks slaughtered nearly 100,000 Greeks.

The Greeks, though often quarreling among themselves, battled on against the Turks and hoped for the eventual support of European governments. In 1827 Great Britain, France, and Russia responded to popular demands at home and directed Turkey to accept an armistice. When the Turks refused, the navies of these three powers trapped the Turkish fleet at Navarino and destroyed it. Russia then declared another of its periodic wars of expansion against the Turks. This led to the establishment of a Russian protectorate over much of present-day Rumania, which had also been under Turkish rule. Great Britain, France, and Russia finally declared Greece independent in 1830 and installed a German prince as king of the new country in 1832. In the end the Greeks had won: a small nation had gained its independence in a heroic war against a foreign empire.

### LIBERAL REFORM IN GREAT BRITAIN

Eighteenth-century British society had been both flexible and remarkably stable. It was dominated by the landowning aristocracy, but that class was neither closed nor rigidly defined. Successful business and professional people could buy land and become gentlemen, while the common people had more than the usual opportunities of the preindustrial world. Basic civil rights for all were balanced by a tradition of deference to one's social superiors. Parliament was manipulated by the king and was thoroughly undemocratic. Only about 6 percent of the population could vote for representatives to Parliament, and by the 1780s there was growing interest in some kind of political reform.

But the French Revolution threw the aris-

tocracy into a panic for a generation, making it extremely hostile to any attempts to change the status quo. The Tory party, completely controlled by the landed aristocracy, was particularly fearful of radical movements at home and abroad. Castlereagh initially worked closely with Metternich to restrain France and restore a conservative balance in central Europe. This same intense conservatism motivated the Tory government at home. After 1815 the aristocracy defended its ruling position by repressing every kind of popular protest.

The first step in this direction was the Corn Law of 1815. During a generation of war with France the British had been unable to import food. As shortages occurred and agricultural prices skyrocketed, a great deal of marginal land had been brought under cultivation. This development had been a bonanza for the landed aristocracy, whose fat rent rolls became even fatter. Peace meant that grain could be imported again and that the price of wheat and bread would go down. To almost everyone except the aristocracy, lower prices seemed highly desirable. The aristocracy, however, rammed the Corn Law through Parliament. This law prohibited the importation of foreign grain unless the price at home rose above eighty shillings per quarter-ton — a level reached only in time of harvest disaster before 1790. Seldom has a class legislated more selfishly for its own narrow economic advantage.

The Corn Law, coming at a time of widespread unemployment and postwar adjustment, led to protests and demonstrations by urban laborers. They were supported by radical intellectuals, who campaigned for a reformed House of Commons that would serve the nation and not just the aristocracy. In 1817, the Tory government responded by temporarily suspending the traditional rights of peaceable assembly and habeas corpus. Two years later Parliament passed the infamous Six Acts, which among other things controlled a heavily taxed press and practically eliminated all mass meetings. These acts followed an enormous but orderly protest at St. Peter's Fields in Manchester, which had been savagely broken up by armed cavalry. Nicknamed the battle of Peterloo, in scornful reference to the British victory at Waterloo, this incident expressed the government's determination to repress and stand fast.

Ongoing industrial development was not only creating urban and social problems but also strengthening the upper middle classes. The new manufacturing and commercial groups insisted on a place for their new wealth alongside the landed wealth of the aristocracy in the framework of political power and social prestige. They called for certain kinds of liberal reform: reform of town government, organization of a new police force, and more rights for Catholics and dissenters. In the 1820s, a less frightened Tory government led by Robert Peel moved in the direction of better urban administration, greater economic liberalism, and civil equality for Catholics. The prohibition on imports of foreign grain was replaced by a heavy tariff. These actions encouraged the middle classes to press on for reform of Parliament, so they could have a larger say in government and perhaps repeal the revised Corn Law – that symbol of aristocratic domination.

The Whig party, though led like the Tories by great aristocrats, had by tradition been more responsive to commercial and manufacturing interests. In 1830, a Whig ministry introduced "an act to amend the representation of the people of England and Wales." Defeated, then passed by the House of Com-

mons, this reform bill was rejected by the House of Lords. But when in 1832 the Whigs got the king to promise to create enough new peers to pass the law, the House of Lords reluctantly gave in rather than see its snug little club ruined by upstart manufacturers and plutocrats. A mighty surge of popular protest had helped the king and lords make up their minds.

The Reform Bill of 1832 had profound significance. The House of Commons had emerged as the all-important legislative body. In the future an obstructionist House of Lords could always be brought into line by the threat of creating new peers. The new industrial areas of the country gained representation in the Commons, and many old "rotten boroughs" – electoral districts with very few voters that the landed aristocracy had bought and sold – were eliminated.

The redistribution of seats reflected the shift in population to the northern manufacturing counties and the gradual emergence of an urban society. As a result of the Reform Bill of 1832, the number of voters increased about 50 percent. Comfortable members of the urban population, as well as some substantial farmers who leased their land, received the vote. Thus the pressures building up in Great Britain were successfully – though only temporarily – released. A major reform had been achieved peacefully, without revolution or civil war. More radical reforms within the system appeared difficult but not impossible.

The principal radical program was embodied in the "People's Charter" of 1838 and the Chartist movement (page 788). Partly inspired by the economic distress of the working class, the Chartists' core demand was universal male (not female) suffrage. They saw complete political democracy and rule by

## THE BRITISH LION IN 1850;

### OR, THE EFFECTS OF FREE TRADE.

FREE TRADE OPTIMISM   *Appearing in* Punch *in
1846 as the Corn Law was being repealed, this cartoon looked to the future and reflected British self-
confidence. Socially and economically advanced Great
Britain had no need for protective tariffs. The British
economy actually did boom after 1850. (The British
Library)*

the common people as the means to a good and just society. Hundreds of thousands of people signed gigantic petitions calling on Parliament to grant all men the right to vote, first and most seriously in 1839, again in 1842, and yet again in 1848. Parliament rejected all three petitions. In the short run the working poor failed with their Chartist demands, but they learned a valuable lesson in mass politics.

While calling for universal suffrage, many working-class people joined with middle-class manufacturers in the Anti-Corn Law League, founded in Manchester in 1839. Mass participation made possible a popular crusade against the tariff on imported grain and against the landed aristocracy. People were fired up by dramatic popular orators such as John Bright and Richard Cobden. These fighting liberals argued that lower food prices and more jobs in industry depended on repeal of the Corn Law. Much of the working class agreed. The climax of the movement came in 1845, when Ireland's potato crop failed and famine seemed likely in England. In 1846, the Tory prime minister Robert Peel joined with the Whigs and a minority of his own party to repeal the Corn Law. Thereafter, free trade became almost sacred doctrine in Great Britain.

The following year the Tories passed a bill designed to help the working classes, but in a different way. This was the Ten Hours Act of 1847, which limited the workday for women and young people in factories to ten hours. Tory aristocrats continued to champion legislation regulating factory conditions. They were competing vigorously with the middle class for the support of the working class. This healthy competition between a still-vigorous aristocracy and a strong middle class was a crucial factor in Great Britain's peaceful evolution. The working classes could make temporary alliances with either competitor to better their own conditions.

## THE REVOLUTION OF 1830 IN FRANCE

Louis XVIII's Constitutional Charter of 1814 – theoretically a gift from the king but actually a response to political pressures – was basically a liberal constitution (page 797). The economic gains of the middle class and the prosperous peasantry were fully protected; great intellectual and artistic freedom was permitted; and a real parliament with upper and lower houses was created. Immediately after Napoleon's abortive Hundred Days, the moderate, worldly-wise king refused to bow to the wishes of diehard aristocrats like his brother Charles, who wished to sweep away all the revolutionary changes and return to a bygone age of royal absolutism and aristocratic pretension. Instead, Louis appointed as his ministers moderate royalists, who sought and obtained the support of a majority of the representatives elected to the lower Chamber of Deputies between 1816 and Louis' death in 1824.

Louis XVIII's charter was anything but democratic. Only about 100,000 of the wealthiest people out of a total population of 30 million had the right to vote for the deputies, who, with the king and his ministers, made the laws of the nation. Nonetheless, the "notable people" who did vote came from very different backgrounds. There were wealthy businessmen, war profiteers, successful professionals, ex-revolutionaries, large landowners from the middle class, Bourbons, and Bonapartists.

The old aristocracy with its pre-1789 mentality was a minority within the voting population. It was this situation that Louis' successor, Charles X (1824–1830), could not abide. Crowned in a lavish, utterly medieval, five-hour ceremony in the cathedral of Reims in 1824, Charles was a true reactionary. He wanted to re-establish the old order in France. Increasingly blocked by the opposition of the deputies, Charles finally repudiated the Constitutional Charter in an attempted coup in July 1830. He issued decrees stripping much of the wealthy middle class of its voting rights, and he censored the press. The reaction was an immediate insurrection. In "three glorious days" the government collapsed. Paris boiled with revolutionary excitement, and Charles fled. Then the upper middle class, which had fomented the revolt, skillfully seated Charles's cousin, Louis Philippe, duke of Orléans, on the vacant throne.

Louis Philippe (1830–1848) accepted the Constitutional Charter of 1814, adopted the red, white, and blue flag of the French Revolution, and admitted that he was merely the "king of the French people." In spite of such symbolic actions, the situation in France remained fundamentally unchanged. As Casimir Périer, a wealthy banker and Louis Philippe's new chief minister, bluntly told a deputy who complained when the vote was extended only from 100,000 to 170,000 citizens: "The trouble with this country is that there are too many people like you who imagine that there has been a revolution in France."[5] The wealthy "notable" elite actually tightened its control as the old aristocracy retreated to the provinces to sulk harmlessly. For the upper middle class there had been a change in dynasty, in order to protect the status quo and the narrowly liberal institutions of 1815. Republicans, democrats, social reformers, and the poor of Paris were bitterly disappointed. They had made a revolution, but it seemed for naught.

## THE REVOLUTIONS OF 1848

In 1848, revolutionary political and social ideologies combined with economic crisis and the romantic impulse to produce a vast upheaval. Only the most advanced and the most backward major countries – reforming Great Britain and immobile Russia – escaped untouched. Governments toppled; monarchs and ministers bowed or fled. National independence, liberal-democratic constitutions, and social reform: the lofty aspirations of a generation seemed at hand. Yet, in the end, the revolutions failed. Why was this so?

### A DEMOCRATIC REPUBLIC IN FRANCE

The late 1840s in Europe were hard economically and tense politically. The potato famine in Ireland in 1845 had echoes on the Continent. Bad harvests jacked up food prices and caused misery and unemployment in the cities. "Prerevolutionary" outbreaks occurred all across Europe: an abortive Polish revolution in the northern part of Austria in 1846, a civil war between radicals and conservatives in Switzerland in 1847, and an armed uprising in Naples, Italy, in January 1848. Revolution was almost universally expected, but it took revolution in Paris – once again! – to turn expectations into realities.

From its beginning in 1830, Louis Philippe's "bourgeois monarchy" was characterized by stubborn inaction. There was a glaring lack of social legislation, and politics was dominated by corruption and selfish special interests. The king's chief minister in the 1840s, François Guizot, was complacency personified. Guizot was especially satisfied with the electoral system. Only the rich could vote for deputies, and many of the deputies were

*DAUMIER: THE LEGISLATIVE BELLY  Protected by freedom of the press after 1830, French republicans and radicals bitterly attacked the do-nothing government of Louis Philippe. Here Daumier, the master of caricature, savagely ridicules the corruption of the Chamber of Deputies and the bloated bellies of its greedy members. (Charles Deering Collection. Courtesy of the Art Institute of Chicago)*

docile government bureaucrats. It was the government's stubborn refusal to consider electoral reform that touched off popular revolt in Paris. Barricades went up on the night of February 22, 1848, and by February 24 Louis Philippe had abdicated in favor of his grandson. But the common people in arms would tolerate no more monarchy. This refusal led to the proclamation of a provisional republic, headed by a ten-man executive committee and certified by cries of approval from the revolutionary crowd.

In the flush of victory, there was much about which Paris revolutionaries could agree. A generation of historians and journalists had praised the First French Republic, and their work had born fruit: the revolutionaries were firmly committed to a republic as opposed to any form of constitutional monarchy, and they immediately set about drafting a constitution for France's Second Republic. Moreover, they wanted a truly popular and democratic republic, so that the healthy, life-giving forces of the common people – the peasants and the workers – could reform society with wise legislation. In practice, building such a republic meant giving the right to vote to every adult male, and this was quickly done. Revolutionary compassion and sympathy for freedom were expressed in the freeing of all slaves in French colonies, abolition of the death penalty, and the establishment of a ten-hour workday for Paris.

Yet there were profound differences within the revolutionary coalition in Paris. On the one hand there were the moderate, liberal republicans of the middle class. They viewed universal manhood suffrage as the ultimate concession to be made to popular forces, and strongly opposed any further radical social measures. On the other hand were the radical republicans. Influenced by the critique of capitalism and unbridled individualism elaborated by a generation of utopian socialists, and appalled by the poverty and misery of the urban poor, the radical republicans were committed to socialism. To be sure, socialism came in many utopian shapes and sizes for the Parisian working poor and their leaders, but that did not make their commitment to it any less real. Finally, wedged in between were individuals like the poet Lamartine and the democrat Ledru-Rollin, who were neither doctrinaire socialists nor stand-pat liberals and who sought to escape an impending tragedy.

Worsening depression and rising unemployment brought these conflicting goals to the fore. Louis Blanc (page 809), who along with the worker Albert represented the republican socialists in the provisional government, pressed for recognition of a socialist "right to work." Blanc asserted that permanent government-sponsored cooperative workshops should be established for workers. Such workshops would be an alternative to capital-ist employment and a decisive. step toward a new social order.

The moderate republicans wanted no such thing. They were willing to provide only temporary relief. The resulting compromise set up national workshops – soon to become a vast program of pick-and-shovel public works – and established a special commission under Louis Blanc to "study the question." This satisfied no one. As bad as the national workshops were, though, they were better than nothing. An army of desperate poor from the French provinces and even from foreign countries streamed into Paris to sign up. The number enrolled in the workshops soared from 10,000 in March to 120,000 by June, and another 80,000 were trying unsuccessfully to join.

While the workshops in Paris grew, the French masses went to the polls in late April. Voting in most cases for the first time, the people elected to the new Constituent Assembly about five hundred moderate republicans, three hundred monarchists, and one hundred radicals who professed various brands of socialism. One of the moderate republicans was the author of *Democracy in America*, Alexis de Tocqueville (1805-1859), who had predicted the overthrow of Louis Philippe's government. To this brilliant observer, socialism was the most characteristic aspect of the revolution in Paris.

This socialist revolution had evoked a violent reaction not only among the frightened middle and upper classes but also among the bulk of the population – the peasants. The French peasants owned land, and, according to Tocqueville, "private property had become with all those who owned it a sort of bond of fraternity."[6] The countryside, Tocqueville wrote, had been seized with a universal hatred of radical Paris. Returning from Normandy to take his seat in the new Constituent Assembly, Tocqueville saw that a majority of the members were firmly committed to the republic and strongly opposed to the socialists, and he shared their sentiments.

The clash of ideologies – of liberal capitalism and socialism – became a clash of classes and arms after the elections. The new government's executive committee dropped Louis Blanc and thereafter included no representative of the Parisian working class. Fearing that their socialist hopes were about to be dashed, the workers invaded the assembly on May 15 and tried to proclaim a new revolutionary state. But the government was ready and used the middle-class National Guard to squelch this uprising. As the workshops continued to fill and grow more radical, the fearful but powerful propertied classes in the assembly took the offensive. On June 22 the government dissolved the national workshops in Paris, giving the workers the choice of joining the army or going to workshops in the provinces.

The result was a spontaneous and violent uprising. Frustrated in their attempts to create a socialist society, masses of desperate men and women were now losing even their life-sustaining relief. As a voice from the crowd cried out when the famous astronomer François Arago counseled patience: "Ah, Monsieur Arago, you have never been hungry!"[7] Barricades sprang up in the narrow streets of Paris, and a terrible class war began. Working men and women fought with the courage of utter desperation, but the government had the army and the support of peasant France. After three terrible "June Days" and the death or injury of more than ten thousand people, the republican army under General Louis Cavaignac stood triumphant in a sea of working-class blood and hatred.

The revolution in France thus ended in spectacular failure. The February coalition of the middle and working classes had in four short months become locked in mortal combat. In place of a generous democratic republic, the Constituent Assembly completed a constitution featuring a strong executive. This allowed Louis Napoleon, nephew of Napoleon Bonaparte, to win a landslide victory in the election of December 1848. The appeal of his great name, as well as the desire of the propertied classes for order at any cost, had produced a semi-authoritarian regime.

## THE AUSTRIAN EMPIRE IN 1848

Throughout central Europe news of the upheaval in France evoked feverish excitement and eventually revolution. Liberals demanded written constitutions, representative government, and greater civil liberties. When governments hesitated, popular revolts followed. Urban workers and students served as the shock troops, but they were allied with middle-class liberals and peasants. In the face of this united front, monarchs collapsed and granted almost everything. The popular revolutionary coalition, having secured great and easy victories, then broke down as it had in France. The traditional forces – the monarchy, the aristocracy, and the regular army – recovered their nerve, reasserted their authority, and took back many though not all of the concessions. Reaction was everywhere victorious.

The revolution in the Austrian Empire began in Hungary. Nationalism had been growing among Hungarians since about 1790, and in 1848 under the leadership of Louis Kossuth the Hungarians demanded national autonomy, full civil liberties, and universal suffrage. When the monarchy in Vienna hesi-

# THE REVOLUTIONS OF 1848

| | |
|---|---|
| February | Revolt in Paris against Louis Philippe's "bourgeois monarchy"; Louis Philippe abdicates; proclamation of a provisional republic |
| February–June | Establishment and rapid growth of government-sponsored workshops in France |
| March 3 | Hungarians under Kossuth demand autonomy from Austrian Empire |
| March 13 | Uprising of students and workers in Vienna; Metternich flees to London |
| March 19–21 | Frederick William IV of Prussia is forced to salute the bodies of slain revolutionaries in Berlin and agrees to a liberal constitution and merger into a new German state |
| March 20 | Ferdinand I of Austria abolishes serfdom and promises reforms |
| March 26 | Workers in Berlin issue a series of socialist demands |
| April 22 | French voters favor moderate republicans over radicals 5–1 |
| May 15 | Parisian socialist workers invade the Constitutional Assembly and unsuccessfully proclaim a new revolutionary state |
| May 18 | Frankfurt Assembly begins writing a new German constitution |
| June 17 | Austrian army crushes working-class revolt in Prague |
| June 22–26 | French government abolishes the national workshops, provoking an uprising |
| | June Days: republican army defeats rebellious Parisian working class |
| October | Austrian army besieges and retakes Vienna from students and working-class radicals |
| December | Conservatives force Ferdinand I of Austria to abdicate in favor of young Francis Joseph |
| | Frederick William IV disbands Prussian Constituent Assembly and grants Prussia a conservative constitution |
| | Louis Napoleon wins a landslide victory in French presidential elections |
| March 1849 | Frankfurt Assembly elects Frederick William IV of Prussia emperor of the new German state; Frederick William refuses and reasserts royal authority in Prussia |
| June–August 1849 | Habsburg and Russian forces defeat the Hungarian independence movement |

tated, Viennese students and workers took to the streets on March 13 and added their own demands. Peasant disorders broke out in parts of the empire. The Habsburg emperor Ferdinand I (1835-1848) capitulated and promised reforms and a liberal constitution. Metternich fled in disguise toward London. The old order seemed to be collapsing with unbelievable rapidity.

The coalition of revolutionaries was not completely stable, though. The Austrian Empire was overwhelmingly agricultural, and serfdom still existed. On March 20, as part of its capitulation before upheaval, the monarchy abolished serfdom with its degrading forced labor and feudal services. Peasants throughout the empire felt they had won a victory reminiscent of France in 1789. Newly free, men and women of the land lost interest in the political and social questions agitating the cities. The government had in the peasants a potential ally of great importance, especially since in central Europe as in France the bulk of the army was made up of peasants.

The coalition of March was also weakened – and ultimately destroyed – by conflicting national aspirations. In March the Hungarian revolutionary leaders pushed through an extremely liberal, almost democratic, constitution granting widespread voting rights and civil liberties, and ending feudal obligations. So far, well and good. Yet the Hungarian revolutionaries were also nationalists with a mission. They wanted the ancient Crown of <u>Saint Stephen</u>, with its mosaic of provinces and nationalities, transformed into a unified centralized Hungarian nation. To the minority groups that formed half the population of the kingdom of Hungary – the Croats, the Serbs, and the Rumanians – such unification was completely unacceptable. Each felt entitled to political

autonomy and cultural independence. The Habsburg monarchy in Vienna exploited the fears of the minority groups, and they were soon locked in armed combat with the new Hungarian government.

In a somewhat different fashion, Czech nationalists in Bohemia and the city of Prague, led by the Czech historian Palacký, came into conflict with German nationalists. Like the minorities in Hungary, the Czechs saw their struggle for autonomy as a struggle against a dominant group – the Germans. Thus the national aspirations of different peoples in the Austrian Empire came into sharp conflict, and the monarchy was able to play off one group against the other.

Nor was this all. The urban working classes of poor artisans and day laborers were not as radical in the Austrian Empire as they were in France, but then neither were the middle class and lower middle class. Throughout Austria and the German states, where Metternich's brand of absolutism had so recently ruled supreme, the middle class wanted liberal reform, complete with constitutional monarchy, limited voting rights, and modest social measures. They wanted a central European equivalent of the English Reform Bill of 1832 and the Corn Law repeal of 1846. When the urban poor rose in arms, as they did in the Austrian cities of Vienna, Prague, and Milan and throughout the German Confederation as well, and presented their own demands for universal voting rights and socialist workshops, the prosperous middle classes recoiled in alarm. As in Paris, the union of the urban poor and the middle class was soon a mere memory, and a bad memory at that.

Finally, the conservative aristocratic forces gathered around Emperor Ferdinand I regained their nerve and reasserted their great

Patron saint of Hungary

strength. The archduchess Sophia, a conservative but intelligent and courageous Bavarian princess married to the emperor's brother, provided a rallying-point. Deeply ashamed of the emperor's collapse before "a mess of students,"[8] she insisted that Ferdinand, who had no heir, abdicate in favor of her eighteen-year-old son, Francis Joseph. Powerful nobles who held high positions in the government, the army, and the church agreed completely. They organized around Sophia in a secret conspiracy to reverse and crush the revolution.

Their first breakthrough came when one of the most dedicated members of the group, Prince Alfred Windischgrätz, bombarded Prague and savagely crushed a working-class revolt there on June 17. Other Austrian officials and nobles began to lead the minority nationalities of Hungary against the revolutionary government proclaimed by the Hungarian patriots. Another Austrian army under General Josef Radetzky reconquered Austria's possessions in northern Italy in late July 1848. Revolution failed as miserably in Italy as everywhere else. At the end of October the well-equipped, predominantly peasant troops of the regular Austrian army attacked the student and working-class radicals in Vienna, and retook the city at the cost of more than four thousand casualties. Thus, the determination of the Austrian aristocracy and the loyalty of its army were the final ingredients in the triumph of reaction and the defeat of revolution.

Only in Hungary were the forces represented by Sophia's son Francis Joseph (1848-1916), crowned emperor of Austria immediately after his eighteenth birthday in December 1848, at first unsuccessful. Yet another determined conservative, Nicholas I of Russia (1825-1855), obligingly lent his iron hand. On June 6, 1849, 130,000 Russian troops poured into Hungary. After bitter fighting – in which the Hungarian army supported the revolutionary Hungarian government – they subdued the country. For a number of years the Habsburgs ruled Hungary as a conquered territory.

## PRUSSIA AND THE FRANKFURT ASSEMBLY

The rest of the states in the German Confederation generally recapitulated the ebb and flow of developments in France and Austria. The key difference was the additional goal of unifying the thirty-eight states of the German Confederation, with the possible exception of Austria, into a single sovereign nation. Therefore events in Germany were extraordinarily complex, since they were occurring not only in the individual principalities but at the all-German level as well.

After Austria, Prussia was the largest and most influential German kingdom. Prior to 1848, the goal of middle-class Prussian liberals had been to transform absolutist Prussia into a liberal constitutional monarchy. Such a monarchy would then take the lead in merging itself and all the other German states into a liberal unified nation. The agitation following the fall of Louis Philippe encouraged Prussian liberals to press their demands. When they were not granted, the artisans and factory workers in Berlin exploded. The autocratic yet paternalistic Frederick William IV (1840-1861), already displaying the instability that later became insanity, vacillated. Humiliated by the revolutionary crowd, which forced him to salute from his balcony the blood-spattered corpses of workers who had fallen in an uprising on March 18, the nearly hysterical king finally caved in. On March 21, he promised to grant Prussia a liberal constitution and to merge it into a new national German state that was to be created. He appointed two wealthy businessmen from the Rhineland – perfect representatives of moderate liberalism – to form a new government.

The situation might have stabilized at this point, if the workers had not wanted much more and the Prussian aristocracy much less. On March 26, the workers issued a series of radical and vaguely socialist demands: universal voting rights, a ministry of labor, a minimum wage, and a ten-hour day. At the same time a wild-tempered Prussian landowner and aristocrat, Otto von Bismarck, joined the conservative clique gathered around the king to urge counterrevolution. While these tensions in Prussia were growing, an elected assembly arrived in Berlin to write a constitution for the Prussian state.

To add to the complexity of the situation, a self-appointed committee of liberals from various German states successfully called for the formation of a national constituent assembly to begin writing a federal constitution for a unified German state. That body met for the first time on May 18 in St. Paul's Church in Frankfurt. The Frankfurt National Assembly was a most curious revolutionary body. It was really a serious middle-class body whose 820 members included some 200 lawyers, 100 professors, many doctors, judges, and officials, and 140 businessmen for good measure.

Called together to write a constitution, the learned body was soon absorbed in a battle with Denmark over the provinces of Schleswig and Holstein. Jurisdiction over them was a hopelessly complicated issue from a legal point of view. Britain's Foreign Minister Lord Palmerston once said that only three people had ever understood the Schleswig-Holstein question, and of those one had died, another

had gone mad, and he himself had forgotten the answer. The provinces were inhabited primarily by Germans but were ruled by the king of Denmark, although Holstein was a member of the German Confederation. When Frederick VII, the new nationalistic king of Denmark, tried to integrate both provinces into the rest of his state, the Germans there revolted.

Hypnotized by this conflict, the National Assembly at Frankfurt debated ponderously and finally called on the Prussian army to oppose Denmark in the name of the German nation. Prussia responded and began war with Denmark. As the Schleswig-Holstein issue demonstrated, the national ideal was a crucial factor motivating the German middle classes in 1848.

Almost obsessed with the fate of Germans under Danish rule, many members of the Frankfurt assembly also wanted to bring the German-speaking provinces of Austria into the new German state. Yet resurgent Austria resolutely opposed any division of its territory. Once this Austrian action made a "big German" state impossible, the Frankfurt assembly completed drafting a liberal constitution. Finally, in March 1849, the assembly elected King Frederick William of Prussia emperor of the new German national state (minus Austria and Schleswig-Holstein).

By early 1849, however, reaction had been successful almost everywhere. Frederick William reasserted his royal authority, disbanded the Prussian Constituent Assembly, and granted his subjects a limited, essentially conservative, constitution. Reasserting that he ruled by divine right, Frederick William contemptuously refused to accept the "crown from the gutter." The reluctant revolutionaries in Frankfurt had waited too long and acted too timidly.

When Frederick William, who really wanted to be emperor but only on his own authoritarian terms, tried to get the small monarchs of Germany to elect him emperor, Austria balked. Supported by Russia, Austria forced Prussia to renounce all its schemes of unification in late 1850. The German Confederation was re-established. After two turbulent years the political map of the German states remained unchanged. Attempts to unite the Germans – first in a liberal national state and then in a conservative Prussian empire – had failed completely.

———◆———

The liberal and nationalistic revolutions of 1848 were abortive. Political, economic, and social pressures that had been building since 1815 exploded dramatically, but very few revolutionary goals were realized. The moderate, nationalistic middle classes were unable to consolidate their initial victories in France or elsewhere in Europe. Instead, they drew back when artisans, factory workers, and radical socialists rose up to present their own much more revolutionary demands. This retreat facilitated the efforts of dedicated aristocrats in central Europe, and made possible the crushing of Parisian workers by a coalition of solid bourgeoisie and landowning peasantry in France. A host of fears, a sea of blood, and a torrent of disillusion had drowned the lofty ideals and utopian visions of a generation. The age of romantic revolution was over.

## NOTES

1. A. J. May, *The Age of Metternich, 1814–1848*, rev. ed., Holt, Rinehart & Winston, New York, 1963, p. 11.

2. H. Kohn, *Nationalism,* Van Nostrand, New York, 1955, pp. 141–142.

3. Quoted by F. D. Klingender, *Art and the Industrial Revolution,* Paladin, St. Albans, England, 1972, p. 117.

4. Quoted by F. B. Artz, *From the Renaissance to Romanticism: Trends in Style in Art, Literature, and Music, 1300–1830,* University of Chicago Press, Chicago, 1962, pp. 276, 278.

5. Quoted by G. Wright, *France in Modern Times,* Rand McNally, Chicago, 1960, p. 145.

6. A. de Tocqueville, *Recollections,* Columbia University Press, New York, 1949, p. 94.

7. M. Agulhon, *1848,* Editions du Seuil, Paris, 1973, pp. 68–69.

8. Quoted by W. L. Langer, *Political and Social Upheaval, 1832–1852,* Harper & Row, New York, 1969, p. 361.

## SUGGESTED READING

All of the works cited in the Notes are highly recommended. May's is a good brief survey, while Kohn has written perceptively on nationalism in many books. Wright's *France in Modern Times* is a lively introduction to French history with stimulating biographical discussions; Langer is a balanced synthesis with an excellent bibliography. Among general studies C. Morazé, *The Triumph of the Middle Classes* (1968), a wide-ranging procapitalist interpretation, may be compared with E. J. Hobsbawm's flexible Maxism in *The Age of Revolution, 1789–1848* (1962). For English history, A. Briggs's socially oriented *The Making of Modern England, 1784–1867* (1967), and D. Thomson's *England in the Nineteenth Century, 1815–1914* (1951), are excellent. Restoration France is sympathetically portrayed by G. de Sauvigny in *The Bourbon Restoration* (1967). T. Hamerow studies the social implications of the dual revolution in Germany in *Restoration, Revolution, Reaction 1815–1871* (1966), which may be compared to H. Treitschke's bombastic, pro-Prussian *History of Germany in the Nineteenth Century* (1915-1919), a classic of nationalistic history, and L. Snyder, *Roots of German Nationalism* (1978). H. Kissinger, *A World Restored* (1957), offers not only a provocative interpretation of the Congress of Vienna but also insights into the mind of Richard Nixon's famous Secretary of State. Compare with H. Nicolson's entertaining *The Congress of Vienna* (1946). On 1848, L. B. Namier's highly critical *1848: The Revolution of the Intellectuals* (1964), and P. Robertson's *Revolutions of 1848: A Social History* (1960), are outstanding. I. Deak, *The Lawful Revolution: Louis Kossuth and the Hungarians, 1848-49* (1979), is a noteworthy study of an interesting figure.

On early socialism and Marxism, there are W. Sewell, Jr.'s *Work and Revolution in France* (1980), and E. Wilson's engrossing survey of nineteenth-century developments, *To the Finland Station* (1953), as well as G. Lichtheim's high-powered *Marxism* (1961) and his *Short History of Socialism* (1970). J. Schumpeter, *Capitalism, Socialism and Democracy* (1947), is magnificent but difficult, a real mind-stretcher. On liberalism, there is R. Heilbroner's entertaining *The Worldly Philosophers* (1967), and G. de Ruggiero's classic *History of European Liberalism* (1959). J. Barzun, *Classic, Romantic and Modern* (1961), skillfully discusses the emergence of romanticism, while R. Stromberg, *An Intellectual History of Modern Europe* (1966), is a readable general survey. The important place of religion in nineteenth-century thought is considered from different perspectives in H. McLeod, *Religion and the People of Western Europe* (1981), and O. Chadwick, *The Secularization of the European Mind in the Nineteenth Century* (1976).

The thoughtful reader is strongly advised to delve into the incredibly rich writing of contemporaries. J. Bowditch and C. Ramsland, eds., *Voices of the Industrial Revolution* (1961), is an excellent starting point, with well-chosen selections from leading economic thinkers and early socialists. H. Hugo, ed., *The Romantic Reader,* is another fine anthology. Jules Michelet's compassionate masterpiece *The People,* a famous historian's anguished examination of French social divisions on the eve of 1848, draws one into the heart of the period and is highly recommended. Alexis de Tocqueville covers some of the same ground less romantically in his *Recollections,* which may be compared with Karl Marx's white-hot "instant history," *Class Struggles in France, 1848-1850* (1850). Great novels that accurately portray aspects of the times are Victor Hugo, *Les Misérables,* an exciting story of crime and passion among France's poor; Honoré de Balzac, *Cousin Bette* and *Père Goriot;* and Thomas Mann, *Buddenbrooks,* a wonderful historical novel that traces the rise and fall of a prosperous German family over three generations during the nineteenth century.

# CHAPTER 24

## LIFE IN URBAN SOCIETY

THE ERA OF INTELLECTUAL and political upheaval that culminated in the revolutions of 1848 was also an era of rapid urbanization. After 1848 Western political development veered off in a novel and uncharted direction, but the growth of towns and cities rushed forward with undiminished force. Thus Western society was urban and industrial in 1900, as surely as it had been rural and agrarian in 1800. The urbanization of society was both a result of the Industrial Revolution and a reflection of its enormous impact. What was life like in the cities, and how did it change? What did the emergence of urban industrial society mean for rich and poor and in between? How did families cope with the challenges and respond to the opportunities of the developing urban civilization? Finally, what changes in thought and culture inspired and gave expression to this new civilization? These are the questions this chapter will investigate.

## TAMING THE CITY

The consequences of economic transformation were, from the beginning, more positive than historians have often recognized. Indeed, given the poverty and uncertainty of preindustrial life, the history of industrialization is probably better written in terms of increasing opportunities than of greater hardships. But does not this relatively optimistic view of the consequences of industrialization neglect the quality of life in urban areas? Were not the new industrial towns and cities awful places where people, and especially the poor, suffered from bad housing, lack of sanitation, and a sense of hopelessness? Did not these drawbacks more than cancel out higher wages and greater opportunity?

## INDUSTRY AND THE GROWTH OF CITIES

Since the Middle Ages European cities had been centers of government, culture, and large-scale commerce. They had also been congested, dirty, and unhealthy. People were packed together almost as tightly as possible within the city limits. The typical city was a "walking city": for all but the wealthiest classes, walking was the only available form of transportation.

Infectious disease spread with deadly speed in cities, and people were always more likely to die in the city than in the countryside. In the larger towns more people died each year than were born, on the average, and urban populations were able to maintain their numbers only because newcomers were continuously arriving from rural areas. Little could be done to improve these conditions. Given the pervasive poverty, absence of urban transportation, and lack of medical knowledge, the deadly and overcrowded conditions could only be accepted fatalistically. They were the urban equivalents of bad weather and poor crops, the price of urban excitement and opportunity.

Clearly, deplorable urban conditions did not originate with the Industrial Revolution. What the Industrial Revolution did was to reveal those conditions more nakedly than ever before. The steam engine freed industrialists from dependence on the energy of fast-flowing streams and rivers, which meant that by 1800 there was every incentive to build new factories in urban areas. Cities had better shipping facilities, and thus better supplies of coal and raw materials. There were also many hands wanting work in the cities, for cities drew people like a magnet. And it was a great advantage for a manufacturer to have other factories nearby to supply his needs and buy his products. Therefore, as industry grew,

MAP 24.1 EUROPEAN CITIES OF 100,000 OR MORE, 1800 AND 1900 *There were more large cities in Great Britain in 1900 than in all Europe in 1800.*

there was also a rapid expansion of already overcrowded and unhealthy cities.

The challenge of the urban environment was felt first and most acutely in Great Britain. The number of people living in cities of 20,000 or more in England and Wales jumped from 1.5 million in 1801 to 6.3 million in 1851, and reached 15.6 million by 1891. Such cities accounted for 17 percent of the total English population in 1801, 35 percent as early as 1851, and fully 54 percent in 1891. Other countries duplicated the English pattern as they industrialized. An American observer was hardly exaggerating when he wrote in 1899 that "the most remarkable social phenomenon of the present century is the concentration of population in cities"[1] (see Map 24.1).

In the 1820s and 1830s, people in Britain and France began to worry about the condi-

tion of their cities. In those years the populations of a number of British cities were increasing by 40 to 70 percent each decade. Manchester, the cotton city, grew by 40 percent between 1811 and 1821, and by 47 percent between 1821 and 1831. The population of the principal Scottish manufacturing city, Glasgow, grew by 30 percent or more each decade between 1801 and 1841. With urban areas expanding at such previously undreamed-of rates, people's traditional fatalistic indifference to overcrowded, unsanitary urban living conditions began to give way to active concern. Something had to be done.

On one point everyone could agree: except on the outskirts, each town and city was using every scrap of land to the fullest extent. Parks and open areas were almost nonexistent. A British parliamentary committee reported in 1833 that "with a rapidly increasing popula-

## A COURT FOR KING CHOLERA.

*FILTH AND DISEASE   This drawing from* Punch *in 1852 tells volumes about the unhealthy living conditions of the urban poor. In the foreground children play with a dead rat and a woman scavenges a* *dungheap. Cheap rooming houses provide shelter for the frightfully overcrowded population. (The British Museum)*

tion, lodged for the most part in narrow courts and confined streets, the means of occasional exercise and recreation in fresh air are every day lessened, as inclosures [of vacant areas] take place and buildings spread themselves on every side."[2] Buildings were erected on the smallest possible lots, in order to pack the maximum number of people into a given space. Narrow houses were built wall-to-wall, in long rows. These row houses had neither front nor back yards, and only a narrow alley in back separated one row from the next. Or

buildings were built around tiny courtyards completely enclosed on all four sides. Many people lived in cellars and attics. The tiny rooms within such buildings were often overcrowded. "Six, eight, and even ten occupying one room is anything but uncommon," wrote a doctor from Aberdeen in Scotland for a government investigation in 1842.

These highly concentrated urban populations lived in extremely unsanitary and unhealthy conditions. Open drains and sewers flowed alongside or down the middle of unpaved streets. Due to poor construction and an absence of running water, the sewers often filled with garbage and excrement. Toilet facilities were primitive in the extreme. In parts of Manchester as many as two hundred people shared a single outhouse. Such privies filled up rapidly, and since they were infrequently emptied, sewage often overflowed and seeped into cellar dwellings.

The extent to which filth lay underfoot and the smell of excrement filled the air is hard to believe; yet it was abundantly documented between 1830 and 1850. One London construction engineer found, for example, that the cellars of two large houses on a major road were "full of night-soil [human excrement], to the depth of three feet, which had been permitted for years to accumulate from the overflow of the cesspools." Moreover, courtyards in poorer neighborhoods sometimes became dunghills, collecting excrement that was sometimes sold as fertilizer. By the 1840s there was among the better-off classes a growing, shocking "realization that, to put it as mildly as possible, millions of English men, women, and children were living in shit."[3]

Who or what was responsible for these awful conditions? The crucial factors were the tremendous pressure of ever more people coupled with the *total* absence of public transportation. People simply had to jam themselves together if they were to be able to walk to shops and factories. Another factor was that government in Great Britain, both local and national, was slow to provide sanitary facilities and establish adequate building codes. This slow pace was probably attributable more to a need to explore and identify what precisely should be done than to rigid middle-class opposition to government action. Certainly Great Britain had no monopoly on overcrowded and unhealthy urban conditions; many continental cities were every bit as bad.

Most responsible of all was the sad legacy of rural housing conditions in preindustrial society, combined with appalling ignorance. As the author of a recent study concludes, there "were rural slums of a horror not surpassed by the rookeries of London. . . . The evidence shows that the decent cottage was the exception, the hovel the rule."[4] Thus housing was far down the newcomer's list of priorities, and it is not surprising that many carried the filth of the mud floor and the dung of the barnyard with them to the city.

Indeed, ordinary people generally took dirt and filth for granted, and some even prized it. As one English miner told an investigator, "I do not think it usual for the lasses [in the coal mines] to wash their bodies; my sisters never wash themselves." As for the men, "their legs and bodies are as black as your hat." When poor people were admitted to English workhouses, they often resisted the required bath. One man protested that it was "equal to robbing him of a great coat which he had had for some years."[5]

## THE PUBLIC HEALTH MOVEMENT

Although cleanliness was not next to godliness in most people's eyes, it was becoming so for some reformers. The most famous of these was Edwin Chadwick, one of the commissioners charged with the administration of relief to paupers under the revised Poor Law of 1834. Chadwick was a good Benthamite — that is, a follower of the radical philosopher Jeremy Bentham (1748–1832). Bentham had taught that public problems ought to be dealt with on a rational, scientific basis and according to the "greatest good for the greatest number." Applying these principles, Chadwick soon saw that much more than economics was involved in the problems of poverty and the welfare budget. Indeed, he soon became convinced that sickness and disease actually caused poverty, simply because a sick worker was an unemployed worker, and orphaned children were poor children. Most important, Chadwick believed that disease could be prevented by quite literally cleaning up the urban environment. That was his "sanitary idea."

Building on a growing number of medical and sociological studies, Chadwick collected detailed reports from local Poor Law officials on the "sanitary conditions of the laboring population." After three years of investigation these reports and Chadwick's hard-hitting commentary were published in 1842 to wide publicity. This mass of evidence proved that disease was related to filthy environmental conditions, which were in turn caused largely by lack of drainage, sewers, and garbage collection. Putrefying, smelly excrement was no longer simply disgusting. For reformers like Chadwick, it was a threat to the entire community. It polluted the atmosphere and caused disease.

The key to the energetic action Chadwick proposed was an adequate supply of clean piped water. Such water was essential for personal hygiene, public bathhouses, street cleaning, firefighting, and industry. Chadwick correctly believed that the stinking excrement of communal outhouses could be dependably carried off by water through sewers at less than one-twentieth the cost of removing it by hand. The cheap iron pipes and tile drains of the industrial age would provide running water and sewerage for all sections of town, not just the wealthy ones. In 1848, spurred on by the cholera epidemic of 1846, Chadwick's report became the basis of Great Britain's first public health law, which created a national

health board and gave cities broad authority to build modern sanitary systems.

The public health movement won dedicated supporters in the United States, France, and Germany from the 1840s on. As in Great Britain, governments accepted at least limited responsibility for the health of all citizens. Moreover, they adopted increasingly concrete programs of action, programs that broke decisively with the age-old fatalism of urban populations in the face of shockingly high mortality. Thus, despite many people's skepticism about sanitation, European cities were making real progress toward adequate water supplies and sewage systems by the 1860s and 1870s. And city dwellers were beginning to reap the reward of better health.

## THE BACTERIAL REVOLUTION

Effective control of communicable disease required more than a clean water supply and good sewers. Victory over disease also required a great leap forward in medical knowledge and biological theory. Reformers like Chadwick were seriously handicapped by the prevailing miasmatic theory of disease – the belief that people contract disease when they breathe the bad odors of decay and putrefying excrement; in short, the theory that smells cause disease. The miasmatic theory was a reasonable deduction from empirical observations: cleaning up filth did produce laudable results. Yet the theory was very incomplete.

Keen observation by doctors and public health officials in the 1840s and 1850s pinpointed the role of bad drinking water in the transmission of disease and suggested that contagion was spread *through* filth and not caused by it. Examples of particularly horrid stenches, such as that of the sewage-glutted Thames River at London in 1858, that did not lead to widely feared epidemics also weakened the miasmatic idea. Another factor was the successful merging of anatomical and clinical approaches to medicine between 1800 and 1850, particularly at the Paris school of medicine. Doctors there recognized a definite connection between the symptoms of certain illnesses observed at the bedside and the diseased organs seen when the body was dissected at autopsy. Medical research began zeroing in on specific diseases in an attempt to find specific treatments. When an improved theory was developed, progress could be rapid.

The breakthrough was the development of the germ theory of disease by Louis Pasteur (1822–1895). Pasteur was a French chemist by profession, not a physician. After important discoveries about the structure of crystals, he turned in 1854 to the study of fermentation. For ages people had used fermentation to make bread and wine, beer and cheese, but without really understanding what was going on. And from time to time beer and wine would mysteriously spoil for no apparent reason. As rapidly growing cities provided a vast, concentrated demand, big brewers and winemakers were seeking ways to prevent spoilage and financial loss. Responding to their calls for help, Pasteur used his microscope to develop a simple test brewers could use to monitor the fermentation process and avoid spoilage. He then investigated various kinds of fermentation.

Pasteur found that fermentation depended on the growth of living organisms. Moreover, he demonstrated that the activity of these organisms could be suppressed by heating the wine or milk – by *pasteurizing* it. The breathtaking implication was that specific diseases were caused by specific living organisms – germs – and that those organisms could be controlled in people as well as in milk and wine. This theory was confirmed in 1868. After three years of intensive research, Pasteur isolated and controlled parasitic micro-organisms that were killing off the silkworms used in France's large silk industry. Once again, scientific research had been stimulated by and had responded to the needs of the emerging industrial society.

By 1870, the work of Pasteur and others had demonstrated the general connection between germs and disease. When in the middle of the 1870s the German country doctor Robert Koch and his coworkers developed pure cultures of harmful bacteria and described their life cycles, the dam broke. Over the next twenty years researchers – mainly Germans – identified the organisms responsible for disease after disease, often identifying several in a single year. At the same time Pasteur and his colleagues concentrated on modifying and controlling the virulence of disease-producing germs. Building on the example of Edward Jenner's pioneering conquest of smallpox, Pasteur and his team developed a number of effective vaccines. The most famous was his vaccination for rabies in 1885, a crucial step in the development of modern immunology.

Acceptance of the germ theory brought about dramatic improvements in the deadly environment of hospitals and in surgery. The English surgeon Joseph Lister (1827–1912) had noticed that patients with simple fractures were much less likely to die than those with compound fractures, in which the skin was broken and internal tissues were exposed to the air. In 1865, when Pasteur showed that air was full of bacteria, Lister immediately grasped the connection between aerial bacteria and the problem of wound infection. He reasoned that a chemical disinfectant applied to a

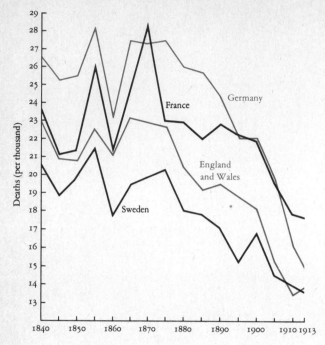

FIGURE 24.1 THE DECLINE OF DEATH RATES IN ENGLAND AND WALES, GERMANY, FRANCE, AND SWEDEN, 1840–1913 *A rising standard of living, improvements in public health, and better medical knowledge all contributed to the dramatic decline of death rates in the nineteenth century.*

wound dressing would "destroy the life of the floating particles." Lister's "antiseptic principle" worked wonders. In the 1880s, German surgeons developed the more sophisticated practice of sterilizing not only the wound but everything – hands, instruments, clothing – that entered the operating room.

The achievements of the bacterial revolution coupled with the ever-more-sophisticated public health movement saved millions of lives, particularly after about 1890. Mortality rates began to decline dramatically in European countries (see Figure 24.1) as the awful death sentences of the past – diphtheria, typhoid and typhus, cholera, yellow fever – became vanishing diseases. City dwellers

benefited especially from these developments. By 1910, the likelihood of death for people of all ages in urban areas was generally no greater than in rural areas, and sometimes it was less. Particularly striking was the decline in infant mortality in the cities after 1890. In many countries, an urban mother was less likely than a rural mother to see her child die before its first birthday by 1910. A great silent revolution had occurred: the terrible ferocity of death from disease-carrying bacteria in the cities had almost been tamed.

## URBAN PLANNING AND PUBLIC TRANSPORTATION

Public health was only part of the urban challenge. Overcrowding, bad housing, and lack of transportation could not be solved by sewers and better medicine; yet in these areas too important transformations improved the quality of urban life after midcentury.

More effective urban planning was one of the keys to improvement. Earlier urban planning had declined by the early nineteenth century; after 1850 it was revived and extended. France took the lead during the rule of Napoleon III (1848–1870), who sought to stand above class conflict and promote the welfare of all his subjects through government action. He believed that rebuilding much of Paris would provide employment, improve living conditions, and testify to the power and glory of his empire. In the baron Georges Haussmann, an aggressive, impatient Alsatian whom he placed in charge of Paris, Napoleon III found an authoritarian planner capable of bulldozing over both buildings and opposition. In twenty years Paris was quite literally transformed.

The Paris of 1850 was a labyrinth of narrow, dark streets, the results of desperate overcrowding. In an area of the central city

APARTMENT LIVING IN PARIS *This realistic contemporary drawing shows how different social classes lived close together in European cities about 1850. Passing the middle-class family on the first floor (American second floor), the economic condition of the tenants declined until one reached abject poverty in the garret. (Bibliothèque Nationale, Paris)*

not twice the size of New York's Central Park lived more than one-third of the city's 1 million inhabitants. Terrible slum conditions and extremely high death rates were facts of life. There were few open spaces and only two public parks for the entire metropolis. Public transportation played a very small role in this enormous walking city.

Haussmann and his fellow planners proceeded on many interrelated fronts. With a bold energy that often shocked their contemporaries, they razed old buildings in order to cut broad, straight, tree-lined boulevards through the center of the city as well as in new quarters on the outskirts. These boulevards, designed in part to prevent the easy construction and defense of barricades by revolutionary crowds, also permitted traffic to flow freely. Their construction also demolished some of the worst slums. New streets stimulated the construction of better housing, especially for the middle classes. Small neighborhood parks and open spaces were created throughout the city, and two very large parks suitable for all kinds of holiday activities were developed on either side of the city. The city also improved its sewers, and a system of aqueducts more than doubled the city's supply of good fresh water.

Haussmann and Napoleon III tried to make Paris a more beautiful city, and to a large extent they succeeded. The broad, straight boulevards, such as those radiating out like the spokes of a wheel from the Arch of Triumph and those centering on the new Opera House, afforded impressive vistas. If for most people Paris remains one of the world's most beautiful and enchanting cities, it is in part because of the transformations of the Second Empire.

The rebuilding of Paris provided a new model for urban planning and stimulated modern urbanism throughout Europe, particularly after 1870. In city after city public au-

thorities mounted a coordinated attack on many of the interrelated problems of the urban environment. As in Paris, improvements in public health through better water supply and waste disposal often went hand in hand with new boulevard construction. Cities like Vienna and Cologne followed the Parisian example of tearing down old walled fortifications and replacing them with broad circular boulevards on which office buildings, town halls, theaters, opera houses, and museums were erected. These ring roads and the new boulevards that radiated out from them toward the outskirts eased movement and encouraged urban expansion. "Zoning expropriation" laws, which allowed a majority of the owners of land in a given quarter of the city to impose major street or sanitation improvements on a reluctant minority, were an important mechanism of the new urbanism.

The development of mass public transportation was also of great importance in the improvement of urban living conditions. Such transportation came late, but in a powerful rush. In the 1870s many European cities authorized private companies to operate horse-drawn streetcars, which had been developed in the United States, to carry riders along the growing number of major thoroughfares. Then, in the 1890s, came the real revolution: European countries adopted another American transit innovation, the electric streetcar.

Electric streetcars were wonderfully cheaper, faster, more dependable, and more comfortable than their horse-drawn counterparts. Service improved dramatically. Millions of Europeans – workers, shoppers, schoolchildren – hopped on board during the workweek. And on weekends and holidays streetcars carried millions on happy outings to parks and countryside, racetracks and music halls. In 1886, the horse-drawn streetcars of Austria-Hungary, France, Germany,

*EXPERIMENTING WITH STEAM   Horses were slow and quickly ruined pulling streetcars. Thus countless inventors sought to adapt steam engines to the demands of urban transit. Yet even the most ingenious steam locomotives, like the one above being introduced before expectant crowds in Paris in 1876, remained dirty, noisy, and undependable. And they frightened horses, which toiled on until relieved by electric motors. (Photo: Caroline Buckler)*

and Great Britain were carrying about 900 million riders. By 1910, electric streetcar systems in the four countries were carrying 6.7 billion riders.[6] Each man, woman, and child was using public transportation four times as often in 1910 as in 1886.

Good mass transit helped greatly in the struggle for decent housing. Just as the new boulevards and horse-drawn streetcars had facilitated the middle-class move to better housing in the 1860s and 1870s, so electric streetcars gave people of modest means access to new, improved housing after 1890. The still-crowded city was able to expand and be-

come less congested. In England in 1901, only 9 percent of the urban population was "overcrowded," in terms of the official definition of more than two persons per room. On the Continent many city governments in the early twentieth century were building electric streetcar systems that provided transportation to new public and private housing developments in outlying areas of the city for the working classes. Poor, overcrowded housing, long one of the blackest blots on the urban landscape, was in retreat – another graphic example of the gradual taming of the urban environment.

## RICH AND POOR AND IN BETWEEN

General improvements in health and in the urban environment had beneficial consequences for all kinds of people. Yet differences in living conditions between social classes remained gigantic.

### SOCIAL STRUCTURE

How much had the almost-completed journey to an urban, industrialized world changed the social framework of rich and poor? The first great change was a substantial and undeniable increase in the standard of living for the average person. The real wages of British workers, for example, which had already risen substantially by 1850, almost doubled between 1850 and 1906. Similar unmistakable increases occurred in continental countries as industrial development quickened after 1850. Ordinary people took a great step forward in the centuries-old battle against poverty, reinforcing efforts to improve many aspects of human existence.

There is another side to the income coin, however, and it must be stressed as well. Greater economic rewards for the average person did *not* eliminate poverty, *nor* did they make the wealth and income of the rich and the poor significantly more equal. In almost every advanced country around 1900, the richest 5 percent of all households in the population received fully one-third of all national income. The richest one-fifth of households received anywhere from 50 to 60 percent of all national income, while the entire bottom four-fifths received only 40 to 50 percent. Moreover, the bottom 30 percent of households received 10 percent or less of all

income. These enormous differences are illustrated in Figure 24.2.

The middle classes were smaller than they are today and accounted for only about 20 percent of the population; thus, statistics show that the upper and middle classes alone received less altogether than the two richest The poorest four-fifths – the working classes, including peasants and agricultural laborers – received less altogether than the two richest classes. And since many wives and teenagers in poor families worked, these figures actually understate the enduring gap between rich and poor. Moreover, income taxes on the wealthy were light or nonexistent. Thus the gap between rich and poor remained enormous at the beginning of the twentieth century. It was probably almost as great as it had been in the age of agriculture and aristocracy, before the Industial Revolution.

The great gap between rich and poor endured, in part, because industrial and urban development made society more diverse and less unified. By no means did society split into two sharply defined opposing classes, as Marx had predicted. Instead, economic specialization enabled society to produce more effectively, and in the process created more new social groups than it destroyed. There developed an almost unlimited range of jobs, skills, and earnings; one group or subclass shaded off into another in a complex, confusing hierarchy. Thus, the tiny elite of very rich and the sizable mass of dreadfully poor were separated from each other by many subclasses, each filled with individuals struggling to rise, or at least to hold their own in the social order. In this atmosphere of competition and hierarchy, neither the middle classes nor the working classes acted as a unified force. The age-old pattern of great economic inequality remained firmly intact.

## THE MIDDLE CLASSES

By the beginning of the twentieth century, the diversity and range within the urban middle class was striking. Indeed, it is more meaningful to think of a confederation of middle classes, loosely united by occupations requiring mental rather than physical skill. At the top stood the upper middle class, composed mainly of the most successful business families from banking, industry, and large-scale commerce. These families were the prime beneficiaries of modern industry and scientific progress. As the incomes of people in the upper middle class rose, and as they progressively lost all traces of radicalism after the trauma of 1848, they were almost irresistibly drawn toward the aristocratic lifestyle.

As the aristocracy had long divided the year between palatial country estates and lavish town houses during "the season," so the upper middle class purchased country places or built beach houses for weekend and summer use. (Little wonder that a favorite scenario in late-nineteenth-century middle-class novels was a mother and children summering gloriously in the country home, with only sporadic weekend intrusions by a distant, shadowy father.) The number of servants was an important indicator of wealth and standing for the middle class, as it had always been for the aristocracy. The first sign of real wealth in a middle-class household was a male servant; two or three were a mark of opulence. (In England well-paid butlers had to be tall; footmen were six inches shorter on the average than butlers and earned only half as much.) Private coaches and carriages, ever an expensive item in the city, were also signs of rising social status. More generally, the rich businessman and certainly his son devoted less time to business and more to "culture" and

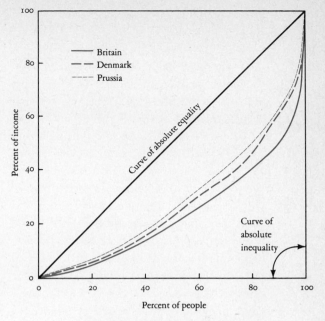

### DISTRIBUTION OF INCOME

| Country | Richest 5% | Richest 10% | Richest 20% | Poorest 60% |
|---|---|---|---|---|
| Britain | 43% | | 59% | |
| Denmark | 30 | 39% | 55 | 31% |
| Prussia | 30 | | 50 | 33 |

FIGURE 24.2 THE DISTRIBUTION OF INCOME IN BRITAIN, DENMARK, AND PRUSSIA IN 1913 *The so-called Lorenz curve is useful for showing the degree of economic inequality in a given society. The closer the actual distribution of income lies to the (theoretical) curve of absolute equality, where each 20 percent of the population receives 20 percent of all income, the more nearly equal incomes are. European society was very far from any such equality before World War I. Notice that incomes in Prussia were somewhat more equal than in Britain. (Source: S. Kuznets,* Modern Economic Growth, *Yale University Press, New Haven, 1966, pp. 208–209)*

easy living than was the case in less wealthy or well-established commercial families.

The topmost reaches of the upper middle class tended to shade off into the old aristocracy to form a new upper class. This was the 5 percent of the population that, as we have seen, received roughly one-third of the national income in European countries before 1914. Much of the aristocracy welcomed this development. Having experienced a sharp decline in its relative income in the course of industrialization, the landed aristocracy had met big business coming up the staircase and was often delighted to trade titles, country homes, and snobbish elegance for good hard cash. Some of the best bargains were made through marriages to American heiresses. Correspondingly, wealthy aristocrats tended increasingly to exploit their agricultural and mineral resources like businessmen. Bismarck was not the only proud noble to make a fortune distilling brandy on his estates.

Below the wealthy upper middle class were much larger, much less wealthy, and increasingly diversified middle-class groups. Here one found the moderately successful industrialists and merchants, as well as professionals in law and medicine. This was the middle middle class, solid and quite comfortable but lacking great wealth. Below them were independent shopkeepers, small traders, and tiny manufacturers – the lower middle class. Both of these traditional elements of the middle class expanded modestly in size with economic development.

Meanwhile the traditional middle class was gaining two particularly important additions. The expansion of industry and technology created an ever-growing demand for experts with specialized knowledge. The most valuable of the specialties became solid middle-class professions. Engineering, for example, emerged from the world of skilled labor as a full-fledged profession of great importance, considerable prestige, and many branches. Architects, chemists, accountants, and surveyors – to name only a few – first achieved professional standing in this period. They established criteria for advanced training and certification and banded together in organizations to promote and defend their interests.

Management of large public and private institutions also emerged as a kind of profession, as governments provided more services and as very large corporations like railroads came into being. Government officials and many private executives were not capitalists in the sense that they owned business enterprises. But public and private managers did have specialized knowledge and the capacity to earn a good living. And they shared most of the values of the business-owning entrepreneurs and the older professionals.

Industrialization also expanded and diversified the lower middle class. The number of independent, property-owning shopkeepers and small businessmen grew and so did the number of white-collar employees – a mixed group of traveling salesmen, bookkeepers, store managers, and clerks who staffed the offices and branch stores of large corporations. White-collar employees were propertyless and often earned no more than the better-paid skilled or even semi-skilled workers did. Yet white-collar workers were fiercely committed to the middle class and to the ideal of "moving up" in society. In the Balkans, for example, clerks let their fingernails grow very long to distinguish themselves sharply from people who worked with their hands. The tie, the suit, and soft clean hands were no-less-subtle marks of class distinction than wages.

Relatively well educated but without complex technical skills, many white-collar groups aimed at achieving professional standing and the accompanying middle-class status. Ele-

*"A CORNER OF THE TABLE"* *With photographic precision this 1904 oil painting by the French academic artist Paul-Emile Chabas (1867–1937) skillfully idealizes the elegance and intimacy of a sumptuous dinner party. (Granger Collection)*

mentary-school teachers largely succeeded in this effort. From being miserably paid part-time workers in the early nineteenth century, teachers rode the wave of mass education to respectable middle-class status and income. Nurses also rose from the lower ranks of unskilled labor to precarious middle-class standing. Dentistry was taken out of the hands of working-class barbers and placed in the hands of highly trained (and middle-class) professionals.

In spite of their growing occupational diversity and conflicting interests, the middle classes were loosely united by a certain style of life. Food was the largest item in the house-

hold budget, for middle-class people liked to eat very well. In France and Italy, the middle classes' love of good eating meant that, even in large cities, activity ground almost to a halt between half past twelve and half past two on weekdays, as husbands and schoolchildren returned home for the midday meal. Around eight in the evening the serious business of eating was taken up once again.

The English were equally attached to big substantial meals, which they ate three times a day if income allowed. The typical English breakfast of bacon and eggs, toast and marmalade, and stewed fruits – not to mention sardines, kidneys, or fresh fish – always astonished French and German travelers, though large-breakfast enthusiasts like the Dutch and Scandinavians were less awed. The European middle classes consumed meat in abundance, and a well-off family might spend fully 10 percent of its substantial earnings on meat alone. In the 1890s even a very prosperous English family – with an income of, say, $10,000 a year when the average working-class family earned perhaps $400 a year – spent fully one-quarter of its income on food and drink.

Spending on food was also great because the dinner party was this class's favored social occasion. A wealthy family might give a lavish party for eight to twelve almost every week, while more modest households would settle for once a month. Throughout middle-class Europe such dinners were served in the "French manner" (which the French had borrowed from the Russian aristocracy): eight or nine separate courses, from appetizers at the beginning to coffee and liqueurs at the end. In summer, a "picnic" was in order. But what a picnic! For a party of ten, one English cookbook suggested five pounds of cold salmon, a quarter of lamb, eight pounds of pickled brisket, a beef tongue, a chicken pie, salads, cakes, and six pounds of strawberries. An ordinary family meal normally consisted of only four courses – soup, fish, meat, and dessert.

The middle-class wife could cope with this endless procession of meals, courses, and dishes because she had both servants and money at her disposal. The middle classes were solid members of what some contemporary observers called the "servant-keeping classes." Indeed, the presence of at least one enormously helpful full-time maid to cook and clean was the best single sign that a family had crossed the vague line separating the working classes from the middle classes. The greater its income, the greater the number of servants a family employed. The all-purpose servant gave way to a cook and a maid, then to a cook, a maid, and a boy, and so on. A prosperous English family far up the line with $10,000 a year in 1900 spent fully one-fourth of its income on a hierarchy of ten servants: a manservant, a cook, a kitchen maid, two housemaids, a serving maid, a governess, a gardener, a coachman, and a stable boy. Domestic servants were the second largest item in the budget of the middle classes. Thus, food and servants absorbed about one-half of income at all levels of the middle classes.

Well-fed and well-served, the middle classes were also well-housed by 1900. Many quite prosperous families rented rather than owned their homes. Apartment living, complete with tiny rooms for servants under the eaves of the top floor, was commonplace (outside Great Britain), and wealthy investors and speculative builders found good profits in middle-class housing. By 1900 the middle classes were also quite clothes-conscious. The factory, the sewing machine, and the department store had all helped to reduce the cost and expand the variety of clothing. Middle-class women were particularly attentive to the fickle dictates of fashion.

Education was another growing expense, as middle-class parents tried to provide their children with ever-more-crucial advanced education. The keystones of culture and leisure were books, music, and travel. The long realistic novel, the heroics of Wagner and Verdi, the diligent striving of the dutiful daughter on an "isn't-it-beautiful" piano, and the "we-wanted-a-change-from-the-seashore" packaged tour to a foreign country were all sources of middle-class pleasure.

Finally, the middle classes were loosely united by a shared code of expected behavior and morality. This code was strict and demanding. It laid great stress on hard work and personal achievement. Men and women who fell into crime or poverty were generally assumed to be responsible for their own circumstances. Traditional Christian morality was reaffirmed by this code and preached tirelessly by middle-class people who took pride in their own good conduct. Drinking and gambling were denounced as vices, sexual purity and fidelity celebrated as virtues. In short, the middle-class person was supposed to know right from wrong and was expected to act accordingly.

### THE WORKING CLASSES

About four out of five people belonged to the working classes at the turn of the century. Many members of the working classes — that is, people whose livelihoods depended on physical labor and who did not employ domestic servants — were still small landowning peasants and hired farm hands. This was especially true in eastern Europe. In western and central Europe, however, the typical worker had left the land. In Great Britain less than 8 percent of the people worked in agriculture, while in rapidly industrializing Germany only one person in four was employed in agriculture and forestry. Even in less-industrialized France less than half of the people depended on the land in 1900.

The urban working classes were even less unified and homogeneous than the middle classes. In the first place, economic development and increased specialization expanded the traditional range of working-class skills, earnings, and experiences. Meanwhile the old sharp distinction between highly skilled artisans and unskilled manual workers was gradually breaking down. To be sure, highly

FIGURE 24.3    THE URBAN SOCIAL HIERARCHY

skilled printers and masons, as well as unskilled dock workers and common laborers, continued to exist. But between these extremes there were ever more semiskilled groups, many of which were composed of factory workers and machine tenders (see Figure 24.3).

In the second place, skilled, semiskilled, and unskilled workers had widely divergent lifestyles and cultural values, and their differences contributed to a keen sense of social status and hierarchy within the working classes. The result was great variety and limited class unity.

Highly skilled workers, who comprised about 15 percent of the working classes, were a real "labor aristocracy." By 1900 they were earning about £2 a week in Great Britain, or roughly $10 a week and $500 per year. This was only about two-thirds the income of the bottom ranks of the "servant-keeping" classes. But it was fully twice as much as the earnings of unskilled workers, who averaged about $5 per week, and substantially more than the earnings of semiskilled workers, who averaged perhaps $7 per week. Other European countries had a similar range of earnings.

The most "aristocratic" of the highly skilled workers were construction bosses and factory foremen, men who had risen from the ranks and were fiercely proud of their achievement. The labor aristocracy also included members of the traditional highly skilled handicraft trades that had not been mechanized or placed in factories. These included makers of scientific and musical instruments, cabinetmakers, potters, jewelers, bookbinders, engravers, and printers. This group as a whole was under constant long-term pressure. Irregularly but inexorably, factory methods were being extended to ever more crafts, and many skilled artisans were being replaced by lower-paid, semiskilled factory workers. Traditional woodcarvers and watchmakers virtually disappeared, for example, as the making of furniture and timepieces was taken out of the shop and put into the factory.

At the same time a contrary movement was occurring. The labor aristocracy was consistently being enlarged by the growing need for highly skilled workers, such as shipbuilders, machine-tool makers, railway locomotive engineers, fine cotton textile spinners, and some metalworkers. Thus, the labor elite was in a state of flux as individuals and whole crafts moved in and out of it.

To maintain their precarious standing, the upper working class adopted distinctive values and strait-laced, almost puritanical, behavior. Like the middle classes, the labor aristocracy was strongly committed to the family and to economic improvement. Families in the upper working class saved money regularly, worried about their children's education, and valued good housing. Despite these similarities, which superficial observers were quick to exaggerate, skilled workers viewed themselves not as aspirants to the middle class but as the pacesetters and natural leaders of all the working classes. Well aware of the poverty and degradation not so far below them, they practiced self-discipline and stern morality.

The upper working class in general frowned on heavy drinking and sexual permissiveness. The organized temperance movement was strong in the countries of northern Europe, such as Great Britain, where a generation advocated tea as "the cup that cheers but does not inebriate." As one German labor aristocrat somberly warned, "the path to the brothel leads through the tavern" and from there quite possibly to drastic decline or total ruin for person and family.[7]

Men and women of the labor aristocracy were quick to find fault with those below them who failed to meet their standards. In 1868, William Lovett, an English labor aristocrat if ever there was one, denounced "this ignorant recklessness and improvidence that produce the swarms of half-starved, neglected, and ignorant children we see in all directions; who mostly grow up to become the burdens and often the pests of society, which the industrious and frugal have to support."[8] Finally, many members of the labor aristocracy had definite political and philosophical beliefs, whether Christian or socialist, or both. Such beliefs further strengthened the stern moral code of the upper working class.

Below the labor aristocracy stood semiskilled and unskilled urban workers. The enormous complexity of this sector of the world of labor is not easily summarized. Workers in the established crafts – carpenters, bricklayers, pipefitters – stood near the top of the semiskilled hierarchy, often flirting with (or having backslid from) the labor elite. A large number of the semiskilled were factory workers, who earned highly variable but relatively good wages and whose relative importance in the labor force was increasing.

The unskilled was the larger group, made

THE LONDON COFFEE STALL *The cities of the nineteenth century teemed with street-sellers. The battered top hat and baggy overcoat of this coffee vendor show how such petty capitalists struggled to reach the lower middle class. (Photo: Caroline Buckler)*

up of day laborers such as longshoremen, wagon-driving teamsters, teenagers, and every kind of "helper." Many of these people had real skills and performed valuable services, but they were unorganized and divided, united only by the common fate of meager earnings. The same lack of unity characterized street vendors and market people – self-employed workers who competed savagely with each other and with the established shopkeepers of the lower middle classes.

One of the largest components of the unskilled group was domestic servants, whose numbers grew steadily in the nineteenth century. In advanced Great Britain, for example, one out of every seven employed persons was

*SERVANTS SEEKING WORK in Moscow bargained with prospective employers (or their agents) in this special hiring yard just outside the ancient city walls. Moscow's bustling "market for servants" was open* *every day of the year and was busiest on Sundays. The shed in the center provided some protection from the weather. (Photo: Caroline Buckler)*

a domestic servant in 1911. The majority were women; indeed, one out of every three girls in Britain between the ages of fifteen and twenty was a domestic servant. Throughout Europe and America, a great many female domestics in the cities were recent migrants from rural areas. As in earlier times, domestic service was still hard work at low pay with limited personal independence. For the full-time general maid in a lower-middle-class family, there was an unending routine of babysitting, shopping, cooking, and cleaning. In the great households the girl was at the bottom of a rigid hierarchy; status-conscious butlers and housekeepers were determined to stand almost as far above her as the wealthy master and mistress.

Nonetheless, domestic service had real attractions for "rough, country girls" with strong hands and few specialized skills. Marriage prospects were better, or at least more varied, in the city. And though wages were low, they were higher and more regular than in hard agricultural work. Finally, as one London observer noted, young girls and other migrants were drawn to the city by "the contagion of numbers, the sense of something going on, the theaters and the music halls, the brightly lighted streets and busy crowds — all, in short, that makes the difference between the Mile End fair on a Saturday night, and a dark and muddy country lane, with no glimmer of gas and with nothing to do."[9]

Many young domestics from the countryside made the successful transition to working-class wife and mother. Yet with an unskilled or unemployed husband and a growing family, such a woman often had to join the broad ranks of working-women in the "sweated industries." These industries resembled the old putting-out and cottage industries of the eighteenth and early nineteenth centuries. The women normally worked at home, though sometimes together in some loft or garret, for tiny merchant-manufacturers. Paid by the piece and not by the hour, these women (and their young daughters), for whom organization was impossible earned pitiful wages and lacked any job security.

Some women did hand-decorating of every conceivable kind of object; the majority, however, made clothing, especially after the advent of the sewing machine. Foot-powered sewing machines allowed the poorest wife or widow in the foulest dwelling to rival and eventually supplant the most highly skilled male tailor. By 1900 only a few such tailors lingered on in high-priced "tailor-made" shops. An army of poor women accounted for the bulk of the inexpensive "ready-made" clothes displayed on department store racks and in tiny shops. All of these considerations graphically illustrates the rise and fall of groups and individuals within the working classes.

The urban working classes sought fun and recreation, and they found it. Across the face of Europe drinking was unquestionably the favorite leisure-time activity of working people. For many middle-class moralists, as well as moralizing historians since, love of drink has been a curse of the modern age — a sign of social dislocation and popular suffering. Certainly, drinking was deadly serious business. One English slum dweller recalled that "drunkenness was by far the commonest cause of dispute and misery in working class homes. On account of it one saw many a decent family drift down through poverty into total want."[10] As in Soviet Russia today, where a worker may earn $200 a month and some of the world's best bread costs only twenty-five cents a loaf but foul vodka costs five dollars a bottle, heavy drinking by only one family member could make the difference between modest dignity and dire, violent poverty for many a working-class family.

Generally, however, heavy "problem" drinking declined by the late nineteenth century, as it became less and less socially acceptable. This decline reflected in part the firm moral leadership of the upper working class. At the same time drinking became more public and social, especially as on-the-job drinking, an ancient custom of field laborers and urban artisans, declined. Cafés and pubs became increasingly bright, friendly places. Working-class political activities, both moderate and radical, were also concentrated in taverns and pubs. Moreover, social drinking by married couples and sweethearts became accepted and widespread for the first time. Greater participation by women undoubtedly helped to civilize the world of drink and hard liquor.

The two other leisure-time passions of the working classes were sports and music halls. By the late nineteenth century there had been a great decline in "cruel sports," such as bull-baiting and cockfighting, throughout Europe. Their place was filled by modern spectator sports, of which racing and soccer were the most popular. There was a great deal of gambling on sports events, and for many a workingman the desire to decipher the racing forms was a powerful incentive toward literacy. Music halls and vaudeville theaters, the working-class counterparts of middle-class opera and classic theater, were enormously

SWEATED INDUSTRY *This photo captures the essence of sweated industry. Women and young boys labor for low wages in a necktie workshop in New York about 1890. (Jacob A. Riis Collection, Museum of the City of New York)*

popular throughout Europe. In the words of one English printer, "It is to the music halls that the vast body of working people look for recreation and entertainment."[11] In 1900 there were more than fifty in London alone. Music-hall audiences were thoroughly mixed, which may account for the fact that drunkenness, pregnancy before marriage, marital difficulties, and mothers-in-law were favorite themes of broad jokes and bittersweet songs.

## THE FAMILY

Urban life wrought many fundamental changes in the family. Although much is still unknown, it seems clear that by the late nineteenth century the family had stabilized considerably after the disruption of the late eighteenth and early nineteenth centuries. The home became more important for both men and women. The role of women and attitudes toward children underwent substantial change, and adolescence emerged as a distinct stage of life. These are but a few of the transformations that affected all social classes in varying degrees.

## PREMARITAL SEX AND MARRIAGE

By 1850, the preindustrial pattern of lengthy courtship and mercenary marriage was pretty well dead among the working classes. In its place the ideal of romantic love had triumphed. As one French observer in a small seaport remarked about 1850: "The young men are constantly letting partners with handsome dowries go begging. When they marry, it's ordinarily for inclination and not for advantage."[12] Couples were ever more likely to come from different, even distant, towns and to be more nearly the same age, further indicating that romantic sentiment was replacing tradition and financial considerations. The calculating practice whereby wealthy old craftsmen took pretty young brides, who as comfortable middle-aged widows later married poor apprentices, was increasingly heard of only in old tales and folk songs.

Sexual experimentation before marriage had also triumphed as had illegitimacy. As we have seen, there was an "illegitimacy explosion" between about 1750 and 1850 (page 698). By the 1840s, as many as one birth in three was occurring outside of wedlock in many large cities. Although poverty and economic uncertainty undoubtedly prevented many lovers from marrying, there were also many among the poor and propertyless who saw little wrong with having illegitimate offspring. As one young Bavarian woman answered happily when asked why she kept having illegitimate children: "It's O.K. to make babies. . . . The king has o.k.'d it!"[13]

Thus, the pattern of romantic ideals, premarital sexual activity, and widespread illegitimacy was firmly established by midcentury among the urban working classes.

It is hard to know how European couples managed sex, pregnancy, and marriage in the second half of the nineteenth century, because such questions were considered improper both in polite conversation and in public opinion polls. Yet there are many telltale clues. The rising rate of illegitimacy was reversed: more babies were born to married mothers. Some observers have argued that this shift reflected the growth of puritanism and a lessening of sexual permissiveness among the unmarried. This explanation, however, is unconvincing.

The percentage of brides who were pregnant continued to be high, and showed little or no tendency to decline. In many parts of urban Europe around 1900 as many as one woman in three was going to the altar an expectant mother. Moreover, unmarried people almost certainly used the cheap rubbers and diaphragms the industrial age had made available to prevent pregnancy, at least in predominantly Protestant countries.

Unmarried young people were probably engaging in just as much sexual activity as their parents and grandparents who had created the illegitimacy explosion of 1750–1850. But toward the end of the nineteenth century, pregnancy usually meant marriage and the establishment of a two-parent household. This important development reflected the growing respectability of the working classes, as well as their gradual economic improvement. Skipping out was less acceptable, and marriage was less of an economic disaster. Thus, the urban working-class couple became more stable, and their stability strengthened the family as an institution.

Economic considerations in marriage long

remained much more important to the middle classes than to the working classes. In France, dowries and elaborate legal marriage contracts were standard practice, and marriage was for many families life's most crucial financial transaction. A popular author advised young Frenchmen that "marriage is in general a means of increasing one's credit and one's fortune and of insuring one's success in the world."[14] This preoccupation with money led many middle-class men, in France and elsewhere, to marry late and to choose women considerably younger and less sexually experienced than themselves. These differences between husband and wife became a source of tension in many middle-class marriages.

A young woman of the middle class found her romantic life carefully supervised by her well-meaning mother, who schemed for a proper marriage and guarded her daughter's virginity like the family's credit. After marriage, middle-class morality sternly demanded fidelity.

Middle-class boys were watched too, but not as vigilantly. By the time they reached late adolescence they had usually attained considerable sexual experience with maids or prostitutes. With marriage a distant, uncertain possibility, it was all too easy for the young man of the middle classes to turn to the urban underworld of whoredom and sexual exploitation to satisfy his desires.

## PROSTITUTION

In Paris alone 155,000 women were registered as prostitutes between 1871 and 1903, and 750,000 others were suspected of prostitution in the same years. Men of all classes visited prostitutes, but the middle and upper classes supplied much of the motivating cash. Thus, though many middle-class men abided by the publicly professed code of stern puritanical morality, many others indulged their appetites for prostitutes and sexual promiscuity.

*My Secret Life,* the anonymous eleven-volume autobiography of an English sexual adventurer from the servant-keeping classes, provides a remarkable picture of such a man. Beginning at an early age with a maid, the author becomes progressively obsessed with sex and devotes his life to living his sexual fantasies. In almost every one of his innumerable encounters all across Europe, this man of wealth simply buys his pleasure. The underlying theme of the rake's progress is the clink of copper, silver, and gold. Usually meetings are arranged in a businesslike manner: regular and part-time prostitutes quote their prices; working-class girls are corrupted by hot meals and warm baths.

At one point, however, he offers a young girl a sixpence for a kiss and gets it. Learning that the pretty, unskilled working girl earns nine pence a day – she fills seed packets at a nursery – he offers her the equivalent of a week's salary for a few moments of fondling. When she finally agrees, he savagely exults that "*her* want was my opportunity."[15] Later he offers more money for more gratification, and when she refuses he tries unsuccessfully to rape her in a hackney cab. On another occasion he takes a farm worker by force: "Her tears ran down. If I had not committed a rape, it looked uncommonly like one." He then forces his victim to take money to prevent a threatened lawsuit, while the foreman advises the girl to keep quiet and realize that "you be in luck if he likes you."

Obviously atypical in its excesses, the encyclopedic thoroughness of *My Secret Life* does mirror accurately the dark side of sex and class in urban society. Thinking of their wives largely in terms of money and social position, the men of the comfortable classes often purchased sex and even affection from poor girls both before and after marriage. Moreover, the great continuing differences between rich and poor made for every kind of debauchery and sexual exploitation, including the brisk trade in poor virgins the author of *My Secret Life* particularly relished. Brutal sexist behavior was part of life – a part the sternly moral women (and men) of the upper working class detested and tried to shield their daughters against. For many poor young women, prostitution, like domestic service, was a stage of life. Having passed through it, they went on to marry men of their own class and establish homes and families.

### KINSHIP TIES

Within working-class homes, ties to relatives after marriage – kinship ties – were normally much stronger than superficial social observers have recognized. Most newlyweds tried to live near their parents, though not in the same house. Indeed, for many married couples in the cities, ties to mothers and fathers, uncles and aunts became more important, and ties to nonrelated acquaintances became weaker.

People turned to their families for help in coping with sickness, unemployment, death, and old age. Although governments were generally providing more welfare services by 1900, the average couple and their children inevitably faced crises. Funerals, for example, were an economic catastrophe, requiring a sudden large outlay for special clothes, carriages, and burial services. Unexpected death or desertion could leave widows and orphans in need of financial aid or perhaps a foster home. Relatives responded to such cries, knowing full well that their time of need and repayment would undoubtedly come.

Relatives were also valuable at less tragic moments. If a couple was very poor, an aged

**THE GREAT SOCIAL EVIL.**

TIME:—Midnight. A Sketch not a Hundred Miles from the Haymarket.

*Bella.* "AH! FANNY! HOW LONG HAVE YOU BEEN GAY?"

*PROSTITUTION was commonly known as "the great social evil" because it was so widespread. This* Punch *cartoon of 1857 shows two weary streetwalkers and involves a play on words. (In the nineteenth century "gays" were prostitutes, not homosexuals.) (The British Museum)*

relation often moved in to cook and mind the children so the wife could earn badly needed income outside the home. Sunday dinners and holiday visits were often shared, as was outgrown clothing and useful information. Often the members of a large family group all lived in the same neighborhood.

## WOMEN AND FAMILY LIFE

Industrialization and the growth of modern cities brought great changes to the lives of European women. These changes were particularly consequential for married women, and most women did marry in the nineteenth century.

The work of most wives became quite distinct and separate from that of their husbands. Husbands became wage earners in factories and offices, while wives tended to stay home and manage the household and care for the children. The preindustrial pattern among both peasants and cottage workers, in which husbands and wives worked together and divided up household duties and childrearing, declined. Only in a few occupations, such as retail trade, did married couples live where they worked and struggle together to make their Mom and Pop operations a success. Factory employment for married women also declined as the early practice of hiring entire families in the factory disappeared.

As economic conditions improved late in the nineteenth century, women generally worked outside the home after marriage only in poor families. One old English worker recalled that "the boy wanted to get into a position that would enable him to keep a wife and family, as it was considered a thoroughly unsatisfactory state of affairs if the wife had to work to help maintain the home."[16] The ideal was a strict division of labor by sex: the wife as mother and homemaker, the husband as wage earner.

This rigid division of labor meant that married women faced great injustice if they tried to move into the man's world, the world of employment outside the home. Husbands were unsympathetic or hostile. Well-paying jobs were off-limits to women, and a woman's wage was almost always less than a man's even for the same work. No wonder some women rebelled by the second half of the nineteenth century and began the long-continuing fight for equality of the sexes and the rights of women. More generally, rigidly separate roles narrowed women's horizons and fenced in their world.

There was a brighter side to the same coin. As home and children became the wife's main concerns, her control and influence there apparently became increasingly absolute throughout Europe. Among the English working classes it was the wife who generally determined how the family's money was spent. In many families the husband gave all his earnings to his wife to tend. She returned to him only a small allowance for carfare, beer, tobacco, and union dues. All the major domestic decisions, from the children's schooling and religious instruction to the selection of new furniture or a new apartment, were hers. In France women had even greater power in their assigned domain. One English feminist noted in 1908 that "though legally women occupy a much inferior status than men [in France], in practice they constitute the superior sex. They are the power behind the throne." Another Englishwoman believed that "in most French households, women reign with unchallenged sway."[17]

Women ruled at home partly because running the urban household was a complicated and extremely demanding task. Twice-a-day food shopping, penny-pinching, economizing, and the growing crusade against dirt – not to mention child raising – were a full-time occupation. Nor were there any laborsaving appliances to help. The wife also ruled at home because a good deal of her effort was directed toward pampering her husband as he expected. In countless humble households she saw that he had meat while she ate bread, that he relaxed by the fire while she did the dishes.

The woman's guidance of the household went hand in hand with the increased emotional importance of home and family. The home she ran was idealized as a warm shelter in a hard and impersonal urban world. By the 1820s one observer of the comfortable middle classes in Marseilles had noted, for example, that "the family father, obliged to occupy himself with difficult business problems during the day, can relax only when he goes home.... Family evenings together are for him a time of the purest and most complete happiness."[18]

In time the central place of the family spread down the social scale. For a child of the English slums in the early 1900s

*home, however poor, was the focus of all love and interests, a sure fortress against a hostile world. Songs about its beauties were ever on people's lips. "Home, sweet home," first heard in the 1870s, had become "almost a second national anthem." Few walls in lower-working-class houses lacked "mottoes" – colored strips of paper, about nine inches wide and eighteen inches in length, attesting to domestic joys: EAST, WEST, HOME'S BEST; BLESS OUR HOME; GOD IS MASTER OF THIS HOUSE; HOME IS THE NEST WHERE ALL IS BEST.[9]*

By 1900 home and family were what life was all about for millions of people of all classes.

One of the most striking signs of deepening emotional ties within the family was the mother's love and concern for her tiny infants. This was a sharp break with the past. It may seem scarcely believable today that the typical mother in preindustrial Western society was very often indifferent toward her baby. This indifference – unwillingness to make real sacrifices for the welfare of the infant – was giving way among the comfortable classes by the later part of the eighteenth century, but the ordinary mother adopted new attitudes only as the nineteenth century progressed. The baby became more important, and women became better mothers.

Women also developed stronger emotional ties to their husbands. Even in the comfortable classes, marriages were increasingly founded on sentiment and sexual attraction rather than money and calculation. Affection and eroticism became more central to the couple after marriage. Gustave Droz, whose book *Mr., Mrs., and Baby* went through 121 editions between 1866 and 1884, saw love within marriage as the key to human happiness. He condemned men who made marriage sound dull and practical, men who were exhausted by prostitutes and rheumatism and who wanted their young wives to be little angels. He urged women to follow their hearts and marry a man more nearly their own age:

*A husband who is stately and a little bald is all right, but a young husband who loves you and who drinks out of your glass without ceremony, is better. Let him, if he ruffles your dress a little and places a kiss on your neck as he passes. Let him, if he undresses you after the ball, laughing like a fool. You have fine spiritual qualities, it is true, but your little body is not bad either and when one loves, one loves completely. Behind these follies lies happiness.[20]*

SUNDAY MORNING
WORKMANS HOME
LEATHER LANE

*A WORKING-CLASS HOME, 1875  Emotional ties within ordinary families grew stronger in the nineteenth century. (Illustrated London News, LXVI, 1875. Photo courtesy of Boston Public Library)*

Many French marriage manuals of the late 1800s stressed that women had legitimate sexual needs, such as "the right to orgasm." Perhaps the French were a bit more enlightened in these matters than other nationalities. But the rise of public socializing by couples in cafés and music halls, as well as franker affection within the family, suggest a more erotic, more pleasurable intimate life for women throughout Western society. This too helped make the woman's role as mother and home-maker acceptable and even satisfying.

## CHILD RAISING

Children benefited from the freer expression of affection within the family circle. Mothers increasingly breast-fed their own infants, for example, rather than paying wet nurses to do so. Breast-feeding involved sacrifice – a temporary loss of freedom, if nothing else. Yet in an age when there was no good alternative to mother's milk, it saved lives. The surge of maternal feeling also gave rise to a wave of specialized books on childrearing and infant hygiene, such as Droz's phenomenally successful best-seller *Mr., Mrs., and Baby.* Droz urged fathers to get into the act, and pitied those "who do not know how to roll around on the carpet, play at being a horse and a great wolf, and undress their baby."[21] Another sign, from France, of increased affection is that fewer illegitimate babies were abandoned as foundlings, especially after about 1850. Moreover, the practice of swaddling – wrapping a baby like a tiny mummy – disappeared completely. Instead, ordinary mothers allowed their babies freedom of movement and delighted in their spontaneity.

The loving care lavished on infants was matched by greater concern for older children and adolescents. They too were wrapped in the strong emotional ties of a more intimate and more protective family. For one thing, European women began to limit the number of children they bore in order to care adequately for those they had. It was evident by the end of the century that the birthrate was declining across Europe, as Figure 24.4 shows, and it continued to do so until after World War Two. The Englishwoman who married in the 1860s, for example, had an average of about six children; her daughter marrying in the 1890s had only four; and her granddaughter marrying in the 1920s had only two or possibly three.

The most important reason for this revolutionary reduction in family size, in which the comfortable and well-educated classes took the lead, was parents' desire to improve their economic and social position and that of their children. Children were no longer an economic asset. By having fewer youngsters, parents could give those they had valuable advantages, from music lessons and summer vacations to long expensive university educations and suitable dowries. A young German skilled worker with only one child

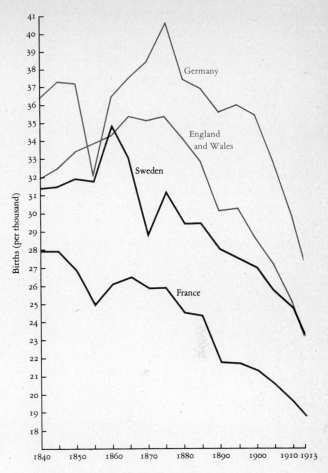

FIGURE 24.4   THE DECLINE OF BIRTHRATES IN ENGLAND AND WALES, FRANCE, GERMANY, AND SWEDEN, 1840–1913   *Women had fewer babies for a variety of reasons, including the fact that their children were increasingly less likely to die before they reached adulthood. Compare with Figure 24.2 on page 847.*

spoke for many in his class when he said, "We want to get ahead, and our daughter should have things better than my wife and sisters did."[22] Thus, the growing tendency of couples in the late nineteenth century to use a variety of contraceptive methods – rhythm, withdrawal, and mechanical devices – certainly reflected increased concern for children.

Indeed, many parents were probably *too* concerned about their children, unwittingly subjecting them to an emotional pressure cooker of almost unbearable intensity. The result was that many children and especially adolescents came to feel trapped and in desperate need of greater independence.

Biological and medical theories led parents to believe that their own emotional characteristics were passed on to their offspring, and that they were thus directly responsible for any abnormality in a child. The moment the child was conceived was thought to be of enormous importance. "Never run the risk of conception when you are sick or over-tired or unhappy," wrote one influential American woman. "For the bodily condition of the child, its vigor and magnetic qualities, are much affected by conditions ruling this great moment."[23] So might the youthful "sexual excesses" of the father curse future generations. Although this was true in the case of syphilis, which could be transmitted to unborn children, the rigid determinism of such views left little scope for the child's individual development.

Another aspect of excessive parental concern was the sexual behavior of the child. Masturbation was viewed with horror, for it represented an act of independence and even defiance. Diets, clothing, games, and sleeping were carefully regulated. Girls were discouraged from riding horses and bicycling because rhythmic friction simulated masturbation. Boys were dressed in trousers with shallow and widely separated pockets. Between 1850 and 1880, there were surgical operations for children who persisted in masturbating. Thereafter until about 1905, various restraining apparatuses were more often used.

These and less blatant attempts to repress the child's sexuality were a source of unhealthy tension, often made worse by the rigid division of sexual roles within the family. It was widely believed that mother and child love each other easily, but that relations between the father and the child are necessarily difficult and often tragic. The father was a stranger; his world of business was far removed from the maternal world of spontaneous affection. Moreover, the father was demanding, often expecting the child to succeed where he himself had failed and making his love conditional on achievement. Little wonder that the imaginative literature of the late nineteenth century came to deal with the emotional and destructive elements of father-son relationships. In the Russian Feodor Dostoevsky's great novel *The Brothers Karamazov* (1880–1881), for example, four sons work knowingly or unknowingly to destroy their father. Later, at the murder trial, one of the brothers claims to speak for all mankind and screams out: "Who doesn't wish his father dead?"

Sigmund Freud (1856–1939), the Viennese founder of psychoanalysis, formulated the most striking analysis of the explosive dynamics of the family, particularly the middle-class family in the late nineteenth century. A physician by training, Freud began his career treating mental illness. He noted that the hysteria of his patients appeared to originate in bitter early childhood experiences, wherein the child had been obliged to repress strong feelings. When these painful experiences were recalled and reproduced under hypnosis or through the patient's free association of ideas, the patient could be brought to understand his or her unhappiness and eventually to deal with it.

One of Freud's most influential ideas concerned the Oedipal tensions, resulting from the son's instinctive competition with the father for the mother's love and affection. More generally, Freud postulated that much of human behavior is motivated by unconscious emotional needs, whose nature and origins are kept from conscious awareness by various mental devices he called defense mechanisms. Freud concluded that much unconscious psychological energy is sexual energy, which is in turn repressed and precariously controlled by rational thinking and moral rules. If Freud exaggerated the sexual and familial roots of adult behavior, that exaggeration was itself a reflection of the tremendous emotional intensity of family life in the late nineteenth century.

The working classes probably had more avenues of escape from such tensions than did the middle classes. Unlike their middle-class counterparts, who remained economically dependent on their families until a long education was finished or a proper marriage secured, working-class boys and girls went to work when they reached adolescence. Earning wages on their own, they could bargain with their parents for greater independence within the household by the time they were sixteen or seventeen. If they were unsuccessful, they could and did leave home, to live cheaply as paying lodgers in other working-class homes. Thus, the young person from the working classes broke away from the family more easily when emotional ties became oppressive. In the twentieth century middle-class youth would follow this lead.

## SCIENCE AND THOUGHT

Major changes in Western thought accompanied the emergence of urban society. Two aspects of these complex intellectual developments stand out as especially significant. Scientific knowledge expanded rapidly and came to influence the Western world-view even more profoundly than it had since the Scientific Revolution and the early Enlightenment. And, between about the 1840s and the 1890s, European literature underwent a shift from soaring romanticism to tough-minded realism.

### THE TRIUMPH OF SCIENCE

As the pace of scientific advance quickened, and as theoretical advances resulted in great practical benefits, science exercised growing influence on human thought. The intellectual achievements of the Scientific Revolution had resulted in few such benefits, and theoretical knowledge had also played a relatively small role in the Industrial Revolution in England. But breakthroughs in industrial technology enormously stimulated basic scientific inquiry, as researchers sought to explain theoretically how such things as steam engines and blast furnaces actually worked. The result was an explosive growth of fundamental scientific discoveries from the 1830s onward. And unlike earlier periods, these theoretical discoveries were increasingly transformed into material improvements for the general population.

A perfect example of the translation of better scientific knowledge into practical human benefits was the work of Pasteur and his followers in biology and the medical sciences. Another was the development of the branch of physics known as thermodynamics. Building on Newton's laws of mechanics and on studies of steam engines, thermodynamics investigated the relationship between heat and mechanical energy. By midcentury, physicists had formulated the fundamental laws of thermodynamics, which were then applied to mechanical engineering, chemical processes, and many other fields. The law of conservation of energy held that different forms of energy – such as heat, electricity, and magnetism – could be converted but neither created nor destroyed. Nineteenth-century thermodynamics demonstrated that the physical world is governed by firm unchanging laws.

Chemistry and electricity were two other fields characterized by extremely rapid progress. Chemists devised ways of measuring the atomic weight of different elements, and in 1869 the Russian chemist Dmitri Mendeleev (1834–1907) codified the rules of chemistry in the periodic law and the periodic table. Chemistry subdivided into many specialized branches, such as organic chemistry – the study of the compounds of carbon. Applying theoretical insights gleaned from this new field, researchers in large German chemical companies discovered ways of transforming the dirty, useless coal-tar that accumulated in coke ovens into beautiful, expensive synthetic dyes for the world of fashion. The basic discoveries of Michael Faraday (1791–1867) on electromagnetism in the 1830s and 1840s resulted in the first dynamo (generator) and opened the way for the subsequent development of electric motors, electric lights, and electric streetcars.

The triumph of science and technology had at least three significant consequences. First, though ordinary citizens continued to lack detailed scientific knowledge, everyday experience and innumerable popularizers impressed the importance of science on the popular mind.

As science became more prominent in popular thinking, the philosophical implications of science formulated in the Enlightenment spread to broad sections of the population. Natural processes appeared to be determined by rigid laws, leaving little room for either divine intervention or human will. Yet scientific and technical advance had also fed the Enlightenment's optimistic faith in human progress, which now appeared endless and automatic to many middle-class minds.

Finally, the methods of science acquired unrivaled prestige after 1850. For many, the union of careful experiment and abstract theory seemed the only reliable route to truth and objective reality. The "unscientific" intuitions of poets and the revelations of saints were hopelessly inferior.

## SOCIAL SCIENCE AND EVOLUTION

From the 1830s onward, many thinkers tried to apply the objective methods of science to the study of society. In some ways these efforts simply perpetuated the critical thinking of the philosophes. Yet there were important differences. The new "social scientists" had access to the massive sets of numerical data that governments had begun to collect, on everything from children to crime, from population to prostitution. In response, they developed new statistical methods to analyze these facts "scientifically" and supposedly to test their theories. And the systems of the leading nineteenth-century social scientists were more unified, all-encompassing, and dogmatic than those of the philosophes. Marx was a prime example (see pages 810–811).

Another extremely influential system builder was the French philosopher Auguste Comte (1798–1857). Initially a disciple of the utopian socialist Saint-Simon, Comte wrote a six-volume *System of Positive Philosophy* (1830–1842) that was largely overlooked during the romantic era. But when the political failures of 1848 completed the swing to realism, Comte's philosophy came into its own. Its influence has remained great to this day.

Comte postulated that all intellectual activity progresses through predictable stages:

*The great fundamental law ... is this: – that each of our leading conceptions – each branch of our knowledge – passes successively through three different theoretical conditions: the Theological, or fictitious; the Metaphysical, or abstract; and the Scientific, or positive. ... The first is the necessary point of departure of human understanding, and the third is the fixed and definitive state. The second is merely a transition.*[24]

By way of example, Comte noted that the prevailing explanation of cosmic patterns had shifted, as knowledge of astronomy developed, from the will of God (the theological) to the will of an orderly Nature (the metaphysical) to the rule of its own unchanging laws (the scientific). Later, this same intellectual progression took place in increasingly complex fields – physics, chemistry, and, finally, the study of society. By applying the scientific, positivist method, Comte believed, his new discipline of sociology would soon discover the eternal laws of human relations. This colossal achievement would in turn enable expert social scientists to impose a disciplined harmony and well-being on less-enlightened citizens. Dismissing the "fictions" of traditional religions, Comte became the chief priest of the religion of science and rule by experts.

Comte's stages of knowledge exemplify the nineteenth-century fascination with the idea of evolution and dynamic development. Thinkers in many fields, like the romantic historians and "scientific" Marxists, shared and applied this basic concept. In geology, Charles Lyell (1797–1875) effectively discred-ited the longstanding view that the earth's surface had been formed by short-lived cataclysms, such as biblical floods and earthquakes. Instead, according to Lyell's principle of uniformitarianism, the same geological processes that are at work today slowly formed the earth's surface over an immensely long time. The evolutionary view of biological development, first proposed by the Greek Anaximander in the sixth century B.C., re-emerged in a more modern form in the work of Jean Baptiste Lamarck (1744–1829). Lamarck asserted that all forms of life had arisen through a long process of continuous adjustment to the demands of the environment.

Lamarck's work was flawed – he believed that characteristics parents acquired in the course of their lives could be inherited by their children – and was not accepted, but it helped prepare the way for Charles Darwin (1809–1892), the most influential of all nineteenth-century evolutionary thinkers. As the official naturalist on a five-year scientific cruise to Latin America and the South Pacific in 1831, Darwin carefully collected specimens of the different animal species he encountered on the voyage. Back in England and convinced by fossil evidence and by his friend Lyell that the earth and life upon it were immensely ancient, Darwin came to doubt the general belief in a special divine creation of each species of animals. Instead, he concluded, all life had gradually evolved from a common ancestral origin in an unending "struggle for survival." After long hesitation, Darwin published his research, which immediately attracted wide attention.

Darwin's great originality lay in suggesting precisely *how* biological evolution might have occurred. His theory is summarized in his title – *On the Origin of Species by the Means of Natural Selection* (1859). Decisively influenced by Malthus's gloomy theory that populations naturally grow faster than their food supplies, Darwin argued that chance differences among the members of a given species help some to survive while others died. Thus, the variations that prove useful in the struggle for survival are selected naturally and gradually spread to the entire species through reproduction. Darwin did not explain why such variations occurred in the first place, and not until the early twentieth century did the study of genetics and the concept of mutation provide some answers.

As the capstone of already-widespread evolutionary thinking, Darwin's theory had a powerful and many-sided influence on European thought. Darwin was hailed as the great scientist par excellence, "the Newton of biology," who had revealed once again the fantastic powers of objective science. Darwin's findings also reinforced the teachings of secularists like Comte and Marx, who scornfully dismissed religious belief in favor of agnostic materialism. In the great cities especially, religion was on the defensive. Finally, many writers applied the theory of biological evolution to human affairs. Herbert Spencer (1820–1903), an English disciple of Auguste Comte, saw the human race as driven forward to ever-greater specialization and progress by the brutal economic struggle that efficiently determined "the survival of the fittest." The poor were the ill-fated weak, the prosperous the chosen strong. Understandably, Spencer and other Social Darwinists were especially popular with the upper middle class.

## REALISM IN LITERATURE

In 1868 Emile Zola (1840–1902), the giant of the realist movement in literature, defended his violently criticized first novel against charges of pornography and corruption of morals. Such accusations were meaningless, Zola claimed: he was only a purely objective scientist using "the modern method, the universal instrument of inquiry of which this age makes such ardent use to open up the future."

*I chose characters completely dominated by their nerves and their blood, deprived of free-will, pushed to each action of their lives by the fatality of their flesh. . . . I have simply done on living bodies the work of analysis which surgeons perform on corpses.*[25]

Zola's literary manifesto articulated the key themes of realism, which had emerged in the 1840s and continued to dominate Western culture and style until the 1890s. Realist writers believed that literature should depict life exactly as it was. Forsaking poetry for prose and the personal, emotional viewpoint of the romantics for strict, scientific objectivity, the realists simply observed and recorded — content to let the facts speak for themselves.

The major realist writers focused their extraordinary powers of observation on contemporary everyday life. Emphatically rejecting the romantic search for the exotic and the sublime, they energetically pursued the typical and commonplace. Beginning with a dissection of the middle classes, from which most of them sprang, many realists eventually focused on the working classes, especially the urban working classes, who had been neglected in imaginative literature before this time. They put a microscope to many unexplored and taboo subjects — raw sex, strikes, violence, alcoholism — and hastened to report that slums and factories teemed with savage behavior. Many shocked middle-class critics denounced realism as ugly sensationalism, wrapped provocatively in pseudo-scientific declarations and crude language.

The realists' claims of objectivity did not prevent the elaboration of a definite worldview. Unlike the romantics, who had gloried in individual freedom and an unlimited universe, realists such as Zola were strict determinists. Human beings, like atoms, were components of the physical world, and all human actions were caused by unalterable natural laws. Heredity and environment determined human behavior; good and evil were merely social conventions.

The realist movement began in France, where romanticism had never been completely dominant, and three of its greatest practitioners – Balzac, Flaubert, and Zola – were French. Honoré de Balzac (1799–1850) spent thirty years writing a vastly ambitious panorama of postrevolutionary French life. Known collectively as *The Human Comedy,* this series of nearly one hundred books vividly portrays more than two thousand characters from virtually all sectors of French society. Balzac pictures urban society as grasping, amoral, and brutal, characterized by a Darwinian struggle for wealth and power. In *Père Goriot* (1835), the hero, a poor student from the provinces, eventually surrenders his idealistic integrity to feverish ambition and society's all-pervasive greed.

*Madame Bovary* (1857), the masterpiece of Gustave Flaubert (1821–1880), is far narrower in scope than Balzac's work but unparalleled in its depth and accuracy of psychological insight. Unsuccessfully prosecuted as an outrage against public morality and religion, Flaubert's carefully crafted novel tells the ordinary, even banal, story of a frustrated middle-class housewife who has an adulterous love affair and is betrayed by her lover. Without moralizing, Flaubert portrays the provincial middle class as petty, smug, and hypocritical.

Zola was most famous for his seamy, animalistic view of working-class life. But he also wrote gripping, carefully researched stories featuring the stock exchange, the big department store, and the army, as well as urban slums and bloody coal strikes. Like many later realists, Zola sympathized with socialism, a sympathy evident in his overpowering *Germinal* (1885).

Realism quickly spread beyond France. In England, Mary Ann Evans (1819–1880), who wrote under the pen name George Eliot, brilliantly achieved a more deeply felt, less sensational kind of realism. "It is the habit of my imagination," George Eliot wrote, "to strive after as full a vision of the medium in which a character moves as of the character itself." Her great novel *Middlemarch: A Study of Provincial Life* examines masterfully the ways in which people are shaped by their social medium as well as their own inner strivings, conflicts, and moral choices. Thomas Hardy (1840–1928) was more in the Zola tradition. His novels, like *Tess of the D'Urbervilles* (1891), depicted men and women frustrated and crushed by fate and bad luck.

The greatest Russian realist, Count Leo Tolstoy (1828–1910), combined realism in description and character development with an atypical moralizing, which came to dominate his later work. Tolstoy's greatest work was *War and Peace,* a monumental novel set against the historical background of Napoleon's invasion of Russia in 1812. Tolstoy probes deeply into the lives of a multitude of unforgettable characters, such as the ill-fated Prince Andrei, the shy, fumbling Pierre, and the enchanting, level-headed Natasha. Tolstoy goes to great pains to develop his fatalistic theory of history, which regards free will as an illusion and the achievements of even the greatest leaders as only the channeling of historical necessity. Yet Tolstoy's central message

GEORGE ELIOT   *Reared in a strict religious atmo-*
*sphere against which she later rebelled, Mary Ann*
*Evans accepted scientific attitudes but never lost a*
*strong moral sense of personal responsibility. Her first*
*novels appeared when she was in her early forties.*
*(Historical Pictures Service)*

is one that most of the people discussed in this chapter would readily accept: human love, trust, and everyday family ties are life's enduring values.

Thoroughgoing realism (or naturalism, as it was often called) arrived late in the United States, most arrestingly in the work of Theodore Dreiser (1871–1945). Dreiser's first novel, *Sister Carrie* (1900), the story of an ordinary farm girl who does well going wrong in Chicago, so outraged conventional morality that the publisher withdrew the book. The

United States subsequently became a bastion of literary realism in the twentieth century, after the movement had faded away in Europe.

———◆———

The Industrial Revolution had a decisive influence on the urban environment. The populations of towns and cities grew rapidly because it was economically advantageous to locate factories and offices in urban areas. This rapid growth worsened longstanding overcrowding and unhealthy living conditions, and posed a frightening challenge for society. Eventually government leaders, city planners, reformers, scientists, and ordinary citizens responded. They took effective action in public health and provided themselves with other badly needed urban services. Gradually they tamed the ferocious savagery of the traditional city.

As urban civilization came to prevail, there were major changes in family life. Especially among the lower classes, family life became more stable, more loving, and less mercenary. These improvements had a price, though. Sex roles for men and women became sharply defined and rigidly separate. Women especially tended to be locked into a subordinate and stereotypic role. Nonetheless, on balance, the quality of family life improved for all family members. Better, more stable family relations reinforced the benefits for the masses of higher real wages, expanding social security systems, greater political participation, and more education.

While the quality of urban and family life improved, the class structure became more complex and diversified than before. Urban society featured many distinct social groups, which existed in a state of constant flux and competition. Thus, the gap between rich and poor remained enormous and really quite traditional in mature urban society, although

there were countless gradations between the extremes. Large numbers of poor women in particular continued to labor as workers in sweated industries, as domestic servants, and as prostitutes in order to satisfy the demands of their masters in the servant-keeping classes. Urban society in the late nineteenth century represented a great step forward for humanity, but it remained very unequal.

Inequality was a favorite theme of realist novelists like Balzac and Zola. More generally, literary realism reflected Western society's growing faith in science, progress, and evolutionary thinking. The emergence of urban, industrial civilization accelerated the secularization of Western thought and the Western world-view.

## NOTES

1. A. Weber, *The Growth of Cities in the Nineteenth Century,* Columbia University Press, New York, 1899, p. 1.

2. Quoted by W. Ashworth, *The Genesis of Modern British Town Planning,* Routledge & Kegan Paul, London, 1954, p. 17.

3. S. Marcus, "Reading the Illegible," in *The Victorian City: Images and Realities,* ed. H. J. Dyos and Michael Wolff, Routledge & Kegan Paul, London, 1973, 1.266.

4. E. Gauldie, *Cruel Habitations: A History of Working-Class Housing, 1780–1918,* George Allen & Unwin, London, 1974, p. 21.

5. Quoted in E. Chadwick, *Report on the Sanitary Condition of the Labouring Population of Great Britain,* ed. M. W. Flinn, University Press, Edinburgh, 1965 (originally published, 1842), pp. 315–316.

6. J. P. McKay, *Tramways and Trolleys: The Rise of Urban Mass Transport in Europe,* Princeton University Press, Princeton, N.J., 1976, p. 81.

7. Quoted by R. P. Neuman, "The Sexual Ques-

tion and Social Democracy in Imperial Germany," *Journal of Social History* 7 (Winter 1974):276.

8. Quoted by B. Harrison, "Underneath the Victorians," *Victorian Studies* 10 (March 1967):260.

9. Quoted by J. A. Banks, "The Contagion of Numbers," in Dyos and Wolff, 1.112.

10. R. Roberts, *The Classic Slum: Salford Life in the First Quarter of the Century,* University Press, Manchester, 1971, p. 95.

11. Quoted by B. Harrison, "Pubs," in Dyos and Wolff, 1.175.

12. Quoted by E. Shorter, *The Making of the Modern Family,* Basic Books, New York, 1975, p. 150.

13. Quoted by J. M. Phayer, "Lower-Class Morality: The Case of Bavaria," *Journal of Social History* 8 (Fall 1974):89.

14. Quoted by T. Zeldin, *France, 1848–1945,* Clarendon Press, Oxford, 1973, 1.288.

15. Quoted by S. Marcus, *The Other Victorians: A Study of Sexuality and Pornography in Mid-Nineteenth-Century England,* Basic Books, New York, 1966, p. 142.

16. Quoted by G. S. Jones, "Working-Class Culture and Working-Class Politics in London, 1870–1900: Notes on the Remaking of a Working Class," *Journal of Social History* 7 (Summer 1974): 486.

17. Quoted by Zeldin, 1.346.

18. Quoted by Shorter, pp. 230–231.

19. R. Roberts, p. 35.

20. Quoted by Zeldin, 1.295.

21. Ibid., 1.328.

22. Quoted by Neuman, p. 281.

23. Quoted by S. Kern, "Explosive Intimacy: Psychodynamics of the Victorian Family," *History of Childhood Quarterly* 1 (Winter 1974):439.

24. A. Comte, *The Positive Philosophy of Auguste Comte,* trans. H. Martineau, J. Chapman, London, 1853, 1. 1–2.

25. Quoted by G. J. Becker, ed., *Documents of Modern Literary Realism,* Princeton University Press, Princeton, N.J., 1963, p. 159.

## SUGGESTED READING

All of the books and articles cited in the Notes are highly recommended; each in its own way is an important contribution to social history and life in the urban society. Note that the *Journal of Social History,* which has a strong European orientation, is excellent both for its articles and for its reviews of new books. T. Zeldin, *France, 1848–1945,* 2 vols. (1973, 1977), is a pioneering social history that opens many doors.

On the European city, D. Pickney, *Napoleon III and the Rebuilding of Paris* (1972), is fascinating, as are G. Masur, *Imperial Berlin* (1970), and M. Hamm, ed., *The City in Russian History* (1976). So also are N. Evenson's beautifully illustrated *Paris: A Century of Change, 1878–1978* (1979), D. Grew's authoritative *Town in the Ruhr: A Social History of Bochum, 1860–1914* (1979), and the essays in J. Merriman, ed., *French Cities in the 19th Century: Class, Power, and Urbanization* (1982). D. Olsen's scholarly *Growth of Victorian London* (1978) complements H. Mayhew's wonderful contemporary study, *London Labour and the Labouring Poor* (1861), reprinted recently. M. Crichton's realistic historical novel on organized crime, *The Great Train Robbery* (1976), is excellent. J. J. Tobias, *Urban Crime in Victorian England* (1972), is a lively, scholarly approach to declining criminal activity in the nineteenth century, with a wealth of detail. G. Rosen, *History of Public Health* (1958), is an excellent introduction to medical developments. For society as a whole, J. Burnett, *History of the Cost of Living* (1969), cleverly shows how different classes spent their money, and B. Tuchman, *The Proud Tower* (1966), draws an unforgettable portrait of people and classes before 1914. J. Laver's handsomely illustrated *Manners and Morals in the Age of Optimism, 1848–1914* (1966), investigates the urban underworld and relations between the sexes. Sexual attitudes are also examined by E. Trudgill, *Madonnas and Magdalenas: The Origin and Development of Victorian Sexual Attitudes* (1976), A. McLaren, *Sexuality and Social Order: Birth Control in Nine-*

teenth-Century France (1982), and J. Phayer, *Sexual Liberation and Religion in Nineteenth Century Europe* (1977).

Women are coming into their own in historical studies. In addition to the general works by Shorter, Wrigley, Stone, and Tilly and Scott cited in Chapter 20, there are a growing number of eye-opening, specialized investigations. These include L. Davidoff, *The Best Circles* (1973), on upper-class society types; O. Banks, *Feminism and Family Planning in Victorian England* (1964); and Patricia Branca, *Women in Europe Since 1750* (1978). L. Holcombe, *Victorian Ladies at Work* (1973), pioneers in examining middle-class women at work. M. Vicinus, ed., *Suffer and Be Still* (1972), and *A Widening Sphere* (1981), are far-ranging collections of essays on women's history, as is R. Bridenthal and C. Koonz, eds., *Becoming Visible: Women in European History* (1976). Feminism is treated perceptively in R. Evans, *The Feminists: Women's Emancipation in Europe, America, and Australia* (1979), and K. Blair, *The Clubwoman as Feminist: True Womanhood Redefined, 1868–1914* (1980). J. Gillis, *Youth and History* (1974), is a good introduction. D. Ransel, ed., *The Family in Imperial Russia* (1978), is an important work on the subject, as is J. Donzelot, *The Policing of Families* (1979), which stresses the loss of family control of all aspects of life to government agencies.

Among studies of special groups, J. Scott, *The Glass-Workers of Carmaux* (1974), is outstanding on skilled French craftsmen, and D. Lockwood, *The Blackcoated Worker* (1958), carefully examines class consciousness in the English lower middle class. Two fine studies on universities and their professors are S. Rothblatt, *Revolution of the Dons: Cambridge and Society in Victorian England* (1968), and F. Ringer, *The Decline of the German Mandarins* (1969). Servants and their employers receive excellent treatment in T. McBride, *The Domestic Revolution: The Modernization of Household Service in England and France, 1820–1920* (1976), and B. Smith, *Ladies of the Leisure Class: The Bourgeoises of Northern France in the Nineteenth Century* (1981), which may be compared with the innovative study by M. Miller, *The Bon Marché: Bourgeois Culture and the Department Store, 1869–1920* (1981).

On Darwin, M. Ruse, *The Darwinian Revolution* (1979), is a good starting point. The masterpieces of the great realist social novelists remain one of the best and most memorable introductions to nineteenth-century culture and thought. In addition to the novels discussed in this chapter, and those cited in the Suggested Reading for Chapters 22 and 23, Ivan Turgenev's *Fathers and Sons* and Zola's *The Dram-Shop (L'Assommoir)* are especially recommended.

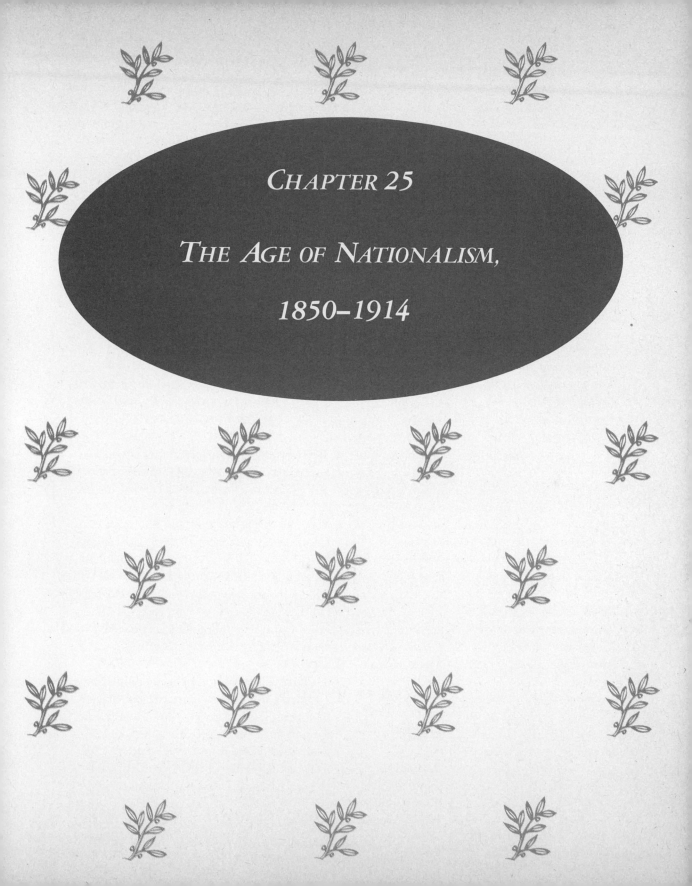

# CHAPTER 25

# THE AGE OF NATIONALISM,

# 1850–1914

*THE REVOLUTIONS OF 1848* closed one era and opened another. Urban industrial society began to take strong hold on the Continent, as it already had in Great Britain. Internationally, the repressive peace and diplomatic stability of Metternich's time was replaced by a period of war and rapid change. In thought and culture soaring romanticism gave way to tough-minded realism. In the European economy the hard years of the 1840s were followed by good times and prosperity throughout most of the 1850s and 1860s. Perhaps most important of all, European society progressively found, for better or worse, a new and effective organizing principle, capable of coping with the many-sided challenge of the dual revolution and the emerging urban civilization. That principle was nationalism – dedication to and identification with the nation-state.

The triumph of nationalism in Europe after 1850 is a development of enormous historical significance. It was by no means completely predictable. After all, nationalism had been a powerful force since at least 1789. Yet it had repeatedly failed to realize its goals, most spectacularly so in 1848. Why, then, did nationalism become in one way or another an almost universal faith in Europe between 1850 and 1914? More specifically, how did nationalism evolve so that it appealed not only to predominantly middle-class liberals but to the broad masses of society as well? These are the weighty questions this chapter seeks to answer.

## NAPOLEON III IN FRANCE

Early nationalism was at least liberal and idealistic and often democratic and radical as well. The ideas of nationhood and popular sovereignty posed an awesome revolutionary threat to conservatives like Metternich. Yet, from the vantage point of the twentieth century, it is clear that nationalism wears many masks: it may be democratic and radical, as it was for Mazzini and Michelet; but it can also flourish in dictatorial states, which may be conservative, fascist, or communist. Napoleon I's France had already combined national devotion with authoritarian rule. Significantly, it was Napoleon's nephew, Louis Napoleon, who revived and extended this merger. It was he who showed how governments could reconcile popular and conservative forces in an authoritarian nationalism. In doing so, he provided a model for political leaders elsewhere.

### THE SECOND REPUBLIC AND LOUIS NAPOLEON

The overwhelming victory of Louis Napoleon Bonaparte in the French presidential elections of December 1848 has long puzzled historians. The nephew of Napoleon I, Louis Napoleon had lived most of his life outside of France and played no part in French politics before 1848. Why did universal manhood suffrage give such an unproven nobody 5.5 million votes, while the runner-up, General Cavaignac of June Days fame, polled only 1.5 million and the other three candidates (including the poet Lamartine) received insignificant support?

The usual explanation is that, though Louis Napoleon had only his great name in common with his uncle, that was enough. According to some historians, the Napoleonic legend – a monument to the power of romanticism between 1820 and 1848 – had transformed a dictator into a demigod in the minds of the unsophisticated French masses.

Another explanation, popularized by Karl Marx, has stressed the fears of middle-class and peasant property owners in the face of the socialist challenge of urban workers. These classes wanted protection. They wanted a tough cop with a big stick on the beat. They found him in Louis Napoleon, who had indeed served briefly as a special constable in London at the height of the Chartist agitation.

These explanations are not wrong, but there was more to Louis Napoleon's popularity than stupidity and fear. In late 1848, Louis Napoleon had a positive "program" for France, which was to guide him throughout most of his long reign. This program had been elaborated earlier in two pamphlets, *Napoleonic Ideas* and *The Elimination of Poverty,* which Louis Napoleon had written while imprisoned for a farcical attempt to overthrow Louis Philippe's government. The pamphlets had been widely circulated prior to the presidential election.

Louis Napoleon believed that the government should represent the people and that it should also try hard to help them economically. How was this to be done? Parliaments and political parties were not the answer, according to Louis Napoleon. Politicians represented special interest groups, particularly middle-class ones. When they ran a parliamentary government, they stirred up class hatreds because they were not interested in helping the poor. This had occurred under Louis Philippe, and it was occurring again under the Second Republic. The answer was a strong, even authoritarian, national leader, like the first Napoleon, who would serve all the people, rich and poor. This leader would be linked to the people by direct democracy and universal male suffrage. Sovereignty would flow from the entire population to the leader, and would not be diluted or corrupted by politicians and legislative bodies.

These political ideas went hand in hand with Louis Napoleon's vision of national unity and social progress. Unlike his uncle, who had reduced unemployment and social tensions by means of foreign wars, Louis Napoleon favored peaceful measures to relieve the awful poverty of the poor. Rather than doing nothing or providing only temporary relief, the state and its leader had a sacred duty to provide jobs and stimulate the economy. All classes would benefit by such action.

Louis Napoleon's political and social ideas were at least vaguely understood by large numbers of French peasants and workers in December 1848. To many common people he appeared to be both a strong man *and* a forward-looking champion of their interests, and that is why they voted for him.

Elected to a four-year term, President Louis Napoleon had to share power with a conservative National Assembly. With some misgivings he signed a bill to increase greatly the role of the Catholic church in primary and secondary education. In France as elsewhere in Europe after 1848, anxious "haves" saw religion as a bulwark against radicalism. As one leader of the church in France put it, "There is only one recipe for making those who own nothing believe in property-rights: that is to make them believe in God, who dictated the Ten Commandments and who promises eternal punishment to those who steal."[1] Very reluctantly, Louis Napoleon also signed another conservative law depriving many poor people of the right to vote. He took these conservative measures for two main reasons: he wanted the assembly to vote funds to pay his personal debts, and he wanted it to change the constitution so he could run for a second term.

The assembly did neither. Thus, in 1851 Louis Napoleon began to organize a conspiracy with key army officers. On December 2, 1851, he illegally dismissed the assembly and seized power in a coup d'état. There was some armed resistance in Paris and other cities, but the actions of the assembly had left the Second Republic with few defenders. Like his uncle, Louis Napoleon called on the French people to legalize his actions. They did. Ninety-two percent voted to make him a strong president for ten years. A year later, 97 percent agreed in a national plebiscite to make him hereditary emperor. For the third time, and by the greatest margin yet, the authoritarian Louis Napoleon was overwhelmingly elected by universal male suffrage to lead the French nation.

## NAPOLEON III'S SECOND EMPIRE

Louis Napoleon – now Emperor Napoleon III – experienced both success and failure between 1852 and 1870. His greatest success was with the economy, particularly in the 1850s. His government encouraged the new investment banks and massive railroad construction that were at the heart of the industrial revolution on the Continent. General economic expansion was also fostered by the government's ambitious program of public works, which included the rebuilding of Paris to improve the urban environment. The profits of businessmen soared with prosperity, and the working classes did not fare poorly either. Their wages more than kept up with inflation, and jobs were much easier to find. France's economy benefited from a worldwide economic boom and other external events, such as gold discoveries in California and Australia. Yet the contribution of Napoleon III's economic policies was real all the same.

Louis Napoleon always hoped that economic progress would reduce social and political tensions. This hope was at least partially realized. Until the mid-1860s there was little active opposition and even considerable support for his government from France's most dissatisfied group, the urban workers. Napoleon III's regulation of pawnshops and his support of credit unions and better housing for the working class were evidence of positive concern in the 1850s. In the 1860s, he granted workers the right to form unions and the right to strike – important economic rights denied by earlier governments.

At first, political power remained in the hands of the emperor. He alone chose his ministers, and they had great freedom of action. At the same time Napoleon III restricted but did not abolish the assembly. To be sure, the French parliament in the 1850s had little power. It could not initiate legislation, and it did not control the budget. Parliamentary sessions were not open to the public, and the government permitted only a dry summary of its debates to be published. Yet the members of the assembly were elected by universal male suffrage every six years. In each district the government put up its candidate and permitted opposition candidates, although it restricted speeches and discussions during the electoral campaigns.

Louis Napoleon and his government took the parliamentary elections very seriously. They tried to entice notable people, even those who had opposed the regime, to stand as government candidates in order to expand its base of support. Moreover, the government rewarded districts that elected government candidates. It used its officials and appointed mayors to spread the word that the election of the government's candidate was the key to roads, schools, tax rebates, and a thousand other local concerns.

In 1857 and again in 1863, Louis Napo-

REBUILDING PARIS *Cutting new boulevards through Paris was like smashing superhighways through cities today. Expensive and time-consuming, it brought massive demolitions, considerable slum clearance, and protests that the old city was being ruined.*

*In addition to expecting economic benefits, Napoleon III rightly believed that broad boulevards would be harder for revolutionaries to barricade than narrow twisting streets. (The Mansell Collection)*

leon's system worked well and produced overwhelming electoral victories. The poet-politician Alphonse de Lamartine was convinced that Louis Napoleon was France's greatest politician since Talleyrand, and possibly even greater than he. Yet in the course of the 1860s Napoleon III's electoral system gradually disintegrated, for several reasons. France's problems in Italy and the rising power of Prussia led to increasing criticism at home from his Catholic and nationalist supporters. With increasing effectiveness, the middle-class liberals who had always detested his dictatorship continued to denounce his rule as a disgrace to France's republican tradition.

Napoleon was always sensitive to the public mood. Public opinion, he once said, always wins the last victory. Thus in the 1860s he progressively "liberalized" his empire. He gave the assembly greater powers and the opposition candidates greater freedom, which

they used to good advantage. In 1869 the opposition, consisting of republicans, monarchists, and liberals, polled almost 45 percent of
the vote.

The following year a sick and weary Louis
Napoleon once again granted France a new
constitution, which combined a basically parliamentary regime with a hereditary emperor
as chief of state. In a final great plebiscite on
the eve of a disastrous war with Prussia, 7.5
million Frenchmen voted in favor of the new
constitution, and only 1.5 million opposed it.
Napoleon III's attempt to reconcile a strong
national state with universal manhood suffrage was still evolving, in a democratic direction.

## NATION BUILDING IN ITALY AND GERMANY

Louis Napoleon's triumph in 1848 and his
authoritarian rule in the 1850s provided the
old ruling classes of Europe with a new model
in politics. As the great Swiss historian Jacob
Burckhardt later noted, "Louis Napoleon had
risked universal suffrage for the elections, and
others followed his lead. The conservative
streak in the rural populations had been recognized, though no attempt had been made to
assess precisely how far it might be extended
from the elections to everything and everybody."[2] To what extent was it possible that
the expanding urban middle classes and even
the growing working classes might, like people in rural areas, rally to a strong and essentially conservative national state? This was
one of the great political questions in the
1850s and 1860s. In central Europe a re-
sounding and definitive answer came with the
national unification of Italy and Germany.

Italy had never been a united nation prior to
1860. Part of Rome's great empire in ancient
times, the Italian peninsula was divided in the
Middle Ages into competing city-states,
which led the commercial and cultural revival
of the West with amazing creativity. A battleground for great powers after 1494, Italy had
been reorganized in 1815 at the Congress of
Vienna. The rich northern provinces of Lombardy and Venetia were taken by Metternich's
Austria. Sardinia and Piedmont were under
the rule of an Italian monarch, and Tuscany
with its famous capital of Florence shared
north central Italy with several smaller states.
Central Italy and Rome were ruled by the papacy, which had always considered an independent political existence necessary to fulfill
its spiritual mission. Naples and Sicily were
ruled, as they had been for almost a hundred
years, by a branch of the Bourbons. Metternich was not wrong in dismissing Italy as "a
geographical expression" (see Map 25.1).

Between 1815 and 1848, the goal of a unified Italian nation captured the imaginations
of increasing numbers of Italians. There were
three basic approaches. The first was the radical program of the idealistic patriot Mazzini,
who preached a centralized democratic republic based on universal suffrage and the will of
the people. The second was that of Gioberti, a
Catholic priest, who called for a federation of
existing states under the presidency of a progressive pope. Finally, there were those who
looked for leadership toward the autocratic
kingdom of Sardinia-Piedmont, much as
many Germans looked toward Prussia.

The third alternative was strengthened by
the failures of 1848, when Austria smashed
and discredited Mazzini's republicanism. Almost by accident, Sardinia's monarch Victor

# IMPRESSIONISM AND URBAN SOCIETY

One of the greatest explosions of artistic genius since the Renaissance found many of its best subjects in the rich diversity of urban society. That explosion occurred in Paris and is known as French impressionism. Despite important individual differences, the impressionist painters wholeheartedly embraced modern life, reflecting western Europe's faith in science, progress, and democracy in the late nineteenth century.

Impressionism grew out of the search for realism in art. The impressionists sought to capture a given moment as the eye perceives it. To do so, they introduced many new techniques and outraged France's conservative artistic establishment. For example, they did not mix colors on the palette, but applied them directly to the canvas in well-defined strokes. Up close such a painting was a jumble, but at a distance the eye "mixed" the colors and saw the ultimate refinement in optical realism. The impressionists were also forerunners of abstract modern art, valuing color and abstract design for their own sake. Impressionism is the crucial bridge between "traditional" and "modern" painting.

The purest and perhaps the greatest of the impressionist painters was Claude Monet (1840–1926). Gare Saint Lazare, painted in 1877 (left), shows his fully developed style. Steam and early morning haze pervade the Paris train station with its vaulted roof of iron and glass, obscuring the buildings beyond. Monet painted this urban industrial scene seven times, at different hours of the day, to catch the ever-changing outdoor light and atmosphere. (Courtesy of the Fogg Art Museum, Harvard University. Bequest – collection of Maurice Wertheim, Class of 1906.)

*RED BOATS AT ARGENTEUIL* (above) Monet. The impressionists were city dwellers who often found the light and open air they admired in the suburbs of Paris. Monet rented a houseboat at the little holiday village of Argenteuil. There he and his friends painted the happy world of sailboats and weekend relaxation, of radiant sunshine and shimmering water shot through with reflections and many shades of blue. (Courtesy of the Fogg Art Museum, Harvard University. Bequest – Collection of Maurice Wertheim, Class of 1906.)

*LE MOULIN DE LA GALETTE À MONTMARTRE (1876)* (below) Renoir (1841-1919). Monet's good friend Auguste Renoir was a joyous painter whose whole work optimistically affirmed the beauty and value of modern life. In this masterpiece, painted for the third impressionist exhibition of 1877, Renoir has transformed a popular outdoor dance hall of the urban masses into a happy fairyland, where beautiful women and gallant men share the enchantment of music and romance. (Cliché des Musées Nationaux, Paris.)

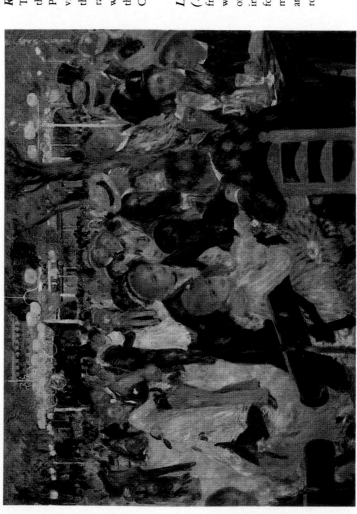

*THE HUMANITY OF DEGAS (1834–1917)*
While Renoir idealized life and women, the great artist Edgar Degas portrayed the range of urban classes and individuals with extraordinary sensitivity and realism. In *At The Races* (left, top), finished about 1870, wealthy, self-confident amateur sportsmen prepare for the starter's gun, while stylish young women rest in an elegant carriage. (Courtesy, Museum of Fine Arts, Boston.) Quite different is Degas's *Women Ironing* (left, bottom), which sympathetically captures the hard work and fatigue of unskilled labor. (Cliché des Musées Nationaux, Paris.)

*BOULEVARD DES ITALIENS* (below) Pissarro (1830–1903). This masterpiece from 1897 by the pure impressionist Camille Pissarro conveys the excitement and vitality of busy Paris boulevards, which brought all social groups together, at least momentarily. The aging Pissarro summed up his method in advice to a young painter: "Don't work bit by bit, but paint everything at once. Paint what you observe and feel." (National Gallery, Washington, D.C.)

*THE STARRY NIGHT* (above) Van Gogh (1853–1890). The tragic Dutchman Vincent van Gogh absorbed impressionism in Paris, but under the burning sun of southern France he went beyond portraying the world of external reality. In works like *The Starry Night* he feverishly painted his own inner world of intense emotion and wild imagination, thereby contributing greatly to the rise of expressionism in modern art. (Collection, the Museum of Modern Art, New York. Acquired through the Lillie P. Bliss Bequest.)

*THE WORLD OF TOULOUSE-LAUTREC (1864–1901)* Wealthy nobleman by birth and grotesque cripple by accident, Henri de Toulouse-Lautrec was drawn to the equally bizarre individuals who made Paris night life the scandal of Europe. *At the Moulin Rouge* (below, left), a group portrait of Lautrec and friends, evokes the atmosphere of Lautrec's favorite cabaret. (Helen Birch Bartlett Memorial Collection, Courtesy of the Art Institute of Chicago.) *A La Mie* (below, right), pictures an aging prostitute and her reptile-like companion. (Courtesy, Museum of Fine Arts, Boston.)

*THE CARD PLAYERS* (overleaf) Cezanne (1839–1906). An immensely important artist, Paul Cezanne rejected his early impressionistic style as too light and delicate. In *The Card Players* (1892) Cezanne shows the dignity of ordinary people in everyday life, as well as the devotion to form and solidity which made him the father of modern abstract art. (The Metropolitan Museum of Art: Bequest of Stephen C. Clark, 1960.)

AUSTRIAN EMPIRE

SWITZERLAND

FRANCE

*Kingdom of Sardinia before 1859*
*To Kingdom of Sardinia, 1859*
*To Kingdom of Sardinia, 1860*
*To Kingdom of Italy, 1866, 1870*
✕ *Major battle*

SAVOY
To France
1860

LOMBARDY

VENETIA
From Austria, 1866

Magenta ✕ •Milan
•Trieste

Turin•

PIEDMONT
Po

•Villafranca
✕ Solferino
Venice•

PARMA

MODENA

•Bologna

Genoa•

ROMAGNA

OTTOMAN EMPIRE

To France
1860 ►

KINGDOM

•Florence

THE MARCHES

NICE

OF

•Nice

Pisa•

TUSCANY

•Marseilles

SARDINIA

A D R I A T I C   S E A

Tiber

PAPAL STATES
(1870)
•Rome

CORSICA
(FRANCE)

•Naples

•Bari

•Taranto

SARDINIA

T Y R R H E N I A N   S E A

KINGDOM OF
THE TWO SICILIES

M E D I T E R R A N E A N   S E A

•Palermo

Straits of Messina

SICILY

0    50    100 Km.
0    50    100 Mi.

*MAP 25.1 THE UNIFICATION OF ITALY,
1859–1870 The leadership of Sardinia-Piedmont
and nationalist fervor were decisive factors in the
dramatic political unification of the Italian peninsula.*

Emmanuel retained the liberal constitution granted under duress in March 1848. This constitution provided for a fair degree of civil liberties and real parliamentary government, complete with elections and parliamentary control of taxes. To the Italian middle classes, Sardinia appeared to be a liberal, progressive state, ideally suited to achieve the goal of national unification. By contrast, Mazzini's brand of democratic republicanism seemed quixotic and too radical. As for the papacy, Pius IX's cautious support for unification had given way to fear and hostility during the upheavals of 1848. For a long generation, the papacy would stand resolutely opposed not only to national unification but to almost all modern trends.

## CAVOUR AND GARIBALDI

Sardinia had the good fortune of being led by a brilliant statesman, Count Camillo Benso di Cavour, the dominant figure in the Sardinian government from 1850 until his death in 1861. Cavour's development was an early sign of the coming tacit alliance between the aristocracy and the solid middle class throughout much of Europe. Beginning as a successful manager of his father's large landed estates in Piedmont, Cavour was also an economic liberal. He turned toward industry and made a substantial fortune in sugar mills, steamships, banks, and railroads. Economically secure, he then entered the world of politics and became chief minister in the liberalized Sardinian monarchy. Cavour's national goals were limited and realistic. Until 1859, he sought unity only for the states of northern and perhaps central Italy in a greatly expanded kingdom of Sardinia. It was not one of his goals to incorporate the papal states or the kingdom of the Two Sicilies, with their very different cultures

and governments, into an Italy of all the Italians. Cavour was a moderate nationalist.

In the 1850s, Cavour worked to consolidate Sardinia as a liberal state capable of leading northern Italy. His program of highways and railroads, of civil liberties and opposition to clerical privilege, increased support for Sardinia throughout nothern Italy. Yet Cavour realized that Sardinia could not drive Austria out of Lombardy and Venetia and unify northern Italy under Victor Emmanuel without the help of a powerful ally. He sought that ally in the person of Napoleon III, who sincerely believed in the general principle of nationality, as well as modest expansion for France.

In a complicated series of diplomatic maneuvers, Cavour in 1854 entered the Crimean War against Russia on the side of Great Britain and France, and tenaciously worked for a diplomatic alliance with Napoleon III against Austria. Finally, he succeeded. In July 1858, Cavour and Napoleon III agreed orally in the utmost secrecy that if Cavour could goad Austria into attacking Sardinia, France would come to Sardinia's "defense."

For a time Cavour feared that an international congress and a diplomatic compromise would thwart his plans. But in the end Austria obligingly issued an ultimatum and declared war. Napoleon III came to Sardinia's defense. Then, after the victory of the combined Franco-Sardinian forces, he did a complete about-face. Nauseated by the gore of war and criticized by French Catholics for supporting the pope's declared enemy, Napoleon III abandoned Cavour. He made a compromise peace with the Austrians at Villafranca in July 1859. Sardinia would receive only Lombardy, the area around Milan. The rest of the map of Italy would remain essentially unchanged. Cavour resigned in a rage.

Yet Cavour's plans were salvaged by popular revolts and Italian nationalism. While the war against Austria had raged in the north, dedicated nationalists in central Italy had risen and driven out their rulers. Nationalist fervor seized the urban masses. Large crowds demonstrated, chanting "Italy and Victor Emmanuel," and singing passionately, "Foreigners, get out of Italy!" Buoyed up by this enthusiasm, the leaders of the nationalist movement in central Italy ignored the compromise peace of Villafranca and called for fusion with Sardinia. This was not at all what France and the other Great Powers wanted, but the nationalists held firm and eventually had their way. Cavour returned to power in early 1860 and worked out a diplomatic deal with Napoleon III. The people of central Italy voted overwhelmingly to join a greatly enlarged kingdom of Sardinia. Cavour had achieved his original goal of a north Italian state (see Map 25.1).

For superpatriots like Giuseppe Garibaldi (1801–1882), the job of unification was still only half done. The son of a poor sailor, Garibaldi personified the romantic, revolutionary nationalism of Mazzini and 1848. As a lad of seventeen he had traveled to Rome and been converted to "the New Italy, the Italy of all the Italians." As he later wrote in his *Autobiography*, "The Rome that I beheld with the eyes of youthful imagination was the Rome of the future – the dominant thought of my whole life." Sentenced to death in 1834 for his part in an uprising in Genoa, Garibaldi escaped to South America. For twelve years he led a guerrilla band in Uruguay's struggle for independence. "Shipwrecked, ambushed, shot through the neck," he found in a tough young woman, Anna da Silva, a mate and companion in arms. Their first children nearly starved in the jungle while Garibaldi, clad in his long red shirt, fashioned a legend not unlike that of the Cuban Ché Guevara in recent times. He returned to Italy to fight in 1848, and led a corps of volunteers against Austria in 1859. By the spring of 1860, Garibaldi had emerged as a powerful independent force in Italian politics.

Partly to use him and partly to get rid of him, Cavour secretly supported Garibaldi's bold plan to "liberate" Sicily. Landing in Sicily in May 1860, Garibaldi's guerrilla band of a thousand "Red Shirts" captured the imagination of the Sicilian peasantry. Outwitting the twenty-thousand-man royal army, the guerrilla leader took Palermo. Then he and his men crossed to the mainland, marched triumphantly toward Naples, and prepared to attack Rome and the pope. But the wily Cavour quickly sent Sardinian forces to occupy most of the Papal States (but not Rome) and to intercept Garibaldi.

Cavour realized that an attack on Rome would bring about war with France, and he also feared Garibaldi's popular appeal. Therefore, he immediately organized a plebiscite in the conquered territories. Despite the urging of some of his more radical supporters, the patriotic Garibaldi did not oppose Cavour, and the people of the south voted to join Sardinia. When Garibaldi and Victor Emmanuel rode through Naples to cheering crowds, they symbolically sealed the union of north and south, of monarch and people.

Cavour had succeeded. He had controlled Garibaldi and had turned popular nationalism in a conservative direction. The new kingdom of Italy, which did not include Venice until 1866 or Rome until 1870, was neither radical nor democratic. Italy was a parliamentary monarchy under Victor Emmanuel, but in accordance with the Sardinian constitution only a small minority of Italians had the right to

GARIBALDI LANDING IN SICILY With a thousand volunteers the flamboyant Garibaldi conquered the kingdom of the Two Sicilies in 1860 and paved the way for Italian unification. (Historical Pictures Service, Chicago)

vote. There was a definite division between the propertied classes and the common people. There was also a great social and cultural gap between the progressive, industrializing north and the stagnant, agrarian south. This gap would increase, since peasant industries in the south would not be able to survive. Italy was united politically. Other divisions remained.

## GERMANY BEFORE BISMARCK

In the aftermath of 1848, while Louis Napoleon consolidated his rule and Cavour schemed, the German states were locked in a political stalemate. With Russian diplomatic support, Austria had blocked the halfhearted attempt of Frederick William IV of Prussia (1840–1861) to unify Germany "from above." This action contributed to a growing tension between Austria and Prussia, as each power sought to block the other within the reorganized German Confederation (pages 801 and 830). Stalemate also prevailed in the domestic politics of the individual states, as Austria, Prussia, and the smaller German kingdoms entered a period of reaction and immobility.

At the same time powerful economic forces were undermining the political status quo. As we have seen, modern industry grew rapidly in Europe throughout the 1850s. Nowhere was this growth more rapid than within the German customs union (Zollverein). Developing gradually under Prussian leadership after 1818 and founded officially in 1834 to stimulate trade and increase the revenues of member states, the customs union had not included Austria. After 1848, it became a crucial factor in the Austro-Prussian rivalry.

Tariff duties were substantially reduced so that Austria's highly protected industry could not bear to join. In retaliation, Austria tried to destroy the Zollverein by inducing the south German states to leave it, but without success. Indeed, by the end of 1853 all the German states except Austria had joined the customs union. A new Germany excluding Austria was becoming an economic reality, and the middle class and business groups were finding solid economic reasons to bolster their idealistic support of national unification. Thus, economic developments helped Prussia greatly in its struggle against Austria's traditional supremacy in German affairs.

The national uprising in Italy in 1859 made a profound impression in the German states. In Prussia, great political change and war — perhaps with Austria, perhaps with France — seemed quite possible. The tough-minded William I of Prussia (1858–1888), who had replaced the unstable Frederick William IV as regent in 1858 and became king in 1861, and his top military advisers were convinced of the need for major army reforms. William I wanted to double the size of the regular army. He also wanted to reduce the importance of the reserve militia, a semipopular force created during the Napoleonic wars. William had contempt for the "dirty reservists," those "civilians in uniform," who lacked efficiency and complete obedience. By drafting every young man into the army for three years, the king and his conservative supporters hoped to promote military attitudes in daily life. Of course, reform of the army meant a bigger defense budget and higher taxes.

Prussia had emerged from 1848 with a parliament of sorts, and by 1859 the Prussian parliament was in the hands of the liberal middle class. The middle class, like the landed aristocracy, was overrepresented by the Prussian electoral system, and it wanted society to be less, not more, militaristic. Above all, middle-class representatives wanted to establish

*OTTO VON BISMARCK   This photo accurately portrays Bismarck's ferocity and determination as a political fighter. Helmets and uniforms were worn by civilian officials as well as soldiers in Prussia. (Bettmann Archive)*

coach." King William considered abdicating in favor of his more liberal son. In the end, he called on Count Otto von Bismarck to head a ministry and defy the parliament. It was a momentous choice.

### BISMARCK TAKES COMMAND

The most important figure in German history between Luther and Hitler, Otto von Bismarck (1815–1898) has been the object of enormous interest and debate. Like his contemporary Abraham Lincoln, Bismarck stood at the very center of a nation's development in a critical era.

A great hero to some, a great villain to others, Bismarck was above all a master of politics. Born into the Prussian landowning aristocracy, the young Bismarck was a wild and tempestuous student, given to duels and drinking. Proud of his Junker heritage – "my fathers have been born and have lived and died in the same rooms for centuries" – and always devoted to his Prussian sovereign, Bismarck had a strong personality and an unbounded desire for power.

Bismarck entered the civil service, which was the only socially acceptable career except the army for a Prussian aristocrat. But he soon found bureaucratic life unbearable and fled to his ancestral estate. The civil servant was like a musician in an orchestra, he said, and "I want to play the tune the way it sounds to me or not at all. . . . My pride bids me command rather than obey."[3] Yet in his drive for power, power for himself and for Prussia, Bismarck was extraordinarily flexible and pragmatic. "One must always have two irons in the fire," he once said. He kept his options open, pursuing one policy and then another as he moved with skill and cunning toward his goal.

Bismarck first honed his political skills as a

once and for all that parliament, not the king, had the ultimate political power. They also wanted to insure that the army was responsible to the people and not "a state within a state." These demands were popular. The parliament rejected the military budget in 1862, and the liberals triumphed so completely in new elections that the conservatives "could ride to the parliament building in a single diplomat. Acquiring a reputation as an ultra-conservative in the Prussian assembly in 1848, he fought against Austria as the Prussian ambassador to the German Confederation from 1851 to 1859. Transferred next to St. Petersburg and then to Paris, Bismarck had an excellent opportunity to evaluate Alexander II and Napoleon III at close range. A blunt, expansive talker, especially after a few drinks, Bismarck's basic goal was well known in 1862 – to build up Prussia's strength and consolidate Prussia's precarious Great Power status.

To achieve this goal, Bismarck was convinced that Prussia had to control completely the northern, predominantly Protestant part of the German Confederation. He saw three possible paths open before him. He might work with Austria to divide up the smaller German states lying between them. Or he might combine with foreign powers – France and Italy, or even Russia – against Austria. Or he might ally with the forces of German nationalism to defeat and expel Austria from German affairs. Each possibility was explored in many complicated diplomatic maneuvers, but in the end the last path was the one Bismarck took.

That Bismarck would join with the forces of German nationalism to increase Prussia's power seemed unlikely when he took office in 1862. Bismarck's appointment made a strong but unfavorable impression. One of the liberal middle-class members of the Prussian parliament expressed enlightened public opinion throughout Prussia and the other German states: "Bismarck, that is to say: government without budget, rule by the sword in home affairs, and war in foreign affairs. I consider him the most dangerous Minister for Prussia's liberty and happiness."[4]

Bismarck's speeches were a sensation and a scandal. Declaring that the government would rule without parliamentary consent, Bismarck lashed out at the middle-class opposition: "The great questions of the day will not be decided by speeches and resolutions – that was the blunder of 1848 and 1849 – but by blood and iron." In 1863 he told the Prussian Parliament, "If a compromise cannot be arrived at and a conflict arises, then the conflict becomes a question of power. Whoever has the power then acts according to his opinion." Denounced for this view that "might makes right," Bismarck and the bureaucracy nevertheless collected taxes and reorganized the army. And for four years, from 1862 to 1866, the voters of Prussia continued to express their opposition by sending large liberal majorities to the parliament.

## THE AUSTRO-PRUSSIAN WAR OF 1866

Opposition at home spurred the search for success abroad. The ever-knotty question of Schleswig-Holstein provided a welcome opportunity. When the Danish king tried again, as in 1848, to bring the provinces into a centralized Danish state against the will of the German Confederation, Prussia joined Austria in a short and successful war against Denmark in 1864. Then, rather than following nationalist sentiment and allowing the conquered provinces to become another medium-sized independent state within the German Confederation, Bismarck maneuvered Austria into a tricky position. Prussia and Austria agreed to joint administration of the conquered provinces, thereby giving Bismarck a weapon he could use either to force Austria into peacefully accepting Prussian domination in northern Germany or to start a war against Austria.

Bismarck knew that a war with Austria would have to be a localized war. He had to be certain that Prussian expansion did not provoke a mighty armed coalition, such as the coalition that had almost crushed Frederick the Great in the eighteenth century. Russia, the great bear to the east, was no problem. Bismarck had already gained Alexander II's gratitude by supporting Russia's repression of a Polish uprising in 1863. Napoleon III – the "sphinx without a riddle," according to Bismarck – was another matter. But Bismarck charmed him into neutrality with vague promises of more territory along the Rhine. Thus, when Austria proved unwilling to give up its historic role in German affairs, Bismarck was in a position to engage in a war of his own making.

The Austro-Prussian War of 1866 lasted only seven weeks. Utilizing railroads to mass troops and the new breechloading needle gun for maximum firepower, the reorganized Prussian army overran northern Germany and defeated Austria decisively at the battle of Königgrätz in Bohemia. Anticipating Prussia's future needs, Bismarck offered Austria realistic, even generous, peace terms. Austria paid no reparations and lost no territory to Prussia, although Venice was ceded to Italy. But the German Confederation was dissolved, and Austria agreed to withdraw from German affairs. The states north of the Main River were grouped in a new North German Confederation led by an expanded Prussia. The mainly Catholic states of the south were permitted to remain independent, while forming military alliances with Prussia. Bismarck's fundamental goal of Prussian expansion was being realized (see Map 25.2).

## THE TAMING OF PARLIAMENT

Bismarck had long been convinced that the old order he so ardently defended should make peace – on its own terms – with the liberal middle class and the nationalist movement. Inspired somewhat by Louis Napoleon, he realized that nationalism was not necessarily hostile to conservative, authoritarian government. Moreover, Bismarck believed that because of the events of 1848 the German middle class could be led to prefer the reality of national unity to a long uncertain battle for truly liberal institutions. During the constitutional struggle over army reform and parliamentary authority, he had delayed but not abandoned this goal. Thus, during the attack on Austria in 1866 he increasingly identified Prussia's fate with the "national development of Germany."

In the aftermath of victory Bismarck fashioned a federal constitution for the new North German Confederation. Each state retained its own local government, but the king of Prussia was to be president of the confederation and the chancellor – Bismarck – was to be responsible only to the president. The federal government – William I and Bismarck – controlled the army and foreign affairs. There was also a legislature, consisting of an upper house whose delegates were appointed by the different states and a lower house. Both houses shared equally in the making of laws. Members of the lower house were elected by universal, equal manhood suffrage. With this radical innovation, Bismarck opened the door to popular participation and went over the head of the middle class directly to the people. All the while, however, ultimate power rested as securely as ever in the hands of Prussia and its king and army.

Events within Prussia itself were even more significant than those at the federal level. In the flush of victory the ultraconservatives expected Bismarck to suspend the Prussian constitution or perhaps abolish the Prussian parliament altogether. Yet he did nothing of

MAP 25.2 THE UNIFICATION OF GERMANY,
1866–1871 *This map deserves careful study. Note
how Prussian expansion, Austrian expulsion from the
old German Confederation, and the creation of a new
German Empire went hand in hand. Austria lost no
territory but Prussia's neighbors in the north suffered
grievously or simply disappeared.*

Sein erster Gedanke von Th. Th. Heine

Ueberschreiten der Geleise verboten!

Fatal! Jetzt kann ich nicht mehr Reserveoffizier sein.

*"His First Thought"* *This 1896 cartoon provides a brilliant commentary on German middle-class attitudes. Suddenly crippled, the man's first thought is "Disaster! Now I can no longer be an army reserve officer." Being a part-time junior officer, below the dominant aristocratic career officers, became a great middle-class status symbol. (Photo: Caroline Buckler)*

For four long years they had opposed and criticized Bismarck's "illegal" measures. And what had happened? Bismarck, the king, and the army had persevered, and in the end these conservative forces had succeeded beyond the wildest dreams of the liberal middle class. In 1866, German unity was in sight, and the people were going to be allowed to participate actively in the new state. Many liberals repented their "sins" and were overjoyed that Bismarck would forgive them.

None repented more ardently or more typically than Hermann Baumgarten, a mild-mannered, thoroughly decent history professor and member of the liberal opposition. In an essay entitled "A Self Criticism of German Liberalism," he confessed in 1866:

*We thought by agitation we could transform Germany. But . . . almost all the elements of our political system have been shown erroneous by the facts themselves. . . . Yet we have experienced a miracle almost without parallel. The victory of our principles would have brought us misery, whereas the defeat of our principles has brought boundless salvation.[5]*

The constitutional struggle was over. The German middle class was bowing respectfully before Bismarck and the monarchial authority and aristocratic superiority he represented. They did not stand upright again in the years before 1914.

### THE FRANCO-PRUSSIAN WAR OF 1870–1871

The rest of the story of German unification is anticlimactic. In 1867, Bismarck brought the four south German states into the customs union and established a customs parliament. But the south Germans were reluctant to go further because of their different religious and political traditions. Bismarck realized that a patriotic war with France would drive the

the sort. Instead, he held out an olive branch to the parliamentary opposition. Marshalling all his diplomatic skill, Bismarck asked the parliament to pass a special indemnity bill to approve after the fact all of the government's spending between 1862 and 1866. Most of the liberals snatched at the chance to cooperate.

south German states into his arms. The French obligingly played their part. The apparent issue – whether a distant relative of Prussia's William I (and France's Napoleon III) might become king of Spain – was only a diplomatic pretext. By 1870 the French leaders of the Second Empire, alarmed by their powerful new neighbor on the Rhine, had decided on a war to teach Prussia a lesson.

As soon as war against France began in 1870, Bismarck had the wholehearted support of the south German states. With other governments standing still – Bismarck's generosity to Austria in 1866 was paying big dividends – German forces under Prussian leadership decisively defeated Louis Napoleon's armies at Sedan on September 1, 1870. Three days later French patriots in Paris proclaimed yet another French republic and vowed to continue fighting. But after five months, in January 1871, a starving Paris surrendered, and France went on to accept Bismarck's harsh peace terms. By this time the south German states had agreed to join a new German Empire. The victorious William I was proclaimed emperor of Germany in the Hall of Mirrors in the palace of Versailles, outside of Paris. Europe had a nineteenth-century German "sun king." As in the 1866 constitution, the king of Prussia and his ministers had ultimate power in the new empire, and the lower house of the legislature was elected popularly by universal male suffrage.

The Franco-Prussian War of 1870–1871, which Europeans generally saw as a test of nations in a pitiless Darwinian struggle for existence, released an enormous surge of patriotic feeling in Germany. Bismarck's genius, the invincible Prussian army, the solidarity of king and people in a unified nation – these and similar themes were trumpeted endlessly during and after the war. The weakest of the Great Powers in 1862 – after Austria, Britain, France, and Russia – Prussia fortified by the other German states had become the most powerful state in Europe in less than a decade. Most Germans were enormously proud, enormously relieved. And they were somewhat drunk with success, blissfully imagining themselves the fittest and best of the European species. Semi-authoritarian nationalism had triumphed. Only a few critics remained dedicated to the liberal ideal of truly responsible parliamentary government.

## THE MODERNIZATION OF RUSSIA

In Russia, unlike Italy and Germany, there was no need to build a single state out of a jumble of principalities. The vast Russian Empire was a great multinational state. In the early nineteenth century, nationalism there was a subversive ideology identified with revolution. After 1853, however, old autocratic Russia was in serious trouble. It became clear to Russia's leaders that the country had to embrace the process of "modernization."

A vague and often overworked term, *modernization* is a great umbrella under which some writers place most of the major developments of the last two hundred or even five hundred years. Yet defined narrowly – as changes that enable a country to compete effectively with the leading countries at a given time – modernization can be a useful concept. It fits Russia after the Crimean War particularly well.

### THE "GREAT REFORMS"

In the 1850s, Russia was a poor agrarian society. Industry was little developed, and almost 90 percent of the population lived on

"FAREWELL," says the triumphant German soldier on the left in this French cartoon. "No, till we meet again," replies the French soldier. "Visits must be returned." German victory and Bismarck's seizure of French territory poisoned Franco-German relations after 1871. (Photo: Caroline Buckler)

the land. Agricultural techniques were backward: the ancient open-field system reigned supreme. Serfdom was still the basic social institution. Bound to the lord on a hereditary basis, the peasant serf was little more than a slave. Individual serfs and serf families were regularly sold, with and without land, in the early nineteenth century. Serfs were obliged to furnish labor services or money payments as the lord saw fit. Moreover, the lord could choose freely among them for army recruits, who had to serve for twenty-five years, and he could punish a serf with deportation to Si-

beria whenever he wished. Sexual exploitation of female serfs by their lords was common.

Serfdom had become the great moral and political question for the government by the 1840s, but it might still have lasted many more years had it not been for the Crimean War of 1853–1856. The war began as a dispute with France over who should protect certain Christian shrines in the Ottoman Empire. Because the fighting was concentrated in the Crimean peninsula in the Black Sea, Russia's transportation network of rivers and wagons failed to supply the distant Russian armies adequately. France and Great Britain, aided by Sardinia, inflicted a humiliating defeat on Russia.

The military defeat marked a turning point in Russian history. The Russian state had been built on the military, and Russia had not lost a major war for a century and a half. This defeat demonstrated that Russia had fallen behind the rapidly industrializing nations of western Europe in many areas. At the very least Russia needed railroads, better armaments, and reorganization of the army if it were to maintain its international position. Moreover, the disastrous war had caused hardship and raised the specter of massive peasant rebellion. Reform of serfdom was imperative. And, as the new tsar, Alexander II (1855–1881), told the serf owners, it would be better if reform came from above rather than below. Military disaster thus forced Alexander II and his ministers along the path of rapid social change and general modernization.

The first and greatest of the reforms was the freeing of the serfs in 1861. Human bondage was abolished forever, and the emancipated peasants received, on the average, about half of the land. Yet they had to pay fairly high prices for their land, and because the land was owned collectively each peasant village was jointly responsible for the payments of all the families in the village. The government hoped that collective responsibility would strengthen the peasant village as a social unit and prevent the development of a class of landless peasants. In practice, collective ownership and responsibility made it very difficult for individual peasants to improve agricultural methods or leave their villages. Thus the effects of the reform were limited, for it did not encourage peasants to change their old habits and attitudes.

Most of the later reforms were also halfway measures. In 1864, the government established a new institution of local government, the *zemstvo*. Members of this local assembly were elected by a three-class system of towns, peasant villages, and noble landowners. A zemstvo executive council dealt with local problems. The establishment of the zemstvos marked a significant step toward popular participation, and Russian liberals hoped it would lead to a national parliament. They were soon disappointed. The local zemstvo remained subordinate to the traditional bureaucracy and the local nobility, who were heavily favored by the property-based voting system. More successful was reform of the legal system, which established independent courts and equality before the law. "Almost overnight it transformed the Russian judiciary from one of the worst to one of the best in the civilized world."[6] Education was also liberalized somewhat, and censorship was relaxed but not removed.

## THE INDUSTRIALIZATION OF RUSSIA

Until the twentieth century, Russia's greatest strides toward modernization were economic rather than political. Industry and transport, both so vital to the military, were transformed in two industrial surges. The first of these came after 1860. The government encouraged and subsidized private railway companies, and construction boomed. In 1860, the empire had only about 1,250 miles of railroads; by 1880, it had about 15,500 miles. The railroads enabled agricultural Russia to export grain and thus earn money for further industrialization. Domestic manufacturing was stimulated, and by the end of the 1870s Russia had a sophisticated and well-developed railway-equipment industry. Industrial suburbs grew up around Moscow and St. Petersburg, and a class of modern factory workers began to take shape.

Industrial development strengthened Russia's military forces and gave rise to territorial expansion to the south and east. Imperial expansion greatly excited many ardent Russian nationalists and superpatriots, who became some of the government's most enthusiastic supporters. Industrial development also contributed mightily to the spread of Marxian thought and the transformation of the Russian revolutionary movement after 1890.

In 1881, Alexander II was assassinated by a small group of terrorists. The era of reform came to an abrupt end, for the new tsar, Alexander III (1881–1894), was a determined reactionary. Russia, and indeed all of Europe, experienced hard times economically in the 1880s. Political modernization remained frozen until 1905, but economic modernization sped forward in the massive industrial surge of the 1890s. As it had after the Crimean War, nationalism played a decisive role. The key leader was Sergei Witte, the tough, competent minister of finance from 1892 to 1903. Early in his career Witte found in the writings of Friedrich List (page 779) an analysis and a program for action. List had stressed the peril for Germany of remaining behind England in the 1830s and 1840s. Witte saw the same threat of industrial backwardness threatening Russia's power and greatness.

*Novgorod Merchants Drinking Tea   This photograph from the late nineteenth century suggests how Russian businessmen were slow to abandon old-fashioned dress and traditional attitudes in the face of change. Stern authoritarians in the family circle and staunchly devoted to church and tsar, Russian businessmen were often suspicious of foreigners as well as of the lawyers and journalists who claimed to speak for the nation's middle class. (BBC Hulton Picture Library)*

Witte moved forward on several fronts. A railroad manager by training, he believed that railroads were "a very powerful weapon . . . for the direction of the economic development of the country."[7] Therefore the government built railroads rapidly, doubling the network to 35,000 miles by the end of the century. The gigantic trans-Siberian line connecting Moscow with Vladivostok on the Pacific Ocean 5,000 miles away was Witte's pride, and it was largely completed during his term of office. Following List's advice, Witte raised high protective tariffs to build Russian industry, and he put the country on the gold standard of the "civilized world" in order to strengthen Russian finances.

Witte's greatest innovation, however, was to use the West to catch up with the West. He aggressively encouraged foreigners to use their abundant capital and advanced technology to build great factories in backward Russia. As he told the tsar, "The inflow of foreign capital is . . . the only way by which our industry will be able to supply our country quickly with abundant and cheap products."[8] This policy was brilliantly successful, especially in southern Russia. There, in the eastern Ukraine, foreign capitalists and their engineers built an enormous and very modern steel and coal industry almost from scratch in little more than a decade. By 1900, only the United States, Germany, and Great Britain were producing more steel than Russia. The Russian petroleum industry had even pulled up alongside that of the United States and was producing and refining half the world's output of oil.

Witte knew how to keep foreigners in line.

Once a leading foreign businessman came to him and angrily demanded that the Russian government fulfill a contract it had signed and pay certain debts immediately. Witte asked to see the contract. He read it and then carefully tore it to pieces and threw it in the wastepaper basket without a word of explanation. It was just such a fiercely independent Russia that was catching up with the advanced nations of the West.

## THE REVOLUTION OF 1905

Catching up partly meant vigorous territorial expansion, for this was the age of Western imperialism. By 1903, Russia had established a sphere of influence in Chinese Manchuria and was casting greedy eyes on northern Korea. When the protests of equally imperialistic Japan went unanswered, the Japanese launched a surprise attack in February 1904. To the world's amazement, Russia suffered repeated losses and was forced to accept a humiliating defeat in August 1905.

As is often the case, military disaster abroad brought political upheaval at home. The business and professional classes had long wanted to match economic modernization with political modernization. Their minimal goal was to turn the last of Europe's absolutist monarchies into a liberal, representative regime. Factory workers, strategically concentrated in the large cities, had all the grievances of early industrialization and were organized in a radical labor movement. Peasants had gained little from the era of reforms and were suffering from poverty and overpopulation. Finally, nationalist sentiment was emerging among the empire's minorities. The politically and culturally dominant ethnic Russians were only about 45 percent of the population, and by 1900 some intellectuals among the subject nationalities were calling for self-rule and au-

tonomy. Separatist nationalism was strongest among the Polish and Ukrainians. With the army pinned down in Manchuria, all these currents of discontent came together in the revolution of 1905.

The beginning of the revolution pointed up the incompetence of the government. On a Sunday in January 1905, a massive demonstration of workers and their families converged peacefully on the Winter Palace in St. Petersburg to present a petition to the tsar. The workers were led by a trade unionist priest named Father Gapon, who had been secretly supported by the police as a preferable alternative to more radical unions. Carrying icons and respectfully singing "God Save the Tsar," the workers did not know Nicholas II had fled the city. Suddenly troops opened fire, killing and wounding hundreds. The "Bloody Sunday" massacre turned ordinary workers against the tsar and produced a wave of general indignation.

Outlawed political parties came out into the open, and by the summer of 1905 strikes, peasant uprisings, revolts among minority nationalities, and troop mutinies were sweeping the country. The revolutionary surge culminated in October 1905 in a great paralyzing general strike, which forced the government to capitulate. The tsar issued the October Manifesto, which granted full civil rights and promised a popularly elected Duma (parliament) with real legislative power. The Manifesto split the opposition. It satisfied most moderate and liberal demands, but the Social Democrats rejected it and led a bloody workers' uprising in Moscow in December 1905. Frightened middle-class moderates helped the government repress the uprising and survive as a constitutional monarchy.

On the eve of the opening of the first Duma in May 1906, the government issued the new constitution, the Fundamental Laws.

The tsar retained great powers. The Duma, elected indirectly by universal male suffrage, and a largely appointive upper house could debate and pass laws, but the tsar had an absolute veto. As in Bismarck's Germany, the emperor appointed his ministers, who did not need to command a majority in the Duma.

The disappointed, predominantly middle-class liberals, the largest group in the newly elected Duma, saw the Fundamental Laws as a great step backwards. Efforts to cooperate with the tsar's ministers soon broke down. The government then dismissed the Duma, only to find that a more hostile and radical opposition was elected in 1907. After three months of deadlock, the second Duma was also dismissed. Thereupon the tsar and his reactionary advisors unilaterally rewrote the electoral law so as to increase greatly the weight of the propertied classes at the expense of workers, peasants, and national minorities.

The new law had the intended effect. With landowners assured half the seats in the Duma, the government finally secured a loyal majority in 1907 and again in 1912. Thus armed, the tough, energetic chief minister, Peter Stolypin, pushed through important agrarian reforms designed to break down collective village ownership of land and to encourage the more enterprising peasants – the so-called "wager on the strong." On the eve of the First World War, Russia was partially modernized, a conservative constitutional monarchy with a peasant-based but industrializing economy.

## THE RESPONSIVE NATIONAL STATE, 1871–1914

For central and western Europe, the unification of Italy and Germany by "blood and iron" marked the end of a dramatic period of nation building. After 1871, the heartland of Europe was organized in strong national states. Only on the borders of Europe – in Ireland and Russia, in Austria-Hungary and the Balkans – did subject peoples still strive for political unity and independence. Despite national differences, European domestic politics after 1871 had a common framework – the firmly established national state. The common themes within that framework were the emergence of mass politics and growing mass loyalty toward the national state.

For good reason, ordinary people – the masses of an industrializing, urbanizing society – felt increasing loyalty to their governments. More and more people could vote. By 1914, universal manhood suffrage was the rule rather than the exception. This development had as much psychological as political significance. Ordinary men were no longer denied the right to vote because they lacked wealth or education. They counted; they could influence the government to some extent. They could feel that they were becoming "part of the system."

Women began to demand the right to vote. The women's suffrage movement achieved its first success in the western United States, and by 1913 women could vote in twelve states. Europe too moved slowly in this direction. In 1914, Norway gave the vote to most women. Elsewhere, women like the English Emmeline Pankhurst were very militant in their demands. They heckled politicians and held public demonstrations. These efforts generally failed before 1914, but they prepared the way for the triumph of the women's suffrage movement immediately after World War One.

As the right to vote spread, politicians and parties in national parliaments represented the people more responsively. Most countries soon had many political parties. The multi-

THE GERMAN REICHSTAG IN 1871 *Bismarck (second from left on the floor) presents the government's program to the new Reichstag. The creation of a national parliament, duly elected by universal* *manhood suffrage, convinced many that Germany was making healthy progress. (Bildarchiv Preussischer Kulturbisitz)*

party system meant that parliamentary majorities were built on shifting coalitions, which were unstable but did give parties leverage. They could obtain benefits for their supporters. Governments increasingly passed laws to alleviate general problems and to help specific groups. Governments seemed to care, and they seemed more worthy of support.

## THE GERMAN EMPIRE

Politics in Germany after 1871 reflected many of these developments. The new German Empire was a federal union of Prussia and twenty-four smaller states. Much of the everyday business of government was conducted by the separate states, but there was a strong national government with a chancellor – Bismarck until 1890 – and a popularly elected parliament, called the Reichstag. Although Bismarck refused to be bound by a parliamentary majority, he tried nonetheless to maintain such a majority. This situation gave the political parties opportunities. Until 1878, Bismarck relied mainly on the National Liberals, who had rallied to him after 1866. They supported legislation useful for further economic and legal unification of the country.

Less wisely, they backed Bismarck's attack on the Catholic church, the so-called *Kulturkampf,* or "struggle for civilization." Like Bismarck, the middle-class National Liberals were alarmed by Pius IX's declaration of papal infallibility in 1870. That dogma seemed to put loyalty to the church above loyalty to the nation. Only in Protestant Prussia did the *Kulturkampf* have even limited success. Catholics throughout the country generally voted for the Catholic Center party, which blocked passage of national laws hostile to the church. Finally, in 1878, Bismarck abandoned his attack. Indeed, he and the Catholic Center party entered into an uneasy but mutually advantageous alliance. The reasons were largely economic.

After a worldwide financial bust in 1873, European agriculture was in an increasingly difficult position. Wheat prices plummeted as cheap grain poured in from the United States, Canada, and Russia. New lands were opening up in North America and Russia, and the combination of railroads and technical improvements in shipping cut freight rates drastically for grain. European peasants with their smaller, less efficient farms could not compete in cereal production, especially in western and southern Germany. The peasantry there was largely Catholic, and the Catholic Center party was thus converted to the cause of higher tariffs to protect the economic interests of its supporters.

The same competitive pressures caused the Protestant Junkers who owned large estates in eastern Germany to embrace the cause of higher tariffs. They were joined by some of the iron and steel magnates of the Prussian Rhineland, who had previously been for free trade. With three such influential groups lobbying energetically, Bismarck was happy to go along with a new protective tariff in 1879. In doing so he won new supporters in parliament – the Center party of the Catholics and the Conservative party of the Prussian landowners – and he held on to most of the National Liberals.

Bismarck had been looking for a way to increase taxes and raise more money for the government. The solution was higher tariffs. Many other governments acted similarly. The 1880s and 1890s saw a widespread return to protectionism. France in particular established very high tariffs to protect agriculture and industry, peasants and manufacturers. Thus, the German government and other governments responded to a major economic problem and simultaneously won greater loyalty.

At the same time, Bismarck tried to stop the growth of German socialism because he genuinely feared its revolutionary language and allegiance to a movement transcending the nation state. In 1878, after two attempts on the life of William I by radicals (though not socialists), Bismarck succeeded in ramming through the Reichstag a law repressing socialists. Socialist meetings and publications were strictly forbidden. The Social Democratic party was outlawed and driven underground. However, German socialists displayed a discipline and organization worthy of the Prussian army itself. Bismarck had to try another tack.

Thus Bismarck's state pioneered with social measures designed to win the support of working-class people. In 1883, he pushed through the parliament the first of several modern social security laws to help wage earners. The laws of 1883 and 1884 established national sickness and accident insurance; the law of 1889 established old-age pensions and retirement benefits. Henceforth, sick, injured, and retired workers could look forward to regular weekly benefits from the state. This national social security system, paid for through compulsory contributions by wage earners and employers as well as grants from the state, was the first of its kind anywhere. It was to be fifty years before similar measures would be taken in the United States. Bismarck's social security system did not wean workers from socialism, but it did protect them from some of the uncertainties of the complex urban industrial world. This enormously significant development was a product of political competition and governmental efforts to win popular support.

Increasingly, the great issues in German domestic politics were socialism and the Marxian Social Democratic party. In 1890 the new emperor, the young, idealistic, and unstable William II (1888–1918), opposed Bismarck's attempt to renew the law outlawing the Social Democratic party. Eager to rule in his own right, as well as to earn the support of the workers, William II forced Bismarck to resign. After the "dropping of the pilot," German foreign policy changed profoundly and mostly for the worse, but the government did pass new laws to aid workers and to legalize socialist political activity.

Yet William II was no more successful than Bismarck in getting workers to renounce socialism. Indeed, socialist ideas spread rapidly, and more and more Social Democrats were elected to the parliament in the 1890s. After opposing a colonial war in German Southwest Africa in 1906 and thus suffering important losses in the general elections of 1907, the German Social Democratic party broadened its base in the years before World War One. In the elections of 1912 the party scored a great victory, becoming the largest single party in the Reichstag. The "revolu-

tionary" socialists were, however, becoming less and less revolutionary in Germany. In the years before World War One, the strength of socialist opposition to greater military spending and imperialist expansion declined greatly. German socialists marched under the national banner.

## REPUBLICAN FRANCE

In 1871, France seemed hopelessly divided once again. The patriotic republicans who proclaimed the Third Republic in Paris after the military disaster at Sedan refused to admit defeat. They defended Paris with great heroism for weeks, living off rats and zoo animals, until they were quite literally starved into submission by German armies in January 1871. When national elections then sent a large majority of conservatives and monarchists to the National Assembly, the traumatized Parisians exploded and proclaimed the Paris Commune in March 1871. Vaguely radical, the leaders of the Commune wanted to govern Paris without interference by the conservative French countryside. The National Assembly, led by the aging politician Adolphe Thiers, would hear none of it. The Assembly ordered the French army into Paris and brutally crushed the Commune. Twenty thousand people died in the fighting. As in June 1848, it was Paris against the provinces, French against French.

Out of this tragedy France slowly formed a new national unity, achieving considerable stability before 1914. How is one to account for this? Luck played a part. Until 1875, the monarchists in the "republican" National Assembly had a majority but could not agree who should be king. The compromise Bourbon candidate refused to rule except under the white flag of his ancestors – a completely un-

THE FACE OF CIVIL WAR *Enraged radicals and anarchists set countless fires as the French army smashed the troops of the Paris Commune, which are pictured here. Most fire bombers were women. Terrible atrocities were committed on both sides. (Photo: Caroline Buckler)*

acceptable condition. In the meantime Thiers' slaying of the radical Commune and his other firm measures showed the fearful provinces and the middle class that the Third Republic might be moderate and socially conservative. France therefore retained the republic, though reluctantly and unenthusiastically. As President Thiers cautiously said, it was "the government which divides us least."

Another stabilizing factor was the skill and determination of the moderate republican leaders in the early years. The most famous of these was Léon Gambetta, the son of an Italian grocer, a warm, easygoing, unsuccessful lawyer turned professional politician. A master of emerging mass politics, Gambetta combined eloquence with the personal touch as he preached a republic of truly equal opportunity. Gambetta was also instrumental in establishing absolute parliamentary supremacy between 1877 and 1879, when the somewhat autocratic President Marie Edmé MacMahon was forced to resign. By 1879, the great majority of members of both the upper and lower houses of parliament were republicans. Although these republicans were split among many parliamentary groups and later several parties – a situation that led to constant coalition politics and the rapid turnover of ministers – the Third Republic had firm foundations after almost a decade.

The moderate republicans sought to preserve their creation by winning the hearts and minds of the next generation. Trade unions were fully legalized, and France acquired a colonial empire. More importantly, under the leadership of Jules Ferry, the moderate republicans of small towns and villages passed a series of laws between 1879 and 1886 establishing free compulsory elementary education for both girls and boys. At the same time, they greatly expanded the state system of public tax-supported schools.

This was a fundamental change. Most elementary and much secondary education had traditionally been in the parochial schools of the Catholic church, which had long been hostile to republics and to much of secular life. Free compulsory elementary education in France became secular republican education. The pledge of allegiance and the national anthem replaced the catechism and the *Ave Maria*. Militant young elementary teachers carried the ideology of patriotic republicanism into every corner of France. In their classes they sought to win the loyalty of the young citizens to the republic, so that France would never again vote en masse for dictators like the two Napoleons.

Although these educational reforms disturbed French Catholics, many of them rallied to the republic in the 1890s. The limited acceptance of the modern world by the more liberal Pope Leo XIII (1878-1903) eased tensions between church and state. Unfortunately, the Dreyfus affair changed all that.

Alfred Dreyfus, a Jewish captain in the French army, was falsely accused and convicted of treason. His family never doubted his innocence and fought unceasingly to reopen the case, enlisting the support of prominent republicans and intellectuals such as the novelist Emile Zola. In 1898 and 1899, the case split France apart. On one side was the army, which had manufactured evidence against Dreyfus, joined by anti-Semites and most of the Catholic establishment. On the other side stood the civil libertarians and most of the more radical republicans.

This battle, which eventually led to Dreyfus's being declared innocent, revived republican feeling against the church. Between 1901 and 1905, the government severed all ties between the state and the Catholic church. The salaries of priests and bishops were no longer paid by the government, and all churches were given to local committees of lay Catholics. Catholic schools were put completely on their own financially, and in a short time they lost a third of their students. The state school system's power of indoctrination was greatly strengthened. In France only the growing socialist movement, with its very different and thoroughly secular ideology, stood in opposition to patriotic, republican nationalism.

## GREAT BRITAIN AND IRELAND

Britain in the late nineteenth century has often been seen as a shining example of peaceful and successful political evolution. Germany had gotten stuck with a manipulated parliament that gave an irresponsible emperor too much power; France had a quarrelsome parliament that gave its presidents too little power. Great Britain, in contrast, seemed to enjoy an effective two-party parliament that skillfully guided the country from classical liberalism to full-fledged democracy with hardly a misstep.

This view of Great Britain is not so much wrong as incomplete. The right to vote, granted to males of the solid middle class in 1832, was further extended to all middle-class men and the best-paid workers by Prime Minister Benjamin Disraeli and the Conservatives via the Second Reform Bill of 1867. The son of a Jewish stockbroker, himself a novelist and urban dandy, the ever-fascinating Disraeli (1804–1881) was willing to risk this "leap in the dark" in order to gain new supporters. The Conservative party, he believed, needed to broaden its traditional base of aristocratic and landed support if it was to survive. After 1867 English political parties and electoral campaigns became more modern, and the "lower orders" appeared to vote as responsibly as their "betters." Hence the

Third Reform Bill of 1884 gave the vote to almost every adult male.

While the House of Commons was drifting toward democracy, the House of Lords was content to slumber nobly. Between 1901 and 1910, however, that bastion of aristocratic conservatism tried to reassert itself. Acting as supreme court of the land, it ruled against labor unions in two important decisions. And, after the Liberal party came to power in 1906, the Lords vetoed several measures passed by the Commons, including the so-called People's Budget. The Lords finally capitulated, as they had done in 1832, when the king threatened to create enough new peers to pass the bill.

Aristocratic conservatism yielded to popular democracy, once and for all. The result was that extensive social welfare measures, slow to come to Great Britain, were passed in a spectacular rush between 1906 and 1914. During those years the Liberal party, inspired by the fiery Welshman David Lloyd George (1863–1945), substantially raised taxes on the rich as part of the People's Budget. This income helped the government pay for national health insurance, unemployment benefits, old-age pensions, and a host of other social measures. The state was integrating the urban masses socially as well as politically.

This record of accomplishment was only part of the story, though. On the eve of World War One the ever-emotional, ever-unanswered question of Ireland brought Great Britain to the brink of civil war. In the 1840s Ireland had been decimated by famine, which fueled an Irish revolutionary movement. Thereafter, the English slowly granted concessions, such as the abolition of the privileges of the Anglican church and rights for Irish peasants. The Liberal prime minister William Gladstone (1809–1898), who had proclaimed twenty years earlier that "my mission is to pacify Ireland," introduced bills to give Ireland self-government in 1886 and in 1893. They failed to pass. After two decades of relative quiet, Irish nationalists in the British Parliament saw their chance. They supported the Liberals in their battle for the People's Budget and received passage of a home-rule bill for Ireland in return.

Thus Ireland, the emerald isle, achieved self-government – but not quite, for Ireland is composed of two peoples. As much as the Irish Catholic majority in the southern counties wanted home rule, precisely that much did the Irish Protestants of the northern counties of Ulster come to oppose it. Motivated by the accumulated fears and hostilities of generations, the Protestants of Ulster refused to submerge themselves in a Catholic Ireland, just as Irish Catholics had refused to submerge themselves in a Protestant Britain.

The Ulsterites vowed to resist home rule in northern Ireland. By December 1913 they had raised 100,000 armed volunteers, and they were supported by much of English public opinion. Thus in 1914 the Liberals in the House of Lords introduced a compromise home-rule law that did not apply to the northern counties. This bill, which openly betrayed promises made to Irish nationalists, was rejected and in September the original home-rule plan was passed but simultaneously suspended for the duration of hostilities. The momentous Irish question had been overtaken by earth-shattering world war in August 1914.

Irish developments illustrated once again the power of national feeling and national movements in the nineteenth century. Moreover, they were proof that governments could not elicit greater loyalties unless they could capture and control that elemental current of national feeling. Though Great Britain had much going for it – power, Parliament, pros-

perity – none of these availed in the face of Irish nationalism in its Catholic and Protestant versions. Similarly, progressive Sweden was powerless to stop the growth of the Norwegian national movement, which culminated in Norway's breaking away from Sweden and becoming a fully independent nation in 1905. In this light, one can also see how hopeless was the case of the Ottoman Empire in Europe in the later nineteenth century. It was only a matter of time before the Serbs, the Bulgarians, and the Rumanians would break away, and they did.

## THE AUSTRO-HUNGARIAN EMPIRE

The dilemma of conflicting nationalisms in Ireland also helps one appreciate how desperate the situation in the Austro-Hungarian Empire had become by the early twentieth century. In 1849 Magyar nationalism had driven Hungarian patriots to declare an independent Hungarian republic, which was savagely crushed by Russian and Austrian armies (pages 829–830). Throughout the 1850s Hungary was ruled as a conquered territory, and Emperor Francis Joseph and his bureaucracy tried hard to centralize the state and "Germanize" the language and culture of the different nationalities.

Then, in the wake of defeat by Prussia in 1866, a weakened Austria was forced to strike a compromise and establish the so-called dual monarchy. The empire was divided in two and the nationalistic Magyars gained virtual independence for Hungary. Henceforth each half of the empire agreed to deal with its own "barbarians" – its own minorities – as it saw fit. The two states were joined only by a shared monarch and common ministries for finance, defense, and foreign affairs. After 1867, the disintegrating force of competing nationalisms continued unabated, for both

Austria and Hungary had several "Irelands" within their borders.

In Austria, ethnic Germans were only one-third of the population, and by the late 1890s many Germans saw their traditional dominance threatened by Czechs, Poles, and other Slavs. A particularly emotional and divisive issue in the Austrian parliament was the language used in government and elementary education at the local level. From 1900 to 1914, the parliament was so divided that ministries generally could not obtain a majority and ruled instead by decree. Efforts by both conservatives and socialists to defuse national antagonisms by stressing economic issues cutting across ethnic lines – which led to the introduction of universal male suffrage in 1907 – proved largely unsuccessful.

One aspect of such national antagonisms was anti-Semitism, which was particularly virulent in Austria. The Jewish populations of Austrian cities grew very rapidly after Jews obtained full legal equality in 1867, reaching 10 percent of the population of Vienna by 1900. Many Jewish businessmen were quite successful in banking and retail trade, while Jewish artists, intellectuals, and scientists, like the world-famous Sigmund Freud, played a major role in making Vienna a leading center of European culture and modern thought. When extremists charged the Jews with controlling the economy and corrupting German culture with alien ideas and ultra-modern art, anxious Germans of all classes tended to listen. The popular mayor of Vienna from 1897 to 1910, Dr. Karl Lueger, combined anti-Semitic rhetoric with calls for "Christian socialism" and municipal ownership of basic services. Lueger appealed especially to the German lower middle class – and to an unsuccessful young artist named Adolf Hitler.

In Hungary, the Magyar nobility in 1867 restored the constitution of 1848 and used it to dominate both the Magyar peasantry and the minority populations until 1914. Only the wealthiest fourth of adult males had the right to vote, making the parliament the creature of the Magyar elite. Laws promoting use of the Magyar (Hungarian) language in schools and government were rammed through and bitterly resented, especially by the Croatians and Rumanians. While Magyar extremists campaigned loudly for total separation from Austria, the radical leaders of the subject nationalities dreamed in turn of independence from Hungary. Unlike most major countries, which were able to harness nationalism to strengthen the state after 1871, the Austro-Hungarian Empire was progressively weakened and eventually destroyed by it.

## THE SOCIALIST MOVEMENT

Nationalism served, for better or worse, as a new unifying principle. But what about socialism? Did the rapid growth of socialist parties, which were generally Marxian parties, dedicated to an international proletarian revolution, mean that national states had failed to gain the support of workers? Certainly, many prosperous and conservative citizens were greatly troubled by the socialist movement. And many historians have portrayed the years before 1914 as a time of ever-increasing conflict between revolutionary socialism on the one hand and a nationalist alliance between conservative aristocracy and the prosperous middle class on the other. This question requires close examination.

### THE SOCIALIST INTERNATIONAL

The growth of socialist parties after 1871 was phenomenal. Neither Bismarck's antisocialist laws nor his extensive social security system checked the growth of the German Social Democratic party, which espoused the Marxian ideology. By 1912, it had attracted millions of followers and was the largest party in the parliament. Socialist parties also grew in other countries, though nowhere else with quite such success. In 1883, Russian exiles in Switzerland founded the Russian Social Democratic party, which grew rapidly in the 1890s and thereafter despite internal disputes. In France various socialist parties re-emerged in the 1880s after the carnage of the Commune. Most of them were finally unified in a single, increasingly powerful Marxian party, called the French Section of the Workers International in 1905. Belgium and Austria-Hungary also had strong socialist parties of the Marxian persuasion.

As the name of the French party suggests, Marxian socialist parties were eventually linked together in an international organization. As early as 1848, Marx had declared in the *Communist Manifesto* that "the working men have no country," and he had urged proletarians of all nations to unite against their governments. Joining the flood of radicals and republicans who fled continental Europe for England and America after the revolutions of 1848, Marx settled in London. Poor and depressed, he lived on his meager earnings as a journalist and the gifts of his friend Engels. Marx never stopped thinking of revolution. Digging deeply into economics and history, he concluded that revolution follows economic crisis, and tried to prove it in *Critique of Political Economy* (1859) and his greatest theoretical work *Capital* (1867).

The bookish Marx also excelled as a practical organizer. In 1864, Marx played an important role in founding the First International of socialists – the International Working Men's Association. In the following years he

SOCIALIST PROPAGANDA, RUSSIAN STYLE   "We work for you; we feed you," groan the masses. "We eat for you," boast the wealthy. Above, the army ("We shoot you"), the church ("We deceive you"), the bureaucracy ("We govern you"), and the monarchy ("We rule over you") all exploit the workers and the peasants. (Courtesy, Thames and Hudson Ltd., from The Nineteenth Century, *edited by Asa Briggs, 1970)*

battled successfully to control the organization and used its annual meetings as a means of spreading his realistic, "scientific" doctrines of inevitable socialist revolution. Then Marx enthusiastically embraced the passionate, vaguely radical patriotism of the Paris Commune and its terrible conflict with the French National Assembly as a giant step toward socialist revolution. This impetuous action frightened many of his early supporters, especially the more moderate British labor leaders. The First International collapsed.

Yet international proletarian solidarity remained an important objective for Marxists. In 1889, as the individual parties in different countries grew stronger, socialist leaders came together to form the Second International, which lasted until 1914. Although the International was only a federation of various national socialist parties, it had great psychological impact. Every three years delegates from the different parties met to interpret Marxian doctrines and plan coordinated action. May 1 – May Day – was declared an annual international one-day strike, a day of marches and demonstrations. A permanent executive for the International was established. Many feared and many others rejoiced in the growing power of socialism and the Second International.

## UNIONS AND REVISIONISM

Was socialism really radical and revolutionary in these years? On the whole, it was not. Indeed, as socialist parties grew and attracted large numbers of members, they looked more and more toward gradual change and steady improvement for the working class, less and less toward revolution. The mainstream of European socialism became militantly moderate; that is, they increasingly combined radical rhetoric with sober action.

Workers themselves were progressively less inclined to follow radical programs. There were several reasons for this. As workers gained the right to vote and to participate politically in the nation state, their attention focused more on elections than on revolutions. And as workers won real, tangible benefits, this furthered the process. Workers were not immune to patriotic education and indoctrination during military service, however ar-

dently socialist intellectuals might wish the contrary. Nor were workers a unified social group, as we have seen in Chapter 24.

Perhaps most important of all, workers' standard of living rose substantially after 1850 as the promise of the Industrial Revolution was at least partially realized. In Great Britain, for example, workers could buy almost twice as much with their wages in 1906 as in 1850, and most of the increase came after 1870. Workers experienced similar increases in most continental countries after 1850, though much less strikingly in late-developing Russia. Improvement in the standard of living was much more than merely a matter of higher wages. The quality of life improved dramatically in urban areas. For all these reasons, workers tended more and more to become militantly moderate: they demanded gains, but they were less likely to take to the barricades in pursuit of them.

The growth of labor unions reinforced this trend toward moderation. In the early stages of industrialization, modern unions were generally prohibited by law. A famous law of the French Revolution had declared all guilds and unions illegal in the name of "liberty" in 1791. In Great Britain, attempts by workers to unite were considered criminal conspiracies after 1799. Other countries had similar laws, and these obviously hampered union development. In France, for example, about two hundred workers were imprisoned each year between 1825 and 1847 for taking part in illegal combinations. Unions were considered subversive bodies, only to be hounded and crushed.

From this sad position workers struggled to escape. Great Britain led the way in 1824–1825, when unions won the right to exist but (generally) not the right to strike. After the collapse of Robert Owen's attempt to form one big union in the 1830s (page 788), new and more practical kinds of unions appeared. Limited primarily to highly skilled workers such as machinists and carpenters, the "new unions" avoided both radical politics and costly strikes. Instead, their sober, respectable leaders concentrated on winning better wages and hours for their members through collective bargaining and compromise. This approach helped pave the way to full acceptance in Britain in the 1870s, when unions won the right to strike without being held legally liable for the financial damage inflicted on employers. After 1890 unions for unskilled workers developed, and between 1901 and 1906 the legal position of British unions was further strengthened.

Germany was the most industrialized, socialized, and unionized continental country by 1914. German unions were not granted important rights until 1869, and until the antisocialist law was repealed in 1890 they were frequently harassed by the government as socialist fronts. Nor were socialist leaders particularly interested in union activity, believing as they did in the iron law of low wages and the need for political revolution. The result was that as late as 1895 there were only about 270,000 union members in a male industrial work force of nearly 8 million. Then, with German industrialization still storming ahead and almost all legal harrassment eliminated, union membership skyrocketed to roughly 3 million in 1912.

This great expansion both reflected and influenced the changing character of German unions. Increasingly, unions in Germany focused on concrete bread-and-butter issues – wages, hours, working conditions – and not on instilling pure socialist doctrine. Genuine collective bargaining, long opposed by socialist intellectuals as a "sellout," was officially recognized as desirable by the German Trade Union Congress in 1899. When employers proved unwilling to bargain, a series of strikes forced them to change their minds.

Between 1906 and 1913, successful collective bargaining was gaining a prominent place in German industrial relations. In 1913 alone, over 10,000 collective bargaining agreements affecting 1.25 million workers were signed. Further gradual improvement, not revolution, was becoming the primary objective of the German trade union movement.

The German trade unions and their leaders were in fact, if not in name, thoroughgoing revisionists. "Revisionism" – that most awful of sins in the eyes of militant Marxists in the twentieth century – was an effort by various socialists to update Marxian doctrines to reflect the realities of the time. Thus, the socialist Edward Bernstein argued in 1899 in his *Evolutionary Socialism* that Marx's predictions of ever-greater poverty for workers and ever-greater concentration of wealth in ever-fewer hands had been proven false. Therefore, Bernstein suggested, socialists should reform their doctrines and tactics. They should combine with other progressive forces to win gradual evolutionary gains for workers through legislation, unions, and further economic development. These views were formally denounced as heresy by the German Social Democratic party and later by the entire Second International. Nevertheless, the revisionist, gradualist approach continued to gain the tacit acceptance of many German socialists, particularly in the trade unions.

Moderation found followers elsewhere. In France the great humanist and socialist leader Jean Jaurès formally repudiated revisionist doctrines in order to establish a unified socialist party, but he remained at heart a gradualist. Questions of revolutionary versus gradualist policies split Russian Marxists.

Socialist parties before 1914 had clear-cut national characteristics. Russians and socialists in the Austro-Hungarian Empire tended to be the most radical. The German party talked revolution and practiced reformism, greatly influenced by its enormous trade union movement. The French party talked revolution and tried to practice it, unrestrained by a trade union movement that was both very weak and very radical. In England, the socialist but non-Marxian Labour party, reflecting the well-established union movement, was formally committed to gradual reform. In Spain and Italy, Marxian socialism was very weak. There anarchism, seeking to smash the state rather than the bourgeoisie, dominated radical thought and action.

In short, socialist policies and doctrines varied from country to country. Socialism itself was to a large extent "nationalized" behind the imposing façade of international unity. This helps explain why, when war came in 1914, socialist leaders almost without exception supported their governments.

◆

From the mid-nineteenth century onward, Western society became nationalistic as well as urban and industrial. Nation states and strong-minded national leaders gradually enlisted widespread support and gave men and women a sense of belonging. Even socialism became increasingly national in orientation, gathering strength as a champion of working-class interests in domestic politics. Yet, while nationalism served to unite peoples, it also drove them apart. Though most obvious in Austria-Hungary and Ireland, this was in a real sense true for all of Western civilization. For the universal national faith, which reduced social tensions within states, promoted a bitter, almost Darwinian competition between states and thus ominously threatened the progress and unity it had helped to build.

## NOTES

1. Quoted by G. Wright, *France in Modern Times,* Rand McNally, Chicago, 1960, p. 179.

2. J. Burckhardt, *Reflections on History,* G. Allen & Unwin, London, 1943, p. 165.

3. Quoted by O. Pflanze, *Bismarck and the Development of Germany: The Period of Unification, 1815–1871,* Princeton University Press, Princeton, N.J., 1963, p. 60.

4. Quoted by E. Eyck, *Bismarck and the German Empire,* W. W. Norton, New York, 1964, p. 59.

5. Quoted by H. Kohn, *The Mind of Germany: The Education of a Nation,* Charles Scribner's Sons & Macmillan, New York, 1960, pp. 156–161.

6. N. Riasanovsky, *A History of Russia,* Oxford University Press, New York, 1963, p. 418.

7. Quoted by T. von Laue, *Sergei Witte and the Industrialization of Russia,* Columbia University Press, New York, 1963, p. 78.

8. Quoted by J. P. McKay, *Pioneers for Profit: Foreign Entrepreneurship and Russian Industrialization, 1885–1913,* Chicago University Press, Chicago, 1970, p. 11.

## SUGGESTED READING

In addition to the general works mentioned in the Suggested Reading for Chapter 23, which treat the entire nineteenth century, G. Craig, *Germany, 1866–1945* (1980), and B. Moore, *Social Origins of Dictatorship and Democracy* (1966), are outstanding.

Among specialized works of high quality, R. Williams, *Gaslight and Shadows* (1957), brings the world of Napoleon III vibrantly alive, while another engaging collective biography by R. Shattuck, *The Banquet Years* (1968), captures the spirit of artistic and intellectual Paris at the end of the century. E. Weber, *Peasants into Frenchmen* (1976), stresses the role of education and modern communications in the transformation of rural France after 1870. E. Thomas, *The Women Incendiaries*

(1966), examines radical women in the Paris Commune. D. Johnson, *France and the Dreyfus Affair* (1967), is a careful examination of the famous case. In *Jean Barois,* Nobel Prize winner R. M. Du Gard accurately recreates in novel form the Dreyfus affair, and Emile Zola's novel *The Debacle* treats the Franco-Prussian War realistically. D. M. Smith has written widely on Italy, and his *Garibaldi* (1956) and *Italy: A Modern History,* rev. ed. (1969), are recommended. P. Schroeder, *Austria, Great Britain and the Crimean War* (1972), is an outstanding and highly original diplomatic study. In addition to the important studies on Bismarck and Germany by Pflanze, Eyck, and Kohn cited in the Notes, F. Stern, *Gold and Iron* (1977), is a fascinating examination of relations between Bismarck and his financial adviser, the Jewish banker Bleichröder. G. Iggers, *The German Conception of History* (1968), and K. D. Barkin, *The Controversy Over German Industrialization, 1890–1902* (1970), are valuable in-depth investigations. H. Glasser, ed., *The German Mind in the Nineteenth Century,* is an outstanding anthology, as is P. Mendes-Flohr, *The Jew in the Modern World: A Documentary History* (1980). P. Gay, *Freud, Jews, and Other Germans* (1978), is brilliant on the development of modern culture. R. Kann, *The Multinational Empire,* 2 vols. (1950, 1964), probes the intricacies of the nationality problem in Austria-Hungary, while S. Stavrianos has written extensively on southeastern Europe, including *The Balkans, 1815–1914* (1963).

In addition to the studies on Russian industrial development by von Laue and McKay cited in the Notes, W. Blackwell, *The Industrialization of Russia,* 2nd. ed. (1982), is recommended. Among fine studies on Russian social development and modernization, T. Emmons, *The Russian Landed Gentry* *and the Peasant Emancipation of 1861* (1968); R. Zelnik, *Labor and Society in Tsarist Russia, 1855–1870* (1971); R. Johnson, *Peasant and Proletarian: The Working Class of Moscow at the End of the Nineteenth Century* (1979); and H. Troyat, *Daily Life in Russia Under the Last Tsar* (1962), are particularly noteworthy. W. E. Mosse, *Alexander II and the Modernization of Russia* (1958), provides a good discussion of midcentury reforms, while C. Black, ed., *The Transformation of Russian Society* (1960), offers a collection of essays on Russian modernization. Ivan Turgenev's great novel *Fathers and Sons* probes the age-old conflict of generations as well as nineteenth-century Russian revolutionary thought. G. Dangerfield, *The Strange Death of Liberal England* (1961), brilliantly examines social tensions in Ireland as well as Englishwomen's struggle for the vote before 1914. W. Arnstein convincingly shows how the Victorian aristocracy survived and even flourished in nineteenth-century Britain in F. Jaher, ed., *The Rich, the Well-Born, and the Powerful* (1973), an interesting collection of essays on social elites in history. The theme of aristocratic strength and survival is expanded in A. Mayer's provocative *Persistence of the Old Regime: Europe to the Great War* (1981). On late-nineteenth-century socialism, C. Schorske, *German Social Democracy, 1905–1917* (1955), is a modern classic; V. Lidtke, *The Outlawed Party* (1966), ably treats the German socialists between 1878 and 1890. H. Goldberg, *The Life of Jean Jaurès* (1962), is a sympathetic account of the great French socialist leader. P. Stearns, who has written several books on European labor history, considers radical labor leaders in *Revolutionary Syndicalism and French Labor* (1971). M. Hanagan, *The Logic of Solidarity* (1980), examines the working class in three French towns between 1870 and 1914.

# CHAPTER 26

## THE WEST AND THE WORLD

*WHILE NATIONALISM* and urban life were transforming Western society, Western society itself was reshaping the world. At the peak of its power and pride, the West entered the third and most dynamic phase of the aggressive expansion that began with the Crusades and continued with the great discoveries and the rise of seaborne colonial empires. An ever-growing stream of products, people, and ideas flowed out from Europe in the nineteenth century. Hardly any corner of the globe was left untouched. The most spectacular manifestations of Western expansion came in the late nineteenth century, when the leading European nations established or enlarged their far-flung political empires. The political annexation of territory in the 1880s – the "new imperialism," as it is often called by historians – was the capstone of a profound underlying economic and technological process. How and why did this many-sided, epoch-making expansion occur, and what were some of its consequences for the West and the rest of the world? These are the questions this chapter seeks to answer.

## BUILDING A WORLD ECONOMY

The Industrial Revolution created, first in Great Britain and then in Europe and North America, a growing and tremendously dynamic economic system. In the course of the nineteenth century that system was extended across the face of the earth. Much of this extension into non-Western areas was peaceful and beneficial for all concerned, for the West had many products and techniques the rest of the world desired. If peaceful methods failed, however, Europeans did not stand on ceremony. They used their superior military power to force non-Western nations to open their doors to trade and investment.

### TRADE AND COMMUNICATIONS

Commerce between nations has always been a powerful stimulus to economic development. Never was this more true than in the nineteenth century, when world trade grew prodigiously. As Figure 26.1 shows, world trade grew modestly until about 1840, and then it took off. After a slowdown in the last years of the century, another surge lasted until World War One. The value of world trade in 1913 was roughly *twenty-five* times what it had been in 1800. This figure actually understates growth, since average prices of both manufactured goods and raw materials were substantially *lower* in 1913 than in 1800. In a general way, the enormous increase in international commerce summed up the growth of an interlocking world economy, centered in and directed by Europe.

Great Britain played a key role in using trade to tie all corners of the world together economically. In 1815, Britain already had a colonial empire, for India, Canada, Australia, and other scattered areas remained British possessions after American independence. The technological breakthroughs of the Industrial Revolution allowed Britain to manufacture cotton textiles, iron, and other goods ever more cheaply and to far outstrip domestic demand for such products. By 1820 Britain was exporting half of its cotton textiles, for example. As European nations and the United States erected protective tariff barriers and began to industrialize, British cotton-textile manufacturers aggressively sought and found other foreign markets. In 1820, Europe bought half of Britain's cotton-textile exports and India bought only 6 percent. By 1850, India bought 25 percent and Europe only 16 percent of a much larger total.

Moreover, after the repeal of the Corn Laws in 1846, Britain's commitment to free trade was unswerving. The decisive argument in the battle against tariffs on imported grain had been, "We must give, if we mean honestly to receive, and buy as well as sell." Until 1914, Britain thus remained the world's emporium, where not only agricultural products and raw materials but also manufactured goods entered freely. Free access to the enormous market of Britain and its empire stimulated business activities around the world.

The growth of trade was facilitated by the conquest of distance. The earliest railroad construction occurred in Europe (including Russia) and in America north of the Rio Grande; other parts of the globe saw the building of rail lines after 1860. By 1920, more than one-quarter of the world's railroads were in Latin America, Asia, Africa, and Australia. Wherever railroads were built, they drastically reduced transportation costs, opened new economic opportunities, and called forth new skills and attitudes. Moreover, in the areas of massive European settlement – North America and Australia – they were built in advance of the population and provided a means of settling the land.

The power of steam revolutionized transportation by sea as well as by land. In 1807, inhabitants of the Hudson Valley in New York saw "the Devil on the way to Albany in a saw-mill," as Robert Fulton's steamship *Clermont* traveled 150 miles upstream in thirty-two hours. Steam power, long used to drive paddle-wheelers on rivers, particularly in Russia and North America, finally began to supplant sails on the oceans of the world in the late 1860s. Lighter, stronger, cheap steel replaced iron, which had replaced wood. Screw propellers superseded paddle wheels, while mighty compound steam engines cut fuel consumption by half. Passenger and freight rates tumbled, and the intercontinental shipment of low-priced raw materials became feasible. In addition to the large passenger liners and freighters of the great shipping

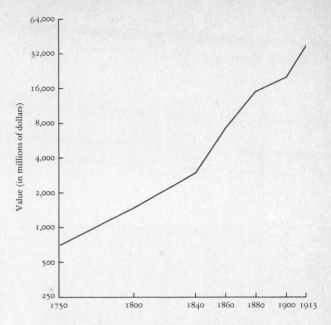

Note: Data show total world exports and total world imports.

*FIGURE 26.1 THE GROWTH OF WORLD TRADE, 1750–1913 IN 1913 DOLLARS The expansion of international commerce encouraged and reflected Western economic development in the nineteenth century. (Source: W. Woodruff, Impact of Western Man: A Study of Europe's Role in the World Economy. St. Martin's Press, New York, 1967, p. 313 and references cited there.)*

companies, there were innumerable independent tramp steamers searching endlessly for cargo around the world.

An account of an actual voyage by a typical tramp freighter will highlight developments in global trade in the nineteenth century. The ship left England in 1910, carrying rails and general freight to western Australia. From there it carried lumber to Melbourne in southeastern Australia, where it took on harvester combines for Argentina. In Buenos Aires it loaded wheat for Calcutta, and in Calcutta took on jute for New York. From New York it carried a variety of industrial products to Australia, before returning to England with lead, wool, and wheat after a

*CHEAP LAND in distant North America was an irresistible magnet for millions of Europeans. This picture shows the special, low-cost sleeping cars for immigrants on the Canadian Pacific Railroad. (Historical Picture Service, Chicago)*

voyage of 72,000 miles to six continents in seventeen months.

The revolution in land and sea transportation helped European pioneers to open up vast new territories and to produce agricultural products and raw materials there for sale in Europe. Moreover, the development of refrigerated railway cars and, from the 1880s, refrigerator ships enabled first the United States and then Argentina, Australia, and New Zealand to ship mountains of chilled or frozen beef and mutton to European (mainly British) consumers. From Asia, Africa, and Latin America came not only the traditional tropical products – spices, tea, sugar, coffee – but new raw materials for industry, such as jute, rubber, cotton, and coconut oil.

Intercontinental trade was enormously facilitated by the Suez and Panama canals. Of great importance too was large and continuous investment in modern port facilities, which made loading and unloading cheaper, faster, and more dependable. Finally, transoceanic telegraph cables inaugurated rapid communications among the financial centers of the world. While a British tramp freighter steamed from Calcutta to New York, a broker in London was arranging, by telegram, for it to carry an American cargo to Australia. World commodity prices were also instantaneously conveyed by the same network of communications.

In surveying these dramatic and impressive developments one must remember that, in terms of value, most *trade* (as opposed to most *shipping*) was among European nations, the United States, and Canada. It was not between Europe and the colonial-tropical lands of Africa, Asia, and Latin America. For example, Britain and Germany, both great world traders, carried on a very large and profitable trade with each other before World War One. Between 1900 and 1913, Britain's second-best customer in the entire world was Germany (after India), and Britain was Germany's largest single customer. Germany sold twice as much to Britain alone as to all of Africa and Asia combined. Before 1914, world trade was centered in the prosperous, tightly integrated European economy.

## FOREIGN INVESTMENT

The growth of trade and the conquest of distance encouraged the expanding European economy to make massive foreign investments. Beginning about 1840, European capitalists started to invest large sums in foreign lands. They did not stop until the outbreak of World War One in 1914. By that year Europeans had invested more than $40 billion abroad. Great Britain, France, and Germany were the principal investing countries, although by 1913 the United States was emerging as a substantial foreign investor. The sums involved were enormous (see Map 26.1). In the decade before 1914, Great Britain was investing 7 percent of its annual national income abroad, or slightly more than it was investing in its entire domestic economy. The great gap between rich and poor meant that the wealthy and moderately well-to-do could and did send great sums abroad in search of interest and dividends.

Contrary to what many people assume, most of the capital exported did *not* go to European colonies or protectorates in Asia and Africa. About three-quarters of total European investment went to other European countries, the United States and Canada, Australia and New Zealand, and Latin America. The reason was simple: Europe found its most profitable opportunities for investment in construction of the railroads, ports, and utilities that were necessary to settle and develop those almost-vacant lands. By loaning money for a railroad in Argentina or in Canada's prairie provinces, for example, Europeans not only collected interest but also enabled white settlers to buy European rails and locomotives, developed sources of cheap wheat, and opened still more territory for European settlement. Much of this investment – such as in American railroads, fully a third of whose capital in 1890 was European, or in Russian railroads, which drew heavily on loans from France – was peaceful and mutually beneficial. The victims were native American Indians and Australian aborigines, who were decimated by the diseases, liquor, and guns of an aggressively expanding Western civilization.

## THE OPENING OF CHINA AND JAPAN

Europe's relatively peaceful development of robust "offshoots" in sparsely populated North America, Australia, and much of Latin America absorbed huge quantities of goods, investments, and migrants. From a Western point of view, that was the most important aspect of Europe's global thrust. Yet Europe's economic and cultural penetration of old, densely populated civilizations was also pro-

To European countries, including Russia

To the United States and Canada

To Asia

To Latin America

To Australia and New Zealand

To Africa

Millions of 1913 dollars

9,000

6,000

3,000

Great Britain

France

Germany

MAP 26.1 EUROPEAN INVESTMENT TO 1914 *Foreign investment grew rapidly after 1850, and Britain, France, and Germany were the major in-* *vesting nations. As the map shows, most European in-* *vestment did not go to the area seized by the "new* *imperialism."*

foundly significant, especially for the non-European peoples affected by it. With such civilizations Europeans also increased their trade and profit. Moreover, as had been the case ever since Vasco da Gama and Christopher Columbus, expanding Western society was prepared to use force to attain its desires, if necessary. This was what happened in China and Japan, two crucial examples of the general pattern of intrusion into non-Western lands.

Traditional Chinese civilization was self-sufficient. For centuries China had sent more to Europe in the way of goods and inventions than it received, and this was still the case in the eighteenth century. Europeans and the English in particular had developed a taste for Chinese tea, but they had to pay for it with hard silver since China was supremely uninterested in European wares. Trade with Europe was carefully regulated by the Chinese imperial government – the Manchu dynasty – which was more interested in isolating and controlling the strange "sea barbarians" than in pursuing commercial exchange. The imperial government refused to establish diplomatic relations with the "inferior" European states, and it required all foreign merchants to live in the southern city of Canton, and to buy and sell only from the local merchant monopoly. Practices considered harmful to Chinese interests, such as the sale of opium and the export of silver from China, were strictly forbidden.

For years the little community of foreign merchants in Canton had to accept the Chinese system. By the 1820s, however, the dominant group, the British, was flexing its muscles. Moreover, in the smoking of opium — that "destructive and ensnaring vice" denounced by Chinese decrees — they had found something the Chinese really wanted. Grown legally in British-occupied India, opium was smuggled into China by means of fast ships and bribed officials. The more this rich trade developed, the greedier British merchants became and the more they resented the patriotic attempts of the Chinese government to stem the tide of drug addiction. By 1836, the aggressive goal of the British merchants in Canton was an independent British colony in China and "safe and unrestricted liberty" in trade. They pressured the British government to take decisive action, and enlisted the support of British manufacturers with visions of vast Chinese markets to be opened.

At the same time the Manchu government decided that the opium trade had to be stamped out for it was ruining the people and stripping the empire of its silver, which was going to British merchants to pay for the opium. The government began to prosecute Chinese drug dealers vigorously and in 1839 sent special envoy Lin Tse-hsü to Canton. Lin Tse-hsü ordered the foreign merchants to obey China's laws, "for our great unified Manchu Empire regards itself as responsible for the habits and morals of its subjects and cannot rest content to see any of them become victims of a deadly poison."[1] The British merchants refused and were expelled, whereupon war soon broke out.

Using troops from India and in control of the seas, the British occupied several coastal cities and forced China to surrender. In the Treaty of Nanking in 1842, the imperial government was forced to cede the island of Hong Kong to Britain forever, pay an indemnity of $100 million, and open up four large cities to foreign trade with low tariffs.

Thereafter the opium trade flourished, and Hong Kong developed rapidly as an Anglo-Chinese enclave. China continued to nurture illusions of superiority and isolation, however, and refused to accept foreign diplomats to Peking, the imperial capital. Finally, there was a second round of foreign attack between 1856 and 1860, culminating in the occupation of Peking by seventeen thousand British and French troops and the intentional burning of the emperor's summer palace. Another round of harsh treaties gave European merchants and missionaries greater privileges and protection. Thus did Europeans use military aggression to blow a hole in the wall of Chinese seclusion and open the country to foreign trade and foreign ideas.

China's neighbor, Japan, had its own highly distinctive civilization and even less use for westerners. European traders and missionaries first arrived in Japan in the sixteenth century. By 1640, Japan had reacted quite negatively to their presence. The government decided to seal off the country from all European influences, in order to preserve its traditional culture and society. It ruthlessly persecuted Japanese Christians and expelled all but a few Dutch merchants, who were virtually imprisoned in a single port and rigidly controlled. When American and British whaling ships began to appear off Japanese coasts almost two hundred years later, the policy of exclusion was still in effect. An order of 1825 commanded Japanese officials to "drive away foreign vessels without second thought."[2]

Japan's unbending isolation seemed hostile and barbaric to the West, particularly to the United States. It complicated the practical problems of shipwrecked American sailors and provisioning of whaling ships and China traders sailing in the eastern Pacific. It also thwarted the hope of trade and profit. Also, Americans shared the self-confidence and dynamism of expanding Western society. They had taken California from Mexico in 1848, and Americans felt destined to play a great role in the Pacific. It seemed, therefore, the United States' duty to force the Japanese to share their ports and behave like a "civilized" nation.

After several unsuccessful American attempts to establish commercial relations with Japan, Commodore Matthew Perry steamed into Edo (now Tokyo) Bay in 1853 and demanded diplomatic negotiations with the emperor. Japan entered a grave crisis. Some Japanese warriors urged resistance, but senior officials realized how defenseless their cities were against naval bombardment. Shocked and humiliated, they reluctantly signed a treaty with the United States that opened two ports and permitted trade. Over the next five years more treaties spelled out the rights and privileges of the Western nations and their merchants in Japan. Japan was "opened." What the British had done in China with war, the Americans had done in Japan with the threat of war.

## WESTERN PENETRATION OF EGYPT

Egypt's experience illustrates not only the explosive power of the expanding European economy and society but also their seductive appeal in non-Western lands. Of great importance in African and Middle Eastern history, the ancient land of the pharaohs had since 525 B.C. been ruled by a succession of foreigners — Persians, Macedonian Greeks, Romans, Byzantine Greeks, Arabs, Mameluks, and Ottoman Turks. In 1798, French armies under young General Napoleon Bonaparte invaded the Egyptian part of the Ottoman Empire and occupied the territory for three years. Into the power vacuum left by the French withdrawal stepped an extraordinary Albanian-born Turkish general, Mohammed Ali.

First appointed governor of Egypt by the Turkish sultan, Mohammed Ali soon disposed of his political rivals and set out to build his own state on the strength of a large, powerful army. He conquered the Sudan to the south of Egypt in order to seize black warriors for a slave army. When this traditional practice did not give the desired results, he decided to build military might on the European model. Mohammed Ali drafted for the first time the illiterate, despised peasant masses of Egypt, and he hired French and Italian army officers to train these raw recruits and their Turkish officers. The government was also reformed, new lands were cultivated, and communications improved. By the time of his death in 1849, Mohammed Ali had established a strong and virtually independent Egyptian state, to be ruled by his family on an hereditary basis, even though Egypt was still officially part of the Turkish empire.

Mohammed Ali's policies of modernization attracted large numbers of Europeans to the banks of the Nile. As one Arab sheikh of the Ottoman Empire remarked in the 1830s, "Englishmen are like ants; if one finds a bit of meat, hundreds follow."[3] The port city of Alexandria, which had fewer than a hundred European residents in 1798, had more than fifty thousand by 1864, most of them Italians,

THE OPENING OF THE SUEZ CANAL *in 1869 revolutionized communications between Europe and
Asia. (BBC Hulton Picture Library)*

Greeks, French, and English. Europeans served not only as army officers but also as engineers, doctors, high government officials, and policemen. Others found their "meat" in trade, finance, and shipping. This was particularly true after 1863, when Mohammed Ali's grandson Ismail began his sixteen-year rule as Egypt's khedive, or prince.

Educated at France's leading military academy and as fluent in French as a Parisian, Ismail was a westernizing autocrat. He dreamed of using European technology and capital to modernize Egypt quickly, and he conquered territory and tried to build a vast empire in northwest Africa. The large irrigation net-

works he promoted caused cotton production and exports to Europe to boom. Ismail also borrowed large sums to install modern communications, and with his support the Suez Canal was completed by a French company in 1869. The Arabic of the masses rather than the Turkish of the conquerors became the official language, and young Egyptians educated in Europe helped spread new skills and new ideas in the bureaucracy. Cairo acquired modern boulevards, Western hotels, and an opera house. As Ismail proudly declared: "My country is no longer in Africa, we now form part of Europe."[4]

Yet Ismail was too impatient and too reckless. His projects were enormously expensive, and the sale of his stock in the Suez Canal to the British government for $20 million did not relieve the situation. By 1876, Egypt owed foreign bondholders a colossal $450 million (up from $16 million when Ismail took power), and the country could not pay the interest on its debt. Rather than let Egypt go bankrupt and repudiate its loans, as had some Latin American countries and U.S. state governments in the early nineteenth century, the governments of France and Great Britain intervened politically in support of the European bankers who held the Egyptian bonds. They forced Ismail to appoint French and British commissioners to oversee Egyptian finances, in order that the Egyptian debt would be paid in full. This was a momentous decision. It implied direct European political control and a loss of Egyptian autonomy. Such direct political control was a sharp break with the previous pattern of trade, investment, and relatively peaceful economic and cultural penetration. Some English critics denounced this action as naked aggression, cloaked in hypocrisy about guarding the Suez Canal, the "life line to India."

Foreign financial control evoked a violent nationalistic reaction among Egyptian religious leaders, young intellectuals, and army officers. In 1879, under the leadership of Colonel Ahmed Arabi, they formed the Egyptian Nationalist Party. Continuing diplomatic pressure, which forced Ismail to abdicate in favor of his weak son Tawfiq (1879–1892), resulted in bloody anti-European riots in Alexandria in 1882. A number of Europeans were killed, and Tawfiq and his court had to flee to British ships for safety. When the British fleet bombarded Alexandria, more riots swept the country, and Colonel Arabi declared that "an irreconcilable war existed between the Egyptians and the English." Britain had superior

military power, and a British expeditionary force decimated Arabi's forces and occupied all of Egypt.

The British said their occupation was temporary, but British armies remained in Egypt until 1956. They maintained the façade of the khedive's government as an autonomous province of the Ottoman Empire, but the khedive was a mere puppet. The able British consul general Evelyn Baring, later Lord Cromer, ruled the country after 1883. Once a vocal opponent of involvement in Egypt, Baring was a paternalistic reformer who had come to believe that "without European interference and initiative reform is impossible here." Baring's rule did result in better conditions for peasants and tax reforms, while foreign bondholders tranquilly clipped their coupons and Egyptian nationalists nursed their injured pride.

In Egypt, Baring and the British reluctantly but spectacularly provided a new model for European expansion in densely populated lands. Such expansion was based on military force, absolute political domination, and a self-justifying ideology of beneficial reform. As we shall see, this model of expansion was to predominate until 1914.

## THE GREAT MIGRATION

A poignant human drama was interwoven with economic expansion: literally millions of people picked up stakes and left their ancestral lands in the course of history's greatest migration. To millions of ordinary people, for whom the opening of China and the interest on the Egyptian debt had not the slightest significance, this great movement was the central experience in the saga of Western expansion. It was, in part, because of this great migration that the West's impact on the world in the nineteenth century was so many-sided, going far beyond economic matters.

## THE PRESSURE OF POPULATION

We have seen that in the early eighteenth century the growth of European population entered its third and decisive stage, which continued unabated until the twentieth century (page 671). Birthrates eventually declined in the nineteenth century, but so did death rates, mainly because of the rising standard of living and secondarily because of the medical revolution. Thus the population of Europe (including Asiatic Russia) more than doubled, from approximately 188 million in 1800 to roughly 432 million in 1900.

These figures actually understate Europe's population explosion, for between 1815 and 1932 more than 60 million people left Europe. These migrants went primarily to the "areas of European settlement" – North and South America, Australia, New Zealand, and Siberia – where they contributed to a rapid growth of numbers. The population of North America (the United States and Canada) alone grew from 6 million to 81 million between 1800 and 1900 because of continuous immigration and the high fertility rates of North American women. Since population grew more slowly in Africa and Asia than in Europe, as Figure 26.2 shows, Europeans and people of European origin jumped from about 22 percent of the world's total to about 38 percent on the eve of World War One.

The growing number of Europeans provided further impetus for Western expansion. It was a driving force behind emigration. As in the eighteenth century, the rapid increase in numbers put pressure on the land and led to land hunger and relative overpopulation in area after area. In most countries migration

*ELLIS ISLAND in New York harbor was the main entry point into the United States after 1892. For millions of migrants the first frightening experience in the new land was being inspected and processed through its crowded "pens." (Culver Pictures)*

Population (in millions)

"European" population as a
percentage of world population

World Population

"European" Population

Percentage of world population

1750    1800    1850    1900    1930    1960 1980 est.

*Note:* "European" population includes Europe and also areas of predominantly European settlement – Asiatic Russia, North America, South America, and Australia/New Zealand.

*FIGURE 26.2    THE INCREASE OF EUROPEAN AND WORLD POPULATIONS, 1750–1975    (Source: W. Woodruff,* Impact of Western Man: A Study of Europe's Role in the World Economy. *St. Martin's Press, New York, 1967, p. 103 and references cited there.)*

increased twenty years after a rapid growth in population, as many children of the baby boom grew up, saw little available land and few opportunities, and migrated. This pattern was especially prevalent when rapid population increase predated extensive industrial development, which offered the best long-term hope of creating jobs within the country and reducing poverty. Thus millions of country folk went abroad, as well as to nearby cities, in search of work and economic opportunity. The case of the Irish, who left en masse for Britain during the Industrial Revolution and for the United States after the potato famine, was extreme but not unique.

Before looking at the people who migrated, let us consider three facts. First, the number of men and women who left Europe increased steadily until World War One. As Figure 26.3 shows, more than 11 million left in the first decade of the twentieth century, over five times the number departing in the 1850s. Although figures on migration are notoriously poor, the outflow of migrants was clearly an enduring characteristic of European society for the entire period.

Second, different countries had very different patterns of movement. As Figure 26.3 also shows, people left Britain and Ireland (which are not distinguished in the British figures) in large numbers from the 1840s on. This emigration reflected not only rural poverty but also the movement of skilled, industrial technicians and the preferences shown to British migrants in the British Empire. Ultimately, about one-third of all European migrants between 1840 and 1920 came from the British Isles. German migration was quite different. It grew irregularly after about 1830, reaching a first peak in the early 1850s and another in the early 1880s. Thereafter it declined rapidly, for Germany's rapid industrialization was providing adequate jobs at home. This pattern contrasted sharply with that of Italy. More and more Italians left the country right up to 1914, reflecting severe problems in Italian villages and relatively slow industrial growth. In sum, migration patterns mirrored social and economic conditions in the various European countries and provinces.

Third, although the United States absorbed the largest number of European migrants, it may surprise Americans to learn that only slightly more than half went to the United States. Asiatic Russia, Canada, Argentina, Brazil, and Australia also attracted large numbers, as Figure 26.4 shows. Moreover, migrants accounted for a larger proportion of the total population in Argentina, Brazil, and Canada than in the United States. Between 1900 and 1910, for example, new arrivals represented 3 percent of Argentina's population each year, as opposed to only 1 percent for the United States. The American assumption that European migration meant migration to the United States is quite inaccurate.

## EUROPEAN MIGRANTS

What kind of people left Europe, and what were their reasons for doing so? Most were poor people from rural areas, though seldom from the poorest classes. Indeed, the European migrant was most often a small peasant landowner or a village craftsman, whose traditional way of life was threatened by too little land, estate agriculture, and cheap factory-made goods. German peasants who left the Rhineland and southwestern Germany between 1830 and 1854, for example, felt trapped by what Friedrich List called the "dwarf economy," with its tiny landholdings and declining craft industries. Selling out and moving to buy much cheaper land in the American Midwest became a common response. Contrary to what is often said, the European migrant was generally not a desperately impoverished landless peasant or urban proletarian, but an energetic small farmer or skilled artisan trying hard to stay ahead of poverty.

Determined to maintain or improve their status, migrants were a great asset to the countries that received them. This was doubly so because the vast majority were young and very often unmarried. Fully two-thirds of those admitted to the United States were under thirty-one years of age, and 90 percent were under forty. They came in the prime of life and were ready to work hard in the new land, at least for a time.

FIGURE 26.3 EMIGRATION FROM EUROPE BY DECADES, 1851–1940 (Source: W. Woodruff, Impact of Western Man: A Study of Europe's Role in the World Economy. St. Martin's Press, New York, 1967, pp. 106–107 and references cited there.)

Many Europeans, especially by the end of the nineteenth century, were truly migrants as opposed to immigrants – that is, they returned home after some time abroad. One in two migrants to Argentina, and probably one in three to the United States, eventually returned to their native land. The likelihood of repatriation varied greatly by nationality. Seven out of eight people who migrated from the Balkans to the United States in the late nineteenth century returned to their countries. At the other extreme, only one person in ten from Ireland and only one in twenty among east European Jews returned to the country of origin.

Once again the possibility of buying land in the old country was of central importance.

ORIGINS

DESTINATIONS

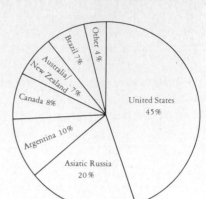

* Not including migrants to Asiatic Russia.

*FIGURE 26.4 ORIGIN AND DESTINATION OF EUROPEAN EMIGRANTS, 1851–1960 (Source: W. Woodruff,* Impact of Western Man: A Study of Europe's Role in the World Economy. *St. Martin's Press, New York, 1967, pp. 108–109 and references cited there.)*

Land in Ireland (as well as in England and Scotland) was tightly held by large, often-absentee landowners, and little land was available for purchase. In Russia, Jews were left in relative peace until the assassination of Alexander II by non-Jewish terrorists in 1881 brought a new tsar and an official policy of pogroms and savage discrimination. Russia's 5 million Jews were already confined to the market towns and small cities of the so-called "Pale of [Jewish] Settlement," where they worked as artisans and petty traders. Most land was held by non-Jews. When, therefore, Russian Jewish artisans began in the 1880s to escape both factory competition and oppression by migrating – a migration that eventually totaled 2 million people – it was basically a once-and-for-all departure. Non-Jewish migrants from Russia, who constituted a majority of those leaving the tsar's empire after 1905, had access to land, and thus returned much more frequently to their peasant vil-

lages in central Russia, Poland, and the Ukraine.

The mass movement of Italians illustrates many of the characteristics of European migration. As late as the 1880s, which was for Italians as for Russian Jews the first decade of substantial exodus, three in every four Italians depended on agriculture. With the influx of cheap North American wheat, the longstanding problems of the Italian village became more acute. And since industry was not advancing fast enough to provide jobs for the rapidly growing population, many Italians began to leave their country for economic reasons. Most Italian migrants were not landless laborers from areas dominated by large estates; such people tended to stay in Italy and turned increasingly toward radical politics. Instead, most were small landowning peasants, whose standard of living was falling because of rural overpopulation and agricultural depression. Migration provided them both an escape valve and a possible source of income to buy more land.

Many Italians went to the United States, but before 1900 more went to Argentina and Brazil. Indeed, two out of three migrants to those two developing countries came from Italy. In Brazil the big coffee planters, faced with the collapse of black slavery, attracted Italians to their plantations with subsidized travel and promises of high wages. In fact, Italian agricultural workers in Brazil were harshly exploited, although many sons and daughters of the first generation eventually did become independent farmers after World War One.

Many Italians had no intention of settling abroad permanently. Some called themselves "swallows": after harvesting their own wheat and flax in Italy, they "flew" to Argentina to harvest wheat between December and April. Returning to Italy for the spring planting, they repeated the exhausting process. This was a very hard life, but a frugal worker could save $250 to $300 in the course of a season. A one-way passage from Latin America to Italy usually cost only $25 to $30, and sometimes as little as $8. Italian migrants also dominated the building trades and the architectural profession in Latin America, and succeeded in giving a thoroughly Italian character to many Latin American cities.

Other Italians migrated to other European countries. France was a favorite destination. In 1911, the Italian-born population of France was roughly a third as large as that in the United States. Like other European nationalities, Italian migrants fanned out in many directions.

Ties of family and friendship played a crucial role in the movement of peoples. There are many examples of people from a given province or village settling together in rural enclaves or tight-knit urban neighborhoods thousands of miles away. Very often a strong individual – a businessman, a religious leader – would blaze the way and others would follow.

Many landless young European men and women were spurred to leave by a spirit of revolt and independence. In Sweden and in Norway, in Jewish Russia and in Italy, these young people felt frustrated by the small privileged classes, who often controlled both church and government and resisted demands for change and greater opportunity. Many a young Norwegian seconded the passionate cry of their national poet, Bjørnson: "Forth will I! Forth! I will be crushed and consumed if I stay."[5]

Many young Jews wholeheartedly agreed with a spokesman of Kiev's Jewish community in 1882, who declared, "Our human dignity is being trampled upon, our wives and daughters are being dishonored, we are looted and pillaged; either we get decent human rights or else let us go wherever our eyes may lead us."[6] Thus, for many, migration was a radical way to "get out from under." Migration slowed down when the people won fundamental political and social reforms, such as the right to vote and social security.

## ASIAN MIGRANTS

Not all migration was from Europe. A substantial number of Chinese, Japanese, Indians, and Filipinos – to name only four key groups – responded to rural hardship with temporary or permanent migration. At least 3 million Asians (as opposed to more than 60 million Europeans) moved abroad before 1920. Most went as indentured laborers to work under incredibly difficult conditions on the plantations or in the goldfields of Latin America, southern Asia, Africa, California, Hawaii, and Australia. White estate owners

THE CHINESE EXCLUSION ACT *This vicious cartoon from a San Francisco newspaper celebrates American laws shutting off Chinese migration. Americans and Europeans generally shared the same attitudes regarding the non-Western world.* (Photo: Caroline Buckler)

very often used Asians to replace or supplement blacks after the suppression of the slave trade.

In the 1840s, for example, there was a strong demand for field hands in Cuba, and the Spanish government actively recruited Chinese laborers. They came under eight-year contracts, were paid about twenty-five cents a day, and were fed potatoes and salted beef. Between 1853 and 1873, when such migration was stopped, more than 130,000 Chinese laborers went to Cuba. The majority spent their lives there as virtual slaves. The great landlords of Peru also brought in more than 100,000 workers from China in the nineteenth century, and there were similar movements of Asians elsewhere.

Such migration from Asia would undoubtedly have grown to much greater proportions if planters and mineowners in search of cheap

labor had had their way. But they did not. Asians fled the plantations and goldfields as soon as possible, seeking greater opportunities in trade and towns. There they came into conflict with other brown-skinned peoples – such as in Malaya and East Africa – and with white settlers in areas of European settlement.

These settlers demanded a halt to Asian migration. One Australian brutally summed up the typical view: "The Chinaman knows nothing about Caucasian civilization. . . . In fact, a Chinaman is a mere dumb animal . . . and could never be anything else. It would be less objectionable to drive a flock of sheep to the poll than to allow Chinamen to vote. The sheep at all events would be harmless."[7] By the 1880s, Americans and Australians were building "great white walls" – discriminatory laws designed to keep Asians out. Thus, a final crucial factor in the migrations before

1914 was the general policy of "whites only" in the open lands of possible permanent settlement. Racism meant that Asian migration was always of secondary importance in the world of expanding European society.

## WESTERN IMPERIALISM

The expansion of Western society reached its apex between about 1880 and 1914. In those years the leading European nations not only continued to send massive streams of migrants, money, and manufactured goods around the world, but also rushed to create or enlarge vast *political* empires abroad. This political empire building contrasted sharply with the economic penetration of non-Western territories between 1816 and 1880, which had left a China or a Japan "opened" but politically independent. By contrast, the empires of the late nineteenth century recalled the old European colonial empires of the seventeenth and eighteenth centuries and led contemporaries to speak of the "new imperialism."

Characterized by a frantic rush to plant the flag over as many people and as much territory as possible, the new imperialism had momentous consequences. It resulted in new tensions between competing European states, and it led to wars and rumors of war with non-European powers. The new imperialism was aimed primarily at Africa and Asia. It put millions of black, brown, and tan peoples directly under the rule of whites. How and why did whites come to rule these peoples?

### THE SCRAMBLE FOR AFRICA

The most spectacular manifestation of the new imperialism was the seizure of Africa, which broke sharply with previous patterns and fascinated contemporary Europeans and Americans.

As late as 1880, European nations controlled only 10 percent of the African continent, and their possessions were hardly increasing. The French had begun conquering Algeria in 1830, and by 1880 substantial numbers of French, Italian, and Spanish settlers lived among the overwhelming Arab majority.

At the other end of the continent, in South Africa, the British had taken possession of the Dutch settlements at Capetown during the wars with Napoleon I. This takeover had led disgruntled Dutch cattlemen and farmers in 1835 to make their so-called Great Trek into the interior, where they fought the Zulu and Kaffir peoples for land. After 1853, while British colonies like Canada and Australia were beginning to evolve toward self-government, the Boers (as the Dutch in south Africa were called) proclaimed their political independence and defended it against British armies. By 1880 Dutch and British settlers, who detested each other, had wrested control of much of South Africa from the Zulus and Kaffirs.

European trading posts and forts dating back to the age of discoveries and the slave trade dotted the coast of West Africa. The Portuguese proudly but ineffectively held their old possessions in Angola and Mozambique. Elsewhere, over the great mass of the continent, Europeans did not rule.

Between 1880 and 1900, the situation changed completely. Britain, France, Germany, and Italy scrambled for African possessions as if their lives depended on it. By 1900, nearly the whole continent had been carved up and placed under European rule: only Ethiopia in northeast Africa and Liberia on the west African coast remained independent. Even the Dutch settler republics of southern

Africa were conquered by the British in the bloody Boer War (1899–1902). In the years before 1914, the European powers tightened their control and established colonial governments to rule their gigantic empires (see Map 26.2).

In the complexity of the European seizure of Africa, certain events and individuals stand out. Of enormous importance was the British occupation of Egypt, which established the new model of formal political control. There was also the role of Leopold II of Belgium (1865–1909), an energetic, strong-willed monarch with a savage lust for distant territory. "The sea bathes our coast, the world lies before us," he had exclaimed in 1861. "Steam and electricity have annihilated distance, and all the non-appropriated lands on the surface of the globe can become the field of our operations and of our success."[8] By 1876 Leopold was focusing on Africa, and he organized in Brussels the International Association for the Exploration and Civilization of Central Africa. Subsequently, Leopold formed a financial syndicate under his personal control to send H. M. Stanley, a sensation-seeking journalist and part-time explorer, to the Congo basin. Stanley established trading stations, signed "treaties" with African chiefs, and planted the flag of Leopold's International Association. Leopold's actions alarmed the French, who quickly sent out an expedition under Pierre de Brazza. In 1880 de Brazza signed a treaty of protection with the chief of the large Teke tribe and began to establish a French protectorate on the north bank of the Congo River.

Leopold's buccaneering intrusion into the Congo area raised the question of the political fate of black Africa – Africa south of the Sahara. By the time the British successfully invaded and occupied Egypt, the richest and most developed land in Africa in 1882,

MAP 26.2 THE PARTITION OF AFRICA *European nations carved up Africa after 1880 and built vast political empires.*

Europe had caught "African fever." There was a gold-rush mentality, and the race for territory was on.

To lay down some basic rules for this new and dangerous game of imperialist competition, Jules Ferry of France and Bismarck of Germany arranged an international conference on Africa in Berlin in 1884 and 1885. The conference established the principle that European claims to African territory had to rest on "effective occupation" in order to be recognized by other states. This principle was very important. It meant that Europeans would push relentlessly into interior regions from all sides, and that no single European power would be able to claim the entire continent. The conference recognized Leopold's personal rule over a neutral Congo Free State and declared all of the Congo basin a free-trade zone. The conference also agreed to work to stop slavery and the slave trade in Africa.

The Berlin conference coincided with Germany's sudden emergence as an imperial power. Prior to about 1880 Bismarck, like many European leaders at the time, had seen little value in colonies. Colonies reminded him, he said, of a poor but proud nobleman who wore a fur coat when he could not afford a shirt underneath. Then, in 1884 and 1885, as political agitation for expansion increased, Bismarck did an abrupt about-face, and Germany established protectorates over a number of small African kingdoms and tribes in Togo, Cameroon, South West Africa, and later in East Africa.

In acquiring colonies Bismarck cooperated against the British with France's Jules Ferry, who was as ardent for empire as he was for

MEDITERRANEAN SEA

MADEIRA IS.
(PORTUGAL)

TANGIER
Casablanca
Algiers
TUNISIA
Tripoli
Cyrene
Cairo

MOROCCO
IFNI

CANARY IS.
(SPAIN)

ALGERIA

LIBYA

EGYPT

ARABIA

RIO DE ORO

SAHARA

RED SEA

FRENCH WEST AFRICA

Nile

GAMBIA
PORTUGUESE
GUINEA

Niger

L. Chad

Khartoum

ERITREA

Adowa

FRENCH SOMALILAND

ANGLO-EGYPTIAN
SUDAN

BRITISH
SOMALILAND

SIERRA LEONE

NIGERIA

Blue Nile

Fashoda

IVORY
COAST

GOLD
COAST

ETHIOPIA

LIBERIA

TOGOLAND

CAMEROONS

Ubangi

White Nile

ITALIAN SOMALILAND

RIO MUNI

FRENCH
EQUATORIAL
AFRICA

Congo

UGANDA

BRITISH
EAST
AFRICA

CABINDA

BELGIAN CONGO

L. Victoria Nyanza

Mombasa

L. Tanganyika

GERMAN
EAST
AFRICA

ZANZIBAR (GR. BR.)

ATLANTIC OCEAN

INDIAN
OCEAN

ANGOLA

L. Nyasa

RHODESIA

NYASALAND

Zambezi

MOZAMBIQUE

GERMAN
SOUTHWEST
AFRICA

BECHUANALAND

MADAGASCAR

TRANSVAAL

ORANGE
FREE STATE

SWAZILAND

UNION OF
SOUTH AFRICA

BASUTOLAND

Capetown

NATAL

ARAB STATES

SAHARA

Egypt

SUDANESE EMPIRES

Ashanti

Ibo

KIKUYU
SWAHILI LANGUAGE

BANTU PEOPLES

AFRICA IN 1878

Bushmen

Hottentots

| | British | | Portuguese |
| | French | | Belgian |
| | German | | Spanish |
| | Italian | | Independent African states |

0        400      800 Km.

0        400      800 Mi.

education. With Bismarck's tacit approval the French pressed vigorously southward from Algeria, eastward from their old forts on the Senegal coast, and northward from de Brazza's newly formed protectorate on the Congo River. The object of these three thrusts was Lake Chad, a malaria-infested swamp on the edge of the Sahara Desert.

Meanwhile, the British began enlarging their west African enclaves and impatiently pushing northward from the Cape Colony and westward from Zanzibar. Their thrust southward from Egypt was blocked in the Sudan by fiercely independent Muslims, who massacred a British force under General Charles "Chinese" Gordon at Khartoum in 1885.

A decade later another British force under General Horatio H. Kitchener moved cautiously and more successfully up the Nile River, building a railroad to supply arms and reinforcements as it went. Finally, in 1898, these British troops met their foe at Omdurman, where Muslim tribesmen charged time and time again only to be cut down by the recently invented machine gun. For one smug participant, the young British officer Winston Churchill, it was "like a pantomime scene" in a play. "These extraordinary foreign figures ... march up one by one from the darkness of Barbarism to the footlights of civilization ... and their conquerors, taking their possessions, forget even their names. Nor will history record such trash." For another more somber English observer, "It was not a battle but an execution. The bodies were not in heaps ... but they spread evenly over acres and acres."[9] In the end eleven thousand fanatical Muslim tribesmen lay dead, while only twenty-eight Britons had been killed.

Continuing up the Nile after the battle of Omdurman, Kitchener's armies found that a small French force under Major Jean-Baptiste Marchand had already occupied the village at Fashoda. Locked in imperial competition ever since Britain had occupied Egypt, France had tried to beat the British to one of Africa's last unclaimed areas – the upper reaches of the Nile. The result was a serious diplomatic crisis, and even the threat of war. Eventually, wracked by the Dreyfus affair (page 901) and unwilling to fight, France backed down and ordered Marchand to withdraw.

The reconquest of the Sudan exemplifies the general process of empire building in Africa. The fate of the Muslim force at Omdurman was eventually inflicted on all native peoples who resisted European rule: they were blown away by vastly superior military force. But however much the European powers squabbled for territory and privilege around the world, they always had the sense to stop short of actually fighting each other for it. Imperial ambitions were not worth a great European war.

## IMPERIALISM IN ASIA

Although the sudden division of Africa was more spectacular, Europeans also extended their political control in Asia. In 1815, the Dutch ruled little more than the island of Java in the East Indies. Thereafter they gradually brought almost all of the three-thousand-mile archipelago under their political authority, though – in good imperialist fashion – they had to share some of the spoils with Britain and Germany. In the critical decade of the 1880s, the French under the leadership of Jules Ferry took Indochina. India, Japan, and China also experienced a profound imperialist impact (see Map 26.3).

Two other great imperialist powers, Russia and the United States, also acquired rich territories in Asia. Russia, whose history since the later Middle Ages has been marked by almost continuous expansion, moved steadily

OMDURMAN, 1898   *The Sudan was conquered and a million square miles was added to the British Empire. (The Mansell Collection)*

forward on two fronts throughout the nineteenth century. Russians conquered Muslim areas to the south in the Caucasus and in central Asia, and also nibbled greedily on China's outlying provinces in the Far East, especially in the 1890s.

The United States' great conquest was the Philippines, taken from Spain in 1898 after the Spanish-American War. When it quickly became clear that the United States had no intention of granting independence, Philippine patriots under Emile Aguinaldo rose in revolt and were suppressed only after long, bitter fighting. (Not until 1933 was a timetable for independence established.) Some Americans protested the taking of the Philippines, but to no avail. Thus another great

Western power joined the imperialist ranks in Asia.

## CAUSES OF THE NEW IMPERIALISM

Many factors contributed to the late-nineteenth-century rush for territory and empire, which was in turn one aspect of Western society's generalized expansion in the age of industry and nationalism. Little wonder that heated controversies have raged over interpretation of the new imperialism, especially since authors of every persuasion have often exaggerated particular aspects in an attempt to prove their own theories. Yet in spite of complexity and controversy, basic causes are clearly identifiable.

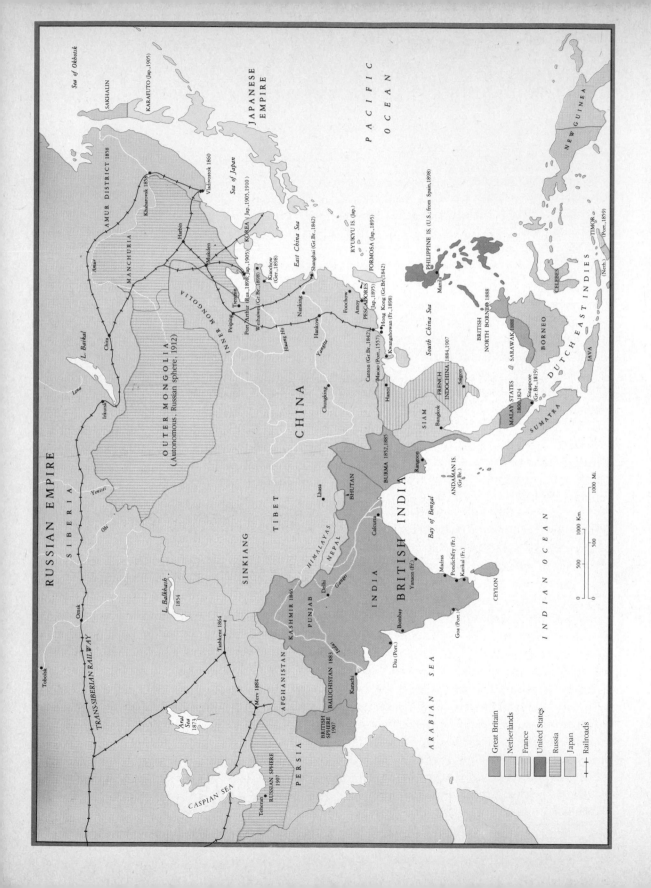

Sea of Okhotsk

SAKHALIN

KARAFUTO (Jap., 1905)

JAPANESE EMPIRE

PACIFIC OCEAN

RUSSIAN EMPIRE

AMUR DISTRICT 1858

Khabarovsk 1858

Vladivostok 1860

Amur

MANCHURIA

Harbin

Mukden

Sea of Japan

KOREA (Jap., 1905, 1910)

NEW GUINEA

China

Peiping

Tientsin

Port Arthur (Rus., 1898, 1905)

Weihaiwei (Gr.Br., 1898)

Kiaochow (Ger., 1898)

Shanghai (Gr.Br., 1842)

East China Sea

RYUKYU IS. (Jap.)

FORMOSA (Jap., 1895)

INNER MONGOLIA

OUTER MONGOLIA
(Autonomous, Russian sphere, 1912)

L. Baikal

Lena

Irkutsk

SIBERIA

Yenisei

Hwang Ho

Nanking

Hankow

Yangtze

Foochow

Amoy

PESCADORES (Jap., 1895)

Hong Kong (Gr.Br., 1842)

Kwangchowan (Fr., 1898)

PHILIPPINE IS. (U.S.: from Spain, 1898)

Manila

TIMOR (Port., 1859)

(Neth.)

CELEBES

CHINA

Chungking

Canton (Gr.Br., 1842)

Macao (Port., 1557)

South China Sea

BRITISH NORTH BORNEO 1888

BORNEO

DUTCH EAST INDIES

Ob

Tobolsk

Omsk

TRANS-SIBERIAN RAILWAY

L. Balkhash

1854

TIBET

SINKIANG

Lhasa

Hanoi

FRENCH INDOCHINA 1884, 1907

Saigon

SIAM

Bangkok

SARAWAK 1888

MALAY STATES 1800, 1824

Singapore (Gr.Br., 1819)

SUMATRA

JAVA

HIMALAYAS

NEPAL

BHUTAN

BURMA 1852, 1885

Rangoon

Bay of Bengal

ANDAMAN IS. (Gr.Br.)

1000 Mi.

Tashkent 1864

Merv 1884

Aral Sea 1873

AFGHANISTAN

KASHMIR 1846

PUNJAB

Indus

Delhi

Ganges

Calcutta

INDIA

BRITISH INDIA

Madras

Pondichéry (Fr.)

Karikal (Fr.)

CEYLON

1000 Km.

500

500

BALUCHISTAN 1883

Karachi

Yanaon (Fr.)

Bombay

Goa (Port.)

Diu (Port.)

INDIAN OCEAN

0

0

RUSSIAN SPHERE 1907

BRITISH SPHERE 1907

PERSIA

Teheran

ARABIAN SEA

CASPIAN SEA

Great Britain

Netherlands

France

United States

Russia

Japan

Railroads

Economic motives played an important role in the extension of political empires, especially the British Empire. By the late 1870s, France, Germany, and the United States were industrializing rapidly behind rising tariff barriers. Great Britain was losing its early lead and facing increasingly tough competition in foreign markets. In this new economic situation Britain came to value old possessions, such as India and Canada, more highly. The days when a leading free-trader like Richard Cobden could denounce "the bloodstained fetish of Empire" and statesman Benjamin Disraeli could call colonies "a millstone round our necks" came to an abrupt end. When continental powers began to grab any and all unclaimed territory in the 1880s, the British followed suit immediately. They feared that France and Germany would seal off their empires with high tariffs and restrictions, and that future economic opportunities would be lost forever.

Actually, the overall economic gains of the new imperialism proved quite limited before 1914. The new colonies were simply too poor to buy much, and they offered few immediately profitable investments. Nonetheless, even the poorest, most barren desert was jealously prized, and no territory was ever abandoned. Colonies became important for political and diplomatic reasons. Each leading country saw colonies as crucial to national security, military power, and international prestige. For instance, safeguarding the Suez Canal played a key role in the British occupation of Egypt, and protecting Egypt in turn led to the bloody reconquest of the Sudan. National security was a major factor in the United States'

decision to take the Panama Canal Zone in 1903.

The widespread belief that great states needed great navies in turn necessitated a string of naval bases and coaling stations around the world.

Many people were convinced that colonies were essential to great nations. "There has never been a great power without great colonies," wrote one French publicist in 1877. "Every virile people has established colonial power," echoed the famous nationalist historian of Germany, Heinrich von Treitschke. "All great nations in the fullness of their strength have desired to set their mark upon barbarian lands and those who fail to participate in this great rivalry will play a pitiable role in time to come."[10]

Treitschke's harsh statement reflects not only the increasing aggressiveness of European nationalism after Bismarck's wars of German unification but also social Darwinian theories of brutal competition between races. As the English economist Walter Bagehot argued, "the strongest nation has always been conquering the weaker . . . and the strongest tend to be best." Thus, European nations, which were seen as racially distinct parts of the dominant white race, had to seize colonies to show they were strong and virile. Moreover, since racial struggle was nature's inescapable law, the conquest of inferior peoples was just. "The path of progress is strewn with the wreck . . . of inferior races," wrote one professor in 1900. "Yet these dead peoples are, in very truth, the stepping stones on which mankind has risen to the higher intellectual and deeper emotional life of to-day."[11] Social Darwinism and racial doctrines fostered imperial expansion.

Finally, certain special-interest groups in each country were powerful agents of expansion. Shipping companies wanted lucrative subsidies. White settlers on dangerous, turbulent frontiers constantly demanded more land and greater protection. Missionaries and humanitarians wanted to spread religion and stop the slave trade. Explorers and adventurers sought knowledge and excitement. Military men and colonial officials, whose role has often been overlooked by writers on imperialism, foresaw rapid advancement and high-paid positions in growing empires. The actions of such groups and the determined individuals who led them thrust the course of empire forward.

Western society did not rest the case for empire solely on naked conquest and a Darwinian racial struggle, or on power politics and the need for naval bases on every ocean. In order to satisfy their consciences and answer their critics, imperialists developed additional arguments.

A favorite idea was that Europeans could and should "civilize" more primitive nonwhites. According to this view, nonwhites would eventually receive the benefits of modern economies, cities, advanced medicine, and higher standards of living. In time, they might be ready for self-government and Western democracy. Thus, French people spoke of their sacred "civilizing mission." Rudyard Kipling (1865–1936), who wrote masterfully of Anglo-Indian life and was perhaps the most influential writer of the 1890s, exhorted Europeans to unselfish service in distant lands:

Take up the White Man's Burden –
  Send forth the best ye breed –
Go bind your sons to exile
  To serve your captives' need,
To wait in heavy harness,
  On fluttered folk and wild –
Your new-caught, sullen peoples
  Half-devil and half-child.[12]

Many Americans accepted the ideology of the white man's burden. It was an important factor in the decision to rule rather than liberate the Philippines after the Spanish-American War. Like their European counterparts, these Americans sincerely believed that their civilization had reached unprecedented heights, and that they had unique benefits to bestow on all "less-advanced" peoples. Another argument was that imperial government protected natives from tribal warfare as well as cruder forms of exploitation by white settlers and businessmen.

Peace and stability under European control also permitted the spread of Christianity – the "true" religion. In Africa, Catholic and Protestant missionaries competed with Islam south of the Sahara, seeking converts and building schools to spread the gospel of Jesus Christ. Many Africans' first real contact with whites was in mission schools. As late as 1942, for example, 97 percent of Nigeria's student population was in mission schools. Some peoples, like the Ibos in Nigeria, became highly Christianized.

Such occasional successes in black Africa contrasted with the general failure of missionary efforts in India, China, and the Islamic world. There, Christians often preached in vain to peoples with ancient, complex religious beliefs. Yet the number of Christian believers around the world did increase substantially in the nineteenth century, and missionary groups kept trying. Unfortunately, "many missionaries had drunk at the well of European racism," and this probably prevented them from doing better.[13]

## CRITICS OF IMPERIALISM

The expansion of empire aroused sharp, even bitter, critics. A forceful attack was delivered in 1902, after the unpopular Boer War, by the radical English economist J. A. Hobson (1858–1940) in his *Imperialism,* a work that influenced Lenin and others. Hobson contended that the rush to acquire colonies was due to the economic needs of unregulated capitalism, particularly the need of the rich to find outlets for their surplus capital. Yet, Hobson argued, imperial possessions do not pay off economically for the country as a whole. Only unscrupulous special-interest groups profit from them, at the expense of both the European taxpayer and the natives. Moreover, the quest for empire diverts attention from domestic reform and closing the gap between rich and poor. These and similar arguments were not very persuasive. Most people then (and now) believed that imperialism was economically profitable for the homeland, and a broad and genuine enthusiasm for empire developed among the masses.

Hobson and many other critics struck home, however, with their moral condemnation of whites imperiously ruling nonwhites. They rebelled against crude Darwinian thought. "O Evolution, what crimes are committed in thy name!" cried one foe. Another sardonically coined a new beatitude: "Blessed are the strong, for they shall prey on the weak."[14] Kipling and his kind were lampooned as racist bullies, whose rule rested on brutality, racial contempt, and the Maxim machine gun. Henry Labouchère, a member of Parliament and prominent spokesman for this position, mocked Kipling's famous poem:

*Pile on the Brown Man's burden!*
*And if ye rouse his hate,*
*Meet his old-fashioned reasons*
*With Maxims up to date,*
*With shells and Dum-Dum bullets*
*A hundred times plain*
*The Brown Man's loss must never*
*Imply the White Man's gain.*[15]

In *Heart of Darkness,* the Polish-born novelist Joseph Conrad (1857–1924) castigated the "pure selfishness" of Europeans in "civilizing" Africa; the main character, once a liberal scholar, turns into a savage racist.

Critics charged Europeans with applying a degrading double standard and failing to live up to their own noble ideals. At home, Europeans had won or were winning representative government, individual liberties, and a certain equality of opportunity. In their empires, Europeans imposed military dictatorships on Africans and Asians, forced them to work involuntarily almost like slaves, and discriminated against them shamelessly. Only by renouncing imperialism, its critics insisted, and giving captive peoples the freedoms Western society had struggled for since the French Revolution, would Europeans be worthy of their traditions. Europeans who denounced the imperialist tide provided colonial peoples with a Western ideology of liberation.

## RESPONSES TO WESTERN IMPERIALISM

To consider the great surge of European expansion from the Western point of view is to see half the story. It is time to try to examine what foreign domination and imperialism meant to those who were ruled.

To peoples in Africa and Asia, Western expansion represented a profoundly disruptive assault. Everywhere it threatened traditional ruling classes, traditional economies, and traditional ways of life. Christian missionaries and European secular ideologies challenged established beliefs and values. Non-Western peoples experienced a crisis of identity, a crisis made all the more painful by the power and arrogance of the white intruders.

*SENEGALESE SCOUTS, 1913    Europeans recruited large numbers of native soldiers to expand and enforce their rule in Africa and Asia. Senegalese scouts were the pride of the French army in black Africa. (Roger-Viollet)*

The initial response of African and Asian rulers was to try to drive the unwelcome foreigners away. This was the case in China, Japan, and the upper Sudan, as we have seen. Violent antiforeign reactions exploded elsewhere, again and again, but the superior military technology of the industrialized West almost invariably prevailed. Beaten in battle, many Africans and Asians concentrated on preserving their cultural traditions at all cost. Others found themselves forced to reconsider their initial hostility. Some (like Ismail of Egypt) concluded that the West was indeed superior in some ways and that it was therefore necessary to reform their societies and copy European achievements. Thus, it is possible to think of responses to the Western impact as a spectrum, with "traditionalists" at one end, "westernizers" or "modernizers" at the other, and many shades of opinion in between. Both before and after European domination, the struggle among these groups was often intense. With time, however, the modernizers tended to gain the upper hand.

When the power of both the traditionalists and the modernizers was thoroughly shattered by superior force, the great majority of Asians and Africans accepted imperial rule. Political participation in non-Western lands was historically limited to small elites, and the masses were used to doing what their rulers told them. In these circumstances Europeans, clothed in power and convinced of their righteousness, governed smoothly and effectively. They received considerable support from both traditionalists – local chiefs, landowners, religious leaders – and modernizers – the Western-educated professional classes and civil servants.

Nevertheless, imperial rule was in many ways a hollow shell built on sand. Support for European rule among the conforming and accepting millions was shallow and weak. Thus, the conforming masses followed with greater or lesser enthusiasm a few determined personalities who came to oppose the Europeans. Such leaders always arose, both when Europeans ruled directly and when they manipulated native governments, for at least two basic reasons.

First, the nonconformists – the eventual anti-imperial leaders – developed a burning desire for human dignity. They came to feel that such dignity was incompatible with foreign rule with its smirks and smiles, its paternalism and condescension. Second, potential leaders found in the Western world the ideologies and justification for their protest. They discovered liberalism with its credo of civil liberty and political self-determination. They echoed the demands of anti-imperialists in Europe and America that the West live up to its own ideals.

More important, they found themselves attracted to modern nationalism, which asserted that every people had the right to control its own destiny. After 1917, anti-imperialist revolt would find another weapon in Lenin's version of Marxian socialism. Thus, the anti-imperialist search for dignity drew strength from Western culture, as is apparent in the development of three major Asian countries, India, Japan, and China.

India was the jewel of the British Empire, and no colonial area experienced a more profound British impact. Unlike Japan and China, which maintained a real or precarious independence, and unlike African territories, which were annexed by Europeans only at the end of the nineteenth century, India was ruled more or less absolutely by Britain for a very long time.

Arriving in India on the heels of the Portuguese in the seventeenth century, the British East India Company had conquered the last independent native state by 1848. The last "traditional" response to European rule – the attempt by the established ruling classes to drive the white man out by military force – was broken in India in 1857 and 1858. Those were the years of the Great Rebellion (which the British called a mutiny), when an insurrection by Muslim and Hindu mercenaries in the British army spread throughout northern and central India before it was finally crushed, primarily by loyal native troops from southern India. Thereafter Britain ruled India directly. India illustrates, therefore, for better and for worse, what generations of European domination might produce.

After 1858, India was ruled by the British Parliament in London and administered by a tiny all-white civil service in India. In 1900 this elite consisted of fewer than 3,500 top officials, for a population of 300 million. The white elite, backed by white officers and native troops, was competent and generally well-disposed toward the welfare of the Indian peasant masses. Yet it practiced strict job discrimination and social segregation, and most of its members quite frankly considered the jumble of Indian peoples and castes to be racially inferior. As Lord Kitchener, one of the

THE BRITISH IN INDIA *This photo suggests not only the incredible power and luxury of the British ruling class in India but its confidence and self-satisfaction as well. As one British viceroy said: "We are all British gentlemen engaged in the magnificent work of governing an inferior race." (BBC Hulton Picture Library)*

most distinguished top military commanders of India, stated:

*It is this consciousness of the inherent superiority of the European which has won for us India. However well educated and clever a native may be, and however brave he may prove himself, I believe that no rank we can bestow on him would cause him to be considered an equal of the British officer.*[16]

When, for example, the British Parliament in 1883 was considering a major bill to allow Indian judges to try white Europeans in India, the British community rose in protest and defeated the measure. The idea that they might be judged by Indians was inconceivable to Europeans, for it was clear to the Europeans that the empire in India rested squarely on racial inequality.

In spite of (perhaps even because of) their strong feelings of racial and cultural superiority, the British acted energetically and introduced many desirable changes to India. Realizing that they needed well-educated Indians to serve as skilled subordinates in the government and army, the British established a modern system of progressive secondary education in which all instruction was in English. Thus, through education and government service the British offered some Indians excellent opportunities for economic and social advancement. High-caste Hindus were particularly quick to respond, and emerged as skillful intermediaries between the British rulers and the Indian people – a new elite profoundly influenced by Western thought and culture.

This new bureaucratic elite played a crucial role in modern economic development, which was a second result of British rule. Irrigation projects for agriculture, the world's third largest railroad network for good communications, and large tea and jute plantations geared to the world economy were all developed. Unfortunately, the lot of the Indian masses improved little, for the increase in production was quite literally eaten up by population increase.

Finally, with a well-educated, English-speaking Indian bureaucracy and modern communications, the British created a unified, powerful state. They placed under the same general system of law and administration the different Hindu and Muslim peoples and the vanquished kingdoms of the entire subcontinent – groups that had fought each other for centuries during the Middle Ages and had been repeatedly conquered by Muslim and Mongol invaders. It was as if Europe, with its many states and varieties of Christianity, had been conquered and united in a single great empire.

In spite of these achievements, the decisive reaction to European rule was the rise of nationalism among the Indian elite. No matter how Anglicized and necessary a member of the educated classes became, he or she could never become the white ruler's equal. The top jobs, the best clubs, the modern-style hotels, and even certain railroad compartments were sealed off to brown-skinned men and women. The peasant masses might accept such inequality as the latest version of age-old oppression, but the well-educated, English-speaking elite eventually could not. For the elite, racial discrimination meant not only injured pride but bitter injustice. It flagrantly contradicted those cherished Western concepts of human rights and equality. Moreover, it was based on dictatorship, no matter how benign.

By 1883, when educated Indians came together to found the predominantly Hindu Indian National Congress, demands were increasing for the equality and self-government Britain enjoyed and had already granted white-settler colonies, such as Canada and Australia. By 1907, emboldened in part by Japan's success (see the next section), the radicals in the Indian National Congress were calling for complete independence. Even the moderates were demanding home rule for India through an elected parliament. Although there were sharp divisions between Hindus and Muslims, Indians were finding an answer to the foreign challenge. The common heritage of British rule and Western ideals, along with the reform and revitalization of the Hindu religion, had created a genuine movement for national independence.

## The Example of Japan

When Commodore Perry arrived in Japan in 1853 with his crude but effective gunboat diplomacy, Japan was a complex feudal society. At the top stood a figurehead emperor, but for more than two hundred years real power had been in the hands of a hereditary military governor, the shogun. With the help of a warrior nobility known as samurai, the shogun governed a country of hardworking, productive peasants and city dwellers. Often poor and restless, the intensely proud samurai were deeply humiliated by the sudden American intrusion and the unequal treaties with Western countries.

When foreign diplomats and merchants began to settle in Yokohama, radical samurai reacted with a wave of antiforeign terrorism and antigovernment assassinations between 1858 and 1863. The imperialist response was swift and unambiguous. An allied fleet of American, British, Dutch, and French warships demolished key forts, which further weakened the power and prestige of the shogun's government. Then, in 1867, a coalition led by patriotic samurai seized control of the government with hardly any bloodshed and restored the political power of the emperor. This was the Meiji Restoration, a great turning point in Japanese development.

The immediate, all-important goal of the new government was to meet the foreign threat. The battle cry of the Meiji reformers was "enrich the state and strengthen the armed forces." Yet how was this to be done? In an about-face that was one of history's most remarkable chapters, the young but well-trained, idealistic but felxible leaders of Meiji Japan dropped their antiforeign attacks. Convinced that Western civilization was indeed superior in its military and industrial aspects, they initiated from above a series of measures to reform Japan along modern lines. They were convinced that "Japan must be reborn with America its mother and France its father."[17] In the broadest sense, the Meiji

"THE RUSSIAN OCTOPUS"  This Japanese cartoon gives an Asian view of Russian imperialism and celebrates Japanese victories in 1904. "The ugly black octopus stretches out its eight arms in all directions," says the cartoon's sly caption, "but sometimes it happens that it gets seriously wounded by a little fish because of its excessive greed." By 1904, Japan was definitely a "big fish" in Asian waters. (The Mansell Collection)

leaders tried to harness the power inherent in Europe's dual revolution, in order to protect their country and catch up with the West.

In 1871, the new leaders abolished the old feudal structure of aristocratic, decentralized government and formed a strong unified state. Following the example of the French Revolution, they dismantled the four-class legal system and declared social equality. They decreed freedom of movement in a country where traveling abroad had been a most serious crime. They created a free, competitive, government-stimulated economy. Japan began to build railroads and modern factories. Thus, the new generation adopted many principles of a free, liberal society; and, as in Europe, such freedom resulted in a tremendously creative release of human energy.

Yet the overriding concern of Japan's political leadership was always a powerful state, and to achieve this more than liberalism was borrowed from the West. The army was completely reorganized along French and German lines, with three-year military service for all males and a professional officer corps. This army of draftees effectively put down disturbances in the countryside, and in 1877 it was used to crush a major rebellion by feudal elements protesting the loss of their privileges. Japan also borrowed rapidly and adopted skillfully the West's science and modern technology, particularly in industry, medicine, and education. Many Japanese were encouraged to study abroad, and the government paid large salaries to attract highly qualified foreign experts. These experts were always carefully controlled, though, and they were replaced by well-trained Japanese as soon as possible.

By 1890, when the new state was firmly established, the wholesale borrowing of the early restoration had given way to more selective emphasis on those things foreign that were in keeping with Japanese tradition. Following the model of the German Empire, Japan established an authoritarian constitution and rejected democracy. The power of the emperor and his ministers was vast, that of the legislature limited.

Japan successfully copied the imperialism of Western society. Expansion not only proved that Japan was strong; it also cemented the nation together in a great mission. Having "opened" Korea with the gunboat diplomacy of imperialism in 1876, Japan decisively defeated China in a war over Korea in 1894 and took Formosa. In the next years Japan competed aggressively with the leading European powers for influence and territory in China, particularly in Manchuria. There Japanese and Russian imperialism met and collided. In 1904, Japan attacked Russia without warning, and after a bloody war Japan emerged with a valuable foothold in China, Russia's former protectorate over Port Arthur (see Map 26.3). By 1910, when it annexed Korea, Japan was a major imperial power, continuously expanding its influence in China in spite of sharp protests from its distant Pacific neighbor, the United States.

Japan became the first non-Western country to use an ancient love of country to transform itself and thereby meet the many-sided challenge of Western expansion. Moreover, Japan demonstrated convincingly that a modern Asian nation could defeat and humble a great Western power. Many Chinese nationalists were fascinated by Japan's achievement. A group of patriots in French-ruled southern Vietnam sent Vietnamese students to Japan to learn the island empire's secret of success. Japan provided patriots in Asia and Africa with an inspiring example of national recovery and national liberation.

## TOWARD REVOLUTION IN CHINA

In 1860, the two-hundred-year-old Manchu dynasty in China appeared on the verge of collapse. Efforts to repel the foreigner had failed, and rebellion and chaos wracked the country. Yet the government drew on its traditional strengths and made a surprising comeback that lasted more than thirty years.

Two factors were crucial in this reversal. First, the traditional ruling groups temporarily produced new and effective leadership. Loyal scholar-statesmen and generals quelled disturbances like the great Tai Ping rebellion. A truly remarkable woman, the empress dowager Tzu Hsi, governed in the name of her young son and combined shrewd insight with vigorous action to revitalize the bureaucracy.

Second, destructive foreign aggression lessened, for the Europeans had obtained their primary goal of commercial and diplomatic relations. Indeed, some Europeans contributed to the dynasty's recovery. A talented Irishman named Robert Hart honestly and effectively reorganized China's customs office and increased the government tax receipts, while a sympathetic American diplomat, Anson Burlingame, represented China in foreign lands and helped strengthen the central government. Such efforts dovetailed with the dynasty's efforts to adopt some aspects of Western government and technology while maintaining traditional Chinese values and beliefs.

The parallel movement toward domestic reform and limited cooperation with the West collapsed under the blows of Japanese imperi-

CRUSHING THE BOXER REBELLION  *A captured Boxer is about to lose his head in a public execution before European troops. (BBC Hulton Picture Library)*

alism. The Sino-Japanese war of 1894–1895 and the subsequent harsh peace treaty revealed China's helplessness in the face of aggression, triggering a rush for foreign concessions and protectorates in China. At its high point in 1898, it appeared that the European powers might actually divide China among themselves, as they had recently divided Africa. Probably only the jealousy each nation felt toward its imperial competitors saved China from partition, although the United States' "Open Door" policy, which opposed formal annexation of Chinese territory, may have helped tip the balance. In any event, the tempo and impact of foreign penetration accelerated dramatically after 1894.

So too did the intensity and radicalism of the Chinese reaction. Like the men of the Meiji Restoration, some modernizers saw salvation in Western institutions. In 1898, the government launched a desperate "hundred days of reform" in an attempt to meet the foreign challenge. More radical reformers like the revolutionary Sun Yat-sen (1866–1925), who came from the peasantry and was educated in Hawaii by Christian missionaries, sought to overthrow the dynasty altogether and establish a republic.

On the other side, some traditionalists turned back toward ancient practices, political conservatism, and fanatical hatred of the "foreign devils." "Protect the country, destroy the foreigner" was their simple motto. Such conservative, antiforeign patriots had often clashed with foreign missionaries, whom they charged with undermining reverence for ancestors and thereby threatening the Chinese family and the entire society. In the agony of defeat and unwanted reforms, secret societies like the Boxers rebelled. In northeastern China, more than two hundred foreign missionaries and several thousand Chinese Christians were killed. Once again the imperialist response was swift and harsh. Peking was occupied and plundered by foreign armies. A heavy indemnity was imposed.

The years after the Boxer Rebellion (1900–1903) were ever more troubled. Anarchy and foreign influence spread, as the power and prestige of the Manchu dynasty declined still further. Antiforeign, antigovernment revolutionary groups agitated and plotted. Finally, in 1912, a spontaneous uprising toppled the Manchu dynasty. After thousands of years of emperors and empires, a loose coalition of revolutionaries proclaimed a Western-style republic and called for an elected parliament. The transformation of China under the impact of expanding Western society entered a new phase, and the end was not in sight.

———◆———

In the nineteenth century the West entered the third and most dynamic phase of its centuries-old expansion into non-Western lands. In so doing Western nations forged an integrated world economy, sent forth millions of emigrants, and established political influence in Asia and vast political empires in Africa. The reasons for this culminating surge were many, but the economic thrust of robust industrial capitalism, an ever-growing lead in technology, and the competitive pressures of European nationalism were particularly important.

Western expansion had far-reaching consequences. For the first time in human history the world became, in many ways, a single unit. Moreover, European expansion diffused the ideas and techniques of a highly developed civilization. Yet the West relied on force to conquer and rule, and it treated non-Western peoples as racial inferiors. Thus non-Western elites, often armed with Western doctrines, gradually responded to the Western challenge. They launched a national, anti-imperialist struggle for dignity, genuine independence, and modernization. This struggle would emerge as a central drama of world history after the great European civil war of 1914–1918, which reduced the West's technological advantage and shattered its self-confidence and complacent moral superiority.

---

## NOTES

1. Quoted by A. Waley, *The Opium War Through Chinese Eyes,* Macmillan, New York, 1958, p. 29.

2. Quoted by J. W. Hall, *Japan, from Prehistory to Modern Times,* Delacorte Press, New York, 1970, p. 250.

3. Quoted by R. Hallett, *Africa to 1875,* University of Michigan Press, Ann Arbor, 1970, p. 109.

4. Quoted by Earl of Cromer, *Modern Egypt,* London, 1911, p. 48.

5. Quoted by T. Blegen, *Norwegian Migration to America,* Norwegian-American Historical Association, Northfield, Minn., 1940, 2.468.

6. Quoted by I. Howe, *World of Our Fathers.* Harcourt Brace Jovanovich. New York, 1976, p. 25.

7. Quoted by C. A. Price, *The Great White Walls Are Built: Restrictive Immigration to North America and Australia, 1836–1888,* Australian National University Press, Canberra, 1974, p. 175.

8. Quoted by W. L. Langer, *European Alliances and Alignments, 1871–1890,* Vintage Books, New York, 1931, p. 290.

9. Quoted by J. Ellis, *The Social History of the Machine Gun,* Pantheon Books, New York, 1975, pp. 86, 101.

10. Quoted by G. H. Nadel and P. Curtis, eds., *Imperialism and Colonialism,* Macmillan, New York, 1964, p. 94.

11. Quoted by W. L. Langer, *The Diplomacy of Imperialism,* 2nd ed., Knopf, New York, 1951, pp. 86, 88.

12. Rudyard Kipling, *The Five Nations,* London, 1903, quoted by the permission of Mrs. George Bambridge, Methuen & Company, and Doubleday & Company, Inc.

13. E. H. Berman, "African Responses to Christian Mission Education," *African Studies Review* 17:3 (1974):530.

14. Quoted in Langer, *Diplomacy of Imperialism,* p. 88.

15. Quoted by Ellis, pp. 99–100.

16. Quoted by K. M. Panikkar, *Asia and Western Dominance,* George Allen & Unwin, London, 1959, p. 116.

17. Quoted by Hall, p. 289.

## SUGGESTED READING

Hall and Hallett, cited in the Notes, are excellent introductions to the histories of Japan and Africa. A. Waley, also cited in the Notes, has written extensively and well on China. K. Latourette, *The Chinese: Their History and Culture,* rev. ed. (1964), is a fine survey with many suggestions for further reading. Howe and Blegen, cited in the Notes,

provide dramatic accounts of Jewish and Norwegian migration to the United States. Most other migrant groups have also found their historians: M. Walker, *Germany and the Emigration, 1816–1885* (1964), and W. Adams, *Ireland and Irish Emigration to the New World* (reissued 1967), are outstanding. Langer's volumes consider the diplomatic aspects of imperialism in exhaustive detail. Ellis's well-illustrated study of the machine gun is fascinating, as is Price on the restriction of Asian migration to Australia. All these works are cited in the Notes.

General surveys of European expansion in a broad perspective include R. Betts, *Europe Overseas* (1968); A. Thornton, *Imperialism in the 20th Century* (1977); T. Smith, *The Patterns of Imperialism* (1981); and W. Woodruff, *Impact of Western Man* (1967), which has an extensive bibliography. D. K. Fieldhouse has also written two fine surveys, *Economics and Empire, 1830–1914* (1970), and *Colonialism, 1870–1945* (1981). G. Barraclough, *An Introduction to Contemporary History* (1964), argues powerfully that Western imperialism and the non-Western reaction to it have been crucial in world history since about 1890. J. A. Hobson's classic *Imperialism* (1902) is readily available, and the Marxist-Leninist case is effectively presented in V. G. Kieran, *Marxism and Imperialism* (1975). Two excellent anthologies on the problem of European expansion are G. Nadel and P. Curtis, eds., *Imperialism and Colonialism* (1964), and H. Wright, ed., *The "New Imperialism,"* rev. ed. (1975).

Britain's leading position in European imperialism is examined in a lively way by B. Porter, *The Lion's Share* (1976); J. Morris, *Pax Britannica* (1968); and D. Judd, *The Victorian Empire* (1970), a stunning pictorial history. B. Semmel has written widely on the intellectual foundations of English expansion, as in *The Rise of Free Trade Imperialism* (1970). G. Himmelfarb, *Darwin and the Darwinian Revolution* (1968), shrewdly considers the philosophy so often used to justify the race for territory. H. Brunschwig, *French Colonialism, 1871–1914* (1966), and W. Baumgart, *Imperialism: The Idea and Reality of British and French Colonial Expansion* (1982), are well-balanced studies. A. Moorehead, *The White Nile* (1971), tells the fascinating story of the European exploration of the mysterious upper Nile. Volumes 5 and 6 of K. Latourette, *History of the Expansion of Christianity,* 7 vols. (1937–1945), examines the powerful impulse for missionary work in non-European areas. D. Headrick stresses Western technological superiority in *Tools of Empire* (1981).

Two unusual and provocative studies on personal relations between European rulers and non-European subjects are D. Mannoni, *Prospero and Caliban: The Psychology of Colonialization* (1964), and F. Fanon, *Wretched of the Earth* (1965), a bitter attack on white racism by a black psychologist active in the Algerian revolution. Novels also bring the psychological and human dimensions of imperialism alive. H. Rider Haggard, *King Solomon's Mines,* portrays the powerful appeal of adventure in exotic lands, while Rudyard Kipling, the greatest writer of European expansion, is at his stirring best in *Kim* and *Soldiers Three.* Joseph Conrad unforgettably probes European motives in *Heart of Darkness,* while André Gide, *The Immoralist,* closely examines European moral corruption in North Africa.

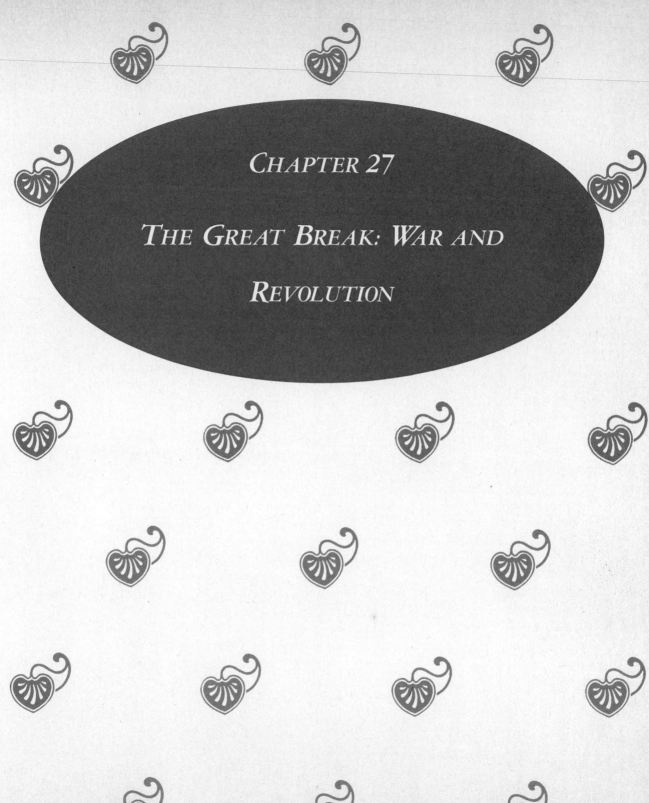

# CHAPTER 27

# THE GREAT BREAK: WAR AND

# REVOLUTION

*IN THE SUMMER OF 1914* the nations of Europe went willingly to war. They believed they had no other choice. Moreover, both peoples and governments confidently expected a short war leading to a decisive victory. Such a war, they believed, would "clear the air," and European society would go on as before.

These expectations were almost totally mistaken. The First World War was long, indecisive, and tremendously destructive. To the shell-shocked generation of survivors, it was known simply as the Great War: the war of unprecedented scope and intensity. From today's perspective it is clear that the First World War marked a great break in the course of Western historical development since the French and Industrial Revolutions. A noted British political scientist has gone so far as to say that even in victorious and relatively fortunate Great Britain, the First World War was *the* great turning point in government and society, "as in everything else in modern British history.... There's a much greater difference between the Britain of 1914 and, say, 1920, than between the Britain of 1920 and today."[1]

This is a very strong statement, but it contains much truth, for all of Europe as well as for Britain. It suggests three questions this chapter will try to answer. What caused the Great War? How and why did war and revolution have such enormous and destructive consequences? And where in the trauma and bloodshed were formed elements of today's world, many of which people now accept and even cherish?

## THE FIRST WORLD WAR

The First World War was so long and destructive because it involved all the Great Powers and because it quickly degenerated into a senseless military stalemate. Like two evenly matched boxers in an old-time hundred-round championship bout, each side tried to wear down its opponent and break its body and spirit. There was no referee to call a draw, only the blind hammering of a life-or-death struggle.

### THE BISMARCKIAN SYSTEM OF ALLIANCES

The Franco-Prussian War and the foundation of the German Empire opened a new era in international relations. France was decisively defeated in 1871 and forced to pay a large war indemnity and give up Alsace-Lorraine. In ten short years, from 1862 to 1871, Bismarck had made Prussia-Germany – traditionally the weakest of the Great Powers – the most powerful nation in Europe (pages 886–891). Had Bismarck been a Napoleon I or a Hitler, for whom no gain was ever sufficient, continued expansion would no doubt sooner or later have raised a powerful coalition against the new German Empire. Yet he was not. As Bismarck never tired of repeating after 1871, Germany was a "satisfied" power. Germany had no territorial ambitions and only wanted peace in Europe.

But how was peace to be preserved? The most serious threat to peace came from the east, from Austria-Hungary and from Russia. Those two enormous multinational empires had many conflicting interests, particularly in the Balkans, where the Ottoman Empire – "the sick man of Europe" – was ebbing fast. There was a real threat that Germany might be dragged into a great war between the two rival empires. Bismarck's solution was a system of alliances to restrain both Russia and Austria-Hungary, to prevent conflict between them, and to isolate a hostile France.

THE CONGRESS OF BERLIN, 1878   With the Austrian representative on his right and with other participants looking on, Bismarck the mediator symbolically seals the hard-won agreement by shaking hands with the chief Russian negotiator. The Great Powers often relied on such special conferences to settle their international disputes. (Bettmann Archive)

A first step was the creation in 1873 of the conservative Three Emperors' League, which linked the monarchs of Austria-Hungary, Germany, and Russia in an alliance against radical movements. In 1877–1878, when Russia's victories over Turkey threatened the balance of Austrian and Russian interests in the Balkans and the balance of British and Russian interests in the Middle East, Bismarck played the role of sincere peacemaker. At the Congress of Berlin in 1878, he saw that Austria obtained the right to "occupy and administer" the Ottoman provinces of Bosnia and Herzegovina to counterbalance Russian gains, while independent Balkan states were also carved from the disintegrating Ottoman Empire.

Bismarck's balancing efforts at the Congress of Berlin infuriated Russian nationalists, which led Bismarck to conclude a defensive military alliance with Austria against Russia in 1879. Motivated by tensions with France, Italy joined Germany and Austria in 1882, thereby forming the Triple Alliance.

Bismarck continued to work for peace in eastern Europe, seeking to neutralize tensions between Austria-Hungary and Russia. In 1881, he capitalized on their mutual fears and cajoled them both into a secret alliance with Germany. This Alliance of the Three Emperors lasted until 1887. It established the principle of cooperation among all three powers in any further division of Turkey, while each state pledged friendly neutrality in case one of the three found itself at war with a fourth power (except Turkey).

Bismarck also maintained good relations with Britain and Italy, while cooperating with France in Africa but keeping France isolated in Europe. In 1887, Russia declined to renew the Alliance of the Three Emperors because of new tensions in the Balkans. Bismarck craftily substituted a Russian-German Reinsurance Treaty, by which both states promised neutrality if the other was attacked.

Bismarck's accomplishments in foreign policy after 1871 were great. For almost a generation he maintained German leadership in international affairs, and he worked successfully for peace by managing conflicts and by restraining Austria-Hungary and Russia with defensive alliances.

## THE RIVAL BLOCS

In 1890, the young, impetuous emperor William II dismissed Bismarck, in part because of the chancellor's friendly policy toward Russia since the 1870s. William then adamantly refused to renew the Russian-German Reinsurance Treaty, in spite of Russian pleas to do so. This fateful departure in foreign affairs prompted long-isolated republican France to court absolutist Russia, offering loans, arms, and friendship. In both countries there were enthusiastic public demonstrations, and in St. Petersburg the autocratic Nicholas II stood bareheaded on a French battleship while a band played the "Marseillaise," the hymn of the Revolution. A preliminary agreement between the two countries was reached in 1891, and in early 1894 France and Russia became military allies. This alliance was to remain in effect as long as the Triple Alliance of Austria, Germany, and Italy: continental Europe was

FIGURE 27.1   THE ALLIANCE SYSTEM AFTER 1871

dangerously divided into two rival blocks.

The policy of Great Britain became increasingly crucial. Long content with "splendid isolation" and no permanent alliances, Britain after 1891 was the only uncommitted Great Power. Could Britain afford to remain isolated, or would it feel compelled to take sides? Alliance with France or Russia certainly seemed highly unlikely. With its vast and rapidly expanding empire, Britain was often in serious conflict with these countries around the world in the heyday of imperialism.

Britain also squabbled with Germany, for Emperor William II was a master of tactless public statements, and Britain found Germany's pursuit of greater world power after about 1897 vaguely disquieting. Nevertheless, many Germans and some Britons believed that their statesmen would eventually formalize the "natural alliance" they felt already united the advanced, racially related Germanic and Anglo-Saxon peoples. Alas, such an understanding never materialized. Instead, the generally good relations that had prevailed between Prussia and Great Britain ever since the mid-eighteenth century, and certainly under Bismarck, gave way to a bitter Anglo-German rivalry.

There were several reasons for this tragic development. The hard-fought Boer War (1899–1902) between the British and the tiny Dutch republics of South Africa had a major impact on British policy. British statesmen saw that Britain was overextended around the world. The Boer War also brought into the open widespread anti-British feeling, as edi-

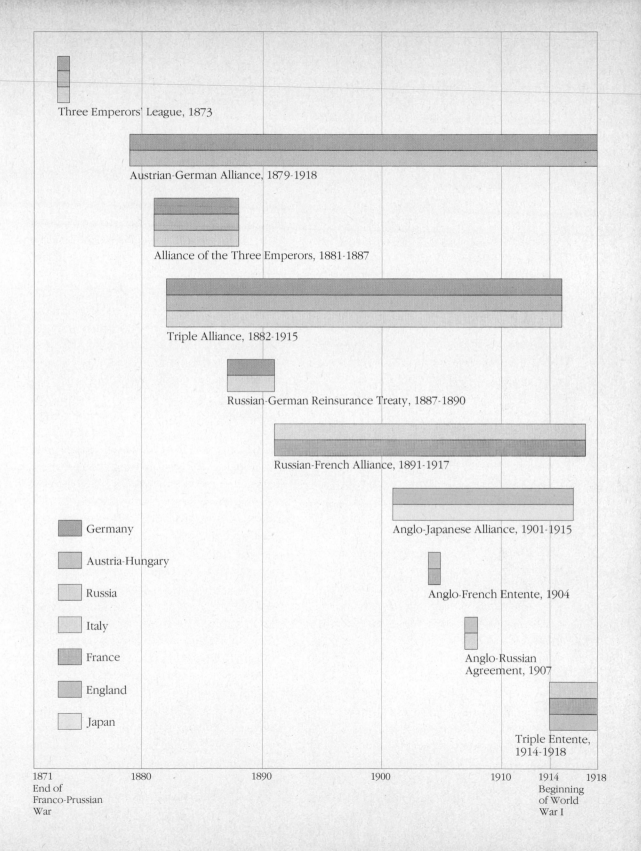

Three Emperors' League, 1873

Austrian-German Alliance, 1879-1918

Alliance of the Three Emperors, 1881-1887

Triple Alliance, 1882-1915

Russian-German Reinsurance Treaty, 1887-1890

Russian-French Alliance, 1891-1917

Anglo-Japanese Alliance, 1901-1915

Anglo-French Entente, 1904

Anglo-Russian
Agreement, 1907

Triple Entente,
1914-1918

Germany

Austria-Hungary

Russia

Italy

France

England

Japan

1871
End of
Franco-Prussian
War

1880

1890

1900

1910

1914
Beginning
of World
War I

1918

torial writers in many nations denounced the latest manifestation of British imperialism. There was even talk of Germany, Austria, France, and Russia forming a grand alliance against the bloated but insatiable British Empire. Therefore British statesmen prudently set about shoring up their exposed position with alliances and agreements.

Britain improved its often-strained relations with the United States and in 1902 concluded a formal alliance with Japan. Britain then responded favorably to the advances of France's skillful foreign minister, Théophile Delcassé, who wanted better relations with Britain and was willing to accept British rule in Egypt in return for British support of French plans to dominate Morocco. The resulting Anglo-French Entente of 1904 settled all outstanding colonial disputes between Britain and France.

Frustrated by Britain's turn toward France in 1904, Germany decided to test the strength of the entente and drive Britain and France apart. First, Germany threatened and bullied France into dismissing Delcassé. However, rather than accept the typical territorial payoff of imperial competition – a slice of French jungle in Africa or a port in Morocco – in return for French primacy in Morocco, the Germans foolishly rattled their swords in 1905. They insisted on an international conference on the whole Moroccan question without presenting precise or reasonable demands. Germany's crude bullying forced France and Britain closer together, and Germany left the Algeciras Conference of 1906 empty-handed and isolated (except for Austria-Hungary).

The result of the Moroccan crisis and the Algeciras Conference was something of a diplomatic revolution. Britain, France, Russia, and even the United States began to see Germany as a potential threat, which might seek to dominate all Europe. At the same time, German leaders began to see sinister plots to "encircle" Germany and block its development as a world power. In 1907, Russia, battered by the disastrous war with Japan and the revolution of 1905, agreed to settle its quarrels with Great Britain in Persia and central Asia with a special Anglo-Russian Agreement. As a result of that agreement, Germany's blustering paranoia increased and so did Britain's thinly disguised hostility.

Germany's decision to add a large, enormously expensive fleet of big-gun battleships to its already expanding navy also heightened tensions after 1907. German nationalists, led by the all-too-persuasive Admiral Tirpitz, saw a large navy as the legitimate mark of a great world power. But British leaders like Lloyd George saw it as a detestable military challenge, which forced them to spend the "People's Budget" on battleships rather than on social welfare. Economic rivalry also contributed to distrust and hostility between the two nations. Unscrupulous journalists and special-interest groups portrayed healthy competition in foreign trade and investment as a form of economic warfare.

Many educated shapers of public opinion and ordinary people in Britain and Germany were increasingly locked in a fateful "love-hate" relationship between the two countries. Proud nationalists in both countries simultaneously admired and feared the power and accomplishments of their nearly equal rival. In 1909, the mass-circulation London *Daily Mail* hysterically informed its readers in a series of reports that "Germany is deliberately preparing to destroy the British Empire."[2] By then, Britain was psychologically if not officially in the Franco-Russian camp. The leading nations of Europe were divided into two hostile blocs, dangerously ill prepared to deal with upheaval on Europe's southeastern frontier.

### The Outbreak of War

In the early years of this century, war in the Balkans was as inevitable as anything can be in human history. The reason was simple: nationalism was destroying the Ottoman Empire and threatening to break up the Austro-Hungarian Empire. The only questions were what kind of wars would occur and where they would lead.

Greece had long before led the struggle for national liberation, winning its independence in 1832. In 1875, widespread nationalist rebellion in the Ottoman Empire had resulted in Turkish repression, Russian intervention, and Great Power tensions. Bismarck had helped resolve this crisis at the 1878 Congress of Berlin, which worked out the partial division of Turkish possessions in Europe. Austria-Hungary obtained the right to "occupy and administer" Bosnia and Herzegovina. Serbia and Rumania won independence, and a part of Bulgaria won local autonomy. The Ottoman Empire retained important Balkan holdings, for Austria-Hungary and Russia each feared the other's domination of totally independent states in the area (see Map 27.1).

After 1878, the siren call of imperialism lured European energies, particularly Russian energies, away from the Balkans. This division helped preserve the fragile balance of interests in southeastern Europe. By 1903, however, Balkan nationalism was on the rise once again. Serbia led the way, becoming openly hostile toward both Austria-Hungary and the Ottoman Empire. The Serbs, a Slavic people, looked to Slavic Russia for support of their national aspirations. To block Serbian expansion and to take advantage of Russia's weak-

*"Immodest England"* This irreverent 1903 French view of King Edward VII reflected widespread hostility toward Britain before the Anglo-French Entente. French newspapers still delight in spreading scandalous rumors about the English royal family. (*L'Impudique Albion* from L'Assiette au Beurre, *1903*)

ness after the revolution of 1905, Austria in 1908 formally annexed Bosnia and Herzegovina with their predominantly Serbian populations. The kingdom of Serbia erupted in rage, but could do nothing without Russian support.

Then in 1912 in the First Balkan War, Serbia turned southward. With Greece and Bulgaria it took Macedonia from the Ottoman Empire and then quarreled with its ally Bulgaria over the spoils of victory – a dispute

MAP 27.1  *THE BALKANS AFTER THE CON-GRESS OF BERLIN, 1878* *The Ottoman Empire suffered large territorial losses but remained a power in the Balkans.*

that led in 1913 to the Second Balkan War. Austria intervened in 1913 and forced Serbia to give up Albania. After centuries, nationalism had finally destroyed the Ottoman Empire in Europe. This sudden yet long-awaited event elated the Balkan nationalists and dismayed the leaders of multinational Austria-Hungary. The former hoped, and the latter feared, that Austria might be next to be broken apart.

Within this tense context, Archduke Francis Ferdinand, heir to the Austrian and Hungarian thrones, and his wife Sophie were assassinated by Bosnian revolutionaries on June 28, 1914, during a state visit to the Bosnian capital of Sarajevo. The assassins were closely connected to the ultranationalist Serbian society, The Black Hand. This revolutionary group was secretly supported by members of the Serbian government and was dedicated to uniting all Serbians into a single state. Although the leaders of Austria-Hungary did not and could not know all the details of Serbia's involvement in the assassination plot, they concluded after some hesitation that Serbia had to be severely punished once and for all. After a month of maneuvering, Austria-Hungary presented Serbia with an unconditional ultimatum, on July 23.

The Serbian government had just forty-eight hours in which to agree to cease all subversion in Austria and all anti-Austrian propaganda in Serbia as well. Moreover, a thorough investigation of all aspects of the assassination at Sarajevo was to be undertaken in Serbia by a joint commission of Serbian and Austrian officials. These demands amounted to virtual control of the Serbian state. When Serbia replied moderately but evasively, Austria began to mobilize and then declared war on Serbia on July 28. Thus, a desperate multinational Austria-Hungary deliberately chose war in a last-ditch attempt to stem the rising tide of hostile nationalism. The "Third Balkan War" had begun (see Map 27.2).

Of prime importance in Austria-Hungary's fateful decision was Germany's unconditional support. Emperor William II and Chancellor Theobald von Bethmann-Hollweg gave Austria-Hungary a "blank check" and urged aggressive measures in early July, even though they realized that war between Austria and Russia was the most probable result. They knew Russian pan-Slavs saw Russia not only as the protector, but also as the eventual liberator, of southern Slavs. As one pan-Slav had said much earlier, "Austria can hold her part of the Slavonian mass as long as Turkey holds hers and vice versa."[3] At the very least a resurgent Russia could not stand by, as in the Bosnian crisis, and simply watch the Serbs be crushed. Yet Bethmann-Hollweg apparently hoped that while Russia (and therefore France) would go to war, Great Britain would remain neutral, unwilling to fight for "Russian aggression" in the distant Balkans. After all, Britain had reached only "friendly understandings" with France and Russia on colonial questions and had no alliance with either power.

In fact, the diplomatic situation was already out of control. Military considerations began to dictate policy. Russia, a vast country, required much longer to mobilize its armies than did Germany and Austria-Hungary. On July 28, as Austrian armies bombarded Belgrade, Russian Foreign Minister Sergei Sazonov ordered a "partial mobilization" against Austria-Hungary. Almost immediately he found that this was impossible. All the complicated mobilization plans of the Russian general staff had assumed a war with both Austria *and* Germany: Russia could not mobilize against one without mobilizing against the other. On July 29, therefore, Russia ordered full mobilization and in effect declared general war. For as the French general Boisdeffre had said to the agreeing Russian tsar when the Franco-Russian military convention was being negotiated in 1892, "mobilization is a declaration of war."[4]

The same tragic subordination of political considerations to military strategy descended on Germany. The German general staff had also thought only in terms of a two-front war. Their plan for war – the Schlieffen plan, the work of Count Alfred von Schlieffen, chief of the German general staff from 1891 to 1906 and a professional military man – called for

MAP 27.2 THE BALKANS IN 1914 *Ethnic boundaries did not follow political boundaries, and Serbian national aspirations threatened Austria-Hungary.*

knocking out France first with a lightning attack through neutral Belgium before turning on Russia.

Thus on August 2, 1914, General Helmuth von Moltke, "acting under a dictate of self-preservation," demanded that Belgium permit German armies to pass through its territory. Belgium, whose neutrality was solemnly guaranteed by all the great states including Prussia, refused. Germany attacked. Thus Germany's terrible, politically disastrous response to a war in the Balkans was an all-out invasion of France by way of the plains of neutral Belgium on August 3. In the face of this act of aggression, Great Britain declared war on Germany the following day. The First World War had begun.

## REFLECTIONS ON THE ORIGINS OF THE WAR

Although few events in history have aroused such interest and controversy as the coming of the First World War, the question of immediate causes and responsibilities can be answered with considerable certainty. Austria-Hungary deliberately started the "Third Balkan War." A war for the right to survive was Austria-Hungary's desperate, if understandable, response to the aggressive, yet understandable, revolutionary drive of Serbian nationalists to unify their people in a single state. In spite of Russian intervention in the quarrel, it is clear from the beginning of the crisis that Germany not only pushed and goaded Austria-Hungary onward but was also responsible for instantly turning a little war into the Great War by means of its sledge-hammer attack on Belgium and France.

After Bismarck's resignation in 1890, German leaders lost control of the international system. They felt increasingly that Germany's status as a world power was declining while that of Britain, France, Russia, and the United States was growing. And indeed the powers of what officially became the Triple Entente – Great Britain, France and Russia – in August 1914 were checking Germany's vague but real aspirations, as well as working to strangle Austria-Hungary, Germany's only real ally. Germany's aggression in 1914 reflected the failure of all European statesmen, not just German leaders, to incorporate Bismarck's mighty empire permanently and peacefully into the international system.

There were other underlying causes. The new overseas expansion – imperialism – did not play a direct role, since the European powers always settled their colonial conflicts peacefully. Yet the easy imperialist victories did contribute to a general European over-confidence and reinforced national rivalries. In this respect it was influential.

The triumph of nationalism was a crucial underlying precondition of the Great War. Nationalism was at the heart of the Balkan wars, in the form of Serbian aspirations and the grandiose pan-German versus pan-Slavic racism of some fanatics. Nationalism drove the spiraling arms race. More generally, as we have seen in Chapter 25, the aristocracy and middle classes arrived at nationalistic compromises, while ordinary people looked toward increasingly responsive states for psychological and material well-being.

Broad popular commitment to "my country right or wrong" weakened groups that thought in terms of international communities and consequences. Thus the big international bankers, who were frightened by the prospect of war in July 1914, and the extreme-left socialists, who believed that the enemy was at home and not abroad, were equally out of step with national feeling.

Finally, the wealthy governing classes underestimated the risk of war in 1914. They had forgotten that great wars and great social revolutions very often go together in history. Metternich's alliance of conservative forces in support of international peace and the domestic status quo had become only a distant memory.

## THE FIRST BATTLE OF THE MARNE

When the Germans invaded Belgium in August 1914, they and everyone else believed that the war would be short, for urban society rested on the food and raw materials of the world economy: "The boys will be home by Christmas." The Belgian army heroically defended its homeland, however, and fell back in good order to join a rapidly landed British army corps near the Franco-Belgian border. This action complicated the original Schlieffen plan of concentrating German armies on the right wing and boldly capturing Paris in a vast encircling movement. Moreover, the German left wing in Lorraine failed to retreat, thwarting the plan to suck French armies into Germany and then annihilate them. Instead, by the end of August dead-tired German soldiers were advancing along an enormous front in the scorching summer heat. The neatly designed prewar plan to surround Paris from the north and west had been thrown into confusion.

French armies totaling 1 million, reinforced by more than 100,000 British troops, had retreated in orderly fashion before Germany's 1.5 million men in the field. Under the leadership of the steel-nerved General Joseph Joffre, the French attacked a gap in the German line at the battle of the Marne on September 6. For three days France threw everything into the attack. At one point the French government desperately requisitioned all the taxis of Paris to rush reserves to the front. Finally, the Germans fell back. Paris and France had been miraculously saved.

## STALEMATE AND SLAUGHTER

The attempts of French and British armies to turn the German retreat into a rout were unsuccessful, and so were moves by both sides to outflank each other in northern France. As a result, both sides began to dig trenches to protect themselves from machine-gun fire. By November 1914, an unbroken line of trenches extended from the Belgian ports through northern France past the fortress of Verdun and on to the Swiss frontier.

In the face of this unexpected stalemate, slaughter on the western front began in earnest. The defenders on both sides dug in behind rows of trenches, mines, and barbed wire. For days and even weeks ceaseless shelling by heavy artillery supposedly "softened up" the enemy in a given area (and also signaled the coming attack). Then young draftees and their junior officers went "over the top" of the trenches in frontal attacks on the enemy's line.

The cost in lives was staggering; the gains in territory minuscule. The massive French and British offensives during 1915 never gained more than three miles of blood-soaked earth from the enemy. In the battle of the Somme in the summer of 1916, the British and French gained an insignificant 125 square miles at the cost of 600,000 dead or wounded, while the Germans lost half a million men. That same year the unsuccessful German campaign against Verdun cost 700,000 lives on both sides. The British poet Siegfried Sassoon (1886–1967) wrote of the Somme offensive: "I am staring at a sunlit picture of Hell."

Terrible 1917 saw General Robert Nivelle's French army almost destroyed in a grand spring attack at Champagne, while at Passchendaele in the fall the British traded 400,000 casualties for fifty square miles of Belgian Flanders. The hero of Erich Remarque's great novel *All Quiet on the Western Front* (1929) describes one such attack:

*We see men living with their skulls blown open; we see soldiers run with their two feet cut off. . . . Still the little piece of convulsed earth in which we lie is held. We have yielded no more than a few hundred*

*PREPARING THE ATTACK* *The great offenses of the First World War required the mobilization of men and material on an unprecedented scale. This photo shows American troops moving up. (U.S. Army Signal Corps)*

*yards of it as a prize to the enemy. But on every yard there lies a dead man.*

Such was war on the western front.

The war of the trenches shattered an entire generation of young men. Millions who could have provided political creativity and leadership after the war were forever missing.

Moreover, those who lived through the holocaust were maimed, shell-shocked, embittered, and profoundly disillusioned. The young soldiers went to war believing in the world of their leaders and elders, the pre-1914 world of order, progress, and patriotism. Then, in Remarque's words, "the first bombardment showed us our mistake, and under it the

THE FRUITS OF WAR *The extent of the carnage, the emotional damage, and the physical destruction were equally unprecedented. Once great cathedrals. standing in ruin symbolized the disaster. (United Press International Photo)*

world as they had taught it to us broke in pieces." For many the sacrifice and comradeship of the battlefield became life's crucial experience, an experience that "soft" civilians could never understand. A chasm opened up between veterans and civilians, making the difficult postwar reconstruction all the more difficult.

## THE WIDENING WAR

On the eastern front slaughter did not degenerate into suicidal trench warfare. With the outbreak of war, the "Russian steamroller" immediately moved into eastern Germany. Very badly damaged by the Germans under Generals Paul von Hindenburg and Erich von

Ludendorff at the battles of Tannenberg and the Masurian Lakes in August and September 1914, Russia never threatened Germany again. On the Austrian front enormous armies seesawed back and forth, suffering enormous losses. Austro-Hungarian armies were repulsed twice by little Serbia in bitter fighting. But with the help of German forces they reversed the Russian advances of 1914 and forced the Russians to retreat deep into their own territory in the eastern campaign of 1915. A staggering 2.5 million Russians were killed, wounded, or taken prisoner that year.

These changing tides of victory and defeat brought neutral countries into the war (see Map 27.3). Italy, a member of the Triple Alliance since 1882, had declared its neutrality in 1914 on the grounds that Austria had launched a war of aggression. Then, in May 1915, Italy joined the Triple Entente of Great Britain, France, and Russia in return for promises of Austrian territory. Bulgaria allied with Austria and Germany, now known as the Central Powers, in September 1915 in order to settle old scores with Serbia. The Austro-Hungarian grand offensive against Italy in June 1916 allowed Russia's most talented commander, General Alexei Brusilov, to reconquer Austria-Hungary's Polish provinces before bogging down once again.

The entry of Italy and Bulgaria in 1915 was part of a general widening of the war. The Balkans, with the exception of Greece, came to be occupied by the Central Powers, and British forces were badly defeated in 1915 trying to take the Dardanelles from Turkey, Germany's ally. More successful was the entente's attempt to incite Arab nationalists against their Turkish overlords. An enigmatic British colonel, soon known to millions as Lawrence of Arabia, aroused the Arab princes to revolt in early 1917. In 1918, British armies from Egypt smashed the Ottoman Empire

MAP 27.3 *THE FIRST WORLD WAR IN EUROPE* *The trench war on the western front was concentrated in Belgium and northern France, while the war in the east encompassed an enormous territory.*

once and for all. In their Middle East campaign the British drew on forces from Australia, New Zealand, and India. Contrary to German hopes, the colonial subjects of the British (and French) did not revolt but loyally supported their foreign masters. Instead, the European war extended around the globe as Great Britain, France, and Japan seized Germany's colonies.

A crucial development in the expanding conflict came in April 1917, when the United States declared war on Germany. American intervention grew out of the war at sea, sympathy for the entente, and the increasing desperation of total war. At the beginning of the war, Britain and France had established a naval blockade to strangle the Central Powers. They refused to accept the traditional distinction under international law between military equipment (contraband) and nonmilitary (noncontraband) articles such as food and clothing. No neutral ship was permitted to sail to Germany with any cargo. The blockade annoyed Americans, but effective propaganda over German atrocities in occupied Belgium and lush profits from selling war supplies to Britain and France blunted American indignation.

Moreover, in early 1915 Germany launched a counterblockade using the murderously effective submarine, a new weapon that violated traditional niceties of fair warning under international law. In May 1915, after sinking about ninety ships in the British war zone, a German submarine sank the British passenger liner *Lusitania,* which was also carrying arms and munitions. More than a thousand lives, among them 139 Americans, were lost. Presi-

Triple Entente and its Allies

Central Powers

Neutral nations

Farthest German-Austrian advance

X  Major battle

Treaty of Brest Litovsk, March 1918

Armistice line, Dec. 1917

R  U  S  S  I  A

Moscow

St. Petersburg

FINLAND

Helsinki

Riga

Masurian Lakes 1914

Tannenberg 1914

Brest-Litovsk

Warsaw

POLAND

Kiev

GALICIA

AUSTRIA-HUNGARY

Vienna

Caporetto 1917

RUMANIA

Bucharest

SERBIA

BULGARIA

Dardanelles

Gallipoli 1915

Sarajevo

MONTENEGRO

ALBANIA

GREECE

OTTOMAN EMPIRE

Constantinople

BLACK SEA

Danube

NORWAY

SWEDEN

DENMARK

Jutland 1916

British blockade line

NORTH SEA

BALTIC SEA

GERMANY

Berlin

Rhine

SWITZERLAND

ITALY

Rome

MEDITERRANEAN SEA

NETHERLANDS

BELGIUM

GREAT BRITAIN

London

IRELAND

FRANCE

Paris

ATLANTIC OCEAN

400 Km.

300 Mi.

200

200

100

Germany, 1914

German offensive, 1914

Farthest German advance, September 1914

Front at beginning of 1915

German offensive, Summer 1918

Armistice line, November 1918

NETHERLANDS

Antwerp

Brussels

BELGIUM

Ghent

Ostend

FLANDERS

Passchendaele

Ypres

Calais

Dover

ENGLISH CHANNEL

Arras

Somme

Amiens

Compiègne

St. Quentin

Aisne

Reims

Château-Thierry

Châlons-sur-Marne

Marne

Seine

Paris

FRANCE

Liège

Meuse

Aix-la-Chapelle

Cologne

Rhine

Ruhr

Coblenz

Moselle

GERMANY

Saar

LORRAINE

LUXEMBOURG

ARDENNES

Sedan

ARGONNE FOREST

Verdun

Nancy

Strasbourg

ALSACE

Épinal

Mulhouse

Basel

100 Km.

50 Mi.

dent Woodrow Wilson protested vigorously. Germany was forced to relax its submarine warfare for almost two years; the alternative was almost certain war with the United States.

Early in 1917, the German military command, confident that improved submarines could starve their island enemy Britain into submission before the United States could come to its rescue, resumed unrestricted submarine warfare. Like the invasion of Belgium, this was a reckless gamble. British shipping losses reached staggering proportions, though by late 1917 shippers came up with the inevitable effective response, the convoy system for safe transatlantic shipping. In the meantime the embattled President Wilson had told a sympathetic Congress and people that "the German submarine warfare against commerce is a warfare against mankind." Thus the last uncommitted great nation, as fresh and enthusiastic as Europe had been in 1914, entered the world war in April 1917, almost three years after it began. Eventually, the United States was to tip the balance in favor of Great Britain and France.

## THE HOME FRONT

Before looking at the last year of the Great War, let us turn our attention to the people on the "home front." The people behind the lines were tremendously involved in the titanic struggle. War's impact on them was no less massive than on the men crouched in the trenches.

### MOBILIZING FOR TOTAL WAR

In August 1914, most people had greeted the outbreak of hostilities enthusiastically. In every country the masses believed that their nation was in the right and was defending itself from aggression. With the exception of a few extreme left-wingers, even socialists supported the war. Tough standby plans to imprison socialist leaders and break general strikes protesting the war proved quite unnecessary in 1914. In Germany, for example, the trade unions voted not to strike, and socialists in the parliament voted money for war credits in order to counter the threat of Russian despotism. A German socialist volunteered for the front, explaining to fellow members of the Reichstag that "to shed one's blood for the fatherland is not difficult: it is enveloped in romantic heroism."[5] William II said that he saw no parties, only good Germans. Everywhere the patriotic support of the masses and the working class contributed to national unity and an energetic war effort.

By mid-October generals and politicians began to realize that more than patriotism would be needed to win the war, whose end was not in sight. Each country experienced a relentless, desperate demand for men and weapons. In France, for example, the generals found themselves needing 100,000 pieces of heavy artillery a day, as opposed to the 12,000 they had anticipated using. This enormous quantity had to come from a French steel industry that had lost three-fourths of its iron resources in the first days of the war, when Germany seized the mines of French Lorraine. In Great Britain shortages of jute for sandbags and flax for tents soon became matters of life and death, while Germany found itself cut off from the Chilean nitrates needed to make explosives. Each belligerent quickly faced countless shortages, for prewar Europe had depended on foreign trade and a great international division of labor. In each country economic life and organization had to change and change fast to keep the war machine from sputtering to a stop. And change they did.

In each country a government of national unity began to plan and control economic and social life in order to wage "total war." Free-market capitalism was abandoned, at least "for the duration." Instead, government planning boards established priorities and decided what was to be produced and consumed. Rationing, price and wage controls, and even restrictions on workers' freedom of movement were imposed by government. Only through such regimentation could a country make the greatest possible military effort. Thus, though there were national variations, the great nations all moved toward planned economies commanded by the established political leadership.

This revolutionary development would burn deeply into the twentieth-century consciousness. The planned economy of "total war" released the tremendous energies first harnessed by the French under Robespierre during the French Revolution. Total war, however, was based on tremendously productive industrial economies not confined to a single nation. The result was an effective — and therefore destructive — war effort on all sides.

Moreover, the economy of total war

blurred the old distinction between soldiers on the battlefield and civilians at home. As President Wilson told Americans shortly after the United States entered the war, there were no armies in the struggle in the traditional sense. Rather, "there are entire nations armed. Thus the men [and women] who remain to till the soil and man the factories are not less a part of the army than the men beneath the battle flags."[6] The war was a war of whole peoples, entire populations, and the loser would be the society that cracked first.

Finally, however awful the war was, the ability of governments to manage and control highly complicated economies strengthened the cause of socialism. With the First World War, socialism became for the first time a realistic economic blueprint as opposed to a utopian program.

Germany illustrates the general trend. It also went farthest in developing a planned economy to wage total war. As soon as war began, Walter Rathenau, the talented, foresighted Jewish industrialist in charge of Germany's largest electrical company, convinced the government to set up a War Raw Materials Board to ration and distribute raw materials. Under Rathenau's direction, every useful material from foreign oil to barnyard manure was inventoried and rationed. Moreover, the board launched successful attempts to produce substitutes, such as synthetic rubber and synthetic nitrates. Without the spectacular double achievement of discovering a way to "fix" nitrogen present in the air and then of producing synthetic nitrates in enormous quantity, the blockaded German war machine would have stalled in a matter of months.

Food was also rationed in accordance with physical need. Men and women doing hard manual work were given extra rations. During the last two years of the war, only chil-

dren and expectant mothers received milk rations. Sometimes mistakes were made that would have been funny if they had not been tragic. In early 1915, German authorities calculated that greedy pigs were eating food that hungry people needed, and ordered a "hog massacre" only to find that there were too few pigs left to eat an abundant potato crop. Germany also failed to tax the war profits of private firms heavily enough. This contributed to massive deficit financing, inflation, the growth of a black market, and the eventual re-emergence of class conflict.

Following the terrible battles of Verdun and the Somme in 1916, the military leaders Hindenburg and Ludendorff became the real rulers of Germany, and they decreed the ultimate mobilization for total war. Germany, said Hindenburg, could win only "if all the treasures of our soil that agriculture and industry can produce are used exclusively for the conduct of the War. . . . All other considerations must come second."[7] This goal, they believed, required that every German man, woman, and child be drafted into the service of the war. Thus, in December 1916 the military leaders rammed through the parliament the Auxiliary Service Law, which required all males between seventeen and sixty to work only at jobs considered critical to the war effort.

Although women and children were not specifically mentioned, this forced-labor law was also aimed at them. Many women already worked in war factories, mines, and steel mills, where they labored like men at the heaviest and most dangerous jobs. With the passage of the Auxiliary Service Law, many more women followed. Children were organized by their teachers into garbage brigades to collect every scrap of useful material: grease strained from dishwater, coffee grounds, waste paper, tin cans, metal door knockers, bottles, rags, hair, bones, and so forth, as well as acorns, chestnuts, pinecones, and rotting leaves. Potatoes gave way to turnips, and people averaged little more than a thousand calories a day. Thus, in Germany total war led to the establishment of history's first "totalitarian" society, and war production increased while some people literally starved to death.

Great Britain mobilized for total war less rapidly and less completely than Germany, for it could import materials from its empire and from the United States. By 1915, however, a serious shortage of shells led to the establishment of a Ministry of Munitions under David Lloyd George. The ministry organized private industry to produce for the war, controlled profits, allocated labor, fixed wage rates, and settled labor disputes. By December 1916, when Lloyd George became prime minister, the British economy was almost totally planned and regulated. More than two hundred factories and 90 percent of all imports were bought and allocated directly by the state. Food was strictly rationed, and the hours for public drinking drastically reduced, while war production soared. Great Britain had followed very successfully in Germany's footsteps.

## THE SOCIAL IMPACT

The social impact of total war on society was no less profound than the economic, though again there were important national variations. The millions of men at the front and the insatiable needs of the military created a tremendous demand for workers. Jobs were available for absolutely everyone. This situation had seldom if ever been seen before 1914, when unemployment and widespread poverty had been facts of urban life. The exceptional demand for labor brought about great and momentous changes.

One such change was greater power and prestige for labor unions. Having proved their loyalty in August 1914, labor unions became an indispensable partner of government and private industry in the planned war economy. Unions cooperated with war governments on work rules, wages, and production schedules in return for real participation in important decisions. This entry of labor leaders and unions into policy-making councils paralleled the entry of socialist leaders into the war governments. Thus did organized labor gain, for the first time, something like real equality with employers in industrial society.

The role of women changed dramatically. In every country large numbers of women left home and domestic service to work in industry, transportation, and offices. By 1917, women formed fully 43 percent of the labor force in Russia. The number of women driving buses and streetcars increased tenfold in Great Britain. Moreover, women became highly visible – not only as munitions workers but as bank tellers, mail carriers, even policewomen.

At first, the male-dominated unions were hostile to women moving into new occupations, believing that their presence would lower wages and change work rules. But government pressure and the principle of equal pay for equal work (until the end of the war) overcame these objections. Women also served as nurses and doctors at the front. In general, the war greatly expanded the range of women's activities and changed attitudes toward them. As a direct result of their many-sided war effort, Britain, Germany, and Austria granted women the right to vote immediately after the war. Women also showed a growing spirit of independence during the war, as they bobbed their hair, shortened their skirts, and smoked in public.

War also promoted greater social equality, blurring class distinctions and lessening the gap between rich and poor. This blurring was most apparent in Great Britain, where wartime hardship was never extreme. In fact, the bottom third of the population generally lived *better* than ever before, for the poorest gained most from the severe shortage of labor. The English writer Robert Roberts recalled how his parents' tiny grocery store in the slums of Manchester thrived as never before during the war, when people who had scrimped to buy bread and soup bones were able to afford fancy cakes and thick steaks. In 1924, a British government study revealed that the distribution of income had indeed shifted in favor of the poorest: only half as many families lived in severe poverty as in 1911, even though total production of goods had not increased. In continental countries greater equality was reflected in full employment, rationing according to physical needs, and a sharing of hardships. There too society became more uniform and more egalitarian, in spite of some war profiteering.

Finally, death itself had no respect for traditional social distinctions. It savagely decimated the young aristocratic officers who led the charge, and it fell heavily on the mass of drafted peasants and unskilled workers who followed. Yet death often spared the aristocrats of labor. Their lives were too valuable to squander at the front, for they were needed to train and direct the newly recruited women and older unskilled men laboring valiantly in war plants at home.

## GROWING POLITICAL TENSIONS

During the first two years of war most soldiers and civilians supported their govern-

ments. Even in Austria-Hungary – the most vulnerable of the belligerents, with its competing nationalities – loyalty to the state and monarchy remained astonishingly strong through 1916. Belief in a just cause, patriotic nationalism, the planned economy, and a sharing of burdens united peoples behind their various national leaders. Furthermore, each government did its best to control public opinion to bolster morale. Newspapers, letters, and public addresses were rigorously censored. Good news was overstated; bad news was repressed or distorted.

Each government used both crude and subtle propaganda to maintain popular support. German propaganda hysterically pictured black soldiers from France's African empire raping German women, while German atrocities in Belgium and elsewhere were ceaselessly recounted and exaggerated by the French and British. Patriotic posters and slogans, slanted news and biased editorials inflamed national hatreds and helped sustain superhuman efforts.

By the spring of 1916, however, people were beginning to crack under the strain of total war. In April 1916, Irish nationalists in Dublin tried to take advantage of this situation and rose up against British rule in their great Easter Rebellion. A week of bitter fighting passed before the rebels were crushed and their leaders executed. Strikes and protest marches over inadequate food began to flare up on every home front. Soldiers' morale began to decline. Russian troops mutinied. Numerous French units refused to fight after General Nivelle's disastrous offensive of May 1917. Only tough military justice and a tacit agreement with his troops that there would be no more grand offensives enabled the new general in chief, Henri-Philippe Pétain, to restore order. A rising tide of war-weariness and defeatism also swept France's civilian popula-

On les aura!

2ᴱ EMPRUNT
DE
LA DÉFENSE NATIONALE
Souscrivez

Daddy, what did YOU do in the Great War?

*WARTIME PROPAGANDA was skillful and effective. Before the draft was introduced to Britain in 1916, the famous poster on the left shamed many able-bodied men into volunteering for military service. The patriotic poster on the right encouraged many French people to buy bonds to finance the war effort. (By courtesy of the Trustees of the Imperial War Museum)*

tion before Georges Clemenceau emerged as a ruthless and effective wartime leader in November 1917. Clemenceau established a virtual dictatorship, pouncing on strikers and jailing without trial journalists and politicians who dared to suggest a compromise peace with Germany.

The strains were worse for the Central Powers. In October 1916, the chief minister of Austria was assassinated by a young social-

ist crying, "Down with Absolutism! We want peace!"[8] The following month, when the feeble old Emperor Francis Joseph died sixty-eight years after his mother Sophia had pushed him onto the throne in 1848 (page 830), a symbol of unity disappeared. In spite of absolute censorship, political dissatisfaction and conflicts among nationalities grew. In April 1917, Austria's chief minister summed up the situation in the gloomiest possible terms. The country and army were exhausted. Another winter of war would bring revolution and disintegration. "If the monarchs of the Central Powers cannot make peace in the coming months," he wrote, "it will be made for them by their peoples."[9] Both Czech and Yugoslav leaders demanded autonomous democratic states for their peoples. The allied blockade kept tightening; people were starving.

The strain of total war and the Auxiliary Service Law was also evident in Germany. In the winter of 1916–1917, Germany's military position appeared increasingly desperate. Stalemates and losses in the west were matched by Russian advances (the Brusilov offense) in the east: hence the military's insistence on the all-or-nothing gamble of unrestricted submarine warfare when the entente refused in December 1916 to consider peace on terms favorable to the Central Powers.

Also, the national political unity of the first two years of war was collapsing as the social conflict of prewar Germany re-emerged. A growing minority of socialists in the parliament began to vote against war credits, calling for a compromise "peace without annexations or reparations." In July 1917 a coalition of socialists and Catholics passed a resolution in the parliament to that effect. Such a peace was unthinkable for conservatives and military leaders. So also was the surge in revolutionary agitation and strikes by war-weary workers that occurred in early 1917. When the bread ration was further reduced in April, more than 200,000 workers struck and demonstrated for a week in Berlin, returning to work only under the threat of prison and military discipline. Thus militaristic Germany, like its ally Austria-Hungary (and its enemy France), was beginning to crack in 1917. Yet it was Russia that collapsed first and saved the Central Powers, for a time.

## THE RUSSIAN REVOLUTION

The Russian Revolution of 1917 was one of modern history's most momentous events. Directly related to the growing tensions of World War One, its significance went far beyond the wartime agonies of a single European nation. The Russian Revolution opened a new era. For some, it was Marx's socialist vision come true; for others, it was the triumph of dictatorship. To all, it presented a radically new kind of state and society.

### THE FALL OF IMPERIAL RUSSIA

Like its allies and its enemies, Russia embraced war with patriotic enthusiasm in 1914. At the Winter Palace, while throngs of people knelt and sang "God Save the Tsar," Tsar Nicholas II (1894–1917) repeated the oath Alexander I had made in 1812 and vowed never to make peace as long as the enemy stood on Russian soil. Russia's lower house, the Duma, voted war credits. Conservatives anticipated expansion in the Balkans, while liberals and most socialists believed alliance with Britain and France would bring democratic reforms. For a moment, Russia was united.

Soon, however the strains of war began to take their toll. The unprecedented artillery barrages used up Russia's supplies of shells and ammunition, and better-equipped German armies inflicted terrible losses. For a time in 1915 substantial numbers of Russian soldiers were sent to the front without rifles; they were told to find their arms among the dead. There were 2 million Russian casualties in 1915 alone. Morale declined among soldiers and civilians. Yet Russia's battered peasant army did not collapse but continued to fight courageously until early 1917.

Under the shock of defeat, Russia moved

toward full mobilization on the home front. The Duma and the organs of local government took the lead, setting up special committees to coordinate defense, industry, transportation, and agriculture. These efforts improved the military situation. Russian factories produced more than twice as many shells in 1916 as in 1915, for example, and monthly shell production in late 1916 was forty times its prewar level. Yet there were many failures, and Russia mobilized less effectively for total war than the other warring nations.

The great problem was leadership. Under the constitution resulting from the revolution of 1905 (pages 895–896), the tsar had retained complete control over the bureaucracy and the army. Legislation proposed by the Duma, which was weighted in favor of the wealthy and conservative classes, was subject to the tsar's veto. Moreover, Nicholas II fervently wished to maintain the sacred inheritance of supreme royal power, which with the Orthodox Church was for him the key to Russia's greatness. A kindly, slightly stupid man, of whom a friend said he "would have been an ideal country gentleman, devoting his life to wife and children, his farms and his sport," Nicholas failed to form a close partnership with his citizens in order to fight the war more effectively. He relied instead on the old bureaucratic apparatus, distrusting the moderate Duma, rejecting popular involvement, and resisting calls to share power.

As a result the Duma, the educated middle classes and the masses became increasingly critical of the tsar's leadership. Following Nicholas's belated dismissal of the incompetent minister of war, demands for more democratic and responsive government exploded in the Duma in the summer of 1915. "From the beginning of the war," declared one young liberal, "public opinion has understood the character and magnitude of the struggle; it has understood that short of organizing the whole country for war, victory is impossible. But the Government has not understood, the Government has rejected every offer of help with disdain."[10] In September parties ranging from conservative to moderate socialist formed the Progressive Bloc, which called for a completely new government responsible to the Duma instead of the tsar. In answer, Nicholas temporarily adjourned the Duma and announced that he was going to the front to lead and rally Russia's armies.

His departure was a fatal turning point. With the tsar in the field commanding the troops, control of the government was taken over by the hysterical empress, Tsarina Alexandra, and a debauched adventurer, the monk Rasputin. A minor German princess and granddaughter of England's Queen Victoria, Nicholas's wife was a devoted mother with a sick child, a strong-willed woman with a hatred of parliaments. Having constantly urged her husband to rule absolutely, Alexandra tried to do so herself in his absence. She seated and unseated the top ministers. Her most trusted adviser was "our Friend Grigori," an uneducated Siberian preacher who was appropriately nicknamed Rasputin – the "Degenerate."

Rasputin began his career with a sect noted for mixing sexual orgies with religious ecstasies, and his influence rested on mysterious healing powers. Alexis, Alexandra's fifth child and heir to the throne, suffered from a rare disease, hemophilia. The tiniest cut meant uncontrollable bleeding, terrible pain, and possible death. Medical science could do nothing. Only Rasputin could miraculously stop the bleeding, perhaps through hypnosis. The empress's faith in Rasputin was limitless. "Believe more in our Friend," she wrote her husband in 1916. "He lives for you and Rus-

FAMILY PORTRAIT *With husband Nicholas II standing behind, the beautiful but tense Alexandra shows one of her daughters, who could not inherit the Russian throne, to her grandmother, Queen Victoria of England, and Victoria's son, the future Edward VII. European monarchs were closely related by blood and breeding before 1914. (Nicholas A. de Basily Collection, Hoover Institution)*

sia." In this atmosphere of unreality, the government slid steadily toward revolution.

In a desperate attempt to right the situation and end unfounded rumors that Rasputin was the empress's lover, three members of the high aristocracy murdered Rasputin in December 1916. The empress went into semipermanent shock, her mind haunted by the dead man's prophecy: "If I die or you desert me, in six months you will lose your son and your throne."[11] Food shortages in the cities worsened, morale declined. On March 8, women in Petrograd (formerly St. Petersburg) calling for bread started riots, which spontaneously spread to the factories and throughout the city. From the front the tsar ordered the troops to restore order, but discipline broke down and the soldiers joined the revolutionary crowd. The Duma responded by declaring a provisional government on March 12, 1917. Three days later Nicholas abdicated without protest.

## THE PROVISIONAL GOVERNMENT

The March revolution was the result of an unplanned uprising of hungry, angry people in the capital, but it was joyfully accepted throughout the country. The patriotic upper and middle classes rejoiced at the prospect of a more determined and effective war effort, while workers happily anticipated better wages and more food. All classes and political parties called for liberty and democracy. They were not disappointed. As Lenin said, Russia became the freest country in the world. After generations of arbitrary authoritarianism the provisional government quickly established equality before the law; freedom of religion, speech, and assembly; the right of unions to organize and strike; and the rest of the classic liberal program.

Yet both the liberal and moderate socialist leaders of the provisional government rejected social revolution. The government formed in May 1917 by the fiery agrarian socialist Alexander Kerensky refused to confiscate large landholdings and give them to peasants, fearing that such drastic action in the countryside would only complete the disintegration of Russia's peasant army. For the patriotic Kerensky, as for other moderate socialists, the continuation of war was still the all-important national duty. There would be plenty of time for land reform later, and all Kerensky's efforts were directed toward a last offensive in early July. Human suffering and war-weariness grew, sapping the limited strength of the provisional government.

From its first day the provisional government had to share power with a formidable rival – the Petrograd Soviet (or "council") of Workers' and Soldiers' Deputies. Modeled on the revolutionary soviets of 1905, the Petrograd Soviet was a huge, fluctuating mass meeting of two to three thousand workers, soldiers, and socialist intellectuals. Seeing itself as a true grass-roots revolutionary democracy, this "counter" or "half" government suspiciously watched the provisional government and issued its own radical orders, further weakening Kerensky's government. The most famous of these orders was "Army Order No. 1," issued to all Russian military forces the very day the provisional government was formed.

Order No. 1 stripped officers of their authority and placed power in the hands of elected committees of common soldiers. Designed primarily to protect the revolution from some counterrevolutionary Bonaparte on horseback, Army Order No. 1 instead led to a total collapse of army discipline. Many an officer was hanged for his sins. Meanwhile, following the foolhardy summer offensive, masses of peasant soldiers began "voting with their feet," to use Lenin's graphic phrase. That is, they began returning to their villages to help their families get a share of the land, land that peasants were simply seizing as they settled old scores in a great agrarian upheaval. All across the country liberty was turning into anarchy in the summer of 1917. It was an unparalleled opportunity for the most radical and most talented of Russia's many socialist leaders, Vladimir Ilyich Lenin (1870–1924).

## LENIN AND THE BOLSHEVIK REVOLUTION

From his youth Lenin's whole life was dedicated to the cause of revolution. Born into the middle class, the seventeen-year-old Lenin became an implacable enemy of imperial Russia when his older brother was executed for plotting to kill the tsar in 1887. As a law student he began searching for a revolutionary faith. He found it in Marxian socialism, which began to win converts among radical intellectuals as industrialization surged forward in Russia in the 1890s. Exiled to Siberia for three years because of socialist agitation, Lenin studied Marxist doctrines with religious intensity. After his release, the young priest of socialism joined fellow believers in western Europe. There he lived for seventeen years and developed his own revolutionary interpretations of the body of Marxian thought.

Three interrelated ideas were central for Lenin. First, turning to the early fire-breathing Marx of 1848 and the *Communist Manifesto* for inspiration, Lenin stressed that capitalism could be destroyed only by violent revolution. He tirelessly denounced all revisionist theories of a peaceful evolution to socialism as betraying Marx's message of unending class conflict. Lenin's second, more original idea was that,

under certain conditions, a socialist revolution was possible even in a relatively backward country like Russia. Though capitalism was not fully developed there, and the industrial working class was small, the peasants were poor and thus potential revolutionaries.

Lenin believed that at a given moment revolution was determined more by human leadership than by vast historical laws. Thus Lenin's third basic idea: the necessity of a highly disciplined workers' party, strictly controlled by a dedicated elite of intellectuals and full-time revolutionaries like Lenin himself. Unlike ordinary workers and trade union officials, this elite would never be seduced by short-term gains. It would not stop until revolution brought it to power.

Lenin's theories and methods did not go unchallenged by other Russian Marxists. At the meetings of the Russian Social Democratic Labor party in London in 1903, matters came to a head. Lenin demanded a small, disciplined, elitist party, while his opponents wanted a more democratic party with mass membership. The Russian party of Marxian socialism promptly split into two rival factions. Lenin's camp was called "Bolsheviks" or "Majority"; his opponents were "Mensheviks" or "Minority." Lenin's majority did not last, but Lenin did not care. He kept the fine-sounding name "Bolshevik" and developed the party he wanted: tough, disciplined, revolutionary.

Unlike most socialists, Lenin did not rally round the national flag in 1914. Observing events from neutral Switzerland, he saw the war as a product of imperialistic rivalries and a marvelous opportunity for class war and socialist upheaval. The March revolution was, Lenin felt, a step in that direction. Since propaganda and internal subversion were accepted weapons of total war, the German government graciously provided the impatient Lenin, his wife, and about twenty trusted colleagues with safe passage across Germany and back into Russia in April 1917. The Germans hoped that Lenin would undermine the sagging war effort of the world's freest society. They were not disappointed.

Arriving triumphantly at Petrograd's Finland Station on April 3, Lenin attacked at once. To the great astonishment of local Bolsheviks, he rejected all cooperation with the "bourgeois" provisional government of the liberals and moderate socialists. His slogans were radical in the extreme: "All power to the Soviets." "All land to the peasants." "Stop the war now." Never a slave to Marxist determinism, the brilliant but not unduly intellectual Lenin was a superb tactician. The moment was now.

Yet Lenin almost overplayed his hand. An attempt by the Bolsheviks to seize power in July collapsed, and Lenin fled and went into hiding. He was charged with being a "German agent," and indeed he and the Bolsheviks were getting money from Germany.[12] But no matter. Intrigue between Kerensky and his commander-in-chief General Lavr Kornilov, a popular war hero "with the heart of a lion and the brains of a sheep," resulted in Kornilov's leading a feeble attack against the provisional government in September. In the face of this rightist "counterrevolutionary" threat, the Bolsheviks were rearmed and redeemed. Kornilov's forces disintegrated, but Kerensky lost all credit with the army and its officer corps, the only force that might have saved him and liberal government in Russia.

### TROTSKY AND THE SEIZURE OF POWER

Throughout the summer the Bolsheviks had appealed very effectively to the workers and soldiers of Petrograd, markedly increasing their popular support. Party membership had soared from 50,000 to 240,000 and in October the Bolsheviks gained a fragile majority in the Petrograd Soviet. Moreover, Lenin had found a strong right arm – Leon Trotsky, the second most important person in the Russian Revolution.

A spellbinding revolutionary orator and independent radical Marxist, Trotsky (1877–1940) supported Lenin wholeheartedly in 1917. It was he who brilliantly executed the Bolshevik seizure of power. Painting a vivid but untruthful picture of German and counterrevolutionary plots, Trotsky first convinced the Petrograd Soviet to form a special Military-Revolutionary Committee in October and make him its leader. Military power in the capital passed into Bolshevik hands. Trotsky's second master stroke was to insist that the Bolsheviks reduce opposition to their coup by taking power in the name not of the Bolsheviks but of the more popular and democratic soviets, which were meeting in Petrograd from all over Russia in early November. On the night of November 6, militants from Trotsky's committee joined with trusty Bolshevik soldiers to seize government buildings and pounce on members of the provisional government. Then on to the Congress of Soviets! There a Bolshevik majority – roughly 390 of 650 turbulent delegates – declared that all power had passed to the soviets and named Lenin head of the new government.

The Bolsheviks came to power for three key reasons. First, by late 1917 democracy had given way to anarchy: power was there for those who would take it. Second, in Lenin and Trotsky the Bolsheviks had utterly determined and truly superior leadership, which both the tsarist government and the provisional government lacked. Third, in 1917 the Bolsheviks

VLADIMIR LENIN *Dramatically displaying both his burning determination and his skill as a revolutionary orator, Lenin addresses the victorious May Day celebration of 1918 in Moscow's Red Square. (Culver Pictures)*

succeeded in appealing to many soldiers and urban workers, people who were exhausted by war and eager for socialism. With time many workers would become bitterly disappointed, but for the moment they had good reason to believe they had won what they wanted.

## DICTATORSHIP AND CIVIL WAR

History is full of short-lived coups and unsuccessful revolutions. The truly monumental accomplishment of Lenin, Trotsky, and the rest of the Bolsheviks was not taking power but keeping it. In the next four years the Bolsheviks went on to conquer the chaos they had helped to create, and they began to build their kind of dictatorial socialist society. The conspirators became conquerors. How was this done?

Lenin had the genius to profit from developments over which he and the Bolsheviks had no control. Since summer a peasant revolution had been sweeping across Russia, as the tillers of the soil invaded and divided among themselves the great and not-so-great estates of the landlords and the church. Peasant seizure of the land – a Russian 1789 – was not very Marxist, but it was quite unstoppable in 1917. Thus Lenin's first law, which supposedly gave land to the peasants, actually merely approved what peasants were already doing. Urban workers' great demand in November was direct control of individual factories by local workers' committees. This too Lenin ratified with a decree in November.

Unlike many of his colleagues, Lenin acknowledged that Russia had lost the war with Germany, that the Russian army had ceased to exist, and that the only realistic goal was peace at any price. The price was very high indeed. Germany demanded in December 1917 that the Soviet government give up all its western territories. These areas were inhabited by Poles, Finns, Lithuanians, and other non-Russians – all those peoples who had been conquered by the tsars over three centuries and put into the "prisonhouse of nationalities," as Lenin had earlier called the Russian Empire.

At first Lenin's fellow Bolsheviks would not accept such great territorial losses. But when German armies resumed their unopposed march into Russia in February 1918, Lenin had his way in a very close vote in the Central Committee of the party. "Not even his greatest enemy can deny that at this moment Lenin towered like a giant over his Bolshevik colleagues."[13] A third of old Russia's population was sliced away by the German meat ax in the Treaty of Brest-Litovsk in March 1918. With peace Lenin had escaped the certain disaster of continued war and could uncompromisingly pursue his goal of absolute political power for the Bolsheviks – now renamed Communists – within Russia.

In November 1917, the Bolsheviks had cleverly proclaimed their regime only a "provisional workers' and peasants' government," promising that a freely elected Constituent Assembly would draw up a new constitution. But the freest elections in Russia's history – both before and after 1917 – produced a stunning setback for the Bolsheviks, who won less than one-fourth of the elected delegates. The Socialist Revolutionaries – the peasants' party – had a clear majority. The Constituent Assembly met for only one day, on January 18, 1918. It was then permanently disbanded by Bolshevik soldiers acting under Lenin's orders. Thus, even before the peace with Germany, Lenin was clearly establishing a one-party government.

The destruction of the democratically elected Constituent Assembly helped feed the flames of civil war. People who had risen up for self-rule in November saw that once again they were getting dictatorship from the capital. For the next three years, "Long live the [democratic] soviets; down with the Bolsheviks" was to be a popular slogan. The officers of the old army took the lead in organizing the so-called White opposition to the Bolsheviks in southern Russia and the Ukraine, in Siberia, and to the west of Petrograd. The Whites came from many social groups and were united only by their hatred of the Bolsheviks – the Reds.

By the summer of 1918, *eighteen* self-proclaimed regional governments – several of which represented minority nationalities – competed with Lenin's Bolsheviks in Moscow. By the end of the year White armies were on the attack. In October 1919, it appeared they might triumph, as they closed in on Lenin's government from three sides. Yet they did not. By the spring of 1920, the White armies had been almost completely defeated, and the Bolshevik Red Army had

# THE RUSSIAN REVOLUTION

| | |
|---|---|
| 1914 | Russia enthusiastically enters the First World War |
| 1915 | Two million Russian casualties |
| | Progressive Bloc calls for a new government responsible to the Duma, not the tsar |
| | Tsar Nicholas adjourns the Duma and departs for the front; control of the government falls to Alexandra and Rasputin |
| December 1916 | Murder of Rasputin |
| March 8, 1917 | Bread riots in Petrograd (St. Petersburg) |
| March 12, 1917 | Duma declares a provisional government |
| March 15, 1917 | Tsar Nicholas abdicates without protest |
| April 3, 1917 | Lenin returns from exile and denounces the provisional government |
| May 1917 | Kerensky forms a moderate socialist government and continues the war |
| | Petrograd Soviet issues Army Order no. 1, granting military power to committees of common soldiers |
| Summer 1917 | Agrarian upheavals: peasants seize estates, peasant soldiers desert the army to join in |
| October 1917 | Bolsheviks gain a majority in the Petrograd Soviet |
| November 6, 1917 | Bolsheviks seize power; Lenin heads the new "provisional workers' and peasants' government" |
| November 1917 | Lenin ratifies peasant seizure of land and worker control of factories; all banks nationalized |
| January 1918 | Lenin permanently disbands the Constituent Assembly |
| February 1918 | Lenin convinces the Bolshevik Central Committee to accept a humiliating peace with Germany in order to pursue the revolution |
| March 1918 | Treaty of Brest-Litovsk: Russia loses one-third of its population |
| | Trotsky as war commissar begins to rebuild the Russian army |
| | Government moves from Petrograd to Moscow |
| 1918–1920 | Great Civil War |
| Summer 1918 | Eighteen competing regional governments; White armies oppose the Bolshevik revolution |
| 1919 | White armies on the offensive but divided politically; they receive little benefit from Allied intervention |
| 1920 | Lenin and Red armies victorious, retaking Belorussia and the Ukraine |

retaken Belorussia and the Ukraine. The following year the Communists also reconquered the independent nationalist governments of the Caucasus. The civil war was over; Lenin had won.

Lenin and the Bolsheviks won for several reasons. Strategically, they controlled the center, while the Whites were always on the fringes and disunited. Moreover, the poorly defined political program of the Whites was vaguely conservative, and it did not unite all the foes of the Bolsheviks under a progressive, democratic banner. For example, the most gifted of the White generals, the nationalistic General Anton Denikin, refused to call for a democratic republic and a federation of nationalities, although he knew doing so would help his cause. Most important, the Communists quickly developed a better army, an army for which the divided Whites were no match.

Once again Trotsky's leadership was decisive. The Bolsheviks had preached democracy in the army and had elected officers in 1917. But beginning in March 1918, Trotsky as war commissar re-established the draft and the most drastic discipline for the newly formed Red Army. Soldiers deserting or disobeying an order were summarily shot. Moreover, Trotsky made effective use of former tsarist army officers, who were actively recruited and given unprecedented powers of discipline over their troops. In short, Trotsky formed a highly disciplined and very effective fighting force.

The Bolsheviks also effectively mobilized the home front. Establishing "war communism" – the application of the "total war" concept to a civil conflict – they seized grain from the peasants, introduced rationing, nationalized all banks and industry, and required everyone to work. Although these measures

contributed to a breakdown of normal economic activity, they also served to maintain labor discipline and to keep the Red Army supplied.

"Revolutionary terror" also contributed to the Communist victory. The old tsarist secret police was re-established as the Cheka, which hunted down and executed thousands of real or supposed foes, like the tsar's family and other "class enemies." At one point, shortly after the government moved from Petrograd to Moscow in March 1918, a circus clown in Moscow was making fun of the Bolsheviks to an appreciative audience. Chekists in the crowd quickly pulled out their guns and shot several laughing people. Moreover, people were shot or threatened with being shot for minor nonpolitical failures. The terror aroused by the secret police became a tool of the government. The Cheka sowed fear, and fear silenced opposition.

Finally, foreign military intervention in the civil war ended up helping the Communists. After Lenin made peace with Germany, the Allies (the Americans, British, and Japanese) sent troops to Archangel and Vladivostok to prevent war materiel they had sent the provisional government from being captured by the Germans. After the Soviet government nationalized all foreign-owned factories without compensation, and refused to pay all of Russia's foreign debts, Western governments and particularly France began to support White armies. Yet these efforts were small and halfhearted. In 1919, Western peoples were sick of war, and few Western politicians believed in a military crusade against the Bolsheviks. Thus, Allied intervention in the civil war did not aid the Whites effectively, though it did permit the Communists to appeal to the patriotic nationalism of ethnic Russians, which was particularly strong among former tsarist army officers. Allied intervention was both too little and too much.

The Russian Revolution and the Bolshevik triumph was, then, one of the reasons why the First World War was such a great turning point in modern history. A radically new government, based on socialism and one-party dictatorship, came to power in a great European state, maintained power, and eagerly encouraged worldwide revolution. Although halfheartedly constitutional monarchy in Russia was undoubtedly headed for some kind of political crisis before 1914, it is hard to imagine the triumph of the most radical proponents of change and reform except in a situation of total collapse. That was precisely what happened to Russia in the First World War.

## THE PEACE SETTLEMENT

In 1918 the guns of world war finally fell silent. After winning great concessions from Lenin in the Treaty of Brest-Litovsk in March 1918, the Germans launched their last major attack against France. Yet this offensive failed like those before it. With breathtaking rapidity the United States, Great Britain, and France decisively defeated Germany militarily. Then, as civil war spread in Russia and as chaos engulfed much of eastern Europe, the victorious Western Allies came together in Paris to establish a lasting peace.

Expectations were high; optimism was almost unlimited. The Allies labored intensively and soon worked out terms for peace with Germany and for the creation of the peacekeeping League of Nations. Nevertheless, the hopes of peoples and politicians were soon disappointed, for the peace settlement of 1919 turned out to be a terrible failure. Rather than creating conditions for peace, it sowed the seeds of another war. Surely this was the ultimate tragedy of the Great War, a war that directly and indirectly cost $332 billion and left 10 million dead and another 20 million wounded. How did it happen? Why was the peace settlement unsuccessful?

### THE END OF THE WAR

In early 1917, the strain of total war was showing everywhere. After the Russian Revolution in March there were major strikes in Germany. In July a coalition of moderates passed a "peace resolution" in the German parliament, calling for peace without territorial annexations. To counter this moderation born of war-weariness, the German military established a virtual dictatorship and aggressively exploited the collapse of Russian armies after the Bolshevik Revolution. Victory in the east having quieted the German moderates, General Ludendorff and company fell on France once more in the great spring offensive of 1918. For a time German armies pushed forward, coming within thirty-five miles of Paris. But Ludendorff's exhausted, overextended forces never broke through. They were decisively stopped in July at the second battle of the Marne, where 140,000 fresh American soldiers saw action. Adding 2 million men in arms to the war effort by August, the late but massive American intervention decisively tipped the scales in favor of Allied victory.

By September, British, French, and American armies were advancing steadily on all fronts, and a panicky General Ludendorff realized that Germany had lost the war. Yet he insolently insisted that moderate politicians shoulder the shame of defeat, and on October 4 the emperor formed a new, more liberal German government to sue for peace. As negotiations over an armistice dragged on, an angry and frustrated German people finally rose up. On November 3, sailors in Kiel mutinied, and throughout northern Germany soldiers and workers began to establish revolutionary councils on the Russian soviet model. The same day Austria-Hungary surrendered to the Allies and began breaking apart. Revolution broke out in Germany, and masses of workers demonstrated for peace in Berlin. With army discipline collapsing, the emperor was forced to abdicate and fled to Holland. Socialist leaders in Berlin proclaimed a German republic on November 9 and simultaneously agreed to tough Allied terms of surrender. The armistice went into effect November 11, 1918. The war was over.

### REVOLUTION IN GERMANY

Military defeat brought political revolution to Germany and Austria-Hungary, as it had to Russia. In Austria-Hungary the revolution was primarily nationalistic and republican in character. Having started the war to preserve an antinationalist dynastic state, the Habsburg Empire had perished in the attempt. In its place independent Austrian, Hungarian, and Czechoslovakian republics were proclaimed, while a greatly expanded Serbian monarchy united the south Slavs and took the name of Yugoslavia. The prospect of firmly establishing the new national states overrode class considerations for most people in east central Europe.

The German revolution of November 1918 resembled the Russian Revolution of March 1917. In both cases a genuine popular uprising toppled an authoritarian monarchy and established a liberal provisional republic. In both countries liberals and moderate socialists took control of the central government, while workers' and soldiers' councils formed a "countergovernment." In Germany, however,

THE FALL OF MONARCHY   Entitled simply "November 1918," this eloquent drawing from a popular German magazine shows the crowns of Europe scattered like driftwood after the final wave of war and revolution. (Photo: Caroline Buckler)

the moderate socialists won and the Lenin-like radical revolutionaries in the councils lost. In communist terms, the liberal, republican revolution in Germany in 1918 was only "half" a revolution: a "bourgeois" political revolution without a communist second installment. It was Russia without Lenin's Bolshevik triumph.

There were several reasons for the German outcome. The great majority of Marxian socialist leaders in the Social Democratic party were, as before the war, really pink and not red. They wanted to establish real political democracy and civil liberties, and they favored the gradual elimination of capitalism. They were also German nationalists, appalled by the prospect of civil war and revolutionary terror. Moreover, there was much less popular support among workers and soldiers for the extreme radicals than in Russia. Nor did the German peasantry, which already had most of the land, at least in western Germany, provide the elemental force that has driven all great modern revolutions, from the French to the Chinese.

Of crucial importance also was the fact that the moderate German Social Democrats, unlike Kerensky and company, accepted defeat and ended the war the day they took power. This act ended the decline in morale among soldiers and prevented the regular army with its conservative officer corps from disintegrating. When radicals headed by Karl Liebknecht and Rosa Luxemburg and their supporters in the councils tried to seize control of the government in Berlin in January, the moderate socialists called on the army to crush the uprising. Liebknecht and Luxemburg were arrested and then brutally murdered by army leaders. Finally, even if the moderate socialists had taken the Leninist path, it is very unlikely they would have succeeded. Civil war in Germany would certainly have followed, and the Allies, who were already occupying western Germany according to the terms of the armistice, would have marched on to Berlin and ruled Germany directly. Historians have often been unduly hard on Germany's moderate socialists.

## THE TREATY OF VERSAILLES

The peace conference opened in Paris in January 1919 with seventy delegates representing twenty-seven victorious nations. There were great expectations. A young British diplomat,

Harold Nicolson, wrote later that the victors "were convinced that they would never commit the blunders and iniquities of the Congress of Vienna [of 1815]." Then "the misguided, reactionary, pathetic aristocrats" had cynically shuffled populations; now "we believed in nationalism, we believed in the self-determination of peoples." Indeed, "we were journeying to Paris . . . to found a new order in Europe. We were preparing not Peace only, but Eternal Peace."[14] The general optimism and idealism had been greatly strengthened by President Wilson's January 1918 peace proposal, the Fourteen Points, which stressed national self-determination and the rights of small countries.

The real powers at the conference were the United States, Great Britain, and France, for Germany was not allowed to participate and Russia was locked in civil war and did not attend. Italy was considered part of the Big Four, but its role was quite secondary. Almost immediately the three great allies began to quarrel. President Wilson, who was wildly cheered by European crowds as the spokesman for a new idealistic and democratic international cooperation, was almost obsessed with creating a League of Nations. Wilson insisted that this question come first, for he passionately believed that only a permanent international organization could protect member states from aggression and avert future wars. Wilson had his way, although Lloyd George of Great Britain and especially Clemenceau of France were unenthusiastic. They were primarily concerned with punishing Germany.

Playing on British nationalism, Lloyd George had already won a smashing electoral victory in December on the popular platform of making Germany pay for the war. "We shall," he promised, "squeeze the orange until the pips squeak." Personally inclined to make

THE TREATY OF VERSAILLES *was signed in the magnificent Hall of Mirrors. The Allies did not allow Germany to participate in the negotiation of the peace treaty. (National Archives)*

a somewhat moderate peace with Germany, Lloyd George was to a considerable extent a captive of demands for a total victory worthy of the sacrifices of total war against a totally depraved enemy. As Rudyard Kipling summed up the general British feeling at the end of the war, the Germans were "a people with the heart of beasts."[15]

France's Georges Clemenceau, "the Tiger," who had broken wartime defeatism and led his country to victory, wholeheartedly agreed. Like most French people, Clemenceau quite frankly wanted old-fashioned revenge. He also wanted lasting security for France. This, he believed, required the creation of a buffer state between France and Germany, the permanent demilitarization of Germany, and vast German reparations. He feared that sooner or later Germany with its 60 million people would attack France with its 40 million, unless the Germans were permanently weakened. Moreover, France had no English Channel (or Atlantic Ocean) as a reassuring barrier against German aggression. Wilson, supported by Lloyd George, would hear none of it. Clemenceau's demands seemed vindictive, violating morality and the principle of national self-determination. By April the conference was deadlocked on the German question, and Wilson packed his bags to go home.

Clemenceau's obsession with security reflected his anxiety about France's long-term weakness. In the end, convinced that France should not break with its allies because France could not afford to face Germany alone in the future, he agreed to a compromise. He gave up the French demand for a Rhineland buffer state in return for a formal defensive alliance with the United States and Great Britain. Under the terms of this alliance, both Wilson and Lloyd George promised that their countries would come to France's aid in the event of a German attack. Thus, Clemenceau appeared to win his goal of French security, as Wilson had won his of a permanent international organization. The Allies moved quickly to finish the peace settlement, believing that necessary adjustments would later be possible within the dual framework of a strong Western alliance and the League of Nations (see Map 27.4).

The Treaty of Versailles between the Allies and Germany was the key to the settlement, and the terms were not unreasonable as a first step toward re-establishing international order. (Had Germany won, it seems certain that France and Belgium would have been treated with greater severity, as Russia had been at Brest-Litovsk.) Germany's colonies were given to France, Britain, and Japan as League of Nations mandates. Germany's territorial losses within Europe were minor,

thanks to Wilson. Alsace-Lorraine was returned to France. Areas of Germany inhabited primarily by Poles were ceded to the new Polish state, in keeping with the principle of national self-determination. Predominantly German Danzig was also placed within the Polish tariff lines, but as a self-governing city under League of Nations protection. Germany had to limit its army to 100,000 men and agree to build no military fortifications in the Rhineland.

More harshly, the Allies declared that Germany (with Austria) was responsible for the war and had therefore to pay reparations equal to all civilian damages caused by the war. This unfortunate and much-criticized clause expressed inescapable popular demands for German blood, but the actual figure was not set and there was the clear possibility that reparations might be set at a reasonable level in the future, when tempers had cooled.

When presented with the treaty, the German government protested vigorously. But there was no alternative, especially in that Germany was still starving because the Allies had not yet lifted their naval blockade. On June 28, 1919, German representatives of the ruling moderate Social Democrats and the Catholic party signed the treaty in the Sun King's Hall of Mirrors at Versailles, where Bismarck's empire had been joyously proclaimed almost fifty years before.

Separate peace treaties were concluded with the other defeated powers – Austria, Hungary, Bulgaria, and Turkey. For the most part, these treaties merely ratified the existing situation in east central Europe following the breakup of the Austro-Hungarian Empire. Like Austria, Hungary was a particularly big loser, as its "captive" nationalities (and some interspersed Hungarians) were ceded to Rumania, Czechoslovakia, Poland, and Yugo-

### Legend

- Boundaries of German, Austrian, and Russian Empires in 1914
- Areas lost by Austro-Hungarian Empire
- Areas lost by Russian Empire
- Areas lost by German Empire
- Areas lost by Bulgaria
- Demilitarized Zone
- Boundaries of 1926

### Map Labels

NORWAY
SWEDEN
DENMARK
NORTH SEA
BALTIC SEA
FINLAND
Helsinki
Stockholm
Tallinn
Leningrad (St. Petersburg)
ESTONIA
Riga
LATVIA
LITHUANIA
Memel
NETHERLANDS
Amsterdam
Brussels
BELGIUM
GERMANY
Berlin
Danzig
EAST PRUSSIA
POLISH CORRIDOR
Vistula
Warsaw
POLAND
Kiev
RUHR
Cologne
Frankfurt
Weimar
Elbe
Prague
LUXEMBOURG
CZECHOSLOVAKIA
GALICIA
Paris
Versailles
LORRAINE
ALSACE
Rhine
Strasbourg
FRANCE
Berne
SWITZERLAND
Geneva
Locarno
S. TYROL
AUSTRIA
Vienna
HUNGARY
Budapest
BESSARABIA
Dniester
Milan
Trieste
Zagreb
RUMANIA
Genoa
Rapallo
Venice
CROATIA
Belgrade
Bucharest
BLACK SEA
ITALY
YUGOSLAVIA
SERBIA
BULGARIA
Rome
Sofia
Istanbul (Constantinople)
MONTENEGRO (To Yugoslavia, 1921)
ALBANIA
Naples
MEDITERRANEAN SEA
GREECE
TURKEY
Athens

0   300 Km.
0   150   300 Mi.

**MAP 27.4  SHATTERED EMPIRES AND TERRITORIAL CHANGES AFTER WORLD WAR ONE** The Great War brought tremendous changes in eastern Europe. New nations were established, and a dangerous power vacuum was created between Germany and Soviet Russia.

slavia. Italy got some Austrian territory. The Turkish empire was broken up. France received Lebanon and Syria, while Britain took Iraq and Palestine, which was to include a Jewish national homeland first promised by Britain in 1917. Officially League of Nations mandates, these acquisitions of the Western powers were one of the more imperialistic elements of the peace settlement. Another was mandating Germany's holdings in China to Japan. The age of Western imperialism lived on. National self-determination was still only for Europeans and their offspring.

## AMERICAN REJECTION OF THE VERSAILLES TREATY

The rapidly concluded peace settlement of early 1919 was not perfect, but within the context of war-shattered Europe it was an acceptable beginning. The principle of national self-determination, which had played such a large role in starting the war, was accepted and served as an organizing framework. Germany had been punished but not dismembered. A new world organization complemented a traditional defensive alliance of satisfied powers. The serious remaining problems could be worked out in the future. Moreover, Allied leaders had seen speed as essential for another reason: they detested Lenin and feared that his Bolshevik Revolution might spread. They realized that their best answer to Lenin's unending calls for worldwide upheaval was peace and tranquillity for war-weary peoples.

There were, however, two great interrelated obstacles to such peace: Germany and the United States. Plagued by communist uprisings, reactionary plots, and popular disillusionment with losing the war at the last minute, Germany's moderate socialists and their liberal and Catholic supporters faced an enormous challenge. Like French republicans after 1871, they needed time (and luck) if they were to establish firmly a peaceful and democratic republic. Progress in this direction required understanding yet firm treatment of Germany by the victorious Western Allies, and particularly by the United States.

However, the United States Senate and, to a lesser extent, the American people rejected Wilson's handiwork. Republican senators led by Henry Cabot Lodge refused to ratify the Treaty of Versailles without changes in the articles creating the League of Nations. The key issue was the league's power – more apparent than real – to require member states to take collective action against aggression.

Lodge and others believed that this requirement gave away Congress's constitutional right to declare war. No doubt Wilson would have been wise to accept some reservations. But, in failing health, Wilson with narrow-minded self-righteousness rejected all attempts at compromise. He instructed loyal Democratic senators to vote against any reservations whatsoever to the Treaty of Versailles. In doing so, Wilson assured that the treaty was never ratified by the United States in any form and that the United States never joined the League of Nations. Moreover, the Senate refused to ratify Wilson's defensive alliance with France and Great Britain. America turned its back on Europe.

Understandable perhaps in the light of American traditions, the Wilson-Lodge fiasco and the new-found gospel of isolationism represented nevertheless a tragic and cowardly renunciation of America's responsibility. Using America's action as an excuse, Great Britain too refused to ratify its defensive alliance with France. Bitterly betrayed by its allies, France stood alone. Very shortly, France was to take actions against Germany that would feed the fires of German resentment and seriously undermine democratic forces in the new republic. The great hopes of early 1919 were turning to ashes by the end of the year. The Western alliance had collapsed, and a grandiose plan for permanent peace had given way to a fragile truce. For this, and for what came later, the United States must share a large part of the guilt.

———◆———

Why did World War One have such revolutionary consequences? Why was it such a great break with the past? World War One was, first of all, a war of committed peoples. In France, Britain, and Germany in particular, governments drew on genuine popular support. This support reflected not only the diplomatic origins of the war but also the way western European society had been effectively unified under the nationalist banner in the later nineteenth century. The relentlessness of total war helps explain why so many died, why so many were crippled physically and psychologically, and why Western civilization would in so many ways never be the same again. More concretely, the war swept away monarchs and multinational empires. National self-determination apparently triumphed, not only in Austria-Hungary but in much of Russia's western borderlands as well. Except in Ireland and parts of Soviet Russia, the revolutionary dream of national unity, born of the French Revolution, had finally come true.

Two other revolutions were products of the war. In Russia the Bolsheviks established a radical regime, smashed existing capitalist institutions, and stayed in power with a new kind of authoritarian rule. Whether the new Russian regime was truly Marxian or socialist was questionable, but it indisputably posed a powerful, ongoing revolutionary challenge within Europe and in Europe's colonial empires.

More subtle, but quite universal in its impact, was an administrative revolution. This revolution, born of the need to mobilize entire societies and economies for total war, greatly increased the power of government. And after the guns grew still, government planning and wholesale involvement in economic and social life did not disappear in Europe. Liberal market capitalism and a well-integrated world economy were among the many casualties of the administrative revolution, and greater social equality was everywhere one of its results. Thus, even in European countries where a communist takeover never came close to occurring, society still experienced a great revolution.

Finally, the "war to end war" did not bring peace but only a fragile truce: in the West the Allies failed to maintain their wartime solidarity. Germany remained unrepentant and would soon have more grievances to nurse. Moreover, the victory of national self-determination in eastern Europe created a power vacuum between a still-powerful Germany and a potentially mighty Communist Russia. A vast area lay open to military aggression from two sides.

## NOTES

1. M. Beloff, *U.S. News and World Report,* 8 March 1976, p. 53.
2. Quoted by J. Remak, *The Origins of World War I,* Holt, Rinehart & Winston, New York, 1967, p. 84.
3. Quoted by W. E. Mosse, *Alexander II and the*

*Modernization of Russia,* Collier Books, New York, 1962, pp. 125–126.

4. Quoted by Remak, p. 123.

5. Quoted by J. E. Rodes, *The Quest for Unity: Modern Germany 1848–1970,* Holt, Rinehart & Winston, New York, 1971, p. 178.

6. Quoted by F. P. Chambers, *The War Behind the War, 1914–1918,* Faber & Faber, London, 1939, p. 444.

7. Ibid., p. 168.

8. Quoted by R. O. Paxton, *Europe in the Twentieth Century,* Harcourt Brace Jovanovich, New York, 1975, p. 109.

9. Quoted by Chambers, p. 378.

10. Ibid., p. 110.

11. Ibid., pp. 302, 304.

12. A. B. Ulam, *The Bolsheviks,* Collier Books, New York, 1968, p. 349.

13. Ibid., p. 405.

14. H. Nicolson, *Peacemaking 1919,* Grosset & Dunlap Universal Library, New York, 1965, pp. 8, 31–32.

15. Ibid., p. 24.

## SUGGESTED READING

Both J. Remak, *The Origins of World War I* (1967), and L. Lafore, *The Long Fuse* (1971), are highly recommended studies of the causes of the First World War. A. J. P. Taylor, *The Struggle for Mastery in Europe, 1848–1919* (1954), is an outstanding survey of diplomatic developments with an exhaustive bibliography. V. Steiner, *Britain and the Origins of the First World War* (1978), and G. Kennan, *The Decline of Bismarck's European Order: Franco-Russian Relations, 1875–1890* (1979), are also major contributions. K. Jarausch's *The Engimatic Chancellor* (1973) is an important recent study on Bethmann-Hollweg and German policy in 1914. C. Falls, *The Great War* (1961), is the best brief introduction to military aspects of the war. B. Tuch-

man, *The Guns of August* (1962), is a marvelous account of the dramatic first month of the war and the beginning of military stalemate. G. Ritter provides an able study in *The Schlieffen Plan* (1958). A. J. P. Taylor, *The First World War* (1963), is a strikingly illustrated history of the war, and A. Horne, *The Prince of Glory: Verdun 1916* (1979), is a moving account of the famous siege.

F. L. Carsten, *War Against War* (1982), considers radical movements in Britain and Germany. The best single volume on the home fronts is still F. Chambers, *The War Behind the War, 1914–1918* (1939). Chambers drew heavily on the many fine books on the social and economic impact of the war in different countries published by the Carnegie Endowment for International Peace under the general editorship of J. T. Shotwell. A. Marwick, *The Deluge* (1970), is a lively account of war and society in Britain, while G. Feldman, *Army, Industry, and Labor in Germany, 1914–1918* (1966), shows the impact of total war and military dictatorship on Germany. Two excellent collections of essays, J. Roth, ed., *World War I* (1967), and R. Albrecht-Carrié, ed., *The Meaning of the First World War* (1965), deftly probe the enormous consequences of the war for people and society. The debate over Germany's guilt and aggression, which has been reopened in recent years, may be best approached through G. Feldman, ed., *German Imperialism, 1914–1918* (1972). M. Fainsod, *International Socialism and the World War* (1935), ably discusses the splits between radical and moderate socialists during the conflict. In addition to Erich Maria Remarque's great novel *All Quiet on the Western Front,* Henri Barbusse, *Under Fire* (1917), and Jules Romains, *Verdun* (1939), are highly recommended for their fictional yet realistic recreations of the war.

A. Ulam's *The Bolsheviks* (1968), which focuses on Lenin, is a masterful introduction to the Russian Revolution, as is B. Wolfe, *Three Who Made a Revolution* (1955), a collective biography of Lenin, Trotsky, and Stalin. Leon Trotsky himself wrote the colorful and exciting *History of the Russian Revolution* (1932), which may be compared with the classic eyewitness account of the young, pro-Bolshevik American John Reed, *Ten Days That*

*Shook the World* (1919). R. Daniels, *Red October* (1969), provides a clear account of the Bolshevik seizure of power, and R. Pipes, *The Formation of the Soviet Union* (1968), is recommended for its excellent treatment of the nationality problem during the Revolution. A. Wildman, *The End of the Russian Imperial Army* (1980), is a fine account of the soldiers' revolt, and G. Leggett, *The Cheka: Lenin's Secret Police* (1981), shows revolutionary terror in action. Boris Pasternak's justly celebrated *Doctor Zhivago* is a great historical novel of the revolutionary era. R. Massie, *Nicholas and Alexandra* (1971), is a moving popular biography of Russia's last royal family and the terrible health problem of the heir to the throne. H. Nicolson, *Peacemaking 1919* (1965), captures the spirit of the Versailles settlement. T. Bailey, *Woodrow Wilson and the Lost Peace* (1963), and W. Widenor, *Henry Cabot Lodge and the Search for an American Foreign Policy* (1981), are also highly recommended. A. Mayer provocatively stresses the influence of domestic social tensions and widespread fears of further communist revolution in *The Politics and Diplomacy of Peacemaking* (1969).

# CHAPTER 28

## THE AGE OF ANXIETY

WHEN ALLIED DIPLOMATS met in Paris in early 1919 with their optimistic plans for building a lasting peace, most people looked forward to happier times. They hoped that life would return to "normal." They hoped that once again life would "make sense" in the familiar prewar terms of peace, prosperity, and progress. These hopes were in vain. The Great Break – the First World War and the Russian Revolution – had mangled too many things beyond repair. Life would no longer fit neatly into the old molds.

Instead, great numbers of men and women felt themselves increasingly adrift in a strange, uncertain, and uncontrollable world. They saw themselves living in an age of anxiety, an age of continuous crisis, which lasted until at least the mid-1950s. In almost every area of human experience people went searching for ways to put meaning back into life. What did the doubts and searching mean for Western thought, art, and culture? How did political leaders try to re-establish real peace and prosperity between 1919 and 1939? And why did they fail? These are questions this chapter will try to answer.

## UNCERTAINTY IN MODERN THOUGHT

A complex revolution in thought and ideas was under way before the First World War, but only small, unusual groups were aware of it. After the war, new and upsetting ideas began to spread through the entire population. Western society began to question and even abandon many cherished values and beliefs that had guided it since the eighteenth-century Enlightenment and the nineteenth-century triumph of industry, science, and evolutionary thought.

Before 1914, most people still believed in progress, reason, and the rights of the individual. Progress was a daily reality, apparent in the rising standard of living, the taming of the city, and the steady increase in popular education. Such developments also encouraged the comforting belief in the logical universe of Newtonian physics, as well as faith in the ability of a rational human mind to understand that universe through intellectual investigation. And just as there were laws of science, so were there laws of society that rational human beings could discover and then wisely act on. Finally, the rights of the individual were not just taken for granted, they were actually increasing. Well-established rights were gradually spreading to women and workers, and new "social rights" like old-age pensions were emerging. In short, before World War One most Europeans had a moderately optimistic view of the world, and with good reason.

From the 1880s on, however, a small band of serious thinkers and creative writers began to attack these well-worn optimistic ideas. These critics rejected the general faith in progress and the power of the rational human mind. One of the most influential of them, who was often ridiculed as a madman before 1914, was the German philosopher Friedrich von Nietzsche (1844–1900).

Nietzsche believed that Western civilization had lost its creativity and decayed into mediocrity. Christianity's "slave morality" had glorified weakness and humility. Furthermore, human beings in the West had overstressed rational thinking at the expense of passion and emotion. Nietzsche viewed the pillars of conventional morality – reason, democracy, progress, respectability – as outworn social and psychological constructs whose influence was suffocating creativity. The only hope of revival was for a few superior individuals to free themselves from the humdrum thinking of the masses and embrace life passionately. Such individuals would become true heroes, supermen capable of leading the dumb herd of inferior men and women. Nietzsche also condemned both political democracy and greater social equality.

The growing dissatisfaction with established ideas before 1914 was apparent in other thinkers. In the 1890s, the French philosophy professor Henri Bergson (1859–1941) convinced many young people through his writing that immediate experience and intuition are as important as rational and scientific thinking for understanding reality. Indeed, according to Bergson, a religious experience or a mystical poem is often more accessible to human comprehension than a scientific law or a mathematical equation.

Another thinker who agreed about the limits of rational thinking was the French socialist Georges Sorel (1847–1922). Sorel frankly characterized Marxian socialism as an inspiring but unprovable religion rather than a rational scientific truth. Socialism would come to power, he believed, through a great, violent strike of all working people, which would miraculously shatter capitalist society. Sorel rejected democracy and believed that the masses of the new socialist society would have to be tightly controlled by a small revolutionary elite.

In the years after 1918, a growing chorus of thinkers, creative writers, and scientists echoed and enlarged on the themes first expressed by the small band of critics between 1880 and 1914. Many prophets of doom bore witness to the decline and decay of Western civilization. The experience of history's most destructive war suggested to many that human beings certainly were a pack of violent, irrational animals quite capable of tearing the individual and his or her rights to shreds.

*"THE WAR, AS I SAW IT"* This was the title of a series of grotesque drawings which appeared in 1920 in Simplicissimus, *Germany's leading satirical magazine. Nothing shows better the terrible impact of World War One than this excellent, profoundly disturbing example of expressionist art. (Photo: Caroline Buckler)*

There was growing pessimism and a general crisis of the mind. People did not know what to think. This disorientation was particularly acute in the 1930s, when the rapid rise of harsh dictatorships and the Great Depression transformed old certainties into bitter illusions.

No one expressed this state of uncertainty better than the French poet and critic Paul Valéry (1871–1945) in the early 1920s. Speaking of the "crisis of the mind," Valéry noted that Europe was looking at its future with dark foreboding:

*The storm has died away, and still we are restless, uneasy, as if the storm were about to break. Almost all the affairs of men remain in a terrible uncertainty. We think of what has disappeared, and we are almost destroyed by what has been destroyed; we do not know what will be born, and we fear the future, not without reason.... Doubt and disorder are in us and with us. There is no thinking man, however shrewd or learned he may be, who can hope to dominate this anxiety, to escape from this impression of darkness.*[1]

In the midst of economic, political, and social disruptions Valéry saw the "cruelly injured mind," besieged by doubts and suffering from anxieties. This was the general intellectual crisis of the twentieth century, which touched almost every field of thought. The implications of new discoveries and ideas in physics, psychology, philosophy, and literature played a central role in this crisis, disturbing "thinking people" everywhere.

## THE NEW PHYSICS

Ever since the scientific revolution of the seventeenth century, scientific advances and their implications have greatly influenced the beliefs of thinking people. By the late nineteenth century, science was one of the main pillars supporting Western society's optimistic and rationalistic view of the world. The Darwinian concept of evolution had been accepted and assimilated in most intellectual circles. "Progressive minds" believed that science, unlike religion and philosophical speculation, was based on hard facts and controlled experiments. Science seemed to have achieved an unerring and almost completed picture of reality. Unchanging natural laws seemed to de-termine physical processes and permit useful solutions to ever more problems. All this was comforting, especially to people who no longer accepted traditional religious beliefs. And all this was challenged by the new physics.

An important first step toward the new physics was the discovery at the end of the century that atoms were not like hard, permanent little billiard balls. They were actually composed of many far smaller, fast-moving particles, such as electrons and protons. The Polish-born physicist Marie Curie (1867–1934) and her French husband discovered that radium constantly emits subatomic particles and thus does not have a constant atomic weight. Building on this and other work in radiation, the German physicist Max Planck (1858–1947) showed in 1900 that subatomic energy is emitted in uneven little spurts, which Planck called quanta, and not in a steady stream as previously believed. Planck's discovery called into question the old sharp distinction between matter and energy; the implication was that matter and energy might be different forms of the same thing. The old view of atoms as the stable, basic building blocks of nature, with a different kind of unbreakable atom for each of the ninety-two chemical elements, was badly shaken.

In 1905, the German-born Jewish genius Albert Einstein (1879–1955) went farther than the Curies and Planck in challenging Newtonian physics. His famous theory of special relativity postulated that time and space are not absolute, but relative to the viewpoint of the observer. To clarify Einstein's idea, consider a person riding on a train. From the viewpoint of an observer outside the train, the passenger's net speed is exactly the same whether the passenger is walking or sitting. From the passenger's viewpoint, walking to the restaurant car is different from sitting in a seat. The closed framework of Newtonian physics was quite limited compared to that of Einsteinian physics, which unified an apparently infinite universe with the incredibly small, fast-moving subatomic world. Moreover, Einstein's theory stated clearly that matter and energy are interchangeable and that all matter contains enormous potential energy.

The 1920s opened the "heroic age of physics," in the apt words of one of its leading pioneers, Ernest Rutherford (1871–1937). Breakthrough followed breakthrough. In 1919, Rutherford showed that the atom could be split. By 1944, seven subatomic particles had been identified, of which the most important was the neutron. The neutron's capacity to pass through other atoms allowed for even more intense experimental bombardment of matter, leading to chain reactions of unbelievable force. This was the road to the atomic bomb.

Although few nonscientists understood the revolution in physics, the implications of the new theories and discoveries, as presented by newspapers and popular writers, were disturbing to millions of men and women in the 1920s and 1930s. The new universe was strange and troubling. It lacked any absolute objective reality. Everything was "relative." Everything depended on the observer's frame of reference. Moreover, the universe was uncertain and undetermined, without stable building blocks. In 1927, the German physicist Werner Heisenberg (1901–1976) formulated the "principle of uncertainty." Heisenberg's principle postulates that because it is impossible to know the position and speed of an individual electron, it is therefore impossible to predict its behavior. Instead of Newton's dependable, rational laws, there

seemed to be only tendencies and probabilities in an extraordinarily complex and uncertain universe.

Moreover, a universe described by abstract mathematical symbols seemed to have little to do with human experience and human problems. When, for example, Max Planck was asked what science could contribute to resolving conflicts of values, his response was simple: "Science is not qualified to speak to this question." Physics, the queen of the sciences, no longer provided people easy, optimistic answers – or, for that matter, any answers at all.

## FREUDIAN PSYCHOLOGY

With physics presenting an uncertain universe so unrelated to ordinary human experience, questions regarding the power and potential of the human mind assumed special significance. The findings and speculations of the leading psychologist, Sigmund Freud (page 864), were particularly disturbing.

Before Freud, poets and mystics had probed the unconscious and irrational aspects of human behavior. But most professional, "scientific" psychologists assumed that a single, unified conscious mind processed sense experiences in a rational and logical way. Human behavior in turn was the result of rational calculation – of "thinking" – by the conscious mind. Basing his insights on the analysis of dreams and of hysteria, Freud developed a very different view of the human psyche beginning in the late 1880s.

According to Freud, human behavior is basically irrational. The key to understanding the mind is the primitive irrational unconscious, which he called the id. The unconscious is driven by sexual, aggressive, and pleasure-seeking desires and is locked in a constant battle with the other parts of the mind: the rationalizing conscious (the ego), which mediates what a person *can* do, and ingrained moral values (the superego), which tell what a person *should* do. Human behavior is a product of a fragile compromise between instinctual drives and the controls of rational thinking and moral values. Since the instinctual drives are extremely powerful, the ever-present danger for individuals and whole societies is that unacknowledged drives will overwhelm the control mechanisms in a violent, distorted way. Yet Freud also agreed with Nietzsche that the mechanisms of rational thinking and traditional moral values can be too strong. They can repress sexual desires too effectively, crippling individuals and entire peoples with guilt and neurotic fears.

Freudian psychology and clinical psychiatry had become an international movement by 1910, but only after 1918 did they receive popular attention, especially in the Protestant countries of northern Europe and in the United States. Many opponents and enthusiasts interpreted Freud as saying that the first requirement for mental health is an uninhibited sex life. Thus after the First World War, the popular interpretation of Freud reflected and encouraged the growing sexual experimentation, particularly among middle-class women. For more serious students, the psychology of Freud and his followers drastically undermined the old, easy optimism about the rational and progressive nature of the human mind.

## PHILOSOPHY: LOGICAL EMPIRICISM AND EXISTENTIALISM

The intellectual crisis of the twentieth century was fully reflected in philosophy, but in two very different ways. In English-speaking countries, the main development was the acceptance of logical empiricism (or logical positivism) in university circles. In continental countries, where esoteric and remote logical empiricism has never won many converts, the primary development in philosophy was existentialism.

Logical empiricism was truly revolutionary. It quite simply rejected most of the concerns of traditional philosophy, from the existence of God to the meaning of happiness, as nonsense and hot air. This outlook began primarily with the Austrian philosopher Ludwig Wittgenstein (1889–1951), who later migrated to England, where he trained many disciples.

Wittgenstein argued in his pugnacious *Tractatus Logico-Philosophicus (Essay on Logical Philosophy)* in 1922 that philosophy is only the logical clarification of thoughts, and therefore the study of language, which expresses thoughts. The great philosophical issues of the ages – God, freedom, morality, and so on – are quite literally senseless, a great waste of time, for statements about them can neither be tested by scientific experiments nor demonstrated by the logic of mathematics. Statements about such matters reflect only the personal preferences of a given individual. As Wittgenstein put it in the famous last sentence of his work: "Of what one cannot speak, of that one must keep silent." Logical empiricism, which has remained dominant in England and the United States to this day, drastically reduced the scope of philosophical inquiry. Anxious people could find few if any answers in this direction.

Highly diverse and even contradictory, existential thinkers were loosely united in a courageous search for human and moral values in a world of terror and uncertainty. They were true voices of the age of anxiety.

Most existential thinkers in the twentieth century have been atheists. Like Nietzsche, who had already proclaimed that "God is dead," they did not believe a supreme being had established humanity's fundamental nature and given life its meaning. In the words of the famous French existentialist Jean-Paul Sartre (1905–1980), human beings simply exist: "They turn up, appear on the scene." Only after they "turn up" do they seek to define themselves. Honest human beings are terribly alone, for there is no God to help them. They are hounded by despair and the meaninglessness of life. The crisis of the existential thinker epitomized the modern intellectual crisis – the shattering of traditional beliefs in God, reason, and progress.

Existentialists did recognize that human beings, unless they kill themselves, must act. Indeed, in the words of Sartre, "man is condemned to be free." There is, therefore, the possibility – indeed, the necessity – of giving meaning to life through actions, of defining oneself through choices. To do so, individuals must become "engaged" and choose their own actions courageously, consistently, and in full awareness of their inescapable responsibility for their own behavior. In the end, existentialists argued, human beings can overcome the absurdity that existentialists saw in life.

Modern existentialism developed first in Germany in the 1920s, when the philosophers Martin Heidegger and Carl Jaspers found a sympathetic audience among disillusioned postwar university students. But it was in France during the years immediately after World War Two that existentialism came of age. The terrible conditions of the war reinforced the existential view of life and the existential approach to it. On the one hand, the armies of the German dictator Hitler had conquered most of Europe and unleashed a hideous reign of barbarism. On the other, men and women had more than ever to define themselves by their actions. Specifically, each individual had to choose whether to join the Resistance against Hitler or to accept and even abet depraved tyranny. The writings of Sartre, who along with Albert Camus (1913–1960), was the leading French existentialist and himself active in the Resistance, became enormously influential. They offered a powerful answer to profound moral issues and the contemporary crisis.

## The Revival of Christianity

Christianity and religion in general had been on the defensive since the late eighteenth century. The loss of faith in human reason and continuous progress led to a renewed interest in the Christian view of the world in the twentieth century. A number of thinkers and theologians began to revitalize the fundamentals of Christianity, especially after World War One. They had a powerful impact on society. Sometimes described as Christian existentialists because they shared the loneliness and despair of atheistic existentialists, they revived the tradition of Saint Augustine. They stressed human beings' sinful nature, the need for faith, and the mystery of God's forgiveness.

This development was a break with the late nineteenth century. In the years before 1914, some theologians, especially Protestant theologians, had felt the need to interpret Christian doctrine and the Bible so that they did not seem to contradict science, evolution, and common sense. Christ was therefore seen primarily as the greatest moral teacher, and the "supernatural" aspects of his divinity were strenuously played down. An important if extreme example of this tendency was the young Albert Schweitzer's *Quest of the Historical Jesus* (1906). A theologian and later a famous medical missionary and a musician of note, Schweitzer (1875–1965) argued that Christ while on earth was a completely natural man whose teachings had been only temporary rules to prepare himself and his disciples for the end of the world, which they were erroneously expecting. In short, some modern theologians were embarrassed by the miraculous, unscientific aspects of Christianity and turned away from them.

The revival of fundamental Christian belief after World War One was fed by rediscovery of the work of the nineteenth-century Danish religious philosopher Søren Kierkegaard (1813–1855), whose ideas became extremely influential. Kierkegaard had rejected formalistic religion and denounced the worldliness of the Danish Lutheran church. He had eventually resolved his personal anguish over his imperfect nature by making a total religious commitment to a remote and majestic God.

Similar ideas were brilliantly developed by the Swiss Protestant theologian Karl Barth (1886–1968), whose many influential writings after 1920 sought to recreate the religious intensity of the Reformation. For Barth, the basic fact about human beings is that they are imperfect, sinful creatures, whose reason and will are hopelessly flawed. Religious truth is therefore made known to human beings only through God's grace. People have to accept God's word and the supernatural revelation of Jesus Christ with awe, trust, and obedience. Lowly mortals should not expect to "reason out" God and his ways.

Among Catholics, the leading existential Christian thinker was Gabriel Marcel (1889–1973). Born into a cultivated French family, where his atheistic father was "gratefully

aware of all that ... art owed to Catholicism but regarded Catholic thought itself as obsolete and tainted with absurd superstitions,"[2] Marcel found in the Catholic church an answer to what he called the postwar "broken world." Catholicism and religious belief provided the hope, humanity, honesty, and piety for which he hungered. Flexible and gentle, Marcel and his countryman Jacques Maritain (1882–1973) denounced anti-Semitism and supported closer ties with non-Catholics.

After 1914, religion became much more relevant and meaningful to thinking people than it was before the war. In addition to Marcel and Maritain, many other illustrious individuals turned to religion between about 1920 and 1950. The poets T. S. Eliot and W. H. Auden, the novelists Evelyn Waugh and Aldous Huxley, the historian Arnold Toynbee, the Oxford professor C. S. Lewis, the psychoanalyst Karl Stern, and the physicist Max Planck were all either converted to religion or attracted to it for the first time. Religion, often of a despairing, existential variety, was one meaningful answer to terror and anxiety. As another famous Roman Catholic convert, the English novelist Graham Greene, explained: "One began to believe in heaven because one believed in hell."[3]

## TWENTIETH-CENTURY LITERATURE

Literature articulated the general intellectual climate of pessimism, relativism, and alienation. Novelists developed new techniques to express new realities. The great nineteenth-century novelists had typically written as all-knowing narrators, describing realistic characters and their relationship to an understandable if sometimes harsh society. In the twentieth century, most major writers adopted the limited, often confused viewpoint of a single individual. Like Freud, these novelists focused their attention on the complexity and irrationality of the human mind, where feelings, memories, and desires are forever scrambled. The great French novelist Marcel Proust (1871–1922) in his semi-autobiographical *Remembrance of Things Past* (1913–1922) recalled bittersweet memories of childhood and youthful love and tried to discover their innermost meaning. To do so, Proust lived like a hermit in a soundproof Paris apartment for ten years, withdrawing from the present to dwell on the past.

Serious novelists also used the "stream-of-consciousness" technique to explore the psyche. In *Jacob's Room* (1922), Virginia Woolf (1882–1941) turned the novel into a series of internal monologues, in which ideas and emotions from different periods of time bubble up as randomly as they do from a patient on a psychoanalyst's couch. William Faulkner (1897–1963), perhaps America's greatest twentieth-century novelist, used the same technique in *The Sound and the Fury,* much of whose intense drama is confusedly seen through the eyes of an idiot. The most famous stream-of-consciousness novel – and surely the most disturbing novel of its generation – is *Ulysses,* which the Irish novelist James Joyce (1882–1941) published in 1922. Into *Ulysses'* account of an ordinary day in the life of an ordinary man, Joyce weaves an extended ironic parallel between his hero's aimless wanderings through the streets and pubs of Dublin and the adventures of Homer's hero Ulysses on his way home from Troy. Abandoning conventional grammar and blending foreign words, puns, bits of knowledge, and scraps of memory together in bewildering confusion, *Ulysses* is like modern life itself: a gigantic riddle waiting to be unraveled.

As creative writers turned their attention from society to the individual and from realism to psychological relativity, they rejected the idea of progress. Some even described "anti-utopias," nightmare visions of things to come. In 1918, an obscure German high school teacher named Oswald Spengler (1880–1936) published *Decline of the West,* which quickly became an international sensation. According to Spengler, every culture experiences a life cycle of growth and decline. Western civilization, in Spengler's opinion, was in its old age, and death was approaching, in the form of conquest by the yellow race. T. S. Eliot (1888–1965), in his famous poem *The Waste Land* (1922), depicted a world of growing desolation, although after his conversion to Anglo-Catholicism in 1927, Eliot came to hope cautiously for humanity's salvation. No such hope appeared in the work of Franz Kafka (1883–1924), whose novels *The Trial* and *The Castle,* as well as several of his greatest short stories, portray helpless individuals crushed by inexplicable hostile forces. The German-Jewish Kafka died young, at forty-one, and so did not see the world of his nightmares materialize in the Nazi state.

The Englishman George Orwell (1903–1950), however, had seen both that reality and its Stalinist counterpart by 1949 when he wrote perhaps the ultimate in anti-utopian literature: *1984.* The action is set in the future, in 1984. Big Brother – the dictator – and his totalitarian state use a new kind of language, sophisticated technology, and psychological terror to strip a weak individual of his last shred of human dignity. As the supremely self-confident chief of the Thought Police tells the tortured, broken, and framed Winston Smith: "If you want a picture of the future, imagine a boot stamping on a human face – forever."[4] A phenomenal best seller,

*1984* spoke to millions of people in the closing years of the age of anxiety.

## MODERN ART AND MUSIC

Throughout the twentieth century, there has been considerable unity in the arts. The "modernism" of the immediate prewar years and the 1920s is still strikingly modern. Manifestations of modernism in art, architecture, and music have of course been highly varied, just as in physics, psychology, and philosophy; yet there are resemblances, for artists, scientists, and original thinkers partake of the same culture. Creative artists rejected old forms and old values. Modernism in art and music meant constant experimentation and a search for new kinds of expression. And although many people find the modern visions of the arts strange, disturbing, and even ugly, the twentieth century, so dismal in many respects, will probably stand as one of Western civilization's great artistic eras.

### ARCHITECTURE AND DESIGN

Modernism in the arts was loosely unified by a revolution in architecture. The architectural revolution not only gave the other arts striking new settings, it intended nothing less than to transform the physical framework of the urban society according to a new principle: functionalism. Buildings, like industrial products, should be useful and "functional": that is, they should serve as well as possible the purpose for which they were made. Thus, architects and designers had to work with engineers, town planners, and even sanitation experts. Moreover, they had to throw away useless ornamentation and find beauty and aesthetic pleasure in the clean lines of practical

*MODERN ARCHITECTURE   Glass, steel, and cool, hard lines characterized the new international style. The Seagram Building in New York (1957) was one of Mies van der Rohe's greatest works. (Joseph E. Seagram and Sons, Inc.; photo: Ezra Stoller)*

constructions and efficient machinery. The Viennese pioneer Adolf Loos (1870–1933) quite typically equated ornamentation with crime, and the Franco-Swiss genius Le Corbusier (1887–1965) insisted that "a house is a machine for living in."[5]

The United States, with its rapid urban growth and lack of rigid building traditions, pioneered in the new architecture. In the 1890s, the Chicago school of architects, led by Louis H. Sullivan (1856–1924), used cheap steel, reinforced concrete, and electric elevators to build skyscrapers and office buildings lacking almost any exterior ornamentation. In the first decade of the twentieth century, Sullivan's student Frank Lloyd Wright (1869–1959) built a series of radically new and truly modern houses featuring low lines, open interiors, and mass-produced building materials. Europeans were inspired by these efforts, and by such other American examples of practical construction as the massive, unadorned grain elevators of the Middle West, those majestic masterpieces of stark functionalism.

Around 1905, when the first really modern buildings were going up in Europe, architectural leadership shifted to the German-speaking countries and remained there until Hitler took power in 1933. In 1911, the twenty-eight-year-old Walter Gropius (1883–1969) broke sharply with the past in his design of the Fagus shoe factory at Alfeld, Germany. A clean, light elegant building of glass and iron, Gropius's new factory represented a jump right into the middle of the century.

After the First World War, the new Ger-

man republic gave Gropius the authority to merge the schools of fine and applied arts at Weimar into a single, interdisciplinary school, the Bauhaus. In spite of intense criticism from conservative politicians and university professors, the Bauhaus brought together many leading modern architects, artists, designers, and theatrical innovators, who worked as an effective, inspired team. Throwing out traditional teaching methods, they combined the study of fine art, such as painting and sculpture, with the study of applied art in the crafts of printing, weaving, and furniture making. Throughout the 1920s the Bauhaus, with its stress on functionalism and good design for everyday life, attracted enthusiastic students from all over the world. It had a great and continuing impact.

Along with Gropius, the Franco-Swiss architect and town planner Le Corbusier had a revolutionary influence on the development of modern architecture. Often drawing his inspiration from industrial forms, such as ocean liners, automobiles, and airplanes, Le Corbusier designed houses with flat roofs, open interior spaces, and clear, clean lines. His famous Savoy Villa at Poissy rested on concrete pillars and seemed to float on air. A true visionary, Le Corbusier sketched plans for a city of the future, with tall buildings surrounded by playgrounds and parks.

Another leader in the modern or "international" style was Ludwig Mies van der Rohe (1886–1969), who followed Gropius as director of the Bauhaus in 1930 and emigrated to the United States in 1937. His classic Lake Shore Apartments in Chicago, built between 1948 and 1951, symbolize the triumph of steel-frame and glass-wall modern architecture, which had grown out of Sullivan's skyscrapers and German functionalism in the great building boom after the Second World War.

## MODERN PAINTING

Modern painting grew out of a revolt against French impressionism. The impressionism of Monet, Renoir, and Pissarro was, in part, a kind of "superrealism." Leaving exact copying of objects to photography, these artists sought to capture the momentary overall feeling, or impression, of light falling on a real-life scene before their eyes. By 1890, when impressionism was finally established, a few artists known as post-impressionists, or expressionists, were already striking out in new directions. After 1905, art took on an abstract, nonrepresentational character, which it has generally retained to the present.

Although individualistic in their styles, post-impressionists were united in their desire to know and depict worlds other than the visible world of fact. Like the early-nineteenth-century romantics, they wanted to portray unseen, inner worlds of emotion and imagination. Like modern novelists, they wanted to express a complicated psychological view of reality as well as an overwhelming emotional intensity. In *The Starry Night* (1889), for example, the great Dutch expressionist Vincent van Gogh (1853–1890) painted the vision of his mind's eye. Flaming cypress trees, exploding stars, and a cometlike Milky Way swirl together in one great cosmic rhythm. Paul Gauguin (1848–1903), the French stockbroker-turned-painter, pioneered in expressionist techniques, though he used them to infuse his work with tranquillity and mysticism. In 1891, he fled to the South Pacific in search of unspoiled beauty and a primitive way of life. Gauguin believed that the form and design of a picture was important in itself, and that the painter need not try to represent objects on canvas as the eye actually saw them.

Fascination with form, as opposed to light,

PICASSO: GUERNICA  *In this rich, complex work a shrieking woman falls from a burning house on the far right. On the left a woman holds a dead child, while toward the center are fragments of a warrior and a screaming horse pierced by a spear. Picasso has used only the mournful colors of black, white, and gray. (Pablo Picasso, Guernica [1937, May–early June]. Oil on canvas. © SPADEM, Paris/VAGA, New York, 1982)*

as characteristic of post-impressionism and expressionism. Paul Cézanne (1839–1906), who had a profound influence on twentieth-century painting, was particularly committed to form and ordered design. He told a young painter, "You must see in nature the cylinder, the sphere, and the cone."[6] As Cézanne's later work became increasingly abstract and non-representational, it also moved away from the traditional three-dimensional perspective toward the two-dimensional plane, which has characterized so much of modern art. The expressionism of a group of painters led by Henri Matisse (1869–1954) was so extreme that an exhibition of their work in Paris in 1905 prompted shocked critics to call them *les fauves*–the wild beasts. Matisse and his followers were primarily concerned not with real objects but with the arrangment of color, line, and form as an end in itself.

In 1907 a young Spaniard in Paris, Pablo Picasso (1881–1973), founded another movement – cubism. Cubism concentrated on a complex geometry of zigzagging lines and sharp-angled, overlapping planes. About three years later came the ultimate stage in the development of abstract, nonrepresentational art. Artists such as the Russian-born Wassily Kandinsky (1866–1944) turned away from nature completely. "The observer," said Kandinsky, "must learn to look at [my] pictures . . . as form and color combinations . . . as a representation of *mood* and not as a representation of *objects*."[7] On the eve of the First World War, extreme expressionism and abstract painting were developing rapidly not only in Paris but also in Russia and Germany. Modern art had become international.

In the 1920s and 1930s, the artistic movements of the prewar years were extended and consolidated. The most notable new developments were dadaism and surrealism. Dadaism attacked all accepted standards of art and behavior, delighting in outrageous conduct. Its name, from the French word *dada,* meaning "hobbyhorse," is deliberately nonsensical. A famous example of dadaism was a reproduction of Leonardo da Vinci's *Mona Lisa* in which the famous woman with the mysterious smile sports a mustache and is ridiculed with an obscene inscription. After 1924, many dadaists were attracted to surrealism, which became very influential in art in the late 1920s and 1930s. Surrealism was inspired to a great extent by Freudian psychology. Surrealists painted a fantastic world of wild dreams and complex symbols, where watches melted and giant metronomes beat time in precisely drawn but impossible, alien landscapes.

Refusing to depict ordinary visual reality, surrealist painters made powerful statements about the age of anxiety. Picasso's twenty-six-foot-long mural *Guernica* (1937) masterfully unites several powerful strands in twentieth-century art. Inspired by the Spanish Civil War, the painting commemorates the bombing of the ancient Spanish town of Guernica by fascist planes, an attack that took the lives of a thousand people – one out of every eight inhabitants – in a single night of terror. Combining the free distortion of expressionism, the overlapping planes of cubism, and the surrealist fascination with grotesque subject matter, *Guernica* is what Picasso meant it to be: an unforgettable attack on "brutality and darkness."

## MODERN MUSIC

Developments in modern music were strikingly parallel to those in painting. Composers too were attracted by the emotional intensity of expressionism. The ballet *The Rite of Spring* by Igor Stravinsky (1882–1971) practically caused a riot when it was first performed in Paris in 1913 by Sergei Diaghilev's famous Russian dance company. The combination of pulsating, barbaric rhythms from the orchestra pit and an earthy representation of love-making by the dancers on the stage seemed a shocking, almost pornographic enactment of a primitive fertility rite.

After the experience of the First World War, when irrationality and violence seemed to pervade the human experience, expressionism in opera and ballet flourished. One of the most famous and powerful examples is the opera *Wozzeck* by Alban Berg (1885–1935), first performed in Berlin in 1925. Blending a half-sung, half-spoken kind of dialogue with harsh, atonal music, *Wozzeck* is a gruesome tale of a soldier driven to murder his mistress by Kafka-like inner terrors and vague suspicions of her unfaithfulness.

Some composers turned their backs on long-established musical conventions. As abstract painters arranged lines and color but did not draw identifiable objects, so modern composers arranged sounds without creating recognizable harmonies. Led by the Viennese composer Arnold Schönberg (1874–1951), they abandoned traditional harmony and tonality. The musical notes in a given piece were no longer united and organized by a key; instead they were independent and unrelated. Schönberg's twelve-tone music of the 1920s arranged all twelve notes of the scale in an abstract, mathematical pattern, or "tone row." This pattern sounded like no pattern at all to the ordinary listener and could be detected only by a highly trained eye studying the musical score. Accustomed to the harmonies of classical and romantic music, audiences generally resisted modern atonal music. Only after the Second World War did it begin to win acceptance.

## MOVIES AND RADIO

Until after World War Two at the earliest, these revolutionary changes in art and music appealed mainly to a minority of "highbrows" and not to the general public. That public was primarily and enthusiastically wrapped up in movies and radio. The long-declining traditional arts and amusements of people in villages and small towns almost vanished, increasingly replaced by standardized, commercial entertainment.

Moving pictures were first shown as a popular novelty in naughty peepshows – "What the Butler Saw" – and penny arcades in the 1890s, especially in Paris. The first "movie houses" date from an experiment in Los Angeles in 1902. They quickly attracted large audiences and led to the production of short, silent action films like the eight-minute *Great Train Robbery* of 1903. American directors and businessmen then set up "movie factories," at first in the New York area and after 1910 in Los Angeles. These factories churned out two short films each week. On the eve of the First World War full-length feature films like the Italian *Quo Vadis* and the American *Birth of a Nation,* coupled with improvements in the quality of pictures, suggested the vast possibilities of screen drama.

During the First World War the United States became the dominant force in the rapidly expanding silent-film industry. In the 1920s, Mack Sennett (1884–1960) and his zany Keystone Cops specialized in short slapstick comedies noted for frantic automobile chases, custard-pie battles, and gorgeous bathing beauties. Screen stars such as Mary Pickford and Lillian Gish, Douglas Fairbanks and Rudolph Valentino became household names, with their own "fan clubs." Yet Charlie Chaplin (1889–1978), a funny little English-

man working in Hollywood, was unquestionably "The King of the Silver Screen" in the 1920s. In his enormously popular role as a lonely tramp, complete with baggy trousers, battered derby, and an awkward, shuffling walk, Chaplin symbolized "the gay spirit of laughter in a cruel, crazy world."[8] Chaplin also demonstrated that, in the hands of a genius, the new medium could combine mass entertainment and artistic accomplishment.

The early 1920s was also the great age of German films. Protected and developed during the war, the large German studios excelled in bizarre expressionist dramas, beginning with *The Cabinet of Dr. Caligari* in 1919. Unfortunately, their period of creativity was short-lived. By 1926, American money was drawing the leading German talents to Hollywood and consolidating American's international domination. Film making was big business, and European theater owners were forced to book whole blocks of American films to get the few pictures they really wanted. This system put European producers at a great disadvantage until "talkies" permitted a revival of national film industries in the 1930s, particularly in France.

Whether foreign or domestic, motion pictures became the main entertainment of the masses until after the Second World War. In Great Britain one in every four adults went to the movies twice a week in the late 1930s, and two in five went once a week. Continental countries had similar figures. The greatest appeal of motion pictures was that they offered ordinary people a temporary escape from the hard realities of everyday life. For an hour or two the moviegoer could flee the world of international tensions, uncertainty, unemployment, and personal frustrations. The appeal of escapist entertainment was especially strong during the Great Depression. Millions flocked to musical comedies featuring glittering stars

MATINEE IDOLS *Fresh and winsome, the Canadian-born Mary Pickford was affectionately known as "America's Sweetheart." Starring in sentimental romances like* Poor Little Rich Girl, Pollyanna, Little Lord Fauntleroy, *she made a fortune and reigned over Hollywood with her second husband, Douglas Fairbanks. Dark and handsome, Italian-born Rudolph Valentino was Hollywood's original "Latin lover." Shown here in his first leading role in the stirring* Four Horsemen of the Apocalypse, *the irresistible Valentino made millions of hearts beat faster until his mysterious death in 1926. (The New York Public Library Picture Collection)*

such as Ginger Rogers and Fred Astaire, and to the fanciful cartoons of Mickey Mouse and his friends.

Radio became possible with the transatlantic "wireless" communication of Guglielmo Marconi (1874-1937) in 1901 and the development of the vacuum tube in 1904, which permitted the transmission of speech and music. But only in 1920 were the first major public broadcasts of special events made in Great Britain and the United States. Lord Northcliffe, who had pioneered in journalism with the inexpensive, mass-circulation *Daily Mail,* sponsored a broadcast of "only one artist ... the world's very best, the soprano Nellie Melba."[9] Singing from London in English, Italian, and French, Melba was heard simultaneously all over Europe on June 16, 1920. This historic event captured the public's imagination. The meteoric career of radio was launched.

Every major country quickly established national broadcasting networks. In the United States, such networks were privately owned and financed by advertising. In Great Britain, Parliament set up an independent, high-minded public corporation, the BBC, which was supported by licensing fees. Elsewhere in Europe the typical pattern was direct control by the government.

Whatever the institutional framework, radio became popular and influential. By the late 1930s, more than three out of every four households in both democratic Great Britain and dictatorial Germany had at least one cheap, mass-produced radio. In other European countries radio ownership was not quite so widespread, but the new medium was no less important.

Radio in unscrupulous hands was particularly well suited for political propaganda. Dictators like Mussolini and Hitler controlled the airwaves and could reach enormous national audiences with their frequent, dramatic speeches. In democratic countries, politicians such as President Franklin Roosevelt and Prime Minister Stanley Baldwin effectively used informal fireside chats to bolster their support.

Motion pictures also became powerful tools of indoctrination, especially in countries with dictatorial regimes. Lenin himself encouraged the development of Soviet film making, believing that the new medium was essential for the social and ideological transformation of the country. Beginning in the mid-1920s, a series of epic films, the most famous of which were directed by Sergei Eisenstein (1898-1948), brilliantly dramatized the communist view of Russian history.

In Germany, Hitler turned to a young and immensely talented woman film maker, Leni Riefenstahl (b. 1902), for a masterpiece of documentary propaganda, *The Triumph of the Will,* based on the Nazi party rally at Nuremberg in 1934. Riefenstahl combined stunning aerial photography, joyful crowds welcoming Hitler, and mass processions of young Nazi fanatics. Her film was a brilliant and all-too-powerful "documentary" of Germany's "Nazi rebirth." The new media of mass culture were clearly potentially dangerous tools of political manipulation.

## THE SEARCH FOR PEACE AND POLITICAL STABILITY

The Versailles settlement had established a shaky truce, not a solid peace. Within the general context of intellectual crisis and revolutionary artistic experimentation, politicians and statesmen struggled to create a stable international order.

The pursuit of real and lasting peace proved difficult. Germany hated the Treaty of Versailles, and France was fearful and isolated. Britain was undependable, and the United States had turned its back on European problems. Eastern Europe was in ferment, and no one could predict the future of Communist Russia. Moreover, the international economic situation was poor and greatly complicated by war debts and disrupted patterns of trade. Yet for a time, from 1925 to late 1929, it appeared that peace and stability were within reach. When the subsequent collapse of the 1930s mocked these hopes, the disillusionment of liberals in the democracies was intensified.

## GERMANY AND THE WESTERN POWERS

Germany was the key to lasting peace. Only under the pressure of the Allies' naval blockade and threat to extend their military occupation from the Rhineland to the rest of the country had Germany's new republican government signed the Treaty of Versailles in June 1919. To Germans of all political parties, the treaty represented a harsh, dictated peace, to be revised or repudiated as soon as possible. The treaty had neither broken nor reduced Germany, which was potentially still the strongest country in Europe. Thus, the treaty had fallen between two stools: too harsh for a peace of reconciliation, it was too soft for a peace of conquest.

Moreover, with ominous implications for the future, France and Great Britain did not see eye to eye on Germany. By the end of 1919, France wanted to stress the harsh elements in the Treaty of Versailles. Most of the war in the west had been fought on French soil, and much of rich, industrialized, northern France had been devastated. The expected costs of reconstruction were staggering, and

French politicians believed that massive reparations from Germany were a vital necessity. If the Germans had to suffer to make the payments, the French would not be overly concerned. Having compromised with President Wilson only to be betrayed by America's failure to ratify the treaty, many French leaders saw strict implementation of all provisions of the Treaty of Versailles as France's last best hope. Large reparation payments could hold Germany down indefinitely, and France would realize its goal of security.

The British soon felt differently. Prewar Germany had been Great Britain's second-best market in the entire world, and after the war a healthy, prosperous Germany appeared to be essential to the British economy. Indeed, many English people agreed with the analysis of the young English economist John Maynard Keynes (1883–1946), who eloquently denounced the Treaty of Versailles in his famous *Economic Consequences of the Peace* (1919). According to Keynes's interpretation, astronomical reparations and harsh economic measures would indeed reduce Germany to the position of an impoverished, second-rate power, but such impoverishment would increase economic hardship in all countries. Only a complete revision of the foolish treaty could save Germany – and Europe. Keynes's attack exploded like a bombshell and became very influential. It stirred deep guilt feelings about Germany in the English-speaking world, feelings that often paralyzed English and American leaders in their relations with Germany between the First and Second World Wars.

The British were also suspicious of France's army – momentarily the largest in Europe – and France's foreign policy. Ever since 1890, France had looked to Russia as a powerful ally against Germany. But with Russia hostile and socialist, and with Britain and the United States unwilling to make any firm commitments, France turned to the newly formed states of eastern Europe for diplomatic support. In 1921, France signed a mutual defense pact with Poland and associated itself closely with the so-called Little Entente, an alliance that joined Czechoslovakia, Rumania, and Yugoslavia against defeated and bitter Hungary. The British and the French were also on cool terms because of conflicts relating to their League of Nations mandates in the Middle East. In late 1920, after serving as France's brilliant ambassador to Great Britain for twenty long years, Paul Cambon mournfully wrote, "I do not believe in the possibility of a rupture but everywhere, on every point, there is disagreement, and the misfortune is that neither in Paris nor in London are they intelligent enough to reduce the disagreements to the essential points and disregard the trifles."[10]

While French and British leaders drifted in different directions, the Allied reparations commission completed its work. In April 1921, it announced that Germany had to pay the enormous sum of $35 billion over many, many years. Facing possible occupation of more of its territory, the young German republic, which had been founded in Weimar but moved back to Berlin, made its first payment in 1921. Then, in 1922, wracked by rapid inflation and political assassinations, and motivated by hostility and arrogance as well, the Weimar Republic announced its inability to pay more. It proposed a moratorium on reparations for three years, with the clear implication that thereafter reparations would either be drastically reduced or eliminated entirely.

The British were willing to accept this offer, but the French were not. Led by their tough-minded, legalistic prime minister, Raymond Poincaré, they decided they either had to call Germany's bluff or see the entire peace settlement dissolve to France's great disadvantage. So, despite strong British protests, France and its ally Belgium decided to pursue a firm policy. In early January 1923, French and Belgian armies began to occupy the Ruhr district, the heartland of industrial Germany, creating the most serious international crisis of the 1920s.

## THE OCCUPATION OF THE RUHR

The strategy of Poincaré and his French supporters was simple. Since Germany would not pay reparations in hard currency or gold, France and Belgium would collect reparations in kind – coal, steel, and machinery. If forcible collection proved impossible, France would use occupation to paralyze Germany and force it to accept the Treaty of Versailles.

Strengthened by a wave of patriotism that temporarily united all political parties, the German government resisted. Believing that French armies could not operate German factories, it ordered the people of the Ruhr to stop working and start resisting – passively – the French occupation. The coal mines and steel mills of the Ruhr grew silent, leaving 10 percent of Germany's total population in need of relief. Although Americans and Britons generally denounced "French aggression," Poincaré and the French did not retreat. Their answer to passive resistance was to seal off not only the Ruhr but the entire Rhineland from the rest of Germany, permitting through only enough food to prevent starvation. They also revived plans for a separate state in the Rhineland.

By the summer of 1923, France and Germany were engaged in a great test of wills. As

**Hände weg vom Ruhrgebiet!**

Kultur Liga

*"HANDS OFF THE RUHR"    The French occupation of the Ruhr to collect reparations payments raised a storm of patriotic protest, including this anti-French poster of 1923. (Internationaal Institut voor Sociale Geschiedenis)*

the German government had anticipated, French armies could not collect reparations from striking workers at gunpoint. But French occupation was destroying Germany and its economy. The Ruhr district, only sixty miles long and twenty-five miles wide, normally produced 80 percent of Germany's steel and coal. The rest of the German economy desperately needed this key area.

Moreover, the occupation of the Ruhr turned rapid German inflation into runaway inflation. Faced with the need to support the striking Ruhr workers and their employers, the German government began to print money to pay its bills. Prices soared. People went to the store with a big bag of paper money; they returned home with a handful of groceries. Workers were paid twice a day or more, so that they could immediately run to shops and buy something before prices went higher. Finally, in mid-November 1923, it took 4 *trillion* marks – as opposed to four marks in 1914 – to equal a single American dollar.

German money lost all value, and so did savings accounts, insurance policies, annuities, mortgages – anything with a stated fixed value. Runaway inflation brought about a social revolution. The accumulated savings of many retired and middle-class people were wiped out. The old middle-class virtues of thrift, caution, and self-reliance were cruelly mocked by catastrophic inflation. People told themselves that nothing had real value any more, not even money. The German middle and lower-middle classes felt cheated and burned with resentment. Many hated and blamed the Western governments, their own government, big business, the Jews, the workers, the communists for their misfortune. They were psychologically prepared to follow radical leaders in a moment of crisis.

In August 1923, as the mark fell and polit-

THE FRUITS OF GERMANY'S INFLATION *In the end, currency had value only as waste paper. Here bank notes are being purchased by the bail for paper mills, along with old rags (Lumpen) and bones (Knochen). (Archiv fur Kunst u. Geschichte/Katherine Young)*

ical unrest grew throughout Germany, Gustav Stresemann assumed leadership of the government. Stresemann adopted a compromising attitude. He called off passive resistance in the Ruhr and in October agreed in principle to pay reparations, but asked for a re-examination of Germany's ability to pay. This was less than France had wanted, but Poincaré accepted Stresemann's proposal. His hard line was becoming increasingly unpopular with French citizens, and it was hated in Britain and the United States. Moreover, occupation was dreadfully expensive, and France's own currency was beginning to lose value on foreign exchange markets.

More generally, in both Germany and France power was finally passing to the moderates, who realized that continued confrontation was a destructive, no-win situation. Thus, after five long years of hostility and tension culminating in a kind of undeclared war in the Ruhr in 1923, Germany and France decided to give compromise and cooperation a try. The British, and even the Americans, were willing to help. The first step was a reasonable compromise on the reparations question.

## HOPE IN FOREIGN AFFAIRS, 1924–1929

The Reparations Commission appointed an international committee of financial experts headed by an American banker, Charles G. Dawes, to reexamine reparations from a broad perspective. The committee made a series of recommendations known as the Dawes Plan (1924), which was accepted by France, Germany, and Britain. German reparations were reduced and placed on a sliding scale, like an income tax, whereby yearly payments depended on the level of German economic prosperity. The Dawes Plan also recommended large loans to Germany, loans that could come only from the United States. These loans were to help Stresemann's government put its new currency on a firm basis and promote German recovery. In short, Germany would get private loans from the United States and pay reparations to France and Britain, thus enabling those countries to repay the large sums they had borrowed from the United States during the First World War.

This circular flow of international payments was complicated and risky. For a time, though, it worked. The German republic experienced a spectacular economic recovery. By 1929, German wealth and income were 50 percent greater than in 1913. With prosperity and large, continuous inflows of American capital, Germany easily paid about $1.3 billion in reparations in 1927 and 1928, enabling France and Britain to pay the United States. In 1929, the Young Plan, named after an American businessman, further reduced German reparations and formalized the link between German reparations and French-British debts to the United States. In this way the Americans, who did not have armies but who did have money, belatedly played a part in the general economic settlement, which though far from ideal facilitated the worldwide recovery of the late 1920s.

The economic settlement was matched by a political settlement. In 1925, the leaders of Europe signed a number of agreements at Locarno, Switzerland. Stresemann, who guided German's foreign policy until his death in 1929, had suggested a treaty with France's conciliatory Aristide Briand, who had returned to office in 1924 after French voters rejected the bellicose Poincaré. By this treaty Germany and France solemnly pledged to accept their common border, and Britain agreed to fight if either country invaded the other. Stresemann also agreed to settle boundary disputes with Poland and Czechoslovakia by peaceful means, and France promised those countries military aid if they were attacked by Germany. For their efforts Stresemann and Briand shared the Nobel Peace Prize in 1926. The effect of the treaties of Locarno was far-reaching. For several years, a "spirit of Locarno" gave Europeans a sense of growing security and stability in international affairs.

Hopes were strengthened by other developments. In 1926, Germany joined the League of Nations, where Stresemann continued his "peace offensive." In 1928, fifteen countries signed the Kellogg-Briand Pact, which "condemned and renounced war as an instrument of national policy." The signing states agreed to settle international disputes peacefully. Often seen as idealistic nonsense because it made no provisions for action in case war actually occurred, the pact was nevertheless a hopeful step. It grew out of a suggestion by Briand that France and the United States renounce the possibility of war between their two countries. Briand was gently and subtly trying to draw the United States back into involvement with Europe. When Secretary of State Frank B. Kellogg proposed a multinational pact, Briand appeared close to success. Thus, the cautious optimism of the late 1920s also rested on the hope that the United States would accept its responsibilities as a great power and contribute to European stability.

## HOPE IN DEMOCRATIC GOVERNMENT

Domestic politics also offered reason to hope. During the occupation of the Ruhr and the great inflation, republican government in Germany had appeared on the verge of collapse. In 1923, communists momentarily entered provincial governments, and in November an obscure nobody named Adolf Hitler leaped on a table in a beer hall in Munich and proclaimed a "national socialist revolution." But Hitler's plot was poorly organized and easily crushed, and Hitler was sentenced to prison, where he outlined his theories and program in his book *Mein Kampf* (*My Struggle*). Throughout the 1920s, Hitler's National Socialist party attracted support only from a few fanatical anti-Semites, ultranationalists, and disgruntled ex-servicemen. In 1928, his party had an insignificant twelve seats in the national parliament. Indeed, after 1923, democracy seemed to take root in Weimar Germany. A new currency was established, and the economy boomed.

The moderate businessmen who tended to dominate the various German coalition governments were convinced that economic prosperity demanded good relations with the Western powers, and they supported parliamentary government at home. Stresemann himself was a man of this class, and he was the key figure in every government until his

death in 1929. Elections were held regularly, and republican democracy appeared to have growing support among a majority of the German people.

There were, however, sharp political divisions in the country. Many unrepentant nationalists and monarchists populated the right and the army. Germany's Communists were noisy and active on the left. The Communists, directed from Moscow, reserved their greatest hatred and sharpest barbs for their cousins the Social Democrats, whom they endlessly accused of betraying the revolution. The working classes were divided politically, but most supported the nonrevolutionary but socialist Social Democrats.

The situation in France had numerous similarities to that in Germany. Communists and socialists battled for the support of the workers. After 1924, the democratically elected government rested mainly in the hands of coalitions of moderates, and business interests were well represented. France's great accomplishment was rapid rebuilding of its war-torn northern region. The expense of this undertaking led, however, to a big deficit and substantial inflation. By early 1926, the franc had fallen to 10 percent of its prewar value, causing a severe crisis. Poincaré was recalled to office, while Briand remained minister for foreign affairs. The Poincaré government proceeded to slash spending and raise taxes, restoring confidence in the economy. The franc was "saved," stabilized at about one-fifth of its prewar value. Good times prevailed until 1930.

Despite its political shortcomings, France attracted artists and writers from all over the world in the 1920s. Much of the intellectual and artistic ferment of the times flourished in Paris. As the writer Gertrude Stein (1874–1946), a leader of the large colony of American expatriates living in Paris, later recalled:

AN AMERICAN IN PARIS *The young Josephine Baker suddenly became a star when she brought an exotic African eroticism to French music halls in 1925. American blacks and Africans had a powerful impact on entertainment in Europe in the 1920s and 1930s. (BBC Hulton Picture Library)*

"Paris was where the twentieth century was."[11] More generally, France appealed to foreigners and the French as a harmonious combination of small businesses and family farms, of bold innovation and solid traditions.

Britain too faced challenges after 1920. The trend toward greater social equality evident during the war continued, however, helping to maintain social harmony. The great problem was unemployment. Many of Britain's best markets had been lost during the war. In June 1921 almost 2.2 million people – 23 percent of the labor force – were out of work, and throughout the 1920s unemployment remained high. Yet the state provided unemployment benefits of equal size to all those without jobs, and supplemented those payments with subsidized housing, medical aid, and increased old-age pensions. These and other measures kept living standards from seriously declining, defused class tensions, and pointed the way toward the welfare state Britain established after World War Two.

Relative social harmony was accompanied by the rise of the Labour party as an aggressive champion of the working classes and of greater social equality. Committed to socialism, the Labour party replaced the Liberal party as the main opposition to the Conservatives. The new prominence of the Labour party reflected the decline of old liberal ideals of competitive capitalism, limited government control, and individual responsibility. In 1924 and 1929, the Labour party under Ramsay MacDonald governed the country with the support of the smaller Liberal party. Yet Labour moved toward socialism gradually and democratically, so that the middle classes were not overly frightened as the working classes won new benefits.

The Conservatives under Stanley Baldwin showed the same compromising spirit on social issues. The last line of Baldwin's greatest speech in March 1925 summarized his international and domestic programs: "Give us peace in our time, O Lord." Thus, in spite of such conflicts as the 1926 strike by hardpressed coal miners, which ended in an unsuccessful general strike, social unrest in Britain was limited in the 1920s and in the 1930s as well. In 1922, Britain granted southern, Catholic Ireland full autonomy after a bitter guerrilla war, thus removing another source of prewar friction. In summary, developments in both international relations and in the domestic politics of the leading democracies gave cause for cautious optimism in the late 1920s.

## THE GREAT DEPRESSION, 1929–1939

Like the Great War, the Great Depression must be spelled with capital letters. Economic depression was nothing new. Depressions occurred throughout the nineteenth century with predictable regularity, as they recur in the form of recessions and slumps to this day. What was new about this depression was its severity and duration. It struck with ever-greater intensity from 1929 to 1933, and recovery was uneven and slow. Only with the Second World War did the depression disappear in much of the world.

The social and political consequences of prolonged economic collapse were enormous. The depression shattered the fragile optimism of political leaders in the late 1920s. Mass unemployment made insecurity a reality for millions of ordinary people, who had paid little attention to the intellectual crisis or to new directions in art and ideas. In desperation, people looked for leaders who would "do something." They were willing to support radical attempts to deal with the crisis by both democratic leaders and dictators.

### THE ECONOMIC CRISIS

There is no agreement among historians and economists about why the Great Depression was so deep and lasted so long. Thus, it is best to trace the course of the great collapse before trying to identify what caused it.

Although economic activity was already declining moderately in many countries by early 1929, the crash of the stock market in the United States in October of that year really started the Great Depression. The American stock-market boom, which had seen stock prices double between early 1928 and September 1929, was built on borrowed money. Many wealthy investors, speculators, and people of modest means had bought stocks by paying only a small fraction of the total purchase price and borrowing the remainder from their stockbrokers. Such buying "on margin" was extremely dangerous. When prices started falling, the hard-pressed margin buyers either had to put up more money, which was often impossible, or sell their shares to pay off their brokers. Thus, thousands of people started selling all at once. The result was a financial panic. Countless investors and speculators were wiped out in a matter of days or weeks.

The general economic consequences were swift and severe. Stripped of their wealth and confidence, battered investors and their fellow citizens started buying fewer goods. Production began to slow down, and unemployment began to rise. Soon the entire American economy was caught in a vicious, spiraling decline.

The financial panic in the United States triggered a worldwide financial crisis, and that crisis resulted in a drastic decline in production in country after country. Throughout the 1920s, American bankers and investors had lent large amounts of capital not only to Germany but to many countries. Many of these loans were short-term, and once panic broke New York bankers began recalling them. Gold reserves thus began to flow out of European countries, particularly Germany and Austria, toward the United States. It became very hard for European businessmen to borrow money, and the panicky public began to withdraw its savings from the banks. These banking problems eventually led to the crash of the largest bank in Austria in 1931 and then to general financial chaos. The recall of private loans by American bankers also accelerated the collapse in world prices, as businessmen around the world dumped industrial goods and agricultural commodities in a frantic attempt to get cash to pay what they owed.

The financial crisis led to a general crisis of production: between 1929 and 1933, world output of goods fell by an estimated 38 percent. As this happened, each country turned inward and tried to go it alone. In 1931, for example, Britain went off the gold standard, refusing to convert bank notes into gold, and reduced the value of its money. Britain's goal was to make its goods cheaper and therefore more salable in the world market. But because more than twenty nations, including the United States in 1934, also went off the gold standard, no country gained a real advantage. Similarly, country after country followed the example of the United States when it raised protective tariffs to their highest levels ever in 1930 and tried to seal off shrinking national markets for American producers only. Within this context of fragmented and destructive economic nationalism, recovery finally began in 1933.

Although opinions differ, two factors probably best explain the relentless slide to the bottom from 1929 to early 1933. First, the international economy lacked a leadership able to maintain stability when the crisis came. Specifically, as a noted American economic historian concludes, the seriously weakened British, the traditional leaders of the world economy, "couldn't and the United States wouldn't" stabilize the international economic system in 1929.[12] The United States, which had momentarily played a positive role after the occupation of the Ruhr, cut back its in-ternational lending and erected high tariffs.

The second factor was poor national economic policy in almost every country. Governments generally cut their budgets and reduced spending when they should have run large deficits in an attempt to stimulate their economies. Since World War Two, such a "countercyclical policy," advocated by John Maynard Keynes, has become a well-established weapon against depression. But in the 1930s, Keynes's prescription was generally regarded with horror by orthodox economists.

*MASS UNEMPLOYMENT*

The need for large-scale government spending was tied to mass unemployment. As the financial crisis led to cuts in production, workers lost their jobs and had little money to buy goods. This led to still more cuts in production and still more unemployment, until millions were out of work. In Britain, unemployment had averaged 12 percent in the 1920s; between 1930 and 1935, it averaged more than 18 percent. Far worse was the case of the United States, where unemployment had averaged only 5 percent in the 1920s. In 1932, unemployment soared to about *one-third* of the entire labor force: 14 million people were out of work. Only by pumping new money into the economy could the government increase demand and break the vicious cycle of decline.

Along with its economic effects, mass unemployment posed a great social problem that mere numbers cannot adequately express. Millions of people lost their spirit and dignity in an apparently hopeless search for work. Homes and ways of life were disrupted in millions of personal tragedies. Young people postponed marriages they could not afford, and birthrates fell sharply. There was an increase in suicide and mental illness. Poverty or the threat of poverty became a grinding reality. In 1932, the workers of Manchester, England, appealed to their city officials – a typical appeal echoed throughout the Western world:

*We tell you that thousands of people . . . are in desperate straits. We tell you that men, women, and children are going hungry. . . . We tell you that great numbers are being rendered distraught through the stress and worry of trying to exist without work. . . .*

*If you do not do this – if you do not provide useful work for the unemployed – what, we ask, is your alternative? Do not imagine that this colossal tragedy of unemployment is going on endlessly without some fateful catastrophe. Hungry men are angry men.*[13]

Mass unemployment was a terrible time bomb preparing to explode.

## THE NEW DEAL IN THE UNITED STATES

Of all the major industrial countries, only Germany was harder hit by the Great Depression, or reacted more radically to it, than the United States. Depression was so traumatic in the United States because the 1920s had been a period of complacent prosperity. The Great Depression and the response to it was a major turning point in American history.

President Herbert Hoover and his administration initially reacted to the stock-market crash and economic decline with dogged optimism and limited action. In May 1930, Hoover told a group of business and farm leaders, "I am convinced that we have now passed the worst and with continued unity of effort we shall rapidly recover." When, however, the full force of the financial crisis struck Europe in the summer of 1931 and boomeranged back to the United States, people's worst fears became reality. Banks failed; un-

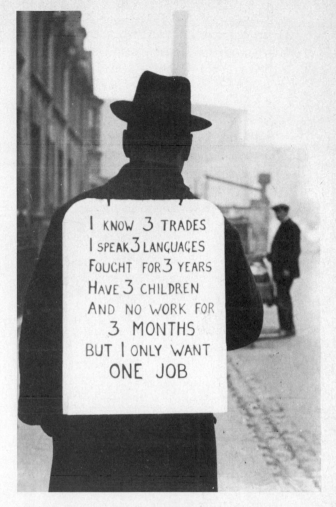

MIDDLE-CLASS UNEMPLOYMENT *An English office worker's unusual sandwich board poignantly summarizes the bitter despair of the unemployed in the 1930s. (BBC Hulton Picture Library)*

employment soared. In 1932, industrial production fell to about 50 percent of its level in 1929. In these tragic circumstances Franklin Delano Roosevelt, a magnetic wheelchair aristocrat previously crippled by polio, won a landslide electoral victory with grand but vague promises of a "New Deal for the forgotten man."

Roosevelt's basic goal was to reform capitalism in order to preserve it. In his words,

"A frank examination of the profit system in the spring of 1933 showed it to be in collapse; but substantially everybody in the United States, in public office and out of public office, from the very rich to the very poor, was as determined as was my Administration to save it."[14] Roosevelt rejected socialism and government ownership of industry in 1933. To right the situation, he chose forceful government intervention in the economy.

In this choice Roosevelt and his advisers were greatly influenced by American experience in World War One. During the wartime emergency, the American economy had been thoroughly planned and regulated. Roosevelt and his "brain trust" of advisers adopted similar policies to restore prosperity and reduce social inequality. Roosevelt was flexible, pragmatic, and willing to experiment. Government intervention and experimentation were combined in some of the New Deal's most significant measures.

The most ambitious attempt to control and plan the economy was the National Recovery Administration (NRA), established by Congress right after Roosevelt took office. The key idea behind the NRA was to reduce competition and fix prices and wages for everyone's benefit. This goal required government, business, and labor to hammer out detailed regulations for each industry. Along with this kind of national planning in the private sector of the economy, the government believed it could sponsor enough public works projects to assure recovery. Because the NRA broke with the cherished American tradition of free competition and aroused conflicts among businessmen, consumers, and bureaucrats, it did not work well. By the time the NRA was declared unconstitutional in 1935, Roosevelt and the New Deal were already moving away from government efforts to plan and control the entire economy.

Instead, Roosevelt and his advisers attacked the key problem of mass unemployment directly. The federal government accepted the responsibility of employing directly as many people as financially possible, something Hoover had consistently rejected. Thus, when it became clear in late 1933 that the initial program of public works was too small, new agencies were created to undertake a vast range of projects.

The most famous of these was the Works Progress Administration (WPA), set up in 1935. At its peak in late 1938, this government agency employed more than 3 million individuals. One-fifth of the entire labor force worked for the WPA at some point in the 1930s. To this day thousands of public buildings, bridges, and highways built by the WPA stand as monuments to energetic government efforts to provide people with meaningful work. The WPA was enormously popular in a nation long schooled in self-reliance and the work ethic. The hope of a job with the government helped check the threat of social revolution in the United States.

Other social measures aimed in the same direction. Following the path blazed by Germany's Bismarck in the 1880s, the U.S. government in 1935 established a national social security system, with old-age pensions and unemployment benefits, to protect many workers against some of life's uncertainties. The National Labor Relations Act of 1935 gave union organizers the green light by declaring collective bargaining to be the policy of the United States. Following some bitter strikes, such as the sit-down strike at General Motors in early 1937, union membership more than doubled, from 4 million in 1935 to 9 million in 1940. In general, between 1935 and 1938 government rulings and social reforms chipped away at the privileges of the wealthy and tried to help ordinary people.

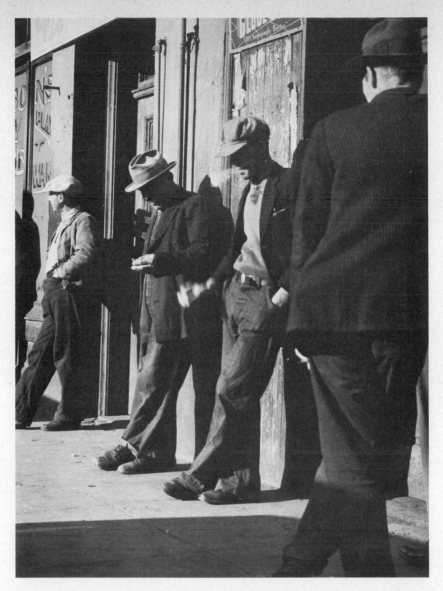

*SAN FRANCISCO, 1934   Standing on the corner, waiting for something to do: this classic photograph by Dorothea Lange captures the frustration and waste of unemployment in the Depression years. (Dorothea Lange, The Oakland Museum)*

Yet in spite of its undeniable accomplishments in social reform, the New Deal was only partly successful as a response to the Great Depression. At the height of the recovery, in May 1937, 7 million workers were still unemployed. The economic situation then worsened seriously in the recession of 1937 and 1938. Production fell sharply, and although unemployment never again reached the 15 million mark of 1933, it hit 11 million in 1938 and was still a staggering 10 million when war broke out in Europe in September 1939.

The New Deal never did pull the United

States out of the depression. This failure frustrated Americans then, and it is still puzzling today. Perhaps, as some have claimed, Roosevelt should have used his enormous popularity and prestige in 1933 to nationalize the banks, the railroads, and some heavy industry, so that national economic planning could have been successful. On the other hand, Roosevelt's sharp attack on big business and the wealthy after 1935 had popular appeal but also damaged business confidence and made the great capitalists uncooperative. Given the low level of profit and the underutilization of many factories, however, it is questionable whether business would have behaved much differently even if the New Deal had catered to it.

Finally, it is often argued that the New Deal did not put enough money into the economy through deficit financing. Like his predecessors in the White House, Roosevelt was attached to the ideal of the balanced budget. His largest deficit was only $4.4 billion in 1936. Compare this figure with deficits of $21.5 billion in 1942 and $57.4 billion in 1943, when the nation was prosperously engaged in total war and unemployment had vanished. By 1945, many economists concluded that the New Deal's deficit-financed public works had been too small a step in the right direction. These Keynesian views were to be very influential in postwar economic policy in Europe and America.

## THE SCANDINAVIAN RESPONSE TO DEPRESSION

Of all the Western democracies, the Scandinavian countries under Socialist leadership responded most successfully to the challenge of the Great Depression. Having grown steadily in the late nineteenth century, Socialists became the largest political party in Sweden and then in Norway after the First World War. In the 1920s they passed important social reform legislation for both peasants and workers, gained practical administrative experience, and developed a unique kind of socialism. Flexible and nonrevolutionary, Scandinavian socialism grew out of a strong tradition of cooperative community action. Even before 1900, Scandinavian agricultural cooperatives had shown how individual peasant families could join together for everyone's benefit. Labor leaders and capitalists were also inclined to work together.

When the economic crisis struck in 1929, Socialist governments in Scandinavia built on this pattern of cooperative social action. Sweden in particular pioneered in the use of large-scale deficits to finance public works and thereby maintain production and employment. Scandinavian governments also increased social welfare benefits, from old-age pensions and unemployment insurance to subsidized housing and maternity allowances. All this spending required a large bureaucracy and high taxes, first on the rich and then on practically everyone. Yet both private and cooperative enterprise thrived, as did democracy. Some observers saw Scandinavia's welfare socialism as an appealing "middle way" between sick capitalism and cruel communism or fascism.

## RECOVERY AND REFORM IN BRITAIN AND FRANCE

In Britain, MacDonald's Labour government and then, after 1931, the Conservative-dominated coalition government followed orthodox economic theory. The budget was balanced, but unemployed workers received barely enough welfare to live. In spite of government lethargy, the economy recovered considerably after 1932. By 1937, total production was about 20 percent higher than in 1929. In fact, for Britain the years after 1932 were actually somewhat better than the 1920s had been, quite the opposite of the situation in the United States and France.

This good but by no means brilliant performance reflected the gradual reorientation of the British economy. After going off the gold standard in 1931 and establishing protective tariffs in 1932, Britain concentrated increasingly on the national rather than the international market. The old export industries of the Industrial Revolution, such as textiles and coal, continued to decline, but the new industries like automobiles and electrical appliances grew in response to British home demand. Moreover, low interest rates encouraged a housing boom. By the end of the decade there were highly visible differences between the old, depressed industrial areas of the north and the new, growing areas of the south. These developments encouraged Britain to look inward and avoid unpleasant foreign questions.

Because France was relatively less industrialized and more isolated from the world economy, the Great Depression came late. But once the depression hit France, it stayed and stayed. Decline was steady until 1935, and the short-lived recovery never brought production or employment back up to predepression levels. Economic stagnation both reflected and heightened an ongoing political crisis. There was no stability in government. As before 1914, the French parliament was made up of many political parties, which could never cooperate for very long. In 1933, for example, five coalition cabinets formed and fell in rapid succession.

The French lost the underlying unity that had made governmental instability bearable before 1914. Fascist-type organizations agitated against parliamentary democracy and looked to Mussolini's Italy and Hitler's Germany for inspiration. In February 1934, French fascists and semifascists rioted and threatened to overturn the republic. At the same time the Communist party and many workers opposed to the existing system were looking to Stalin's Russia for guidance. The vital center of moderate republicanism was sapped from both sides.

Frightened by the growing strength of the fascists at home and abroad, the Communists, the Socialists, and the Radicals formed an alliance – the Popular Front – for the national elections of May 1936. Their clear victory reflected the trend toward extremism. The number of Communists in the parliament jumped dramatically from 10 to 72, while the Socialists, led by Léon Blum, became the strongest party in France with 146 seats. The really quite moderate Radicals slipped badly, and the conservatives lost ground to the semifascists.

In the next few months Blum's Popular Front government made the first and only real attempt to deal with the social and economic problems of the 1930s in France. Inspired by Roosevelt's New Deal, the Popular Front encouraged the union movement and launched a far-reaching program of social reform, complete with paid vacations and a forty-hour workweek. Popular with workers and the lower middle class, these measures were quickly sabotaged by rapid inflation and cries of revolution from fascists and frightened conservatives. Wealthy people sneaked their money out of the country, labor unrest grew, and France entered a severe financial crisis. Blum was forced to announce a "breathing spell" in social reform.

The fires of political dissension were also fanned by civil war in Spain. The Communists demanded that France support the Spanish republicans, while many French conservatives would gladly have joined Hitler and Mussolini in aiding the attack of Spanish fascists. Extremism grew, and France itself was within sight of civil war. Blum was forced to resign in June 1937, and the Popular Front quickly collapsed. An anxious and divided France drifted aimlessly once again, preoccupied by Hitler and German rearmament.

———◆———

After the First World War, Western society entered a complex and difficult era – truly an age of anxiety. Intellectual life underwent a crisis marked by pessimism, uncertainty, and fascination with irrational forces. Rejection of old forms and ceaseless experimentation characterized art and music, while motion pictures and radio provided a new, standardized entertainment for the masses. Intellectual and artistic developments that had been confined to small avant-garde groups before 1914 gained wider currency along with the insecure state of mind they expressed.

Politics and economics were similarly disrupted. In the 1920s, statesmen groped to create an enduring peace and rebuild the prewar prosperity, and for a brief period late in the decade they even seemed to have succeeded. Then the Great Depression shattered the fragile stability. Uncertainty returned with redoubled force in the 1930s. The international economy collapsed, and unemployment struck millions. The democracies turned inward as they sought to cope with massive domestic problems and widespread disillusionment. Generally speaking, they were not very successful. The old liberal ideals of individual rights and responsibilities, elected government, and economic freedom seemed ineffective and outmoded to many, even when they managed to survive. And in many countries they were abandoned completely.

---

## NOTES

1. P. Valéry, *Variety,* trans. Malcolm Cowley, Harcourt, Brace, New York, 1927, pp. 27–28.

2. G. Marcel, as quoted by S. Hughes, *The Obstructed Path: French Social Thought in the Years of Desperation, 1930–1960,* Harper & Row, New York, 1967, p. 82.

3. G. Greene, *Another Mexico,* Viking Press, New York, 1939, p. 3.

4. G. Orwell, *1984,* New American Library, New York, p. 220.

5. C. E. Jeanneret-Gris (Le Corbusier), *Towards a New Architecture,* J. Rodker, London, 1931, p. 15.

6. Quoted by A. H. Barr, Jr., *What Is Modern Painting?,* 9th ed., Museum of Modern Art, New York, 1966, p. 27.

7. Ibid., p. 25.

8. R. Graves and A. Hodge, *The Long Week End: A Social History of Great Britain, 1918–1939,* Macmillan, New York, 1941, p. 131.

9. Quoted by A. Briggs, *The Birth of Broadcasting,* Oxford University Press, London, 1961, 1.47.

10. Quoted by R. Butler in C. L. Mowat, ed., *The New Cambridge Modern History,* 2nd ed., Cambridge University Press, Cambridge, England, 1968, 12.229.

11. Quoted by R. J. Sontag, *A Broken World, 1919–1939,* Harper & Row, New York, 1971, p. 129.

12. C. P. Kindleberger, *The World in Depression, 1929–1939,* University of California Press, Berkeley, 1973, p. 292.

13. Quoted by S. B. Clough et al., eds., *Economic History of Europe: Twentieth Century,* Harper & Row, New York, 1968, pp. 243–245.

14. Quoted by D. Dillard, *Economic Development of the North Atlantic Community,* Prentice-Hall, Englewood Cliffs, N.J., 1967, p. 591.

## SUGGESTED READING

Among general works, R. Sontag's *A Broken World, 1919–1939* (1971), and E. Wiskeman, *Europe of the Dictators, 1919–1945* (1966), are particularly recommended. The former has an excellent bibliography. A. Bullock, ed., *The Twentieth Century* (1971), is a lavish visual feast combined with penetrating essays on major developments since 1900. Crucial changes in thought before and after World War One are discussed in three rewarding intellectual histories: G. Masur, *Prophets of Yesterday* (1961); H. S. Hughes, *Consciousness and Society* (1956); and M. Biddiss, *Age of the Masses: Ideas and Society Since 1870* (1977). J. Rewald, *The History of Impressionism,* rev. ed. (1961) and *Post-Impressionism* (1956), are excellent, as are the works of A. H. Barr, Jr., cited in the Notes. P. Collaer, *A History of Modern Music* (1961), and H. R. Hitchcock, *Architecture: 19th and 20th Centuries* (1958), are good introductions, while T. Wolfe, *From Bauhaus to My House* (1981), is a lively critique of modern architecture. L. Barnett, *The Universe and Dr. Einstein* (1952), is a fascinating study of the new physics. P. Rieff, *Freud* (1956), and M. White, ed., *The Age of Analysis* (1955), open up basic questions of twentieth-century psychology and philosophy. P. Gay, *Weimar Culture* (1970), is a brilliant exploration of the many-sided artistic renaissance in Germany in the 1920s. M. Marrus, ed., *Emergence of Leisure* (1974), is a pioneering inquiry into an important aspect of mass culture. H. Daniels-Rops, *A Fight for God,* 2 vols. (1966), is a sympathetic history of the Catholic church between 1870 and 1939.

C. Maier, *Recasting Bourgeois Europe* (1975), is an ambitious comparative study of social classes and conflicts in France, Germany, and Italy after World War One. R. Wohl, *The Generation of 1914* (1979); R. Kuisel, *Capital and State in Modern France: Renovation and Economic Management* (1982); and W. McDougall, *France's Rhineland Diplomacy, 1914–1924* (1978), are three more important studies on aspects of the postwar challenge. M. Childs, *Sweden: The Middle Way* (1961), applauds Sweden's efforts at social reform. W. Neuman, *The Balance of Power in the Interwar Years, 1919–1939* (1968), perceptively examines international politics after the Locarno treaties of 1925. In addition to the contemporary works discussed in the text, the crisis of the interwar period comes alive in R. Crossman, ed., *The God That Failed* (1950), in which famous Western writers tell why they were attracted to and later repelled by communism; Ortega y Gassett's renowned *The Revolt of the Masses* (1932); and F. A. Hayek's *The Road to Serfdom* (1944), a famous warning of the dangers to democratic freedoms. In addition to C. Kindleberger's excellent study of the Great Depression cited in the Notes, there is J. Galbraith's very lively and understandable account of the stock-market collapse, *The Great Crash* (1955). Novels best portray the human tragedy of economic decline. W. Holtby, *South Riding,* and W. Greenwood, *Love on the Dole* (1933), are moving stories of the Great Depression in England; H. Fallada, *Little Man, What Now?* (1932), is the classic counterpart for Germany. Also highly recommended as commentaries on English life between the wars are R. Graves, *Goodbye to All That,* rev. ed. (1957), and G. Orwell, *The Road to Wigan Pier* (1972). Among French novelists André Gide painstakingly examines the French middle class and its values in *The Counterfeiters,* while Albert Camus, the greatest of the existential novelists, is at his unforgettable best in *The Stranger* and *The Plague.*

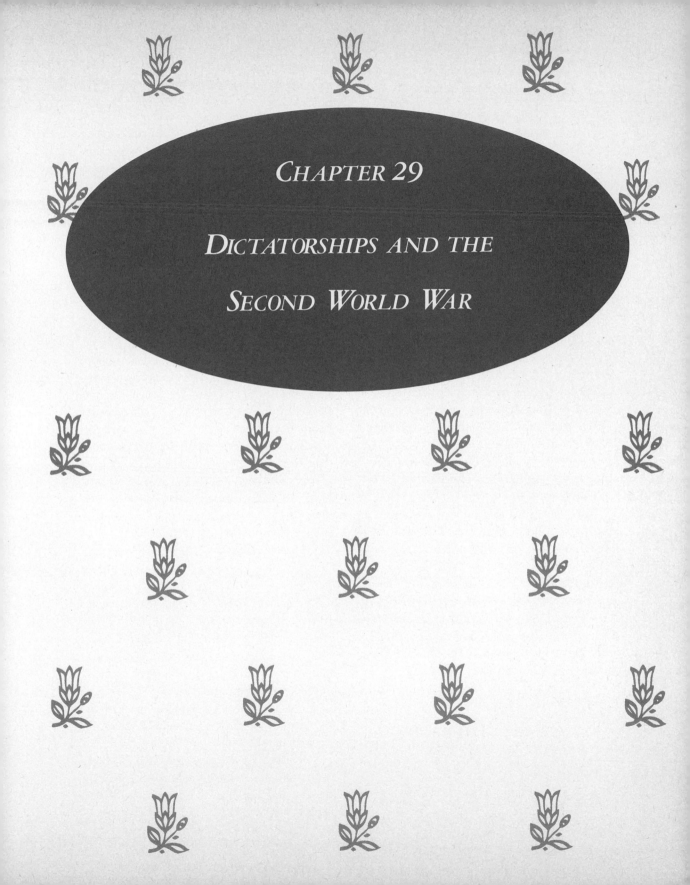

# CHAPTER 29

# DICTATORSHIPS AND THE

# SECOND WORLD WAR

*THE ERA OF ANXIETY* and economic depression was also a time of growing strength for political dictatorship. Popularly elected governments and basic civil liberties declined drastically in Europe. On the eve of the Second World War, liberal democratic government survived only in Great Britain, France, the Low Countries, the Scandinavian nations, and neutral Switzerland. Elsewhere in Europe, various kinds of "strong men" ruled. Dictatorship seemed the wave of the future. Thus, the decline in liberal political institutions and the intellectual crisis were related elements in the general crisis of European civilization.

The era of dictatorship is a highly disturbing chapter in the history of Western civilization. The key development was not simply the resurgence of dictatorship but the rise of a new kind of tyranny — the modern totalitarian state. Modern totalitarianism reached its fullest realization in Communist Russia and Nazi Germany in the 1930s. Stalin and Hitler mobilized their peoples for enormous undertakings and ruled with unprecedented severity.

Today we want to believe that the era of totalitarian dictatorship was a terrible accident, that Stalin's slave labor camps and Hitler's gas chambers "can't happen again." But one cannot be sure: it was all very recent and very powerful. What was the nature of the twentieth-century totalitarian state? How did totalitarianism affect ordinary people, and why did it lead to another world war? These are the questions this chapter seeks to answer.

## AUTHORITARIAN AND TOTALITARIAN STATES

The modern totalitarian state differed from the old-fashioned authoritarian state. Com-

pletely rejecting liberal values and drawing on the experience of total war, the totalitarian state exercised much greater control over the masses, and mobilized them for constant action. The nature of this control may be examined by comparing the old and new forms of dictatorship in a general way, before entering the strange world of Stalin's Russia and Hitler's Germany.

### CONSERVATIVE AUTHORITARIANISM

The traditional form of antidemocratic government in European history has been conservative authoritarianism. Like Catherine the Great in Russia and Metternich in Austria, the leaders of such governments have tried to prevent major changes and preserve the existing social order. To do so, they have relied on obedient bureaucracies, vigilant police departments, and trustworthy armies. Popular participation in government has been forbidden or else severely limited to such natural allies as landlords, bureaucrats, and high church officials. Liberals, democrats and socialists have been persecuted as radicals and have often found themselves in jail or exile.

Yet old-fashioned authoritarian governments were limited in their power and in their objectives. Lacking modern technology and communications, they lacked the power to control many aspects of their subjects' lives. Nor did they wish to do so. Preoccupied with the goal of mere survival, these government's demands were largely limited to taxes, army recruits, and passive acceptance. As long as the people did not try to change the system, they often had considerable personal independence.

After the First World War this kind of authoritarian government revived, especially in the less-developed eastern part of Europe. There, the parliamentary regimes that had been founded on the wreckage of empires in 1918 fell one by one. By early 1938 only economically and socially advanced Czechoslovakia remained true to liberal political ideals. Conservative dictators also took over in Spain and Portugal.

There were several reasons for this development. These lands lacked a strong tradition of self-government, with its necessary restraint and compromise. Moreover, many of these new states were torn by ethnic conflicts that threatened their very existence. Dictatorship appealed to nationalists and military leaders as a way to repress such tensions and preserve national unity. Large landowners and the church were still powerful forces in these largely agrarian areas, and they often looked to dictators to save them from progressive land reform or communist agrarian upheaval. So did some members of the middle class, which was small and weak in eastern Europe. Finally, though some kind of democracy managed to stagger through the 1920s in Austria, Bulgaria, Rumania, Greece, Estonia, and Latvia, the Great Depression delivered the final blow in those countries by 1936.

Although some of the authoritarian regimes adopted certain Hitlerian and fascist characteristics in the 1930s, their general aims were not totalitarian. They were concerned more with maintaining the status quo than with forcing society into rapid change or war. This tradition lives on today, especially in some of the military dictatorships of Latin America.

Hungary was a good example of conservative authoritarianism. In the chaos of collapse in 1919, Béla Kun formed a Lenin-like government, but communism in Hungary was soon crushed by foreign troops, large landowners, and hostile peasants. Thereafter, a combination of great and medium-sized landowners instituted a semi-authoritarian regime, which maintained the status quo in the 1920s. Hungary had a parliament, but elections were carefully controlled. The peasants did not have the right to vote, and an upper house representing the landed aristocracy was reestablished. There was no land reform, no major social change. In the 1930s, the Hungarian government remained conservative and nationalistic. Increasingly, it was opposed by a Nazi-like fascist movement, the Arrow Cross, which demanded radical reform and totalitarian measures.

Another example of conservative authoritarianism was newly independent Poland, where democratic government was overturned in 1926 when General Joseph Pilsudski established a military dictatorship. Poland was torn by bitter party politics and sandwiched between Russia and Germany. Pilsudski silenced opposition and tried to build a strong state. His principal supporters were the army, big industrialists, and dedicated nationalists.

In Yugoslavia, King Alexander (1921–1934) proclaimed a centralized dictatorship in 1929 to prevent ethnic rivalries among Serbs, Croats, and Slovenes from tearing the country apart. An old-style authoritarian, Alexander crushed democracy, jailed separatists, and ruled through the bureaucracy.

Another example of conservative authoritarianism was Portugal, at the westernmost end of the European peninsula. Constantly shaken by military coups and uprisings after a republican revolution in 1910, very poor and backward Portugal finally got a strong dictator in Antonio de Oliveira Salazar in 1932. A devout Catholic, Salazar gave the church the strongest possible position in the country, while controlling the press and outlawing most political activity. Yet there was no attempt to mobilize the masses or to accomplish great projects. The traditional society was firmly maintained, and that was enough.

## MODERN TOTALITARIANISM

Although both are dictatorships, modern totalitarianism and conservative authoritarianism differ. They may be thought of as two distinct types of political organization that in practice sometimes share certain elements.

Modern totalitarianism burst on the scene with the revolutionary total war effort of 1914–1918. The war called forth a tendency to subordinate all institutions and all classes to one supreme objective: victory. Nothing, absolutely nothing, had equal value. People were called to make ever greater sacrifices, and their personal freedom was constantly reduced by ever greater government control. As the outstanding French thinker Elie Halévy put it in 1936, the varieties of modern totalitarian tyranny – fascism, Nazism, and communism – may be thought of as "feuding brothers" with a common father, the nature of modern war.[1]

The crucial experience of World War One was carried further by Lenin and the Bolsheviks during the Russian civil war. Lenin showed how a dedicated minority could make a total effort and achieve victory over a less-determined majority. Lenin also demonstrated how institutions and human rights might be subordinated to the needs of a single group – the Communist party – and its leader, Lenin. Thus, Lenin provided a model for single-party dictatorship, and he inspired imitators.

Building on its immediate origins in World War One and the Russian civil war, modern totalitarianism reached maturity in the 1930s in Stalinist Russia and Nazi Germany. Both had several fundamental characteristics of modern totalitarianism.

Armed with modern technology and communications, the true totalitarian state began as a dictatorship exercising complete political power, but it did not stop there. Increasingly, the state took over and tried to control just as completely the economic, social, intellectual, and cultural aspects of life. Although such unlimited control could not be fully realized, the individual's freedom of action was greatly reduced. Deviation from the norm even in art or family behavior could become a crime. In theory, nothing was politically neutral, nothing was outside the scope of the state.

This grandiose vision of total state control broke decisively not only with conservative authoritarianism but also with nineteenth-century liberalism and democracy. Indeed, totalitarianism was a radical revolt against liberalism. Liberalism sought to limit the power of the state and protect the sacred rights of the individual. Moreover, liberals stood for rationality, harmony, peaceful progress, and a strong middle class. All of that disgusted totalitarians as sentimental slop. They believed in will power, preached conflict, and worshiped violence. They believed that the individual was infinitely less valuable than the state and that there were no lasting rights, only temporary rewards for loyal and effective service. Only a single powerful leader and a single party, both unrestrained by law or tradition, determined the destiny of the totalitarian state.

Unlike old-fashioned authoritarianism, modern totalitarianism was based not on elites but on the masses. As in the First World War, the totalitarian state sought and sometimes won the support and even the love of ordinary people. Modern totalitarianism built on politically alert masses, on people who had already become engaged in the political process, most notably through commitment to nationalism and socialism. Its character as a mass movement gave totalitarianism much of its elemental force.

The final shared characteristic of real totalitarian states was their boundless dynamism.

NAZI MASS RALLY, 1936 *This picture captures the spirit of modern totalitarianism. The uniformed members of the Nazi party have willingly merged themselves into a single force and await the command of the godlike leader. (Wide World Photos)*

The totalitarian society was a fully mobilized society, a society moving toward some goal. It was never content merely to survive, like an old-fashioned military dictatorship or a decaying democracy. Paradoxically, totalitarian regimes never reached their goals. Or, more precisely, as soon as one goal was achieved at the cost of enormous sacrifice, another arose at the leader's command to take its place. Thus, totalitarianism was in the end a *permanent* revolution, an *unfinished* revolution, in which rapid, profound change imposed from on high went on forever.

## TOTALITARIANISM OF THE LEFT AND THE RIGHT

The two most-developed totalitarian states — Stalin's Communist Russia and Hitler's Nazi Germany — shared all the central characteristics of totalitarianism. But although those regimes may seem more alike than not, there were at least two major differences between them.

Communism as practiced in Soviet Russia grew out of Marxian socialism. Nazism in Germany grew out of extreme nationalism

*VICIOUS ANTI-SEMITISM was visible in all European countries before World War One. This 1898 French cartoon shows the Jewish banker Rothschild worshipping gold and exploiting the whole world. Jews were also denounced as revolutionary socialists intent upon destroying private property and the middle class. (Historical Pictures Service, Chicago)*

bilities for regeneration. Socialism, with its concern for social justice and human progress, is linked to the living core of Western civilization and the Judeo-Christian tradition. Stalin's communism was an ugly perversion of socialism, but even in its darkest moments it had the potential for reforming itself and creating a more humane society. Nazism, however, had no such potential. Based on the claptrap phobias of anticapitalism, anti-Semitism, and racism, its elements could be found in many a European city before the First World War. Totally negative and devoid of even perverted truth, it promised only destruction and never rebirth.

## STALIN'S RUSSIA

and racism. This distinction meant that private property and the middle class received very different treatment in the two states. In Soviet Russia the socialist program of the radical left was realized: all large holdings of private property were taken over by the state, and the middle class lost its wealth and status. In Germany big landowners and industrialists on the conservative right were attacked but managed to maintain their private wealth. This difference in property and class relations has led some scholars to speak of "totalitarianism of the left" – Stalinist Russia – and "totalitarianism of the right" – Nazi Germany.

More important were the differing possi-

Lenin established the basic outlines of a modern totalitarian dictatorship in Russia after the Bolshevik Revolution and during the civil war. Joseph Stalin (1879–1953) finished the job. A master of political infighting, Stalin cautiously consolidated his power and eliminated his enemies in the mid-1920's. Then in 1928, as undisputed leader of the ruling Communist party, he launched the first five-year plan – "the revolution from above," as he so aptly termed it.

The five-year plans were extremely ambitious. Often incorrectly considered a mere set of economic measures to speed up Soviet Russia's industrial development, the five-year plans actually marked the beginning of a renewed attempt to mobilize and transform Soviet society along socialist lines. The goal was to create a new way of life and to generate new attitudes and new loyalties. The means Stalin and the small Communist party elite chose were constant propaganda, enormous sacrifice, and unlimited violence and state control. Thus, the Soviet Union in the 1930s became a dynamic, modern totalitarian state.

## FROM LENIN TO STALIN

By spring 1921, Lenin and the Bolsheviks had won the civil war, but they ruled a shattered and devastated land. Many farms were in ruins, and food supplies were exhausted. In southern Russia drought combined with the ravages of war to produce the worst famine in generations. By 1920, according to the government, from 50 to 90 percent of the population in seventeen provinces was starving. Industrial production also broke down completely. In 1921, for example, output of steel and cotton textiles was only about 4 percent of what it had been in 1913. The revolutionary Trotsky later wrote that "the collapse of the productive forces surpassed anything of the kind history had ever seen. The country, and the government with it, were at the very edge of the abyss."[2] The Bolsheviks had destroyed the economy as well as their foes.

In the face of economic disintegration and rioting by peasants and workers, the tough but ever-flexible Lenin changed course. In March 1921, he announced the New Economic Policy, or NEP, which re-established limited economic freedom in an attempt to rebuild agriculture and industry. During the civil war, the Communists had simply seized grain without payment. Lenin in 1921 substituted a grain tax on the country's peasant producers, who were permitted to sell their surpluses in free markets. Peasants were also encouraged to buy as many goods as they could afford from private traders and small handicraft manufacturers, both of whom were allowed to reappear. Heavy industry, railroads, and banks, however, remained wholly nationalized. Thus, NEP saw only a limited restoration of capitalism.

Lenin's New Economic Policy was shrewd and successful, from two points of view. Politically, it was a necessary but temporary compromise with Russia's overwhelming peasant majority. Flushed with victory after their revolutionary gains of 1917, the peasants would have fought to hold onto their land. With fond hopes of immediate worldwide revolution fading by 1921, Lenin realized that his government was not strong enough to take it from them. As he had accepted Germany's harsh terms at Brest-Litovsk in 1918, Lenin made a deal with the only force capable of overturning his government.

Economically, NEP brought rapid recovery. In 1926, industrial output had surpassed the level of 1913, and Russian peasants were producing almost as much grain as before the war. Counting shorter hours and increased social benefits, workers were living somewhat better than they had in the past.

As the economy recovered and the government somewhat relaxed its censorship and repression, an intense struggle for power began in the inner circles of the Communist party, for Lenin had left no chosen successor when he died in 1924. The principal contenders were the stolid Stalin and the flamboyant Trotsky.

The son of a shoemaker, Joseph Dzhugashvili – later known as Stalin – studied for the priesthood but was expelled from his theological seminary, probably for his rude rebelliousness. By 1903 he had joined the Bolsheviks. In the years before the First World War he engaged in many revolutionary activities in the Transcaucasian area of southern Russia, including a daring bank robbery to get money for the Bolsheviks. This raid gained Lenin's attention and approval. Ethnically a Georgian and not a Russian, Stalin in his early writings focused on the oppression of minority peoples in the Russian Empire.

Stalin was a good organizer but a poor speaker and writer, with no experience outside of Russia.

Leon Trotsky, a great and inspiring leader who had planned the 1917 takeover (pages 973–974) and then created the victorious Red Army, appeared to have all the advantages. Yet it was Stalin who succeeded Lenin. Stalin won because he was more effective at gaining the all-important support of the party, the only genuine source of power in the one-party state. Rising to general secretary of the party's Central Committee just before Lenin's first stroke in 1922, Stalin used his office to win friends and allies with jobs and promises. Stalin also won recognition as commissar of nationalities, a position that gave him the important task of governing many of Russia's minorities.

The "practical" Stalin also won because he appeared better able than the brilliant Trotsky to relate Marxist teaching to Russian realities in the 1920s. First, as commissar of nationalities, he built on Lenin's idea of granting minority groups a certain degree of freedom in culture and language while maintaining rigorous political control through carefully selected local Communists. Stalin could loudly claim, therefore, to have found a way to solve the ancient problem of ethnic demands for independence in the multinational state. And of course he did.

Second, Stalin developed a theory of "socialism in one country," which was more appealing to the majority of Communists than Trotsky's doctrine of "permanent revolution." Stalin argued that Russia had the ability to build socialism on its own. Trotsky maintained that socialism in Russia could succeed only if revolution occurred quickly throughout Europe. To many communists, Trotsky's views seemed to sell Russia short and to promise risky conflicts with capitalist countries by recklessly encouraging revolutionary movements around the world. Stalin's willingness to break with NEP and push socialism at home appealed to young militants. In short, Stalin's theory of "socialism in one country" provided many in the party with a glimmer of hope in the midst of the capitalist-appearing NEP, which they had come to detest.

With cunning skill Stalin gradually achieved absolute power between 1922 and 1927. First, he allied with Trotsky's personal enemies to crush Trotsky, who was expelled from the Soviet Union in 1929 and eventually murdered in Mexico in 1940, undoubtedly on Stalin's order. Stalin then aligned with the moderates, who wanted to go slow at home, to suppress Trotsky's radical followers. Finally, having defeated all the radicals, he turned against his allies, the moderates, and destroyed them as well. Stalin's final triumph came at the Party Congress of December 1927, which condemned all "deviation from the general party line" formulated by Stalin. The dictator was then ready to launch his "revolution from above" – the real Russian revolution for millions of ordinary citizens.

## THE FIVE-YEAR PLANS

The Party Congress of 1927, which ratified Stalin's seizure of power, marked the end of the New Economic Policy and the beginning of the era of socialist five-year plans. The first five-year plan had staggering economic objectives. In just five years, total industrial output was to increase by 250 percent. Heavy industry, the preferred sector, was to grow even faster; steel production, for example, was to jump almost 300 percent. Agricultural production was slated to increase by 150 percent, and one-fifth of Russia's peasants were scheduled to give up their private plots and join

СО ЗНАМЕНЕМ ЛЕНИНА ПОБЕДИЛИ МЫ В БОЯХ ЗА ОКТЯБРЬСКУЮ РЕВОЛЮЦИЮ.
СО ЗНАМЕНЕМ ЛЕНИНА ДОБИЛИСЬ МЫ РЕШАЮЩИХ УСПЕХОВ В БОРЬБЕ ЗА ПОБЕДУ
СОЦИАЛИСТИЧЕСКОГО СТРОИТЕЛЬСТВА.
С ЭТИМ ЖЕ ЗНАМЕНЕМ ПОБЕДИМ В ПРОЛЕТАРСКОЙ РЕВОЛЮЦИИ ВО ВСЕМ МИРЕ.
(С т а л и н. Политический отчет ЦК XVI съезду ВКП (б).)

*"THE 5-YEAR PLAN IN 4 YEARS" This typical 1930 poster shows the fatherly Stalin leading the superhuman industrialization effort against his evil foreign foes. Lukewarm supporters at home were branded as the treasonous agents of those Catholics, capitalists, social democrats, Mensheviks, Fascists, and the like, pictured on the left. (John R. Freeman)*

socialist collective farms. In spite of warnings from moderate Communists that these goals were unrealistic, Stalin raised them higher as the plan got under way. By 1930, a whirlwind of economic and social change was sweeping across the country.

Stalin unleashed his "second revolution" for a variety of interrelated reasons. There were, first of all, ideological considerations. Like Lenin, Stalin and his militant supporters were deeply committed to socialism as they understood it. Since the country had recovered economically and their rule was secure, they burned to stamp out NEP's private traders, independent artisans, and few well-to-do peasants. Purely economic motivations

were also important. Although the economy had recovered, it seemed to have stalled in 1927 and 1928. A new socialist offensive seemed necessary if industry and agriculture were to grow rapidly.

Political considerations were most important. Internationally, there was the old problem remaining from prerevolutionary times of catching up with the advanced and presumably hostile capitalistic nations of the West. As Stalin said in 1931, when he pressed for ever greater speed and sacrifice: "We are fifty or a hundred years behind the advanced countries. We must make good this distance in ten years. Either we do it, or we shall go under."[3]

Domestically, there was what Communist

writers in the 1920s called the "cursed problem" – the problem of the Russian peasants. For centuries Russian peasants had wanted to own the land, and finally they had it. Sooner or later, the Communists reasoned, the peasants would become conservative little capitalists and pose a threat to the regime. Therefore, Stalin decided on a preventive war against the peasantry, in order to bring it under the absolute control of the state.

That war was collectivization – the forcible consolidation of individual peasant farms into large, state-controlled enterprises. Beginning in 1929, peasants all over the Soviet Union were ordered to give up their land and animals and to become members of collective farms, although they continued to live in their own homes. As for the kulaks, the better-off peasants, Stalin instructed party workers to "liquidate them as a class." Stripped of their land and livestock, the kulaks were generally not even permitted to join the collective farms. Many either starved or were deported to forced-labor camps for "re-education."

Since almost all peasants were in fact poor, the term *kulak* soon meant any peasant who opposed the new system. Whole villages were often attacked. One conscience-stricken colonel in the secret police confessed to a foreign journalist: "I am an old Bolshevik. I worked in the underground against the Tsar and then I fought in the Civil War. Did I do all that in order that I should now surround villages with machine-guns and order my men to fire indiscriminately into crowds of peasants? Oh, no, no!"[4]

Forced collectivization of the peasants led to economic and human disaster. Large numbers of peasants slaughtered their animals and burned their crops in sullen, hopeless protest. Between 1929 and 1933, the number of horses, cattle, sheep, and goats in the Soviet Union fell by at least one-half. Nor were the state-controlled collective farms more productive. The output of grain barely increased between 1928 and 1938, when it was almost identical to that of 1913. Communist economists had expected collectivized agriculture to pay for new factories. Instead, the state had to invest heavily in agriculture, building thousands of tractors to replace the slaughtered draft horses. Collectivized agriculture was unable to make any substantial financial contribution to Soviet industrial development in the first five-year plan. The human dimension of the tragedy was shocking. Collectivization created man-made famine in 1932–1933, and many perished. Indeed, Stalin confided to Churchill at Yalta in 1945 that 10 million people had died in the course of collectivization.

Yet collectivization was a political victory of sorts. By the end of 1932, fully 60 percent of Russian peasant families had been herded onto collective farms; by 1938, 93 percent. Regimented and indoctrinated as employees of an all-powerful state, the peasants were no longer even a potential political threat to Stalin and the Communist party. Moreover, the state was assured of grain for bread for urban workers, who were much more important politically than the peasants. Collective farmers had to meet their grain quotas first and worry about feeding themselves second. Many collectivized peasants drew much of their own food from tiny, grudgingly tolerated garden plots that they worked in their off hours. No wonder some peasants joked, with that grim humor peculiar to the totalitarian society, that the initials then used by the Communist party actually stood for "The Second Serfdom, That of the Bolsheviks."

The industrial side of the five-year plans was more successful – indeed, quite spectacular. The output of industry doubled in the first five-year plan and doubled again in the second. Soviet industry produced about four times as much in 1937 as it had in 1928. No other major country had ever achieved such rapid industrial growth. Heavy industry led the way; consumer industry grew quite slowly. Steel production – a near-obsession with Stalin, whose name fittingly meant "man of steel" in Russian – increased roughly 500 percent between 1928 and 1937. A new heavy industrial complex was built almost from scratch in western Siberia. Industrial growth also went hand in hand with urban development. Cities rose where nomadic tribes had grazed their flocks. More than 25 million people migrated to cities and industrial centers during the 1930s.

The great industrialization drive, concentrated between 1928 and 1937, was an awe-inspiring achievement purchased at a cost of enormous sacrifice. The sudden creation of dozens of new factories required a great increase in investment and a sharp decrease in consumption. Few nations had ever invested more than a sixth of their yearly net national income. Soviet planners decreed that more than a third of net income go for investment. This meant that only two-thirds of everything being produced could be consumed by the people *and* the increasingly voracious military. The money was collected from the people by means of heavy, hidden sales taxes.

There was, therefore, no improvement in the average standard of living. Indeed, the most careful studies show that the average nonfarm wage apparently purchased only about *half* as many goods in 1932 as in 1928. After 1932, real wages rose slowly, so that in 1937 workers could buy about 60 percent of what they had bought in 1928. Thus, rapid industrial development went hand in hand with an unprecedented decline in the standard of living for ordinary people.

Two other factors contributed importantly to rapid industrialization: firm labor discipline and foreign engineers. Between 1930 and 1932, trade unions lost most of their power. The government could assign workers to any job anywhere in the country, and individuals could not move without the permission of the police. When factory managers needed more hands, they called on their counterparts on the collective farms, who sent them millions of "unneeded" peasants over the years.

Foreign engineers were hired to plan and construct many of the new factories. Highly skilled American engineers, hungry for work in the depression years, were particularly important until newly trained Soviet experts began to replace them after 1932. The gigantic mills of the new Siberian steel industry were modeled on America's best. Those modern mills were eloquent testimony to the ability of Stalin's planners to harness even the skill and technology of capitalist countries to promote the surge of socialist industry.

## LIFE IN STALINIST SOCIETY

The aim of Stalin's five-year plans was to create a new kind of society and human personality, as well as a strong industrial economy and a powerful army. Stalin and his helpers were good Marxian economic determinists. Once everthing was owned by the state, they believed, a socialist society and a new kind of human being would inevitably emerge. They were by no means totally successful, but they did build a new society, whose broad outlines exist to this day. For the people, life in Stalinist society had both good and bad aspects.

The most frightening aspect of Stalinist society was brutal, unrestrained police terrorism. First directed primarily against the peasants after 1929, terror was increasingly turned on leading Communists, powerful adminis-

*ADULT EDUCATION   Illiteracy, especially among women, was a serious problem after the Russian Revolution. This early photo shows how adults successfully learned to read and write throughout the Soviet Union. (Sovfoto/Eastfoto)*

trators, and ordinary people for no apparent reason. As one Soviet woman later recalled: "We all trembled because there was no way of getting out of it. Even a Communist himself can be caught. To avoid trouble became an exception."[5] A climate of fear fell upon the land.

In the early 1930s, the top members of the party and government were Stalin's obedient servants, but there was some grumbling in the party. At a small gathering in November 1932 even Stalin's wife complained bitterly about the great misery of the people. Stalin showered her with insults, and she died that same night, apparently by her own hand. In late 1934, Stalin's number-two man, Sergei Kirov, was suddenly and mysteriously mur-

dered. Although Stalin himself probably ordered Kirov's murder, he used the incident to launch a reign of terror.

In August 1936, sixteen prominent old Bolsheviks confessed to all manner of plots against Stalin in spectacular public trials in Moscow. Then, in 1937, lesser party officials and newer henchmen were arrested. In addition to party members, union officials, managers, intellectuals, army officers, and countless ordinary citizens were struck down. Local units of the secret police were even ordered to arrest a certain percentage of the people in their district. In all, at least 8 million people were probably arrested.

Stalin's mass purges were truly baffling, and many explanations have been given for them. Possibly Stalin believed that the old Communists, like the peasants under NEP, were a potential threat to be wiped out in a preventive attack. Yet why did leading Communists willingly confess to crimes they could not possibly have committed? Their lives had been devoted to the party and the socialist revolution. In the words of the German novelist Arthur Koestler, they probably confessed "in order to do a last service to the Party," the party they loved even when it was wrong. Some of them were subjected to torture and psychological brainwashing. It has been argued that the purges indicate that Stalin was sadistic or insane, for his bloodbath greatly weakened the government and the army. Others see the terror as an aspect of the fully developed totalitarian state, which must by its nature always be fighting real or imaginary enemies. At the least, the mass purges were a message to the people. No one was secure. Everyone had to serve the party and its leader with redoubled devotion.

Another aspect of life in the 1930s was constant propaganda and indoctrination. Party activists lectured workers in factories and peasants on the collective farms, while newspapers, films, and radio broadcasts endlessly recounted socialist achievements and capitalist plots. Art and literature became highly political. Whereas the 1920s had seen considerable experimentation in modern art and theater, the intellectual elite were ordered by Stalin to become "engineers of human minds." Writers and artists who could effectively combine genuine creativity and political propaganda became the darlings of the regime. They often lived better than top members of the political elite. It became increasingly important for the successful writer and artist to glorify Russian nationalism. Russian history was rewritten, so that early tsars like Ivan the Terrible and Peter the Great became worthy forerunners of the greatest Russian leader of all — Stalin.

Stalin seldom appeared in public, but his presence was everywhere — in portraits, statues, books, and quotations from his "sacred" writings. Although the government persecuted religion and turned churches into "museums of atheism," the state had both an earthly religion and a high priest — Marxian socialism and Joseph Stalin.

Life was hard in Stalin's Soviet Russia. The standard of living declined substantially in the 1930s. The masses of people lived primarily on black bread and wore old, shabby clothing. There were constant shortages in the stores, although very heavily taxed vodka was always readily available. A shortage of housing was a particularly serious problem. Millions were moving into the cities, but the government built few new apartments. In 1940, there were approximately 4 people per room in every urban dwelling, as opposed to 2.7 per room in 1926. A relatively lucky family received one room for all its members, and shared both a kitchen and a toilet with others on the floor. Less fortunate workers, kulaks, and class enemies built scrap-lumber shacks or underground dugouts in shantytowns.

Life was hard, but by no means hopeless. Idealism and ideology had real appeal for many Russians, who saw themselves heroically building the world's first socialist society while capitalism crumbled in the West. This optimistic belief in the future of Soviet Russia also attracted many disillusioned Western liberals to communism in the 1930s.

On a more practical level, Soviet workers did receive some important social benefits, such as old-age pensions, free medical services, free education, and day-care centers for children. Unemployment was almost unknown. Finally, there was the possibility of personal advancement.

The key to improving one's position was

specialized skills and technical education. Rapid industrialization required massive numbers of trained experts, such as skilled workers, engineers, and plant managers. Thus, the state provided tremendous incentives to those who could serve its needs. It paid the mass of unskilled workers and collective farmers very low wages, but it dangled high salaries and many special privileges before its growing technical and managerial elite. This elite joined with the political and artistic elites in a new upper class, whose members were rich, powerful, and insecure, especially during the purges. Yet the possible gains of moving up outweighed the risks. Millions struggled bravely in universities, institutes, and night schools for the all-important specialized education. One young man summed it up: "In Soviet Russia there is no capital except education. If a person does not want to become a collective farmer or just a cleaning woman, the only means you have to get something is through education."[6]

## WOMEN IN SOVIET RUSSIA

Women's lives were radically altered by Stalinist society. Marxists had traditionally believed that both capitalism and the middle-class husband exploited women. The Russian Revolution of 1917 immediately proclaimed complete equality of rights for women. In the 1920s, divorce and abortion were made very easy, and women were urged to work outside the home and liberate themselves sexually. A prominent and influential Bolshevik feminist, Alexandra Kollontai, went so far as to declare that the sexual act had no more significance than "drinking a glass of water." This observation drew a sharp rebuke from the rather prudish Lenin, who said that "no sane man would lie down to drink from a puddle in the gutter or even drink from a dirty glass."[7] After Stalin came to power, sexual and familial liberation was played down, and the most lasting changes for women involved work and education.

The changes were truly revolutionary. Young women were constantly told that they must be fully equal with men, that they could and should do anything men could do. Russian peasant women had long experienced the equality of backbreaking physical labor in the countryside, and they continued to enjoy that equality on collective farms. With the advent of the five-year plans, millions of women also began to toil in factories and on heavy construction, building dams, roads, and steel mills in summer heat and winter frost. Yet most of the opportunities open to men through education were also opened to women. Determined women pursued their studies and entered the ranks of the better-paid specialists in industry and science. Medicine practically became a woman's profession. By 1950, 75 percent of all doctors in Soviet Russia were women.

Thus Stalinist society gave women great opportunities, but demanded great sacrifices as well. The vast majority of women simply *had* to work outside the home. Wages were so low that it was almost impossible for a family or couple to live only on the husband's earnings. Moreover, the full-time workingwoman had a heavy burden of household tasks in her off-hours, for most Soviet men in the 1930s still considered the home and the children the woman's responsibility. Finally, rapid change and economic hardship led to many broken families, creating further physical, emotional, and mental strains for women. In any event, the often-neglected human resource of women was ruthlessly mobilized in Stalinist society. This too was an aspect of Soviet totalitarianism.

Before turning to Hitler's Germany, it is necessary to look briefly at Mussolini's role in Italy. Like all the other emerging dictators, Mussolini hated liberalism, and he destroyed it in Italy. But that was not all. Mussolini and his supporters were the first to call themselves fascists – revolutionaries determined to create a certain kind of totalitarian state. As Mussolini's famous slogan of 1926 put it: "Everything in the state, nothing outside the state, nothing against the state." But Mussolini in power, unlike Stalin and Hitler, did not in fact create a real totalitarian state. His dictatorship was rather an instructive hybrid, a halfway house between conservative authoritarianism and modern totalitarianism.

## THE SEIZURE OF POWER

Before the First World War, Italy was a liberal state moving gradually toward democracy. But there were serious problems. Much of the Italian population was still poor, and class differences were extreme. Many peasants were more attached to their villages and local interests than to the national state. Moreover, the papacy and many devout Catholics, as well as the socialists, were strongly opposed to the heirs of Cavour and Garibaldi, middle-class lawyers and politicians who ran the country largely for their own benefit.

The war worsened the political situation. Having fought on the side of the Allies almost exclusively for purposes of territorial expansion, Italian nationalists were bitterly disappointed with Italy's modest gains at Versailles. Workers and peasants also felt cheated: to win their support during the war, the government had promised social and land reform, which it did not deliver after the war.

Encouraged by the Russian Revolution of 1917, radical workers and peasants began occupying factories and seizing land in 1920. These actions scared and radicalized the property-owning classes. The Italian middle classes were already in an ugly mood, having suffered from inflation during the war. Moreover, after the war, the pope lifted his ban on participation by Catholics in Italian politics, and a strong Catholic party quickly emerged. Thus, by 1922 almost all the major groups in Italian society were opposed – though for different reasons – to the liberal parliamentary government.

Into these crosscurrents of unrest and frustration stepped the blustering, bullying Benito Mussolini (1883–1945). Son of a village schoolteacher and a poor blacksmith, Mussolini began his political career as a socialist leader and radical newspaper editor before World War One. In 1914, powerfully influenced by antiliberal cults of violent action, the young Mussolini urged that Italy join the Allies, for which he was expelled from the Italian Socialist party by its antiwar majority. Later Mussolini fought at the front and was wounded. Returning home in 1919, he organized bitter war veterans like himself into a band of "fascists" – from the Italian word for a union of forces.

At first, Mussolini's progam was a radical combination of nationalist and socialist demands, including territorial expansion, benefits for workers, and land reform for peasants. As such, it competed with the better-organized Socialist party and failed to get off the ground. When Mussolini saw that his violent verbal assaults on the rival socialists won him growing support from the frightened middle class, he shifted gears in 1920. In thought and action Mussolini was a striking example of the turbulence of the age of anxiety.

Mussolini and his growing private army of

MUSSOLINI *loved to pose and show off. He was sure he had irresistible sex appeal for millions of Italian women. (National Archives, Washington)*

convince themselves that they were not just opposing the "reds" but making a real revolution of their own. Many believed that they were not only destroying parliamentary government but forming a strong, dynamic movement that would help the little people against the established interests.

With the government breaking down in 1922, largely because of the chaos created by his direct-action bands, Mussolini stepped forward as the savior of order and property. Striking a conservative note in his speeches and gaining the sympathetic neutrality of army leaders, Mussolini demanded the resignation of the existing government and his own appointment by the king. In October 1922, to force matters, a large group of Fascists marched on Rome to threaten the king and force him to call on Mussolini. The threat worked. Victor Emmanuel III (1900–1946), who had no love for the old liberal politicians, asked Mussolini to form a new cabinet. Thus, after widespread violence and a threat of armed uprising, Mussolini seized power "legally." He was immediately granted dictatorial authority for one year by the king and the parliament.

### THE REGIME IN ACTION

Mussolini became dictator on the strength of Italians' rejection of parliamentary government, coupled with fears of Russian-style revolution. Yet what he intended to do with his power was by no means clear until 1924. Some of his dedicated supporters pressed for a "second revolution." Mussolini's ministers, however, included old conservatives, moderates, and even two reform-minded socialists. A new electoral law was passed giving two-thirds of the representatives in the parliament to the party that won the most votes, which allowed the Fascists and their allies to win an

Black Shirts began to grow violent. Typically, a band of Fascist toughs would roar off in trucks at night and swoop down on a few isolated socialist organizers, beating them up and force-feeding them almost deadly doses of castor oil. Few people were killed, but socialist newspapers, union halls, and local socialist party headquarters were destroyed. Mussolini's toughs pushed communists and socialists out of the city governments of northern Italy.

Mussolini, a skillful politician, refused to become a puppet of frightened conservatives and capitalists. He allowed his followers to overwhelming majority in 1923. Then, in 1924, five of Mussolini's Fascist thugs kidnapped and murdered Giacomo Matteotti, the young leader of the socialists in the parliament. In the face of this outrage, the opposition demanded that Mussolini's armed squads be dissolved and all violence be banned.

Although he may or may not have ordered Matteotti's murder, Mussolini stood at the crossroads in a severe political crisis. After some hesitation, he charged forward. Declaring his desire to "make the nation fascist," he imposed a series of repressive measures. Freedom of the press was abolished, elections were fixed, and the government ruled by decree. Mussolini arrested his political opponents, disbanded all independent labor unions, and put dedicated Fascists in control of Italy's schools. Moreover, he created a Fascist youth movement, Fascist labor unions, and many other Fascist organizations. By the end of 1926, Italy was a one-party dictatorship under Mussolini's unquestioned leadership.

Yet Mussolini did not complete the establishment of a modern totalitarian state. His Fascist party never became all-powerful. It never destroyed the old power structure, as the Communists did in Soviet Russia, or succeeded in dominating it, as the Nazis did in Germany. Membership in the Fascist party was more a sign of an Italian's respectability than a commitment to radical change. Interested primarily in personal power, Mussolini was content to compromise with the old conservative classes that controlled the army, the economy, and the state. He never tried to purge these classes or even move very vigorously against them. He controlled and propagandized labor, but left big business to regulate itself, profitably and securely. There was no land reform.

Mussolini also came to draw on the support of the Catholic church. In the Lateran Agreement of 1929 he recognized the Vatican as a tiny independent state, and he paid the church a large sum of money. The pope expressed his satisfaction and urged Italians to support Mussolini's government.

Nothing better illustrates Mussolini's unwillingness to harness everyone and everything for dynamic action than his treatment of women. He abolished divorce and told women to stay at home and produce children. To promote that goal, he decreed a special tax on bachelors in 1934. In 1938, women were limited by law to a maximum of 10 percent of the better-paying jobs in industry and government. Italian women, as women, appear not to have changed their attitudes or behavior in any important way under Fascist rule.

It is also noteworthy that Mussolini's government did not persecute Jews until late in the Second World War, when Italy was under Nazi control. Nor did Mussolini establish a truly ruthless police state. Only twenty-three political prisoners were condemned to death between 1926 and 1944. In spite of much pompous posing by the chauvinist leader, and in spite of mass meetings, salutes, and a certain copying of Hitler's aggression in foreign policy after 1933, Mussolini's Italy – though undemocratic – was never really totalitarian.

## HITLER'S GERMANY

The most frightening and horrible totalitarian state was Nazi Germany. A product of Hitler's evil genius as well as Germany's social and political situation and the general attack on liberalism and rationality in the age of anxiety, Nazi Germany emerged rapidly after Hitler came to power in 1933. The Nazis quickly smashed or took over most independent organizations, mobilized the economy, and began brutally persecuting the Jewish population. From the start, all major decisions were in the hands of the aggressive dictator Adolf Hitler.

## THE ROOTS OF NAZISM

Nazism grew out of many complex developments, of which the most influential were extreme nationalism and racism. These two ideas captured the mind of the young Hitler, and it was he who dominated Nazism for as long as it lasted.

Born the fourth child of a successful Austrian customs official and an indulgent mother, Adolf Hitler (1889–1945) spent his childhood happily in small towns in Austria. A good student in grade school, Hitler did poorly on reaching high school, and dropped out at age fourteen after the death of his father. After four years of unfocused loafing, Hitler finally left for Vienna to become an artist. Denied admission to the Imperial Academy of Fine Arts because he lacked talent, the dejected Hitler stayed on in Vienna. There he lived a comfortable, lazy life on his generous orphan's pension and found most of the perverted beliefs that guided his life.

In Vienna Hitler soaked up extreme German nationalism, which was particularly strong there. Austro-German nationalists, as if to compensate for their declining position in the Austro-Hungarian Empire, believed Germans to be a superior people and the natural rulers of central Europe. They often advocated union with Germany and violent expulsion of "inferior" peoples as the means of maintaining German domination of the Austro-Hungarian Empire.

Hitler was deeply impressed by Vienna's mayor Karl Lueger, whom he called "the mightiest mayor of all times." Lueger claimed to be a "Christian socialist." With the help of the Catholic trade unions, he had succeeded in winning the support of the little people of Vienna for an attack on capitalism and liberalism, which he held responsible for un-Christian behavior and excessive individualism. A master of mass politics in the urban world, Lueger showed Hitler the enormous potential of anticapitalist and antiliberal propaganda.

From Lueger and others, Hitler eagerly absorbed virulent anti-Semitism, racism, and hatred of Slavs. He was particularly inspired by the racist ravings of an ex-monk named Lanz von Liebenfels. Preaching the crudest, most exaggerated distortions of the Darwinian theory of survival, Liebenfels stressed the superiority of Germanic races, the inevitability of racial conflict, and the inferiority of the Jews. Liebenfels even anticipated the breeding and extermination policies of the Nazi state: he claimed that the master race had to multiply its numbers by means of polygamy and breeding stations, while it systematically sterilized and liquidated inferior races. Anti-Semitism and racism became Hitler's most passionate convictions, his explanation for everything. He believed inferior races – the Slavs and the Jews in particular – were responsible for Austria's woes. The Jews, he claimed, directed an international conspiracy of finance capitalism and Marxian socialism against German culture, German unity, and the German race. Hitler's belief was totally irrational, but he never doubted it.

Although he moved to Munich in 1913 to avoid being drafted into the Austrian army, the lonely Hitler greeted the outbreak of the First World War as a salvation. He later wrote in his autobiography *Mein Kampf* that, "overcome by passionate enthusiasm, I fell to my knees and thanked heaven out of an overflowing heart." The struggle and discipline of war gave life meaning, and Hitler served bravely as a dispatch carrier on the western front.

When Germany was suddenly defeated in 1918, Hitler's world was shattered. Not only was he a fanatical nationalist, but war was his reason for living. Convinced that the Jews and the Marxists had "stabbed Germany in the back," he vowed to fight on. And in the bitterness and uncertainty of postwar Germany, his wild speeches began to attract attention.

In late 1919, Hitler joined a tiny extremist group in Munich called the German Workers' party. In addition to denouncing Jews, Marxists, and democrats, the German Workers' party promised unity under a uniquely German "national socialism," which would abolish the injustices of capitalism and create a mighty "people's community." By 1921, Hitler had gained absolute control of this small but growing party. Moreover, Hitler was already a master of mass propaganda and political showmanship. Party members sported badges and uniforms, gave victory salutes, and marched like robots through the streets of Munich. But Hitler's most effective tool was the mass rally, a kind of political revival meeting. Songs, slogans, and demonstrations built up the tension until Hitler finally arrived. He then often worked his audience into a frenzy with wild, demagogic attacks on the Versailles treaty, the Jews, the war profiteers, and Germany's Weimar Republic.

Party membership multiplied tenfold after early 1922. In late 1923, when the Weimar Republic seemed on the verge of collapse, Hitler decided on an armed uprising in Munich. Inspired by Mussolini's recent easy victory, Hitler had found an ally in General Ludendorff of First World War fame. After Hitler had overthrown the Bavarian government, Ludendorff was supposed to march on Berlin with Hitler's support. The plot was poorly organized, however, and it was crushed

ADOLF HITLER   A lonely, unsuccessful misfit before 1914, Hitler found his mission in World War One and its aftermath. He emerged as a spellbinding speaker and a master of the politics of hate and violence. (Bettmann Archive)

by the police, backed up by the army, in less than a day. Hitler was arrested, tried, and sentenced to five years in prison. He had failed for the moment. But Nazism had been born, and it did not die.

### HITLER'S ROAD TO POWER

At his trial Hitler violently denounced the Weimar Republic and skillfully presented his own program. In doing so he gained enormous publicity and attention. Moreover, he learned from his unsuccessful uprising. Hitler concluded that he had to undermine rather than overthrow the government, that he had to use its tolerant democratic framework to come to power *legally*. He forced his more violent supporters to accept his new strategy. Finally, Hitler used his brief prison term – he was released in less than a year – to dictate his autobiography, *Mein Kampf*. There, he expounded on his basic themes – "race," with

*"HITLER, OUR LAST HOPE"* So reads the very effective Nazi campaign poster, which is attracting attention with its gaunt and haggard faces. By 1932 almost half of all Germans, like these in Berlin, had come to agree. (Bildarchiv Preussischer Kulturbisitz)

the stress on anti-Semitism; "living space," with a sweeping vision of war and conquered territory; and the leader-dictator (the führer) with unlimited, arbitary power. Hitler's followers had their bible.

In the years of prosperity and relative stability between 1924 and 1929, Hitler concentrated on building his National Socialist German Workers' party, or Nazi party for short. By 1928, the party had a hundred thousand highly disciplined members, and Hitler's absolute control of them was unquestioned. To appeal to the middle class, Hitler de-emphasized the anticapitalist elements of national socialism.

The Nazis were still a small splinter group in 1928, when they received only 2.6 percent of the vote in the general elections and twelve Nazis won seats in the parliament. There, the Nazi deputies pursued the legal strategy of using democracy to destroy democracy. As Hitler's talented future minister of propaganda Joseph Goebbels (1897–1945) explained in 1928 in the party newspaper: "We become Reichstag deputies in order to paralyze the spirit of Weimar with its own aid. . . .

We come as enemies! As the wolf breaks into the sheepfold, so we come."[8]

In 1929, the Great Depression began striking down economic prosperity, one of the barriers that had kept the wolf at bay. Unemployment jumped from 1.3 million in 1929 to 5 million in 1930; that year Germany had almost as many unemployed as all the other countries of Europe combined. Industrial production fell by one-half between 1929 and 1932. By the end of 1932, an incredible 43 percent of the labor force was unemployed, and it was estimated that only one in every three union members was working full-time. No factor contributed more to Hitler's success than the economic crisis. Never very interested in economics before, Hitler began promising German voters economic as well as political and military salvation.

Hitler focused his promises on the middle and lower middle class – small businessmen, office workers, artisans, and peasants. Already disillusioned by the great inflation of 1923, these people were seized by panic as bankruptcies increased, unemployment soared, and the dreaded Communists made dramatic election gains. The middle and lower middle classes deserted the conservative and moderate parties for the Nazis in great numbers.

The Nazis also appealed strongly to German youth. Indeed, in some ways the Nazi movement was a mass movement of young Germans. Hitler himself was only forty in 1929, and he and most of his top aides were much younger than other leading German politicians. "National Socialism is the organized will of the youth," proclaimed the official Nazi slogan, and the battle cry of Gregor Strasser, a leading Nazi organizer, was, "Make way, you old ones."[9] In 1931, almost 40 percent of Nazi party members were under thirty, compared to 20 percent of Social Democrats. Two-thirds of Nazi members were

under forty. National recovery, exciting and rapid change, and personal advancement: these were the appeals of Nazism to millions of German youths.

In the election of 1930, the Nazis won 6.5 million votes and 107 seats, which made them second in strength only to the Social Democrats, the moderate socialists. The economic situation continued to deteriorate, and Hitler kept promising he would bring recovery. In 1932, the Nazi vote leaped to 14.5 million, and the Nazis became the largest party in the Reichstag.

Another reason Hitler came to power was the breakdown of democratic government as early as May 1930. Unable to gain the support of a majority in the Reichstag, Chancellor (chief minister) Heinrich Brüning convinced the president, the aging war hero General Hindenburg, to authorize rule by decree. The Weimar Republic's constitution permitted such rule in emergency situations, but the rather authoritarian, self-righteous Brüning intended to use it indefinitely. Moreover, Brüning was determined to overcome the economic crisis by cutting back government spending and ruthlessly forcing down prices and wages. Brüning's ultraorthodox policies not only intensified the economic collapse in Germany, they also convinced the lower middle classes that the country's republican leaders were stupid and corrupt. These classes were pleased rather than dismayed by Hitler's attacks on the republican system. After President Hindenburg forced Brüning to resign in May 1932, the new government headed by Franz von Papen continued to rule by decree.

The continuation of the struggle between the Social Democrats and Communists, right up until the moment Hitler took power, was another aspect of the breakdown of democratic government. The Communists foolishly refused to cooperate with the Social Demo-

## EVENTS LEADING TO WORLD WAR TWO

| | |
|---|---|
| 1919 | Treaty of Versailles |
| | J. M. Keynes, *Economic Consequences of the Peace* |
| 1919–1920 | U.S. Senate rejects the Treaty of Versailles |
| 1921 | Germany is billed $35 billion in reparations |
| 1922 | Mussolini seizes power in Italy |
| | Germany proposes a moratorium on reparations |
| January 1923 | France and Belgium occupy the Ruhr |
| | Germany orders passive resistance to the occupation |
| October 1923 | Stresemann agrees to reparations with re-examination of Germany's ability to pay |
| 1924 | Dawes Plan: German reparations reduced and put on a sliding scale; large U.S. loans to Germany recommended to promote German recovery; occupation of the Ruhr ends |
| | Adolf Hitler, *Mein Kampf* |
| 1924–1929 | Spectacular German economic recovery; circular flow of international funds enables sizable reparations payments |
| 1925 | Treaties of Locarno promote European security and stability |
| 1926 | Germany joins the League of Nations |
| 1928 | Kellogg-Briand Pact renounces war as an instrument of international affairs |
| 1929 | Young Plan further reduces German reparations |
| | Crash of U.S. stock market |
| 1929–1933 | Depths of the Great Depression |

crats, even though the two parties together outnumbered the Nazis in the Reichstag, even after the elections of 1932. German Communists (and the complacent Stalin) were blinded by their ideology and their hatred of the socialists. They were certain that Hitler's rise represented the last agonies of monopoly capitalism and that a Communist revolution would quickly follow his taking power. The socialist leaders pleaded, even at the Russian embassy, for at least a temporary alliance with the Communists to block Hitler, but to no avail. Perhaps the Weimar Republic was already too far gone, but this disunity on the left was undoubtedly another nail in its coffin.

Finally, there was Hitler's skill as a politician. A master of mass propaganda and psychology, he had written in *Mein Kampf* that

## Events Leading to World War Two (continued)

| | |
|---|---|
| 1931 | Japan invades Manchuria |
| 1932 | Nazis become the largest party in the Reichstag |
| January 1933 | Hitler appointed chancellor |
| March 1933 | Reichstag passes the Enabling Act, granting Hitler absolute dictatorial power |
| October 1933 | Germany withdraws from the League of Nations |
| July 1934 | Nazis murder Austrian chancellor |
| March 1935 | Hitler announces German rearmament |
| June 1935 | Anglo-German naval agreement |
| October 1935 | Mussolini invades Ethiopia and receives Hitler's support |
| 1935 | Nuremburg Laws deprive Jews of all rights of citizenship |
| March 1936 | German armies move unopposed into the demilitarized Rhineland |
| July 1936 | Outbreak of civil war in Spain |
| 1937 | Japan invades China |
| | Rome-Berlin Axis |
| March 1938 | Germany annexes Austria |
| September 1938 | Munich Conference: Britain and France agree to German seizure of the Sudetenland from Czechoslovakia |
| March 1939 | Germany occupies the rest of Czechoslovakia; the end of appeasement in Britain |
| August 1939 | Russo-German nonaggression pact |
| September 1, 1939 | Germany invades Poland |
| September 3, 1939 | Britain and France declare war on Germany |

the masses were "the driving force of the most important changes in this world" and were themselves driven by hysterical fanaticism and not by knowledge. To arouse such hysterical fanaticism, he believed that all propaganda had to be limited to a few simple, endlessly repeated slogans. Thus, in the terrible economic and political crisis, he harangued vast audiences with passionate, irrational oratory. Men moaned and women cried, seized by emotion. And many uncertain individuals, surrounded by thousands of entranced listeners, found security and a sense of belonging.

At the same time Hitler excelled at dirty, backroom politics. That, in fact, brought him to power. In 1932, he cleverly succeeded in gaining the support of key people in the army and big business. These people thought they could use Hitler for their own advantage, to get increased military spending, fat contracts, and tough measures against workers. Conservative and nationalistic politicians like Papen thought similarly. They thus accepted Hitler's demand to join the government only if he became chancellor. There would be only two other National Socialists and nine solid conservatives as ministers, and in such a coalition government, they reasoned, Hitler could be used and controlled. On January 30, 1933, Hitler was legally appointed chancellor by President Hindenburg.

## THE NAZI STATE AND SOCIETY

Hitler moved rapidly and skillfully to establish an unshakable dictatorship. His first step was to continue using terror and threats to gain more power "legally." He immediately called for new elections, and applied the enormous power of the government to restrict his opponents. In the midst of a violent electoral campaign, the Reichstag building was partly destroyed by fire. Although the Nazis probably set the fire, Hitler screamed that the Communist party was responsible. On the strength of this accusation, he convinced President Hindenburg to sign dictatorial emergency acts that practically abolished freedom of speech and assembly, as well as most personal liberties.

When the Nazis won only 44 percent of the vote in the elections, Hitler immediately outlawed the Communist party and arrested its parliamentary representatives. Then, on March 23, 1933, the Nazis pushed through the Reichstag the so-called Enabling Act, which gave Hitler absolute dictatorial power for four years. Only the Social Democrats voted against this bill, for Hitler had successfully blackmailed the Center party by threatening to attack the Catholic church.

Armed with the Enabling Act, Hitler and the Nazis moved to smash or control all independent organizations. Meanwhile Hitler and his propagandists constantly proclaimed that their revolution was legal and constitutional. This stress on legality, coupled with the divide-and-conquer technique, disarmed the opposition until it was too late for effective resistance.

The systematic subjugation of independent organizations and the creation of a totalitarian state had massive repercussions. The Social Democrat and Center parties were soon dissolved, and Germany became a one-party state. Only the Nazi party was legal. Elections were farces. The Reichstag was jokingly referred to as the most expensive glee club in the country, for its only function was to sing hymns of praise to the Führer. Hitler and the Nazis took over the government bureaucracy intact, installing many Nazis in top positions. At the same time they created a series of overlapping Nazi party organizations, responsible solely to Hitler. Thus Hitler had both an established bureaucracy for normal business and a private, personal "party government" for special duties.

In the economic sphere, strikes were forbidden and labor unions were abolished, replaced by a Nazi Labor Front. Professional people — doctors and lawyers, teachers and engineers—also saw their previously independent organizations swallowed up in Nazi associations. Nor did the Nazis neglect cultural and intellectual life. Publishing houses were put under Nazi control, and universities and writers were quickly brought into line. Democratic, socialist, and "Jewish" literature was put on ever-growing blacklists. Passionate students and pitiful professors burned forbidden books in public squares. Modern art and architecture were ruthlessly prohibited. Life became violently anti-intellectual. As Hitler's cynical minister of propaganda, Joseph Goebbels, put it: "When I hear the word 'culture' I reach for my gun."[10] By 1934, a totalitarian state characterized by frightening dynamism and obedience to Hitler was already largely in place.

By 1934 only the army retained independence, and Hitler moved brutally and skillfully to establish his control there too. He realized that the army, as well as big business, was suspicious of the Nazi storm troopers (the SA), the quasi-military band of 3 million toughs in brown shirts who had fought Communists and beaten up Jews before the Nazis took power. These unruly storm troopers expected top positions in the army and even talked of a "second revolution" against capitalism. Needing the support of the army and big business, Hitler decided that the SA leaders had to be eliminated. On the night of June 30, 1934, he struck.

Hitler's elite personal guard – the SS – arrested and shot without trial roughly one thousand SA leaders and assorted political enemies. While his propagandists spread lies about SA conspiracies, the army leaders and President Hindenburg responded to the purge with congratulatory telegrams. Shortly thereafter, the army leaders swore a binding oath of "unquestioning obedience . . . to the Leader of the German State and people, Adolf Hitler." The purge of the SA was another decisive step toward unlimited totalitarian terror. The SS, the elite guard that had loyally murdered the SA leaders, grew rapidly. Under its methodical, inhuman leader Heinrich Himmler (1900–1945), the SS joined with the political police, the Gestapo, and began expanding its network of special courts and concentration camps. Nobody was safe.

From the beginning the Jews were a special object of Nazi persecution. By the end of 1934, most Jewish lawyers, doctors, professors, civil servants, and musicians had lost their jobs and right to practice their professions. In 1935, the infamous Nuremberg Laws classified as Jewish anyone having one or more Jewish grandparents and deprived Jews of all rights of citizenship. By 1938, roughly one-quarter of Germany's half-million Jews had emigrated, sacrificing almost all their property in order to leave Germany.

Following the assassination of a German diplomat in Paris by a young Jewish boy trying desperately to strike out at persecution, the attack on the Jews accelerated. A well-organized wave of violence destroyed homes, synagogues, and businesses, after which German Jews were rounded up and made to pay for the damage. It became very difficult for Jews to leave Germany. Some Germans privately opposed these outrages, but most went along or looked the other way. Although this lack of response partly reflected the individual's helplessness in the totalitarian state, it was also a sign of the great popular support Hitler's government enjoyed.

### HITLER'S POPULARITY

Hitler had promised the masses economic recovery – "work and bread" – and he delivered. Breaking with Brüning's do-nothing policies, Hitler immediately launched a large public works program to pull Germany out of the depression. Work began on superhighways, offices, gigantic sports stadia, and public housing. In 1936, as Germany rearmed rapidly, government spending began to concentrate on the military. The result was that unemployment dropped steadily, from 6 million in January 1933 to about 1 million in late 1936. By 1938 there was a shortage of workers, and women eventually took many jobs previously denied to them by the antifeminist Nazis. Thus everyone had work, and between 1932 and 1938 the standard of living for the average employed worker rose by more than 20 percent. The profits of business also increased. For millions of people, economic recovery and Nazi rule went hand in hand.

For the masses of ordinary German citizens, who were not Jews, Slavs, gypsies, Jehovah's Witnesses, or Communists, Hitler's government meant greater equality and exceptional opportunities. It must be remembered that in 1933 the position of the traditional German elites – the landed aristocracy, the wealthy capitalists, and the well-educated professional classes – was still very strong. Barriers between classes were generally high. Hitler's rule introduced vast changes in this pattern. For example, stiff educational requirements, which favored the well-to-do, were greatly relaxed. The new Nazi elite was composed largely of young and poorly educated dropouts, rootless lower-middle-class people like Hitler, who rose to the top with breathtaking speed.

More generally, the Nazis, like the Russian Communists, tolerated privilege and wealth only as long as they served the needs of the party. Big business was constantly ordered around, to the point that "probably never in peacetime has an ostensibly capitalist economy been directed as non- and even anti-capitalistically as the German economy between 1933 and 1939."[11] Hitler brought about a kind of social revolution, which was enthusiastically embraced by millions of modest middle- and lower-middle-class people and even by many workers.

Hitler's extreme nationalism, which had helped him gain power, continued to appeal to Germans after 1933. Ever since the wars against Napoleon, many Germans had believed in a special mission for a superior German nation. The successes of Bismarck had furthered such feelings, and near-victory in World War One made nationalists eager for renewed expansion in the 1920s. Thus, when Hitler went from one foreign triumph to another and a great German empire seemed within reach, as we shall see, the majority of the population was delighted and praised the Führer.

By no means all Germans supported Hitler, however, and a number of German groups actively resisted him after 1933. Tens of thousands of political enemies were imprisoned, and thousands were executed. Opponents of the Nazis pursued different goals, and under totalitarian conditions they were never unified, which helps account for their ultimate lack of success. In the first years of Hitler's rule, the principal resisters were the Communists and the Social Democrats in the trade unions. But the expansion of the SS system of terror after 1935 smashed most of these leftists. A second group of opponents arose in the Catholic and Protestant churches. However, their efforts were directed primarily at preserving genuine religious life, not at overthrowing Hitler. Finally, in 1938 (and again in 1942–1943) some high-ranking army officers, who feared the consequences of Hitler's reckless aggression, plotted against him, unsuccessfully.

## NAZI EXPANSION AND THE SECOND WORLD WAR

Although economic recovery and increased opportunities for social advancement won Hitler support, they were only by-products of Nazi totalitarianism. The guiding concepts of Nazism remained space and race – the territorial expansion of the superior German race. As Germany regained its economic strength and as independent organizations were

July 8, 1936

STEPPING STONES TO GLORY.

DAVID LOW *was a genius of a political cartoonist and his biting criticism of appeasing leaders appeared shortly after Hitler remilitarized the Rhineland. Appeasement also appealed to millions of ordinary citi-* zens, *who wanted to avoid at any cost another great war. (Cartoon by David Low by arrangement with the Low Trustees and the London* Evening Standard*)*

brought under control, Hitler formed alliances with other dictators and began expanding. German expansion was facilitated by the uncertain, divided, pacific Western democracies, which tried to buy off Hitler to avoid war. Yet war was inevitable, in both the west and the east, for Hitler's ambitions were essentially unlimited. On both fronts the Nazis scored enormous success until late 1942, establishing a vast empire of death and destruction.

### AGGRESSION AND APPEASEMENT, 1933–1939

Hitler's tactics in international politics after 1933 strikingly resembled those he used in domestic politics between 1924 and 1933. When Hitler was weak, he righteously proclaimed that he intended to overturn the "unjust system" established by the treaties of Versailles and Locarno – but only by legal means. As he grew stronger, and as other leaders showed their willingness to compromise, he increased his demands and finally began attacking his independent neighbors (see Map 29.1).

Hitler realized that his aggressive policies had to be carefully camouflaged at first, for Germany's army was limited by the Treaty of Versailles to only a hundred thousand men. As he told a group of army commanders in February 1933, the early stages of his policy of "conquest of new living space in the East and

### Legend

- Germany in 1933
- Remilitarized in 1936
- Annexed in 1938
- Satellite states, March 1939
- Conquered by Germany in September 1939
- Annexed by Soviet Union in September 1939

SWEDEN

ESTONIA

*BALTIC SEA*

Riga

LATVIA

Memel · Annexed, March 1939

LITHUANIA

*NORTH SEA*

Minsk

Danzig

EAST PRUSSIA

Hamburg

Bremen

Berlin

Oder

Warsaw

POLAND

SOVIET

Brest-Litovsk · Pinsk

Elbe

GERMANY

Vistula

NETHERLANDS

RUHR

Cologne

BELGIUM

RHINELAND

WHITE RUSSIA

UNION

Weimar

Rhine

LUXEMBOURG

SAAR
Gained by plebiscite, 1935

SUDETENLAND

Prague

BOHEMIA

CZECHOSLOVAKIA

SUDETENLAND

MORAVIA

SLOVAKIA

RUTHENIA

FRANCE

Danube

Munich

Vienna

To Hungary, March 1939

SWITZERLAND

AUSTRIA

Budapest

HUNGARY

RUMANIA

ITALY

YUGOSLAVIA

Danube

*ADRIATIC SEA*

0    100    200 Km.
0    100    200 Mi.

MAP 29.1  THE GROWTH OF NAZI GERMANY,
*1933–1939  Until March 1939, Hitler brought
ethnic Germans into the Nazi state; then he turned on
the Slavic peoples he had always hated.*

its ruthless Germanization" had serious dangers. If France had real leaders, Hitler said, "it will not give us time but attack us, presumably with its eastern satellites."[12] Thus Hitler loudly proclaimed his peaceful intentions to all the world. Nevertheless, he felt strong enough to walk out of a sixty-nation disarmament conference and withdraw from the League of Nations in October 1933. Stresemann's policy of peaceful cooperation was dead; the Nazi determination to rearm was out in the open.

Following this action, which met with widespread approval at home, Hitler moved to incorporate independent Austria into a Greater Germany. Austrian Nazis climaxed an attempted overthrow by murdering the Austrian chancellor in July 1934. They were unable to take power, however, because a worried Mussolini, who had initially greeted Hitler as a fascist little brother, massed his troops on the Brenner Pass and threatened to fight. When in March 1935 Hitler established a general military draft and declared the "unequal" disarmament clauses of the Treaty of Versailles null and void, other countries appeared to understand the danger. With France taking the lead, Italy and Great Britain protested strongly and warned against future aggressive actions.

Yet the emerging united front against Hitler quickly collapsed. Of crucial importance, Britain adopted a policy of appeasement, granting Hitler everything he could reasonably want (and more) in order to avoid war. The first step was an Anglo-German naval agreement in June 1935, which broke Germany's isolation. The second step came in March 1936, when Hitler suddenly marched his armies into the demilitarized Rhineland, brazenly violating the treaties of Versailles and Locarno. This was the last good chance to stop the Nazis, for Hitler had ordered his troops to retreat if France resisted militarily. But an uncertain France would not move without British support, and the occupation of German soil by German armies seemed right and just to Britain. Its strategic position greatly improved, Germany was suddenly the strongest military power in Europe.

British appeasement, which practically dictated French policy, lasted far into 1939. It was motivated by British feelings of guilt toward Germany and the pacifism of a population still horrified by the memory of the First World War. Like many Germans, British statesmen seriously underestimated Hitler. They believed that they could use him to stop Russian communism. A leading member of Britain's government personally told Hitler in November 1937 that it was his conviction that Hitler "not only had accomplished great things in Germany itself, but that through the total destruction of Communism in his own country ... Germany rightly had to be considered as a Western bulwark against Communism."[13] Such rigid anticommunist feelings made an alliance between the Western powers and Stalin against Hitler very unlikely.

As Britain and France opted for appeasement and Russia watched all developments suspiciously, Hitler found powerful allies. In 1935, the bombastic Mussolini decided that imperial expansion was needed to revitalize fascism. From Italian colonies on the east coast of Africa he attacked the independent African kingdom of Ethiopia. The Western powers and the League of Nations piously condemned Italian aggression, which angered Mussolini, without saving Ethiopia from defeat. Hitler, who had secretly supplied Ethiopia with arms to heat up the conflict, supported Italy energetically and thereby overcame Mussolini's lingering doubts about the Nazis. The result of this cooperation was an alliance in 1936 between Italy and Germany; the so-called Rome-Berlin Axis. Japan, which had been expanding into Manchuria since 1931, quickly joined the alliance between Italy and Germany.

At the same time Germany and Italy intervened in the long, complicated Spanish Civil War, where their support eventually helped General Francisco Franco's fascist movement defeat republican Spain. Spain's only official aid came from Soviet Russia, for public opinion in Britain and especially in France was hopelessly divided on the Spanish question.

By late 1937, as he was proclaiming his peaceful intentions to the British and their gullible prime minister, Neville Chamberlain, Hitler told his generals his real plans. His "unshakable decision" was to crush Austria and Czechoslovakia at the earliest possible moment, as the first step in his long-contemplated drive to the east for "living space." By threatening Austria with invasion, Hitler forced the Austrian chancellor in March 1938 to put local Nazis in control of the government. The next day German armies moved in unopposed, and Austria became two more provinces of Greater Germany.

Simultaneously, Hitler began demanding that the pro-Nazi, German-speaking minority of western Czechoslovakia – the Sudetenland – be turned over to Germany. Yet democratic Czechoslovakia was prepared to defend itself. Moreover, France had been Czechoslovakia's ally since 1924; and if France fought, Soviet Russia was pledged to help. As war appeared inevitable – for Hitler had already told the leader of the Sudeten Germans that "we must always ask so much we cannot be satisfied" – appeasement triumphed again. In September 1938, Chamberlain flew to Germany three times in fourteen days. In these negotiations – known as the Munich Conference – to which Russia was deliberately not invited, Chamberlain and the French agreed with

Hitler that the Sudetenland should be ceded to Germany immediately. Returning to London, Chamberlain told cheering crowds that he had secured "peace with honor . . . peace for our time." Sold out by the Western powers, Czechoslovakia gave in.

Confirmed once again in his opinion of the Western democracies as weak and racially degenerate, Hitler accelerated his aggression. In a shocking violation of his solemn assurances that the Sudetenland was his last territorial demand, Hitler's armies occupied the rest of Czechoslovakia in March 1939. The effect on Western public opinion was electrifying. For the first time there was no possible rationale of self-determination for Nazi aggression, since Hitler was seizing Czechs and Slovaks as captive peoples. Thus, when Hitler used the question of German minorities in Danzig as a pretext to smash Poland, a suddenly militant Chamberlain declared that Britain and France would fight if Hitler attacked his eastern neighbor. Hitler did not take these warnings seriously, and he pressed on.

In an about-face that stunned the world, Hitler offered and Stalin signed a Russo-German nonaggression pact in August 1939, whereby each dictator promised to remain neutral if the other became involved in war. Even more startling was the attached secret protocol, which ruthlessly divided eastern Europe into German and Russian zones, "in the event of a political territorial reorganization." Although this top-secret protocol sealing the destruction of Poland and the Baltic states became known only after the war, the non-aggression pact itself was enough to make Britain and France cry treachery, for they too had been negotiating with Stalin. But Stalin had remained very distrustful of Western intentions. Moreover, Britain and France had offered him military risk without gain, while Hitler had offered territorial gain without risk. For Hitler, everything was set. He told his generals on the day of the nonaggression pact: "My only fear is that at the last moment some dirty dog will come up with a mediation plan." On September 1, 1939, German armies and warplanes smashed into Poland from three sides. Two days later, finally true to their word, Britain and France declared war on Germany. The Second World War had begun.

## HITLER'S EMPIRE, 1939–1942

Using planes, tanks, and trucks in a lightning attack, Hitler's armies crushed Poland in four weeks. While Soviet Russia quickly took its part of the booty — the eastern half of Poland and the Baltic states of Lithuania, Estonia, Latvia — French and British armies dug in in the west. They expected another war of attrition and economic blockade.

In spring 1940, the lightning attack struck again. After quickly occupying Denmark, Norway, and Holland, German motorized columns broke through southern Belgium, split the Franco-British forces, and trapped the entire British army on the beaches of Dunkirk. By heroic efforts the British managed to withdraw their troops but not their equipment to England.

France was taken by the Nazis. The aging Marshal Henri-Philippe Pétain formed a new French government — the so-called Vichy government — to accept defeat, and German armies occupied most of France. By July 1940, Hitler ruled practically all of western continental Europe, and Italy and Soviet Russia were his allies. Only Britain, led by the uncompromising Winston Churchill (1874–1965), remained unconquered. Churchill proved to be one of history's greatest wartime leaders, rallying his fellow citizens with stirring speeches, infectious confidence, and bulldog determination.

Germany sought to gain control of the air, the necessary first step for a naval invasion of Britain. In the Battle of Britain up to a thousand German planes attacked British airfields and key factories in a single day, dueling with British defenders high in the skies. Losses were heavy on both sides. Then in September Hitler angrily and foolishly changed his tactics, turning from military objectives to indiscriminate bombing of British cities in an attempt to break British morale. British factories increased production of their excellent fighter planes; antiaircraft defense improved with the help of radar; and the heavily bombed people of London defiantly dug in. In September-October 1940, Britain was beating Germany three-to-one in the air war. There was no possibility of immediate German invasion of Britain.

In these circumstances the most reasonable German strategy would have been to attack Britain through the eastern Mediterranean, taking Egypt and the Suez Canal and pinching off Britain's supply of oil. Moreover, Mussolini's early defeats in Greece had drawn Hitler into the Balkans, where Germany quickly conquered Greece and Yugoslavia while forcing Hungary, Rumania and Bulgaria into alliances with Germany by April 1941. This reinforced the logic of a thrust into the eastern Mediterranean. But Hitler was not a reasonable person. His lifetime obsession with a vast east European empire for the master race irrationally dictated policy. By late 1940 he had already decided on his next move, and in June 1941 German armies suddenly attacked the Soviet Union along a vast front. With Britain still unconquered, Hitler's decision was a wild irrational gamble, epitomizing the violent, unlimited ambitions of modern totalitarianism.

Faithfully fulfilling all his obligations under the Nazi-Soviet Pact and even ignoring warnings of impending invasion, Stalin was caught off guard. Nazi armies moved like lightning across the Russian steppe. By October 1941, Leningrad was practically surrounded, Moscow beseiged, and most of the Ukraine conquered; yet the Russians did not collapse. When a severe winter struck German armies outfitted in summer uniforms, the invaders were stopped.

While Hitler's armies dramatically expanded the war in Europe, his Japanese allies did the same in Asia. Engaged in a general but undeclared war against China since 1937, Japan's rulers had increasingly come into diplomatic conflict with the Pacific Basin's other great power, the United States. When the Japanese occupied French Indochina in July 1941, the United States retaliated by cutting off sales of vital rubber, scrap iron, oil, and aviation fuel. Tension mounted further, and on December 7, 1941, Japan attacked the U.S. naval base at Pearl Harbor in Hawaii. Hitler immediately declared war on the United States, even though his treaty obligations with Japan did not require him to do so.

As Japanese forces advanced swiftly into southeast Asia after the crippling surprise attack at Pearl Harbor, Hitler and his European allies continued the two-front war against the Soviet Union and Great Britain. Not until late 1942 did the Nazis suffer their first major defeats, as we shall see in the next chapter. In the meantime Hitler ruled a vast European empire stretching from the outskirts of Moscow to the English Channel. Hitler and the top Nazi leadership began building their "New Order," and they continued their efforts until their final collapse in 1945. In doing so, they showed what Nazi victory would have meant.

Hitler's New Order was based firmly on the guiding principle of Nazi totalitarianism: racial imperialism. Within this New Order

the Nordic peoples – the Dutch, the Norwegians, and the Danes – received preferential treatment, for they were racially related to the Germans. The French, an "inferior" Latin people, occupied the middle position. They were heavily taxed to support the Nazi war effort, but were tolerated as a race. Once Nazi reverses began to mount in late 1942, however, all the occupied territories of western and northern Europe were exploited with ever-increasing intensity. Shortages and suffering afflicted millions of people.

Slavs in the conquered territories to the east were treated with harsh hatred as "subhumans." At the height of his success in 1941–1942, Hitler painted for his intimate circle the fantastic details of a vast eastern colonial empire, where the Poles, Ukranians, and Russians would be enslaved and forced to die out, while Germanic peasants resettled their abandoned lands. Himmler and the elite corps of SS volunteers struggled loyally, sometimes against the German army, to implement part of this general program even before victory was secured. In parts of Poland the SS arrested and evacuated Polish peasants to create a German "mass settlement space." Polish workers and Russian prisoners of war were transported to Germany, where they did most of the heavy labor and were systematically worked to death. The conditions of Russian slave labor in Germany were so harsh that four out of five Russian prisoners did not survive the war.

Finally, Jews were condemned to extermination, along with gypsies, Jehovah's Witnesses, and captured Communists. By 1939 German Jews had lost all their civil rights, and after the fall of Warsaw the Nazis began deporting them to Poland. There they and Jews from all over Europe were concentrated in ghettos, compelled to wear the Jewish star, and turned into slave laborers. But by 1941,

*PRELUDE TO MURDER   This photo captures the terrible inhumanity of Nazi racism. Frightened and bewildered families from the soon-to-be destroyed Warsaw ghetto are being forced out of their homes by German soldiers for deportation to concentration camps. There they face murder in the gas chambers. (Collection Viollet)*

Himmler's SS was carrying out the "final solution of the Jewish question" – the murder of every single Jew. All over Hitler's empire Jews were arrested, packed like cattle onto freight trains, and dispatched to extermination camps.

There the victims were taken by force or deception to "shower rooms," which were actually gas chambers. These gas chambers, first perfected in the quiet, efficient execution of 70,000 mentally ill Germans between 1938 and 1941, permitted rapid, hideous, and thoroughly bureaucratized mass murder. For fifteen to twenty minutes there came the terrible screams and gasping sobs of men,

women, and children choking to death on poison gas. Then, only silence. Special camp workers quickly tore the victims' gold teeth from their jaws and cut off their hair for use as chair stuffings. The bodies were then boiled for oil to make soap and the bones were crushed to produce fertilizers. At Auschwitz, the most infamous of the Nazi death factories, as many as 12,000 human beings were slaughtered each day. On the turbulent Russian front the SS death squads forced the Jewish population to dig giant pits, which became mass graves as the victims were lined up on the edge and cut down by machine guns. The extermination of the European

Jews was the ultimate monstrosity of Nazi racism and racial imperialism. By 1945, 6 million Jews had been murdered in cold blood.

———◆———

The tremendous practical and spiritual maladies of the age of anxiety led in many lands to the rise of dictatorships. Many of these dictatorships were variations on conservative authoritarianism, but there was also a fateful innovation – the modern totalitarian regime, most fully developed in Communist Russia and Nazi Germany. The totalitarian regimes utterly rejected the liberalism of the nineteenth century. Inspired by the lessons of total war and Lenin's one-party rule, they tried to subordinate everything to the state. Although some areas of life escaped them, state control increased to a staggering, unprecedented degree. The totalitarian regimes trampled on basic human rights with unrestrained brutality and police terror. Moreover, they were armed with the weapons of modern technology, rendering opposition almost impossible.

Both Communist Russia and Nazi Germany tried to gain the *willing* support of their populations. Monopolizing the means of expression and communication, they claimed to represent the masses and to be building new, more equal societies. Many people believed them. Both regimes also won enthusiastic supporters by offering tough, ruthless people from modest backgrounds enormous rewards for loyal and effective service. Thus these totalitarian dictatorships rested on considerable genuine popular support, as well as on police terror. This combination gave them their awesome power and dynamism. That dynamism was, however, channeled in quite different directions. Stalin and the Communist party aimed at building their kind of socialism and the new socialist personality at home. Hitler and the Nazi elite aimed at unlimited territorial and racial aggression on behalf of a master race; domestic recovery was only a means to that end. Unlimited aggression made war inevitable, first with the Western democracies and then with Germany's totalitarian neighbor. It plunged Europe into the ultimate nightmare.

———

## NOTES

1. E. Halévy, *The Era of Tyrannies,* Doubleday, Garden City, N.Y., 1965, pp. 265–316, esp. p. 300.

2. Quoted by P. C. Roberts, " 'War Communism': A Re-examination," *Slavic Review* 29 (June 1970): 257.

3. Quoted by A. G. Mazour, *Soviet Economic Development: Operation Outstrip, 1921–1965,* Van Nostrand, Princeton, N.J., 1967, p. 130.

4. Quoted by I. Deutscher, *Stalin: A Political Biography,* 2nd ed., Oxford University Press, New York, 1967, p. 325.

5. Quoted by H. K. Geiger, *The Family in Soviet Russia,* Harvard University Press, Cambridge, 1968, p. 123.

6. Ibid., p. 156.

7. Quoted by B. Rosenthal, "Women in the Russian Revolution and After," in *Becoming Visible: Women in European History,* ed., R. Bridenthal and C. Koonz, Houghton Mifflin, Boston, 1976, p. 383.

8. Quoted by K. D. Bracher, in T. Eschenburg et al., *The Path to Dictatorship, 1918–1933,* Doubleday, Garden City, N.Y., 1966, p. 117.

9. Quoted by K. D. Bracher, *The German Dictatorship: The Origins, Structure and Effects of National Socialism,* Praeger, New York, 1970, pp. 146–147.

10. Quoted by R. Stromberg, *An Intellectual History of Modern Europe,* Appleton-Century-Crofts, New York, 1966, p. 393.

11. D. Schoenbaum, *Hitler's Social Revolution: Class and Status in Nazi Germany, 1933–1939,* Doubleday, Garden City, N.Y., 1967, p. 114.

12. Quoted by Bracher, *German Dictatorship*, p. 289.

13. Ibid., p. 306.

## SUGGESTED READING

The historical literature on totalitarian dictatorships is rich and fascinating. H. Arendt, *The Origins of Totalitarianism* (1951), is a challenging interpretation. E. Weber, *Varieties of Fascism* (1964), stresses the radical social aspirations of fascist movements all across Europe. F. L. Carsten, *The Rise of Fascism*, rev. ed. (1982), and W. Laqueur, ed., *Fascism* (1976), are also recommended. On Germany, F. Stern, *The Politics of Cultural Despair* (1963), and G. Mosse, *The Crisis of German Ideology* (1964), are excellent complementary studies on the origins of Nazism. The best single work on Hitler's Germany is K. Bracher, *The German Dictatorship: The Origins, Structure and Effects of National Socialism* (1970). A Bullock's *Hitler* (1953) is a totally engrossing biography of Der Führer. In addition to *Mein Kampf, Hitler's Secret Conversations, 1941–1944* (1953) reveals the dictator's wild dreams and beliefs. Among countless special studies, E. Kogon, *The Theory and Practice of Hell* (1958), is a chilling examination of the concentration camps; M. Mayer, *They Thought They Were Free* (1955), probes the minds of ten ordinary Nazis and why they believed Hitler was their liberator; and A. Speer, *Inside the Third Reich* (1970), contains the fascinating recollections of Hitler's wizard of the armaments industry. G. Mosse, *Toward the Final Solution* (1978), is a powerful history of European racism. Jørgen Haestrup, *Europe Ablaze* (1978), is a monumental account of wartime resistance movements throughout Europe.

Richard Stites, *The Women's Liberation Movement in Russia: Feminism, Nihilism, and Bolshevism, 1860–1930* (1978); S. Fitzpatrick, *Cultural Revolution in Russia, 1928–1931* (1978); K. Geiger, *The Family in Soviet Russia* (1968); and I. Deutscher, *Stalin: A Political Biography* (1967), are all highly recommended, as is Deutscher's sympathetic three-volume study of Trotsky. S. Cohen, *Bukharin and the Bolshevik Revolution* (1973), examines the leading spokesman of moderate communism, who was destroyed by Stalin. R. Conquest, *The Great Terror* (1968), is an excellent account of Stalin's purges of the 1930s. A. Solzhenitsyn, *The Gulag Archipelago* (1974), passionately condemns Soviet police terror, which Solzhenitsyn traces back to Lenin. A. Koestler, *Darkness at Noon* (1956), is a famous fictional account of Stalin's trials of the Old Bolsheviks. R. Medvedev, *Let History Judge* (1972), is a penetrating and highly recommended history of Stalinism by a Russian dissident. Three other remarkable books are J. Scott, *Behind the Urals* (1942, 1973), the eyewitness account of an American steelworker in Russia in the 1930s; S. Alliluyeva, *Twenty Letters to a Friend* (1967), the amazing reflections of Stalin's daughter, now living in America; and M. Fainsod, *Smolensk Under Soviet Rule* (1958), a unique study based on Communist records captured first by the Germans and then by the Americans.

E. R. Tannebaum, *The Fascist Experience* (1972), is an excellent study of Italian culture and society under Mussolini. I. Silone, *Bread and Wine* (1937), is a moving novel by a famous opponent of dictatorship in Italy. Two excellent books on Spain are H. Thomas, *The Spanish Civil War* (1961), and E. Malefakis, *Agrarian Reform and Peasant Revolution in Spain* (1970). In the area of foreign relations, G. Kennan, *Russia and the West Under Lenin and Stalin* (1961), is justly famous, while A. L. Rowse, *Appeasement* (1961), powerfully denounces the policies of the appeasers. R. Paxton, *Vichy France* (1973), tells a controversial story extremely well, and J. Lukac, *The Last European War* (1976), skillfully — and infuriatingly — argues that victory by Hitler could have saved Europe from both Russian and American domination.

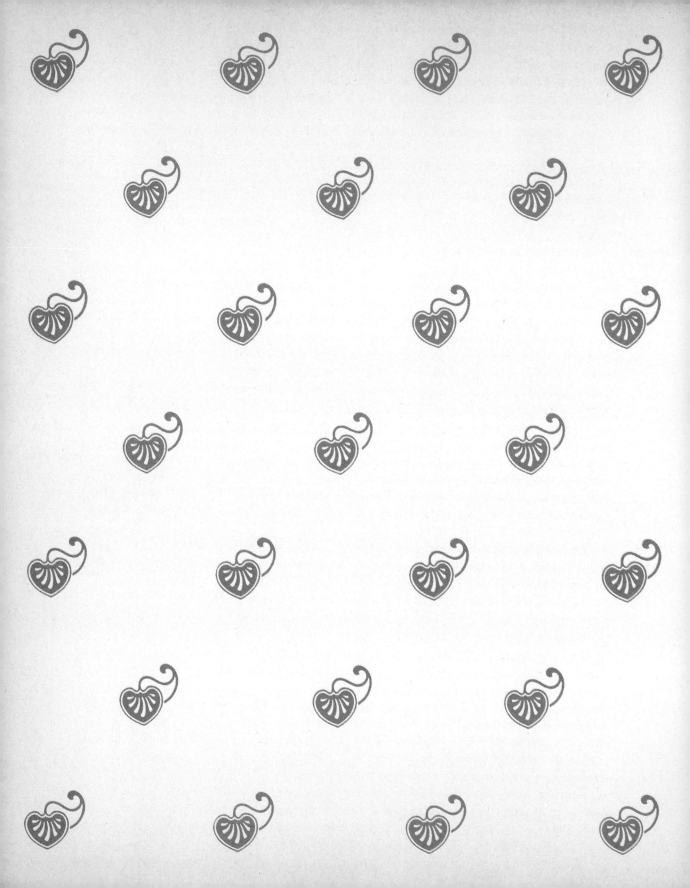

# CHAPTER 30

# THE RECOVERY OF EUROPE AND

# THE AMERICAS

IN 1942, when Hitler's empire stretched across Europe and the Nazi "New Order" was taking shape, Western civilization was in danger of dying. A terrible, triumphant barbarism was striking at the hard-won accomplishments and uneven progress of many generations. From this low point, European society staged a truly astonishing recovery.

The Nazis and their allies were utterly defeated. Battered western Europe then experienced a great renaissance, and the western hemisphere with its strong European heritage also made exemplary progress. Soviet Russia eventually became more humane and less totalitarian. Yet there was also a tragic setback. The Grand Alliance against Hitler gave way to an apparently endless cold war, in which conflict between East and West threatened world peace and troubled domestic politics.

How and why did Europe recover from the depths of despair in one of the most extraordinary periods of rebirth in its long history? What were the causes of the cold war? How did the course of that international struggle influence domestic politics? These are some of the more important questions this chapter seeks to answer.

## ALLIED VICTORY AND THE COLD WAR, 1942–1950

The recovery of Western society depended on the defeat of the Nazis and their Italian, Balkan, and Japanese allies. On this point the twenty-six allied nations, led by Britain, the United States, and Soviet Russia, were firmly agreed. The Grand Alliance — to use Winston Churchill's favorite term — functioned quite effectively in military terms to achieve this overwhelming objective. By the summer of 1943, the tide of battle had turned, and Allied victory was only a matter of time.

Yet victory was flawed. The Allies could not cooperate politically when it came to peacemaking. Motivated by different goals and hounded by misunderstandings, the United States and Soviet Russia soon found themselves at loggerheads. By the end of 1947, Europe was rigidly divided. It was West versus East in the cold war.

### THE GRAND ALLIANCE

Chance, rather than choice, brought together the anti-Axis coalition. Stalin had been cooperating fully with Hitler between August 1939 and June 1941, and only the Japanese attack on Pearl Harbor in December 1941 and Hitler's immediate declaration of war had overwhelmed powerful isolationism in the United States. The Allies' first task was to try to overcome their mutual suspicions and build an unshakable alliance on the quicksand of accident. By means of two interrelated policies they succeeded.

First, President Roosevelt accepted Churchill's contention that the United States should concentrate first on defeating Hitler. Only after victory in Europe would the United States turn toward the Pacific for an all-out attack on Japan, the lesser threat. Therefore, the United States promised and sent large amounts of military aid to Britain and Russia, and American and British forces in each combat zone were tightly integrated under a single commander. America's policy of "Europe first" helped solidify the anti-Hitler coalition.

Second, within the European framework, the Americans and the British put immediate military needs first. They consistently postponed tough political questions relating to the eventual peace settlement. Thus, in December 1941 and again in May 1942, Stalin asked the United States and Britain to agree to Russia's moving its western border of 1938 further west at the expense of Poland, in effect ratifying the gains Stalin had made from his deal with Hitler in 1939.

Stalin's request ran counter to the moralistic Anglo-American Atlantic Charter of August 1941. In good Wilsonian fashion, the Atlantic Charter had called for peace without territorial expansion or secret agreements, and free elections and self-determination for all liberated nations. Stalin thus received only a military alliance and no postwar commitments in 1942. Yet the United States and Britain did not try to take advantage of Russia's precarious position in 1942, promising an invasion of continental Europe as soon as possible. They feared that hard bargaining would anger Stalin and encourage him to consider making a separate peace with Hitler.

Both sides found it advantageous to paper over their long-standing differences by stressing military operations and the total defeat of the Axis. At a conference in Casablanca, Morocco, in January 1943 to plan a massive Allied offensive, Churchill and Roosevelt adopted the principle of the "unconditional surrender" of Germany and Japan. Stalin agreed to it shortly thereafter. The policy of unconditional surrender had profound implications. It cemented the Grand Alliance together, denying Hitler any hope of dividing his foes. It probably also discouraged Germans and Japanese who might have tried to overthrow their dictators in order to make a compromise peace. And, most important, it meant that Russian and Anglo-American armies would almost certainly come together to divide all of Germany, and all of Europe, among themselves.

The military resources of the Grand Alliance were awesome. The strengths of the United States were its mighty industry, its large population, and its national unity. Even before Pearl Harbor, President Roosevelt had called America the "arsenal of democracy" and given military aid to Britain and Russia. Now the United States geared up rapidly for all-out war production, and drew heavily on a generally cooperative Latin America for resources. It not only equipped its own armies but eventually gave its allies about $50 billion of arms and equipment. Britain received by far the most, but about one-fifth of the total went to Russia in the form of badly needed trucks, planes, and munitions.

Too strong to lose and too weak to win when it stood alone, Britain too continued to make a great contribution. The British economy was totally and effectively mobilized, and the sharing of burdens through rationing and heavy taxes on war profits maintained social harmony. Moreover, as 1942 wore on, Britain could increasingly draw on the enormous physical and human resources of its empire and the United States. By early 1943, the Americans and the British combined small aircraft carriers with radar-guided bombers to rid the Atlantic of German submarines. Britain, the impregnable floating fortress, became a gigantic front-line staging area for the decisive blow to the heart of Germany.

As for Soviet Russia, so great was its strength that it might well have defeated Germany without Western help. In the face of the German advance, whole factories and whole populations were successfully evacuated to eastern Russia and Siberia. There, war production was reorganized and enormously expanded, and the Red Army was increasingly well supplied. The Red Army was also well led, for a new generation of talented military leaders quickly arose to replace those so recently purged. Most important of all, Stalin drew on the massive support and heroic determination of the Soviet people. Broad-based Russian nationalism, as opposed to narrow Communist ideology, became the powerful unifying force in what was appropriately called "the Great Patriotic War of the Fatherland."

Finally, the United States, Britain, and Soviet Russia were not alone. They had the resources of much of the world at their command. And, to a greater or lesser extent, they were aided by a growing resistance movement against the Nazis throughout Europe, even in Germany. Thus, although Ukrainian peasants often welcomed the Germans as liberators, the barbaric occupation policies of the Nazis quickly drove them to join and support behind-the-lines guerrilla forces. More generally, after Russia was invaded in June 1941, Communists throughout Europe took the lead in the underground resistance, joined by a growing number of patriots and Christians. Anti-Nazi leaders from occupied countries established governments-in-exile in London, like that of the "Free French" under the intensely proud General Charles de Gaulle. These governments gathered valuable secret information from resistance fighters and even organized armies to help defeat Hitler.

## THE TIDE OF BATTLE

Barely halted at the gates of Moscow and Leningrad in 1941, the Germans renewed their Russian offensive in July 1942. This time they drove toward the southern city of Stalingrad, in an attempt to cripple communications and seize the crucial oilfields of Baku. Reaching Stalingrad, the Germans slowly occupied most of the ruined city in a month of

*MAP 30.1   WORLD WAR TWO IN EUROPE The map shows the extent of Hitler's empire at its height, before the battle of Stalingrad in late 1942, and the subsequent advances of the Allies until Germany surrendered on May 7, 1945.*

incredibly savage house-to-house fighting.

Then, in November 1942, Soviet armies counterattacked. They rolled over Rumanian and Italian troops to the north and south of Stalingrad, quickly closing the trap and surrounding the entire German Sixth Army of 300,000 men. The surrounded Germans were systematically destroyed, until by the end of January 1943 only 123,000 soldiers were left to surrender. Hitler, who had refused to allow a retreat, had suffered a catastrophic defeat. In the summer of 1943, the larger, better-equipped Soviet armies took the offensive and began moving forward (See Map 30.1).

In late 1942, the tide also turned in the Pacific and in North Africa. By early summer of 1942, Japan had established a great empire in east Asia. Unlike the Nazis, the Japanese made clever appeals to local nationalists, who hated European imperial domination and preferred Japan's so-called Greater Asian Co-Prosperity Sphere.

Then in the battle of the Coral Sea, in May 1942, Allied naval and air power stopped the Japanese advance and also relieved Australia from the threat of invasion. This victory was followed by the battle of Midway Island, in which American pilots sank all four of the attacking Japanese aircraft carriers and established American naval superiority in the Pacific. In August 1942, American marines attacked Guadalcanal in the Solomon Islands. Badly hampered by the policy of "Europe first" — only 15 percent of Allied resources were going to fight the war in the Pacific in early 1943 — the Americans, under General Douglas MacArthur and Admiral Chester Ni-

SOVIET UNION

Russian front, Nov. 1942

Russian front, Dec. 1941

Russian front, Spring 1944

BLACK SEA

TURKEY

SYRIA

CYPRUS

PALESTINE
(Br. Mandate)

TRANS-
JORDAN
(Br. Mandate)

Suez

Cairo

Nile

EGYPT

El Alamein
(Summer 1942)

Moscow

Tula

Smolensk

Kiev

Minsk

UKRAINE

Riga

FINLAND

Helsinki

Leningrad

Stockholm

SWEDEN

BALTIC SEA

NORWAY

Oslo

DENMARK

Copenhagen

Berlin

Elbe

GERMANY

Warsaw

Posen

Krakow

SLOVAKIA

Russian front, Feb. 1945

HUNGARY

Budapest

Vienna

SWITZERLAND

CROATIA

SERBIA

Bologna

Italian front, Feb. 1945

RUMANIA

Bucharest

Sofia

BULGARIA

ALBANIA

GREECE

Athens

CRETE

MEDITERRANEAN SEA

Monte Cassino
(May 1944)

Salerno (Sep. 1943)

Sicily
(July 1943)

MALTA (GR. BR.)

Rome

ITALY

LIBYA

Western front, Feb. 1945

Battle of the Bulge
(Dec. 1944)

Paris

FRANCE

Vichy

VICHY FRANCE
(occupied Nov. 1942)

NETHERLANDS

BELGIUM

Dunkirk

Invasion of Normandy
(June 6, 1944)

GREAT
BRITAIN

Battle of Britain
(Fall 1940)

London

NORTHERN
IRELAND

IRELAND

NORTH SEA

ATLANTIC OCEAN

Rommel defeated in Tunisia
(May 1943)

TUNISIA

ALGERIA
(Vichy France)

Madrid

SPAIN

PORTUGAL

Lisbon

Gibraltar (Gr. Br.)

SP. MOROCCO

Casablanca (Nov. 1942)

FRENCH MOROCCO

Don

Volga

Stalingrad

Yalta

Ankara

400 Mi.

400 Km.

200

200

0

0

Hitler's Greater Germany

Allied with Germany

Occupied by Germany and its allies

Grand Alliance

Neutral nations

Major battle

WAR IN THE PACIFIC    A Japanese ship burns off
the coast of New Guinea as an attacking B-25 roars
overhead. The lights along the shoreline are fires
caused by United States bombers. (Air Force Photo)

mitz, and the Australians nevertheless began
"island hopping" toward Japan. Japanese
forces were on the defensive.

In North Africa, the war had been seesaw-
ing back and forth since 1940. In May 1942,
combined German and Italian armies, under
the brilliant General Erwin Rommel, attacked
British-occupied Egypt and the Suez Canal for
the second time. After a rapid advance they
were finally defeated by British forces at the
battle of El Alamein, only seventy miles from
Alexandria. In October, the British counterattacked in Egypt, and almost immediately

thereafter an Anglo-American force landed in
Morocco and Algeria. These French possessions, which were under the control of
Pétain's Vichy French government, quickly
went over to the Allies.

Having driven the Axis powers from
North Africa by the spring of 1943, Allied
forces maintained the initiative by invading
Sicily and then mainland Italy. Mussolini was
deposed by a war-weary people, and the new
Italian government publicly accepted unconditional surrender in September 1943. Italy, it
seemed, was liberated. Yet Mussolini was res-

cued by German commandos in a daring raid and put at the head of a puppet government. German armies seized Rome and all of northern Italy. Fighting continued in Italy.

Indeed, bitter fighting continued in Europe for almost two years. Germany, less fully mobilized for war than Britain in 1941, applied itself to total war in 1942 and enlisted millions of prisoners of war and slave laborers from all across occupied Europe in that effort. Between early 1942 and July 1944, German war production actually *tripled*. Although British and American bombing raids killed many German civilians, they were surprisingly ineffective from a military point of view. Also, German resistance against Hitler failed. After an unsuccessful attempt on Hitler's life in July 1944, thousands of Germans were brutally liquidated by SS fanatics. Terrorized at home and frightened by the prospect of unconditional surrender, the Germans fought on with suicidal stoicism.

On June 6, 1944, American and British forces under General Dwight Eisenhower landed on the beaches of Normandy in history's greatest naval invasion. Having tricked the Germans into believing that the attack would come near the Belgian border, the Allies secured a foothold on the coast of Normandy. In a hundred dramatic days, more than 2 million men and almost a half-million vehicles pushed inland and broke through German lines. Rejecting proposals to strike straight at Berlin in a massive attack, Eisenhower moved forward cautiously on a broad front. Not until March 1945 did American troops cross the Rhine and enter Germany.

The Russians, who had been advancing steadily since July 1943, reached the outskirts of Warsaw by August 1944. For the next six months they moved southward into Rumania, Hungary, and Yugoslavia. In January 1945, Red armies again moved westward through Poland, and on April 26 they met American forces on the Elbe River. The Allies had closed their vise on Nazi Germany and overrun Europe. As Soviet forces fought their way into Berlin, Hitler committed suicide in his bunker, and on May 7 German commanders capitulated.

Three months later the United States dropped atomic bombs on Hiroshima and Nagasaki. Mass bombing of cities and civilians, one of the terrible new practices of World War Two, had ended in the final nightmare – unprecedented human destruction in a single blinding flash. The Japanese surrendered. The Second World War, which had claimed the lives of more than 50 million soldiers and civilians, was over.

## THE ORIGINS OF THE COLD WAR

Total victory was not followed by genuine peace. The most powerful allies – Soviet Russia and the United States – began to quarrel as soon as the unifying threat of Nazi Germany disappeared. Though the hostility between the eastern and western superpowers was a tragic disappointment for millions of people, it was not really surprising. It grew sadly but logically out of military developments, wartime agreements, and long-standing political and ideological differences.

The conference Stalin, Roosevelt, and Churchill had held in the Iranian capital of Teheran in November 1943 was of crucial importance in determining subsequent events. There, the Big Three had jovially reaffirmed their determination to crush Germany and searched for the appropriate military strategy. Churchill, fearful of the military dangers of a direct attack and anxious to protect Britain's political interests in the eastern Mediterranean, argued that American and British forces should follow up their North African and Ital-

*HIROSHIMA, AUGUST 1945 A single atomic bomb leveled 90 percent of this major city and claimed 130,000 casualties. Hiroshima has never regained its earlier prosperity. (U.S. Army Air Forces)*

ian campaigns with an indirect attack on Germany through the Balkans. Roosevelt, however, agreed with Stalin that an American-British frontal assault through France would be better. This agreement was part of Roosevelt's general effort to meet Stalin's wartime demands whenever possible. As Roosevelt reportedly told his friend William Bullitt, formerly American ambassador to the Soviet Union, before the Teheran conference, "I have just a hunch that Stalin doesn't want anything but security for his country, and I think that if I give him everything I possibly can and ask nothing from him in return, *noblesse oblige,* he won't try to annex anything and will work for a world of democracy and peace."[1]

At Teheran, the Normandy invasion had

been set for the spring of 1944. Although military considerations probably largely dictated this decison, it had momentous political implications: it meant that the Russian and the American-British armies would come together in defeated Germany along a north-south line and that only Russian troops would liberate eastern Europe. Thus the basic shape of postwar Europe was already emerging. Real differences over questions like Poland were carefully ignored.

When the Big Three met again at Yalta on the Black Sea in southern Russia in February 1945, rapidly advancing Soviet armies were within one hundred miles of Berlin. The Red Army had occupied not only Poland but also Bulgaria, Rumania, Hungary, most of Yugoslavia, and much of Czechoslovakia. The temporarily stalled American-British forces had yet to cross the Rhine into Germany. Moreover, the United States was far from defeating Japan. Indeed, it was believed that the invasion and occupation of Japan would cost a million American casualties – an estimate that led to the subsequent decision to drop atomic bombs in order to save American lives. In short, Russia's position was strong and America's weak.

There was little the increasingly sick and apprehensive Roosevelt could do but double his bet on Stalin's peaceful intentions. It was agreed at Yalta that Germany would be divided into zones of occupation and would pay heavy reparations to the Soviet Union in the form of agricultural and industrial goods, though many details remained unsettled. At American insistence, Stalin agreed to declare war on Japan after Germany was defeated. He also agreed to join the proposed United Nations, which the Americans believed would help preserve peace after the war; it was founded in April 1945 in San Francisco. For Poland and eastern Europe – "that Pandora's Box of infinite troubles," according to American Secretary of State Cordell Hull – the Big Three struggled to reach an ambiguous compromise at Yalta: East European governments were to be freely elected but pro-Russian. As Churchill put it at the time, "The Poles will have their future in their own hands, with the single limitation that they must honestly follow in harmony with their allies, a policy friendly to Russia."[2]

The Yalta compromise over eastern Europe broke down almost immediately. Before the war was over, Soviet Russia demanded and obtained from the Rumanian king the appointment of an obedient Communist as prime minister. Even before the Yalta Conference, Bulgaria and Poland were in the hands of Communists, who arrived home in the baggage of the Red Army. Minor concessions to non-Communist groups thereafter did not change this situation. Elsewhere in eastern Europe, pro-Russian "coalition" governments of several parties were formed, but the key ministerial posts were reserved for Moscow-trained Communists.

At the postwar Potsdam Conference of July 1945, the long-ignored differences over eastern Europe finally surged to the fore. The compromising Roosevelt had died and been succeeded by the inflexible President Harry Truman, who demanded immediate free elections throughout eastern Europe. Stalin refused pointblank. "A freely elected government in any of these East European countries would be anti-Soviet," he admitted simply, "and that we cannot allow."[3]

Here, then, is the key to the much-debated origins of the cold war. American ideals, pumped up by the crusade against Hitler, and American politics, heavily influenced by millions of voters from eastern Europe, demanded free elections in Soviet-occupied eastern Europe. On the other hand, Stalin,

THE BIG THREE AT YALTA  In 1945 a triumphant Winston Churchill, an ailing Franklin Roosevelt, and a determined Joseph Stalin met at Yalta, in southern Russia, to plan for peace. Wartime cooperation soon gave way to bitter hostility. (National Archives, Washington)

who had lived through two enormously destructive German invasions, wanted absolute military security from Germany and its potential eastern allies, once and for all. Suspicious by nature, he believed that only Communist states could truly be devoted allies, and he feared that free elections would result in independent and quite possibly hostile governments on his western border. Moreover, by the middle of 1945 there was no

way short of war that the United States and its western allies could really influence developments in eastern Europe, and war was out of the question. Stalin was bound to have his way.

## WEST VERSUS EAST

The American response to Stalin's conception of security was to "get tough." In May 1945,

Truman abruptly cut off all aid to Russia. In October, he declared that the United States would never recognize any government established by force against the free will of its people. In March 1946, former British Prime Minister Churchill ominously informed an American audience, "From Stettin in the Baltic to Trieste in the Adriatic, an iron curtain has descended across the continent." Soon emotional, moralistic denunciations of Stalin and Communist Russia re-emerged as a popular American political game. At the same time the United States demobilized with incredible speed, perhaps because, according to some historians, it felt so secure with its atomic bomb. When the war against Japan ended in September 1945, there were 12 million Americans in the armed forces; by 1947 there were only 1.5 million, as opposed to 6 million for Soviet Russia. "Getting tough" really meant "talking tough."

Stalin's agents quickly reheated the "ideological struggle against capitalist imperialism," proving as adept as the Americans at verbal abuse. Moreover, the large, well-organized Communist parties of France and Italy obediently started to uncover American plots to take over Europe, and aggressively challenged their own governments with violent criticisms and large strikes. The Soviet Union also put pressure on Iran and Turkey, and while Greek Communists battled Greek royalists, another bitter civil war raged in China. By the spring of 1947, it appeared to many Americans that Stalin wanted much more than just puppet regimes in Soviet-occupied eastern Europe. Stalin seemed determined to export communism by subversion and guerrilla warfare throughout Europe and around the world as well.

The American response to the escalating conflict was the Truman Doctrine, which was aimed at "containing" communism in areas already occupied by the Red Army. Truman told Congress in March 1947: "I believe it must be the policy of the United States to support free people who are resisting attempted subjugation by armed minorities or by outside pressure." As a first step, Truman asked Congress for large-scale military aid to Greece and Turkey. Then in June, Secretary of State George C. Marshall offered all the nations of Europe economic aid – the so-called Marshall Plan – to help them rebuild.

Stalin refused Marshall Plan assistance for all of eastern Europe. He purged the last remaining non-Communist elements from the "coalition" governments of eastern Europe and established Soviet-style, one-party Communist dictatorships. The seizure of power in Czechoslovakia in 1948 was particularly brutal and antidemocratic, greatly strengthening Western fears of limitless Communist expansion. In 1949, therefore, the United States formed an anti-Soviet military alliance of western governments, the North Atlantic Treaty Organization (NATO); in response Stalin formally united his satellites in the Warsaw Pact. Europe was divided into two hostile blocs.

In late 1949, the Communists triumphed in China, frightening and infuriating many Americans, who saw an all-powerful worldwide communist conspiracy extending even into the upper reaches of the American government. When the Russian-backed Communist forces of northern Korea invaded southern Korea in 1950, President Truman's response was swift. American-led United Nations armies intervened. The cold war had spread around the world and become very hot.

It seems clear that the rapid descent from victorious Grand Alliance to bitter cold war was intimately connected with the tragic fate of eastern Europe. When the east European

"ON A 'STRENGTH-GIVING' DIET"   *This typical example of Soviet cold war "humor" from* Izvestia *in 1960 shows the revenge-seeking West German beast of Bonn, complete with U.S. knife, French fork, and British napkin, being served a Polaris missile. (Photo: Caroline Buckler)*

later began to claim the spoils of victory, a helpless but moralistic United States refused to cooperate and professed outrage. One cannot help but feel that western opposition immediately after the war came too late and probably encouraged even more aggressive measures by the always suspicious Stalin. And it helped explode the quarrel over eastern Europe into a global confrontation, which quickly became institutionalized.

## THE WEST EUROPEAN RENAISSANCE

As the cold war divided Europe into two blocs, the future appeared very bleak on both sides of the Iron Curtain. Economic conditions were the worst in generations, and millions of people lived on the verge of starvation. Politically, Europe was weak and divided, a battleground for cold war ambitions. Moreover, long-cherished European empires were crumbling in the face of Asian and African nationalism. Yet Europe recovered, and the western nations led the way. In less than a generation western Europe achieved unprecedented economic prosperity and regained much of its traditional prominence in world affairs. It was an amazing rebirth – a true renaissance.

### THE POSTWAR CHALLENGE

After the war, economic conditions in western Europe were terrible. Simply finding enough to eat was a real problem. Runaway inflation and black markets testified to severe shortages and hardship. The bread ration in Paris in 1946 was little more than it had been in 1942 under the Nazi occupation. Rationing

power vacuum after 1932 had lured Nazi racist imperialism, the appeasing western democracies had quite mistakenly done nothing. They had, however, had one telling insight: how, they had asked themselves, could they unite with Stalin to stop Hitler without giving Stalin great gains on his western borders? After Hitler's invasion of Soviet Russia, the western powers preferred to ignore this question and hope for the best. But when Stalin of bread had to be introduced in Britain in 1946 for the first time. Both France and Italy produced only about half as much in 1946 as before the war. Many people believed that Europe was quite simply finished. The prominent British historian Arnold Toynbee felt that, at best, west Europeans might seek to civilize the crude but all-powerful Americans, somewhat as the ancient Greeks had civilized their Roman conquerors.

Suffering was most intense in defeated Germany. The major territorial change of the war had moved Soviet Russia's border far to the west. Poland was in turn compensated for this loss to Russia with land taken from Germany (see Map 30.2). To solidify these boundary changes, 13 million people were driven from their homes in eastern Germany (and other eastern countries) and forced to resettle in a greatly reduced Germany. In the last days of the war a captured British airman watched this "migration of a vast peasant population. . . . They were a pitiful sight, frozen, hungry, shoes and clothes falling apart, dragging themselves along to an unknown destination, hoping only that it might be beyond the reach of the Russian army."[4] The Russians were also seizing factories and equipment as reparations, and even tearing up railroad tracks and sending the rails to the Soviet Union. The command "Come here, woman," from a Russian soldier was the sound of terror, the prelude to rape.

In 1945 and 1946, conditions were not much better in the western zones. The western allies also treated the German population with great severity at first. By February 1946, the average daily diet of a German in the Ruhr had been reduced to two slices of bread, a pat of margarine, a spoonful of porridge, and two small potatoes. Countless Germans sold many of their possessions to American soldiers to buy food. Cigarettes replaced worthless money as currency. The winter of 1946-1947 was one of the coldest in memory, and there were widespread signs of actual starvation. By the spring of 1947, refugee-clogged, hungry, prostrate Germany was on the verge of total collapse and threatening to drag down the rest of Europe.

Yet western Europe was not finished. The Nazi occupation and the war had discredited old ideas and old leaders. All over Europe many people were willing to change and experiment in hopes of building a new and better Europe out of the rubble. New groups and new leaders were coming to the fore to guide these aspirations. Progressive Catholics and revitalized Catholic political parties – the Christian Democrats – were particularly influential.

In Italy the Christian Democrats emerged as the leading party in the first postwar elections in 1946, and in early 1948 they won an absolute majority in the parliament in a landslide victory. Their very able leader was Alcide De Gasperi, a courageous antifascist and former Vatican librarian, firmly committed to political democracy, economic reconstruction, and moderate social reform. In France too the Catholic party provided some of the best postwar leaders, like Robert Schuman. This was particularly true after January 1946, when General de Gaulle, the inspiring wartime leader of the Free French, resigned after having re-established the free and democratic Fourth Republic. Western Germany also found new and able leadership among its Catholics. In 1949, Konrad Adenauer, the former mayor of Cologne and a long-time anti-Nazi, began his long, highly successful democratic rule; the Christian Democrats became West Germany's majority party for a generation. In providing effective leadership

MAP 30.2   EUROPE AFTER 1945   *Both the So-*
*viet Union and Poland took land from Germany,*
*which was then permanently divided by the cold war.*

for their respective countries, the Christian Democrats were inspired and united by a common Christian and European heritage. They steadfastly rejected totalitarianism and narrow nationalism and placed their faith in close cooperation.

The socialists and the communists, active in the resistance against Hitler, also emerged from the war with increased power and prestige, especially in France and Italy. They too provided fresh leadership and pushed for social change and economic reform with considerable success. Thus, in the immediate postwar years, welfare measures such as family allowances, health insurance, and increased public housing were enacted throughout much of Europe. In Italy social benefits from the state came to equal a large part of the average worker's wages. In France large banks, insurance companies, public utilities, coal mines, and the Renault auto company were nationalized by the government. Britain followed the same trend. The voters threw out Churchill and the Conservatives in 1945, and the socialist Labour party under Clement Attlee moved toward establishment of the "welfare state." Many industries were nationalized, and the government provided each citizen with free medical service and taxed the middle and upper classes heavily. The Labour government was also committed to providing everyone a job and avoiding economic depression.

The massive economic aid the United States provided under the Marshall Plan speeded western Europe's economic recovery. Offered to all of Europe but accepted only by the western nations, Marshall Plan aid was intended to create the economic prosperity on which stable democratic societies could be built. The plan's requirement that the participating countries coordinate their efforts for maximum effectiveness led to the establishment of the Organization of European Economic Cooperation (OEEC). Over the next five years the United States furnished foreign countries roughly $22.5 billion, of which seven-eighths was in the form of outright gifts rather than loans. Thus America assumed its international responsibilities after the Second World War, exercising the leadership it had shunned in the tragic years after 1919.

### ECONOMIC "MIRACLES"

As Marshall Plan aid poured in, the battered economies of western Europe began to turn the corner in 1948. Impoverished West Germany led the way with a spectacular advance after the western Allies permitted Adenauer's government to reform the currency and stimulate private enterprise. Other countries were not far behind. The outbreak of the Korean War in 1950 further stimulated economic activity, and Europe entered a period of rapid, sustained economic progress. By 1963, western Europe was producing more than two-and-one-half times as much as it had before the war. Never before had the European economy grown so fast. For politicians and economists, for workers and business leaders, it was a time of astonishing, loudly proclaimed economic "miracles."

There were many reasons for western Europe's brilliant economic performance. American aid helped the process get off to a fast start. Europe received equipment to repair damaged plants and even whole new specialized factories when necessary. Thus, critical shortages were quickly overcome. Moreover,

*BERLIN DIGS OUT* What was once a great newspaper building stands as a ghostly gutted-out shell in
this altogether typical postwar scene from 1945. But
the previously impassable street has been partially
cleared of rubble and traffic has begun to move again.
In the midst of ruins life refuses to die. (U.S. Army
Signal Corps)

since European nations coordinated the distribution of American aid, many barriers to European trade and cooperation were quickly
dropped. Aid from the United States helped,
therefore, to promote both a resurgence of
economic liberalism with its healthy competition and an international division of labor.

As in most of the world, economic growth
became a basic objective of all west European

governments, for leaders and voters were determined to avoid a return to the dangerous
and demoralizing stagnation of the 1930s.
Governments generally accepted Keynesian
economics (page 1014) and sought to stimulate
their economies, and some also adopted a
number of imaginative strategies. Those in
Germany and France were particularly successful and influential.

Under Minister of Economy Ludwig Erhard, a roly-poly, cigar-smoking ex-professor, postwar West Germany broke decisively with the totally regulated, straight-jacketed Nazi economy. Erhard bet on the free-market economy. He and his teachers believed not only that capitalism was more efficient but also that political and social freedom could thrive only if there were real economic freedom. Erhard's first step was to reform the currency and abolish rationing and price controls in 1948. He boldly declared, "The only ration coupon is the Mark."[5] At first profits jumped sharply, prompting businessmen to quickly employ more people and produce more. By the late 1950s, Germany had a prospering economy and full employment, a strong currency and stable prices. Germany's success aroused renewed respect for free-market capitalism and encouraged freer trade within Europe.

In France the major innovation was a new kind of planning. Under the guidance of Jean Monnet, an economic pragmatist and apostle of European unity, a planning commission set ambitious but flexible goals for the French economy. It used Marshall aid money and the nationalized banks to funnel money into key industries, several of which were state-owned. At the same time, the planning commission and the French bureaucracy encouraged private enterprise to "think big." The often-cautious French business community responded, investing heavily in new equipment and modern factories. Thus, France combined flexible planning and a "mixed" state and private economy to achieve the most rapid economic development in its long history. Throughout the 1950s and 1960s, there was hardly any unemployment in France. The average person's standard of living improved dramatically. France too was an economic "miracle."

Other factors also contributed to western Europe's economic boom. In most countries after the war, there were large numbers of men and women ready to work hard for low wages and the hope of a better future. Germany had millions of impoverished refugees, while France and Italy still had millions of poor peasants. Expanding industries in those countries thus had a great asset to draw on. More fully urbanized Britain had no such rural labor pool; this lack, along with a welfare socialism that stressed "fair shares" rather than rapid growth, helps account for its fairly poor postwar economic performance.

In 1945, impoverished Europe was still rich in the sense that it had the human skills of an advanced industrial society. Skilled workers, engineers, managers, and professionals knew what could and should be done, and they did it.

Many consumer products had been invented or perfected since the late 1920s, but few Europeans had been able to buy them during the depression and war. In 1945 the electric refrigerator, the washing machine, and the automobile were rare luxuries. There was, therefore, a great potential demand, which the economic system moved to satisfy.

Finally, ever since 1919 the nations of Europe had suffered from high tariffs and small national markets, which made for small and therefore inefficient factories. In the postwar era European countries junked many of these economic barriers and gradually created a large unified market – the Common Market. This action, which stimulated the economy, was part of the postwar search for a new European unity.

## POLITICAL RECOVERY

Western Europe's political recovery was spectacular. Republics were re-established in

France, West Germany, and Italy. Constitutional monarchs were restored in Belgium, Holland, and Norway. These democratic governments took root once again and thrived. To be sure, only West Germany established a two-party system on the British-American model; states like France and Italy returned to multiparty politics and shifting parliamentary coalitions. Yet the middle-of-the road parties – primarily the Christian Democrats and the Socialists – dominated and provided continuing leadership. National self-determination was accompanied by civil liberties and great individual freedom. All of this was itself an extraordinary achievement.

Even more remarkable was the still-unfinished, still-continuing movement toward a united Europe. The Christian Democrats with their shared Catholic heritage were particularly committed to "building Europe," and other groups shared their dedication. Many Europeans believed that narrow, exaggerated nationalism had been a fundamental cause of both world wars, and that only through unity could European conflict be avoided in the future. Many west Europeans also realized how very weak their countries were in comparison with the United States and the Soviet Union, the two superpowers that had divided Europe from outside and made it into a cold war battleground. Thus, the cold war encouraged some visionaries to seek a new "European nation," a superpower capable of controlling western Europe's destiny and reasserting its influence in world affairs.

The close cooperation among European states required by the Marshall Plan led to the creation of both the OEEC and the Council of Europe in 1948. European federalists hoped that the Council of Europe would quickly evolve into a true European parliament with sovereign rights, but this did not happen.

Britain, with its empire and its "special relationship" with the United States, consistently opposed giving any real political power – any sovereignty – to the council. Many old-fashioned continental nationalists and communists felt similarly. The Council of Europe became little more than a multinational debating society.

Frustrated in the direct political approach, European federalists turned toward economics. As one of them explained, "Politics and economics are closely related. Let us try, then, for progress in economic matters. Let us suppress those obstacles of an economic nature which divide and compartmentalize the nations of Europe."[6] In this they were quite successful.

Two far-seeing French statesmen, the planner Jean Monnet and Foreign Minister Robert Schuman, courageously took the lead in 1950. The Schuman Plan called for a special international organization to control and integrate all European steel and coal production. West Germany, Italy, Belgium, the Netherlands, and Luxembourg accepted the French idea in 1952; the British would have none of it. The immediate economic goal – a single competitive market without national tariffs or quotas – was rapidly realized. By 1958, coal and steel moved as freely among the six nations of the European Coal and Steel Community as among the states of the United States. The more far-reaching political goal was to bind the six member nations so closely together economically that war among them would become unthinkable and virtually impossible. This brilliant strategy did much to reduce tragic old rivalries, particularly that of France and Germany, which practically disappeared in the postwar era.

The coal and steel community was so successful that it encouraged further technical and economic cooperation among "the Six." In 1957, the same six nations formed Euratom to pursue joint research in atomic energy. The same year they also signed the Treaty of Rome, which created the European Economic Community, generally known as the Common Market. The treaty's first goal was to reduce gradually all tariffs among the Six and create a large free-trade area. The Treaty of Rome also called for the free movement of capital and labor, and it envisioned common economic policies and institutions.

An epoch-making stride toward unity, the Common Market was a tremendous success. Tariffs were rapidly reduced, and the European economy was stimulated. Companies and regions specialized in what they did best. Western Europe was being united in a single market almost as large as that of the United States. Many medium-sized American companies rushed to Europe, for a single modern factory in, say, Belgium or southern Italy had a vast potential market of 170 million customers.

The development of the Common Market fired imaginations and encouraged hopes of rapid progress toward political as well as economic union. In the 1960s, however, these hopes were frustrated by a resurgence of more traditional nationalism. Once again, France took the lead. Mired in a bitter colonial war in Algeria, the country turned in 1958 to General de Gaulle, who established the Fifth French Republic and ruled as its president until 1969. A towering giant both literally and figuratively, de Gaulle was dedicated to reasserting France's greatness and glory. Once he had resolved the Algerian conflict, he labored to recreate a powerful, truly independent France, which would lead and even dictate to the other Common Market states. De Gaulle personified the political resurgence of

FRENCH PRESIDENT DE GAULLE welcomed the young President Kennedy to Paris in 1961. De Gaulle strongly challenged American leadership in Western Europe. (Wide World Photos)

the leading nations of western Europe, as well as declining fears of the Soviet Union in the 1960s. Viewing the United States as the main threat to genuine French (and European) independence, he withdrew all French military forces from the "American-controlled" NATO command, which had to move from Paris to Brussels. De Gaulle tried to create financial difficulties for the United States by demanding gold for the American dollars

France had accumulated. France also developed its own nuclear weapons. Within the Common Market, de Gaulle in 1963 and again in 1967 vetoed the application of the pro-American British, who were having second thoughts and wanted to join. More generally, he refused to permit the scheduled advent of majority rule within the Common Market, and he forced his partners to accept many of his views. Thus, throughout the 1960s the Common Market thrived economically, but it remained a union of revitalized sovereign states.

## DECOLONIALIZATION

The postwar era saw the total collapse of colonial empires. Between 1947 and 1962, almost every colonial territory gained independence. Europe's long expansion, which had reached a high point in the late nineteenth century, was completely reversed (see Map 30.3). The spectacular collapse of Western political empires fully reflected old Europe's eclipsed power after 1945. Yet the new nations of Asia and Africa have been so deeply influenced by Western ideas and achievements that the "westernization" of the world has continued to rush forward.

Modern nationalism, with its demands for political self-determination and racial equality, spread from intellectuals to the masses in virtually every colonial territory after the First World War. Economic suffering created bitter popular resentment, and thousands of colonial subjects had been unwillingly drafted into French and British armies. Nationalist leaders stepped up their demands. By 1919, one high-ranking British official mournfully wrote: "A wave of unrest is sweeping over the Empire, as over the rest of the world. Almost every day brings some disturbance or other at our Imperial outposts."[7] The Russian Revolution

also encouraged the growth of nationalism, and Soviet Russia verbally and militarily supported nationalist independence movements.

Furthermore, European empires had been based on an enormous power differential between the rulers and the ruled, a difference that had declined almost to the vanishing point by 1945. Not only was western Europe poor and battered immediately after the war, but Japan had demonstrated that whites were not invincible. With its political power and moral authority in tatters, Europe's only choices were to give in gracefully or to wage risky wars of reconquest.

Most Europeans regarded their empires very differently after 1945 than before 1914, or even before 1939. Empire had rested on self-confidence and a sense of righteousness; Europeans had believed their superiority to be not only technical and military but spiritual and moral as well. The horrors of the Second World War and the near-destruction of Western civilization destroyed such complacent arrogance and gave opponents of imperialism the upper hand in Europe. After 1945 most Europeans were willing to let go of their colonies more or less voluntarily and to concentrate on rebuilding at home.

India played a key role in decolonialization and the end of empire. India was Britain's oldest, largest, and most lucrative nonwhite possession, and Britain had by far the largest colonial empire. Nationalist opposition to British rule coalesced after the First World War under the leadership of the British-educated lawyer Mahatma Gandhi (1869–1948), who preached nonviolent "noncooperation" against the British. Indian intellectuals effec-

NORTH KOREA 1948
SOUTH KOREA 1948
From Japan

PHILIPPINES 1946

NORTH VIETNAM 1954
SOUTH VIETNAM 1954
Unified 1974
KAMPUCHEA (CAMBODIA) 1954
LAOS 1949
MALAYSIA 1963
SINGAPORE 1965

INDONESIA 1949

BURMA 1947

PAKISTAN 1947
BANGLADESH 1973

INDIA 1947

PAKISTAN 1947

SRI LANKA (CEYLON) 1948

INDIAN OCEAN

Date is year independence was achieved.
Shading indicates former ruler

Great Britain
France
Netherlands
Italy
Belgium
Portugal
United States

SOUTHERN YEMEN 1967

KUWAIT 1961

SYRIA 1944
IRAQ 1947
JORDAN 1946

DJIBOUTI 1977

SOMALIA 1960

MAURITIUS 1968

ETHIOPIA 1944

KENYA 1963
UGANDA 1962
TANZANIA 1964
MALAWI 1964

MALAGASY REPUBLIC 1960

SWAZILAND 1968

CYPRUS 1960
LEBANON 1944
ISRAEL 1948

EGYPT 1954

SUDAN 1956

CENTRAL AFRICAN REPUBLIC 1960
ZAIRE 1960
RWANDA 1962
BURUNDI 1962
ZAMBIA 1964
ZIMBABWE 1980
MOZAMBIQUE 1974
LESOTHO 1966
BOTSWANA 1966
SOUTH AFRICA (Republic 1961)

MALTA 1964
TUNISIA 1957

LIBYA 1951

CHAD 1960

CAMEROUN 1960
GABON 1960
ANGOLA 1975

ITALY

ALGERIA 1962

NIGER 1960

DAHOMEY 1960
NIGERIA 1960

EQUATORIAL GUINEA 1968
REPUBLIC OF CONGO 1960
NAMIBIA (occupied by South Africa)

GREAT BRITAIN
NETHERLANDS
BELGIUM
FRANCE

MOROCCO 1956

MAURITANIA 1960

MALI 1960

VOLTA 1960
IVORY COAST 1960
GHANA 1957
TOGO 1960

PORTUGAL

SENEGAL 1960
GAMBIA 1965
GUINEA-BISSAU 1974
GUINEA 1958
SIERRA LEONE 1961

ATLANTIC OCEAN

0   800 Km.
0   800 Mi.

tively argued the old liberal case for equality and self-determination. In response, Britain's rulers gradually introduced political reforms and limited self-government. When the war ended, independence followed very rapidly. The new Labour government was determined to leave India: radicals and socialists had always opposed imperialism, and the heavy cost of governing India had become an intolerable financial burden. The obstacle posed by conflict between India's Hindu and Muslim populations was resolved in 1947 by creating two states, predominantly Hindu India and Muslim Pakistan.

If Indian nationalism drew on Western parliamentary liberalism, Chinese nationalism developed and triumphed in the framework of Marxist-Leninist totalitarianism. In the turbulent early 1920s, a broad alliance of nationalist forces within the Russian-supported Kuomintang – the National People's party – was dedicated to unifying China and abolishing European concessions. But in 1927 Chiang Kai-shek (1887–1975), the successor to Sun Yat-Sen (page 942) and the leader of the Kuomintang, broke with his more radical Communist allies, headed by Mao Tse-tung.

In 1931, Mao Tse-tung (1893–1976) led his followers on an incredible five-thousand-mile march to remote northern China and dug in. Even war against the Japanese army of occupation could not force Mao and Chiang to cooperate. By late 1945, the long-standing quarrel erupted in civil war. Stalin gave Mao some aid, and the Americans gave Chiang much more. Winning the support of the peasantry by promising to expropriate the big landowners, the tougher, better-organized Communists forced the Nationalists to withdraw to the island of Taiwan in 1949.

Mao and the Communists united China's 550 million inhabitants in a strong centralized state, expelled foreigners, and began building a new society along Soviet lines, with mass arrests, forced-labor camps, and ceaseless propaganda. The peasantry was collectivized, and the inevitable five-year plans concentrated quite successfully on the expansion of heavy industry.

Most Asian countries followed the pattern of either India or China. Britain quickly gave Sri Lanka (Ceylon) and Burma independence in 1948; the Philippines became independent of the United States in 1946. The Dutch attempt to reconquer the Netherlands East Indies was unsuccessful, and in 1949 Indonesia emerged independent.

The French similarly sought to re-establish colonial rule in Indochina, but despite American aid they were defeated in 1954 by forces under the Communist and nationalist guerrilla leader Ho Chi Minh (1890–1969). At the subsequent international peace conference, French Indochina gained independence. Vietnam was divided into two hostile independent states, one communist and one anticommunist. Civil war soon broke out between the two.

In Africa, Arab nationalism was an important factor in the ending of empire. Sharing a common language and culture, Arab nationalists were also loosely united by their opposition to the colonial powers and to the migration of Jewish refugees to Palestine. The British, whose occupation policies in Palestine were condemned by Arabs and Jews, by Russians and Americans, announced their withdrawal from Palestine in 1948. The United Nations voted for the creation of two states, one Arab and one Jewish. The Arab countries immediately attacked the new Jewish nation and suffered a humiliating defeat. Thousands of Arab refugees fled Palestine.

This Arab defeat triggered a nationalist revolution in Egypt in 1952, when a young army officer named Gamal Abdel Nasser

*WORKING THE LAND    China's peasants, like these girls preparing for planting, worked on state-run collective farms after the Communists abolished private ownership of land. (Magnum Photo Library © Marc Riboud Magnum)*

(1918–1970) drove out the pro-Western king. In 1956 Nasser abruptly nationalized the Suez Canal, the last symbol and substance of Western power in the Middle East. Infuriated, the British and French, along with the Israelis, invaded Egypt. This was, however, to be the dying gasp of imperial power: the moralistic, anti-imperialist Americans joined with the Russians to force the British, French, and Israelis to withdraw.

The failure of the Western powers to unseat Nasser in 1956 in turn encouraged Arab nationalists in Algeria. Algeria's large French population considered Algeria an integral part of France. It was this feeling that made the ensuing war so bitter and so atypical of decolonialization. In the end, General de Gaulle, who had returned to power as part of a movement to keep Algeria French, accepted the principle of Algerian self-determination. In 1962, after more than a century of French rule, Algeria became independent and the European population quickly fled.

In most of Africa south of the Sahara, decolonialization proceeded much more smoothly. Beginning in 1957, Britain's colonies won independence with little or no bloodshed. In 1960 the clever de Gaulle offered the leaders of French black Africa the choice of a total break with France or immediate independence within a kind of French commonwealth. Heavily dependent on France for economic aid and technology, all but one of the new states chose association with France. Throughout the 1960s and 1970s, France (and its west European partners) successfully used economic and cultural ties with former colonies, such as special trading privileges with the Common Market and heavy investment in French-based education, to maintain a powerful European presence in black Africa. Radicals charged France (and Europe generally) with "neo-colonialism," designed to perpetuate European economic domination indefinitely. In any event, enduring aid and influence in black Africa was an important manifestation of western Europe's political recovery and even of its possible emergence as a genuine superpower.

## RECENT TRENDS

Events in the late 1960s and 1970s suggested that the period of unprecedented postwar recovery was finally over, and that an uncertain new era had probably begun. In 1968, a mini-revolution in France signaled the re-emergence of serious social and political conflict in western Europe and the United States after a generation of relative peace. Serious economic problems also reappeared. Most countries in the late 1960s began to suffer from rapid inflation. Governments' inability to control this inflation led to fears that the new economic orthodoxy – Keynesian economics – had not possessed the secret to permanent, stable prosperity after all.

The international monetary system, so instrumental in the postwar boom, also broke down. That system, created by the Bretton Woods Agreement of 1944, was based on the American dollar, which was supposed to be "as good as gold" since foreign governments could always exchange dollars for gold. Beginning in the 1950s, however, the United States constantly spent more abroad than it earned. By early 1971, the United States had only $11 billion in gold left in Fort Knox, and Europe had accumulated 50 billion American dollars. The result was a classic, long-overdue "run on the bank" in 1971, as holders of dollars tried to exchange their dollars for gold. President Richard Nixon was forced to stop the sale of American gold. The free-market price of gold soared, and the value of the dollar declined. The dollar, no longer "as good as gold," became just another currency, and great uncertainty arose about international trade and finance.

Furthermore, the postwar boom in Europe had been fueled by cheap oil from the Middle East. Following an Arab-Israeli war in 1973 and reflecting the desire to gain greater profit from their natural resources, the Arab states quadrupled the price of oil. This act increased inflation, worsened the worst recession since 1945, and signaled the end of an era of cheap energy.

Yet in the face of all these challenges the Common Market did not collapse. The fall of the dollar standard showed the world that western Europe was once again America's economic equal. Moreover, the Common Market continued to exert a powerful attraction. In 1973, Britain, Denmark, and Ireland finally joined; Greece, Portugal, and Spain applied for membership in 1977 and in 1981 Greece joined officially as negotiations with Portugal and Spain continued. Although a United States of Europe is still far in the future, the nations of the Common Market are cooperating more and more closely in many international undertakings and negotiations. The Common Market decided in 1977, for example, to go ahead with plans for a nuclear breeder reactor to produce electric power, and it has developed a common policy on peace in the Middle East and economic negotiations with the Third World. The movement toward European unity is still very much alive.

Democracy has remained strong in Europe, unlike much of the world, and even appears to be expanding its sway. Both Spain and Portugal scrapped their aging dictatorships in 1974 and committed themselves to building democratic governments. Greece also established parliamentary rule. More difficult to interpret is an apparent trend toward a more liberal Western communism and toward communist participation in west European governments. The large Communist parties of France and Italy have openly criticized the Soviet Union for its inattention to human rights, and both claim to be stalwart democrats worthy of trust. In Italy, the Communists have begun working with the Christian Democrats in parliament on economic and social problems. In France, Communists actually entered the cabinet after the victory of a socialist, François Mitterrand, in the presidential elections of 1981. Whether these developments signal a great "historic compromise" or merely a passing phase, only time will tell.

## SOVIET EASTERN EUROPE

While western Europe surged ahead economically, regaining political independence as American influence gradually waned, eastern Europe followed a different path. Soviet Russia first tightened its grip on the "liberated" nations of eastern Europe under Stalin and then refused to let go. Economic recovery in eastern Europe proceeded, therefore, along Soviet lines, and political and social developments were largely determined by changes in the Soviet Union. Thus one must look primarily at Soviet Russia to understand the achievements and failures of east European peoples after the Second World War.

### STALIN'S LAST YEARS

The unwillingness of the United States to approve of what Stalin did with territories occupied by the triumphant Red Army was at least partly responsible for the outbreak and institutionalization of the cold war. Yet Americans were not the only ones who felt disappointed and even betrayed by Stalin's postwar actions.

The Great Patriotic War of the Fatherland had fostered Russian nationalism and a relaxation of totalitarian terror. It also produced a rare but real unity between Soviet rulers and most Russian people. When an American correspondent asked a distinguished sixty-year-old Jewish scientist who had decided to leave Russia for Israel in 1972 what had been the best period in Russian history, he received a startling answer: the Second World War. The scientist explained: "At that time we all felt closer to our government than at any other time in our lives. It was not *their* country then, but *our* country. . . . It was not *their* war, but *our* war."[8] Having made such a heroic war effort, the vast majority of the Soviet people hoped in 1945 that a grateful party and government would grant greater freedom and democracy. Such hopes were soon crushed.

Even before the war ended, Stalin was moving his country back toward rigid dictatorship. As early as 1944, the leading members of the Communist party were being given a new motivating slogan: "The war on Fascism ends, the war on capitalism begins."⁹ By early 1946, Stalin was publicly singing the old tune that war was inevitable as long as capitalism existed. Stalin's invention of a new foreign foe was mainly an excuse for re-establishing totalitarian measures, for the totalitarian state cannot live without enemies. Unfortunately, as the rebel Russian historian Andrei Amalrik has argued, Stalin's language at home and his actions in eastern Europe were so crudely extreme that he managed to turn an imaginary threat into a real one, as the cold war took hold.

One of Stalin's first postwar goals was to repress the millions of Soviet citizens who were outside Soviet borders when the war ended. Many had been captured by the Nazis; others were ordinary civilians who had been living abroad. Many were opposed to Stalin; some had fought for the Germans. Determined to hush up the fact that large numbers of Soviet citizens hated his regime so much that they had willingly supported the Germans and refused to go home, Stalin demanded that all these "traitors" be returned to him. At Yalta, Roosevelt and Churchill agreed, and they kept their word. American and British military commanders refused to recognize the right of political asylum under any circumstances.

Roughly 2 million people were delivered to Stalin against their will. Most were immediately arrested and sent to forced-labor camps, where about 50 percent perished. The revival of many forced-labor camps, which had accounted for roughly one-sixth of all new construction in Soviet Russia before the war, was further stimulated by large-scale purges of many people who had never left the Soviet Union, particularly in 1945 and 1946.

Culture and art were also purged. Rigid anti-Western ideological conformity was reimposed in violent campaigns led by Stalin's trusted henchman, Andrei Zhdanov. Zhdanov denounced many artists, including the composers Sergei Prokofiev and Dimitri Shostakovich and the outstanding film director Sergei Eisenstein. The great poet Anna Akhmatova was condemned as "a harlot and nun who mixes harlotry and prayer" and, like many others, driven out of the writers' union, which practically insured that her work would not be published. In 1949, Stalin launched a savage verbal attack on Soviet Jews, who were accused of being pro-Western and antisocialist.

In the political realm Stalin reasserted the Communist party's complete control of the government and his absolute mastery of the party. Five-year plans were reintroduced to cope with the enormous task of economic reconstruction. Once again heavy and military industry were given top priority, and consumer goods, housing, and still-collectivized agriculture were neglected. Everyday life was very hard: in 1952 the wages of ordinary people still bought 25 to 40 percent *less* than in 1928. In short, it was the 1930s all over again in Soviet Russia, although police terror was less intense than during that era's purges.

Stalin's prime postwar innovation was to export the Stalinist system to the countries of eastern Europe. The Communist parties of eastern Europe had established one-party states by 1948, thanks to the help of the Red Army and the Russian secret police. Rigid ideological indoctrination, attacks on religion, and a lack of civil liberties were soon facts of life. Industry was nationalized, and the middle class was stripped of its possessions. Economic life was then faithfully recast in the Stalinist mold. Forced industrialization, with five-year plans and a stress on heavy industry, lurched forward without regard for human costs. For the sake of ideological uniformity, agriculture had to be collectivized; this process went much faster in Bulgaria and Czechoslovakia than in Hungary and Poland. Finally, the satellite countries were forced to trade heavily with Soviet Russia on very unfavorable terms, as traditional economic ties with western Europe were forcibly severed.

Only Josip Tito (1892–1980), the popular resistance leader and Communist chief of Yugoslavia, was able to resist Russian economic exploitation successfully. Tito openly broke with Stalin in 1948, and, since there was no Russian army in Yugoslavia, he got away with it. Tito's successful proclamation of Communist independence led the infuriated and humiliated Stalin to purge the Communist parties of eastern Europe. Hundreds of thousands who had joined the party after the war were expelled. Popular Communist leaders who, like Tito, had led the resistance against Germany, were made to star in reruns of the great show trials of the 1930s, complete with charges of treason, unbelievable confessions, and merciless executions. Thus did history repeat itself as Stalin sought to create absolutely obedient instruments of domination in eastern Europe.

## KHRUSHCHEV AND DE-STALINIZATION

In 1953, the aging Stalin finally died, and a new era slowly began in Soviet eastern Europe. Even as they struggled for power, Stalin's heirs realized that changes and reforms were necessary. There was, first of all, widespread fear and hatred of Stalin's political terrorism, which had struck both high and low with its endless purges and unjust arrests. Even Stalin's secret-police chief, Lavrenti Beria, publicly favored a relaxation of controls in an unsuccessful attempt to seize power. Beria was arrested and shot, after which the power of the secret police was curbed and many of its infamous forced-labor camps were gradually closed. Change was also necessary for economic reasons. Agriculture was in bad shape, and shortages of consumer goods were discouraging hard work and initiative. Finally, Stalin's aggressive foreign policy had led directly to an ongoing American commitment to western Europe and a strong Western alliance. Soviet Russia was isolated and contained.

On the question of just how much change should be permitted, the Communist leadership was badly split. The conservatives led by Stalin's long-time foreign minister, the stone-faced Vyacheslav Molotov, wanted to make as few changes as possible. The reformers, led by Nikita Khrushchev, argued for bold innovations. Khrushchev (1894–1971), who had joined the party as an uneducated coal miner in 1918 at twenty-four and had risen steadily to a high-level position in the 1930s, was emerging as the new ruler by 1955.

To strengthen his position and that of his fellow reformers within the party, Khrushchev launched an all-out attack on Stalin and his crimes at a closed session of the Twentieth Party Congress in 1956. In gory detail he described to the startled Communist delegates how Stalin had tortured and murdered thousands of loyal Communists, how he had trusted Hitler completely and bungled the country's defense, and how he had "supported the glorification of his own person with all conceivable methods." For hours Soviet Russia's top leader delivered an attack whose content would previously have been dismissed as "anti-Communist hysteria" in many circles throughout the Western world.

*LENIN AVENUE, VOLGOGRAD    Devastated Sta-
lingrad was completely rebuilt and then renamed
Volgograd as part of Khrushchev's de-Stalinization
campaign. Seen here are the massive apartment blocks,*
*the gigantic boulevard, and the stress on public trans-
portation as opposed to private automobiles, which are
all quite characteristic of Soviet urban style. (Sovfoto/
Eastfoto)*

Khrushchev's "secret speech" was read to Communist party meetings throughout the country and strengthened the reform movement. The liberalization – or de-Stalinization, as it was called in the West – of Soviet Russia was genuine. The Communist party jealously maintained its monopoly on political power, but Khrushchev shook it up and brought in new blood. The economy was made more responsive to the needs and even some of the desires of the people, as some resources were shifted from heavy industry and the military toward consumer goods and agriculture. Stalinist controls over workers were relaxed, and independent courts rather than the secret police judged and punished nonpolitical crimes.

Russia's very low standard of living finally began to improve, and continued to rise throughout the 1960s. By 1970, Russians were able to buy twice as much food, three times as much clothing, and twelve times as many appliances as in 1950. (Even so, the standard of living in Soviet Russia was only about half that of the wealthier west European countries in 1970, and well below that of east European countries as well.)

De-Stalinization created great ferment among writers and intellectuals, who hungered for cultural freedom. The poet Boris

Pasternak (1890–1960), who survived the Stalinist years by turning his talents to translating Shakespeare, finished his great novel, *Doctor Zhivago,* in 1956. Published in the West but not in Russia, *Doctor Zhivago* is both a literary masterpiece and a powerful challenge to communism. It tells the story of a prerevolutionary intellectual who rejects the violence and brutality of the revolution of 1917 and the Stalinist years. Even as he is destroyed, he triumphs because of his humanity and Christian spirit. Pasternak was forced by Khrushchev himself to refuse the Nobel prize in 1958 – but he was not shot. Other talented writers followed Pasternak's lead, and courageous editors let the sparks fly.

The writer Alexander Solzhenitsyn (b. 1918) created a sensation when his *One Day in the Life of Ivan Denisovich* was published in Russia in 1962. Solzhenitsyn's novel portrays in grim detail life in a Stalinist concentration camp – a life to which Solzhenitsyn himself had been unjustly condemned – and is a damning indictment of the Stalinist past.

Khrushchev also de-Stalinized Soviet foreign policy. "Peaceful coexistence" with capitalism was possible, he argued, and great wars were not inevitable. Khrushchev made positive concessions, meeting with U.S. President Dwight Eisenhower at the first summit meeting since Potsdam and agreeing in 1955 to real independence for a neutral Austria after ten long years of Allied occupation. Thus there was a relaxation of cold war tensions. At the same time Khrushchev began wooing the new nations of Asia and Africa – even if they were not communist – with promises and aid. He also proclaimed that there could be different paths to socialism, thus calling a halt to the little cold war with Tito's Yugoslavia.

De-Stalinization stimulated rebelliousness in the east European satellites. Having suffered in silence under Stalin, Communist reformers and the masses were quickly emboldened to seek much greater liberty and national independence. Poland took the lead in March 1956: riots there resulted in the release of more than nine thousand political prisoners, including the previously purged Wladyslaw Gomulka. Taking charge of the government, Gomulka skillfully managed to win greater autonomy for Poland while calming anti-Russian feeling.

Hungary experienced a real and very tragic revolution. Led by students and workers – the classic urban revolutionaries – the people of Budapest installed the liberal Communist reformer Imre Nagy as their new chief in October 1956. Soviet troops were forced to leave the country. One-party rule was abolished, and the new government promised free elections, freedom of expression, and massive social changes. Worst of all from the Russian point of view, Nagy declared Hungarian neutrality and renounced Hungary's military alliance with Moscow. As in 1849, the Russian answer was to invade Hungary with a large army and to crush, once again, a national, democratic revolution.

Fighting was bitter until the end, for the Hungarians hoped that the United States would fulfill its earlier propaganda promises and come to their aid. When this did not occur because of American unwillingness to risk a general war, the people of eastern Europe realized that their only hope was to strive for small domestic gains while following Russia obediently in foreign affairs. This cautious approach produced some results. In Poland, for example, the peasants were not collectivized and Catholics were allowed to practice their faith. Thus eastern Europe profited modestly from Khrushchev's policy of de-Stalinization, and could hope for still greater freedom in the future.

## THE BREZHNEV ERA

In October 1962, a remarkable poem entitled "Stalin's Heirs" by the popular young poet Yevgeny Yevtushenko (b. 1933) appeared in *Pravda,* the official newspaper of the Communist party and the most important one in Soviet Russia. Yevtushenko wrote:

*Some of his heirs are in retirement pruning their*
*    rosebushes,*
*    and secretly thinking that their time will come*
*    again.*
*Others even attack Stalin from the rostrum but at*
*    home, at night-time, think back to bygone*
*    days....* [10]

Like Solzhenitsyn's novel about Stalin's concentration camps, published a month later, this very political poem was authorized by Communist party boss Khrushchev himself. It was part of his last, desperate offensive against the many well-entrenched conservative Stalinists in the party and government, who were indeed "secretly thinking their time will come again." And it did.

Within two years Khrushchev had fallen in a bloodless palace revolution. Under Leonid Brezhnev (b. 1906), Soviet Russia began a period of limited "re-Stalinization" which has not yet ended. The basic reason for this development was that Khrushchev's Communist colleagues saw de-Stalinization as a dangerous, two-sided threat. How could Khrushchev denounce the dead dictator without eventually denouncing and perhaps even arresting his still-powerful henchmen? In a heated secret debate in 1957, when the conservatives had tried without success to depose the menacing reformer, Khrushchev had pointed at two of Stalin's most devoted followers, Molotov and Kaganovich, and exclaimed: "Your hands are stained with the blood of our party leaders and of innumerable innocent Bolsheviks!" "So are yours!" Molotov and Kaganovich shouted back at him. "Yes, so are mine," Khrushchev replied. "I admit this. But during the purges I was merely carrying out your order.... I was not responsible. You were." [11] Moreover, the widening campaign of de-Stalinization posed a clear threat to the dictatorial authority of the party. It was producing growing, perhaps uncontrollable, criticism of the whole Communist system. The party had to tighten up while there was still time. It was clear that Khrushchev had to go.

Another reason for conservative opposition was Khrushchev's foreign policy. Although he scored some diplomatic victories, notably with Egypt and India, Khrushchev suffered a humiliating defeat in the Cuban missile crisis in 1962. Seeing a chance to change the balance of military power decisively, Khrushchev ordered missiles with nuclear warheads installed in Fidel Castro's Communist Cuba. U.S. President John F. Kennedy countered with a naval blockade of Cuba, and after a very tense diplomatic crisis, Khrushchev was forced to remove the Russian missiles in return for American pledges not to disturb Castro's regime. Khrushchev looked like a bumbling buffoon; his influence, already slipping, declined rapidly after the Cuban fiasco.

After Brezhnev and his supporters took over in 1964, they started talking cautiously of Stalin's "good points" and ignoring his crimes. Their praise of the whole Stalinist era, with its five-year plans and wartime victories, demonstrated that no real break with the past had occurred. They denounced anti-Stalinist writers such as Solzhenitsyn and sent some other liberal intellectuals to prison as a severe warning to all. The government carefully watched the tiny Russian protest movement of urban intellectuals, which had grown out of the more liberal atmosphere of de-Stalini-

THE INVASION OF CZECHOSLOVAKIA *Russian tanks enter Prague in 1968 and stand ready to annihilate any opposition. Dubček fell and the Russians maintained their control of eastern Europe. (Wide World Photos)*

zation and was calling for greater freedom. Russian leaders also launched a massive arms buildup, determined never to suffer Khrushchev's humiliation in the face of American nuclear superiority.

To eastern Europe the 1960s brought modest liberalization and more consumer goods, as well as somewhat greater national autonomy, especially in Poland and Rumania. Czechoslovakia had moved more slowly than its neighbors, but in January 1968 the reform elements in its Communist party finally triumphed. Under the new Communist leader, Anton Dubček, the government introduced major economic and political reforms. Local decision making by trade unions, managers, and consumers replaced rigid bureaucratic planning. Mindless ideological conformity gave way to exciting free expression. Enormously popular with the people, Dubček promised to build a new and profoundly democratic socialist society.

Although Dubček remembered the lesson of Hungary and constantly proclaimed military loyalty to the Warsaw Pact of Communist states, the determination of the Czech reformers to build "socialism with a human face" frightened hard-line Communists. Such a Czechoslovakia would certainly set a dangerous example for the peoples of eastern Europe and Soviet Russia, and would probably be drawn toward the democratic West. Thus 500,000 Russian and east European allied troops suddenly occupied Czechoslovakia in August 1968. The dejected Czechs made no attempt to resist. Soon unbending orthodox Communist dictators ruled once again.

Shortly thereafter, Brezhnev declared the so-called Brezhnev Doctrine, according to which Soviet Russia had the right to intervene in any socialist country whenever it saw the need. Predictably, the Russian invasion of Czechoslovakia raised a storm of protest. Many Communist parties in western Europe were harshly critical of it. None of this altered the fact that Stalin's empire was still solidly in place, and that developments in eastern Europe would continue to follow those in Soviet Russia.

The invasion of Czechoslovakia — perhaps the crucial event of the Brezhnev era — brought further re-Stalinization of Soviet Russia, though with collective rather than personal dictatorship and without uncontrolled terror. This compromise seemed to suit the leaders and most of the people. Whether westerners liked it or not, Soviet Russia appeared quite stable in the 1970s.

A rising standard of living for ordinary people contributed greatly to stability. By 1974, two-thirds of the nation's families had television sets, almost 60 percent had sewing and washing machines, and about half had some kind of refrigerator. There were still long lines and many shortages, but long-suffering Soviet consumers compared the present

with the recent past and not with conditions abroad. The enduring differences between the life of the elite and the life of ordinary people also reinforced the system. Ambitious individuals still had tremendous incentive to do as the state wished, in order that they might gain access to special well-stocked stores, attend special schools, and travel abroad.

Another source of stability was that ordinary Russians remained more intensely nationalistic than almost any people in the world. The party leaders successfully identified themselves with this patriotism, stressing their role in saving the motherland during the Second World War and protecting her now from foreign foes. By playing on nationalist feelings, de-Stalinization was very easily reversed. Many ordinary Russians considered an attack on Stalin to be an attack on the great sacrifices they had willingly made for the nation. Similarly, ordinary Russians took enormous pride in their country's military power, and young men accepted an inescapable three-year hitch in the army without question. The cult of Lenin, which replaced the cult of Stalin, also had nationalistic overtones, which neutralized the general cynicism about Communist ideology.

Finally, the strength of the government was expressed in the re-Stalinization of culture and art. Free expression and protest disappeared. In 1968, when a small group of dissenters appeared in Red Square to protest the invasion of Czechoslovakia, they were arrested before they could unfurl their banners. This was to be the high point of dissent, for in the 1970s Brezhnev and company made certain that liberalism did not infect Soviet intellectuals. The slightest acts of nonconformity were severely punished, but with sophisticated, cunning methods.

Most frequently, dissidents were blacklisted

and thus rendered unable to find a decent job, since the government was the only employer. This fate was enough to keep most in line. More determined but unrenowned protesters were quietly imprisoned in jails or mental institutions. Celebrated nonconformists such as Solzhenitsyn were permanently expelled from the country. Once again Jews were persecuted as a "foreign" element, though some were eventually permitted to emigrate to Israel.

As the distinguished Russian dissident historian Roy Medvedev summed it up:

*The technology of repression has become more refined in recent years. Before, repression always went much farther than necessary. Stalin killed millions of people when arresting 1000 would have enabled him to control the people. Our leaders . . . found out eventually that you don't have to put people in prison or in a psychiatric hospital to silence them. There are other ways.*[12]

Thus the worst aspects of Stalin's totalitarianism had been eliminated, but rule by a self-perpetuating Communist elite in the Soviet Union appeared as solid as ever throughout the 1970s.

The 1980s, however, opened on an uncertain note in the satellite empire. A spectacular resurgence of liberalism and nationalism in Poland crystallized around protests by workers and a remarkable free trade union called Solidarity. The almost-universal dissatisfaction of the Polish people with more than thirty years of communist rule, and their profound longing for "rebirth," were clear for all to see. Finally, after some major economic and cultural reforms were announced and as the power of the Polish Communist party waned and the Soviet Union demanded countermeasures, the Polish army took control of the government in December 1981. The generals imposed strict martial law, arrested thousands

of Solidarity members, and talked of revitalizing the Polish Communist party. It was widely feared in the West that the Soviet Union had once again managed to use puppets and raw force to maintain its oppressive system in eastern Europe.

## THE WESTERN HEMISPHERE

One way to think of what historians used to call the New World is as a vigorous offshoot of Western civilization, an offshoot that has gradually developed its own characteristics while retaining European roots. From this perspective, one can see many illuminating parallels and divergences in the histories of Europe and the Americas. So it has been in the recent past.

Thus the western hemisphere experienced a spectacular many-sided postwar recovery, somewhat similar to that of Europe although it began earlier, especially in Latin America. Cold war conflicts also exercised a tremendous influence on domestic politics in the western hemisphere. Yet here too the timing was different, for the full force of the impact came only in the 1960s, when the cold war was assuming a secondary role in western Europe. Moreover, profound differences continued to exist between predominately English-speaking Canada and the United States, on the one hand, and Latin America on the other.

### POSTWAR PROSPERITY IN THE UNITED STATES

The Second World War cured the depression in the United States and brought about the greatest boom in American history. Unemployment practically vanished as millions of new workers, half of them women, found jobs. Personal income doubled and the well-being of Americans increased dramatically. Yet the experience of the 1930s weighed heavily on people's minds, feeding fears that peace would bring renewed depression.

In fact, conversion to a peacetime economy went smoothly, marred only by a spurt of inflation accompanying the removal of government controls. Moreover, the U.S. economy continued to advance fairly steadily for a long generation. Though cold-war fears and anxieties dominated American relations with the rest of the world, the warm glow of economic prosperity soothed and satisfied at home.

This helps explain why postwar domestic politics consisted largely of modest adjustments to the status quo until the 1960s. After a flurry of unpopular postwar strikes, a conservative Republican Congress chopped away at the power of labor unions by means of the Taft-Hartley Act of 1947. But Truman's upset victory in 1948 demonstrated that Americans had no interest in undoing Roosevelt's social and economic reforms. The Congress proceeded to increase social security benefits, subsidize middle- and lower-class housing, and raise the minimum wage. These and other liberal measures extended and consolidated the New Deal. But major innovations – whether in health or civil rights – were decisively rejected, and in 1952 the Republican party and the voters turned to General Eisenhower, a national hero and self-described moderate.

The federal government's only major new undertaking during "the Eisenhower years" was the interstate highway system, a suitable symbol of the basic satisfaction of the vast majority. Some Americans feared that the United States was becoming a "blocked soci-

ety," obsessed with stability and incapable of wholesome change. This feeling contributed in 1960 to the election of the young, attractive John F. Kennedy, who promised to "get the country moving again." President Kennedy captured the popular imagination with his flair and rhetoric, revitalized the old Roosevelt coalition, and modestly expanded existing liberal legislation before he was struck down by an assassin's bullet in 1963.

## THE CIVIL RIGHTS REVOLUTION

Belatedly and reluctantly, complacent postwar America experienced a genuine social revolution: after a long and sometimes bloody struggle, blacks (and their white supporters) threw off a deeply entrenched system of segregation, discrimination, and repression. This movement for civil rights advanced on several fronts. Eloquent lawyers from the National Association for the Advancement of Colored People challenged school segregation in the courts, and in 1954 won a landmark decision in the Supreme Court that "separate educational facilities are inherently unequal." While state and local governments in the south were refusing to comply, blacks were effectively challenging institutionalized inequality with bus boycotts, sit-ins, and demonstrations. As Martin Luther King told the white power structure, "We will not hate you, but we will not obey your evil laws."[13]

Blacks also used their growing political power in key northern states to gain the support of the liberal wing of the Democratic party. All these efforts culminated after the liberal landslide that elected Lyndon Johnson in 1964. The Civil Rights Act of 1964 categorically prohibited discrimination in public services and on the job. In the follow-up Voting Rights Act of 1965, the federal govern-

THE MARCH ON WASHINGTON  This stunning aerial shot captures on film the dramatic climax of the civil rights struggle, the spectacular mass demonstration at the Lincoln Memorial in August 1963, which was organized by Martin Luther King and other black leaders. The march was supported by President Kennedy, who was assassinated just three months later. (Associated Press Photo)

ment firmly guaranteed all blacks the right to vote. By the 1970s, there were substantial numbers of elected black officials in all the southern states, proof positive that dramatic changes had occurred in American race relations.

Black voters and political leaders enthusiastically supported the accompanying surge of new liberal social legislation in the mid-1960s. President Johnson, reviving the New Deal approach of his early congressional years, solemnly declared "unconditional war on poverty." Congress and the administration created a host of antipoverty projects, such as the domestic peace corps, free preschools for slum children, and community-action programs. Although these programs were directed to all poor Americans – the majority of whom are white – they were also intended to extend greater equality for blacks to the realm of economics. Johnson's ambitious initiatives scored some successes, but economic disadvantages proved less easily remedied than legal and political ones.

### The Trauma of Vietnam

President Johnson wanted to go down in history as a master reformer and healer of old wounds. Instead, he opened new ones with the Vietnam war.

American involvement in Vietnam had its origins in the ideology of the cold war. From the late 1940s onward, most Americans and their leaders continued to view the world in terms of a constant struggle to stop the spread of communism. There were exceptions, to be sure, as well as lively debates over nuances and tactics. Yet anticommunism remained the basis of U.S. foreign policy on all continents. Therefore, after the defeat of the French in Indochina in 1954, when Vietnam

became two hostile states, communist North Vietnam and anticommunist South Vietnam, the Eisenhower administration instinctively provided aid to the new South Vietnamese government. President Kennedy greatly increased the number of American "military advisers," to 16,000, and had the existing South Vietnamese leader deposed in 1963 when he refused to follow American directives.

Having successfully portrayed his opponent Barry Goldwater as a trigger-happy extremist in a nuclear age during the 1964 campaign, President Johnson proceeded to expand the American role in the Vietnam conflict enormously. As Johnson explained to his ambassador in Saigon, "I am not going to lose Vietnam. I am not going to be the President who saw Southeast Asia go the way China went."[14] American strategy was to "escalate" the war sufficiently to break the will of the North Vietnamese and their southern allies, but without resorting to "overkill" that might lead to war with the entire communist bloc. Thus the South received colossal U.S. military aid, American forces grew steadily to a half-million men, and the United States bombed North Vietnam with ever-greater intensity. But there was no invasion of the north, nor were essential seaborne military supplies from the Soviet Union ever disrupted. In the end, the strategy backfired. It was the Americans themselves who grew weary of the war.

The undeclared war in Vietnam, fought nightly in all its horror on American television, divided the nation. Supporters saw the war as part of a defense against communist totalitarianism in all poor countries. Critics increasingly denounced it as an immoral, unsuccessful, and unnecessary intrusion into a complex and distant civil war. There were mass protests, often led by college students.

Then in 1968, as the antiwar movement peaked, a chastened President Johnson tacitly admitted defeat: he called for negotiations with North Vietnam and announced that he would not run for re-election.

President Nixon cleverly tried to conceal this defeat by bombing heavily and extending the war to Cambodia while negotiations continued and American troops were gradually withdrawn. In January 1973, he and Henry Kissinger finally concluded a deceptive peace agreement, which allowed remaining American forces to complete their withdrawal before the civil war resumed. For two years the government of South Vietnam seemed to hold its own, but in the wake of the Watergate paralysis of government and Nixon's resignation it suddenly collapsed. After more than thirty-five years of battle, the Vietnamese communists had unified their country.

Defeat in Vietnam had a traumatic effect on the United States. Because American action in Vietnam was financed by massive deficit spending, it set off a wave of inflation, which eventually halted the expensive war on domestic poverty and even discredited all social reform. Not only did Vietnam leave a heritage of division; it also badly shook American self-confidence. Defeat and widespread denunciation left the United States uncertain about its proper role in world affairs. The long-dominant belief that the interests of the United States required an unending global struggle against the spread of communism had been gravely damaged. But by the early 1980s no alternative concept had won general support.

## ECONOMIC NATIONALISM IN LATIN AMERICA

Although the countries of Latin America share a European heritage, and specifically a Spanish-Portuguese heritage, their striking differences make it difficult to generalize meaningfully about recent Latin Americn history. Yet a growing economic nationalism seems unmistakable. As the early nineteenth century saw Spanish and Portuguese colonies win wars of political independence, recent history has been an ongoing quest for genuine economic independence through local control and industrialization. This quest has sometimes brought Latin American countries into sharp conflict with Europe and the United States, in turn encouraging a new feeling of solidarity with Africa, Asia, and Third World causes.

To understand the rise of economic nationalism, one must remember that Latin American countries developed as producers of foodstuffs and raw materials, which were exported to Europe and the United States in return for manufactured goods and capital investment. This exchange was mutually beneficial, especially in the later nineteenth century, and the countries that participated most actively, like Argentina and southern Brazil, became the wealthiest and most advanced. There was, however, a heavy price to pay. Latin America became very dependent on foreign markets, products, and investments. Industry did not develop and large landowners profited most, further enhancing their social and political power.

The old international division of labor, disrupted by the First World War but reestablished in the 1920s, was finally destroyed by the Great Depression – a historical turning point as critical for Latin America as for the United States. Prices and exports of Latin American commodities collapsed as Europe and the United States drastically reduced their purchases and raised tariffs to protect domestic producers. With foreign sales plummeting,

Latin American countries could not buy industrial goods abroad. Latin America suffered the full force of the global economic crisis.

The result in the larger, more important Latin American countries was a profound shift in the direction of economic nationalism after 1930. The more popularly based governments worked to reduce foreign influence and gain control of their own economies and natural resources. They energetically promoted national industry by means of high tariffs, government grants, and even state enterprise. They favored the lower-middle and urban working classes with social benefits and higher wages in order to increase their purchasing power and gain their support. These efforts at recovery were fairly successful. By the late 1940s, the factories of Argentina, Brazil, and Chile could generally satisfy domestic consumer demand for the products of light industry. In the 1950s, some countries began moving into heavy industry. Economic nationalism and the rise of industry are particularly striking in the two largest and most influential countries, Mexico and Brazil, which together account for half the population of Latin America.

*MEXICO* Overthrowing the elitist, upper-class rule of the tyrant Porfiro Díaz, the spasmodic, often-chaotic Mexican Revolution of 1910 culminated in 1917 in a new constitution. This radical nationalistic document called for universal suffrage, massive land reform, benefits for labor, and strict control of foreign capital. Actual progress was quite modest until 1934, when a charismatic young Indian from a poor family, Lazaro Cárdenas, became president and dramatically revived the languishing revolution. Under Cárdenas, many large estates were divided up among small farmers or returned undivided to Indian communities.

Meanwhile, because foreign capitalists were being discouraged, Mexican businessmen built many small factories and managed to thrive. The government also championed the cause of industrial workers. In 1938, when Mexican workers became locked in a bitter dispute with British and American oil companies, Cárdenas nationalized the petroleum industry – to the astonishment of a world unaccustomed to such actions. Finally, the 1930s saw the flowering of a distinctive Mexican culture, which proudly embraced its long-despised Indian past and gloried in the modern national revolution.

In 1940 the official, semiauthoritarian party that has governed Mexico continuously since the revolution selected the first of a series of more moderate presidents. Steadfast in their radical, occasionally anti-American rhetoric, these presidents used the full power of the state to promote industrialization through a judicious mixture of public, private, and even foreign enterprise. The Mexican economy grew rapidly, at about 6 percent per year from the early 1940s to the late 1960s, with the upper and middle classes reaping the lion's share of the benefits.

*BRAZIL* After the fall of Brazil's monarchy in 1889, politics was largely dominated by the coffee barons and by regional rivalries. These rivalries and deteriorating economic conditions allowed a military revolt led by Getulio Vargas, governor of one of Brazil's larger states, to seize control of the federal government in 1930. Vargas, who proved to be a consummate politician, fragmented the opposition and established a mild dictatorship that lasted until 1945. Vargas's rule was generally popular, combining as it did effective economic nationalism and moderate social reform.

Somewhat like President Franklin Roosevelt in the United States, Vargas decisively

JOSÉ CLEMENTE OROZCO (1883–1949) *was one of the great and committed painters of the Mexican Revolution. Orozco believed that art should reflect the "new order of things" and inspire the common people — the workers and the peasants. This vibrant central* *mural in the National Palace in Mexico City, one of Orozco's many great wall paintings, depicts a brutal Spanish conquest and a liberating revolution. (Palacio Nacional, Mexico City)*

tipped the balance of political power away from the Brazilian states to the ever-expanding federal government, which became a truly national government for the first time. Vargas and his allies also set out to industrialize Brazil and gain economic independence. While the national coffee board used mountains of surplus coffee beans to fire railroad locomotives, the government supported Brazilian manufacturers with high tariffs, generous loans, and labor peace. This probusiness policy did not prevent new social legislation: workers received shorter hours, pensions, health and accident insurance, paid vacations, and other benefits. Finally, Vargas shrewdly upheld the nationalist cause in his relations with the giant to the north. Early in the Second World War, for example, he traded U.S. military bases in Brazil for American construction of Brazil's first huge steel-making complex. By 1945, when the authoritarian Vargas fell in a bloodless military coup calling for greater political liberty, Brazil was modernizing rapidly.

Modernization continued for the next fifteen years. The economy boomed. Presidential politics were re-established, while the military kept a watchful eye for extremism among the civilian politicians. Economic nationalism was especially vigorous under the flamboyant President Kubitschek (1956–1960), a doctor of German-Czech descent. The government borrowed heavily from international bankers to promote industry and built the extravagant new capital of Brasilia in the midst of a wilderness. When Brazil's creditors demanded more conservative policies to stem inflation, Kubitschek delighted the nationalists with his firm and successful refusal. His slogan was "Fifty Years' Progress in Five," and he seemed to mean it.

The Brazilian and Mexican formula of national economic development, varying degrees of electoral competition, and social reform was shared by some other Latin American countries, notably Argentina and Chile. By the late 1950s optimism was widespread, if cautious. Economic and social progress seemed to promise less violent, more democratic politics. These expectations were profoundly shaken by the Cuban revolution.

## THE CUBAN REVOLUTION

Although many aspects of the Cuban revolution are obscured by controversy, certain background conditions are clear. First, after achieving independence in 1898, Cuba was for many years virtually an American protectorate. The Cuban constitution gave the United States the legal right to intervene in Cuban affairs, a right that was frequently exercised until Roosevelt renounced it in 1934. Second, and partly because the American army had often been the real power, Cuba's political institutions were weak and its politicians were extraordinarily corrupt. Under the strongman Fulgencio Batista, an opportunistic ex-sergeant who controlled the government almost continually from 1933 to 1958, graft and outright looting were a way of life. Third, Cuba was one of Latin America's most prosperous and advanced countries by the 1950s, but its sugar-and-tourist economy was dependent on the United States. Finally, the enormous differences between rich and poor in Cuba were typical of Latin America. But Cuba also had a strong Communist party, which was highly unusual.

Fidel Castro, a magnetic leader with the gift of oratory and a flair for propaganda, managed to unify anti-Batista elements in a revolutionary front. When Castro's guerrilla forces triumphed in late 1958, the new government's goals were unclear. Castro had promised a "real" revolution but had always laughed at charges that he was a communist. As the regime consolidated its power in 1959 and 1960, it became increasingly clear that "real" meant "communist" in Castro's mind. Wealthy Cubans, who owned three-quarters of the sugar industry and many profitable businesses, fled to Miami. Soon the middle class began to follow.

Meanwhile relations with the Eisenhower administration – which had indirectly supported Castro by refusing to sell arms to Batista after March 1958 – deteriorated rapidly. Thus, in April 1961, newly elected President Kennedy went ahead with a pre-existing CIA plan to use Cuban exiles to topple Castro. But the Kennedy administration lost its nerve and abandoned the exiles as soon as they were dumped ashore at the Bay of Pigs. This doomed the invasion and the exiles were quickly captured, to be ransomed later for $60 million.

The Bay of Pigs invasion – a triumph for Castro and a humiliating, roundly criticized fiasco for the United States – had significant consequences. It freed Castro to build his version of a communist society, and he did. Political life in Cuba featured "anti-imperialism," an alliance with the Soviet bloc, the dictatorship of the party, and a vigorously promoted Castro cult. Revolutionary enthusiasm was genuine among party activists, much of Cuba's youth, and some of the masses some of the time. Prisons and emigration silenced opposition. The economy was characterized by all-pervasive state ownership, collective farms, and Soviet trade and aid. Early efforts to industrialize ran aground, and sugar production at pre-Castro levels continued to dominate the economy. Socially, the regime

pursued equality and the creation of a new socialist personality. In short, revolutionary totalitarianism came to the Americas.

The failure of the United States' halfhearted effort to derail Castro heightened both hopes and fears that the Cuban revolution could spread throughout Latin America. As leftists were emboldened to try guerrilla warfare, conservatives became more rigid and suspicious of calls for change. In the United States, fear of communism aroused heightened cold-war-style interest in Latin America. Using the Organization of American States to isolate Cuba, the United States in 1961 pledged $10 billion in aid over ten years to a new hemispheric "Alliance for Progress." The Alliance was intended to promote long-term economic development and social reform, which American liberals typically assumed would immunize Latin America from the Cuban disease.

## THE NEW AUTHORITARIANISM IN LATIN AMERICA

U.S. aid did contribute modestly to continued Latin America economic development in the 1960s, although population growth cancelled out two-thirds of the increase on a per capita basis. Democratic social reforms – the other half of the Alliance for Progress formula – proceeded slowly, however. Instead, the era following the Cuban revolution saw the rise of extremism and a new kind of conservative authoritarianism. By the 1980s, only four Latin American countries – Costa Rica, Venezuela, Colombia, and Mexico – retained some measure of democratic government. Brazil, Argentina, and Chile are more representative of the general trend.

Influential Brazil led the way. Intense political competition in the early 1960s prompted President João Goulart to swing to

JUAN AND EVA PERÓN  *Perón appealed to Argentina's workers and industrialists with his social programs and economic nationalism. His beautiful wife Eva was a consummate politician in her own right. Here they are shown parading triumphantly at Perón's presidential inauguration for another six-year term in 1952. (United Press Photo)*

the left to gain fresh support. Castroism appeared to spread in the impoverished northeast, and mass meetings of leftists were answered by huge demonstrations of conservatives. Meanwhile Goulart called for radical change, proposing that the great landed estates be broken up and that Brazil's many illiterates receive the right to vote. When Goulart and his followers appeared ready to use force to implement their program, army leaders took over in 1964. The right-wing military government banned political parties

and ruled by decree. It showed little sign of giving up power in the early 1980s, as Brazil industrialized rapidly and strove for status as a great power.

In Argentina, the military intervened in 1955 to oust the dictatorial populist and economic nationalist Juan Perón, but it had restored elected government. Then, worried by a Peronist revival and heartened by the Brazilian example, the army took control in 1966 and again in 1976 after a brief civilian interlude. Each military takeover was followed by an escalation of repression, and culturally and economically advanced Argentina came to resemble a genuine police state.

If events in Argentina were discouraging, Chile was tragic. Chile has a population of predominantly European origin and a long tradition of democracy and moderate reform. Thus when Salvador Allende, a doctor and the Marxist head of a coalition of Communists, Socialists, and Radicals, won a plurality of 36 percent of the vote – only 2 percent more than the runner-up nationalist – in fair elections in 1970, he was duly elected president by the Congress. Allende completed the nationalization of the American-owned copper companies – the great majority of Chileans had already embraced economic nationalism – and proceeded to socialize private industry, accelerate the breakup of landed estates, and radicalize the poor.

Marxism in action evoked a powerful backlash in Chile. The middle class fought back, and by 1973 Chile seemed headed for civil war. Then, with enormous conservative support and some U.S. backing, the traditionally impartial army struck in a well-organized coup. Allende died, probably murdered, and thousands of "leftists" were arrested, or worse, as the military imposed a harsh despotism and settled down for a long rule.

The revival of antidemocratic authoritarianism in Latin America is clearly a major development. Interpretations, however, vary widely. At one level, military government is clearly part of a determined conservative resurgence, which has at least temporarily squelched not only the Marxist and socialist challenge but most liberal and moderate reform as well. Instructed by the Cuban experience, the upper and middle classes had no intention of playing dead: if dictatorship was necessary to protect privilege and property, so

be it. Military governments effectively defended private capital and halted or reversed radical change. (Some blamed it all on Washington, the CIA, and American corporations, steadfastly ignoring the obvious decline of U.S. power, influence, and direct investment in Latin America.)

Yet some observers saw in the new military governments something more than the traditional weakness of Latin American democracy and cold-war fears of communism. They noted that military takeovers grew out of intense crises that threatened national unity as well as the upper classes. In such circumstances, the politically conscious officer corps saw the military as the only institution capable of preventing chaos in the foreseeable future.

Moreover, the new authoritarians were determined modernizers. Eager to catch up with the advanced countries, they were often deeply committed to nationalism, industrialization, technology, and even modest social progress. In a larger sense, Latin America seemed to be moving closer to Asia and Africa, where a multitude of authoritarian governments and military leaders have declared themselves best suited to meet the enormous challenges of the late twentieth century.

◆

The recovery of Europe and the Americas during and after World War Two is one of the most remarkable chapters in the long, uneven course of Western civilization. Although the dangerous tensions of the cold war frustrated fond hopes for a truly peaceful international order, the transition from imperialism to decolonialization proceeded rapidly, surprisingly smoothly, and without serious damage to western Europe. Instead, genuine political democracy gained unprecedented strength in the West, and economic progress quickened the pace of ongoing social and cultural transformation. Thus the tremendous promise inherent in Western society's fateful embrace of "the dual revolution," which had begun in France and England in the late eighteenth century and which had momentarily halted in the agonies of the Great Depression and the horrors of Nazi totalitarianism, was largely if perhaps only temporarily realized in the shining achievements of the postwar era.

## NOTES

1. William Bullitt, "How We Won the War and Lost the Peace," *Life,* XXV (30 August 1948):94.

2. Quoted by N. Graebner, *Cold War Diplomacy, 1945–1960,* Van Nostrand, Princeton, N.J., 1962, p d17.

3. Ibid.

4. Quoted by A. Crawley, *The Spoils of War: The Rise of Western Germany Since 1945,* Bobbs-Merrill, New York, 1973, p. 10.

5. Quoted in J. Hennessy, *Economic "Miracles,"* André Deutsch, London, 1964, p. 5.

6. P. Van Zeeland, in *European Integration,* ed. C. G. Haines, Johns Hopkins Press, Baltimore, 1957, p. xi.

7. Lord Milner, quoted by R. von Albertini, "The Impact of Two World Wars on the Decline of Colonialism," *Journal of Contemporary History* 4 (January 1969):17.

8. Quoted by H. Smith, *The Russians,* Quadrangle/New York Times, New York, 1976, p. 303.

9. Quoted by D. Treadgold, *Twentieth Century Russia,* Houghton Mifflin, Boston, 5th ed., 1981 p. 442.

10. Quoted by M. Tatu, *Power in the Kremlin: From Khrushchev to Kosygin,* Viking Press, New York, 1968, p. 248.

11. Quoted by I. Deutscher, in *Soviet Society,* ed. A. Inkeles and K. Geiger, Houghton Mifflin, Boston, 1961, p.41.

12. Quoted by Smith, pp. 455–456.

13. Quoted by S. E. Morison et al., *A Concise History of the American Republic,* Oxford University Press, New York, 1977, p. 697.

14. Ibid., p. 735.

## SUGGESTED READING

B. H. Liddell Hart, *The History of the Second World War* (1971), is a good overview of military developments. Three dramatic studies of special aspects of the war are A. Dallin, *German Rule in Russia, 1941–1945* (1957), which analyzes the effects of Nazi occupation policies on the Soviet population; L. Collins and D. La Pierre, *Is Paris Burning?* (1965), a best-selling account of the liberation of Paris and Hitler's plans to destroy the city; and J. Toland, *The Last 100 Days* (1966), a lively account of the end of the war. Great leaders and matchless stylists, Winston Churchill and Charles de Gaulle have both written histories of the war in the form of memoirs. Other interesting memoirs are those of Harry Truman (1958); Dwight Eisenhower, *Crusade in Europe* (1948); and Dean Acheson, *Present at the Creation* (1969), a beautifully written defense of American foreign policy in the early cold war. W. A. Williams, *The Tragedy of American Diplomacy* (1962), and G. Kolko, *The Politics of War* (1968), claim, on the contrary, that the United States was primarily responsible for the conflict with the Soviet Union. A. Fontaine, a French journalist, provides a more balanced approach in his *History of the Cold War,* 2 vols. (1968). V. Mastny's thorough investigation of Stalin's war aims, *Russia's Road to the Cold War* (1979), is highly recommended.

R. Mayne, *The Recovery of Europe, 1945–1973,* rev. ed. (1973), and N. Luxenburg, *Europe Since World War II,* rev. ed., (1979), are recommended general surveys, as are two works by W. Laqueur, *Europe*

*Since Hitler* (1972), and *A Continent Astray, 1970–1978* (1979). T. White, *Fire in the Ashes* (1953), is a vivid view of European resurgence and Marshall Plan aid by an outstanding journalist. Postwar economic and technological developments are carefully analyzed by D. S. Landes, *The Unbound Prometheus: Technological Change and Industrial Development in Western Europe from 1750 to the Present* (1969). A. Shonfield, *Modern Capitalism* (1965), provides an engaging, optimistic assessment of the growing importance of government investment and planning in European economic life. F. R. Willis, *France, Germany, and the New Europe, 1945–1967* (1968), is useful for postwar European diplomacy. Three outstanding works on France are J. Ardagh, *The New French Revolution* (1969), which puts the momentous social changes since 1945 in human terms; G. Wright, *Rural Revolution in France: the Peasantry in the Twentieth Century* (1964); and D. L. Hanley et al., eds., *France: Politics and Society Since 1945* (1979). R. Dahrendorf, *Society and Democracy in Germany* (1971), and H. S. Hughes, *The United States and Italy* (1968), are excellent introductions to recent German and Italian history. A. H. Halsey, *Change in British Society,* 2nd ed. (1981), is good on recent developments. H. Seton-Watson, *The East European Revolution* (1965), is a good history of the communization of eastern Europe, and S. Fischer-Galati, ed., *Eastern Europe in the Sixties* (1963), discusses major developments. P. Zinner, *National Communism and Popular Revolt in Eastern Europe* (1956) and *Revolution in Hungary* (1962), are excellent on the tragic events of 1956. H. Schwartz, *Prague's 200 Days* (1969), is an engrossing account of events in Czechoslovakia in 1968. W. Connor, *Socialism, Politics and Equality: Hierarchy and Change in Eastern Europe and the USSR* (1979), and J. Hough and M. Fainsod, *How the Soviet Union is Governed* (1978), are important general studies. A. Amalrik, *Will the Soviet Union Survive Until 1984?* (1970), is a fascinating interpretation of contemporary Soviet society and politics by a Russian who paid for his criticism with prison and exile. A. Lee, *Russian Journal* (1981), and H. Smith, *The Russians* (1976), are excellent journalistic yet comprehensive reports by perceptive American observers.

R. von Albertini, *Decolonialization* (1971), is a good history of the decline and fall of European empires. The tremendous economic problems of the newly independent countries of Asia and Africa are discussed sympathetically by B. Ward, *Rich Nations and Poor Nations* (1962), and R. Heilbroner, *The Great Ascent* (1953).

Two excellent general studies on Latin America are J. E. Fagg, *Latin America: A General History,* 3rd. ed. (1977), and R. J. Shafer, *A History of Latin America* (1978). Both books have detailed suggestions for further reading. D. Collier, ed., *The New Authoritarianism in Latin America* (1979), is an excellent introduction to contemporary political developments.

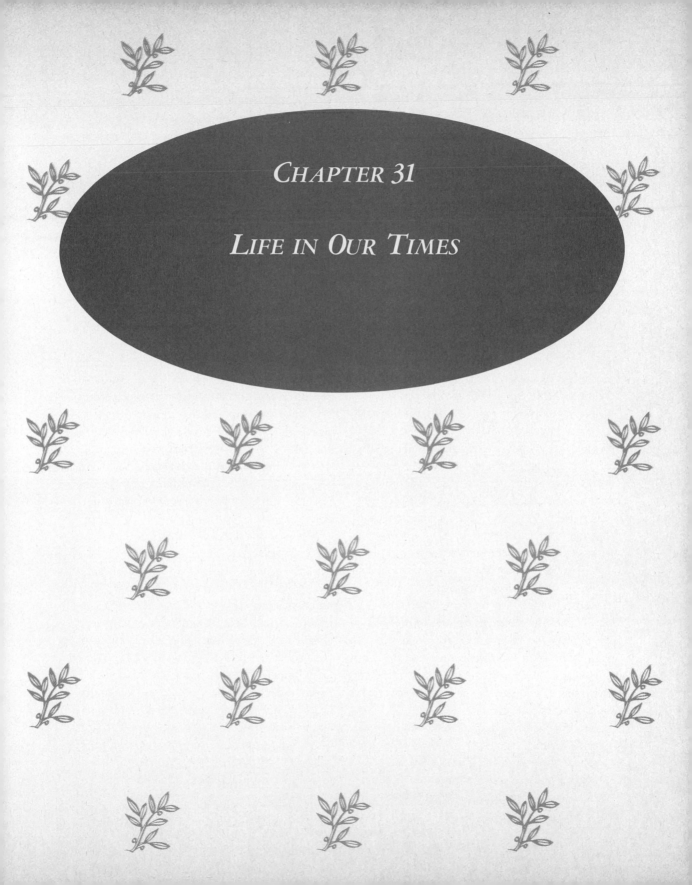

# CHAPTER 31

## LIFE IN OUR TIMES

*WHILE EUROPE* staged its astonishing political and economic recovery from the Nazi nightmare, the patterns of everyday life and the structure of Western society were changing no less rapidly and remarkably. This will come as no surprise. Thinking about modern life, one immediately thinks about the inventions and new technologies – the atomic bomb, television, computers, jet planes, contraceptive pills, to name only a few – that have so profoundly affected human existence. One also thinks of the new attitudes and demands of different groups in society, which are reflected in such phenomena as the ever-expanding role of government, the revolt of youth in the late 1960s, the women's movement, and concern about damage to the environment. Rapid social change is clearly a fact of modern life in the Western world.

It is by no means easy to make sense out of all these changes. Many "revolutions" and "crises" are merely passing fads, sensationally ballyhooed by the media today but forgotten tomorrow. Some genuinely critical developments, such as those involving the environment or the family, are complex and contradictory, making it hard to understand what is really happening, much less to explain why. In short, we are simply too close to what is going on and lack vital perspective. It is, therefore, most difficult to interpret intelligently the life we all think we know best – the life of our own times. As Voltaire once said, "The man who ventures to write contemporary history must expect to be attacked both for everything he has said and everything he has not said."[1]

Yet the historian must take a stand. How have Western society and everyday life changed since World War Two and why? What have these changes meant to people? These are the questions this chapter seeks to answer. The focus will be on three interrelated matters of particular significance: the spectacular development of science and technology, the gradual emergence of a new kind of society, and the evolving position of women and the role of the family.

## SCIENCE AND TECHNOLOGY

Ever since the scientific revolution of the seventeenth century and the Industrial Revolution at the end of the eighteenth century, scientific and technical developments have powerfully influenced attitudes, society, and everyday life. Never has this influence been stronger than since about 1940. Fantastic pipedreams of science fiction a brief century ago have become realities. Submarines pass under the North Pole, and astronauts walk on the moon. Skilled surgeons replace their patients' failing arteries with plastic tubing. Millions of people around the world simultaneously watch a historic event on television. And the end is not in sight.

The reason science and technology have been so productive and influential is that for the first time in history they have been effectively joined together on a massive scale. This union of "pure theoretical" science with "applied" science or "practical" technology had already made possible striking achievements in the late nineteenth century in some select fields, most notably organic chemistry, electricity, and preventive medicine. Generally, however, the separation of science and technology still predominated in the late 1930s. Most scientists were university professors, who were little interested in such practical matters as building better machines and inventing new products. Such problems were the concern of tinkering technicians and engineers, who were to a large extent trained on the job. Their accomplishments and discoveries owed much more to careful observation and trial-and-error experimentation than to theoretical science.

During World War Two, however, scientists and technicians increasingly marched to the sound of the same drummer. Both scientific research and technical expertise began to be directed at difficult but highly practical military problems. The result was a number of spectacular breakthroughs, such as radar and the atomic bomb, that had immediate wartime applications. After the war this close cooperation between pure science and applied technology continued with equal success. Indeed, the line between science and technology became harder and harder to draw.

The consequences of the new intimate link between science and technology were enormous. Seventeenth-century propagandists for science such as Francis Bacon had predicted that scientific knowledge of nature would give human beings the power to control the physical world. With such control, they believed, it would be possible to create material abundance and genuine well-being. The successful union of science and technology created new industries and spurred rapid economic growth after 1945, making this prediction finally come true for the great majority of people in Europe and North America.

At the same time, however, the unprecedented success of science in controlling and changing the physical environment has produced unexpected and unwanted side effects. Chemical fertilizers have poisoned rivers in addition to producing bumper crops. A great good like the virtual elimination of malaria-carrying mosquitoes with DDT dramatically lowered the death rate in tropical lands, but it

LORD RUTHERFORD *The great British physicist Ernest Rutherford shows the apparatus he used to split the atom in 1919. Until World War II science was still relatively inexpensive, impractical, and independent. (Cavendish Laboratory, University of Cambridge)*

also contributed to a population explosion in those areas.

The list of such unwelcome side effects is very long. By the late 1960s, concern about the undesirable side effects of technological change had brought into being a vigorous environmental movement. In 1977, French university students were convinced that only the economic problems of inflation and unemployment were as serious for society as damage to the environment; every other problem came far behind. Fully one-third of all students said they would vote for an "ecologist candidate" for president of France. The ability of science and technology to control and alter nature has proved to be a two-edged sword, which must be wielded with great care and responsibility.

### THE STIMULUS OF WORLD WAR TWO

Just before the outbreak of World War Two, a young Irish scientist and Communist named John Desmond Bernal wrote a book entitled *The Social Function of Science.* Bernal argued that the central government should be the source of funds for scientific research, and that these funds should be granted on the basis of the expected social and political benefits. Most scientists were horrified by Bernal's proposals, which were contradictory to their cherished ideals. Scientists were committed to designing their own research without any regard to its immediate usefulness. As late as 1937, the great physicist Ernest Rutherford could state that the work he and his colleagues were doing at Cambridge University in nuclear physics had no conceivable practical value for anyone and he expressed delight that such was the case. Nor did university scientists drool over government grants, since many had independent incomes to help finance their still-inexpensive equipment and experiments.

The Second World War changed this pattern. Pure science lost its impractical innocence. Most leading university scientists went to work on top-secret projects for their governments to help fight the war. The development of radar by British scientists was a particularly important outcome of this new kind of sharply focused research.

As early as 1934, the British Air Ministry set up a committee of scientists and engineers to study the problem of air defense systematically. Calculations by a leading British expert on radio waves suggested that the idea of a "death ray" so powerful it could destroy an attacking enemy aircraft was nonsense, but that detection of enemy aircraft by radio waves was theoretically possible. Radio waves emitted at intervals by a transmitter on the ground would bounce off flying aircraft, and a companion receiver on the ground would hear this echo and detect the approaching plane. Experiments went forward, and by 1939 the British had installed a very primitive radar system along the southern and eastern coasts of England.

Immediately after the outbreak of war with Germany in September 1939, the British military enlisted leading academic scientists in an all-out effort to improve the radar system. The basic problem was developing a high-powered transmitter capable of sending very short wavelengths, which could be precisely focused in a beam sweeping the sky like a searchlight. In summer 1940, British physicists made the dramatic technical breakthrough that solved this problem of short-wave transmission. The new and radically improved radar system that was quickly installed played a key role in Britain's victory in the battle for air supremacy in the fall of 1940. During the war many different types of radar were developed – for fighter planes, for bombers, for detection of submarines.

Since 1945, war-born microwave technology has generated endless applications, especially in telecommunications. Microwave transmission very conveniently carries long-distance telephone conversations, television programs, and messages to and from satellites.

The air war also greatly stimulated the development of jet aircraft and computers. Al-

ATOMIC WEAPONS *were the ultimate in state-directed scientific research. In this awesome photo the mushroom cloud of an American atomic bomb rises over the Pacific island of Bikini. (Joint Army Navy Task Force)*

though the first jet engines were built in the mid-1930s, large-scale government-directed research did not begin until right before the war. The challenge was to build a new kind of engine – a jet engine – capable of burning the low-grade "leftovers" of petroleum refining, thereby helping to overcome the desperate shortage of aviation fuel. The task proved extremely difficult and expensive. Only toward the end of the war did fast high-flying jet fighters become a reality. Quickly adopted for both military and peacetime purposes after the war, jet airplanes contributed to the enormous expansion of commercial aviation in the 1950s.

The problems of air defense spurred further research on electronic computers, which had barely come into existence before 1939. Computers calculated the very complex mathematical relationships between fast-moving planes and antiaircraft shells, so as to increase the likelihood of a hit.

Wartime needs led to many other major technical breakthroughs. Germany had little oil and was almost completely cut off from foreign supplies; Germany's scientists and engineers found ways to turn coal into gasoline so the German war machine did not sputter to a halt. Long ignored after petroleum became cheap and abundant in the postwar era, this wartime advance is being restudied in both Europe and North America in this era of undependable and expensive foreign oil.

The most spectacular result of directed scientific research during the war was the atomic bomb. In August 1939, Albert Einstein wrote to President Franklin Roosevelt stating that recent work in physics suggested that

*it may become possible to set up a nuclear chain reaction in a large mass of uranium, by which vast amounts of power and large quantities of new*

*radium-like elements would be generated. . . . This new phenomenon would also lead to the construction of bombs, and it is conceivable – though much less certain – that extremely powerful bombs of a new type may thus be constructed.*[2]

This letter and ongoing experiments by nuclear physicists led to the top-secret Manhattan Project and the decision to build the atomic bomb.

The American government spared no expense to turn a theoretical possibility into a practical reality. A mammoth crash program went forward in several universities and special laboratories, the most important of which was the newly created laboratory at Los Alamos in the wilds of New Mexico. The Los Alamos laboratory was masterfully directed from 1942 by J. Robert Oppenheimer (1904–1967), a professor and theoretical physicist. Its sole objective was to design and build an atomic bomb. Toward that end Oppenheimer assembled a team of brilliant American and European scientists and managed to get them to cooperate effectively. After three years of intensive effort, the first atomic bomb was successfully tested in early 1945. In August 1945 two bombs were dropped on Hiroshima and Nagasaki, ending the war with Japan.

The atomic bomb showed the world both the awesome power and the heavy moral responsibilities of modern science and its high priests. As one of Oppenheimer's troubled colleagues exclaimed as he watched the first mushroom cloud rise over the American desert: "We are all sons-of-bitches now!"[3]

### THE RISE OF BIG SCIENCE

The spectacular results of directed research during World War Two inspired a new model for science – Big Science. By combining theoretical work with sophisticated engineering in a large organization, Big Science can attack extremely difficult problems. Solution of these problems leads to new and better products for consumers and to new and better weapons for the military. In any event, the assumption is that almost any conceivable technical goal may be attained. Big Science is extremely expensive. Indeed, its appetite for funds is so great that it can be financed only by governments and large corporations. Thus, the ties between science and tax-paying society have grown very close.

Science has become so "big" largely because its equipment has become ever more complex and expensive. Because many advances depend directly on better instruments, the trend toward bigness goes on unabated. This trend has been particularly pronounced in atomic physics, perhaps the most prestigious and influential area of modern science. When Rutherford first "split the atom" in 1919, his equipment cost only a few dollars. In the 1930s, the price of an accelerator, or "atom smasher," reached $10,000, and the accelerators used in high-energy experiments while the atomic bomb was being built were in the $100,000 range. By 1960, however, when the west European nations pooled their resources in the European Council for Nuclear Research (CERN) to build an accelerator outside of Geneva — an accelerator with power in billions rather than millions of electron volts — the cost had jumped to $30 million.

These big accelerators have done an amazingly good job of prying apart atoms, and over two hundred different particles have been identified so far. Yet new answers produce new questions, and the logic of ever-more-sophisticated observations demands ever-more-powerful accelerators. In order to catch up with western Europe's "superCERN" accelerator, the Fermi laboratory outside of Chicago is building a comparable accelerator with a power of a trillion electron volts at a cost of $400 million dollars, with society — through the U.S. Congress — footing the bill.

Astronomers have followed physicists in the ways of Big Science. Their new eye is the radio telescope, which picks up radio emissions rather than light. The largest of these very costly radio telescopes sits atop a mountain and has a bowl a thousand feet wide to focus the radio signals from space. The receiver is suspended on cables stretched across the bowl below. Aeronautical research and development have also attained mammoth proportions. The cost of the Anglo-French *Concorde,* the first supersonic passenger airliner, has gone into the billions. The biggest area of Big Science is space research. By 1967, the U.S. National Aeronautics and Space Administration was spending $5 billion a year just for its experiments, although NASA's budget declined substantially in the 1970s.

Even ordinary science has become big and expensive by historical standards. The least costly laboratory capable of doing useful research in either pure or applied science now requires around $200,000 a year.

Populous, victorious, and wealthy, the United States took the lead in Big Science after World War Two. Between 1945 and 1965, spending on scientific research and development in the United States grew five times as fast as the national income. By 1965, fully 3 percent of all income in the United States was spent on science. While large American corporations maintained impressive research laboratories, fully three-quarters of all funds spent on scientific research and development in the United States was coming from the government by 1965. It was gener-

*THE APOLLO PROGRAM   Astronauts Neil Armstrong, Michael Collins, and Edwin Aldrin, Jr., took off from Florida on July 16, 1969 in the Apollo II spacecraft. Astronaut Armstrong was the first man to set foot on the moon, four days later, on July 20. His footprint in the lunar dust brought to reality another fantasy of science fiction. The astronauts splashed down in the Pacific Ocean, and recovery was made by the U.S.S. Hornet on July 24. (National Aeronautics and Space Administration)*

ally accepted that government should finance science heavily. One wit has pointed out that by the mid-1960s the "science policy" of the supposedly conservative Republican party in the United States was almost identical to that of the supposedly revolutionary Communist party of the Soviet Union.

One of the reasons for the similarity was that science was not demobilized in either country after the war. Indeed, scientists remained a critical part of every major military establishment and, since 1945 as during World War Two, a large portion of all scientific research has gone for "defense." Jet bombers gave way to rockets, battleships were overtaken by submarines with nuclear warheads, and spy planes were replaced with spy satellites. All such new weapons demanded breakthroughs no less remarkable than those of radar and the first atomic bomb. Roughly one-quarter of all men and women trained in science and engineering in the West – and perhaps more in the Soviet Union – have been employed full-time in the design and production of weapons to kill other men and women.

The rapid expansion of government-financed research in the United States attracted many of Europe's best scientists in the 1950s and 1960s. Thoughtful Europeans lamented this "brain drain." In his best seller *The American Challenge* (1967), the French journalist Jean-Jacques Servan-Schreiber warned that Europe was falling hopelessly behind the United States in science and technology. The only hope was to copy American patterns of research before the United States achieved an absolute stranglehold on computers, jet aircraft, atomic energy, and indeed most of the vital dynamic sectors of the late twentieth-century economy.

As the United States entered its time of troubles with the Vietnam War and began spending relatively less on scientific research, Europe did respond to the American challenge. By pooling their efforts and spending more on science and engineering, and specifically by concentrating on such projects as the *Concorde* supersonic passenger airliner and the peaceful uses of atomic energy, European countries created their own Big Science. By the late 1970s and early 1980s many European nations were devoting a substantial percentage of their income to research and development and had achieved equality with the United States in many fields of scientific endeavor (see Figure 31.1).

## THE LIFE OF SCIENTISTS AND TECHNOLOGISTS

The rise of Big Science and of close ties between science and technology have greatly altered the lives of scientists. The scientific community is, first of all, much larger than ever before: of all the scientists who have ever lived, nine out of ten are alive today. The astonishing fact is that the number of scientists has been doubling every fifteen years for the past three centuries. There are, therefore, about four times as many scientists today as when the Second World War ended, just as there are a *million times* as many scientists as there were in 1670. Scientists, technologists, engineers, and medical specialists count in modern society, in part because there are so many of them.

One important consequence of the bigness of science is its high degree of specialization. With close to a hundred thousand scientific journals currently being published, no one can possibly master a broad field like physics or medicine. Instead, a field like physics is constantly dividing and subdividing into new specialties and subdisciplines. The fifty or hundred men and women who are truly abreast of the latest developments in a highly specialized field form an international "invisible college." Cooperating and competing, communicating through special journals and conferences, the leading members of these invisible colleges keep the problems of the subdiscipline under constant attack. Thus, intense specialization has undoubtedly increased the rates at which both basic knowledge is acquired and practical applications are made.

Highly specialized modern scientists and technologists must normally work as members of a team. The problems and equipment of Big Science are simply too complicated and expensive for a person to work effectively as

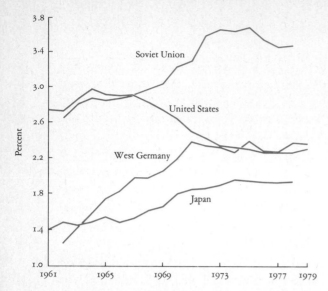

FIGURE 31.1 RESEARCH AND DEVELOPMENT EXPENDITURES AS A PERCENTAGE OF GNP IN THE UNITED STATES, SOVIET UNION, WEST GERMANY, AND JAPAN, 1961–1979 *While the United States spent less of its national income on research and development after the early 1960s, European nations and Japan spent more. This helped Europe and Japan narrow or even close the technological gap that had existed since the end of World War II. (Source: Data Resources, Inc.)*

an individual researcher. The collaborative "team" character of much of modern scientific research – members of invisible colleges are typically the leaders of such teams – has completely changed the work and lifestyle of modern scientists. Old-fashioned, prewar scientists were like professional golfers – lonely individuals who must make all the shots themselves. Modern scientists and technologists are more like the members of American professional football organizations. There are owners and directors, coaches and assistant coaches, overpaid stars and unsung heroes, veterans and rookies, kickoff specialists and substitutes, trainers and water boys, and even

mini-skirted beauties prancing on the sidelines.

If this parallel seems fanciful, consider the research group of Luis Alvarez at the high-energy physics Radiation Laboratory of the University of California at Berkeley in the late 1960s. This group consisted of more than two hundred people. At the top were Alvarez and about twenty Ph.D.s, followed by twenty graduate research assistants and fourteen full-time engineers. Almost fifty people were categorized as "technical leadership" – computer programmers, equipment operators, and so on. Finally, there were more than a hundred "technical assistants" – primarily scanners who analyzed photographs showing the tracks of particles after various collisions. A laboratory like that of CERN outside Geneva resembles a small city of several thousand people – scientists, technicians, and every kind of support personnel. A great deal of modern science and technology goes on, therefore, in large well-defined bureaucratic, organizations. The individual is very often a small cog in a great machine, a member of a scientific army.

The advent of large-scale scientific bureaucracies has led to the emergence of a new group, science managers and research administrators. Such managers generally have scientific backgrounds, but their main tasks are scheduling research, managing people, and seeking money from politicians or financial committees of large corporations. This last function is particularly important, for there are limits to what even the wealthiest governments and corporations will spend for research. Competition for funds is always intense.

Many science managers are government bureaucrats. These managers dole out funds and "referee" the scientific teams that are actually playing on the field. Is the *Concorde* supersonic jet too noisy to land in New York City? Does saccharin cause cancer, and should it be banned? The list of potential questions is endless. The number of such referees and the penalties they are imposing are both exploding, driven by public alarm about undesirable side effects of technological advance. More generally, the growth of the scientific bureaucracy suggests how scientists and technologists permeate the entire society and many aspects of life.

Two other changes in the lives of scientists may be noted briefly. One is the difficulty of appraising an individual's contribution to a collaborative team effort. Who deserves the real credit (or blame) for a paper coauthored by a group of twenty-five physicists? Even in a field like chemistry, which is still relatively "small" in its research techniques, more than two-thirds of all papers now have two or more authors. Questions of proper recognition within the team effort are thus very complicated and preoccupying to modern scientists.

Second and relatedly, modern science has become highly, even brutally, competitive. This competitiveness is well depicted in Nobel Prize winner James Watson's fascinating book *The Double Helix,* which tells how in 1953 Watson and an English colleague discovered the structure of DNA, the vital molecule of heredity. A brash young American Ph.D. in his twenties, Watson seemed almost obsessed by the idea that some other research team would find the solution first and thereby deprive him of the fame and fortune he desperately wanted. With so many thousands of like-minded researchers in the wealthy countries of the world, it is hardly surprising that scientific and technical knowledge rushes forward.

## TOWARD A NEW SOCIETY

The prodigious expansion of science and technology has greatly affected the peoples of the Western world. By creating new products and vastly improved methods of manufacturing and farming, it has fueled rapid economic growth and rising standards of living. Moreover, especially in Europe, scientific and technological progress, combined with economic prosperity, have gone a long way toward creating a whole new society since World War Two.

This new society has been given many catchy titles. Some call it "the technocratic society," a society of highly trained specialists and experts. For others, fascinated by the great increase in personal wealth, it is "the affluent society" or "the consumer society." For those struck by the profusion of government-provided social services, it is simply "the welfare state." For still others, it is "the permissive society," where established codes of conduct no longer prevail. In fact, contemporary Western society is all of these: technocratic, affluent, welfare-oriented, and permissive. These characteristics result from changes in the class structure and indicate undeniable social progress.

### THE CHANGING CLASS STRUCTURE

Since 1945, European society has become more mobile and more democratic. Old class barriers have been relaxed, and class distinctions have become fuzzier.

Changes in the structure of the middle class, directly related to the expansion of science and technology, have been particularly influential in the general drift toward a less rigid class structure. The model for the mid-

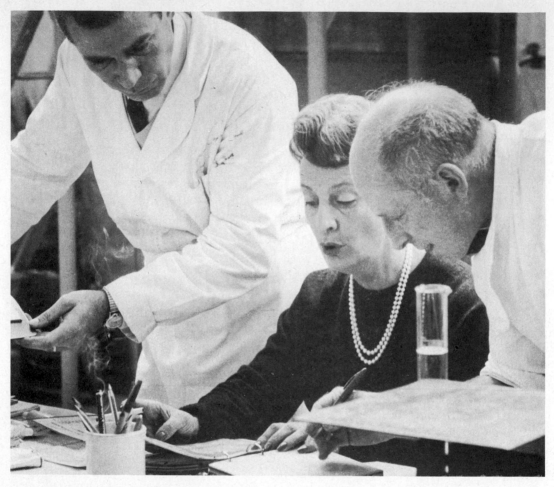

*A MODERN MANAGER Despite lingering discrimination, women are increasingly found in the new middle class of salaried experts, be they in business, science, or technology. (Niépce-Rapho)*

dle class in the nineteenth and early twentieth centuries was the independent, self-employed individual, who owned a business or practiced a liberal profession like law or medicine. Many businesses and professional partnerships were tightly held family firms. Marriage into such a family often provided the best opportunity for an outsider to rise to the top. Ownership of property, usually inherited property, and strong family ties were the usual keys to wealth and standing within the middle class.

This traditional pattern, which first changed in the United States and the Soviet Union (for very different reasons) before the Second World War, has declined drastically in western Europe since 1945. A new breed of managers and experts has risen to replace traditional propertyowners as the leaders of the middle class. Within large bureaucratic corporations and government, men and women increasingly advance as individuals and on the basis of merit (and luck). Ability to serve the needs of a large organization, which usually depends on special expertise, has largely replaced inherited property and family connections in determining an individual's social position in the middle and upper middle class. Social mobility for individuals, both upward and downward, has increased. At the same time, the middle class has grown massively and has become harder to define.

There are a number of reasons for these developments. Rapid industrial and technological expansion created in large corporations and government agencies a powerful demand for technologists and managers capable of responding effectively to an ever-more-complicated world. This growing army of specialists – the backbone of the new middle class – can be led effectively only by like-minded individuals, of whom only a few at best can come from the old owning families.

Second, the old propertied middle class has lost control of many of its formerly family-owned businesses. Even very wealthy families have had to call on the general investing public for capital, and heavy inheritance taxes have forced sales of stock, further diluting family influence. Many small businesses (including family farms) simply passed out of existence, and their ex-owners joined the ranks of salaried employees. In Germany in 1950, for example, 33 percent of the labor force were self-employed and 20 percent were white-collar workers. By 1962, the percentages for these two groups were exactly reversed. Moreover, the wave of nationalization in western and eastern Europe after the Second World War automatically replaced capitalist owners with salaried managers and civil servants in state-owned companies.

Top managers and ranking civil servants represent, therefore, the model for a new middle class of salaried specialists. Well paid and highly trained, often with backgrounds in science or engineering or accounting, these experts increasingly come from all social classes, including the working class. Pragmatic and realistic, they are primarily concerned with efficiency and practical solutions to concrete problems. They tend not to be very interested in the old ideological debates about capitalism and socialism, confidently assuming that their skills are indispensable in either system or any combination of the two.

Indeed, the new middle class of experts and managers is an international class, not much different in socialist eastern Europe than in capitalist western Europe and North America. Everywhere successful managers and technocrats can pass on the opportunity for all-important advanced education to their children, but they cannot pass on the positions they have attained. Thus the new middle class, which is based largely on specialized skills and high levels of education, is more open, democratic, and insecure than the old propertied middle class.

The structure of the traditional lower classes has also become more flexible and open. There has been a massive exodus from farms and the countryside. One of the most traditional and least mobile groups in European society has drastically declined: since 1945, the number of peasants has declined by at least 50 percent in almost every European country. Meanwhile, because of rapid technological change, the industrial working class has ceased to expand, stabilizing at slightly less than one-half of the labor force in wealthy advanced countries. Job opportunities for white-collar and service employees, however, have expanded rapidly. Such employees bear a greater resemblance to the new middle class of salaried specialists than to industrial workers, who are themselves becoming better educated and more specialized. Developments within the lower classes have contributed, therefore, to the breakdown of rigid social divisions.

## SOCIAL SECURITY REFORMS AND RISING AFFLUENCE

While the demands of modern technology have been breaking down rigid class divisions, European governments since 1945 have reduced class tensions with a series of social security reforms. Many of these reforms simply strengthened social security measures first pioneered in Bismarck's Germany before World War One. Unemployment and sickness benefits were increased and extended, as were retirement benefits and old-age pensions. Other programs were new.

Britain's Labour government took the lead immediately after the Second World War in establishing a comprehensive national health system; other European governments followed the British example. Depending on the system, patients either received completely free medical care or paid only a very small portion of the total cost.

Most countries also introduced family allowances – direct government grants to parents to help them raise their children. Lower-paid workers generally received the largest allowances, and the rate per child often kept increasing until the third or fourth child. These allowances helped many poor families make ends meet. Most European governments also gave maternity grants and built inexpensive public housing for low-income families and individuals. Other social welfare programs ranged from cash bonuses for getting married in Belgium and Switzerland to subsidized vacations for housewives in Sweden.

It would be wrong to think that the expansion of social security services after World War Two has provided for every human need "from cradle to grave," as early advocates of the "welfare state" hoped and critics feared. But these social reforms do provide a humane floor of well-being below which very few individuals drop in advanced countries of northern and western Europe. (Social benefits are greatest in the wealthiest nations, such as Sweden, West Germany, Britain, and less in poorer areas of southern and eastern Europe.)

These reforms have also promoted greater social and economic equality. They are expensive, and paid for in part by high taxes on the rich. In Britain, for example, where social security benefits for the population at large and taxes on the rich have both become quite high, the top 5 percent of the population received about 14 percent of national income after taxes in 1957, as opposed to fully 43 percent in 1913. Thus, extensive welfare measures have leveled society both by raising the floor and by lowering the ceiling.

The rising standard of living and the spread of standardized, mass-produced consumer goods also work to level Western society. A hundred years ago, food and drink cost roughly two-thirds of the average family's income in western and northern Europe; today it takes only about a third to two-fifths of that family's income. Consumption of traditional staples like bread and potatoes has actually declined almost everywhere in Europe since 1945, yet because incomes have risen rapidly, people eat more meat, fish, and dairy products. The long-elusive goal of adequate and good food has been attained almost universally in advanced countries.

But progress introduces new problems. Today people in Europe and North America eat too much rather than too little, giving rise to an endless proliferation of diet foods and diet fads. Another problem is that modern consumers are often remarkably ignorant of basic nutrition. They stuff themseves with candy, soft drinks, French fries, and spongy white bread, and frequently get poor value for their money. Finally, the traditional pleasures of eating good food well prepared are suffering catastrophic declines in the age of fast-food franchises and mass-produced, hopelessly standardized burgers and buns.

The phenomenal expansion of the automobile industry exemplifies even more strikingly the emergence of the "consumer society." In the United States automobile ownership was commonplace far down the social scale by the mid-1920s, whereas only the rich could generally afford cars in Europe before the Second World War. In 1948, there were only 5 million cars in western Europe, and most ordinary people dreamed at most of stepping up from a bicycle to a motorcycle. With the development of cheaper, mass-produced cars, this situation changed rapidly. By 1957, the number of cars had increased to 15 million, and automobiles had become a standard item of middle-class consumption. By 1965, the number of cars in western Europe had tripled again to 44 million, and car ownership had come well within the range of better-paid workers.

Europeans took great pleasure in the products of the "gadget revolution" as well. Like Americans, Europeans filled their houses and apartments with washing machines, vacuum cleaners, refrigerators, dishwashers, radios, TVs, and stereo sets. The purchase of these and other consumer goods has been greatly facilitated by installment purchasing, which allows people to buy on credit. Before World War Two, Europeans had rarely bought "on time." But with the expansion of social security safeguards, reducing the need to accumu-

late savings for hard times, ordinary people are increasingly willing to take on debt. This change has far-reaching consequences.

Household appliances have become quite essential for most families. Middle-class women have to do much of their own housework, for young girls avoid domestic service like the plague. Moreover, more women than ever before work outside the home, and they need machines to help do house chores as quickly as possible. The power tools of "do-it-yourself" work have also become something of a necessity, for few dependable artisans are now available for household repairs.

Leisure and recreation occupies an important place in consumer societies. Indeed, with incomes rising and the workweek shrinking from roughly forty-eight hours right after the war to about forty-one hours today, leisure has become big business. In addition to ever-popular soccer matches and horse races, movies, and the more recent numbing addiction to television, individuals have at their disposal a vast range of commercialized hobbies, most of which can soak up a lot of cash. Newsstands are full of specialized magazines about everything from hunting and photography to knitting and antique collecting. Interest in "culture," as measured by attendance at concerts and exhibitions, has also increased. Even so, the commercialization of leisure through standardized manufactured products is striking.

The most astonishing leisure-time development in the consumer society has been the blossoming of mass travel and tourism. Before the Second World War travel for pleasure and relaxation was a rather aristocratic pastime. Most people had neither the time nor the money for it. But with month-long paid vacations required by law in most European countries, and widespread automobile ownership, beaches and ski resorts have become accessible to middling people and many workers. At certain times of year, hordes of Europeans surge to the sea or the mountains, and woe to the traveler who has not made arrangements well in advance. Packaged tours with cheap group flights and bargain hotel accommodations have made even distant lands easily accessible. One-fifth of West Germany's population travels abroad each year. A French company, the Club Méditerranée, has grown rich building imitation Tahitian paradises around the world. At Swedish nudist colonies on secluded west African beaches, secretaries and salesmen from Stockholm fleetingly worship the sun in the middle of the long northern winter. Truly, consumerism has come of age.

## RENEWED DISCONTENT AND THE STUDENT REVOLT

For twenty years after 1945, Europeans were preoccupied with the possibilities of economic progress and consumerism. There was little social tension, and ideological conflict went out of style. In the late 1960s, however, sharp criticism and discontent re-emerged. It was a common complaint that Europeans were richer but neither happier nor better. These doubts and disappointments persist to this day.

Simmering discontent in eastern Europe is not hard to understand. The gradual improvement in the standard of living stands in naked contrast to the ongoing lack of freedom in political and intellectual life, and makes that lack of freedom all the more distasteful. It is doubtful that such dissatisfaction will produce any major improvement in the foreseeable future, given the refinement of the techniques of repression in eastern Europe,

but discontent will almost certainly continue to smolder.

The reappearance of discontent in western Europe is not so easily explained. Since the mid-1950s, west European society has been prosperous, democratic, and permissive. Yet this did not prevent hostility to the existing order from growing among some children of the new society. Radical students, in particular, rejected the materialism of their parents and claimed that the new society was repressive and badly flawed. Though these criticisms and the movements they sparked were often ridiculed by the older generation, they reflected real problems of youth, education, and a society of specialists. They deserve closer attention.

In contrast to the United States, high school and university educations in Europe were limited for centuries to a small elite. That elite consisted mainly of young men and women from the well-to-do classes, along with a sprinkling of scholarship students from humble origins. Whereas 22 percent of the American population was going on to some form of higher education in 1950, only 3 to 4 percent of west European youths were doing so. Moreover, European education was still directed toward traditional fields: literature, law, medicine, and pure science. Its basic goal was to pass on culture and pure science to an elite, and, with the exception of law and medicine, applied training for specialists was not considered very important.

After World War Two public education in western Europe began to change dramatically. Enrollments exploded. By 1960 there were at least three times as many students going to some kind of university as there had been before the war, and the number continued to rise sharply until the 1970s. Holland had ten thousand university students in 1938 and a hundred thousand in 1960. In France 14 percent of young people went to a university in 1965, as opposed to 4.5 percent in 1950. With an increase in scholarships and a growing awareness that higher education was the key to success, European universities became more democratic, opening their doors to more students from the lower middle and lower classes. Finally, in response to the prodigious expansion of science and technology, the curriculum gradually changed. All sorts of new "practical" fields – from computer science to business administration – appeared alongside the old liberal arts and sciences.

The rapid expansion of higher education created problems as well as opportunities for students. Classes were badly overcrowded, and there was little contact with professors. Competition for grades became very intense. Moreover, although more "practical" areas of study were added, they were added less quickly than many students wanted. Thus many students felt that they were not getting the kind of education they needed for the modern world and that basic university reforms were absolutely necessary. The emergence of a distinctive "youth culture" also brought students into conflict with those symbols of the older generation and parental authority – professors and school officials.

These tensions within the exploding university population came to a head in the late 1960s and early 1970s. Following in the footsteps of their American counterparts, European university students rose to challenge their university administrations and even their governments. The most far-reaching of these revolts occurred in France in 1968. It began at the stark new University of Nanterre in the gloomy industrial suburbs of Paris. Students demanded both changes in the curriculum and a real voice in running the university. The

movement spread to the hallowed halls of the medieval Sorbonne in the heart of Paris. Students occupied buildings and took over the university. This takeover led to violent clashes with police, who were ordered in to break up a demonstration that was fast becoming an uprising.

The student radicals appealed to France's industrial workers for help. Rank-and-file workers ignored the advice of their cautious union officials, and a more or less spontaneous general strike spread across France in May 1968. It seemed certain that President de Gaulle's Fifth Republic would collapse. In fact, de Gaulle stiffened, declaring he was in favor of reforms but would oppose "bedwetting." Securing the firm support of French army commanders in West Germany, he moved troops toward Paris and called for new elections. Thoroughly frightened by the protest-turned-upheaval and fearful that a successful revolution could lead only to an eventual communist takeover, the masses of France voted for a return to law and order. De Gaulle and his party scored the biggest electoral victory in modern French history. The mini-revolution collapsed. By the early 1970s student protest in France and the rest of Europe had generally subsided.

The student protest of the 1960s, which peaked in 1968 in France, was due to more than overcrowded classrooms and outdated courses. It reflected a rebirth of romantic revolutionary idealism, which repudiated the quest for ever more consumer goods as stupid and destructive. The student revolt was also inspired by the Vietnam War, which served to radicalize many students in Europe and America. These students believed that the war in Vietnam demonstrated that Western civilization was immoral and imperialistic. Finally, the students of the late 1960s were a com-

STUDENT DEMONSTRATION IN PARIS *These rock-throwing students in the Latin Quarter of Paris are protesting against the government. Throughout May 1968 students often clashed with France's tough riot police in bloody street fighting. (Wide World Photos)*

pletely new generation: they had never known anything but prosperity and tranquillity, and they were bored with both.

The student revolt was also motivated by new perceptions about the new society of highly trained experts. Students realized that higher specialized education was necessary for success in life. Yet some reflective young peo-

ple feared that universities would soon do nothing but turn out docile technocrats both to stock and to serve "the establishment." These students also feared being locked into unsatisfying work in large, rigid organizations after graduation, or being rendered obsolete and unwanted by some new technical development.

Some student intellectuals saw the class of highly trained specialists they would enter as the new exploited class in society. The remedy to this situation, they believed, was "participation" – the democratizing of decisionmaking *within* large, specialized bureaucratic organizations. Only in this way would such organizations serve real human needs and not merely exploit the individual and the environment. Thus, the often unrealistic and undisciplined student radicals tried to answer a vital question: how is our complex new society of specialized experts to be made humane and responsive?

## WOMEN AND THE FAMILY

The growing emancipation of women in Europe and North America is unquestionably one of the most important developments in modern society. To be sure, there has been a good deal of semihysterical and irresponsible writing and discussion about women. Almost everyone is interested in the subject, and it lends itself well to the shallow sensationalism that characterizes so much of modern journalism. What is clear is that women today are demanding and winning new rights. Having shared fully in the postwar education revolution, women are better educated than ever before. Women are moving into areas of employment formerly closed to them. Married women in particular are much more likely to work outside the home than they were a few short years ago. Women no longer fatalistically accept childbearing and childrearing, for modern techniques of contraception have given them effective control over their bodies and the number and spacing of their offspring. In short, women are becoming more equal and independent, less confined and

stereotyped. A major transformation is in process.

The changing position of women is altering the modern family. Since the emancipation of women is far from complete, it is impossible to say at this point whether some major revolution is in process within the family. Certainly the family is evolving, but scare headlines about its impending demise are contradicted by much of the evidence. This will be apparent if we examine women's traditional role in the home and then women's new roles outside the home. We shall also look at problems of health care and old age that have special implications for women.

### MARRIAGE AND MOTHERHOOD

Before the Industrial Revolution most men and women married late, and substantial numbers never married at all. Once a woman was married, though, she normally bore several children, of whom a third to a half would not survive to adulthood. Moreover, many women died in childbirth. With the growth of industry and urban society, people began to marry earlier, and fewer remained unmarried. As industrial development led to higher incomes and better diets, more children survived to adulthood, and population grew rapidly in the nineteenth century. By the late nineteenth century, contraception within marriage was spreading.

In the twentieth century, and especially since World War Two, these trends have continued. In the last thirty or forty years women have chosen to marry ever earlier. In Sweden, for example, the average age of first marriage has dropped steadily from twenty-six in the early 1940s to twenty-three in the late 1960s. Moreover, more than nine out of ten women marry at least once, usually in their early

*A Contemporary Family* *This scene sums up some important changes taking place within the family. The young father feeds and talks with the baby, while the student-mother concentrates on the education essential for successful employment. (Niépce-Rapho)*

twenties. Marriage has never been more in vogue than in the contemporary era. The triumph of romantic attraction over financial calculation has been made complete, and perhaps never before have young couples expected so much emotional satisfaction from matrimony.

After marrying early, the typical woman in Europe, the United States, and Canada has her children quickly. Whereas women in the past very often had children as long as they were fertile, women in Europe and North America now have about 80 percent of their children before they are thirty. As for family size, the "baby boom" that lasted several years after 1945 made for fairly rapid population growth of 1 to 1.5 percent per year in many European countries. Since the 1960s, however, the long-term decline in birthrates has resumed. Surveys in northern and western Europe reveal that most women now believe that two instead of three children is ideal.

Women must have 2.1 children on the average if total population is to remain constant over the long term. Indeed, the number of births has fallen so sharply that total population is actually declining in four European countries. More people are dying each year than are being born in Austria, East Germany, West Germany, and Luxembourg. The United States has followed the same trend; the birthrate declined from 25 per thousand in 1957 to 15 per thousand in 1973, and has remained at about that level. Since the American death rate has remained unchanged, the rate of population growth from natural increase (that is, excluding immigration) has declined by two-thirds, from 1.5 percent to .5 percent per year in the last twenty years. The population of Africa, Asia, and Latin America is still growing very rapidly from natural increase, but that is no longer true for most European countries and countries of European ancestry.

The culmination of the trends toward early almost-universal marriage and small family size in wealthy societies has revolutionary implications for women. An examination of these implications will suggest why the emancipation of women — sooner or later — has almost assuredly been built into the structure of modern life.

The main point is that motherhood occupies a much smaller portion of a woman's life than it used to even eighty years ago. The average woman's life expectancy at birth has increased from about fifty years to about seventy-five years in this century. At the same time women are increasingly compressing childbearing into the decade between their twentieth and thirtieth birthdays, instead of bearing children until they are in their late thirties. About half of today's women, and

more than half in some Western nations, have had their last baby by the age of twenty-six or twenty-seven. When the youngest child troops off to kindergarten, the mother has more than forty years of life in front of her.

This is a momentous change. Throughout history most married women have been defined to a considerable extent as mothers. Motherhood was very demanding: pregnancy followed pregnancy, and there were many children to nurse, guide, and bury. Now, however, the years devoted to having babies and caring for young children represent at most a seventh of the average woman's life. Motherhood has become a relatively short phase in most women's total life span. Perhaps a good deal of the frustration that many women feel today is due to the fact that their traditional role as mothers no longer absorbs the energies of a lifetime, and that new roles in the male-dominated world outside the family are opening up slowly.

A related revolutionary change for women is that the age-old biological link between sexual intercourse and motherhood has been severed. As everyone knows, women have gained effective control of pregnancy with oral contraceptives and intrauterine devices, and no longer have to rely on undependable males and their undependable methods. Less well known is the reason for birth control being absolutely necessary in the advanced countries today.

Women today are capable of having children for many more years than their forebears. The age of menarche — the age at which girls begin to menstruate and become fertile — has dropped from about seventeen years in the early nineteenth century to about thirteen years today. At the same time the age at onset of menopause has risen. At the beginning of the eighteenth century, menopause occurred at about age thirty-six, on average; it occurs at about fifty today. These physiological changes are poorly understood, but they are apparently due to better diets and living standards, which have also substantially increased people's height and size. In any event, modern women have of necessity separated their sexual lives from their awesome reproductive power. In doing so, women have become free to pursue sensual pleasure for its own sake. The consequences of this revolutionary development will be working themselves out for a long time.

## WOMEN AT WORK

For centuries before the Industrial Revolution ordinary women were highly productive members of society. They often labored for years before marriage to accumulate the necessary dowry. Once married, women worked hard on farms and in home industries while bearing and caring for their large families. With the growth of modern industry and large cities, young women continued to work as wage earners. But once a poor woman married, she typically stopped working in a factory or a shop, struggling instead to earn money at home by practicing some low-paid craft as she looked after her children. In the middle classes, it was an extremely rare and tough-minded woman who worked outside the home for wages, although charity work was socially acceptable.

Since the beginning of the twentieth century and especially since World War Two, the situation has been changing dramatically once again. Opportunities for women of modest means to earn cash income within the home have practically disappeared. Piano teachers, novelists, and part-time typists may still work at home as independent contractors, but the ever-greater complexity of the modern wage-

based economy and its sophisticated technology means that almost all would-be wage earners must turn elsewhere. Moreover, motherhood takes less and less time, so that the full-time mother-housewife has less and less economic value for families. Thus the reduction of home-centered work and child care has resulted in a sharp rise all across Europe and North America in the number of married women who are full-time wage earners.

In communist countries the trend has gone farthest. In the Soviet Union most married women work outside the home; women account for almost half of all employed persons there. In noncommunist western Europe and North America there is a good deal of variety, depending on whether married women have traditionally worked outside the home, as in France or Sweden, or stayed at home, as in Belgium and Switzerland. Nevertheless, the percentage of married women who work has risen in all countries, from a range of roughly 20 to 25 percent in 1950 to a range of 35 to 60 percent today. The trend is still upward. This rise has been particularly dramatic in the United States, where married women are twice as likely to be employed today as they were in 1952.

The dramatic growth of employment among married women is a development whose ultimate effects may be imagined only dimly. Nevertheless, it seems clear that the rising employment of married women is a powerful force in the drive for women's equality and emancipation. Take the critical matter of widespread discrimination between men and women in pay, occupation, and advancement. The young unmarried woman of seventy years ago generally accepted such injustices. She thought of them as temporary nuisances, and looked forward to marriage and motherhood for fulfillment. Today a married wage earner in her thirties has a totally different perspective. Employment is a permanent condition within which she, like her male counterpart, seeks not only income but psychological satisfaction as well. Sexism and discrimination quickly become loathsome and evoke a sense of injustice of the kind that drives revolutions and reforms. The "movement" spreads, winning converts among the young and newly awakened.

Rising employment for married women has been a factor in the decline of the birthrate (see Figure 31.2). Women who work have significantly fewer children than women of the same age who do not. Moreover, survey research shows that young women who have worked, and intend to work again, revise downward the number of children they expect to have after the first lovable but time-consuming baby is born. One reason is obvious: raising a family while holding down a full-time job is a tremendous challenge and often results in the woman being grossly overworked. The fatiguing, often frustrating multiple demands of job, motherhood, and marriage simply become more manageable with fewer children.

Another reason for the decline of the birthrate is that motherhood interrupts a woman's career. The majority of women in Western countries prefer or are forced to accept — interpretations vary — staying at home for a minimum of two or three years while their children are small. The longer the break in employment, the more a woman's career suffers. Women consistently earn less than men partly because they are employed less continuously and thus do not keep moving steadily up the bureaucratic ladders of large organizations.

Because most Western countries do little to help women in the problem of re-

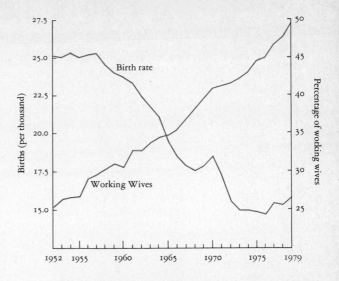

Note: Data for working wives includes only women with husbands present.

FIGURE 31.2 THE DECLINE OF THE BIRTHRATE AND THE INCREASE OF WORKING WIVES IN THE UNITED STATES, 1952– 1979 *The challenge of working away from home has encouraged American wives to prefer fewer children and has helped lower the birthrate.*

employment after their children are a little older, some women advocate the pattern of career and family typically found in communist eastern Europe. There, women are usually employed continuously until they retire. There are no career-complicating interruptions for extended mothering. Instead, a woman in a communist country receives as her right up to three months of maternity leave to care for her newborn infant and recover her strength. Then she returns to her job, leaving her baby in the care of a state-run nursery or, more frequently, a retired relative or neighbor. Some west European countries are beginning to provide well-defined maternity leaves as part of their social security systems. The United States lags far behind in this area.

What the increasing numbers of career-minded women with independent, self-assertive spirits mean for marriage and relations between the sexes is by no means clear. As we have seen, marriage remains an almost universal experience. Moreover, the decline of informal village and neighborhood socializing with the advent of the automobile and suburban living has made most wives and husbands more dependent than ever on their mates (and their children) for their emotional needs. Never has more been demanded from hearth and home.

The great increase in life expectancy for males and females has itself made marriage more stable, at least in one sense. The average couple will live together for forty years before the death of one dissolves the union, as opposed to less than twenty years together at the beginning of the century. And husbands are slowly getting the message that the old rule of leaving the dishes and diapers exclusively to wives needs rewriting, especially in two-income families.

At the same time there are contrary trends. Everywhere the divorce rate keeps moving up: it has doubled in the United States in ten years. Studies of marriage consistently show that working women are considerably more likely to get divorced than nonworking women. The independent working woman can more easily afford to leave if dissatisfied, while the no-income career housewife is practically locked into her situation.

Since the very late 1960s the marriage rate has plunged in a few advanced nations, notably Sweden, which has often led the way in social trends, and the United States. Does this decline mean only that young women and men are postponing marriage because of less robust economic conditions? Or does it mean that marriage, after its long rise, is finally in retreat in the face of growing careerism and acceptance of new and less structured relations between (and within) the sexes? Only time will tell, but it is by no means impossible that a radical break with the past is now taking place in marriage patterns and family relationships.

## HEALTH CARE AND GROWING OLD

The great increase in the number of elderly people in advanced countries is one of the major developments of our time. In 1900, a newborn female baby in western Europe could expect to live about fifty-two years and a male baby about forty-nine. In 1970, life expectancy at birth was seventy-five years for females and sixty-eight years for males. For the first time in history the vast majority of newborn infants, not just the lucky ones, will live to be senior citizens. This is certainly a great human achievement, but large numbers of elderly people also present new challenges for society, and especially for women.

One challenge that accompanies growing old for most women is several years of widowhood toward the end of life. Not only does the average woman outlive the average man by six or seven years, but the average woman marries a man two or three years her senior. The death of a spouse, which will happen far more often to women than to men, is commonly a shattering experience. During the first year after the death of a spouse, a widow or a widower in the United States is ten times more likely to die than other people in the same age group. The problems of growing old gracefully in good health, therefore, have special significance for women: their welfare depends on taking care not only of themselves but of their mates from the weaker sex as well.

Probably the most serious obstacle to preserving good health into ripe old age is that men and women vastly overestimate the powers of medical science. In the age of very sophisticated technology, they think it can do anything, especially if enough money is spent on it. In fact, the contribution of doctors and hospitals to good health has been and will continue to be quite limited. The key to good health lies elsewhere.

One must understand first why death has struck later and later in life over the last three centuries, so that a newborn infant will live more than twice as long today as in the seventeenth century. In the first place, half of the reduction in mortality that has occurred over the last three centuries occurred before 1900. That reduction was caused in roughly equal measure by more and better food and by the control of infectious diseases borne through air and water. The mid-nineteenth-century sanitary revolution, which introduced safe water supplies, efficient sewage systems, and improved food and personal hygiene, accounted for most of the decline in infectious disease. Preventive medicine in the form of vaccinations after Pasteur's breakthrough played a welcome but quite secondary role in the decline of infectious disease before 1900.

The second half of the increase in human life expectancy has come in the twentieth century. It has largely been due to a great reduction in the rate of death during the first year of an infant's life. In 1900, between 160 and 250 of every 1,000 European children still did not reach their first birthday. Now only 10 to 30 of every 1,000 die in the first year. Mortality in early childhood also declined sharply in this century. Better care by mothers because of better knowledge, and preventive medicine in the form of vaccinations against infectious diseases, have been the key to healthier babies and small children, although pediatricians have made some contribution.

Doctors and hospitals have been able to do much less for the rest of us, however, and especially for the elderly. Medical science has made little progress in controlling the major causes of death in adults: heart disease, cancer, and stroke. An adult male in the United States who managed to reach age sixty-five in 1900 could expect to live thirteen more years; an adult male of sixty-five today may expect fifteen more years, or only two more years than his great-grandparent. To date, society has spent ever greater sums on the care of people growing old, but with only very modest results.

Modern society, oversold on the limitless possibilities of scientific progress in every domain, cannot understand the lack of improvement in the health of older people. People alternately blame the greed of the medical profession, the stinginess of government aid, and the deterioration of the environment. In fact, the individual must accept a large portion of the responsibility for illness and disease.

Ninety-nine percent of the population in advanced countries is born healthy. Having survived the old scourges of childhood because of high standards of living and preventive medicine, we are often made sick through our own bad habits. Consider the central finding of one careful five-and-a-half year study of seven thousand adults in the United States.[4] The study showed that life expectancy and health are significantly related to seven simple health habits: (1) eating three regular meals a day and avoiding snacks, (2) having breakfast every day, (3) performing moderate exercise two or three times a week, (4) sleeping seven or eight hours a night, (5) forgoing smoking, (6) maintaining moderate weight, and (7) avoiding alcohol or using it only in moderation. A forty-five-year-old man who practices three or fewer of these habits may expect to live to be sixty-seven; one who adheres to six or seven may expect to live eleven more years to age seventy-eight.

In short, a great deal of sickness, disease, premature aging, and untimely death may be prevented. One problem is teaching people how to prevent illness, for less than .5 percent of all money spent on health in the United States is spent on health education. Yet in spite of this scandalous situation the individual can learn many essential facts quite easily.

Simply practicing the seven habits mentioned above is a good start. In addition, individuals can improve their diets by eating less fat, sugar, and highly refined carbohydrates. They can eat more vegetables and foods rich in fiber, have annual checkups, and take as few drugs, legal and otherwise, as possible. The chances of growing old gracefully will be vastly improved.

## THE FUTURE IN PERSPECTIVE

What about the future? For centuries astrologers and scientists, experts and ordinary people, have been trying to answer this question. Although it may seem that the study of what has been has little to say about what will be, the study of history over a long period is actually very useful in this regard. It helps put the future in perspective.

In 1931 a distinguished Harvard professor of genetics examined the prospects for the human race in an article read by millions. Among his predictions was that "in the year 2500 the population of the world should be about 3,500 millions, or about twice the figures of today."[5] In fact, the population of the world reached 4 billion in the 1970s and outside the highly developed countries of Europe and North America is still growing rapidly. The six-century projection of the learned expert was proved dead wrong in less than fifty years.

History is full of such erroneous predictions, a few of which we have mentioned in this book. Yet lack of success has not diminished the age-old desire to look into the future. Self-proclaimed experts even pretend that they have created a new science of futurology. With great pomposity they often act as if their hunches and guesses about future human developments were inescapable realities. Yet the study of history teaches healthy skepticism regarding such predictions, however ingenious or apparently scientific they may be. Past results suggest that most such predictions will simply not come true, or not in the anticipated way. Thus, history provides some psychological protection from the fantastic visions of the modern astrologers.

This protection is particularly valuable today because a great many projections into the future are quite pessimistic, just as they were very optimistic in the 1950s and 1960s. Many people in the Western world seem convinced that conditions are going to get worse rather than better. They fear, for example, that continuous rapid inflation will permanently cripple the economy, that pollution will destroy the environment, and that the traditional family will disappear. Many experts and politicians have been predicting that the "energy crisis" means disaster, in the form of lower standards of living at best and the collapse of civilization at worst. It is heartening to know that most such predictions will almost certainly not prove true, just as the same knowledge of likely error is sobering in more optimistic ages.

One of the most frightening and pessimistic predictions currently in vogue is that the northern nations of Europe and North America will increasingly find themselves locked in a life-and-death struggle with the poor, overpopulated southern nations of Africa, Asia, and South America. This North-South conflict, it is predicted, will replace the cold war struggle of East and West with a much more dangerous international class and race conflict of rich versus poor, white versus colored. Such, it is said, is the bitter legacy of Western imperialism.

As Map 31.1 shows, there is indeed an enormous gap between the very wealthy nations of noncommunist western Europe and North America and the very poor nations of much of Africa and Asia. Yet closer examination does not reveal a growing split between two sharply defined economic camps. On the contrary, there are five or six distinct categories of nations in terms of wealth and income. The communist countries of eastern Europe form something of a middle-income group, as do the major oil-exporting states, which, contrary to common belief, are still behind the wealthier countries of western Europe. Poverty in parts of Latin America is severe, but, as the map shows, standards of living are substantially higher there than in much of Africa and Asia, both of which encompass considerable variation.

When one considers differences in culture, religion, politics, and historical development, the supposed split between "rich" and "poor" nations breaks down still further. Thus, a global class war between rich and poor appears unlikely in the foreseeable future. A more reasonable expectation is continuing pressure to reduce international economic differences through taxation and welfare measures, as has already occurred domestically in the wealthy nations. Such pressure may well bring at least modest success, for the wealthy nations generally realize that an exclusively Western viewpoint on global issues is unrealistic and self-defeating. The true legacy of Western imperialism is one small world.

It is this that makes the nuclear arms race so ominous. Not only do the United States and the Soviet Union possess unbelievably destructive, ever-expanding nuclear arsenals, but Great Britain, France, China, and India all have "the bomb," and probably Israel and South Africa as well. Other countries have the capacity or the desire to "go nuclear." Thus

MAP 31.1  ESTIMATED WORLD PER CAPITA INCOME IN 1979  (Larger Countries)

some gloomy experts predict that by 1990 twenty or thirty states will have nuclear weapons. In a world increasingly plagued by local wars and ferocious regional conflicts, they conclude that nuclear war is almost inevitable and speculate that the human race is an "endangered species."

Such predictions and the undeniable seriousness of the arms race appear to be jolting Western populations out of their customary fatalism regarding nuclear weapons, at least temporarily. Efforts to reduce or even halt the nuclear buildup in the Soviet Union and the NATO alliance are blossoming again. Moreover, the current revival of the antinuclear movement is drawing on broad popular support and enlisting creditable mainstream leaders, such as Catholic bishops in the United States and Protestant clergy in West Germany. An optimist can hope that comparable concern in non-Western areas may yet develop to help create the global political will necessary to control nuclear proliferation before it is too late.

Whatever does or does not happen, the study of history puts the future in perspective in other ways. We have seen that every age has its problems and challenges. Others before us have trod these paths of crisis and uncertainty. This knowledge helps save us from exaggerated self-pity in the face of our own predicaments.

Perhaps our Western heritage may even inspire us with pride and measured self-confidence. We stand, momentarily, at the end of the long procession of Western civilization winding through the ages. Sometimes the procession has wandered, or backtracked, or

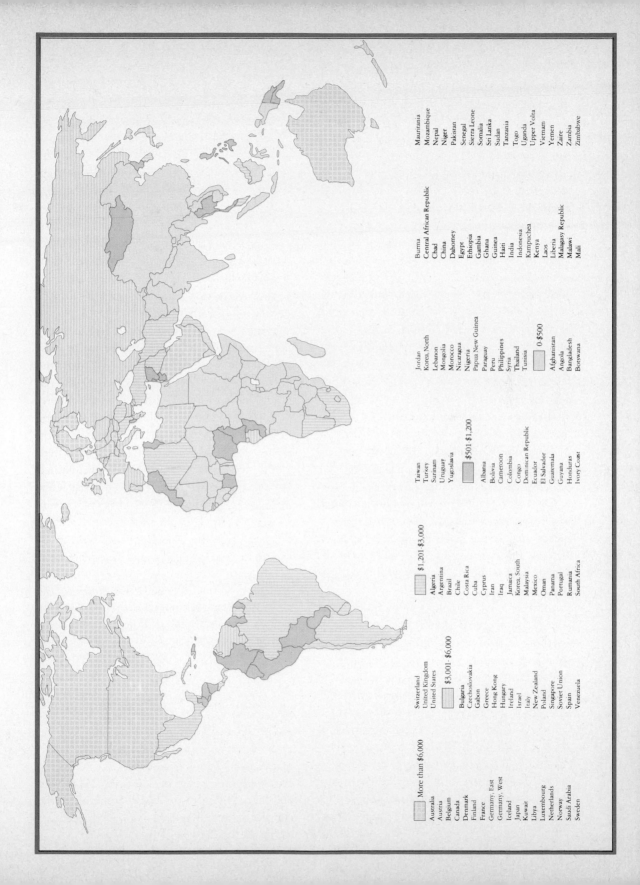

More than $6,000

Australia
Austria
Belgium
Canada
Denmark
Finland
France
Germany, East
Germany, West
Iceland
Japan
Kuwait
Libya
Luxembourg
Netherlands
Norway
Saudi Arabia
Sweden

Switzerland
United Kingdom
United States

$3,001–$6,000

Bulgaria
Czechoslovakia
Gabon
Greece
Hong Kong
Hungary
Ireland
Israel
Italy
New Zealand
Poland
Singapore
Soviet Union
Spain
Venezuela

$1,201–$3,000

Algeria
Argentina
Brazil
Chile
Costa Rica
Cuba
Cyprus
Iran
Iraq
Jamaica
Korea, South
Malaysia
Mexico
Oman
Panama
Portugal
Rumania
South Africa

Taiwan
Turkey
Surinam
Uruguay
Yugoslavia

$501–$1,200

Albania
Bolivia
Cameroon
Colombia
Congo
Dominican Republic
Ecuador
El Salvador
Guatemala
Guyana
Honduras
Ivory Coast

Jordan
Korea, North
Lebanon
Mongolia
Morocco
Nicaragua
Nigeria
Papua New Guinea
Paraguay
Peru
Philippines
Syria
Thailand
Tunisia

0–$500

Afghanistan
Angola
Bangladesh
Botswana

Burma
Central African Republic
Chad
China
Dahomey
Egypt
Ethiopia
Gambia
Ghana
Guinea
Haiti
India
Indonesia
Kampuchea
Kenya
Laos
Liberia
Malagasy Republic
Malawi
Mali

Mauritania
Mozambique
Nepal
Niger
Pakistan
Senegal
Sierra Leone
Somalia
Sri Lanka
Sudan
Tanzania
Togo
Uganda
Upper Volta
Vietnam
Yemen
Zaire
Zambia
Zimbabwe

done terrible things. But it has also carried the efforts and sacrifices of generations of toiling, struggling ancestors. Through no effort of our own, we are the beneficiaries of those sacrifices and achievements. Now that it is our turn to carry the torch onward, we may remember these ties of solidarity to our forebears.

To change the metaphor, we in the West are like a card player who has been dealt many good cards. Some of them are obvious, like our technical and scientific heritage or our commitments to human rights and the individual. Others are not so obvious, sometimes half-forgotten or even hidden up the sleeve. One thinks, for example, of the Christian Democrats, the moderate Catholic party, which emerged after World War Two to play such an important role in the west European renaissance. Or one thinks of the dismantling of colonial empires, which was a victory of Western ideals of liberty and nationhood as well as a defeat for Western imperialism. We hold a good hand.

Our study of history, of mighty struggles and fearsome challenges, of shining achievements and tragic failures, gives a sense of what is the essence of life itself: the process of change over time. Again and again we have seen how peoples and societies evolve, influenced by such things as ideas, human passions, and material conditions. As sure as anything is sure, this process of change over time will continue as the future becomes the present and then the past. And students of history are better prepared to make sense of this unfolding process because they have already observed it. They know how change goes forward on the basis of existing historical forces, and their projections will probably be as good as those of the futurologists. Students of history are also prepared for the new

and unexpected in human development, for they have already seen great breakthroughs and revolutions. They have an understanding of how things really happen.

---

## NOTES

1. Quoted by W. Laqueur, *Europe Since Hitler,* Penguin Books, Baltimore, 1972, p. 9.

2. Quoted by J. Ziman, *The Force of Knowledge: the Scientific Dimension of Society,* Cambridge University Press, Cambridge, England, 1976, p. 128.

3. Quoted by S. Joulmin in *The Twentieth Century: A Promethean Age,* ed. A. Bullock, Thames & Hudson, London, 1971, p. 294.

4. J. Knowles, "The Responsibility of the Individual," *Daedalus* 106 (Winter 1977):61–62.

5. E. M. East, in *Scientific Monthly,* April 1931; also in *Reader's Digest* 19 (May 1931):151.

---

## SUGGESTED READING

J. Ziman, *The Force of Knowledge: The Scientific Dimension of Society* (1976), which has an excellent bibliography, is a penetrating look at science by a leading physicist. C. P. Snow, *The Two Cultures and the Scientific Revolution,* rev. ed. (1963), explores the gap between scientists and nonscientists in a widely discussed book. A. Toffler, *Future Shock* (1970), is an interesting but exaggerated best seller, which claims that many contemporary psychological problems are due to overly rapid technical and scientific development. J. Ellul, *The Technological Society* (1964), is also highly critical of technical progress, while D. S. Landes, *The Unbound Prometheus: Technological Change and Industrial Development in Western Europe from 1750 to the Present* (1969), remains enthusiastic. Two more stimulating works on technology are J. J. Servan-Schreiber,

*The World Challenge* (1981), and H. Jacoby, *The Bureaucratization of the World* (1973).

In addition to studies cited in the Suggested Reading for Chapter 30, A. Simpson, *The New Europeans* (1968), is a good guide to contemporary Western society. Two engaging books on recent intellectual developments are J. Barzun, *The House of Intellect* (1959), and R. Stromberg, *After Everything: Western Intellectual History Since 1945* (1970). L. Wylie, *Village in the Vauclause,* rev. ed. (1964), and P. J. Hélias, *The Horse of Pride* (1980), provide fascinating pictures of life in the French village. A. Kriegel, *The French Communists* (1972) and *Eurocommunism* (1978), are also recommended. A. Touraine, *The May Movement* (1971), is sympathetic toward the French student revolt, while the noted sociologist R. Aron, *The Elusive Revolution* (1969), is highly critical. F. Zweig, *The Worker in an Affluent Society* (1961), probes family life and economic circumstances in the British working class

on the basis of extensive interviews. R. E. Tyrrell, ed., *The Future That Doesn't Work* (1977), is a polemical but interesting attack on socialist policies in Britain. W. Hollstein, *Europe in the Making* (1973), is a fervent plea to integrate Europe by a former top official of the Common Market. Three magazines, *Encounter, Commentary,* and *The Economist,* often carry interesting and intelligent articles on major social and political trends.

E. Sullerot, *Women, Society and Change* (1971), is an outstanding introduction to women's evolving role. R. Patia, ed., *Women in the Modern World* (1967), compares women's situation in many countries. Two other influential books on women and their new awareness are S. de Beauvoir, *The Second Sex* (1962), and B. Friedan, *The Feminine Mystique* (1963). These may be compared with C. Lasch, *Haven in a Heartless World* (1977), and A. Cherlin, *Marriage, Divorce, Remarriage* (1981), which interpret changes in the American family.

# NOTES ON THE ILLUSTRATIONS

*Page 20* The stone pillar containing the law code of Hammurabi is in the collection of the Louvre in Paris.

*Page 34* The Hittite Atarluhas from Carchemish is in the British Museum.

*Page 50* Mosaic floor of the ancient Beth Alpha Synagogue in Israel.

*Page 52* The relief of Assurbanipal feasting, from Nineveh, is now in the British Museum.

*Page 64* Shown here is the east stairway of the apadana (audience hall) of Darius and Xerxes, with Darius' palace in the background. Achaemenid period.

*Page 77* This figure is 6½ inches high, made of gold and ivory about 1600–1500 B.C.

*Page 78* The Melian relief, depicting the return of Odysseus, was made of terracotta in the fifth century B.C. Greek.

*Page 103* Young warrior making libation before departure. Attic red figure technique, c. 500 B.C.

*Page 127* Dieties of Palmyrene in bas-relief, gypsum. Selukos Nikator crowning the Tyche of Dura.

*Page 160* Relief shows a school in Trier on the northern frontier of the Roman empire, about the third century A.D.

*Page 169* This helmet, found in Lancashire, is now in the British Museum. The crown is embossed with combat scenes and a visor in the form of a face.

*Page 204* Roman mosaic from the Bardo Museum, Tunis, illustrating a great estate.

*Page 215* Vandal landowner, in a mosaic from Carthage, sixth century, in the British Museum.

*Page 218* From *Vie de Saint Denis,* MS. Nov. Acq. Fr. 1098, fol. 50, in the Bibliothèque Nationale, Paris.

*Page 235* Detail from Madonna enthroned with saints and angels, c. 1380–1390 by Agnolo Gaddi, a Florentine active 1369–1396. Wood.

*Page 237* Emperor Justinian and his court, A.D. 546–548, in mosaic at San Vitale, Ravenna, Italy.

*Page 242 Above.* Samson destroying the temple of the Philistines, miniature from Rashid-ad-Zdin's *Universal History* (1306–1314). *Below.* Muhammed and follower fleeing from Mecca to Medina, watched by Christ, miniature from thirteenth-century Arabic manuscript. Both in the Edinburgh University Library.

*Page 248* The Dome of the Rock, built in 691 by the Caliph Omar on the site of King Solomon's and Herod's temples in Jerusalem.

*Page 267* The scribe Ezra rewriting the sacred records. Early eighth century, from the Codex Amiatinus (fol. 5r), Biblioteca Laurenziana, Florence.

*Page 269* Upper cover of the binding of the Lindau Gospels, c. 870.

*Page 271* Conant took this design from some of Walter Horn's early studies on the plan of St. Gall.

*Page 273* Illustration from the North Italian Coden Paneth, MS. 28, in the Medical Library at Yale University.

*Page 288* Woodcut from the Nuremberg Chronicle, 1493.

*Page 294* From *Gouvernment des princes,* MS. 5062, fol. 149.

*Page 296* This house stands on the corner of Edmund Street in Exeter, Devon, having been moved in one piece in 1961 from its original site in the city.

*Page 665* *Les Glaneuses* by Jean François Millet (1814–1875), French genre and landscape painter of the Barbizon school. The original can be seen in the Louvre.

*Page 674* Colored engraving, 1746.

*Page 686* Frontispiece from a map of "the most Inhabited part of Virginia containing the whole province of Maryland with part of Pensilvania, New Jersey and North Carolina drawn by Joshua Fry and Peter Jefferson in 1775," in Thomas Jeffrey's *American Atlas,* 1776, in The British Library.

*Page 700* *Peasant Family* by Giacomo Ceruti, Italian painter active c. 1750.

*Page 702* After an engraving by R. Lehman of the foundlings' home called La Rota.

*Page 709* *Famille de paysans,* c. 1640, by Louis Le Nain, French painter (1593–1648). The original can be seen in the Louvre.

*Page 715* Engraving, 1746.

*Page 717* "The Remarkable Effects of Vaccination," an anonymous nineteenth-century Russian cartoon in the Clements C. Fry Collection of Medical Prints and Drawings, Yale Medical Library.

*Page 734* This portrait of Louis XVI by Joseph-Siffrein Duplessis, French portrait painter (1725–1802), hangs in the Marie Antoinette Gallery at Versailles.

*Page 738* This drawing by Persin de Prieur, "Premier assaut contre La Bastille," can be seen in the Musée Carnavalet, Paris.

*Page 744* "Fin Tragique de Louis XVI," drawn from life by Fious; engraving by Sarcifu. Louis XVI was executed on 21 January 1793 in the Place de Louis XV, renamed the Place de la Révolution, and now called the Place de la Concorde.

*Page 748* "Un Comité révolutionnaire sous la Terreur," after Alexandre Évariste Fragonard, French historical painter (1780–1850).

*Page 755* "Con razón o sin ella," by Francisco José de Goya y Lucientes (1746–1828), Plate 2 in *Los desastres de la guerra,* 1863. Etching. A Spanish painter, etcher, and lithographer, Goya was the chief master of the Spanish school in the eighteenth century.

*Page 767* James Hargreaves (d. 1778), English inventor, weaver, and mechanic, invented the spinning jenny about 1765.

*Page 771* Engraving by Henry Beighton, 1717, of the atmospheric steam engine invented about 1705 by Thomas Newcomen, English blacksmith (1663–1729).

*Page 773* Honoré Daumier (1808–1879), *The Third-Class Carriage.* Oil on canvas. Daumier was both a caricaturist and a serious painter.

*Page 778* The Cockerill works at Seraing, Belgium, at night. Lithograph by E. Toovey, Brussels, 1852.

*Page 786* From *Parliamentary Papers,* 1842, vol. XV.

*Page 790* "Emigrants' Arrival at Cork – A Scene on the Quay," woodcut from *Punch,* 1851.

*Page 800* "La balance politique," 1815, print in the Bibliothèque Nationale. *From left,* two Englishmen, Prussian, Metternich, Russian, Talleyrand.

*Page 803* *Count Clemens von Metternich* (1773–1859) by Sir Thomas Lawrence, English painter (1769–1830).

*Page 813* Eugene Delacroix (1798–1863), French painter and leader of the Romantic school.

*Page 817* *Liszt am Klavier,* 1840, by Josef Danhauser, German painter (1805–1845).

*Page 822* From *Punch,* 1846. The humorous weekly *Punch* – founded in 1841 by the British journalist and sociologist Henry Mayhew (1812–1887) and others – is the most famous of its kind. Its cartoons and caricatures became a powerful vehicle of political and social comment.

*Page 825* *The Legislative Belly,* lithograph by Honoré Daumier (1808–1879).

*Page 838* "The Court for King Cholera," cartoon from *Punch,* XXIII (1852), 139.

*Page 843* Cross-section of a Parisian house, about 1850, from Edmund Texier, *Tableauade Paris,* Paris, 1852, vol. I, p. 65.

*Page 845* Opening of steam-propelled tramways by the locomotive *Harding* in Paris between the railroad stations of Montparnasse and Austerlitz. From *L'Illustration,* 19 August 1876.

*Page 849* *Un Coin de Table,* 1904, by Paul-Émile Chabas, French painter (1869–1937). Oil on canvas.

*Page 854* Market for servants, situated just outside the ancient boundary wall (the Kitai Yard) of Moscow and open every day of the year, Sundays being the busiest. From *The Illustrated London News,* 1 November 1850, p. 458. England had no fully illustrated newspaper until the first number of the weekly *Illustrated London News* appeared on 14 May 1842, with 16 printed pages and 32 woodcuts.

*Page 856* Necktie workshop in a Division Street tenement photographed about 1889 by Jacob A. Riis, American (Danish-born) social worker and writer (1849–1914).

*Page 859* From *Punch,* XXXIII (1857), 114.

*Page 870* George Eliot c. 1864 in an etching by Paul Rajon after the portrait from life by Sir Frederick

Burton, Irish watercolor painter (1816-1900). The original portrait is in the National Portrait Gallery, London.

*Page 879* Demolition of part of the Latin Quarter in 1860. Engraving from a drawing by Félix Thorigny.

*Page 894* Merchants of Nijni-Novgorod drinking tea. From *L'Illustration,* 29 August 1905.

*Page 914* Immigrant sleeping car, Canadian Pacific Railroad, September 1888.

*Page 921* Ellis Island pens, photographed in 1907.

*Page 940* Japanese cartoon of Russian expansion, about 1904.

*Page 949* *The Congress at Berlin in 1878* by Anton von Werner, German painter of portraits and historical subjects (1843-1915).

*Page 1001* *Guernica,* 1937, by Pablo Picasso, Spanish painter and sculptor (1881-1973). The original oil on canvas, 11 ft. 5½ in. high by 25 ft. 5¾ in. wide, is in the Museo del Prado, Madrid.

*Page 1004* Mary Pickford (1893-1979) photographed by Hartsook in 1918. Rudolph Valentino (1895-1926) as he appeared in *Four Horsemen of the Apocalypse* (1921).

*Page 1017* Scene in San Francisco in 1934, photographed by Dorothea Lange.

*Page 1027* 100,000 Nazi Storm Troopers gathered in the Luitpodarena in Nuremberg, Germany, to hear Adolf Hitler on Brown Shirt Day at the Nazi Party convention, 20 September 1936.

*Page 1028* French caricature by C. Leavdre, 1898.

*Page 1031* Poster by Deni, 1930, now in the British Museum.

*Page 1049* The cartoon 'Stepping Stones to Glory" by Sir David Low (1891-1963) appeared in the London *Evening Standard* on 8 July 1936.

*Page 1064* Rabaul Harbor, New Britain. U.S. Air Force North American B-25 passing over Japanese ship.

*Page 1072* The *Deutscher Verlag* building in Berlin after impassable street had been cleared of rubble, photographed on 6 July 1945.

*Page 1077* Photographed at Orly Airport outside Paris on 31 May 1961.

*Page 1089* Column of Russian tanks in a side street near the Old Town Square in Prague, photographed 28 August 1968.

*Page 1091* Civil rights marchers gathered at the Lincoln Memorial in Washington, D.C., in August 1963.

*Page 1097* Muro Central in the Palacio Nacional, Mexico City, painted 1929-1935 by José Clemente Orozco (1883-1949), Mexican painter of the modernist school.

*Page 1100* President Juan Perón and his wife Eva riding down the Avenida de Mayo in Buenos Aires on 4 June 1952 after Perón's inauguration for another six-year term.

*Page 1109* First atomic bomb test at Bikini Atoll, in photograph released 26 July 1946.

*Page 1112* Astronaut Edwin E. Aldrin, Jr., leaving the lunar module. Apollo 11 was launched in Florida on 16 July 1969. Astronauts Neil A. Armstrong and Aldrin landed on the moon on 20 July while Michael Collins circled in the main spacecraft until rejoined by the others on 21 July. The astronauts returned to Earth on 24 July, when they were picked up in the Pacific Ocean.

*Page 1122* Students in the Boulevard Saint Michel in Paris protesting the closing of the suburban Nanterre University, photographed on 3 May 1968.

# INDEX

Abdurrahman, of Omayyad dynasty, 248
Abélard, Peter, 367
Abraham, 43, 44
Absolutism: described, 556–557; in France, 557–572; decline of in Spain, 572–575; Puritan, in England, 580–581; in Austria, 569–600; in Prussia, 600–606; in Russia, 611–616; and the baroque, 622; influence of Enlightenment on, 650–658; falls in France, 741
Abstract expressionism, 1000–1002
*Ab Urbe Condita* (Livy), 183
Acropolis, 72, 93, 94–95
Act for the Submission of the Clergy, 492
Act in Restraint of Appeals, 492
Actium, battle of, 172, 184
Acton, Sir John, 814
A.D., dating method, 267
*Adages, The* (Erasmus), 448
Adenauer, Konrad, 1071
Adrian VI, pope, 498
Adriatic Sea, 144
Aediles, 150
Aegean, Sea, 70
Aemilius Stephanus, 199
*Aenid* (Virgil), 183
Aequi, 147
Aeschylus, 95–96
Africa: impact of early Egypt on, 41; Portugal in, 510–511; and slave trade, 541–542, 544; Western imperialism in, 927–930; and responses to imperialism, 935–937; end of imperialism in, 1078–1082
*Against the Murderous, Thieving Hordes of the Peasants*

(Luther), 478
*Agamemnon* (Aeschylus), 95
*Age of Louis XIV* (Voltaire), 643
Agincourt, battle of, 399
Agriculture: Neolithic origins, 6–11; Hammurabi's Code on, 21–22; in early Egypt, 23; ancient Israel, 47, 49–50; ancient Greece, 72, 98; Hellenistic, 125–126; Roman, 161–162, 195–196, 203–204; in early Europe, 220–221; contribution of monasteries to, 236; medieval, 320–323, 344; bad 14th-century harvests, 388; in late Middle Ages, 415; in Germany after Thirty Years' War, 536; growth of estate, 594; "slash-and-burn," 607; by 17th century, 662–664; open-field system, 664–666; new rotation of crops, 666–667; new methods' origins, 667–670; enclosure debate, 670–671; in New World, 684–686; role in Industrial Revolution, 764, 765; effect of Industrial Revolution on, 851; collective, in Russia, 1032
Agrippa, Menenius, 151
Aguinaldo, Emile, 931
Ahaz, 54
Ahmose (pharaoh), 29
Ahriman, 62
Ahuramazda, 61, 62
Aiguillon, duke of, 739
Ailred of Rievaulx, 427
Akhenaten, 29–31, 45
Akhmatova, Anna, 1084
Akkad, 11, 15; people of, 17, 18
Alamanni, 199
Alaric, 233
Albania, 954

Bentham, Jeremy, 839
*Beowulf,* 267-268
Berg, Alban, 1002
Bergson, Henri, 991
Beria, Lavrenti, 1085
Berlin, 830, 831
Bernal, John Desmond, 1108
Bernard (at Citeaux), 305
Bernard of Clairvaux, 427, 499
Bernini, 564
Berno, abbot of Cluny, 304
Bessarion, John, 426
"Bess of Hardwick," *see* Hardwick, Elizabeth
Bethmann-Hollweg, Theobald van, 954-955
Bible: Mesopotamian influence on, 15, 18-19; Old Testament, 43, 44, 45-47, 48, 50; New Testament, 226-227; Mohammed's familiarity with, 246; Wycliff's reliance on, 409; Luther's translation, 479; Tyndale's, 489; King James Version, 549-550
Big Science, 1110-1113
Bill of Rights, American, 724, 732
Bill of Rights, English, 583, 732
Birth control, 697-698, 863, 1123, 1125-1126
*Birth of a Nation* (film), 1003
Birthrate, decline in, 863, 921, 1125, 1127
Bismarck, Otto von: in Revolution of 1848, 831; in unification of Germany, 886-891; as chancellor of German Empire, 897-899; calls imperialism conference, 928-930; and European system of alliances, 948-950
Black Death, *see* Bubonic plague
Black Hand, The, 954
Blacks: in Renaissance, 441-443; and civil rights movement, 1092-1093. *See also* Slavery
Blake, William, 782
Blanc, Louis, 809, 826, 827
Blenheim, battle of, 571
Bloch, Marc, 666
Blood, Council of, 526-527
Bloodletting, 712-713, 714
Blum, Léon, 1019-1020
Boccaccio, Giovanni, 336, 392, 428-429
Bodin, Jean, 613
Boeotia, 72, 73, 77-78, 104
Boers, 927
Boer Wars, 927-928, 950-952
Boghazköy, 33
Bohemia, 531-532, 533, 597-598, 802
Boisdeffre, General, 955
Boleyn, Anne, *see* Anne Boleyn
Bologna, Concordat of, 522
Bologna, University of, 365
Bolsheviks, 972-978
Bonaparte, Louis Napoleon, *see* Napoleon III
Bonaparte, Napoleon, *see* Napoleon I
Bonhomme, Jacques, 411
Boniface, *see* St. Boniface
Boniface VIII, pope, 381-383
*Book of Common Order* (Knox), 495
*Book of Common Prayer* (Cranmer), 494
*Book of the First Navigation and Discovery of the Indies* (Columbus), 511
Books, first printing from movable type, 437-439

Borgia, Cesare, 452
Borgia, Rodrigo, *see* Alexander VI, pope
Borgia family, 471
Borodino, battle of, 758
Bosch, Jerome, 450
Bosnia, 949, 953-955
Bossuet, Jacques, 560
Boston Tea Party, 729
Botany, beginnings in Hellenistic period, 136
Botticelli, 430
Boulton, Matthew, 770
"Bourgeois," meaning of word, 289
Bourgeoisie, in Marxian socialism, 810
Bourges, Pragmatic Sanction of, 456, 600
Boutham, England, 295
Boxer Rebellion, 943
Boyars, 609, 611-613
Brahe, Tycho, 631
Brandenburg, elector of, 600-602
Brassey, Thomas, 774
Brazil, 922, 925, 1096-1098, 1099-1100
Brazza, Pierre de, 928
Breast-feeding, *see* Nursing of babies
Breitenfeld, battle of, 533
Brest-Litovsk, Treaty of, 975, 1029
Brethren of the Common Life, 471
Brezhnev, Leonid, 1088-1091
Brezhnev Doctrine, 1090
Briand, Aristide, 1010, 1011
Bright, John, 823
Britain, *see* England; Great Britain
Britain, Battle of, 1053
British College of Surgeons, 718
British Empire, *see* Great Britain
British West Indies, 684
Britons, conquest by Germanic tribes, 221-222
Bronze Age, 28-29, 75-78
*Brothers Karamazov, The* (Dostoevsky), 864
Brunel, Isambard Kingdom, 774
Brunelleschi, Filippo, 431, 433, 441
Bruni, Leonardo, 427
Brüning, Heinrich, 1043
Brusilov, Alexei, 960, 968
Bubonic plague (Black Death): spread of in 14th century, 388, 389; pathology of, 389-393; consequences of, 393; disappears, 673
Bulgaria: in time of Rome, 181; independence from Ottoman Empire, 903; in Balkan wars, 953; in W.W. I, 960; and 1919 peace treaty, 982; forced into alliance with Germany, 1053; Russia occupies, 1067
Bullitt, William, 1066
Burckhardt, Jacob, 88
"Burgher," meaning of word, 289
Burgundians, 217, 455
Burke, Edmund, 742
Burlingame, Anson, 941
Bury St. Edmunds, 342
Bussy, Sir William, 410
Byblos, 40-41, 42
Byron, George Gordon, 814, 818
Byzantine Empire: 200, 237-242; compared with Germanic West, 238-239; Justinian's law codes, 239-240; intellectual

life, 240–242
Byzantium, 206, 238

Cabal, 582
*Cabinet of Dr. Caligari, The* (film), 1003
Cabinet system, 583–584
Cabot, John, 515
Cabral, Pedro Alvares, 511
Caesar, Julius, 164, 167, 170, 171–172, 179
Cairo, modernization of, 919
Calais, 402
Calendar, 161
Caligula, 185, 188
Callisthenes, 110
Calvin, John: debt to Luther, 479; life and ideas, 485–487; influence on Knox, 495; quoted, 585; reaction to Copernican theory, 631
Calvinism: tenets of, 485–487; in France, 522, 523–524; in Netherlands, 526; in Germany, 530–531, 534; and Puritanism, 578–579; and the Dutch, 585
Cambon, Paul, 1007
Cambridge University, 367, 371
Cambyses, 62
Campania, 144, 149
Camus, Albert, 995
Canaan, 43
Canada, 515; developed by Colbert for French Empire, 566; British colony, 912; immigration in, 921, 922
Cannae, battle of, 155
Cannon, 516–517
Canon law, 223
Canossa, 309
Canterbury Cathedral, 375, 471
*Canterbury Tales,* 404, 468
Canton, foreign merchants in, 917
Canute, 285, 351
*Capital* (Marx), 905
Capitalism: medieval, 300–301; and cottage industry, 676; and Industrial Revolution, 765, 780–781; and foreign investment, 915; Roosevelt's efforts to reform, 1015–1018
Capitoline Hill, 146
Caracalla, 197
Caraffa, Cardinal, 499, 502
Caravels, 517
Cardenas, Lazaro, 1096
Cardinals, 307. *See also* Papacy
Caribbean islands, 513, 682
Carlsbad Decrees, 801
Carolingian dynasty: rise of, 257–260; chart of, 259; Charlemagne's empire, 260–262; government of, 262–264; Charlemagne becomes Holy Roman emperor, 264–265; cultural revival of, 265–266, 269–274; collapse of, 274–276
Carthage, 42, 154–157
Cartier, Jacques, 515
Casablanca Conference, 1061
Cassian, John, 234
Cassiodorus, 234–235, 236
Castiglione, Baldassare, 433, 435, 439–440
Castile, 459
*Castle, The* (Kafka), 997
Castlereagh, Robert Stewart, 797, 779, 801, 820
Castro, Fidel, 1098–1099

Catal Hüyük, 9
Catapult, 134
Cateau-Cambrésis, Treaty of, 519
Cathedrals: as centers of bishops' authority, 224; as origin of towns, 289; and medieval schools, 365, 366; building and uses of, 371–378
Catherine II (the Great), empress of Russia, 616, 622, 648, 718; early life of, 651–652; as enlightened absolutist, 652–654; organizes League of Armed Neutrality, 730
Catherine de' Medici, 520, 522–523, 524
Catherine of Aragon, queen of England, 458, 491, 494
Catherine of Siena, 407
Catholic church, *see* Roman Catholic church
Catholicism, *see* Roman Catholic church
Catholic League, 533
Catholic Reformation, 496–503
Cato, Marcus, 159
Caucasus, 653
*Causes of Plants* (Theophrastus), 136–163
Cavaignac, Louis, 827, 876
Cave paintings, 6
Cavour, Camillo Benso di, 882–883
Celibacy, of clergy, 305–306, 469
Cellini, Benvenuto, 426–427, 433
Celts: invade Italy, sack Rome, 148–149; as native Britons, 221; to Wales, 222; Christianity of, compared to Roman, 222
Census, Roman, 179
Central Powers, 960, 967
CERN (European Council for Nuclear Research), 1111, 1114
Cervantes, 575
Cézanne, Paul, 1001
Chadwick, Edwin, 782, 839–840
Chaeronea, 74, 79, 00, 00
Chamberlain, Neville, 1052
Champagne, 957
Champaigne, Philippe de, 559
Chaplin, Charlie, 1003
Chariot racing, Roman, 194–195
"Charity schools," 705
Charlemagne: described, 260–261; as warrior/expansionist, 261–262; style of governing, 262–263; crowned Holy Roman emperor, 264–265; stimulates learning, 265–274; dies, empire collapses, 274–276
Charles II (the Bald), Holy Roman emperor, 275, 276
Charles V, Holy Roman emperor: and Titian, 432; wars with Italy, 455; vast patrimony, 462; outlaws Luther, 476; and ideas of empire, 480–482; and German reaction to Luther, 484; and war over Italy, 498; and Council of Trent, 499; commissions exploration, 513; and the Netherlands, 525–526; and slave trade, 541
Charles VI, Holy Roman emperor, 600
Charles I, king of England, 578–580
Charles II, king of England, 581–582, 680
Charles III (the Simple), king of France, 284
Charles IV, king of France, 395
Charles V, king of France, 408
Charles VI, king of France, 403
Charles VII, king of France, 400–401, 403, 455–456
Charles VIII, king of France, 455
Charles IX, king of France, 522–523, 524
Charles X, king of France, 823–824

18th, 19th-century Ireland, 789–792; in 20th-century Russia, 1029, 1032

Faraday, Michael, 866

Farming, see Agriculture

Farnese, Alexander, 528, 529, 530

Facism: in France, 1020; in Spain, 1020; as variety of totalitarianism, 1026; in Italy, 1037–1039; in Germany, 1039–1048

Fasces, 146

Faulkner, William, 588, 997

Federalists, 732

Ferdinand I, emperor of Austria, 801, 829–830

Ferdinand II, Holy Roman emperor, 531, 533, 597

Ferdinand III, Holy Roman emperor, 598

Ferdinand II, king of Spain, 378, 451, 458, 459

Ferdinand of Syria, see Ferdinand II, Holy Roman emperor

Fermi laboratory, 1111

Ferry, Jules, 901, 928–929, 930

Fertile Crescent, 8 (map)

Fertilizers, medieval, 321

Feudalism, 255–257, 279–280

Fiammetta's Tale (Boccaccio), 336

Films, see Motion pictures

Finance, 357–360, 1082

First Continental Congress, 729–730

First (Communist) International, 905

First World War, see World War I

Fischer von Erlach, J. B., 618

Fisher, John, 492

Five-year plans (Russia), 1028, 1030–1033, 1084

Flagellants, 393

Flanders: textile industry, 298; and Hundred Years' War, 395; Louis XIV invades, 570

Flaubert, Gustave, 869

Flavians, 188–189, 190

Florence, 880; effect of Black Death on, 393; in Renaissance, 423–424, 426; as city-state, 452, 454, 455

Florida, 682

Fontenelle, Bernand de, 639–640, 641, 648

Food, see Diet

Foreign investment, 915

Formosa, Japan takes from China, 941

Fortescue, Sir John, 404

Forum Romanum, 145

Fouché, Joseph, 753

Foulon, Joseph François, 737

Foundling homes, 701–702

Four Horsemen of the Apocalypse (Dürer woodcut), 672

Fourier, Charles, 809

Fourteen Points, 980

Fourteenth century, disasters of, 388–418

France: development of modern state, 350–351, 352–353, 354 (map); medieval finances, 358; medieval law, 360; 13th-century dispute with papacy, 381–383; papal court in Avignon, 383, 407–408; Hundred Years' War, 395–404; failure to develop representative assembly, 403–404; peasants' revolt, 411; invades Italy, 454–455; recovery under Charles VII, affirms autonomy of French church from papacy, 455–457; angered by Habsburg-Burgundian marriage, 480; loses Habsburg-Valois wars, start of religious wars, 519; Renaissance revival of monarchy, 520–522; concludes Concordat of Bologna with papcy, 522; Calvinism in, 522; religious

riots, civil war, 522–524; Edict of Nantes signed, 525; in Thirty Years' War, 534; and Richelieu, 558–560; under Louix XIV, 560–572; the philosophes, 639–650; competition for colonial empire, 680, 681–682; in Seven Years' War, 682–683; aid for American Revolution, 730; first phase of revolution, 733–739; National Assembly, 737, 739; limited monarchy, 739–742; war with Austria-Prussia, 742; monarchy falls, second phase of revolution, 743–749; Thermidorean reaction of the Directory, 749–750; Napoleon's reign, 750–758; industrialization, 775, 780; restoration of Bourbon monarchy, 797; Napoleon returns from exile, defeated, exiled again, 799–800; utopian socialism in, 808–810; romantic movement in, 815–816; supports Greek nationalist war, 820; Revolution of 1830, 823–824; Revolution of 1848, Second Republic, 825–827; Louis Napoleon in power, 827, 876–880; becomes emperor, 878; in Crimean War, 882; in 1870–71 war with Prussia, 890–891; Third Republic falls, Thiers crushes Paris Commune, 899; stability to 1914, 899–901; Dreyfus affair, 901–902; in Egypt, 918, 919, 920; in Africa, 927, 928–930; reasons for imperialism, 931–934; defeated in 1871, 948; courts Russia, 950; courts Britain, 952; Germany plans to attack, 955; in W.W. I, 957–968, 978–979; at peace conference, 980–984; German reparations, 1006–1010; occupies Ruhr, 1007–1010; attracts artists, 1011–1012; Great Depression in, 1019–1020; and Nazi Germany's expansionism, 1051–1053; falls to Germany, 1053; post-W.W. II conditions, 1070–1071; recovery, 1076, 1078; in Algeria, 1077, 1081–1082; in Indochina, 1080; 1968 student revolt in, 1121

Francesca, Piero della, 431

Francis II, Holy Roman emperor, 755

Francis I, king of France, 457, 498, 520, 522

Francis II, king of France, 522

Francis Ferdinand, archduke of Austria, 954

Francis Joseph, emperor of Austria, 830, 903, 967

Franco, Francisco, 1052

Franco-Prussian War of 1870–71, 890–891, 948

Frankfort, H., 27

Frankfurt National Assembly, 831

Franks: invade Gaul, Spain, 199; most enduring of Germanic kingdoms, 217; and Salic Law, 219; Arabs in kingdom, 248; Carolingians and kingdom of, 260, 261, 262

Frederick, prince of the Palatinate, 533

Frederick I (Barbarossa), Holy Roman emperor, 274, 355, 359, 380, 451

Frederick II (Hohenstaufen), Holy Roman emperor, 311, 359–360, 371, 380–381

Frederick III, Holy Roman emperor, 610

Frederick I, king of Prussia, 602, 618

Frederick II (the Great), king of Prussia, 618, 652, 654; imitates Versailles, 565; early years, 605; follows father's militarism, absolutism, 606; and Voltaire, 643; as enlightened absolutist, 651; starts War of Austrian Succession, 682

Frederick III, elector of Prussia (the Ostentatious), see Frederick I, king of Prussia

Frederick VII, king of Denmark, 831

Frederick of Saxony, 474–475

Frederick William I, king of Prussia, 602–605

Frederick William III, king of Prussia, 756

Frederick William IV, king of Prussia, 830–832, 885

French Academy, 559

French Revolution: causes of, 733–736; moderate first phase,

736-742; France/Austro-Prussian war as result of, 743; monarchy falls, second phase of, 743-748; Reign of Terror, 748-749; Thermidorean reaction, the Directory, 748-750; rise of Napoleon, 750-751

Freud, Sigmund, 864-865, 904, 993-994

Freudian psychology, 864-865, 993-994

Froissart, Jean, 397, 398

Fronde, 560

Fugger family, 474

Fulda, abbey of, 258

Fulton, Robert, 913

Fundamental Laws, 895-896

Fur-collar crime, 410-411

Fust, Johann, 437

Future, perspective on, 1131-1134

Gabelle, 455

Gabriel, 244

Gaiseric, 225

Galen, 249, 710-711

Galileo, 632-634

Galliani, Abbé, 209

Gallican liberties, 456

Gama, Vasco da, 511, 519

Gambetta, Léon, 901

Gandhi, Mahatma, 1078

*Gargantua* (Rabelais), 449

Garibaldi, Giuseppe, 883

Gasoline, from coal, 1110

Gattinara, Chancellor, 481

Gaugin, Paul, 1000

Gaul: under Rome, 172, 179, 195, 197, 198; Franks invade, 199

Gauls: migration of, 32; invade Italy, sack Rome, 148-149

Gedrosian Desert, 111

Gelasius I, pope, 238-239

*General History of the Indies* (Oviedo), 518

General Motors strike, 1016

Geneva, Calvinist theocracy in, 485-487

Genius, concept of, 433

Genoa, 285, 423

Gentz, Friedrich von, 742

Geoffrey, son of Henry II, 336

Geoffrey of Lorraine, 379

Geoffrin, Madame, 648

Geography, Hellenistic, 135-136

Geometry, Hellenistic, 134

George I, king of England, 565, 583-584

George II, king of England, 584

George III, king of England, 730

*Georgics* (Virgil), 182

Gerald of Wales, 333

Géricault, Théodore, 812

German Confederation of the Rhine: formed, 755-756, 801; in Revolution of 1848, 829-832; and unification of Germany, 885-888; dissolved, 888

German Empire: formed, 891; events from 1871 to 1914, 897-899; wins Franco-Prussian War, 948; system of alliances, rival blocs before 1914, 948-953; supports Austria-Hungary in Balkan Wars, 954; plans to attack France, then Russia, 955; invades neutral Belgium, W.W. I starts, 956; in W.W. I, 957-968, 978-979

Germanic peoples, 950; migration of, 214-217; society of, 217-221; conquer Britain, 221-222; prevail in West, 238; Martel attempts to unite, 258

German Workers' Party, *see* Nazism

Germany: Rome in, 179-181, 189, 195, 197; Carolingians in, 261-262; and development of Holy Roman Empire, 353-357; neglected by Frederick II, 360; Luther and Protestant Reformation in, 473-477; Protestantism's impact on, 477-484; arena of Habsburg-Valois conflict, 480; and Charles V, 481-482; and Luther's ideas, 483-484; and Thirty Years' War, 530-536; after war, 534-536; serfdom in eastern, 594; and Seven Years' War, 682; Napoleon in, 754, 755-756; industrialization of, 775, 776-779, 780; German Confederation formed, 801; romantic movement in, 812-818; and Revolution of 1848, 830-832; unification as German Empire, 885-891; as national state, 897-899; trade with British, 915; emigration from, 922, 923; in Africa, 927, 928-930; in Asia, 930; reasons for imperialism, 931-934; system of alliances, rival blocs before 1914, 948-953; supports Austria-Hungary in Balkan wars, 954; plans to attack France, then Russia, 955; invades neutral Belgium, W.W. I starts, 956; in W.W. I, 957-968; Brest-Litovsk treaty with Russia, 975; war ends, revolution, 979-980; reparations issue, 1006-1010; occupation of Ruhr, 1007-1010; Weimar Republic's government, 1011; Great Depression, 1013-1015; Nazi, as totalitarian state, 1026-1028, 1039-1048; expansionism, 1049-1053; British, France declare war on, 1053; in W.W. II, 1053-1056, 1060-1065; post-W.W. II conditions, 1071; economic recovery in West Germany, 1073, 1076

*Germany in Her Deepest Humiliation* (pamphlet), 756

*Germinal* (Zola), 869

Germ theory of disease, 841

Gertrude of Saxony, 339

Gesith, 219

Gestapo, 1047

Gheslin de Busbecq, Ogier, 519

Ghiberti, Lorenzo, 431, 433

Ghirlandaio, 431

Ghirshman, Roman, 58

Gibbon, Edward, 189-190, 192, 195, 206-207, 703

Gioberti, Vincenzo, 880

Giotto, 431

Girondists, 744, 745

Gish, Lillian, 1003

Gladiators, Roman, 193-194

Gladstone, William, 902-903

Glanvill, 318

*Gleaners, The* (Millet painting), 665

Glorious Revolution, 582-583

Godfrey of Bouillon, 379

Goebbels, Joseph, 1042-1043

Goethe, Johann W., 815

Gold, 510, 515, 1082; standard, 1014

Golden Horde, 609

Goldwater, Barry, 1094

Gomulka, Wladyslaw, 1087

Gordon, Charles, 930

Gospel book of Lindisfarne, 266

Gothic cathedrals, 371-378

Hôtel-Dieu, 714–715
House of Commons, *see* Parliament, English
House of Lords, *see* Parliament, English
Hugh, abbot of Cluny, 304, 344
Hugh, bishop of Lincoln, 327
Hugo, Victor, 815–816
Huguenots, 487, 524, 525, 559, 566–567
*Human Comedy, The* (Balzac), 869
Humanism: secular, 427–428, 468; Christian, 444–450, 468, 469
*Hunchback of Notre Dame, The* (Hugo), 815
Hundred Years' War, 395–404
Hungary: in Roman era, 181; Habsburgs conquer from Otto-man Turks, 598–600; nobles thwart Habsburgs, 60; Mag-yars dominate, 802; part in Austrian Revolution of 1848, 827–830; as part of Austro-Hungarian Empire, 903–904; independent republic proclaimed, 979; 1919 peace treaty, 982–984; Little Entente formed against, 1007; as example of conservative authoritarianism, 1025; forced into alliance with Germany, 1053; Russia occupies, 1067; revolt in, 1087. *See also* Austro-Hungarian Empire
Huns, 198, 216
Hurrians, 29, 31
Hus, John, 409, 475, 476
Hutton, Ulrich von, 479
Huxley, Aldous, 996
Hydrostatics, science of, founded, 134–135
Hyksos, 24, 28–29
Hyphasis River, 111

Iaroslave, prince of Kiev, 607
Iberian Peninsula: pluralism of, 459; politically united by Isa-bella, Ferdinand, 459–462. *See also* Portugal; Spain
ibn Thabit, Zaid, 244
Ice Age, 7
Ideograms, 16–17
*Iliad,* 78–79, 92
Illegitimacy: in 17th, 18th centuries, 697, 698–699; urban, in 1900, 857
*Imitation of Christ, The* (Thomas à Kempis), 471
Immigration, *see* Migrations
Immunology, 841
Imperialism, pre-Roman: Mesopotamian, 14–16; ancient Egyptian, 29; Hittite, 31, 33, 34–35; Assyrian, 51–56; Per-sian, 57, 59–61, 62–65
Imperialism, Western: 18th-century competition for colonial empires, 680–690; of late 19th century, 912–943; "new," 927–943; in Africa, 927–930; in Asia, 930–931; causes of, 931–934; critics of, 934–935; responses to, 935–943; col-lapses in Asia, Africa, 1078–1082
Impressionism, 1000
Inca empire, 514
Incest, Germanic practice, 258
Income: in 18th-century colonies, 685; of handloom weavers, 766; Industrial Revolution's effect on British, 774–775, 783–784; 1900 urban, 846, 851
Income tax, in 1900, 846
Indentured servants, 684
*Index of Prohibited Books,* 502
India, 687; Alexander enters, 111; Ptolemies, Seleucids trade with, 121, 122; and Seven Years' War, 682; British colony, 912; West in, 930; response to imperialism, 937–939; key

role in ending of imperialism, divided into two nations, 1078, 1080
Indian National Congress, 939
Indians, American, 513, 728; enslavement of, 541, 544; and Spanish settlers, 688–689; effect of European expansion on, 915
Individualism, in the Renaissance, 426–427
Indochina, 930, 1080
Indo-Europeans, 31–32, 35, 144
Indulgences, 475, 501
Industrial Revolution: in England, 764–775; origins of, 764–765; and first factories, 765–768; energy problems in, 768–770; Watt's steam engine, 770–772; coming of railroads, 772–774; and economic growth, 774–775; spreads, 775–780; Continent lags in industrializing, 775–776; agents of, 776–780; capital-labor relations, 780–788; factory owners, 780–781; workers, 781–784; working conditions, 784–787; growth of unions, 787–788; population pressures, 788–789; nonindustrialization, famine in Ireland, 789–792; effect on urban growth, 836–837; effect on urban class structure, 846–856; in Russia, 893–895
Industry: Hellenistic, 124–125; in Roman Empire, 197, 202–203; growth limited in colonies, 684; cottage, 675–679, 698, 765–766; revolution in, 764–788; Russian, under five-year plans, 1032–1033
Infanticide: under Hebrew law, 49; in ancient Greece, 85; Islam proscribes female, 246; in Middle Ages, 333; in Ren-aissance, 440–441; in 18th century, 701
Infantry, 53, 614
Infants: nursing of, in 18th century, 700–701; changing pat-terns of care for, 861; caring for, in 1900, 862–863
Inflation: in late Roman Empire, 202, 203; after Thirty Years' War, 536; in Germany in 1920s, 1009
Inheritance: Hebrew, 49; Muslim, 245–246
Innocent I, pope, 225
Innocent III, pope, 311, 363, 367, 381, 440
Innocent IV, pope, 311
Innocent VIII, pope, 470
Inquests (English inquiries), 352
*Inquiry into the Nature and Causes of the Wealth of Nations* (Adam Smith), 805
Inquisition: Spanish, 461–462; Roman, 502–503
*Institutes* (Justinian), 240
*Institutes of the Christian Religion, The* (Calvin), 485–487
International Association for the Exploration and Civilization of Central Africa, 928
International Working Men's Association, 905
Investment, foreign, 915
Ionians, 100, 101
Iran, *see* Persian Empire
Iraq, 984
Ireland: early monasteries in, 234; and Church of Ireland, 495–496; and potatoes as staple food, 710; nonindustriali-zation, famine in, 789–792; struggle with Britain over home rule, 902–903; emigrants from, 923, 924; 1916 upris-ing in, 966; Catholic south granted autonomy, 1012; joins Common Market, 1082
Irnerius, 365
Iron: increased use of, 321; monasteries produce, 344; pro-duction stagnates, 769–770; and Industrial Revolution, 772
Iron Curtain, 1069
Irrigation, 10, 11; in Ptolemaic Egypt, 125

Isabella, queen of England, 395

Isabella, queen of Spain, 378, 451, 458, 459–462

Isabella of Este, duchess of Mantua, 443

Isis, 25, 29–31; cult of, 128–129

Islam, 19: Hebrew influence on, 45, 47; rise, expansion of, 242–249; and Christian Crusades, 378–381; in Spain, 242, 247–248, 459, 460; and Ottoman Turks, 599

Ismail, khedive of Egypt, 919–920

Isolationism, American, 984

Israel: creation of ancient, 45; religion in, 45–47; life in, 47–51; falls to Assyrians, 52; prediction of Messiah in, 185; creation of modern, 1080; defeated in Egypt in war over Suez Canal, 1081; in war with Arabs, 1082. *See also* Hebrews; Jews

Italy: geography of, 142–144; early peoples in, 144–145; Roman conquest of, 146–149; maritime cities destroy Muslim fleet, prosper, 285; as 14th-century center of trade, 298; German emperors in, 355–357; origins of Renaissance in, 422–426; city-states, 452–455; Napoleon's victories in, 751; unification of, 880–885; in Egypt, 918; emigration from, 922, 924–925; in Africa, 927; in Triple Alliance, 949; in W.W. I, 960; at peace conference, 980, 984; under Mussolini, 1037–1038; in W.W. II, 1051–1052, 1053, 1064–1065; post-W.W. II conditions, 1071; recovery in, 1076. *See also* Rome

*Ius civile,* 151

*Ius gentium,* 151

Ius naturale, 151

Ivan I, Russian prince, 610

Ivan III, prince of Moscow, 610–611

Ivan IV (the Terrible), tsar of Russia, 611–613

Jacobins, 743, 744

*Jacob's Room* (Woolf), 997

*Jacquerie,* 411

Jacques de Vitry, 411

Jamaica, 513

James I, king of England, 546, 549–550, 576–577

James II, king of England, 582

James V, king of Scotland, 495

Janissary corps, 599

Japan: industrializes, 775; and Russian war, 895; West's intrusion in, 917–918; emigrants from, 925–927; and response to imperialism, 939–941; becomes imperialistic, 941; in W.W. I, 960; gains colonies from Germany in 1919, 982; joins Italy, Germany alliance, 1052; attacks U.S., in W.W. II, 1054–1056, 1060–1065

Jaspers, Carl, 995

Java, Dutch in, 930

Jeanne d'Albret, 538

Jefferson, Thomas, 725, 730, 739

Jehovah, *see* Yahweh

Jena, battle of, 756

Jenner, Edward, 718, 841

Jeremiah, 46, 50

Jericho, 8, 9, 10 (illus.)

Jerusalem: as Hebrew capital, 44–45; Assyrian siege of, 53–54; Roman siege of, 189; and Crusades, 378–381

Jesuits, 501, 502, 533, 616

Jesus Christ: life, teachings of, 184, 185–186; his nature debated, 223; his teachings in Bible, 226–227; dating method based on birth, 267. *See also* Christianity

Jet aircraft, 1108–1110

Jews: in antiquity, 42–51; and Hellenism, 120–121; and Augustus, 179; and rise of Christianity, 184–188; Rome reconquers, enslaves in Judaea, 189; Romans' hatred of, 205; in medieval Europe, 289–290, 358; attacked in 14th century, 413; in Spain, 460–462; welcomed to England by Cromwell, 581; dominate banking in France, 780; Dreyfus affair, 901; and anti-Semitism in 19th-century Austria, 904; as migrants, 923; promised national homeland by Britain, 984; and Nazis' anti-Semitism, 1011, 1028, 1040, 1047, 1054–1056; in Palestine after W.W. II, 1080; in Russia, 1084

Jiménez, Francisco, 460, 468, 471

Joan of Arc, 400–402

Joanna of Castile, 462, 480

Joffre, Joseph, 957

John, archbishop of Plano Carpini, 609

John, king of England, 336, 353, 362, 364

John II, king of Portugal, 511

John XII, pope, 305

John of Salisbury, 311, 365, 375, 427

John of Spoleto, 408

John the Baptist, 185

Johnson, Lyndon, 1092–1095

Johnson, Samuel, 812

Joliet, Louis, 566

Jordanes, 198

Joseph (biblical), 27

Joseph II, king of Austria, 656

Joyce, James, 997

Judaea, 184–186, 189

Judah, 44, 45, 52

Judaism: beliefs of, 45–47; and rise of Christianity, 184–188

Judeo-Christian tradition, 725

Jugurtha, 170

Julio-Claudians, 188–189

Julius Caesar, *see* Caesar, Julius

Julius II, pope, 429, 471, 473, 491, 498

Junkers, 605, 651

Jury system, 361

Justices of the peace, in Tudor England, 458

Justinian, 217, 237, 240–241

Justinian Code, 240, 364, 365, 451

Jutes, 222

Kaaba, 244

Kadesh, battle of, 34

Kaffirs, 927

Kafka, Franz, 997

Kaganovich, Lazar, 1088

Kalah, 55

Kandinsky, Wassily, 1000

Karlsruhe, 619

Kassites, 31, 33

Kaunitz, Eleonora von (Metternich's wife), 802

Kay, John, 678

Kazan, 612

Keats, John, 814

Kellogg, Frank B., 1011

Kellogg-Briand Pact, 1010

Kennedy, John F., 1088, 1092, 1094

Kepler, Johannes, 632

Kerensky, Alexander, 971, 973
Keynes, John Maynard, 634, 1006, 1014
Khan, Jenghiz, 609
Khans (rulers of Russia), 609
Khartoum, battle of, 930
Khrushchev, Nikita, 1085-1088
Khwarizmi, Al-, 249
Kierkegaard, Søren, 996
Kiev, principality of, 607-609
"Killing nurses," 701
King, Martin Luther, 1092
*King James Bible,* 549-550
Kingship, *see* Monarchy
Kinship ties, 5
Kipling, Rudyard, 934, 935, 981
Kirov, Sergei, 1034
Kissinger, Henry, 1095
Kitchener, Horatio H., 930, 937-938
Knighthood, 330-331, 334, 378, 397-398
Knox, John, 495, 538
Koch, Robert, 841
Koestler, Arthur, 1035
Kollontai, Alexandra, 1036
Königgrätz, battle of, 888
Koran, 244-246
Korea, 895, 941, 1069, 1073
Kornilov, Lavr, 973
Kossuth, Louis, 827
Kubitschek, president of Brazil, 1098
Kulaks, 1032
*Kulturkampf,* 898
Kun, Béla, 1025
Kuomintang, 1080
Kush, 41

Labor: effect of Industrial Revolution on, 766-767, 780, 781-788; child, 767, 785-787; in 1900, 851-855; and socialism, 906-908; in W.W. I, 965; collective bargaining established, 1016. *See also* Unions, labor
Laborers, Statute of, 393, 411-412
Labouchère, Henry, 935
Labour party, British, 1012, 1018, 1073, 1080
Laconia, 72
Lafayette, marquis de, 733, 739
Laissez-faire, economic doctrine, 806
Lake Chad, 930
Lake Shore Apartments, Chicago, 1000
Lamarck, Jean Baptiste, 867
Lamartine, Alphonse de, 815, 826, 879
Lancaster, House of, 457
Language: Indo-European, 31-32; role in modern philosophy, 994
Languedoc, 388
LaRochelle, 559
La Salle, Robert, 566
Lascaris, Jonus, 426
Las Casas, Bartholomé de, 541, 542
*Last Supper, The,* 431
Lateran Agreement of 1929, 1039
Lateran Council, 361, 473, 498
Lateran Palace, 223
Lateran Synod of 1059, 307

Latifundia, 168, 195
Latin America: economic nationalism in, 1095-1098; Cuban revolution, 1098-1099; new authoritarianism in, 1099-1101. *See also* South America
Latin language, 209-210, 240, 270, 428
Latium, 144, 145, 148, 149, 155
Latvia, Russian annexation of, 1053
Laud, William, 579
Law, John, 735
Law: Hammurabi's Code, 18, 19-23; Mosaic, 19, 20, 46; in ancient Greece, 74; Draco's code, 86, 152; in polis contrasted with Hellenistic cities, 116; Roman, 149, 150, 151, 152, 160; of Germanic tribes, 219-220; beginnings of canon, 223; Roman, preserved by Byzantines, 239-240; Justinian's codes, 240, 364, 365, 451; medieval developments in, 291; Roman curia as court of, 311; monks studying, 343; Constitutions of Melfi, 359; in medieval Europe, 360-364, 365-367; Napoleon's civil code of 1800, 752
Law of the Twelve Tables, 152
Lawrence of Arabia, 960
*Laws, The* (Plato), 102
Layard, A. H., 56
Lay investiture, 308-310
League of Armed Neutrality, 730
League of Cambrai, 455
League of Nations, 980, 982, 984, 1051
Leakey, Louis, 4
Leakey, Mary, 4
Leakey, Richard, 4
Learning: revival of in Carolingian age, 266-272; effect of printing on, 438-439
Lech River, battle at, 285
Le Corbusier, 998, 1000
Ledru-Rollin, Alexandre, 826
*Leech Book of Bald, The,* 343
Lefèvre d'Etaples, Jacques, 445
Legislative Assembly (France), 743
Legnano, battle of, 357
Le Havre, founded, 520
Leisure, *see* Recreation
*Lélia* (Sand) 816
Le Nain, Louis, 567
Lenin, Vladimir Ilyich, 972-978, 1005, 1026, 1028, 1029
Le Nôtre, André, 563
Leo I, pope, 225
Leo III, pope, 264-265
Leo IX, pope, 306, 307
Leo X, pope, 429, 455, 457, 471, 474, 498
Leo XIII, pope, 901
Leonardo da Vinci, see da Vinci, Leonardo
Leopold II (of Austria), Holy Roman emperor, 617, 656
Leopold II, king of Belgium, 928
Lepidus, 172
Leprosy, 287
Lérins, 234
Lesbos, 83
Lescot, Pierre, 520
Lespinasse, Julie de, 649
Le Tellier, François, 568
Leuctra, 104
Le Vau, Louis, 563
*Leviathan* (Hobbes), 580

Lewis, C. S., 996
*Libation Bearers, The* (Aeschylus), 95
Liberalism: central ideas of, 724–725, 805–807; roots of, 725–726; attraction of, 726–727
Liberia, 927
Liberty, concept of, 724–725, 805
*Liberty Leading the People* (Delacroix painting), 816
Libyans, 41
Licinian-Sextian rogations, 152
Licinius, 152
Liebenfels, Lanz von, 1040
Liebknecht, Karl, 980
Liège, industrialization of, 777
Life expectancy, 1125
*Life of the Emperor Augustus* (Seutonius), 261
"Limeys," English sailors, 708
Lisbon, and Portuguese commerce, 511, 514
List, Friedrich, 779, 893, 923
Lister, Joseph, 841–842
Liszt, Franz, 817
Literacy: in ancient Israel, 49; among Hellenistic women, 133; under Charlemagne, 270; in Middle Ages, 334, 365; growth of in 17th, 18th centuries, 705
Literature: Roman, 165, 181–184; Byzantine, 240–241; Bede, *Beowulf*, 267–269; development of vernacular, 404–406; writings of Northern Renaissance, 445–450; Montaigne, 544–546; Elizabeth, Jacobean, 546–550; French, encouraged by Richelieu, 559; French classicism, 567–568; of the Enlightenment, 642–647; romantic movement in, 814–816; realism in, 868–871; 20th century, 996–998; Russian, 1086–1087
Lithuania, 612, 1053
Little Entente, 1007
Liverpool and Manchester Railway, 772–773
Livy, 146, 151, 159, 183
Lloyd George, David, 902, 952, 980–982
Locarno treaties, 1010
Locke, John, 583, 642, 726
Lodge, Henry Cabot, 984
Loftus, W. K., 11
Logical empiricism, 994
Lollards, 409, 489
Lombard, Peter, 369
Lombards, 217; invasion of Rome, 225; defeated by Carolingians, 260, 262
Lombardy, and unification of Italy, 880–882
London: 12th-century, described, 295–297; Foundling Hospital, 702, Crystal Palace exposition in, 774; filth in, 839. *See also* Cities
London *Daily Mail,* 952, 1005
Long Parliament, 579
Loos, Adolf, 998
Lords, House of, *see* Parliament, English
Lorenzo the Magnificent, 429
Lorraine, 948, 982
Los Alamos laboratory, 1110
Lot, Ferdinand, 208–209
Lothair, Carolingian ruler, 275
Louis VI, king of France, 352–353, 372–373
Louis VII, king of France, 372–373
Louis VIII, king of France, 353, 358
Louis IX, king of France, 353, 358, 360, 380

Louis XI, king of France, 451, 457, 480
Louis XII, king of France, 455, 469
Louis XIII, king of France, 558, 560
Louis XIV, king of France, 681; as supreme example of absolutist monarch, 560; early years, personality, 561; building and use of Versailles, 562–565; economics under, 565–567; arts in reign of, 567–568; wars under, 568–572; death of, 572; provides refuge for James II, 582; hatred of Dutch, 584–585; and Peace of Utrecht, 682
Louis XV, king of France, 654–655
Louis XVI, king of France, 655; dominated by nobility, 736; accepts constitutional monarchy, 741; tries to flee, arrested, 742; imprisoned, 743; guillotined, 744–745
Louis XVIII, king of France: 797, 799, 800, 823
Louis Napoleon, *see* Napoleon III
Louis Philippe, king of France, 824–825
Louis the German, 275–276
Louis the Pious, 274–275, 276
Louise of Savoy, 538
Louisiana, 682, 688
Louvre, 520
Lovett, William, 852
Low Countries, *see* Netherlands
Loyalists, in American Revolution, 730
Loyola, Ignatius, 501–502
Lucretia, 159–160
Luddites, 782
Ludendorff, Erich von, 959–960, 964, 978, 1041
Lueger, Karl, 904, 1040
Lully, Jean-Baptiste, 568
Lunéville, Treaty of, 754
Lupercalia, 228–229
*Lusitania,* 960
Luther, Martin: and printing, 439; use of Lefèvre's texts, 445; early years, 473–474; launches Protestant Reformation, 474–476; his theology, 476–477, 478–479; and impact of his beliefs, 477–479, 482–484; reaction to Copernican theory, 631
Lutheranism: in Scandinavia, 496; in France, 522; in Germany, 530–531, 534; supported by Richelieu, 559
Lützen, battle of, 533
Luxemburg, Rosa, 980
Lycurgan regimen, 85–86
Lydia, 60
Lyell, Charles, 867
Lyons, 197
*Lyrical Ballads* (Wordsworth/Coleridge), 814

MacArthur, Douglas, 1062
*Macbeth* (Shakespeare), 546, 549
Macaulay, Thomas, 546, 716
MacDonald, Ramsay, 1012, 1018
Macedonia: victory over Greeks, 104–105; conquests under Alexander, 110–111; after Alexander's death, 111–112; Roman conquest of, 157; Serbia takes from Ottoman Empire, 953
Machiavelli, Niccoló: Livy's influence on, 183; despised masses, 433; life, work, 436–437; and Renaissance kings, 451–452; Borgia hero of *The Prince,* 452; on the church, 468
MacMahon, Marie Edmé, 901
*Madame Bovary* (Flaubert), 869
Magellan, Ferdinand, 513

Magic "cures," 137
Magna Carta, 363
Magnetic compass, 517
Magyars, 277, 279, 285, 802, 903-904
Maintenon, Madame de, 566
Malaria, 287
Malaya, 926
Malthus, Thomas, 806
Managers, as emerging social elite, 1116-1117
Manchu dynasty, 916-917, 941, 943
Manchuria, 895, 941
Manetho, 28
Manhattan Project, 1110
Manicheanism, 62
Manila, 682
Manorial system, 257, 319-321
Manuel, king of Portugal, 511
Manufacturing, *see* Industrial Revolution; Industry
Mao Tse-tung, 1080
Maps, improvements in, 517
Marathon, battle of, 88
Marcel, Gabriel, 996
Marchand, Jean-Baptiste, 930
Marconi, Guglielmo, 1005
Marcus Aurelius, 190
Marduk (Babylonian god), 16, 18-19
Margaret, regent of the Netherlands, 526
Margaret of Austria, 538
Margaret of Valois, 524
Maria Theresa, queen of Austria, 651, 656, 682, 718
Maria Theresa, queen of France, 561
Marie Antoinette, queen of France, 741
Maritain, Jacques, 996
Marius, 167
Markets: medieval, 293-294; effect of Industrial Revolution on, 773
Marne, first battle of, 957; second battle of, 978
Marquette, Jacques, 566
Marriage: under Hammurabi's Code, 22-23; in ancient Israel, 47-49; in ancient Athens, 100; Roman, 159-160; Muslim, 245-246; Charlemagne decrees on, 258; in Middle Ages, 335-336; in 14th century, 413-415; in 16th, 17th centuries, 540; late, in 17th, 18th centuries, 694-695; new patterns in late 18th century, 698-699; urban in 1900, 857-858, 859-862; modern changes in, 1123-1125, 1126-1128. *See also* Family; Women
Marseilles, bubonic plague in, 389
Marshal, William, 335
Marshall, George C., 1069
Marshall Plan or economic aid to Europe, 1069, 1073
Marsiglio of Padua, 408-409, 476
Martel, Charles, 248, 254, 256, 258
Martin, John, 814
Martin V, pope, 409
Marx, Karl, 670, 780, 782; life and views of, 810-811; London years, 905-906; and Russian Revolution, 968; doctrine studied by Lenin, 972
Marxian socialism, 810-811, 972, 1027-1028. *See also* Communism
Mary, queen of Scots, 495, 528, 529, 538
Mary I, queen of England, 491, 492, 494, 539
Mary II (William and Mary), queen of England, 582, 583

Mary, Virgin, 329
Maryland, planter class in, 684
Mary of Burgundy, 481
Masaccio, 431
Massachusetts, beginnings of American Revolution in, 729
Mass transportation, 839, 844-845
Masturbation, 716, 864
Masurian Lakes, 960
*Mathematical Principles of Natural Philosophy* (Newton), 634
Mathematics: Mesopotamian, 17-18; Hellenistic, 134-135; Byzantine, 241-242; Arabic, and use of zero, 249
Matisse, Henry, 1000
Matteotti, Giacomo, 1039
Matter, and energy, 993
Matthias, Holy Roman emperor, 531
Maupéou, René de, 655
Maximilian I, Holy Roman emperor, 455, 480
Mazarin, Jules, 560
Mazzini, Guiseppe, 807, 808, 880, 882
Mecca, 242, 244, 245, 246
Mechanics: Archimedes' inventions, 134-135; Galileo's, 632-634; Newton's, 634-635
Mecklenburg, dukes of, 533
Medes, 55, 58-59, 60
Medici, Catherine de', queen of France, 520, 522-523, 524
Medici, Cosimo de', 433, 452, 454
Medici, Giovanni de', *see* Leo X, pope
Medici, Lorenzo de', 452, 455
Medici, Marie de', 558
Medici, Piero de', 455
Medici family, 430, 437
Medicine: Mesopotamian, 18; and Hippocrates, 101; Hellenistic, 136-137; Byzantine, 241 (illus.), 242; Arabic, 249; Carolingian, 272-274; monks practicing, 343, 344; in medieval Sicily, 367; and bubonic plague, 391; in 18th century, 674, 712-718; early views of, on nutrition, 710-711; 19th-century bacterial revolution, 840-842; Freudian psychology, 864-865; and longer life spans, 1129-1130
Medieval, *see* Middle Ages
Mediterranean Sea: and Egypt, 24; colonization around, 73 (map); influence on Greece, 81-82; as Christian "highway," 225; in Pirenne's thesis, 254
Medvedev, Roy, 1091
Meiji Restoration, 939
*Mein Kampf* (Hitler), 1011, 1040, 1041-1042, 1044-1045
Melanchthon, Philip, 477
Melba, Nellie, 1005
Melfi, Constitutions of, 359
Melton, William, 489
Memling, Hans, 450
Menarche, age of, 1125-1126
Mencken, H. L., 18
Mendeleev, Dmitri, 866
Menes, 24
Menopause, age of, 1125-1126
Mental illness, 715-716, 864-865, 993-994
Mercantilism: as principle of Spanish colonial government, 515; as practiced by Colbert, 565-566; as colonial economic warfare, 680-689; Adam Smith's criticism of, 805-806
Merchants: in ancient Israel, 51; in cottage industry, 675-679
*Merchant's, Tale, The* (Chaucer), 336

Merici, Angela, 501
Merovech, 217
Merovingian dynasty, 217, 257
Mesopotamia, 11-23; spread of culture of, 8 (map), 14-19; influence of geography on, 11-13; society of, 13-14; thought and religion in, 17-19; Hammurabi Code, daily life in, 19-23; impact on Egypt, 24; religion compared to Judaism, 46; Jews captive in, 51; under Rome, 197; Sassanids overrun, 199
Messenia, 72, 84-85
Messiah, coming of the, 184, 185, 186
Messina, 154
Metallurgy: in China, 8; Etruscan, 145
*Metaphysics* (Aristotle), 103
Metternich, Klemens von, 820; and Napoleon, 758; and balance of power, 797-799; conservative policies, life of, 801-805; opposes Greek national war, 818; flees in 1848, 829
Mexico, 513, 918, 1096
Meyer, Eduard, 61, 148
Miasmatic theory of disease, 840
Michael, tsar of Russia, 613
Michelangelo, 429, 431, 432, 433
Michelet, Jules, 402, 807, 808
Mickey Mouse, 1005
Microwave technology, 1108
Middle Ages, 253-420; origins in Roman Empire, 198, 203; birth of, debate over date, 254-255; rise of Carolingian dynasty, 257-260; Charlemagne's empire, 260-265; intellectual revival of, 265-272; health, medical care during early, 272-274; Carolingian empire collapses, 274-276; Viking invasions, 276-279; nature of feudalism, 279-280; High Middle Ages, 284-383; 10th, 11th-century decline in disorder, 284-285; church movements for peace, 286; population growth, 286-287; economic recovery, rise of towns, 287-297; revival of trade, 297-300; commercial revolution, 300-302; revival, reform of Christian church, 302-312; life during, 316-346; peasants in, 316-330; nobility in, 330-339; monasteries in, 339-346; rejected by Renaissance, 422
Middle class: origins in Middle Ages, 287, 290-291; and Calvinist values, 579; new industrial, 780; effect of growth on representative government, 796; as political factor in England, 823; in 19th-century reform efforts in France, 823-824; in cities of 1900, 846, 847-851; changes in modern, 1115-1118
*Middlemarch* (Eliot), 869
Middleton, Sir Gilbert de, 410
Midway Island, battle of 1062
Midwives: Hebrew, 49; in Middle Ages, 331-332
Mies van der Rohe, Ludwig, 1000
Migrants, 923-927
Migrations: of Indo-Europeans, 31-33; of barbarians in 3rd century, 198-199; of Germanic peoples, 214-217; of Vikings in early Middle Ages, 276; of Greeks to Italy in Renaissance, 425-426; of Europeans in 16th century, 508-519, 541-544; of Irish to America, 789, 791; of 19th-century Europeans, 920-925; of 19th-century Asians, 925-927
Milan: prosperity in 14th century, 423; as city-state, 452, 454; Spain in, 519; in Revolutions of 1848, 829
Militarism: of Assyrians, 52-54; of Prussians, 602-605
Mill, John Stuart, 178
Millet, Jean François, 666
Mines Act of 1842, 787

Mining: Hellenistic, 124-125; use of steam in, 770, 772; use of women and children in, 786
Minoans, 76-77
Mirandola, Pico della, 427
*Missi dominici,* 262
Missionaries, 934
Mitanni, 29, 31, 35
Mithraism, 187
Mitterrand, François, 1083
Modern life: science and technology, 1106-1115; emergence of a new society, 1115-1123; women and the family, 1123-1131; perspective on the future, 1131-1134
Modern society: movies and radio in, 1003-1005; changing class structure, 1115-1118; social security, welfare reforms, 1118; rising affluence, 1118-1120; renewed discontent, student revolts, 1120-1123; changing roles of women and marriage, 1123-1128; longer life spans, 1128-1131
Modern thought: uncertainty in, 990-992; the new physics, 992-993; Freudian psychology, 993-994; modern philosophies, 994-995; revival of Christianity, 995-996; modern literature, music, art, 996-1102
Mohammed: religious visions, founding of Islam, 242; life, teachings of, 244-246; as seen in Pirenne's thesis, 255
Mohammed II, sultan, 510, 516
Mohammed Ali, 918-919
Mohammedanism, *see* Islam
Molière, 165, 568
Molotov, Vyacheslav, 1085, 1088
Moltke, Helmuth von, 955
*Mona Lisa,* 1002
Monarchy: in Mesopotamia, 13-14; in ancient Egypt, 24-26, 29-31; under Hittites, 33-34; under Cyrus the Great, 59-61; in ancient Greece, 75, 76; Hellenistic, 111-113; 114-117; evolution of Roman, 176-179, 190, 198, 200, 203; Carolingians and papal decision on, 260; development of western, 350-364; in the Renaissance, 451-452, 461-462; Charles V's ideas of, 481-482; absolutist, 556-565, 568-575; development of modern English, 581-584; and influence on differing East-West systems, 595; Enlightenment's influence on, 650-658; fall of, in France, 733-750
Monasteries: development of, 234-235; Benedictine, 235-237; 9th-century design for, 271 (illus.); 11th-century revival of, 302-305; in Middle Ages, 339-346, 365; in Spain, 574
Monet, Claude, 774, 1000
Monetary systems: Hellenistic, 121; in late Roman Empire, 202, 203
Mongols, 609-611
Monks, *see* Monasteries
Monnet, Jean, 1075, 1076
Monogamy, among Hebrews, 48
Monotheism, 29-31, 45-47, 129
Monroe Doctrine, 801
Montague, Lady Mary Wortley, 717
Montaigne, Michel de, 544-546
Montesquieu, Charles-Louis, Baron de, 642-643, 648, 658, 726
Montezuma, 513
Moors, 249
Morality: 1900 middle-class code of, 850-851; upper-working-class code of, 852
More, Thomas, 445-448, 468, 492
Mortality rates, 842, 921
Mosaic law, 19, 20, 46

Moscow, 758; rise of, 609-611; 1905 uprising in, 895
Moses, 43
Motherhood, see Family; Women
Motion: Galileo's work on, 632-634; Newton's synthesis of findings on, 634-636
Motion pictures, 1003-1005
Mountain (French political group), 744-746
Mount Olympus, 74
Movies, see Motion pictures
Mozambique, 927
*Mr., Mrs., and Baby* (Droz), 861, 862
Mun, Thomas, 680
Munich, 1041
Münster, 488
Mursilis I, 33
Mursilis II, 34
Music: French classicism, 568; baroque, 617; romanticism, 816-818; modern, 1002
Music halls, 855-856
Muslims: victory at Guadelete, 217; rise, expansion of, 242-249; in Pirenne's thesis, 254-255; checked by Charlemagne, 261; sack Rome, 277; in Spain, 277-279; accelerate feudalism, 279; at battle of Omdurman, 930; and British in India, 937, 938, 939
Mussolini, Benito, 1005; in power, 1037-1039; opposes Hitler, then joins, attacks Ethiopia, 1051-1052; defeats in Greece, 1053; deposed, 1064-1065
Mycenaeans, 32, 75-78
*My Secret Life* (anonymous) 858-859
Mystery plays, 327, 378
Mystery religions, 127-129

Nagasaki, bombing of, 1965
Nagy, Imre, 1087
Nahum, 56
Nanking, Treaty of, 917
Naples: University of, 359; as city-state, 452, 454, 455; Spain in, 519; and unification of Italy, 880, 883
Napoleon I, emperor of France: rules France, 751-754; England defeats at battle of Trafalgar, 754; becomes emperor, 754-755; European wars of, 754-756; defeated in Russia, abdicates, 758; returns from exile, defeated at Waterloo, exiled again, 779-800; in Egypt, 918
Napoleon III, emperor of France: as Louis Napoleon, wins election in 1848, 827; and rebuilding of Paris, reasons for election, 876-877; as president of Second Republic, 877-878; as emperor, 878-880; and Cavour, 882, 883; and Bismarck, 887, 888
*Napoleonic Ideas* (Napoleon), 877
Nasser, Gamal Abdel, 1080-1081
National Aeronautics and Space Administration (NASA) 1111
National Assembly of France, 737, 739, 741, 743, 877
National Association for the Advancement of Colored People, 1092
National Convention (France), 744
Nationalism: stimulated by Hundred Years' War, 404; concept of state in Renaissance, 451-452; in Hungary, 600; and French Republic's success in war, 749; concept of, 807-808; triumphs in Europe, 876-908; in France, 876-880; in Italy, 880-885; in Germany, 885-891; and the modernizing of Russia, 891-896; from 1871 to 1914, 896-

904; vs. socialism, 904-908; as a cause of W.W. I, 956; Nazism grows out of, 1027-1028; German, in Vienna, 1040; Hitler's 1048; spreads to colonial territories, 1078-1082; economic, in Latin America, 1095-1098
National Labor Relations Act, 1016
National People's party, China, 1080
National Recovery Administration, 1016
National Socialist German Workers' party, see Nazism
*National System of Political Economy* (List), 779
Nations, see Nationalism; State
NATO (North Atlantic Treaty Organization), 1069, 1077
Nature: romanticism's concern with, 812; modern environmental movement, 1107-1108
Navarino, battle of, 820
Navarre, 459, 460
Navigation: 15th-century developments in, 517; problems of as factor in scientific revolution, 635-636; instruments developed for, 636
Navigation Acts, 680-681, 684-686
Nazism: as variety of totalitarianism, 1026-1028; and Germany, 1039-1048; and expansionism, 1048-1054; and racial imperialism, 1054-1056
Neanderthal Man, 4, 6
Near East: origins of Western world in, 4-37; kingdoms and empires, 40-67
Nefertiti, 29
Negroes, see Blacks
Nelson, Horatio, 754
Neolithic Age, 6-11
Nero, 188
Nerva, 190
Netherlands: ravaged by Louis XI, 480; under Charles V, 525-526; revolt of, 526-528; southern provinces (Belgium) under Habsburgs, northern provinces (Holland) form United Provinces, declare independence, turn to English for help, 528-529; independence of United Provinces recognized at Peace of Westphalia, 534; in 17th century, 584-586; new farming system in, 667-668; and competition for colonial empire, 680-681; declares war on Britain, 730; and First Coalition against France, 743, 745, 746, 749; as part of Napoleon's Grand Empire, 756; united under enlarged Dutch monarchy, 797
Newcomen, Thomas, 770
New Deal, 1015-1018, 1092
New Economic Policy, 1029, 1030, 1031
Newfoundland, discovery of, 515
New Harmony, Indiana, 788
New Jersey, 684
New Testament, see Bible
Newton, Isaac, 634-635, 640-641, 643, 865
Nicaean council, 223
Nicholas II, pope, 306
Nicholas V, pope, 427
Nicholas I, tsar of Russia, 830
Nicholas II, tsar of Russia, 895, 950, 968-971
Nicoliasm, 306, 308
Nicolson, Harold, 980
Nieman River, 756
Nietzsche, Friedrich von, 990-991, 995
Nigeria, missionaries in, 934
Nijmegen, Treaty of, 570
Nikon, Patriarch, 613

Nile River, 23–24, 930
*1984* (Orwell), 997
Ninety-five Theses, Luther, 475–476
Nineveh, 51, 55, 56
Nippur, 12 and illus.
Nitrogen-storing crops, 666–667
Nivelle, Robert, 957, 966
Nixon, Richard, 1082, 1095
Nobel Peace prize, 1010
Nobility: in Mesopotamia, 13–14; in medieval Europe, 330–339; fur-collar crime by, 410–411; absolute monarchy's mastery over, 556; Richelieu breaks power of French, 558–559; Louis XIV humbles, 561, 562, 564, 565; in eastern Europe, 592–596; of Hungary thwarts Habsburgs, 600; Prussian, 600, 602; Russian, 609, 611–615; under Catherine the Great, 653; in France under Louis XV, 654; as second estate in France, 735
Nomads: Paleolithic, 5; Neolithic, 7–8; Mesopotamian, 11; Hebrew, 47; Bedouins, 242, 244
Nördlingen, battle of, 534
Normandy: origin of word, 277; rise of, 284; in Hundred Years' War, 399–400; in W.W. II, 1065
Normans: in England, 351–352; in Sicily, 358
North Africa, in World War II, 1064
North America: European exploration of, 510–519; French, Spanish, British fight over, 680–684; farming in, high standard of living, 684–686; revolution of British colonies, 727–732; railroads as aid to settlement of, 913; immigration as factor in population growth, 921; discrimination against Asian emigrants, 925–927. *See also* Canada; United States
North Atlantic Treaty Organization (NATO), 1069, 1077
Northcliffe, Lord, 1005
North German Confederation, 888
Northumbrian culture, 266
Norway: 215; and Reformation, 496; women's suffrage in, 896; breaks from Sweden, 903; migration from, 925; Socialist party's growth in, 1018; Nazis occupy, 1053; post-W.W. II recovery, 1076
Notre Dame cathedral, 375, 701
Novgorod, 610
NRA (National Recovery Administration), 1016
Nubia, 24, 29, 41
Nunneries, *see* Convents
Nuremberg Laws, 1047
Nursing of babies, 333, 700–701, 862
Nutrition: and European diet, 707–712; need to improve knowledge of, 1130–1131. *See also* Diet

Octavian, *see* Augustus
October Manifesto, 895
Odeleric, 340
Odilo, abbot of Cluny, 305
Odo, abbot of Cluny, 304
*Odyssey*, 78–79
Oedipal complex, 864–865
*Oedipus at Colonus* (Sophocles), 96
*Oedipus the King* (Sophocles), 96
OEEC (Organization of European Economic Corporation), 1073, 1076
Oil, price of, 1082
Old age, 1128–1131

Old Believers, 613
Oldenbarneveldt, Jan van, 585
Old Testament, *see* Bible
Oleg (Varangian ruler), 607
Oligarchy, 75
Olivares, Count, 574
Omayyad dynasty, 247, 248
Omdurman, battle of, 930
*On Airs, Waters, and Places* (Hippocrates), 101
"On Cannibals" (Montaigne), 545
*On Christian Liberty* (Luther), 477
*On Conoids and Spheroids* (Archimedes), 135
"On Cruelty" (Montaigne), 545
*On Female Disorders,* 274
*On Floating Bodies* (Archimedes), 134
*On Plane Equilibriums* (Archimedes), 134
*On Pleasure* (Valla), 428
"On Solitude" (Montaigne), 544
*On Spirals* (Archimedes), 135
"On the Dignity of Man" (Mirandola), 427
*On the False Donation of Constantine* (Valla), 428
*On the Heaven* (Aristotle), 103
*On the Measurement of a Circle* (Archimedes), 135
*On the Origin of Species by the Means of Natural Selection* (Darwin), 4, 867–868
*On the Physical Elements* (Hildegard), 274
*On the Revolutions of the Heavenly Spheres* (Copernicus), 630
*On the Sphere and Cylinder* (Archimedes), 135
*One Day in the Life of Ivan Denisovich* (Solzhenitsyn), 1087
"Open Door" policy, 942
Open-field agricultural system, 321, 664–666
Opium trade, 917
Oppenheimer, J. Robert, 1110
Orangerie, at Versailles, 564
Oratories of Divine Love, 471
Orderic Vitalis, 340
*Oresteia, The* (Aeschylus), 95
Organization of European Economic Corporation (OEEC), 1073, 1076
Origins of Western world, 4, Paleolithic (Old Stone) Age, 5–6; Neolithic (New Stone) Age, 6–11; Mesopotamians, 10–22; Sumerians, 11–14; Babylonians, Egyptians, 23–31; Indo-European mass migrations,
Orléans, 401
Orlov, Gregory, 652
Orthodox Christianity, *see* Eastern Orthodox church; Greek Orthodox church
Orwell, George, 997
Osiris, 25, 29–31
Ostrogoths, 215, 216, 217
O'Sullivan, John Louis, 808
*Othello* (Shakespeare), 546, 549
Othman, 244
Otto I, German king, 285
Ottoman Turks: as threat to Europe, 510; Habsburgs drive out of Hungary, 598–600; history of, 599; driven from Greece, 818–820; in Egypt, 918–920; empire dying, 948, 949, 953; destroyed, 954, 960
Overseas expansion: 508–519; 541–544; by Vikings, 510; by Turks, 510; by Portugal, 510–511; Columbus, 511–513; Spanish, 513–514; Dutch, 514–515; English-French, 515; colonial administration, 515; economic effects of Spain's,

516; stimuli for, 516–517; motives for, 517–519; slave trade in, 541–544
Ovid, 163, 166
Oviedo, 518
Owen, Robert, 788
Oxford University, 367, 371

Pacific, World War II in, 1062–1064
Paganini, Niccolò, 817
Paine, Thomas, 730, 742
Painting, *see* Art
Pakistan, creation of, 1080
Palaces, as symbols of absolutism, 617–618
Palacký, Francis, 808, 829
Palatine Hill, 145
Paleolithic Age, 5–6
Palestine: ancient, 43–45; attacked by Assyrians, 51, 52; Islam controls, 242; Arabs and Jews in, 1080
Palm, Johann Philipp, 756
Palmerston, Lord, 831
Panama, isthmus of, 682
Panama Canal, 914
Panama Canal Zone, 933
Pankhurst, Emmeline, 896
*Pantagruel* (Rabelais), 449
Papacy: first popes, 225; alliance with Carolingians, given Papal States, 260; and crowning of Charlemagne, 264–265; 11th-century reform of, 305–312; cardinals elect pope, 307; Gregory VII's reforms, 307–308; and lay investiture controversy, 308–310; further Gregorian reforms, 311–312; and Frederick I, 357; and the Crusades, 378–381; and 13th-century dispute with English, French kings, 381–383; and Babylonian Captivity, schism, 407–408; conciliar movement, 408–410; Renaissance popes, 427, 429; French break with, 456; living style of 16th-century popes, 470–471; Luther challenges authority of, 475–476; and reform, 498–499; in Italian unification, 880, 882, 883; Pius IX declares dogma of papal infallibility, 898; in pre-W.W. I Italy, 1037; Italy recognizes Vatican as independent state, 1039
Papal States, 260, 407, 452, 498, 883
Papen, Franz von, 1043, 1046
Paper, and printing, 437
Paris: students in medieval, 367; prostitutes in, 697; uprising of poor in, during revolution, 737–739; rebuilt, 842–844; surrenders to Bismarck forces, 891; Commune, 899; as artistic center, 1011–1012. *See also* France
Paris, Peace of (1814), 797
Paris, Peace of (1815), 800
Paris, Treaty of 1763, 682
Paris, Treaty of 1783, 732
Parlement of Paris, 360, 654, 655, 736
Parliament, English: Hundred Years' War stimulates development of, 403–404; and Tudors, 458; and Stuarts, 577–580; under Cromwell, 580–581; in Restoration, 581–582; triumph of, 583–584; in American Revolution, 729, 730; and 19th-century reform movement, 820–823; Lords vs. Commons in 1901 to 1910, 902; rules India, 937, 938
Parthenon, 93, 94
Passchendaele, 957
Pasternak, Boris, 1086–1087
Pasteur, Louis, 389, 841, 865
Pasteurization, 841

Paston, John, 414
Paston, Margaret, 414
Patriarchs, Greek Orthodox, establishment of position, 239
Patricians, 150, 151–154
Paul III, pope, 499, 501, 502
Paul VI, pope, 307
Paul of Tarsus, *see* St. Paul
Paul the Deacon, 270
Pavia, battle of, 498
Pax Romana, 176, 183, 184
Peace of Augsburg, 484, 485
Peace of Paris of 1814, 797
Peace of Paris of 1815, 800
Peace of Utrecht, 571–572, 682
Peace of Villafranca, 882, 883
Peace of Westphalia, 534, 584
Pearl Harbor, attack on, 1054, 1060
Peasantry: in ancient Egypt, 27; in ancient Athens, 86; in feudal society, 257; in medieval Europe, 316–330; revolts of, 411–413, 477–479; and Lutheran movement, 477; in eastern Europe, 592–596; in east Germany, 600; in Russia, 609, 611–614; as third estate in France, 736; conditions among Irish, 789–792; Russian, 1032; recent decline of, 1117
Peel, Robert, 821, 823
Peking, 917, 943
Peloponnesian War, 91
Peloponnesus peninsula, 76
Penitentials, 229
Penn, William 581
Pennsylvania, 684
*People, The* (Michelet), 808
People's Budget, 902
People's Charter, 821
*Père Goriot* (Balzac), 869
Pereire, Emile, 780, 809
Pereire, Isaac, 780, 809
Pergamene monarchy, 112
Pergamum, 112, 116 (illus.)
Pericles, 89–90, 91, 93
Périer, Casimir, 824
Perón, Juan, 1100
Perry, Matthew, 918, 939
Persepolis, 110
Persian Empire, 57–65; map, 55; influence of Assyrians on, 56–57; geography of, 57–58; background of, 58–59; creation of, 59–61; religion in, 61–62; becomes world empire, 62–65; in Greek wars, 88–89; Alexander the Great overthrows, 110
Persian Gulf, 11
*Persian Letters, The* (Montesquieu), 642
Peru, 514, 926
Pétain, Henri-Philippe, 966, 1053
Peter I (the Great), tsar of Russia: imitates Versailles, 565; his reign, 614–616; builds St. Petersburg, 620–622; abolishes hereditary succession, 651
Peter III, tsar of Russia, 652, 682
Peterloo, battle of, 821
Peter of Dreux, 337
Peter the Hermit, 379
Petrarch, Francesco, 183, 422
Petri, Olaus, 496

Petrograd Soviet of Workers' and Soldiers' Deputies, 971
Pharaohs, 24–26, 29–31
Pharmacists, in 18th century, 712–713
Phidias, 94
Philinus, 137
Philip I, king of France, 308, 310
Philip II (Augustus), king of France: pope compels to take back wife, 311; accomplishments as king, 353; and taxes, 358; gains Normandy, 363; and medieval education, 367, 371; on Crusade, 380
Philip III, king of France, 353
Philip IV (the Fair), king of France, 381–383, 389, 451
Philip VI, king of France, 395
Philip II, king of Macedonia, 104, 110
Philip II, king of Spain: Iberian peninsula united by, 462; marriage to Mary I of England, 494; and state finances, 516; inherits Low Countries, Spain, 525, 526; "pacifies" Low Countries, 526–528; as defender of Catholicism, 529; his Armada defeated by England in 1588, 530
Philip III, king of Spain, 530, 574
Philip IV, king of Spain, 574
Philip V, king of Spain, 688
Philip of Burgundy, 462, 480
Philippe de Beaumanoir, 364
Philippines, 682, 925, 931, 1080
Philistines, 42, 45
Philosophes: ideas of, 642–646; political thinking of, 650
*Philosophical Dictionary* (Voltaire), 644
Philosophy: Greek, 88, 100–103; Hellenistic, 129–131; Greek, passed to West by Arabs, 249; medieval scholastic, 368–369; and the Enlightenment, 639–647; the French philosophes, 642–646; liberalism, 725–726, 805–807; conservatism, 802; radical theories, 805–811; determinism, 869; modern, 990–992; logical empiricism, 994; existentialism, 994–995
Phoenicians, 42, 43 (illus.), 51, 73 (map), 154
Physicians: Hippocrates, 101; in early Middle Ages, 273; Galen, 710–711; in 18th century, 713–714; women as, in Soviet Russia, 1036
Physics: Aristotelian, 103, 629–630; Galileo's experimental method, 632–633; Newton's law, 634–635; development of thermodynamics, 865–866; modern advances in, 992–993
*Physics* (Aristotle), 103
Piankhy, 41
Picasso, Pablo, 1000, 1002
Pickford, Mary, 1003
Picts, 221–222
Pilgrimages, Christian, 330
Pillnitz, Declaration of, 742–743
Pilsudski, Joseph, 1025
Pinel, Philippe, 716
Pippin I, 257
Pippin II, 257
Pippin III, 258, 260
Pirenne, Henri, 254, 288–289
Pisa, 285
Pisistratus, 87
Pissarro, 1000
Pitt, William, 682
Pius II, pope, 427, 470
Pius VII, pope, 752
Pius IX, pope, 883, 898

Pizzaro, Francisco, 514
Plague, 208, 269
Planck, Max, 992, 993, 996
Plantagenet, Richard, 333
Plantations, in New World, 684
Plataea, 89
Plato, 73, 102
Plautus, 165
Plays, Athenian, 95–97
Plebeians, 150, 151–154
Plutarch, 93, 114, 132, 134
Poincafe, Raymond, 1007, 1009, 1011
Poitiers, battle of, 397–398, 399
Poitiers, Diane de, 520
Poland: serfdom in, 594; conflicts with Russia, 612, 613, 614; partitioning of in 18th century, 653–654; and nationalism, 895; gains territory in 1919, 982; signs pact with France, 1007; as example of conservative authoritarianism, 1025; Nazis, Russians occupy, 1053; Russia occupies all, 1067; revolt in, 1087; and Solidarity movement, 1091
Polis, 72–75, 114, 115, 149
Politeuma, 120
*Politics* (Aristotle), 103
Poltava, battle of, 615, 620
Polybius, 142, 157, 164, 240
Polygamy: among Hebrews, 47–48; Koran on, 245, 246; among Germanics, 258; theories of, concerning Vikings, 276; 16th-century reformers' attitude toward, 541
*Pomerium,* 146
Pomeroy, Sarah, 132
Pompey, 167, 170, 171
Pontius Pilate, 184, 185, 186
Popes, *see* Papacy
Popular Front, 1019–1020
Population: growth in neolithic times, 9; of Roman Empire, 179; of ancient Rome, 193; growth in Europe, 11th to 13th centuries, 286–287; in 1377 England, 289; decline in 14th century, 388; effect of Black Death on, 392–393; losses in Germany in Thirty Years' War, 534–535; in 17th-century Amsterdam, 668; 18th-century growth, 671–675; in colonial America, 685; 19th-century growth, 789; growth in Ireland, 789; toll of Great Famine in Ireland, 791; Malthusian theory of, 806; growth in 19th-century English cities, 837; 19th-century explosion as impetus for Great Migration, 921–923
Port Arthur, 941
Portugal: dominated by Castile, Aragon, 459; united to Spanish crown, 462; and oversea exploration, 510–511; as example of conservative authoritarianism, 1025; dictatorship scrapped, 1083
Poseidon, 94
Postumus, 198
Potsdam Conference, 1067
Pottery: Chinese, 8, 10; in early Egypt, 24; Hellenistic, 125
Poussin, Nicholas, 567
Power, *see* Energy
Praetor, 150
Praetorian Guard, 188, 189 (illus.)
Pragmatic Sanction of Bourges, 456, 600
Prague, "defenestration of," 533, 829
*Praise of Folly, The* (Erasmus), 439, 448
Predestination, 246

Premarital sex, 697-699, 857-858
Presbyterian Church of Scotland, 487, 495, 705
Pre-Socratics, 100-101
Priesthood: in Mesopotamia, 13; in Egypt, 31; early Hebrew, 45; in early Iran, 61
Priestley, Joseph, 742
Primogeniture: Hebrew, 49; theories regarding Vikings, 276; among Spanish colonists, 689
*Prince, The* (Macchiavelli), 436-437, 452
*Principia* (Newton), 634, 642
Printing, 437-439, 479
Procopius, 240-241
Professional class, rise of, 848
Progress: Enlightenment's concept of, 640, 647
*Progress of the Human Mind* (Condorcet), 647
Prokofiev, Sergei, 1084
Proletariat, in Marxian socialism, 810
Propaganda: during W.W. I, 966; radio and movies used for, 1005; Stalin's use of, 1028, 1035; Hitler's use of, 1041, 1044-1045
Propylaea, 93
Prostitution: in Mesopotamia, 21; in ancient Athens, 99; Koran laws on, 245-246; in 16th century, 538-539; among poor in 17th, 18th centuries, 696-697; urban, in 1900, 858-859
Protectorate, English, 580-581
Protestantism: Luther establishes, 474-476; ideas of, 476-477; identification with French industrialism, 781; in modern age, 995-996
Protestant Reformation, 473-496; Luther's early years, 473-474; the Ninety-five Theses, 474-476; Protestant thought, 476-477; social impact of, 477-480; effect on political situation in Germany, 480-484; growth of, 484-496; Calvinism, 485-486; Anabaptists, 487-488; in England, 488-495; in Scotland, Ireland, 495-496; in Scandinavia, 496
Protestant Union, 533
Proudhon, Pierre Joseph, 810
Proust, Marcel, 997
Prussia: serfdom in, 593; rise of absolutism in 17th century, 600-606; and Seven Years' War, 682; compulsory education in, 705; issues Declaration of Pillnitz, 742-743; and First Coalition against France, 743, 745, 746, 749; at war with Napoleon, 756, 758; gains territory from France, 797; and balance of power struggle after Napoleon's defeat, 799; forms Holy Alliance, 801; and 1848 Revolution, 830-832; and unification of Germany, 885-891; develops rivalry with Britain, 950
Psychology, Freudian, 864-865, 993-994
Ptolemies: as successors to pharaohs, 112; wars over Syria, 117; rule of, 119; trade under, 121-122; mining under, 124-125; agriculture under, 125-126; culture under, 135
Ptolemy, Claudius, 134
Ptolemy, king of Egypt, 132, 135, 136
Ptolemy Lagus, 112
Public health, 674, 706; development of in 19th century, 839-840
Public transportation, 839, 844-845
Puerto Rico, 513, 689
Pugachev, Emelian, 652-653
Punic wars, 154-157
Punt (monarchy), 41
Purges, Stalin's, 1034-1035

Purging, medical, 712-713, 714
Puritans: Calvinism as model for, 487; their desire to purify English church, 494-495; urge new translation of Bible, 549; rise to power in England, 578-579; Cromwell and the Protectorate, 580-581
Pushkin, Alexander, 816
"Putting-out" system, 675-679, 740, 765-766
Pyramids, 25-26
Pyrenees, Treaty of, 575
Pyrrhus, 154

Quackery, medical, 137, 716
Quadruple Alliance, 758, 797
Quaestors, 150
Quakers, 781
Quebec, 515, 682
*Quest of the Historical Jesus, The* (Schweitzer), 996
Quiberon Bay, 682
*Quo Vadis* (film), 1003

Rabelais, François, 449-450
Racine, Jean, 568
Racism: and theories of Rome's decline, 207-209; origins of North American, 541-544; and Asian migrants, 925-927; and imperialism, 933-934; of British in India, 939; Nazism grows out of, 1027-1028; and Nazism, 1040, 1054
Radar, invention of, 1108
Radetzky, Josef, 830
Radiation Laboratory, University of California at Berkeley, 1114
Radical political concepts: liberalism, 805-807; nationalism, 807-808; utopian socialism, 808-810; Marxian socialism, 810-811
Radio, 1005
*Raft of the Medusa, The* (Géricault painting), 812
Railroads: invention, spread of, 772-774; in Russia, 893, 894; facilitate trade, 913; investment in, 915
Rákóczy, Francis, 600
Ralph, archbishop of Tours, 364
Rameses II, 34
Rape: Renaissance attitudes toward, 440; of servant girls in 17th, 18th centuries, 696
Rasputin, 969-970
Rastrelli, Bartolomeo, 622
Rathenau, Walter, 964
Rats, and bubonic plague, 673-674
Razin, Stenka, 614
Realism, in literature, 868-871
*Reconquista,* 248, 459, 460
Recreation: in 14th century, 416-417; in Rome, 165-167; of middle classes in 1900, 850; of working classes, 855-856; motion pictures and radio, 1003-1005; modern, 1119-1120
"Red Shirts," 883
*Reflections on the Revolution in France* (Burke), 742
Reformations: Protestant, 473-496; Catholic and Counter, 496-503
Reform Bill of 1832, 821
Refrigerated transportation, 914
Reichstag, 897, 1043, 1046
Reign of Terror, in French Revolution, 748-749
Relativity, Einstein's theory of, 992-993

Religion: Mesopotamian, 12–13, 16, 18–19; in ancient Egypt, 25–26; 29–31; Jewish, 45–47; early Iranian, 61–62; in ancient Greece, 74–75; Hellenistic, 126–129; Roman, 163, 166–167; early Christianity, 184–188, 204–206, 222–236; rise of Islam, 242–249; 11th-century revival, reform in Christianity, 302–312; as center of medieval life, 327–330; Islam driven from Spain, 460; Great Schism ends Christian unity, 473–496; 16th-century practice of, 482–483; as motive for explorations, 517–518; 16th-century wars over, 519–520; English dissension over, 578–583; Dutch toleration of, 585–586; Vikings in Russia convert to Eastern Orthodox Christianity, 607; influence on baroque arts, 616–617; and science, 637–638, 868; and the Enlightenment, 640–641, 644–645, 646; in modern age, 995–996; in communist Russia, 1035

Remarque, Erich, 957–959
*Remembrance of Things Past* (Proust), 997
Remus, 145
Renaissance: defined, 422; Italian origins of, 422–426; hallmarks of, 426–429; art and artists during, 429–433; social change during, 433–444; in the North, 444–450; politics and the state in, 451–462; contribution to scientific revolution, 635
Renoir, 1000
Reparations, World War I, 1006–1010
Representative government, 724–725
*Republic, The* (Plato), 102
Republicanism, of 19th-century liberals, 807
Republic of South Africa, 1082
*Res Gestae* (Augustus), 178
Resistance movement, World War II, 995
Restoration, English, 581–582
Revolutionary era: ideas of liberty, equality, 724–727; American Revolution, 727–733; French Revolution, 733–750; Industrial Revolution, 764–788; Industrial and French Revolutions fuse, dual revolution, 796; revolution in France, 1830, 823–824; 1848 revolutions in Europe, 824–832
Rhineland, 982, 1007, 1051
Rhine River, as Roman-German frontier, 181
Ricardo, David, 806, 811
Richard I (the Lion-Hearted), king of England, 344, 362, 364, 380
Richard II, king of England, 409, 413
Richard III, king of England, 458
Richard Plantagenet, duke of York, 290
*Richard II* (Shakespeare), 546
Richelieu, Cardinal (Armand Jean du Plesis), 533, 534, 558–560
Riddles, Anglo-Saxon, 268–269
Riefenstahl, Leni, 1005
Rigord, 353
*Rite of Spring, The* (Stravinsky), 1002
Roads: Assyrian, 55; Persian, 63–64; Roman, 181, 192, 196
Robespierre, Maximilien, 742, 743, 744–749
Robin Hood, 410
Roger I of Sicily, 358
Roger II of Sicily, 358–359, 367
Rogers, Ginger, 1005
Rollo, 284
Roma et Augustus, cult of, 179
Roman Catholic church: bishops of Rome first popes, 225; Roman tradition prevails at Synod of Whitby, 226; schism

with Greek Orthodox church, 238–239; alliance with Carolingians, 260; crowns Charlemagne first Holy Roman emperor, 264–265; 10th, 11th-century peace moves, 286; revival, reform in, 302–312; as center of medieval life, 327–330; 14th-century decline in prestige, 406–410; Babylonian Captivity, 407–408; Great Schism, 408; conciliar movement, 408–410; linchpin of Spanish monarchy, 460–462; church's condition from 1400 to 1517, 468–473; Luther breaks with, 473–476; England breaks with, 488–495; Catholic and Counter Reformations, 496–503; and Council of Trent, 499–501; establishment of Sacred Congregation of Holy Office, Roman Inquisition, 502–503; becomes "national" religion of France, 522; and the Thirty Years' War, 530–534; England denies succession to members of, 583; and science, 631, 633–634, 638; in conflict with Republican France, 741–742; signs concordat with Napoleon, 752; Bismarck attacks, 898; France severs ties with, 901–902; and modern thinkers, 996; in Mussolini's Italy, 1039. *See also* Papacy
*Romance of Tristan and Isolde, The,* 336
Roman Empire: beginnings, 154–159, 167, 168; under Augustus, 176–184; army of, 178; administration of provinces, 179; expansion of, 179–181; under Julio-Claudians, Flavians, 188–189; age of Five Good Emperors, 189–192; emperors after Augustus, events listed, 191; changes in army, 192; life in provinces, Golden Age, 195–198; disruptions of 3rd century, 198–200; reconstruction, 200–203; divided into eastern, western halves, 200; farms' decline in, 203–204; Christianity's ascendancy in, 204–206; theories of decline, 206–210; Germanic tribes invade, take over, in Europe, 215–220; Byzantine Empire's identification with, 238; Charlemagne's identification with, 264–265. *See also* Rome
Romanesque architecture, 372
Romanov dynasty, 613
Romantic love, 857, 861–862
Romantic movement, 811–818
Rome: Stoicism's influence on, 131; Hellenistic quacks' influence on, 137; rise of, 142–172; achievement of, 142; geography of Italy, 142–144; and Etruscans, 144–146; conquest of Italy, 146–149; Gauls invade, 148–149; political system, 149–151; senate in, 150; social conflict in, 151–154; overseas conquests by, 154–157; opposing attitudes develop, 157–167; Cato as symbol of traditionalism, 159–163; daily life in, 160–161; agriculture in, 161–162; slavery in, 162–163; religion in, 163; Scipio as symbol of Greek culture, 164–167; urban life in, 165–167; problems of late republic, 167–172; rise of Julius Caesar, death of republic, 171–172; Augustus in power, 176–184; expansion into northern, western Europe, 179–181; literary flowering, 181–184; entry into Jewish affairs, 184–185; city life in Golden Age, 192–195; during Babylonian Captivity, 407; Renaissance in, 426, 427, 429; France invades, 455; sacked, 455; part of Italy in 1870, 883. *See also* Papacy; Roman Empire
Rome, Treaty of, 1077
Rome-Berlin Axis, 1052
Romilles, 571
Rommel, Erwin, 1064
Romulus, 145
Romulus Augustus, 238
Roosevelt, Franklin D., 1005, 1110; and New Deal, 1015–1018; in W.W. II, 1060–1065; at Teheran Conference, 1065–1067, at Yalta Conference, dies, 1067

Schönberg, Arnold, 1002
Schönbrunn palace, 617
Schools, *see* Education
Schuman, Robert (statesman), 1071, 1076
Schumann, Robert (composer), 817
Schweitzer, Albert, 996
Science: Greek theories, 100–103; Hellenistic, 133–136; Byzantine, 242; Arabic, 249; revolution in, 628–639; Aristotelian view, 629–630; Copernicus's theory, 630–631; Tycho Brahe's observations, 631; Kepler's laws, 632; Galileo's work, 632–634; Newton's synthesis, 634–635; causes of revolution in, 635–638; consequences of revolution, 638–639; bacterial revolution, 840–842; Freudian psychology, 864–865; triumphs in modern thought, 865–866; growth of social sciences, 866–868; the new physics, Einstein, 992–993; contemporary, 1106–1115; brings environmental problems, 1107–1108; stimulated by military needs, 1108–1110; rise of big, 1110–1113; life of scientists, 1113–1115
Scientific instruments: development of, 635–636; cost of, 1111
Scientific method, 632, 637
Scientific revolution, 628–639
Scientists, modern, 1113–1115
Scipio Aemilianus, 157, 159, 164–166, 167
Scipio Africanus, 155–157
Scotland, 222; and Protestant Reformation, 485, 495; people's identification with England's industrialization, 781. *See also* Great Britain
Scott, Sir Walter, 814, 815
Sculpture, Greek, 93–95
"Sea Peoples," 35, 40
Second Continental Congress, 730
Second Empire, French, 878
Second International, 906
"Second Treatise on Civil Government" (Locke), 583, 642
Second World War, *see* World War II
*Secret History* (Procopius), 240
Secularism: in the Renaissance, 428; of the Enlightenment, 639
Seleucid dynasty, 112, 117, 120, 121, 122, 157
Seleucus, 112
Semites: Mesopotamian culture spread by, 14–15; in Egypt, 28
Senate, Roman, 150, 177
Seneca, 544
Sennacherib, King, 52, 53–54
Sennett, Mack, 1003
*Sententiae* (Lombard), 369
Separation of powers in government, 732–733
September Massacres, 743
Serapion, 137
Serapis, cult of, 128
Serbia: in Roman era, 181; breaks from Ottoman Empire, 903; in Balkan wars, 953–955; in W.W. I, 960; unites with south Slavs to form Yugoslavia, 979
Serfdom: in Sparta, 84; origins in Roman Empire, 203–204; in feudal society, 257; in medieval Europe, 318–319; rural, in England, disappears, 413; in eastern Europe, 592–596; under Habsburgs, 598; in eastern Germany, 600; in Russia, 612, 613, 615; under Catherine the Great, 653; in Austria, 656; in 18th century, 666; abolished by Napoleon, 756; abolished in Russia, 892

Servan-Schreiber, Jean Jacques, 1113
Servants: young girls in 17th, 18th centuries, 696–697; as indicator of wealth, 847, 850; domestic, in 19th century, 853–855
Servetus, Michael, 487
Seven Years' War, 651, 654, 682–684, 730
Severan dynasty, 198
Seville, as port for American riches, 514
Sex: homosexuality in Greece, 83–84, 99–100; Charlemagne's decrees on, 258, 261; tensions of Middle Ages, 336; in Renaissance, 440; premarital, in 17th, 18th centuries, 697–699; premarital, in 1900, 857–858; and marriage manuals, 862; and Freud's theories, 864–865; in Stalinist Russia, 1036. *See also* Prostitution
Sextus, 152
Seymour, Jane, 492
Sforza, Francesco, 454
Sforza family, 443, 452
Shabbathai Ben Abraham, 274
Shakespeare, William, 397, 546–549
Shalmaneser, 51
Sheriffs, 351–352, 361
Shipping, 913–914
Ships: Phoenician, 43 (illus.); Hellenistic, 122; Roman war, 155 (illus.); Viking, 275, 277 (illus.); 14th-century change in design, and spread of plague, 389; 15th-century changes in design, 517; Dutch, 585 (illus.); steam, 913; refrigerated, 914; submarines in W.W. I, 960
Shogun, 939
Shostakovich, Dimitri, 1084
Shrewsbury, countess of, *see* Hardwick, Elizabeth
Siberia, Muscovy capture of, 614
*Sic et Non* (Abélard), 367
Sicily: geography of, 142; Roman and Carthage compete for control of, 154–155; as feudal state, 358–360; medicine in, 367; Spain in, 519; and unification of Italy, 880, 883
*Siderus Nuncius* (Galileo), 633
Sieges: used by Assyrians, 53–54; engines, 134
Sieyès, Abbé, 751
Sigismund, Holy Roman emperor, 409
Silesia, 682
Silva, Anna da, 883
Silver, 513, 514, 515, 536, 572, 574, 688
Simon de Montfort, 381
Simony, 304, 305, 308, 501
Sino-Japanese War (1894–95), 942
*Sister Carrie* (Dreiser), 870
Sistine Chapel, 432, 470
Six Acts, 821
Sixtus IV, pope, 427, 470
Sixtus V, pope, 529
Siyalk, 58–59
Skepticism: defined, 544; origins in Montaigne's writings, 544–546
Slavery: in Mesopotamia, 14; in early Egypt, 27, 29; under Hittites, 33; of Hebrews in Egypt, 43; in ancient Israel, 50; in ancient Greece, 86, 88, 98; in Hellenistic world, 122–123; in Rome, 161, 162–163, 168, 195, 208; in medieval Europe, 318; in the Renaissance, 441–444; in 15th through 18th centuries, 541–544; 574; under Ottomans, 599; Britain gains control of trade in, 682; in 18th-century Virginia, 684; West agrees to work to stop, 928